THE WORLD ALMANAC OF
WORLD WAR II

THE WORLD ALMANAC OF
WORLD WAR II

The Complete and Comprehensive Documentary of World War II

Edited by Brigadier Peter Young

First Revised Edition

World Almanac
An Imprint of Pharos Books
New York, New York

A Bison Book

Copyright © 1981 by Bison Books Corporation

First published in the United States in 1981 as
The World Almanac Book of World War II

First revised edition published in 1986.

Library of Congress Cataloging-in-Publication Data

The World almanac of World War II : the
   complete and comprehensive documentary of
   World War II / edited by Peter Young. — 1st
   revised ed.
         p.   cm.
      Previously published: New York : World
   Almanac, 1986.
      ''A Bison book.''
      ISBN 0-88687-712-1
      1. World War, 1939–1945—
   Chronology.   2. World War, 1939–1945—
   Equipment and supplies.   3. World War,
   1939–1945—Biography.
   I. Young, Peter, 1915–
   D743.5.W67   1992
   940.53—dc20   92-20216
                                       CIP

Printed in the United States of America

World Almanac
An Imprint of Pharos Books
A Scripps Howard Company
200 Park Avenue
New York, NY 10166

10 9 8 7 6 5 4 3

CONTENTS

INTRODUCTION BY BRIGADIER PETER YOUNG

World War II was the greatest cataclysm in history. Tens of millions of people died in battle. Millions more were murdered simply because of the ethnic or religious group they belonged to. Millions still more were innocent civilians, who were caught up in a conflict of which they knew little and understood less. For those who lived through the war, the conflict was complex and, for most, largely unintelligible apart from the anxieties and hardships which the war thrust upon them. To most people living today who were born after the war came to an end, the events seem far away and still less comprehensible. Nevertheless, as the greatest collective human endeavor ever undertaken, it demands understanding. The war was fought, with varying intensity, on every continent of the

military historians in the world, John Keegan of the Royal Military Academy, Sandhurst, whose book, *The Face of Battle*, is considered to be one of the finest military histories to have appeared in the last decade. He was assisted in this task by Catherine Bradley of New Hall, Cambridge University. The world conflict introduced a series of new weapons, and many more weapons from earlier wars were used by the armies, navies and air forces of the great and lesser powers. An analysis of these weapons was prepared by William Newby-Grant, a leading small arms and artillery expert from the Royal Military Academy, Sandhurst, and Ian V. Hogg, perhaps the world's foremost authority on small arms and artillery. The naval section was written by Antony Preston, editor of *Defence* Magazine and author of dozens of naval histories, considered by many to be the world's most outstanding historian of ships and naval actions. The aircraft section was prepared by John Pimlott, expert historian of the Royal Military Academy, Sandhurst. The entire work was supervised by its general editor S. L. Mayer, recently of the University of Southern California, who has written or edited over 20 books on military history and World War II. The editor-in-chief of this almanac is Brigadier Peter Young, who served in the British Army at

globe and it has touched and sometimes scarred the lives of all those who lived through its terrors or those who live today. All of us live in the shadow of World War II. It is for that reason that this book was undertaken.

The principal part of this almanac is a chronology of the major events leading up to World War II, a detailed day-by-day analysis and commentary about what took place on every front; the final section of the chronology covers the immediate postwar years up until the start of the Korean War in 1950. This chronology was largely prepared by Donald Sommerville, historian of University College, Oxford University. It is followed by a biographical dictionary of the most important people who played a role in the war. This was prepared by one of the most outstanding

Dunkirk, Vaagso, the Dieppe Raids, D-Day and the last stages of the Burma campaign. One of Britain's most decorated war heroes, Brigadier Young went on to write and edit some 25 military histories during and after his period as Director of Historical Studies at the Royal Military Academy, Sandhurst.

This book has been designed and set out to be useful both to the general reader and the specialist. The main chronological section is subdivided by subject headings, so that the events and significance of a particular campaign can be followed in detail by a newcomer to the subject. Equally a specialist already familiar with certain aspects of the history of the war will now have a world-wide framework to illuminate and extend previous knowledge. The value of the biographical and weapons sections is perhaps greatest for cross reference, but they can also be used to suggest new areas for study and research. Where better to begin this than in the facts and analysis of the chronology section? Like most reference works this almanac is not designed to be read straight through from beginning to end (does anyone read a dictionary like that?), but by judicious use of the subheadings and index this book can serve many purposes. The biography of a general serving in North Africa in 1942 can lead to his career in other theaters at other times, and similarly Allied aircraft used over Europe also played their part in the Pacific war.

The biographical section is organized simply in alphabetical order. In the weapons sections each major class of equipment is dealt with in turn so that, for example, machine guns of all nations are dealt with together. In the chronology most of the campaigns are dealt with on a day-to-day basis with appropriate geographical headings. A few campaigns are discussed month by month because their significance is best understood by an account of their cumulative effects over a period of time. Particularly important individual actions are, of course, included within this treatment. As well as military developments there are also series of entries on political changes, resistance work and many other subjects like inter-allied planning. There are many published accounts in all these fields as well as a mass of official histories and records, but unfortunately their versions of any one story often differ. The editors have made every effort to reconcile these discrepancies to reach a reliable synthesis, but clearly opinions may differ as to which variant is best.

Whatever conclusions are reached on particular issues we are all the stepchildren of the Second World War. Its legacy haunts us if we gaze across the Berlin Wall into Communist-controlled Europe, if we look across the Taiwan Straits toward the People's Republic of China, or if we look at the maps of Africa or the Middle East. The Arab-Israeli conflicts were a direct result of World War II. So were the Korean and Vietnam Wars. The waxing and waning of the Cold War between the Western nations and the Soviet Union and its client states is a constant reminder of the importance of World War II in the daily headlines. It has been said that were it not for the peace settlement of World War I, that World War II would never have taken place. It is certainly true that the unfulfilled aspirations of nations and peoples at the end of World War I were the hair-trigger pulled by the dictators who arose from the ashes of that terrible conflict. This, almost inevitably, led to the still greater horrors of World War II. In 1945 national aspirations and a natural human desire for a better life created the conflicts between nations and within them that we face today. It can only be hoped that the lessons taught by World War II, among the most important of which is that uncontrolled craving for world hegemony can only lead to a third world war, have been sufficiently understood. It is the purpose of this book to add to the knowledge of the Second World War in the fervent hope that a third one may never take place.

Hitler at a Nuremberg Rally in 1934.

CHRONOLOGY

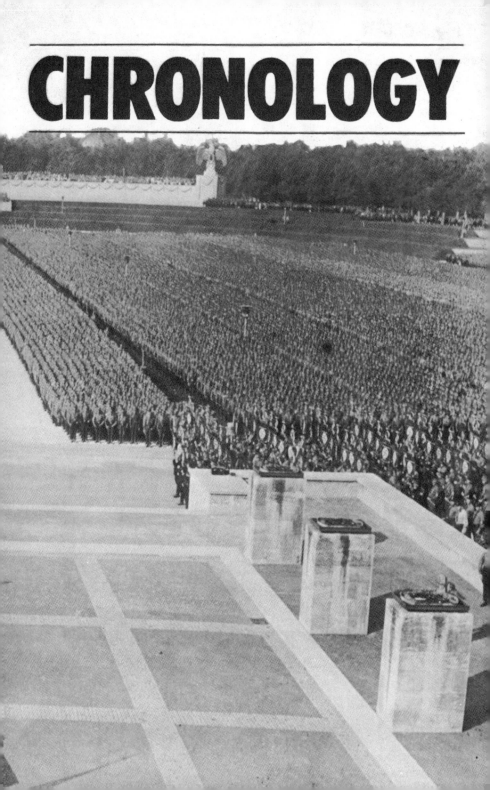

CHRONOLOGY

THE APPROACH TO WAR

JUNE 1919
The Treaty of Versailles is concluded. This treaty, and the similar Treaty of St Germain between Austria-Hungary and the Allies together help to foster some of the grievances and weaknesses which will form the causes of World War II. Germany is to be largely disarmed and the Rhineland is to be occupied by Allied forces. Considerable reparations are to be paid but the amount of the burden is not yet fixed. The map of Europe is substantially redrawn. From the wreck of the former Austro-Hungarian Empire a whole group of new states is created. Each of these states has grievances against the others and none has a wholly homogeneous population. Poland too has been created and will fight successfully in 1920 to retain its independence against the Soviets. Japan (still allied with Britain) gains a mandate over islands in the Pacific; in the Marshalls, Marianas and Carolines. The Charter of the League of Nations is part of the Versailles agreement but its scope is left substantially weakened by the refusal of the United States Congress to ratify it.

SEPTEMBER 1919
A young German army political-instruction officer named Adolf Hitler is ordered to investigate a small right-wing political party, the German Workers' Party (DAP), in Munich. He joins it, becomes its leading public speaker and by July 1921 is its leader. He changes its title to the National Socialist German Workers' Party (NSDAP). He obtains money from army political funds to purchase a newspaper, the *Völkischer Beobachter* (this title can be translated as Racist Observer). Hitler leaves the army in April 1920 but retains some of his former contacts, especially with a Major Roehm. His program, with its radical tone and its combination of anti-Communism and nationalist opposition to Versailles, is designed to have wide appeal. His technique and the reforms advocated are backed unashamedly with violence.

NOVEMBER 1921–FEBRUARY 1922
The leading naval powers meet in Washington to discuss limitation of their forces. The conference was originally planned as a general disarmament meeting but the French refused to discuss army reductions because the guarantees of their security which had formed part of the Versailles agreement have not come into force because of the United States' refusal to ratify. The battleship-building race which had been about to begin is halted. The British and Americans accept parity in their main forces. The Japanese are to have about two-thirds of this strength and the French and Italians about one-half of the Japanese force. Although none of the signatories, with the possible exception of the United States, is particularly happy with the terms they all conform, largely because of economic pressure. The effects for the Japanese are particularly important. They feel that in a sense they have been denied an equal position in the world by the Western Powers and are, therefore, impelled to look more toward Asian affairs. More- or less-overtly racist immigration measures taken by the Western countries during the next few years contribute to this hurt attitude. The almost total dependence of the Japanese on outside sources for their raw materials can only increase this tendency to·look for foreign gains and be wary of restrictions.

OCTOBER 1922
Mussolini's Fascists stage a 'March on Rome' to demand power. They succeed and the party blackshirts begin operations to eliminate opposition.

JANUARY 1923
France and Belgium occupy the Ruhr in an attempt to enforce the payment of reparations in which Germany has fallen behind. In 1921 a provisional figure of 132,000,000,000 marks has been set (equivalent to $33,000,000,000 or £6,850,000,000). One of the reasons for Germany's failure to keep up with payments is the decline in the value of the mark. In 1918 it stood at four marks to the dollar, in the summer of 1921 at 75, in 1922 at 400, it is now over 7000 and by July it will be 160,000. The peak is not until November 1923 when the rate will be 130,000,000,000 marks to the dollar.

NOVEMBER 1923
The financial weakness in Germany contributes to political unrest, to the benefit of the more-radical parties. One such is Hitler's NSDAP in Munich. In conjunction with the wartime leader General Ludendorff he attempts a *putsch* to seize power in Bavaria. It fails, partly because it is ill planned and led, but mainly because the army is not brought in to the scheme. Hitler is tried early in 1924 and is sentenced to serve two years. He stays in prison for nine months and spends his time writing *Mein Kampf*. This book explains his political ideas, notably his anti-Communism, his violent anti-Semitism and his intention to look for *Lebensraum* for Germany

in Eastern Europe. His connection with Ludendorff brings him some prominence. From the failure of the *putsch* he learns the importance of maintaining an appearance of legality which he will try to keep up until the war begins. The appearance of legality does not prevent the party thugs from intimidating opponents.

JANUARY 1924
The first national congress of the Kuomintang is held. This party represents the growing forces of Chinese nationalism. Its leader at this stage is Sun Yat-sen but General Chiang Kai-shek has an increasing influence. It is only loosely a party in the Western sense, with little formal structure. It draws support from a variety of groups in Chinese society, generally among the more affluent. Its army is the main basis of its power. The Chinese Communist Party was founded in 1922 and it also has a growing appeal. The Communists and the Kuomintang are not yet confirmed enemies.

APRIL 1924
The Dawes Plan provides new arrangements for the payment of German reparations and forms the background to the stabilization of the German currency. About $250,000,000 is to be paid each year and much of the money to finance this, and Germany's economic recovery, is to be borrowed from abroad.

APRIL 1925
Field Marshal von Hindenburg becomes president of Germany.

OCTOBER 1925
The Locarno treaties are concluded. By these agreements Britain and Italy promise to guarantee the Franco-German frontier against violation by either side. No similar promise is made for Germany's eastern borders. This is a blow to the French because their policy has been to try to keep Germany contained by the threat of attack from the west and by having allies in the Little Entente (Czechoslovakia, Yugoslavia and Rumania) in the east. Britain prefers to be friendly toward Germany and wants to avoid being entangled in Balkan problems. In this way armaments can be kept low and there will be no need to call for help from the British Empire.

SEPTEMBER 1926
Germany joins the League of Nations. This step illustrates the progress being made by the Weimar regime during this comparatively untroubled period. Although the radical parties of the left and right have a considerable following, they are not yet a major force in German affairs.

APRIL 1927
Shanghai falls to the Kuomintang. Chiang Kai-shek chooses to have the support of the rich merchants of the port rather than the Communists and eliminates many of their officials there.

AUGUST 1928
The Kellogg-Briand Pact is signed. By its terms the United States, Great Britain, France, Germany, Italy and Japan agree to renounce aggressive war.

JUNE 1929
A committee of experts under the chairmanship of the American banker Owen Young presents the Young Plan for the final settlement of the German reparations bill. It fixes the amount which is owed and gives a date by which payments are to be completed. Although the terms are less harsh than those previously fixed they are not as good as the German authorities hoped. They are, however, accepted. Hitler joins with the Nationalist Party, led by the industrialist Hugenberg, in opposing the settlement. This campaign brings new financial backing for the Nazis and makes Hitler a national figure.

23 OCTOBER 1929
The New York Stock Exchange collapses. A worldwide economic depression begins. There has been a worldwide tendency for agricultural overproduction which combined with a decline in international trade has led to protectionist measures. The economic system has been unbalanced by the reparations and other war debts. The debts have been largely covered by loans from the United States but, because of protection, other countries have been unable to sell in the United States and therefore have had to borrow still more. This borrowing will now come to an end.

APRIL 1930
The London Naval Treaty is agreed. By its terms there are to be no new battleships before 1937. Limitations are also agreed to cover submarines, cruisers and destroyers.

MAY 1930
The Japanese Prime Minister Inukai is assassinated by a group of young army officers because of his support for the London Treaty. The militants had hoped for parity with Britain

and the United States. The fixing of the number of cruisers allowed to Japan as an arbitrary fraction of that of Britain and the United States is seen as particularly obnoxious. This murder is only one token of a growing anarchy within the Japanese ruling class. Various pressure groups and 'patriotic' societies are developing in which junior officers are becoming deeply involved. They are prepared to take the law into their own hands and act without regard for the more cautious policies which some Japanese statesmen and many of the Japanese people prefer.

SEPTEMBER 1930
In the German elections the Nazis become the second-largest party. They receive 20 percent of the vote. The Communists also do well. The Nazis are still a long way from being in a dominant position but they have taken over from Hugenberg's National Party as the leading party of the right.

MAY 1931
The principal Austrian bank, the Credit-Anstalt, fails. This is a result of French-led financial pressure because of the Austro-German negotiations for a customs union, which the French think is a prelude to German unification. In July a German bank, the Darmstadter-National, also fails. These failures only increase the economic problems in Germany, which are acute anyway because of the depression. The plan for the customs union has to be abandoned. This is a real humiliation for the government and a bonus for the nationalist parties. Although reparations payments are suspended for a year and then abandoned altogether, this is of little consequence for the German unemployed.

SEPTEMBER 1931
Following an incident at Mukden on the South Manchurian Railroad (the railroad line was sabotaged), the Japanese army sends forces to occupy south and central Manchuria. Chinese resistance is comparatively weak and by early in 1932 the conquest is complete. From the speed of the army reaction it seems likely that the incident at Mukden has not been entirely accidental. The Japanese government is not consulted by the army and can do little except follow on. The Japanese constitution provides that any government must have serving officers as navy and army ministers and this means that if either service is set on a course of action it can bring down a government which tries to oppose it.

China appeals to the League of Nations soon after the attack begins, the League calls on Japan to withdraw and appoints a Commission to investigate the rights and wrongs of the situation. This is the first time the League has been asked to intervene in a case where a great power is involved and the eventual failure of the intervention illustrates only too clearly the weakness of the League.

JANUARY 1932
In Shanghai a boycott of Japanese goods by the Chinese leads to riots and then fighting, with Japanese troops protecting the Japanese enclave in the Treaty port. Early in February the Japanese bring their forces up to four divisions and by March control the port and the area around it.

FEBRUARY 1932
Japan declares the independence of the former Manchuria as the puppet state Manchukuo. The puppet government is headed by a descendant of the Manchu emperors. The Japanese make little attempt either to make themselves popular or to give the Manchukuo government even the appearance of power. There is much direct, open economic exploitation in which the power of the Japanese-owned railroad company is extended considerably. The opium trade is also encouraged.

MARCH–APRIL 1932
There are presidential elections in Germany in which Hitler stands unsuccessfully against Hindenburg. During April the Nazi SA is banned after plans for a coup are discovered. Hitler denies knowledge of these plans and insists that the Party continues to work within the electoral system.

Above: Chancellor Hitler and President Hindenburg meet in 1934. Goering stands behind Hitler wearing steel helmet.

MAY 1932
The conservative leader Franz von Papen becomes chancellor. The leading member of his Cabinet is General Schleicher.

JUNE 1932
The ban on the SA is lifted after the Nazis have promised to give some support to the government. Later, in July, the Nazis become the largest party in the Reichstag after elections in which the thugs of the SA have done much to intimidate opponents. The Nazis now hold 230 out of 608 seats but this is not a majority. Papen remains chancellor but in September his government is defeated by a combination of the Nazis and Communists.

NOVEMBER 1932
After the new elections the Nazis are still the largest party in the Reichstag, but their share of the vote has declined from 37 percent to 33 percent. The Communist vote increases. General Schleicher is worried by this and by Papen's failure to put together a solid parliamentary majority. Papen resigns believing that he will be recalled once coalition negotiations with the Nazis fail.

DECEMBER 1932
President Hindenburg is ready to recall Papen when Schleicher declares that the army has no confidence in him. Instead Schleicher himself becomes chancellor.

JANUARY 1933
Adolf Hitler becomes chancellor of Germany. In the political maneuverings during the month it becomes clear that Schleicher cannot construct a coalition government and that Hitler, Papen and the other right-wing parties probably can. The president refuses to give Schleicher powers to rule without the Reichstag and he is forced to resign. Papen becomes vice-chancellor in the new Hitler government and his supporters hold many of the key posts. The coalition talks with the Center Party fail, as the Nazis hope, and Hitler is able to call for elections for March.

FEBRUARY 1933
On the night of the 27th the Reichstag is set on fire. Four Communists are tried and executed for this crime but it seems likely that the Nazis have a hand in it. Whoever is responsible it works to the Nazis' advantage. The intimidation campaign against their opponents is stepped up, backed by the Prussian police who are now controlled by Goering and packed with Nazi nominees. A special presidential decree, granted after the fire, increases these powers.

MARCH 1933
In the elections the Nazis poll 43 percent of the vote but even with the support of the Nationalists they only have a bare majority. Most of the Communist deputies are arrested along with some of the Social Democrats. When the Reichstag assembles the Nazis have succeeded, with support from the Vatican, in winning the votes of the mainly Catholic Center Party for a special constitutional law. This Enabling Act is passed on the 23rd and with it Hitler becomes independent of the presidential power. A token of the ability the Nazis now have to eliminate all opposition is that in this month the first concentration camp, Dachau, is established near Munich.

Japan announces that it intends to leave the League of Nations. This follows the report of the investigating commission on Manchuria. Although it concedes that Japan had important interests to protect and may have been provoked, it also makes no bones about accusing Japan of aggression. Japan's exit from the League only makes the position of the more militant sections of opinion stronger. Money is granted for army modernization plans.

OCTOBER 1933
Hitler leaves the League of Nations and ends German participation in the disarmament conferences, ostensibly because other countries have refused to reduce their military to the German level.

JANUARY 1934
Germany and Poland conclude a nonaggression pact. This is a setback for France's system of Eastern European alliances.

MARCH 1934
Mussolini makes agreements with Hungary and Austria. German and Italian policy on Austria is entirely different. Mussolini does not want to see any form of union between the German-speaking nations and, therefore, supports Chancellor Dollfuss in opposition both to socialism and Nazism.

JUNE 1934
On the Night of the Long Knives Hitler destroys his enemies, particularly within the SA. Ernst Roehm, the leader of the SA, Gregor Strasser, who leads the working-class left of the Nazi party, and General Schleicher are the most

Above: Nazis boycott Jewish businesses.

prominent of the victims. The SA is subjected to tighter party control and Himmler's SS becomes more important. The purge takes place on the night of the 30th. Over 1000 people are executed.

JULY 1934
The Austrian Nazis stage a coup and assassinate Chancellor Dollfuss. Mussolini sends troops to the Italian border and Hitler does not intervene. The Austrian authorities recover and Schuschnigg is the new chancellor.

AUGUST 1934
President Hindenburg dies. Hitler proclaims himself Fuehrer and chancellor. The Armed Forces are prevailed upon to swear personal allegiance to the new head of state.

SEPTEMBER 1934
The Soviet Union joins the League of Nations. Stalin is obviously disturbed by the possibility of a threat from the new Germany.

OCTOBER 1934
King Alexander of Yugoslavia and Foreign Minister Barthou of France are assassinated by a Croat terrorist group. The assassins have Italian backing and the aim is to disrupt the Franco-Yugoslav alliance. The Yugoslav regency which follows is indeed weak and open to German and Italian pressure. Barthou has been distinguished also by his opposition to Hitler.

OCTOBER 1934–NOVEMBER 1935
The Chinese Communists move their main forces from Kiangsi to Shensi province in the Long March. Some groups travel as much as 6000 miles. There are many casualties on the way but the regime established in Shensi is better placed to fight off the Kuomintang and to draw recruits. The Communists are strongly in favor of war with the Japanese.

DECEMBER 1934
The Japanese abrogate the Washington Naval Treaty.

There is a clash between Italian and Abyssinian troops in a disputed area of the border between Italian Somaliland and Abyssinia.

JANUARY 1935
In a referendum the people of the Saar region vote overwhelmingly for union with Germany. This is an important success for the Nazis.

MARCH 1935
Hitler introduces compulsory military service and announces the existence of a German air force. This is in direct contravention of the Versailles Treaty. The so-called Nuremberg decrees are issued, which greatly increase the persecution of the Jews in Germany.

APRIL 1935
At Stresa, Britain, France and Italy join in condemning breaches of the Versailles Treaty. There is little substance to this agreement. The Anglo-German naval talks which soon follow and the growing Italian involvement in Africa will end this brief anti-German unity.

The Neutrality Act is passed in the United States. This prevents financial assistance being given to any country involved in war and states that no protection can be offered to US citizens who enter a war zone. The War Policy Act of May 1937 modifies these provisions a little, giving the president some discretion in their application.

MAY 1935
France and the USSR conclude a mutual assistance pact. Later in the year a similar pact is made between Czechoslovakia and the Soviets. The Franco-Soviet agreement is not ratified for nine months. The British are still reluctant to think of the Soviets as friends against Germany and although Foreign Secretary Eden visits Moscow later in the year, no agreement is made.

JUNE 1935
The Anglo-German Naval Agreement is signed. Germany is to be allowed to build a fleet of up to 35 percent of the British fleet. U-Boats are

permitted.

This contravenes both the Versailles Treaty and the Stresa agreement. France is not told of the talks until a late stage and the subsequent protests are ignored.

A more general naval conference is also held in London later in the year and proposals to continue the limitations on size and numbers of ships are produced, but these are never finally agreed.

OCTOBER 1935

Italy moves against Abyssinia in force. Britain and France lead the League of Nations into imposing sanctions against Italy in November, but these are halfhearted. Oil supplies are left unhindered and nothing is done to close the Suez Canal to Italian troopships. Mussolini is nonetheless driven to look toward Germany for support. In turn Germany receives a free demonstration of the ineffectiveness of the League and some indication of what can be achieved by determination and brute force.

DECEMBER 1935

There is an important series of anti-Japanese riots by Chinese students in Peking. These reflect the popular Chinese feeling. The Kuomintang has been growing stronger and its army better trained in the recent months but Chiang Kai-shek has been using his forces principally to fight the Communists and not the Japanese.

FEBRUARY 1936

A far-reaching plot by a group of younger officers to seize power in Japan only just fails. They have planned a program of assassinations, to be followed by the imposition of a new Cabinet on the emperor. Not all the killings are carried out and after a few days' confusion senior politicians regain control. Although trials and executions follow the dangerous scope for independent action at junior levels is made only too clear.

MARCH 1936

In Hitler's first foreign-policy triumph the Rhineland, demilitarized by the provisions of Versailles and the Locarno agreement, is re-occupied by German troops. The French and British governments do little more than briefly protest. To take the step, Hitler has had to overcome opposition from his generals and by being proved right his supremacy over them and his self-esteem are confirmed. Implicitly this act suggests that Germany and not France is now the leading power on the continent of Europe

and that France lacks the will to protect its allies to the east.

MAY 1936

The war in Abyssinia comes to an end with the occupation of Addis Ababa and the flight of Haile Selassie. The Italians formally annex the country.

JULY 1936

Sanctions against Italy come to an end.

The Spanish Civil War begins. This is important to wider issues of international relations for several reasons. It sharpens the ideas of a Fascist-Communist conflict and brings Italy and Germany closer together. It weakens the ties between France and the USSR because France refuses to help the Republicans. The British reputation for hypocrisy is confirmed with Britain once again content to take only ineffective steps to prevent foreign interference in the war. It also provides several shattering demonstrations of the power of the new Luftwaffe. The war will continue until 1939.

NOVEMBER 1936

The Anti-Comintern Pact is concluded by Germany and Japan. Italy joins later. Secret clauses of the pact make it clear that the main aim is to threaten the USSR from both west and east. It is not, however, a formal alliance since the Japanese do not want to be drawn in to a future European war. They hope that by strengthening Germany against the Soviets that Britain will be distracted from Asian affairs.

DECEMBER 1936

Chiang Kai-shek is arrested by one of his generals, Chang Hseuh-liang, while visiting some troops employed in blockading the Communist Shensi province. After complicated negotiations involving the Communist Chou En-lai Chiang is eventually released but he has been compelled to agree to take a more definitely anti-Japanese line. A recent defeat for a Japanese-backed warlord in Suiyuan province has shown that the Japanese can be beaten.

JANUARY 1937

Hitler formally abrogates all of the provisions of the Versailles Treaty in a Reichstag speech, claiming that it is impossible for a great power to accept restrictions of this nature.

MAY 1937

Neville Chamberlain becomes prime minister of Britain.

JUNE 1937

The purges of the Soviet Communist Party are extended to take in the army. About 35,000 officers will be arrested and executed or will simply disappear during the coming months. Three of the five marshals of the Soviet Union, 13 out of 15 army commanders, all the military district commanders and well over half of all officers of general rank will be included. The most prominent casualty is Marshal Tukhachevsky who has been working to convert the army to run on the most modern lines with the emphasis on independent tank forces. These ideas are abandoned after his fall.

JULY 1937

There is an outbreak of fighting near Peking at the Marco Polo bridge. There is some evidence that this incident has been provoked by junior officers on both sides but during the next few weeks the fighting spreads throughout north China. Peking and Tientsin are controlled by the Japanese before the end of the month. Throughout this time negotiations are continuing and not ungenerous offers of settlement are made by the Japanese, but by early August Chiang Kaishek has decided to fight.

AUGUST–NOVEMBER 1937

There is heavy fighting around Shanghai in which the Japanese, for some time seriously outnumbered, are very hard pressed. During September the Communist forces in Shansi score an important, morale-boosting victory over the Japanese 5th Infantry Division. By early November the Japanese forces in Shanghai have been increased and, aided by landings nearby to threaten the Chinese rear, they drive the Chinese back. They begin to advance toward Nanking.

During October and November there are further Japanese proposals for a settlement but these come to nothing. Equally abortive is a conference of Far East powers held in Brussels in November. The Japanese do not attend because they see it as an attempt by the West to deny them the profits of their strength. Although Chiang has hoped for at least economic help, he gets little satisfaction from the conference. The United States maintains its isolation policy and the Europeans are not prepared to act unless the United States does.

NOVEMBER 1937

Hitler holds an important conference in which he explains his intentions for Germany during the next few years. A record of the conference is kept by Colonel Hossbach and is known as the Hossbach Memorandum. Hitler explains his aim to look for *Lebensraum* in Eastern Europe and specifically accepts that it will probably be necessary to use force to attain this. In the short term he is considering action against Austria and Czechoslovakia. He is not certain of the timing of these moves, preferring to wait on opportunity, but he intends that the whole process be over by between 1943 and 1945 because by that time he will be past his peak and other nations will be catching Germany's lead in arms.

Private discussions between Britain and France decide that nothing should be done about any German move against Austria. France maintains that its treaty obligations will compel it to fight for Czechoslovakia. Britain would not be able to keep out of such a war for fear of a French defeat. The British policy is, therefore, to try to obtain an agreement between Germany and Czechoslovakia and the only way to achieve this is to put pressure on the Czechs to make concessions. This pressure now begins.

DECEMBER 1937

The Japanese forces advancing from Shanghai reach and capture Nanking. The Japanese now offer new, rigorous terms to Chiang Kai-shek but these are not accepted. Many Japanese are prepared to look for peace and consider less harsh terms. The fighting is a growing economic burden and the heavy involvement is an unwelcome commitment to the Army General Staff who would prefer to prepare to fight the USSR. The army is, however, not easy to control. The incident on 12 December when the American gunboat *Panay* is sunk, the air attack in August on the British ambassador's car and, worst of all, the several days rampage of murder and rape which follow the capture of Nanking, all provide evidence of the army's lack of restraint.

FEBRUARY 1938

British Foreign Secretary Eden resigns. He resigns over a quarrel concerning policy toward Italy but this is only part of his disagreement with Chamberlain over how to combat Hitler.

Early in the month Hitler also reorganizes his administration. In January War Minister Blomberg was dismissed for marrying a lady with an unsuitable background and the Army Commander in Chief Fritsch was sacked on trumped-up charges that he is homosexual. At the start of February Hitler announces the abolition of the War Ministry and its replacement by a new organization, Armed Forces High Command,

Above: US airman at the waist gun of a B-17.

Above: A German infantryman with MG 15.

Above: German mountain troops in the USSR.

Above: An 81mm mortar team in the Ukraine.

Map Legend

PRE-1914 BOUNDARIES
BOUNDARIES AFTER TREATY OF VERSAILLES, 1919
TERRITORIES LOST BY GERMANY
UNDER LEAGUE OF NATIONS CONTROL
DEMILITARISED ZONE

ESTONIA
SWEDEN
RIGA
LATVIA
BALTIC SEA
DENMARK
COPENHAGEN
MEMEL
LITHUANIA
NORTH SEA
KÖNIGSBERG
KAUNAS
MINSK
GREAT BRITAIN
NETHERLANDS
AMSTERDAM
DANZIG
East Prussia
RUSSIA
LONDON
HAMBURG
BERLIN
Vistula
Bug
BRUSSELS
BELGIUM
COLOGNE
Rhine
LEIPZIG
WARSAW
POLAND
PARIS
LUX.
Saar
FRANKFURT
PRAGUE
LVOV
FRANCE
MUNICH
CZECHOSLOVAKIA
BERN
VIENNA
Danube
BUDAPEST
SWITZ.
AUSTRIA
AUSTRIA-HUNGARY
GENEVA
HUNGARY
RUMANIA
MILAN
ITALY
YUGOSLAVIA
BELGRADE
RUMANIA
SERBIA
BUCHAREST

MILES 0 250
KM 0 400

Below: German 5cm Granatwerfer 36 mortar.

BRUSSE
BEL
PARIS

**March 1935
Saar Basin to Germany
(by plebiscite)**

FRANCE

BORDEAUX

SPAIN
MADRID

MARSEILLES
BARCELONA

GERMANY, 1934
BOUNDARY OF GERMANY, 3 SEPT. 1939
Slovakia, German protectorate

MILES 0 400
KILOMETERS 0 600

Left: The effects of the Versailles Treaty.   Above: A British Beaufighter aircraft takes off.

March 1939
Annexed by Germany

August 1939
Russo-German
non-aggression
pact signed

March 1936
Rhineland remilitarized

October 1938
Occupied by Germany

March 1939
To Hungary

March 1938
Annexed by Germany

October 1938
To Hungary

March 1939
Occupied by Germany

May 1939
'Pact of Steel' signed by
Germany & Italy

April 1939
Occupied by Italy

SWEDEN

DENMARK

COPENHAGEN

BALTIC
SEA

MEMEL

RIGA

LATVIA

LITHUANIA

KAUNAS

MOSCOW

R U S S I A

KÖNIGSBERG

EAST
PRUSSIA

MINSK

Belorussia

HAMBURG

BERLIN

DANZIG

Vistula

Bug

G E R M A N Y

WARSAW

P O L A N D

KIEV

Dnieper

Rhineland

Sudeten-
land

PRAGUE

CZECHOSLOVAKIA

LVOV

Ukraine

Siegfried
Line

MUNICH

VIENNA

BERCHTESGADEN

AUSTRIA

BUDAPEST

HUNGARY

ODESSA

Crimea

R U M A N I A

MILAN

BUCHAREST

BLACK SEA

ITALY

BELGRADE

YUGOSLAVIA

Danube

ROME

ADRIATIC
SEA

SOFIA

BULGARIA

ISTANBUL

ANKARA

NAPLES

TIRANE

ALBANIA

GREECE

TURKEY

Above: German expansion 1934–39.

Above: A German assault gun in Athens.

Above: British prisoners in the desert.

Above: German gains 1939–40.

Above: T-34 tanks bogged down and abandoned during the fall of 1941.

Above: The war in the USSR and North Africa 1941–42.

Above: A desert foxhole with MG 34.   *Maps: Germany's retreat and final defeat.*

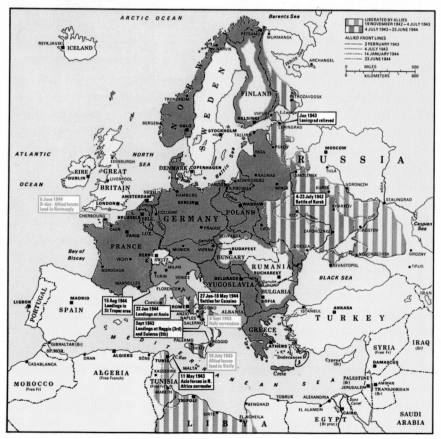

Above: Winter fighting in the USSR.

Above: German engineer carrying mines.

Right: A Fletcher *Class destroyer in 1945.*
Far right, top: A Vought Kingfisher on its catapult on the battleship Alabama.
Far right, middle: The Mahan *Class destroyer* Drayton *pictured in 1941.*
Far right, bottom: Crewmen fit an auxiliary fuel tank to a P-51 Mustang fighter.
Below: Japanese expansion in the Pacific and China, 1934–41.

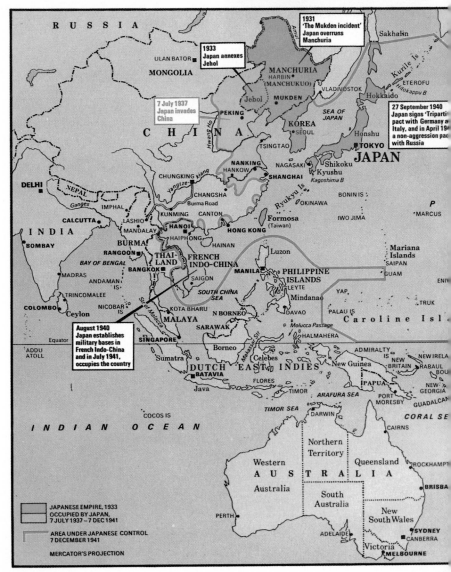

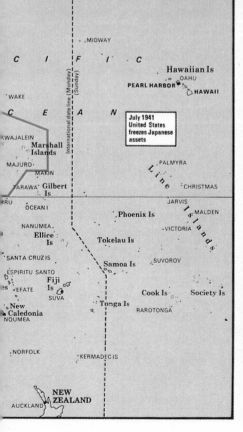

Map labels:

MIDWAY

C · I · F · I · C

International date line (Monday)
(Sunday)

Hawaiian Is
OAHU
PEARL HARBOR
HAWAII

WAKE

O · C · E · A · N

KWAJALEIN

Marshall
Islands

MAJURO

MAKIN

July 1941
United States
freezes Japanese
assets

PALMYRA

Line Islands

TARAWA Gilbert
Is

CHRISTMAS

RU OCEAN I

JARVIS

Phoenix Is

MALDEN

NANUMEA

VICTORIA

Ellice
Is

Tokelau Is

SANTA CRUZ IS

SUVOROV

ESPIRITU SANTO

Samoa Is

es EFATE Fiji
Is
SUVA

Cook Is

Society Is

New
Caledonia
NOUMEA

Tonga Is

RAROTONGA

NORFOLK

KERMADEC IS

NEW
ZEALAND
AUCKLAND

Right: Douglas Dauntless aircraft prepare to take off from the USS Ranger.
Far right, top: A Mustang fighter over England. The pilot has six victories.
Far right, middle: Batmen on the USS Wasp *guide aircraft in to land.*
Far right, bottom: Ships of the US Task Forces assembled to invade Okinawa.
Below: Pacific Theater operations 1941–42.

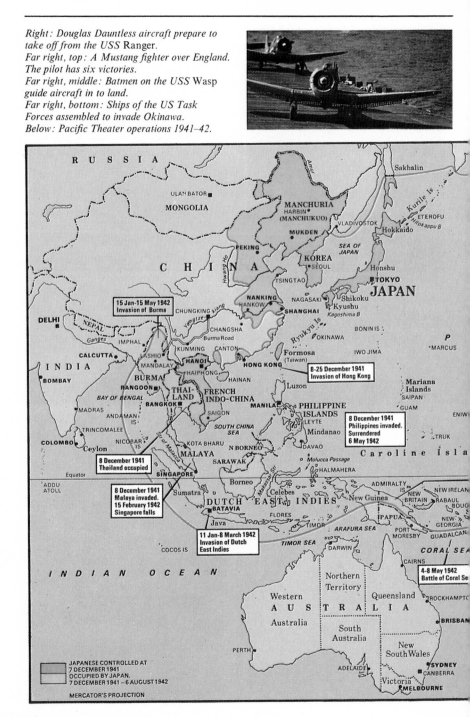

Map labels:

RUSSIA
Amur
Sakhalin
Kurile Is
ETEROFU
Hitokappu B
ULAN BATOR
MONGOLIA
MANCHURIA
HARBIN
(MANCHUKUO)
VLADIVOSTOK
MUKDEN
Hokkaido
PEKING
SEA OF JAPAN
Hwang Ho
C H I N A
KOREA
SEOUL
Honshu
TSINGTAO
TOKYO
JAPAN
NANKING
NAGASAKI
Shikoku
Kyushu
HANKOW
SHANGHAI
Kagoshima B

**15 Jan-15 May 1942
Invasion of Burma**

CHUNGKING
Yangtze Kiang
DELHI
NEPAL
CHANGSHA
Burma Road
Ryukyu Is
OKINAWA
BONIN IS
P
MARCUS
Ganges
IMPHAL
LASHIO
KUNMING
CANTON
Formosa
(Taiwan)
IWO JIMA
CALCUTTA
MANDALAY
HANOI
HONG KONG

**8-25 December 1941
Invasion of Hong Kong**

INDIA
BURMA
HAIPHONG
HAINAN
Luzon
Mariana Islands
SAIPAN
BOMBAY
RANGOON
THAI-LAND
FRENCH INDO-CHINA
BAY OF BENGAL
BANGKOK
SAIGON
MANILA
PHILIPPINE ISLANDS
GUAM
ENIWI
MADRAS
ANDAMAN IS
SOUTH CHINA SEA
LEYTE

**8 December 1941
Philippines invaded.
Surrendered
6 May 1942**

TRINCOMALEE
Mindanao
TRUK
COLOMBO
NICOBAR IS
KOTA BHARU
N BORNEO
DAVAO
Caroline Isla
Ceylon
MALAYA
SARAWAK
Molucca Passage
HALMAHERA

**8 December 1941
Thailand occupied**

Equator
SINGAPORE
Borneo
Makassar Str
ADMIRALTY IS
NEW IRELAN
ADDU ATOLL
Sumatra
Celebes
New Guinea
NEW BRITAIN
RABAUL
BOUG

**8 December 1941
Malaya invaded.
15 February 1942
Singapore falls**

DUTCH EAST INDIES
FLORES
PAPUA
NEW GEORGIA
GUADALCAN
BATAVIA
Java
PORT MORESBY

**11 Jan-8 March 1942
Invasion of Dutch
East Indies**

TIMOR
ARAFURA SEA
COCOS IS
TIMOR SEA
CORAL SEA
DARWIN

**4-8 May 1942
Battle of Coral Se**

INDIAN OCEAN
CAIRNS
Northern Territory
Western Australia
Queensland
ROCKHAMPTO
A U S T R A L I A
Australia
South Australia
BRISBAN
PERTH
New South Wales
ADELAIDE
SYDNEY
CANBERRA
Victoria
MELBOURNE

JAPANESE CONTROLLED AT
7 DECEMBER 1941
OCCUPIED BY JAPAN,
7 DECEMBER 1941–6 AUGUST 1942

MERCATOR'S PROJECTION

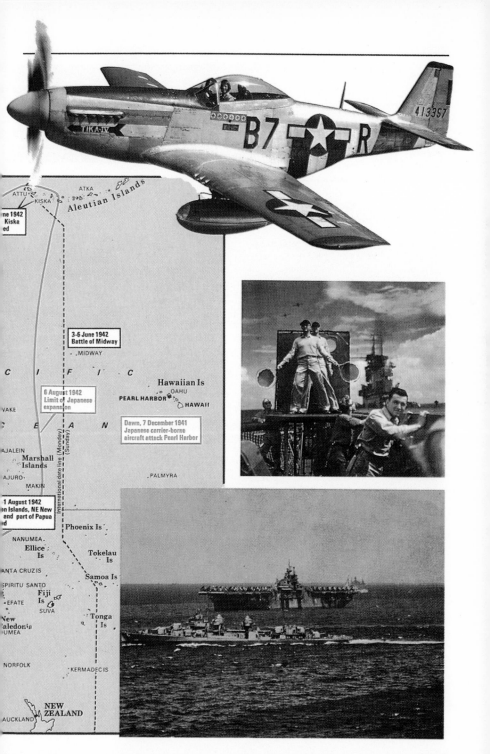

TIKA IV

B7-R 413357

Map labels

ATTU
KISKA
ATKA
Aleutian Islands

ne 1942
Kiska
ed

3-6 June 1942
Battle of Midway

MIDWAY

P A C I F I C

Hawaiian Is
OAHU
PEARL HARBOR
HAWAII

6 August 1942
Limit of Japanese
expansion

Dawn, 7 December 1941
Japanese carrier-borne
aircraft attack Pearl Harbor

WAKE

O C E A N

AJALEIN
Marshall
Islands
AJURO
MAKIN

PALMYRA

1 August 1942
on Islands, NE New
and part of Papua
ed

NANUMEA
Ellice
Is

SANTA CRUZ IS

SPIRITU SANTO
EFATE

New
aledonia
UMEA

Fiji
Is
SUVA

Phoenix Is

Tokelau
Is

Samoa Is

Tonga
Is

NORFOLK

KERMADEC IS

NEW
ZEALAND
AUCKLAND

International date line (Monday)
(Sunday)

Right: LST.449 seen during a landing operation in the Southwest Pacific.
Far right, top: The cruiser Savannah *at Algiers. Two Liberty ships burn behind.*
Far right, middle: A GI inspects a crashed Zero at Munda, New Georgia.
Far right, bottom: An Atlantic convoy seen from the battleship Arkansas *in February 1944.*
Below: The US counteroffensive 1942–44.

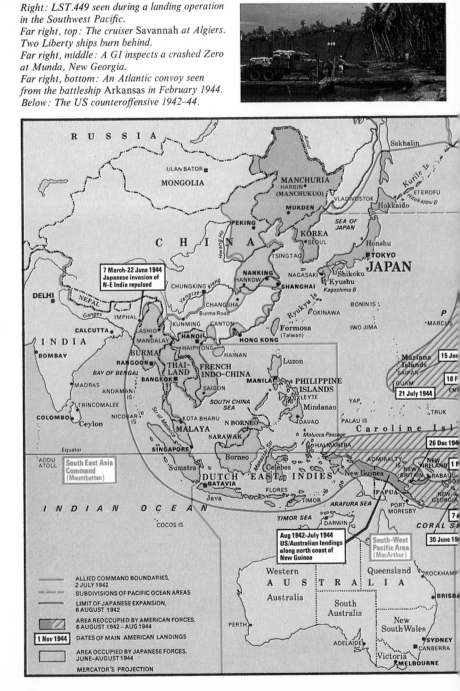

RUSSIA
Sakhalin
ULAN BATOR
MONGOLIA
Kurile Is
ETEROFU
Shinokappu B
MANCHURIA
HARBIN
(MANCHUKUO)
VLADIVOSTOK
Hokkaido
MUKDEN
PEKING
KOREA
SEOUL
SEA OF JAPAN
Honshu
C H I N A
TSINGTAO
TOKYO
Shikoku
JAPAN

7 March–22 June 1944
Japanese invasion of
N-E India repulsed

NANKING
HANKOW
NAGASAKI
Kyushu
Kagoshima B
SHANGHAI
CHUNGKING Kiang
Yangtze
CHANGSHA
BONIN IS
Burma Road
DELHI
NEPAL
IMPHAL
KUNMING
CANTON
RYUKYU Is
OKINAWA
MARCUS
Ganges
CALCUTTA
LASHIO
MANDALAY
HANOI
HAIPHONG
HONG KONG
Formosa
(Taiwan)
IWO JIMA
I N D I A
BOMBAY
BURMA
HAINAN
Luzon
Mariana
Islands
15 Jur
SAIPAN
RANGOON
**THAI-
LAND**
**FRENCH
INDO-CHINA**
MANILA
**PHILIPPINE
ISLANDS**
GUAM
18 F
EN
BAY OF BENGAL
BANGKOK
SAIGON
LEYTE
21 July 1944
MADRAS
ANDAMAN
IS
Mindanao
YAP
TRUK
TRINCOMALEE
NICOBAR
IS
KOTA BHARU
N BORNEO
DAVAO
PALAU IS
C a r o l i n e   I s l
COLOMBO
Ceylon
SOUTH CHINA
SEA
Molucca Passage
Equator
MALAYA
SARAWAK
HALMAHERA
26 Dec 194
ADDU
ATOLL
South East Asia
Command
(Mountbatten)
SINGAPORE
Borneo
Sumatra
DUTCH   EAST   INDIES
New Guinea
ADMIRALTY
IS
NEW
IRELAND
1 F
NEW
BRITAIN
RABAUL
BO
BATAVIA
Java
FLORES
PAPUA
NEW
GEORGIA
I N D I A N   O C E A N
TIMOR
PORT
MORESBY
7
COCOS IS
Makassar Str
Celebes
TIMOR SEA
ARAFURA SEA
CORAL S
DARWIN
30 June 19

Aug 1942–July 1944
US/Australian landings
along north coast of
New Guinea

South-West
Pacific Area
(MacArthur)

Western
Queensland
ROCKHAMP
A U S T R A L I A
Australia
BRISB
South
Australia
PERTH
New
South Wales
ADELAIDE
SYDNEY
CANBERRA
Victoria
MELBOURNE

ALLIED COMMAND BOUNDARIES,
2 JULY 1942
SUBDIVISIONS OF PACIFIC OCEAN AREAS
LIMIT OF JAPANESE EXPANSION,
6 AUGUST 1942
AREA REOCCUPIED BY AMERICAN FORCES,
6 AUGUST 1942–AUG 1944
1 Nov 1944   DATES OF MAIN AMERICAN LANDINGS
AREA OCCUPIED BY JAPANESE FORCES,
JUNE–AUGUST 1944
MERCATOR'S PROJECTION

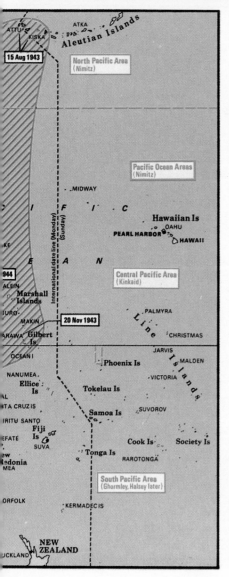

Right: Wrecked Japanese aircraft seen at an airfield near Tokyo in 1945.
Far right, top: A Martin Mariner flying boat seen in bright prewar color scheme.
Far right, middle: The USS Trippe *seen in 1940. She carries four 5-inch guns.*
Far right, bottom: Stuart tanks of a US armored division seen in China in 1945.
Below: The final stages of the Pacific war.

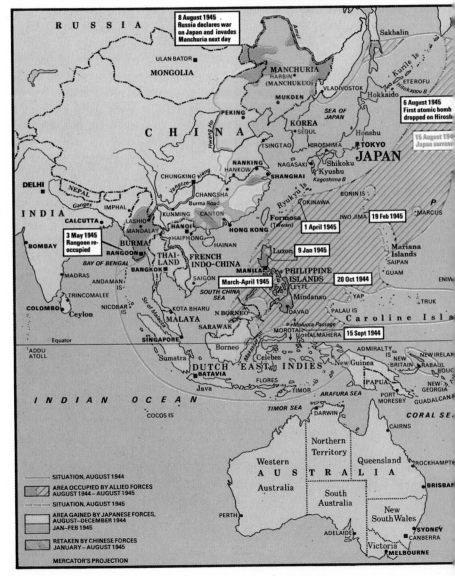

R U S S I A

8 August 1945
Russia declares war
on Japan and invades
Manchuria next day

Sakhalin

ULAN BATOR

MONGOLIA

MANCHURIA
HARBIN
(MANCHUKUO)

Kurile Is.

ETEROFU
Tokappu B

VLADIVOSTOK

Hokkaido

6 August 1945
First atomic bomb
dropped on Hirosh

PEKING

SEA OF
JAPAN

C H I N A

KOREA
SEOUL

Honshu

15 August 194
Japan surrend

Hwang Ho

TSINGTAO

HIROSHIMA

TOKYO
JAPAN

NANKING
HANKOW

NAGASAKI

Shikoku
Kyushu
Kagoshima B

CHUNGKING

Yangtze Kiang

SHANGHAI

DELHI

NEPAL

CHANGSHA

Ryukyu Is.

BONIN IS

Ganges

IMPHAL

Burma Road

OKINAWA

MARCUS

I N D I A

CALCUTTA

KUNMING

CANTON

Formosa
(Taiwan)

IWO JIMA

19 Feb 1945

P

LASHIO
MANDALAY

HANOI

HONG KONG

1 April 1945

3 May 1945
Rangoon re-
occupied

HAIPHONG

BURMA

THAI-
LAND

FRENCH
INDO-CHINA

HAINAN

Luzon

9 Jan 1945

Mariana
Islands
SAIPAN

BOMBAY

MADRAS

BAY OF BENGAL

BANGKOK

SAIGON

MANILA

PHILIPPINE
ISLANDS

20 Oct 1944

GUAM

ANDAMAN
IS

March-April 1945

LEYTE

YAP

ENIW

SOUTH CHINA
SEA

Mindanao

TRINCOMALEE

NICOBAR
IS

KOTA BHARU

N BORNEO

DAVAO

PALAU IS

TRUK

C a r o l i n e   I s l a

COLOMBO

Ceylon

MALAYA

SARAWAK

Molucca Passage

MOROTAI

HALMAHERA

15 Sept 1944

Equator

SINGAPORE

Borneo

ADMIRALTY
IS

NEW
BRITAIN

NEW IRELAN

ADDU
ATOLL

Sumatra

Celebes

New Guinea

RABAUL
BOUC

DUTCH   EAST   INDIES

BATAVIA

FLORES

PAPUA

NEW
GEORGIA

Java

TIMOR

PORT
MORESBY

GUADALCAN

I N D I A N   O C E A N

COCOS IS

ARAFURA SEA

CORAL SE

TIMOR SEA

DARWIN

CAIRNS

ROCKHAMPT

Northern
Territory

Queensland

Western
Australia

A U S T R A L I A

BRISBAN

South
Australia

PERTH

New
South Wales

ADELAIDE

SYDNEY
CANBERRA

Victoria

MELBOURNE

SITUATION, AUGUST 1944

AREA OCCUPIED BY ALLIED FORCES
AUGUST 1944 – AUGUST 1945

SITUATION, AUGUST 1945

AREA GAINED BY JAPANESE FORCES,
AUGUST–DECEMBER 1944
JAN–FEB 1945

RETAKEN BY CHINESE FORCES
JANUARY – AUGUST 1945

MERCATOR'S PROJECTION

ATTU · KISKA ᐧ ATKA

Aleutian Islands

MIDWAY

P A C I F I C

International date line (Monday)
(Sunday)

Hawaiian Is
OAHU
PEARL HARBOR
HAWAII

KE

E A N

ALEIN

Marshall
Islands

JURO
MAKIN

ARAWA Gilbert
Is

PALMYRA

Line

CHRISTMAS

OCEAN I

JARVIS

Phoenix Is

MALDEN

NANUMEA

Ellice
Is

Tokelau Is

VICTORIA

Islands

TA CRUZ IS

IRITU SANTO

SUVOROV

Samoa Is

EFATE

Fiji
Is

SUVA

Cook Is

Society Is

ew
edonia
MEA

Tonga Is

RAROTONGA

ORFOLK

KERMADEC IS

NEW
ZEALAND

UCKLAND

31

Above: US Marine artillery on Bougainville.

Above: Jungle fighting on New Guinea.

Above: Scenes of devastation in Hiroshima after the atomic attack.

(OKW). Keitel is appointed to head it. This is a serious demotion for the army. Instead of having a Ministry of their own they are now only a department (OKH) within a larger organization. More seriously for the future, the army expertise in strategic planning and in policy advice is put at a distance from Hitler, further confirming his supremacy and isolation. Foreign Minister Neurath and Papen, who is ambassador in Vienna, are also dismissed to be replaced by reliable Nazis. Brauchitsch becomes Commander in Chief of the army. The army does succeed in obtaining a court of inquiry on the Fritsch case in which he is cleared of the charges against him but this is not held until after the *Anschluss* when Hitler's position is impregnable.

Also this month Austrian Chancellor Schuschnigg visits Hitler and is browbeaten into giving greater recognition to the Austrian Nazis. The Nazi Seyss-Inquart is to become interior minister.

MARCH 1938

The Germans annex Austria in the *Anschluss*. Hitler acts because early in the month Chancellor Schuschnigg has tried to organize a plebiscite to strengthen his hand against the Austrian Nazis. At the last minute Schuschnigg is prepared to cancel the plebiscite and resigns. The Nazis demand that Seyss-Inquart be made Chancellor, they take to the streets to seize control of government offices and President Miklas gives in. Even so, on the morning of 12 March German troops cross the border. Mussolini, once so opposed to German penetration of Austria, does nothing. On 13 March Austria is proclaimed a province of the German Reich (contravening Versailles). The arrests begin – more than 70,000 in Vienna alone. In a plebiscite held later under Nazi auspices 99.75 percent of the 'vote' is in favor of the new situation. Hitler is even able to claim that his action is in line with the principles of self-determination advocated by President Wilson and enshrined in the Versailles terms.

APRIL 1938

In a series of battles in Shantung province the Japanese North China Army loses heavily to the Chinese Nationalist forces.

MAY 1938

A partial Czech mobilization is announced because of reports of German military preparations. Britain and France back the Czechs with a warning to Germany. Although supporting the Czechs in public, the British and French are annoyed at having to risk war on the basis of some tenuous rumors. They fail to realize that the German attitude is more concilliatory for a while, although Hitler is furious at having thus to climb down.

JUNE–JULY 1938

The Japanese attack west from Kaifeng but their advance is halted near Chengchow by massive flooding caused by the Chinese breaching the dikes along the Yellow River. The Japanese lose a considerable number of casualties in this flood but it is also estimated that as many as 1,000,000 Chinese peasants have died. Many more are made homeless.

In July there is an important Soviet-Japanese clash on the border of Manchukuo near Lake Hassan. This has been provoked by the Japanese. Both sides reinforce and in the fierce fighting which follows the Japanese lose heavily.

SEPTEMBER 1938

The Munich Crisis. The Czechoslovakian state created by Versailles has in 1938 a population of about 14,000,000 of whom 3,000,000 are German speaking. These Germans live principally in the area known as the Sudetenland. Agitation for union of this area with Germany is led by Konrad Henlein's Sudeten German Party with strong Nazi support. There has been trouble in the past and more occurs following an inflammatory speech by Hitler on 12 September. By 15 September the Czechs have control of the situation and Henlein has fled to Germany. Chamberlain flies to Germany, despite Hitler's hand in the trouble, in an attempt to find a solution. He has a plan which he has only discussed with a few advisers and not with the French for ceding to Germany areas where more than half of the population supports this. This is acceptable to Hitler. The French have up to this stage been resigned to fighting for Czechoslovakia but under British pressure they join in making President Beneš agree to this plan. Hitler now says that this is not enough. Chamberlain returns to Germany on the 22nd and after talks he again wishes to give in to Hitler but he is opposed by the British Cabinet on his return. On the 23rd the Czechs mobilize. On the 27th the British Fleet is sent to its war stations. Negotiations have been going on behind the scenes and an appeal has been sent to Mussolini to mediate, convincing Hitler of Anglo-French weakness. Chamberlain and Daladier go to Munich on the 29th and accept proposals put forward by Mussolini but drafted by the German Foreign Office which amount virtually to

Hitler's last demands. Just before leaving, Chamberlain has Hitler sign a vague friendship agreement and with this he proclaims on his return home that he has secured 'peace for our time.'

Chamberlain's policy has dominated the Anglo-French side of the negotiations. He seems to have believed that fundamentally Hitler is a normal, reasonable and responsible statesman who will keep his word. He is, therefore, able to regard the Czech problem as a small central-European issue and the French guarantee as a way of dragging Britain into war for comparatively minor reasons. France is presented with a choice of staying aligned with Britain or fighting for the Czechs. The Czechs are, therefore, abandoned. Some historians argue that to have gone to war at this time would have been foolish because Britain and France were most unprepared. This argument is not convincing. At this time Czechoslovakia is perhaps the only country in Europe which is ready for war. The Czech army has almost as many as trained troops as the German army and is as well, if not better, equipped. The Czech frontier defenses are stronger than the French Maginot Line and are far more comprehensive. At the height of the crisis the Germans can only allocate five divisions to the Western Front to meet the whole of the French army. Certainly Britain and France are weak in the air, but the necessity for a long campaign against the Czechs would almost certainly have prevented heavy attacks from the Luftwaffe. The argument that time is gained for rearmament is also weak. German production continues to be greater and their lead is extended by September 1939.

Above: Hitler and Chamberlain (right) at Munich, 29 September 1938.

OCTOBER 1938

President Beneš of Czechoslovakia resigns as the Germans move in to the Sudetenland. President Hacha takes over. Czechoslovakia is now split into three fairly autonomous provinces: Bohemia-Moravia, Slovakia and Ruthenia. Poland joins in the dismemberment, taking the long-disputed Teschen area from the Czechs.

The Japanese Central China Army completes its advance up the Yangtze to Hankow and captures the city. The battles of this campaign are the fiercest of the whole war between China and Japan. Chiang Kai-shek and the Nationalist government move to Chungking. In a separate campaign the Japanese forces make landings near Hong Kong and advance inland to take Canton. The Japanese now control all China's major ports, cutting the Nationalists off from most of their support from the outside world. Some supplies can still come in through French Indochina or over the Burma Road but the main route and source for these is now through the USSR.

The Japanese end their major military operations against Chiang, believing that he has been reduced to a merely local power.

NOVEMBER 1938

The Japanese announce the establishment of the New Order for East Asia. Effectively this means that Japan is to be the dominant economic power, with the Western countries perhaps allowed access to what is left over. Britain and the United States, who have already been worried by Japanese conduct in China, now become more-definitely opposed to the Japanese expansion.

The partition of Czechoslovakia continues, with Hungary now getting a share. This is achieved by the German-sponsored Vienna Award which the Czechs cannot resist. A large area of Ruthenia and 1,000,000 people are given to Hungary.

In Germany itself the persecution of the Jews is stepped up. On the night of 9/10 November, following the murder of a German diplomat in Paris by a young Jew, Jewish homes and businesses throughout Germany are attacked by Nazi thugs in what becomes known as the *Kristallnacht.* There is worldwide condemnation.

DECEMBER 1938

France and Germany reach a friendship agreement similar to Chamberlain's Munich paper. Germany disavows interest in Alsace-Lorraine and during the coming months Hitler will quote this as proof of his peaceful intentions.

FEBRUARY 1939
Japanese troops occupy Hainan Island. In Britain this is seen as a threat to communications between Hong Kong and Singapore.

MARCH 1939
Germany completes the destruction of Czechoslovakia. Following internal political troubles early in the month President Hacha dismisses the Ruthenian and Slovak governments. This is an unexpected opportunity for Hitler. Hacha is summoned to Berlin and forced to capitulate while at the same time the Slovak parliament is pressured into accepting an independence proclamation. German troops begin to move in, and on 15 March Hitler proclaims the establishment of the Protectorate of Bohemia and Moravia. Hungary also takes the opportunity to take some land in the Carpatho-Ukraine. Britain and France do nothing, saying that the guarantees they gave at Munich were to the whole of Czechoslovakia and that these are rendered invalid by the secession of Slovakia.

Germany's gains continue with an ultimatum presented to Lithuania that the district around Memel be ceded. This is done on 22 March. On 23 March an economic agreement is concluded with Rumania which gives Germany considerable access to oil at privileged terms.

The only Allied response is the granting to Prime Minister Daladier of special powers by the French Parliament and at the end of the month the issue of a British and French guarantee to Poland. Although by the terms of this offer Poland is to decide when it should be put into action, from the British and French point of view it is seen more as a device for putting pressure on Poland to reach a reasonable compromise with Hitler. Unfortunately, this agreement can only make contact with the USSR more difficult without putting anything very strong in its place.

APRIL 1939
Britain and France issue guarantees to Greece and Rumania against both Germany and Italy. The Italian attack on Albania begins early in the month. On 18 April Litvinov approaches the Western powers with proposals for talks. Toward the end of the month Hitler rejects a mediation attempt by President Roosevelt. He revokes the 1934 Nonaggression Pact with Poland, the 1935 Anglo-German Naval Agreement and in a typically violent speech demands that Danzig be returned to Germany and that Poland give Germany ground for a road through the Polish Corridor linking with Danzig and the German province of East Prussia.

MAY 1939
Britain introduces conscription.

Germany and Italy announce the agreement of a formal alliance, 'The Pact of Steel.' This is signed in Berlin on the 22nd.

Although Foreign Minister Litvinov is replaced by Molotov early in the month talks between the USSR and Britain and France begin later. Litvinov has been regarded as more in favor of collective security policies and contact with the West.

There are British proposals to limit Jewish entry to Palestine and to work to establish a joint Jewish and Arab government. These are resisted chiefly by the Zionist movement.

MAY–AUGUST 1939
There is more fighting between the USSR and Japan. The incident this time is on the border between Manchukuo and Outer Mongolia near the Khalka River. The Japanese are the first to reinforce and they gain the upper hand for a while. The Soviets then increase their strength and, led by General Zhukov, they win a major victory by 20 August. This defeat and the simultaneous political developments in Europe seriously worry the Japanese and they come to terms. This indication of the efficiency of the Red Army is little noticed in Europe.

JUNE–JULY 1939
Formal talks start in Moscow between the Soviets and British and French representatives. Britain and France are trying to arrange help for Poland and Rumania. Stalin's attitude is rather different. In essence he seems to be prepared to fight Hitler now only if he is granted a free hand in the future in Eastern Europe. He wants Poland, for example, to allow Soviet troops on her territory. The British and French feel that they are being asked to blackmail Poland and the talks do not make much progress for the moment.

Late in July there is an important meeting in Warsaw between a British and a Polish representative at which the British are given two Polish Enigma coding machines. These are based on the German versions of the machine and give a valuable start to the code-breaking effort which will be a vital tool for Allied commanders in the future.

At the end of the month a further step is taken toward war in the Far East when the United States announces its intention to withdraw from the 1911 commercial treaty with Japan.

12 AUGUST 1939

An Anglo-French military mission begins talks in Moscow. They continue until 19 August but no agreement is reached because of the dispute about Soviet troops being allowed into Poland.

15 AUGUST 1939

British forces in Egypt are reinforced by the arrival of Indian troops at Suez.

19 AUGUST 1939

The German navy sends 14 U-Boats to patrol positions in the North Atlantic because of the tense international situation. The pocket battleships *Graf Spee* and *Deutschland* are sent off on 21 and 24 August. Supply ships are also sent out to cooperate with these units.

20 AUGUST 1939

German-Soviet negotiations have been proceeding for some time at growing speed and Hitler now sends a personal message to Stalin asking if he will receive Foreign Minister Ribbentrop. An economic agreement has already been prepared.

21 AUGUST 1939

The Soviet-German economic agreement is signed and Stalin announces that he will see Ribbentrop for further talks.

23-24 AUGUST 1939

The Soviet-German Nonaggression Pact is concluded and signed in Moscow. Secret terms of the agreement define the countries' spheres of interest. Poland is to be divided approximately in half, Germany is to be allowed to control Lithuania and the USSR is allotted Finland, Estonia and Latvia. Later this will be revised to place Lithuania in the Soviet sphere and to give more of Poland to Germany.

There is an exchange of messages between Chamberlain and Hitler in which Chamberlain warns that Britain is prepared to help Poland with force and Hitler says that he can never renounce his interest in Danzig and the Corridor. Forster, the Nazi leader in Danzig, is proclaimed head of state by the Danzig Senate.

25 AUGUST 1939

Hitler orders the German attack on Poland to begin on 26 August but he cancels it at the last moment on hearing that Britain and Poland have signed a formal alliance and that Mussolini refuses to join a war at this stage. Britain and France are trying independently to talk to Hitler through Mussolini. They only succeed in exposing their disunity since France is notably more intransigent than Britain. The British are still looking for a compromise over Danzig.

26-30 AUGUST 1939

There is intense diplomatic activity in the major European capitals. The Swede Dahlerus is used as an emissary by the Germans and shuttles to and fro from London with various proposals. Hitler offers to negotiate if the Poles immediately send a representative with full powers to Berlin. The Poles are prepared to negotiate but realize only too well the pressure that will be put on any diplomat negotiating in Berlin.

31 AUGUST 1939

Hitler decides to invade Poland on 1 September. Mussolini proposes a European conference and the Polish Ambassador in Berlin makes another futile offer to negotiate. Hitler signs the order at noon and the German troops move up to the frontier. At 2000 hours the German radio station at Gliewitz is 'attacked.' The attackers are members of the SS in Polish uniforms and they leave behind some bodies (of concentration-camp inmates) in Polish uniforms to convince the world that Poland is the aggressor.

1 SEPTEMBER 1939

Poland At 0445 hours the German forces invade Poland without a declaration of war. The operation is code named *Fall Weiss* (Plan White). The Germans put 53 divisions into the attack, including their six armored and all their motorized units. Of the divisions left on the Western Front only about 10 are regarded by the Germans as being fit for any kind of action. General Brauchitsch, the Commander in Chief, will be left in full charge of the campaign and, indeed, will only meet Hitler on a few occasions in the course of the battles. Bock leads Army Group North and Rundstedt leads Army Group South. Bock's army commanders are Küchler (Fourth Army) and Kluge (Third Army). Rundstedt's men are Blaskowitz (Eighth Army), Reichenau (Tenth Army) and List (Fourteenth Army). Guderian and Kleist lead Panzer Corps. Air support comes from Kesselring's and Löhr's Air Fleets which have around 1600 aircraft. Rundstedt's troops, advancing from Silesia, are to provide the main German attacks. Blaskowitz on the left is to move toward Poznan, List on the right toward Krakow and the Carpathian flank, while the principal thrust is to be delivered by Reichenau who is to advance in the center to the Vistula between Warsaw and Sandomierz. Küchler from East Prussia is to move south toward Warsaw and the line of the Bug to the east. Kluge is to cross the Polish Corridor and join Küchler in moving south.

The Poles have 23 regular infantry divisions prepared with seven more assembling, one weak armored division and an inadequate quantity of artillery. They also have a considerable force of cavalry. (Although it is commonly believed, it is not true that cavalry will be used later in the campaign to charge German tanks.) The reserve units were only called up on 30 August and are not, therefore, mobilized as yet. In the air almost all the 500 Polish planes are obsolete and will be able to do very little to blunt the impact of the German attack. During this period the Germans also strike at Warsaw, Lodz and Krakow by air. The Polish Commander in Chief, Marshal Rydz-Smigly, has deployed the stronger parts of his army in the northwestern half of the country, including large forces in the Poznan area and in the Polish Corridor. Although there are few natural barriers favoring defense in the western half of the country (the dry summer weather confirms this), he hopes to hold the Germans to only gradual gains. By thus stationing his forces well forward and by the attacking tactics adopted, Rydz-Smigly has risked a serious defeat. Many units will be overrun before their reinforcements from the reserve mobilization can arrive.

All along the front the superior training, equipment and strength of the Germans quickly brings them the advantage in the first battles. At sea, as in the air, the story of Polish inferiority and crushing early attacks is much the same. Three of the four Polish destroyers manage to leave for Britain before hostilities begin and later one submarine also escapes. On the first day the old pre-Dreadnought battleship *Schleswig-Holstein* bombards the Polish naval base at Westerplatte.

Diplomatic Relations Britain and France immediately demand a German withdrawal from Poland. The British army is mobilized. Italy announces that she will not take any military initiative.

Britain, Home Front Because of the fear of air attacks the evacuation of young children from London and other supposedly vulnerable areas is begun.

2 SEPTEMBER 1939

Poland Rundstedt's troops are already over the River Warta in many places after rapid but expensive victories in the frontier battles. Krakow is now near the front line. In the north Kluge's Fourth Army make contact with the Third Army from East Prussia. The Luftwaffe is spreading chaos in the Polish rear. The Polish regular troops have been stationed too far forward so the German advance is soon in their rear areas, preventing the movement of reserves and completely dislocating any communications left unscathed by the Luftwaffe's repeated attacks in support of the ground forces.

Diplomatic Relations Throughout the day there are frantic talks in London and Paris attempting to decide how to oppose Germany. Mussolini again declares Italian neutrality and calls for a peace conference. Germany announces that Norwegian neutrality will be respected.

The British Parliament is openly opposed to the passive line that Chamberlain's government is taking and in the evening the Cabinet decides to present an ultimatum to Germany. A French ultimatum is also to be sent.

3 SEPTEMBER 1939

Diplomatic Relations The British ultimatum to Germany expires at 1100 hours and at 1115 hours Chamberlain broadcasts to announce that war has begun. Australia and New Zealand also declare war immediately. Chamberlain forms a War Cabinet which includes Churchill as First Lord of the Admiralty (Navy Minister) and Eden as Secretary for the Dominions. Churchill and Eden have been the most prominent opponents of an appeasement policy. At 1135 hours, as if to confirm the state of war, there is an air-raid warning in London but it is a false alarm.

In the afternoon, at 1700 hours, the French follow suit and declare war in fact before their ultimatum expires.

Poland The Polish Lodz Army is now in retreat after being beaten in the frontier battles with Army Group South. General Reichenau's forces have crossed the Warta in some areas while List's troops are converging on Krakow.

Battle of the Atlantic The liner SS *Athenia* is torpedoed off the northwest coast of Ireland by *U.30* as the *Athenia* is believed to be an auxiliary cruiser. There are 112 dead including 28 American citizens. Britain believes that this is the start of unrestricted submarine warfare but in fact after this the German naval authorities impose even stricter controls. The controls are gradually removed after about the middle of October.

At this stage 39 of the German fleet of 58 U-Boats are at sea. Doenitz, the submarine chief, had hoped for a fleet of 300 before contemplating war with Britain. Two U-Boats are sunk this month. Allied shipping losses are 53 ships, of which 41 of 153,800 tons are sunk by German submarines.

CHRONOLOGY

4 SEPTEMBER 1939
Europe, Air Operations The first attacks by RAF Bomber Command go in against German warships in the Heligoland Bight. The *Admiral Scheer* is hit three times but the bombs do not explode. Of the 24 attacking aircraft six are lost. There is no question at this stage of attacking targets in Germany. For the next few months only leaflets are dropped and when the question is raised in Parliament in October the government reply is that there can be no thought of bombing industry in the Ruhr because it is private property!
Poland In the north the Polish Modlin Army begins to retreat after putting up a stubborn defense around Mlawa. In the south General Reichenau's forces have already advanced more than 50 miles.

5 SEPTEMBER 1939
United States, Politics The United States proclaims its neutrality. On 12 September naval patrols to protest this status are begun.
South Africa, Politics After a dispute in the existing Cabinet over whether to join the war. Smuts forms a new ministry and on 6 September South Africa declares war on Germany.

6 SEPTEMBER 1939
Poland Reichenau's Tenth Army continues to lead the German advance, having already penetrated to the east of Lodz. Krakow is taken by troops of List's Fourteenth Army. The Polish government and supreme command leave Warsaw. They issue orders for their forces to retire to the line of the Rivers Narew, Vistula and San.

7 SEPTEMBER 1939
Western Front French patrols cross the frontier into Germany near Saarbrucken. The French mobilization is too slow and their tactical system too inflexible to permit any grander offensive operation. These gentle probings continue until 17 September when a larger advance is meant to be made but is in fact cancelled because the Polish collapse makes it pointless.
Poland The Polish naval base at Westerplatte surrenders after renewed German bombardment. The Polish command decides that it will be impossible to hold the line of the Narew although the order to do so has only been in force for one day. The forces in the Narew area are to retire to the Bug.
Battle of the Atlantic The first British Atlantic convoys set out. The convoy system has already been reintroduced on the east coast. Although escorts can only be provided as far as 12.5

degrees West they do provide effective protection against U-Boats. Many of the faster ships and some particularly slow ones do not sail in convoy at this stage or later in the war. During 1939 almost all the U-Boat successes are from such 'independents.'

8 SEPTEMBER 1939
Poland Advance units of a part of Reichenau's force reach the southeastern suburbs of Warsaw late in the day. Other sections of Tenth Army are heavily engaged around Radom. List's Fourteenth Army reaches the San north and south of Přzemyśl. In the north Guderian's Panzer Corps is attacking along the line of the Bug east of Warsaw.

9 SEPTEMBER 1939
Poland The German 4th Panzer Division mounts an attack in the southeast suburbs of Warsaw but is beaten off. The German command believes that almost all the Polish forces have retired east of the Vistula but in fact unfought units from the Poznan Army and part of the Pomorze Group have joined together around Kutno. About 10 Polish divisions are assembled in this area under the command of General Kutrzeba. They now begin a counterattack over the Bzura against the German Eighth Army. The battles which follow will be the hardest fought of the campaign. For the first two or three days the Poles gain some success.

10 SEPTEMBER 1939
Diplomatic Relations Canada declares war on Germany.
Western Front The first major units of the BEF begin to land in France. Field Marshal Lord Gort is in command. Small advance parties have been arriving since 4 September. In the first month 160,000 men, 24,000 vehicles and 140,000 tons of supplies are sent to France.

11 SEPTEMBER 1939
Poland The German forces cross the River San north and south of Přzemyśl. The battle on the Bzura continues but the leaders of the German Army Group South, Rundstedt and his Chief of Staff, Manstein, are beginning to assemble reinforcements for Eighth Army.
Allied Planning The first meeting of the Anglo-French Supreme War Council takes place.

12 SEPTEMBER 1939
Poland Some of List's troops are fighting near Lvov while others are moving north from their bridgeheads over the San.

13 SEPTEMBER 1939
Poland A small German force begins to cross the Vistula just south of Warsaw. The Bzura battles are now going badly for the Polish forces. The heaviest fighting will be over by 15 September but some engagements will continue until the 19th. Although the Germans will take their largest single haul of 150,000 prisoners in this battle, by 19 September units of two Polish brigades and elements of others will manage to escape to Warsaw.

France, Politics Prime Minister Daladier forms a War Cabinet in which he is responsible for foreign affairs as well as his normal duties.

14 SEPTEMBER 1939
Poland German troops enter Gdynia. Guderian's XIX Panzer Corps reaches Brest Litovsk.

16 SEPTEMBER 1939
Poland Warsaw is now surrounded but a surrender demand is refused. Part of List's army is still fighting west of Lvov while other units are advancing north to link with Guderian's forces who are maintaining their attack along the Bug.

17 SEPTEMBER 1939
Poland Soviet troops enter Poland. Naturally because of the German attack there is almost no defense in the east. The Soviets employ two Army Groups or Fronts. The Poles have only 18 battalions in the east of their country.

Battle of the Atlantic The British aircraft carrier *Courageous* is sunk by *U.29* while on anti-submarine patrol off the southwest of Ireland. The carrier *Ark Royal* had a lucky escape on 14 September from a submarine attack while similarly misemployed. After these incidents the carriers are withdrawn from such work. *Courageous* has been one of the most effective of the British carriers.

18 SEPTEMBER 1939
Poland, Politics The Polish president, Moscicki and the Commander in Chief Rydz-Smigly enter Rumania and are interned. They leave behind messages telling their troops to fight on.

19 SEPTEMBER 1939
Poland The Soviet advance reaches the Hungarian frontier. In the north Vilna is taken. The Soviets link up with the Germans at Brest Litovsk which is given up to the Soviets according to the provisions of the secret agreement of 23 August.

21 SEPTEMBER 1939
Rumania The Rumanian prime minister, Calinescu, is murdered by the Iron Guard, a Fascist organization.

22 SEPTEMBER 1939
Poland The rapidly advancing Soviet troops take Lvov.

23 SEPTEMBER 1939
Japan, Politics Admiral Nomura becomes foreign minister in General Abe's recently appointed government. Between now and their fall in January 1940 some conciliatory moves are made toward the United States. These are not reciprocated and this strengthens the beliefs and standing of the more militant Japanese politicians.

25 SEPTEMBER 1939
Poland The Germans step up their bombardment of Warsaw and add heavy air attacks to it. Hitler wishes to complete the conquest as soon as possible and since the garrison is fairly strong it is necessary to force them to submit by terrorizing the civilian population. The bombing continues until the surrender.

Germany, Home Front Food rationing is introduced.

Above: Hitler enters Danzig, 20 September 1939.

26 SEPTEMBER 1939

Battle of the Atlantic After a near miss in an air attack German propaganda machine claims that the *Ark Royal* has been sunk. This is the first of several such false claims made during the coming months.

27 SEPTEMBER 1939

Poland Warsaw surrenders after two days of vicious bombardment. There are 150,000 prisoners.

Germany, Planning Hitler tells his service chiefs that he plans to attack in the west as soon as possible. He has reached this decision entirely on his own. The army's opposition is very strong.

Britain, Home Front Chancellor of the Exchequer Sir John Simon presents his first War Budget. Income tax is raised from 5/6d (25½p) to 7/6d (37½p) in the pound.

28 SEPTEMBER 1939

Poland The fortress of Modlin surrenders to the Germans and elsewhere the Polish resistance is nearly over.

29 SEPTEMBER 1939

Diplomatic Relations A Soviet-German Treaty of Friendship is announced. By its terms Poland is partitioned. The Soviet Union gets slightly more land but the Germans now control the majority of the population and the industrial and mining centers.

The Soviets begin to put real pressure on the Baltic states. A Soviet-Estonian Mutual Assistance Pact is signed, giving the USSR the use of bases in Estonia. A similar agreement is concluded with Latvia on 5 October and with Lithuania on 10 October. Vilna is ceded to Lithuania. These pacts are designed to ensure Soviet control of the Baltic, particularly in the event of future German aggression.

30 SEPTEMBER 1939

Poland, Politics A new Polish government is formed in Paris. Raczkiewicz is the new president and General Sikorski the Commander in Chief of the Armed Forces.

OCTOBER 1939

Atomic Research President Roosevelt, after receiving advice from Einstein, sets up the Advisory Committee on Uranium. The research at this stage is still fairly slowly paced.

1 OCTOBER 1939

German Raiders The first news of the German pocket-battleships *Graf Spee* and *Deutschland* reaches the Admiralty. On 30 September the *Graf Spee* sank its first merchant ship. Before the battle of December *Graf Spee* will sink nine ships of 50,000 tons altogether, a totally inadequate return for such a valuable unit.

In October Allied shipping losses are 196,000 tons. Five U-Boats are sunk.

Poland Admiral Unrug's Polish garrison on the Hela Peninsula surrenders after a gallant fight. As well as land attacks they have endured a considerable naval bombardment.

2 OCTOBER 1939

World Affairs The Pan-American Conference, with 21 countries participating, establishes a 300-mile security zone off the American coast in which any act of war is to be interpreted as a hostile act against the nearby American country. The belligerents will, of course, ignore this.

3 OCTOBER 1939

France The I Corps of the BEF takes over responsibility for an appropriate section of the Franco-Belgian frontier.

Poland The last significant units of the Polish army surrender near Luck. The Germans have taken 700,000 prisoners and the Soviets 200,000. Polish casualties have been severe. The Germans have lost 10,000 dead and 30,000 wounded. Many Poles have escaped and will gradually find their way to the West.

Although tank units have played a notable part in the campaign, it is interesting to note that the contemporary German official appreciations lay more stress on the traditional-style infantry battles. The tank forces are seen at this stage, except by enthusiasts like Guderian, as little more than useful auxiliaries who can help the infantry do the real work. The first plans for the attack in the west will reflect this official attitude.

5 OCTOBER 1939

German Raiders Eight British and French hunting groups are formed to hunt for the *Graf Spee*. At this stage the British and the French can afford to divert considerable forces to such a task.

5–23 OCTOBER 1939

Diplomatic Relations The Soviets continue their moves to strengthen their position in the Baltic by asking the Finnish government for new talks on altering their boundaries. The Soviets want the cession of some territory near Leningrad, control of the islands in the Gulf of Finland, use of the port of Hanko and other rearrangements of the border in the far north near Murmansk. In return they offer rather more land than they demand in the Suomussalmi area. The Finns only feel able to offer a much smaller range of concessions. There are talks on 12–14 and 23 October but there is little change in the terms offered by either side. The Soviet demands are probably based on genuine worries about the security of Leningrad and Murmansk but, understandably, the Finns believe that to give in would only invite more extreme claims. On 6 October the Finns mobilize their standing military forces. On 10 October they call up their reserves and begin the evacuation of some frontier districts.

6 OCTOBER 1939
Diplomatic Relations In a major speech to the Reichstag Hitler speaks of his desire for peace with Britain and France. Hitler says that up to now he has done nothing more than correct the unjust Versailles Treaty and that he has no war aims against France or Britain. He blames warmongers like Churchill for the present state of affairs and calls for a European conference to meet to resolve the few remaining differences. On 10 and 12 October Daladier and Chamberlain respectively reject the offer. Chamberlain says that to consider such terms would be to forgive Germany for all aggression.

8 OCTOBER 1939
Baltic States In accordance with the Soviet-German agreement, 'Reich Germans' are evacuated from the Baltic States to what the Nazis believe is their racial home in Germany.

9 OCTOBER 1939
Germany, Planning Hitler issues Directive No 6. Its message is simple: 'Should it become evident in the near future that England, and, under her influence, France also, are not disposed to bring the war to an end, I have decided, without further loss of time to go over to the offensive.'

The offensive is to be directed across the Low Countries and is intended to defeat strong sections of the French and British armies when these arrive to help the Dutch and Belgians. The ground taken is to provide protection for the Ruhr and to give bases for the air war against Britain. The aims of the plan are, therefore, limited when compared with the Schlieffen Plan of 1914 or with the scheme which is actually adopted in May 1940. There is no mention of completely defeating France.

This order is a further blow to the autonomy of the German army. Their view is that, although it lies within Hitler's authority as head of state and Commander in Chief of the Wehrmacht to order an attack to be prepared as soon as possible, the army should be asked where and how this attack should take place. Even the normally subservient Keitel argues against Hitler on this issue.

10 OCTOBER 1939
Germany, Planning Admiral Raeder mentions to Hitler for the first time the possibility of invading Norway to secure naval and especially submarine bases (*see* 8 December 1939 and 27 January 1940). Churchill is, at this time, arguing in the British Cabinet that Norwegian coastal waters should be mined to interfere with German iron-ore traffic.

14 OCTOBER 1939
War at Sea The British battleship *Royal Oak* is sunk at anchor in the main fleet base at Scapa Flow by *U.47* commanded by Kapitänleutnant Prien. This is a major blow to British prestige as well as an indication of a very serious real weakness in the defenses.

19 OCTOBER 1939
Germany, Planning OKH issues *Fall Gelb* (Plan Yellow) in response to Hitler's Directive of 9 October. It provides for a holding action on the French border with the main attack being sent through central Belgium and some attention being devoted to the Dutch. It is reissued in a slightly modified form on 29 October with the main thrust shifted slightly south and less strength being sent against Holland. It is clear that neither Hitler nor any of the senior commanders is particularly happy with it and there is much debate as to how it should be modified. This continues until mid-February 1940 when those voices calling for a radical change manage to have their way. General Manstein will lead this movement.

Poland Hitler officially incorporates western Poland into the German Reich. The first Jewish ghetto is established in Lublin.

31 OCTOBER–9 NOVEMBER 1939
Diplomatic Relations There are three further sets of discussions between the Soviets and the Finns over the recent Soviet demands. No agreement is reached. The Finnish negotiators wish to accept some concessions but their government sees the Soviet attempts to bargain as a sign of weakness. Marshal Mannerheim opposes this view. In fact, because Molotov has explained the nature of the talks in a public

speech, the Soviets are probably even more firmly committed with prestige at stake. Although it is not apparent to the Finns, there will be no more serious talks.

NOVEMBER 1939
Allied Intelligence Polish and French cryptanalysts working in France begin occasionally to read the Luftwaffe Enigma transmissions. This is the first such breakthrough of which later developments will give the British invaluable intelligence. The Luftwaffe is the least security conscious of the German services.

Battle of the Atlantic The German submarine campaign is less effective this month, sinking only 21 ships of 51,600 tons. More than twice this tonnage is sunk by mines.

4 NOVEMBER 1939
United States, Politics A modification of the Neutrality Acts passes into law in the United States. Although by its terms the ban on American ships and citizens in clearly defined war zones is confirmed, it does provide for supply of arms to belligerents on a 'Cash and Carry' basis. Such arms must be ordered from private companies, paid for on the nail and transported to the war zone in the buyer's own ships. British naval strength means that, as is intended, only the Allies will benefit from this. Within a few days both the British and the French establish Purchasing Missions in Washington.

5 NOVEMBER 1939
Germany, Planning Brauchitsch meets Hitler to discuss the plans for the attack in the west. He argues very strongly that it should not take place as scheduled on 12 November because of weaknesses in the army. Hitler shouts him down.

General Halder, Brauchitsch's Chief of Staff, leads a group which has planned to overthrow Hitler if he is not persuaded to abandon the plan and timing of the attack. Although fairly detailed plans have been made for an army takeover, Halder has received few firm promises of support from the senior officers he has sounded out. The more junior officers tend to follow the Nazi line more closely and, from their positions, can see little wrong with Hitler's leadership. Halder, in any case, is unwilling as a senior serving officer to murder the head of state in wartime. This, combined with the poor prospects of success and a chance remark of Hitler's that suggests that he knows of a plot, persuades Halder to cancel the preparations.

It is important to note that the army opposition to Hitler is at this time not really based on moral principle but rather on resentment of his usurpation of their function as strategic planners and advisers.

7 NOVEMBER 1939
Germany, Planning The German attack in the west is postponed because of bad weather. This postponement will be repeated another 14 times until 16 January 1940.

Diplomatic Relations Queen Wilhelmina of the Netherlands and King Leopold of Belgium issue an appeal for peace. King George VI and President Lebrun reply on 12 November.

8 NOVEMBER 1939
Germany, Home Front A bomb explodes in the Burgerbraukeller in Munich shortly after Hitler has left after speaking there. It has in fact been planted by the Nazis themselves as an excuse for measures against what remains of the German Left and as anti-British propaganda.

Germany, Intelligence Two officers of the British Secret Intelligence Service (MI6), Major Stevens and Captain Best, are kidnapped at Venlo on the German-Dutch border. They have been lured there by a German agent who has promised that they will meet a disaffected German general. Unfortunately, one is carrying a list of British agents with him and from this, other indiscretions and from their interrogation, the Germans are able to arrest many British agents in Czechoslovakia and other occupied territory. The Venlo Incident is a serious setback for British Intelligence.

Poland Hans Frank is appointed Governor General of Poland by the Germans. He quickly encourages the persecution of the Jews.

16 NOVEMBER 1939
Czechoslovakia, Resistance After some recent unrest, martial law is declared in Prague. There are many shootings and deportations.

17 NOVEMBER 1939
Czechoslovakia, Politics A Czechoslovak National Committee is established in Paris. It is recognized by Britain and France in mid-December.

Allied Planning The Supreme Allied Council meeting in Paris endorses General Gamelin's Plan D (*see* 10 May 1940).

21 NOVEMBER 1939
War at Sea The brand-new British cruiser *Belfast* is seriously damaged by a mine in the Firth of Forth.

23 NOVEMBER 1939

War at Sea One of the first batch of magnetic mines to be dropped by air by the Germans lands on the mud flats at Shoeburyness. A British expert succeeds in defusing it and it can therefore be examined to devise countermeasures. These mines have been in use since 16 October and already they have been responsible for the loss of 50,000 tons of shipping.

German Raiders Between Iceland and the Faroes the British armed merchant cruiser *Rawalpindi*, armed with only four 6-inch guns, meets the German battlecruiser *Scharnhorst* and is blown out of the water. *Scharnhorst* has been sailing in the company of *Gneisenau* and because of this meeting they turn back from their raiding mission. They evade searches by many British ships during the next few days and return to base safely. Their escape is made easier by the German ability to read many of the British naval codes.

26–29 NOVEMBER 1939

Diplomatic Relations Relations between the Soviet Union and Finland continue to deteriorate. On the 26th there are attacks on Finland in the Soviet press and an official complaint concerning a spurious border incident. The Finnish reply to this is to suggest that both sides should pull their forces back from the border. The Soviets denounce this as ridiculous, saying that they would have to retreat to the suburbs of Leningrad to comply. On the 28th the Soviets renounce their nonaggression pact with Finland. Orders are issued to the Red Army to invade on the 30th. On the 29th the Soviets break off diplomatic relations while the Finns at last offer new discussions.

The approach of war can only be described as a failure for the Finnish government. They have no outside help, they are not well armed and the Soviets have no other worries for the moment. It should have been obvious that the Soviets meant business and that the correct interpretation of their willingness to negotiate was a desire to avoid war and not a sign of weakness.

30 NOVEMBER 1939

Finland The Russo-Finnish War begins. The Soviets invade Finland. Helsinki is bombed. The Finnish army can only muster about 150,000 men in nine divisions, with a tenth being formed. There are also a number of smaller independent units but their reserves of manpower are small. They have little heavy equipment and virtually no tanks. They are handicapped here in having relied on their limited domestic arms production

since late 1938 in an attempt to confirm their neutrality. Ammunition is an especially pressing problem and even toward the end of the war shell production will be only about 10 rounds per day for each gun in the army. The air force has about 100 planes which are not very modern. These weaknesses are partly offset by the training and morale of the Finnish troops. They are especially adept in rapid cross-country movement in winter conditions. Such conditions do, however, partly devalue the normal defensive strength of much of the terrain in the Karelian Isthmus, interspersed as it is with river lines and marshy ground. There are also some fairly strong fortifications in this area but the system is by no means comprehensive.

The Soviet forces present a very different picture. Their divisions are larger, with artillery components three times as strong as their Finnish equivalents and each is accompanied by more tanks than the entire Finnish army possesses. Independent tank and artillery units add even more weight. At the start the Soviets employ 26 divisions (not all at full strength), mustered in four armies. Seventh Army, the strongest with 12 divisions, attacks the five Finnish divisions on the Karelian Isthmus. Eighth Army advances in the area immediately to the north of Lake Ladoga, Ninth Army attacks from Soviet Karelia in the direction of the head of the Gulf of Bothnia and Fourteenth Army moves out from Murmansk in the far north. Despite this lavish deployment in greater strength than the Finns expect, the Soviets are not well prepared for the winter conditions and the coordination between their infantry and other arms is not at all good. Their preparations have been rushed.

The Soviets announce that their action is in support of the Finnish People's Government whose existence is now announced This puppet organization is led by Otto Kuusinen, an exile who has long been a member of the Comintern.

DECEMBER 1939

Battle of the Atlantic Allied shipping losses are 73 ships of 189,900 tons. U-Boats sink 25 of these ships at a cost of one of their number.

1 DECEMBER 1939

Finland The legitimate Finnish government is reorganized. Dr Ryti becomes prime minister.

2 DECEMBER 1939

Finland Finland appeals to the League of Nations to mediate in their quarrel with the Soviets. The League meets between 9–11 December and agrees to intervene. The Soviets refuse to recognize this offer and are expelled on 14 December. This is one of the few times that the League has attempted to take a decisive stand. Of course it is now quite useless.

In the fighting there are Soviet landings with naval support near Petsamo and other units of Fourteenth Army are attacking overland nearby. Elsewhere the slow advance of the Soviet forces continues. The Finnish defenses have not yet been reached in most areas.

3 DECEMBER 1939
Finland The Soviet Eighth Army achieves a small success near Suojärvi. The Finns pull back a little in this sector. They also send a small reinforcement to the forces opposing the advance of the Soviet 54th Division of Ninth Army near Kuhmo.

4 DECEMBER 1939
War at Sea The British battleship *Nelson* is damaged by a magnetic mine off Loch Ewe. This is the last major success for this weapon. The Germans have been employing this and other types of mine to good effect. By the end of the year the Allied shipping lost to mines will amount to 79 ships of 262,700 tons.

5 DECEMBER 1939
Finland Forward units of the Soviet Seventh Army reach the main Finnish defenses, the Mannerheim Line, on the Karelian Isthmus. Mannerheim is the Finnish Commander in Chief. Already the Finns are learning to exploit the poor management of the Soviet advance. They are developing tactics to master the Soviet tanks by separating them from their supporting infantry and emerging from concealed positions during the night to destroy them in close combat.

7 DECEMBER 1939
Finland In the area north of Lake Ladoga the Finnish positions at Kollaa are attacked. Farther north Soviet troops enter Suomussalmi on the east side of Lake Kianta after it has been evacuated by the Finns.

8 DECEMBER 1939
Germany, Planning Raeder again talks to Hitler of invading Norway. Rosenberg, the Nazi Party's political and racial 'expert' also introduces the head of the tiny Norwegian National Unity Party to Hitler. His name is Vidkung Quisling (*see* 27 January 1940).

8–9 DECEMBER 1939
Finland The Finns bring the attacks of the Soviet Ninth Army in the Kuhmo sector to a halt on 8 December. Near Suomussalmi they have a similar success on the 9th. A brilliant night attack is also mounted on Eighth Army units near Kollaa.

11 DECEMBER 1939
Finland The Soviet 163rd Division is cut off in Suomussalmi by the attacks of the Finnish 9th Brigade.

12–15 DECEMBER 1939
Finland The Finns send in a series of attacks against the Soviet Eighth Army. The 139th Division at Tolvajärvi is virtually destroyed and the 75th Division is also hard hit. The Finns capture much invaluable equipment. Finnish attacks near Kollaa meet with less success.

13 DECEMBER 1939
Battle of the River Plate The British Commodore Harwood has brought his squadron to the River Plate estuary hoping that the *Graf Spee* will come hunting there. Harwood has the heavy cruiser *Exeter* and the light cruisers *Ajax* and *Achilles*. When Langsdorff does appear in *Graf Spee* there is a fierce two-hour battle. *Exeter* is very badly damaged, *Ajax* also heavily hit and *Achilles* less so. *Graf Spee* has received some damage as well and Langsdorff decides to break off the action. He heads for Montevideo to make quick repairs and have his wounded treated. *Ajax* and *Achilles* take station off the port.
War at Sea In the North Sea the British submarine *Salmon* torpedoes the German cruisers *Leipzig* and *Nürnberg*. *Leipzig* will only return to service in 1941 but solely as a training ship. *Nürnberg* will be out of action until May 1940.

Above : Finnish infantry in a defensive position.

16 DECEMBER 1939

Finland The main forces of Seventh Army have now advanced to the Mannerheim Line and a major Soviet attack, therefore, begins. The first efforts are subsidiary moves against the northeast end of the Line. They continue for two days without success.

17 DECEMBER 1939

Battle of the River Plate Since 13 December the British Admiralty has been sending ships speeding to Montevideo. Only the heavy cruiser *Cumberland* has arrived so far. Local British diplomats try to have the *Graf Spee* held for a few more days until stronger forces arrive and at the same time contrive to give the impression that heavy units, including the battlecruiser *Renown*, are already in position. Langsdorff, an extremely humane man, therefore decides to scuttle his ship rather than fight a hopeless battle. *Graf Spee* is sunk outside the port with an audience of thousands lining the waterfront. On 20 December Langsdorff kills himself.

17–22 DECEMBER 1939

Finland The main Soviet attacks go in against the Mannerheim Line around Summa. The same pattern is repeated for the first three days. The advancing tanks penetrate into the Finnish positions during each day. The infantry are held off and the tanks mostly destroyed during the nights by the Finnish troops who then emerge from their defenses. The attacks on 20–22 December are less forceful.

On 20 December the Soviet 122nd Division is cut off by Finnish attacks while advancing toward Salla from positions near the White Sea.

23 DECEMBER 1939

Finland A Finnish counterattack on the Karelian Isthmus is sharply rebuffed.

Allied Preparations The first Canadian troops arrive in the United Kingdom. A heavily protected convoy has brought over 7500 men of the 1st Canadian Division.

World Affairs The Pan-American Conference protests about the fighting inside the 'security zone' during the River Plate Battle.

25–27 DECEMBER 1939

Finland The Soviets repeat their earlier attacks on the north end of the Mannerheim Line with little success.

27 DECEMBER 1939

Western Front The first Indian army troops arrive to join the BEF in France.

27 DECEMBER 1939–6 JANUARY 1940

Finland The Finns inflict a series of defeats on the Soviet Eighth and Ninth Armies. On 27–28 December the 163rd Division, which has been holding a tenuous position around Suomussalmi, is attacked and largely broken up. Help was expected to arrive from the 44th Division but this unit has been unable to move forward. It is in turn cut off on 2 January and by 6 January has been broken into small groups.

The Soviet Eighth Army suffers equally heavily. The Finnish offensive against these units also begins on 27 December and continues to achieve success until about 5 January. By this time the Soviet 18th and 168th Divisions have been cut off but they have not been destroyed. Instead they have formed themselves into 'hedgehog' defensive positions which the Finns cannot break without heavy weapons. The Soviet forces receive some supplies by air.

The Finnish tactic in all these operations is to isolate the individual Soviet columns as they move along the forest tracks by moving around them with small units. Each column can then be harassed and wiped out in turn. The Soviets are not able to counter these tactics because their troops are not as well trained or equipped for cross-country skiing.

28 DECEMBER 1939

Britain, Home Front Meat rationing begins.

War at Sea The British battleship *Barham* is hit by a torpedo from *U.30* while cruising off northwest Scotland. Repairs will take three months to complete.

JANUARY 1940

Battle of the Atlantic At this time Doenitz has only 32 operational U-Boats which means that only six or eight can be on patrol on any one occasion. The rest will either be in transit or in port. Of course, a larger force can be concentrated after a lull in operations.

During January the U-Boats sink 40 ships of 111,200 tons. The total Allied losses are 73 ships of 214,500 tons. The main U-Boat successes are in the North Sea and particularly in the Moray Firth area.

4 JANUARY 1940

Germany, Home Front Goering is given overall control of German war industry.

5 JANUARY 1940

Britain, Politics There is a ministerial reshuffle. Oliver Stanley replaces Leslie Hore-Belisha at the War Office (that is, the Army Ministry),

Lord Reith becomes Minister for Information and Sir Andrew Duncan comes to the Board of Trade.

7 JANUARY 1940
Finland General Timoshenko takes command of all the Soviet forces. His troops on the Karelian Isthmus are now organized in two armies, Seventh and Thirteenth. The Finns are in the process of a reorganization also. During January they will be able to form, but only partially equip, two new divisions. Additional defenses are being constructed behind the Mannerheim Line.

Timoshenko immediately institutes a program of training for his forces, emphasizing cooperation between all arms. New equipment is also arriving for the Soviet forces. Their already dominant artillery is being strengthened and among the new tanks are some of the latest KV types. Intensive patrolling to investigate the Finnish lines is also begun.

In the fighting north of Lake Ladoga the Finnish pressure on the Soviet 18th and 168th Divisions continues but their defensive positions known as *mottis* to the Finns, are strong. The Finns will have to keep forces committed against these *mottis* until the end of the war.

8 JANUARY 1940
Britain, Home Front Bacon, butter and sugar are all put on the ration list and will only be available in small quantities.

10 JANUARY 1940
Western Front Two German officers carrying copies of the plan for the attack in the west are forced down when their plane strays off course over Belgium. They land at Mechelen. They are unable to destroy their documents and the Belgian authorities pass on details to the British and French. At this stage Hitler plans to attack on 17 January, but this will be postponed.

11 JANUARY 1940
France, Home Front The government announces that Friday will be a 'meatless day' and that no beef, veal or mutton will be sold on Mondays or Tuesdays.

14 JANUARY 1940
Japan, Politics Prime Minister Abe and all his Cabinet resign and Admiral Mitsumasa Yonai is chosen to form a new government.

15 JANUARY 1940
Western Front The Mechelen incident (*see* 10

January) has been followed by much diplomatic activity. For a time the British and French have believed that they will be invited to move troops into Belgium even before a German attack but this possibility is now firmly ruled out by the Belgian government.
Finland The Soviet forces begin to bombard the Finnish lines around Summa. This softening-up process continues until the end of the month, giving the defending Finnish troops little rest and doing considerable damage to their vital defenses.

16 JANUARY 1940
Germany, Planning Hitler decides to cancel the German attack in the west until the spring. The loss of the plans at Mechelen and the continuing bad weather are the principal reasons.

19 JANUARY 1940
Finland There is an unsuccessful Finnish attack against the positions of the Soviet 122nd Division at Salla.

25 JANUARY 1940
Canada, Politics Parliament is dissolved for an election on 28 March because of recent controversy over the alleged weakness of war preparations.

27 JANUARY 1940
South Africa, Politics A peace resolution introduced into the South African Parliament by the opposition leader General Hertzog is defeated by 81 votes to 59.
Germany, Planning The German plans for invading Norway are put on a more formal basis with the allocation of the code name *Weserübung* (*see* 21 February).

28 JANUARY 1940
Finland The Finnish 9th Division attacks the Soviet 54th Division near Kuhmo and succeeds in splitting the Soviet force into three separate groups. The Finns are not able to press their attacks home. They are further distracted by relief attempts by the Soviet 23rd Division. These are held off, as is an advance by Soviet ski troops between 10–13 February. This force is wiped out.

29 JANUARY 1940
Finland In diplomatic exchanges made via Sweden it emerges that the Soviets are prepared to negotiate with the legitimate Finnish government and, implicitly, to abandon support for the puppet communist regime.

FEBRUARY 1940

Battle of the Atlantic Allied shipping losses amount to 226,900 tons, of which submarines sink 45 ships of 169,500 tons. Again, about half of the U-Boat successes are in the North Sea.

1 FEBRUARY 1940

Japan, Politics A record budget is presented to the Japanese Diet. Almost half is to be devoted to military expenditure.

1–8 FEBRUARY 1940

Finland There are new Soviet attacks against the Mannerheim Line, especially in the Summa sector. There is an extensive preliminary bombardment to add to the artillery efforts of the past two weeks. The Soviet Seventh and Thirteenth Armies have 14 divisions and six tank brigades in the advance, with strong reserves. The Finnish 3rd Division, holding the Summa sector, takes much of the weight. During these days there is no attempt at a breakthrough but almost continuous heavy pressure is maintained. By the 8th the Finns are very tired and their artillery is running short of ammunition. Throughout this period the diplomatic exchanges via Sweden continue, but achieve nothing in the face of Soviet refusals to modify their terms.

5 FEBRUARY 1940

Allied Planning In their Supreme War Council the British and French decide to intervene in Norway and send help to Finland. They plan to begin with landings at Narvik and three other towns on or about 20 March. They rely on the Norwegians and Swedes acquiescing and doing nothing to maintain their neutrality. By comparison with the contemporary, typically meticulous German plans, these Allied preparations are vague, irresolute and amateurish. The pretext of going to help Finland is most unconvincing and it is the obvious intention to devote most effort to stopping the Swedish iron ore reaching Germany.

9 FEBRUARY 1940

Germany, Planning General Manstein is appointed to command the German XXXIII Army Corps. Although this promotion is well deserved it seems that the German High Command hopes to shift Manstein to a less influential post than his present appointment as Chief of Staff to Rundstedt at Army Group A. He has had considerable influence in policy making and has been the leading figure arguing for a radical change in the plans for the attack on the west

(*see* 17 February 1940).

11 FEBRUARY 1940

Diplomatic Relations The Germans and Soviets sign a further trade and economics agreement. The Soviets will supply raw materials, especially oil and food, in return for manufactured products of all kinds, including arms.

Finland The Soviet 123rd Division succeeds in breaking into the Finnish defenses on the Mannerheim Line near Summa.

12 FEBRUARY 1940

Finland A counterattack late in the day by the Finnish 5th Division fails to expel the Soviet forces from their hold on the Summa position.

In the diplomatic negotiations the Soviets raise their terms a little further to match their growing military success.

14 FEBRUARY 1940

Finland The British government announces that it will allow volunteers to go and help the Finns. This is, of course, far too late.

War at Sea The British government announces that all British merchant ships in the North Sea will be armed. On 15 February the Germans reply that all such ships will be treated as warships.

15 FEBRUARY 1940

Finland The Soviets take Summa. The Finnish forces are ordered to retire from the Mannerheim Line to their intermediate position.

16 FEBRUARY 1940

Norway Acting on instructions from Churchill, the British destroyer *Cossack* (Captain Vian) enters Norwegian territorial waters and removes 299 British prisoners from the German transport *Altmark*. *Altmark* has entered Norwegian waters on 14 February and, according to International Law the prisoners should have been released. The *Altmark*'s Captain has denied that he is carrying prisoners. The Norwegians have made no real attempt to search and in fact have provided a torpedo boat as escort. The British action is of course also contrary to international law and although very popular at home, it serves to convince the Germans that the British are contemplating sterner measures against Norway. This gives further impetus to the German plans for an invasion.

17 FEBRUARY 1940

Germany, Planning General Manstein visits Hitler and discusses with him the plan for the armored attack through the Ardennes which Manstein has devised. Hitler has been thinking along these lines himself and is very impressed with Manstein's work.

Finland The Soviet advance has completely cleared the Mannerheim Line. All the Finnish defenders are now established in their second line of defense. The Finnish 23rd Division, brought forward from the reserve, has been slow to arrive because of air attacks.

19 FEBRUARY 1940
Finland The Finnish intermediate defense line is broken in some places by Soviet tank attacks.

21 FEBRUARY 1940
Germany, Planning The preparations for an attack on Norway move forward another stage with the appointment of General Falkenhorst to command. He has been selected by the OKW staff without consulting the Army High Command (*see* 1 March).

Occupied Europe Work begins on the construction of the concentration camp at Auschwitz.

22 FEBRUARY 1940
Finland The Soviets begin to occupy the islands in the Gulf of Finland. The Finns evacuate Koivisto after blowing up the coast-defense guns there.

24 FEBRUARY 1940
Germany, Planning Revised orders for the attack in the west are issued. OKH has been conducting exercises throughout the winter and especially in the early days of this month because of dissatisfaction with the attack plan. Following Manstein's conversation with Hitler on the 17th and an OKH presentation to him on the 18th it has been decided to revise the plans to emphasize the role of Army Group A and an attack through the Ardennes. As far as technique goes the plans are fairly traditional. The emphasis is still not yet fully on the possibilities of the Panzer advance. Rundstedt and Bock, who will be the principal commanders are, despite their considerable abilities, wedded to the conventional infantry-based ideas. Although the direction of the attack is certainly bold, the old school see early problems when it becomes necessary to cross the Meuse. The tank enthusiasts, like Guderian, are more concerned about exploiting the advance after the crossing.

26 FEBRUARY 1940
Finland After the failure of counterattacks

against the Soviet penetrations, the Finnish command orders their forces to retreat to their third, final line of defense.

29 FEBRUARY 1940
Finland The Finns decide that they must give in to the Soviet demands but their note to that effect is not sent immediately because of British and French reactions to the news. The French government has become deeply committed to a policy of supporting Finland and persuades the British to join in making rash promises that cannot possibly be kept.

MARCH 1940
Battle of the Atlantic The German U-Boat campaign is less effective this month because many of them are withdrawn to prepare for the Norwegian campaign. The Allies lose 45 ships altogether, 23 to submarine attack. Three U-Boats are sunk.

1 MARCH 1940
Germany, Planning The final directive for the invasion of Norway and Denmark is issued. On 3 March the date for the attack is set as 17 March but this will be altered to early April.

2 MARCH 1940
Finland The Soviet forces begin major attacks on the new Finnish defense line. Pressure is exerted against all points but is strongest at the north and south ends. Vuosalmi in the north is attacked by Thirteenth Army forces while the reserve corps of Seventh Army is advancing over the sea ice toward the west side of Viipuri Gulf.

3 MARCH 1940
Finland The Soviets begin attacks on Viipuri, Finland's second city.

5–7 MARCH 1940
Finland The Finns correctly deduce on 5 March that the British and French promises are valueless and, therefore, tell the Soviets that they agree to meet their terms. A Finnish delegation is sent to Moscow, led by Ryti and Paasikivi, and arrives on 7 March.

8 MARCH 1940
Finland The Soviets capture part of Viipuri. Their pressure on the Finnish defenses northeast of the city is beginning to wear down the Finnish resistance.

11 MARCH 1940
Finland The final terms of the armistice be-

tween the USSR and Finland are concluded. Finland is to give up the whole of the Karelian Isthmus, including Viipuri, territory in the 'waist' of the country near Salla, the Rybachiy Peninsula near Murmansk and is to grant a lease on the port of Hanko to the Soviets. Petsamo is returned to the Finns. When the recent Soviet military successes are taken into account these terms can be described as fairly moderate.

In a final bid to prevent the Finns agreeing to an armistice Chamberlain and Daladier announce that Britain and France will send help to Finland. The plan to do so is shelved when the Finns conclude their agreement with the Soviets and with it is abandoned the scheme to block the supply of Swedish iron ore to Germany.

13 MARCH 1940

Finland After the Finnish delegation have received formal permission from their government, the treaty with the Soviets is signed in Moscow in the early hours of the morning. The ceasefire is at noon.

The Finns have never had more than 200,000 men in the fight and have lost 25,000 dead and 45,000 wounded. Altogether the war has absorbed, on the Soviet side, 1,200,000 men, 1500 tanks and 3000 planes. Official sources put their losses at 48,000 dead and 158,000 wounded but this may well be a considerable understatement. This disparity in losses suggests to Allied and Axis observers that the effects of Stalin's officer purges have still not been overcome. This impression of inefficiency contributes to Hitler's decision to invade the USSR and makes the British and Americans a little reluctant to send supplies to the Soviets when the Germans do invade because they expect that the Germans will win quickly.

14 MARCH 1940

Australia, Politics Prime Minister Menzies forms a new coalition Cabinet to improve the direction of the war effort.

16 MARCH 1940

War at Sea There is a German air raid on the British fleet base at Scapa Flow. One cruiser is slightly damaged. The raid is more notable for causing the first civilian casualties in Britain.

18 MARCH 1940

Axis Diplomacy Hitler and Mussolini meet at the Brenner Pass. Mussolini says that he is ready to join Germany and its allies in the war against France and Britain.

20 MARCH 1940

France, Politics Daladier, the French prime minister, is forced to resign. On 21 March Paul Reynaud forms the new government. Daladier has been criticized for failing to bring effective help to Finland. In France this has been seen as a way for the Allies to seize the initiative in the war and take the fighting away from French soil and, by association, avoid all the horrors of World War 1.

28 MARCH 1940

Allied Planning In their Supreme War Council the British and French decide to make a formal agreement that neither will make a separate peace.

In the same meeting it is also decided to mine Norwegian coastal waters and, if the Germans seem ready to interfere, to send a military expedition to Norway. The contingency plan prepared for such an eventuality has had to be abandoned, however, because the excuse for landings in Norway was to have been a clause in the constitution of the League of Nations allowing transit for troops if they were going to the aid of a victim of aggression. This is now invalid, of course, because of the Finnish surrender. The operation is timed to start on 5 April but is later deferred to 8 April – a vital difference in view of the timing the Germans fix for their own landings (*see* 1 April).

Canada, Politics Mackenzie King's Liberal Party is returned to power in the Canadian elections.

30 MARCH 1940

China A Japanese-sponsored puppet government is established in Nanking. The Japanese have been able to persuade Wang Ching-wei, formerly a respected Nationalist politician, to lead this body.

31 MARCH 1940

German Raiders The first German armed merchant cruiser, *Atlantis*, sails for operations against Allied shipping. Up to seven vessels will be in service later in 1940 and 1941. Generally these ships are better armed than their British equivalents and must therefore be hunted down by real cruisers. They cause considerable disruption. Their total successes in their period of operation are 87 ships of more than 600,000 tons, which is approximately one-fifth of British losses in this time.

The *Atlantis* will be the most successful raider. In a cruise lasting until 22 November 1941 she will sink 22 ships of 145,700 tons.

CHRONOLOGY

APRIL 1940

Atomic Research Following a memorandum presented by Professor Rudolf Peierls and Dr Otto Frisch the British government establishes the Maud committee to supervise further nuclear work (*see* June 1941).

Battle of the Atlantic This month U-Boats only sink seven ships at a cost of five of their number. This poor return is because they are heavily involved in the Norwegian campaign. Allied shipping losses are still considerable, however. Fifty-eight ships of 158,200 tons are sunk.

1 APRIL 1940

Germany, Planning Hitler approves the plans for the invasion of Norway. On the 2nd he fixes the date for the operation as 9 April.

3 APRIL 1940

Britain, Politics Lord Chatfield resigns his post as Minister for the Co-ordination of Defence. Although he has had a distinguished naval career, he has not been a success in this job. Churchill is appointed to chair the Ministerial Defence Committee – a significant increase in his responsibilities. The decision-making machinery is still clumsy, however, and there is need for an even stronger directing hand and for more provision for interservice cooperation.

One of Churchill's first acts in his new post is to obtain final consent for the mining of the Norwegian Leads.

In the same Cabinet reshuffle Lord Woolton becomes Minister of Food. Perhaps his most famous initiative in this office is the invention of the 'Woolton Pie' – intended to be a nourishing and appetizing use of ration materials. It will not be widely liked.

5 APRIL 1940

Diplomatic Relations Britain and France send a note to Norway announcing that they reserve the right to act to deprive Germany of Norwegian resources.

Britain, Politics In a major public speech Chamberlain proclaims that Hitler has 'missed the bus' – a most unfortunately timed remark.

7 APRIL 1940

Norway The German warships begin to leave their home ports for the invasion of Norway. The British have detected the concentration of shipping in Kiel but because they have no previous information to compare this with they fail to appreciate the significance. Some of the German units are sighted and attacked by British aircraft, however. Independently British

units are preparing to sail for their own mining operations. In the evening the main forces of the Home Fleet sail. The whole of the German surface fleet is committed to this operation, sailing at different times in six groups. They plan to land at Narvik, Trondheim, Bergen, Kristiansand, Oslo and a small detachment at Egersund. The battlecruisers *Scharnhorst* and *Gneisenau* sail with the Narvik group but are to go on to operate against shipping in the Arctic. A large part of the U-Boat fleet is also involved in the campaign but they achieve very little, partly because they use torpedoes with magnetic exploders which do not function properly in high latitudes. This error is discovered during the campaign and is later rectified.

The ships carry units of three divisions for the assault. Three more are earmarked for a second wave. Only one, 3rd Mountain Division, is regarded by the Germans as being of best quality. They have air support from 500 transport planes, over 300 bombers and 100 fighters. For this air support to be effective it will be necessary quickly to take airfields in north Denmark and Norway itself. This difficult task will be achieved.

8 APRIL 1940

Norway Early in the morning the British destroyer *Glowworm* meets part of the German force bound for Narvik off Trondheim Fiord. After ramming the heavy cruiser *Hipper*, *Glowworm* is sunk. About midday the German transport *Rio de Janeiro* is sunk by a British submarine in the Skaggerak and many German soldiers are rescued by Norwegian fishing boats. Despite these and other indications the Norwegian authorities only alert the coastal forces in the evening. The British naval forces at sea are of course alerted, but are not kept up to date with all the information available to London and are, therefore, deployed too far out to sea to hope for interceptions of a landing force. Instead they guard against a raid out toward the Atlantic. The troops embarking at Rosyth for the Anglo-French expedition to Narvik are sent back onshore and their cruiser transports sail. In fact these troops could easily have reached their objectives before the German landings, or at least have been on hand for an attempt on Narvik early in the campaign when this would have been most worthwhile.

9 APRIL 1940

Denmark Two German divisions under the command of General Kaupitsch invade Denmark. Copenhagen is taken within 12 hours.
Norway The German landings begin. The

group of ships intended for Oslo meet increasing resistance as they sail up the Oslo Fiord. At the Oscarsborg Narrows the brand-new heavy cruiser *Blücher* is sunk. The troops are compelled to land below this point but are, however, soon in the town. Airborne units take some casualties in a simultaneous landing at Oslo airport. Fog disrupts the German landings at Kristiansand but eventually the troops get ashore. At Stavanger the vital airfield is quickly taken by airborne attack but much of the airborne force's equipment is sunk offshore by a Norwegian destroyer.

At Bergen surprise is also achieved but the cruiser *Königsberg* is damaged by a coastal battery. To the north, Trondheim is taken practically without a shot. The most questionable part of the German plan is the move on Narvik. By a combination of luck and bad weather they pass the British patrols en route and once up the fiord quickly sink the two old coast-defense ships. Offshore there is an engagement between the battlecruiser *Renown* and *Scharnhorst* and *Gneisenau* in which, despite the disparity of force, *Gneisenau* is damaged before the German ships break off the action. A British destroyer force is on the way to Narvik. Off Kristiansand the cruiser *Karlsruhe* is sunk by a British submarine. Overall the Germans have succeeded brilliantly in getting their forces ashore and their hold on Stavanger airport will prove crucial later in the campaign. Their airpower is already restricting British operations, having sunk one destroyer and damaged the battleship *Rodney*.

10 APRIL 1940
Norway First Battle of Narvik. Captain Warburton-Lee leads five destroyers in a surprise attack up Narvik Fiord. There are 10 German destroyers in various inlets off the main fiord but in a series of quick, confused actions both sides lose two ships. The British have one more seriously damaged while the Germans have four vessels hit – two very badly.

The German pocket battleship *Lützow* is badly damaged by submarine attack while homeward bound. Other German merchant ships from a convoy for Oslo are also sunk.

The German cruiser *Königsberg* is dive bombed by land-based British naval aircraft while in Bergen harbor and sinks. This is the first major warship to be sunk by this method of attack. This is very much an isolated success for the British air forces in this campaign since only one carrier is with the Home Fleet at this stage, the others being in the Mediterranean.

The Norwegian government and Royal Family have left Oslo and Quisling has been installed to lead a puppet government. With their seizure of so many of the country's large towns the Germans have taken most of the stocks of arms at the Norwegian mobilization centers. The Norwegians, therefore, have even less chance for resistance than might have been expected.

11 APRIL 1940
Norway A new Commander in Chief, General Ruge, is appointed for the Norwegian Army. He replaces General Laake, who has resigned.

12 APRIL 1940
Norway *Gneisenau*, *Scharnhorst* and *Admiral Hipper* are located by air reconnaissance southwest of Stavanger on their way home. Attacks by British land-based and carrier aircraft fail. Despite this escape the German navy has lost heavily in the campaign so far and will lose more ships at Narvik on 13 April.

On land the German forces are pushing out from Oslo in all directions. They take Kongsberg to the southwest of the capital.

Above: Wrecked ships in a Norwegian fiord.

CHRONOLOGY

13 APRIL 1940
Norway Second Battle of Narvik. All eight German destroyers remaining in the fiord are sunk by a British force which includes the battleship *Warspite* as well as nine destroyers. A U-Boat is also sunk by the *Warspite*'s scout plane. The German commander, Captain Bey, has missed several opportunities to get at least some of his ships away during the previous few days. Now, as later in his career when in command of the *Scharnhorst*, he is not decisive enough. Hitler is very worried by the situation in Norway and is only just prevented by his staff from issuing a series of very rash orders, particularly to the troops in Narvik.

14 APRIL 1940
Norway The Norwegian forces are fighting a series of delaying actions in the Glomma Valley and around Lake Mjösa against the German forces advancing north from Oslo. There are small British landings at Namsos and Harstad. The British and French are considering a number of possible strategies with the object of freeing Trondheim and Narvik. During the next few days, however, direct assaults on these places will be ruled out. Instead the chosen plan for the Trondheim area will involve a buildup at Namsos and Andalsnes and for Narvik preparations at Harstad.

15 APRIL 1940
Norway Quisling resigns and is replaced for the moment by Ingolf Christensen as the head of the German-sponsored puppet government.

The main body of the 24th British Guards Brigade arrives at Harstad.

16 APRIL 1940
Norway The British 146th Brigade lands at Namsos during the night and is immediately moved inland to Steinkjer.

17 APRIL 1940
Norway The British heavy cruiser *Suffolk* carries out a fairly effective bombardment of the German-held Stavanger airfield but is severely damaged by air attacks while retiring. Late in the day the first British forces land at Andalnses.

18–19 APRIL 1940
Norway The British 148th Brigade lands at Andalsnes during 18 April. General Paget is in command. During the night part of the 5th *Demi-brigade Chasseurs Alpins* lands at Namsos. There has, however, been a mistake made with the equipment for this force and they lack some of the bindings necessary for their skis. This sort of elementary error is typical of the muddled way the whole Norwegian campaign has been conducted and will go on being conducted on the Allied side.

The units of the British 146th Brigade which have advanced from Namsos to Steinkjer are forced to retreat on the 19th by German troops who have support from the warships in Trondheim Fiord.

20 APRIL 1940
Norway Namsos is heavily bombed by the Germans and the harbor installations, such as they are, are severely damaged. The port is ruined as a landing place. There is no natural cover from air attacks and, of course, the Germans have complete air superiority. The German forces advancing from Oslo reach the Norwegian positions at Lillehammer and Rena.

21 APRIL 1940
Norway The Norwegian forces are pushed out of Lillehammer by German attacks on both sides of Lake Mjösa.

22–24 APRIL 1940
Norway The British 148th Brigade is attacked north of Lillehammer by the superior German force advancing up the Gudbrandsdal. On each day the British troops are forced to retreat. On the night of 23 April the British 15th Brigade lands at Molde and Andalsnes and is soon moving forward to relieve the 148th Brigade. On 24 April the German forces in the Osterdal reach Rendal. In the north Narvik is bombarded in an attempt to bring about the surrender of the German garrison. If this looks likely a landing is to be made. The battleship *Warspite*, a heavy cruiser and three light cruisers are used but despite this concentration of force the commanding general decides that the naval guns will not have sufficiently disrupted the German positions because of their unsuitable, flat trajectory of fire. The naval commander is Admiral of the Fleet Lord Cork. This officer has been brought back to active service at Churchill's request and his position is somewhat anomalous. He is senior in the service to even the commander of the Home Fleet but is using ships from that fleet for his mission. His seniority poses problems in his relations with the military commanders who are at times reluctant to insist on measures which their military knowledge makes them believe essential. Churchill and his political colleagues have done little to clarify this situation.

25–27 APRIL 1940
Norway The fighting in the Gudbrandsdal continues. The British 15th Brigade and the Norwegian units put up a fierce resistance but are repeatedly forced back. The Germans advance even more rapidly in the Osterdal. In the north the Norwegian forces begin attacks toward Narvik.

On 27 April the British decide to evacuate their forces from Namsos and Andalsnes, giving up any attempt to reach Trondheim. Andalsnes is heavily attacked from the air.

28 APRIL 1940
Norway A further detachment of French mountain troops arrives at Harstad.

29–30 APRIL 1940
Norway King Hakkon and his government are evacuated from Molde on the British cruiser *Glasgow* and taken to Tromso where they arrive on 1 May. The Norwegian gold reserves go with them. During 29 April the German units which have moved up the Osterdal link with their Trondheim force at Dragset. The British and French forces in the Gudbrandsdal are fighting south of Dombas when the order to retire reaches them. The Norwegian troops in this area will be forced to surrender when their Allies leave.

30–31 APRIL 1940
Norway During the night the British begin to evacuate their troops from Andalsnses.

MAY 1940
Battle of the Atlantic The U-Boat effort this month is again fairly small. Only 13 ships of 55,500 tons are sunk this way. The start of the German campaign in western Europe is, however, marked by an increase in air and mining activity. The total Allied losses are 101 ships of 288,400 tons. New corvette-type escort vessels are beginning to come into service with the British forces. These ships are slower than is ideal and very uncomfortable for their crews in rough Atlantic weather but they are, nonetheless, of vital importance because they have good range and can be built quickly.

On 16 May the British Admiralty decide to close the Mediterranean to normal British merchant shipping. This adds more than 20,000 miles to the round trip from Britain to Suez and since many of the convoys on this route will carry important troop and arms convoys they must be escorted strongly. After the French surrender, Freetown will be the only port available on the west coast of Africa but the facilities there will be inadequate to cope with all the traffic. There will be considerable strain on British resources.

1 MAY 1940
Norway The evacuation of Andalsnes is completed. Altogether 4400 men have been taken off but much equipment has been lost.

2 MAY 1940
Norway The Germans reach Andalsnes. The Allies begin to leave Namsos. Before dawn 5400 French and British troops have been evacuated. Small French and British forces are landed at Mosjoen to try to help block the road north to Narvik.

5 MAY 1940
Norway The German forces continue to advance north from Trondheim. More Allied troops arrive in the north at Tromso and Harstad. This contingent is from the French Foreign Legion and the exiled Polish forces.

7–8 MAY 1940
Britain, Politics There is a major debate in the House of Commons on the conduct of the war and especially of the Norwegian campaign. At the vote Chamberlain's government has a majority of 281–200 but when compared to former support this is not sufficient to allow the government to continue to claim to be representative. Chamberlain resigns. In fact the errors of the Norwegian campaign have been at least as much Churchill's as any others. However, in a wider sense the responsibility is Chamberlain's for failing to establish a coherent decision-making structure to see that plans were properly coordinated and that subordinates worked sensibly and efficiently.

For a while on 8 May it seems that Lord Halifax will be the next prime minister. Most of the Conservative majority in Parliament would prefer to have Halifax, and the Labour minority are also ready to support him. The problem is that as a peer he sits in the House of Lords and this is not ideal for a national leader. At the meeting of senior Conservatives Halifax's own worries about this leave Churchill the only alternative. He visits the King and officially takes office on 10 May.

Even when he is established as the choice for prime minister he still has to win the confidence of his own party. The civil service and the military leaders are also suspicious of him. By a combination of his oratory, his forceful energy, far surpassing Chamberlain's in all his work, and the soundness of his administrative decisions, he quickly attains an unrivalled position. He will not always be easy to work with and often produces wild, impractical ideas but in the major issues, his handling is essentially very sound. Part of his success is owed to the way he delegates responsibility for home affairs to others, for he is less able in this capacity.

8 MAY 1940
Soviet Union, Command Timoshenko replaces Voroshilov as commissar for defense. Training programs are soon introduced to correct some of the defects which have appeared during the Finnish war.

9 MAY 1940
France, Politics Reynaud has been growing more and more unhappy with the leadership of Gamelin, the Supreme Commander. He has been unable to dismiss him because he is supported in Cabinet by Daladier, who remains influential although he is no longer prime minister. These quarrels now come to a head but no announcement is made pending the formation of a new government. The German attack on 10 May will cause the changes to be deferred.
Western Front The Belgian army is placed on alert because of recent tension and signs of German troop movements. The Luftwaffe has been successful in keeping Allied reconnaissance flights away from the German preparations.

10 MAY 1940
Western Front The Germans begin their attack in the west. Their plans are for Leeb's Army Group C to hold the frontier opposite the Maginot Line while Rundstedt's Army Group A makes the main attack, with most of the armor, through the Ardennes and Bock's Army Group B sends a secondary advance through Belgium and Holland to draw the main British and French forces north so that Rundstedt can hit their flank. Neither the Belgians nor the Dutch have given the Allies any real cooperation in planning a joint defense because they do not wish to compromise their neutrality or provoke the Germans into attacking. The Allied Plan D is consequently less well elaborated than the German scheme. It provides for the First Army Group, the BEF and the Seventh Army to advance to the line of the River Dyle and the Meuse above Namur, to be joined there by the Belgian forces and on the left to link with the Dutch. General Gamelin is the Supreme Commander, General Georges commands the armies

on the Northeast Front, General Billotte the French First Army Group and General Lord Gort the BEF. Gort has the right to appeal to the British government if he believes that his orders from the French leaders threaten the existence of his force.

In theory the two sides are fairly evenly matched on the ground, the Germans having 136 divisions and the four Allies together 149. In tanks the Allied strength is somewhat greater and a number are of superior quality. Of course the Germans have the advantage that all their forces come under a single command and conform to one tactical system. In the air the Germans are very much stronger, with over 3000 combat planes facing less than 2000 of the Allies to which the British home-based bombers, about 500, can be added. Later more RAF fighters and bombers will take part in the battle, both from bases in France and England. Most of the Allied planes are of inferior types. The German organization and command are immeasurably superior. Their tanks are concentrated efficiently in armored divisions which are almost invariably energetically, and sometimes brilliantly, led. The higher command is not always ready to accept armored innovation but both individually and collectively it is still superior to the rambling Allied arrangements. Gamelin will take little real control of the operations and several of the French general officers will perform inadequately. The Allied troops of all nations are often poorly equipped and poorly led at more junior levels also. The tanks, especially the powerful French force, are mostly deployed in small infantry support units and will be let down by their poor mobility and defeated in detail. Although the British believe in the idea of the armored division they have not yet deployed one in France. (The 1st Armored Division will be ordered to France, incomplete, on 11 May.)

The distribution of the Allied forces also leaves much to be desired. The strongest and best-trained units are in the force to be sent forward in to Belgium with the best parts of the small reserve in support. Bilotte's First Army Group includes almost all the armored units which the French army has formed. All three of the light armored divisions and two of the three heavy armored divisions are with the force which advances into Belgium and the infantry of the BEF and the French First Army are the best on the Allied side. The forces covering the Ardennes are weakest because the terrain in this sector is judged to be too difficult to allow a significant German attack. They have almost no reserves. The Maginot line forces are stronger. In effect, the flanks are strong and the center, where the German attack falls, is weak.

On the first day Rundstedt's forces immediately begin their advance through the Ardennes with the three armored corps in the van. Kleist has two Panzer corps under command, Guderian's and Reinhardt's and they are heading for Sedan and Montherme. Hoth's corps is making for Dinant. The advance is rapid and the little opposition, mostly French cavalry, is thrown aside.

Far more spectacular and a far greater claim on Allied attention are the efforts of Bock's Army Group B. There are parachute landings deep inside Holland which do much to paralyze Dutch resistance. German units cross the Maas near Arnhem in sudden early-morning attacks and, more exciting still, the fort at Eben Emael is put out of action by a German airborne force which lands its gliders literally on top of it. The fort is meant to cover the crossings of the Albert Canal nearby and this is not achieved. The Luftwaffe gives powerful support.

The British and French react quickly to these attacks as soon as they hear of them from the Belgians. By the evening much of the Dyle line has been occupied but the troops find that there are no fortifications to compare with the positions they have prepared along the Franco-Belgian frontier during the Phony War. Some of the reserve is therefore committed to strengthen the line. Some of the advance forces of Giraud's Seventh Army make contact with the Germans in southern Holland and are roughly handled.

Above: German troops fire at a Dutch aircraft.

At the end of the day the German advance has gone almost according to plan and the Allies are acting in the manner best calculated to improve the German success. Already it is becoming apparent that the Belgian and Dutch armies are going to fail to hold out long enough to receive British and French help. The main blow against the British and French has not yet fallen but it is being well prepared.

Norway British forces are sent south from Harstad to Mo-i-Rana to join the small units trying to delay the German advance to relieve the Narvik force. Some of these units are now engaged at Mosjoen.

Iceland British troops land on the island. They are the advance elements of a force which is to set up a destroyer and scout-plane base to help in the convoy battles in the Atlantic. Equally, they will prevent the Germans using the island to aid their U-Boat campaign.

11 MAY 1940
Western Front The German offensive continues at high speed. The advance in Holland is very rapid and even more of the Dutch army is put out of action. In Belgium the Germans are approaching the British and French positions which are now strongly held. Eben Emael falls to German attacks after some fruitless resistance. Rundstedt's forces advance nearer to the Meuse.
Caribbean British and French troops land on the Dutch islands of Aruba and Curaçao to protect the oil installations there, and also the approach to the Venezuelan fields.

12 MAY 1940
Western Front The French Seventh Army advancing into Holland is engaged with the German advance near Tilburg and is thrown back. In their main armored thrust the Germans enter Sedan without a fight. The French forces in the area retire to the left bank of the Meuse where they have substantial artillery support deployed to deny the crossing to the Germans. Other tank forces reach the Meuse farther north.

13 MAY 1940
Western Front The German Panzer divisions cross the Meuse in two places at Sedan and Dinant. The French troops opposing them have not prepared their positions properly and are quickly demoralized and terrorized by heavy dive-bomber attacks. At Sedan Guderian is right at the front, urging his troops on and at Dinant the young commander of the 7th Panzer Division, General Rommel, is also doing well. Farther north the Germans take Liège and in

Holland the defense has now been totally disrupted. The advancing German ground troops have linked with the paratroops at Moerdijk. Queen Wilhelmina and the Dutch Government are taken to London at different times during the day. Giraud's Seventh Army is in full retreat.

Norway The Allied forces start their advance toward Narvik from Harstad. The first landings on the way, at Bjerkvik 10 miles north of Narvik, are successfully carried out by French troops.

Britain, Home Front Prime Minister Churchill makes the first of a famous series of inspirational speeches in a radio broadcast. He says, 'I have nothing to offer you but blood, toil, tears and sweat.'

14 MAY 1940

Western Front After a surrender demand has been submitted but before it has expired, Rotterdam is very heavily bombed by the Luftwaffe. The Dutch Commander in Chief, General Winkelmans, decides that he must surrender.

The German armor pours across the Meuse at Sedan and Dinant. French tank units in both areas, but especially at Sedan fail to put in any concerted counterattacks and are brushed aside. There are considerable air attacks on the German bridgeheads by both British and French bombers. Many of the attacking planes are shot down. Once across the river the Germans drive west, cutting a huge gap between Corap's Ninth and Huntziger's Second Army. Huntziger has no orders on which way to retreat. Corap's Army is falling apart.

Britain, Home Front Recruiting begins for a volunteer home-defense force from men in reserved occupations or too old or young for military service. This force is to be called the Local Defence Volunteers. In July the far more-effective title of Home Guard is chosen.

Norway A transport carrying a large part of the British 24th Guards Brigade to join the holding forces south of Narvik is bombed and sunk by the Germans. Much equipment is lost.

15 MAY 1940

Western Front The Dutch army capitulates at 1100 hours. General Bilotte, commanding the French First Army Group, decides to abandon the Dyle line in the face of Reichenau's attacks. His superior, General Georges, concurs with the decision and is now in fact beginning to lose his nerve. At this stage Gamelin, the Supreme Commander, remains oblivious and confident. The German tank forces push forward, urged on all the time by their commanders who are up

with the leaders and in complete control of the situation. Their momentum is maintained by this leadership. The optimistic atmosphere at French GHQ is partly dispelled by the news that Guderian's tanks have reached Montcornet less than 15 miles from Laon. Guderian is ordered to halt here but after vigorous complaints he is allowed another day's march.

Britain, Planning This is a vital, symbolic day for several reasons. At crucial meetings of the Chiefs of Staff Committee and the War Cabinet, Air Marshal Dowding argues strongly against sending any more RAF fighters to France. Despite strong opposition Dowding has way. The decision is taken also to send the first strategic bombing raid against the Ruhr. Finally on this day Churchill sends the first in a long series of telegrams to Roosevelt, signing himself as Former Naval Person. He asks consistently for American aid, works to develop a good relationship with Roosevelt and above all to bring America closer to active participation in the war. Not the least of Churchill's achievements as prime minister will be the way he cultivates this friendship. Already in this first message he presents a shopping list which includes old destroyers and aircraft as well as other arms.

16 MAY 1940

Western Front The British and French forces which advanced into Belgium only a few days ago, begin to retreat to their former positions behind the line of the Scheldt. Units of Hoth's XV Panzer Corps, with Rommel's 7th Division well to the fore, have reached just east of Cambrai and to the south Guderian's forces are moving on St Quentin. Again a halt order is issued to the German tank forces because some of the more conservative minds at army headquarters cannot accept that the Panzers can advance so far without exposing their flanks. In fact the speed of the advance has itself protected them and thrown the French into confusion. Perhaps the best indication of the German success is the conversation between Churchill, on a visit to Paris, and Gamelin. Churchill asks where the strategic reserve is and is appalled to receive the answer that there is none, or at least none left. Outside the room where this meeting takes place French government employees are beginning to burn secret files.

United States, Politics Roosevelt asks Congress to authorize the production of 50,000 military planes per year and for a $900,000,000 extraordinary credit to finance this massive operation.

17 MAY 1940

Western Front Reichenau's troops enter Brussels. Antwerp and the islands at the mouth of the Scheldt are also being abandoned but have not yet been taken by the Germans. The British and French forces in Belgium have now fallen back to the River Dendre. The Belgian government has moved to Ostend. In the main German attacks Guderian's forces, exploiting the loophole in their orders allowing reconnaissance in force, reach the Oise south of Guise. On their left flank the French 4th Armored Division led by Colonel de Gaulle sends in an attack northward from around Laon. The Luftwaffe attacks them fiercely and prevents any real gains.

General Gort is now worried by the growing threat to his right flank and rear areas and, therefore, forms a scratch force to defend this area. General Mason-Macfarlane is put in command. He has up till now been Gort's Chief of Intelligence. Gort can be criticized for weakening this important department at such a vital stage.

Norway The British cruiser *Effingham* goes aground and is lost while carrying men and stores to join the forces south of Narvik.

18 MAY 1940

Western Front St Quentin and Cambrai are taken by German Panzer units. Farther north Reichenau's Sixth Army takes Antwerp.

France, Politics Reynaud appoints a new Cabinet in an attempt to strengthen the French conduct of the war. He himself takes the Ministry of Defense, Marshal Pétain is deputy prime minister and Mandel is minister of the interior. General Weygand, even older than Gamelin but far more vigorous, has been recalled from the Middle East to take over the Supreme Command. Although these changes probably do strengthen Reynaud's team, especially his own new office, they will turn out to have been ill-advised. Some of the new men, Pétain in particular, will become deeply pessimistic about the outcome of the war and will in time bring Reynaud down when he himself would have preferred to fight on.

Holland, Home Front Artur Seyss-Inquart is appointed Reich Commissioner for Holland. He will take up office on 29 May.

Britain, Home Front Tyler Kent, a clerk at the US Embassy in London, and Anna Wolkoff, a Russian emigrée, are arrested on spying charges. Kent has had access to the correspondence between Churchill and Roosevelt, and Wolkoff has helped pass it to Germany via Italian diplomats. Kent's diplomatic immunity is waived by the United States ambassador. Wolkoff has had connections with a pro-Fascist organization, the Right Club.

19 MAY 1940

Western Front Most of the German Panzer forces halt in positions between Péronne and St Quentin to regroup but some of Guderian's troops are still pushing forward. Rommel's 7th Panzer Division also makes a small advance in the direction of Arras. De Gaulle's 4th Armored Division again attacks north from around Laon. It makes very good progress against gradually stiffening resistance but is ordered to retire before any real gains can be achieved.

The possibility that it will be necessary to evacuate the BEF is raised for the first time in telephone conversations between London and the commanders in the field. The government are still optimistic at this stage. The main British forces are now in positions along the Scheldt.

20 MAY 1940

Western Front The German armored advance again makes considerable progress. The most spectacular gains are made by Guderian's XIX Corps. Amiens is taken in the morning and in the evening Abbeville is captured. Advance units even reach the coast at Noyelles. The Germans have now driven a corridor at least 20 miles wide from the Ardennes to the Channel. The obvious need is for the British and French to cut through this corridor before its walls can be strengthened to cut off irrevocably the forces to the north. Before his dismissal Gamelin was planning such an attack, but it has been cancelled following his sacking only to be revived now by Weygand. The delay imposed by these changes of mind prevents it from retaining even a slim chance of success.

21 MAY 1940

Western Front Rommel's division is sharply attacked around Arras by British tank forces. The attack does very well at first largely because of the comparative invulnerability of the Matilda tanks to the standard German antitank weapons. After some panic on the German side the attack is halted, principally because of the fire of a few 88mm guns. The British force is too small to repeat the advance or to shake free from this setback.

Weygand visits the commanders of the northern armies to try to coordinate attacks from north and south of the German corridor to the coast. By a series of accidents he misses seeing Gort, and Bilotte, to whom he has given the fullest explanation of his plans, is killed in a car accident before he can pass them on. The attack will never take place. The small British effort has already been made. The Belgians will try to free some more British units for a later effort but this will not be possible. The French themselves, both north and south, are already too weak.

Norway The French, Polish and Norwegian forces moving in on Narvik advance another stage and gain positions on the northern side of Rombaksfiord.

Germany, Planning In a conference Admiral Raeder mentions to Hitler for the first time that it may be necessary to invade Britain. The German navy has made some preliminary studies before this but they have not been based on the availability of French bases. Little real thought is given to the possibility at this stage even after this conference.

22 MAY 1940
Western Front The German forces on the Channel coast turn their attacks to the north toward Boulogne and Calais. The Belgian forces retreat to the Lys.

Allied Planning Churchill is again in Paris discussing plans for an Allied offensive. Once more Weygand proposes an attempt to cut the German line to the Channel by attacks from the north and south. It is agreed that this should be attempted but in reality there is little with which to implement the plans.

Britain, Home Front Parliament passes an Emergency Powers Act giving the government sweeping powers over the persons and property of British citizens.

23 MAY 1940
Western Front General Rundstedt, commanding Army Group A, orders his tank forces to halt their advance. Despite this order 2nd Panzer Division are attacking Boulogne and inland the British evacuate Arras. Owing to this retreat the planned Allied counteroffensive is postponed. It is becoming clear to the British generals in France that an evacuation by sea is probably going to be necessary.

Britain, Home Front The former leader of the British Union of Fascists, Sir Oswald Mosley, is arrested. Also detained is a Member of Parliament, Captain Ramsay. Ramsay has been connected with the Right Club (*see* 18 May).

United States, Politics President Roosevelt wins the Democratic primary in Vermont and is now certain to receive his party's nomination for the November elections.

24 MAY 1940
Western Front The German attacks on Boulogne continue. Farther along the coast they are also attacking Calais. The Royal Navy is active in support of the British forces in both towns. During the day and later in the night destroyers are used to evacuate 5000 men from Boulogne and over the next three days two light cruisers and seven destroyers are in support near Calais. There are also German attacks on the line of the Lys and around Tournai. The plans for an Allied counteroffensive depend on the Belgians being able to take over a longer section of the front but with this pressure they will not be able to do so.

The partial halt of the main German armored forces already made by Rundstedt is confirmed by Hitler. They have reached the line Gravelines-Omer-Béthune. Although the ground north of here is not well suited to armored action the Allied defenses are weak. The pause, which lasts until the morning of the 27th, gives the French and British time to strengthen this position and is generally seen as being the move which makes the evacuation of the BEF possible. The motives for Hitler's decision can only be guessed. Certainly the armored forces are in need of a rest. Equally, Goering is pressing for the Luftwaffe to be given a bigger share of the action and the consequent glory. There may also be some truth in the suggestions that Hitler is deliberately being soft on the British in the hope that they can be persuaded to come to terms in the near future.

Allied Planning The Supreme War Council decides to end its involvement in Norway. They agree to capture Narvik and destroy the port facilities before they will evacuate. Ironically the airfield at Bardufoss has only just received its first complement of British aircraft and already the campaign is seeming less one-sided, showing what might have been done. The Norwegians are not yet told of the decision to leave.

25 MAY 1940
Western Front The Belgian forces are driven out of Menin by attacks of units from Army Group B. The last pockets of resistance in Boulogne are eliminated.

At 1700 hours Gort cancels the preparations he has been making to join Weygand's offensive. Later in the day Weygand in turn cancels the whole scheme, blaming Gort for this decision. In fact the French forces on the Somme have not made any attacks, as has been claimed, and the French forces with the northern armies are in no condition to do so.

26 MAY 1940
Western Front, Dunkirk The position of the Belgian army is becoming increasingly grave. It is clear that it is unable to stay in the fight for much longer. The British forces are beginning to fall back on Dunkirk and in the evening the order is issued to begin Operation Dynamo, the evacuation from Dunkirk. Admiral Ramsay, who commands the Royal Navy forces based at Dover, is appointed to command the operation. The scope of the operation is not made clear to the local French commanders at first and they feel, with some justice, that they are being abandoned.

Norway The British cruiser *Curlew* is sunk by air attack off Harstad.

British Command General Dill becomes Chief of the British General Staff. His predecessor General Ironside takes over as Commander in Chief of Home Forces.

27 MAY 1940
Western Front, Dunkirk The German armor resumes its attacks, trying to cut off the British and French forces around Lille. A desperate defense enables most of them to get away to positions nearer the coast. There is also trouble nearer the coast where the Belgian resistance is becoming increasingly weak. In the Dunkirk evacuation only a little is achieved with less than 8000 men being landed in Britain.

27–28 MAY 1940
Norway The Allied assault on Narvik gets under way. The attacking troops are led by the French General Béthouart. The town is taken after a brisk fight. When bad weather at the Bardufoss airfield grounds the Allied fighters, the attack is briefly held up because the ships providing bombardment support then have to fight off the Stukas alone.

28 MAY 1940
Western Front, Dunkirk King Leopold agrees to the surrender of the Belgian army without consulting the other Allies or his government (now in Paris). The capitulation becomes effective at 1100 hours and it is only by a desperately hurried redeployment of the British and French forces that the Germans are prevented from reaching Nieuport, and from there the Dunkirk beaches. A corps of French First Army is holding out in Lille but they are now cut off from the main British and French forces in the evacuation area. There is fierce fighting around Cassel and Poperinghe where Rundstedt's men again press forward. The evacuation continues, with 17,800 men being brought off at a cost of one destroyer and several other less important vessels.

Above: Lines of soldiers waiting at Dunkirk.

CHRONOLOGY

29 MAY 1940

Western Front, Dunkirk The German forces continue to press all round the contracting Dunkirk perimeter. By the end of the day most of the remaining British troops and a large proportion of the French are inside the final canal positions. The evacuation from Dunkirk and over the beaches goes on. The Luftwaffe increases the strength of its attacks despite the efforts of the RAF to give protection. A further 47,310 men are evacuated but three destroyers are sunk and seven others damaged. At least 15 other vessels are sunk. The French are now beginning to allow their troops to be evacuated and have sent some ships to assist. Owing to the destroyer losses and the demand for them in other operations the Admiralty decides that the more modern types must be withdrawn.

30 MAY 1940

Western Front, Dunkirk There is something of a lull in the land battle around Dunkirk because of confusion and disagreement in the German command. The Panzer forces begin to withdraw from the front line to take up positions to the south for the next stage of the Battle of France. The evacuation, of course, continues with 53,823 men being taken off. The small ships over the beaches do most of the lifting but transfer their loads to larger vessels for the trip to England. One destroyer is sunk during the day, the French *Bourrasque*, three others are hit and at least nine of the smaller ships are also sunk. This total does not include the smallest vessels whose losses are also considerable. General Brooke, who has commanded the British II Corps with distinction, is one of the evacuees.

31 MAY 1940

Western Front, Dunkirk This is the most successful day of the Dunkirk evacuation, with 68,014 men being taken to Britain. The ships lost include one destroyer and six more are damaged. General Gort returns to Britain after handing over command of the remnant of the BEF to General Alexander as ordered. There are considerable air battles over the beaches at various stages during the day in which the RAF claim to shoot down 38 German aircraft for the loss of 28. In fact the true figures are nearer equality.
Norway The British blocking force is evacuated from Bodo.
Britain, Home Front A series of measures, including the removal of all direction signs from crossroads, is taken to counter worries about fifth-column and parachute attacks.

United States, Politics President Roosevelt introduces a 'billion-dollar defense program' which is designed to boost the United States' military strength significantly.

JUNE 1940

Battle of the Atlantic Allied shipping losses this month increase dramatically to 140 ships of 585,500 tons. A considerable proportion of these losses occur at Dunkirk and during other evacuation operations. The normal shipping routes are also less protected because many vessels suitable for escort work have to be used in the evacuations.

The Atlantic convoys can now be given escorts as far as 15 degrees West. U-Boats sink 58 ships of 284,100 tons.

1 JUNE 1940

Western Front, Dunkirk Despite increased Luftwaffe attacks a total of 64,429 men are evacuated from Dunkirk. However, German planes sink four destroyers and damage five more as well as several of the Channel ferries and other ships, which form the backbone of the evacuation fleet. The RAF sends eight large patrols to give cover but most of the damage is done in the intervals between them. On the ground the Germans increase their efforts, breaking the defensive perimeter along the canals at Bergues and forcing retreats in other sectors also. During the night the British authorities decide that the air attacks have made the evacuation too dangerous to continue by day.

Above: A crowded troopship in a French port.

Norway The British and French tell the Norwegians that they are about to begin their evacuation. They have delayed giving this information on the grounds of security but by doing so they have encouraged the Norwegians to openly resist the Germans, which can only be costly when the Allies leave.

2 JUNE 1940

Western Front, Dunkirk During the day the Dunkirk perimeter, now manned entirely by French forces, is largely driven in but the Germans still cannot penetrate to the town. The beach area is only about two miles long after this advance, however. Both before dawn and after dark the evacuation continues, with 26,256 men being taken off, including the last British units to leave. Just before midnight the evacuation dies to a trickle. There are still plenty of ships but the French troops have not been given proper orders about where to go and which piers are in use. Many more have gone to earth in and around the town and will take no further part in military operations.

3 JUNE 1940

Western Front, Dunkirk During the day the German attacks around Dunkirk continue. Again they force forward, contracting the perimeter, and despite a brave counterattack they reach to within two miles of the harbor. The British and French naval authorities are led to believe that there are only about 30,000 soldiers left in the beachhead and plan the night's operations accordingly. In the course of the night 26,175 men are evacuated but as the rearguard are marching down to the ships an enormous crowd of French stragglers begins to appear out of cellars and other hiding places. When the last ship leaves at 0340 hours on 4 June there are still 40,000 men left for the Germans to capture.

4 JUNE 1940

Western Front, Dunkirk Early in the morning the Germans enter Dunkirk and capture all the remaining French soldiers. The official figure for those evacuated is 338,226 of which 112,000 are French. Almost all heavy equipment has been lost and many of the troops are without rifles and basic kit. Against the original expectation that a maximum of perhaps 50,000 men might be taken off it has been something of a triumph, but at some cost. The British and French navies have lost at least 80 merchant craft and warships as well as many small vessels. Nine destroyers have been sunk. From a force of 180 in September 1939 the Royal Navy now has only 74 destroyers not in dock for essential repairs. The Home Fleet has three capital ships and eight cruisers under repair also, although this is not because of Dunkirk. The credit for the unexpected success of the operation must lie in part with the British land and naval commanders but the Germans must also be included. Despite the brilliance of their campaign, many of the most senior commanders have not fully realized the potential of their armor and have handled it hesitantly, granting vital time for Gort and his subordinates to redispose their force. The RAF has also suffered heavily, with 80 pilots being killed in the operation. The German losses in the air have been a little heavier but German reserves are, of course, much larger.

Britain, Home Front Churchill delivers perhaps the most famous of his great wartime speeches. His message is, 'We shall fight on the beaches . . . We shall never surrender.' Already he is talking of the time when '. . . The New World, with all its power and might, steps forth to the rescue and the liberation of the Old.' This message seems to suggest that France will be beaten, leaving Britain to fight alone. This is not perhaps the best way to encourage the French.

4–8 JUNE 1940

Norway The Allied evacuation gets under way. During these days the Harstad force is taken off. The total number evacuated is 24,500. The considerable base organization which has been built up has to be dismantled.

5 JUNE 1940

Western Front The German attack on the line of the Somme begins. The French have used the period of the Dunkirk battle to make some defensive preparations but not enough to compensate for the weakness of their forces. These are now organized as Army Groups Three and Four. Army Group Three holds the Somme near the coast and Army Group Four the line of the Aisne. The German attack is code named *Fall Rot*. Their tank forces, now organized in two Panzer Groups and one Panzer Corps, are given the leading role. The heaviest fighting at first is in the sector between Amiens and the sea where Hoth's Panzer Corps is heading the drive.

France, Politics In a Cabinet reshuffle Daladier is dropped and the newly promoted General de Gaulle is made Under-Secretary for Defense.

6 JUNE 1940

Western Front The French line along the

Somme between Amiens and the coast is broken by the attacks of XV Panzer Corps after a vigorous struggle. Rommel's 7th Panzer Division makes the largest gains. Between Amiens and Péronne Kleist's Group is still being held, but farther inland Guderian's divisions are seizing bridgeheads over the Aisne in preliminary attacks.

7 JUNE 1940
Western Front In their advance on the coastal sector the Germans take Montdidier, Noyon and Forges-les-Eaux. They are now only 20 miles from the Seine at Rouen.

Norway The British cruiser *Devonshire* carries the king of Norway and his government from Tromso to Britain.

8 JUNE 1940
German Raiders The German battlecruisers *Scharnhorst* and *Gneisenau* operate off the Norwegian coast. Their aim is to attack the various convoys carrying the evacuation from Norway to Britain. They sink three empty ships and then find the aircraft carrier *Glorious* and two destroyers. Despite a gallant defense by the destroyers there is no time for *Glorious* to escape or launch her aircraft, and although *Scharnhorst* is damaged all three British ships are sunk. The British Admiralty has been careless in providing too few escorts for these waters, and it is by no means inconceivable that *Scharnhorst* and *Gneisenau* might have achieved a still greater victory by intercepting the simultaneous troop convoys. Admiral Marschall, in command of the German operation, decides to return to base because of the damage to *Scharnhorst*.

9 JUNE 1940
Norway The king and his prime minister order the loyal Norwegian forces to cease fighting at midnight.

Western Front The German forces reach the Seine at Rouen and take the city. Dieppe and Compiègne are both captured. Guderian's forces are now in full attack against the French positions around Reims. They have been joined by Kleist's Panzer Group who have been switched east after being held between Amiens and Péronne. In the fighting the French defenders manage to hold most of their positions but take heavy losses.

10 JUNE 1940
Italy Unable to resist the opportunity to take a share of the glory, Mussolini issues declarations of war to Britain and France. Neither the Italian

economy nor the Italian people are particularly well prepared for war. Their fleet is, however, of considerable strength and strategic significance. They have two battleships immediately available, with four more modern ships nearly completed. They also have a powerful force of cruisers and destroyers and the largest submarine force in the world, 116 strong. These forces, when all the battleships are available, will be comfortably stronger than the British and French forces in the Mediterranean, the more so when Britain is fighting alone. The only class of ship which the Italians do not have is the aircraft carrier. Two British ships of this type are in the Mediterranean at this time.

The Italian army is not as formidable as the fleet. Although of considerable size its units are usually understrength and, as the coming battles will show, badly led and dreadfully equipped.

Diplomatic Relations Prime Minister Reynaud appeals to President Roosevelt to intervene in the war in Europe. This appeal is repeated on 13 June but without success.

Norway The Allied campaign comes to an end. Strategically the campaign has been most significant for the naval losses on each side and the transformation it has helped to bring about in the potential of the available bases for the German fleets. The Allies have lost one carrier, two cruisers, nine destroyers and many smaller craft, also many ships were damaged. These losses do nothing to help the British ability to protect the trade routes. The Germans have lost three cruisers, 10 destroyers and several submarines. This forms a large proportion of their fleet and this loss cannot be replaced at all quickly. It certainly subtracts considerably from the Kriegsmarine's limited ability to help protect, for example, an invasion of Britain.

Manpower losses in the Norwegian campaign are about 5600 for the Germans and 6100 military deaths for the Allies as well as many civilian casualties.

Western Front The Germans are across the Seine west of Paris. Elements of the French Tenth Army are still fighting around St Valéry along with some British forces. Some of these units are evacuated from the town. East of Paris the German advance is also very rapid. Evacuations also begin at Le Havre. In the next three days 11,059 British and some French will be taken off, some to go to Cherbourg but the bulk is bound for Britain. East of Paris the German forces begin to gain ground south of the Aisne.

11 JUNE 1940
Western Front Paris is declared an open city.

Most of what remains of the French forces are retreating in confusion south of the Seine and Marne. The German tank forces take Reims.

Mediterranean The first actions of the war in this theater are some air skirmishes in North Africa and over Malta.

11–13 JUNE 1940

Allied Diplomacy Churchill is again in France meeting Reynaud and Weygand at Briare. Churchill is unable to instill much of his own fighting spirit into the French leaders. Reynaud would prefer to fight on but has little support. The British are determined to prevent the Germans from obtaining control of the French navy.

12 JUNE 1940

Mediterranean A British cruiser and destroyer force shells the Italian base at Tobruk. The main force of Admiral Cunningham's Mediterranean Fleet is in support. An Italian force of cruisers is sent to engage the bombardment group but does not make contact. In a different action off Crete the cruiser *Calypso* is sunk by an Italian submarine. Turin and Genoa are bombed by the RAF.

Western Front Guderian's troops take Châlons-sur-Marne. Here and elsewhere the German advance continues to be very rapid. St Valéry on the Channel coast is taken. A large part of the British 51st Highland Division is captured.

12–22 JUNE 1940

Baltic States On 12 June the Soviet government issues an ultimatum to Lithuania demanding territory and the establishment of a new government. Kaunas and Vilna are occupied by Soviet troops on 15 June and a new government installed on 16 June. Similar demands are made of Estonia and Latvia. These are met on 20 and 22 June respectively. There have been Soviet garrisons based in the Baltic States since October 1939.

13 JUNE 1940

Western Front The French forces west of Paris are now retreating to the Loire. The British decide to abandon attempts to rebuild a BEF in France and begin to evacuate the British and Canadian troops which still remain in the country.

United States, Politics Roosevelt signs a new $1,300,000,000 Navy bill providing for much extra construction.

Arms Supply In response to Churchill's pleas in his telegrams to President Roosevelt, surplus stocks of artillery weapons and rifles have been assembled from US government stores. The first shipment now leaves the USA on the SS *Eastern Prince* for the voyage to Britain. The US Neutrality Laws have been subverted by first 'selling' the arms to a steel company and then reselling them to the British government.

14 JUNE 1940

Western Front Paris falls to the Germans. New instructions are issued to the German armies. While most of the armored forces are to continue their advance into the center of the country, Guderian's two corps are to swing east to cut off any attempt by the Maginot garrisons to retreat. Army Group C, General Leeb, attacks and breaks through the Maginot defenses in some sectors.

Mediterranean A force of French cruisers and destroyers shells the Italian ports of Genoa and Vado.

15 JUNE 1940

Western Front Strasbourg and Verdun are taken in the converging German advance on the Maginot defenses. On the Channel coast evacuations begin from Cherbourg. In the next three days 30,630 British and Canadian troops are taken off without loss.

United States, Politics Another Navy bill passes into law. This provides for a much-expanded air corps, with 10,000 planes and 16,000 more aircrew.

16 JUNE 1940

Western Front Dijon is taken and to the east Guderian's units have reached the Saône. The Maginot Line is breached near Colmar in Alsace. On the Channel coast there are more evacuations. From St Malo during the next two days 21,474 Allied troops are taken off and from Brest 32,584. The evacuations from St Nazaire and Nantes take three days and carry 57,235 away but over 3000 are lost when the *Lancastria* is sunk by German bombers.

Allied Diplomacy France asks Britain to be released from the obligation not to make a separate peace. In return the British make an offer to establish a state of union between the two countries, but this rather wild scheme is rejected by the French. Reynaud has lost the support of his Cabinet and resigns. Pétain is chosen to replace him.

17 JUNE 1940

Western Front Pontarlier, almost on the Swiss

border, is reached by Guderian's forces. Other units have nearly reached the Loire and still more are advancing in Brittany and Normandy.
France, Politics The Pétain Cabinet takes office. Weygand is Minister of Defense. They announce that they are asking Germany for armistice terms. The British government understands that these will only be accepted on the condition that the French Fleet does not fall into German hands. Equally it is the German policy to stop the French Fleet and colonies from joining Britain and this is the reason for their comparative leniency in allowing the establishment of Vichy as a focus for the loyalty for the French. French representatives in the USA do allow the British to take up arms orders they have made under the 'Cash and Carry' rules.
Britain, Home Front Churchill broadcasts saying that the Battle of France is over and that the Battle of Britain is about to begin. His message is 'Let us so bear ourselves that, if the British Empire and Commonwealth last for a thousand years, men will still say, "This was their finest hour."'

18 JUNE 1940
Western Front The German advance continues inexorably. The 7th Panzer Division takes Cherbourg, 5th Panzer Brest. Among the other towns captured are Le Mans, Briare, Le Creusot, Belfort, Dijon and Colmar.
Europe, Air Operations The RAF bomb Hamburg and Bremen.
France, Politics General de Gaulle, as yet comparatively unknown to the majority of his countrymen, broadcasts from London urging the French to fight on, saying that only a battle and not the whole war has been lost.

19 JUNE 1940
Western Front On the Loire Nantes and Saumur are taken. In Brittany Brest falls and in central France, between the Saône and the Loire, the Germans are approaching Lyons. There are more evacuations from the west coast. In the following week 19,000, mostly Poles, are taken off from Bayonne and St Jean-de-Luz. Since Dunkirk 144,171 British, 18,246 French, 24,352 Poles, 4938 Czechs and a few Belgians have got away.

20 JUNE 1940
German Raiders The German battlecruiser *Gneisenau* is seriously damaged in a torpedo attack by the British submarine *Clyde* off Trondheim.
Western Front Lyons and Vichy are captured.

Diplomatic Relations The French delegation sets out for the armistice talks which are to be held at Compiègne in the same railroad carriage and on the same site as the negotiations which ended World War I.
United States, Politics President Roosevelt strengthens his Cabinet by bringing in two prominent Republicans. Henry Stimson becomes Secretary for War and Frank Knox becomes Secretary for the Navy. Stimson is strongly against America's isolationist tradition and will be a champion of Lend-Lease.

21 JUNE 1940
Diplomatic Relations The German armistice terms are given to the French delegation. The Germans will permit no discussion. In addition to the provisions for establishing a vestigial French State and for demobilizing the French Armed Forces there are stringent financial clauses. The French are allowed to consult briefly with their government.
Western Front There are Italian attacks in some of the Alpine passes which are easily beaten off despite the weakness of the French forces which are left in these areas.
War in the Air R V Jones, who heads British Scientific Intelligence, gives evidence to an important investigating committee concerning a German radio navigation aid code named *Knickebein*. Churchill gives orders for countermeasures to be developed. Vital progress in this field is soon made and plays a large part in mitigating the effects of the German Blitz in the coming months. Henry Tizard, who, more than any other, has been responsible for organizing the British use of radar, resigns because his advice is disregarded. His resignation confirms the position of the less reliable Frederick Lindemann (Lord Cherwell) as Churchill's principal scientific advisor.

22 JUNE 1940
Diplomatic Relations General Huntziger, who leads the French delegation, signs the armistice with Germany in the Compiègne railroad carriage specially taken out of its museum. It is perhaps appropriate that Huntziger, who led the Second Army at Sedan at the start of the campaign, should be involved in the final act. The French forces which have been driven out of the Maginot Line but are still resisting, finally surrender on Weygand's order.

23 JUNE 1940
France, Politics Pierre Laval is appointed Deputy Premier by Pétain. Incidentally de

Gaulle is also officially cashiered by General Weygand on this day.

24 JUNE 1940
Diplomatic Relations The Franco-Italian armistice is concluded.

24–30 JUNE 1940
United States, Politics In the Republican Party convention at Philadelphia Wendell Willkie is selected as the presidential candidate after the sixth ballot by a margin of 654 to 318 over Senator Taft. The convention is overwhelmingly in favor of a policy of nonintervention in the war.

25 JUNE 1940
United States, Home Front New considerably increased taxes are introduced which bring an additional 2,200,000 people into the tax roll who have never formerly payed income tax. These increases of course reflect the armament expenditure.
Diplomatic Relations The Franco-German armistice comes into force.

The Japanese put pressure on the French authorities in Indochina to block the transit of supplies to the Chinese Nationalists. They wish the rail line into China to be closed and a Japanese mission to be allowed in to inspect this.

26 JUNE 1940
Rumania The Soviets present an ultimatum to Rumania demanding the cession of territory in Bessarabia and Northern Bukovina. Germany reluctantly intervenes to help persuade the Rumanians to give in. They do so on 27 June.

27 JUNE 1940
Diplomatic Relations A confidential meeting is held between British and Australian representatives and the United States' Secretary of State Cordell Hull. The British and Australians ask for help in standing up to Japan. They wish the USA to take economic measures or to move more units of the fleet to Malaysian and Philippine waters or to offer to mediate between China and Japan. Hull is unable to agree to any of these moves which would involve a more active foreign policy than the American public is prepared to contemplate at this time.

28 JUNE 1940
France, Politics General de Gaulle is recognized by Britain as 'Leader of All Free Frenchmen.'
North Africa Marshal Balbo, Italian Governor and Commander in Chief in Libya, is killed by 'friendly' antiaircraft fire while flying over Tobruk during a British air raid. Marshal Graziani is appointed to replace him.

30 JUNE 1940
Western Front The German forces begin to occupy the Channel Islands, the only British territory which they will conquer.

JULY 1940
Battle of the Atlantic The period between now and October 1940 will become known to the U-Boat crews as *Die Gluckliche Zeit* (the Happy Time). During these months each submarine will sink an average of eight Allied ships each patrol. (By early in 1941 this figure will be down to two and will only rise again briefly early in 1942.) This is the period when the U-Boat ace commanders will make their names. Endras, Prien, Schepke and Kretschmer will be the best known. Almost exactly two-thirds of the U-Boat successes will be among 'independents.'

From 17 July all convoys bound for the British west coast are routed north of Ireland and any ships going to the east coast will travel north of Scotland. Of course, such radical changes cause problems of organization for the escort forces and congestion in the ports now emphasized.

In July the U-Boats sink 38 of a total Allied loss of 105 ships. There are now 28 operational U-Boats with 23 more in training.

1 JULY 1940
United States, Politics Roosevelt signs a further Navy bill providing for the construction of 45 more ships and providing $550,000,000 to finance these and other projects.

2 JULY 1940
Germany, Strategy An Armed Forces High Command, OKW, order is issued entitled 'The War Against England.' It begins 'The Fuehrer and Supreme Commander has decided that a landing in England is possible.' In response to this order Goering gives instructions for an intensified air blockade with especial attention to be given to attacks on shipping. The Luftwaffe has two air fleets in Northern France.
War at Sea/Home Front The British merchant ship *Arandora Star* is sunk off the coast of Ireland by a U-Boat. Of the 1200 people aboard 800 are drowned. They are among the 8000 'enemy aliens' who are to be deported from Britain for internment abroad.

As in the later cases of Japanese-Americans in the United States, the British internment policy is both harsh and foolish. Among those interned in Britain are many Jewish refugees from Hitler, including important scientists and many more who want to work for Britain. Hysterical fears of a Fifth Column are the main reason for the internment policy. It is gradually relaxed after August 1940.

3 JULY 1940

Britain, Planning There have been some suggestions, supported by Admiral Pound, the First Sea Lord, that the British Fleet should be withdrawn from the Eastern Mediterranean. The idea is squashed by Churchill. This is a brave decision when it has not yet been established that the Italians are likely to misuse their considerable resources and when the problem of the French Fleet has not yet been resolved.

War at Sea The British government and Admiralty are desperately worried by the status of the French navy and fear that it will fall into German hands. They therefore take action to prevent this. At Plymouth and Portsmouth two French battleships, nine destroyers and many smaller ships are taken over with a little bloodshed in some minor skirmishes. At Mers-el-Kebir near Oran there is an entirely different story. Here the British Admiral Somerville has been sent with the two battleships and one battlecruiser of Force H supported by an aircraft carrier. Somerville has been ordered to present various alternative schemes for the demobilization of the French ships and their removal to distant ports. The French Admiral Gensoul has four battleships and a large complement of supporting vessels. The deadline in Somerville's orders expires before the negotiations have achieved an agreement and he feels compelled to open fire. The *Bretagne* is sunk and two more battleships badly damaged. The *Strasbourg* and five destroyers steam out of the port and succeed in getting away to Toulon. Negotiations are proceeding in Alexandria between the British and French commanders there.

4 JULY 1940

East Africa The Italians advance from Abyssinia into the Sudan occupying Kassala and Gallabat just over the border. The Italians use more than two brigades at Kassala which is defended by only two companies of the Sudan Defense Force.

Rumania A new Cabinet is formed. The prime minister is Gigurtu and the Foreign Minister Manoilescu who represents the Iron Guard. On 5 July Rumania adheres to the Axis system. The

policies of the new government are clearly pro-German and anti-Semitic.

Battle of Britain The Luftwaffe attacks a Channel convoy south of Portland and the Stuka bombers sink five of the nine ships involved.

5 JULY 1940

France, Politics Marshal Pétain's government, now based in Vichy, breaks off diplomatic relations with Britain because of the action taken against the French navy. There is an attempt to raid Gibraltar with torpedo planes but without success.

6 JULY 1940

Mediterranean The carrier *Ark Royal* sends planes to attack the battleship *Dunkerque*, lying damaged at Mers-el-Kebir. Further hits are achieved. *Dunkerque* and the escaped *Strasbourg* are the principal concern of the British since these are modern ships built specifically to be superior to the German pocket battleships.

6–10 JULY 1940

Mediterranean There are various convoy operations covered by the main forces of each side. The Italian squadron, led by Admiral Campioni, has two battleships active along with eight heavy and 12 light cruisers. Admiral Somerville's Force H is still stronger than usual from the Mers-el-Kebir operation with three battleships and one carrier and Admiral Cunningham's Mediterranean Fleet has at this stage a similar strength. All the convoys pass safely. There is some action on 9 July however. Force H is attacked by high-altitude bombers without loss and Cunningham's force and the Italian squadron are involved in a brief surface action in which the battleship *Giulio Cesare* is damaged by a hit from the *Warspite* after which the Italians break off.

7 JULY 1940

War at Sea The French commander in Alexandria, Admiral Godefroy, agrees to allow his ships to be demobilized. The French force here consists of the battleship *Lorraine*, three heavy cruisers, one light cruiser, three destroyers and a submarine.

7–8 JULY 1940

War at Sea The battleship *Richelieu* is attacked in Dakar Harbor during the night by a small British unit. On 8 July the damage done is increased by a hit from a torpedo bomber from the carrier *Hermes*. The *Jean Bart* in Casablanca is also attacked. De Gaulle criticizes the British for these actions. This is the first sign that he will maintain French independence and be a stormy partner.

9 JULY 1940
France, Politics Marshal Pétain is granted powers to make and alter the constitution by vote of the French parliament. He is opposed by only four votes, three in the Chamber and one in the Senate.

10 JULY 1940
Battle of Britain There are more actions over the Channel in which there are losses on both sides. The Germans also send 70 planes to raid dock targets in South Wales. In the British reckoning this is the first day of the battle.

11 JULY 1940
France, Politics President Lebrun resigns and Pétain becomes head of state after an overwhelming vote in his favor in parliament. His first decree shows his new style and pretensions. It begins 'Nous, Philippe Pétain.'

11–24 JULY 1940
Battle of Britain The principal events are attacks by aircraft from Luftflotten 2 and 3 against shipping in the Channel. The RAF responds cautiously to these probing actions and the losses are 48 for the RAF and 93 for the Luftwaffe. On balance this favors the RAF because of the time granted to improve aircraft stocks, but in fighters alone the casualties are about equal and the Luftwaffe has superior numbers.

13 JULY 1940
Germany, Planning Hitler issues Directive 15 on the air war with Britain. The offensive is to begin at full strength on 5 August. Goering in fact will not be able to have his plans ready by this date. This lack of efficiency will waste vital days of the fine summer weather. The RAF is to be rapidly driven from the skies and the air supremacy necessary if an invasion is to be attempted is to be achieved.

In a conversation with some of his generals Hitler makes his first real mention of the future necessity to attack Russia. He suggests that England is only fighting on because of the hope of Soviet help.

13–15 JULY 1940
East Africa The Italian forces in Abyssinia move over the border into Kenya to attack the

small town of Moyale. After a brief resistance the outnumbered garrison withdraws.

15 JULY 1940
Baltic States Plebiscites conducted in Estonia, Lithuania and Latvia are announced to show a unanimous desire for union with the USSR.

15–18 JULY 1940
United States, Politics In the Democratic Party convention at Chicago Roosevelt is nominated as the presidential candidate without any real opposition. Henry Wallace is chosen to run for vice-president.

16 JULY 1940
Germany, Planning Hitler issues his Directive 16. It begins, 'I have decided to begin to prepare for, and if necessary to carry out, an invasion of England.' It goes on to explain the importance of the air battles for the achievement of this aim. Some commentators think that the tentative phrasing of the Directive indicates uncertainty in Hitler's mind over the desirability of the operation. It is certainly true that it could have been issued sooner after the end of the Battle of France. At this stage in the planning the German army's views are dominant. They wish the Channel crossing to take place on a wide front with landings all along the south coast of Britain. They envisage that the force to be employed will be at least 25 and perhaps 40 divisions. They hope that the crossing can be protected by the Luftwaffe and mines on its flanks. This is not a very realistic plan.

Japan, Politics Prime Minister Yonai resigns because of military pressure and on 17 July a new Cabinet headed by Prince Konoye is appointed. Matsuoka is the new Foreign Minister and will be very influential. The Cabinet also includes a number of supporters of a more aggressive policy. The most important is General Tojo who becomes Minister of War.

18 JULY 1940
Diplomatic Relations In response to Japanese pressure and because of their present weakness, the British government closes the Burma Road to the passage of supplies to the Chinese Nationalists. The monsoon season is just beginning in Burma, so there is little real loss to the Chinese, and the road will be reopened in October when the better weather begins.

19 JULY 1940
Britain, Home Front General Brooke is appointed to be Commander in Chief, Home

Forces replacing General Ironside. This is purely an army position and does not give authority over the other services as the title might suggest. Brooke is more of a success in the job than Ironside and produces more realistic plans for dealing with invasion. Ironside is promoted to field marshal.

Diplomatic Relations In a speech to the Reichstag Hitler issues what he describes as 'a final appeal to common sense,' urging that Britain make peace. The British Foreign Secretary, Lord Halifax, replies on 22 July 'we shall not stop fighting till freedom for ourselves and others is secure.'

United States, Politics President Roosevelt signs the 'Two-Ocean Navy Expansion Act.' This orders construction of 1,325,000 tons of warships and 15,000 naval planes. Including the existing ships, the fleet will comprise 35 battleships, 20 carriers and 88 cruisers.

Mediterranean There is an action between two Italian cruisers and the Australian cruiser *Sydney* and five destroyers. The Italian *Bartolomeo Colleoni* is damaged by *Sydney* and then sunk by destroyer attack. Later *Sydney* is hit by *Bande Nere* before the Italians flee.

21 JULY 1940

Germany, Planning In an OKH conference Hitler again says that Germany must prepare to attack the Soviet Union. Although the generals would prefer to deal with Britain first, they raise no objections. Later in the month Jodl tells an OKW planning section that Germany will attack in the east in the spring of 1941 and that planning for the movement of the armed forces to Eastern Europe should be begun.

Baltic States The Soviet Union formally annexes all three states and they become constituent republics of the USSR.

22 JULY 1940

Britain, Planning The British government believes strongly that there will be uprisings against Hitler's rule that will contribute greatly to the overthrow of his power and will make a British return to the continent possible. The Special Operations Executive is created to work clandestinely to encourage these developments. Although events will not turn out as the British imagine, SOE will make a considerable contribution to the development of the various resistance movements in occupied Europe. This will be despite the lack of funds and equipment allowed to the department by the three services. Officially SOE is to be a part of the Ministry for Economic Warfare. The later American OSS will be modelled partly on SOE.

23 JULY 1940

Allied War Production The British Purchasing Mission in the United States reaches agreement that it will be allowed to buy up 40 percent of the United States' production of aircraft.

Czechoslovakia, Politics A provisional government is formed in London and is recognized by Britain. Dr Beneš is president and Mgr Šramek is prime minister.

25 JULY 1940

United States, Policy The United States prohibits the export of oil and metal products in certain categories, unless under license, to countries outside the Americas generally and to Britain. This move is seen as an anti-Japanese measure, particularly because of Japan's needs for foreign oil. From this time Japanese fuel stocks begin to decline. There are similar problems with other raw materials. Japanese attention is, therefore, drawn south from China to the resources of the Netherlands East Indies, and Malaysia.

25–29 JULY 1940

Battle of Britain There are various attacks on British convoys in the Channel. On the 25th aircraft from Kesselring's Luftflotte 2 attack one convoy in the Dover Straits very fiercely. They have help from German light naval forces. These are driven off during the day but return to do damage during the night. The British lose 11 of the 21 ships in the convoy. On 26 July the British Admiralty order that no ships are to pass Dover during daylight. This is not a direct response to the previous day's losses but has been under preparation for some time because of the extra organization involved. On 27 July Kesselring sinks two destroyers and damages one in Channel operations. On 28 July all destroyers are withdrawn from Dover to Portsmouth. This is a significant achievement for the Luftwaffe implying that they may be able to dominate the Channel Narrows during the hours of daylight. On 29 July another destroyer is sunk and the whole eastern half of the Channel is placed out of bounds for RN destroyers in daylight. Minesweeping operations continue, however, ensuring that access can be gained if necessary. In the air operations the RAF loses 18 planes and the Germans 52.

26 JULY 1940

Japan, Policy The Japanese government formally adopts policy documents giving top priority to solving their China problem by blocking supplies reaching the Chinese through Indochina and to securing their own raw materials by a more aggressive stance in the Dutch East Indies.

28 JULY 1940

War at Sea There is an engagement in the South Atlantic between the German auxiliary cruiser *Thor* and the similar but less well-armed British merchant cruiser *Alcantara*. *Thor* is only lightly hit but *Alcantara* is forced to break off and head for Rio. Only proper British cruisers are adequate to catch and fight such useful German vessels.

31 JULY 1940

British War Production Fighter output for July is found to be 50 percent above the target figures. Since 1 May 1200 have been made. This is more than have been made in Germany and the RAF is therefore closing the Luftwaffe's advantage.

AUGUST 1940

Battle of the Atlantic Changes are introduced in the British naval codes which, for a time, set back the work of B Dienst, the German cryptanalysis service, which has previously been able to glean a considerable quantity of very up-to-date and useful intelligence from the British radio transmissions. The British work on the German Enigma coding machine is not yet giving the marvellous results that will be achieved later.

The German potential for Atlantic operations is strengthened by the entry into maritime service of long-range Condor aircraft from bases near Bordeaux. On the 17th Hitler declares a total blockade of the British Isles in which neutral ships may be sunk at sight. In the month's operations the U-Boats sink 56 ships of 267,600 tons out of a total Allied and neutral loss of 397,200 tons. One minor consolation for the British is the first sinking of a U-Boat by a depth charge dropped by a plane (*U.51* on 16 August). These modified weapons will not come into widespread use until the spring of 1941 until which time the less effective antisubmarine bombs will be used.

1 AUGUST 1940

Germany, Planning Hitler issues his Directive 17 on the invasion of Britain. The army plans have now been revised to take some note of naval problems and on account of these it is laid down that preparations are to be complete by 15 September for the operation to take place between the 19th and 26th. The order is to be given about 14 days after the main Luftwaffe offensive to gain air supremacy has begun.

Japan, Politics A public policy declaration is made concerning Japan's support for a 'New Order' in East Asia.

1–10 AUGUST 1940

Battle of Britain On each day there are German attacks on shipping in the Channel. The air fighting is heaviest on 8 August when the Germans lose 31 planes and the RAF 20. Overall the losses are less favorable than on that occasion for the Luftwaffe with the RAF total loss being 27 planes and the Luftwaffe's 62.

2 AUGUST 1940

Mediterranean The carrier *Ark Royal* with Force H attacks the Italian base on Sardinia at Cagliari. The old carrier *Argus* which is also based on Gibraltar, is at sea to fly off a cargo of Hurricanes to Malta.

Britain, Politics Lord Beaverbrook, Minister of Aircraft Production is taken into the inner circle of Churchill's War Cabinet.

3 AUGUST 1940

East Africa The Italians invade British Somaliland. In Abyssinia the Italians have a total force of 350,000 men of whom 70 percent are native troops. The British forces in East Africa, also including many colonial troops, are less than 25,000 men of whom only four battalions are in Somaliland. The Italians allot seven times this force to the invasion along with an overwhelmingly superior artillery contingent. General Nasi is in command. There are three main lines of advance: toward Zeila in the north, Hargeisa in the center and Odweina on the right.

5 AUGUST 1940

Germany, Strategy The first operational plans for the German invasion of the Soviet Union are presented to General Halder, the Chief of Staff at OKH, by one of his officers, General Marcks. They envisage a two-pronged attack with the major effort being directed toward Moscow and a minor advance being made toward Kiev. Work continues on the plans at both OKH and OKW (*see* 17 September).

East Africa Zeila in the north of British Somaliland and Hargeisa on the main road to Berbera are both taken by the Italians.

6 AUGUST 1940

East Africa Odweina is taken by the Italians.

CHRONOLOGY

9 AUGUST 1940

France, Politics General de Gaulle announces that he has the support of the French New Hebrides colony. Later in the month Chad, French Equatorial Africa, Cameroun and several of the French Pacific islands also declare for the Free French. The leader of the Free French forces who brings the Cameroons over to de Gaulle is Captain de Hautecloque who will later change his name and be better known as Leclerc. This is in order to avoid persecution of his family. Another prominent officer who joins de Gaulle is General Larminat who is in command at Brazzaville.

China The British government announces that it is abandoning the British presence in Shanghai and Tientsin province. The forces concerned move out later in the month.

10 AUGUST 1940

Britain, Planning The decision is taken to send a large part of the country's total stock of tanks out to the Middle East although there is the threat of a German invasion. Churchill takes much of the credit for this brave decision which, although not his idea, is necessarily carried out on his instructions.

11 AUGUST 1940

Battle of Britain There are German air raids on Weymouth and Portland. The RAF loses 32 planes and the Luftwaffe 38.

East Africa In British Somaliland the Italians advance to and attack the main British positions on the Hargeisa-Berbera road at Tug Argan. General Godwin-Austen has arrived to command the small British force.

12 AUGUST 1940

Battle of Britain There are German raids on Portsmouth and the British airfields in Kent at Manston, Lympne and Hawkinge. The radar station at Ventnor on the Isle of Wight is attacked and damaged, putting it out of action for two weeks. This leaves a significant gap in the British radar cover. The Germans fully understand the technical capabilities of radar, but they do not envisage that its contribution to fighter defense can be as great as is in fact the case. The Germans have no precise equivalent of the British operations direction rooms in the sector stations which are essential to the proper interpretation and dissemination of radar information and which enable senior ground officers to manage their squadrons efficiently. The Germans believe too that the radar masts are more difficult to destroy than they really are.

The losses for the day are 22 British and 31 German.

Soviet Union The power of the commissars in the Red Army is reduced. Formal military ranks are restored and the military commanders are made solely responsible for operational decisions.

East Africa A British mission is sent into Abyssinia from the Sudan to organize resistance, especially in the Gojjam district, and to prepare for the return of the emperor to the country. The mission is led by a Colonel Sandford and one of the officers later employed on this task will be Major Wingate.

13 AUGUST 1940

Battle of Britain This is *Adlertag* (Eagle Day) which is to mark the beginning of the all-out German offensive against the RAF. The RAF is to be crippled and driven out of the sky over southern England within four days and to be out of the fight completely in four weeks.

At this stage the RAF has something over 600 modern fighters with trained crews, half deployed in southern England. There are adequate numbers of new planes in reserve stocks but trained pilots are in far shorter supply. A limited number can be borrowed from the navy and bomber crew can be employed if absolutely necessary, but these expedients can not make much difference. The Luftwaffe has between 600 and 700 operational Me 109s, just over 1000 twin-engined bombers and 350 each of Stukas and Me 110s. This preponderance in numbers is somewhat illusory since the number of attacking bombers usually has to be limited to the strength of the available fighter escort for which it will emerge that the Me 109 is the only suitable aircraft. The Me 110s can usually manage to look after themselves by defensive tactics if they do nothing else. The bombers are all weakly armed and the Stukas especially are dreadfully vulnerable without escorts. Neither side has a very accurate appreciation of the other's strength. This and the inflated claims of casualties inflicted is a less serious error for the RAF, since it must merely keep on defending against whatever attacks are made rather than for the Luftwaffe which must judge from its Intelligence appreciations which forces to send and which targets to attack.

Until now the fighting has gone, if anything, in the RAF's favor. They have lost 150 fighters for 228 German planes shot down since 12 July. These figures are not entirely conclusive since the German fighter losses are only about half their total and, if these roughly equal fighter losses continue, then the process of attrition will leave the RAF crippled and the Germans with fighters and bombers to spare. Although the claims of German aircraft shot down are greatly, if honestly, exaggerated (the claims of German propaganda are less honestly meant), this danger is horribly clear to the RAF. It is obvious above all that they must, as far as possible, avoid simple fighter-to-fighter battles while inflicting maximum casualties on the bombers and keeping them from bombing with perfect accuracy. The tactics adopted by Air Marshal Dowding who leads Fighter Command and Air Marshal Park, his principal lieutenant, who commands 11 Fighter Group in southeast England, are to send relatively small formations to disrupt and harry the German bomber forces. Air Marshal Leigh-Mallory commanding 12 Group in the Midlands and eastern England, with strong prompting from one of his subordinates, Squadron Leader Bader, advocates that large fighter groups be assembled before attacks are made in order to ensure something closer to parity of numbers. It seems likely that these tactics are mistaken, principally because the forces closer to the coast lack the time to assemble 'big wings' at sufficient altitude. Also with this system it is more difficult to maintain the necessary reserves and to avoid the risk of planes being caught on the ground.

The events of Eagle Day go strongly in favor of the RAF. The Germans fly about 1500 sorties, 1000 by fighters, and the British about 700 exclusively by fighters. The Germans lose 45 planes, the British only 13 and from these six pilots are able to return to their units and new machines. This will be a factor throughout the battle. Instances will occur when RAF pilots shot down in the morning will be flying in combat once more in the afternoon. Since the German losses mostly occur away from home, they have no such benefit. The number of sorties flown by the fighters on each side at this stage shows the strain which will be put on these units. If the Germans are to continue to fly twice as many fighter missions as bomber missions, then they will be compelled to keep almost all their fighters in the front line unless they are willing to reduce the strength of the bomber attacks. If they do not make such reductions, then the comparative shortage of reserve planes will tell against them since pilots otherwise combat-ready will be grounded because of battle-damage to their planes or simply because of fatigue. Since the RAF has only about half of its fighter squadrons in the front line and is miserly in the way it exposes them to losses, it will be better able to rest units and to cover up for its

losses. This is a further advantage of Dowding's and Park's tactics. The battle of course continues.

14 AUGUST 1940
Science and Technology Sir Henry Tizard heads a British scientific mission to the United States, carrying with him details of all of Britain's most advanced thinking in several vital fields. There are ideas on jet engines, explosives, gun turrets and above all a little device called the cavity magnetron. This valve is vital for the development of more advanced types of radar, including the versions used in proximity fuses later and the types working on centimetric wavelengths which will be vital at sea in the U-Boat war. The US Official History will later describe this collection as the 'most valuable cargo ever brought to our shores.'

Battle of Britain The weather is less good for flying, and the Luftwaffe therefore confines itself to small-scale operations which include raids on Hastings and Southampton. About 500 sorties are flown by each side. The RAF loses eight planes, the Germans 19.

15 AUGUST 1940
Battle of Britain The Germans fly almost 1800 sorties, the greatest number they will achieve during the battle, and the RAF almost 1000. The attacks of Kesselring and Sperrle from northern France are joined according to plan by Stumpff's forces from Norway and Denmark which send attacks against targets in northeast England. The distances to be flown here prevent any Me 109s from giving cover, and the Me 110s which are sent to fill the escort's role have to be fitted with extra fuel tanks in lieu of their rear gunners, further reducing their already limited combat capability. The Luftwaffe believes that because of the earlier attacks Dowding will have been forced to station all his few remaining fighters in the south and will have nothing left to meet this assault. In fact the Germans suffer heavily, losing 23 aircraft from a force of about 150, shooting no enemy aircraft down and doing little damage with their bombs. In the south the day's events are much less one-sided. In several engagements the RAF comes off worse but not in all. By the end of the day the overall score shows the RAF as having lost 34 planes, all fighters, and the Germans 75 altogether. Several RAF airfields have been damaged but not yet seriously enough to prevent rapid repairs.

Goering takes two important and misguided decisions. He decides that because the RAF has been so reduced in strength it is wasting effort to continue to attack any radar stations. This seems to contradict his other decision that the escorting fighters must fly a considerable portion of their strength very close to the bomber formations because of bomber casualties and poor morale among their crews. This drastically reduces the fighters' effectiveness and increases the number needed to escort each raid. It is strongly resented by the fighter pilots.

15–16 AUGUST 1940

East Africa The British forces pull out of their positions around Tug Argan in British Somaliland after a notable defense.

16 AUGUST 1940

Battle of Britain The Luftwaffe flies 1715 sorties and the RAF 776. In the fighting the Germans lose 45 planes and the British 21 in the air and a number on the ground. Among the targets attacked by the Germans are several Fighter Command airfields and these are quite heavily damaged.

Hitler intervenes in the quarrel between his army and naval staffs as to whether the invasion of Britain should be conducted on a broad front, as the army prefers or the narrow front more suited to naval limitations. He orders them to reach a compromise. The army has previously talked of using 40 divisions in the first three days of the operation, but now consider using 13.

Italy The RAF sends attacks against the Fiat works in Turin and the Caproni works in Milan.

United States, Politics Roosevelt announces that there have been conversations with the UK on the acquisition of bases for western hemisphere defense. He does not disclose as yet that Britain wants some old US destroyers in return.

16–19 AUGUST 1940

East Africa In British Somaliland the British forces embark at Berbera for evacuation to Aden. Altogether nearly 5700 service personnel and civilians are taken off by RN cruisers and destroyers.

The British have suffered 260 casualties in the brief campaign and the Italians 2050. Churchill criticizes the performance of the British forces despite this balance. They are defended, however, by General Wavell, whose Middle East command they are part of. Wavell has recently been in London and has made a bad impression on Churchill and the arguments about this issue do not improve Churchill's feeling toward him.

17 AUGUST 1940

North Africa Admiral Cunningham leads three battleships and several other vessels of the British Mediterranean Fleet to bombard the Italian positions at Bardia and Fort Capuzzo. Air attacks on the ships are beaten off.

Europe, Air Operations The RAF sends a raid against the armament works at Leuna. Although at this stage of the war the RAF intends to hit only military targets, it cannot achieve the necessary accuracy in night bombing.

Greece Following recently increased tension with Italy, the Greek armed forces are partially mobilized with a call-up in some districts. Among the provocations is the sinking of the Greek cruiser *Helle* by an Italian submarine.

Battle of Britain There are no major German attacks even though the weather is reasonably good. In response to pleas from Dowding the Air Ministry agrees to give Fighter Command some extra pilots from other RAF branches and to shorten the training period for new pilots even though this has obvious disadvantages.

18 AUGUST 1940

Battle of Britain The Germans make another big effort. Their targets are still mostly airfields but not all the attacks are well organized. Biggin Hill escapes comparatively lightly, but Kenley is so disrupted that part of the fighter force has to be withdrawn to another airfield. The Germans lose very heavily, 71 aircraft to Fighter Command's 27. The British originally claim that 155 have been shot down. Owing to heavy losses the Stuka is withdrawn from attacks on targets inland.

20 AUGUST 1940

Britain, Home Front Churchill produces another of his famous fighting speeches. His message is a tribute to the RAF fighter pilots: 'Never in the field of human conflict was so much owed by so many to so few.'

Of more concrete importance to the course of the war is an official announcement that bases will be leased to the United States.

21 AUGUST 1940

World Affairs Leon Trotsky is assassinated in Mexico. Trotsky has been an enemy of Stalin throughout the latter's career, and it seems that the assassin has been working on Soviet orders.

24 AUGUST 1940

Battle of Britain After a lull of five days of poor weather the Germans again resume major operations. Their bombers now have really strong escorts and it is in consequence very difficult for the British fighters to get among the formations. The small airfield at Manston is so badly damaged that it cannot be used. There is also a damaging attack on Portsmouth. The losses for the day are nearer the figures required by the Germans, with the Luftwaffe losing 38 and the RAF 22. During the night the Germans continue their efforts, sending 170 bombers on various missions. Some of these, unable to find their targets, scatter their bombs aimlessly on South London despite specific orders to avoid this – a serious and significant error. During the night only two German bombers are lost.

25 AUGUST 1940

Battle of Britain The main German attack is against the fighter airfield at Warmwell. The attack is heavily escorted and, despite powerful British fighter forces being sent, the Germans only lose one bomber and each side loses 11 fighters. In total the Germans lose 20 aircraft and the British 16. This ratio favors the Germans in the long run. During the night the Germans attack Birmingham and other targets.

In response to the events of the previous night the RAF bombs Berlin. This is something of a shock to the German leaders who have claimed extravagantly that this is impossible.

26 AUGUST 1940

Battle of Britain The German attacks continue. They send three major raids against RAF airfields and one on Portsmouth. One of the airfield raids gets through almost undamaged but all the others are engaged heavily by the RAF. The day's losses are 31 RAF fighters and 19 German bombers and 26 fighters. According to the original timetable Hitler ought to decide now whether the invasion should be attempted.

27 AUGUST 1940

Battle of the Atlantic The Coastal Command of the RAF establishes an air base on Iceland to help in convoy protection. At this stage there are only outdated Fairey Battle aircraft situated there, but this base will soon be expanded.

28 AUGUST 1940

Battle of Britain After a lull on the 27th, the Germans attack again. They lose 30 aircraft and Fighter Command 20. One attack is made by fighters alone and the British commanders are tricked into engaging it on the assumption that it is a mixed formation. During the night there is the first of a series of four raids on Liverpool. Around 160 aircraft are sent each night.
Battle of the Atlantic The British AMC *Dunvegan Castle* is sunk by a U-Boat.

29 AUGUST 1940

Battle of Britain There are more German fighter sweeps but no major efforts by the day-bomber force. The losses are 17 German and nine British aircraft.

30 AUGUST 1940

Battle of Britain The Germans attack airfields in Kent and an aircraft factory at Luton. The important Biggin Hill sector station is severely hit as is the Luton airport. The Germans lose 36 planes and the RAF 26. Hitler announces that he will make a decision on Operation Sealion about 10 September. This will mean that the landings will be on 21 September.
Diplomatic Relations In the Balkans, Hungary and Bulgaria have been recently trying to pick a quarrel with Rumania so that, following the example of the Soviet Union, they can seize portions of Rumanian territory. The Germans do not wish their grain and oil supplies to be threatened by a Balkan war and, therefore, intervene to adjudicate the dispute. A conference is called at Vienna and by the Vienna Award Hungary is given a large part of Transylvania and Bulgaria is given southern Dobruja. Rumania can only acquiesce.

31 AUGUST 1940

Battle of Britain The Germans maintain their concentrated attacks on the British airfields. Biggin Hill is almost put out of action and Debden and Hornchurch are severely hit. The RAF loses 39 aircraft in the air and several more are hit on the ground. The Luftwaffe losses are 41. Goering is now in measurable distance of achieving his objective of superiority over southeast England. The RAF airfields at Biggin Hill, Manston, West Malling, Lympne and Hawkinge are all more or less out of the fight. There are only two RAF sector stations in commission south of the Thames and three more airfields which might be used for that role. There is no reason why these might not be similarly damaged, three having been already hit. This is the RAF's most difficult period of the battle.

SEPTEMBER 1940

Battle of the Atlantic British problems in coastal waters increase when German E-Boats now begin major operations off the east coast. (There have been a few E-Boat sorties earlier in the summer.) The majority of sinkings by U-Boats are still occurring off the Irish coast with 70 percent being achieved by surface attack by night. The U-Boats sink 59 ships out of a total loss of 100 of 448,600 tons.

CHRONOLOGY

1 SEPTEMBER 1940

East Africa In Kenya the Italians capture the small town of Buna in the northeast of the country.

1–6 SEPTEMBER 1940

Battle of Britain The German attacks on the British airfields continue but with less strength than in the two previous days. Effort is wasted on less vital aircraft factories. On 4 September they attack a bomber factory at Weybridge and on 6 September a more important plant at Brooklands. By the end of this period the RAF fighters are flying more sorties per day than the combined total of the German bombers and fighters. The RAF loses 120 planes and the Luftwaffe 148. If the RAF losses on the ground are added or if some allowance is made for German planes crashing on the way home it seems that the Germans are getting the better of the fighting. However, it is clear that Park is keeping his force in existence through the troubles and is not yet beaten. There are also night attacks on Bristol, Liverpool and London.

2 SEPTEMBER 1940

United States, Policy Following the agreement made in July and later detailed negotiations, a deal is now ratified between Britain and the USA by which Britain gets 50 old destroyers, veterans of World War I, but desperately needed for escort work, in return for bases granted to the United States in the West Indies and Bermuda. The first of the ships is taken over by a RN crew on 9 September and reaches the UK on the 28th. Considerable modification will be necessary to make the ships ready for service. This is an important stage in Roosevelt's efforts to develop a more active foreign policy and accustom the American public to actively supporting the Allies.

Mediterranean Admiral Cunningham's fleet is reinforced by the battleship *Valiant* and the carrier *Illustrious* from Gibraltar. He now has three battleships and two carriers. The composition of the Gibraltar based Force H varies greatly from time to time because of the uncertainty regarding the behavior of the French Fleet. The Italians now have five battleships in commission, including two modern ships.

3 SEPTEMBER 1940

Germany, Planning The operational orders for the invasion of Britain are issued. It is confirmed that the decision to go will be taken 10 days before the invasion is to take place. S-Day is now scheduled for 21 September.

The Sealion plan now provides for elements of 11 divisions to make the assault. Two airborne divisions are to be sent in at once, but the other nine will start 6700 strong and will only reach full strength after several days. About 250 tanks are to accompany the assault. Four divisions of the Sixteenth Army with airborne support are to land near Folkestone, two of the Ninth Army near Eastbourne and three more of the Ninth Army, also with airborne support, at Brighton. These beachheads will not be mutually supporting in the early stages.

At this time the defending British forces have only made a partial recovery from the equipment losses at Dunkirk. There are perhaps four divisions fully equipped and about eight more in a reasonable state. In addition, there are various mobile brigade groups. There are about 350 cruiser and heavy tanks in the country and about 500 antitank guns.

4 SEPTEMBER 1940

United States, Policy The United States warns the Japanese government against making aggressive moves in Indochina.

4–6 SEPTEMBER 1940

Rumania There are political upheavals following the recent losses of territory by the Vienna Award. On the 4th King Carol gives General Antonescu full powers. Parliament is dissolved on the 5th and the constitution suspended, and on the 6th the king abdicates in favor of Prince Michael. Later in the month it is announced that the fascist Iron Guard is to be the only legal political party.

7 SEPTEMBER 1940

Battle of Britain The British authorities decide that they have information that a German invasion is likely in the next few days and accordingly they issue an invasion warning. This warning is in the form of the signal word Cromwell which means that invasion is imminent and its issue causes some wild measures to be taken. In fact this signal has been chosen because its true meaning corresponds most nearly to the needs of bringing about a higher state of readiness. No other code word has this effect.

The Germans alter the tactics of their air offensive and send a major daytime raid against London. This gives the RAF a welcome respite from the airfield attacks which have been so damaging during the last few days. The German attack on London follows from a suggestion of Hitler which coincides with Goering's own theories. The German tactic is that the RAF will be forced to commit its carefully hoarded reserves and that they can then be destroyed. Kesselring's 2nd Air Fleet is to attack London by day with its 500 bombers (including some brought from Norway and Denmark) and 600 fighters. Sperrle is to attack by night with about 300 bombers, as all his fighters have been switched to Kesselring. In addition there are about 100 Me 110s and over 200 Stukas. The British have about 350 aircraft in their front-line squadrons with more in reserve. Park is modifying his tactics slightly to cope with the bigger German formations and now intends pairing his squadrons where possible.

In the afternoon the Germans send 300 bombers and 600 fighters to attack targets in the London dock area. The British interceptions are not well managed because the change of tactics comes as a surprise. The Luftwaffe loses 41 aircraft and Fighter Command 28 shot down and several more damaged. The bombing is most effective. During the night Sperrle follows up the attack with 250 bombers with the still-blazing fires to guide them to their target. The damage is very serious. There is little the RAF can do at night to achieve interceptions although the first airborne radar sets are coming into operation. Despite the damage done it is clear that the casualties and the disruption of civilian life are not as great as prewar fears suggested. There is no question of the Germans achieving a decisive result in these operations. These attacks become known as 'The Blitz' by the British people.

8 SEPTEMBER 1940

Battle of Britain There is relatively little activity, but the day is important because of a decision by Dowding that the Fighter Command units in southeast England should have the right to select the best pilots to keep their experienced squadrons up to strength despite the effects this will have on the other parts of the Command and on planning for the future.

9 SEPTEMBER 1940

Battle of Britain The Germans send about 200 bombers, well escorted, to bomb London. They are intercepted by strong RAF forces and many are compelled to drop their bombs before reaching their targets. The air battle is very fierce. The British lose 19 planes and the Germans 28.

United States, Politics A new $5,500,000,000 appropriations bill becomes law in the United States. Contracts are placed for 210 new vessels for the navy, including seven battleships and 12 carriers.

West Africa Six French warships leave Toulon bound for Dakar. They are reported to the British forces too late, and reach Dakar despite the efforts of the squadrons now en route to Dakar to attack on behalf of the Free French.

10 SEPTEMBER 1940

Battle of Britain Hitler decides that the Luftwaffe has not yet won clear air supremacy and puts off his decision on Sealion until 14 Sep-

Above: A Messerschmitt Bf 109, the Luftwaffe's standard fighter in 1940.

tember, which means that the invasion is now scheduled for 24 September. In the air this is a quiet day.

10–20 SEPTEMBER 1940

Albania The Italians increase their force in Albania by 40,000 men in preparation for their proposed attack on Greece.

11 SEPTEMBER 1940

Battle of Britain The air fighting goes well for the Germans. They send a raid to London which gets through to the target and they also do significant damage to a Spitfire factory at Southampton. In the fighting the RAF comes off worst, losing 25 aircraft to the German loss of 29. Buckingham Palace is hit by a bomb but none of the Royal family is hurt. In fact, this is of benefit to national morale since it gives the impression that punishment is being shared fairly.

13 SEPTEMBER 1940

North Africa The Italian forces begin a cautious offensive from Libya into Egypt. They have five divisions in the attack with another eight in rear areas in Libya. Marshal Graziani is in command. The British Western Desert Force of two divisions is led by General O'Connor. On the first day the Italians occupy Sollum as the British pull back.

During the months since the Italian declaration of war there have been no actions of any size, but the Italian numerical superiority has been morally undermined by much offensive patrolling by the British forces. These harassing tactics are now employed to good effect against the Italian offensive.

Battle of Britain The British bring heavy units of the Royal Navy nearer to the likely invasion area. The battleships *Nelson* and *Rodney* join the *Hood* at Rosyth and the *Revenge* is at Plymouth. There are, of course, strong cruiser and destroyer forces in relevant positions.

East Africa Italian troops from Ethiopia penetrate up to 20 miles into Kenya in a tentative advance.

14 SEPTEMBER 1940

Battle of Britain Hitler decides that Goering needs four or five consecutive days of fine weather to hammer home his advantage. Accordingly he defers his decision on the invasion once more, until 17 September, which in turn means that the invasion cannot take place until 27 September. This is a final date because 8 October might be the only day when

conditions will be suitable for the landing; this is dangerously near winter for the exploitation stage of the invasion. There can almost certainly be no further postponement.

The daytime attacks on London are repeated again after two quieter days. The night attacks have been continuing without respite. The fighting goes well for the Luftwaffe with 14 planes lost on either side. With some justification it appears to the Luftwaffe leaders that the RAF is almost beaten.

15 SEPTEMBER 1940

Battle of Britain Kesselring makes another great effort against London. He plans two main raids but they cannot be timed to catch the RAF fighters refuelling because his strength is sufficiently reduced that he must send the same fighters on both occasions. He can muster about 400 fighters but less than 200 bombers in the morning attack. The fighting is very heavy with the Germans being harried all the way to London, then being heavily engaged over London and all the way back to the coast. The bombers are not able to drop their loads with any accuracy at all. The afternoon shows a similar story but the fighter battles are more intense and the bombers bomb nearer to their targets as a consequence. Although the fighter combats have gone about equally the German bomber losses are very severe, bringing the German loss for the day to 60 aircraft for a bag of 26 from the RAF. Many more German bombers have been damaged or have crewmen dead or wounded. Their morale suffers as they meet up to 300 RAF fighters in one raid after their leaders have told them that the RAF as a whole has less than this number. Although it is not apparent at the time or for several weeks afterward, this is the last real attempt by the Luftwaffe to destroy the resistance of Fighter Command.

USSR, Home Front The USSR modifies its conscription laws. From now on 19–20 year olds will be conscripted.

Canada, Home Front Following legislation passed in August single men between 21–24 are called up.

16 SEPTEMBER 1940

North Africa The Italians take Sidi Barrani as their cautious advance into Egypt begins to grind to a halt.

United States, Home Front The Selective Service Bill becomes law. It permits compulsory induction into the armed forces for all males between the ages of 21–35.

16–17 SEPTEMBER 1940
Mediterranean Aircraft from the carrier *Illustrious*, escorted by the battleship *Valiant*, attack Benghazi during the night. Four Italian ships are sunk in the harbor, including two destroyers. The cruiser *Kent* is detached from the force while returning to Alexandria in order to shell Bardia and is badly damaged in an attack by torpedo planes.

17 SEPTEMBER 1940
Battle of Britain Hitler postpones Operation Sealion until further notice. The German invasion flotillas are attacked during the night by RAF Bomber Command and a fair degree of damage is done. The German night attacks include a raid on Clydeside in which the cruiser *Sussex* is damaged.
Germany, Planning General Paulus, the Deputy Chief of the Army General Staff, presents a further plan for the attack on the Soviet Union. This version envisages three thrusts for Leningrad, Moscow and Kiev, but the emphasis is still on the central advance to the Soviet capital. Further consideration over the coming weeks confirms to the General Staff that this priority is correct (*see* 5 December).

18 SEPTEMBER 1940
North Africa The advance of the Italian Tenth Army comes to a halt, officially because of supply difficulties. They occupy themselves building various fortified camps and make little effort to keep in touch with the British forces which have pulled back before their superior strength.
Battle of Britain During the day there is a German attack by 50 bombers on targets in London. There is heavy fighting in which the RAF loses 12 planes and the Luftwaffe 19.

19 SEPTEMBER 1940
Battle of Britain The German invasion fleet begins to disperse from the Channel ports. The later reports of the German navy show that 1918 barges have been assembled, of which 214 have been sunk or damaged. Similarly 21 out of 170 transports have been lost.
Axis Diplomacy Ribbentrop meets Mussolini and Ciano in Rome and warns them not to attack Greece or Yugoslavia. The Italian leaders dutifully reply that they will conquer Egypt first.

19–24 SEPTEMBER 1940
Battle of Britain The German attacks continue with minor raids in which they lose 59 planes and shoot down 22.

20–22 SEPTEMBER 1940
Battle of the Atlantic The convoy HX-72 is successfully attacked by a U-Boat group. Altogether 12 ships of 78,000 tons are sunk, seven of them during the night of 21–22 September by Schepke's *U.100* without him even being detected by the convoy escorts.

21 SEPTEMBER 1940
Australia, Politics The election results are declared. Menzies remains prime minister. Labor is the largest party in both the House and the Senate but has no overall majority.
It is announced that a 9th Australian Division will be raised.
The Blitz As the night attacks on London continue, the government officially allows the subway stations to be used as air-raid shelters. This has been happening for some time.

22 SEPTEMBER 1940
Indochina The Japanese enter Indochina after concluding a long period of negotiation with the Vichy government. The Japanese aim is to prevent aid reaching the Chinese through Indochina. There are to be 6000 troops stationed in the country and they are to have transit rights.
Finland Finland agrees to allow transit rights to German troops en route to north Norway in return for arms supplies.

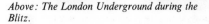

Above: The London Underground during the Blitz.

23–24 SEPTEMBER 1940
Europe, Air Operations During the night the RAF bombs Berlin.

23–25 SEPTEMBER 1940
French West Africa British and Free French forces try to bring the port of Dakar over to the Allied cause. The operation is code named Menace. The British are led by Admiral J Cunningham and the French by General de Gaulle. The forces involved include three small Free French warships but the main power is provided by two British battleships and one carrier. There are 3600 Free French troops aboard the various transports and a further 4300 British who, for political reasons, are not to be used unless absolutely necessary. The Vichy forces include the battleship *Richelieu* (unfinished), two cruisers and some destroyers and submarines. Admiral Landriau commands these vessels and Governor Boisson is in overall charge. On the first day of the operation there are talks between de Gaulle and the Vichy representatives, but these fail to reach any agreement and the Vichy warships begin an exchange of fire. There is damage done on both sides and one Vichy submarine sunk. An attempt by the Free French forces to land in Rufique Bay is beaten off. On 24 September the battleship *Resolution* is hit by shellfire and on 25 September is seriously damaged by a torpedo. On 25 September the *Barham* takes a 15-inch hit from *Richelieu*. Following these setbacks the operation is abandoned on Churchill's orders.

24–25 SEPTEMBER 1940
Mediterranean As a retaliation for the events at Dakar, Vichy air forces attempt on both days to raid Gibraltar. Little damage is done.

25 SEPTEMBER 1940
Norway Terboven, the Reichs Commissioner, deposes the King of Norway formally and appoints Quisling to lead the new Norwegian government.

25–30 SEPTEMBER 1940
Battle of Britain The German attacks in this period are sent mostly against aircraft factories. Factories in Bristol, Southampton and Yeovil are all hit but the defending fighters exact a high price. The RAF loses 82 planes and the Luftwaffe 143.

26 SEPTEMBER 1940
United States, Policy An embargo is imposed on the export of all scrap iron and steel to Japan.

27 SEPTEMBER 1940
Axis Diplomacy Germany, Italy and Japan sign an agreement promising that each will declare war on any third party which joins the war against one of the three. It is stated that this agreement does not affect either Germany's or Japan's relations with the USSR. This treaty is known as the Tripartite Pact. All the signatories hope that the pact will deter the United States from joining the war in Europe or taking a more active line in the Far East.

OCTOBER 1940
Battle of the Atlantic During the month the British shipping losses are 103 ships of 443,000 tons of which the U-Boats sink 352,400 tons. Convoys are now provided with escorts as far as 19 degrees west (about 300 miles east of Ireland). The Canadian forces provide similar cover in their waters. There are, however, still very few escorts and the cover is not strong. Following a few earlier attempts to coordinate operations by a group of U-Boats the wolf-pack tactics now begin to be widely used. There is little that can be done against these or against the U-Boats' favorite technique of attacking on the surface from within the center of a convoy at night. The submarines present only a small, insignificant, profile to visual search and radar is not yet advanced enough to conquer this deficiency. The listening devices with which escorts are equipped are not able to discern the difference between the sound of a submarine and the sound of the ships of the convoy, and Asdic (Sonar) is only effective against submerged submarines. Even if they are sighted, the U-Boats are often able to escape into the darkness because they are faster on the surface than the corvettes which form a large part of the escort forces.

Battle of Britain The Germans only send in a few raids by bombers in daylight. They do, however, send sweeps by fighters and fighter-bombers at altitudes which make interceptions difficult for the RAF and at which the Me 109 is superior to both the Spitfire and Hurricane. The night attacks of the Blitz continue, with London still bearing the brunt, but Liverpool, Manchester and Birmingham are also attacked.

By the end of the month bad weather is beginning to put an end to the day operations, and in fact 31 October is regarded by the British as the end of the Battle of Britain.

Germany, Planning To aid their preparations for an attack on the Soviet Union, German reconnaissance planes begin flights over Soviet territory at great altitude to spy out troop dispositions. The Soviets either are not aware or choose to ignore these air space violations.

1 OCTOBER 1940

Finland The Germans and Finns reach another agreement strengthening their ties. The Germans promise arms and the Finns grant rights to the Germans to purchase their nickel production from the mines in the Petsamo region.

3 OCTOBER 1940

Britain, Politics Neville Chamberlain resigns his position in the War Cabinet. His offices are taken up by Herbert Morrison, Lord President of the Council, and Sir John Anderson, Home Secretary. Kingsley Wood and Bevin are brought into the War Cabinet.

4 OCTOBER 1940

Axis Diplomacy Hitler and Mussolini meet. Hitler warns Mussolini against undertaking new campaigns and offers help in Africa, which Mussolini declines.
British Command Sir Charles Portal is chosen to be the new Chief of the Air Staff. The former chief, Sir Cyril Newall, becomes governor of New Zealand.

5 OCTOBER 1940

United States, Politics The Tripartite Pact is condemned by Navy Secretary Knox and he announces that he is calling up some of the naval reserve.

6 OCTOBER 1940

Rumania Antonescu assumes command of the Iron Guard, adding further strength to his position. On 7 October German troops enter Rumania ostensibly to help reorganize the army. Hitler's main aim is in fact to protect the oil fields.

7 OCTOBER 1940

France The Germans order all Jewish people in the occupied part of France to register immediately with their authorities.

9 OCTOBER 1940

Britain, Politics Following Chamberlain's resignation Churchill is chosen as the new leader of the Conservative Party. This is an impressive achievement because he was little liked by many in the party at the time of his selection as prime minister. He has succeeded in winning their loyalty despite the hard times he has presided over. His attention to party affairs illustrates his concern for the forms of parliamentary democracy.

9–20 OCTOBER 1940

Battle of the Atlantic During this time there are 11 German submarines operating in the North Atlantic and they succeed in sinking 39 ships. Convoy SC-7 of 30 ships is attacked between 17–19 October and loses 21 vessels and HX-79 of 49 ships loses 12 between 19–20 October. Following these losses the British decide to increase their convoy escorts and this can only be done by dismantling some of the antiinvasion measures.

10 OCTOBER 1940

Luxembourg The Germans run a plebiscite in Luxembourg. When the results are counted they find that 97 percent of the population is opposed to their occupation. The experiment is not repeated elsewhere.

11 OCTOBER 1940

The Blitz Liverpool is heavily attacked in the continuing German bombing campaign. Four ships in the port are sunk and other damage is inflicted.
Finland The demilitarization of the Åland Islands is agreed in a Finnish-Soviet convention.
France, Politics Pétain broadcasts to the French people, advocating that they abandon their traditional ideas on who are their friends and who are their enemies.

11–12 OCTOBER 1940

Mediterranean The British light cruiser *Ajax* is attacked during the night by first three then four Italian destroyers. Two of the attackers are sunk and two damaged.

12 OCTOBER 1940

Germany, Planning Operation Sealion is deferred until the spring of 1941. It will never take place.

15 OCTOBER 1940

Italy, Planning The Italian War Council makes the final decision for an attack on Greece. Hitler is not to be told beforehand and instead is to be presented with a *fait accompli*. The Italians hope for the campaign to be over within two weeks. Operations will start at the end of the month.
Germany, Planning Goering issues orders to give priorities for the German night offensive against Britain. The priorities are firstly London, secondly aircraft factories and third industry in the Midlands and all air bases.

16 OCTOBER 1940

United States, Home Front Registration begins for the draft according to the provisions of the

Selective Service Act. The first drafts will be balloted on 29 October.

16–19 OCTOBER 1940
Diplomatic Affairs There are discussions between the Japanese and the authorities in the Dutch East Indies concerning the supply of oil. It is agreed to supply the Japanese with 40 percent of the production for the next six months. There are British attempts to block this agreement.

18 OCTOBER 1940
China The Burma Road is reopened to the passage of supplies to Chiang Kai-shek's forces.
Vichy France Anti-Semitic laws are introduced whereby Jews are to be excluded from public service and from positions of authority in industry and the media.

20 OCTOBER 1940
Persian Gulf Italian planes from bases in East Africa bomb oil refineries in Bahrain and Saudi Arabia.

20–21 OCTOBER 1940
Red Sea There is a surface action between four Italian destroyers and the escorts of a British convoy. The convoy is escorted by a light cruiser, one destroyer and five smaller vessels. The Italians lose one ship.

23 OCTOBER 1940 ·
Axis Diplomacy Hitler meets General Franco at Hendaye in southern France. Hitler tries to persuade Franco to join the war and offers as bait the allocation of Gibraltar and territory in North Africa. Franco is uncertain about how to proceed and successfully muddles the issue, leaving Hitler no better informed as to what is Spanish policy but without causing offense.

24 OCTOBER 1940
Belgium, Politics An exile government is established in London. Its leading members include Camille Gutt, Hubert Pierlot and Paul-Henri-Spaak.

26 OCTOBER 1940
Battle of the Atlantic The 42,000-ton liner *Empress of Britain* is damaged by a bomb attack off the coast of Ireland. On 28 October *U.32* completes the job and sinks the damaged ship.

27 OCTOBER 1940
Axis Diplomacy At 2100 hours the Italians tell the Germans of their decision to invade Greece.

28 OCTOBER 1940
Greece and Albania An Italian ultimatum is presented to the Greeks during the night. It amounts to a declaration of war. At dawn, before the ultimatum expires, the Italians begin to cross the border into Greece. Patras is bombed.

General Prasca leads eight of the 10 Italian divisions in Albania in the advance. They attack along three lines with the main effort being in the center from the Dhrina and Vijosë valleys. General Papagos, the Greek Commander in Chief, has not deployed his main forces close to the border to avoid giving any provocation to the Italians. He too hopes to use eight divisions with the possibility of reinforcements being brought from the troops watching the Bulgarian border.

The greatest obstacle to the Italians for the first two or three days is the very bad weather which grounds their air support. The Italians have chosen a very unwise time of the year for their attack.

Hitler and Mussolini meet at Florence. Hitler conceals his anger at not being kept informed of the Italian plans and says that German troops are available if it is necessary to keep the British out of Greece and away from the Rumanian oil.
France, Politics Laval becomes Foreign Minister of the Vichy government.

NOVEMBER 1940
Battle of the Atlantic The German submarine force has now been joined in the Atlantic by 26 Italian vessels, but this strong force proves to be very inefficient. The shipping losses are 97 ships of 385,700 tons of which U-Boats account for 32 ships.
The Blitz Among the targets for the German air raids this month are Coventry, Birmingham, Southampton, Bristol and Liverpool. London continues to be hit also. Civilian casualties are 4500 dead and 6200 seriously hurt.
Europe, Air Operations Among the RAF targets are Berlin, Essen, Munich, Hamburg and Cologne. Bomber Command drops 1300 tons of bombs.

1 NOVEMBER 1940
Greece and Albania The Italian advance reaches the Kalamas River in the Epirus district. A small British bomber unit is sent to help the Greeks. This force is increased at Churchill's order during the next few days. About half the RAF strength from Egypt is sent. The British government believes that it is vital to fulfill the guarantees given to Greece to bolster neutral opinion, especially in the Balkans and Turkey.

3 NOVEMBER 1940
The Blitz This is the first night since 7 September that there is no raid on London. There have been 57 consecutive nights of attack and after tonight 10 more will follow. An average of 165 planes has attacked each night dropping 13,600 tons of high explosive and many incendiaries.

Battle of the Atlantic Two British AMCs, the *Laurentic* and the *Patroclus* are sunk by Kretschmer's *U.99*.

4 NOVEMBER 1940
Greece and Albania The first Greek counterattacks begin in the northern sector of the front. The Italian offensive, despite its numerical strength, is already in difficulties.

5 NOVEMBER 1940
United States, Politics President Roosevelt is elected for an unprecedented third term. His majority in the popular vote is 10 percent – 27,000,000 to Willkie's 22,000,000. In the Congressional elections the Democrats lose four Senate seats and gain eight seats in the House. They retain their majority in both chambers.

Battle of the Atlantic The German pocket battleship *Admiral Scheer* finds the British convoy HX-84 of 37 ships while on a sortie into the Atlantic. At this point in its route the convoy is only escorted by a single AMC, the *Jervis Bay*, which, although totally outgunned, engages the *Scheer* to gain time for the convoy to scatter. *Jervis Bay* is, of course, sunk but only five ships of the convoy fail to get away. The British suspend convoy sailings until 17 November but their pursuit fails to find the German ship which has moved toward the south Atlantic.

Scheer has left port on October 23 and will return on 1 April 1941 after sinking 16 ships of 99,000 tons in addition to *Jervis Bay*.

6 NOVEMBER 1940
Greece and Albania The Italian advance in the coastal sector reaches Igoumenitsa.

6–7 NOVEMBER 1940
East Africa General Slim's 10th Indian Brigade attacks and captures Gallabat from the Italians on the 6th but withdraws again on the 7th after losses to the supporting tanks and in the air. The Italians reoccupy the position.

7 NOVEMBER 1940
West Africa Colonel Leclerc leads a Free French force in landings north of Libreville. There is some fighting but by 14 November French Equatorial Africa has been brought over to the Free French.

8–10 NOVEMBER 1940
Greece and Albania The Italian 3rd Alpini Division is trapped in the area of the Pindus Gorges by the Greek counterattacks. The Greeks take over 5000 prisoners.

9 NOVEMBER 1940
Britain, Politics Neville Chamberlain, the former prime minister, dies at the age of 71.

10 NOVEMBER 1940
Greece and Albania The Italian Undersecretary for War, General Soddu, replaces General Prasca as the Commander in Chief in Albania.

11 NOVEMBER 1940
Battle of Britain In a postscript to the main actions a force of Italian bombers, protected by biplane fighters, is sent to attack Harwich. They are intercepted and lose six planes for no loss to the RAF. The Italians make other attacks, mostly by night, on east-coast ports during the next nine weeks.

11–12 NOVEMBER 1940
Mediterranean The British Mediterranean Fleet attacks the Italian base at Taranto. During the night 21 Swordfish aircraft attack in two waves and gain three torpedo hits on the brand new battleship *Littorio* and one each on *Caio Duilio* and *Conte di Cavour*. Two other ships are damaged. The aircraft have come from the carrier *Illustrious* and only two are lost. This brilliant attack will certainly be studied by other navies and the potential for such an attack on an enemy fleet in harbor is clear to the Japanese.

In other operations in the few preceding days the Mediterranean Fleet has carried troops to Malta and been strengthened by another battleship, making five in all. The Gibraltar based Force H attacked Cagliari with aircraft from *Ark Royal* on 9 November.

12 NOVEMBER 1940
Germany, Planning Hitler issues Directive 18. Although talks are being conducted with the Soviets (Molotov is in Berlin), the planning for the attack on the Soviet Union is to continue as are the preparations for the attack, code named Marita, on Greece, and Felix, the advance through Spain to Gibraltar.

12–13 NOVEMBER 1940
Dutch East Indies Agreements are concluded

between the Japanese and the principal oil companies whereby the Japanese are to receive 1,800,000 tons of oil annually from the Dutch East Indies.

14 NOVEMBER 1940
British Command The new British Commander in Chief for the Far East, Air Marshal Brooke-Popham, arrives in Singapore.

The Blitz There is an especially heavy and effective German attack on Coventry involving 449 planes. Factories and historic buildings are badly damaged. Some historians have since suggested that, by a combination of scientific and cryptographic Intelligence, the British authorities were able to take precautions against this raid but that they did not do so in order to protect their sources. This is not the case. Warning has been received during the afternoon of the 14th and the few precautions possible at this short notice have been taken by the relevant authorities.

14–16 NOVEMBER 1940
Greece and Albania By the 14th all the Greek forces are in full attack against the Italian invaders. Reinforcements have been brought from the troops facing Bulgaria.

British aid to Greece begins to arrive. Four cruisers ferry 3400 troops and airfield staff from Alexandria to Piraeus. By 20 November another 4000 have arrived.

15 NOVEMBER 1940
Atlantic US flying boats begin patrols from bases in Bermuda.

Greece and Albania The Greek counteroffensives continue with especial success for the advance from western Macedonia in the area around Mount Morava.

17 NOVEMBER 1940
British Command Air Marshal Dowding is replaced at Fighter Command by Air Marshal Sholto Douglas. Dowding is sent to work for the Ministry of Aircraft Production in the section dealing with orders for American planes. Later he will be denied the promotion to Marshal of the Royal Air Force which his distinguished services during the Battle of Britain more than entitle him to expect. Air Marshal Park will also be treated in a shabby fashion and will shortly be replaced at 11 Group by Leigh Mallory. Park will receive no comparable command in the future. A new RAF Command for army Cooperation is created, to be led by Air Marshal Barratt.

18–19 NOVEMBER 1940
Battle of the Atlantic In an Atlantic operation a U-Boat approaching a convoy is detected by a Sunderland flying boat fitted with an Air to Surface Vessel (ASV1) radar set. This is the first time such a location has been achieved by airborne radar in operational conditions.

19 NOVEMBER 1940
Greece and Albania The Greeks claim to have driven the Italians back behind the Kalamas River. There is heavy fighting near Koritza.

20 NOVEMBER 1940
Hungary Prime Minister Count Teleki and Foreign Minister Csaky agree in Vienna to bring Hungary in to the Tripartite Pact's provisions.

21 NOVEMBER 1940
Greece and Albania The Greeks enter Koritza. They capture 2000 prisoners and some heavy equipment. Almost all the invading Italian forces have now been driven back to Albania.

United States, Home Front The Dies report on German and Communist espionage and subversive activities is published. As in the similar investigations which have been made in Britain, the strength of these disruptive elements is wildly overestimated and accompanied with calls for preventive measures.

Australia, Politics The government presents its war budget for the coming year. Twenty percent of the national income is to be devoted to war expenditure and is to be financed by considerable increases in taxation.

23 NOVEMBER 1940
Britain, Production and Supply The new British Ambassador to the United States, Lord Lothian, talks in New York of the possibility of Britain running out of ready money and securities to pay for arms and says that Britain will need financial help in 1941. In fact by April 1941 British reserves of gold and dollars will be as low as $12,000,000 – a mere pittance when set against arms expenditure.

Balkans, Politics In a meeting in Berlin Antonescu agrees to join the Axis powers. There are also talks on preparation for a German attack on Greece by the forces based in Rumania. Germany has been putting pressure on all the Balkan states since the Italian invasion of Greece in an attempt to ensure the stability of food and oil supplies. Hungary succumbed to the pressure on 20 November. Bulgaria and Yugoslavia have not joined the Tripartite Pact but progress has been made in the talks.

24 NOVEMBER 1940
Balkans, Politics The prime minister of the German puppet state of Slovakia, Tuka, joins the Tripartite Pact powers in a meeting in Berlin.

26 NOVEMBER 1940
Poland, Home Front Work begins on the creation of a Jewish ghetto in Warsaw in which the Germans intend to herd the local Jewish population under dreadful living conditions. The Germans describe the move as a 'health measure.'
Mediterranean Aircraft from the British carrier *Eagle* raid Tripoli. In another operation the carrier *Illustrious* attacks targets on Rhodes.

27 NOVEMBER 1940
Mediterranean There is a naval battle off Sardinia. Admiral Somerville, who is covering a Malta convoy, has the *Renown, Ark Royal*, four cruisers and nine destroyers. He will be joined later by *Ramillies*, three cruisers and five destroyers. Admiral Campioni leads two battleships, seven heavy cruisers and 16 destroyers. There is a brief gun battle in which the cruiser *Berwick* and one Italian destroyer are hit. Despite their superior gunpower the Italians then break off the action.

27 NOVEMBER–4 DECEMBER 1940
Rumania, Home Front There are riots and other civil disturbances. The Iron Guard begin the trouble with the arrest and execution of various prominent persons including the former Prime Minister Jorga. The army later clamps down with German help.

30 NOVEMBER 1940
China, Politics Japan officially recognizes the puppet Nanking government led by President Wang Ching-wei.
Greece and Albania The Greek advance from Macedonia continues. They win an important victory near Pogradec.

DECEMBER 1940
War at Sea Bad weather hampers the main U-Boat operations with only one convoy, HX-90, being attacked during the month. There are some successes for the U-Boats off Portugal and West Africa. They sink 37 ships out of a total loss of 82.
The Blitz British civilian casualties this month are 3800 dead with 5250 injured. German targets include London, Sheffield and Liverpool. The attack on London on 29/30 December is heavy and destructive.

2 DECEMBER 1940
British Command Various command changes for the Royal Navy are announced. Admiral Tovey is to succeed Admiral Forbes as Commander in Chief, Home Fleet. Forbes goes to Plymouth Command. Admiral Harwood becomes Assistant Chief of the Naval Staff.

3 DECEMBER 1940
Britain, Production and Supply Britain announces that it has placed a first order with US yards for the construction of 60 merchant ships.

4 DECEMBER 1940
Greece and Albania The Greek forces continue their advance and enter Premeti.

5 DECEMBER 1940
Germany, Planning An outline plan for the attack on the Soviet Union is presented to Hitler by the army. As in the last version it provides for a three-pronged attack, with the center force moving toward Moscow being strongest. Hitler agrees to allow planning to go ahead on this basis but suggests some modifications (*see* 18 December). He also orders planning for the attack on Greece to continue.

6 DECEMBER 1940
Italian Command Marshal Badoglio resigns his post as Italian Commander in Chief. His successor is General Count Cavallero.
Greece and Albania The Greek advance north along the coast continues to go well. Sarandë is taken.

8 DECEMBER 1940
Greece and Albania The Greek forces capture Argyrocastro and Delvino.

9 DECEMBER 1940
North Africa The British begin an offensive in the western desert. General O'Connor leads two divisions, 7th Armored and 4th Indian, in the attack. They are supported by 7th Royal Tank Regiment (RTR) against whose Matilda tanks the Italians will have no answer. General Wavell is in Supreme Command in Egypt. The British force has few reserves and therefore the attack has comparatively limited objectives at first. General Graziani is the Italian Commander in Chief and he has deployed the seven divisions of General Gariboldi's Tenth Army in forward positions in Egypt. O'Connor's men began their advance from Mersa Matruh, 70 miles from the Italian front, three days previously and achieve

complete surprise when they make their attack. The Italians have done 'little since mid-September but build a series of fortified camps in which they now sit. These camps do not give any real support to each other and will be very easily isolated.

The British attack is in the form of a left hook around behind the Italian coastal positions and owes much to the careful training which the troops have received in desert warfare. The Matildas are used to break into first the Nibeiwa camp and then the Tummar West camp which both fall during this first day.

Italian Command There are command changes and redistribution of ships and squadrons in the Italian navy. Admiral Riccardi replaces Admiral Cavagnari as Undersecretary of State and Head of Supermarina. Admiral Iachino replaces Campioni as Fleet Commander in Chief.

Greece and Albania Pogradec falls to the Greek advance.

10 DECEMBER 1940

United States, Policy Roosevelt announces an extension of the export-license system. Iron ore, pig iron and many important iron and steel manufactures are brought within the system. Like previous measures this is aimed at Japan. The changes come into effect at the end of the year.

Germany, Strategy OKW issues a directive ordering the transfer of X Fliegerkorps to south Italy and Sicily. Field Marshal Milch has been in Rome during the past few days to discuss the measures to help the Italian navy.

North Africa Sidi Barrani falls to the British attack. There are 20,000 prisoners already in the offensive. The coast road to the west has been cut by 7th Armored Division at Buq Buq.

11 DECEMBER 1940

North Africa Sollum is bombarded by ships from Cunningham's fleet. Wavell's attacks have ruined five of the seven Italian divisions they have met and they are all rapidly retreating from Egypt. Some 14,000 more prisoners are taken, many of whom come from the Catanzaro Division which is expelled from positions near Buq Buq.

12 DECEMBER 1940

North Africa Wavell is not able to follow up his success as vigorously as he would have wished because 4th Indian Division is about to be withdrawn for service in the Sudan.

Balkans, Politics A treaty of friendship is signed in Belgrade by Yugoslavian and Hun-garian representatives. By this token of good relations with a German client the Yugoslavs hope to improve their own relations with Germany.

13 DECEMBER 1940

Germany, Planning Hitler issues Directive 20 giving orders for the further preparation of the invasion of Greece, Operation Marita. The German forces in Rumania are accordingly increased.

Vichy, Politics Pétain dismisses and arrests Laval and appoints Flandin as foreign minister in his place. Laval is released on 17 December after the German ambassador has intervened.

North Africa A small British force has entered Libya and now cuts the road leading west from the important Italian position at Bardia.

16–24 DECEMBER 1940

Mediterranean There are further British and Italian fleet operations. Valona in Albania is shelled by the British battleships *Valiant* and *Warspite*. The Italians are also active in support of their armies in Albania with Lukova, just north of the Corfu Channel being shelled. The British carrier *Illustrious* attacks airfields on Rhodes and sends strikes against Italian convoys.

17 DECEMBER 1940

United States, Politics President Roosevelt gives a press conference outlining a scheme which he plans to introduce to bring further aid to Britain which he will call Lend-Lease. His argument is that if a neighbor's house is on fire it is only sensible to lend him a hose to stop the fire spreading to your own house, and that it would be stupid to think of asking for payment in such circumstances.

North Africa The British forces occupy Fort Capuzzo, Sollum and three other Italian positions near the Egypt-Libya border. The Italian garrisons of these places have withdrawn to the Bardia fortress.

18 DECEMBER 1940

Germany, Planning Hitler issues Directive 21. Its message is simple: 'The German Armed Forces must be prepared, even before the conclusion of the war against England, to crush Soviet Russia in a rapid campaign.' The projected operation is given the code name Barbarossa.

Hitler has modified the draft plans prepared by the army in one important respect. Although three lines of attack are still suggested, Hitler's scheme reduces the importance which has been laid on the advance to Moscow. He suggests that after the first battles the center group should swing north to help clear the Baltic States and Leningrad before moving on the capital. The preparations are to be ready by 15 May 1941.

19 DECEMBER 1940
Finland, Politics President Risto Ryti takes office. His predecessor, Dr Kallio, dies suddenly the same day.

20 DECEMBER 1940
Bulgaria, Politics New anti-Semitic laws are introduced. Bulgaria's Jewish population at this point is about 50,000 people. There are also measures against Free Masons and other so-called secret societies.

23 DECEMBER 1940
Britain, Politics Lord Halifax becomes British ambassador to the United States. Anthony Eden takes over as foreign secretary. David Margesson becomes secretary for war (army minister).
Greece and Albania The Greeks continue their advance, occupying Himarra.

25 DECEMBER 1940
German Raiders The German cruiser *Admiral Hipper* meets and attacks a British troop convoy 700 miles west of Cape Finisterre. The escort for the convoy consists of three cruisers and the carriers *Argus* and *Furious*. In the engagement which develops, the British cruiser *Berwick* is hit but the *Hipper* is forced to withdraw to Brest with engine trouble, sinking one ship on the way. This is the only return for a cruise lasting one month.

27 DECEMBER 1940
German Raiders The German raider *Komet* shells the phosphate production installations on the island of Nauru in the Central Pacific while flying a Japanese flag. Both *Komet* and *Orion* have been active in this area for some days and have sunk several of the ships engaged in the specialized phosphate trade.

28 DECEMBER 1940
Greece and Albania The Greeks bring their offensive to an end for the moment in order to consolidate their gains and improve communications with the front.

29 DECEMBER 1940
United States, Home Front In one of his famous 'fireside chat' broadcasts President Roosevelt describes how he wishes the United States to become the 'arsenal of democracy' and to give full aid to Britain regardless of threats from other countries.

JANUARY 1941
Battle of the Atlantic There are now 22 operational submarines in the German fleet but there are 67 more on trials or in training. A total of 21 ships of 126,800 tons is sunk by U-Boats in January. A large proportion of this success is achieved after the convoys have dispersed, usually beyond 20 degrees west. German aircraft are also very active, both in scouting for the U-Boats and in their own right. They sink 15 ships themselves. The total shipping losses for the Allies are 76 ships of 320,200 tons. The first types of radar sufficiently sensitive to detect submarines on the surface are beginning to be used by the British escort forces but it will take some time for all problems to be ironed out.
The Blitz The principal targets for the German bombing this month are London, Bristol, Cardiff and Portsmouth. The casualties are 1500 dead and 2000 injured.
British Air Operations Among the targets for the RAF this month are Bremen, Hamburg, Brest and Wilhelmshaven.

1 JANUARY 1941
Balkans, Politics Ribbentrop, the German foreign minister, meets Filov, the Bulgarian prime minister, in Berlin to discuss arrangements for allowing the passage of German troops across Bulgaria. No agreement is reached but Bulgaria is now nearer to acquiescing to German pressure to join the Tripartite Pact.
Mediterranean The strength of the German X Fliegerkorps in Sicily is now 96 bombers and 25 fighters. At full strength there will be 270 bombers, 150 of them Stukas, 40 fighters and 20 scout planes. At this time the RAF has only 15 Hurricanes in Malta.

2 JANUARY 1941
United States, Production Roosevelt announces a program to produce 200 7500-ton freighters to standardized designs. They will be known as Liberty ships.

3 JANUARY 1941
North Africa The Allied force, renamed XIII Corps, has been increased by the arrival of the 6th Australian Division to replace the 4th Indian Division previously withdrawn to the Sudan. The new force leads the attack on Bardia which

now begins. The 16th and 17th Brigades provide the assault units. They have considerable tank and artillery support. In addition three battleships of the Mediterranean Fleet also shell the Italian positions. The attack goes in against the west and southwest of the fortress and progress is very rapid. Around 30,000 prisoners are taken in the first 24 hours.

4 JANUARY 1941
Albania The Greeks begin a new offensive. They drive westward toward Valona from their positions in the mountains. The Greeks are, however, outnumbered by the Italians and find it difficult to make significant gains.

5 JANUARY 1941
North Africa Bardia is taken along with 40,000 prisoners and large numbers of guns, tanks and other vehicles. General Bergonzoli is withdrawing toward Tobruk with the still considerable remnants of his force. There have been less than 500 Allied casualties in the attack.

6 JANUARY 1941
United States, Home Front President Roosevelt, in his State of the Union message, talks of four essential freedoms, of speech and worship and from fear and want. He again refers to the United States as the 'arsenal of democracy.'
North Africa Advance units of the Allied force reach the outer defenses of Tobruk after taking El Adem airfield to the south. The encirclement of Tobruk will not be complete in any strength, however, until 9 January. Patrols to examine the Italian defenses begin immediately. The Tobruk garrison is 25,000 men with 220 guns and 70 tanks. General Mannella is in command. There are other Italian units still in positions farther west in Libya.

8 JANUARY 1941
United States, Politics Roosevelt presents his budget to Congress. It outlines total expenditure of $17,500,000,000 with $10,800,000,000 going on defense.
Albania The Greeks begin to attack Klisura in their continuing offensive. Their progress farther north is less good, especially around Berat.
Mediterranean There is a British air raid on Naples by Wellington bombers in which the battleship *Giulio Cesare* is badly hit while moored in the harbor. The *Vittorio Veneto* is hit also but scarcely damaged.

10 JANUARY 1941
United States, Politics The Lend-Lease Bill is introduced to Congress. There is considerable opposition. Among the prominent opponents of the bill are Senators Wheeler and Nye, former Ambassador Kennedy and Charles Lindbergh. (*see* 11 March).
Mediterranean Off Pantelleria a British convoy is attacked, first by two Italian torpedo boats, one of which is sunk for no loss to the convoy, and then by 40 German Stuka and Ju 88 bombers. The carrier *Illustrious* is hit six times by dive bombers. *Warspite* dodges several attacks but other ships are also damaged. This is the first action by the German X Fliegerkorps. *Illustrious* retires to Malta. All the British forces from Gibraltar and Alexandria have been out covering convoys for Greece and Malta. More troops and 18 fighters are brought to Malta.
Axis Politics Soviet-German pacts on frontiers in Eastern Europe and on trade are signed in Berlin and Moscow. Food and raw materials are to be exchanged for industrial equipment. The economic benefits to Germany of the agreement with the Soviet Union will continue until the very day that Operation Barbarossa begins.
Albania The Greek forces take Klisura after the four Italian divisions in that sector have been pulled back.

11 JANUARY 1941
Mediterranean The British cruisers *Southampton* and *Gloucester* leave Malta for Gibraltar. *Gloucester* is damaged and *Southampton* sunk by a Stuka attack.
Germany, Planning Hitler issues Directive 22 outlining his plans for limiting British gains in the Mediterranean. It includes the order for the establishment of the Afrika Korps.

12 JANUARY 1941
Malta British aircraft based on Malta attack Catania airfield on Sicily in an attempt to prevent German and Italian planes from attacking Malta while temporary repairs are carried out on the crippled aircraft carrier *Illustrious*.

14–15 JANUARY 1941
Greece General Wavell and Air Marshal Longmore are in Athens for talks with Prime Minister Metaxas and the Greek Commander in Chief, General Papagos. The Greeks ask for nine divisions and a substantial air component to be sent to support their forces. The Greeks have the equivalent of 13 divisions facing the larger Italian force in Albania and four facing the Bulgarians. At this stage the Germans have 12 divisions in Rumania and more in Bulgaria. To meet such a force Wavell is able to offer only

a small contribution now, but more later.

16–19 JANUARY 1941
Mediterranean There are German and Italian attacks on Malta and especially the damaged carrier *Illustrious*. On 16 January a force of about 80 Stukas attacks and, although 10 are shot down, they hit the carrier again as well as the cruiser *Perth*. The harbor facilities are also badly hit. On 18 January the attacks are repeated but the island's airfields are the principal target. On 19 January slight damage is done to *Illustrious*. On 23 January the emergency repairs are complete and the ship is able to make for Alexandria with 24 knots available if necessary. Later the *Illustrious* will proceed to the United States for full repairs.

19 JANUARY 1941
East Africa The British forces in the Sudan begin their offensive against the Italians in Eritrea. The British force is led by General Platt and includes 4th and 5th Indian Divisions and units of the Sudan Defense Force. The Italian troops in the various border positions amount to 17,000 men and are led by General Frusci. There is the equivalent of four more divisions in the interior of the country. Kassala is taken immediately.

19–20 JANUARY 1941
Axis Politics Hitler and Mussolini meet at the Berghof. Mussolini is unwilling to accept German help in Albania but is prepared to accept some aid in Africa. Hitler says that he will attack Greece if it seems that Britain is going to come in.

20–24 JANUARY 1941
Rumania, Home Front There is a revolt of the Iron Guard which is put down on the order of General Antonescu with the help of the Rumanian and German armies.

21 JANUARY 1941
North Africa The 6th Australian Division begins the attack on Tobruk. The town is already isolated by the advance of the British 7th Armored Brigade which is heading for Martuba and Mechili. The southeast corner of the Italian position is assaulted and after a heavy bombardment the Italian defense is quickly broken. Fort Palastrino is taken later in the day and General Mannella also captured.

22 JANUARY 1941
North Africa The remainder of the garrison of Tobruk surrenders after demolishing some of the harbor facilities. There are 27,000 prisoners. Much equipment is also captured and in fact it will prove possible to put the port into service fairly quickly. The Allied casualties have been less than 500 men.

East Africa In Eritrea the Italian forces are falling back toward Agordat in the face of Platt's attacks. There is also some skirmishing along the border between Kenya and Italian Somaliland.

23 JANUARY 1941
Balkans, Politics The Bulgarian prime minister agrees to bring his country into the Tripartite Pact as soon as military arrangements with the Germans can be completed.

24 JANUARY 1941
North Africa There is a brief tank engagement near Mechili. The British 4th Armored Brigade and the Italian force suffer about equal losses before the Italians retire. The Italian forces in Libya are now split, with one group around Mechili and one on the coast at Derna. These positions do not give each other any support. The 19th Australian Brigade is moving on Derna while Mechili is to be encircled by 4th and 7th Armored Brigades.

26 JANUARY 1941
North Africa The Italians pull out of Mechili. The British blocking force from 4th Armored Brigade is carelessly handled and does nothing to prevent their escape.

Albania There is an Italian counterattack near Klisura which has a slight local success.

27 JANUARY 1941
Albania Ciano and other senior members of the Italian government arrive in Albania to take up active army commands. This bizarre measure is presumably designed to boost morale.

East Africa The British advance into Eritrea reaches Agordat and a battle gradually develops in this area.

29 JANUARY 1941
Greece, Politics Prime Minister Metaxas dies. His successor is Alexander Korizis. Korizis is less decisive than Metaxas and does not have as good a relationship with the Greek Commander in Chief, General Papagos. Although he is, if anything, more ready to accept British help this change does not contribute to the smooth running of the discussions with the British.

North Africa The Italians pull out of Derna and

begin a precipitate retreat toward the west along the coast road.

East Africa Allied forces cross the border from Kenya into Italian Somaliland. General Cunningham is in command and his forces are 11th and 12th East African Divisions and 1st South African Division. The main attack will not begin until 10 February.

29 JANUARY–27 MARCH 1941

Allied Planning There are secret staff talks in Washington between British and American representatives. They produce conclusions code named ABC1 which state that Allied policy in the event of war with Germany and Japan should be to put the defeat of Germany first. In March an American mission visits Britain to select sites for bases for naval and air forces in case of war with Germany. Preliminary work to equip these bases will begin later in the year. The talks mark an important stage in the development of .cooperation between the US and Britain. As well as their important decisions they accustom the staffs to working with each other.

30 JANUARY 1941

North Africa Derna is taken by the 19th Australian Brigade.

31 JANUARY 1941

Germany, Planning After consultations with army and army group staffs the Army High Command has now prepared the first operational plans for the German invasion of the Soviet Union. The deployment plan for the forces is also ready. These schemes are presented to Hitler at a conference on 3 February. He again tries to draw attention away from the central drive toward Moscow which the Army planners think essential.

FEBRUARY 1941

Battle of the Atlantic Although the operational U-Boat strength is at its lowest mark of the war at 22 vessels, the sinkings increase this month to 39 ships of 196,800 tons. Aircraft are also more effective, sinking 27 vessels. The total Allied shipping loss is 403,400 tons. More than half of the U-Boat successes are stragglers from convoys or independents. This reflects the growing strength and deterrent effect of the convoy escorts. On 6 February Hitler issues orders confirming the aims of the offensive. There are changes in the British organization. On 7 February the Western Approaches Command HQ is moved to Liverpool where it will be in closer touch with the organizations controlling

merchant shipping and better able to supervise the training of the escort forces. On the 17th Admiral Noble takes over the command.

British Air Operations Among the targets for the RAF this month are Dusseldorf, Wilhelmshaven, Brest and Cologne. Only 1400 tons of bombs are dropped in these operations – a mere fraction of later efforts.

The Blitz The German attacks continue. Their range of targets includes heavy attacks on Swansea for the first time. The civilian casualties are 789 dead and 1068 injured.

1 FEBRUARY 1941

East Africa In Eritrea Agordat falls to Platt's forces after a vigorous three-day battle. Frusci's troops are falling back to the mountain positions around Keren after suffering some losses. To the south Barentu has also been captured by the Indian troops.

United States, Command There is a major reorganization of the US Navy. It is now to be formed in three fleets, the Atlantic, the Pacific and the Asiatic. Admiral King is appointed to command the new Atlantic Fleet. There is to be a significant strengthening of the forces in the Atlantic.

Japan, Home Front Japan announces that it will be necessary to introduce rice rationing.

1–14 FEBRUARY 1941

War at Sea The heavy cruiser *Admiral Hipper* goes on a commerce-destroying raid in the north Atlantic from Brest. The convoy SLS-64 of 19 ships is attacked on 12 February. Seven of the ships are sunk. One independent is also attacked. *Hipper* then returns to Brest.

2 FEBRUARY 1941

North Africa The Australian forces have already advanced well to the west of Derna on the coast and are discovering that the Italians are withdrawing at speed. Wavell agrees with O'Connor that 7th Armored Division should be sent hurrying across the center of Cyrenaica in an attempt to cut the Italians off. Supplies are being assembled to support this move but because the Italian retreat is so rapid the advance will have to start before the preparations are complete.

East Africa The British carrier *Formidable*, on her way to the Mediterranean to replace the damaged *Illustrious*, sends its planes to attack the harbor installations at Mogadishu.

3 FEBRUARY–22 MARCH 1941

German Raiders The German battlecruisers

Above: A German Panzer IV in North Africa during the early campaigns in 1941.

Scharnhorst and *Gneisenau* go on a commerce-destroying expedition in the Atlantic under the command of Admiral Lutjens. On the night of 3 February they pass through the Denmark Strait. On 8 February they approach the convoy HX-106 but do not attack because the escort includes the old battleship *Ramillies.* Similarly, on 8 March SL-67 escapes because the battleship *Malaya* is present. Hitler has ordered that no risk of damage to the ships is to be run if this can be avoided. On 22 February five ships from a dispersed convoy are sunk and on 15–16 March 16 more are destroyed. During this encounter the British battleship *Rodney* comes up but cannot close the range and engage.

After this the British hunt is extensive but the Germans reach French waters on 22 March. As well as the dispersing convoys found, one other ship has been sunk, bringing the total to 22 ships of 115,600 tons. Considerable disruption to the British convoy system has been caused.

4 FEBRUARY 1941
North Africa The British advance across Cyrenaica has now begun. Msus is taken and the forces then move toward Antelat. In the north the Italian retreat is continuing.
East Africa The British forces begin to attack the strong Italian positions around Keren. There are 30,000 Italian troops in this area. In the first phase of the battle, which lasts until 7 February, the 11th Indian Brigade manages to take Cameron Ridge but is thrown back from other positions by Italian counterattacks.

5 FEBRUARY 1941
North Africa The first British armored units reach the coast road near Beda Fomm with armored cars and light tanks after their drive across Cyrenaica. Heavier tank units are following rapidly. The retreating Italian columns are

engaged and about 5000 men are captured. In the north the Australians take Barce.

6 FEBRUARY 1941
North Africa Benghazi is taken by Australian units following the Italian retreat. The Italian forces are streaming back along the coast road to Beda Fomm and during the day they make desperate attacks on the British blocking force there. These attacks are repulsed with heavy loss but the small British force is compelled to give some ground.

7 FEBRUARY 1941
North Africa Large-scale surrenders begin at Beda Fomm after the Italians have made fruitless attempts to break through to continue their retreat. Eventually about 25,000 more Italians will be taken, along with 200 guns and 120 tanks. Since the start of the campaign two months previously a force of no more than two divisions has destroyed 10 Italian divisions and taken 130,000 prisoners for the loss of 555 dead and 1400 wounded. Many of the British vehicles now desperately need repairs. This will have an important effect later. In the evening Agedabia falls to the British forces.

8 FEBRUARY 1941
Balkans, Politics The German and Bulgarian staffs agree on the detailed arrangements for German troops to enter Bulgaria.

9 FEBRUARY 1941
North Africa The British advance comes to a halt at El Agheila. There is little Italian opposition to prevent a further move, but Wavell is being compelled to withdraw troops which will be sent to Greece. He is also responsible for the campaign in East Africa and for making some provision for the defense of Palestine. In the near future, this will demand more of his attention because of German activity in Iraq and Syria.
Mediterranean In an audacious attack the battleship *Malaya* and the battlecruiser *Renown* from Force H bombard the harbor at Genoa. The carrier *Ark Royal* also takes part in the operation, sending aircraft to attack Leghorn and La Spezia. Five ships in Genoa are sunk and 18 damaged. The Italians fail to attack the British force.

10 FEBRUARY 1941
Britain, Strategy Churchill formally instructs Wavell to regard help for Greece as having a higher priority than exploiting the success in

Africa. He mentions the important effect on American opinion of being seen to fulfill promises to smaller nations. Colonel Bill Donovan has recently been on a tour of the Balkans on Roosevelt's behalf and is known to value the idea of fighting the Germans there. The British also hope to make a good impression on Turkey and perhaps even establish a Balkan coalition against Hitler.

East Africa The attacks of 4th Indian Division at Keren go on with renewed effort. The fighting is fierce over the next two days but Italian counterattacks prevent the Indian troops from making any gains. A long lull follows for the rest of the month while the British commanders bring up more forces and supplies for the formal offensive which will be necessary to break the Italian positions.

11 FEBRUARY 1941
East Africa General Cunningham's forces extend their advance from Kenya into the Italian Somaliland and take Afmadu.
France, Politics Darlan is nominated to be successor and deputy to Pétain. He is to hold office as Foreign Minister, Minister of the Interior and Minister of Information as well as his rank as Commander in Chief of the Navy.

12 FEBRUARY 1941
North Africa General Rommel arrives in Tripoli. Nominally more important is the appointment of the new Italian Commander in Chief for Libya, General Gariboldi. The first units of what will become the Afrika Korps begin to land at Tripoli on 14 February. The advance guard is a battalion of light infantry and an antitank unit. Field Marshal Kesselring is in Rome as the German representative.
Soviet Command General Zhukov is appointed Chief of the General Staff and Deputy Commissar for Defense. General Meretskov is now to lead the Red Army's training directorate.

13 FEBRUARY 1941
East Africa The carrier *Formidable* attacks Massawa. This raid is repeated on 21 February and 1 March because the *Formidable* cannot pass through the Suez Canal to join the Mediterranean Fleet owing to mines which have been dropped by German planes. These are being cleared.

14 FEBRUARY 1941
Balkans, Politics Hitler meets the Yugoslav Premier Cvetković and his foreign minister at Berchtesgaden to urge them to join the Tri-

partite Pact. They still refuse to commit their country, in the hope that Hitler will soon be preoccupied with relations with the Soviet Union and that they can get aid from Britain and the USA.
East Africa The 22nd East African Brigade takes Kismayu with fire support from the cruiser *Shropshire* and other smaller vessels. Elsewhere in Somaliland the British advance is also rapid.

16 FEBRUARY 1941
East Africa In Italian Somaliland the 1st South African Brigade begins an important battle to seize crossings over the lower reaches of the river Juba.

17 FEBRUARY 1941
Balkans, Politics Under German pressure Turkey and Bulgaria sign a friendship agreement by which Turkey accepts that the movement of German troops through Bulgaria is not an act of war. This more or less confirms that there is no possibility of Turkey being persuaded to ally with Britain.

18 FEBRUARY 1941
East Africa In Abyssinia South African forces advancing from Kenya attack the town of Mega. It is quickly captured along with 1000 prisoners.

19 FEBRUARY 1941
East Africa Emperor Haile Selassie, who was brought back to Abyssinia in January to help organize resistance to the Italians, arrives at Dangilla along with Wingate's Gideon Force. During the next two weeks they harass the Italian troops around Bahrdar Giorgis and Burye with considerable success. The Italians have four brigades in the area and the Gideon Force is only 1700 strong.

19–23 FEBRUARY 1941
Greece On 19 February Eden, Dill (the Chief of the General Staff) and the local commanders, Wavell and Cunningham, meet in Cairo to discuss whether they can send help to Greece and if so how much. The British political leaders are strongly in favor of sending all that can be spared and Wavell, the military commander who is responsible, believes that this can be done effectively and is, therefore, prepared to recommend it.

On 22 February the British leaders are in Athens to meet King George and Premier Korizis. On 23 February the Greeks agree to accept a force which at this stage is intended to be 100,000 men with suitable artillery and tank support. The Greeks are very reluctant to accept anything less since it would not be enough to fight the Germans off and would only encourage them to attack. The disposition of the British and Greek forces is also discussed. The British prefer a position along the line of the Aliakmon River but the Greeks are unwilling to give up the territory which this line does not cover. No final decision is made – a serious ommission in the light of later events.

20 FEBRUARY 1941
North Africa The British and German patrols make contact for the first time in the desert, near El Agheila. The first brief action is on the 24th.

21 FEBRUARY 1941
Soviet Union, Politics Changes in the Central Committee of the Communist Party are announced. Among those to be dismissed are the former ambassador to the United States, Maxim Litvinov.

23 FEBRUARY 1941
East Africa In Somaliland the main Italian forces defending the line of the Juba River have been defeated. General Cunningham's troops are now advancing very rapidly toward Mogadishu. There is a small Free French landing in Eritrea.

25 FEBRUARY 1941
East Africa Mogadishu is taken by the British forces after an advance of over 230 miles in the past three days. Considerable stocks of fuel and other supplies are captured.
Mediterranean The Italian light cruiser *Diaz* is sunk by a British submarine while forming part of the escort for a Naples-Tripoli convoy.

26 FEBRUARY 1941
Balkans, Politics Eden and Dill continue their Middle East mission with a visit to Ankara, but they get no real response to their efforts to interest the Turks in an alliance.

27 FEBRUARY 1941
War at Sea The Italian merchant cruiser *Ramb I* is sunk by the New Zealand cruiser *Leander* off the Maldive Islands. *Ramb I* sailed from Massawa on 20 February.

28 FEBRUARY 1941
East Africa Asmara, Eritrea, is bombed by British planes. The RAF has now established superiority in this area.

MARCH 1941
Battle of the Atlantic The threat posed by the German attacks is formally recognized by Churchill when he issues his Battle of the Atlantic Directive on 6 March. Measures are immediately put in hand to strengthen the British forces and a high-level Battle of the Atlantic Committee begins meeting to monitor progress. It includes political, military and scientific leaders and will be important in bringing about better coordination between these specialities. Although enemy submarines and aircraft both sink 41 ships during the month and although the total of 139 ships of 529,700 tons is comparable with the worst times of the previous German offensive in 1917, there is some compensation in the sinking by the escort forces of six U-Boats, one fifth of the operational fleet (*see* 7 and 16–17 March).

Churchill's later comment on the events of the following months is most revealing. 'How willingly would I have exchanged a full-scale attempt at invasion for this shapeless, measureless peril, expressed in charts, curves and statistics.'
British Air Operations The Halifax bomber comes into service with Bomber Command. Among the targets for the RAF this month are Kiel, Hamburg, Bremen and Brest, of special interest because of the entry of the German battlecruisers later in the month. Bomber command flies about 1900 sorties, 39 aircraft fail to return and 36 more crash.
The Blitz The strength of the German attacks increases again with the coming of better weather. London is the target for three major raids. Merseyside is attacked twice, and Glasgow, Bristol and Plymouth are also heavily hit. In the first three months of the year the Luftwaffe has lost 90 bombers. The British night fighters and AA defenses are becoming stronger.

1 MARCH 1941
United States, Preparations The US Navy forms a Support Force for the Atlantic Fleet. The main part of this unit is made up from three destroyer squadrons of 27 ships.
Balkans, Politics Prime Minister Filov brings Bulgaria into the Tripartite Pact.
North Africa Kuffra in southeast Libya is taken by a Free French force from Chad. Colonel Leclerc is in command. The French force has received some help from units of the British Long Range Desert Group.

2 MARCH 1941
Balkans Following the treaty agreement on the

previous day German troops begin to move into Bulgaria in force. These German units are part of List's Twelfth Army.

4 MARCH 1941

Norway There is a British Commando raid on the Lofoten Islands. The 500-strong force is carried by naval units which include two light cruisers and five destroyers. Ten ships are sunk in the operation and 215 German prisoners taken. There are also 300 Norwegian volunteers who are taken to Britain. The operation is a success but the Germans take fierce reprisals when the British force withdraws. Many members of the Norwegian resistance movement do not approve of such raids for this reason.

Balkans Hitler meets Prince Paul of Yugoslavia secretly at Berchtesgaden to ask him once again to join the Tripartite Pact. Paul returns to Yugoslavia convinced that he must decide very soon between Britain and Germany. Talks in the next few days convince him that Britain has little help to offer.

General Wilson, who is to command the British force being prepared for Greece, arrives in Athens to arrange the final details with the Greek staff. A major convoy is about to leave Alexandria with the first large contingent. The British have only just discovered that the Greek forces in Macedonia have not retired to the Aliakmon Line and will not be able to persuade them to do so because of the damage to morale that would result if territory is obviously given up without a fight after the German move into Bulgaria. Although understandable, this is not a very realistic attitude. Wilson is further hindered by the Greek insistence that he remains incognito inside the British Embassy in order not to provoke the Germans. In fact the German consulate in Piraeus overlooks the port area which will be used to land the British forces, so they are well aware what is happening.

6 MARCH 1941

Holland, Resistance Following strikes during February over the arrest of Jews and attempts to send workers to jobs in Germany the Germans condemn 18 Dutch resistance members. These are the first such victims in Holland. The Communists have played a notable part in organizing the strikes.

7 MARCH 1941

Battle of the Atlantic The British destroyer *Wolverine* sinks the German submarine *U.47* in a convoy engagement. The *U.47* is commanded by the ace captain, Prien, one of three leading

U-Boat captains who will be killed or captured in the next few weeks.

9 MARCH 1941

Albania The Italians launch an offensive along the front between the Rivers Devoli and Vijosë. There are a few local successes initially. The Italians have assembled 12 divisions for the attack and Mussolini himself has crossed to Albania to supervise its progress. There is little subtlety in the tactical plan and much that is reminiscent of World War I. The Greek intelligence of the direction of the attack is good and their defenses well prepared.

10 MARCH 1941

East Africa Since taking Mogadishu General Platt's troops have advanced 600 miles north from there into Abyssinia and only now come into contact with any Italian forces. Their encounter is at Dagabur, only 100 miles south of Jijiga.

11 MARCH 1941

United States, Politics The Lend-Lease Bill becomes law when signed by President Roosevelt. It passed the House on 8 February by 260 votes to 165, and passed the Senate on 8 March by 60 to 13. Important amendments have been made by Congress. A time limit has been placed on the operation of the act – until June 1943 – but a motion originally passed in the House forbidding US warships to give convoy protection to foreign ships has been defeated. Also to be allowed are transfers of ships to other countries solely on the presidential authority without reference to Congress.

Essentially the act means that Britain can continue to order American materials without necessarily having the cash to pay for them. They are to be paid for after the war. At this stage it makes little difference to the quantity of supplies going to Britain. British war production is greater than America's and will continue to be so until some time after Pearl Harbor. Most of the items supplied for the rest of 1941 will in fact be paid for in cash. There is little difference too in the quantity supplied when compared with 1940 but in some commodities, such as food and fuel oil, the United States' contribution will be of very great value.

Although justly described as one of the most generous acts of any nation's history, Lend-Lease is not entirely disinterested. Britain is compelled to go on paying cash for as long as this is possible and this means that many British assets in the United States must be sold at well below their true value. Britain is also forbidden to export anything containing materials supplied under Lend-Lease nor can items wholly produced in Britain be exported if equivalent items are being supplied under Lend-Lease. These restrictions and the keenness with which they are enforced will do much to destroy the little that remains of Britain's export trade. Although there will be some relaxation of the rules in 1944, a considerable barrier will have been placed against a British postwar economic recovery.

12 MARCH 1941
United States, Politics President Roosevelt presents an Appropriations Bill for Lend-Lease to Congress for $7,000,000,000. It passes into law on 27 March.

13 MARCH 1941
Albania The Italian attacks toward Klisura continue but are now being held comfortably by the Greek defense.

Germany, Planning Hitler issues a directive for the invasion of the Soviet Union which gives administrative control of any captured territory to the SS. This and later orders concerning the treatment of commissars and ordinary prisoners will lead to many dreadful atrocities. It also ruins the previously quite good chance that the Germans will receive worthwhile support from those who have reason to bear Stalin's government no love.

14 MARCH 1941
East Africa Wingate and Haile Selassie establish new headquarters at Burye. The main Italian force in their area is now at Debra Markos. The Italians are negotiating with a local chief called Ras Hailu and are preparing an attack with him.

15 MARCH 1941
East Africa The British attacks toward Keren, Eritrea, are renewed. Both 4th and 5th Indian Divisions are now involved. The first attacks by 4th Indian go fairly well but not all the gains can be held.

United States, Politics In an important speech Roosevelt promises that the United States will supply Britain and the Allies 'aid until victory' and that there will be an 'end of compromise with tyranny.'

16 MARCH 1941
East Africa A small British force arriving by sea from Aden in two light cruisers, two destroyers and seven other vessels lands and captures the port of Berbera. The capture takes only a little time and immediately afterward they begin to advance inland. There are also British gains in the battle around Keren. The 5th Indian Division, which has been unable to advance on the first day, now takes the Dologorodoc position south of the Keren road. The next five days are dominated by Italian efforts to mount counterattacks.

Albania The Italian offensive is called off. In the past few days they have incurred 12,000 casualties and taken absolutely no ground. However, the Greeks have been compelled by the Italian offensive to do nothing to strengthen their forces which face the German threat elsewhere.

16–17 MARCH 1941
Battle of the Atlantic Kretschmer's *U.99* and Schepke's *U.100* are both sunk in a convoy battle. These sinkings, combined with the loss of Prien 10 days previously, are a severe blow to the morale of the U-Boat crews as well as a serious military loss because of their unusual ability. The sinking of *U.100* is symbolic as being achieved with the aid of new radar equipment. Kretschmer is captured after his ship is sunk.

17 MARCH 1941
East Africa General Cunningham's northward advance reaches Jijiga which has been evacuated by the Italians.

19 MARCH 1941
Balkans, Politics The Germans repeat their demands on Yugoslavia. They now give the Yugoslavs five days to make a decision.

Battle of the Atlantic The British battleship *Malaya* is seriously damaged by a torpedo from *U.106* when with a convoy in the Atlantic. The *Malaya* goes to New York for repairs – the first major British warship to receive such help.

20 MARCH 1941
Balkans, Politics In a meeting of the Royal Council in Belgrade it becomes clear that Regent Paul is ready to agree to Hitler's demand that Yugoslavia join the Tripartite Pact and allow free passage of German troops. Four ministers resign in protest.

East Africa The British force advancing from Berbera takes Hargeisa.

21 MARCH 1941
East Africa Troops of the 11th African Division attack Italian positions in the Marda Pass west of Jijiga. After some resistance the Italians

fall back despite the strength of their position.

22 MARCH 1941

East Africa In the advance west from Jijiga the Allied forces overrun another defensive position at the Babile Pass.

24 MARCH 1941

North Africa El Agheila is recaptured from the British by Rommel's forces. General O'Connor and his experienced desert troops have been withdrawn and General Neame has been left to hold Libya with the understrength and in-experienced 2nd Armored Division, 9th Australian Division and an Indian Brigade. The tanks available are mostly old and more or less worn out. Collectively the Allied units have neither the desert experience of O'Connor's veterans nor the professionalism of Rommel's troops. Rommel has one German division, 5th Light, with a strong tank component and part of four Italian divisions. Rommel has been for-bidden to attack by the German High Command and has been told that he will receive no extra forces. He will ignore his instructions.

25 MARCH 1941

Balkans, Politics The Yugoslav Prime Minister Cvetković and the Foreign Minister Cincar-Marković sign the Tripartite Pact in Vienna. The reality of the situation and the influence of German pressure is made only too clear by the cold tone of the occasion. Germany agrees to respect Yugoslav sovereignty and not to demand passage for troops. There are disturbances in Belgrade when the agreement is known.
East Africa The 5th Indian Division renews its advance toward the Italian blocking position on the Keren road.

26 MARCH 1941

Mediterranean A night attack by explosive boats of a special Italian unit penetrates Suda Bay in Crete and sinks one tanker and cripples the British cruiser *York*.
East Africa The British forces occupy Harar, Abyssinia.

26–29 MARCH 1941

Mediterranean Battle of Cape Matapan. Following claims by German aircraft to have sunk two of the British Mediterranean Fleet's battleships and with the promise of German air support and reconnaissance, Admiral Iachino leads the Italian Fleet in a sortie into the Aegean to disrupt the British convoys to Greece. He has one battleship, six heavy cruisers, two

light cruisers and 13 destroyers. They leave port on 26 March. On 27 March the British forces set out. Admiral Pridham-Wippell leads four light cruisers and four destroyers from the Piraeus and Admiral Cunningham the main body of three battleships, one carrier and nine destroyers from Alexandria.

On 28 March there is a long-range engagement between Pridham-Wippell's force and some of the Italian cruisers. The Italians suspect that a large British force is present and begin to retire. In the afternoon Swordfish aircraft from the *Formidable* attack the Italian ships, hitting the battleship *Vittorio Veneto* and the cruiser *Pola*. The *Vittorio Veneto* is able to proceed at reduced speed but the *Pola* is stopped. In the evening Iachino sends the cruisers *Zara* and *Fiume* and four destroyers back to help the *Pola*. The British ships are pressing on in pursuit hoping to come up with the damaged *Vittorio Veneto* when, during the night, they find the three Italian cruisers and their escorts on their radar. The British approach to close range, without being sighted in return, and in a brief gun battle the cruisers and two of the destroyers are shot to pieces and sunk before they have the chance to fire a shot. On 29 March the British give up the chase and return to port.

In the whole operation the British lose two aircraft. The training of the British forces pays off superbly and the steady process of British success over the previous months has now achieved a position of almost complete moral superiority which will inhibit any further Italian initiative.

26 MARCH–4 APRIL 1941

East Africa The Italian forces and their new local allies attack Wingate's Gideon force around Burye. They are beaten off despite their superior strength.

27 MARCH 1941

Balkans, Politics There is a coup in Yugoslavia. The council of Regency and Prince Paul are deposed and the 17-year-old King Peter takes over nominal charge of the government. The rising is led by air force officers and their Chief of Staff, General Simović, who becomes the new head of government. British agents have had a hand in bringing the rising about. The change is very popular among the Serbian sections of the population (almost all the leaders of the armed forces are Serbian) but less so among the Croats. In an immediate angry response to the change of government Hitler issues Directive 25 which orders planning for the invasion of Yugoslavia to begin. It is to be mounted as soon as possible and the invasion of Greece is to take place at the same time. Hitler accepts that it may be necessary to defer Barbarossa to allow these new operations to take place.

East Africa The Allied advance clears the Italian road blocks in the Keren position. The Italian force begins to withdraw toward Asmara. The Indian divisions have lost 4000 casualties in the Keren battles and the Italians 3000 dead as well as many wounded.

28 MARCH 1941

Balkans, Allied Planning The British Chief of Staff, General Dill, is in Belgrade for talks with the Yugoslav authorities, but there is little he can offer them and no agreements of any importance are reached.

29 MARCH 1941

East Africa Cunningham's South African troops take Diredawa, Abyssinia, in their advance west to Addis Ababa. The local Italian population has appealed to the British for help because of atrocities committed by deserters from the native forces after the Italian part of the garrison has withdrawn.

30 MARCH 1941

North Africa Correctly discerning that the British forces are weakly dispersed in positions which prevent mutual support, Rommel brings his forces forward from El Agheila toward Mersa Brega. Only part of 2nd Armored Division is ready to oppose him. The bulk of the Australian Division is near Benghazi and the remainder is back at Tobruk.

Germany, Planning Hitler approves the army plans for the attack on Yugoslavia, to begin on 6 April. Hitler also speaks to a conference of 250 top commanders who will have important parts in the Barbarossa operation. He makes it plain to them that the war in the east is to be conducted along different lines to any previous operation. There is to be no talk of proper 'knightly' behavior and commissars and Communists are to be treated with utmost severity.

United States, Politics The United States takes German, Italian and Danish ships into 'protective custody,' effectively confiscating them.

31 MARCH 1941

North Africa Rommel's forces attack the positions of infantry units from the British 2nd Armored Division at Mersa Brega. A fierce battle develops, in which the British come off worst but are able to halt the German advance

for the moment. The few tanks with 2nd Armored Division do not join the battle.

Mediterranean The British cruiser *Bonaventure* is sunk by a torpedo-boat attack in the Eastern Mediterranean.

APRIL 1941

Battle of the Atlantic The German U-Boat fleet now has 32 operational boats which means that about 20 are on patrol at any one time. There are a further 81 boats on trial or in training in the Baltic. In the Atlantic the trend is for the U-Boats to hunt farther west looking for unescorted ships to attack but the British are countering this by providing escorts as far as 35 degrees West (more than halfway across). Fuelling bases for the British escorts have now been established on Iceland. The number of aircraft based on Iceland has also been increased to give even more protection. On 15 April RAF Coastal Command is brought under the operational control of the Admiralty which will lead to an increase in its effectiveness in the battle against the U-Boats. This month the U-Boats sink 43 ships of 249,000 tons but only 10 of these are from convoys. The only convoy battles are round SC-26 and HX-121. It is a good month for German aircraft – they sink 116 ships in all theaters. The total Allied loss from all causes is 195 ships of 687,000 tons.

The Blitz There are two very heavy German attacks on London on 16/17 April and 19/20 April with about 700 planes being involved in each raid. Other targets are Plymouth, Coventry and Birmingham. Some Luftwaffe units are withdrawn for service in the Balkans.

British Air Operations Brest is attacked seven times by RAF bombers and among the other targets for Bomber Command are Kiel, Wilhelmshaven, Emden and Mannheim.

1 APRIL 1941

North Africa The British withdraw from Mersa Brega, abandoning almost the only available defensive position before the wide open spaces of the Cyrenaica Plateau.

East Africa Asmara, the capital of Eritrea, is taken by the British forces led by General Platt.

1-3 APRIL 1941

Iraq, Politics On 1 April a coup begins and by 3 April a new government has been installed. The Regent Faisal escapes to Transjordan. The coup is led by the nationalist politician Rashid Ali and a group of officers calling themselves the 'Golden Square.' They are opposed to the British presence in the country. The British react quickly and soon troops are being sent from India and the Middle East to ensure access to the vital oil supplies.

2 APRIL 1941
North Africa The German advance begins to gather momentum. Adegabia is taken and the Germans now have the option of striking out across Cyrenaica on various routes or following the coast. In fact they will split their force and follow almost all these options. The German units divide into three columns taking two main routes to Msus and Mechili. Italian forces and a small German unit are sent along the coast to Benghazi under a German commander. Rommel flies from column to column in his scout plane, urging the advance on.

Wavell comes up to the front from Cairo and decides that O'Connor must be brought back from convalescence to replace Neame. In fact when he arrives O'Connor agrees to act only as an adviser. The exiguous British tank force is split up on Wavell's order and is further weakened by breakdowns, giving the Germans every opportunity to continue their advance.
Mediterranean The carrier *Ark Royal* flies a small contingent of Hurricane fighters to Malta.
Hungary, Politics Prime Minister Count Teleki commits suicide because he does not wish to lead his country in collaboration with Germany. The regent, Admiral Horthy, and the new prime minister, László Bárdossy, continue to work with the Germans.
United States, Politics Roosevelt orders the transfer of 10 coastguard cutters to the Royal Navy. These are very useful vessels for escort work, having a long range and good seakeeping qualities. They will be in RN service by June.

4 APRIL 1941
North Africa Rommel's offensive develops further. There are three main lines of advance. Benghazi, on the coast, is taken by the Italian forces and the accompanying German battalion. The force heading for Msus is making only slow progress but the third group, the most southerly, with part of 5th Light and the Italian Ariete Division, is going well toward Mechili.
United States, Politics Roosevelt agrees to allow RN warships to be repaired in the US. Among the first ships to benefit from this order are the battleships *Malaya* and *Resolution*. RN warships are also to be allowed to refuel in the US when on combat missions.
German Raiders The German raider *Thor* meets and sinks the British AMC *Voltaire* in the central Atlantic.

5 APRIL 1941
Yugoslavia A Soviet-Yugoslav Nonaggression Pact is agreed and is signed in the early hours of the 6th but is too late to have any effect in halting the imminent German attack.
North Africa The Axis advance continues. On the coast Barce is taken while inland Tengeder falls and Mechili is threatened.

6 APRIL 1941
Balkans German forces invade Yugoslavia and Greece. The attack begins with advances by List's Twelfth Army from Bulgaria and with bombing raids on Belgrade and targets in Greece. The initial forces from the Twelfth Army, will be joined over the next few days by Kleist's First Panzer Group also part of Twelfth Army, Weich's Second Army and other German, Hungarian and Italian forces. As well as infantry forces the Germans employ six armored and four motorized divisions. The Yugoslav Army has 28 infantry and three cavalry divisions but these are widely dispersed in a cordon defense of the frontier and only five infantry and two cavalry units will do any real fighting. The Germans also have overwhelming air support of around 1000 planes from Fliegerkorps IV and VIII. Apart from the forces facing the Italians in Albania, in Greece the Allies have seven weak Greek divisions, the New Zealand Division, part of the 6th Australian Division and one British armored brigade. There are about 80 RAF planes. General Wilson commands the British and Anzac forces which are based on positions known as the Aliakmon Line. There is a mixed tank and infantry force holding the route into Greece from Yugoslavia by the so-called Monastir Gap. Some of the Greek force are also on the Aliakmon Line but rather more are in frontier positions known as the Metaxas Line in Macedonia and Thrace.

The main German attack on the first day falls on these advanced Greek troops. One German corps, XXX, attacks the center and right of the line. A second corps attacks the left of the line but sends more of its force into Yugoslavia toward Strumica. The third corps moves into Yugoslavia farther north heading for Skopje. There is heavy fighting on the Greek border but the Yugoslav frontier is crossed easily by the Germans. During the night of the 6th there is an important air raid on the port of the Piraeus in which a British ammunition ship blows up, sinking many other vessels and extensively damaging the port installations.
North Africa The German and Italian advance is maintained. On the coast the Australian

Division is beginning to pull back to Tobruk from Derna. General O'Connor has now arrived at the front to advise Neame but both are captured during the night by a German patrol. O'Connor, the architect of Beda Fomm, is an especially serious loss.

War at Sea The German battlecruiser *Gneisenau* is badly hit by a British torpedo plane while on exercise just outside the port of Brest. On the night of 10/11 April the same ship is hit another four times by bombs during a British raid. The *Scharnhorst* is also in the port undergoing engine repairs. Neither battlecruiser will be able to join The *Bismarck* in its cruise in May.

East Africa Addis Ababa, Abyssinia, is taken in the continuing Allied advance. The Duke of Aosta is withdrawing to the north toward Amba Alagi with the remains of the main Italian force. General Frusci is in tactical command of these troops. Elsewhere in the country the Italians have about 80,000 more men. General Nasi commands in the Gondar area with half this force and General Gazzera in the south and southwest with the rest. The port of Massawa in Eritrea is attacked by the Allied forces with support from British naval vessels lying offshore.

7 APRIL 1941

Greece As well as the frontal pressure on the Metaxas Line its left flank is being threatened by a German armored division which is moving south into Greece after having reached Strumica in the advance in Yugoslavia. The Greek Commander in Chief, General Papagos, further weakens the Aliakmon Line by sending forward a Greek force from it to try to block this last German advance.

Yugoslavia After a rapid advance troops from XL Panzer Corps enter Skopje late in the day.

Battle of the Atlantic US naval and air bases open in Bermuda. The carrier *Ranger* and other ships are to be based there as the Central Atlantic Neutrality Patrol. These forces will be considerably increased by three battleships and two carriers later in April and during May and June.

North Africa On the coast Derna is overrun in the continuing Axis advance. Inland near Mechili an armored battle begins between the German 5th Panzer Regiment and the remnants of the British 2nd Armored Division.

8 APRIL 1941

Yugoslavia The German offensive is extended with the start of attacks by Kleist's First Panzer Group. They advance west over the Bulgarian border and by evening have destroyed the Yugoslav forces on the frontier and have advanced as far as Nis.

East Africa Massawa falls to the Allied forces. Seventeen large Axis merchant ships are taken, in the port along with many smaller military and civilian vessels. The 4th Indian Division, which has played a large part in the Allied campaign in Eritrea, is immediately prepared for shipping to Egypt where the Allied forces are under great pressure. The priority in the East African campaign is now to clear the road between Asmara and Addis Ababa. Forces are being sent to this task from both ends of the road.

North Africa Mechili falls to the German attacks in the morning and Rommel immediately begins to organize an advance to Tobruk.

9 APRIL 1941

Greece The resistance of the Greek forces in the Metaxas Line has been weakened on the 8th and now collapses. Thessaloniki is taken by the 2nd Panzer Division. The Greek Second Army, the force defending the Metaxas Line, surrenders. Other German units have taken Monastir in Yugoslavia and are moving south through the Monastir Gap. It will not be possible to hold a strong attack here, although Wilson has strengthened the defending force and it will, therefore, be necessary to withdraw from some of the Aliakmon positions. This is discussed with Papagos and he concurs.

Yugoslavia The German Second Army joins the attack on Yugoslavia. Two corps move south over the Austrian border, quickly taking Maribor. The third corps, XLVI Panzer, is based in Hungary and begins to seize crossings over the Drava. The two corps from Kleist's force which began the attack on Yugoslavia have now moved through the southern part of the country and into Greece.

10 APRIL 1941

Yugoslavia The advance of the German Second Army gathers speed. Zagreb is captured. The German advance is helped by the desertion of many Croat troops from the Yugoslav army. During the day Zagreb radio proclaims the establishment of an independent Croatian republic. The Croatian nationalist leader, Pavelić, is in Rome.

North Africa Rommel's troops begin to attack Tobruk with a small improvised force but are beaten off.

10–12 APRIL 1941

Greece On the 10th the Germans begin their attacks through the Monastir Gap. The attacks are repeated with growing strength over the following two days and on the 12th the defending British and Australian forces pull back. The Germans have very powerful air support throughout. During this time the Allied forces to the east are pulling back from the Aliakmon Line to a position hinging on Mount Olympus.

11 APRIL 1941

Yugoslavia The Italian Second Army, led by General Ambrosio, begins a cautious advance from the Trieste area toward Ljubljana but Weich's forces arrive there first. Other Italian units begin to advance south along the Dalmatian coast. The German XLI Corps also begins an advance over the Rumanian border toward Belgrade. The Hungarians also join in with an advance from the Szeged area toward Novi Sad. They are held up more by resistance from Yugoslav civilians than by the Yugoslav army.

North Africa The isolation of Tobruk is now complete, all the remainder of the Allied force having retreated to the Egyptian border. The German attack on Tobruk continues but the combination of Australian infantry and British artillery defending proves too strong for them and they fail to break through.

War at Sea Roosevelt tells Churchill that the US Navy will extend the American Defense Zone up to the line of 26 degrees West. The Red Sea is declared to be no longer a 'combat zone' and under the terms of US law US ships may now carry cargos to ports there including supplies for the British in Egypt.

United States, Politics President Roosevelt creates the Office of Price Administrations under the direction of Leon Henderson. It is given the task of controlling prices and profits and balancing civilian and defense needs. This bureau will play an important part in holding back many increases in prices and containing inflation despite the pressures that will develop in the war economy.

12 APRIL 1941

Yugoslavia In the evening Belgrade surrenders to General Kleist's forces who have advanced down the Morava valley from Nis. They only reach Belgrade a little before other German units from the north and east.

13 APRIL 1941

Diplomatic Affairs The USSR and Japan sign a five year Neutrality Agreement. For Stalin this is an invaluable piece of diplomacy which, backed by secret information from Soviet spies in Tokyo, will allow him to transfer forces from Siberia to face a possible German attack. These

moves begin now and will be particularly important during the final German advance on Moscow later in the year.

The agreement represents a complete change in Japanese policy and marks the growing concern of the Japanese military leaders and statesmen to look south to the resources of the East Indies. The agreement has been negotiated almost alone by Foreign Minister Matsuoka, in Moscow on the way back from a European visit. Although it conforms well to the other Japanese leaders' ideas, they are upset at Matsuoka's brash and independent attitude.

Greece Although the withdrawal to the Mount Olympus position is not yet complete the British and Greeks decide that they must retreat farther to shorter lines near Thermopylae.

13–17 APRIL 1941

North Africa There are more German and Italian attacks on Tobruk but again they are beaten off. The Italian Ariete Division performs particularly badly in these operations.

14 APRIL 1941

Yugoslavia, Politics King Peter leaves Yugoslavia and flies to Athens. The Simović government joins him there on the 15th.

Diplomatic Affairs There are secret talks in New York between the Americans and the Icelandic consul. The Icelandic officials agree to do nothing to resist an American occupation to replace the present British force.

14–18 APRIL 1941

Greece From the 14th the Allied forces on the Olympus position are attacked by the advancing Germans. In the Monastir Gap the rearguards are also under pressure throughout this time as they try to retire through Kozani. On 16 April Wavell gives orders, on the basis of the situation both in North Africa and Greece, that the sailing of the 7th Australian Division and the Polish Brigade from Egypt is to be cancelled. This is effectively a decision to abandon the Greek campaign and indeed Papagos is already suggesting that the British leave Greece in order to minimize the damage to his country. On the 18th the Greek Prime Minister Korizis commits suicide. The campaign continues however, with the Olympus position having been abandoned on that day. The rearguard will be considerably harried by the Luftwaffe as they fall back to Thermopylae.

15 APRIL 1941

United States, Politics Harry Hopkins is

appointed to be Roosevelt's personal representative in charge of running the Lend-Lease program.

16 APRIL 1941
Yugoslavia Ante Pavelić is sworn in to head the new Croat republic. Over the next few months his Ustaše followers, Roman Catholic Croats, will murder about 500,000 people, most of them Orthodox Serbs, who will be presented with a choice between rebaptism and death. Many Jews are also killed. Unusually the local Catholic priests will be involved in the massacres. Elsewhere in Occupied Europe the Catholic clergy will have a fine record in resistance work.

Mediterranean An important German convoy of five transports escorted by three Italian destroyers is attacked by four British destroyers near Kerkinnah Island. One of the British ships is sunk in the engagement but all the Axis vessels go down. About 1250 of the 3000 German troops are rescued by Axis forces.

17 APRIL 1941
Yugoslavia On the Dalmatian coast the Italians enter Dubrovnik.

The former prime minister, Cincar-Marković (deposed 27 March), signs an armistice with the Germans. In the course of overrunning the country the Germans have lost less than 200 dead.

19 APRIL 1941
Iraq A British convoy begins to land troops from the 20th Indian Brigade at Basra. A small British contingent has already been sent in by air to protect the air base at Shaibah, near Basra. Later in the month this force will be sent on to the Habbaniyah airfield. By a treaty of 1930 the British are entitled to send troops across Iraq to and from Palestine and with no prospect of immediate German help of any size Rashid Ali's new government cannot object at first to the British landings. In diplomatic exchanges they unsuccessfully oppose any addition to the British force. British reinforcements in fact arrive at Basra on the 29th. By this time the Iraqis will have decided to fight.

Britain, Home Front The first registration of women for war work under a new Employment Order begins.

19–21 APRIL 1941
Greece On the 19th Wavell is in Athens to meet General Wilson and General Blamey, the commander of the Australian forces. They decide that it will probably be necessary to evacuate their troops from Greece, but promise the Greeks that they will keep fighting as long as the Greeks themselves do so. On the 21st Papagos recommends that the Allies leave and permission for the evacuation is given from London.

On the ground the Allied forces still active have all passed through the Thermopylae position by the 20th. On that day, however, the Greek forces in Epirus that have been fighting the Albanian campaign are forced to surrender to the SS Adolf Hitler Division.

19–22 APRIL 1941
East Africa The 1st South African Brigade has been sent north from Addis Ababa along the road to Asmara in Eritrea and now comes up to Italian positions south of Dessie. The fighting lasts for four days before the Italians fall back before the advance.

21 APRIL 1941
North Africa Three battleships from the Mediterranean Fleet shell Tripoli on their return from escorting a Malta convoy. Cunningham has only undertaken this operation under protest and with direct orders from Churchill. At first Churchill wished to try to block the port by sinking the battleship *Barham* in the entrance to Tripoli Harbor.

22–24 APRIL 1941
Greece The German forces begin to arrive at the Thermopylae position on the 22nd but do not mount a large attack until the 24th when they are held off. By the 24th the position has largely served its delaying function and during the night of the 24th the defending troops fall back, leaving a further rearguard at Thebes. On the 23rd King George and his government are evacuated to Crete and on the night of the 24th the main evacuation begins, with 11,000 men being taken off.

23 APRIL 1941
German Raiders The German raider *Thor* returns to Brest after a cruise of 322 days in which 11 merchant ships and one British auxiliary cruiser have been sunk and two more auxiliaries damaged.

24 APRIL 1941
United States, Politics Roosevelt formally orders US warships to report the movements of German warships west of Iceland. This is happening unofficially already. The information

is usually passed one way or another to the British.

25 APRIL 1941
Germany, Planning Hitler issues Directive 28 giving the order for Operation *Merkur*, the airborne attack on Crete.

25–29 APRIL 1941
Greece There is little fighting until the 26th when the main German advance is again halted by the Allied rearguard, this time at Thebes. There are, however, two German attempts to move into the Peloponnese to interfere with the evacuations going on there. A paratroop force is dropped at Corinth to take the vital canal bridge but it is blown up before they can do so. At the west end of the Gulf of Corinth there is more success for the Germans as the Adolf Hitler Division begins to cross over to Patras. The Thebes rearguard falls back during the night of the 26th and the Germans enter Athens on the 27th.

Meanwhile the evacuation of the Allied forces has been going on. The few port facilities and the beaches at Rafina, Nauplia, Monemvasia and Kalamata are all used, as well as other sites. The British Mediterranean Fleet provides a force of six cruisers, 20 destroyers and about 30 other ships. The evacuation generally goes very well except for incidents at Nauplia and Kalamata. On the 27th a transport is bombed off Nauplia and two destroyers that come to the rescue are also sunk. Many of the soldiers on all three ships are lost. Also at Nauplia a burning merchant ship blocks the pier on the last night and 1700 men have to be left behind. At Kalamata a German force bursts into the town on the 28th but is eventually defeated by the 7000 troops waiting for evacuation. The naval force off the port sees the fighting and withdraws before the Germans are subdued. About 5000 troops are taken off on the 28/29th, the last night, bringing the total evacuated to just over 50,000 at a cost of two destroyers and four transports. It has taken Germany less than a month to overrun Greece and Yugoslavia.

The strategic importance of the German campaign lies particularly in its relationship to the preparations for the attack on the USSR. It has often been suggested, although probably incorrectly, that the Balkan campaign delayed Barbarossa during a period of fine summer weather that might have been invaluable to the Germans later in the year. As well as questions of equipment, training and the weather in Poland that probably contributed most to the timing of the attack, it should be noted that the campaign in Greece was part of the long-intended German strategic program and that any disruption to the program was caused by the independent Yugoslavian situation. The 'postponement' of Barbarossa which Hitler ordered in response to the Yugoslav coup did not change the date fixed for the attack, but changed the date by which preparations were to be complete – a rather different thing. Very few of the forces employed in Yugoslavia were irreplaceable in the Barbarossa order of battle, and there is evidence to suggest that after the Yugoslavian campaign they were only sent back to their Barbarossa positions slowly. If an earlier Barbarossa attack had been required, the units used in Yugoslavia could have taken part or been replaced, temporarily, from the reserve.

26 APRIL 1941
East Africa The Allied forces take Dessie with 8000 Italian prisoners.

27 APRIL 1941
North Africa General Paulus arrives in North Africa on an inspection tour of Rommel's force. He has orders from OKH to try to bring Rommel under control and sort out a situation which, from Germany, seems very confused. He immediately halts preparations for more attacks on Tobruk. German reconnaissance units enter Egypt and occupy the Halfaya Pass, one of the few routes from Egypt by which the Cyrenaica plateau can be reached.
Mediterranean The carrier *Ark Royal* flies a further 23 Hurricanes to Malta. A small convoy also arrives at the island with some supplies from Gibraltar and some reinforcements which are to join the Mediterranean Fleet at Alexandria.

29 APRIL 1941
East Africa Advance forces from 5th Indian Division reach the north side of the Italian position at Amba Alagi, in Abyssinia.

30 APRIL 1941
North Africa After General Paulus has decided to allow a further effort against Tobruk the heaviest German attack yet goes in after a bombardment by artillery and many Stuka bombers. A salient in the western sector of the perimeter around the Ras el Madauar hill is gained by the attack but vigorous defense halts it there.

MAY 1941
War at Sea Partly because of captures made

during the month, the British code-breaking service begins to be able to decipher German naval messages regularly and promptly. This is not a continuous process, however. The code is altered daily and major changes are made every month. The keys to these changes are given only a limited issue and thus a U-Boat setting out for a planned six-week cruise would only be given the machine settings for a little more than this period. Captures are, therefore, of very limited value as well as being very difficult to achieve.

A new Newfoundland Escort Force, largely provided by the Canadian Navy, is established and after HX-126 and OB-318 have lost heavily in mid-ocean, a continuous escort is provided for eastbound convoys from Halifax. This begins with HX-129 which sets out on 27 May. The escort is provided in stages from Canada, Iceland and finally from Britain. Obviously these new requirements increase the strain on the escort forces and call for very careful organization so that, for example, destroyers with a comparatively limited margin of endurance are not kept waiting at a rendezvous for a convoy which has been delayed by bad weather or attack. The Allies lose 58 ships of 325,500 tons to the U-Boats during May, more than half of which fall to a six-strong group operating in the weakly protected waters off Freetown. During this operation *U.107* sinks 14 ships in one patrol – a record total for the whole war. The total Allied shipping loss is 139 ships.

The Blitz In the first week there are several heavy attacks on Liverpool in which 18 vessels are sunk in the harbor and 25 badly damaged. The port installations are reduced to 75 percent of their normal handling capacity. Belfast and the Clyde ports are also attacked. The raid on London on the night of 10–11 May is the last major attack for three years. The Houses of Parliament are damaged in this attack, the heaviest made on a British city in the whole campaign. On the night of 30–31 May Dublin is bombed in error by the Luftwaffe.

British Air Operations Among the targets for Bomber Command this month are Brest, Hamburg, Bremen and Cologne. Bomber Command is now able to send over 350 sorties on selected nights. In the month's operations 2690 sorties are flown, 2840 tons of bombs are dropped and 76 aircraft are lost.

Europe, Resistance The first three British Special Operations Executive (SOE) agents to become active are parachuted into France.

1 MAY 1941

Iraq Fighting begins when Iraqi soldiers make a small attack on the British outpost at Rutba (west of Baghdad, about 125 miles from the Transjordan border).

Iraqi forces are also established in positions around the Habbaniyah airfield. The Iraqi forces amount to about four divisions in total. two are in the Baghdad area.

North Africa Rommel's attack on Tobruk continues. He attempts to widen and deepen the gap already won in the defenses but the Australian forces fight fiercely and largely contain the attacks.

2 MAY 1941

Iraq The British airfield at Habbaniyah is attacked by considerable Iraqi ground forces. The British have about 80 obsolescent aircraft at Habbaniyah, many of them training types. Despite their age and unsuitability they are immediately employed against the Iraqi forces with considerable success. The British are, therefore, encouraged to hold Habbaniyah although their ground force there is very small.

There are also some skirmishes at several points near the Persian Gulf, especially at Basra where there are riots and some shooting in opposition to further British landings.

North Africa The fighting at Tobruk continues with little change in the positions on either side.

3 MAY 1941

East Africa The British forces begin attacks from the north against the Italian positions at Amba Alagi. These positions guard passes in the road between Asmara and Addis Ababa. They are based on a number of steep and rugged hills and there are numerous caves. The position is very strong.

Iraq There are British attacks on the Iraqi positions around Habbaniyah and by air on the Iraqi Rashid airfield.

4 MAY 1941

North Africa Rommel halts his attack on Tobruk. The Germans will continue to hold the enclave in the perimeter that they have just won but will not be able to extend it at any time later in the siege. For both sides life at Tobruk settles down into a style not unlike the trench warfare of World War I. The ground is very hard, however, and this makes digging particularly difficult so that trenches are often shallow at first. This means that their occupants must stay virtually motionless throughout the burning heat of the day. Neither side is well placed with regard to supplies or other personal comforts. Both sides soon adopt a policy of offensive night patrolling which means that there can be no relaxation.

Iraq The main events are again British air operations. An airfield at Mosul which is being used by a small German force is one RAF target. The German force is receiving supplies from and via Syria with the cooperation of the Vichy authorities.

East Africa The Italian forces around Amba Alagi are driven off three hills in the west of their position by attacks from the 29th Indian Brigade.

5 MAY 1941

East Africa Emperor Haile Selassie triumphantly returns to his capital, Addis Ababa. In the battles at Amba Alagi the Italian Middle Hill position is taken.

5–6 MAY 1941

North Africa Supplies are brought to the besieged garrison in Tobruk by destroyer for the first time. From now until the end of the siege two destroyers will be used on such missions on most nights and at about weekly intervals reinforcements will be brought in and the wounded evacuated.

6 MAY 1941

Iraq The British forces consolidate their hold on Habbaniyah airfield, driving the Iraqis back from Sin el Dhibban toward Fallujah, nearer the capital. The 21st Indian Brigade arrives at Basra.

Soviet Union, Politics The Praesidium of the Supreme Soviet nominates Stalin President of the Council of People's Commissars. Previously Stalin has been content to hold only the office of general secretary of the Communist Party.

6–12 MAY 1941

Mediterranean For the first time for many months the British try to run a convoy through the Mediterranean from Gibraltar to Egypt. Churchill is the driving force behind this decision and has ordered the operation because he wishes the supplies and tanks carried in the ships to form the basis of an offensive in the desert as soon as possible.

The operation is code named Tiger. There are five transports. On 6 May they pass Gibraltar and are joined by one battleship, a carrier from Force H and another battleship which is to go on to join the Mediterranean Fleet. With these heavy units are four cruisers and seven destroyers. Six more destroyers join the convoy from Gibraltar on 6 May. Also on 6 May two convoys leave Alexandria for Malta with an

escort of five cruisers and three destroyers.

Cunningham takes the whole of the Mediterranean Fleet out in support with three battleships, his single carrier, three cruisers and 19 destroyers. On the night of 7/8 May part of Cunningham's force shells the harbor at Benghazi, sinking two ships.

On 8 May there are air attacks on the eastward and westward bound convoys. The carrier with each convoy engages the attacking Italian planes. On 9 May one of the Tiger transports sinks on a mine. Force H begins to return to Gibraltar. On the night 10/11 May Benghazi is again shelled. By 12 May all the ships have reached their destinations. Tiger has brought 238 tanks and 43 Hurricanes to Egypt for the loss of 57 tanks.

7 MAY 1941

Battle of the Atlantic In a special operation mounted for the purpose the German trawler *München*, a weather ship, is captured northeast of Iceland and secret papers relating to the Enigma coding machine are taken.

Iraq General Quinan takes command of the British forces in Iraq.

8 MAY 1941

German Raiders The British heavy cruiser *Cornwall* finds and sinks the German raider *Pinguin* near the Seychelles. The *Pinguin* has sunk 28 ships of 136,550 tons during its cruise.

8–10 MAY 1941

East Africa The Amba Alagi fighting continues. On the 8th the Indian forces take the Falagi Pass and three small peaks south of Amba Alagi itself. On the 10th the Gumsa position is taken.

9–11 MAY 1941

Battle of the Atlantic After sinking two ships from the convoy OB-318, *U.110* is forced to surface by a depth-charge attack and is boarded and captured. Code books and an Enigma cipher machine are recovered. As well as providing useful information for general code breaking work, in this case the books are of considerable use in the imminent operations involving the *Bismarck* and her supply ships. On 11 May *U.110* sinks from the depth charge damage while on the way to Iceland. Throughout the war the Germans do not discover that *U.110* has been captured. (It should be noted that the code details captured do not include the main code which will be used by the *Bismarck*. None of the *Bismarck*'s messages will be successfully decoded by the British at the time.)

10 MAY 1941
Iraq British-led forces from the Jordanian Arab Legion take Rutba. A stronger detachment, Habforce, is being prepared for a move to Rutba. Part of this force, to be known as Kingcol, will then move on to relieve Habbaniyah.

10–11 MAY 1941
Diplomatic Affairs Rudolf Hess, the deputy leader of the Nazi Party and second in line to Goering as heir to Hitler, flies to Britain on a bizarre peace mission. He lands by parachute at Eaglesham near Glasgow, hoping to contact the Duke of Hamilton whom he met at the 1936 Olympics. He believes that there is a considerable body of British opinion that is opposed to Churchill but is also anti-Communist and therefore prepared to consider making common ground on these terms with Germany. He is immediately disowned by the German authorities (he has left a note explaining himself to Hitler) and this prompt reaction detracts from the propaganda value that the episode might have had for the British.

13 MAY 1941
Germany, Politics Martin Bormann is appointed to take Hess' former position. He is given the title of party chancellor, an important step in his rise to power.
Middle East, Politics The exiled Mufti of Jerusalem broadcasts from Baghdad summoning all Islamic countries to join the fight against Britain.

14 MAY 1941
East Africa The South African force advancing north from Addis Ababa has now joined the Amba Alagi battle and moves to attack the Italian Triangle position. The attacks are held during the day but the Italians retire at night. Italian morale is now very low, largely because of the fierce and undisciplined conduct of some of the Ethiopian guerrilla forces supporting the Allies.

15 MAY 1941
Yugoslavia, Politics An independent Kingdom of Croatia is established with Italian backing. On 18 May the Duke of Spoleto is proclaimed king. He will never visit his kingdom.
Iraq and Syria The British government announces that German planes are arriving in Syria and using Syrian bases to move on to Iraq. The RAF, therefore, bombs Palmyra and Damascus airfields. These attacks continue over

the next few days.

15–16 MAY 1941
North Africa In preparation for the major offensive which the tanks from the Tiger convoy (*see* 6–12 May) will allow, Wavell begins an operation code named Brevity. It is designed to capture Halfaya Pass and gain ground leading to the more open areas of the Cyrenaica Plateau. Churchill's habit of describing the recently arrived tanks as 'Tiger Cubs' indicates the importance which he attaches to the coming offensive and foreshadows the rigor with which he will punish failure. The information which has been received from the interception of German signals, especially from the recent reports of General Paulus on the situation in Africa, has convinced Churchill that the German forces are weak and overextended.

General Gott commands the Brevity operation. His plan calls for mixed columns to advance to Halfaya Pass and Fort Capuzzo and for a tank force to move to Sidi Aziz. On the first day the forces on the coast reach and capture Halfaya, but the 22nd Guards Brigade is held up in heavy fighting at Capuzzo. The tank force on the left makes good ground initially but the approach of the German 8th Panzer Regiment makes the British decide to withdraw on the 16th.

15–19 MAY 1941
Crete There are powerful German air attacks on the island. These are, of course, in preparation for the coming landing and are designed to subdue the garrison and compel the RAF to withdraw its few aircraft from Crete.

18 MAY 1941
Iraq After outflanking an Iraqi blocking force the British relieving group, Kingcol, reaches Habbaniyah airfield.
Syria General Dentz broadcasts, warning his troops in Vichy-controlled Syria to meet force with force. Airfields in Syria are bombed again by the RAF.

18–22 MAY 1941
Battle of the Atlantic On 18 May the battleship *Bismarck* leaves Gdynia in company with the heavy cruiser *Prinz Eugen* for an Atlantic cruise under the command of Admiral Lutjens. Various supply ships are already at sea. On 20 May the two ships are reported in the Kattegat. The information reaches London with the cooperation of Intelligence officers of the Swedish navy. On 21 May British reconnaissance aircraft find the German ships near Bergen. Later in the

day the battleship *Prince of Wales* and the battlecruiser *Hood* put to sea from Scapa Flow. On 22 May British planes report correctly that the Germans have also put to sea and the Commander in Chief of the British Home Fleet, Admiral Tovey, therefore, sets out with the battleship *King George V* and the carrier *Victorious*. The battlecruiser *Repulse* joins this force later in the day. Tovey plans to reinforce the patrols watching the Faeroes–Iceland passage while Holland in the *Hood* goes to give further strength to the forces in the Denmark Strait (*see* 23–27 May).

19 MAY 1941

East Africa The Duke of Aosta surrenders with the 7000 remaining Italian troops at Amba Alagi. The Allied forces have now killed or captured 230,000 of the Italian East Africa force. About 80,000 remain.

Iraq The British forces based at Habbaniyah airfield begin to operate more aggressively, attacking and capturing Fallujah. The British airfield is bombed by German planes.

20 MAY 1941

Crete The German attack begins. There are airborne landings by forces of 7th Paratroop Division from Fliegerkorps XI. General Student is in command and has 5th Mountain Division in reserve. There is massive air support from Fliegerkorps VIII which has over 400 bombers and 200 fighters. Altogether the Germans employ about 23,000 troops. The garrison consists mostly of troops recently evacuated from Greece. There are strong Australian and New Zealand contingents among the 32,000 British and Empire troops and about 10,000 Greeks. All units are short of equipment and heavy weapons. General Freyberg is in command.

The attack begins with heavy air raids and these are followed in the morning by airborne landings at Máleme and Caneá. In the afternoon there are further landings at Rétimo and Heráklion. It is clear to both Allies and Germans that the battle for the island depends on control of the airfields and it is round these that the German attack concentrates. There is heavy fighting in all sectors, with the German forces suffering heavy losses. At Rétimo and Heráklion the defending forces are successful in holding off the Germans and although fighting in these areas continues for several days it will not effect the outcome of the battle. The German forces near Caneá are made to retreat inland but are not neutralized. At Máleme the fighting is very fierce

and by the end of the day the airfield is virtually no man's land. The commander of the New Zealand battalion holding the airfield is slightly out of touch with the situation of his whole force, through no fault of his own, and decides to withdraw during the night. This comparatively minor move effectively decides the whole battle. The Germans recognize their lack of success in the other sectors and soon rush reinforcements in to the Máleme airfield.

The British Mediterranean Fleet is cruising off the island to prevent any German force arriving by sea.

Battle of the Atlantic The US merchant ship *Robin Moor* is sunk in the Atlantic by a U-Boat. On 21 May Roosevelt describes the incident as 'an act of intimidation' to which 'we do not propose to yield.'

21 MAY 1941

Mediterranean The carriers *Ark Royal* and *Furious* fly off a cargo of 48 Hurricanes to Malta. In the air fighting since January the Germans have lost 62 aircraft and the Italians 15. The British losses in the air have been 32 machines, as well as an equal number destroyed on the ground.

21–23 MAY 1941

Crete During the 21st the Germans consolidate their hold on Máleme. The first troops of the 5th Mountain Division are flown in. During the night the nearby New Zealand forces counterattack and although they have some success they do not penetrate to the airfield. There is little change in the Allied positions during the 22nd but in the face of the growing strength and complete air superiority, Freyberg cancels a further counterattack on the night of the 22nd

Above: Ju 52 aircraft carried paratroops during the successful attack on Crete.

and orders a withdrawal instead. During the 23rd the Germans continue to exploit their hold on Máleme, sending in artillery units and fighter aircraft.

In the naval battles offshore one British destroyer is lost to air attack on the 21st, but during the night a German convoy attempting to reach the island is intercepted and turned back without loss by a force of cruisers and destroyers. On the 22nd a second convoy is turned back but is not pursued far because the Luftwaffe intervenes. In various actions during the day the battleship *Warspite* is badly damaged and two cruisers and one destroyer are sunk. Admiral Cunningham, ashore in Alexandria, orders the fleet to return after being wrongly informed that ammunition for the battleship's antiaircraft guns is in very short supply. During the night of 22/23 May the Máleme airfield is bombarded by Lord Mountbatten's 5th Destroyer Flotilla but the destroyers *Kelly* and *Kashmir* are sunk on the 23rd by the Germans while they are withdrawing. King George of Greece is evacuated from the island to Egypt on 22/23 May.

23–27 MAY 1941
Battle of the Atlantic The German battleship *Bismarck* and her consort, *Prinz Eugen*, are sighted in the Denmark Strait by the patrolling British cruisers *Norfolk* and *Suffolk*. British radar equipment plays an important part in the interception. On 24 May the *Hood* and the *Prince of Wales* come up and engage the German ships. The *Hood* is sunk very quickly and a short while later the *Prince of Wales* breaks off the action after receiving some damage. Only three men from the *Hood*'s complement of 1416 are saved. Various theories try to explain how the *Hood* was destroyed so quickly. Certainly the ship's armor was inadequate by 1941 standards and the *Hood* was long overdue for her planned modernization. It is possible that a shell from the *Bismarck* penetrated the magazine but a more plausible explanation is that a shell set fire to some antiaircraft rocket ammunition and that this fire spread to the magazine.

The *Prince of Wales* is very new and has sailed from Scapa with some dockyard men still aboard working on the guns. In the action one of the guns jams and cannot be used. This contributes to the decision to break off the action. There has been no time for the crew to train properly and this state of affairs will prevail for the rest of the ship's life. Although the ships of the *King George V* Class are generally sound, they all require a generous working-up period before they are fully efficient.

However, the defects of the ships are not the only reasons for the *Bismarck*'s success. Admiral Holland led his ships into the battle in such a way that not all their heavy guns could bear, nor does he seem to have made full allowance for the possible effects of plunging long-range fire on the comparatively thin deck armor of the *Hood*.

After the action the British cruisers continue to shadow the German ships. The *Bismarck* has been hit three times, which has caused the loss of some fuel and the contamination of more. Lutjens therefore decides to put in to Brest. The British battleships *Rodney* and *Ramillies* leave the convoys they have been escorting to join the hunt. Force H, with the battlecruiser *Renown* and the carrier *Ark Royal*, puts to sea from Gibraltar. During the night of 24–25 May aircraft from the Home Fleet carrier *Victorious* attack, and hit *Bismarck* with one torpedo. The damage is negligible. Later in the night *Prinz Eugen* slips away to operate independently, and later still contact is lost between the shadowing British cruisers and the *Bismarck*. For much of 25 May, therefore, the British commanders are in the dark as to *Bismarck*'s position but Lutjen's breaks radio silence to report and is picked up on the British direction-finding equipment. This information is passed to Admiral Tovey but is at first misinterpreted, perhaps because the radio bearings are plotted on an unsuitable navigation chart. Tovey now has *King George V* and *Rodney*, but both are short of fuel and by this mistake they lose their chance of meeting the *Bismarck* unless her speed can be reduced. During the operation the British have been most worried to protect the convoy lanes and block the *Bismarck*'s return home by the northern routes. The best dispositions to prevent the *Bismarck* reaching Brest have not been made. Nonetheless Force H has been hurrying north over the past few days and when on 26 May a Catalina aircraft finds *Bismarck* only 700 miles from Brest it is clear that the aircraft of the *Ark Royal* offer the best chance of slowing the German ship so that she can be caught. The first strike launched from the *Ark Royal* finds and attacks the British cruiser *Sheffield* by mistake owing to the bad weather. The attack fails because of defects in the magnetic exploders of the torpedoes, so simple contact types are substituted for a second strike. The 15 Swordfish find the correct target and score two hits. One hit wrecks the German battleship's steering and practically brings her to a halt. During the night the *Bismarck* is further harried by torpedo and gunfire attacks by five British destroyers. It is not clear whether they score any torpedo hits.

On 27 May *Rodney* and *King George V* come up and in a gun battle lasting less than two hours, the *Bismarck* is reduced to a hulk. She is finished off with torpedoes from the cruisers *Dorsetshire* and *Norfolk*.

24 MAY 1941

Crete The Allied forces in the Caneá area are now in positions around Galatas. The German buildup at Máleme continues.

East Africa In southern Abyssinia Soddu falls to the Allied forces. In this area General Gazzera leads seven weak Italian divisions. The attacking Allied force is made up of the 11th and 12th African Divisions.

25–26 MAY 1941

Crete The German forces begin to advance westward toward Galatas. The fighting is very intense and the town changes hands several times during the two days. Toward the end of the 26th Freyberg raises the question of a withdrawal from the island. During the night of the 26th most of the Allied forces withdraw from the Galatas position amid some confusion about the exact nature of their orders. On the 26th aircraft from the carrier *Formidable* attack the Stuka base at Scarpanto in the Italian Dodecanese. The carrier is hit twice by air attacks.

27 MAY 1941

Crete The Germans take Caneá and Suda. The Allied forces are now largely split up and moving in a disorganized manner in the direction of Sfakia to be evacuated. The evacuation is authorized by Wavell after he has consulted with London. The battleship *Barham* is damaged by air attack.

North Africa Rommel has reinforced his troops on the Egyptian border and his two panzer regiments retake Halfaya Pass in a converging attack. The Germans begin work to fortify their new position, especially by digging in their 88mm guns.

Iraq British forces begin to advance from their positions around Habbaniyah and Fallujah toward the capital, Baghdad.

28 MAY 1941

Iraq The Allied forces occupy Ur. The 20th Indian Brigade has made this advance from Basra but can go no further for the moment because repairs to roads and railroad tracks are needed.

28 MAY–1 JUNE 1941

Crete The Allied forces fight some small,

rearguard actions to cover their retreat to the evacuation beaches at Sfakia. Evacuations from Sfakia take place each night. Also, on the night of 28/29 May, the Heraklion garrison of 4000 men is taken off by a force of cruisers and destroyers. These ships are heavily attacked while withdrawing. Two destroyers are sunk and the two cruisers involved are hit. During 1 June the cruiser *Calcutta* is also sunk by the German aircraft. Altogether 18,600 men are taken off but casualties and prisoners in the battle for the island amount to another 15,000 from the land forces and 2000 from the navy. About 600 more men will escape from the island by various routes later. The largest groups of prisoners are the 5000 men who are captured when the Germans take Sfakia on 1 June and the garrison of Rétimo who do not receive evacuation instructions because of a communications breakdown. The ships lost include three cruisers and six destroyers. In addition, two battleships, one carrier and numerous cruisers and destroyers have been hit. In all the operations in Greece and Crete 44 transports are lost. The Germans admit casualties of 7000 from their force – a very high proportion of them deaths – and Hitler decides that such large-scale airborne attacks should not be repeated even although the result has been a brilliant success.

30 MAY 1941

Iraq Although the main Allied force is held up at Ur and the small British force from Habbaniyah is only advancing very slowly, Rashid Ali gives up the struggle and flees to Iran. An armistice is agreed on the 31st. The British right to station troops in the country is confirmed and the Iraqis undertake to do nothing to help the Axis.

JUNE 1941

Battle of the Atlantic German submarines sink 61 ships of 310,000 tons this month. Owing to the diversion of German aircraft to take part in Barbarossa there is a drop in Allied shipping losses to air attack. The total Allied loss from all causes is 432,000 tons (109 ships). The first escort carrier, the *Audacity*, enters British service. Five more ships of this class are being converted in the UK and six in the USA under Lease-Lend arrangements. The work on these British ships will provide useful information for the construction of later US vessels of this class. The U-Boats' task is also being made more difficult by Allied scientists. Radar working on the 10cm wavelength is now gradually coming into service. This is sufficiently sensitive to detect a submarine periscope over 1000 yards away in the best conditions.

Atomic Research The British Maud Committee reports that they believe that it will be possible to make an atomic bomb using the isotope Uranium 235. Research in the US is also proceeding, as yet at a more gentle pace but substantial funds will be authorized later in the year. Following the Maud report, the British soon move to set up a formal research program under the code name Tube Alloys (*see* 18 June 1942.)

The Blitz Manchester is the target for almost the only major German attack during the month. Much of the strength of the Luftwaffe is being withdrawn early in the month to be ready to support the attack on the Soviet Union.

British Air Operations Brest is attacked five times during the month, as are targets in the Ruhr, the Rhineland and ports in northwest Germany. RAF Fighter Command conducts a series of fighter sweeps over northern France.

1 JUNE 1941
Iraq British forces enter Baghdad. Regent Emir Abdul Illah, the uncle of King Faisal, returns to the country.

North Africa Air Marshal Tedder takes command of the RAF forces in the Middle East. The majority of the German 15th Panzer Division has now joined Rommel's force.

Battle of the Atlantic The US Coastguard begins patrol operations off the southern Greenland coast. Only four ships are involved at this stage.

Britain, Home Front It is announced that measures for clothes rationing are being prepared.

2 JUNE 1941
North Africa Vichy grants the Axis powers the use of the port of Bizerta for unloading non-military supplies for their forces stationed in North Africa.

3 JUNE 1941
Iraq British forces enter Mosul. A few German pilots are captured.

3–23 JUNE 1941
German Raiders British forces successfully intercept and sink nine German supply ships. Seven of them have been sent to sea to cooperate with the *Bismarck* and the remaining two have been working with the merchant raiders. These interceptions all occur because of the British ability to decode some German signals.

4 JUNE 1941
World Affairs The former kaiser of Germany, Wilhelm, dies at home in Doorn, Holland.

Iraq A new Iraqi Cabinet is formed under British auspices. British forces are now moving through the country establishing control of key points. Some of the British troops will be ready to move into Syria later in the month.

5 JUNE 1941
United States, Politics The US Army Bill for 1942 is introduced into Congress. It calls for appropriations amounting to $10,400,000,000. It will be passed on 28 June.

6 JUNE 1941
United States, Politics A new law comes into force allowing the government to take over foreign ships laid up in the United States.

Mediterranean The carriers *Ark Royal* and *Furious* again carry a cargo of Hurricanes from Gibraltar to within flying distance of Malta.

8 JUNE 1941
Syria At 0200 hours British and Free French forces invade Syria. The British have been increasingly worried by reports of a German presence in Syria in recent weeks. In fact, although German aircraft did use Syrian bases during the fighting in Iraq, they have all now left at the request of the Vichy authorities. The Allied attack goes in nonetheless.

The attacking force is commanded by General Wilson and includes 7th Australian Division, 4th Indian Brigade and Free French units. The defending Vichy forces are rather stronger, with 45,000 men under the command of General Dentz. The Allied force advances along several lines from positions in Palestine and Transjordan. There is little resistance at first.

General Catroux, who has been appointed by General de Gaulle to head the Free French forces, issues a proclamation calling optimistically for Dentz and his men to change sides. The British announce that they seek no territorial gains.

9 JUNE 1941
Syria The Allied advance continues to make good progress. Tyre, Marjayoun and El Quneitra are all taken in the advance from Palestine. In the drive from Transjordan Dera'à is taken.

There is a naval battle off the Syrian coast between forces which eventually include four British and two Vichy destroyers. The French are forced to retire but inflict some damage.

10 JUNE 1941
Syria Australian forces advancing along the coast north of Tyre begin improvising crossings over the Litani River. A commando raid on the 9th failed to take an important bridge in this sector.
East Africa An Indian battalion lands and captures Assab, the last Red Sea port held by the Italians. There is fighting southwest of Addis Ababa near Galla Sidamo.

13 JUNE 1941
War at Sea The German pocket battleship, *Lützow*, is damaged by a torpedo attack from a British Beaufort aircraft off the Norwegian port of Lindesnes. *Lützow* returns to port and will be in dock until January 1942.
Syria On the coast the Australian forces begin attacks around Sidon. The town falls on the 15th.
Vichy France The Vichy government announces that more than 12,000 Jews have been arrested and are 'interned' in concentration camps because of a 'Jewish plot' to hinder Franco-German cooperation. The anti-Semitic laws in Vichy are being extended to include the expropriation of Jewish business without compensation.
Soviet Union, Politics The news agency Tass issues an official denial that there is tension between Germany and the USSR. It states that 'there could be no misunderstanding between the two countries.'

14 JUNE 1941
Mediterranean The carriers *Ark Royal* and *Victorious* fly another cargo of Hurricanes to Malta. Of the 47 sent 43 arrive.
United States, Politics President Roosevelt freezes all German and Italian assets in the United States.

15 JUNE 1941
North Africa A major British offensive, Operation Battleaxe, begins. The aim is to relieve Tobruk. Wavell is still reluctant to attack, largely because the tanks which recently arrived on the Tiger convoy have had many mechanical faults and the time taken for repairs means that the troops have had a very short training period. Although the two divisions involved, 4th Indian and 7th Armored, are both experienced formations, they are not at full strength and have been further weakened by changes in command. General Beresford-Pierse is in charge of the attack.
Three columns are sent forward, one to Halfaya Pass, one to Capuzzo along the edge of

the escarpment and one inland to Hafid Ridge. The attack of Matilda tanks is beaten off at Halfaya by the emplaced 88's, and without tank support the infantry units there can achieve nothing. A force of lighter cruiser tanks similarly loses heavily at Hafid Ridge. Some success is achieved at Capuzzo, however.
The German radio intelligence gives them excellent tactical information and their dispositions of 5th Light forward and 15th Panzer watching Tobruk are more than adequate. On the whole Rommel is content to defend on the first day and, indeed, by the end of the day the British tank losses already leave them at a disadvantage.
Syria A counterattack by the Vichy forces succeeds in retaking part of the town of Marjayoun and some nearby positions. However, both to the west on the coast, where Sidon is taken, and to the east in the approaches to Damascus, where Kiswe falls, the Allied advance is still going well.

16 JUNE 1941
North Africa Nominally the British attack continues but the initiative has really passed to the Germans. The British 7th Armored Brigade loses heavily in a running battle with 5th Light while 4th Indian Division has to fight hard to hold off 15th Panzer. Halfaya remains in German hands.
Syria The Vichy counterattacks continue. El Quneitra is retaken.
United States, Politics President Roosevelt orders that all German and Italian consulates in the country should be closed, along with the offices of other German agencies. On 19 June Italy and Germany take similar action regarding American offices in their countries.

17 JUNE 1941
North Africa Rommel attempts to move his tank forces together early in the day to threaten the now-weakened British armor guarding the inland flank. After some confusion the whole British force begins to withdraw and Wavell is left to signal the failure of Battleaxe to Churchill.
Syria Australian troops take Jezzine, just inland from Sidon. The Habforce group, which had an important role in the fighting in Iraq and is now made up of a cavalry brigade and some small infantry units, is ordered to begin an advance from Iraq due west along the main oil pipeline leading to Palmyra.
Germany, Planning Hitler decides that the attack on the Soviet Union will commence on 22 June 1941.

18 JUNE 1941
Diplomatic Affairs A German-Turkish treaty of friendship for 10 years is concluded by the Turkish government and the German ambassador in Ankara, Von Papen.

19–20 JUNE 1941
Syria There is heavy fighting just outside Damascus at Mezze where the Vichy forces manage to cut off and eventually eliminate an Indian battalion.

20 JUNE 1941
Finland, Politics All reservists under the age of 45 are called up.
Battle of the Atlantic A German U-Boat sights the American battleship *Texas* within the area that Germany has declared is the operational area for U-Boats. However, after checking with the U-Boat Command, the *Texas* is not attacked.

21 JUNE 1941
East Africa British forces take Jimma, southwest of Addis Ababa. About 15,000 prisoners are taken. Although Jimma has been General Gazzera's main base, he escapes capture with a small part of his force. A further 4000 prisoners were taken earlier after an action at crossings of the Omo River, and many more were rounded up in smaller groups.
Syria Damascus falls to the Allied forces after the Vichy garrison has been evacuated. Habforce begins to advance into Syria from Iraq.

22 JUNE 1941
Eastern Front Operation Barbarossa, the German attack on the Soviet Union, begins. Despite the massive preparations spread over many months and the numerous indications Stalin receives from many sources, the Soviet forces are taken almost completely by surprise and lose very heavily in the first encounters.

The Germans have assembled almost 140 of their own divisions (figures vary in different sources), including 17 Panzer and 13 motorized units. Army Group North, commanded by Field Marshal Leeb, has 26 divisions and includes two infantry armies and Hoeppner's Fourth Panzer Group. Field Marshal Bock leads the largest German force, Army Group Center, with 51 divisions in two infantry armies and Guderian's Second and Hoth's Third Panzer Groups. Army Group South is led by Field Marshal Runstedt and includes 41 German divisions in three armies and one Panzer Group as well as 14 Rumanian and two Hungarian divisions. German units from Nor-

way in General Falkenhorst's Norway Army will join the attack in alliance with the 21 divisions of the Finnish army who are keen to regain the territory lost to the USSR in 1940. There are more German units in general reserve and others allocated for security duties in captured territory. Altogether, the Germans deploy over 3,000,000 men, 7100 guns and 3300 tanks. Each army group has support from a complete Luftflotte. The total strength is 2770 aircraft, almost the same as in France but now spread over a much larger front. Of the 3300 tanks deployed in the attack only 1400 are Mark III or IV types. This is a rather greater proportion of high-grade machines than in 1940 but Hitler's wish to have many of them armed with better guns has not been met. The increase in the number of Panzer divisions compared with 1940 has been achieved by a reorganization made in September 1940, when tank establishment was halved so that the number of divisions could be doubled. The strongest Panzer division in May 1940 had 300 tanks; now the strongest has 199. The new Panzer divisions have made considerable demands on scarce supplies of other vehicles also. As well as the tank force there is now a significant number of assault guns (250), mustered in special infantry-support battalions. The assault guns are formidable machines but they are administered and commanded by the artillery rather than the Panzer arm and will come to compete with the true tanks for scarce production resources.

The logistic preparations for Barbarossa have been particularly difficult for the German High Command. It has only been possible to assemble even a bare sufficiency of motor transport by using German, French and other captured types, which will, of course, cause many problems with spares and maintenance. The captured vehicles, especially the French, will be found to be notably unreliable. In addition to the motor transport the forces moving into the USSR still employ 625,000 horses. A further difficulty for the Germans is that the Soviet railroad system runs on a different gauge and must be converted if German rolling stock is to be used in captured areas. The Soviet forces also have their problems. Out of a total Red Army strength of over 230 divisions, about 170 are in the western part of the Soviet Union and 134, 32 of them armored, are with the formations facing the Germans. The total Soviet tank strength is around 24,000 machines but only a quarter of these are in running order. The Red Air Force has about 8000 aircraft facing the Germans but, again, many are obsolete or in poor repair. In all classes of equipment the most modern Soviet designs are simple and durable and at least as good as the German equivalent.

There are important gaps in the German's information about Soviet strength and equipment. They underestimate badly the manpower the Soviets have available and take too little account of the speed with which the Soviets will prepare new army and militia units. They also believe that the Soviets have a total of 10,000 tanks and they have no real information about the superior T34 and KV1 tanks. There are 1475 of these in the various armored divisions. The KV type is almost invulnerable to the German tanks' guns.

However, the considerable Soviet resources are less formidable than their extent suggests. Following the purges of the late 1930's a large part of the remaining senior leadership of the Red Army has been made up from the 'Cavalry Army' clique, old associates of Stalin not always distinguished for their military talents. Marshal Budenny typifies this group, perhaps owing his preferment to his position as one of Stalin's favorite drinking companions.

The Winter War with Finland exposed many weaknesses within the Red Army and led to many changes. Some, like the re-creation of the mechanized corps in September 1940, are undoubtedly sensible but others have been wasteful. All the changes, sensible or not, have been made in an atmosphere of haste which has made assimilating them more difficult. Training has also been poor. Some of the tank drivers and mechanics have had about an hour's instruction altogether on their new T34's and KV1's. Soviet deployment is also very weak. Some units which

are supposedly part of the front line are as much as 200 miles away in barracks or on training grounds. Other formations, Tenth Army of the Western Front is the best example, are too far forward in dangerously exposed salients. Plans are under way to bring reinforcements from the units deployed in the Far East but these have not yet become effective. Thus, despite Soviet manpower resources and useful stocks of equipment, the weakness of their tactical system, training and deployment means that they could hardly be worse placed.

Marshal Timoshenko is Commissar for Defense and General Zhukov is Chief of the General Staff. In the line from north to south are Kuznetsov's Northwest Front, Pavlov's West Front, Kirponos' Southwest Front and Tyulenev's South Front. The balance of forces differs from the Germans in showing a slight preponderance in the south. Kuznetsov, Pavlov and Kirponos will all be replaced early in the campaign.

The German plan is for an advance by all three army groups. Leeb is to go for Leningrad, Bock for Smolensk and Rundstedt for Kiev. Army Group Center is to be prepared to give support to the flanks of the thrust rather than to press toward Moscow after Smolensk. This decision has been Hitler's own and is generally regarded by later military critics as unsound. Equally controversial is the timing of the attack. Since the war it has often been argued that despite errors in Hitler's direction of the campaign, the main reason why the German army did not reach Moscow and win the war in the autumn and early winter was the weather and that, if Barbarossa had been begun earlier in

Above: Barbarossa *1941. The Germans relied extensively on horse-drawn transport.*

the year, Moscow would have fallen. However, it is by no means certain that even with a few weeks' grace the Germans would have been able to finish off their Moscow attack. Also, it is almost certain that Barbarossa could not have been started any earlier. The Greek campaign did not cause any delay and the Yugoslav campaign almost none (*see* 25–29 April). The real causes of delay were that the winter and spring of 1940 was particularly wet, flooding the rivers of Poland and softening the ground. Even in early June the Bug was well over its banks in many places on the front of Army Group Center. It should not be forgotten also that any delay meant that the Germans could add tanks and lorries to their units. All this discussion is somewhat academic. The Germans were in no particular hurry because they believed that they could win in a matter of weeks, and foreign military opinion agreed with them. The Red Army proved everyone wrong.

On the first day of the attack almost everything goes the German way. The attack begins at 0300 hours with advances on the ground and simultaneous air strikes. The Luftwaffe begins its operations very early in order to be over the Soviet bases exactly at zero hour. By noon the Soviet Air Force has lost around 1200 planes. The land battle is equally successful. Army Group North's Panzer spearhead advances 40 miles during the day and Army Group Center captures most of the Bug bridges intact. During the first four days Manstein's LVI Panzer Corps with Army Group North will advance 185 miles; Guderian's Panzer Group will make 270 miles in the first week. Other forces will do equally well. One setback for Army Group Center is that, although they win control of the town of Brest Litovsk, they will not be able to take the medieval citadel or use the communications network centering there for several days.

Britain, Politics Churchill broadcasts saying that help will be given to the Soviet Union. He says, 'Any state who fights Nazism will have our aid. . . . It follows therefore that we shall give whatever help we can to Russia.'

22–29 JUNE 1941

Syria There is heavy fighting in and around Marjayoun in which the Australians eventually drive the Vichy forces into retreat.

23 JUNE 1941

Eastern Front The German attacks continue to make astonishing progress. The tank and motorized forces are already forging ahead. In the north Fourth Panzergruppe has advanced

almost 50 miles. Hoth's forces have gone a little farther and taken bridges over the Niemen. Guderian's tanks have done slightly less well but have still made deep penetrations on either side of Brest Litovsk. Kleist's First Panzer Group has made some ground also but the Soviet defense in their southern sector is stronger. The Luftwaffe continues to batter the Red Air Force and disrupt the already exiguous Soviet communications.

Syria The advance of the British force from Iraq reaches Palmyra but the Vichy garrison holds out.

23–29 JUNE 1941

War at Sea The largest convoy battle to date occurs around HX-133. Ten U-Boats are concentrated to attack the convoy, which at first has four escorts. The escort group is later reinforced by nine more ships from other convoys (which, partly in consequence, lose two freighters) and in the ensuing battles HX-133 loses five ships. Two U-Boats are sunk. This ratio of losses would be favorable to the British in the long run if it could be repeated.

24 JUNE 1941

Eastern Front The German attacks continue to make rapid gains. Vilna and Kaunas have been taken and Brest Litovsk, which is now far behind the front line, is also assaulted.

United States, Politics At a press conference President Roosevelt announces that he intends to send aid to the USSR.

25 JUNE 1941

Eastern Front Already the Germans are threatening to complete the first of their great encircling operations. The Soviet salient around Bialystok, containing forces of Third and Fourth Armies, is menaced by an envelopment southwest of Grodno while a far deeper cordon is to be drawn closed at Minsk in a few days.

Sweden, Politics The government announces that it will allow the Germans to move forces up to one-division strong through Sweden from Norway to Finland.

Eastern Front In the north Daugavpils is taken in the German advance and Hoeppner's forces begin working to take bridgeheads over the Dvina. In the advance of Army Group Center the first encirclement is closed by Hoth's and Guderian's forces near Baranovichi.

26 JUNE 1941

Diplomatic Affairs Finland declares war on the USSR.

CHRONOLOGY

26–30 JUNE 1941
Mediterranean In two operations, first by *Ark Royal* alone and then by *Ark Royal* and *Victorious* together, 57 Hurricanes are flown off to Malta. More planes are embarked but cannot be sent because of malfunctions in the launching equipment of the carriers.

27 JUNE 1941
Diplomatic Affairs Hungary declares war on the USSR.

29 JUNE 1941
Eastern Front Hoth's and Guderian's forces, join up near Minsk, completing the isolation of another huge pocket around Gorodische. Elsewhere the German armies are maintaining their advances and the Soviet position is further stretched by the start of joint German-Finnish attacks in the Karelian Isthmus and farther north near Petsamo.

30 JUNE 1941
Eastern Front Bobryusk is taken by Second Panzer Group and operations begin to cross the Berezina. Troops from Army Group South take Lwow while to the north other units make deeper advances toward Kiev.
Soviet Union, Politics The formation of a new State Committee of Defense is announced in Moscow. The members will be Stalin, Molotov, Voroshilov, Malenkov and Beria. Stalin is very much in charge.

JULY 1941
Battle of the Atlantic Allied shipping losses are much less severe this month. Only 22 ships of 94,200 tons are sunk by U-Boats out of a total of 121,000 tons. The strength of the U-Boat fleet is increasing, however. There are now 63 boats operational and a further 93 in training. About 20 new boats will be commissioned during the month and only one of the operational fleet will be lost. The strength of the British escort forces is increasing also. Outward convoys to North America and convoys to West Africa can now be given continuous escort and the Gibraltar convoys have their escorts strengthened. Until this time the U-Boats have been able to take supplies from German ships sheltering in the Canary Island harbors but British diplomatic pressure on the Spanish government now brings this to an end.

On the technical side the British ability to track U-Boats from their radio messages is becoming greater. A U-Boat which finds a convoy must signal to assemble a pack for an attack but if the position of the sighting U-Boat can be plotted by radio direction finding it may perhaps be driven away or sunk and the whole pack left blind. There is no way the Germans can avoid this.

British Air Operations There are several attacks on general targets in the Ruhr and the Rhineland. Berlin is also hit. There are more operations against ports in France and Germany (*see* 24 July). RAF bombers drop 4380 tons – the highest total achieved until mid-1942. Over 3800 sorties are flown and 188 aircraft are lost.

1 JULY 1941
Middle East General Auchinleck is appointed to command the British forces in the Middle East. General Wavell takes Auchinleck's old post as Commander in Chief in India. Churchill has finally tired of Wavell with the failure of the Battleaxe offensive. The British government recognizes that the Commander in Chief, Middle East, has had heavy political responsibilities up to now in addition to his military duties and to avoid the distraction which this has caused in the past Oliver Lyttleton is appointed minister of state, resident in the Middle East.
Eastern Front Units of Army Group North take Riga while to the south other German troops are already well beyond the Dvina, making for Ostrov. West of Minsk the Berezina has been crossed and the advance continues.
Syria Troops from General Slim's 10th Indian Division move into northern Syria from Iraq.
Battle of the Atlantic Aircraft from the United States Navy start antisubmarine patrols from bases in Newfoundland.

2 JULY 1941
Japan, Policy An Imperial Conference (a meeting of Japanese government and military leaders and the Emperor to explain policy to the Emperor and nominally to take important decisions – in fact these are already taken at the Liaison Conferences between the politicians and the military leaders) records the decision that attempts should be made to take bases in Indochina even at the risk of war. The US authorities very soon know of this determination through their code-breaking service which has managed to work out the key to the major Japanese diplomatic code and some other minor operational codes. The information gained from the diplomatic code is circulated under the code name Magic.
Eastern Front After a rapid concentration and regrouping Hoeppner's Fourth Panzer Group attacks with renewed vigor toward Ostrov.

In the south the Rumanian Third and Fourth Armies and the German Eleventh Army begin full-scale attacks.

3 JULY 1941
Soviet Union, Home Front Stalin broadcasts for the first time since the German invasion. The reason for his delay in responding is not clear. He calls for total effort and a policy of scorched earth before the German advance, and guerilla warfare in their rear. He defends the 1939 non-aggression pact on the grounds of his desire for peace. The broadcast is the first of many to emphasize patriotic nationalism.
East Africa In southern Abyssinia the Italian resistance comes to an end with the surrender of General Gazzera and 7000 troops to a Belgian unit. In the northwestern Gondar area there are more Italian surrenders around Debra Tabor.
Syria Deir el Zor falls to the troops from 10th Indian Division. The Vichy fort at Palmyra surrenders to Habforce after a long defense.

4 JULY 1941
United States, Home Front In an Independence Day broadcast Roosevelt says that the United States 'will never survive as a happy and fertile oasis of liberty surrounded by a cruel desert of dictatorship.'

5 JULY 1941
Eastern Front The German Sixth Army breaches the Soviet defense line west of Zhitomir. Kleist's First Panzer Group begins to move through the gap but is somewhat held back by orders from Hitler. Farther north in the attacks east of Minsk the German advance reaches the Dniepr.

6 JULY 1941
Eastern Front Rumanian forces take Chernovtsy and are welcomed by the civilian population on entering the city. The Soviets claim to have carried out successful counterattacks in Latvia and in Belorussia.

7 JULY 1941
Iceland American forces land on the island to take over the task of garrisoning it and protecting nearby shipping from submarine attack. The US troops are from General Marston's 1st Marine Brigade and the transport ships are from Admiral Breton's TF 19, which also includes two battleships, two cruisers and 12 destroyers.

8 JULY 1941
Yugoslavia The Germans and Italians formally announce their plans for the dismemberment of Yugoslavia. Croatia is to be 'independent.' The province of Ljubljana, part of Dalmatia and some of the Adriatic islands are to be annexed by Italy. Bosnia is to be under Italian protection. Germany takes Montenegro, Carinthia and Cariola. Hungary also takes some territory.
Eastern Front In the advance on Leningrad, Hoeppner's Fourth Panzer Group takes Pskov.

8–10 JULY 1941
Syria There is a series of sharp fights just inland from Sidon at Jezzine and Mazzrat-ech-Chouf.

9 JULY 1941
Eastern Front The pockets earlier surrounded by Army Group Center have now all been wiped out. At least 300,000 prisoners have been taken and more than 40 divisions have been eliminated from the Soviet Order of Battle. Second and Third Panzer Groups are united to form Fourth Panzer Army and the forces of this new formation have now crossed both the Dniepr and the Dvina, aiming to encircle Smolensk.
Syria The Australian troops advancing north along the coast take Damour. There is now no obstacle blocking their approach to Beirut. Homs also falls to the Allied advance. General Dentz asks for an armistice on behalf of the Vichy forces.

10 JULY 1941
Eastern Front Units of the Soviet Fifth Army counterattack southwest of Korosten. Kleist's Panzer Group holds the attack amid heavy fighting. Four Italian divisions leave Italy bound for the Eastern Front.
United States, Politics Roosevelt submits new appropriations measures to Congress. He asks for \$4,770,000,000 for the army. On 11 July he asks for \$3,323,000,000 for the navy and the Maritime Commission.

11 JULY 1941
Syria Despite instructions from Vichy forbidding him to do so, General Dentz accepts the Allied armistice terms. The cease-fire begins 2100 hours. The casualties in the campaign have been about 2500 on the Allied side and 3500 from the Vichy forces. In addition the Vichy authorities have had a number of prisoners flown out to Europe including a few after the armistice terms forbidding this have been agreed.
Eastern Front First Panzer Group renews its advance toward Kiev and reaches to within 15 miles of the city. The Soviet State Defense

Committee establishes three new command areas for the Red Army. Marshal Voroshilov is to command in the north (Northwest Front), Marshal Timoshenko the central West Front, and Marshal Budenny the Southwest Front.

United States Roosevelt appoints William Donovan to head a new civilian intelligence agency with the title 'coordinator of defense/information.' This appointment will lead to the creation of the Office for Strategic Services (OSS) which will in turn develop into the modern CIA.

12 JULY 1941

Eastern Front Moscow is bombed for the first time.

Diplomatic Affairs Britain and the Soviet Union sign an agreement in Moscow providing for mutual assistance and forbidding the making of a separate peace.

North Africa General Bastico replaces General Gariboldi as Commander in Chief of the Italian, and nominally the German, forces in North Africa.

14 JULY 1941

Eastern Front The German advance continues and the Luga River is reached in the northern sector.

Mediterranean A force of German Ju 88 bombers attacks Suez from bases in Crete causing damage to harbor installations and to ships unloading.

15 JULY 1941

Eastern Front The Soviets counterattack for the next three days in the Lake Ilmen area to gain time for the building of further fortifications round Leningrad. The attacking forces lose heavily in their efforts because the troops are very inexperienced.

16 JULY 1941

Eastern Front The Finnish attacks north of Lake Ladoga take Sortavala and reach the Lake to the southeast of the town, cutting off Soviet forces to the west. The Soviets will be able to get some of their troops away by boat. The German attacks by Army Group South surround a Soviet pocket south of Uman.

Germany, Planning At an important meeting Hitler, Goering, Bormann and Rosenberg decide on plans for the exploitation of the territory being captured from the Soviets. Rosenberg is put in charge of a new ministry with the task of organizing the new lands for Germany's economic benefit and eliminating Jews and Communists.

Vichy, Politics General Weygand is appointed Governor General of Algeria.

16–18 JULY 1941

Japan, Politics In order to remove Matsuoka from the Foreign Ministry, Prince Konoye resigns on 16 July and re-forms his Cabinet on 18 July with Baron Hiranuma as deputy prime minister and Admiral Toyoda as foreign minister. Already personally unpopular, Matsuoka is removed because he has been urging that the Neutrality Agreement with the Soviets should be abandoned and that Japan should join with Germany in the attack on the USSR. The other Japanese leaders do not wish to take such a decisive step, and have decided that without Matsuoka and his known liking for Hitler they have a better chance of reaching an agreement with the US over the pressing problem of the oil resources.

17 JULY 1941

Eastern Front The Germans develop an important bridgehead over the Dniepr near Mogilev.

In an attempt to stiffen resistance the political commissars are restored to the Soviet army and navy units.

18 JULY 1941

Czechoslovakia, Politics Britain formally recognizes the Beneš government as the legal provisional government. A friendship and mutual assistance agreement between the Czechs and the Soviets is signed in London.

19 JULY 1941

Eastern Front Guderian receives orders that after the Smolensk battle is over he is to move his force south to join the Kiev battle. This proposal is very much Hitler's idea. Guderian objects strongly, arguing that it will be far better to continue the attack toward Moscow.

Battle of the Atlantic The United States Atlantic Fleet forms TF 1 for the protection of the American forces on Iceland and support for convoys bound there. The carrier *Wasp* flies a cargo of P-40 fighters to the island. Early in August flying boats begin patrols from Iceland. The USN commits up to 25 destroyers to the Iceland operation as well as heavier forces. They are ordered to provide escorts for ships of any nationality sailing to and from Iceland.

Europe, Resistance At midnight there is a BBC broadcast by 'Colonel Britton' urging the creation of resistance forces with the slogan 'V for Victory.' The BBC has been introducing programs to Europe with the Morse signal for V for some time. Following this resistance members paint V signs on walls and German posters and it becomes a symbol for all Western European resistance movements.

21 JULY 1941

United States, Politics Roosevelt asks Congress to extend the draft period from one year to 30 months and to make similar increases in the terms of service for the National Guard. These measures pass the Senate on 7 August and the House on 12 August only after considerable debate. Indeed, the Bill is only passed by one vote (203–202) in the House, so it would be wrong to say that American political opinion is strongly in favor of a more militant policy at this stage.

Eastern Front There are more German air attacks on Moscow. The Soviet authorities announce that they have withdrawn their forces from the line of the Dniestr.

21–27 JULY 1941

Mediterranean A major operation, code named Substance, is mounted by the British Gibraltar forces to bring supplies to Malta. There are seven transports in the convoy and they are covered by Force H which has been specially reinforced for the occasion. In addition to *Renown*, *Ark Royal*, a cruiser and eight destroyers, the Home Fleet has sent *Nelson*, three cruisers and nine destroyers. The whole force sets out on 21 July. On 22 July part of the convoy is located by Italian planes but the Italian fleet stays in port, expecting only a repeat of the previous carrier operations to fly planes to Malta. On 23 July one destroyer is sunk and one cruiser and three destroyers are hit in Italian air attacks. On 24 July one transport is hit before entering Malta. Empty ships from previous trips join Force H for the return to Gibraltar where they arrive on 27 July.

24 JULY 1941

Japanese Policy In line with the Imperial Conference decision of 2 July, the Japanese presented an ultimatum to the representatives of the Vichy government on the 19th demanding bases in southern Indochina. This demand is now conceded. The Japanese forces begin to occupy the bases on the 28th. It is very clear that the main use for such bases would be in an invasion of Malaya, the East Indies or the Philippines.

British Air Operations The *Scharnhorst* is hit

five times by bombs from a force of 15 Halifax bombers while lying in the port of La Pallice. The repairs will not be complete until 1942. Since *Prinz Eugen* has been hit earlier in the month and *Gneisenau* is under repair, this means that none of the German heavy ships in and around Brest is fit for operations in the near future.

26 JULY 1941

Diplomatic Affairs Japanese assets in the United States and Britain are frozen. On 28 July Japan retaliates with similar measures. Also on 28 July Japanese assets in the Dutch East Indies are frozen and oil deals cancelled. On 29 July Japan freezes Dutch assets. This means that almost 75 percent of Japan's foreign trade is at a standstill and that 90 percent of its oil supplies have been cut off.

Philippines Roosevelt orders that the Philippine army be entirely incorporated in to the US Army for the duration of the tension with Japan. General MacArthur, who has been leading the Filipino forces, is appointed to command the US forces in the area as well.

27 JULY 1941

Eastern Front The Soviet forces in and around Smolensk are cut off by the German pincer movement. In the north the Baltic port of Kallinn is attacked by the Germans.

30 JULY 1941

China The US gunboat *Tutuila* is damaged by an attack by Japanese bombers in Chungking. Japan apologizes for the incident but it does nothing to ease the strained relations between the two countries.

30 JULY–4 AUGUST 1941

Norway On 30 July planes from the British Home Fleet carriers *Victorious* and *Furious* attack German shipping and installations near Kirkenes and Petsamo. Little damage is done and 15 of the 57 attacking aircraft are lost to antiaircraft fire and the German fighters. There is a further small operation by *Victorious* alone against Tromso on 4 August.

31 JULY 1941

Eastern Front Sixteenth Army from the German Army Group North continues the advance reaching the south side of Lake Ilmen. In southern Finland Finnish attacks toward Viipuri and Vuosalmi begin.

North Africa The Axis forces are reorganized. General Cruewell now commands the Afrika

Korps (DAK) with Rommel in charge of the new Panzer Group Africa. The 5th Light is renamed as 21st Panzer Division and Rommel, therefore, has two Panzer divisions and one German infantry division in his force. In addition there are seven Italian divisions.

31 JULY–4 AUGUST 1941

Mediterranean There is a small British supply operation from Gibraltar to Malta. Force H gives cover. While on this operation destroyers from Force H and aircraft from the *Ark Royal* attack Alghero in Sardinia. When the operation is complete the battlecruiser *Renown* returns to the UK for a refit. *Nelson* remains as Admiral Somerville's flagship.

AUGUST 1941

Battle of the Atlantic This is another month of moderate success for the German U-Boat fleet. They sink only 23 ships of 80,300 tons for the loss of three of their number. The U-Boat effort in the North Atlantic is now concentrated rather closer to the UK than has been the recent practice because of the longer patrols this allows the smaller boats. The total Allied shipping loss is 41 ships of 130,700 tons.

British Air Operations Bomber Command raids many towns in Germany including Hanover, Frankfurt, Mannheim, Hamburg, Berlin and Karlsruhe. There are also sweeps by fighters and fighter-bombers over northern France and the Low Countries. Rotterdam is among the targets for these operations.

It has recently become apparent that the results of the British bombing offensive have been very poor. The Butt Report is prepared from studying photographs taken at the moment of bomb release during the June and July operations. This report is presented during August. It shows that on moonlit nights, of the planes which claim to have bombed their targets, only 40 percent have dropped their bombs within five miles. On dark nights less than seven percent have achieved this 'accuracy.' As there are no navigational aids available to overcome the problem yet, the whole policy of precision attacks is seriously questioned.

1 AUGUST 1941

Diplomatic Affairs President Roosevelt forbids the export of oil and aviation fuel from the United States except to Britain, the British Empire and the countries of the Western Hemisphere. This decision hits very hard indeed against Japan because Japan has no oil of her own and is left with only strictly limited stocks.

The position is such that Japan must either change her foreign policy very radically or decide very quickly to go to war and try to gain access to the oil of the East Indies. Roosevelt's decision confirms the steps taken recently when Japanese assets were frozen.

Eastern Front The fighting is especially heavy near Vitebsk and Orsha. The Soviets attack along the northern edge of the Pripet Marshes from west of Gomel with the aim of striking into the German rear areas. In most sectors the Germans can withstand the attacks.

2 AUGUST 1941

Eastern Front The German forces in the northern sector begin to attack Staraya Russa just south of Lake Ilmen on the right of their drive toward Leningrad.

United States, Politics US Lend-Lease aid begins to be sent to the Soviet Union.

3 AUGUST 1941

Eastern Front In the south another German encircling move closes near Pervomaysk on the River Bug.

5 AUGUST 1941

Eastern Front The fighting around Smolensk comes to an end. The Germans claim to have taken 310,000 prisoners and to have killed many of the 700,000-strong Soviet force. The Soviets admit far lower losses. The German figures are probably more accurate.

Vichy, Politics Admiral Darlan is promoted to be in charge of Vichy policy in North Africa. Weygand is to be his subordinate.

6 AUGUST 1941

Diplomatic Affairs Konoye's government presents proposals involving some concessions in China and Indochina to the US, asking in return for the end of the freeze on Japanese assets. The proposals are not acceptable to the US and when the rejection is made known to the Japanese they propose that Konoye and Roosevelt meet to discuss the issues at stake. This question is not resolved until after Roosevelt and Churchill meet at Placentia Bay (*see* 9–12 August).

7–8 AUGUST 1941

Soviet Air Operations During the night the Soviets raid Berlin with a small force. Berlin is bombed on six more occasions by the Soviets in this month.

9 AUGUST 1941

Eastern Front Army Group South, with forces

from Eleventh and Seventeenth Armies, begins attacks along the line of the River Bug.

9–12 AUGUST 1941
Allied Diplomacy Churchill and Roosevelt meet at Placentia Bay in Newfoundland. Both are accompanied by their military staffs. The discussions cover the situation in Europe and the Far East. It is agreed to send strong warnings to the Japanese and it is understood that America will almost certainly enter the war if Japan attacks British or Dutch possessions in the East Indies or Malaya. A message is also sent to Stalin, proposing a meeting in Moscow to make formal arrangements for the provision of supplies to the Soviet Union.

The conference is best remembered for the agreement later called the Atlantic Charter. This is a statement of the principles governing the policies of Britain and America and states that all countries should have the right to hold free elections and be free from foreign pressure.

Although its noble intentions will have comparatively little influence on the course of the war it is important as setting out the reasons why the United States might go to war and as a description of the aims of such a war.

The conference is important also because of the opportunity it gives the British and American staffs to get to know each other and to work together.

11 AUGUST 1941
Eastern Front The Finnish attacks south of Lake Ladoga reach Vuosalmi.

12 AUGUST 1941
Eastern Front Hitler issues Directive 34. Army Group North is ordered to continue its efforts in the direction of Leningrad. Army Group South is to begin the battle for the Crimea, Kharkov and the Donets. Army Group Center is to halt for the moment to bring help to the other forces.

Vichy, Politics In a broadcast Marshal Pétain says that Germany is fighting 'in defense of civilization' in the war against the Soviet Union. He announces new measures for the suppression of political parties and the creation of a stronger police force and special courts. Admiral Darlan is to be appointed to the Ministry of Defense.

12–18 AUGUST 1941
North Africa The Australian government has been pressing for their troops in Tobruk to be relieved and so in various night operations 6000 fresh troops from a Polish Brigade are sent in and 5000 of the Australians brought out. The fast minelayers *Abdiel* and *Latona* are prominent in these moves. A cruiser and two destroyers are also employed.

14–17 AUGUST 1941
Eastern Front The Soviets evacuate their Black Sea naval base of Nikolayev. Eight destroyers of the Black Sea Fleet cover the operation. Of the ships under construction in the port, 13 are far enough advanced to be towed away but one battleship and 10 other vessels on the stocks have to be blown up. The Black Sea Fleet is very active in support of land operations whenever possible.

Above: Soviet BT-7 tanks on parade. They carried a 45mm gun and were lightly armored.

CHRONOLOGY

17 AUGUST 1941
Diplomatic Affairs The United States presents a formal warning to the Japanese along the lines agreed at Placentia Bay. The text of the note has been toned down somewhat from the draft originally agreed with the British and Dutch, so they do not present their notes in order not to be seen to disagree with the American line. No decision has yet been taken on the Japanese proposal of a meeting between Roosevelt and Konoye, but on 3 September the Japanese will be told that it cannot take place. The Americans are worried that Konoye would not be able to make the Japanese military keep to any agreement that might be made.

Eastern Front The attacks of Army Group South reach the Dniepr at Dnepropetrovsk. The town is captured. In the northern sector Novgorod on the shores of Lake Ilmen is also taken.

18 AUGUST 1941
Eastern Front Budenny, commanding the Soviet southern armies, begins to withdraw as many of his troops as possible behind the line of the Dniepr. In the north the Germans take Kingisepp, on the Luga west of Narva. In this sector there is also heavy fighting near Novgorod. In the central sector there are fierce engagements near Gomel.

19 AUGUST–10 SEPTEMBER 1941
Arctic There are various British naval operations. The population of Spitsbergen is evacuated and the Norwegians taken to Britain and the Soviets to the USSR. The first small supply convoy is sent from Iceland to the Soviet Union. The carrier *Argus* also brings a cargo of Hurricanes to the Soviet Union, complete with RAF pilots who will fly them in combat for the first few weeks. The carrier *Victorious* sends air attacks against German installations in and around Tromso on both 3 and 7 September but little damage is done.

21 AUGUST 1941
Eastern Front In the north the Germans take Chudovo, northeast of Novgorod, cutting the main rail link between Leningrad and Moscow. In the Finnish attacks farther north Kexholm is taken from the Soviets. In the central sector the Soviets pull out of Gomel after a long struggle and a series of counterattacks. In the south the Germans take Kherson on the lower Dniepr.

23 AUGUST 1941
Eastern Front Second Panzer Group and Second Army from the German Army Group Center begin attacks south to link up east of Kiev with the forces of Army Group South. Most of the German generals are opposed to this move and would prefer to maintain the drive toward Moscow but Hitler insists on this change in strategy.

German Raiders The German merchant cruiser *Orion* returns from its cruise and arrives in the Gironde Estuary. The cruise has lasted 510 days and six ships of 39,000 tons have been sunk, as well as seven more in company with the raider *Komet*.

24 AUGUST 1941
Eastern Front General Konev leads a new Soviet counterattack in the Gomel area. It makes little progress. In the north the Finnish attacks continue to press forward and Viipuri is surrounded.

24–25 AUGUST 1941
Mediterranean Force H carries out another offensive operation. Aircraft from *Ark Royal* attack the Italian airfield at Tempio in northern Sardinia. Mines are also laid off Leghorn. The battleship *Nelson* is in support. The Italian battleships *Vittorio Veneto* and *Littorio* also come out but they move against a suspected Malta operation and there is no contact. The cruiser *Bolzano* is torpedoed by the submarine *Triumph*.

25 AUGUST 1941
Iran British and Soviet forces move into Iran. They have been worried by reports of German 'tourists' being in the country and have decided to demand that Iran accept their 'protection' of its oil supplies. The British land forces are led by General Quinan and their naval support by Admiral Arbuthnot. They advance in two areas, to seize the oil installations near Abadan, and from northeast of Baghdad to take similar sites around Kermanshah. The Soviet forces advance in three columns under General Novikov's command. One column moves on Tabriz while the other two advance on either side of the Caspian. There is little opposition to either the British or the Soviet forces.

There are British landings at Bandar Shapur, Abadan and Khoramshahr in the Persian Gulf area. Two small Iranian warships are sunk and several Axis merchant ships are seized. The British forces moving on Kermanshah, commanded by General Slim, and all three Soviet columns soon make good progress. The Soviets bomb Tabriz.

26 AUGUST 1941
Eastern Front There is a brief, unsuccessful Soviet counterattack against the German positions near Velikiye Luki.

26 AUGUST 1941
Iran The British forces take complete control of the Abadan area while the Soviets moving down from the north enter Tabriz. The Soviets bomb Teheran.

27 AUGUST 1941
Eastern Front The Germans begin full-scale attacks against the Baltic port of Tallinn.
Iran In the advance on Kermanshah the British take Shahabad and in the south they are preparing to attack Ahwaz. The Iranian government resigns.
Battle of the Atlantic While on an operation south of Iceland *U.570* surfaces immediately below a Coastal Command Hudson bomber and is surrendered. *U.570* is taken to Iceland and eventually will enter British service as HMS *Graph*.
Vichy, Politics Laval and a prominent pro-German newspaper editor are shot and wounded near Versailles by a young member of a resistance group. This incident is taken as an excuse by the Vichy government to round up many of its opponents, describing them as communists.

28 AUGUST 1941
Iran, Politics A new government led by Ali Furughi takes office and gives orders to cease fire. Negotiations with the British and the Soviets are under way.
Eastern Front The Soviets announce that the great dam over the Dniepr at Zaporozhye has been destroyed.

28–29 AUGUST 1941
Eastern Front The Soviets evacuate their garrison, X Rifle Corps, from Tallinn by sea. Several convoys attempt to get through to Kronstadt but losses to mines and air attacks are very severe on both days. Almost all the transports are sunk, along with many of the escorting vessels from the Baltic Fleet. On 29 August the Finnish forces farther north take Viipuri. The Finns are preparing to halt their advance when they reach their former frontier positions. This decision will contribute much to the Soviet ability to defend Leningrad.

29 AUGUST 1941
Iran The fighting comes to an end. On 31

August the Soviet and British troops link up at Kazvin. The final terms are agreed by the Iranian government on 9 September. The British and Soviets are to occupy certain key points but agree to keep out of Teheran.
Yugoslavia General Milan Nedić is appointed to lead the puppet Serbian government backed by Germany.

30 AUGUST 1941
Eastern Front In the Leningrad sector the Germans take Mga, cutting the last railroad link between Leningrad and the rest of the USSR.

SEPTEMBER 1941
War at Sea Allied shipping losses increase this month to 84 ships of 285,900 tons. U-Boats account for 53 ships of 202,800 tons. There are important convoy battles around SC-42, which loses 20 ships and one escort. SL-97 and HG-73 suffer heavily also. Some U-Boats are sent to the Mediterranean later in the month.
During the month there are several important developments in the maritime policy of the United States.
British Air Operations Among the targets for Bomber Command this month are Stettin, Hamburg and Cologne. The north German ports and Brest are again hit because of their naval value but little damage is done to the ships, which are the main targets. The usual daylight sweeps by light forces over northern France continue.
North Africa Italian agents of the Servizio Informazione Militare steal the 'Black Code' from the US Embassy in Rome. This theft is to be of great value because the US Military Attaché in Cairo, Colonel Fellers, is accustomed to send accurate and detailed reports to Washington concerning Eighth Army's plans and dispositions. This source of intelligence lasts until June 1942.
Yugoslavia Tito's Partisans begin active resistance operations in southwest Serbia.
Mihajlović gets word out to the west that he is organizing resistance and is hailed as a hero by the Allied press.

1 SEPTEMBER 1941
Eastern Front The attacking German forces are now within artillery range of Leningrad itself. To the east of the city the advance is nearing the south shore of Lake Ladoga.
Battle of the Atlantic The US Atlantic Fleet forms a Denmark Strait patrol. At first two heavy cruisers and four destroyers are allocated to this duty, but this force is increased later. The

US Navy is now allowed to escort convoys in the Atlantic comprising ships of any nation provided an American merchant ship is present.

4 SEPTEMBER 1941
Battle of the Atlantic In a convoy operation the US destroyer *Greer* is attacked by a German U-Boat and is not damaged and in return attempts to sink the submarine with depth charges. In fact the *Greer* has been brought into action by the reports of a British aircraft and has been mistaken, not unreasonably, for a British ship by the German commander. Roosevelt, however, presents the incident to the American public as an example of German aggression.

6 SEPTEMBER 1941
Japan, Policy Konoye gives in to military pressure and an Imperial Conference decides that, in view of the declining oil stocks, war preparations should be completed by mid-October and that if no agreement is reached by then that the decision to go to war should be taken. Konoye continues to make some conciliatory proposals to the US but is judged insincere despite the advice of Grew, the Ambassador in Tokyo, that if no agreement is reached the moderate Konoye may be replaced by a military dictatorship.

Occupied Europe By order of Heydrich, who heads the German security services (SD, a division of the SS) and the security police, all Jews over the age of six are to wear a distinguishing Star of David badge. This measure is only one token of the increasing barbarity with which the Jews are being treated. Experiments are being conducted at the Auschwitz concentration camp with various methods of exterminating large numbers of people. The gas Cyclon-B is being tested. The extermination camps will not begin full-scale operations until early in 1942 when the mass transportation of Jews begins.

8 SEPTEMBER 1941
Eastern Front Between Lake Ladoga and Lake Onega the continuing Finnish attacks cross the Svir and take Lodenoye Pole, cutting the railroad track south from Murmansk. At this time of year it is still possible to use Archangel as the entrepôt for British and American supplies to the Soviet Union but later in the winter the Soviets will be unable to fulfill their promise to attend to the icebreaking. It will, therefore, be necessary to build a railroad track to Murmansk.

8–14 SEPTEMBER 1941
Mediterranean A further 69 Hurricanes are flown to Malta in two operations by Force H, involving first the *Ark Royal* alone and then both the *Ark Royal* and *Furious*.

9 SEPTEMBER 1941
Eastern Front A Spanish volunteer 'Blue Division' arrives to begin service on the Leningrad Front with the German forces.

10 SEPTEMBER 1941
Eastern Front Guderian's southward attack on the Soviet forces east of Kiev reaches Konotop. Kleist's First Panzer Group begin to break out of their bridgehead over the Dniepr around Kremenchug.

11 SEPTEMBER 1941
Battle of the Atlantic Owing to the *Greer* incident on 4 September, Roosevelt is able to order US warships to 'shoot on sight' in waters 'the protection of which is necessary for American defense.' In fact this is more or less what is happening already.

12 SEPTEMBER 1941
Eastern Front Guderian's and Kleist's forces link up near the small town of Lokhvitsa, cutting off the huge Soviet forces in the pocket between there and Kiev, 100 miles to the west. At least 600,000 men are encircled. North of Kiev Chernigov, on the banks of the Desna, is evacuated in the face of attacks by the German Second Army.

The first snowfall on the Eastern Front is reported.

Norway, Home Front The Quisling government bans the Boy Scouts and other youth organizations. Boys are to be obliged to join youth sections of the Nasjonal Samling Party.

12–22 SEPTEMBER 1941

North Africa There is another series of relief operations to Tobruk. The fast transports bring in about 6300 men and a large quantity of supplies, and take out 6000 of the Australian garrison. The new troops are from General Scobie's 70th British Division.

15 SEPTEMBER 1941
Eastern Front The Germans capture Schlüsselburg on the south shore of Lake Ladoga, east of Leningrad, completely isolating the city from overland contact with the rest of the Soviet Union. Some supplies can still be carried in by boat across Lake Ladoga. There are sufficient stores for only about one month in the city even

Above: A German machine-gun post in a Russian town.

with very poor ration allowances. The siege will not be raised fully until early in 1944 and several hundred thousand civilians will die of starvation in the city.

United States, Politics The Attorney General rules that the Neutrality Act does not prevent US ships from carrying war material to British possessions in the Near and Far East or in the Western Hemisphere.

16 SEPTEMBER 1941
Iran The Allies have decided to occupy Teheran because the Shah has not done enough, in their view, to expel all Axis nationals from the country. The Shah abdicates in favor of the Crown Prince, Mohammad Reza Pahlavi. The British and Soviet forces arrive in the capital on 17 September.

17 SEPTEMBER 1941
Battle of the Atlantic The US Navy increases its commitment to escort Atlantic convoys. It takes over responsibility for some of the Halifax–UK convoys and for most of the Iceland traffic. Canadian forces are escorting the others as far as 22 degrees west when the British take over on all routes.
Eastern Front There is heavy fighting with some German successes in the outskirts of Kiev.

18 SEPTEMBER 1941
United States, Politics Roosevelt asks Congress for an additional $5,985,000,000 for Lend-Lease.

19 SEPTEMBER 1941
Eastern Front Kiev finally falls to the Germans after more than 40 days of fighting. The Soviet losses in this battle have probably been in excess of 500,000 men. The Germans have lost about 100,000.

Yugoslavia, Resistance Tito and Mihajlovič meet to discuss resistance but they quarrel. Mihajlovitch sees Tito as an anti-Royalist troublemaker who wants to muscle in on the Serbian territory that Mihajlovitch regards as his own preserve. Tito in turn sees Mihajlovitch as a bourgeois representative of an already discredited officer corps. They meet again on 26 October but cannot resolve their differences. Their supporters soon begin fighting.

20 SEPTEMBER 1941
Battle of the Atlantic An aircraft from the British escort carrier *Audacity* shoots down an Fw Condor which is trying to shadow the convoy OG-74. This is the first success for the escort-carrier class. Escort carriers will not be readily available for convoy operations until the spring of 1943. Even with the *Audacity* in escort, OG-74 loses six from 27 ships.
Mediterranean Italian midget submarines are sent to attack shipping in Gibraltar harbor and succeed in sinking two ships.

23 SEPTEMBER 1941
United States, Politics At a press conference Roosevelt announces that the United States is thinking of arming its merchant shipping against possible German attacks.

24 SEPTEMBER 1941
Mediterranean The first German U-Boat to enter the Mediterranean passes Gibraltar. Six boats of the first group will arrive in the next two weeks. Later in the year about half the German U-Boat force will be engaged in the Mediterranean. Their most notable successes will be the sinking of the battleship *Barham* and the carrier *Ark Royal*.
Eastern Front The advance of the tank forces of Army Group South reaches to within 40 miles of Kharkov.
Allied Diplomacy Fifteen governments sign the Atlantic Charter at ceremonies in London and Washington. They include the UK, USA, USSR, the countries of the British Empire and many of the exiled governments of Europe.

24–30 SEPTEMBER 1941
Mediterranean Operation Halberd is launched in a major effort to carry supplies from Gibraltar to Malta. There are nine transports in the convoy and their escorts and covering force include three battleships, one carrier, five cruisers and 18 destroyers. On 26 September Admiral Iachino leads two battleships, six cruisers and 14 destroyers of the Italian Fleet out to intercept.

The remainder of the Italian Fleet stays in port, ostensibly because of fuel shortage. On 27 September both sides fail to find the main enemy force by air reconnaissance. The British battleship *Nelson* receives slight damage by a hit from an Italian torpedo plane, but the heavy ships do not make contact. One transport is sunk by air attack but the rest reach Malta with a close escort of cruisers and destroyers. Pantellaria is shelled by part of the British force and an Italian submarine is sunk by a destroyer. Among the 50,000 tons of supplies brought to Malta is a enough food to last for several months.

25 SEPTEMBER 1941
Eastern Front The Germans have now isolated the Soviet forces in the Crimea and begin attacks near Perekop with support from parachute troops.

27 SEPTEMBER 1941
Eastern Front In the fighting in the approaches to the Crimea the Germans take Perekop.
East Africa The 4000-strong Italian garrison at Wolchefit surrenders to the besieging 25th East African Brigade. The Italians here have been very short of food because they have been isolated from their main body at Gondar by guerrilla activity.
Czechoslovakia, Home Front Von Neurath, the German governor of Bohemia and Moravia, resigns his post. Heydrich replaces him. On 28 September Heydrich imposes martial law on six districts. On 29 September Prime Minister Elias is arrested. There are many more strict measures taken at Heydrich's order and he quickly gains a justly vile reputation.
United States, Production The first batch of 14 Liberty ships is launched in the various constructing yards. Another 312 are on order. The total tonnage of these vessels is 2,200,000 tons.

28 SEPTEMBER–1 OCTOBER 1941
Allied Planning The conference suggested at Placentia by Churchill and Roosevelt takes place in Moscow. Harriman is the United States' representative and Beaverbrook the British delegate. Molotov takes the leading part on the Soviet side. On 1 October a joint declaration is made that the Soviet Union will continue to receive an increasing amount of help from both Britain and America.

29 SEPTEMBER–11 OCTOBER 1941
Arctic The convoy PQ-1 passes from Iceland to Archangel with 10 merchant ships escorted by one cruiser and two destroyers. There is no

German attack. At the same time QP-1 passes from Archangel to Scapa Flow. This is the start of the regular traffic.

30 SEPTEMBER 1941
Eastern Front Now that the Kiev battle is complete, Guderian's Second Panzer Army has been moved north again to form the right wing of the German attack on Moscow. Guderian's troops now begin this attack with an advance from around Glukhov northeast toward Orel and Bryansk.
In the south Kleist's Panzer Group attacks east of the Dniepr from Dnepropetrovsk. The Soviet line is quickly broken. Some of the attacking units head toward Donetsk while others move in a more southerly direction toward the Sea of Azov at Berdyansk.

OCTOBER 1941
Battle of the Atlantic German U-Boat strength is now 198 vessels of which 80 are operational. This month they sink 156,500 tons of Allied shipping out of a total loss of 218,300 tons. The diversion of U-Boats to the Mediterranean continues and this partly accounts for the lower Allied loss than in September.
British Air Operations Hamburg, Stuttgart, the Ruhr towns and several of the north German ports are the main targets for Bomber Command this month. Over 2600 sorties are flown, 3000 tons of bombs dropped and 126 planes lost.

1 OCTOBER 1941
Eastern Front The Finnish attacks west of Lake Onega capture Petrozavodsk.

2 OCTOBER 1941
Eastern Front The German attack on Moscow, Operation Typhoon, officially begins. Hoth's Third and Hoeppner's Fourth Panzer Groups, Second, Fourth and Ninth Armies all join the advance, which was started two days previously by Guderian's forces on the right wing. The Germans have considerably superior forces on the ground and an even greater preponderance in the air. The main efforts are by the tank units. Guderian's force is already making good progress toward Bryansk and Orel while Hoth and Hoeppner plan an encircling movement to link at Vyazma.
Australia, Politics The Country Party government falls. The new prime minister is John Curtin of the Labor Party.

4 OCTOBER 1941
Eastern Front Units of Hoeppner's Panzer

Group attack near Vyazma from the south while Hoth's forces are attacking the still-intact Soviet line between Vyazma and Rzhev. On the right wing of the attack Guderian's forces are increasing their threat to Orel and Bryansk. Large Soviet forces west of Bryansk and Vyazma are in danger of being cut off.

6 OCTOBER 1941
Eastern Front In the south the right wing of Kleist's attacks reaches Berdyansk, on the Sea of Azov, cutting off more than 100,000 Soviet troops. The German Eleventh Army is attacking along the coast to link with Kleist's force. The German advances in the Moscow sector continue.

The Soviet position around Vyazma and Bryansk grows more desperate. Large pockets have been isolated and are being reduced south of Bryansk and west of Vyazma. Other German forces are attacking well to the east of both these towns.

8 OCTOBER 1941
Eastern Front The Germans occupy Mariupol on the Sea of Azov. In the Moscow sector the Vyazma and Bryansk battles continue. In these engagements about 600,000 Soviet troops will be taken, along with massive quantities of equipment. The main German efforts are now in northeasterly attacks toward Tula and Kaluga in the south and Rzhev and Kalinin in the north. Heavy rain begins to fall along the front. This will prove to be an ever-increasing hindrance to the German mobile operations.

9 OCTOBER 1941
United States, Politics Roosevelt asks Congress to allow US merchant ships to be armed and to repeal certain sections of the Neutrality Act.

10 OCTOBER 1941
Eastern Front General Zhukov returns to Moscow from his duties at Leningrad to take control of the defense of the capital.

12 OCTOBER 1941
Eastern Front The German advance on Moscow continues with the capture of Kaluga despite the poor weather and the increasing determination of the Soviet defenders. The Soviets evacuate the town of Bryansk but the fighting round the isolated pockets nearby continues.

12–26 OCTOBER 1941
North Africa There is a further series of relief

operations to Tobruk. Just over 7000 troops are taken in to the fortress and just under 8000 are taken out. The minelayer *Latona* is lost to a Stuka attack and one destroyer is damaged.

13 OCTOBER 1941
Eastern Front The Soviet forces are driven out of Vyazma and the resistance of the nearby pocket is almost over.

14 OCTOBER 1941
Eastern Front The German attack northwest of Moscow reaches Kalinin. The Soviet defense between here and Tula, southwest of the capital, is very stubborn.

15 OCTOBER 1941
Poland, Home Front The German authorities decree that any Jews found outside the ghettos will be executed automatically.

15–16 OCTOBER 1941
Eastern Front The Soviets evacuate Odessa, which has been holding out although for several weeks it has been well behind the German lines. About 35,000 men from three divisions are taken off. One transport is sunk by air attack on 16 October but the rest reach Sevastopol safely. Two cruisers and four destroyers and many smaller craft are involved. Most units of the Black Sea Fleet are now based in Sevastopol.

The 16 October is remembered in Moscow as a day of panic. Foreign diplomats and much of the government staff are moved to Kuibyshev. Many senior party members lead a less official exodus in official cars and on the trains.

16 OCTOBER 1941
Japan, Politics Prime Minister Konoye resigns and is replaced by War Minister Tojo. Tojo himself takes the offices of prime minister, war minister and home affairs minister. Shigenori Togo is foreign minister and Admiral Shimada is navy minister. These changes mark the increasing ascendency of the party which intends to go to war. The decision to go to war has not yet finally been taken, and it has been suggested that Tojo has taken the Home Affairs Ministry himself in order to be able to prevent any violent opposition if a decision for peace is reached.
Vichy Politics Daladier, Reynaud and Blum, all former prime ministers of France, are arrested on Pétain's orders to face charges that they were responsible for the French defeat.

16–17 OCTOBER 1941
Battle of the Atlantic During the night *U.568*

hits the US destroyer *Kearny* with a torpedo in a convoy battle involving British, Canadian and United States' ships. There are 11 dead on the *Kearny*.

18 OCTOBER 1941
Eastern Front In the continuing German advance on Moscow, Mozhaysk is taken by troops from Fourth Panzer Group.

18–21 OCTOBER 1941
Mediterranean On 18 October Malta's air forces are augmented by a force of strike planes flown in from Gibraltar. On 21 October two cruisers and two destroyers arrive in Malta to add their efforts to the threat which Malta poses to the Axis supply lines to Africa. For the next few weeks, as the British prepare for a new offensive in North Africa, an increasing portion of the Axis supplies will be lost.

19 OCTOBER 1941
Eastern Front Stalin announces that he is remaining in Moscow, although most of the government has left, and that the city will be defended with every effort. Harsh punishments are to be imposed on looters and defeatists. Work is proceeding at a hectic pace on three fixed defense lines around the city. In the south the German advance along the coast of the Sea of Azov reaches Taganrog.

20 OCTOBER 1941
Eastern Front In the Moscow sector there is heavy fighting near Mozhaysk and at Malayaroslavets.

In the south the German attacks also make progress capturing Donetsk (also known as Stalino).

France, Resistance The German commander in Nantes is shot by resistance workers. Fifty hostages are shot in reprisal. There is a similar incident similarly punished in Bordeaux on 22 October.

Above: The destroyer Reuben James, *sunk by a U-Boat on 31 October.*

23 OCTOBER 1941
Eastern Front The Soviet command system is reorganized. Zhukov takes over responsibility for the northern half of the front and Timoshenko for the south.

24 OCTOBER 1941
Eastern Front A joint attack by the German Sixth and Seventeenth Armies succeeds in taking Kharkov.

25 OCTOBER 1941
War at Sea The British battleship *Prince of Wales* leaves the Clyde for the Far East. Admiral Phillips is aboard on the way to take command of the new Far East Fleet which is to be created around *Prince of Wales*. On 28 November *Prince of Wales* and *Repulse* both arrive at Colombo. The carrier *Indomitable* is intended to join them, but will be accidentally damaged on 3 November in the West Indies while training.

27 OCTOBER 1941
Eastern Front In the south the Germans capture Kramatorsk.

28 OCTOBER 1941
Eastern Front Most of the German attacks toward Moscow are now being halted, partly by their own weakness but even more by the weather. By day the soft and muddy ground hinders movement, and by night the severe frosts weaken the inadequately clad German troops and damage and halt their vehicles. The final major effort of this phase of attacks is a push by Guderian's forces near Tula, but this makes little progress. Farther north another brief German attack manages to take Volokolamsk.

29 OCTOBER 1941
Eastern Front The first of the Soviet reserve divisions from Siberia go into the line west of Moscow.

30 OCTOBER 1941
Eastern Front The German offensive in the Moscow sector comes to a halt until the winter weather sets in fully, giving permanently hard ground and restoring some mobility to the German tank forces.

31 OCTOBER 1941
Battle of the Atlantic While forming part of the escort of the convoy HX-156 the US destroyer *Reuben James* is sunk by a U-Boat. This is the first sinking of a US warship and 100 sailors are lost.

NOVEMBER 1941

Battle of the Atlantic Allied shipping losses are the lowest of the war so far at 104,600 tons. U-Boats only sink 13 ships of 62,200 tons. At the start of the month there are 10 U-Boats in the Mediterranean with more on the way. Ironically the sinking of the *Ark Royal* by two of the U-Boats makes submarine operations near Gibraltar more difficult since the carrier's surviving aircraft are based ashore and used solely for antisubmarine work. British air strength on the main convoy routes is now being augmented by Catapult Aircraft Merchant Ships (CAMS). The first action by an aircraft from one of these is on 1 November.

British Air Operations The targets for RAF Bomber Command include Kiel, Hamburg and Emden. British aircraft losses have been high and have risen in recent weeks; in the light of the Butt Report (*see* August) the practicality of the bomber offensive is being increasingly questioned. On the night of 7/8 November these problems come to a head when, of a force of 400 planes sent to Berlin, the Ruhr, Cologne and Boulogne, 37, or nearly 10 percent, fail to return. After this Churchill gives orders to conserve the bomber force until the spring brings better weather and equipment. In the last few months it is probably true to say that more Bomber Command personnel have been killed than German civilians.

Mediterranean/North Africa More than 60 percent of the Axis supplies sent to North Africa are lost in transit. Only about 30,000 tons arrive, compared with an average over the past few months of more than 70,000 tons. Both Rommel and Auchinleck are hoping to prepare for an offensive and the supply situation is crucial.

Yugoslavia, Resistance Throughout the month the Germans are very active in anti-Partisan operations. This is their first major drive against the resistance forces in Yugoslavia.

1 NOVEMBER 1941

Eastern Front In the Crimea Simferopol, an important communications center, falls to the German Eleventh Army.

Marshal Shaposhnikov becomes Chief of Staff of the Soviet forces.

2 NOVEMBER 1941

United States, Politics The coastguard is placed under the control of the navy.

3 NOVEMBER 1941

Eastern Front In the Leningrad sector there are further German attacks in the continuing effort to complete the isolation of the city. Their aim in this phase is to take Tikhvin, an important railroad center, 100 miles east of the city. During this battle there will be repeated Soviet counterattacks but they will be foolishly directed against some of the strongest German positions.

At the junction between Army Group Center and Army Group South, Kursk falls to the Germans.

4 NOVEMBER 1941

Eastern Front In the Crimea the German attacks are now making good progress. Feodosia is captured by the 170th Division.

5 NOVEMBER 1941

Diplomatic Affairs After discussion the Japanese decide to make further peace attempts, setting their deadline for the end of any negotiations at the end of November. The terms they offer are rejected by the United States because they contain no repudiation of the Tripartite Pact and because the Japanese intend to maintain bases in some parts of China. The outcome of the Japanese discussions and their diplomatic plans continue to be intercepted by the US code-breaking service.

6 NOVEMBER 1941

Production and Supply President Roosevelt announces that a loan of $1,000,000,000 is to be given to the USSR to help finance the acquisition of Lend-Lease supplies.

German Raiders The German blockade runner *Odenwald*, carrying a cargo of rubber from Japan, is captured in the American Security Zone off the Brazilian coast by the US cruiser *Omaha*. This is the first success for the increasingly extensive US patrols in the Atlantic.

Soviet Union, Home Front In a major public speech delivered to celebrate the anniversary of the 1917 Revolution, Stalin calls on the peoples of the Soviet Union to increase their efforts to defend 'holy Russia.' He claims that the German forces are worn out having taken almost 5,000,000 casualties compared to 1,800,000 for the Red Army.

8–9 NOVEMBER 1941

Mediterranean In a night battle the British Force K from Malta, two cruisers and two destroyers, attacks an Italian convoy sinking all seven transports and one of its escorts. The Italian covering force of heavy cruisers and destroyers does not engage.

9 NOVEMBER 1941

Eastern Front In the Leningrad sector Tikhvin

is taken by the Germans, cutting the rail route into the city. In the Crimea Yalta falls to the German attack.

10 NOVEMBER 1941

World Affairs In a public speech Churchill announces that 'should the United States become involved in war with Japan, a British declaration of war will follow within the hour.'

11 NOVEMBER 1941

East Africa The final battle to eliminate the Italian presence in Abyssinia begins. The regular Allied forces, aided by local guerrillas, attack Chilga to the west and Kulkaber to the southeast of the main Italian Gondar position. The attacks are beaten off for the moment.

12 NOVEMBER 1941

Eastern Front There is an important conference of German commanders at Orsha at which General Halder presents plans for continuing the attack on Moscow. The generals who will have to execute the scheme are not entirely happy with it but their opposition is fairly half-hearted and the plan is agreed. Three Panzer groups and three infantry armies are to take part.

12–14 NOVEMBER 1941

Mediterranean A further 34 Hurricanes are flown off from the British carriers *Argus* and *Ark Royal* to Malta on the 12th. On the 13th the force is returning to Gibraltar when two U-Boats, *U.81* and *U.205*, make attacks. *Ark Royal* is hit once and badly damaged. It seems at first that the damage has been brought under control but on the 14th, when the carrier has been brought to within 25 miles of Gibraltar, a fire breaks out and she is abandoned to sink. As in some carrier losses early in the Pacific war, poor damage control seems largely to have been responsible.

13 NOVEMBER 1941

United States, Politics Changes in the Neutrality Laws pass Congress. US merchant ships may now be armed and enter war zones. These administration-sponsored measures only pass by a small margin even after the *Kearny* incident and other developments in the Atlantic have been carefully presented as German aggressions. The small margin shows that the US is not yet ready to go to war.

15 NOVEMBER 1941

Eastern Front The German Moscow offensive is renewed. The main effort is to be made by the

tank forces which are to drive converging attacks toward the capital from just to the north and to the south. Guderian's Second Panzer Group attacks from around Tula to the south of the capital, while just north of the city both Third and Fourth Panzer Groups are involved in the advance toward the Moscow-Volga Canal. The infantry armies on the flanks, and particularly Fourth Army occupying the front between the armored thrusts, are to make supporting holding attacks.

The Soviet strategy for this winter period is to try to build up reserves for a counterattack from the forces that are being brought from Siberia, while doing just enough to hold the German advances. To some extent, therefore, the inward movement of the German tank attacks will be permitted during the next few days while the Soviet reserves are built up on the outer flanks.

All the German units are very seriously under strength both from the losses in the fighting since June and from the more recent ravages of the weather. This winter will turn out to be the most severe in the Soviet Union throughout the period for which records have been kept and the German troops and their equipment are badly prepared for it. Losses of manpower through frostbite and of equipment through other effects of the cold – lubricating oil freezing solid and metal parts like rifle bolts becoming brittle and breaking – have already helped reduce Panzer divisions to tank strengths appropriate for battalions. The losses will continue.

16 NOVEMBER 1941

Eastern Front The German forces continue to overrun the Crimea. Kerch falls to one wing of the attack while Sevastopol is now being besieged by other forces. The Soviet resistance in Sevastopol will become very stubborn.

In the Moscow sector the new German drive makes some slow advances.

17 NOVEMBER 1941

Eastern Front Rosenberg, the Nazi Party 'racial expert' and ideologist, is appointed to head a new Reich Ministry for Occupied Eastern Territories. His jurisdiction includes the Baltic States and White Russia and his task is to exploit these areas for German economic benefit and to rid them of the 'undesirable elements' of their populations, such as Jews and Communist supporters. Throughout their occupation the German authorities treat the population with ever-increasing brutality. This plays into the hands of the Soviet authorities who are trying to organize partisan bands and ensure the continued loyalty of the people to the Soviet state.

In the fighting at the front the advance of First Panzer Group continues to go well in the southern sector near Rostov, but the Soviet Ninth and Thirty-seventh Armies begin a counterattack on the flank of the German drive. General Timoshenko is in overall charge of the Soviet forces in the south.

18 NOVEMBER 1941

North Africa A new British offensive, Operation Crusader, begins with an advance by XXX Corps over the Egyptian border into Libya. The British forces in the desert are now organized as Eighth Army with General Cunningham in command. They have about 450 cruiser tanks and 132 infantry models in their main forces with more in the Tobruk garrison. They also have good reserve stocks of all equipment. The cruiser tanks are concentrated in XXX Corps which leads the British attack. There are problems with the reliability and gun power of the British tanks and, far more importantly, defects in the tactical training of their armored units. General Cunningham has no experience of commanding tank units. The Germans have about 180 Mk III and IV tanks with another 220 of the much weaker Italian and other German models. On or near the frontier there are garrisons in fortified areas on the coastal routes to west and east with 21st Panzer supporting them. The bulk of the Italian force is farther back, around Tobruk and to the south. 15th Panzer and the German Afrika Division are also near Tobruk. Rommel was intending to attack Tobruk on 21 November and has, therefore, enough supplies for a short sharp battle, but not for the prolonged brawl which will in fact ensue. The British deception measures have been good and because of this and his determination to attack Tobruk, Rommel will not react promptly to the British attack. He is in fact returning to North Africa from Rome when the British moves begin.

The rather vague British plan is to advance round the inland flank to the area of Gabr Saleh and Sidi Rezegh, draw the Germans into making attacks and destroy their tank forces. On the first day 7th Armored Division and other XXX Corps units advance virtually unmolested to Gabr Saleh.

Eastern Front One of Guderian's infantry divisions loses heavily in fighting near Venev in a counterattack sent in by one of the fresh Soviet Siberian divisions. There is a series of similar brief Soviet attacks against Guderian's force during the next few days which do much to confine the German attempts to advance.

Pacific A force of 11 Japanese submarines leaves their home ports to go to take up stations off Hawaii or to take part in other scouting missions. A further nine vessels sails toward Hawaii from Kwajalein.

British Command General Brooke is chosen to replace General Dill as Chief of the Imperial General Staff (the British Army Staff). General Dill will go to Washington to lead the British military mission there and General Paget becomes Commander in Chief, Home Forces in place of Brooke. These appointments take effect in December.

19 NOVEMBER 1941

North Africa The British 7th Armored Brigade advances easily to Sidi Rezegh but the other parts of 7th Armored Division are heavily engaged. The 4th Armored Brigade loses heavily in an attack by part of 21st Panzer and 22nd Armored Brigade equally heavily in a wasteful, unnecessary and badly conducted attack on the Italian Ariete Division at Bir el Gubi. Both British and Germans would have done better to concentrate their forces. The British have more than 40 tanks out of action already whereas the Germans have lost only a handful.

German Raiders The Australian light cruiser *Sydney* finds a suspicious ship in an area about 170 miles west of Western Australia. After an exchange of signals the *Sidney* rashly approaches close to the ship which opens fire with guns and torpedoes crippling the cruiser with the first salvo. The ship is in fact the German raider *Kormoran*. *Sydney* manages to fight back and both ships later sink. The *Kormoran* has sunk 11 ships of 68,300 tons during its cruise. News of the battle only becomes known when some of the crew of the *Kormoran* are found later. There are no survivors from *Sydney*.

20 NOVEMBER 1941

North Africa Both British and Germans still fail to concentrate their tank forces properly. The British 4th Armored Brigade is again mauled, this time by 15th Panzer. The 7th Armored Brigade is still active around Sidi Rezegh and 22nd Armored Brigade is moving to join 4th Armored. General Cunningham feels sufficiently in control of the situation to order the Tobruk garrison to begin break-out attacks, but in fact Rommel is beginning to appreciate the extent of the British aims and orders his panzer divisions toward Sidi Rezegh at the end of the day.

Vichy, Politics It is announced that General

Weygand has retired from his posts in North Africa. He has been removed after German pressure.

20–25 NOVEMBER 1941
Diplomatic Affairs The Japanese make proposals for an interim settlement with the United States. The proposals are unacceptable but Secretary Hull prepares a negotiating reply. This is not delivered because Chiang Kai-shek's government are successful in making the British and Dutch worried about the concessions offered to the Japanese in China.

21 NOVEMBER 1941
North Africa Both German tank divisions attack the 7th Armored Brigade at Sidi Rezegh and by the end of the day the British force has about 20 tanks left. A break-out attempt by the Tobruk garrison is brought to a halt when the expected help from 7th Armored Brigade cannot arrive. The British 4th and 22nd Armored Brigades are moving toward Sidi Rezegh.
Eastern Front Rostov is captured by the German forces after a particularly fierce battle.
East Africa The Allied attacks on Kulkaber southeast of Gondar are renewed with greater force and after a stout resistance the Italian defenders surrender. The Italians are now confined to the immediate area of Gondar.

21–22 NOVEMBER 1941
Mediterranean There are considerable Axis convoy operations because of the growing supply difficulties of their forces in North Africa. Two of the escorting cruisers are badly hit, one by a British torpedo plane and the other by submarine attack. The British Malta naval forces search for the Italian ships but cannot find them.

22 NOVEMBER 1941
North Africa There is a very confused tank battle around Sidi Rezegh in which 21st Panzer forces the British 7th and 22nd Armored Brigades to withdraw away from Tobruk. The 4th Armored Brigade loses heavily in a separate action with 15th Panzer. The New Zealand Division, part of XIII Corps, begins to move into the battle to help the British tanks. The Germans now hold the initiative, however, since they have over 170 tanks left and the British less than 150.
German Raiders The raider *Atlantis* is found and sunk by the cruiser *Devonshire* while replenishing a U-Boat off the west African coast. *Atlantis* has sunk 22 ships of 145,700 tons during

Above: Soviet cavalry in the Moscow sector.

her cruise. On 1 December the German supply ship *Python* is also sunk in this area by a British cruiser. Doenitz had hoped to send a force of U-Boats to work off South Africa but with the loss of these sources of supply this will not now be possible. The British successes are based on code-breaking information.

23 NOVEMBER 1941
Eastern Front In the Moscow sector the German offensive continues to make gradual gains. Progress is made on a 50-mile front northwest of the city. In these attacks Klin is captured by three of Hoth's Panzer Divisions. Some of the German forces are less than 35 miles from Moscow.
North Africa There are more violent battles southeast of Sidi Rezegh. The fighting is especially in the afternoon when both German panzer divisions and the Ariete Division make a headlong charge against the British armor and two South African Brigades which have now joined the tanks. The losses on the German side bring their force down to less than 100 tanks. German infantry casualties are also heavy. To the Afrika Korps the day becomes known as '*Totensonntag*,' 'the Sunday of the Dead.' The British losses are also high and General Cunningham has now lost confidence in the outcome of the battle. This brings Auchinleck, the more resolute British Commander in Chief, forward to take more interest in the tactical moves. Rommel does not take part in the day's main fighting but is involved farther north around Gambut where the New Zealand infantry capture the Afrika Korps Headquarters and much of Rommel's communications equipment.

23–25 NOVEMBER 1941
Mediterranean An Axis convoy bringing fuel

from Greece to Benghazi is attacked by the Malta-based Force K and loses two freighters. The British Mediterranean Fleet puts to sea to cover the operation and on the 25th the battleship *Barham* is torpedoed and blows up in an attack delivered by *U.331*.

24 NOVEMBER 1941

Eastern Front The Germans evacuate Rostov because of the threat to their rear from the continuing Soviet counterattacks in this sector. Field Marshal Rundstedt is personally responsible for this move which has been expressly forbidden by Hitler.

North Africa Rommel believes that the British armor has largely been destroyed in the fighting of the 23rd and, ignoring the New Zealand infantry, decides to collect his armor and advance along the Trigh el Abd to the Egyptian frontier. This move becomes known as 'the dash to the wire.' Although it causes some panic (the 'Matruh Stakes') in Eighth Army's rear echelons, the German forces take some losses from harrying attacks and more significantly have loosened their grip on the British tank units. Rommel and the senior generals with him are out of touch with the situation.

Battle of the Atlantic The British cruiser *Dunedin* is sunk by *U.124* in the central Atlantic.

25 NOVEMBER 1941

Eastern Front In the Moscow sector, northwest of the capital, the Germans take Istra.

Pacific The US Navy begins to establish compulsory convoying of merchant vessels.

East Africa The British forces take Tadda Ridge, seven miles from Gondar.

25–26 NOVEMBER 1941

North Africa The German panzer divisions dissipate their strength in attacks on British positions around Capuzzo and Sidi Azeiz. Toward the end of the 26th Rommel realizes that the British armor is quietly regrouping in the Sidi Rezegh area and that the New Zealand infantry are continuing to move toward Tobruk. He therefore begins to move his tank forces back in that direction. On the 26th also General Cunningham is relieved of command of Eighth Army. Auchinleck's Chief of Staff, General Ritchie, takes over, but Auchinleck himself will take a closer interest in the tactical control of the battle.

26–27 NOVEMBER 1941

Diplomatic Affairs Roosevelt and Hull decide to present a stiff 10-point note of final terms to

the Japanese. It demands that the Japanese leave China and Indochina and recognize the Chinese Nationalist Government. The Americans promise in return to negotiate new trade and raw materials agreements.

On the 26th the Japanese carrier force leaves its bases to move across the Pacific to Pearl Harbor. On the 27th the US authorities issue a war warning to their overseas commanders.

27 NOVEMBER 1941

Eastern Front In the southern sector the Soviet forces have now reoccupied Rostov as their offensive goes on. The German First Panzer Group are retreating toward Taganrog.

In the Moscow sector Guderian's forces have been fighting around Kashira for three days, but it is agreed that they cannot continue their drive toward Moscow unless reinforced. This is as close as they will get. They will be able to maintain limited attacks for a few days, however.

North Africa The advance of the 4th and 6th New Zealand Brigades links up with forces from the Tobruk garrison at El Duda early in the day. Later on there are evenly fought tank engagements in the Sidi Rezegh area.

The German Afrika Division zbv is renamed 90th Light Division. The famous trio of 15th Panzer, 21st Panzer and 90th Light, which are together associated with the name Afrika Korps, is thus complete.

27–28 NOVEMBER 1941

East Africa Early on the 27th the Allied attack on Gondar goes in and quickly makes progress despite the very rugged terrain. General Nasi, commanding the Italian forces, decides to ask for terms. These are agreed and the 22,000 Italians surrender on the 28th. Mussolini's East African Roman Empire has ceased to exist.

28–30 NOVEMBER 1941

North Africa There is renewed heavy fighting around Sidi Rezegh with the German tank forces trying to wipe out the link between the New Zealand infantry and the Tobruk garrison. By the end of the 30th, after a very confused battle and losses on both sides, one of the New Zealand brigades has been forced out of the fight.

29 NOVEMBER 1941

Eastern Front In the Moscow sector German tank forces commanded by General Reinhardt reach the Moscow-Volga Canal and manage to cross it in the Dmitrov area. The Germans here are coming up against some of the fresh Siberian units and more of the German tank force is being tied down here because of the fierce Soviet resistance.

Mediterranean The British forces in Malta are strengthened by the arrival of a further two cruisers and two destroyers.

29 NOVEMBER–1 DECEMBER 1941

Japan, Policy On 29 November a Japanese government liaison conference decides that the final terms are unacceptable and that Japan must go to war. This decision is confirmed on 1 December at a meeting in the presence of the Emperor Hirohito. As Japanese custom requires, he remains silent throughout the meeting merely giving his assent to his ministers' decisions.

30 NOVEMBER 1941

Eastern Front Field Marshal Rundstedt is relieved of his command of Army Group South for refusing to cancel his orders for retreat in the Rostov sector. Reichenau is the new commander. On the Soviet side Stalin gives his approval to Zhukov's plans and preparations for the coming counteroffensive in the Moscow sector.

Pacific & East Indies Japanese naval forces are reported to be on the move by British units based in Borneo. There are various other reports during the next few days of Japanese movements, which lead to an increase in tension in Malaysia and the East Indies but draw no eyes toward Hawaii.

German Raiders The raider *Komet* arrives back in Hamburg after a cruise of 516 days in which three ships of 31,000 tons have been sunk along with seven more in company with *Orion*.

Battle of the Atlantic A British Whitley bomber sinks *U.206* in the Bay of Biscay with the aid of Air-to-Surface-Vessel radar (ASV). This is the first success achieved with this equipment. It also marks a period of greater British efforts to interfere with the German traffic across the Bay.

DECEMBER 1941

War at Sea With the beginning of the war with Japan total Allied shipping losses soar this month to 285 ships of 583,700 tons. It is again a poor month for the German submarines with much of their effort being still devoted to the comparatively unrewarding waters of the Mediterranean and off Gibraltar. (*See* 14–23 December for one important Gibraltar convoy.) Ten U-Boats are lost during the month.

During 1941 Allied shipping losses have been 1229 ships of 4,300,000 tons. Britain has

received just over 30,000,000 tons of dry cargo during the year compared to a peacetime average of around 50,000,000 tons. As well as the losses, ships in convoy tend to sail slower, by longer routes, and are often unavoidably sent to crowded ports, unsuitable for their particular cargo. The British have already imposed strict rationing controls, of course, but the continuing shortfall in imports means that these must be made even more rigorous if the war effort is to continue.

Occupied Europe The '*Nacht und Nebel*' Decree (Night and Fog) is issued to the German secret services. This allows them to arrest and hold anyone they judge is a danger to German security, without being required to give any information about who they are holding or why. In future those arrested by the Gestapo will virtually vanish leaving their friends and relatives with the terrible dilemma about whether to inquire and risk being implicated in their 'crimes.'

British Air Operations The bomber effort is less intense this month but Aachen, Cologne, Bremen and Brest are all attacked while light forces are active over northern France.

1 DECEMBER 1941

North Africa Rommel's forces manage to make the remaining New Zealand force at Sidi Rezegh retreat, but the German units are now becoming very tired and have had many of their senior officers captured or killed. Although Eighth Army has been severely mauled it is still very much in the fight and unlike the Axis units it is still receiving generous supplies and replacement tanks.

Eastern Front There is a brief Soviet counterattack in the Moscow sector near Tula.

Malaya The British authorities declare a State of Emergency following reports of Japanese preparations for an attack.

2 DECEMBER 1941

Eastern Front In the Moscow sector some small German forces reach the northern suburbs of the capital and come within sight of the Kremlin less then 20 miles away. There are renewed efforts, on Hitler's direct order, by Kluge's forces to the west of the city. The weather continues to grow colder with blizzards being added to the previous hard frosts and heavy snow. Both Bock, commanding Army Group Center, and Brauchitsch, the Commander in Chief, are ill and unable to perform their duties fully effectively.

Pacific A special code order 'Climb Mount

Niitaka' is transmitted by Japanese naval headquarters to the ships of the carrier force steaming across the ocean to Hawaii. The order confirms that negotiations have broken down and that the carriers are to execute the Pearl Harbor attack.

East Indies The British battleship *Prince of Wales* and the battlecruiser *Repulse* arrive in Singapore. Their arrival is noted by the Japanese but is now too late for them to have the planned deterrent effect.

2–6 DECEMBER 1941

North Africa The very confused fighting continues. Rommel's forces are trying simultaneously to maintain the confinement of the Tobruk garrison in fighting around El Duda, to inflict losses on the British armor regrouping farther south toward Bir el Gubi and to send some help to the Axis garrisons at Bardia, Sollum and Halfaya Pass which are still holding out against XIII Corps' 4th Indian Division. The Germans are not strong enough to accomplish all this and their efforts only increase their weakness.

4 DECEMBER 1941

Britain, Home Front A new National Service Bill is passed by Parliament. Its provisions include compulsory direction and conscription for female labor.

South China Sea The Japanese landing force bound for Malaya sets out from Hainan.

5 DECEMBER 1941

Eastern Front Hitler agrees that the German Moscow offensive should be halted, as the growing weakness of the German forces prevents there being any possibility of further gains.

Mediterranean Hitler orders the transfer of the whole of Fliegerkorps II from the Eastern Front to the Mediterranean. The aim is to reduce the effectiveness of the attacks of the British Malta forces on the Axis supply convoys and by this and more direct intervention to help the forces in North Africa.

Allied Diplomacy General Sikorski, the head of the exiled Polish government is in Moscow to see Stalin. A friendship and mutual aid agreement between the Soviets and the Poles is signed by the two leaders.

6 DECEMBER 1941

Eastern Front In the early hours the Soviets begin a major counteroffensive all along the 500 miles of the Moscow sector. Fresh troops and tanks have been added to the Kalinin, West and Southwest Fronts. Among the units prominent in the attack are First Shock and Twentieth Armies in the advance against the Klin area and Tenth Army which leads the move against Guderian's troops east of Tula. The Soviet intention with these attacks, and others on their immediate flanks, is to cut through the panzer wings of Army Group Center and then to isolate and destroy it. Among the Soviet commanders in the attack are Zhukov, who has planned and commands the whole effort, Rokossovsky, Kuznetsov and others who will be among the Red Army's best war leaders in the years to come. From the beginning the attacks meet with considerable success against the weak and overextended German forces.

Diplomatic Affairs President Roosevelt makes a final appeal to the Japanese Emperor for peace. This is misunderstood and resented by the Japanese leaders who believe it wrong for the Emperor to be given the burden of such decisions. There is no Japanese reply. Late in the day the Japanese begin transmitting what is to be their final message to the US Government. The first 13 parts of the note are intercepted by the US code-breaking service, quickly translated and passed to the president. Although the crucial 14th and last part is not yet available, Roosevelt correctly interprets the message as meaning war. The message is not seen at this stage by General Marshall or Admiral Stark.

It is also known in the US that a Japanese agent in Honolulu has been asked for a special situation report on the US Pacific Fleet, but since similar requests to agents elsewhere have also been intercepted no special interpretation is put on this order.

Pacific Japanese forces leave Palau bound for the attack on the Philippines.

7 DECEMBER 1941

Diplomatic Affairs The 14th part of the Japanese signal, stating specifically that relations are being broken off, reaches Washington in the morning and is decoded by the US authorities around 0900 hours. A little after 1000 the order to the Japanese Embassy in Washington to deliver the main message at 1300 is similarly intercepted by the Americans. It is quickly realized that this timing coincides roughly with dawn at Pearl Harbor. Various delays ensue while General Marshall is found (it is a Sunday and he has gone for a morning ride) and then there are errors in the method of transmission of the warning message. It arrives in Headquarters in Oahu just before midday local time, when it is far too late.

There are also delays in the preparation of the

The battleship Pennsylvania *and the destroyers* Cassin *and* Downes *after the Japanese attack.*

Japanese note at their Embassy in Washington. The decoding and translation proceeds at a leisurely pace until the order giving the time for delivery arrives – the Embassy has had no previous hint that urgency is required. There is also delay in obtaining an appointment for the ambassador to see Secretary Hull. He eventually does so and delivers the message at 14.30. Hull has, of course, already seen the American version and has just received first reports of events at Pearl Harbor.

The British receive no official indications of what is afoot from the Japanese until three hours later, when their Ambassador in Tokyo is given a copy of the Japanese note. Both the British and US ambassadors in Tokyo are given declarations of war a further three hours later.

Pearl Harbor At 0755 local time Japanese carrier aircraft attack the main base of the US Pacific Fleet at Pearl Harbor. There is complete tactical and strategic surprise.

The Japanese have sent six carriers, *Akagi*, *Kaga*, *Hiryu*, *Soryu*, *Zuikaku* and *Shokaku*, with a total of 423 planes embarked to make the attack. The pilots are brilliantly trained and their equipment is good. Admiral Nagumo commands and he has, in addition to the carriers, two battleships and two heavy cruisers in his force along with destroyers and other supporting vessels including tankers.

Two waves of attacks are sent in. Commander Fuchida leads the first strike with 40 torpedo bombers (with special shallow running torpedoes), 51 dive bombers, 50 high-level bombers and 43 fighters. The second wave is of similar total strength but with extra dive bombers replacing the torpedo aircraft. All eight US battleships in port are damaged, five of them sinking. (*Arizona* is a total loss; *Oklahoma* will be raised but scrapped; *California*, *Nevada* and *West Virginia* will be rebuilt and will rejoin the fleet later in the war.) Three cruisers and three destroyers are also sunk. The Americans lose 188 aircraft from the island's airfields. The Japanese lose 29.

Although what is regarded at the time as the main force of the US Pacific Fleet has been destroyed, it is perhaps more relevant to recount what escapes the Japanese attack. By a combination of coincidences all three carriers serving with the Pacific Fleet at this time are absent when the Japanese attack, and of necessity they will become the major element in the USN forces. The base installations at Pearl Harbor including the massive oil storage tanks also escape unhurt because Nagumo unwisely disregards the advice of his staff to send in a third

attack. The Americans are, therefore, left with their base intact and the nucleus of a more modern fleet still in being.

One aspect of the Japanese attack plan is a complete failure. They have sent off five midget submarines to try to penetrate the American anchorage but all of these are lost. One is attacked by the destroyer *Ward* at about 0630 but, since it has not been unknown for destroyers to make false submarine reports, no great stir is caused. When compared with the wonderful successes of their airmen, the failure of the Japanese submarine service is especially disappointing and this has a disproportionate effect on the later Japanese naval effort. The submarine service will find its work devalued and there will be no Japanese equivalent of the U-Boat offensive in the Atlantic. The tactical doctrine of the Japanese submarine service is also faulty in its emphasis on attacking enemy warships and disregarding commerce destroying. It will be the US Navy which will mount an increasingly effective submarine offensive, destroying a growing proportion of the Japanese merchant marine and preventing the Japanese gaining anything like the desired benefit from the resources of Malaysia and the East Indies because of their inability to ship the raw materials back to Japanese factories and refineries. It is ironic that access to these resources is the principal Japanese war aim and that, although they will be taken, they will be of disappointingly little use. It should be noted that it will be some time before the US submarine campaign begins to be effective because of depth keeping and fuse defects in their torpedoes which will take time to remedy. (The Germans had similar trouble off Norway in 1940.)

The sighting report of the *Ward* is not the only warning received by the US authorities. Even more exact warning comes from one of Oahu's five radar stations. Two conscientious operators stay on watch for longer than the prescribed early morning period and just after 0700 they detect the Japanese strike approaching. Their reports are disregarded by the junior officer they contact who believes that they must be American aircraft. To add to this is the information from the diplomatic radio traffic that a deadline for action is imminent, and a mass of lower level radio information that some Japanese moves are about to take place. No radio intelligence is received concerning the position of the Japanese carriers, but no sinister interpretation is placed on this silence. A similar radio pattern has occurred during previous Japanese moves against Indochina in which the carriers were not involved. It is, therefore, easy to assume that, although the Japanese may be up to something, the carriers may not be involved. The US commanders at the Pearl Harbor base have been kept fully informed of the intelligence situation, and their general conclusion has been that, since none of the evidence points more specifically to Pearl Harbor than elsewhere, it is unnecessary to order a very high state of readiness. Instead, US aircraft are found parked wingtip to wingtip on the island's airfields; there are no torpedo nets to protect the fleet anchorage; partly because it is a Sunday officers and crew from the ships are ashore and few antiaircraft guns are manned; many ammunition boxes for AA guns are kept locked because peacetime custom decrees that every round must be accounted for. Admiral Kimmel, Commander in Chief US Pacific Fleet, and General Short, commanding US Army forces in Hawaii, will be dismissed for this catalog of errors.

At the highest level of the US command criticism is also deserved. The proverbially poor relations between the US Army and Navy are one cause of the difficulty. More understandably the misguided audacity of the Japanese is a very real surprise. The American leaders all find it easier to believe that the Japanese might attack Singapore, for example, since this would leave the US Government with the political problem of whether it could declare war to help Britain defend colonies, when the whole idea of empire is ideologically obnoxious to American opinion and without an attack on American territory.

The Pearl Harbor attack leaves the Allies with the three US carriers and the two doomed British battleships at Singapore as the only active capital ships left to face the Japanese. Counting Dutch and Free French ships the Allies have only a slight inferiority in cruisers, destroyers and submarines, but the Allied forces are widely dispersed and there will be problems of coordination and command.

Japanese Forces and Plans The Japanese Army has 51 divisions of which 11 can be spared from duties in China, Indochina and at home to join the offensive against the Allies. The Japanese navy has 10 battleships, six large and four smaller carriers, 36 cruisers, 113 destroyers and 63 submarines. There is no independent air force but the navy has about 1000 aircraft, half of them carrierborne, which will be committed along with about half of the army's 1500 planes.

It is clear that with such forces the Japanese cannot hope to win an all-out war against the United States and the British Empire. Instead their aim is to take advantage of the distraction provided by the war in Europe and seize the resource producing areas of Malaya and the East Indies. They will then be self-sufficient and will hope to defend a fortified perimeter around their conquests so fiercely that Britain and the United States will make peace. As well as the economic and militaristic pressure supporting the plan, there is also an element of broader Asian nationalism which sees value in the Asian Co-Prosperity Sphere which is to be created.

The attack on Pearl Harbor has been planned to disable the US Navy for the time required for the creation of the defensive perimeter. Admiral Yamamoto, who commands the Japanese Combined Fleet and has been responsible for the planning of the attack, is, however, deeply pessimistic about the eventual outcome. He sees the Pearl Harbor success as illusory and as granting only six months respite before Japan is swamped by US production. In greater detail the plan provides in the first phase for four divisions of Twenty-fifth Army to advance into Malaya to take Singapore after landing in Thailand; for two divisions of Fifteenth Army to move into Burma from Thailand; for two and a half divisions of Fourteenth Army to take the Philippines; and for other units to take Hong Kong, Guam, Wake, and the Makin Islands. The second and subsequent phases will see the

---

Note. The chronological account of the war in the Pacific is made considerably more complicated by the International Date Line and the many time zones. Events will normally be listed under the appropriate local date and time. A comparison of the local, Washington and London times of the opening events of the Japanese offensive shows the high degree of co-ordination involved.

	Local time	Washington time	London time
Landings in Malaya	01.00, 8 Dec	12.30, 7 Dec	17.30, 7 Dec
Pearl Harbor	07.55, 7 Dec	12.55, 7 Dec	17.55, 7 Dec
First air attack on Luzon	09.30, 8 Dec	20.30, 7 Dec	01.30, 8 Dec
Opening attack on Hong Kong	08.00, 8 Dec	19.00, 7 Dec	24.00, 7 Dec

The first military act of the Pacific war was several hours before the Japanese landings in Malaya when a British reconnaissance plane was shot down near the Japanese invasion force.

same forces being regrouped and moving on to Borneo, Sumatra and Java; the Bismarcks and New Guinea; and into Burma in strength.

Pacific As well as the Pearl Harbor attack there are Japanese air raids on Guam and Wake and a bombardment of Midway by two destroyers.

Eastern Front Already stricken by illness and now demoralized by the Soviet counteroffensive, Brauchitsch offers his resignation to Hitler. No formal acceptance of the resignation is made, but Brauchitsch will take no more important decisions.

8 DECEMBER 1941

World Affairs The United States and Britain declare war on Japan. In his address to Congress President Roosevelt describes the events at Pearl Harbor as forming part of 'a date which will live in infamy.' Roosevelt does not ask Congress to declare war on Germany and Italy. Australia, New Zealand, the Netherlands, the Free French, Yugoslavia and several South American countries all declare war on Japan also. China declares war on Germany, Italy and Japan.

Philippines The Japanese offensive here begins in the morning with air attacks and a landing on Batan Island north of Luzon by a small force who soon overcome the tiny garrison and begin work on an airfield. The main air attacks come in about midday, having been delayed by fog over the Japanese airfields in Formosa. Almost 200 aircraft are involved and they catch most of the defending aircraft on the ground and destroy about 100, leaving 17 B-17 bombers and less than 40 fighters in operating condition. There are also attacks by 22 planes from the carrier *Ryujo* against Davao on Mindanao. The first of the Japanese landing forces bound for the Philippines leaves Palau. General MacArthur commands the 130,000 strong Allied force on the Philippines. About 20,000 of his men are American, the rest being from the Philippine army. They are comparatively poorly equipped and trained. Many are unavoidably dispersed to garrisons on the various islands. The largest units are on Luzon as part of either Wainwright's North Luzon Force or the smaller South Luzon Force led by General Parker. MacArthur has hoped to use his aircraft to delay and disrupt Japanese landings which he recognizes his ground forces are too weak to repel. He then plans to retreat into the Bataan Peninsula and to hold out there until help can be brought from the main forces of the Pacific Fleet. The losses at Pearl Harbor and his own losses in aircraft mean that neither part of this plan can

work properly.

Malaysia Not long after midnight Japanese transports appear off Kota Bharu and landings begin. Before dawn there is also a small bombing raid on Singapore and by early morning the Japanese have also begun landings at Singora and Patani in Thailand. Units of the Japanese 5th Division land here while at Kota Bharu the troops are from 18th Division. Tank units are landed at Singora and Patani also. The British have almost no tanks in Malaya. In Malaya the British have three divisions and numerous fortress troops but only one division is free for active operations against the Japanese, since the other units are guarding possible landing places or airfields. The British force is poorly trained and too dependent on movement with motor transport by road. General Percival is in command. The RAF has 158 planes in Malaya when operations begin but many are lost on the first day. The airfield at Kota Bharu is also abandoned on the first day, but the runway is left untouched and stocks of fuel and bombs are not destroyed. The battleships *Prince of Wales* and *Repulse* sail from Singapore with four destroyers on the afternoon of the 8th. Admiral Phillips is in command. The Japanese have two battleships and six heavy cruisers covering their landings as well as many smaller ships. Admiral Kondo is in command.

The British have hoped to forestall Japanese landings at Singora and Patani by an advance into Thailand, but have not ordered this before the Japanese attack because such an advance into a neutral country could have upset opinion in the United States. Once the Japanese land it is too late to begin this plan and so a more limited alternative involving delaying actions at Jitra in northern Malaya and an advance into Thailand to a position known as The Ledge is ordered. There is delay in putting the plan into operation and more delay is imposed by the resistance of the Thai border guards who know nothing of events farther north. Thus by the end of the day the Japanese are well ashore at all three of their landing places and the British have been delayed in their counter moves and have lost heavily in the air.

Wake Island There are Japanese air attacks on the island on the 8th and over the following two days. A small landing force leaves Kwajalein on the 8th, escorted by a cruiser and six destroyers.

Hong Kong The Japanese 38th Division begins an attack at 0800 hours local time. General Maltby commanding the garrison has only six battalions and 28 guns with which to make a defense. His plan is to fall back from the border to a line across the neck of the Kowloon Peninsula known as the Gindrinkers Line and to try to hold out there for as long as he can. Delaying actions will be fought for the first two days to cover the retreat to this line.

Shanghai The Japanese occupy the whole of the city and capture the small US garrison in the American section.

Eastern Front The Soviet counteroffensive in the Moscow sector continues to make considerable headway despite desperate German defense. The Red Army forces are advancing successfully in the Leningrad sector also.

8–11 DECEMBER 1941

North Africa On the 8th Rommel decides to give up attempts to stay in the fight around Tobruk. There are only about 40 tanks left in the German divisions and 90th Light is down to a strength equivalent to two battalions. The German retreat is well controlled and the whole force is back around Gazala on the 11th. The siege of Tobruk is raised completely on the 10th. About 34,000 men have been taken in to replace the garrison during the siege and a similar number taken out as well as 7000 wounded and 7000 prisoners. In the various supply operations two destroyers have been lost and many other ships sunk or damaged.

9 DECEMBER 1941

Eastern Front In the Moscow sector the Soviet drive against Guderian's forces succeeds in reaching and capturing Elets. In the Leningrad sector the Soviets retake Tikhvin and force the Germans into a brief but hurried retreat. General Meretskov commands the Soviet forces here. Although tremendous efforts are being made by the citizens and garrison of the city and by Meretskov's forces outside, only the merest trickle of supplies is getting in. Rations are already well below starvation level and during this month perhaps 50,000 of the population will die.

Malaysia There are more Japanese landings at Kota Bharu, Singora and Patani. In Thailand the Japanese occupy Bangkok.

9–10 DECEMBER 1941

South China Sea On the afternoon of the 9th *Prince of Wales* and *Repulse* are sighted by a Japanese submarine while heading north toward the Japanese landing areas. They turn back later in the day when Japanese aircraft are sighted, since Admiral Phillips knows that no British fighter protection will be available farther north. About midnight reports of a Japanese landing at

Kuantan are sent to Admiral Phillips and he alters course in that direction. He decides not to signal his intentions to avoid giving away his position, believing that the staff at Singapore will realize that he will make this move and send fighters to Kuantan at first light. In the early hours of the 10th the British ships are sighted and attacked by a Japanese submarine. The attack is not noticed and the submarine later reports their position. In the morning the landings at Kuantan are found not to exist and just before midday Japanese aircraft from Indochina find and attack Phillips' force. About 90 Japanese planes are involved and in two hours both British capital ships have been sunk. This disaster leaves the Allies without a battleship active in the whole Pacific theater.

Gilbert Islands On the 9th small Japanese forces occupy Tarawa and on the 10th Makin.

10 DECEMBER 1941

Philippines There are Japanese landings and air attacks on Luzon. The naval base at Cavite is badly hit and important weapon stocks destroyed in the air attacks. On the north coast, at Aparri, 2000 men of the Tanaka Detachment land from one cruiser, six destroyers and other ships while in the northeast of the island at Vigan a similar number, the Kanno Detachment, also goes ashore covered by a slightly larger naval force.

Marianas A Japanese force commanded by Admiral Goto lands and captures the island of Guam which is defended by only 300 US troops.

Hong Kong The Japanese forces have now advanced up to the main defense line and succeed in capturing an important position at its west end.

Malaysia The British force which has advanced into Thailand from Kroh reaches The Ledge position where they are to prepare to meet the Japanese advance, only to find that the Japanese have arrived first and are stronger. The British attack is thrown back.

11 DECEMBER 1941

World Affairs Germany and Italy declare war on the United States. Congress replies with declarations of war and votes that US forces may be dispatched to any part of the world. The term of service of those enlisted under the Selective Service Act is extended until six months after the end of the war. The German declaration of war can only be regarded as one of Hitler's greatest mistakes, since without it US participation in the European war has still been in doubt.

Eastern Front The Soviet propaganda machine

begins to announce the Red Army's successes in the Moscow counteroffensive. The gains on the ground continue to be impressive with Guderian's troops being forced back from Stalinogorsk. Many of the already weakened German units have suffered so heavily in the few days of the Soviet offensive that they are virtually out of the fight.

Wake Island An attempted Japanese landing is beaten off and two destroyers sunk by the small defending force of 450 marines. Admiral Kimmel prepares to send his carriers to bring help and more aircraft to the island.

11–12 DECEMBER 1941
Malaya The positions of the 11th Indian Division at Jitra are attacked by the Japanese units which have advanced from Singora. The Indian division has already lost heavily in some outpost actions and the Jitra position is abandoned after a further brief fight.

12 DECEMBER 1941
Philippines The Japanese Kimura Detachment, 2500 men of the 16th Infantry Division, lands in south Luzon at Legaspi. There are further Japanese air attacks on the few remaining US aircraft on the island.

13 DECEMBER 1941
Hong Kong The British forces withdraw from their positions on the mainland on to Hong Kong island.
Burma The British evacuate their airfield at Victoria Point in the extreme south of the country on the Kra Isthmus. The Japanese move in.

13–16 DECEMBER 1941
North Africa Some of the British forces have closed up to the Gazala position by the 13th but lose heavily to sharp German counterattacks. Rommel realizes that, despite these successes, he cannot make a permanent stand here because of the weakness of his forces. He therefore begins the long retreat through Cyrenaica to the next defensible position at El Agheila. The withdrawal begins on the 16th.

13–19 DECEMBER 1941
Mediterranean There is much naval activity by both sides. On the 13th two Italian cruisers carrying a cargo of fuel to North Africa are attacked and sunk off Cape Bon by three British and one Dutch destroyer. Also on the 13th the Italians begin a major convoy operation to bring supplies to Benghazi covered by their main fleet

including four battleships. Two transports are sunk by a British submarine on the 13th and the *Vittorio Veneto* similarly damaged on the 14th. The Italians abandon this effort. On the 15th *U.557* sinks a cruiser off Alexandria. Later on the 15th the British begin an operation to bring supplies to Malta from Egypt. Including the forces that set out from Malta six cruisers and 16 destroyers are involved. On the 16th the Italians start a second convoy again covered by four battleships with five cruisers and 21 destroyers also in the escort. Admiral Iachino commands the Italian force and Admiral Vian the British. On the 17th the British Force K from Malta joins with Vian's Force B from Alexandria. On the night of the 17th the covering forces of the two convoys meet in an action known as the First Battle of Sirte, but the fighting is indecisive because most attention is paid to protecting the convoys. On the 18th the British convoy reaches Malta, and Force B turns back to Egypt while Force K searches for the Italian ships. During the night, however, Force K runs into a minefield and loses one cruiser and one destroyer and has both the other cruisers present damaged. On the same night three Italian midget submarines penetrate into the Mediterranean Fleet anchorage at Alexandria, taking advantage of the net defenses being opened to allow Force B to return. Their charges are placed under the battleships *Queen Elizabeth* and *Valiant*. Both ships sink to the bottom of the harbor, but because it is comparatively shallow and they come to rest on an even keel the Italians do not realize the brilliant extent of their success. Thus, in the actions of one night, the Mediterranean Fleet is deprived of its Malta striking force and of both its battleships. As well as being a serious blow to British strength in the Mediterranean it compounds the Allied lack of capital ships for all theaters.

14 DECEMBER 1941
Malaya The Japanese forces from Patani have now pushed on beyond The Ledge to Kroh.

14–23 DECEMBER 1941
Battle of the Atlantic On the 14th the convoy HG-76 sails from Gibraltar for the UK. There are 32 ships in the convoy and the escort includes the escort carrier *Audacity* and 12 other ships. The escort is led by perhaps the most famous of the British escort leaders, Commander (later Captain) Walker. During the convoy's passage 12 U-Boats are involved in attacks, but five are sunk and in addition two Condor aircraft are shot down. This success is tempered by the

sinking of the *Audacity* on the 21st. One destroyer and two merchant ships are also lost to the attacks which are called off by Doenitz on the 23rd.

15 DECEMBER 1941
Eastern Front In their attacks northwest of Moscow the Soviets have reached Klin and Kalinin and they claim to have taken both towns. Elsewhere the remorseless pressure of their offensive continues to wear the defending German units out.

Malaya The British forces have fallen back to Gurun and once more lose heavily to a Japanese attack. The Japanese cannot take Gurun, however.

Hong Kong The Japanese attempt to ferry a small force over to Hong Kong Island from Kowloon but are pushed back.

16 DECEMBER 1941
Borneo Early in the day there are Japanese landings at Miri, Seria and Lutong. The oil plants are set on fire before the small British and Dutch forces retreat. The Japanese force is from 16th Infantry Division and they have considerable naval support.

16–17 DECEMBER 1941
Malaya There is a second wave of Japanese landings. Over the next few days the 5th and 18th Divisions will be brought up to full strength and the Imperial Guards Division will begin to arrive. On the 16th the British forces withdraw from Penang on the west coast and on the 17th they pull back from their main defensive position at Gurun. They will now retreat south of the Perak River fighting delaying actions on the way.

17 DECEMBER 1941
Eastern Front In contrast to the continuing Soviet attacks on all other fronts, in the Crimea German attacks by LIV Corps begin against the fortress city of Sevastopol.

United States Command Admiral Nimitz is appointed to command the US Pacific Fleet relieving Admiral Kimmel. It will be a few days until Nimitz can arrive in Hawaii, and Admiral Pye takes temporary command until he does so. These changes do not help with the attempts to relieve Wake which are under way.

Battle of the Atlantic The British cruiser *Dunedin* is sunk by a U-Boat.

18 DECEMBER 1941
Eastern Front Following Rundstedt's dismissal at the beginning of the month, a second of the

German army group commanders is replaced. Field Marshal Bock has been ill like Brauchitsch and is replaced by Kluge.

18–19 DECEMBER 1941
Hong Kong During the night there are Japanese landings on Hong Kong Island along a front between North Point and the Lei U Mun Channel. The attacking force gets well established and British counterattacks over the following days, especially on the 20th, are unsuccessful.

19 DECEMBER 1941
German Command Hitler formally removes Brauchitsch from his post of Commander in Chief of the army. Hitler directly assumes the responsibilities of this post himself, telling Halder that 'anyone can do this little matter of operational command.'

At first Hitler is remarkably successful, applying his considerable talents to mastering a range of detailed information relating to his task. It is generally agreed that his orders to stand fast, which he repeats throughout this winter campaign on the Eastern Front, will help save the German Army from an even more disastrous defeat.

The Germans will be able to retreat into admittedly isolated defensive localities based around what shelter can be obtained in the many villages. The Soviets will be unable to prevent Luftwaffe supply operations and will lack the heavy weapons or tanks necessary to break into the German defenses.

Hitler's clear perception of his own place in this defensive success will only serve to convince him further of his own ability as a general and of the useless weakness of the army leaders. He will also remain convinced to the end that no retreat is a sufficient tactical answer to any attack in any circumstances. His belief in the army's failure also encourages him to expand the forces of the Waffen SS. Although these units will almost always fight fanatically in the German cause, their leaders often lack the training and experience of their army counterparts because they have been selected for Nazi Party reasons. The priority of equipment that the SS receives also means that more experienced army formations will end up going short.

North Africa The Axis retreat through Cyrenaica continues. The following Allied troops reach Derna.

United States, Manpower The Selective Service Act is amended, making it compulsory for all men 18–64 to register and for those 20–44 to be subject to military service. The Act is signed by Roosevelt on 22 December.

19–20 DECEMBER 1941
Philippines During the night the Japanese land near Davao on Mindanao. The carrier *Ryujo* is in support and the landing force is made up of 500 men from the 56th Infantry Regiment.

19–25 DECEMBER 1941
Eastern Front In the Crimea the German attacks on Sevastopol continue, and by the 23rd the outer ring of forts around the town has been captured after heavy fighting. The garrison is being strengthened, however, in various Soviet naval operations during this time. Altogether over 14,000 men are brought in as well as supplies.

20 DECEMBER 1941
Eastern Front In the Moscow sector the Soviet offensive continues to inflict considerable losses on the defending forces. Northwest of the capital Volokolamsk is retaken.
United States Command Admiral King is appointed to be Commander in Chief, US Fleet.
Germany, Home Front Goebbels broadcasts an appeal for contributions of winter clothing for the troops serving in the USSR.

21–23 DECEMBER 1941
Philippines There are Japanese landings on Luzon at Lingayen Gulf. The landing force is made up from 48th Infantry Division specially reinforced with other units including tanks. They have considerable air and naval support. The defending forces are not able to make a very strong resistance and the Japanese soon establish a strong perimeter for their beachhead.

22–23 DECEMBER 1941
Wake Island The Japanese return to the attack with stronger forces. Wake has been bombarded from the air since the first successful defense with planes from the carriers *Hiryu* and *Soryu* joining in on the 21st and 22nd. Just before midnight on the 22nd the Japanese are able to land some 200 men on the island and, although the garrison fights back, they are compelled to surrender later on the 23rd. The carriers of the US Pacific Fleet have been sent on a mission to Wake but they are still several hundred miles away when the island surrenders.

22 DECEMBER 1941–7 JANUARY 1942
Allied Planning The British and American leaders meet in Washington at the Arcadia Conference. There are long discussions between Churchill and Roosevelt, their Chiefs of Staff and other political leaders from both countries. The two main conclusions of the conference are to confirm the policy of beating Germany first agreed early in 1941 and to establish the Combined Chiefs of Staff as the directing body for the whole Allied military effort. The idea for the Combined Chiefs of Staff is General Marshall's and arises from his belief that a Supreme Commander should be appointed to control the operations against the Japanese in the East Indies and Malaya. Wavell will be selected for this task (*see* 3 January) and it is decided that he should be responsible to a combined Allied authority. The Combined Chiefs of Staff will meet in Washington. The American Chiefs will participate personally and General Dill will lead the British Military Mission. The general strategic program is agreed also. This provides for a US buildup in Britain in preparation for future land operations against Germany. The bomber offensive is to continue. It is accepted that there will be further losses in the Pacific but these are to be held to a minimum by stout defense. The British come to the conference rather better prepared than the Americans, not unnaturally since they have been fighting longer. The American military delegation is also a little unbalanced since Admiral King has only just taken over at the head of the US Navy. The US military leaders will feel afterward that they have been unfairly dominated and will also worry about Churchill's personal influence on Roosevelt.

23 DECEMBER 1941
Burma There are the first Japanese air attacks on Rangoon. The Allied air forces in Burma only have two fighter squadrons at this stage, one from the RAF and one from Chennault's American Volunteer Group.
Borneo There are Japanese landings at Kuching, the capital of Sarawak. Two transports are sunk and two damaged by a Dutch submarine. A second submarine sinks a Japanese destroyer but is then sunk in turn. The small British force at Kuching resists until 25 December and then withdraws.
North Africa The Axis forces evacuate Benghazi. The Allied advance has reached Barce.

24 DECEMBER 1941
Philippines The Japanese land 7000 men of the 16th Infantry Division at Lamon Bay in southeast Luzon. In north Luzon the American forces have taken up the first of five delaying positions

planned to block the advance of the Japanese from Lingayen Gulf toward the Bataan Peninsula. MacArthur's intention from the first has been to retire to this area and await help and reinforcements from across the Pacific. Such help cannot now arrive but MacArthur has no other options open.

Atlantic Free French forces landed from three corvettes and a submarine occupy the islands of St Pierre and Miquelon off the Canadian coast. Official opinion in the United States is offended by this move because the US still has relations with Vichy.

24–25 DECEMBER 1941
Sulu Archipelago Japanese forces land on Jolo.

25 DECEMBER 1941
Eastern Front The Soviet offensives continue to achieve successes. The German forces are now down to 75 percent of their strength in June. Their losses in tanks have been especially severe. Guderian has less than 40 tanks in his whole command. In Hoeppner's Panzer Group only one of the four armored divisions has more than 15 tanks.

North Africa The advancing Allied forces reach Benghazi and Agedabia as the Axis retreat continues.

Hong Kong The British forces in Hong Kong capitulate in the evening.

Philippines The US forces in north Luzon are attacked on their second line of defense at the Agno River.

26 DECEMBER 1941
Eastern Front The German attacks on Sevastopol are continuing, but other German units of Eleventh Army are threatened by Soviet landings in the eastern Crimea at Kerch.

26–28 DECEMBER 1941
Arctic There is a British commando raid on the Lofoten Islands. On December 26 a force of 260 men is landed on Moskenesoy to destroy the fish-oil factory there. On 27 December there are landings on Vaagso and Maaloy nearby by almost 600 troops. Again fish factories and radio stations are the targets. The raids are a success with various merchant and patrol craft being sunk and 243 volunteers being taken to join the Norwegian forces in Britain. The raid also contributes to fears of Hitler's about a British invasion of Norway. In the short term Doenitz will be ordered to station U-Boats to guard against this and in the long term considerable German forces will be sent to idle in Norway.

27 DECEMBER 1941
Philippines Manila is declared an open city by the American authorities while in the fighting to the north the American forces have now fallen back to their third line running east and west from Paniqui.

British Command General Pownall replaces Air Marshal Brooke-Popham as Commander in Chief Far East. This command will shortly be superseded by Wavell's ABDA to which Pownall will become Chief of Staff.

28 DECEMBER 1941
Eastern Front The German attacks on Sevastopol make some gains in the Fort Stalin area where 22nd and 24th Divisions are leading the offensive. The German commanders believe that they will soon take the city.

Philippines The US forces have now fallen back to the line Tarlac-Cabanatuan and are attacked there.

Malaya The British forces withdraw from Ipoh under pressure from the Japanese advance. The next defended positions will be at Kampar and the crossings of the River Slim.

Burma General Hutton is appointed to command the British forces.

28–30 DECEMBER 1941
North Africa In a series of brisk engagements the British 22nd Armored Brigade takes severe losses as the retreating Germans turn and counterattack. The German performance in this retreat through Cyrenaica and in their retreat after Alamein, contrasts strongly with the behaviour of the British and Allied forces when they have the same experience. In March 1941 and January 1942 when the Allied front breaks there is great confusion and often panic in the rear areas. The Afrika Korps in retreat is trained and orderly.

29 DECEMBER 1941
Eastern Front There are new Soviet landings in the eastern Crimea at Feodosia. The forces moved to here and Kerch will be a serious threat to the German Eleventh Army and it will be compelled to halt attacks on Sevastopol while it deals with them. The Soviet units involved are Fifty-first and Forty-fourth Armies.

30 DECEMBER 1941
Philippines The US forces fall back from Tarlac to their last prepared line before the Bataan Peninsula. They must attempt to hold this position just north of Clark Field so that the troops retiring before the Japanese landings in

south Luzon can pass through Manila to Bataan.
Eastern Front The continuing Soviet advance on the Moscow sector recaptures Tula.
Malaya The Japanese advance has now reached nearly to Kampar in the west and Kuantan in the east.

31 DECEMBER 1941
Eastern Front Although the battles since June have seen huge losses for the Red Army – at least 5,000,000 casualties, 3,000,000 prisoners, 20,000 tanks and 30,000 guns destroyed – the Soviets are still very much in the fight. They will maintain the initiative until well into the spring of 1942, but by then the resources that have been carefully assembled during the autumn of 1941 will have been dissipated in attacks. Although the Germans have already lost severely in the winter offensive and will continue to do so, there will be no Soviet breakthrough and instead a gradual growth in German manpower and equipment levels.
United States Command General Brett takes command of US forces in Australia.

JANUARY 1942
Battle of the Atlantic The German U-Boat fleet now has 91 vessels operational with another 158 on training missions or on trials. The operational boats are distributed with 64 in the Atlantic theater, 23 in the Mediterranean and four in the Arctic. This month Allied shipping losses in all theaters amount to 106 ships of 419,900 tons; 48 ships are sunk in the Atlantic and 62 ships fall to Axis submarines of all nations. From later in the month until March Doenitz is compelled by Hitler to deploy a significant number of his fleet off Norway to guard against an invasion. This is one useful result for the Allies of the British commando raid on the Lofotens at the end of 1941. The most important development in the maritime war during the month is the move of the German submarines to the East Coast of America (*see* 13 January 1942).
British Air Operations RAF Bomber Command makes many attacks during the month. Targets include Emden, Hamburg, Bremen and Brest (aimed at the *Scharnhorst, Gneisenau* and *Prinz Eugen*).
Mediterranean Fliegerkorps II makes heavy attacks on Malta throughout the month, ensuring that British forces based there can do little against the Axis supply routes going to North Africa. In any case the Italians provide very strong (up to four battleships and many cruisers) escorts for all convoys sent to North Africa. The British send three small convoys to Malta.

1 JANUARY 1942
World Affairs The first step is taken toward the establishment of the United Nations when representatives of 26 countries meet in Washington to endorse the principles of the Atlantic Charter. They agree (1) to employ all their resources against the Axis powers and (2) to make no separate peace.
Eastern Front German forces counterattack near Kerch in the Crimea. The attacks of the Kalinin Front retake Staritza.

2 JANUARY 1942
Eastern Front In the advance of the West Front south of Moscow Maloyaroslavets is retaken from the Germans.
North Africa The Axis garrison of Bardia on the Egyptian border surrenders. It has held out since almost the start of the Crusader offensive.
Philippines Japanese forces occupy Manila. Their American and Filipino opponents establish themselves on the approaches to the Bataan Peninsula.
Malaya British and Empire forces continue to be compelled to retreat southward. The 15th Indian Brigade is forced back from around Kampar.

3 JANUARY 1942
Allied Command By the authority of the Arcadia Conference Chiang Kai-shek is named Commander in Chief of Allied forces in China. General Wavell is appointed to the newly established ABDA (American-British-Dutch-Australian) Command. His task is to hold the 'Malay Barrier' (the line from Malaya through the Dutch East Indies to Borneo).

4 JANUARY 1942
Malaya The 11th Indian Division prepares to attempt to hold the line of the River Slim but is coming under increasingly heavy Japanese air attack as the new Japanese bases in Thailand become operational.
New Britain Japanese air forces attack Rabaul.

5 JANUARY 1942
Eastern Front Stalin refuses advice from Zhukov and his other military advisers and orders offensives on all fronts rather than concentrating against Army Group Center. Zhukov has argued that Soviet resources are not sufficient to allow such diverse operations and that, although early successes may be achieved, there will be no reserve of strength to break into German fortified positions. This will turn out to be an accurate prediction.

Philippines Late in the day American forces begin to make final withdrawals to the main Bataan position.

6 JANUARY 1942
North Africa The British 1st Armored Division becomes operational in Cyrenaica. The inexperience of this formation is to be an important factor in the coming operations. The German retreat through Cyrenaica comes to an end. The British advance has reached Mersa Brega and El Agheila.

7 JANUARY 1942
United States, Politics President Roosevelt submits the budget for 1943 to Congress. The total of the appropriations is $59,000,000,000. Production in 1942 is to be 60,000 planes, 45,000 tanks and 8,000,000 tons of shipping; in 1943, 125,000 planes, 75,000 tanks and 11,000,000 tons of shipping.

Malaya Japanese tanks and infantry totally disrupt the defenses of 11th Indian Division around Trolak and Kampong Slim. The two brigades most heavily engaged are reduced to about 20 percent of their normal strength.

8 JANUARY 1942
Malaya General Wavell, visiting Singapore, orders the Allied forces to withdraw to positions south of the Muar River where the next stand is to be made.

Eastern Front West of Moscow the Soviet forces are now attacking Mozhaysk.

8–10 JANUARY 1942
Malaya There is a third wave of Japanese landings bringing in more troops. There is the usual lavish escort for the convoys.

9 JANUARY 1942
Eastern Front The Soviet Northwest, Volkhov and Kalinin Fronts launch a new offensive in the Valdai Hills area west and northwest of Moscow. The Soviet advance is very rapid at first despite fierce German resistance.

Philippines The first period of Japanese attacks on Bataan begins.

11 JANUARY 1942
East Indies Japanese forces begin their invasion of the Dutch East Indies. They make landings on the small island of Tarakan and Minahassa. General Yamashita and Admiral Takahashi are in command.

The Japanese plan for the invasion of the East Indies envisages a three-pronged attack. The

landings at Tarakan are from the Central Force which is to take Borneo. The Western Force will advance from Sarawak and make landings on Sumatra and Java. The Eastern Force is to begin with landings on the Celebes and at Amboina, before attacking Bali, Timor and the eastern part of Java.

Pacific The carrier *Saratoga* is severely damaged in an attack by the Japanese submarine *I.6* near Hawaii.

12 JANUARY 1942
North Africa Rommel agrees with a proposal from his subordinates that they should prepare a surprise counteroffensive against the British. To preserve security neither the German nor Italian High Command are told of the plans. Even during the retreat in December the Germans were receiving new supplies of tanks and more arrived on 5 January. The British forces are going to be reduced by the withdrawal of the two Australian divisions to face the Japanese, and 7th Armored Brigade will also go. Other units earmarked for Eighth Army will be diverted in transit.

Yugoslavia, Politics General Simović resigns and Professor Yovanović becomes Premier of the exile government with Colonel Mihajlović as Minister for War.

East Indies After fierce fighting Tarakan is taken by the Japanese. Tarakan and Manado in the Celebes are quickly made into air bases to support the Japanese advance.

Malaya Japanese troops enter Kuala Lumpur.

13 JANUARY 1942
Battle of the Atlantic The German U-Boats begin operations off the US East Coast. The move is code named Paukenschlag (Drum Roll). Doenitz has faced arguments from his superiors in the German Navy who do not favor the operation, and he has had the difficulty that only the larger 740-ton U-Boats are really suitable for such long-range patrols. When Doenitz gives the order for the attack to begin there are 11 U-Boats in position and 10 more en route, and together they sink 150,000 tons during the first month. Intelligence sources have given reasonable warning of the attack but the U-Boats find virtually peace-time conditions in operation. Ships sail with lights at night; lighthouses and buoys are still lit; there is no radio discipline – merchant ships often give their positions in clear language; there are destroyer patrols (not convoys with escorts) but these are regular and predictable and their crews are naturally inexperienced. The US Navy refuses to take the

advice on trade protection offered by the British, and the British are annoyed that many of their ships making for the convoy assembly points in Nova Scotia are among the victims.

Philippines Japanese attacks on Bataan continue and, although they make progress on the east side of the peninsula, they are still held in the west.

War Crimes Allied representatives meeting in London announce that Axis war criminals will be punished after the war.

15 JANUARY 1942

Arctic The German battleship *Tirpitz* is moved to Norwegian waters.

Burma Units of the Japanese 55th Division move into Burma north of Mergui.

Malaya Japanese forces have now penetrated south of Malacca. The Japanese 5th Division is heavily engaged with Australian troops at Batu Anam on the River Muar. Troops from the Japanese Imperial Guards Division break into the coastal section of the Allied position where 45th Indian Brigade is stationed.

16 JANUARY 1942

Eastern Front Field Marshal Leeb is removed from command of Army Group North and replaced by General Kuchler. All three German Army Group commanders have, therefore, been removed since the start of December; two of the Panzer Group commanders, Guderian and Hoeppner, have also gone, as well as 33 other officers commanding divisions or higher formations. All have been removed because of Hitler's annoyance over their requests to make withdrawals. Hitler now completely dominates German military planning and decision making.

Malaya The fighting on the Muar continues with more Japanese gains.

United States, Politics Donald Nelson is appointed head of the newly created War Production Board.

17 JANUARY 1942

South Africa, Politics The South African Parliament rejects a motion calling for independence from Britain and accords General Smuts a vote of confidence.

Eastern Front Field Marshal von Reichenau dies of a stroke while returning to Germany from the Eastern Front.

North Africa British forces take Halfaya and capture 5500 German and Italian troops. The garrison at Halfaya has been isolated since the start of the Crusader offensive, but has held out under the command of a remarkable German

leader, Major the Reverend Bach.

Arctic The convoy PQ-8 is attacked by U-Boats. This is the first such attack on an Arctic convoy. One destroyer and one merchant ship are sunk by *U.454*.

18 JANUARY 1942

Eastern Front South and Southwest Fronts provide the attacking units and the aim is to cross the Donets and wheel south to the Sea of Azov, trapping German units against it. The German Sixth and Seventeenth Armies are the defending units.

In the Moscow sector the Valdai Hills offensive is still going well for the Red Army. They have reached to within 70 miles of Smolensk and also threaten Velikiye Luki. In the Crimea the German forces are recovering from the disruption caused by the Soviet landings at the end of December and have resumed their attacks to take Feodosia.

19 JANUARY 1942

Eastern Front Von Bock is appointed to succeed von Reichenau in command of Army Group South. The Russians recapture Mozhaysk in the central sector after a fierce street battle. There are also Soviet paratroop landings south of Smolensk now and over the next few days. The paratroops will help establish partisan groups to strike at German rear areas.

20 JANUARY 1942

Occupied Europe At a conference held in Berlin, which will become known as the Wannsee Conference, Heydrich presents plans to Hitler for the 'Final Solution' to the 'Jewish Problem.' These plans provide for the transportation of all Europe's Jews to extermination camps. Hitler gives his approval. Eichmann will be in charge of the department of the SS responsible for the execution of the plan (*see* March 1942).

New Britain Japanese aircraft from four carriers make major attacks on Rabaul.

21 JANUARY 1942

North Africa Rommel's second offensive begins. Cautious German advances quickly reveal faulty British dispositions. The German attacks are therefore pressed home with great success. This ability to respond quickly to fleeting opportunity is one of the secrets of the Afrika Korps' strength. The Germans employ about 100 tanks in their drive with the German tank units advancing to El Agheila on the inland flank while German and Italian infantry move along the coast. The British forces in the forward defensive positions are a Guards Brigade and part of 1st Armored Division. They are taken by surprise.

Malaya The Allied forces are beginning to retreat south of the Muar after taking heavy losses. The 45th and 15th Brigades have been virtually destroyed in the fighting. Japanese air raids on Singapore increase in intensity. The few defending Hurricane fighters are outmatched by the Japanese Zeros.

China General Stilwell is nominated as Chief of Staff to Chiang Kai-shek.

22 JANUARY 1942
North Africa The German attack gathers pace, taking Antelat and Agedabia. The Axis troops in Africa are formally renamed Panzer Army Africa.

23 JANUARY 1942
Pacific There are Japanese landings at Rabaul in New Britain, at Balikpapan in Borneo, near Kavieng on New Ireland and on Bouganville in the Solomons. After Rabaul is taken it becomes a major Japanese naval base.

24 JANUARY 1942
Eastern Front In the Soviet offensive south of Kharkov the advance has now crossed the Donets. Barvenkovo is taken.

Philippines On the Bataan Peninsula the US forces begin withdrawals to a second defense line.

Above: MacArthur's HQ on Corregidor.

East Indies Four Dutch and American destroyers attack the Japanese transports off Balikpapan, sinking five ships. There are Japanese landings at Kendari in the Celebes where an important airfield is captured.

25 JANUARY 1942
North Africa The British 2nd Armored Brigade is largely destroyed in fighting around Msus as the German advance continues.

Burma General Wavell, visiting Rangoon, gives orders for the defense of Moulmein although the local commander would prefer to retire.

Malaya Batu Pahat, the last defensive position near the Muar River, is abandoned by the Allied forces. Wavell has authorized Percival to retreat to Singapore.

26 JANUARY 1942
United States, Politics The Board of Inquiry established to investigate the Pearl Harbor disaster publishes its findings. Admiral Kimmel (then Commander in Chief US Fleet) and General Short (then Commander in Chief Hawaiian Department) are judged guilty of deriliction of duty. Both have already been dismissed.

North Africa Rommel's offensive recaptures Msus.

Western Europe The first American troops arrive in the British Isles.

27 JANUARY 1942
Britain, Politics Churchill opens a major House of Commons debate with a report of recent negotiations of measures for Allied cooperation. He describes the Combined Chiefs of Staff Committee, the Pacific Council and the plans for US land forces to come to Britain. The debate clears the air of various criticisms of the conduct of the war and a vote of confidence is opposed by only one member.

Eastern Front Timoshenko's troops continue their advance into the Ukraine and capture Lozovaya. They now threaten Dnepropetrovsk which is the main supply base for Army Group South. The German defense is now stiffening and by 31 January the Soviets will be halted.

Borneo A Japanese force lands and captures Pemangkat and the nearby airfield.

27-28 JANUARY 1942
Malaysia The British carrier *Indomitable* flies a cargo of 48 Hurricane fighters to Java. From here they will move on to reinforce the defenses of Singapore. The 22nd Indian Brigade is cut off

in fighting near Layang Layang south of Kluang.

29 JANUARY 1942
North Africa Rommel retakes Benghazi and continues to advance.

Diplomatic Affairs Britain and the USSR sign a treaty of alliance with Iran. Many supplies from the Western Allies later use this route to Russia.

United States, Command General Harmon becomes Chief of Staff, USAAF, succeeding General Spaatz who will now lead Air Force Combat Command.

30 JANUARY 1942
Philippines Japanese pressure on the American positions on Bataan is maintained. As well as striking against the main defense lines, amphibious landings have been made at various points on the coast. Amboina, the second largest naval base in the Dutch East Indies, is attacked by the Japanese.

Burma The Japanese 55th Division begins attacks on Moulmein.

31 JANUARY 1942
Malaya The last Australian-British forces are withdrawn from the Malayan mainland to Singapore.

Burma In Burma there is more heavy fighting at Moulmein causing British troops to retire northward. The town falls to the Japanese.

FEBRUARY 1942
Battle of the Atlantic On 1 February the Germans begin to use a new cipher, Triton, for the radio traffic of their U-Boats operational in the Atlantic. This will not be broken by the British until almost the end of the year. Since the German codes were first broken regularly, however, the British have improved their radio direction finding techniques and their photo-reconnaissance capabilities. They are still able to read most of the other German naval codes and, from all these sources and the insight their long period of knowledge has given, are still able to make useful guesses about the German moves.

The submarine campaign off the United States continues with great success and is being extended to take in the Caribbean also. One of the few battles about this time is round ON-67 when five U-Boats sink eight ships in three days – with six of the casualties being large tankers. Altogether Axis submarines sink 85 ships of 476,500 tons this month out of a total Allied loss of 154 ships of 679,600 tons (54 ships of 181,200 tons are sunk in the Pacific).

British Air Operations RAF bombers mount various attacks on targets in Germany and France, especially in the middle and at the end of the month. Keil, Mannheim and Cologne are among the targets. (*See* 14 and 22 February for important developments.)

Mediterranean Malta is bombed on many occasions, day and night, throughout the month. The problems of supplying the island and keeping the forces there up to strength are now more difficult now that the airfields of Cyrenaica are in German hands, preventing air cover being given to convoys. Equally without Cyrenaican airfields the RAF finds it more difficult to strike at Rommel's supplies.

1 FEBRUARY 1942
Pacific American naval task forces under Halsey and Fletcher attack air bases in the Marshall and Gilbert Islands. The aircraft carrier USS *Enterprise* is damaged.

Norway, Politics Quisling is appointed to head the Nazi puppet government.

North Africa General Ritchie orders Eighth Army to withdraw to the Gazala line.

3 FEBRUARY 1942
East Indies The Japanese begin major attacks on Java. Surabaya and other Dutch bases are hit. All defending aircraft are destroyed. In New Guinea, Port Moresby is bombarded.

North Africa British forces evacuate Derna.

4 FEBRUARY 1942
East Indies Japanese aircraft repel Dutch and American ships attempting attacks in the Makassar Straits. Two American cruisers are damaged. The Japanese have now completed the capture of Amboina despite brave resistance by the mixed Australian and Dutch garrison.

Malaya Japanese demands for the surrender of Singapore are rejected. British reinforcements continue to arrive despite the desperate situation. Wavell hopes that the island can be held for some time while Allied forces elsewhere in the East Indies are being built up.

6 FEBRUARY 1942
Allied Planning The first meeting of the Combined Chiefs of Staff takes place in Washington. (*See* Arcadia Conference, 22 December 1941.)

Philippines Japanese reinforcements land on Luzon. The fighting on Bataan has been less severe for a few days.

7 FEBRUARY 1942
Germany, Production The German minister of

munitions, Todt, is killed in an air crash. Speer, Hitler's architect, is appointed to replace him. The German war industries have been fairly inefficiently run until Todt's brief appointment when more sensible priorities were established. At this time, when compared with Britain or the USSR, Germany is not well mobilized for war. As yet the German people have had no real cuts in their standard of living when compared with peace-time conditions. This is gradually changing under the impetus of Todt's measures and the effect of the first defeats in the USSR. Speer will prove to be brilliant at continuing and extending the process.

North Africa Rommel's forces stop their advance near Gazala. In a lightning campaign they have recovered almost all of the ground so dearly won by the British at the end of 1941. They have completely disrupted the British 1st Armored Division and severely damaged Eighth Army morale.

Eastern Front The Soviet forces attack Rzhev in the battles west of Moscow.

8 FEBRUARY 1942

Philippines General Homma, commanding Japanese forces on Luzon, discontinues his main attacks and awaits further reinforcements. However, heavy fighting continues on some sectors for several weeks.

Malaya After dark and following a considerable bombardment, Japanese troops of the 5th, 18th and Imperial Guards Divisions make successful landings on Singapore. The landings are made in the northwest of the island in the sector defended by 22nd Australian Brigade. The garrison of the island is about 85,000 strong, including administrative units. The attacking Japanese force is considerably smaller. The guns of the Singapore fortress can only make a small contribution to the defense because their positions and the ammunition supplied are designed with a seaborne attack in mind.

10 FEBRUARY 1942

Malaya The fighting on Singapore Island continues. Owing to a confusion of orders, the Allied forces fall back farther than is necessary and abandon some good defensive positions on the Jurong Line.

Burma Japanese troops begin to cross the Salween near its mouth at Martaban and Pa-an. Reinforcements are ready to follow.

Allied Planning There is the first meeting of the Pacific War Council in London. Representatives of Britain, New Zealand, Australia and Holland are present.

11 FEBRUARY 1942

Malaya A final Allied counterattack on Singapore Island is driven off with heavy losses and the Allied troops begin to pull back to their final perimeter around the town itself.

11–12 FEBRUARY 1942

English Channel The German battlecruisers *Scharnhorst* and *Gneisenau* and the heavy cruiser *Prinz Eugen* run home from Brest up the English Channel. By a combination of luck and slackness British forces only make a few piecemeal attacks. Both battlecruisers are damaged by mines however. The damage to *Scharnhorst* is serious and when *Gneisenau* is in dock to have her slighter hurts repaired she is seriously hit in a bombing raid. The operation is code named Cerberus and Admiral Ciliax is in command. Although it is a notable insult to British naval power, the British strategic position is improved by it since it is easier to guard against any attack from the German ships when they are in German or Norwegian bases.

13 FEBRUARY 1942

Eastern Front The Russian offensives continue in all sectors against increasing German resistance. Despite this Russian spearheads have now reached White Russia.

Germany, Planning Operation Sea Lion, the invasion of Britain, is finally formally cancelled by the German High Command. (Until now it has merely been postponed.)

14 FEBRUARY 1942

British Air Operations The Area Bombing Directive is issued to RAF Bomber Command. The attacks 'should now be focused on the morale of the enemy civil population and, in particular, of the industrial workers.' It is understood that the aiming points for the attacks will be the inflammable residential districts rather than the factories, and that the desired effects will be produced by destroying the workers' houses rather than the means of production.

East Indies Japanese paratroops land at Palembang on Sumatra. Other units of Admiral Ozawa's Western Force are en route to Sumatra by sea.

15 FEBRUARY 1942

Malaya The Allied forces are now confined into a small area around Singapore town. Certain categories of ammunition are in short supply and there is little water because the Japanese hold the reservoir area. The Allied

Above: Yamashita accepts Percival's surrender.

commanders decide to seek terms. General Yamashita accepts General Percival's surrender. The Japanese losses in the whole Malayan campaign have been less than 10,000 men. The British have lost 138,000. Japanese forces have been far better trained and led, and have had the crucial advantages of overwhelming air power and the few tanks present. They have expected to complete the campaign in 100 days; they have taken 70. The Malayan campaign has been the greatest disaster in British military history.

East Indies The Japanese forces attacking Palembang receive reinforcements and compel the garrison to retreat before they have finished destroying the great oil refinery.

Burma Because the Japanese are now over the Salween in force, the outpost units of 17th Indian Division are pulled back west of the Bilin.

16 FEBRUARY 1942
Japan, Politics General Tojo outlines Japanese war aims to the Diet. He speaks of 'a new order of coexistence and coprosperity on ethical principles in Greater East Asia.'

Battle of the Atlantic German U-Boats shell important oil installations at Aruba. Seven tankers are sunk by torpedoes.

16–19 FEBRUARY 1942
Burma There is fighting along the Bilin River as the Japanese continue to attempt to advance.

19 FEBRUARY 1942
United States, Command General Eisenhower is appointed Chief of the War Plans Division of the US Army General Staff.

Vichy, Politics General Gamelin and two former prime ministers of France, Reynaud and Blum are put on trial at Riom by the Vichy authorities, charged with being responsible for the French defeat in 1940. The defendants are largely successful in shifting the blame as it appears from the evidence toward the whole of the military establishment. This is a victory because a large part of the Vichy government is taken from such sections of society. The trial is never concluded.

Britain, Politics Churchill announces changes in his War Cabinet. Sir Stafford Cripps, formerly ambassador in Moscow, replaces Arthur Greenwood and Sir Kingsley Wood.

Australia One hundred and fifty carrierborne aircraft attack Darwin in Northern Australia, damaging the harbor installations and sinking a number of warships. Four carriers from the Pearl Harbor force lead the attack.

East Indies The Japanese invade Bali.

20 FEBRUARY 1942
East Indies The aircraft carrier USS *Lexington*, escorted by cruisers and destroyers, attempts to attack Rabaul but is driven off by Japanese forces. Portugese Timor is invaded by the Japanese.

21 FEBRUARY 1942
Burma The 17th Indian Division begins to fall back to the Sittang through Kyaikto.

Arctic The pocket-battleship *Admiral Scheer* and the cruiser *Prinz Eugen* leave Germany for bases in Norway.

22 FEBRUARY 1942
British Air Operations Air Marshal Harris is appointed to lead RAF Bomber Command. He will become a controversial figure but his early record will be good. He will succeed in reviving Bomber Command morale and developing a policy suited to the limitations of the force. He will be especially good at the public relations side of his job. The bomber offensive will be the only weapon with which Britain can strike directly at Germany until 1944, and it will be important to convince the British people and the leaders of the USSR that as much as possible is being done.

Philippines General MacArthur is ordered to leave the Philippines and establish his headquarters in Australia.

Burma Japanese troops attack the positions of 17th Indian Division around Mokpalin on the River Sittang. There is heavy fighting near the one bridge over the river.

23 FEBRUARY 1942
Burma The only accessible bridge over the Sittang is demolished, leaving a large part of the 17th Indian Division cut off on the east bank. Most of the men manage to escape but all heavy equipment is lost.

CHRONOLOGY

24 FEBRUARY 1942
Wake Island An American task force led by Admiral Halsey in the USS *Enterprise* successfully attacks Wake Island.

Eastern Front The German resistance to Russian attacks grows firmer, but in the northern sector the Russians have surrounded II Corps of the German Sixteenth Army just south of Lake Ilmen in the Demyansk area. Air supply (an average of 270 tons a day) will enable this unit to hold out until relieved in April.

25 FEBRUARY 1942
Burma and East Indies The ABDA Command is dissolved. General Wavell again becomes Commander in Chief India. The Dutch General Ter Poorten takes command in Java.

26 FEBRUARY 1942
Allied Politics Litvinov, speaking in Washington, demands effort from the Allies, saying that, 'only by simultaneous offensive operations on two or more fronts can Hitler's armed forces be disposed of.'

Eastern Front The Soviets inflict heavy casualties on the German Sixteenth Army around Staraya Russa.

Burma The Japanese infiltrate west of the Sittang. They now threaten the Rangoon–Mandalay railroad.

27–29 FEBRUARY 1942
Battle of the Java Sea An Allied squadron, commanded by Admiral Doorman, comprising five cruisers and 11 destroyers of four nationalities, tries to intercept an invasion force bound for Java and, in a series of running battles, is almost totally eliminated. The Japanese, aided by their superior torpedo equipment and night-fighting skills, suffer only slight damage. Their force includes four cruisers and 14 destroyers. Admiral Takagi is in command.

28 FEBRUARY 1942
France British commandos raid the German radar station at Bruneval, taking away equipment for examination.

MARCH 1942
Battle of the Atlantic The U-Boat campaign off the United States is stepped up. Of the 111 operational U-Boats 80 are deployed for the Atlantic. Axis submarines sink 95 ships this month, 35 of them in US or West Indian waters. Of these 35 half are large tankers. Two U-Boats off Freetown sink 11 ships. Toward the end of the month the first submarine tanker or

milch cow leaves Lorient to join the U-Boat fleet. During the next few months there will be two or three of these on station at any time, effectively doubling the radius of the German U-Boats. Total Allied shipping losses are 273 ships of 834,200 tons of which 534,000 tons are sunk in the North Atlantic. In the war against Japan 252,000 are lost. The US Navy is still arguing against British advice and saying that the weak convoys that would be all they would be able to organize would be worse than none. Many of the US forces deployed in the Atlantic before December 1941 are now, of course, in the Pacific, but about 35 British escorts and some Coastal Command aircraft are now operating off the US or in the Caribbean.

British Air Operations There are several important landmarks for Bomber Command this month. The *Gee* navigational aid comes into large-scale service (it has been tested in 1941). The Lancaster bomber is first used on operations in the raid on Lubeck on the 28th, which is itself important as being the first demonstration of Harris' new policy. Lubeck is chosen because it is a medieval town with narrow streets and timber framed houses and will, therefore, burn well. Other RAF targets include Essen, Cologne and Kiel.

War Crimes The large-scale transportation of Jews to the Nazi extermination camps gets fully under way. The five extermination camps, Auschwitz, Chelmno, Treblinka, Sobibor and Belsec, should be distinguished from the 'ordinary' concentration camps. The extermination camps' sole mission is to kill, whereas the concentration camps expect to work their inmates to death amid foul conditions and rations much less than the minimum for survival.

Auschwitz, the largest of the extermination camps, will be able to deal with over 12,000 people in a day. The occupants of the Polish ghettos will form the largest proportion of the camps' victims during the first months – 2,600,000 of Poland's 3,000,000 Jews will be killed during the war. For German occupied territory as a whole at least 5,500,000 will be murdered by the Nazis or their local accomplices.

Mediterranean German air attacks on Malta continue throughout the month, as do British efforts to transport supplies to the island (*see* 6 and 20–23 March).

United States, Home Front The American authorities begin to transport almost 100,000 Japanese-Americans from their homes on the West Coast to internment camps in the midwest. This measure is in fact almost totally unnecessary as the performance of some Japanese-American regiments later in the war, particularly in Italy, shows only too well.

Eastern Front The mud of the spring thaws checks movement all along the front. Both Russians and Germans are becoming too exhausted to make important gains.

1 MARCH 1942

Burma The Chinese Fifth Army is being concentrated around Toungoo, on the Sittang 150 miles from Rangoon. Chennault's 'Flying Tigers,' who have done sterling work in the defense of Rangoon, move to the RAF bomber base at Magwe.

Eastern Front A new Soviet push begins in the Crimea. In a staff analysis General Halder estimates that German losses in the war with the USSR have reached 1,500,000.

East Indies The remainder of Doorman's squadron, retreating from Java, fight actions in the Sunda Strait in which they lose three cruisers and four destroyers. There are almost unopposed Japanese landings on Java at Kragan, Merak and Eretenwetan.

2 MARCH 1942

Philippines Japanese troops land on Mindanao. Targets on Mindanao, Cebu and Negros are also bombarded by Japanese warships.

Burma The Japanese begin to cross the Sittang in force.

East Indies Japanese troops capture Batavia on Java.

3 MARCH 1942

Eastern Front German announcements mention the difficulties of Sixteenth Army which is still partially encircled.

4 MARCH 1942

Central Pacific Halsey's task force attacks Marcus Island.

China General Stilwell establishes US China Headquarters at Chunking.

5 MARCH 1942

British Command General Brooke replaces Admiral Pound as Chairman of the British Chiefs of Staff Committee. Brooke works well with Churchill and his all-round qualities are an improvement on Pound's more strictly maritime viewpoint.

Burma General Alexander arrives in Rangoon to take command and orders counterattacks.

New Guinea Japanese invasion forces leave Rabaul bound for New Guinea.

6 MARCH 1942

Burma Counterattacks fail to relieve Pegu. Alexander confirms the order for the evacuation of Rangoon.

Mediterranean The carrier *Eagle* ferries 18 Spitfires to Malta. Seven Blenheim bombers are also flown in. These Spitfires are the first of Britain's best fighter planes that can be spared for service overseas.

6–12 MARCH 1942

Arctic While the convoy PQ-12 is sailing to the USSR the German battleship *Tirpitz* makes a sortie from Trondheim to try to attack it. The British Home Fleet with the carrier *Victorious* is out also and, although it is given accurate instructions from the Admiralty, there is no contact between the various forces. This is one instance when it has been correct for the Admiralty to 'interfere' in the conduct of operations in the way that will attract criticism concerning the PQ-17 operation.

7 MARCH 1942

East Indies On Java, Japanese troops take Surabaya and Lembang.

New Guinea The Japanese invasion fleet begins landings on New Guinea in the Salamaua area.

Burma Rangoon is evacuated. British troops retiring north from here and Pegu have to fight through road blocks on the way. As Rangoon is the only significant port in Burma, all supplies for the Allies must now come overland from India. Late in the day units of the Japanese 33rd Division occupy Rangoon.

9 MARCH 1942

United States, Command Admiral Harold Stark is appointed to command US naval forces in European waters. He relieves Admiral Ghormley. Admiral King, Commander in Chief of the US Navy, takes over Stark's work as Chief of Naval Operations on 26 March.

East Indies The Japanese army in Java has virtually complete control of the island. The Dutch government has been evacuated and General Ter Poorten has agreed to surrender the 100,000 Allied troops.

10 MARCH 1942

New Guinea Japanese naval units are attacked near Lae by aircraft launched from the carriers USS *Lexington* and *Yorktown*.

11 MARCH 1942

Philippines General MacArthur leaves Luzon with the famous declaration 'I shall return!' On orders from Washington he hands over his command to General Wainwright.

Burma General Stilwell is appointed to command the Chinese Fifth and Sixth Armies (the equivalent of European divisions) presently concentrating around Mandalay and in the Shan States.

Mediterranean The British cruiser *Naiad* is sunk by *U.565* 50 miles north of Sollum.

12 MARCH 1942

Pacific American forces land at Noumea in New Caledonia to garrison the island and build a base. They include the first 'Seabees' to see active service.

The Japanese consolidate their conquests in the Solomon Islands.

East Indies The Dutch forces formally surrender to the Japanese. Units of the Japanese Imperial Guards Division land in northern Sumatra.

14 MARCH 1942

Australia US troops begin to arrive in Australia in large numbers.

15 MARCH 1942

Eastern Front Hitler announces that Russia will be 'annihilatingly defeated' in the coming summer campaign. German casualties since the start of the year have now reached 250,000.

17 MARCH 1942

Allied Command General MacArthur arrives in Australia to take Supreme Command of Allied Forces in the Southwest Pacific.

19 MARCH 1942

Burma General Slim arrives in Burma to take operational command of the British forces now to be organized as I Burma Corps.

20–23 MARCH 1942

Mediterranean There is an important British convoy operation to supply Malta, but because of British losses in late 1941 and the demands of the Far East there is only a relatively small escort. Four merchant ships are in the convoy and the escort, led by Admiral Vian, has five light cruisers and 17 destroyers to face perhaps the whole Italian navy. On the 22nd the Italians send out the battleship *Littorio*, two heavy cruisers, one light cruiser and eight destroyers. They attack the convoy during the afternoon but, despite their very superior strength (one of the British cruisers and several of the destroyers must stay as close escort and AA defense for the

convoy), they are beaten off in an action involving smoke screens and torpedo attacks. Because of the German and Italian air attacks only 5000 tons of cargo is landed in Malta from the three ships that reach port.

21 MARCH 1942

Eastern Front The units of the German Sixteenth Army surrounded at Demyansk begin attempts to break out.

24 MARCH 1942

Burma General Alexander and Chiang Kaishek meet to discuss plans for the cooperation of Chinese and British forces. Japanese troops attacking near Toungoo achieve considerable success.

Philippines Japanese artillery and aircraft again attack American positions on Bataan and Corregidor.

27 MARCH 1942

Burma RAF aircraft and the remainder of the volunteer American squadrons are withdrawn from Burma. Japanese attacks on the Chinese 200th Division at Toungoo continue.

British Command Admiral Somerville takes command of the British Far East Fleet based in Ceylon.

Australia, Command General Blamey arrives back in Australia with some of the troops from North Africa. He is appointed to command Allied land forces in Australia.

28 MARCH 1942

France British commandos raid St Nazaire. At considerable cost the dock gates are badly damaged. The St Nazaire dock is the only one in Western France capable of accommodating the *Tirpitz*.

29 MARCH 1942

British Air Operations An unusually successful raid on Lubeck causes Hitler to order reprisals. These 'Baedeker Raids' begin in April.

Burma At the request of General Stilwell, British forces attack Boungde to relieve pressure on the Chinese at Toungoo.

Arctic A British convoy for Murmansk is engaged unsuccessfully by German surface forces. The *Tirpitz* and the other heavy units of the German fleet are now based in Norway posing a further threat to convoys.

30 MARCH 1942

Pacific, Command The Joint Chiefs of Staff divide the Pacific into two commands. Admiral

Nimitz is to control the Pacific Ocean Zone and General MacArthur the Southwest Pacific (including Australia, New Guinea, the Bismarcks and the Solomons). This division presages the later controversy between the two as to how the reconquest should be attempted.

31 MARCH 1942

Indian Ocean Admiral Somerville's Eastern Fleet sails from Ceylon to avoid the coming attack by the main Japanese carrier forces of which intelligence has been received. Somerville is well aware that the aircraft from his three carriers are not a match for the Japanese in an open fight. However, they have been well trained in night operations (at this stage of the war neither Japanese nor Americans are similarly trained) and have radar mounted in planes to assist target acquisition. Somerville therefore plans to avoid action by day and search for the Japanese each night.

Burma Chinese forces withdraw from Toungoo.

APRIL 1942

Battle of the Atlantic The U-Boat campaign off America continues to score many important successes. The loss of tankers is especially worrying. On 1 April a partial convoy system off the US East Coast is begun. The number of Halifax–UK convoys sailing has to be reduced so that more British and Canadian escorts can be sent to join the US forces. Axis submarines sink 74 ships during the month out of a total Allied loss of 132 ships of 674,500 tons. Only seven ships are sunk in the Pacific while in the Indian Ocean 150,000 tons is lost largely because of the foray early in the month by the Japanese carrier force.

Eastern Front In the course of the month the German forces receive massive help from their allies. Italy, Rumania, Hungary, Slovakia and Spain all send units and in all 51 divisions are added to the German Order of Battle.

British Air Operations RAF Bomber Command attacks increase in intensity this month. The range of targets includes industrial areas in Germany and France and several of the Atlantic ports in France and Norway. Cologne, Hamburg and Rostock are all heavily hit. There are also offensive fighter sweeps over occupied France practically every day. Like Lubeck in the attack during March, Rostock has been chosen for its inflammable nature and its easy-to-find position on the Baltic. It is an important pointer for the future that, although attacked four times this month, industry in Rostock is soon back at full production.

Mediterranean Air attacks, despite RAF retaliation against Sicilian airfields, make Malta's situation still more desperate. Toward the end of the month British submarines are forced to abandon their base at Malta. One destroyer is lost in the harbor and it is virtually closed because of the lack of minesweepers and the damage to the dockyard. During the month the RAF force in Malta loses 126 planes on the ground and 20 more in the air. Very few are left. The converse of Malta's weakness is that Rommel loses only one percent of the supplies shipped to Africa by the Axis. He receives 150,000 tons.

1 APRIL 1942

Philippines The Japanese resume major attacks on Bataan. The American and Filipino forces have 24,000 men sick because of short (one-quarter) rations and tropical diseases.

Mediterranean, British Command The cruiser *Bande Nere* is sunk by the submarine *Urge* north of Sicily.

Admiral Cunningham leaves the command of the British Mediterranean Fleet to serve on the Combined Chiefs of Staff Committee in Washington.

Burma The Chinese troops near Toungoo are forced to continue their retreat. The British at Prome are also heavily attacked.

New Guinea There are Japanese landings on New Guinea at Sorong and Hollandia. As yet there is almost no opposition to the Japanese forces on New Guinea which continue their buildup for about three weeks.

2 APRIL 1942

Burma The British Burma Corps retreats from Prome to avoid being surrounded.

3 APRIL 1942

Burma Mandalay is heavily bombed. British forces continue to withdraw up the Irrawaddy Valley.

Philippines After a lull on the 2nd, the final Japanese assault on Bataan begins. There is a long bombardment before the attack goes in and the exhausted defenders are thrown back.

4 APRIL 1942

Indian Ocean A Catalina seaplane from Ceylon sights the Japanese fleet of Admiral Kondo. As well as four battleships of the *Kongo* Class, the Japanese fleet includes their main carrier forces with Admiral Nagumo leading *Akagi*, *Soryu*, *Hiryu*, *Shokaku* and *Zuikaku*. Somerville's intelligence predicted that the Japanese attack would be on 1st or 2nd and after being ready then, he has now retired to Addu Attoll to replenish. HMS *Hermes*, *Cornwall* and *Dorsetshire* have been sent on other missions. The Japanese attack cannot now be parried, so the order is given for shipping to disperse from Colombo.

5 APRIL 1942
Indian Ocean Believing that the British will still be in port, the Japanese carriers launch 130 planes against Colombo. A small British air strike against the carriers is completely unsuccessful. Later Japanese scout planes sight the heavy cruisers HMS *Dorsetshire* and HMS *Cornwall*. New strikes are mounted by the Japanese which find and sink these ships. The Japanese squadron continues its hunt for the main British force without success.
Philippines The Japanese attacks on Bataan continue. Mount Samat is taken after heavy fighting in which the US 21st Division loses heavily. Japanese detachments leave Luzon bound for Cebu Island.
War at Sea US Task Force 39 arrives in Scapa Flow with the aircraft carrier USS *Wasp* and the battleship USS *Washington*. These forces are to aid the British Home and Gibraltar squadrons while Operation Ironclad is being carried out against Madagascar.

6 APRIL 1942
Indian Ocean A Japanese force with cruisers and a small carrier attacks shipping in the Bay of Bengal causing heavy damage. The 83,000 tons of shipping sunk are largely the vessels dispersed from Colombo on the 4th. The attacks are extremely efficiently carried out.
Solomons The Japanese land at Bougainville.
Burma Chiang Kai-shek visits the Chinese Divisions and gives orders for the defense of positions around Pyinmana in the Sittang Valley.

7 APRIL 1942
Burma The Japanese 18th Infantry Division arrives in Rangoon by sea from Singapore.
Philippines The Japanese continue to make gains, particularly in the eastern sector of Bataan. The American and Filipino forces are now behind a line running inland from Limao. Roosevelt authorizes the commanders to take any necessary steps. Wainwright withdraws as much of his force as possible to the fortress island of Corregidor in Manila Bay.

8 APRIL 1942
Mediterranean It is a particularly bad day for

Malta. The worst air attacks of the war take place.
Philippines The American resistance on Bataan collapses under the fierce Japanese attacks. The destruction of equipment is ordered as a preparation for surrender.

9 APRIL 1942
Indian Ocean Trincomalee is attacked by planes from Nagumo's carriers with damage being inflicted. The small British carrier HMS *Hermes* is attacked and sunk.

In their operations in the Indian Ocean the Japanese forces have sunk 112,000 tons of merchant shipping along with one carrier, two cruisers and four smaller RN ships. This is the high-water mark of the Japanese carrier forces' success. Their limitations are now beginning to appear. It is notable that in the attacks on Colombo and Trincomalee, the efficiency of the Japanese strike has been sharply reduced by the small defense forces (even though these have been quickly overcome) when compared with the carriers' early successes.
Philippines General King unconditionally surrenders US forces on Luzon. Seventy-five thousand men are captured, 12,000 of them American. The prisoners are marched to San Fernando, 100 miles away, many thousands dying because of ill-treatment on the way.

Fighting continues in isolated areas of Luzon and the other islands with some US and Filipino units operating in a guerrilla role. General Wainwright holds out on Corregidor.
Burma The British troops take positions between Taungdwingyi and Minhla on the Irrawaddy. Both the Allies and the Japanese are preparing offensives, but the Japanese are ready

Above: Japanese tanks advance in Burma.

first because they have been more quickly reinforced.

Eastern Front German attempts to relieve the units of Sixteenth Army trapped around Demyansk make some progress. In the Crimea renewed Russian attacks achieve little.

10 APRIL 1942

Indian Ocean The British Far East Fleet is withdrawn from bases in Ceylon to the Persian Gulf because of the superior Japanese forces which are in fact mostly returning to the Pacific.

Philippines The Japanese land on Cebu with about 12,000 men. The small American forces retire inland.

British Air Operations The RAF drops its first two-ton bombs over Essen.

11 APRIL 1942

Burma The new Japanese offensive begins with attacks on the British positions.

Eastern Front Russian landings in the Crimea at Eupatoriya are strongly held by the German Eleventh Army.

12 APRIL 1942

Burma Despite receiving help from 38th Chinese Division, the British positions on the Irrawaddy are threatened by the Japanese capture of Migyaungye.

13 APRIL 1942

British Command Rear Admiral Lord Mountbatten, despite his junior rank, has been appointed Chief of Combined Operations with a seat on the British Chiefs of Staff Committee. This appointment, only now announced, has been effective since 18 March.

Burma The Japanese achieve a breakthrough in the British defenses. Allied forces take new positions at Magwe. The Chinese Sixth Army, previously positioned in the Shan States, is ordered to Mandalay.

14 APRIL 1942

Battle of the Atlantic The destroyer *Roper* sinks *U.85*. This is the first submarine kill by an American ship.

Vichy, Politics Laval forms a new government in Vichy. Pétain is to remain as head of state.

Burma The demolition of oil installations around Yenangyaung is begun in order to deny them to the Japanese.

Allied Planning The British government and its military advisers provisionally accept the American plan 'Bolero' for the American build-up in Britain in preparation for a second front.

15 APRIL 1942

Burma Following their breakthrough on the 13th the Japanese continue to drive northward, isolating one of Slim's divisions.

16 APRIL 1942

Philippines With resistance on Cebu now being overcome, the Japanese also land 4000 troops on Panay.

Malta King George VI awards Malta the George Cross, for the collective heroism of the Maltese people in the face of the Axis air attacks.

17 APRIL 1942

Burma Unsuccessful attempts are made to relieve the 1st Burma Division trapped around Magwe. Further north the Japanese hold the main road in the Irrawaddy Valley at Yenang-yaung. The Chinese forces in the Sittang Valley and at Mauchi come under heavy pressure.

18 APRIL 1942

Eastern Front Von Leeb is removed from command of Army Group North attacking Leningrad.

Burma The Chinese 55th Division, retreating from Mauchi, is effectively destroyed by the Japanese 56th Division. This leaves the road to Lashio undefended for the moment. Lashio is the terminus of the Burma Road. In the Sittang Valley the Chinese are forced to withdraw.

Pacific Bombers from the USS *Hornet* raid targets in Japan. Under the command of Colonel Doolittle, 16 B-25 Mitchell bombers take off from the *Hornet* about 650 miles from Japan, raid Tokyo and other targets and fly on to China. Technically the raid is extremely difficult. The bombers fly practically unarmed because of the need to lighten them to give extra range and the ability to take off from a carrier deck. The USS *Enterprise* accompanies the *Hornet* to give fighter cover. This is not in fact needed because, although the carriers are sighted, the Japanese wait for them to come within the range of lighter bombers before launching their attack. Little material damage is done, but the effect on the morale of both sides is enormous. The Japanese immediately begin to bring more fighter forces home to strengthen their defenses. The attack contributes most importantly of all to the Japanese decision to revise their strategy and expand their perimeter. The direct results of this decision will be the Battles of the Coral Sea and Midway.

20 APRIL 1942

Mediterranean The USS *Wasp*, escorted by

HMS *Renown*, two cruisers and six destroyers, ferries 47 Spitfire fighters to Malta. Unfortunately of the 46 which arrive, 30 are destroyed immediately after landing.
Burma British and Chinese forces retreat in both the Sittang and Irrawaddy Valleys.

21 APRIL 1942

Eastern Front The German pocket at Demyansk is relieved after being cut off from all apart from air support for two and a half months. This success for air supply will probably contribute to Hitler's decision to attempt it at Stalingrad at the end of the year.
France, Politics General Giraud reaches Switzerland after escaping from German captivity. He will return to the unoccupied part of France.
Burma There is heavy fighting near Taunggyi in which the Chinese Sixth Army is engaged.

22 APRIL 1942

Burma British forces including the 7th Armored Brigade take up positions around Meiktila. Chinese troops of 200th Division are sent from there to bolster the position at Taunggyi, but inattention to General Stilwell's orders by another formation makes this position dangerous.

23 APRIL 1942

Burma The remains of Chinese Sixth Army begins to retreat from Taunggyi toward Yunnan Province. The Allied forces in the Sittang and Irrawaddy Valleys are forced to retreat because the Japanese 56th Division has forged on from Taunggyi toward Lashio, threatening the left flank of the Allied Armies.

24 APRIL 1942

German Air Operations Exeter is bombed by the Luftwaffe in the first of the 'Baedeker Raids,' so called because they are aimed at historic towns selected from the Baedeker Guide book in retaliation for the RAF raid on Lubeck on 28 March.

25 APRIL 1942

Burma Although the Japanese fail to hold Taunggyi which is now defended by Chinese Fifth Army, they continue to move toward Lashio. To the west, General Alexander orders that the forces around Meiktila should withdraw north of the Irrawaddy.
German Air Operations The Germans bomb Bath. In the next few days Norwich, York, Hull and Exeter are all hit.

26 APRIL 1942

Philippines Fighting continues on Mindanao where Filipino forces resist the Japanese invaders, who now receive further reinforcements.
Germany, Politics Hitler, speaking in the Reichstag, foretells major victories for Germany in the summer and calls for supreme effort. His absolute power is extended and confirmed.

28 APRIL 1942

Burma The Chinese 28th Division, now moving from Mandalay, is ordered to defend Lashio.

29 APRIL 1942

New Guinea Japanese preparations are now well in hand for an amphibious attack on Port Moresby (Operation Mo).
Philippines The Japanese forces continue to bombard Corregidor and on Mindanao, with reinforced strength and air support, they push back the defenders.
Burma The Japanese enter Lashio. China is now cut off by land and all supplies from the Allies must go by air.

General Alexander decides to withdraw to new positions in the Chindwin and Irrawaddy Valleys.

30 APRIL 1942

Southwest Pacific The carriers *Shokaku, Zuikaku* and *Shoho* sail from Truk for the Coral Sea to take part in Operation Mo.
Burma After withdrawing north of the Irrawaddy, British forces destroy the bridge at Ava.

MAY 1942

Battle of the Atlantic The efforts of the *milch cows* mean that there is the large number of between 16 and 18 U-Boats off the US coast during the month. Their only easy successes are off Florida, and they are gradually moving south to the Caribbean and the Gulf of Mexico where there are as yet no convoys. British and Canadian ships are being moved to strengthen the US forces in this area however. From the middle of the month a fairly complete convoy system covers all the US coast north of Florida. There is also one pack operation against ONS-92 on the main convoy routes. Axis submarines sink 125 ships of 607,200 tons this month out of a total of 705,000 tons.
British Air Operations RAF targets this month include Stuttgart and Mannheim as well as day and night attacks on strategic installations in France. All these operations are overshadowed by the raid on Cologne on the night of the 30/31st.

Mediterranean Air attacks on Malta are again severe, but the defending forces are now being strengthened. The RAF attacks airfields in Sicily at Catania and Augusta on several occasions.

1 MAY 1942

Philippines More Japanese forces have landed on Mindanao and fighting is therefore heavy. Corregidor is bombed and shelled.
Burma Mandalay falls to the Japanese.

2 MAY 1942

Solomons The Australian garrison of Tulagi, a small island near Guadalcanal, is evacuated.
Battle of the Coral Sea The buildup to the Coral Sea Battle begins. The principal aim of the Japanese plans is the capture of Port Moresby. The Japanese forces are divided into five groups to accomplish this and other subsidiary tasks. These forces include the large carriers *Zuikaku* and *Shokaku* under the command of Admiral Takagi which are to provide overall cover. A second group with the small carrier *Shoho* and four heavy cruisers, Admiral Goto, is to help first with close support for the landings on Tulagi (to establish a seaplane base) and then with the main operations. Admiral Inouye commanding at Rabaul, from where the main invasion force is to set out, is in command.

Largely because of American ability to read the Japanese codes, Admiral Nimitz is able to order a concentration of Allied task forces to oppose the Japanese who in turn believe that there can be at most one enemy carrier in the area. The withdrawal from Tulagi already mentioned is designed to encourage the Japanese attacks by feigning weakness. The Allied ships come from three task forces. Task Force 17 (Admiral Fletcher) with the carrier USS *Yorktown*, Task Force 11 (Admiral Fitch) with the carrier USS *Lexington* and Task Force 44 (Admiral Crace) with Australian and American cruisers. At first only Task Force 17 is in operation.
Philippines Despite the Japanese buildup on Mindanao, they can only make slow progress with their attacks.
Arctic The cruiser HMS *Edinburgh*, already damaged by *U.456*, is sunk by destroyers in the Barents Sea while escorting the Arctic convoy QP-11.

3 MAY 1942

Solomons The Japanese land at Tulagi.
Philippines There are further Japanese landings on Mindanao which cannot be beaten off.

4 MAY 1942

Battle of the Coral Sea Aircraft from the *Yorktown*, 100 miles south of Guadalcanal, attack the Japanese forces off Tulagi. The *Yorktown* then returns south to join the rest of the Allied forces.
Philippines On Mindanao there is reduced activity, but in Manila Bay the bombardment of Corregidor becomes most intense.
Burma Akyab is evacuated by the British. Chinese forces are defeated at Wanting on the Burma Road and at Bhamo on the Irrawaddy.

5 MAY 1942

Battle of the Coral Sea Takagi's carriers enter the Coral Sea from the west. Fletcher is refuelling but fortunately for him the Japanese make no contact.
Madagascar British forces land near Diego Suarez supported by a battleship and two carriers. The US Government, previously sensitive to Vichy opinion, openly backs the British action as necessary to secure the island against Axis, 'especially Japanese' use.
Philippines Just before midnight the Japanese land on Corregidor. Most of the gun emplacements on the island have been put out of action by the Japanese bombardment. Nonetheless the Japanese lose heavily to the defensive fire before they consolidate their landing.
Burma General Stilwell, in Burma with his Chinese troops, learns of the true extent of the Japanese advance further north on the Irrawaddy and decides that his forces must also retire toward India, not China. Japanese forces have in fact entered China via the Burma Road.
Japan, Planning Imperial Headquarters orders the navy to prepare for an attack and landing on Midway Island.

6 MAY 1942

Philippines General Wainwright on Corregidor surrenders with 15,000 American and Filipino troops. On Mindanao there are further Japanese attacks.

7 MAY 1942

Battle of the Coral Sea Fletcher sends Task Force 44 to attack the Japanese transports bound for Port Moresby. The Japanese sight these ships and unsuccessfully launch heavy attacks on them with land-based aircraft. The Japanese also sight the American tanker the *Neosho* and the destroyer USS *Sims*. They are attacked and sunk but the *Neosho* has been mistaken for a carrier. The Americans also record a success, locating Goto's covering force and sinking the small carrier *Shoho*. An attempt by Takagi late in the day to locate and attack the American carriers is a failure, with 21 aircraft lost for no result (a small group are sufficiently confused to attempt to land on the *Yorktown*). The Japanese transports turn back to Rabaul to await the outcome of the carrier action.

Philippines General Wainwright, in Japanese custody, broadcasts from Luzon to announce the surrender of Corregidor and invites the remaining US forces in the Philippines to do likewise. Despite the US losses the campaign has not been an unqualified failure. General Homma was initially allocated 50 days to complete the campaign, but his crack troops have in fact been campaigning now for five months when they might have been employed elsewhere. One feature of the struggle has been the loyalty of the Filipinos. This has been contrary to Japanese expectations and contrasts significantly with some of the British Burmese Regiments.

Madagascar Vichy commanders at Diego Suarez surrender to Admiral Syfret and General Sturges.

8 MAY 1942

Battle of the Coral Sea Reconnaissance aircraft from each fleet sight their enemy virtually simultaneously and all the carriers dispatch strikes. The *Lexington* is badly hit and abandoned (she is later finished off by an American destroyer) and the *Yorktown* is damaged. The *Shokaku* is seriously hurt. The Japanese losses in aircraft have been especially severe and with them have gone irreplaceable, highly trained pilots. The Japanese are forced to abandon their attack on Port Moresby and this, the first real check to the Japanese advance means that the action can be justly described as a strategic victory for the Americans. This is the first major naval battle fought without visual contact between the main bodies of opposing forces.

Eastern Front The first real German attacks of the year begin slowly with an offensive by 22nd Panzer Division of Eleventh Army in the Crimea aimed at clearing the Kerch Peninsula.

9 MAY 1942

Mediterranean Sixty-four British Spitfires are ferried to Malta by forces including USS *Wasp* and HMS *Eagle*. Unlike on 20 April adequate arrangements have been made to have them quickly and safely refuelled and rearmed so that they are not immediately neutralized. *Wasp* returns to the US after this operation.

Philippines The Japanese forces on Mindanao press home their attacks near Dalirig, practically finishing the defenders' resistance.

10 MAY 1942

Philippines General Sharp, commanding the remaining American forces, gives the order to surrender. A few small groups keep fighting for a few weeks.

11 MAY 1942

Burma Part of the retreating British forces fight a sharp action at Kalewa before continuing on to the Imphal area.

Canada, Politics Following a referendum on 27 April the Canadian Parliament passes legislation to introduce full conscription.

Mediterranean The British destroyers HMS *Lively*, *Kipling* and *Jackal* are sunk by German aircraft from a specially trained force based on Crete.

12 MAY 1942

Eastern Front Russian attacks near Kharkov

Above: The crew of the Lexington *abandon ship during the Battle of the Coral Sea.*

begin. This offensive is a renewal of the attempts made in January to trap German forces against the Sea of Azov.

13 MAY 1942
Burma Japanese troops, pursuing the Chinese Sixth Army, cross the Salween on the way to Kengtung.
Eastern Front Russian troops begin to withdraw from Kerch in the face of German attacks. About 80,000 manage to get away.

14 MAY 1942
Midway The first indications of the coming Japanese attack reach the American code breakers.

15 MAY 1942
Burma The first British forces reach India in the retreat from Burma. The British casualties from the campaign have been about 30,000 from a force of 45,000. Many of these 'casualties' are Burmese deserters. The Chinese losses cannot be computed, but must have been enormous. There were about 95,000 Chinese engaged and only one formation, 38th Division, remains as a viable fighting unit. The Japanese losses of less than 8000 reflect their superior training, tactics, equipment and air power. With the monsoon season beginning the Japanese can be well satisfied with having so rapidly overrun Burma and with cutting China off from surface communication.
Arctic The cruiser HMS *Trinidad* is sunk by German bombers while escorting an Arctic convoy.
New Guinea Australian reinforcements are dispatched to Port Moresby.
Eastern Front Troops from Manstein's Eleventh Army capture Kerch. The Russians lose 150,000 men, including many taken prisoner.
United States, Home Front Gasoline rationing begins in 17 states. The weekly ration is three gallons for nonessential vehicles.

18 MAY 1942
Mediterranean The carriers HMS *Argus* and *Eagle* of Force H ferry 17 Spitfires to Malta. Admiral Harwood is appointed to command the British Mediterranean Fleet.

19 MAY 1942
Eastern Front After strongly resisting the Russian attacks for several days, the Germans mount a major counterattack near Kharkov, in the Ukraine.

23 MAY 1942
Eastern Front The German Sixth Army from the north and Group Kleist (Seventeenth Army and First Panzer Army) work to encircle elements of the Russian Sixth and Fifty-seventh Armies west of the Donets.

25 MAY 1942
Midway Two light carriers and two cruisers leave port in Hokkaido to carry out diversionary raids in the Aleutian Islands. US forces are also on the move with submarines leaving Hawaii for patrol positions related to the Midway operation.
Burma Part of the Chinese 38th Division manage to reach India.

26 MAY 1942
North Africa Rommel begins a new offensive with holding attacks on the Gazala Line made by the Italian infantry. The British forces have extensively fortified this position in front, leaving their armor free to attack outflanking moves such as those now being attempted. Rommel sends all his armor, both Italian and German, in a wide right hook south of Bir Hacheim. The Italian Trieste Division gets lost and blunders into 150th Brigade between Trigh Capuzzo and Trigh el Abd.
The balance of forces is very much in the Allies' favor. The Germans and the Italians have respectively 400 and 230 tanks but are very short of infantry, especially German infantry. The British have about 850 tanks operational and 150 in reserve. About a quarter of these are the new American Grant type which at last gives the British tanks a weapon which can fire a high-explosive shell against antitank gun positions. The British dispositions are faulty, however, with the armor too widely dispersed.
Midway Admiral Nagumo's 1st Carrier Fleet leaves the Inland Sea. He has the carriers *Akagi*, *Kaga*, *Soryu* and *Hiryu*, with two battleships, cruisers and destroyers as escort. The US Task Force 16, based around the *Enterprise* and *Hornet*, returns to Pearl Harbor from the South Pacific where the Japanese believe it still to be.

27 MAY 1942
Midway The Midway Invasion Fleet puts to sea from Saipan and Guam with transports carrying 5000 men escorted by cruisers and destroyers. The invasion force for the Aleutians also sails in two groups from Ominato. USS *Yorktown* arrives in Pearl Harbor and repairs begin immediately.
Czechoslovakia, Resistance Resistance fighters

attempt to assassinate Reichsprotektor Heydrich in Prague. He dies of his wounds on 4 June.

North Africa Rommel's armor turns north and rapidly defeats 3rd Indian and 7th Motorized Brigade. In various engagements with British armor both sides lose heavily but the British are better able to absorb such losses. Ariete are meant to eliminate the Free French at Bir Hacheim but fail to do so and 90th Light swing furthest to the east in a diversionary role.

28 MAY 1942

North Africa The Afrika Korps is in trouble. Some of Rommel's panzers halt, out of gasoline, on the Rigel Ridge but some, although short of supplies, continue to attack toward Acroma. There is more fighting with British armor especially near Bir el Harmat.

Midway The Japanese continue their preparations. The remainder of the Japanese forces set out. Admiral Yamamoto is in supreme command. Under his direct control he has seven battleships, one small carrier, cruisers and destroyers. Admiral Kondo's Second Fleet consists of two battleships, one light carrier and two seaplane carriers with escorts. Admiral Kakuta's force (see 25 May) has two light carriers and their escorts. The Japanese plan is complex. Kakuta is to cover landings on the Aleutians before the main operation begins in order to make sure that there are no American forces near Midway. Even without this diversion the main forces which are to attack and capture Midway are expected to achieve complete surprise and finish the conquest before any assistance can come up. Yamamoto believes that once Midway is taken, the American Fleet will come in force to dispute the capture. They can then be beaten before new American production swamps the Japanese. The plan is therefore for Nagumo's carriers to pound the Midway defenses and then await the American Fleet. Kondo is to give close support to the landings and Yamamoto's battleships are to be disposed in general reserve.

The Americans make preparations. Task Force 16 sails from Oahu with the carriers *Enterprise* and *Hornet* with escorts. Fletcher's Task Force 17 follows later with repairs to *Yorktown* completed miraculously quickly.

29 MAY 1942

Eastern Front The Germans complete their encircling maneuver west of the Donets. The Russians have lost 250,000 men. They have badly underestimated the German strength and preparedness. In fact the Germans had intended in any event to pinch out the Russian salient and the Russian attacks between 12 and 19 May only made this operation more worthwhile.

North Africa There is heavy fighting around the 'Knightsbridge' road junction, but the British fail to develop a coordinated attack and the German antitank guns are as usual most effective. The Italian Trieste Division which had blundered into 150th Brigade on the 26th has now managed to clear a path through their position. This path is to be a lifeline for the Afrika Korps.

30 MAY 1942

North Africa Rommel pulls all his tanks back into the 'Cauldron' – a tight defensive semicircle backing on to the minefields and, while holding the main British attacks, works to eliminate 150th Brigade and free his supply lines.

Midway Four Japanese submarines arrive to patrol off Pearl Harbor but too late to intercept the American carriers. Two more carry supplies to the French Frigate Shoals to help set up a seaplane base to supplement the Japanese reconnaissance but they find the Americans there first.

30–31 MAY 1942

British Air Operations Bomber Command sends more than 1000 bombers to raid Cologne. This enormous effort has only been made possible by scraping together every plane from operational squadrons and training units. The planes from the training units are flown by pupils and instructors. The raid is a considerable military and propaganda success. Only 40 of the 1046 bombers are lost and 45,000 people are made homeless in Cologne.

31 MAY 1942

Midway In a desperate attempt to reinforce the Pacific Fleet the battleships *Colorado* and *Maryland* sail from San Francisco.

31 MAY–1 JUNE 1942

North Africa The Afrika Korps overruns 150th Brigade and frees its supply route.

JUNE 1942

Battle of the Atlantic Throughout the month there are about a dozen U-Boats in the Caribbean and some more in waters off Brazil. Doenitz is hindered in his task by orders from Hitler to watch for an Allied move to take bases in the Atlantic islands. On the British side important developments include the entry into service of some aircraft fitted with Leigh lights for work in the Bay of Biscay. Some convoy escorts are now being refuelled at sea which eases routing problems since one of the previous limitations has been the restricted range of the escorts. The total Allied loss is 173 ships of 834,200 tons of which submarines sink 144 ships of 700,200 tons.

British Air Operations There are two RAF 1000 bomber raids this month on Essen and Bremen. Other targets include Emden, Osnabruck, St Nazaire, Le Havre and Dieppe. Bomber Command drops 6950 tons of bombs, the largest total achieved until February 1943, flying 5000 sorties and losing 240 aircraft.

This level of losses is about the average for the rest of this year. With each crew doing a tour of 30 operations and a rate of loss of about one in 20, the prospects for those involved are clearly not good. The normal front-line strength of the Command is about 420 aircraft, half of them Wellingtons and less than 100 Halifaxes and Lancasters. The numerical strength will remain similar for the rest of the year but quality will improve.

North Africa The British Intelligence Service contrives, late in the month, to break the 'Black Code' used by the American military attache in Cairo. The code is therefore correctly judged to be insecure (*see* September 1941) and is changed, cutting off a major source of intelligence for Rommel.

Mediterranean RAF bombers attack many targets in Italy as well as enemy ground forces in Egypt and Libya. Oil installations at Ploësti are raided by US Liberators on 12 June.

Yugoslavia, Resistance There is a third period of German anti-Partisan operations in Montenegro throughout the month.

1 JUNE 1942

Midway The USS *Saratoga* sails from San Diego after repairing the torpedo damage caused on 11 January, but is too late to take part in the battle. Various groups of US submarines, 25 in all, are in position in the waters round Midway.

1–2 JUNE 1942

Western Europe Essen is raided by 1036 RAF bombers. Thirty-five fail to return. The raid is not very effective.

2 JUNE 1942

North Africa Rommel sends 90th Light and the Trieste Division south to take Bir Hacheim and free his flank. The French resistance there is extremely stubborn and even when 15th Panzer

and Rommel's heavy artillery come up they still hold out.

Eastern Front German forces renew the bombardment of Sevastopol. Among their 1300 artillery weapons are the two 60cm 'Karl' mortars and the even more enormous 80cm 'Dora' gun. They are also supported by the Fliegerkorps VII.

Midway The US carrier groups from Pearl Harbor join forces northeast of Midway. Altogether the three carriers have about 250 aircraft, approximately the same as the Japanese main force.

Diplomatic Affairs Chinese Foreign Minister Soong and Cordell Hull sign a Lend-Lease agreement.

Aleutians Kakuta's light carriers attack Dutch Harbor, but with their knowledge of Japanese intentions against Midway, the Americans are not of course distracted.

3 JUNE 1942

Midway The Midway Invasion Group and their heavy supports (Admiral Kondo) are found by air reconnaissance from Midway and are unsuccessfully attacked by a group of Flying Fortresses from the island.

Malta Another batch of 31 Spitfires is flown from HMS *Eagle* to Malta; 27 arrive safely.

4 JUNE 1942

Midway Believing that the Americans will not yet have left Hawaii, 14 Japanese submarines patrol between Midway and Hawaii. The Japanese operations around Midway begin according to plan with 108 aircraft from the carrier force being sent to attack the island. The American forces on the island detect the strike on the way in and send off one of their own. The Japanese massacre the defending fighters but in their commander's view, fail to inflict sufficient damage on the island. He signals for a second strike to be prepared. The mixed bag of aircraft attacking the Japanese carriers are also roughly handled, losing 17 of 52 and scoring no hits.

The US carriers begin searching for Nagumo at dawn and the first strikes are launched around 0800. At 0700 the Japanese begin to rearm their reserve planes for a second attack on Midway but, reports of the American Fleet, vague at first, begin to arrive during the next hour and a quarter. When the presence of an enemy carrier is finally confirmed, Nagumo is presented with a terrible problem. His decks are cluttered with aircraft, torpedoes and bombs, his defending fighters need fuel, having just finished repelling the attack from Midway, and his first strike force is shortly due to return. He decides to recover all his aircraft first and then send a coordinated strike against the American ships.

At about 0930, the first American carrier planes come into action. The American strike is badly coordinated and at this stage only the 41 torpedo bombers attack. Thirty-five are shot down and no hits achieved. They have managed, however, to lure almost all the Japanese Zeros down to low level and the tight cruising formation of the Japanese ships has been disrupted, weakening their AA defense. Just before 1030, when the Japanese have at last organized their strike, the American dive-bombers arrive, and within five minutes *Akagi*, *Kaga* and *Soryu*, their decks packed with aircraft ready to take off, have all been fatally hit. *Hiryu* is at this stage undamaged and launches strikes which find and critically damage the *Yorktown*. Late in the afternoon planes from *Enterprise* and *Hornet* inflict similar damage on the *Hiryu*. All four Japanese carriers sink or are scuttled within the next 24 hours.

5 JUNE 1942

North Africa The British, having lost the best opportunity, mount attacks on 'The Cauldron.' One armored brigade, 32nd Army Tank Brigade, blunders into a minefield and loses 60 out of 70 of its tanks and another, 22nd Armored Brigade, loses touch with the infantry and artillery which it should be supporting. Over the next few days all these units are defeated in detail. The tank forces available to the two armies are now about equal in numbers but in quality the Germans are far ahead.

Above: Damage on the Yorktown *at Midway.*

World Affairs The United States declares war on Bulgaria, Hungary and Rumania.

5–7 JUNE 1942

Midway At first Yamamoto thinks of closing in to try and fight a surface action but abandons the idea and retreats on 6 June. *Yorktown* is sunk by a Japanese submarine on 7 June. Midway ranks as one of the most decisive victories of the war. With the lost Japanese carriers have gone many irreplaceable pilots. The only large carriers the Japanese have left are *Shokaku* and *Zuikaku* which are still refitting after the Coral Sea Battle. The American success is perhaps the clearest example of the whole war of a victory based on superior intelligence. The urgency with which the carriers were rushed from the Coral Sea and repaired and replenished at Pearl Harbor was based entirely on the code-breaking information. The Japanese, by contrast, produced an overelaborate plan with their forces wastefully dispersed. Their four 'light' carriers, for example, could carry up to 140 aircraft and the survivors from the air groups of *Shokaku* and *Zuikaku* could have brought the main force up to full strength – there was room for 50 more planes. The Japanese scouting was marred by ill-luck and poor reporting and the timing of the American attacks in the morning was most fortunate especially when they had not been well organized.

After Midway the American strategic position and the strength and quality of their forces can only improve. The Japanese have lost the initiative.

6 JUNE 1942

Aleutians The Japanese successfully land a small force on Kiska Island. On 7 June they also take Attu.

7 JUNE 1942

Eastern Front Major German attacks on Sevastopol begin. The Soviet Black Sea Fleet is heavily involved in bringing supplies to the town. The Russian garrison consists of seven infantry divisions and three marine brigades, all badly understrength. The Germans have nine divisions, two of them Rumanian.

9 JUNE 1942

Czechoslovakia The village of Lidice is obliterated as a reprisal for the assassination of Heydrich (*see* 27 May). More than 100 Czechs have already been killed and on 24 June the village of Levzasky is also destroyed. Altogether the Germans murder more than 1000 people in direct reprisals.

Mediterranean Another consignment of 32 Spitfires is flown to Malta. The number sent in during the last few weeks shows how fierce the fighting for the island is.

Allied Planning The British and Americans appoint Combined Boards for Production and for Food. They are to meet in Washington under the supervision of Donald Nelson and Oliver Lyttleton.

10 JUNE 1942

North Africa During the day the Free French defenders of Bir Hacheim still hold out and at night 2700 of them are successfully evacuated.

Pacific The carrier *Wasp* and the battleship *North Carolina* with cruisers and destroyers pass the Panama Canal to join the Pacific Fleet. There are now four large US carriers in the Pacific.

11 JUNE 1942

Allied Diplomacy Litvinov and Hull sign an additional Lend-Lease agreement in Washington.

North Africa Rommel's forces break out from 'The Cauldron' and attack the line of ridges between Knightsbridge and El Adem. Ritchie is compelled to fight there as he has foolishly left the bulk of his infantry still in the Gazala Line and because his massive base organization outside Tobruk is threatened.

11–16 JUNE 1942

Mediterranean There are two major convoy operations to supply Malta. Admiral Curteis leads Operation Harpoon from Gibraltar and Admiral Vian Operation Vigorous from Egypt. The Harpoon force passes Gibraltar on the 11th and has six merchant ships escorted by the battleship *Malaya*, the carriers *Eagle* and *Argus*, four cruisers and 17 destroyers. Several other merchantmen sail independently. The first air attacks, by German and Italian forces, are on the 14th when one merchantman is sunk and one cruiser hit. On the 15th the convoy goes on with only a close escort of cruisers and destroyers and is engaged by a similar Italian force. There are also many air attacks and altogether two destroyers and three merchant ships are sunk and four of the escorts damaged. Two merchant ships reach Malta.

Operation Vigorous is even less successful. Admiral Vian has received reinforcements from the Eastern Fleet, so he can lead eight cruisers and 26 destroyers to cover the 11 merchant ships. The convoy sets out on the 11th and the first air attacks are on the 13th. On the night of the 14th

Axis torpedo boats join in, damaging a cruiser and sinking a destroyer. On the 15th there are more air attacks in which two destroyers are sunk and a cruiser hit. The merchant convoy has now been reduced to six ships. Ammunition is running short after the many attacks and it is known that the battleships *Littorio* and *Vittorio Veneto* are approaching with a cruiser and destroyer escort. The convoy, therefore, turns back. The *Littorio* is damaged later by air attack and the heavy cruiser *Trento* sunk by a submarine, providing some consolation for the failure. Also during the operation almost all the German aircraft from North Africa have been involved in the attacks, giving Eighth Army some respite. However, on the 16th there is a further loss when the cruiser *Hermione* is sunk by *U.205*.

12 JUNE 1942

North Africa The Guards Brigade at Knightsbridge comes under particularly heavy pressure and British counterattacks are badly directed. The British lose 100 tanks, leaving only 70 operational, half the number Rommel has. The battle is now decided. A further advantage for Rommel is that, since the Germans have taken the ground on which the battle has been fought, they are able to recover and repair many damaged tanks. This is another area where the Germans have usually been superior in the desert.

13 JUNE 1942

North Africa The South African and British infantry begin to pull out of the Gazala Line and the Guards abandon Knightsbridge.

15 JUNE 1942

North Africa Early in the day part of 15th Panzer Division blocks the main road east of Tobruk just too late to catch the South African Division. In the evening the main body of 21st Panzer reaches Sidi Rezegh.

16 JUNE 1942

North Africa The British evacuate the position of El Adem, finally conceding any chance of forming a front west of Tobruk.

17 JUNE 1942

North Africa In an attack on the main German forces near Sidi Rezegh 4th Armored Brigade loses one-third of its tanks.

18 JUNE 1942

Allied Planning/Atomic Research Churchill

arrives in the USA for talks with President Roosevelt and his advisers. There is much discussion of the plans for a Second Front, but it is becoming clear that the conditions for Operation Sledgehammer (the Second Front in France in 1942) are going to be impossible to meet. This is confirmed during July. Churchill raises the possibility for an attack on French North Africa, to be known at first as Gymnast and later as Torch, with the president. (*See* 22 July.)

As well as the discussions on the Second Front, Churchill and Roosevelt talk about the future of atomic research. They agree that Britain and the United States should share their knowledge but that for the future the work should mostly be concentrated in the US. At a lower level relations between those involved in the project have not been good and these troubles continue, especially since the American work is now beginning to make better progress (*see* 17 September 1942).

North Africa Although his forces are now exhausted, Rommel issues orders for an attack on Tobruk to be begun on 20 June. He plans to attack in the southeast sector with 15th and 21st Panzer and Ariete and to drive straight to the harbor. Kesselring brings in every bomber available in the Mediterranean to support the attack. The garrison, though lavishly supplied, is made up of a hodgepodge of units and is not as forcefully led by the South African General Klopper as the Australians were during the former siege.

20 JUNE 1942
North Africa Rommel's attack on Tobruk begins with fierce dive-bomber attacks early in the morning. His ground forces advance quickly and by the afternoon are through the main positions, reaching the harbor in the evening.

Above: Tobruk harbor, 21 June 1942.

Eastern Front Amid bitter fighting the Germans penetrate to Sevastopol Harbor.

21 JUNE 1942
North Africa The garrison of Tobruk surrenders to the Germans and Italians. There are 30,000 prisoners and mountains of stores of every kind. One German soldier even records how his comrades sent home parcels of Australian bully beef. More importantly the captured stores, 3,000,000 rations and 500,000 gallons of gasoline, are a vital addition to the Afrika Korps' scanty reserves. Rommel wishes to drive on to Egypt, chasing his beaten enemy. He puts this suggestion to Hitler and Mussolini despite the objections of Kesselring, who prefers to carry out Operation Herkules against Malta. Rommel has his way and, as the hero of the hour, is promoted Field Marshal by Hitler. The fall of Tobruk has one consequence that Rommel could not have foreseen, however. On the 21st, while in a meeting with Roosevelt, Churchill is given the news and accepts a generous offer of immediate help. The result is that 300 Sherman tanks and 100 self-propelled guns are quickly sent off to Eighth Army and in fact play a vital role at El Alamein.

22 JUNE 1942
Vichy, Politics Vichy Prime Minister Laval broadcasts on the desirability of a German victory and urges Frenchmen to work hard in German industry.

23 JUNE 1942
North Africa The leading German troops cross the border into Egypt. Eighth Army meanwhile is withdrawing to Mersa Matruh in considerable confusion.

25 JUNE 1942
Eastern Front The Soviets retreat from Kupyansk on the Oskol River east of Kharkov.
North Africa Auchinleck sacks General Ritchie from command of Eighth Army and takes direct control of the battle himself.
United States, Command General Eisenhower is appointed to command US Land Forces in Europe.

26 JUNE 1942
North Africa The Afrika Korps has about 60 tanks and the Italian Littorio Division about 40 more. The British have about 200 tanks in operation at this moment and have several fresh formations in position around Mersa Matruh. Despite this imbalance of forces the German

advance continues.

Western Europe The RAF 'thousand raid' has Bremen as its target. This is the last such raid at this time. The training squadrons must return to normal duty if the future of Bomber Command is not to be seriously disrupted.

27 JUNE 1942

Arctic The convoy PQ-17 leaves Reykjavik for Archangel. There are 36 freighters and a tanker. The close escort consists of 6 destroyers and 13 smaller ships. The 35 ships of QP-13 have also left Murmansk and Archangel on their return journey.

North Africa The Allied forces around Mersa Matruh at first fight back strongly against the German attacks, but later in the day they are compelled to withdraw.

28 JUNE 1942

North Africa The German 90th Light Division takes Mersa Matruh and again a large quantity of stores and equipment are captured. The Eighth Army and the German and Italian forces are intermingled in a great stream heading back toward El Alamein where Auchinleck has decided to make a stand.

Arctic The Home Fleet leaves Scapa Flow to provide distant cover for PQ-17. There are two battleships, *Duke of York* and *Washington*, and one carrier, the *Victorious*, with cruisers and destroyers.

Eastern Front The main German summer offensive gets under way. Bock's Army Group South begins to drive east from around Kursk toward Voronezh.

30 JUNE 1942

Arctic The close cover for PQ-17 leaves Iceland with four cruisers, two American, and three destroyers. QP-13 is sighted by the Germans but is not attacked.

Eastern Front The Russian High Command orders the evacuation of Sevastopol. The Black Sea Fleet, much weakened by recent operations, attempts to comply with little success.

JULY 1942

Battle of the Atlantic The convoy system off the East Coast of America is extended during the month south from Florida. These convoys will be very effective in the months to come, losing only 39 ships up to December 1942. Other changes in the Allied system this month include the establishment of a CHOP (CHange of OPerational control) Line in mid-Atlantic clearly marking the boundaries of responsibility of the eastern and western routing authorities. High Frequency Direction Finding (HF/DF) sets are now being fitted in the escort vessels. These will become standard and will supplement the shore radio direction finding services. Eleven U-Boats are lost this month. Axis submarines sink 96 ships of 476,100 tons out of a total Allied loss of 128 ships of 618,100 tons. There is some return to operations in the Atlantic away from the American coast with U-Boats being active off Sierra Leone.

Allied Supply The United States finalizes arrangements with various South American countries for the supply of raw rubber to replace the sources captured by the Japanese. These agreements are extended in October.

British Air Operations RAF targets this month include Danzig, Bremen, Hamburg and the Ruhr. There are daylight attacks on targets in France in which the USAAF participates from 4 July onward. Bomber Command drops 6400 tons.

1 JULY 1942

North Africa The German advance reaches the defended area around El Alamein. The British 4th Armored Brigade arrives at Alam el Onsol only just before the German 90th Light Division. To the south there is particularly fierce fighting at the west end of the Ruweisat Ridge where 15th and 21st Panzer Divisions are pressing forward to Point 64. These attacks continue with little progress until 4 July.

Arctic The German intelligence service, B Dienst, has intelligence of PQ-17. Early in the day PQ-17 is sighted by *U.255* and *U.408*. Eight other U-Boats join the operation.

2 JULY 1942

Arctic QP-13 and PQ-17 pass each other. Reports of the sighting of both convoys and some of the covering forces are not properly reconciled by the Germans causing some confusion in their dispositions. There are unsuccessful air and submarine attacks on PQ-17. Farther south the *Tirpitz*, the *Hipper* and six destroyers leave their base at Trondheim.

Britain, Politics In the House of Commons, a motion of censure on the direction of the war is defeated by 476 votes to 25. Churchill's speech winding up the debate does much to reassure MPs. The principal criticism is that Churchill has too heavy a burden with the conduct of the war and the business of government both being his direct responsibility. Churchill's reply is that Parliament should either change the government or support it, but should not meddle with its

CHRONOLOGY

composition.

Allied Supply The British Board of Trade announces an agreement to control the supply of wheat involving the USA, UK, Argentina, Australia and Canada.

3 JULY 1942

Arctic The *Lützow* and the *Admiral Scheer* leave Narvik with a destroyer escort and proceed to join *Tirpitz* at Altafiord. On the way however, *Lützow* and three destroyers run aground.

North Africa The Italian Ariete Division, attacking toward Alam Nayil, is almost totally destroyed by 2nd New Zealand Division and their supporting artillery.

4 JULY 1942

Eastern Front The siege of Sevastopol comes to an end. The Germans take 90,000 prisoners and have lost 24,000 casualties. The Russian death toll is impossible to estimate.

Arctic The Germans score their first successes against PQ-17. Admiral Pound, the First Sea Lord, orders the convoy to scatter and the close cover and escort to retire. He believes that the German heavy ships will inevitably attack and, since the convoy is now comfortably within the range of German aircraft, it cannot be protected by the Home Fleet. The Admiralty messages are badly worded, but the commanders on the spot, although inclined to disobey, eventually conform to the orders.

United States Air Operations Airfields in Holland are the first targets for USAAF planes operating over Europe. Six planes join a RAF attack.

5 JULY 1942

Arctic Thirteen vessels from PQ-17 are sunk. The German heavy units make an abortive sortie, returning when the successes of the Luftwaffe and the U-Boats make their presence unnecessary. QP-13 in the Denmark Strait sails into a 'friendly' minefield, losing four ships.

Eastern Front Hoth's Fourth Panzer Group reaches the Don near Voronezh. On their left the attacks of Weich's Second Army also make some progress.

7 JULY 1942

Eastern Front The Germans capture Voronezh. Other units of Army Group South, including Sixth Army, continue to drive along the Donets Corridor.

Mediterranean British aircraft raid targets in southern Italy including Messina and Reggio Calabria.

United States Command General Spaatz is appointed to command US air forces in Europe.

Arctic Another eight ships of PQ-17 are sunk. From 9 July onward stragglers begin to arrive in Russian ports both singly and in groups. The ships which reach Russia deliver 896 vehicles, 164 tanks, 87 aircraft and 57,000 tons of general cargo. Twenty-four ships are lost altogether, with 3350 vehicles, 430 tanks, 210 aircraft and 96,000 tons of other equipment. The Germans lose five planes. There are no more Arctic convoys until September. PQ-17 has been a disaster.

Although Admiral Pound could not know of the restrictive conditions placed by Hitler on the operation of the German heavy ships his decision to order the convoy to scatter has probably been premature. The system of control from the Admiralty has not been to blame. Pound has had all the information and the necessary authority to make such a decision because he has access to the latest intelligence.

9 JULY 1942

Eastern Front The Germans reorganize their command system in the south. Army Group South is divided into two. Army Group A (General List) is composed of First Panzer Army, Seventeenth Army and Eleventh Army. Army Group B (General Bock) has Fourth Panzer Army, Second Army and Sixth Army. This reorganization is designed to expedite the progress of the Caucasus offensive now being prepared. The plan is for Army Group A to advance from positions south of the Donets, capture Rostov, cross the Don and after over-running the oilfields, to come to a halt on a line from Batumi on the Black Sea to Baku on the Caspian. Army Group B at this stage is ordered to advance north of the Don and establish a protective front for Army Group A (but *see* 17 July and 29 July for changes to this plan). Army Group A's attacks begin immediately. Army Group B's forces are already under way and their advance now reaches Rossosh cutting the Moscow–Rostov railway.

10 JULY 1942

North Africa The Australian 9th Division, recently arrived at the front, attacks the positions of the Italian Sabratha Division around Tell el Eisa and Rommel is forced to send reinforcements. In a series of spoiling attacks in the next few days, Auchinleck concentrates against the weak and unreliable Italians forcing the German armor to burn precious fuel motoring to their aid.

12 JULY 1942
Eastern Front The Soviet High Command appoint Marshal Timoshenko to a newly constituted Stalingrad Front. The Germans reach Lisichansk and Kanteminovka.

13 JULY 1942
Eastern Front Misled by early success, Hitler alters the strategic plan for his summer offensive and designates Stalingrad as a major objective for Army Group B which previously has been given only a covering role.

14 JULY 1942
North Africa There are British attacks, by units of 1st Armored Division, to the south of Ruweisat Ridge. Little ground is gained and losses on both sides are severe.

14–19 JULY 1942
Mediterranean Supplies are carried to Malta by submarine and fast transport. HMS *Eagle* flies 31 Spitfires to the island. Italian submarines are also engaged in supply work for their forces in North Africa which are critically short of supplies.

15 JULY 1942
India and China The first supplies flown 'Over the Hump' reach Chiang Kai-shek's forces.
North Africa In the operations south of the Ruweisat Ridge the Germans regain some ground but lose heavily to British artillery fire. The British artillery in North Africa has generally up to now been ill-organized and wastefully dispersed, so that its comparatively lavish resources have produced inadequate results. These faults are gradually remedied in the next few months.

16 JULY 1942
Eastern Front The Russians claim that in the fighting since 15 June, the Germans have lost 900,000 men. Although this claim is wildly exaggerated, the Russian resistance has stiffened as the Germans near Rostov and press toward the Volga.

17 JULY 1942
Eastern Front Hitler again interferes with the German dispositions. He fears that Army Group A will not be able to force its way across the Don, and therefore switches Fourth Panzer Army to join these operations. Naturally Army Group B, deprived of its spearhead, now makes much slower progress.
North Africa Desperate counterattacks by German and Italian forces halt a British advance around Miteirya Ridge. Rommel's supply difficulties continue to increase and he suggests a retreat to Cavallero and Kesselring.

19 JULY 1942
Eastern Front The German forces of Army Groups A and B continue to make rapid progress. In the last few days they have captured Kamensk and Voroshilovgrad and have reached the Don as far east as Tsimlyansky.
Battle of the Atlantic The final two U-Boats sent to operate off the United States' East Coast are ordered to other areas after a period of no success because of the improved convoy operations.

21 JULY 1942
New Guinea Japanese troops of General Horii's Eighteenth Army land at Gona. The Allies have also planned landings here but are forestalled.
North Africa Rommel sends reports to OKW giving details of his shortages of men, equipment and supplies. The British through *Ultra* are aware of his position and have therefore decided to mount a major attack. Eighth Army has more than 300 tanks and the Germans and Italians about 50 each. As the actions during the last two or three weeks have worn out the Italians, Auchinleck decides to complete the job by attacking the Afrika Korps directly. At first there is some progress in infantry attacks, but as happens all too often, the supporting armor fails to arrive in the right place at the right time. The Australian and New Zealand infantry especially (perhaps the best troops in Eighth Army) are growing increasingly disillusioned because of these failures.
United States Command Admiral Leahy is appointed as President Roosevelt's personal Chief of Staff.

22 JULY 1942
North Africa Although the British forces attacking south of Ruweisat take heavy losses, including the decimation of 23rd Armored Brigade, Rommel decides that the drain on his strength in the past fourteen days has been too great to permit further attacks. Both sides now wish a pause to rest and regroup. The British are far better placed to receive reinforcements being so close to their base in the Nile Delta. Malta too is recovering its strength to attack Axis communications.
New Guinea The Japanese forces begin to advance along the Kokoda Trail from Buna. A small Australian force prepares to defend

Kokoda itself.

Allied Planning Roosevelt agrees with the British that 'Sledgehammer' (the Second Front in 1942) is not possible and instructs his negotiators in London to agree 'another place for US troops to fight in 1942.' The plan to invade North Africa, previously mooted as 'Gymnast' is adopted in talks over the next few days and renamed 'Torch.'

23 JULY 1942

New Guinea The advancing Japanese make contact with Australian defensive positions on the Kokoda Trail near Wosida. By 27 July the Australians have been pushed back to Kokoda itself.

Eastern Front There is heavy fighting along the Don from Rostov to Tsimlyansk, especially around Novocherkassk.

World Affairs In a broadcast US Secretary of State Cordell Hull urges the formation of an international peace-keeping organization by the United Nations after the war.

25 JULY 1942

Eastern Front Army Group A completes the capture of Rostov.

27 JULY 1942

Eastern Front Army Group B, and especially Paulus' Sixth Army, battles to clear the Don elbow of Russian troops. The important position at Kalach is attacked.

28 JULY 1942

Eastern Front Following the fall of Rostov, now officially admitted by the Russians, Stalin begins to implement measures to bolster the resistance of the Red Army with increasingly harsh discipline and by granting officers higher status and authority.

29 JULY 1942

New Guinea After heavy fighting for three days Kokoda is taken by the Japanese who have been reinforced. Help was sent to the Australians during the fight but the supply planes turned back at the last minute when they were told incorrectly that the airstrip was in Japanese hands. Since this is the only airfield in the interior of the island, its loss is crucial.

Allied Production A combined British and American Production and Resources Board is established in London to control allocations of material and industrial priorities. Harriman, the US Lend-Lease Representative in the UK, and Lyttleton, the UK Minister of Produc-

tion, are to be the senior members.

Eastern Front The attacks of Army Group A south of the Don continue to make good progress with Proletarskaya being captured. Hitler is not satisfied with the progress of Sixth Army in the Don elbow and again alters his dispositions, returning Fourth Panzer Army to Army Group B. The series of alterations to the strategic plan which Hitler has found necessary are generally held to have crippled the German chances of decisive success in this campaign. Fourth Panzer Army has wasted much effort moving from front to front and Stalingrad has gradually assumed an ever more dominant position in the German plan, leaving Army Group A with a massive, strategically vital, task and inadequate resources.

30 JULY 1942

Canada, Politics Parliament passes a Bill introducing full conscription.

East Indies The Japanese occupy some small islands between Timor and New Guinea in a move designed to support their campaign against Port Moresby.

Eastern Front German troops advancing from Rostov take Bataisk on the south side of the Don.

31 JULY 1942

Solomons American bombers attack targets on Tulagi and Guadalcanal where the Japanese are building an airfield.

AUGUST 1942

Battle of the Atlantic The total Allied shipping losses in all theaters are 123 ships of 661,100 tons of which submarines sink 108 ships of 544,400 tons. The U-Boats are now operating again on the main North Atlantic convoy routes. Other U-Boat concentrations are off Brazil and Venezuela, with some still in the Caribbean and the Gulf of Mexico. A further group operates off Freetown. The narrow channels in Caribbean waters mean that there are many targets for the U-Boats there, but that making attacks is difficult. The protection of traffic off Brazil is made easier by Brazil's entry into the war on 22 August following many German provocations and especially the sinking of five ships off Bahia on the 16th and 17th by *U.507*. Bases can be provided for the Allied forces in Brazil. The German prospects are improved by the fitting of Metox radar search receivers to some of their boats. These are effective against radar on the 1.5-meter wavelength.

Allied Air Operations RAF Bomber Command continues its campaign with attacks on Duisburg, Mainz and Frankfurt. The first independent raids by US heavy bombers are made on targets in occupied France (*see* 17 August). Altogether US planes drop 170 tons of bombs and also take a small part in the offensive sweeps made by other units of the RAF against communications targets in France.

During August a Pathfinder Force for Bomber Command is established. This unit is to have responsibility for marking targets for the main force to bomb. Harris has opposed its formation as unnecessary and as bad for the morale of Bomber Command as a whole. Harris is certainly wrong in his opposition and, because of the Pathfinder Force and the technique it develops, accuracy will improve. In the short term there is a setback for bombing accuracy as the Germans have now begun completely effective jamming of the navigational aid *Gee*. It will still be useful for homing aircraft to their bases.

Mediterranean This month the air attacks on Malta are somewhat less fierce.

United States, Production This month the carrier USS *Independence* and the battleship USS *Iowa* are launched – an indication of how American warship production will soon swamp the Japanese. Between now and the end of the year four more carriers and another battleship are also launched.

1 AUGUST 1942

Eastern Front The forces of Army Group A continue to advance, capturing the town of Salsk and reaching the Kuban River near Kropotkin. There is more fierce fighting in the bend of the Don near Kalach and Kletskaya.

3 AUGUST 1942

Eastern Front Army Group B continues to attack Kletskaya. Fourth Panzer Army, having crossed the Don at Tsimlyansky, is now driving east around Kotelnikovo. First Panzer Army is mounting two attacks from its position on the Kuban, east toward Stavropol and south toward Maykop.

British Command Churchill and General Brooke arrive in Cairo to investigate what is wrong with the Eighth Army and to provide new commanders. Churchill feels that with the lavish resources sent to Eighth Army far more should have been achieved.

5 AUGUST 1942

Eastern Front The German attacks continue, with Army Group A making some progress near the Kuban River.

5–13 AUGUST 1942

Battle of the Atlantic The convoy SC-94 is attacked by a U-Boat pack during its passage across the Atlantic. This marks the return of the U-Boats to large-scale operations on the main north Atlantic routes. SC-94 loses 11 ships, but two of the attacking U-Boats are sunk and four damaged.

6 AUGUST 1942

British Command After much discussion of various proposals, General Alexander is chosen to command in the Middle East and General Gott to have tactical control of Eighth Army.

Eastern Front Army Group B is beginning to wear down the Russian defenses in the Don elbow. Seventeenth Army from Army Group A manages to capture Tikhoretsk.

7 AUGUST 1942

North Africa General Gott is killed on the flight back to Cairo and General Montgomery is chosen to replace him.

Palestine Sir John Grigg announces the creation of a Palestine Regiment in the British Army. This unit will be made up of separate Arab and Jewish battalions. The training provided for service in these units will provide valuable experience for the postwar operations of both sides.

Aleutians The Japanese-held island of Kiska is bombarded by an American naval task force.

Solomons The American landings begin. An amphibious task force (Admiral Turner) carries General Vandegrift's 1st Marine Division to land on Guadalcanal. Smaller detachments also land on Tulagi and Gavutu. Admiral Fletcher with three carriers is in support. The landings on Guadalcanal meet little opposition at first. The subsidiary operations are, however, heavily opposed.

8 AUGUST 1942

Solomons The remainder of the first American wave lands on Guadalcanal. The forces advancing inland easily overrun the Japanese airstrip which is renamed Henderson Field. The capture of Tulagi and Gavutu is completed. Because of the intense air and submarine activity, Fletcher decides, probably incorrectly, to withdraw his carriers but the cruisers and transports near Guadalcanal remain.

Allied Command Roosevelt and Churchill agree that General Eisenhower shall lead Operation Torch.

Eastern Front Army Group A continues to drive south as well as consolidate its gains near the Kuban River. Army Group B captures Surovniko.

9 AUGUST 1942
Solomons Just after midnight a Japanese cruiser squadron led by Admiral Mikawa enters Sealark Channel (later renamed Ironbottom Sound) south of Savo Island. The defending allied force, led by Admiral Crutchley, is not nearly so well trained or equipped for night fighting and is decisively beaten, losing four cruisers and sinking none.

The Japanese have failed, however, in their aim of attacking the transports unloading off Lunga Point. The transports are withdrawn because of the Japanese threat. The Marines are left very short of heavy equipment and with only about half their supplies.

Eastern Front From Army Group A, First Panzer Army captures Maykop and Seventeenth Army, Krasnodar. The oil installations at Maykop have been demolished however.

10 AUGUST 1942
Solomons The Japanese heavy cruiser *Kako* is sunk by a US submarine while returning to Rabaul from the Savo Island battle.

11 AUGUST 1942
Mediterranean A large convoy of 14 merchant ships en route to Malta is sighted by Axis reconnaissance aircraft. The importance of Operation Pedestal is well shown by the massive escort provided for such a comparatively small convoy. Admiral Syfret leads two battleships, four carriers, seven cruisers, 32 destroyers and other smaller craft. As well as supplies from the convoy, more aircraft are flown to Malta from HMS *Furious* which then turns back to Gibraltar. The carrier HMS *Eagle* is sunk by *U.73*, but an air attack on the convoy in the evening is unsuccessful.

New Guinea The Australian forces are pushed out of Deniki on the Kokoda Trail and retreat for five miles toward Templeton's Crossing near the summit of the Trail.

Vichy, Politics In a public speech, the Vichy Prime Minister, Pierre Laval, says, 'The hour of liberation for France is the hour when Germany wins the war.'

Eastern Front The Soviet position at Kalach on the west bank of the Don falls to the Germans.

12 AUGUST 1942
Mediterranean The convoy and the covering forces of Operation Pedestal are attacked constantly throughout the day. One merchant-

man is sunk in the morning, and in the early evening, shortly before the main covering force withdraws on schedule, the carrier *Indomitable* is damaged and a destroyer sunk. Later a cruiser and two freighters are sunk and two more cruisers, a transport and a vital tanker, the *Ohio*, are damaged.

New Hebrides The Americans land strong reinforcements on Espiritu Santu to build a base to support the Guadalcanal campaign.

Allied Diplomacy Churchill arrives in Moscow for talks essentially to apologize to Stalin that there will be no Second Front in 1942.

12–13 AUGUST 1942
New Guinea A strong Japanese detachment lands at Buna.

13 AUGUST 1942
Eastern Front Troops from Fourth Panzer Army advance southeast toward Elista.

North Africa Montgomery, supposedly only on a visit to the front, assumes command of the Eighth Army. Alexander replaces Auchinleck on 15 August. Montgomery starts at once to prepare his defenses for a German attack.

Mediterranean Very early in the morning the cruiser HMS *Manchester* is sunk, as are five more freighters from the Pedestal convoy. Later another two are sunk but four reach Malta and a fifth, the tanker *Ohio*, is towed into Valetta on 15 August. *Ohio* carries vital fuel for the island's striking forces.

14 AUGUST 1942
Eastern Front Sixth Army has almost completely cleared the Don Elbow of Russian resistance, but from the German point of view too many potential prisoners have escaped to the east because of the lack of mobile forces.

15 AUGUST 1942
Eastern Front The Germans make further gains in the Caucasus, especially around Georgivesk.

Guadalcanal The Marines are busy preparing the airstrip and consolidating their perimeter around it. They receive a small consignment of supplies by sea.

16–17 AUGUST 1942
New Guinea More Japanese reinforcements for the Kokoda Trail land near Buna.

17 AUGUST 1942
Gilbert Islands A Japanese seaplane base on Makin Island is raided by US Marines.

Allied Air Operations Rouen is the target for the first all-American bombing raid over Europe.

Between now and the end of 1942 the US Eighth Air Force will fly 1547 sorties and lose 32 aircraft. This loss is less than two percent, but all the raids have British fighter escort and none penetrates Germany. The buildup of the Eighth Air Force is badly delayed by the transfer of many aircraft to north Africa after Operation Torch in November. Thus there is no real test for the theories of the American airmen that their aircraft can bomb unescorted and with great accuracy. It will emerge even in the few operations that are undertaken this year that the much vaunted Norden bombsight, although excellent in good training conditions, is less impressive in the overcast skies of Europe.

Eastern Front The Germans capture Pyatigorsk and Yessentuki in the Caucasus where there are important power stations.

18 AUGUST 1942

Eastern Front Because partisan activity has been so intense, Hitler issues a directive ordering harsh measures and giving more power to SS Special Units.

Guadalcanal The first Japanese reinforcements land at Taivu. This detachment, about 1000 strong, led by Colonel Ichiki, immediately marches toward the American positions. At this stage the Japanese believe there are only 3000 Americans on the island. There are in fact more than 10,000 and Henderson Field is now ready to receive aircraft.

19 AUGUST 1942

Western Europe There is a major raid by Canadian and British troops on Dieppe. The troops involved are the 2nd Canadian Division (General Roberts) and Nos 3 & 4 Commando with a handful of Americans and Free French – in all 6000 men. The raid is designed to provide battle experience for the troops and to gain information about German defense methods which might be useful in the future. The raid is a disaster. Almost none of the installations marked for destruction is reached and only a proportion of the landing force can be evacuated. The casualty list is long: 3600 men, 106 aircraft, a destroyer, 30 tanks, and 33 landing craft. The Germans lose about 600 men and about 50 planes. The lessons of the operation, however bitter, are very important both on the general points of how difficult it is to capture a defended port, or how important is a preliminary bombardment, to the more detailed lessons relating to equipment for beach landings.

20 AUGUST 1942

Guadalcanal Henderson Field receives its first aircraft – a group of 31 fighters is flown in from the escort carrier *Long Island*.

21 AUGUST 1942

Eastern Front Army Group A penetrates almost as far as Novorossiysk on the Black Sea. Troops from Army Group B cross the Don near Kletskaya.

Guadalcanal Ichiki's force makes a series of wild attacks across the Tenaru River in which they are eventually wiped out. The US forces receive useful shipments of supplies and some reinforcements.

22 AUGUST 1942

World Affairs Brazil declares war on Italy and Germany after several Brazilian ships have been sunk in the past week.

23 AUGUST 1942

Eastern Front Army Group B reaches the Volga on a five-mile front between Rynak and Erzovka. The Soviets continue to resist.

German mountain troops climb Mount Elbrus in the Caucasus but it is merely a propaganda victory. In terrain like this everything is on the side of a stubborn defense.

Battle of the Eastern Solomons Both the Japanese and the Americans send major warships to cover attempts to ferry supplies to Guadalcanal. The main American squadron, Task Force 61 (Admiral Fletcher) consists of the carriers *Saratoga, Enterprise* and *Wasp*. The Japanese are operating characteristically in several separate groups. Admiral Nagumo has the carriers *Zuikaku* and *Shokaku*, and Admiral Hara has the smaller *Ryujo*. Fletcher sends off a strike but it fails to find any targets. Both forces are now alert for the next day's fight.

24 AUGUST 1942

Battle of the Eastern Solomons In the morning American scout planes sight *Ryujo* and a strike is dispatched. While it is on its way *Shokaku* and *Zuikaku* are also sighted and Fletcher tries to redirect his attack. Only a few of his planes receive this message and most carry on to sink *Ryujo*. Shortly after this strikes from Nagumo's carriers find the *Enterprise* and although she is damaged, aircraft can still be landed on. At the end of the day both carrier groups retire without attempting to achieve a decisive result.

Germany, Home Front Hitler appoints Thierack as Minister of Justice with powers to set aside any or all written law.

24–25 AUGUST 1942

New Guinea Japanese assault troops from Buna land on Goodenough Island in preparation for a later move into Milne Bay.

25 AUGUST 1942

Eastern Front There is heavy fighting along the Terek River in the Caucasus particularly around Mozdok.

Solomons Despite the setback received on 24 August, the Japanese transports continued on toward Guadalcanal. Two are damaged and a destroyer is sunk by American aircraft and after that they turn back. The Japanese now recognize the difficulty of daylight operations because of Henderson Field's aircraft, and for the moment revert to using fast destroyers to bring in supplies during the night.

Britain, Home Front HRH The Duke of Kent (King George's younger brother), a serving officer in the RAF, is killed in a plane crash in the north of Scotland.

25–26 AUGUST 1942

New Guinea Japanese troops landing in Milne Bay are fiercely resisted by the Australian and American garrison. Despite the arrival of reinforcements on 27 August, no real progress is made by the Japanese. On the Kokoda Trail the Japanese do gain some ground near Isurava.

26 AUGUST 1942

Eastern Front The Russians announce that a successful offensive on the Moscow front began two weeks ago. Their claim of a 15- or 20-mile penetration on a 75-mile front is exaggerated however.

26–27 AUGUST 1942

Soviet Air Operations Soviet aircraft raid Berlin and other German cities. The attack is repeated on 30 August.

27 AUGUST 1942

Eastern Front Around Stalingrad the Soviet perimeter is gradually drawing in, and in the far south the Germans have crossed the River Terek and captured Prochladrii.

Solomons The aircraft carrier USS *Saratoga* is damaged in an attack by the Japanese submarine *I.26* and is out of action until the end of October. The *Wasp* is now the only operational US carrier left in the Pacific.

28 AUGUST 1942

Eastern Front There is a small Russian attack near Leningrad.

28–29 AUGUST 1942

Guadalcanal The Japanese receive important reinforcements run in during the night by Admiral Tanaka's 2nd Destroyer Flotilla now known to the Marines as the 'Tokyo Express.'

30 AUGUST 1942

Guadalcanal The American air group at Henderson Field receives 18 more fighters and 12 dive bombers.

30–31 AUGUST 1942

North Africa Rommel's forces begin a final attack designed to clear the British out of Egypt. Already, however, British preparations have been more extensive than he realizes. Much has been done to reconstitute formations shattered earlier in the summer and the British intelligence is effective, enabling Montgomery to improve on the good dispositions established by Auchinleck. Rommel has received some reinforcements, particularly the German 164th Division and a parachute brigade. He is desperately short of supplies and decides to mount his attack on the strength of promises of future shipments. As well as helping the Royal Navy strike at the supply routes, the RAF is dominant over the desert and causes Rommel many casualties.

As usual the cutting edge of Rommel's attack is the German tank formations and these are sent, shortly before midnight, to break through the British minefields between Alam Nayil and Qaret el Himeimat. Once this is done, the plan is for them to push east of Alam Halfa and then turn north. The British minefields are more elaborate and better defended than Rommel's staff have anticipated and progress is slow. Indeed, by 0800 hours on 31 August Rommel wishes to call off the attack but is persuaded not to. Instead he orders an earlier turn north and a direct attack on Alam Halfa Ridge but this is beaten off. The Afrika Korps has been bombarded all day by the improved British artillery and by the RAF. This continues day and night for the remainder of the battle, allowing the Germans no rest.

31 AUGUST 1942

United States, Home Front Claude Wickard, the Agriculture Secretary, warns that it will probably be necessary to introduce meat rationing. Roosevelt has already spoken on 28 August about the possibility of introducing a meatless day.

New Guinea General Hyakutake, commanding Seventeenth Army, decides to evacuate the troops who have landed in Milne Bay and concentrate on the Guadalcanal operation. This evacuation is completed by 7 September, but at least 1000 Japanese have died. This is the first significant setback the Japanese have received on land.

Guadalcanal General Kawaguchi and 1200 troops land on the island.

Eastern Front The Germans have thrust forward to within 16 miles of Stalingrad despite tenacious Russian resistance.

SEPTEMBER 1942

Battle of the Atlantic The German U-Boats operate in much the same areas as in August. Their attacks off Trinidad remain important for the next two months, but these are the last easy gains to be made off the American coast. Convoys in this area will only be started in October. The North Atlantic convoys are reorganized to run from New York to the UK rather than from Sydney and Halifax in Canada. This makes fitting the main convoys with the coastal convoys easier. The first Support Groups are formed to aid the escort forces. These are groups of escort vessels, ideally including an escort carrier, which are to be sent to help the escort of any particularly hard-pressed convoy. They are particularly valuable for their high standard of training and teamwork. There are also increases in the number of Leigh Light aircraft in service with RAF Coastal Command. One notable convoy battle occurs around ON-127 (*see* 10–14 September).

The total Allied shipping losses during the month are 114 ships of 567,300 tons of which submarines sink 98 ships of 485,400 tons.

Western Europe Allied air attacks continue. British targets are to include Bremen, Duisburg and Wilhelmshaven. The American targets are in France and the Low Countries. Bomber Command drops more than 6000 tons of bombs during the month. As yet the USAAF can only make a small contribution (about 200 tons).

Mediterranean British naval and air forces based on Malta and Egypt sink one-third of the supply ships sent to the German and Italian forces. Rommel's supply position remains dreadfully weak and, to his fury, many of the supplies and vehicles which do land are sent to inactive Italian units in Libya. Only one-third of Italy's 1940 merchant fleet remains in operation; the rest has either been sunk or captured.

1 SEPTEMBER 1942

Eastern Front There is fierce fighting in the Stalingrad area where German units have now reached the suburbs in some sectors. The Russian Sixty-second Army is in danger of being cut off.

North Africa The German attack today is much weaker. One Panzer Division is out of fuel and the other, 15th Panzer, makes no real progress, although it gives the British 8th Armored Brigade an expensive lesson in the use of antitank guns.

Japan, Politics The Foreign Minister, Togo, resigns and his office is taken over for the moment by Prime Minister Tojo. Masayuka Tani is appointed to the Foreign Ministry on 17 September.

Eastern Front Troops of Eleventh Army cross from Kerch and land on the Taman Peninsula. There are both German and Rumanian units involved.

2 SEPTEMBER 1942

Eastern Front Troops from Eleventh and Seventeenth Armies advance near Novorossiysk. First Panzer Army is approaching Grozny but its progress is slow.

North Africa Rommel gives orders to withdraw back to the start line and Montgomery, probably quite correctly, refuses to follow up with his own armor.

2–3 SEPTEMBER 1942

New Guinea The Japanese Army is reinforced by 1000 more men from Rabaul who land at Buna.

3 SEPTEMBER 1942

North Africa The New Zealand Division, in position around Alam Nayil, is ordered to attack southward to threaten the retreat of the German forces but fails to get far in heavy fighting during the next two days.

4 SEPTEMBER 1942

Eastern Front Over 1000 German planes are involved in attacks in the Stalingrad sector. The Germans reach the Volga south of the city.

4–5 SEPTEMBER 1942

Guadalcanal Again the Japanese receive reinforcements during the night. Two old American destroyers being used as transports are sunk by the Japanese destroyers.

6 SEPTEMBER 1942

Eastern Front Army Group A captures Novorossiysk.

North Africa The battle of Alam Halfa is over and the Germans are back in their original positions. They discover that large reinforcements for Montgomery are on the way and that, unless they also receive considerable help, Eighth Army will win in the end. Rommel sets his forces to prepare elaborate fixed defenses of barbed wire, minefields and booby traps. The Eighth Army is busy regrouping, absorbing new equipment and training for the coming assault.

7–8 SEPTEMBER 1942
Guadalcanal A force of Marine Raiders, about 600 strong, lands to attack the Japanese base at Taivu. They do considerable damage and disrupt Japanese preparation for an attack on the main American position.

8 SEPTEMBER 1942
New Guinea The Australian forces are pushed back once more in the Owen Stanley Range. This time the position near Efogi has to be abandoned.
Vichy, Politics General de St Vincent, Military Governor of Lyons, is dismissed by the Vichy authorities for refusing to help arrest Jews in his area.

9 SEPTEMBER 1942
Eastern Front Hitler sacks General List from command of Army Group A and from now on he directs it personally.
Guadalcanal The commander of the Japanese Seventeenth Army, General Hyakutake, lands at Tassafaronga with elements of 2nd Infantry Division.

10 SEPTEMBER 1942
Madagascar There are renewed operations on the west coast of Madagascar. The British now intend to occupy the whole island and therefore make landings at Majunga.

10–14 SEPTEMBER 1942
Battle of the Atlantic The increasing skill of the U-Boat commanders is shown in the operations against the convoy ON-127. Every U-Boat from a group of 13 manages to make at least one attack. Only one U-Boat is damaged and 12 freighters and one destroyer are sunk.

12 SEPTEMBER 1942
War at Sea *U.156*, en route to the area of the Cape of Good Hope, sinks the liner *Laconia* just south of the Equator. *Laconia* is carrying servicemen's wives and children and Italian prisoners of war. Kapitan Leutnant Hartenstein surfaces and helps the survivors and sends radio messages to the Allied authorities in plain language. *U.156* is, however, attacked by an American plane. Doenitz, therefore, gives orders that there are to

be no further similar rescue attempts by U-Boats. He also arranges for Vichy ships from Dakar to be sent to finish the rescue work. This *Laconia* Order forms one of the counts against Doenitz at Nuremberg.
Eastern Front The Soviet perimeter around Stalingrad is now only about 30 miles long. In this desperate situation General Chuikov is appointed to command Sixty-second Army, soon to be besieged in Stalingrad. Chuikov performs superbly throughout the battle. His orders are responsible for the Russian close quarter style of fighting which so effectively disrupts the normally fluid all-arms cooperation of the German forces. His firm and abrasive character are also essential to the defense.
Guadalcanal The Japanese begin major attacks especially around 'Bloody Ridge.' The attacking units are from General Kawaguchi's 35th Brigade. The Americans receive valuable reinforcements of aircraft flown in from the carrier *Wasp*.

13 SEPTEMBER 1942
North Africa British units of the Long Range Desert Group attack airfields at Benghazi and Barce. There are also amphibious landings at Tobruk which are beaten off with heavy casualties.
Guadalcanal The Japanese attacks are very fierce. They are only held off with difficulty and because of effective American artillery support.

13–18 SEPTEMBER 1942
Arctic The convoy PQ-18 passes to the USSR with none of the disasters of its predecessor. It is provided with a large escort including an escort carrier. Thirteen ships are lost, but the Germans lose two U-Boats and 20 planes.

14 SEPTEMBER 1942
Guadalcanal Kawaguchi's attacks peter out, with 1200 casualties lost.
New Guinea The Japanese have their final success on the Kokoda Trail when they move the Australians back to Imita Ridge, only about 30 miles from Port Moresby.
Solomons The Japanese submarine *I.19* sinks the USS *Wasp* with three torpedoes. A destroyer is also sunk and the battleship *North Carolina* is damaged.
Aleutians American bombers attack the Japanese held island of Kiska. The attacks are repeated during the next few days.

16 SEPTEMBER 1942
New Guinea The Japanese attacks are brought

to a halt before Ioribaiwa and with the benefit of local air superiority and the American troops who are now arriving at Port Moresby, the Allies can plan an offensive.

Eastern Front There is heavy fighting in Stalingrad around the Mamayev Kurgan Hill. It is taken and retaken several times by each side during the next few days, and throughout the battle will be the scene of many extremely fierce confrontations.

17 SEPTEMBER 1942

Atomic Research All atomic research in the United States is placed under military control and General Groves is appointed to direct the program. Groves is deeply worried about security; partly for this reason and partly through simple chauvinism he is strongly opposed to sharing any information with the British (*see* December 1942).

Madagascar The terms suggested by the British for an armistice are rejected by the Vichy Governor General.

18 SEPTEMBER 1942

Guadalcanal Six transports bring supplies and the 7th Marine Regiment to reinforce the American position. The American strength is now about 23,000 men and they have adequate supplies.

New Guinea In response to superior orders and because of the difficulty of supplying the forward troops, General Horii begins to pull some of his men back to the area around Buna and Gona.

Madagascar There are British landings on the east coast at Tamatave.

20 SEPTEMBER 1942

Eastern Front In the Caucasus the town of Terek is captured by the Germans.

21 SEPTEMBER 1942

Sweden, Politics In the national elections the pro-Nazi candidates do very badly.

23 SEPTEMBER 1942

Madagascar British troops take the capital, Tananarive.

North Africa Rommel flies back to Germany for medical treatment. General Stumme takes command in Africa with General Von Thoma to lead the armor. In the past few months there have been many high-level German casualties in Africa. Some of the new men have been brought in from the Russian campaign and do not fit in well with the old hands of Afrika Korps.

New Guinea The Australians go over to the

attack. More American reinforcements land at Port Moresby and General Blamey (the Australian Commander in Chief) takes personal charge with orders from MacArthur to invigorate the conduct of the campaign.

23–26 SEPTEMBER 1942

Eastern Front The Russians mount a small counterattack in the northwest of Stalingrad from the district of Orlovka. This attack makes some progress but is fiercely resisted by the German troops.

24 SEPTEMBER 1942

German Command General Halder is dismissed by Hitler after many arguments during the summer. The new Chief of Staff at OKH with responsibility for the Russian front is General Zeitzler.

German Raiders In one of the most notable small actions of the war the Liberty ship *Stephen Hopkins*, armed with only one 4-inch gun, fights an attack by the much more powerful German raider *Stier*. Both ships sink. In its cruise *Stier* has sunk four ships of 29,400 tons.

24–25 SEPTEMBER 1942

Guadalcanal During their habitual night supply operations, two Japanese destroyers and one cruiser are damaged.

25 SEPTEMBER 1942

United States, Production In Washington the Maritime Commission announces that 488 cargo ships have been built in the last year.

27 SEPTEMBER 1942

New Guinea The Japanese begin to withdraw back down the Kokoda Trail in the face of Australian attacks.

28–29 SEPTEMBER 1942

Eastern Front In a small attack, Russian forces cross the Volga near Rzhev in the central sector.

29 SEPTEMBER 1942

Madagascar British forces land at Tuléaron, in the southwest of the island.

OCTOBER 1942

Battle of the Atlantic Allied shipping losses increase this month to 637,800 tons from all causes. Axis submarines account for 619,000 tons, or 94 ships, of this. The increase is partly because escorts have to be diverted, especially later in the month, to cover the 10 Torch convoys on their way to Morocco and Algeria. The period of German successes off the east coast of America is coming to an end. The last good pickings for the U-Boats are in the area near Trinidad.

Allied Air Operations The Allied bomber offensive continues. Among the German targets for RAF Bomber Command are Flensburg, Essen and Cologne. British and American aircraft attack targets in France by night and day, including Le Creusot and Fives-Lille. There are heavy attacks by RAF aircraft based in Britain on targets in Italy, including Genoa, Turin and Milan. The RAF drops 4100 tons of bombs and the US Eighth Air Force 300 tons.

1 OCTOBER 1942

Eastern Front There is heavy fighting along the Black Sea coast north of Tuapse. Inland the Germans are still battling toward Grozny. There are German gains in the Orlovka sector of Stalingrad.

New Guinea General MacArthur issues orders for the Allied advance on Gona and Buna. Australian forces have already begun to move forward along the Kokoda Trail. A US force is to move over the parallel Kapa Kapa Trail to join the Australians in cutting off the Japanese retreat at the Kumusi River. There are also to be landings along the north coast between Milne Bay and Cape Nelson, especially at Wanigela.

United States, Home Front Fuel oil is now rationed in most parts of the country.

2 OCTOBER 1942

United States, Home Front President Roosevelt is granted power to control wages, salaries and agricultural prices from 1 November by the Stabilization of the Cost of Living Act which now becomes law.

War at Sea The British cruiser *Curaçao* is sunk off Ireland after a collision with the liner *Queen Mary* which is being used as a troop transport. Like the other giant ocean liners, the *Queen Mary* is normally unescorted for the major part of any voyage, relying on speed to keep out of trouble. Only in waters close to the British Isles are escorts provided.

South Pacific American forces begin to build a base on Funafuti Atoll in the Ellice Islands.

4 OCTOBER 1942

Eastern Front Paulus begins a new series of attacks within Stalingrad – his fourth major effort. This will be the fiercest and longest lasting of the German offensives. They have been reinforced by combat-engineer and police units to increase their street fighting expertise. The

Soviets are developing their skills also and will attempt to direct the German advances into specially prepared killing zones. The German attacks are sent against the Soviet posts in the Barrikady, Krasnye Oktyabr and Tractor Factories.

New Guinea The Australian forces following up the Japanese retreat along the Kokoda Trail take Effogi and continue the advance to Kagi and Myola.

5 OCTOBER 1942

Solomons Aircraft from the carrier *Hornet* attack Japanese shipping gathering off Bougainville but only achieve slight success.

6 OCTOBER 1942

United States, Production and Supply An additional Lend-Lease agreement is signed in Washington by representatives of the USA and the USSR. Between now and July 1943 it is planned to deliver 4,400,000 tons of supplies to the Soviet Union, 75 percent by sea, the rest through Iran.

Eastern Front Army Group A captures the oil-producing center of Malgobek near Mozdok, in the Caucasus. The advance continues toward the Terek.

New Guinea A small party from the US 32nd Division begins to move over the Kapa Kapa Trail. This route is about 25 miles southwest of the Kokoda Trail and the terrain is even worse.

7 OCTOBER 1942

Guadalcanal The 1st Marine Division attacks west from the American beachhead in an attempt to free Henderson Field from all but the heaviest Japanese artillery fire by taking positions at the mouth of the Matanikau River.

Eastern Front In Stalingrad there are particularly fierce fights near the Tractor Factory.

War Crimes Britain and the United States announce that a United Nations Commission is to be established to investigate Axis war crimes. It is to be a condition of any armistice that war criminals are to be handed over to be tried.

7 OCTOBER–13 NOVEMBER 1942

War at Sea A group of four U-Boats operating off the South African coast sink 170,000 tons of shipping. This is a very clear illustration of the wide scope and effect of submarine operations and of the difficulty of protecting shipping in distant waters.

8 OCTOBER 1942

Guadalcanal Despite heavy rain, there is heavy

fighting west of the American beachhead along the River Matanikau.

Belgium, Home Front German decrees are issued ordering the registration for war work of all males between the ages of 18–50 and of all unmarried women between 21–35.

9 OCTOBER 1942

Soviet Command The command authority of the commissars in the Red Army is taken away. They are still to have an important role in morale and propoganda, but responsibility for military decisions now rests entirely with the commanding officers.

Guadalcanal The American attacks west of the Matanikau continue and succeed in wiping out a Japanese battalion. The attacks are halted after this largely because of intelligence reports that the Japanese plan to renew their attacks on the main part of the American beachhead.

Madagascar British East African forces begin moving south from the capital, Tananarive, to link up with the troops landed in the south at the end of September.

11 OCTOBER 1942

Eastern Front For the first time in almost two months there is a complete lull in the Stalingrad sector.

11–12 OCTOBER 1942

Battle of Cape Esperance Both sides mount supply operations to the forces on Guadalcanal. The covering squadrons of cruisers and destroyers meet off Cape Esperance and a confused night action ensues. The American force consists of four cruisers and four destroyers led by Admiral Scott. The Japanese squadron, commanded by Admiral Goto, has three cruisers and two destroyers. Although the Americans have the crucial advantage of radar, communications between their ships are poor and their actions are not well coordinated. Likewise the Japanese are not well led and they fail to make best use of their superior torpedo equipment. At various stages in the battle both sides fire on their own ships. The Americans lose one destroyer, and two cruisers and another destroyer are seriously damaged. The Japanese come off worse, losing a cruiser and a destroyer and having their other two cruisers damaged. Their remaining two destroyers are sunk by air attack by planes from Henderson Field during 12 October.

Both sides' transports get through. On the 11th the Japanese land various supplies including artillery and tanks, and on the 13th the

Americans land 3000 more men from the Americal Division.

12 OCTOBER 1942

Battle of the Atlantic *U.597* is sunk in the Atlantic by a British Liberator bomber. This is the first success scored by the single RAF Coastal Command squadron of these invaluable long-range aircraft. Despite the obvious utility of these planes a second squadron is not established until March 1943, largely because the aircraft are claimed for the strategic-bomber forces.

13 OCTOBER 1942

Eastern Front In the southern part of Stalingrad XLVIII Panzer Corps of Fourth Panzer Army has reached the Volga, but to the north many of the large factory buildings are still stubbornly held. There are Soviet counterattacks in the factory areas.

13–14 OCTOBER 1942

Guadalcanal As the bombers based on Henderson Field have become so effective, the Japanese bring up the battleships *Kongo* and *Haruna* to bombard the airfield during the night. About 50 aircraft are destroyed, more than half the complement. Taking advantage of the disruption caused to the American air cover, a group of destroyers and transports led by Admiral Tanaka lands 4500 men and large quantities of supplies at Tassafaronga. Henderson Field is shelled again. During 14 October some aircraft manage to leave Henderson Field and damage three Japanese transports which are trying to unload.

14 OCTOBER 1942

Eastern Front Hitler decides that all offensive action should be suspended except in Stalingrad and a small area of the Caucasus along the middle reaches of the Terek River. In Stalingrad the Soviet forces in and around the Tractor Factory are nearly broken by attacks from five German divisions which are assisted by heavy air support. A newly arrived Russian Guards Division joins the defending troops. Throughout the battle the Soviets will be deliberately niggardly in giving help to Sixty-second Army because they want to build up reserves for a counterattack.

New Guinea There is an important action on the Kokoda Trail at Templeton's Crossing. The battle lasts until 16 October.

War at Sea The German raider *Komet* is sunk in the Channel by a British force.

15 OCTOBER 1942

Eastern Front In Stalingrad the German attacks in the area of the Tractor Factory continue to make ground, reaching the Volga a little to the north of the main complex.

16 OCTOBER 1942

Solomons Aircraft from the carrier *Hornet* raid Japanese supply bases on Santa Isabel. On Guadalcanal the Japanese are preparing for a major attack by an increasing bombardment of the American positions.

Madagascar The British forces take Ambositra, 140 miles south of Tananarive.

17 OCTOBER 1942

New Guinea The Australian advance along the Kokoda Trail is temporarily held up at Eora Creek by strong Japanese resistance. The Australian 16th Brigade has now taken over from 25th Brigade at the head of the advance. One regiment of the US 32nd Division is airlifted from Port Moresby to Wanigela on the north coast.

Burma Orders are given to the 14th Indian Division, advancing slowly into the Arakan, to reach a line between Rathedaung and Buthidaung by the start of December in preparation for further operations toward Akyab.

18 OCTOBER 1942

United States Command Admiral Halsey replaces Admiral Ghormley in charge of the South Pacific Command Area.

Stalingrad After two days in which the Soviets have largely succeeded in holding the German advance, renewed attacks in the Krasnye Oktyabr area make some gains.

War Crimes Following some incidents in the raid on Dieppe and the more-recent, smaller landings in the Channel Islands, in which German prisoners have been shot while tied up, Hitler issues orders that all prisoners taken from Commando or other similar units are to be shot immediately.

New Guinea The American force moving over the Kapa Kapa Trail begins to arrive at Pongani. By 21 October the whole of one regiment has made this journey but after the rigors of the trip they are in no condition to fight. Its efforts have been wasted since it has proved possible to fly troops from Port Moresby to the north coast.

20 OCTOBER 1942

United States, Home Front Congress passes the largest tax bill in the country's history. The measures are designed to raise $6,881,000,000.

21 OCTOBER 1942

Guadalcanal The Japanese forces under General Maruyama are now 20,000 strong and begin a series of attacks against the American positions. The main units are from the 2nd Infantry Division. The plan is for the primary attacks to be delivered northward between the Lunga and Tenaru Rivers while secondary attacks are to be made on the western outposts along the Matanikau. Japanese Intelligence has little information on the strength and dispositions of the US forces. When this shortcoming is added to the difficulties of the inland approach march for the main attacks, the whole Japanese effort proves to be badly planned and badly coordinated.

The offensive opens with a brief, unsuccessful attack across the Matanikau supported by tanks and heavy artillery fire.

Eastern Front The focus for the German effort in Stalingrad is now the Barrikady Factory and housing estate. Over the next two days over half of it is taken in a series of vicious engagements. There are German gains in the Red October area.

New Guinea The Australian troops fighting their way along the Kokoda trail have succeeded in closing up to the main Japanese positions at Eora. MacArthur issues orders trying to speed their progress.

21–30 OCTOBER 1942

Operation Torch Although 21 U-Boats are operating off Gibraltar and the Moroccan coast, they are engaged with the convoy SL-125 and do not sight any of the transports which are now en route. There are occasional sightings of some of the warship groups bound for North Africa, but they are sufficiently vague and scattered to prevent the Germans and Italians making a correct appreciation of the situation.

22 OCTOBER 1942

Guadalcanal The Japanese again attack over the Matanikau with a strong force of tanks and infantry, but are beaten back with heavy losses inflicted largely by the well-organized American artillery. These actions are repeated on 23 October at a lower intensity.

Eastern Front The first winter snow falls at Stalingrad.

New Guinea There are Australian landings on Goodenough Island which has been largely abandoned by the Japanese since their defeat at Milne Bay.

23 OCTOBER 1942

Operation Torch General Clark lands in

Algeria for talks with the French General Mast and with the American diplomat Robert Murphy. Murphy has been conducting delicate negotiations with many of the French leaders in Morocco and Algeria. The most important supporters of the Allied cause are Generals Mast and Béthouart who are Chiefs of Staff at Algiers and Casablanca respectively. The Allies have had less success with the more senior French officials and soldiers and none at all with the admirals, who have remained profoundly anti-British since Mers-el-Kebir and Dakar. This particular conference is intended to confirm to Mast the importance to the Allies of his help and to ascertain that he is prepared to accept the authority of General Giraud. Giraud is still in Vichy but is to be smuggled out before the invasion starts. Mast agrees to accept Giraud but in reality he is an unsatisfactory choice and unlikely to command widespread loyalty. For his own part Giraud prefers to be regarded as a soldier rather than as a politician.

Burma The bulk of the British force has advanced to Cox's Bazar but forward units have reached Buthidaung. There they come into contact with a Japanese formation which has pushed up from Akyab. After a brief fight the Japanese hold the position.

23–24 OCTOBER 1942
Battle of El Alamein Montgomery's attack begins shortly before midnight after meticulous preparation. Units have received precise training in night movement and mine clearance. An elaborate and extensive artillery plan has been worked out, and complicated measures of deception have been taken to confuse the enemy as to the time and place of the attack. The plan is for the infantry of XXX Corps to push through the minefields and the enemy infantry positions and then for X Corps, of two armored divisions, to move through and hold off the counterattacks while the infantry clears and widens the gap behind. In the final phase the German armor will be fought and destroyed in the open. Eighth Army has a superiority of about two to one in tanks, guns and men as well as a considerable advantage in the air. Most important, however, is the question of supplies. The German armor has been dispersed into two groups because, if concentrated, it might not have enough fuel to motor to the site of an attack. All along the front Italian and German units have been mixed so there is a reliable German contingent everywhere.

The main attack in fact falls on the German 164th Division and the Italian Trento Division who are supported by Littorio and 15th Panzer. Diversionary attacks at first make sure that 21st Panzer stays in the south. During the opening night and day of the battle the British forces make some progress but do not manage to keep to their timetable to force their armor through the minefields. General Stumme, who commands in Rommel's absence, dies of a heart attack during a visit to the front and in the very confused situation the German reaction is somewhat lethargic. On the afternoon of 24 October Rommel receives word to return from Germany.

24–25 OCTOBER 1942
Guadalcanal The Japanese offensive continues. The secondary operations in the Matanikau sector continue on both days with partially successful Japanese infiltrations of the left wing of the American force. The main operations against the south of the American perimeter begin after dark on the 24th and continue throughout the night. They fail and similar unimaginative efforts on the night of the 25th are thrown back with heavy losses.

25 OCTOBER 1942
El Alamein Montgomery intervenes decisively in the battle to ensure that X Corps pushes forward vigorously. Although by the end of the day they have lost perhaps 250 tanks, this can be accepted since 15th Panzer has less than 40 left. When Rommel arrives in the evening the 9th Australian Division in the north has already started attacking toward the sea. They make important gains which attract Rommel's attention.

Above: British antitank gun under fire, Alamein.

CHRONOLOGY

Eastern Front After a period devoted to regrouping, the Germans renew their offensive with attacks by III Panzer Corps south of the Terek River in the Caucasus.

Battle of Santa Cruz The Japanese navy mounts a major operation in support of the offensive on Guadalcanal, sending four battleships and the carriers *Shokaku, Zuikaku, Zuiho* and *Junyo* as well as numerous cruisers and destroyers. The carriers are to send aircraft to Henderson Field once the army has captured it and only a report to that effect has brought it so close to the island. The Americans have two carriers in the operation, the *Enterprise* and the *Hornet*, but unlike the Japanese their one battleship is in close attendance to provide supporting antiaircraft fire. As at Midway, the Japanese force is split into several groups (in this instance four). The battleships are separate from the carriers which themselves have fewer defensive guns than their American counterparts. The *Junyo*, with 55 aircraft, is even in a separate group from the rest of the carriers. A second disadvantage in the design of the Japanese carriers is that their bridges are too small to accommodate the admiral's staff necessary if no other large ships are in company. However, despite these disadvantages, the Japanese have 212 planes on their carriers and the Americans 171. Both sides will receive help, especially in scouting, from land-based aircraft.

The American patrols are first to find the enemy but a strike launched later goes astray. Both sides prepare for action on the 26th.

26 OCTOBER 1942

Battle of Santa Cruz Both sides launch strikes about 0700 hours. Just after 0900 hours the Japanese attack reaches and seriously damages the *Hornet* which sinks later. The American attacks have been launched at the extreme range of the aircraft (the Japanese have longer range) and so no fuel can be used forming up for a coordinated attack. Some of the American planes attack Admiral Abe's Vanguard Group, damaging the cruiser *Chikuma*, and the remainder inflict severe punishment on *Shokaku*. A second wave of Japanese attacks manages to severely damage the *Enterprise*, but many aircraft from this group and from a third less successful strike from *Junyo* are shot down by the massive barrage of the *South Dakota*. Although the *Enterprise* is made partially effective. Kinkaid decides to withdraw.

Although this has been an undoubted Japanese victory, leaving the damaged *Enterprise* as the only American carrier in the Pacific,

the Japanese losses in aircrew have again been severe, with the undamaged *Zuikaku* virtually out of action because of this. The Japanese withdraw also, partly because of lack of fuel, and partly because their aircraft strength has been too reduced to make any attack on Henderson Field worthwhile.

El Alamein The British attack is making little progress and Montgomery halts most of his forces to regroup. Rumors of this reach Churchill and he is furious that the battle seems to be abandoned so soon. However, it is far from over. The main events of the day are German counterattacks. Rommel orders up 21st Panzer and Ariete from the south. Believing that the main Allied attack is now coming along the coast, he tries to counter there with 15th Panzer and moves 90th Light forward to support.

Eastern Front In the Caucasus the town of Nalchik, southeast of Pyatigorsk, falls to the Germans. Four Soviet divisions are being threatened by the attacks of III Panzer Corps here.

27 OCTOBER 1942

El Alamein While the British command is mostly concerned with regrouping, what Rommel intends as a major counterattack by his armor is beaten off by a small British force at Kidney Ridge. He also attacks farther north, with equally little success.

Eastern Front In Stalingrad the Germans gain ground in the area between the Red October and Barrikady Factories. From their new positions they are able to bring the landing stages on the west bank of the Volga under direct machine-gun fire. The remaining Soviet-held areas of the city are now on average about 300 yards deep. Their largest holdings are on the Mamayev Kurgan Hill and in the Barrikady Factory. The Red October Factory and almost all of the Tractor Factory are now in German hands. What remains to the Soviets, however, is very strongly held and fortified.

The Soviet policy has been to commit only small parts of divisions at a time, but German Intelligence has assumed that when these parts have been destroyed the whole unit can be written off. They thus overestimate the Soviet losses and underestimate the size of the Soviet reserves. The Soviet practice of briefly blooding newly assembled divisions in the Moscow sector also contributes to the faulty German appreciations. The Germans tend to assume that these divisions are being held in the central sector when in fact they have been moved south after a brief spell in the front line.

Guadalcanal The Japanese offensive is called off. They have suffered 3500 casualties. The various attacking groups have not been properly coordinated and, therefore, have been defeated in detail. Both sides are now nearly exhausted but the Japanese have lost the initiative.

28 OCTOBER 1942

Operation Torch Murphy tells General Mast that the invasion will take place early in November. Mast protests that he will be unable to organize the Allied sympathizers by then or arrange for Giraud to be accepted, but he promises to do his best. It is, of course, a considerable risk to give this information to Mast but it will be worthwhile.

28–29 OCTOBER 1942

El Alamein The attacks of the Australian division make some progress during the night in the northern sector and draw more German forces, principally from 90th Light, to oppose them. On the morning of the 29th Montgomery is persuaded to alter the direction of the next phase of his attack, Supercharge, to bear more on the Italians now alone opposite Kidney Ridge.

28–30 OCTOBER 1942

Malta The British carrier *Furious* flies off another cargo of Spitfires to Malta from Gibraltar. Malta is getting very short indeed of food and armaments, and the only supplies which are being brought in are the small quantities carried by a few submarines and one fast minelayer. The Germans and Italians are well aware that stocks are low on Malta and this knowledge contributes to their belief a few days later that the buildup of shipping in Gibraltar presages a supply operation to the island.

29 OCTOBER 1942

New Guinea The Australian forces send in a final attack against the Japanese positions at Eora, forcing the Japanese out only a little before they had intended to retire. General Vasey takes over command of the 7th Australian Division from General Allen who has been judged to be insufficiently forceful.

Guadalcanal The Japanese are dismayed by their heavy losses and begin to pull some of their units back along the coast to the west of the American bridgehead. The Americans are preparing to follow up.

Madagascar East African troops take Fianarantsoa, the most important town in the south of the island, and continue their advance toward the final areas of resistance from the Vichy forces.

30 OCTOBER 1942

New Guinea The Australian advance has reached Alola, about 10 miles south of Kokoda. One brigade is sent directly toward Kokoda while a second takes a more easterly route to Oivi.

30–31 OCTOBER 1942

El Alamein The Australians and 90th Light continue their slogging match north and east of Tell el Eisa.

NOVEMBER 1942

Battle of the Atlantic This month the U-Boat operations are again more successful than the last with 729,100 tons or 119 ships being sunk. The total loss from all causes is 807,700 tons, of which 131,000 tons are sunk in the Pacific and Indian Oceans. This is the third best month of the war for the Axis forces. In the various operations 13 German and 4 Italian submarines are lost. The main focus of the U-Boat campaign is beginning to turn to the central North Atlantic once more despite the efforts which are made against the Allied shipping near North Africa. At the start of the month the Germans have about 110 vessels on active operations.

Allied Air Operations Bomber Command's raids on Germany are less intense this month. Among the targets are Hamburg and Stuttgart. In France Allied targets include Le Havre, St Nazaire and La Pallice. RAF bombers from Britain heavily raid Genoa and Turin four times. Airfields on Sicily and Sardinia are also raided by theater forces. The RAF drops 2600 tons of bombs in the main operations and the Eighth Air Force just over 650.

Atomic Research Work begins on the first atomic pile at the University of Chicago under the direction of Enrico Fermi.

Yugoslavia, Resistance The Yugoslav National Anti-Fascist Liberation Council meets openly at Bihać in Croatia, protected by the Partisan forces. The Partisans are now solidly enough established to begin to create the apparatus of government, with courts and other administrative bodies in operation.

1 NOVEMBER 1942

Guadalcanal Two Marine regiments begin to attack west across the Matanikau River. During the last few days engineers have built bridges to help supply the attack. There is fairly heavy fighting. Other American units begin to advance east of the bridgehead toward Koli Point where a Japanese landing is expected.

Eastern Front The German advance in the Caucasus region stumbles on. Alagir, an important road junction 30 miles west of Ordzhonikidze, is taken by First Panzer Army.

1–2 NOVEMBER 1942

El Alamein Montgomery's Supercharge Operation gets under way. The infantry attacks to clear the final minefields are held up and when the armor reaches open ground during the 2nd it takes heavy losses from the prepared positions of 15th Panzer. The British can afford these largely inevitable losses, however, since later in the day when 21st Panzer joins the battle Rommel has only about 35 tanks in action with little ammunition and less fuel. He therefore signals to Hitler that he cannot prevent a breakthrough and must withdraw.

1–12 NOVEMBER 1942

Guadalcanal During this period the Japanese destroyer force bringing supplies to the island is especially active. Nearly 70 missions are run by its various ships. The force is known to the Americans as the Tokyo Express. Admiral Tanaka takes command of these operations on 5 November.

2 NOVEMBER 1942

New Guinea Kokoda is recaptured by men of the Australian 25th Brigade. With possession of the Kokoda airstrip it will now be possible to ease the strain on the men by supplying them by air rather than having everything carried up to Kokoda over the terrible switchback terrain of the trail.

Guadalcanal The US advance to the west continues slowly with some success around Cruz Point.

3 NOVEMBER 1942

El Alamein The German and Italian forces begin to withdraw but some are halted because Hitler orders no retreat. In the south the Italian infantry is already committed to the move back. Rommel is astonished by the lack of pressure from the British, who are in fact trapped in confused traffic jams in the paths through the minefields.

Guadalcanal During the early hours of the morning a Japanese force about 1500 strong is put ashore at Koli Point to the east of the American perimeter. It is engaged by the American force in the area but these troops are

soon forced to pull back. At the end of the day the Americans prepare to halt their attacks to the west in order to send reinforcements toward Koli Point.

United States, Politics In congressional elections the Republicans make some gains but do not win control. They gain nine extra seats in the Senate, 42 in the House and four more state governorships.

4 NOVEMBER 1942

El Alamein The British X Corps finally reaches open ground. There is considerable fighting in which Ariete, 90th Light and even German headquarters units all suffer heavily before breaking off to retreat. General von Thoma is captured while leading an attack. During the night, when the remnants of Rommel's forces are retreating to Fuka, the Eighth Army fails to advance at all despite Montgomery's orders to do so. The battle so far has been an almost unqualified success for the British, whatever shortcomings there may develop in the pursuit. Eighth Army has taken 30,000 prisoners, at least 1000 guns and the remains of 450 tanks. The German divisions can barely muster a regiment each and the Italian formations are ruined. The British and Commonwealth troops have about 13,500 casualties, with 150 tanks destroyed and 300 damaged.

Guadalcanal There are US landings at regimental strength at Aola, 25 miles east of the main perimeter. Among the forces landed are construction troops who have orders to build an airfield. This effort will fail, as the local commanders have claimed it will, because of the difficult ground. Raider units move out from this landing in a fighting patrol toward the main position.

Battle of the Atlantic The first meeting of the Cabinet Anti-U-Boat Warfare Committee takes place in London. Churchill himself takes the chair and the other members include the service chiefs, other government ministers and several important scientists in the fields of radar and operational research. This combination of the highest-level political, military and scientific personnel in one decision-making body is symbolic of the sort of coordination which the British and Americans are able to bring to their war efforts. None of the Axis powers achieves a system in any way comparable.

Operation Torch A group of 19 German and 21 Italian submarines begins to take up patrol positions in the western Mediterranean because of the shipping concentrations which have been sighted off Gibraltar. During the next two weeks they achieve some successes but lose six of their number.

5 NOVEMBER 1942
North Africa Rommel retreats from Fuka. Some of the Italian infantry in particular take heavy punishment. The main pursuit is held up by lack of fuel and by an old minefield which in fact is a dummy laid months previously by the British themselves.

Eastern Front The German attacks south of the Terek in the Caucasus are being worn down, but the advance still goes on and has now reached nearly to Ordzhonikidze.

Operation Torch General Eisenhower arrives in Gibraltar and sets up his headquarters. Admiral Cunningham will command the naval forces. General Doolittle and Air Marshal Welsh will command the air forces. General Anderson will lead the British First Army which will be the main ground formation.

Madagascar The Vichy forces ask for an armistice. The terms are agreed and signed on 6 November.

New Guinea The Australian forces begin attacks against Oivi. The Japanese intend to fight a rearguard action here while their main force retires across the Kumusi River.

6 NOVEMBER 1942
Egypt Many of the pursuing British forces are short of fuel because not enough can be got through the chaos around Alamein. The 7th Armored Division does catch and destroy what is left of 21st Panzer, which is completely stranded and out of fuel. Later in the day heavy rain falls which means that the only practical route of advance is now along the coast road.

7 NOVEMBER 1942
Operation Torch General Giraud, who has been brought from southern France secretly in the British submarine *Seraph*, arrives in Gibraltar for talks with General Eisenhower. The Allies wish to involve a more prominent French figure than de Gaulle or any of the North Africans in their operation in the hope of minimizing resistance from forces loyal to Vichy. They have been told by local sympathizers that Giraud will be suitable but in fact he is not likely to command wide support. Giraud believes that he has been summoned to take command of the whole operation but Eisenhower, of course, cannot agree to this.

Guadalcanal The US Marines begin attacks to the east of their main perimeter in the direction of Koli Point. There are two columns in the advance. There are Japanese landings after dark to the west of the American holdings. The troops brought in are the first from the 38th Infantry Division.

Egypt The pursuing British forces enter Mersa Matruh but most of Rommel's divisions have slipped away, albeit in total disorder.

8 NOVEMBER 1942
Operation Torch The Allied invasion of French North Africa begins. There are three main sectors of operations. The Western Task Force has sailed direct from the United States and sends in landings at three places on a 200-mile front around Casablanca. There are 35,000 troops from the US 2nd Armored, 3rd Infantry and part of the 9th Infantry Divisions. General Patton commands the ground forces. The naval forces involved include two battleships, one fleet carrier, four escort carriers and numerous cruisers and destroyers, led by Admiral Hewitt. The Center Task Force, to land in and near Oran, is led by General Fredendall and Commodore Troubridge. There are 39,000 troops from the US 1st Infantry and Armored Divisions. The naval force includes two escort carriers as well as many smaller ships. The Eastern Task Force lands at Algiers and is led by Admiral Burrough and General Ryder. There are 52 warships and 33,000 soldiers. The troops are from the US 34th Infantry Division with parts of 9th Infantry and 1st Armored also present. The only large British assault force, 78th Division, is landed here. In support of the whole operation and on guard against the still-formidable Italian Fleet is the British Force H from Gibraltar under Admiral Syfret with three battleships, three fleet carriers and a strong force of cruisers and destroyers.

At Algiers the landings make good early progress and quickly capture the town. Admiral Darlan, who is there on a visit on private business, is captured also. At Oran the landing is not so successful and an attempt to rush the harbor costs two destroyers. By nightfall, however, the landing is well established and the airfield at Tafaraiu is in Allied hands with an American-manned Spitfire force already in position. The fighting is fiercest at Casablanca. The battleship *Jean Bart*, armed but immobile, fights a gunnery duel with the *Massachusetts*. The French destroyer flotilla in the port also fights but its ships are soon driven off or sunk. Of the other landings of the Western Task Force, those at Safi go well but at Port Lyautey there is more fighting. Altogether there are 1800 Allied casualties.

All the landings receive some help from

French supporters. This help is most effective at Algiers where General Mast does much to make the French reaction hesitant enough not to hinder the actual landings. His superior, General Juin, is not actively opposed to the Allies but feels that it may be necessary for the good of the French mainland to make some show of resisting the landings. Mast and the Allied leaders are surprised when they learn that Darlan is in Algiers. As one of the principal leaders of the Vichy government he is likely to command widespread support, as being a representative of constituted French authority, and if his undoubted influence over the navy is also considered his importance is obvious. Negotiations with him begin immediately. In Casablanca General Béthouart is less successful in his efforts. General Noguès is less sympathetic to the Allied cause and the commanding admiral of the strong naval force, Admiral Michelier, is deeply anti-British.

Although most of the merchant shipping and naval support is provided by the British, the Allies have taken pains to present Torch to the French as mainly a US operation. Therefore almost all of the assault troops are American, and all the political and military contacts with the French have been made by the Americans. On the other hand, the British have better relations with the Spanish and Portuguese and have been responsible for ensuring that a German move through Spain to Gibraltar will not be aided by the Spanish. The various broadcasts put out during the day confirm these arrangements. Roosevelt and Eisenhower broadcast to the French, and the British lead in giving public assurances that Spanish neutrality will be respected. Although de Gaulle has not been told of the operation he buries his annoyance for the moment and also makes a

Above: A US Ranger battalion in the Tunisian hills soon after the Torch landings.

suitable approving broadcast.

All U-Boats in the Atlantic with sufficient fuel (25 in all) are ordered to North Africa. Among their successes is the sinking of the escort carrier *Avenger* by *U.155* on 15 November.

Eastern Front The Soviet forces in the Caucasus have gone over to the attack on the Terek front and are threatening to cut off some units of III Panzer Corps.

9 NOVEMBER 1942

French North Africa At Casablanca the US forces secure their beachheads and at Port Lyautey there is more heavy fighting between French tanks and General Truscott's troops. The town of Oran still holds out, but General Anderson, who has landed to take command of First Army at Algiers, is able to send armored columns rushing to the east. Prime Minister Laval agrees to allow the Germans to use airfields in Tunisia, and the first German troops are flown in immediately. The British planners of Torch, particularly Admiral Cunningham, wished to make landings as far west as Bône and Bizerta, but this was vetoed by the American Chiefs of Staff. In retrospect this decision seems to have been an error.

General Giraud arrives in Algiers but General Clark realizes now that Darlan is likely to command more loyalty and, therefore, continues to press him to declare for the Allies. Publicly Pétain is strongly opposed to the Allied landings but secretly he is giving some encouragement to Darlan to negotiate with them.

Egypt and Libya The New Zealand Division enters Sidi Barrani, leading the pursuit of Rommel's forces.

9–10 NOVEMBER 1942

New Guinea The Australian 25th Brigade takes Gorari after a fierce battle. The Japanese force at Oivi is, therefore, cut off and with it General Horii.

10 NOVEMBER 1942

French North Africa Oran falls to the US attack and to the east, at Casablanca, Patton's men begin to move into the town. Admiral Darlan broadcasts orders to all the French forces in North Africa to stop fighting the Allies. A similar appeal to sail and join the Allies is sent to the powerful French Fleet at Toulon.

Hitler, Laval and Ciano meet at Munich to discuss the situation in Africa and, as Hitler wishes, they decide to hold on to as much as possible. Churchill, speaking in London, describes recent events in Africa as marking 'the

end of the beginning' of the Allied efforts.

Eastern Front In response to intelligence reports of a Soviet buildup, some German units from XLVIII Panzer Corps are sent from around Stalingrad to bolster the reserves supporting Third Rumanian Army to the north.

10–11 NOVEMBER 1942

Guadalcanal The Japanese forces around Koli Point are dispersed by American attacks. Attacks to the west of the perimeter are renewed on the 10th but are halted the next day when information about Japanese convoys comes in.

11 NOVEMBER 1942

French North Africa The French authorities sign an armistice. Casablanca is occupied. The British 11th Brigade begins to move east from Algiers in strength and Bougie is taken by a landing by 36th Brigade. These forward forces have little air cover and several of the ships at Bougie carrying important equipment are sunk by the Luftwaffe during the next few days. The Germans now have over 1000 troops in Tunisia.

France Hitler orders German troops to move into Vichy.

Eastern Front In Stalingrad Paulus' last major attack begins. There is, as usual, vicious fighting with heavy casualties on both sides. Despite some new German tactics the Soviets are able to fragment the German effort so that within two days all central control is lost and the offensive degenerates into a series of unconnected actions. Some German groups are able to penetrate to the Volga while others are cut off from support. The German command is unable to follow the course of the battle and thus the Soviet small-unit expertise gradually prevails. The offensive continues for six days. The Soviets are having problems with their supplies because floating blocks of ice on the Volga are making the river crossing almost impossible.

Egypt and Libya The advance units of Eighth Army reach Halfaya Pass, move into Libya and take Bardia without opposition. The New Zealand Division is forced to halt to reorganize on the Egyptian frontier.

War at Sea Two Japanese merchant raiders attack the Indian minesweeper *Bengal* and the tanker *Ondina* in the Indian Ocean. In the ensuing action *Bengal* sinks the *Hokoku Maru* and drives the *Aikoku Maru* off despite an enormous disparity of force. Both Japanese ships have six 6-inch guns, while the *Bengal* has one 3-inch and the *Ondina* one 4-inch. This action ranks with that of the *Stephen Hopkins* as one of the most remarkable defenses made by small ships during the war.

11–13 NOVEMBER 1942

New Guinea The advancing Australians are heavily engaged around Gorari during this time. When the Japanese finally manage to pull back across the Kumusi River they leave behind 600 dead. General Horii is drowned during the retreat. This battle signals the collapse of organized Japanese resistance outside their beachhead at Gona and Buna.

12 NOVEMBER 1942

Tunisia and Algeria A combined sea and airborne assault takes Bône and the nearby airfield. The first German supply ships begin docking in Bizerta despite the efforts of the local French commanders to block the harbor and prevent this.

Guadalcanal A large American convoy landing supplies and reinforcements is compelled to retire on the approach of large Japanese naval forces. There are many Japanese air attacks on land and shipping targets.

Libya Units of the British 1st and 7th Armored Divisions enter Tobruk.

United States, Home Front The draft age is lowered from 20 to 18. Roosevelt estimates that the US armed forces will embody nearly 10,000,000 men by the end of 1943.

12–13 NOVEMBER 1942

Eastern Front In the Caucasus the Germans extricate 13th Panzer Division from a brief Soviet encirclement south of the Terek but are still under considerable pressure in this sector.

13 NOVEMBER 1942

Algeria The Allied troops at Bône are reinforced. The British 36th Brigade has now passed Djidjelli in their advance from Algiers. A formal agreement is signed by Admiral Darlan and General Clark recognizing Darlan as head of the French civil government in North Africa. The agreement is ratified by Eisenhower, Noguès and Juin. Giraud is to command the French armed forces.

Battle of Guadalcanal The Japanese send a large convoy of 11 transports carrying 11,000 men and escorted by Tanaka's 11 destroyers. To give cover to the operation and to bombard Henderson Field Admiral Abe leads two battleships, two cruisers and 14 destroyers. The Japanese carriers are at sea farther to the north providing more protection. Admiral Callaghan, with five cruisers and eight destroyers, moves to

intercept Abe's squadron.

Just before 0200 hours the two forces blunder into each other. In an action lasting about half an hour two Japanese cruisers are sunk and almost all their other ships are damaged. The Americans lose two cruisers and four destroyers. Once more the Americans fail to make proper use of their radar equipment, partly because various ships have sets with different capabilities, and communications are poor. The Japanese transport convoy turns away. Later in the day the battleship *Hiei*, badly damaged during the night, is torpedoed by American aircraft and has to be scuttled.

14 NOVEMBER 1942

Tunisia The French commander, General Barré, begins to move his troops away from the coastal towns in preparation for going over to the Allies.

14–15 NOVEMBER 1942

Battle of Guadalcanal Tanaka turns south with his destroyers and transports early on the 14th and immediately comes under heavy air attack. Seven of the transports and two warships are lost. The attacking aircraft mostly come from Henderson Field but some are from the carrier *Enterprise*. Tanaka continues his advance, however, and during the night there is a further battle off Savo Island. The Japanese covering force is now led by Admiral Kondo with the battleship *Kirishima*, four cruisers and nine destroyers. The Americans have brought up TF 64 (Admiral Lee) with the battleships *Washington* and *South Dakota* and four destroyers. Shortly before midnight the engagement begins. *South Dakota* is hit and forced out of the battle but later a devastating seven-minute burst of fire from *Washington* sinks *Kirishima*. Control of the seas round Guadalcanal is now passing gradually to the Americans but in this case Tanaka's remaining transports manage to reach Tassafaronga. Of the troops who have survived the earlier attacks more are killed while landing. After this defeat the Japanese are forced to make considerable use of submarines to transport supplies. Already many of their men are ill and hungry.

15 NOVEMBER 1942

Tunisia and Algeria The British 36th Brigade captures Tabarka on the coast road to Bizerta. US paratroops take the airfield at Youks les Bains near Tebéssa. The German buildup has been very rapid and there are now 10,000 troops taking up positions in Tunisia. They have over 100 combat planes in bases long established by the French, convenient for the front and with all-weather runways. The Allied air forces are forced to use temporary landing grounds farther from the front.

New Guinea Having built rudimentary bridges over the Kumusi the Australians are able to advance to take Wairopi and Ilimow.

16 NOVEMBER 1942

Tunisia A British parachute battalion takes Souk el Arba and 36th Brigade farther north takes Djebel Abiod. Late in the day the paratroops have reached nearly to Béja.

General de Gaulle announces that he and his Free French supporters do not accept Darlan's authority. Many British politicians are worried, too, about cooperating with a former member of the Vichy government. The Americans have been always much more ready to favor Vichy than the British and, therefore, see nothing wrong with such a useful arrangement.

17 NOVEMBER 1942

Libya The vanguard of Eighth Army has reached Derna on the coast and Mechili inland.

New Guinea A Japanese convoy lands 1000 fresh troops at Buna. The Japanese positions around Gona, Buna and Sanananda have been strongly fortified since September and are now well garrisoned also.

Burma General Wavell decides to cancel the proposed major amphibious operation against Akyab and instead, on 19 November, issues orders for a more limited advance by 14th Indian Division down the Mayu Peninsula perhaps to be followed by a shorter seaborne operation against Akyab.

17–20 NOVEMBER 1942

Malta A convoy, code named Stoneage, passes from Gibraltar to the island. None of the four freighters is lost and of the three cruisers and 10 destroyers which form the escort only one vessel is hit. The long period of heavy attacks on the island is over and the siege has come to an end.

18 NOVEMBER 1942

Guadalcanal The US forces begin moving west from their perimeter once more. The attacks are not particularly forceful but do continue for five days before the next lull. The Americans are not again compelled to close up to their original perimeter.

Tunisia The British Brigade at Djebel Abiod drives off a German attack. The parachute force is now at Sidi Nsir.

Vichy, Politics Pétain grants power to Laval

allowing him to issue decrees solely on his own authority. Pétain is gradually becoming less and less important in the Vichy government, although his enormous prestige remains.

19 NOVEMBER 1942

Eastern Front The Soviet winter offensive begins along the Don. The German forces throughout the southern Soviet Union are hopelessly overextended. Stalingrad has drawn German troops like moths to a candle while both to their left and right are unreliable allies. The Soviets have been planning a grand attack with fresh divisions for weeks. They intend a pincer move with armies from the Southwest Front (Vatutin) and the Don Front (Rokossovsky) attacking southward from the Don, especially between Kletskaya and Kotovskiy, and the Stalingrad Front (Yeremenko) whose armies are to attack westward from south of the city. Zhukov is in overall command. Only the northern claw of the pincer attacks at this stage. The Soviets have assembled more than 500,000 infantry, 900 new T34 tanks, and have the support of masses of artillery and over 1000 attack planes. The units deployed in the northern pincer are Fifth Tank Army, Twenty-first Army and part of First Guards Army. The unfortunate victims are the seven divisions of the Rumanian Third Army who come under murderous pressure and can do little to prevent a major breakthrough around Kletskaya. In the Caucasus the Germans are in trouble also. The Soviets win an important engagement near Ordzhonikidze. Bad weather largely ends major operations here but the Soviets manage a series of small gains in the next few weeks.

Tunisia French forces at Medjez el Bab resist German attacks and are reinforced by the British and Americans. The Germans, now led by General Nehring, have brought forward tanks and infantry. General Barré openly joins the Allies.

Libya Eighth Army enters Benghazi.

New Guinea The US troops from Pongani begin their attack on Buna, believing it to be only lightly held. In reality the Americans are easily pushed back by the well-prepared Japanese forces. The Australians are closing up to Gona and a mixed Allied force is moving on Sanananda.

Battle of the Atlantic Admiral Horton takes over the British Western Approaches Command from Admiral Noble. Although Noble has been an able leader, he does not have the forceful spirit which Horton brings to the job. The German U-Boat leaders soon notice the change.

CHRONOLOGY

20 NOVEMBER 1942

Eastern Front The southern claw of the Soviet pincer round Stalingrad begins its attacks. The attacking units are from Fifty-first, Sixty-fourth and Fifty-seventh Armies. The principal victims here are the Rumanian Fourth Army and part of the German Fourth Panzer Army (the other part is in the city and will be surrounded). The attack is held up for a time by energetic counterattacks by the 29th Panzergrenadier Division, but eventually the Soviet numbers tell.

Vichy, Politics Laval broadcasts once more in support of Germany. He says that Germany will win the war and that the alternative is to be ruled by 'Jews and Communists.' At a press conference on 13 December he confirms these views announcing, 'I must say without any ambiguity, that I want Germany's victory.'

New Guinea An Australian advance succeeds in breaking into the Japanese position at Gona but the attacking force is later driven out. The Australian and American attacks on the Japanese positions continue intermittently for the next 10 days, but with small success.

21 NOVEMBER 1942

Eastern Front The Rumanian Third Army is in a desperate condition. The Soviets have 34 divisions in the advance and have broken through on a 50-mile front. Tank units from Rokossovsky's Don Front are advancing rapidly toward Kalach. The German command is disorganized. Sixth Army's staff is being forced to move because of the Soviet advance and General Manstein, who has been ordered to take command of a new Army Group Don, is making a long train journey to take up his post.

23 NOVEMBER 1942

Eastern Front The important bridge over the Don at Kalach is captured by Soviet forces coming from the north in a surprise attack. After crossing this bridge advance units link up with tank forces of Fifty-first Army and the encirclement of Stalingrad begins. The Soviets believe that they have about 85,000 Germans cut off in the city when in fact the total is nearer 300,000. Five Rumanian divisions of Third Army's seven surrender around Raspopinskaya.

The Soviets intend, as their first priority, methodically to destroy the Stalingrad garrison before continuing their offensive to the west. Zhukov supports this unambitious scheme because he is well aware of the limitations of the Soviet forces in wide-ranging operations. Despite this priority, the false assessment of German positions leaves the siege forces short.

Libya After a sharp action around Agedabia the Axis troops fall back to the El Agheila position. Montgomery halts his advance to reorganize his forces, which have now chased their enemy almost 600 miles in 14 days. The British advance has been perhaps too cautious although German demolitions and booby traps have been one cause of delay.

France, Politics Darlan announces that French West Africa now accepts his authority.

24 NOVEMBER 1942

Eastern Front Manstein arrives at Army Group A Headquarters. He has been summoned south from Leningrad to restore the situation but the forces allocated to him to create Army Group Don are either practically nonexistent or shut in Stalingrad. The whole of Sixth Army and most of Fourth Panzer Army are surrounded, and have orders from Hitler to maintain their positions with the help of air supply. Five of the seven divisions of the Third Rumanian Army have surrendered. Almost the only significant German unit available to Manstein is a division holding the important position at Elista which ought to be maintained as a link with Army Group A in the Caucasus. The other German Army Group commanders and the High Command cooperate with Manstein's request for reserves only with reluctance and his buildup is, therefore, slow.

It is not at all clear to Manstein how he should proceed even when his forces are assembled. The Soviets already have over 1000 antitank guns in positions round Stalingrad and with such opposition a breakout may be impossible. Even if a breakout is possible Manstein cannot be sure that it is desirable. Since the Soviets would have no need to continue to invest the city they could devote their forces to further wide encirclements, to which the Germans would be especially vulnerable with Sixth Army and the relieving force concentrated at the tip of an exposed salient. In this situation the whole of Manstein's forces and also Army Group A in the Caucasus might well be endangered. In fact this large threat will not materialize for the moment because of the more limited Soviet intentions, but it must remain in Manstein's thoughts.

Hitler's orders to hold on to Stalingrad are based on a wild claim by Goering that Stalingrad can be supplied by air. Sixth Army would need at least 700 tons of supplies each day and for this 500 planes would be necessary as well as good weather and low losses. There are 300 planes available and their airfields are in poor condition and under threat from the Soviet advance. There is no possibility of Goering keeping his promise although the attempt will be made and almost 500 planes lost before the end of the siege. They will manage to take out 42,000 wounded men and some important specialists.

In the central sector, west of Moscow, there are Soviet attacks around Rzhev and Velikiye Luki.

25 NOVEMBER 1942

Greece, Resistance   Led by British SOE agents, resistance workers from two rival Greek organizations join forces to blow up an important viaduct on the Athens–Salonika railroad at Gorgopotamos. Many of Rommel's supplies have in the past used this route.

26 NOVEMBER 1942

Eastern Front   The Soviets claim to have taken Krasnoye, Generalov and Selo on the Don. For the next few days there is something of a lull on the outer ring round Stalingrad. The Soviets are concentrating on the German pocket inside and the Germans are busy assembling strength for a counterattack.

Tunisia   The Germans are driven out of Medjez el Bab by the British 78th Division. The German-held airfield at Djedeida is raided by a US tank battalion.

26–27 NOVEMBER 1942

New Guinea   Despite losing a destroyer to air attack the Japanese manage to reinforce their troops at Buna.

27 NOVEMBER 1942

France   The German II SS Panzer Corps occupies Toulon but the French Fleet is scuttled by order of Admiral Laborde. Three battleships, seven cruisers and 62 other craft go down, including 16 submarines.

Tunisia   Tebourba, 15 miles west of Tunis, is captured by the Allied forces while another column approaches Bizerta.

28 NOVEMBER 1942

Eastern Front   The Soviets make considerable gains on the central sector near Rzhev.

Tunisia   British and American forces at brigade strength take Djedeida, but German troops are moving on their rear from St Cyprien.

Indian Ocean   Free French forces occupy the island of Réunion.

29 NOVEMBER 1942

Tunisia   A British parachute battalion lands at Depienne and moves toward Oudna. The Allied forces occupying Djedeida come under heavy pressure and begin to fall back.

Churchill broadcasts from London, warning the Italian people that they must chose between a full-scale Allied attack and a revolt against Mussolini.

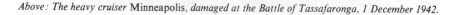

Above: The heavy cruiser Minneapolis, *damaged at the Battle of Tassafaronga, 1 December 1942.*

CHRONOLOGY

30 NOVEMBER 1942

New Guinea The American forces attacking Buna make their first real gains.

Burma The advance of the British 123rd Brigade in the Arakan has now reached Bawli Bazar. Terrible weather, which would normally be expected to clear during November, has been impeding the advance and making road construction difficult.

German Raiders The German raider *Thor* is destroyed by fire in Yokohama Harbor. In a cruise lasting from January–October 1942, *Thor* sank 10 ships of 56,000 tons.

30 NOVEMBER–1 DECEMBER 1942

Battle of Tassafaronga The regular night run of the Tokyo Express again develops into a major battle. Tanaka has eight destroyers and the US Admiral Wright has five heavy cruisers and seven destroyers. Although radar helps Wright get off the first shells and torpedoes the American fire is ineffective, with one Japanese destroyer sinking later. In the Japanese reply one cruiser is sunk and three very seriously damaged. Despite these successes Tanaka is reprimanded for failing to deliver his supplies to the starving Japanese forces on the island.

DECEMBER 1942

Battle of the Atlantic This month the U-Boats sink 60 ships of 330,000 tons in the Atlantic convoy battles. The most important development during the month is the change in the standard of the Allied intelligence information that occurs in the second week when the U-Boat cipher Triton is broken for the first time. For several months there will be delays, often of three or four days or sometimes as much as a week, before new settings on the code machine can be broken. Even when messages can be decoded promptly it will not always be possible to route convoys away from U-Boat concentrations. One problem here is the shortage in Britain of bunker fuel for the merchant fleet. There are only two months' reserves outside RN stocks.

During 1942 Allied shipping losses have been 7,790,000 tons of which less than 7,000,000 tons has been replaced by new construction. The German U-Boat strength has increased to 212 operational boats despite a shortfall of 15 percent in production. Eighty percent of the Allied loss has fallen to submarines. British resources in shipping and British needs for imports and the transport of supplies to forces overseas remain greater than those of the US for the moment. During Torch Britain has been lending more shipping to the US than she has been borrowing. During 1942 Britain has consumed 2,400,000 tons of supplies more than has been landed. The year 1943 will see the American production begin to show fruit and will see a complete change in the patterns of Allied shipping and losses.

Allied Air Operations British bomber targets in Germany include Frankfurt, Duisburg and Munich. In France American attacks are made on Abbeville and Rouen as well as other joint British and American raids with lighter forces. RAF bombers from bases in Britain attack Turin on three occasions while targets raided by the British and American forces from North Africa include Naples (five times), Palermo and Taranto. RAF Bomber Command drops 3000 tons in these operations and the US Eighth Air Force based in Britain drops 370 tons.

The navigational aid *Oboe* comes into service with the RAF. It gives accurate and reliable results, but its range is comparatively limited, reaching only as far as the Ruhr from bases in Britain. Only a very limited number of planes can be operated on the system at a time so it is used mostly for target marking. Theoretically it is very vulnerable to jamming, but the Germans only begin this in August 1943. More advanced versions of *Oboe*, which enter service from late in 1943, remain almost immune to interference until the end of the war.

1 DECEMBER 1942

French North Africa In Tunisia there is a strong German counterattack near Tebourba which the Allies manage to beat off after taking heavy casualties. German forces in Tunisia are now 15,000 strong. The buildup is to continue. Two German infantry divisions and most of 10th Panzer Division will arrive soon. The Italians have shipped 90,000 tons of supplies to Tunisia since Operation Torch began and the German air-transport fleet is also very active. Allied attacks are taking a considerable, and increasing, toll of these shipments. The efforts made to strengthen Tunisia also mean that Rommel is forced to make do with a poorer allowance for his troops to the east.

Darlan broadcasts from Algiers announcing that, because the Chief of State, Marshal Pétain, is a prisoner, he has assumed the responsibilities of the French government.

General Spaatz is transferred to command the Allied Air Forces in Northwest Africa. General Eaker takes his place with Eighth Air Force in Britain. Many of the supplies which would otherwise have come to Eighth Air Force are now being sent to North Africa where Twelfth Air Force will be established.

Britain, Home Front The House of Commons receives the Report on Social Insurance prepared by the Beveridge Committee. The report proposes far-reaching measures of social reform which are designed to eliminate poverty in Britain. The laws which will emerge from the consideration of the report are the foundation of Britain's modern welfare system.

United States, Home Front Gasoline rationing is introduced throughout the country.

1–2 DECEMBER 1942

Mediterranean Axis supply problems are well illustrated by events during these two days. There are four Italian convoys at sea which are threatened by a British squadron of three cruisers and two destroyers. Three of the convoys are recalled. The four freighters and one of the escorts of the fourth convoy are sunk and two more escorts damaged. The British later lose one destroyer to an air attack. During December the Italians will try to convoy over 200,000 tons of cargo to Tunis and Tripoli, but of this 90,000 tons (32 ships) will be lost to British and Allied naval and air attacks.

2 DECEMBER 1942

Atomic Research The first manmade, self-sustaining chain reaction is achieved in the atomic pile at Chicago University.

New Guinea The Australians capture part of the Gona defenses. A further Japanese reinforcement convoy for Buna is turned away by air attacks but the troops carried are landed along the coast to the west. General Eichelberger has been sent by MacArthur to investigate the lack of progress at Buna and he decides to relieve General Harding of command of the US forces there.

3 DECEMBER 1942

Tunisia Djedeida and Tebourba are taken by German troops from 10th Panzer Division after a series of attacks.

3–4 DECEMBER 1942

Guadalcanal Tanaka leads 10 destroyers in a supply operation. Only about 300 of the 1500 containers dropped reach the Japanese forces ashore.

4 DECEMBER 1942

Italy The US Ninth Air Force attacks Naples, sinking two cruisers in the harbor and causing other damage. This is the first US raid on the mainland of Italy.

United States, Politics Roosevelt receives a petition from 244 Congressmen supporting the establishment of a Jewish homeland in Palestine.

5 DECEMBER 1942

New Guinea There is a strong US attack on Buna which is halted by defensive fire after a few scattered gains have been made.

6 DECEMBER 1942

Tunisia The Allied forces are pushed back near Medjez el Bab by renewed German attacks which continue for the next four days.

New Guinea After more vicious fighting the Allied troops manage to reach the beach on the east side of Buna. The Australian forces again attack at Gona but with little success. Japanese attempts to push a relieving force along the coast from farther west make some progress.

7 DECEMBER 1942

New Guinea There are fierce Japanese counterattacks at Buna which are only just beaten off by the US forces.

Eastern Front There are several Soviet attacks to gain bridgeheads over the River Chir and threaten the German airfields which are the bases for the supply operation to Stalingrad. The German 11th Panzer Division is in the area and in a sequence of maneuver battles it brings the Soviet advance to a halt, but only at considerable cost.

7–8 DECEMBER 1942

Guadalcanal A Japanese supply operation, involving seven destroyers led by Captain Sato, is abandoned because of attacks by American PT boats.

8 DECEMBER 1942

Tunisia German forces led by General Gause occupy Bizerta, capturing four French destroyers, nine submarines and three other warships.

Britain, Home Front Parliament lowers the age for conscription by six months, to 18.

8–9 DECEMBER 1942

New Guinea In yet another horrible engagement the Japanese positions at Gona are stormed by Australian troops from 21st Brigade.

9 DECEMBER 1942

Guadalcanal The exhausted 1st Marine Division is relieved by General Patch's XIV Corps. The Marines begin to leave for Australia and, as

Above: Japanese casualties on Guadalcanal.

not all Patch's force is assembled, there is a continued lull in the land fighting.

10 DECEMBER 1942
Eastern Front A small German counterattack in the Rzhev area makes a little ground.

10–11 DECEMBER 1942
Tunisia In the continuing German attacks Medjez el Bab is now the objective but the advancing columns are finally beaten off. The Allied force is still very thin on the ground and many of the troops are showing their inexperience.

11 DECEMBER 1942
Libya Eighth Army begins to advance once more.

11–12 DECEMBER 1942
Guadalcanal Tanaka again leads a Japanese supply operation with 11 destroyers. One destroyer is sunk, and of 1200 containers dropped overboard to float in to the island, only 200 are collected by the Japanese forces. The remainder are mostly punctured and sunk by machine-gun fire from American PT boats.

12 DECEMBER 1942
Eastern Front Although the Germans have a bridgehead over the Don at Nizhne Chirskaya, only 25 miles from the nearest of the forces trapped in the Stalingrad pocket, Manstein has decided to begin his relieving attack farther south, around Kotelnikovo. The code name for the operation is *Wintergewitter* (Winter Storm). General Hoth is in tactical charge of the attack

which, with initial armor superiority, makes good progress at first. The Germans have assembled a total of 13 divisions for the operation, including three Panzer units. The Soviet line, held by Fifty-first Army, is comparatively weak because its next major moves are planned both farther north and farther south. In fact Second Guards Army, which is intended to participate in the next attack to the north, is quickly summoned to take up positions on the Myshkova River. This reinforcement for the Soviet rear cannot arrive for a few days, and Fifty-first Army is left to delay the German advance.
Tunisia Italian midget submarines sink four ships in Algiers Harbor. There is more heavy fighting near Medjez el Bab.

13 DECEMBER 1942
Libya Eighth Army captures Mersa Brega. Rommel begins to pull out of the El Agheila position.
Tunisia There are heavy US air raids on Bizerta and Tunis. On the ground the fighting dies down for the moment.

14 DECEMBER 1942
Eastern Front The German relieving attack toward Stalingrad is still making good progress. The airlift to the city today supplies 180 tons. This is the largest effort which will be managed on any day during the siege.
Libya The El Agheila line is attacked by 7th Armored Division while the New Zealanders attempt an outflanking maneuver.
New Guinea Japanese reinforcements land about 30 miles west of Gona and begin to march along the coast toward the Australians' flank. There are renewed US attacks on Buna village which is taken easily after a brief Japanese resistance. The far tougher obstacle of the Buna Government Station still remains in Japanese hands.
Madagascar Eden and de Gaulle agree that the administration of the island should be handed over to the Free French. General le Gentilhomme will be High Commissioner.

15–25 DECEMBER 1942
Solomons In addition to their usual duties Tanaka's flotilla carries out several missions to help build an airfield on Munda (New Georgia) to support the operation on Guadalcanal.

16 DECEMBER 1942
Eastern Front The Soviets begin the next phase (*Saturn*) of their winter offensive even though

the German drive toward Stalingrad is still going forward slowly. The Soviet blow falls on the Italian Eighth Army on the middle Don and this force is almost immediately shattered. As in the Soviet offensive in November, there are very few German units in the immediate area of the attacks. There are also Soviet attacks along the Chir against Army Detachment Hollidt. The German relieving attack toward Stalingrad is still going well but the Soviet breakthrough to the north threatens the sort of wide encirclement that has been particularly worrying to Manstein for the past few weeks.

Libya Because of the progress of the New Zealanders to their rear, the Axis force at El Agheila splits into small groups to break away.

Guadalcanal The Tokyo Express is again in operation. The destroyer *Kagero* is damaged by US dive bombers. On land the US forces begin to move on Mount Austen.

Burma In the Arakan the British forces have assembled two brigades to attack the Japanese lines between Maungdaw and Buthidaung, but the Japanese forces pull out before the blow can fall. They move south to a shorter, more defensible line between Gwedauk and Kondan.

17 DECEMBER 1942
Eastern Front The Volga freezes over and the Soviets are able to send supplies easily to Sixty-second Army on the west bank in Stalingrad. This has been difficult for the past few weeks because of fast-moving blocks of ice floating down river. Hoth's attacks to relieve the city are still going fairly well, with his leading tank units now having reached the Aksai River.

Libya Rommel leaves a rearguard to cover his main forces while they consolidate at Buerat.

Tunisia There are heavy US air attacks on Tunis and Gabes and other German air bases.

18 DECEMBER 1942
New Guinea Cape Endiadere, east of Buna, is taken by the Allies. Australian forces are now leading the attack here, and with newly arrived tank support they are able to come to grips with the Japanese defenses on more favorable terms than in the recent past. The battle continues.

Libya There is a brisk engagement at Nofilia.

19 DECEMBER 1942
Eastern Front The Soviets take Kontemirovka. The Italian Eighth Army has practically ceased to exist as a fighting formation. Owing to the success of this attack, Paulus is ordered by Manstein to attempt a breakout immediately, but he refuses. The chief of staff of Sixth Army,

General Schmidt, an ardent Nazi, is instrumental in bringing about this decision. General Hoth's attacks to relieve the city are gradually making less and less ground. They are now being held near the Myshkova River.

Guadalcanal The American forces on Mount Austen meet heavy resistance.

20 DECEMBER 1942
Eastern Front The Soviets claim to have reached nearly to Millerovo, 70 miles northeast of Voroshilovgrad. The Rostov-Voronezh railroad has been cut and severe pressure is now being brought to bear on Army Detachment Hollidt, the northern wing of Manstein's force. Manstein tries to get Zeitzler at OKH to arrange for a breakout by Paulus. Zeitzler gives little help and Paulus now pleads that he is too short of fuel to attempt it in any case. There is some truth to this argument, but not to make some sort of effort is senseless.

21 DECEMBER 1942
Eastern Front The Red Army makes a deep advance with the troops of General Golikov's Voronezh Front. Manstein appeals to Hitler to order Paulus to break out, but Hitler quotes Paulus' reports of fuel shortage and refuses.

Burma The British forces advancing toward Akyab capture Alethangyaw.

22 DECEMBER 1942
Eastern Front The Soviet advances are very rapid and they retake several towns, including Morozovsk, Nikolkoe and Fydorovka.

Tunisia The British V Corps of First Army begins an attack just north of Medjez el Bab. The fiercest fighting centers around Longstop Hill. There is very heavy rain which does much to hinder the attack.

Burma General Lloyd orders his 47th Brigade to advance down both sides of the Mayu Peninsula while the 123rd Brigade is to send the bulk of its force toward Rathedaung. A small detachment is to move farther inland in the direction of Kyauktaw. These dispositions are less than ideal because of the dispersion they bring about.

23 DECEMBER 1942
Eastern Front While Manstein has been fighting to have Paulus ordered to break out, Hoth has been dutifully battling his way forward. Today, however, the Soviet defense line on the Myshkova River finally wears Hoth's attacks to a halt. The troops in Stalingrad can hear the fighting but it comes no closer.

CHRONOLOGY

24 DECEMBER 1942
Eastern Front The Soviets drive Hoth back. Despite stubborn resistance Generalovsky is taken. In Stalingrad fresh forces attached to Sixty-second Army retake the Red October Factory.
French North Africa Admiral Darlan is shot in his office by a fanatic called Bonnier de la Chapelle who supports both royalist and Gaullist policies.
The fighting in Tunisia continues. Although Longstop is once again taken by a British Guards battalion, Eisenhower, Anderson and Allfrey (commanding V Corps) decide to end their attacks for the moment.
New Guinea The Allied forces break into the new defensive positions of the Japanese near Buna, but the casualties are heavy and the last serviceable tanks of the small group which has been in support for the last few days are also lost.
Burma Japanese advances in two areas of the Chin Hills are repelled by Allied troops.

25 DECEMBER 1942
Libya The Axis garrison of Sirte, already outflanked, withdraws because of pressure to the front.
New Britain The Japanese base at Rabaul is attacked by bombers from Guadalcanal, causing damage to harbor installations.
Tunisia The German forces retake Longstop Hill. There is continued sporadic activity for the next few days, but this soon dies down with bad weather and supply problems hindering both sides.
Burma Patrols from the 123rd Brigade reach Rathedaung and report that the Japanese have moved out. In fact this is not the case and Japanese reinforcements are on their way.

26 DECEMBER 1942
Eastern Front Manstein's forces are in full retreat south of the Don and the Soviet advance nears Kotelnikovo.
France, Politics General Giraud is chosen as French high commissioner for North Africa. Darlan's assassin is executed.

27 DECEMBER 1942
Guadalcanal The US attacks on Mount Austen are restarted. The attacking troops, from the 132nd Infantry Regiment, lose heavily and are brought to a halt despite considerable artillery preparation.
Eastern Front As well as their continuing advance on the Stalingrad fronts, the Soviets are also on the move in the Caucasus, especially

around Nalchik where there are six armies attacking under the command of Maslennikov and Tyulenev. Von Kleist is beginning to withdraw, fearful of being cut off if the advance of the Stalingrad armies reaches Rostov to the north.
Under German auspices the captured General Vlasov forms the Smolensk Committee to organize Russian opponents of Stalin. This body will later become known as the Liberation Army. The Germans give little real support to Vlasov and fail to understand his position as both a patriotic Russian and an opponent of Stalinism.

27–28 DECEMBER 1942
Burma Part of the 123rd Indian Brigade tries to occupy Rathedaung but is thrown back by the recently reinforced Japanese forces there.

28 DECEMBER 1942
Atomic Research Roosevelt confirms the policy of noncooperation with the British that his advisers have been recommending. He orders that no information should be given to the British unless it happens to be in an area in which British scientists are directly involved. Among the American worries is the question of the postwar peaceful use of atomic energy and the fear that the British may be too concerned with using American research for this. That one of the leading British workers is also research director for a major British chemical and industrial company only confirms this fear.
The British are upset at Roosevelt's decision feeling that it contradicts former agreements and does not recognize the important early work done by the British. Churchill raises the matter with Hopkins at the Casablanca conference and again with Roosevelt in Washington in May. (*See* 20 July for further developments.)
Vichy, Politics In a broadcast Pétain describes the Free French leaders as having betrayed French Africa to the British and Americans.

29 DECEMBER 1942
Eastern Front The Soviets recapture Kotelnikovo after a bitter fight and make other gains all along the front.
Libya The advance elements of Eighth Army come to a halt before the Axis' Buerat position.

30 DECEMBER 1942
Eastern Front The Soviets retake Remontnoe, 40 miles northwest of Elista.

30–31 DECEMBER 1942
Battle of the Barents Sea The Germans send

heavy surface ships to try to intercept the Arctic convoy JW-51B. On 30 December Admiral Kummetz sets out from north Norway with the pocket battleship *Lützow* and the heavy cruiser *Admiral Hipper* with an escort of six destroyers. The British escorts for the convoy are in three groups. Captain Sherbrooke commands the close escort of seven destroyers and five other warships. Admiral Burnett leads a close-covering force of two light cruisers and two destroyers. Admiral Fraser is also at sea with the battleship *Anson* and an escort, but is forbidden to risk air attack near Norway and will not take part in the action.

On 31 December the *Hipper* and the *Lützow* move toward the convoy on separate courses. *Hipper* approaches three times and *Lützow* twice, but Sherbrooke's destroyers use smoke-screens and the threat of torpedo attack to keep the German ships ineffective at a distance. One British destroyer is sunk and one badly damaged. Burnett's cruisers are able to intervene during the *Hipper*'s third approach, damaging the German ship and sinking one destroyer. After this the German force withdraws. The German leaders have been hampered by instructions not to risk serious damage to their ships and have, therefore, shown a disastrous lack of initiative despite their overwhelming strength. The enterprise with which the British ships have been handled has done the rest.

31 DECEMBER 1942

Eastern Front Troops of the Soviet Fifth Shock Army, driving southwest from Nizhne Chirskaya, expel the Germans from Tormosin. Army Detachment Hollidt can do little to halt such strong attacks.

Guadalcanal The Japanese High Command decide to evacuate the island. The orders are issued on 4 January.

Libya A Free French force under the command of General Leclerc advances from Chad into the South Fezzan. They will continue to move north and join up with Eighth Army during January 1943.

JANUARY 1943

Battle of the Atlantic The German U-Boat fleet now has 212 operational boats and a further 181 on training or trials missions. This month the Allied shipping losses are fairly moderate at 50 ships of 261,400 tons of which total submarines account for 37 ships of 203,100 tons. Bad weather in the Atlantic and effective evasive routing by the convoy authorities helps keep the losses down. One successful action for the Germans is against the tanker convoy TM-1 which loses seven of its nine ships in attacks just to the south of the Azores. Radar failures hamper the escort. At the end of the month Liberators in Coastal Command service begin to be fitted with 10-centimeter ASV radar. This offers an enormous improvement in performance over the earlier types and cannot be detected by the search receivers presently fitted in the U-Boats. It is similar to the H2S radar entering service with the strategic bomber forces.

Allied Air Operations The Allied air offensive is directed this month principally against the German U-Boat bases and production centers. Among the manufacturing towns attacked are Essen, Cologne and Dusseldorf. The first USAAF raid on Germany is against Wilhelmshaven on 27 January. Targets in France for the USAAF include St Nazaire and Brest. Altogether the Americans drop 547 tons of bombs. The British effort is still much greater. The RAF drops more than 1000 tons in four raids on Lorient alone. The navigational aid H2S is used for the first time over Hamburg on 30/31 January. There is also the first daytime raid on Berlin, by a force of RAF Mosquitoes on the 30th. The Casablanca Directive sets forth future bombing policy for both the British and American strategic forces.

The average daily availability of Bomber Command aircraft is now about 515 compared with about 500 a year before. The quality of the force has much improved. There are now 178 Lancasters and 104 Halifaxes in the heavy bomber force and 17 Mosquitoes are also in service. The number of Wellingtons is now down to 128. The navigational aids Gee, Oboe and H2S are all available and will be improved. General Eaker's Eighth Air Force has about 80 bombers and is gradually gaining experience.

JANUARY–APRIL 1943

Yugoslavia, Resistance The German forces mount their fourth offensive against Tito's Partisans. There are actions throughout Hercegovina, Montenegro and in Dalmatia. Although Tito's forces lose heavily and there is much destruction of the homes and livelihood of his supporters, the Partisans remain in the fight.

1 JANUARY 1943

Eastern Front After vicious street fighting the Soviets capture Velikiye Luki in the central sector. Other important positions taken include Elista and Chikola.

New Guinea Heavy attacks against the Japanese positions at Buna continue. Some of the garrison withdraw as the situation becomes hopeless.

2 JANUARY 1943
New Guinea Troops from Eichelberger's I Corps storm the Japanese posts at Buna. Fighting continues, however, around Sanananda.

Guadalcanal Once again the Americans mount a formal attack on the Japanese positions on Mount Austen. Some progress is made but the Gifu strongpoint remains in Japanese hands.

3 JANUARY 1943
Eastern Front The Soviet Caucasus offensive is now well under way. Mozdok and Malgobek are both retaken by troops from Fifty-eighth and Forty-fourth Armies. Farther north Manstein is fighting hard to keep the Soviets from cutting Kleist off in the Caucasus and at Stalingrad Sixth Army continues to suffer. The inadequate attempts to ferry supplies in by air are proving very costly indeed and the route to Stalingrad is littered with wrecked German transport aircraft.

4 JANUARY 1943
Eastern Front The Soviet advance goes on. They capture Nalchik in the Caucasus and Chernyshkovskiy on the River Chir.

New Georgia The Japanese base at Munda is bombarded by the US TF 67 (Admiral Ainsworth). A second group of cruisers and destroyers is in support. Proximity fuses for AA ammunition are used for the first time by one of the bombarding vessels.

5 JANUARY 1943
Tunisia British forces make small gains near Djebel Azzag west of Mateur.

Eastern Front The Russians capture Prokhladny in the Caucasus and consolidate their gains farther north by taking Morozovsk and Tsimlyansk.

Guadalcanal The Americans are unaware that the Japanese are beginning to execute their planned withdrawal. The Japanese stand on Mount Austen continues despite the growing American strength.

Tunisia The US Fifth Army led by General Clark becomes operational.

6 JANUARY 1943
German Command Following the fiasco of the attack on the convoy JW-51B (*see* 30–31 December 1942), Admiral Raeder resigns his post as Commander in Chief of the navy.

7 JANUARY 1943
Guadalcanal The Americans send fresh troops against Mount Austen and begin to make final dispositions in all sectors for new advances.

New Guinea A Japanese convoy lands supplies and reinforcements at Lae despite air attacks.

8 JANUARY 1943
Eastern Front Rokossovsky, commanding the Don Front Armies besieging Stalingrad, and Voronov, the Stavka representative, issue a summons to surrender to the Germans. Paulus' sense of resistance is stiffened by his chief of staff, Schmidt, a convinced Nazi, and he ignores the demand. In terms of manpower the German defenders are if anything superior, but the Russians are well fed and clothed and have adequate supplies of fuel and ammunition. The Germans have virtually nothing and are already weakened by hunger and cold. Farther south Zimovniki falls to Russian attack.

Madagascar The Free French take over the administration of the island.

9 JANUARY 1943
New Guinea The Australian 17th Brigade is airlifted to Wau to establish a forward base for the next phase of the Allied offensive which will take place when the capture of Buna and Sanananda is achieved and consolidated. In that sector the Americans take Tarakena village but are held up when they try to advance nearer to Sanananda.

10 JANUARY 1943
Eastern Front The Russians begin an offensive all round Stalingrad. They nominally have seven armies and the Germans the equivalent of two, but Russian armies are only the same size as a German corps. Sixty-second and Sixty-fourth on the east and southeast of the circle are particularly under strength. All the Russian forces move to the attack but the main effort is by Sixty-fifth and Twenty-first Armies to the west. The attack goes in after the usual fierce barrage and the Germans are soon on the retreat.

Guadalcanal An American offensive begins, accompanied by heavy air and artillery bombardments. The Gifu strongpoint is again attacked by the 35th Infantry Regiment. The Americans now have well over 50,000 men on Guadalcanal and the Japanese less than 15,000, all of whom are desperately short of food. During the night eight Japanese destroyers attempt to bring supplies. One is damaged by PT boats.

New Guinea The American forces make some

progress in their drive on Sanananda and make a small advance near Tarakena.

11 JANUARY 1943
Eastern Front The Siege of Leningrad is partially broken. A narrow corridor is opened south of Lake Ladoga by concerted attacks by the Leningrad garrison and the troops of the Volkhov Front.

In the Caucasus the Russians take Georgivesk, Pyatigorsk and Mineralnye Vody. Slightly farther north Kuberle, on the railroad line from Zimovniki to Proletarskaya, also falls.
Guadalcanal The Americans take the Japanese 'Sea Horse' position but the Gifu strongpoint continues to hold out.

12 JANUARY 1943
Aleutians Amchitka Island is occupied by a small American force (General Jones), but the destroyer *Worden* is lost in an accident.
New Guinea The Japanese positions north and west of Gona are attacked by Australian infantry and tanks.
Eastern Front The Soviet Voronezh and Bryansk Fronts (Generals Golikov and Reiter) attack the Hungarian Second and the German Second Army respectively. The Hungarian defenses are quickly shattered and the Russians are soon driving toward Kharkov. Farther south, Manstein's Army Group Don is also under heavy pressure as the Russians attempt to cut off the Caucasus by an advance to Rostov. Even more dangerous for the Germans is the possibility that the Russians may be able to drive south from around Kharkov, cutting off both Manstein and Kleist. Almost all the supplies for these German units have to come through Dnepropetrovsk, which the Russians in fact nearly reach in mid-February.

13 JANUARY 1943
Eastern Front The Soviet attacks in the Stalingrad sector are making good progress and reach the Rossoshka River late in the day.
Guadalcanal The Americans develop their offensive farther, advancing westward along the north coast as well as attacking parallel to this advance farther inland.
New Guinea The American General Eichelberger takes overall command of the fighting troops.

14 JANUARY 1943
Libya and Tunisia The personnel of 21st Panzer Division are withdrawn from Rommel's defense line and are sent to Gabes to re-equip. They are to be used to defend Tunisia from the western attack.
Eastern Front The Soviets capture Pitomnik airfield, the larger of the two which have been held by the Germans in Stalingrad. The Soviet forces have advanced across the Chervlennaya and Rossoshka Rivers. On the Voronezh Front, the Red Army advance continues but could be more forceful if more troops were available. The sacrifices of Sixth Army are not, therefore, entirely valueless.
Guadalcanal A small group of Japanese reinforcements lands near Cape Esperance to prepare positions in that area to cover the planned evacuation.

14–24 JANUARY 1943
Allied Planning Churchill and Roosevelt meet in Casablanca accompanied by their Chiefs of Staff. There is some danger of a split between the British and Americans. The Americans feel, with some justice, that the British are doing too little against the Japanese, and the British believe, also with reason, that the Americans are gradually abandoning their commitment to the Germany-first policy. After several days' discussion between the Chiefs of Staff, these differences are smoothed over and broad guidelines agreed. The fact that the agreement is produced principally by the Chiefs of Staff is important because the American military has felt previously that Churchill has been able to convince Roosevelt to adopt policies with which they have not been in full agreement (Torch is the best example). The U-Boat offensive and supplies for Russia are now to have first priority and preparations for a landing in Europe are to be continued but this is unlikely to take place before 1944. The operations in the Pacific are to continue also and once North Africa is cleared the forces there are to move on to Sicily and Italy rather than be idle. The attack on Germany is also to be carried on by strategic bombing and an important directive ordering this is issued. At a press conference on 24 January Roosevelt announces that the Allies are fighting for the 'unconditional surrender' of Germany, Italy and Japan and this stand is immediately endorsed by Churchill. This policy has since been criticized as perhaps having helped prolong the war. This is uncertain but it is clear that neither leader has at this stage given much thought to considering the implications of the idea. The main failing of the conference is not at first apparent. All the plans are based on false estimates of the available quantity of shipping. Shipping shortages very soon affect

British plans for Burma and later this is also a problem for Mediterranean operations.

15 JANUARY 1943
Libya Montgomery is now ready to advance again and the Germans are quickly forced to retire from the Buerat position.

16 JANUARY 1943
Eastern Front There is continuous heavy fighting in all sectors. In the Caucasus, Kleist's Army Group A continues to pull back in good order. Manstein is still fighting to defend Rostov, and in the north the Russians continue to try to clear and widen the supply route to Leningrad. This route is nowhere wider than six miles and it is so much under German fire that it becomes known as the 'corridor of death.' At Stalingrad the Germans now hold only about 250 square miles of territory, about half as much as five days ago.
Guadalcanal A new phase of American attacks begins. The advance goes west and southwest of the American perimeter. Japanese positions overlooking the upper part of the Matanikau River are captured.
New Guinea In converging attacks near Sanananda the American 163rd Infantry Regiment and the Australian 18th Brigade both make progress.

17 JANUARY 1943
Eastern Front Again there are Russian gains along the front from Orel to the Caucasus. Millerovo and Zimovniki are captured. Around Stalingrad there is a slight lull as the Russians regroup for the final push.

Above: Soviet troops in the ruins of Stalingrad.

New Guinea The Australians penetrate the Japanese position at Sanananda but the Japanese continue to resist here and against the Americans at Giruwa.

18 JANUARY 1943
Eastern Front The Russians succeed in clearing the supply corridor into Leningrad but can do nothing to extend it. In the Caucasus they take Cherkessk and Divnoe (70 miles east of Elista).
Burma Troops from 14th Indian Division attack the Japanese positions at Donbaik in the Arakan without success.
Tunisia Tiger tanks are used for the first time in this theater at Bou Arada. Neither the British nor the Americans have anything which can face them on equal terms.

18–19 JANUARY 1943
Aleutians Two American cruisers and four destroyers bombard Attu Island.

19 JANUARY 1943
Eastern Front The Russian offensive on the Voronezh Front continues to make rapid progress. Valuyki and Urazavo are captured, while in the rear a pocket of Hungarian troops are driven from Ostrogozhsk. So far the Russians have taken more than 50,000 prisoners on this front but only 2500 are German.
New Guinea General Yamagata orders his forces to pull out of Sanananda but fierce fighting continues.
Libya Eighth Army's offensive continues. Tarhuna is captured and the German defense line between there and the sea is outflanked.

20 JANUARY 1943
Eastern Front Army Group A is forced back all along its lines and the Soviets take Nevinnomyssk and Proletarskaya.
Guadalcanal The Japanese resistance on Mount Austen weakens. The garrison of the Gifu strongpoint has lost heavily to artillery fire.
Libya Troops from 51st Highland Division take Homs as the Germans fall back.

21 JANUARY 1943
Allied Strategic Bombing The Casablanca Directive is issued to the British and American strategic bombing forces in Europe by the Combined Chiefs of Staff. It sets out the priorities for the continuing Allied attacks. Most of the reasoning is in line with the precision bombing ideas of the American leaders. As yet the US Air Forces have too few resources to carry out the full scheme and RAF Bomber

Command is probably not yet able to attack with enough accuracy. The RAF Command will continue its area bombing policy.

Eastern Front The Soviets recapture Voroshilovsk between Stavropol and Armavir. In Stalingrad the Germans lose Gumrak Airport and are now completely cut off.

New Guinea The Japanese resistance at Sanananda and Giruwa is now almost completely overcome, and the Australians and Americans have only a few pockets left to wipe out.

22 JANUARY 1943

Eastern Front The final phase of the Red Army assault on Stalingrad begins characteristically with a massive bombardment followed by infantry attacks.

In the Caucasus, Salsk falls to the Russians.

Guadalcanal The American attacks are renewed and begin to make progress, especially toward Kokumbona. The Japanese fight well but the American aircraft, artillery and naval forces combine in a fierce and telling bombardment.

Libya The retreating German forces pull out of Tripoli after evacuating large quantities of stores and destroying many of the port installations.

New Guinea The last Japanese are cleared from Papua by the Allied forces. The Japanese have lost about 7000 killed in the campaign, and the Allies about half this number.

23 JANUARY 1943

Libya Eighth Army enters Tripoli and is able to start using the port by the end of the month.

Eastern Front Golikov's forces try to extend the front of their advance northward by attacking Voronezh with increased strength.

Armavir in the Caucasus is taken by the Soviet forces.

Guadalcanal The Americans begin to make more rapid gains but fail to realize that this is mainly because of Japanese withdrawals toward the Cape Esperance position. The Gifu strongpoint finally falls to the Americans.

24 JANUARY 1943

Eastern Front Manstein asks Hitler's permission to order Paulus to surrender since it has now become clear that the mobile forces of Army Group A will be able to escape from the Caucasus whatever happens at Stalingrad. Permission for the surrender is refused. Farther west, troops from Vatutin's Southwest Front capture Starobelsk.

Solomons A US naval task force attacks Kolombangara Island in the New Georgia group.

On Guadalcanal the Americans push forward to the west of Kokumbona.

25 JANUARY 1943

Tunisia American forces advance to Maknassy, threatening Sfax and Gabes.

Eastern Front The attacking Russian forces meet in the middle of Stalingrad. There are two pockets of German resistance remaining, holding 36 square miles in all.

Farther north, Voronezh also falls to the Russians.

26 JANUARY 1943

Libya and Tunisia After a series of quarrels with the Italian High Command, to whom he is nominally responsible, Rommel is told that he is to be relieved by the Italian General Messe. Rommel does not hand over the command at this stage.

27 JANUARY 1943

Allied Air Operations Fifty-five US bombers raid Wilhelmshaven, losing three of their number but claiming to have shot down 22 German planes. This is the first raid by the USAAF over a German target; previously they have been allocated easier objectives in France while they gained experience.

The American bomber leaders believe that their Fortress and Liberator aircraft will be able to defend themselves in unescorted daylight missions over Germany and that they can bomb specific industrial targets with considerable and damaging accuracy. The fortunate results of this first raid help to confirm these erroneous beliefs for the moment.

28 JANUARY 1943

Eastern Front The Soviets take Kastornoye east of Voronezh near which a detachment of German Second Army is cut off.

Germany, Home Front A decree for the further mobilization of civilian men and women is issued by Sauckel, the Director-General of Labor.

New Guinea The Japanese carry out an unsuccessful attack on the detachment of the Australian 3rd Division at Wau.

29 JANUARY 1943

Germany and Occupied Europe, Home Front The Austrian Ernst Kaltenbrunner is appointed to head the SD. (The previous chief was

Heydrich assassinated in June 1942 – see above.)
Eastern Front The Russians continue their advances on all the southern fronts. Kropotkin in the Caucasus and Novyy Oskol north of Valuyki are captured.

29–30 JANUARY 1943
Solomons The US TF 18 (Admiral Giffen), covering a supply operation to Guadalcanal, is attacked by Japanese aircraft off Rennel Island and the heavy cruiser *Chicago* is sunk.

30 JANUARY 1943
Eastern Front The Russians take Tikhoretsk in the Caucasus and clear the Maykop oilfields. Seventeenth Army in the Kuban Peninsula is now becoming separated from First Panzer Army which is managing to retreat toward Rostov.

In Stalingrad the Russians find Paulus' Headquarters in the southern pocket and begin to surround them. Paulus is created Field Marshal by Hitler.
Germany, Home Front It is the tenth anniversary of Hitler's régime and special speeches are made in Berlin by Goebbels and Goering to mark the occasion. The RAF also mark the occasion by mounting the first daylight raid on Berlin by a group of Mosquito bombers whose attacks are timed to coincide with the speeches.
German Command Doenitz is appointed as Commander in Chief of the German navy.
Guadalcanal The US advance continues but the Japanese resistance, especially along the River Bonegi, is very heavy.
Tunisia The re-equipped German 21st Panzer Division makes easy gains around Faid, throwing back inexperienced French and American troops.
France, Home Front The Vichy régime begins the formation of a sort of French version of the Gestapo, called the Milice, which rapidly acquires an odious reputation. Its commander is Joseph Darnand.

31 JANUARY 1943
Italian Command Marshal Cavallero resigns and General Ambrosio takes over as Chief of the Italian General Staff.
Eastern Front Paulus surrenders himself and the southern pocket of Germans in Stalingrad. General Strecker's northern group still holds out.

FEBRUARY 1943
Battle of the Atlantic Allied shipping losses increase to 73 ships of 403,100 tons in all theaters. Submarines sink 63 ships of 359,300 tons. There are now about 100 U-Boats at sea in the Atlantic at any one time. In the month's operations the Germans lose 19 vessels. During the month the first success is recorded for the new 10cm radar. However, Coastal Command has only one squadron of modified VLR Liberator bombers for the main convoy routes; although Bomber Command makes many attacks on U-Boat pens, this is not an adequate substitute for the transfer of aircraft to maritime service since the pens can not be penetrated with the bombs available at this time. During the month Air Marshal Slessor takes command of RAF Coastal Command. (*See* 4–9 and 21–25 February for typical convoy actions.)
Allied Air Operations Targets for the Allied bomber offensive are again mostly connected with the U-Boat war. Lorient and St Nazaire are most heavily raided and other targets include Hamburg, Bremen and Wilhelmshaven. Allied bombers based in the Mediterranean attack Turin, Spezia, Milan, Palermo, Naples and other targets.

1 FEBRUARY 1943
Eastern Front The Russians capture Svatovo between Kupyansk and Starobelsk as their drive toward Kharkov continues.
Guadalcanal An American force lands at Verahue near Cape Esperance, but despite this interference the Japanese evacuation begins.

Above: Abandoned German tanks at Peskovatka, a village near Stalingrad.

The Americans are aware of the Japanese naval activity but believe that it heralds a new offensive. Instead 5000 men are evacuated by a force of 20 destroyers, one of which is sunk by air attack.

Burma In the Arakan the British forces renew their attack on Donbaik but can make no progress.

2 FEBRUARY 1943

Eastern Front The last German troops in Stalingrad surrender. Of the approximately 280,000 Germans originally surrounded in the city, 90,000 are prisoners and about 40,000 have been evacuated, mostly seriously wounded. The Luftwaffe has lost 500 transport planes in the fruitless supply operation and other equipment losses have been huge. The Soviets later announce that they have removed 147,000 German and 47,000 Soviet corpses from the city for reburial. The prisoners are badly treated by the Russians, and only 5000 ever return to Germany, the last in 1955. On the Russian side much of the credit for the success of the operations in the city must go to Chuikov for his forceful leadership and the tactics he has developed. Zhukov's has been the dominant influence over the wider strategic plans.

Guadalcanal The Americans succeed in crossing the Bonegi River at the coast.

Mediterranean The British submarine *Turbulent* sinks an Italian tanker near Palermo and prevents important fuel supplies reaching the Italian naval squadron based on Sicily.

3 FEBRUARY 1943

Eastern Front The Russians capture Kuschevka on the Soskya River 50 miles south of Rostov. In the drive to Kharkov Kupyansk is taken.

Germany, Home Front The loss of Stalingrad is announced. Three days of national mourning begin on 4 February.

Guadalcanal The US forces consolidate their lines running inland from Tassafaronga. Patrols penetrate much nearer to Cape Esperance.

4 FEBRUARY 1943

Eastern Front The Russian advance continues on all fronts. Shcigny, 40 miles east of Kursk, is taken as is Kanevskaya, only 30 miles from the Sea of Azov to the east of Tikhorestsk. The German Seventeenth Army is now cut off in the Kuban and must be supplied by sea from the Crimea.

Libya and Tunisia The first units of Eighth Army cross the border into Tunisia.

Guadalcanal A squadron of one cruiser and 22 destroyers led by Admiral Koyanagi manages to evacuate 5000 more Japanese troops from the island. Four ships are damaged by air attacks. On the ground the American 147th Regiment advances west of Tassafaronga.

4–9 FEBRUARY 1943

Battle of the Atlantic The convoy SC-118 is attacked by 20 U-Boats during this time and loses 20 of its 63 ships. There are 10 escorts at first, 12 later, and they sink three submarines and badly damage two more.

5 FEBRUARY 1943

Italy, Politics Mussolini dismisses Count Ciano from the Foreign Ministry and takes over responsibility for it himself.

Eastern Front The Russians take Stary Oskol and Izyum. In the Caucasus they make several landings successfully at Myoshako, but are driven off at Anopa.

6 FEBRUARY 1943

United States Command Europe and North Africa are separated in the US command structure. General Andrews is appointed to the new European Theater Command and General Eisenhower remains in charge in North Africa.

Eastern Front In the Caucasus the Russians reach Bataysk south of Rostov and capture Yeysk on the Sea of Azov. Lisichansk on the Donets also falls and the Russians cross the river farther upstream at Izyum and reach Barvenkovo. Manstein flies to see Hitler, who eventually agrees to allow a retreat behind the River Mius.

7 FEBRUARY 1943

Eastern Front The Russians take Azov at the mouth of the Don and in the Ukraine they also capture Kramatorsk just south of Slavyansk.

Guadalcanal The US 161st Regiment continues to lead the American advance but for the moment moving cautiously.

8 FEBRUARY 1943

Burma The first Chindit raid begins. This force, more properly called 77th Indian Brigade, is led by General Wingate and its task is to penetrate behind enemy lines, causing damage and disruption. Above all the expedition is designed to demonstrate that the British and Indians can take on the Japanese in the jungle. The expedition begins at Imphal and sets out toward Tamu.

Eastern Front The Russians capture Kursk.

CHRONOLOGY

9 FEBRUARY 1943
Eastern Front The Russians take Belgorod and the small town of Shebekino to the southeast.
Guadalcanal The American 161st and 132nd Regiments link up at Tenaro too late to stop the last Japanese forces leaving the island. The final 2000 men have been evacuated by 18 destroyers on 8 February.

In the campaign the Japanese have lost about 10,000 killed to the Americans' 1600. The losses in ships and planes have been about equal but in effect this favors the Americans. Strategically it has been a major Japanese defeat, but only a fraction of the Japanese army has been involved, and, judging by their resistance, the next American campaigns will be very hard indeed.

10 FEBRUARY 1943
Eastern Front The Russians capture Volchansk and Chuguyev only 20 miles east of Kharkov.

11 FEBRUARY 1943
Eastern Front Lozovaya falls to Vatutin's troops from the Southwest Front.

12 FEBRUARY 1943
Eastern Front The Soviet progress is still rapid. In the Caucasus they take Krasnodar. North and west of the Don Shakhty, Kommunarsk and Krasnoarmeskoye are all captured.

13 FEBRUARY 1943
Eastern Front The Soviets capture Novocherkassk.

14 FEBRUARY 1943
Tunisia The Axis forces begin a major attack on the US II Corps positions west of Faid. The attacking troops are mostly from 10th and 21st

Above: Wingate, center right, at a briefing.

Panzer Divisions from General von Arnim's Fifth Panzer Army. General Zeigler is in direct command. This attack is only begun after considerable high-level debate. Rommel is still holding command of what is now known as First Italian Army and he and Arnim have both produced plans of attack. Rommel urges an aggressive attack toward Tébessa but Arnim's more limited plan is the one adopted at this stage. In the attack the inexperienced American forces around Sidi Bou Zid are given a vicious lesson.
Burma The Chindits cross the Chindwin in two groups at Auktaung and Tonhe. Wingate is leading the larger northern group.
Eastern Front The Russians capture Rostov and Voroshilovgrad and among other less important gains they take Drasny Sulin, north of Shakhty.

15 FEBRUARY 1943
Tunisia Rommel joins in the Axis attack, sending a detachment of 15th Panzer and some Italian armor against Gafsa which is taken. Most of Rommel's forces have had to be left in the Mareth line where the last of his rearguard is now arriving from Libya.

16 FEBRUARY 1943
Eastern Front After fierce fighting for several days, the Russians complete the capture of Kharkov when Hausser's II SS Panzer Corps are forced to withdraw despite an order from Hitler to hold on.
Tunisia Some of Montgomery's forward units capture Medenine on the approaches to the Mareth line.

17 FEBRUARY 1943
Tunisia Both von Arnim's and Rommel's attacks are making good progress. The northern wing is now approaching Sbeitla, having virtually destroyed two-thirds of US 1st Armored Division including two tank battalions. Rommel to the south enters Fériana. The limited attack that von Arnim envisaged has certainly come off; he diverts 10th Panzer Division toward Foundouk, which has in fact been abandoned, instead of pressing on vigorously toward Sbeitla. Having observed the weak American command and the understandable inexperience of the American troops, Rommel wants to be more ambitious. He puts his plans to the Italian and German High Command, who fail to make a quick decision.
Eastern Front Hitler flies to Manstein's Headquarters at Zaporozhye. He stays until 19

February and is eventually persuaded to agree to Manstein's plans for a counterattack.

18 FEBRUARY 1943
Southwest Pacific A new American Army becomes operational, the Sixth, led by General Krueger.

Tunisia The Germans enter Sbeitla, already abandoned by the Allies. The debate over what to attempt next continues in the Axis camp.

18–19 FEBRUARY 1943
Aleutians A US Task Group (Admiral Mc-Morris) with two cruisers and four destroyers shells Japanese positions on Attu Island.

19 FEBRUARY 1943
Solomons American reinforcements are being landed on Guadalcanal in preparation for the next move to the Russell Islands which are now reported abandoned by the Japanese.

Tunisia The next phase of the Axis attack begins. It is to be more ambitious than the first, but on the orders of the Italian High Command it is to be directed toward Le Kef, as the Allies in fact expect, and not Tébessa, as Rommel wishes. There are two wings to the assault. One, involving units of 15th Panzer, goes in from Kasserine toward Thala, and the other by 21st Panzer is already beyond Sbeitla aiming north for Sbiba. Rommel has managed to have Arnim ordered to put 10th Panzer under his command, but Arnim does not release the whole division and keeps the Tiger battalion especially. The Allies have prepared to meet attacks in both passes, and as a result resistance is fairly strong.

20 FEBRUARY 1943
Eastern Front The Russians capture Pavlograd and are involved in fierce fighting at Krasnograd. They fail to realize that, although they are making rapid progress toward the Dniepr, they are in fact driving in to a salient which is strongly held on both flanks.

Tunisia The German attacks on Sbiba are held by the defending British and American units of which the most prominent is a British Guards Brigade. The attack through Kasserine Pass is held at first, but later the detachment of 15th Panzer is joined by units from 10th Panzer and the assault goes home. Later in the day the Germans drive to within 10 miles of Thala despite the resistance of the British 26th Armored Brigade which has come up.

The Allied command in the theater is re-organized and General Alexander is appointed to lead the newly constituted 18th Army Group.

21 FEBRUARY 1943
Solomons In Operation 'Cleanslate' troops from General Hester's 43rd Division occupy Banika and Pavuvu in the Russell Islands without resistance from the Japanese. By the end of the month there are 9000 American troops on these islands.

21–22 FEBRUARY 1943
Tunisia Rommel is at the front urging 10th Panzer on in its advance toward Thala, but the British armor holds out well during the day despite inferior tanks and by the evening the front is still three miles south of the town. A detachment of 15th Panzer is sent on a diversionary move toward Tébessa, but it too is held by units of US 1st Armored Division. The Sbiba attack achieves nothing.

During the night a fierce fight develops in the British position before Thala in which both sides lose heavily. Also during the night an American artillery regiment (General Irwin) arrives in support after an 800-mile march from Oran accomplished in four days. At dawn this new support and a small counterattack by the British convince Rommel that the Allied reserves are arriving too quickly, and in the afternoon he pulls back. Rommel's attack has come very close to a major success, and it is interesting to speculate what might have been achieved if his own, less expected, plan had been chosen. The German troops have been astonished at the lavish scale of equipment of the American units they have overrun. Although the inexperience of the Americans has been very obvious, it is clear that they are learning very quickly, and already their artillery is formidably well organized. One factor in the battle which is to recur in other campaigns is the difference in the Allied performance from 22 February onward when the weather improves for flying. The British system for controlling air support has been well worked out and is adopted by the Americans from now on – another example of the American's ability to learn quickly from experience.

On the Axis side the operation has been hampered by divided command and the desert veterans of 15th and 21st Panzer Divisions have proved less able than usual in the unfamiliar mountain terrain. Rommel is certainly worn out and perhaps they are too.

21–25 FEBRUARY 1943
Battle of the Atlantic The convoy ON-166 is attacked and loses 14 ships of 85,000 tons. One U-Boat is sunk by the escorts.

CHRONOLOGY

22 FEBRUARY 1943

Eastern Front Manstein's counteroffensive begins. However, in the salient the Russians continue to press forward, one unit even coming within 12 miles of Manstein's headquarters before running out of fuel. All the Russian units have advanced so quickly that they are very short of both fuel and ammunition. By brilliant handling of his reserves, Manstein has assembled considerable forces for the attack despite being outnumbered by about seven to one. First and Fourth Panzer Armies are to attack northward from a line to the west of Krasnoarmeskoye, and Group Kempf, including principally II SS Panzer Corps, is to drive south from Krasnodar.

23 FEBRUARY 1943

Eastern Front The Russians capture Sumy and Lebedin northeast of Kharkov, but farther south the German counteroffensive is beginning to make real progress, especially with the attack toward Barvenkovo by XLVIII Panzer Corps.

24 FEBRUARY 1943

Tunisia Rommel is appointed to command Army Group Afrika which is to include von Arnim's Fifth Panzer Army and the First Italian Army of General Messe. This is a remarkable choice because, although a single commander is clearly required, Kesselring for one has certainly detected Rommel's tiredness. On the ground the Germans are pulling back skillfully to the Eastern Dorsale, leaving behind booby traps.

25 FEBRUARY 1943

Eastern Front The Soviet attack in the Caucasus continues and east of Krasnodar Mingrelsk is captured.

26 FEBRUARY 1943

Tunisia Units from 10th and 21st Panzer Divisions under von Arnim's command attack the British positions at Medjez el Bab. This comes to nothing but prevents Rommel from concentrating as quickly as he wishes for an attack on Eighth Army before the Mareth line. At this stage Montgomery only has two divisions forward because his supply organization has not yet been completed. Montgomery knows that he is vulnerable and has only advanced so far as a diversionary move to help with the Kasserine operations.

27 FEBRUARY 1943

Eastern Front Manstein's forces attacking from the south are now on a line from Lozovaya to Kramatorsk.

28 FEBRUARY 1943

Norway, Resistance The Norsk Hydro power station near Ryukan is badly damaged by a sabotage team of Norwegian soldiers who have been parachuted in from Britain. This plant is known to be being used by the Germans to produce 'heavy water,' vital in atomic research.

MARCH 1943

Battle of the Atlantic In later British Admiralty appreciations, the first 20 days of this month are described as the period when the Germans came closest to defeating the convoy system and winning the battle. The total Allied shipping loss for the whole month is 120 ships of 693,400 tons, of which submarines sink 627,400 tons. Of the 108 ships falling to submarines, 72 are in North Atlantic convoys. The German U-Boat fleet loses 15 boats but only six of these in convoy battles. The fiercest actions are around HX-229 and SC-122 (*see* 14–20 March). One problem for the Allied forces is the change in the German coding machine introduced on 8 March. By adding a fourth rotor to the standard Enigma machine the number of different settings is increased and the Germans hope that this will confirm the security of their communications. In fact the Allied coding services begin to operate as successfully as before after a brief delay. On the Allied side important developments are the reorganization of the slower north Atlantic convoys, shifting their terminus from New York to Halifax, and the return of the support groups to the Atlantic after their service with Operation Torch. The first operation by a support group is that around the convoys immediately after HX-229 and SC-122. By the end of the month there are five support groups available, including three escort carriers. A fourth escort carrier, *Dasher*, is lost in an explosion on the 27th.

Allied Air Operations RAF Bomber Command mounts 10 major attacks on targets in Germany, dropping more than 8000 tons of bombs. Berlin and Essen are heavily hit. The attacks on U-Boat facilities continue. The American targets include Vegesack and Wilhelmshaven while the RAF again hit St Nazaire very hard. The navigational aid 'Oboe' is used for the first time in the raid on Essen on 5–6 March when 442 aircraft attack with considerable effect. This raid marks the beginning of what Air Marshal Harris calls the 'Battle of the Ruhr.' This is the first of three 'battles' which Bomber Command will fight during the next year.

1 MARCH 1943

Eastern Front The Russians are on the offensive

north of Moscow and capture the important town of Demyansk.

Burma The Chindit force is making slower progress than has been hoped, partly because it has been concerned to find clearings for supply drops, when in fact it later discovers that it is possible to recover supplies dropped in jungle areas.

2 MARCH 1943

Tunisia American forces re-enter Sbeitla and move on to Fériana. Farther north the British hold off German attacks.

2–4 MARCH 1943

Battle of the Bismarck Sea A Japanese convoy of eight transports carrying 7000 troops of General Nakano's 51st Division, escorted by eight destroyers and led by Admiral Kimura is sighted en route from Rabaul to Lae. It is attacked by planes from General Kenney's Fifth Air Force on all three days, but especially on 3 March. PT-Boats join the attack on 4 March. All the transports and four destroyers and at least 3500 men are lost. In the air the Australians and Americans lose five planes but shoot down 25. The Japanese regard the battle as a major disaster and a serious setback to their prospects in New Guinea.

3 MARCH 1943

Eastern Front The Red Army enters Rzhev as the Germans pull out after several days of fierce fighting. They also capture Lgov on the River Seim west of Kursk. The first phase of Manstein's counteroffensive is over in the south. The Russians have been pushed back behind the Donets everywhere south of Zmiyev, and have lost heavily. Their casualties include approximately 20,000 dead so far, but only 9000 prisoners. From this a deeper truth becomes evident – the Germans are now too short of manpower to hold the ring strongly when they do manage to encircle large Soviet units. Manstein still has the initiative, but there is little time before the spring thaw halts movement all along the front.

Tunisia There is a small skirmish between 15th Panzer and the British forces at Medenine as both sides try to scout the opposing lines.

Burma After a setback on 2 March, the southern Chindit group succeeds in cutting the Mandalay–Myitkyina railroad just north of Kyaikthin.

4 MARCH 1943

Tunisia Montgomery is able to bring a second infantry division and an armored brigade up to Medenine where the British position is now fairly secure. A formal defense line has been established, backed by a strong antitank gun screen and including some of the new and very effective 17-pounder weapons. Intelligence has warned of the coming Axis attack, and this is confirmed when 10th and 21st Panzer are sighted moving up.

Eastern Front The Soviets take Olenino and Chertolino to the west of Rzhev and in the Kursk area they take Sevsk and Sudzha. The next phase of Manstein's offensive begins and now the objective is Kharkov and the Soviet troops nearby. Part of the SS Panzer Corps attacks westward from Poltava and units of Fourth Panzer Army attack northward from a line on the Berestovaya River west of Izyum.

5 MARCH 1943

Strategic Bombing Bomber Command sends 443 aircraft to attack Essen. Fourteen aircraft are lost. This is the first attack of Air Marshal Harris' Battle of the Ruhr, and from now until 12 July 1943 when the battle ends there will be 43 major attacks mounted by Bomber Command in which 1000 aircraft will be lost.

Eastern Front Hoth's Fourth Panzer Army inflicts heavy casualties on three Russian Corps west of Izyum, but cannot continue its attack because the Donets is blocked by floating ice which prevents bridging operations.

6 MARCH 1943

Eastern Front In the central sector the Russians capture Gzhatsk on the approaches to Vyazma south of Rzhev.

Tunisia In the morning the Germans mount a major attack on Medenine but are driven off. In the afternoon the attack is renewed half-heartedly but to no effect. The British and New Zealanders are surprised by the inept performance of their veteran opponents – for the antitank gunners it has been almost like shooting on a range. The Germans lose 50 of their tanks for absolutely nothing and now have only about 100 left. Rommel has not wanted to attack now and has taken little to do with the planning. He would have preferred to withdraw to Wadi Akarit.

United States, Home Front Roosevelt appoints a top-level committee to look into the manpower problems of US industry. Among the committee members are Byrnes and Baruch.

Burma The Chindits make a series of demolitions on the railroad between Nankan and Bongyaung.

Solomons The Americans send three cruisers and seven destroyers to bombard the Japanese airfields at Munda and Vila. Little damage is done to these targets, but two Japanese destroyers are met and sunk.

7 MARCH 1943
Eastern Front Fourth Panzer Army has been shifted slightly westward and now begins to attack northeast from around Krasnograd, joining the SS Panzer Corps.

8 MARCH 1943
Eastern Front The Soviets take Sychevka on the central sector between Rzhev and Vyazma.

9 MARCH 1943
Tunisia Rommel leaves Africa for good. On his way home he meets Mussolini in Rome and Hitler in East Prussia but is not able to persuade either of them to withdraw from Africa.
Eastern Front Hausser's SS troops begin to attack Kharkov from the west and north. South of the city the small town of Taranovka is strongly held by the Soviet 25th Guards Division despite vicious attacks by LXVIII Panzer Corps.
New Guinea There are heavy Japanese attacks on Wau as a prelude to a spell of intensive effort in the air.

10 MARCH 1943
Burma The Chindits are now operating in several columns and cross the Irrawaddy in two places, at Tagaung and Tigyaing farther north.
Tunisia The Germans organize an attack with air support on the Free French outpost at Ksar Rhilane southeast of Mareth but are beaten off by Leclerc's men.
United States Command Chennault is promoted and his command in China is to be enlarged and named Fourteenth Air Force.

11 MARCH 1943
United States, Politics The Americans extend the Lend-Lease agreements for another year. Their value for the two years until the end of February 1943 is reported to have been $9,632,000,000.
Eastern Front The SS Corps enters Kharkov in force and penetrates to the center of the town after fierce fighting.

12 MARCH 1943
Eastern Front While fighting continues in Kharkov, the Germans send a unit east to Chuguyev to cut off some of the Red Army forces south of the city. In the central sector the Germans are retreating on a wide front and the Soviets retake Vyazma without a fight.

Above: An Allied merchant ship in flames after being torpedoed by a U-Boat.

Tunisia The 2nd New Zealand Division and the 8th Armored Brigade are secretly moved south from Medenine, and begin to concentrate west of Wilder's Gap in preparation for an outflanking move round the Mareth Line across the Dahar region.

14–20 MARCH 1943
Battle of the Atlantic In a series of convoy battles, the largest during the war, 21 ships of 140,800 tons are sunk from the convoys SC-122 and HX-229. The slower SC convoy is sailing in front and gradually the two coalesce into one mass of about 100 ships. About 20 U-Boats out of a pack of 40 manage to make attacks and, despite the efforts of the escort, no U-Boats are sunk. The German intelligence service, B Dienst, has provided good information on the routes of these convoys.

15 MARCH 1943
New Guinea The US Seventh Fleet (Admiral Carpender) is formed to control naval operations around the island.
Eastern Front The Germans complete the conquest of Kharkov when the last Red Army defenders withdraw from the tractor factory. In the central sector the Soviets take Kholm and Zharkovskiy, respectively north and east of Velikiye Luki.

16–17 MARCH 1943
Tunisia Eighth Army is involved in sharp skirmishes on the approaches to the Mareth Line as it clears the way for its coming full-dress attack.

17 MARCH 1943
Burma The 123rd Indian Brigade is attacked by the Japanese just north of Rathedaung in the Arakan and is forced to fall back. General Koka leads the Japanese attack with units of 55th and 33rd Divisions being involved.

18 MARCH 1943
Eastern Front Troops from SS Division *Gross Deutchsland* attack Belgorod in the last act of Manstein's offensive. In this phase the Soviets have lost 40,000 casualties and at least 600 tanks. The whole operation has been an unqualified technical success for the Germans, but cannot make up for their 1,000,000 dead since November 1942. As activity begins to die down all along the front in the mud of the spring thaw, German and Soviet attention begins to be drawn toward the Soviet salient around Kursk.
Tunisia General Patton's II US Corps takes Gafsa and pushes forward toward El Guettar.
Burma Wingate's column crosses the Irrawaddy south of Inywa, the last group to do so. The Japanese have now assembled considerable forces to hunt the Chindits and their operations are being increasingly circumscribed. In the Arakan the more regular British operations are not going well either. Htizwe falls to a pincer attack and on the Mayu Peninsula a British attack on Donbaik fails.

19 MARCH 1943
Tunisia The New Zealand Corps begins to move off toward Ksar Rhilane.

20 MARCH 1943
Tunisia The New Zealanders speed up their march, abandoning concealment, and reach the Tebaga Gap in the evening. During the night the main attack on the Mareth Line begins with a heavy bombardment of the positions of the Young Fascist Division near the coast, followed up rapidly by the assaulting infantry of 50th Division.

The Mareth Line is held by the usual mixture of German and Italian units with the 30 tanks of 15th Panzer in reserve. The Americans at Gafsa are being watched by 10th Panzer, and 21st Panzer is at Gabes in general reserve.

21 MARCH 1943
Tunisia The New Zealanders at Tebaga are held up by a mixed Italian force. In the main attack by morning the British have managed to establish a small force across the natural antitank obstacle of Wadi Zigzaou, but ground conditions prevent any real buildup during the day.

22 MARCH 1943
Tunisia Although the British have managed to reinforce their bridgehead over Wadi Zigzaou during the night, a counterattack by 15th Panzer causes heavy losses, effectively ending the attack there. At the Tebaga Gap 21st Panzer and 164th Light Divisions are more than enough to hold the New Zealanders.
Eastern Front The Soviets capture Durovo to the northeast of Smolensk.

23 MARCH 1943
Tunisia For the moment the Germans halt the American advance near El Guettar, but 10th Panzer Division loses heavily in trying to exploit early successes. Already the American tactical performance is much improved. Montgomery decides to transfer his main attack to the Tebaga

CHRONOLOGY

Gap and therefore sends 1st Armored Division and General Horrocks off to join the New Zealanders. This move is slowed by traffic problems.

24 MARCH 1943
Burma The various Chindit columns join up between Baw and Pago, but Wingate is ordered to break off the operation and return to India. His forces split up into small groups and most succeed in reaching base by early April. One returns later via China. Losses have been heavy – about one-third of the force – but many lessons have been learned and the value to morale and propaganda has been high.
Tunisia Montgomery sends 4th Indian Division on a short outflanking move toward Ksar el Hallouf and then Beni Zelten. In difficult terrain their progress is too slow to affect the outcome of the battle, however.

25 MARCH 1943
Tunisia By nightfall 1st Armored Division has nearly reached the Tebaga Gap. Von Arnim is worried about this attack and the threat from the Americans at Maknassy, and therefore begins to pull his German and Italian infantry out of the Mareth Line.

26 MARCH 1943
Vichy, Politics Laval organizes a cabinet reshuffle to consolidate his power.
Tunisia Throughout the day the Axis forces in the Tebaga Gap are fiercely attacked from the air and on the ground. By the evening the German defenses have been worn practically to nothing and 1st Armored Division heads for El Hamma by the light of the moon.
Bering Sea Admiral McMorris' squadron of two cruisers and four destroyers meets a considerably superior Japanese force of four cruisers and five destroyers (Admiral Hosogaya) off the Komandorski Islands. In a traditional-style gun engagement a cruiser from each side is badly damaged before Hosogaya breaks off the fight, just when his superiority is beginning to tell.

27 MARCH 1943
Tunisia In the early hours of the morning the Germans manage to construct a weak defensive front around El Hamma which holds the British off until the Axis infantry from Mareth escape toward Wadi Akarit. There is also a new American attack near Fondouk.

28 MARCH 1943
Tunisia The German and Italian forces are arriving at the Wadi Akarit position from Mareth. The Italian formations are least weakened but have lost heart completely. Of the Germans, 90th Light is in fairly good order, 21st and 15th Panzer have both lost heavily and 164th Light is very weak indeed. The Mareth battle stands as probably the most imaginative of Montgomery's actions and has only been marred by some confused leadership on 27 March when Horrocks and Freyberg were uncertain as to who was to take charge.

29 MARCH 1943
Tunisia The last Axis units reach Wadi Akarit as the New Zealanders enter Gabes. General Messe reports to the Italian High Command that the Akarit position, although naturally probably the strongest in North Africa (at least in Rommel's opinion), has not received much preparation and may be vulnerable to a rapid attack. Characteristically Montgomery does not attempt this.

31 MARCH 1943
New Guinea A US battalion occupies positions around Morobe at the mouth of the Waria River.
Eastern Front The Soviets take Anastasyevsk in the Kuban north of Novorossiysk.

APRIL 1943
Battle of the Atlantic There are various changes in the Allied situation. The north Atlantic convoys become solely a British and Canadian responsibility from 1 April while the US Navy is to look after the more southerly routes. The British aircraft strength is augmented both for operations over the Bay of Biscay and in VLR aircraft for the main convoy routes. There are no VLR aircraft operating from western Atlantic bases.

The German submarine strength has now become 425 boats of which 240 are operational. The Allied losses are 64 ships of 334,700 tons in total and to submarines, 56 ships of 327,900 tons. There is something of a lull at the start of the month, but among the later operations are attacks on ONS-5 (*see* 28 April–6 May) and HX-233 which loses only one ship and sinks one U-Boat with the help of a support group. There is some success toward the end of the month and in early May for a small group off Freetown. Fifteen U-Boats are lost during the month.
Allied Air Operations The Allied bomber offensive continues to increase in intensity. Bomber Command mounts 10 major attacks on Germany, dropping close to 10,000 tons of bombs. Essen and Duisburg are most heavily hit.

Attacks on U-Boat bases continue also. Lorient, St Nazaire and Brest are the main targets. The US Eighth Air Force drops nearly 1000 tons of bombs altogether.

In the Mediterranean Allied forces are again active. La Spezia is heavily attacked in connection with the U-Boat offensive. Allied aircraft strike at communications in Italy and Sicily and shoot down numerous transport aircraft flying to North Africa. Italian and German naval units are also involved in the supply operations. Despite Allied attacks 28,000 men are landed along with 19,000 tons of supplies and other equipment.

3 APRIL 1943
Tunisia The Germans continue to hold off the attacks by Patton's troops around El Guettar.

5 APRIL 1943
Burma The Japanese on the Mayu peninsula continue to advance northwestward, in the direction of Indin.

5–6 APRIL 1943
Tunisia In his usual methodical style Montgomery is now ready to attack the Wadi Akarit Line. The defenses there have been improved in the past few days and are now occupied mostly by the Italian infantry with 15th Panzer and part of 90th Light in reserve. Most of the Axis armor is farther north, engaging Patton's Corps around El Guettar. Montgomery has been persuaded to begin his attack with a silent night advance by 4th Indian Division against the Djebel Fatnassa position. This gets under way on the evening of 5 April and soon makes good progress. The follow-up attack in the morning is badly co-ordinated, however, and an untidy battle develops during the day as the Axis reserves are drawn in.

7 APRIL 1943
Solomons In an attempt to set back American preparations, Yamamoto decides to mount an all-out air offensive to be known as Operation I. The Eleventh Air Fleet based on Rabaul, Kavieng and Buin is reinforced by the pilots and aircraft from the carriers *Zuikaku, Shokaku, Junyo* and *Hiyo*, leaving the fleet with almost no trained pilots. The attacks begin with a raid against Guadalcanal and Tulagi by 180 planes in which a destroyer and two other vessels are sunk.
Tunisia The Axis forces are retreating rapidly from the Wadi Akarit position. Advance units of Eighth Army meet patrols from Patton's Corps on the road toward Gafsa.

7–11 APRIL 1943
Axis Planning Hitler and Mussolini meet at Salzburg. Among the subjects for their discussion is, of course, the situation in North Africa, but they decide they must hold on.

8 APRIL 1943
United States, Home Front In an attempt to combat inflation Roosevelt forbids certain wage and price increases and orders workers not to change their jobs in some industries unless this is beneficial to the war effort.
Burma General Kawabe replaces General Iida in command of the Japanese forces, now to be organized as the Burma Area Army. The Japanese are planning to extend their hold on northern Burma and among the logistic preparations that accompany this is the construction of new rail lines. About 60,000 Allied POWs are employed on this work – about 15,000 of them die through ill treatment.

9 APRIL 1943
Tunisia British troops from Eighth Army take Mahares, 50 miles north of Gabes, as the Axis forces continue to retreat.

10 APRIL 1943
Tunisia The leading elements of Eighth Army enter Sfax as the Axis retreat continues apace. The British IX Corps only now succeeds in breaking out from Fondouk Pass too late to cut the retreat.
Sardinia A force of 84 Liberator bombers raids La Maddalena sinking the heavy cruiser *Trieste* and damaging the *Gorizia*.

11 APRIL 1943
New Guinea There are vigorous Japanese air attacks on Allied shipping, especially in Oro Bay where two freighters are sunk.
Eastern Front The Germans are now planning in earnest for an attack on the Kursk salient. The idea is too obvious for any hope of surprise, and so it is clear that a massive attack must be prepared if there is to be any chance of success. The German generals are divided in their opinions. Kluge, commanding Army Group Center, and Zeitzler and Keitel of the General Staff are in favor. Guderian, now Inspector-General of Armored Troops, and Manstein who in fact originally suggested the idea, are opposed to it.

12 APRIL 1943
War Crimes The Germans announce the discovery of a group of mass graves in the Katyn

Forest. The bodies of 4100 Polish officers, murdered by the Soviets, are found.

Tunisia The retreating Axis forces are now reaching Enfidaville where they will halt.

New Guinea In the continuing Japanese air offensive Port Moresby is attacked by 174 aircraft, but little significant damage is done.

14 APRIL 1943

Tunisia The Axis forces are now established in their final defensive positions of the campaign. They occupy the ring of hills around Bizerta and Tunis from about Cape Serrat to Enfidaville. The Eighth Army units coming up from the south begin to put pressure on Djebel Garci and Takrouna.

New Guinea A Japanese raid on shipping in Milne Bay marks the end of the recent flurry of air activity. Two transports are sunk. The Japanese air forces have lost heavily.

15 APRIL 1943

Aleutians America begins preparations for an attack on Attu Island. It is to be carried out by 7th Division which has in fact been training for North Africa.

16 APRIL 1943

War Crimes The Polish government in London issues a statement on the Katyn massacre asking for Red Cross investigation.

17 APRIL 1943

Eastern Front The only real activity is in the Kuban Peninsula where the Russians continue to press Seventeenth Army back.

Allied Air Operations In one of the Eighth Air Force's largest operations yet 115 B-17 bombers are sent to attack Bremen aircraft factories. Sixteen aircraft fail to return.

18 APRIL 1943

War Crimes The Russians make an announcement on the Katyn massacre alleging predictably that the Germans have concocted the whole story.

Tunisia A massive convoy of 100 transport planes leaves Sicily with supplies for the Axis forces, but at least half are shot down by Allied fighters.

Bougainville An aircraft carrying the Commander of the Japanese Combined Fleet, Admiral Yamamoto, is shot down by Lightning fighters over Bougainville. Yamamoto is killed. The operation is only possible because of the interception of a coded message announcing a visit by Yamamoto. The decision to try to intercept his plane goes to the highest level. In fact the Japanese do not deduce that their codes are insecure so the risk is worthwhile. As well as suffering the loss of their leading strategist, the Japanese national morale suffers when the death is announced in May. The Americans, of course, make no announcement, since this would obviously suggest to the Japanese how they got the information that Yamamoto was aboard that particular plane. Technically it has been a very difficult operation well performed.

19 APRIL 1943

Tunisia Another German effort to fly in supplies suffers disastrous losses.

Poland, Resistance The remaining population of the Warsaw ghetto rises against the Germans. In October 1940 there were probably almost 500,000 Jews who had been herded into the ghetto. By July 1942, when the extermination policy began in earnest, there were 380,000 left, and by October 1942, 70,000 left. Most of the rest have been taken to be murdered in Treblinka.

20 APRIL 1943

Japan, Politics The Japanese Cabinet is reorganized, with Shimegitsu becoming Foreign Minister.

Tunisia Montgomery mounts a series of attacks on the Axis positions near Enfidaville, but these are very strong and the attacks fail with heavy casualties.

21 APRIL 1943

Japanese Command Admiral Koga is appointed to succeed Yamamoto in command of the Japanese Combined Fleet.

Tunisia A German attack around Medjez el Bab is driven off with loss.

22 APRIL 1943

Tunisia A series of Allied attacks begins on the various German hill positions. The US II Corps, now led by Bradley, attacks Hill 609 in 'Mousetrap Valley,' intending to advance to Mateur. The British V Corps attacks 'Longstop' and 'Peter's Corner' and the British IX Corps also attacks between Goubellat and Bou Arada. Montgomery has been ordered to stop his attacks along the coast. Another German air supply effort is decimated – 30 transports are shot down.

23 APRIL 1943

New Guinea Australian troops occupy positions around Mubo without opposition.

24 APRIL 1943

Poland, Resistance The SS begins all-out operations against the Jews in the Warsaw ghetto. Buildings are burned or blown up but resistance continues among the rubble or in the sewers. Any Jews captured are either shot immediately or sent off to the extermination camps.

26 APRIL 1943

Aleutians The Japanese-held harbors on Attu are bombarded by an American squadron led by Admiral McMorris.

Allied Diplomacy The Russians break off relations with the Polish exile government because of the allegations concerning the Katyn massacre. Relations have been poor for some time in any case as Stalin's attitude toward a postwar Poland has become more clear. On 30 April in an attempt to patch up the quarrel, the Poles drop the call for a Red Cross enquiry.

Tunisia Longstop Hill is taken by British V Corps, much aided by the excellent cross-country performance of their Churchill tanks.

South Pacific New plans are agreed for the American Solomon Islands operations, code named 'Cartwheel.' Halsey's South Pacific Area forces are to advance through New Georgia and Bougainville. MacArthur's Southwest Pacific Area is to continue its advance northwest along the coast of New Guinea until he and Halsey can join to isolate the Japanese bases at Rabaul and Kavieng.

27 APRIL 1943

Tunisia The British take Djebel Bou Aoukaz after a vicious battle.

28–29 APRIL 1943

Tunisia There is heavy fighting around Djebel Bou Aoukaz in the British sector as the German 8th Panzer Regiment counterattacks. In the American sector some progress is made in the Mousetrap Valley.

28 APRIL–6 MAY 1943

Battle of the Atlantic There is a series of engagements around the convoy ONS-5. The convoy has 42 merchant ships and is attacked by 51 U-Boats; in running battles most of the way across the Atlantic it loses 13 vessels. Of the attacking U-Boats seven are sunk and five seriously and 12 slightly damaged. This is an important success for the escorts since the ratio of one U-Boat for two merchantmen is very acceptable. There has been little air support for the convoy, which is unusual for such a successful operation.

30 APRIL 1943

Operation Husky As part of the deception plan for the invasion of Sicily (Operation Husky), a British submarine, *Seraph*, releases a corpse into the sea off the Spanish port of Huelva hoping that it will be picked up and the papers carried passed to the Germans. The body purports to be that of a Major Martin of the Royal Marines and he is carrying letters from General Nye, Vice-Chief of the British General Staff, and Admiral Mountbatten, Chief of Combined Operations, to Eisenhower, Alexander and Cunningham referring to Allied plans for an invasion of Greece. The Germans do receive the information and it contributes to their lack of appreciation of the true Allied strategy.

Tunisia The Germans retake Djebel Bou Aoukaz but at heavy cost to their armor. Farther north the Americans gain a foothold on Hill 609. Alexander decides to switch veteran units from Eighth Army to join a renewed attack between Bou Aoukaz and Ksar Tyr.

MAY 1943

Battle of the Atlantic Allied shipping losses decline again to 58 ships of 299,400 tons, of which submarines sink 50 ships of 264,900 tons. The Germans lose 41 U-Boats and on 22 May Doenitz decides to withdraw his forces from the north Atlantic routes (*see* 22 May). Typical convoy battles might be those of HX-237 which loses three ships but sinks three U-Boats helped by the escort carrier *Biter*, or SC-129 which loses two and sinks two, again with *Biter*'s help. From the German side the month has looked hopeful at the start, with four groups, 13–17 strong, on patrol in the Atlantic and another 18 in the Mediterranean. Doenitz is being forced, because of increasing British air operations, to order his boats to reverse their previous procedure while crossing the Bay of Biscay and to surface by day and try to fight the air attacks.

On the Allied side one important change of organization is the creation of the US Tenth Fleet under the direct command of Admiral King to supervise US antisubmarine operations. This unit has no ships of its own but is important in coordinating the actions of the various US commands.

Allied Air Operations The Battle of the Ruhr continues. More than 2000 tons of bombs are dropped on Dortmund on 23/24 May, the heaviest raid yet, and other major targets include Essen, Duisburg, and Wuppertal. The USAAF concentrates on the U-Boat war dropping 2800 tons of bombs on a range of objectives including St Nazaire, Antwerp and Kiel. A

CHRONOLOGY

specially trained RAF squadron attacks the Mohne and Eder Dams (*see* 16–17 May).

Allied aircraft based in the Mediterranean fly about 25,000 missions in support of operations in Tunisia (until the German surrender) and against targets in Sicily, Sardinia and southern Italy.

MAY–JUNE 1943

Greece, Resistance The British and the Americans encourage the Greek resistance to increase its operations as part of the plan to draw German attention away from Sicily and Operation Husky. Two extra German armored divisions are sent to Greece. Once they have arrived an important viaduct on the Athens–Thessaloniki railroad is destroyed, so that if the tanks are moved away they will have to do so under their own power at the cost of much wear and tear. SOE agents help the resistance workers. The rail line is blocked for four months.

1 MAY 1943

Tunisia The Americans manage to complete the capture of Hill 609 but are held there.

3 MAY 1943

Tunisia The American 1st Division finally fights its way out of Mousetrap Valley and captures Mateur, but the Germans manage to improvise a new defense line and the advance is halted.

United States, Command General Andrews, US General commanding the European Theater, is killed in an air accident. General Devers is selected to replace him.

4 MAY 1943

Burma The Japanese have now infiltrated between Buthidaung and Maungdaw, disrupting British communications.

5 MAY 1943

Eastern Front In the Kuban the Soviets advance once more, capturing Krymsk and Neberjaisk.

Tunisia Late in the day Djebel Bou Aoukaz is taken once more by the British forces. The V Corps is now commanded by Horrocks and includes 6th and 7th Armored Divisions and 4th Indian Division.

6 MAY 1943

Tunisia Supported by a massive artillery and air bombardment, V Corps destroys what is left of 15th Panzer and breaks through toward Tunis. Farther north the Americans are also on

the move, heading for Bizerta, Ferryville and Protville in three separate thrusts. The French XIX Corps are approaching Pont du Fahs.

7 MAY 1943

Tunisia The Allied forces burst forward all along the line. Tunis and Bizerta are both captured at about the same time in the afternoon by the British and Americans respectively.

Solomons US forces lay mine barrages in the waters around New Georgia to isolate it from Japanese supplies. Three destroyers are sunk by these mines on 8 May.

Burma The British are forced to retire from Buthidaung, which is taken by the Japanese.

8–9 MAY 1943

Tunisia The Axis forces are trying to retire to the Cape Bon Peninsula for a final stand, but during the night 6th Armored Division drives from Hammam Lif toward Hammamet, right in among the retreating troops and completing their disorganization.

10 MAY 1943

Eastern Front Hitler gives his consent for Operation Citadel, the attack on Kursk, to go ahead despite news of Soviet defensive preparations. Later Hitler defers the starting date from 13 June to early July in order to allow extra Panther tanks to be supplied to the attacking units.

Tunisia The last organized Axis resistance is overcome. There is no hope of evacuation and wholesale surrenders begin.

11 MAY 1943

Aleutians The American 7th Division (General Brown) begins to land on Attu supported by Admiral Kinkaid's Task Force 16. All units get ashore safely but are held up by the Japanese and the difficult terrain when they try to advance inland. There are strong naval forces in support including three battleships, one escort carrier and numerous cruisers and destroyers.

The ships provide effective fire support throughout the operation.

Burma The British pull 26th Division back from Maungdaw which the Japanese occupy on 14 May. The 1943 Arakan campaign is over. The British have lost 3000 killed and seriously wounded, more than twice as many as the Japanese. Above all the morale of the British force could hardly be poorer and their health is also weak. Generals Irwin and Lloyd are relieved and Slim is appointed to command Fourteenth Army on 15 May.

12 MAY 1943
Tunisia General von Arnim surrenders to the Allies as the mopping up continues. General Messe is promoted to Field Marshal by Mussolini in the hope that he will be encouraged to hold out.

Solomons Admiral Ainsworth leads four cruisers and seven destroyers in two groups to shell Vila and Munda. Other vessels also lay mines near New Georgia.

12–25 MAY 1943
Allied Planning Roosevelt and Churchill meet in Washington for the 'Trident' Conference. The Americans come to this better prepared for detailed argument than they have been in the past and are determined to get a firm commitment by the British to a cross-Channel invasion. The British feel that their commitment to this has never been in doubt and that the American insistence in planning so formally so far ahead will deprive the Allies of any strategic flexibility, especially in the Mediterranean. The invasion of Sicily has already been agreed but the British wish to be able to exploit this on the Italian mainland and perhaps also to act in the Balkans. The Americans feel that this is motivated by dubious postwar political aims and their Chiefs of Staff are opposed on strategic grounds as well. Admiral King has always wanted and striven for priority to be given to the Pacific, and Marshall is worried about doing anything which might detract from the cross-Channel operation which he believes is essential.

From the British point of view a major complaint is that despite the agreed Germany-first policy, the Americans have committed a larger share of their army and airforce to the Pacific as well as the bulk of their navy. The British feel that the shortage of shipping which is the major limiting factor for European operations can be put down to this. (In fact an important contributory element of this shortage is the decision taken at Casablanca in January to give priority to the building of escorts for the Battle of the Atlantic and not to landing craft.) Compromises are reached on all headings. The Americans do not have to accept any real limitations on their Pacific operations and the British get a provisional agreement to exploit any Italian successes. Perhaps the most significant decision taken by the conference is to set a target date for D-Day – 1 May 1944. The British General Morgan, is appointed to prepare plans for the invasion. He is given the designation COSSAC (Chief of Staff to the Supreme Allied Commander).

13 MAY 1943
Tunisia Marshal Messe orders the surrender or the remaining German and Italian troops. Altogether 250,000 have been captured in the last few days, half of them German.

Aleutians The American forces are still being contained virtually in their landing areas although they now outnumber the Japanese by about four to one. Bad weather has been hindering the US air support and the terrain is very difficult.

15 MAY 1943
Eastern Front The Germans attempt a small attack in the Leningrad sector but fail to make any progress.

Aleutians One American attack at Massacre Bay is beaten off, but a second in the north of Attu does better although there are casualties from badly aimed American bombing as well as Japanese fire.

Soviet Diplomacy The Soviet authorities decide to dissolve the Comintern to 'prove' to the West that Russia no longer has any expansionist aims. The dissolution is announced on 22 May.

16 MAY 1943
Aleutians The Americans continue their attacks near Holtz Bay on Attu. The Japanese are forced to pull back by weight of numbers.

Poland, Resistance In the last act of the extermination of the Warsaw ghetto, the SS blow up the synagogue. Stroop, the SS commander, boasts that since the rising began 14,000 Jews have been killed in the ghetto and a further 40,000 have been sent to Treblinka to be killed.

16–17 MAY 1943
The Dambusters Raid During the night a specially trained RAF squadron, No 617, led by Wing Commander Guy Gibson, undertakes a precision attack on the dams on the Möhne and Eder Rivers. They use specially designed bombs and unique techniques to attack targets which are reckoned to supply the majority of the electricity used in the Ruhr and a great deal of the water. A third target, the Sorpe dam, is not attacked. The operation has only been possible by training an elite squadron for this one mission and the losses, eight of nineteen planes, are too high to bear repetition. The damage is far slighter than has been hoped and both dams are fairly quickly repaired. The operation certainly does not prove that such precision attacks are either possible on a large scale, or likely to have the greatest effects.

CHRONOLOGY

16–25 MAY 1943
Eastern Front The Germans mount a series of counterattacks in the Kuban area but these are fairly comfortably held by the Soviet forces.

17 MAY 1943
Yugoslavia, Resistance The Germans begin their fifth major offensive against Tito's Partisans, code name Operation *Schwarz* and commanded by General Lüters. The main striking forces for the operation are to be provided by the SS Division Prinz Eugen and two formations specially brought in, 1st Mountain Division and 4th Brandenburg Regiment. Various other Axis formations are to hold an encircling ring and altogether there are 120,000 against Tito's 20,000 at most.

18 MAY 1943
Aleutians On Attu the American forces advancing from the north and south of the island link up and prepare to attack what they believe are the last Japanese positions on the approach to Chicagof Harbor.
World Affairs A United Nations Food Conference begins in Hot Springs, Virginia. It sits until 3 June and produces various resolutions calling for fairer distribution of resources in the postwar world.

19 MAY 1943
Aleutians On Attu the Americans advance along Clevesy Pass toward Chicagof.

20 MAY 1943
Aleutians Fighting continues on Attu in the Clevesy Pass area where the Japanese hold the high ground and have to be prised out of every position.

21 MAY 1943
Free French Forces Admiral Godefroy, commanding the small French squadron interned in Alexandria, decides to join the Allies.

21–25 MAY 1943
United States, Home Front More than 150,000 people are made homeless as rivers in the Mississippi system burst their banks.

21–27 MAY 1943
Aleutians The Americans make some progress on Attu each day. The fighting is especially fierce from 24–27 May when the Japanese are gradually driven off a feature known as Fish Hook Ridge. On 27 May work is begun on an airfield at Alexai Point.

22 MAY 1943
Battle of the Atlantic Doenitz orders all U-Boats on patrol in the north Atlantic to break off operations against the convoys. The losses have grown too high and although the Germans continue to hope for a revival of their fortunes by technical developments, the battle has effectively been won. Some boats are moved south to the Caribbean and to waters off the Azores. It is only by diverting his operations to less vital areas that Doenitz is able to continue his campaign, even at a reduced level.

The causes of the Allied victory are several: radar, aircraft and code-breaking information figure prominently. The U-Boats can perform their operations best on the surface and when they are able to signal to each other. Air cover prevents them reaching their patrol positions quickly and they cannot shadow a convoy on the surface and signal its position without being detected and attacked. Messages from the U-Boat Command can be decoded and U-Boat patrols avoided and the favored tactics for night attacks are made difficult when radar ends the U-Boats concealment. Altogether the Allies' performance has been impressively coordinated, with scientists designing and airmen and sailors operating the weapons so quickly produced by industry. The only question over the Allied performance has been the way the maritime air services have had to compete with the strategic bomber forces for long-range aircraft. The Germans have been slow to realize the potential of their submarine force as the rate of building even as late as 1941 shows. Equally, they have been slower in fitting scientific developments into their operations.

26 MAY 1943
Canada, Home Front Meat rationing is introduced throughout the country.

27 MAY 1943
Allied Planning Churchill and General Marshall leave Washington for North Africa for talks with General Eisenhower on what is to be attempted in the coming Italian campaign. Marshall wishes to avoid any commitment that could interfere with a later cross-Channel operation, while Churchill is keen for opportunities in the Mediterranean to be exploited and Italy knocked out of the war.
Yugoslavia, Resistance British officers are dropped to rendezvous with Tito's Partisan forces in Montenegro near Mount Durmitor. For some time the SOE have been receiving reports that General Mihajlović and his Četniks

are cooperating with the Germans, but only now are they able to contact Tito and the real resistance. Tito's forces are in trouble at this time. They are hemmed in by superior German, Italian and Bulgarian forces and have been under attack for 10 days but are beginning now to concentrate their force in preparation for fighting their way out. One reason for this slowness has been the desire to keep the appointment with the British.

France, Resistance The Comité National de la Résistance meets in Paris for the first time. This nationwide organization for the various resistance groups has largely been the achievement of de Gaulle's lieutenant, Jean Moulin. Politically this is of considerable benefit to de Gaulle's position with the Allies.

Eastern Front In the Kuban another Soviet attack goes in but fails to penetrate the German defenses.

29 MAY 1943

Aleutians On Attu the Japanese mount a final fanatical attack on the Americans who are now established in Chicagof. The fighting is extremely vicious.

30 MAY 1943

Aleutians The Americans complete the capture of Attu. The Japanese have lost 2350 killed including many suicides and only 28 wounded have been captured. The American losses are also fairly heavy, 600 dead and 1200 wounded in capturing what is really a very unimportant position.

France, Politics De Gaulle arrives in Algiers for talks with General Giraud to reconcile their differences.

31 MAY 1943

Mediterranean Pantelleria is shelled by a British cruiser and two destroyers. It has already been bombed several times in the past few days.

JUNE 1943

Battle of the Atlantic The German U-Boats operate principally in waters west of the Azores against US–Gibraltar convoys. The U-Boats are now sailing in groups across the Bay of Biscay to improve their chances of beating off air attacks but this tactic is not successful and from the middle of the month they are ordered to submerge while on passage except when charging their batteries. Seventeen U-Boats are sunk during the month but Allied losses to submarines are only 20 ships out of a total 28.

Important changes are introduced in the British naval codes which almost completely end the ability of B Dienst to intercept British messages. The Germans still remain convinced that their codes are secure, preferring to blame radio direction finding and spies in the French ports for any lack of security.

Allied Air Operations RAF Bomber Command drops more than 15,000 tons of bombs, principally on targets in the Ruhr. Dusseldorf is the victim of one particularly heavy raid on 11 June and Oberhausen, Mulheim and Cologne are also strongly attacked. The US Eighth Air Force drops 2500 tons on Bremen, Keil, Wilhelmshaven and Cuxhaven. During the month the BBC issues several warnings to the population in France and the Low Countries to stay away from factories producing goods for Germany.

In the Mediterranean the main Allied bombing effort is directed early in the month against Pantelleria and Lampedusa. Later Sicilian and Sardinian targets are most common.

1 JUNE 1943

United States, Home Front More than 500,000 coal miners go on strike after protracted wage negotiations break down. Most return to work by 7 June when talks resume. A further strike begins on 21 June but most of the men have returned to work by early July.

3 JUNE 1943

France, Politics De Gaulle and Giraud agree on the composition of a Committee of National Liberation under their joint presidency. The members are to include Massigli, Jean Monnet and André Philip.

France, Resistance The Michelin tire works at Clermont-Ferrand are badly damaged in a sabotage operation conducted by local resistance workers and SOE agents.

4–11 JUNE 1943

Mediterranean Pantelleria is very heavily bombarded by air and from the sea.

8 JUNE 1943

Pacific The battleship *Mutsu* sinks in Hiroshima Bay after an internal explosion.

9 JUNE 1943

Eastern Front There is a Soviet attack on the Mius River sector which gains some ground. The Germans are repulsed in a similar limited effort near Lisichansk.

10 JUNE 1943

Strategic Bombing The Joint Chiefs of Staff

issue the Pointblank Directive to the commanders of the British and American heavy bomber forces in Europe. It sets out formal instructions for the priorities and aims of the bomber offensive which will last until D-Day. The instructions mostly reflect American thinking on precision attacks on specific target systems with particular reference to the German aircraft industry. There is also some mention of attacks to damage civilian morale. The leaders of the US Air Forces and Air Marshal Harris are all able to read into the directive permission to continue with their favored types of operations. There will be little coordination between the British and American forces. The American daylight precision attacks will not come near achieving their objectives until the advent of the Mustang escort fighter and the British night area bombing will also have disappointing results. German industrial production will prove to be astonishingly resilient and the morale of the workers will not suffer notably despite the damage to their homes. It is being discovered in Germany that factories that seem badly hit will often be untouched in their vital machinery and that once the rubble is cleared production can be resumed almost immediately.

11 JUNE 1943
Mediterranean Pantelleria's 11,000-strong Italian garrison surrenders without a fight on the approach of an Allied assault force. More than 5000 tons of bombs have been dropped on this one small island in the last month and although the damage has been great, it has been far less than has been expected. This is an important indication of the difficulties in store for the main strategic-bombing campaign.

12 JUNE 1943
Mediterranean King George VI arrives in North Africa to visit the troops. He visits Malta on 20 June.

The island of Lampedusa surrenders to the Allies. Like Pantelleria it has been heavily bombarded. The smaller islands of Linosa and Lampione are surrendered on 13 and 14 June respectively.
Solomons There is a major air battle near Guadalcanal in which the attacking Japanese forces lose heavily. This is only one of a series of such encounters about this time.

16 JUNE 1943
Solomons US fighters from Henderson Field claim to have shot down 93 aircraft from a Japanese force attacking shipping assembled for

the coming operations against New Georgia.
Operation Husky The first convoys for the invasion of Sicily leave the United States. On 17 June the first units of the supporting naval force set out from the British Home Fleet base at Scapa Flow.

18 JUNE 1943
British Command The British government announces that General Wavell is to be the next viceroy of India in succession to Lord Linlithgow in October. General Auchinleck becomes Commander in Chief in India immediately but a separate East Asia Command is to be created. By these 'promotions' Churchill is planning to remove Wavell and Auchinleck from important military responsibility because he has lost confidence in them.

20 JUNE 1943
New Guinea General Krueger establishes his Sixth Army HQ at Milne Bay. A Japanese attack on 17th Australian Brigade in the Mubo area is unsuccessful.

20–24 JUNE 1943
Allied Air Operations RAF bombers attack Friedrichshaven on the night of 20/21 June, fly to Africa, and attack Spezia on the way back on 23/24 June. This is the first such 'shuttle-service' attack.

21 JUNE 1943
New Georgia The 4th Marine Raider Battalion lands at Segi Point at the southern tip of New Georgia. There is no Japanese garrison there and the marines are reinforced without incident on 22 June.

22 JUNE 1943
France, Politics After several days of hard bargaining the Committee of National Liberation decide that Giraud will retain command of the French forces in North Africa and that de Gaulle will lead elsewhere. This is in effect a victory for de Gaulle.

23 JUNE 1943
Australia, Politics In the House of Representatives a censure motion on the government is beaten by one vote. Prime Minister Curtin announces that he will advise the Governor General to dissolve Parliament.

23–24 JUNE 1943
New Guinea There are American landings on Woodlark Island.

26 JUNE 1943
New Guinea The Allied force at Morobe prepares for an amphibious move north along the coast.

27 JUNE 1943
New Georgia The marines are ferried slightly farther up the coast from Segi Point to begin an overland advance on Viru Harbor.

28–29 JUNE 1943
New Guinea Kiriwina and Woodlark are occupied by further US forces who start work immediately on airfield construction.

29 JUNE 1943
Solomons A squadron of cruisers and destroyers shells the Japanese base at Shortland while other vessels lay mines in the area. Some of the US convoys bound for New Georgia are sighted by the Japanese but they mistakenly believe that they are merely carrying supplies to Guadalcanal.

30 JUNE 1943
Solomons There are American landings on several islands in the New Georgia group, particularly Rendova. The forces involved come principally from General Hester's 43rd Division and are supported directly by Admiral Turner's Task Force 31 and by land-based aircraft commanded by Admiral Fitch. All landings are successful but resistance is heavy on Vangunu and progress is difficult.
New Guinea A mixed Australian and American unit known as McKechnie Force lands at Nassau Bay near Salamaua from Morobe and immediately is involved in heavy fighting to consolidate and extend a bridgehead.
Eastern Front There are numerous small-scale engagements in many locations all along the front. The armies are becoming more active again as the ground hardens and the winter's losses are being made good as far as is possible.

JULY 1943
Battle of the Atlantic The British offensive over the Bay of Biscay is stepped up and succeeds in sinking 20 U-Boats out of the 37 lost this month. There are also successes for US hunter-killer escort groups sent to the Gibraltar and Azores area. These are based around the escort carriers *Bogue*, *Santee* and *Cove*. The Germans achieve some successes off Brazil, southeast and West Africa. Allied losses are 61 ships of 365,400 tons in all theaters, 46 ships falling to submarines.
Europe, Air Operations This month RAF

Bomber Command drops about 16,000 tons of bombs and Eighth Air Force about 3600. Hamburg is the principal target. Essen and other cities in the Ruhr are also attacked by the RAF. American objectives include towns in France, Norway and Germany.

In the early part of the month the main target of the Allied Mediterranean air forces is Sicily. Later, Naples, Bari and Rome are among the objectives. The raid on Rome on 19 July is particularly heavy – 1100 tons of bombs are dropped by 700 aircraft. In all the raids on Italian cities leaflets are dropped urging an Italian surrender.
China, Air Operations Targets for the Fourteenth Air Force include Hankow, Pailochi, Hainan and Hong Kong.

1 JULY 1943
Axis Diplomacy Marshal Antonescu comes to visit Mussolini to suggest that Italy, Rumania and Hungary should leave the war together. This would clearly be a sensible policy for Mussolini to attempt but he is afraid to give any lead and in meetings with Hitler over the next few weeks he is too frightened to speak out.
New Guinea The marines from Segi Point capture Viru.

2 JULY 1943
Solomons The American buildup on Rendova continues but the Japanese garrison still holds out. During the night a Japanese naval force bombards the American positions on the island with little effect.

3 JULY 1943
New Guinea After heavy fighting in the Mubo area, the Australians advancing from Wau join up with the Americans from the Nassau Bay landing force in the region of the Bitoi River.
New Georgia US forces land at Zanana about eight miles east of Munda. There is no Japanese resistance and the beachhead is quickly consolidated.

4 JULY 1943
Solomons The American force advancing from Zanana toward Munda is held up by heavy Japanese resistance. The Japanese land 1200 men from three destroyers at Vila on Kolombangara.
Poland, Politics General Sikorski is killed in an air crash near Gibraltar. Mikolajczyk replaces him as prime minister of the London exile government and General Kukiel becomes Commander in Chief. Neither of these men is as

capable as Sikorski. The commander of the Polish Home Army, Grot-Rowecki, was arrested by the Germans in Warsaw on 30 June. His replacement is Bor-Komorowski who, although personally a fine man, is less suited for the job.

5 JULY 1943

Eastern Front Both sides have assembled huge ground and air forces for what is to be the largest tank engagement of the war, the Battle of Kursk. The Germans hope to cut off the Kursk salient and create a huge gap in the Soviet front which can then be exploited. The Soviets are well aware of the general German intentions from local reconnaissance and high-level espionage information and have decided, after much debate, to follow Zhukov's advice and stand on the defensive rather than attack first themselves.

Altogether the Soviets and the Germans have concentrated 2,000,000 men, 6000 tanks and 5000 aircraft to take part in the operation with the Soviets having a slight numerical superiority in all categories. In artillery the Soviets have a significant advantage. As far as the quality of the equipment is concerned, in every class the Red Army is receiving newer and better designed weapons than has been the case in the past. The excellent T-34 tank, already in service, is being supplemented by new assault gun models. These qualitative improvements are particularly significant for the Red Air Force, which now has much more advanced fighter and ground-attack aircraft. The Germans have delayed the planned starting date of the battle at Hitler's command, in order to allow larger numbers of the new

Above: German trucks under air attack at Kursk.

Panther tank to be supplied to the units taking part. The heavy Tiger tanks and the even more massive Elefant assault guns are also to have an important role in the attack. All these models are basically very effective designs but the conditions of the battle, and minor design errors and teething troubles for the new Panthers and Elefants, will limit their performance and to some extent set aside the advantage of skill which the German tank crews and small-unit commanders still maintain.

The northern wing of the German pincer is led by General Model and is spearheaded by XLVII Panzer Corps of Ninth Army. The somewhat stronger southern wing is commanded by General Hoth and includes Fourth Panzer Army and Operational Group Kempf. Manstein and Kluge are in overall charge of the southern and northern army groups respectively. Model's attack falls on Rokossovsky's Central Front and Hoth's on Vatutin's Voronezh Front. Konev's Steppe Front is in reserve to carry out the planned counteroffensive when the Germans have shot their bolt. Zhukov is supervising the defense in the north and Vasilievsky in the south.

In all areas the Soviets have prepared elaborate fixed defenses of minefields, other obstacles and antitank guns. Even before the German attack starts they fire a disruptive bombardment which causes the Germans considerable loss. When the attack is launched at dawn on 5 July the progress made is slow in both sectors and many tanks are lost. Soviet casualties are also considerable but at this stage few of their tanks are engaged.

5–6 JULY 1943

Solomons During 5 July a further US force of regimental strength lands in the north of New Georgia at Rice Anchorage. The fighting on the Zanana–Munda track continues. During the night a force of Japanese destroyers brings almost 3000 more troops to Vila. Admiral Ainsworth, with three cruisers and four destroyers, engages a part of the Japanese squadron and sinks a destroyer but loses the cruiser *Helena*. A second Japanese destroyer is sunk by aircraft on 6 July. Bougainville is also raided by US bombers on 6 July. In New Georgia the fighting along the Barike River continues to be fierce.

6 JULY 1943

Eastern Front The bitter fighting of the Battle of Kursk continues. In the north the Germans make about six miles. The Elefant assault guns employed here suffer heavily from infantry attacks as their support is destroyed and their lack of machine guns prevents effective self-defense. In the south excellent artillery and air support helps achieve rather more – about 10 miles is gained. A heavy downpour restricts the advance here a little, especially on the left on the lower ground allocated to the front of XLVIII Corps.

Aleutians The Japanese positions on Kiska are bombarded by four cruisers and four destroyers led by Admiral Giffen. This attack is repeated several times by smaller forces over the next few days.

7 JULY 1943

Eastern Front In the northern sector of the Battle of Kursk the Germans can only make a very small advance. For the rest of the battle Model is able to push forward less than a mile a day. In the south the Germans come close to a breakthrough on the front of XLVIII Corps around Syrtzevo but Soviet armored counter-attacks arrive in time to hold the Germans up in what soon becomes a slogging match.

New Guinea The Japanese positions at Mubo are heavily bombed and are further threatened by the Australian capture of Observation Hill about one mile away.

8 JULY 1943

Solomons On New Georgia the US forces make some progress near the Barike River.

Eastern Front The fierce fighting in the Battle of Kursk continues. The position in the south is still quite hopeful for the Germans despite their considerable losses but gradually their force is being worn down and in the very confused situation command and weapon-handling skills are becoming devalued.

North Atlantic Strong forces of the British Home Fleet cruise off Norway but they are not noticed by the Germans. This operation is designed to draw attention away from Mediterranean operations.

9 JULY 1943

Eastern Front The vicious attrition at Kursk continues, with the Germans becoming more and more bogged down in local encircling operations against stubborn strongpoints and at the same time having to fight off increasing Soviet tank forces which are beginning to arrive.

Sicily The Allied landing force for Operation Husky is being concentrated around Malta but the bad weather is proving troublesome. The defense of Sicily is entrusted to General Guzzoni's Italian Sixth Army. He has about 240,000 men, of whom a quarter are German. The Italian troops are all demoralized and poorly equipped, and many are tied down to fixed coastal defenses. The Allies have about 1200 transports and 2000 landing craft which will land elements of eight divisions (more than on D-Day). By the third day 150,000 will be ashore and eventually 480,000, of whom slightly more than half will be British will be landed. General Eisenhower is the Supreme Commander and his deputy, General Alexander, will lead 15th Army Group. This is composed of Patton's Seventh Army and Montgomery's Eighth Army. The naval commander is Admiral Cunningham with Admirals Ramsay and Hewitt controlling the British and American landings respectively. Tedder commands the Allied air forces which provide 3700 aircraft for direct supporting operations.

The Allies have mounted a considerable deception operation pointing both to Greece and Sardinia (*see* 30 April 1943 for one famous incident). This has been fairly successful. Hitler believes that Sardinia will be the target and has moved an airborne corps to the south of France to guard against this as well as taking precautions in Greece. Mussolini correctly expects that Sicily will be next but he is reluctant to call for the German help necessary to strengthen the defenses there.

The attack begins on the night of 9 July with airborne landings. Partly because of the strong winds and partly because of inexperience, the paratroops from Genl Ridgway's 82nd Airborne Division are scattered over a huge area. Although the paratroops in the British sector are dropped more accurately many gliders are released too early and more than a third come down in the sea. The airborne troops are not able, therefore, to seize all their objectives but they do cause considerable disruption.

Solomons The Americans on New Georgia are able to begin formal full-scale attacks toward Munda. The Japanese defend fiercely, however, and only a small advance is made. The Americans send reinforcements to Rendova and the Japanese to Kolombangara.

10 JULY 1943

Eastern Front In the north Model's attacks finally grind to a halt in the Battle of Kursk. In the south the unrelenting German pressure has seriously worried Vatutin and help is sent from Konev's Steppe Front – principally the Fifth Guards Tank Army.

Sicily The main Allied landings for Operation Husky begin. Patton's Seventh Army lands in the Gulf of Gela between Licata and Scoglitti. They meet only slight opposition and quickly take Gela, Licata and Vittoria. The British landings between Syracuse and the southwest tip of the island are unopposed and Syracuse is taken by the end of the day.

The bad weather has helped put the Italian coastal divisions off their guard and the Allied bombardment has helped complete their demoralization. New equipment has also been used, including LST's and LCT's which enable the armor to be put ashore with the assaulting infantry.

Solomons The American advance on New Georgia is largely being held by the Japanese and because of the difficult terrain supply is becoming a problem for the combat troops.

New Guinea The Australians and Americans manage to link up in another sector, cutting the Japanese in Mubo off from Salamaua.

11 JULY 1943

Eastern Front The vicious fighting continues in the southern sector in the Battle of Kursk. It is now more strictly a tank battle with the air and other supporting forces unable to intervene effectively. Visibility on the battlefield has become so poor because of dust and smoke that the Germans can make nothing of their advantage in long-range gunnery.

Sicily The British continue to advance almost unopposed. Palazzolo is taken and on the coast the only halt is late in the day at Priolo. The Americans are more seriously attacked, however. The Hermann Goering Panzer Division moves down toward Gela from its positions around Caltagirone. The American landings have suffered rather more than the British from the weather and few tanks and antitank guns have been landed. It is, therefore, only with the help of naval gunfire that the German attack is beaten off when it has almost reached the beaches. British battleships and cruisers are also in action shelling Favignana and Marsala during the night.

12 JULY 1943

Eastern Front In the Battle of Kursk the Fourth Panzer Army, led by the II SS Panzer Corps, makes one final effort in the direction of Prokhorovka but cannot break through the fresh Soviet forces. Army Group South is now being threatened near Taganrog and Stalino, and in the north of the salient a Soviet counteroffensive begins toward Orel even as Kluge orders Model to withdraw some of his panzers to meet such a threat. At the end of the day Hitler

orders that the battle be discontinued. This new Soviet attack involves troops of the West and Bryansk Fronts in two thrusts west from Novosil and south from between Kozelsk and Sukhinichi.

In this battle the Germans have conceded the strategic initiative to the Soviets for good. Their shortage of manpower has compelled them to attack on a limited front and to commit almost all of their tank force to one effort. The Soviet losses in the battle so far have probably been rather greater than the German's but they can afford it. The Luftwaffe losses have been severe and its dominance is now over. The Germans must also send troops to Italy but Hitler still forbids his Generals to make necessary withdrawals.

Sicily In the morning the Hermann Goering Division continues its attack on the American positions without success and in the afternoon is drawn off to face the more threatening British advance. However, the Americans are now coming under increasing pressure from elements of 15th Panzergrenadier Division which have been brought from the west of the island.

In the British sector the advance on Augusta continues against German and Italian resistance. Lentini is captured.

12–13 JULY 1943

Solomons Admiral Ainsworth's Task Force with three cruisers and 10 destroyers meets a Japanese squadron of one cruiser and nine destroyers led by Admiral Izaki off Kolombangara. The Japanese make good use of their torpedo equipment, sinking one destroyer and damaging two cruisers. However, the Japanese cruiser is virtually blown out the water by the radar-directed gunfire of the American cruisers.

13 JULY 1943

Solomons The Americans continue to reinforce their troops on Rendova and New Georgia. On New Georgia their attacks make a little more progress against fierce resistance.

New Guinea The Japanese positions at Mubo are overrun and their force is practically wiped out.

13–14 JULY 1943

Sicily Augusta is captured by the British 5th Division on 13 July and other British units are engaged by the Hermann Goering Division around Vizzini. During the night Dempsey's XIII Corps begin a major effort to reach Catania, attacking from around Lentini. Commandos and paratroops are sent in to capture two vital river bridges. The commandos land by sea and manage to take the nearer bridge but the paratroops suffer heavy casualties and are driven off on 14 July. By coincidence the German 1st Paratroop Division is dropped near the commandos' positions and can therefore begin its task of strengthening the Axis front immediately. On 14 July the main British and American forces succeed in advancing fairly evenly all along the front. American units take Biscani airfield and Niscemi and the British capture Vizzini.

Eastern Front Despite the formal order to abandon the battle, Hoth's forces continue to make local efforts in the southern part of the Kursk salient. To the north both of the Soviet pincers make good progress toward Orel.

15 JULY 1943

United States, Politics Roosevelt creates a new office of economic warfare, headed by Leo Crowley, to replace the previous board.

Eastern Front Rokossovsky's Central Front goes over to the offensive, joining the attacks toward Orel. In the south of the Kursk salient Manstein's forces begin to pull back to their start lines followed up all the time by Soviet pressure.

Sicily General Patton forms a provisional corps to move on the west of the island while Bradley's II Corps drives north. In Catania the Axis forces fall back behind the Simeto River.

Solomons General Griswold replaces General Hester in charge of the operations in New Georgia. There is a fierce air battle over Rendova in which the Americans lose three aircraft and shoot down more than 40.

16 JULY 1943

Diplomatic Affairs Roosevelt and Churchill issue a special joint statement calling for an Italian surrender and suggest to the Italian people that they get rid of Mussolini. In Italy some of the Fascist politicians are beginning to plot to accomplish exactly this.

Sicily The American 3rd Division attacks Agrigento and Porto Empedocle. The Canadian 1st Division takes Caltagirone and advances on Piazza Armerina against strong resistance. Units of the British 50th Division succeed in crossing the Simeto River and later are reinforced by armor.

17 JULY 1943

Eastern Front The Soviet drive north and west of Orel is gradually slowed down by German tank forces. In the south of the Kursk salient the German fighting withdrawal continues. Farther

Above: Jungle fighting in the Southwest Pacific.

south still, Malinovsky's Southwest Front opens attacks around Voroshilovgrad.

Solomons The Americans mount a large air raid on Bougainville. Shipping offshore and the airfields between Buin and Faisi are attacked. One destroyer is sunk.

New Guinea Units from the Australian 3rd and the American 41st Divisions move toward Salamaua. This is merely a holding action in preparation for a later move against Lae and the Markham valley.

Sicily The Americans take Agrigento and Porto Empedocle.

18 JULY 1943

Sicily The Americans capture Caltanisetta and push on north to cut the Palermo–Enna road. To the east of Enna the Canadians take Valguarnerna. On the east coast strong German resistance halts Dempsey's force just north of the River Simeto.

19 JULY 1943

Axis Politics Hitler and Mussolini meet at Feltre in northern Italy. Hitler hardly lets Mussolini speak and does little but demand more effort from the Italians. Mussolini realizes that Italy cannot fight much longer, but face to face with Hitler he will not admit it. The angry criticism of Mussolini's government following the heavy Allied air raids on Rome illustrates the Italian war weariness.

Sicily The American forces advance quickly to north and west, meeting little resistance. On the east coast the British attack is held and Montgomery therefore directs the weight of his attack somewhat further inland toward Gerbini, Agira and Leonforte.

Eastern Front The Soviets continue to push forward in both sides of the Kursk salient. In the north they threaten Bolkhov.

20 JULY 1943

Atomic Research Roosevelt issues a firm order that atomic information should be shared with the British. Discussions between the British and American staffs follow and in August at the Quebec Conference, a formal agreement is signed by which Britain and the United States agree to share their knowledge, not to use atomic weapons against each other, not to use atomic weapons without the other's consent and not to give information to any third party. The British deny any right to exploit atomic knowledge after that war except to the extent judged fair by the US President (*see* September 1944.)

Sicily On the south the Americans reach Menfi and in the center of the island Enna is captured by the Canadians who also advance to Leonforte.

Eastern Front Troops of Popov's Bryansk Front clear the Germans out of Mtsensk.

Solomons On New Georgia fresh American forces arrive in the front line. The supply problem is not so acute now because of new road construction. Two Japanese destroyers are sunk while on a supply mission.

21 JULY 1943

Italy The Allied advance on Sicily continues. The British take Gerbini, the Canadians Leonforte and the Americans Corleone and Castelvetrano. The Italian naval base at Crotone on the mainland is bombarded.

Eastern Front The Soviets capture Bolkhov.

21–22 JULY 1943

Solomons A small American force is sent to Vella Lavella to examine the possibility of major landings, thus by-passing Kolombangara. On New Georgia, Griswold lays plans for a large offensive.

22 JULY 1943

Sicily The Americans enter Palermo and have now cut off 50,000 Italian troops in the west of the island but the mobile forces including most of the Germans are escaping to the northeast corner.

Aleutians Major US naval forces bombard Kiska. Two battleships and four cruisers as well as lighter forces are involved.

23 JULY 1943

Sicily The Americans occupy Trapani and Marsala and on the north coast they reach Termini Imerese.

Eastern Front In the south of the Kursk salient the Germans are now back in their original positions.

24 JULY 1943

Italy, Politics The Fascist Grand Council meets for the first time since December 1939. The debate and voting go against Mussolini but it is not yet clear what is to happen next.

Sicily On the north coast the American 45th Division takes Cefalu and inland other American units advance toward Nicosia.

24 JULY–2 AUGUST 1943

Europe, Air Operations Hamburg is raided in the most effective attacks of the European campaign. The RAF mounts major operations on four nights: 24/25 July, 27/28 July, 29/30 July and 2/3 August. On the first three of these nights about 780 bombers drop 2300 tons of bombs each night and on the fourth night 425 bombers drop 940 tons. The USAF joins in on 25 and 26 July and the RAF sends small forces on every other night. Altogether about 50,000 civilian deaths are caused and as many injuries. About 800,000 people are made homeless. The attack on 27/28 July includes many incendiary weapons and a fire storm is raised for the first time. A fire storm occurs when the fires in a given area become so intense that they devour all the oxygen nearby and suck more into themselves, creating hurricane-force winds which both feed the fires and move them along at great speed. The Allied bombers only raise firestorms on a handful of occasions during the war including the atomic bomb attack on Hiroshima on 6 August 1945.

Tactically the raids are important for the RAF as they are the first time that 'window' is used. This consists of strips of metal foil dropped from supporting aircraft which confuses the German radar system by giving false echoes. It is very successful at first but improved radar nullifies some of its benefits during later months. A token of the growing strength of Bomber Command is that it is able to mount major attacks on other targets even during this period. The attacks on Hamburg and other later efforts make up the second of Air Marshal Harris' 'battles.'

This period also sees intensive operations by the US forces against other targets, including many German aircraft factories. The Eighth Air Force loses 88 planes in these operations.

25 JULY 1943

Italy, Politics Mussolini is summoned to a meeting with the king in the afternoon and is told that he is being relieved of his offices. He is arrested on leaving the meeting. Marshal Badoglio is chosen to form the new government.

Sicily The Americans in the north are now meeting stronger resistance. In the center the British and Canadians are attacking Agira from two directions. Allied reinforcements are being brought over to the island from North Africa including the US 9th and the British 78th Divisions.

New Georgia The American offensive begins with units of the 25th Division supplementing the efforts of 43rd and 37th Divisions. Little progress is made, however, except near a feature called Bartley Ridge.

26 JULY 1943

Italy, Politics Marshal Badoglio forms a new cabinet and declares martial law throughout Italy. He professes his loyalty to the Axis but in reality he is looking for a way to end the war.

New Georgia The American attacks continue to make slow progress with heavy air and artillery support. Tanks and flame throwers are also employed.

27 JULY 1943

Sicily There is heavy, but inconclusive, fighting at Agira and Nicosia.

28 JULY 1943

Aleutians Late in the day the Japanese evacuate almost all the remainder of the Kiska garrison without being spotted. The Americans bombard Kiska on three occasions between now and their landing on 15 August as well as dropping 1300 tons of bombs.

Sicily The Americans take Nicosia and the Canadians Agira.

Solomons On New Georgia the American attacks continue, now directed principally toward Horseshoe Hill. Two Japanese destroyers are sunk by aircraft near Rabaul.

29 JULY 1943

Britain, Home Front The minister of labor, Ernie Bevin, announces that women up to 50 must now register for war work. This is a sign of the strain on manpower resources produced by Britain's more complete mobilization for war production. As the war continues this will become more pronounced and will be an important factor in Britain's negotiations with the Allies.

Sicily The British 78th Division arrives at the front and attacks toward Paterno.

Eastern Front The III Panzer Corps counterattacks the Soviet positions on the River Mius north of Taganrog but with little effect.

30 JULY 1943

Sicily The American forces are heavily engaged on the outskirts of Santo Stefano and Troina. On the British front Catenanouva is taken. Off the west coast the Egadi Islands surrender.

31 JULY 1943

Sicily The US 45th Division takes Santo Stefano. The British and Canadians are now moving toward Regalbuto and Centuripe.

AUGUST 1943

Battle of the Atlantic A further 25 U-Boats are sunk this month although U-Boat activity is at a lower level. Among the casualties in July and August are 10 U-Tankers which are important for the distant operations which now form the main effort of the German submarine command. One development is the German attempt to fight back against the Allied forces in the Bay of Biscay. Long-range fighters will be sent from Britain to try to counter this. Allied shipping losses for the month are not much over 100,000 tons.

Europe, Air Operations The heavy-bomber forces of the USAAF and the RAF concentrate on German targets. The RAF attacks on Hamburg continue intermittently, between now and November there are 14,500 sorties in 30 major raids. This month Bomber Command drops 19,000 tons and Eighth Air Force 3600 tons. Among the targets are Nuremberg, Berlin and Bochum. Milan, Turin and Genoa are also hit by bombers based in Britain. Milan is attacked four times, 4000 tons of bombs are dropped altogether. There are particularly important attacks on Schweinfurt and Peenemunde (*see* 17–18 August). Lighter aircraft of both Allies attack communications and airfields in Occupied Territory.

Italian communications are the main targets in many fairly small raids in the Mediterranean. Major efforts are also made against Rome and Foggia and on 1 August Ploesti in Rumania is hit by a strong American Liberator group but losses are heavy. From a force of 177 bombers, 50 fail to return.

1 AUGUST 1943

France, Politics The Free French reorganize their leadership. Giraud will now preside in the

National Liberation Committee only when purely military matters are discussed. De Gaulle is to be president of the Committee at all other times.

Japan, Politics Tokyo announces that Burma is now independent and has declared war on the United States and Britain. The head of the puppet government, Ba Maw, signs a secret treaty with the Japanese.

Sicily There is heavy fighting around Troina, Regalbuto and Centuripe. The terrain in the northeast of the island is very rugged which greatly helps defense.

2 AUGUST 1943
Aleutians The Americans bombard Kiska with battleships and cruisers, yet again unaware that the Japanese have gone.

Sicily The Canadians take Regalbuto and the British 78th Division fights its way into Centuripe.

Solomons The Americans on New Georgia are now fighting on the edge of the Munda airfield. The Japanese have decided not to reinforce the island any more and are concentrating instead on Kolombangara. They are able to withdraw some of their forces to Kolombangara from New Georgia.

Eastern Front On the Orel front the Soviets take Znamenskaya.

4 AUGUST 1943
Eastern Front The Soviets enter Orel and to the south of the Kursk salient Konev's and Vatutin's forces have completed their regrouping and begin to attack toward Belgorod. The attack falls on the junction between Fourth Panzer Army and Eighth Army.

Sicily The British attack Catania while the Americans are still battling to take Troina.

4–5 AUGUST 1943
Solomons The Americans complete the capture of Munda and its airfield.

5 AUGUST 1943
Eastern Front The attacks of Konev's armies make rapid progress, capturing Belgorod and advancing to the southwest. In the Orel sector the Germans are also being pushed back after Second Panzer Army suffered such heavy losses that it has been incorporated in Ninth Army.

Sicily The British take Catania and Paterno a few miles inland.

6 AUGUST 1943
Sicily The American 1st Division finally captures Troina after a bitter fight. The British are now attacking the important position of Adrana.

Eastern Front The Soviets capture Zolochev, northwest of Kharkov.

6–7 AUGUST 1943
Solomons Six US destroyers meet four Japanese destroyers carrying men and supplies to Kolombangara in Vela Gulf. Three of the Japanese ships are sunk.

6–8 AUGUST 1943
Axis Politics German and Italian representatives meet at Verona. Foreign Ministers Ribbentrop and Guaniglia and the Chiefs of Staff Keitel and Ambrosio are present. The Italians try to assure the Germans that they are not negotiating with the Allies. The fact that neither of the leading German delegates is in the first rank of the Nazi hierarchy shows that the Germans attach little importance to the conference.

7 AUGUST 1943
Sicily The British capture Adrana and advance toward Bronte.

8 AUGUST 1943
Sicily In an amphibious operation supported by one cruiser and three destroyers, the Americans land a small force east of Sant Agata. The Germans pull back and Sant Agata falls to the main US forces, as does Cesaro inland. On the British sector Bronte and Acireale are taken.

New Georgia Although Munda has been captured, fighting on the island continues. The Americans are trying to prevent more Japanese escaping to Kolombangara.

9 AUGUST 1943
Denmark, Resistance Scavenius, the Danish prime minister, refuses to accept the German demand that saboteurs be tried in German courts.

10 AUGUST 1943
Eastern Front Khotinets, east of Orel, falls to the Soviets. Their offensives farther south continue to make good progress despite skillful German defense.

10–11 AUGUST 1943
Sicily The cruiser *Philadelphia* and six destroyers support another amphibious operation on the north coast. The landing is east of Cape Orlando, at Brolo, but again the Germans fall back quickly.

11 AUGUST 1943

Eastern Front The Soviets manage to cut the Poltava–Kharkov railroad about 30 miles west of Kharkov.

12 AUGUST 1943

Eastern Front In the Kharkov sector Chuguyev falls to the Soviets. The threat to Poltava is more serious, however, for if it is taken not only will the garrison of Kharkov be almost certainly cut off, but the German forces farther south will also be in grave danger. The III Panzer Corps is therefore brought back north from the Taganrog area.

13 AUGUST 1943

Borneo The US Fifth Air Force sends 380 planes to raid the oilfields at Balikpapan from its bases in Australia.

Eastern Front The Soviets are now very close to Kharkov, having taken Bolshaya and Danilovka. A new offensive has been begun in the Smolensk area and Spas-Demensk, west of Kirov, is taken.

13–24 AUGUST 1943

Allied Planning The British and American military leaders meet in Quebec and are joined by Roosevelt and Churchill to discuss future Allied strategy.

General Morgan's plans for the invasion of Europe are presented and accepted as the basis of more detailed work. Britain is committed to producing Mulberry Harbors – artificial ports which will be placed off the French beaches. Churchill accepts that the Supreme Commander for the invasion should be an American. In the Mediterranean the British are pleased that some exploitation of the defeat of Italy is provided for. The Pacific operations will continue, as agreed before, with the US authorities in full control. There is some difficulty in devising plans for Burma, however. It is decided to prepare another Chindit operation and to continue with the policy of sending aid to Chiang Kai-shek. Admiral Mountbatten is selected to lead a new Southeast Asia Command (SEAC).

14 AUGUST 1943

United States, Home Front New regulations for the draft come into force. There is a revised list of important occupations and, together with having dependents, will now be the deciding factor in any deferment of call up.

Sicily American and British units converge on Randazzo and capture it. The Allies are now advancing rapidly in most sectors.

15 AUGUST 1943

Eastern Front On the Bryansk Front, Karachev falls to Popov's troops after a fierce fight.

Aleutians An American assault force supported by three battleships lands 34,000 US and Canadian troops on Kiska. The Japanese have gone.

Solomons Vella Lavella is occupied by 4500 men from General McLure's 25th Division. The naval force is commanded by Admiral Wilkinson who leads Task Force 31.

New Guinea Japanese aircraft attack Tsili Tsili where the Allies now have an air base.

Sicily On the east coast the British enter Taormina as the Allied advance continues. A further American amphibious operation on the north coast arrives after the Germans have pulled back.

16 AUGUST 1943

Sicily The British attempt a small seaborne attack on the east coast but it is too late to cut off any of the retreating Germans. In the evening US forward patrols reach the outskirts of Messina.

Eastern Front The Soviets take Zhidra, northeast of Bryansk.

16–23 AUGUST 1943

New Guinea The Japanese airfields around Wewak are subjected to a series of attacks by planes of Fifth Air Force from Australia. Many Japanese aircraft are destroyed on the ground for small losses to the attackers.

17 AUGUST 1943

Solomons A small force of Japanese reinforcements is landed on Vella Lavella and there is a small inconclusive action between American destroyers and the Japanese transport force.

Sicily General Patton's troops enter Messina a few hours before the British. The campaign in Sicily is over. One disappointment for the Allies is the extent of the evacuations the Germans and Italians have managed. They have shipped 40,000 German troops with 50 tanks, 100 guns and a large quantity of supplies as well as 62,000 Italians across the Messina Strait. The Germans have lost about 10,000 men killed or captured plus many wounded. The British and Americans have suffered about 7000 killed and 15,000 wounded. More than 100,000 Italians have been taken. Although the campaign has been a political success in as much as Mussolini has been brought down, the escape of so many Germans makes the campaign in Italy a daunting prospect. Critics have suggested that the

Allies could have made more imaginative use of their sea power, not only around the island but in attacks on the Italian mainland. It has been suggested also that the Allies would have done better to follow up their success on Sicily with an immediate move to the Italian mainland. Although this is a plausible idea, it does not take account of the wider strategic debate between the British and Americans.

17–18 AUGUST 1943
Europe, Air Operations The Americans mount a large daylight raid on the ball-bearing manufacturing centers at Schweinfurt and Regensburg on 17 August. Fifty-one aircraft are lost, one-fifth of the attacking force. Such losses are insupportable. During the night the German rocket research and manufacturing establishment at Peenemunde is attacked by nearly 600 RAF bombers. Forty-one are lost but important damage is done. The setback to the rocket program has been estimated variously but was probably about two months. This raid provides a good example of the effectiveness of window. The Mosquitos dropping window cause about 200 German fighters to operate over Berlin.

18 AUGUST 1943
Italy US cruisers and destroyers bombard Palmi and Gioai Taura on the Italian mainland.

19 AUGUST 1943
Diplomatic Affairs The Italians have made approaches to the Allies to negotiate a surrender. General Bedell Smith, Eisenhower's Chief of Staff, and General Strong, his chief of Intelligence, arrive in Lisbon to continue the talks with approaches to the British ambassador there, Sir Samuel Hoare. The leading Italian representative is General Castellano. (*See* 3 and 8 September.)
German Command The Chief of Staff of the Luftwaffe, Jeschonnek, commits suicide after being criticized for the effects of the attacks on Peenemunde and Schweinfurt.

20 AUGUST 1943
Eastern Front The Soviets take Libedin, to the west of Kharkov.
New Guinea Allied forces fight fiercely to take Babdubi Ridge, southwest of Salamaua.

21 AUGUST 1943
Australia, Politics Premier Curtin's Labour Party wins the election.
New Guinea Australian troops occupy Komiatum, six miles southwest of Salamaua.

22 AUGUST 1943
Eastern Front The Germans begin to pull out of Kharkov after a stubborn defense. Manstein, commanding Army Group South, refuses to hold out any longer because he believes that it would sacrifice Army Detachment Kempff in a rerun of the very costly Stalingrad offensive.

22–28 AUGUST 1943
Central Pacific US forces occupy various islands in the Ellice group, including Nukufetau and Namumea, without opposition. Work is begun on airfields.

23 AUGUST 1943
Eastern Front There are special Soviet celebrations to mark the capture of Kharkov.
Farther south the Soviets are pushing forward beyond Voroshilovgrad.

23–24 AUGUST 1943
New Guinea Four American destroyers bombard Finschafen in support of air operations against Wewak.

24 AUGUST 1943
Germany, Politics Himmler is appointed Minister of the Interior. Neurath resigns his post as Protector of Bohemia and Moravia. Frisch replaces him.

24–25 AUGUST 1943
Denmark, Resistance There are several bomb incidents in Copenhagen and many strikes in the shipyards.

25 AUGUST 1943
Battle of the Atlantic German Hs 293 glider bombs are used unsuccessfully for the first time against an escort vessel, hunting U-Boats in the Bay of Biscay. The attack is repeated on 28 August with better results.
Solomons The battle for New Georgia is over. The last Japanese resistance at Bairoko is wiped out. However, many of the Japanese have succeeded in getting away to Arundel or Kolombangara.
Eastern Front The Soviets capture Zenkov and Akhtyrka to the west and northwest of Kharkov respectively.

26 AUGUST 1943
Diplomatic Affairs The United States, Britain and Canada give limited recognition to the French Committee of National Liberation. On 27 August the Soviet Union and China follow suit.

27 AUGUST 1943
Solomons US forces land on Arundel. Troops of 43rd Division occupy the Nauro Peninsula in the southeast of the island without a fight.
Eastern Front In the continuing Soviet offensives, Kotleva is captured by Vatutin's troops and Sevsk by Rokossovsky's Central Front.

28 AUGUST 1943
Denmark, Resistance The Danish government refuse to accept a German ultimatum and resign. The German commander, General von Hanneken, takes over. On 29 August he proclaims martial law and there is some fighting in various parts of the country. The Germans manage to capture one or two of the Danish Navy's few small ships but most are scuttled and a few are sailed to Sweden. The Danish government has been very successful until now in mitigating the effects of the German occupation while rigorously avoiding collaboration.

29 AUGUST 1943
Eastern Front The Soviets take Lyubotin, just west of Kharkov.

30 AUGUST 1943
Eastern Front The Soviets announce two more important captures. Sokolovsky has taken Yelna, on the approach to Smolensk, and in the south Taganrog has also fallen.

31 AUGUST 1943
Eastern Front Advancing south of Sevsk the Soviets capture Glukhov and Rylsk.

31 AUGUST–1 SEPTEMBER 1943
Central Pacific US carriers attack Marcus Island. The carriers *Independence*, *Essex* and *Yorktown* are involved. Losses on both sides are slight. The carriers are from the newly formed Fast Carrier Task Force. At last the new American ships are beginning to come into action in large numbers.

SEPTEMBER 1943
Battle of the Atlantic Doenitz sends his forces back to the North Atlantic convoy routes. New groups are sent out equipped with new radar search receivers, better AA armament and acoustic homing torpedoes. They have orders to try to sink convoy escorts rather than merchant ships. In the new operations six merchantmen and three escorts are sunk but so are three U-Boats. The U-Boat commanders give highly optimistic reports of the effectiveness of the new torpedoes because of their tendency to explode

at the end of their run whether they have hit anything or not. The Allies also have an acoustic torpedo in service and soon develop a device known as 'foxer' which causes the German type to head into a ship's wake. Nine U-Boats are sunk during the month in all operations and the Allied shipping losses are 29 ships of 156,400 tons.
Pacific US submarines sink 160,000 tons of Japanese shipping. This is by no means an unusual monthly total. The drain on Japanese reserves is becoming ever more noticeable.
Europe, Air Operations Bomber Command drops 14,000 tons of bombs on various targets including Berlin, Mannheim and Hanover. American heavy bombers drop 5400 tons and their objectives include Paris, Stuttgart and Nantes. US medium bombers drop 2800 tons on airfields and marshalling yards in Occupied Europe. The deceptive effect of window is now being augmented by electronic countermeasures against the German radar.
The Mediterranean forces make more than 15,000 sorties over Italy, concentrating on airfields and communications targets. During the first few days of the Salerno operation more than 1000 sorties per day are flown.

1 SEPTEMBER 1943
Central Pacific US forces land on Baker Island and within a week have prepared an airstrip to support their coming campaign in the Gilbert Islands.
Solomons The US force on Vella Lavella is making good progress and reaches Orete Cove.
Eastern Front Th Soviets capture Dorogobuzh, midway between Smolensk and Vyazma. They also make progress in the south around Taganrog.

2 SEPTEMBER 1943
Eastern Front The Soviets announce a number of important gains in the Donets sector. Lisichansk, Kommunarsk and other important centers are taken. There are also significant advances on the Bryansk Front with Glushkovo and Sumy being captured.
Italy The British battleships *Valiant* and *Warspite* shell the Italian mainland defenses around Reggio.

3 SEPTEMBER 1943
World Affairs General Castellano signs the Italian surrender at Cassibili in Sicily. No announcement is made until arrangements are made to forestall a German takeover can be worked out.
Italy At dawn units of XIII Corps from

CHRONOLOGY

Montgomery's Eighth Army land on the Italian mainland to the north of Reggio after a heavy bombardment. There is almost no resistance. By the end of the day Reggio, Catona and San Giovanni are taken by the main forces and Mélito and Bagnara by commandos.

Eastern Front The Soviets take Putivl to the northeast of Konotop. They have now cut the Bryansk–Konotop railroad. In the south, in the Donets basin, Ilovask is taken.

4 SEPTEMBER 1943

New Guinea The Allies land on Huon Gulf, east of Lae. The troops are 20th and 26th Brigades from 9th Australian Division. There is little Japanese resistance. The naval forces include 10 US destroyers, led by Admiral Barbey.

Solomons The US forces on Arundel which have so far been quietly consolidating their beachhead now begin to move out.

5 SEPTEMBER 1943

Eastern Front The main Soviet drives in the Bryansk and Donets sectors make considerable gains. Artemovsk in the south and Khutov and Mikhailovsky farther north are all in Soviet hands.

New Guinea The US 503rd Parachute Regiment lands in the Markham Valley at Nadzab, in the rear of Lae. They are joined by Australian units from Tsili Tsili. The complete Australian 7th Division is to be flown in.

6 SEPTEMBER 1943

Italy The Eighth Army continues to advance slowly up the toe of Calabria, capturing Palmi and Delianuova. There is little German resistance but demolitions cause much delay.

Eastern Front It is another successful day for the Red Army in the south and on the Central Front. Makeyevka, just west of Stalino, Kromatorsk and Slavyansk are taken as is the important railroad town of Konotop.

Solomons The Japanese on Arundel begin to fight back strongly.

New Guinea Two brigades of the Australian 9th Division advancing west toward Lae meet strong Japanese resistance on the river crossings. The third brigade of the division, 24th Brigade, is landed.

6–9 SEPTEMBER 1943

Arctic The *Tirpitz* and *Scharnhorst* make a sortie to bombard Spitzbergen, successfully destroying the few small installations there. The base is reestablished on 15 October

7 SEPTEMBER 1943

Italy The Eighth Army take Bova Marina.

Eastern Front The Soviets take Baturin, east of Konotop, and Zvenkov in the Kharkov sector. The Germans begin to evacuate Stalino.

8 SEPTEMBER 1943

Italy The Eighth Army takes Locri and land at Pizzo.

World Affairs The Italian surrender is announced, first by Eisenhower and then by Badoglio. The main body of the Italian Fleet sails from La Spezia and Genoa with three battleships, six cruisers and nine destroyers. They are to be surrendered to the Allies.

Eastern Front The Soviets move in to occupy Stalino and also take Yasinovataya nearby and Krasnoarmeisk.

Solomons Both the Americans and Japanese reinforce their troops on Arundel as the fighting there continues.

New Guinea The Australians advancing on Lae from the east win an engagement at Saingaua but are held for the moment on the line of the River Busu. The Japanese begin to withdraw from Salamaua as the Australians push forward in that sector also. Lae is shelled by four US destroyers.

9 SEPTEMBER 1943

Italy The Allies land at Salerno and Taranto. The British 1st Airborne Division lands by sea at Taranto and seizes the port without opposition but the main landings at Salerno are more difficult. The landing forces are from General Clark's Fifth Army. On the left flank groups of US Rangers and British Commandos land respectively at Maiori and Vietri, with orders to advance north and capture passes through the hills toward Naples. Both landings are successful. The British X Corps under General Mc-Creery, made up of 46th and 56th Divisions, lands on the beaches immediately to the south of Salerno. There are some mistakes made and German resistance is strongest here but the troops manage to get ashore fairly well. The Southern Assault Force is taken from General Dawley's VI US Corps with the 36th Division forming the first wave and landing north and south of Paestum. American losses on the approach are fairly heavy because they adhere more strictly than the British to Clark's order that there is to be no supporting bombardment. Once they land, however, the resistance is less intense.

The landings at Taranto are covered by Admiral Power with the battleships *Howe* and

King George V and an Allied cruiser squadron led by Commodore Agnew. The Salerno landings are much more complex. Admiral Cunningham commands the whole operation and the main covering force is led by Admiral Willis with four battleships and two carriers. Admiral Vian leads a support group of five small carriers and Admiral Hewitt is in direct command of the landings.

In the south Eighth Army continues to advance fairly slowly because of demolitions and poor roads.

Italian Surrender The battleship *Roma* is sunk by a glider bomb launched from a German aircraft while en route to Malta with the main body of the Italian Fleet. Several other ships are damaged by similar attacks. Admiral Zara sails from Taranto with the battleships *Andrea Doria* and *Caio Duilio* as well as other vessels. There is some fighting in the Rome area between Italian and German troops but the Italian plans have not been well prepared and the government has to leave the city, allowing the Germans to take over.

Eastern Front Advancing westward beyond Konotop, the Soviets take Bakhmach after a brisk fight. The German Seventeenth Army begins to pull out of its forward position in the Kuban.

New Guinea The Australians manage to force some small units across the Busu River.

10 SEPTEMBER 1943

Malta The Italian fleet, including five battleships, arrives to surrender. Many smaller craft reach other Allied ports and some are scuttled in their home ports.

Italy The American sector of the Salerno landings is fairly quiet today, with the front being pushed further inland. In the British sector Montecorvino airfield and Battipaglia are occupied in the morning but the Germans concentrate most of their local reserves here, including a number of tanks from 16th Panzer Division and retake the positions by nightfall.

The German forces south of the beachhead, including those engaging Montgomery, withdraw north to reinforce the German cordon. They rely on small parties, demolitions and Montgomery's natural caution to hold up Eighth Army's advance.

Aegean Castelrosso in the Dodecanese is occupied by the British. Two British officers are dropped on Rhodes to contact the Italian commander there, General Campione. However, on 11 September he surrenders to the German forces on the island.

Eastern Front The Soviets mount a seaborne attack in the Sea of Azov and capture Mariupol. Inland on the Donets sector they take Barvenkovo, Volnovakha and Chaplino. They also land troops in Novorossiysk and a major engagement begins there.

New Guinea The Australian 7th Division is now in position at Nadzab and begins to advance on Lae. Forward elements have reached Heath's Plantation.

Solomons The Americans are having to fight unexpectedly hard for Arundel Island and therefore send more reinforcements to their troops there.

10–30 SEPTEMBER 1943

Corsica and Sardinia On 10 September the

Above: A DUKW unloads from an LST at Salerno, 9 September 1943. A 40mm AA gun is in the foreground. The fighting at Salerno became very fierce.

Germans begin to evacuate their garrison from Sardinia, moving first to Corsica and then the Italian mainland. Several of the transport ships are sunk on 21 September by Allied air and submarine attacks. Various fairly small French contingents land on Corsica from 14 September onward. They harass the retreating Germans and inflict some damage.

11 SEPTEMBER 1943

Italy The pattern of the previous day is repeated at Salerno. Early on both the British and American Corps advance with some success but both are later pushed back. The German reinforcements are beginning to come up and in the bridgehead morale is poor because of the lack of progress.

There are major German air attacks on the landings throughout the day despite the efforts of the Allied air forces. The cruiser *Savannah* is badly damaged by a glider bomb.

Troops from British 1st Airborne Division take Brindisi without opposition. These units and those at Taranto have been sent simply to seize the ports and have virtually no transport to enable them to push north. The only opposition in that direction is the understrength German 1st Parachute Division, which is about a quarter of the British strength. The main forces of Eighth Army move into Catanzaro and advance toward Crotone.

Solomons The American 27th Infantry Regiment lands on Arundel.

New Guinea As the Japanese garrison of Salamaua pulls back the Australians take the airfield and enter the town.

12 SEPTEMBER 1943

Italy Eighth Army takes Crotone and continues its advance. At Salerno the first major German counterattacks begin late in the day. The British are driven out of Battipaglia once more and in Molina Pass the unit which has replaced the Commandos is under heavy pressure from part of the Hermann Goering Panzer Division.

Mussolini is rescued from Gran Sasso in the Abruzzi Mountains by a German parachute detachment led by Otto Skorzeny. He is taken to Germany. The Germans have been trying to organize such an operation since Mussolini was arrested but he has never been kept for long in one place. The operation even now is technically very difficult and is executed with great daring.

Eastern Front The Soviet attacks continue in all sectors but with renewed vigor near Bryansk. On the Donets front Stary Kermenchik is taken.

The Germans begin to evacuate Seventeenth Army from the Kuban. Altogether 255,000 troops, 27,000 civilians and army supplies are withdrawn by 9 October.

New Guinea Salamaua is taken by troops from the Australian 5th Division. Farther north the Japanese at Lae are beginning to be hemmed in.

13 SEPTEMBER 1943

Italy There are now signs that a wedge can be driven between the British and American beachheads at Salerno and so the Germans now attack the US sector as well with units from 16th Panzer and 29th Panzergrenadier Divisions. The US forces are driven out of Persano and the line is penetrated in several places. In one area the Germans reach within a mile of the beaches. Naval gunfire is important in preventing the attacks from achieving a decisive success. The cruiser *Uganda* is damaged by glider bombs. Unloading from the ships in the southern sector is stopped and hurried plans are made for evacuation. Alexander and Eisenhower are extremely annoyed at this and make arrangements for more rapid reinforcement. Therefore, part of General Ridgway's 82nd Airborne Division is dropped on the beaches in the evening. The remainder drop on 14 September. Farther south Montgomery's forces continue to push forward. Cosenza is taken.

China, Politics Chiang Kai-shek becomes president of China.

Solomons The Americans land a small force on Sagekarasa.

13–22 SEPTEMBER 1943

Greece The Italian Acqui Division resists the Germans in Cephalonia and surrenders only when 1500 have been killed and the Germans then kill 5000 more and deport the rest to labor camps.

14 SEPTEMBER 1943

Italy The Germans maintain pressure on the Salerno beachhead but Allied air support and, even more importantly, naval gunfire prevent any significant success. Eighth Army is still driving forward in the south, having reached Bari in the east and beyond Belvedere in the west.

Solomons On Vella Lavella the US and New Zealand attacks make good progress but it is necessary to reinforce the battalion on Sagekarasa because of Japanese attacks.

Eastern Front The Germans announce the evacuation of Bryansk but fighting there continues. In the south there is also heavy fighting for the Kuban town of Novorossiysk.

15 SEPTEMBER 1943

Italy There is something of a lull at Salerno as the Germans regroup. They now have available the equivalent of about four divisions, including perhaps 100 tanks. The Allies have seven divisions and twice as much armor and can now make practical plans to expand the beachhead. The battleships *Valiant* and *Warspite* join the bombarding forces. Alexander visits the beachhead on the morning of the 15th and firmly squashes any remaining ideas of withdrawal. He decides, too, to replace General Dawley in charge of VI Corps.

Eighth Army's advance continues, gradually quickening in pace. A group of war correspondents actually drives on ahead by minor roads and tracks and makes contact with Fifth Army.

The island of Procida in Naples Bay is taken by the Allies.

Italy, Politics Mussolini issues a proclamation resuming his authority.

New Guinea The Australians have now crossed the Busu in force and built bridges. The front line is within two miles of Lae.

Aegean Cos in the Dodecanese is occupied by British paratroops and a squadron of Spitfires flown in.

Eastern Front Rokossovsky's forces take Nezhin, on the railroad from Konotop to Kiev. To the north of Bryansk the Germans are pushed out of Dyatkovo.

16 SEPTEMBER 1943

Italy Vietinghoff orders another attack on the British between Salerno and Battipaglia but it is driven off. By midday Kesselring has authorized a withdrawal to the Volturno line. In the afternoon the battleship *Warspite*, which has been providing gunnery support, is hit by two glider bombs and seriously damaged. Forward units of Fifth and Eighth Armies join up but the bulk of Eighth Army is well behind and busy transferring to the east side of the peninsula. The battle for Salerno is over but it has been a very close thing.

Aegean British forces occupy Leros and Samos.

Eastern Front The Soviets take Novgorod Seversky and Romny, north and south of Konotop respectively, on the flanks of their advance toward Kiev. Lozovaya, a railroad junction northeast of Pavlograd, is taken and Novorossiysk, in the Kuban, falls to the Soviets after a terrible struggle.

New Guinea Lae is taken by the converging attacks of Australian 9th and 7th Divisions. Many of the Japanese garrison are able to slip away into the jungle, and head for the north coast of the Huon Peninsula. In a major air attack on Wewak the Japanese lose many planes.

17 SEPTEMBER 1943

Eastern Front The Soviets complete the capture of Bryansk. They also take Bezhitsa, a little to the north, and Trubchevsk, to the south, as they advance across the River Desna on a broad front. In the south on the Sea of Azov, Berdyansk is taken.

Italy Fifth Army is beginning to push out the boundaries of its beachhead once more. Altavilla and Battipaglia are attacked again by the Germans in order to cover their withdrawal which is now beginning.

Yugoslavia, Resistance A senior British liaison mission arrives and is sent to visit Tito. It is led by Brigadier Fitzroy Maclean who is Churchill's personal representative. It is to follow up the reports of the representatives sent in May and June and to confirm that Tito is doing more against the Germans than Mihajlović.

17–19 SEPTEMBER 1943

Central Pacific Tarawa is attacked on the 17th and 19th by land-based Liberator bombers. On the 18th aircraft from the carriers *Lexington*, *Princeton* and *Belleau Wood* (Admiral Pownall) also carry out attacks.

18 SEPTEMBER 1943

Aegean British forces occupy Simi, Stampalia and Icaria. The Germans attack Antimachia airfield on Cos.

Eastern Front In the drive toward Kiev, Priluki, Lubny and Romodan are taken. Farther south there are gains all along the front, including Pavlograd, Krasnograd, Pologi and Nogaysk.

Solomons The fighting continues on Arundel. General Barrowclough, a New Zealander, takes command on Vella Lavella.

19 SEPTEMBER 1943

Eastern Front In the Smolensk sector the Soviets take Yartsevo and Dukovshina to the northeast of the city.

Italy Auletta is captured by 5th British Division, Eighth Army.

20 SEPTEMBER 1943

New Guinea The Australians advancing up the Markham Valley take Kaiapit after a hard struggle.

United States, Home Front In the continuing debate about the drafting of fathers of families, General Marshal and Admiral King tell a

Senate Committee that failure to do so will probably prolong the war.

Eastern Front Yeremenko's troops take Velizh, northwest of Smolensk, and Kholm, farther north.

Italy Canadian troops from Eighth Army enter Potenza after being held up by a tiny German force. General Lucas takes over command of VI Corps from Dawley.

20–21 SEPTEMBER 1943

Solomons The Americans on Sagekarasa find their enemy have been evacuated on the 20th, and on Arundel a similar discovery is made on the 21st.

21 SEPTEMBER 1943

Eastern Front The Soviets take Demidov, north of Smolensk. Troops from Central Front take Chernigov and Sinelnikovo, a little to the east of Dnepropetrovsk, is also captured.

Italy Fifth Army wheels to the left as Eighth Army moves to the east side of the country. The Germans are falling back everywhere except in the vital passes leading to Naples.

22 SEPTEMBER 1943

Arctic Six British midget submarines are sent to attack *Tirpitz* in Altenfiord. Only two manage to place their charges but *Tirpitz* is put out of action until March 1944.

Eastern Front The Soviets take Anapa in the Kuban and Novomoskovosk, just north of Dnepropetrovsk. There is fierce fighting at Poltava as the Germans begin to pull out.

Italy Eighth Army is reinforced by 78th Division and 8th Indian Division who land at Bari and Brindisi but they cannot immediately advance up the coast in any great strength. Fifth Army is preparing to advance also. The British X Corps has the task of clearing the way to Naples and the US VI Corps moving in the first instance toward Benevento.

New Guinea The Australian 20th Brigade are landed at Katika, just north of Finschafen. The landing is supported by a naval bombardment. Admiral Barbey leads the naval force and a strong air group also provides cover.

23 SEPTEMBER 1943

Corsica Free French forces occupy Bonifaccio. They now control more than half of the island.

Italy The British X Corps begins formal attacks to clear the passes toward Naples. Although more than three divisions are employed against little more than a regiment, the terrain and tenacious German defense prevent very much

progress. The attacks continue.

Italy, Politics Mussolini proclaims the foundation of the Italian Social Republic. Parts of northern Italy are given up to wholly German control by this administration.

Eastern Front The Soviets take Poltava and to the north, between Bryansk and Gomel, they enter Unecha east of Klintsy.

New Guinea The Australian 20th Brigade advances south toward Finschafen and reaches a Japanese defense position on the River Bumi.

24 SEPTEMBER 1943

New Guinea The Australians break the Japanese defenses on the River Bumi. Finschafen airfield is captured. Offshore Japanese aircraft attempt to attack supply convoys but achieve little.

Eastern Front The Soviets capture Borispol just east of Kiev and farther north the Germans begin to evacuate Smolensk and Roslavl. Smolensk has been one of the strongest positions in the Soviet Union.

25 SEPTEMBER 1943

Britain, Politics There is a Cabinet reshuffle because of the death on 23 September of Sir Kingsley Wood, then Chancellor of the Exchequer. Atlee becomes Lord President of the Council, Sir John Anderson Chancellor, Lord Cranbourne Dominions Secretary and Lord Beaverbrook Lord Privy Seal.

Allied Diplomacy A Lend-Lease agreement is signed by United States and Free French representatives at Algiers.

Solomons The Japanese begin to evacuate Kolombangara. Their garrison there has been made useless by the American capture of the other islands in the New Georgia group.

Eastern Front The Soviets take Smolensk and Roslavl – arguably their most important success since the end of the Kursk battle. From here to the south the Germans are retreating behind the Dniepr, where they have been ordered to make a stand by Hitler. This retreat has been entirely forced and so there has been less benefit than if it had been done earlier as Manstein recommended.

26 SEPTEMBER 1943

Corsica The Free French occupy Ghisonaccia airfield.

Italy The attack of the British X Corps today meets no resistance because the Germans have withdrawn, having won enough time for their forces farther inland to pull back. They have left behind many demolitions and booby traps which prove a real hindrance. To the east, patrols from XIII Corps (Eighth Army) enter Canosa on the Ofanto River.

New Guinea The Japanese mount a series of counterattacks on the Australians around Finschafen but they are unsuccessful.

27 SEPTEMBER 1943

Corfu The Germans take full control of the island, having practically wiped out the Italian garrison.

Eastern Front The Red Army moves into the suburbs of Dnepropetrovsk and in the Kuban the German enclave is further reduced with the capture of Temryuk the last port they have held.

Italy Advance detachments of Eighth Army enter Foggia and capture the airfields without a fight. Melfi is taken by Canadian units. The main body of Eighth Army is still not ready to move.

27–28 SEPTEMBER 1943

New Guinea On both days there are heavy Allied air attacks on the Japanese airfields around Wewak.

27–30 SEPTEMBER 1943

Italy, Resistance The people of Naples rise against the Germans and fight them for three days, taking heavy losses. The battle only ends as the Allied armies approach.

28 SEPTEMBER 1943

Italy Units of British X Corps emerge into the plain of Naples at Nocera and push on. Inland US VI Corps is advancing near Avellino and has taken Teora despite having to advance over difficult roads.

29 SEPTEMBER 1943

Italy The US 3rd Division begins to attack Avellino. In the X Corps sector the advance reaches beyond Pompeii.

World Affairs General Eisenhower and Marshal Badoglio sign the full armistice agreement aboard HMS *Nelson* at Malta.

Eastern Front The Soviet forces take Kremenchug after the usual fierce battle. Farther north, Rudnya on the Smolensk–Vitebsk railroad, is taken.

30 SEPTEMBER 1943

Italy Advance units of X Corps reach the outskirts of Naples. Inland the Americans take Avellino.

Eastern Front The Soviets take Krichev on the River Sozh.

OCTOBER 1943

Europe, Air Operations Bomber Command drops 13,000 tons of bombs in nine large operations. Targets include Munich, Kassel and Frankfurt. Heavy bombers of Eighth Air Force drop 4700 tons on targets including Emden, Bremen and Anklam. The USAAF raid on Schweinfurt is very significant (*see* 14 October). USAAF medium bombers drop 850 tons on various French airfields. RAF medium and light forces are also active against railroads and airfields. The last Wellington bombers are taken out of front-line service with RAF Bomber Command and are replaced by four-engined heavy bombers.

Pacific, Air Operations There are many Allied attacks in all areas. Rabaul is perhaps the target most heavily hit, being raided five times. In all operations Allied pilots claim to have shot down 780 Japanese aircraft. This is an exaggeration but gives some idea of the extent of the attacks.

China, Air Operations During the month Fourteenth Air Force attacks Haiphong, Hainan, Kwanchow and Quangyen.

Battle of the Atlantic From early in the month the Allies are able to use bases in the Azores and thus cover areas of the Atlantic which their land-based aircraft have been unable to patrol previously. The efforts of the newly equipped U-Boats continue, especially against the convoys ONS-18 and ON-202 but have little success. The U-Boat fleet is still large at 175 operational boats and 237 in training but a further 26 are lost during the month. In September and October nine merchant ships have been lost in north Atlantic convoys and 25 U-Boats have been sunk while attempting to attack.

1 OCTOBER 1943

Italy Naples is taken by Fifth Army. Eighth Army begins to advance its main forces once again. For the moment only two divisions, 78th and 1st Canadian of XIII Corps, are sent forward, V corps is kept back in reserve for the moment.

Owing to the success achieved by the delaying actions so far, Hitler orders Kesselring to hold a line south of Rome during the coming months rather than retire farther north.

1–6 OCTOBER 1943

Eastern Front The Soviets cross the Dniepr in several places north and, more particularly, south of Kremenchug. Konev is in command here and farther north beyond Kiev Vatutin organizes similar work. Bridges are quickly improvised.

CHRONOLOGY

2 OCTOBER 1943

New Guinea Finschafen is taken by troops from the Australian 20th Brigade. The 23rd Brigade, which has advanced overland from Lae, also reaches the town.

2–3 OCTOBER 1943

Italy The US VI Corps takes Benevento on the 2nd at the same time as the advance units of 78th Division on the east coast cross the Biferno. During the night commandos land near Termoli and take the town. The Germans send 16th Panzer Division from positions on the Volturno to meet this attack. The commandos succeed in joining up with 78th Division as the battle continues.

3 OCTOBER 1943

Aegean The Germans land on Cos. They complete the capture on 4 October and take 1400 British and 3150 Italians prisoner.

4 OCTOBER 1943

Corsica The liberation of the island is completed when the Free French forces enter Bastia.

New Guinea Australian troops manage to capture Kumpu as they extend their advance into the Ramu valley from the Markham Valley.

Arctic German shipping off the Norwegian coast near Bodo is attacked by aircraft from the US carrier *Ranger* operating with the British Home Fleet. Four freighters are sunk and seven badly damaged at little cost. The battleships *Duke of York* and *Anson* are in support.

British Command Admiral Pound resigns his post as First Sea Lord because of ill health. He dies on 21 October. His position is taken by Admiral Andrew Cunningham after Admiral Fraser has refused the job.

Solomons The Japanese complete the evacuation of Kolombangara. Despite the attention of American destroyers, 9400 men of General Sasaki's garrison have been got away by Admiral Ijuin's ships. A number of small boats have been lost, along with about 1000 men.

5 OCTOBER 1943

Italy Fifth Army takes Aversa and Maddaloni. Forward units of X Corps reach the Volturno. In the battle around Termoli, 16th Panzer comes into action and for a time pushes the British back.

5–6 OCTOBER 1943

Central Pacific Wake Island is shelled and bombed on both days by ships and planes from Admiral Montgomery's Task Force 14. There

are six carriers, seven cruisers and 25 destroyers in this force. The carrier aircraft fly 738 sorties.

6 OCTOBER 1943

New Britain Small parties of US troops land secretly around Cape Gloucester to spy out the land.

Italy Fifth Army takes Caserta, drives on to the Volturno and captures Capua. On the east coast the British gain the upper hand in the fighting around Termoli.

6–7 OCTOBER 1943

Solomons The American 25th Division lands unopposed at Vila on Kolombangara on the 6th. The whole island is occupied by the 9th. During the night of 6/7 October two Japanese destroyers are sent to evacuate 600 men from Vella Lavella. Six more destroyers escorting them are engaged by three American ships. In a torpedo action each side loses one destroyer and both the other American vessels are damaged.

7 OCTOBER 1943

Aegean Two British cruisers and two destroyers intercept a German convoy bound for Cos and sink seven transports and one escort.

Eastern Front In a new offensive in the north the Soviets take Nevel. At the western end of the Kuban Peninsula Taman is captured. Along the Dniepr to the south of Kiev there is something of a lull as the Soviets bring up supplies and build bridges.

Italy The Germans withdraw from contact with the 78th Division around Termoli and pull back behind the Trigno. Montgomery does not feel able to follow them closely at this stage.

8 OCTOBER 1943

Italy Eighth Army takes Larino and Guglionesi inland from the coast on either side of the Biferno. Fifth Army has now come up to the Volturno line and plans an attack for 12 October.

9 OCTOBER 1943

Eastern Front Petrov's forces complete the occupation of the Kuban but most of Seventeenth Army have escaped to the Crimea. Seventeenth Army is to be sent to join the right of the German line to the south of Zaporozhye but will in fact be too late to move out of the Crimea when the front around Melitopol is broken in the next few days.

10 OCTOBER 1943

Eastern Front The Soviets take Dobrush, just to the east of Gomel.

Italy Troops from Fifth Army enter Portelandalfo, north of Benevento.

11 OCTOBER 1943

Eastern Front The Soviets capture Novobelitsa on the outskirts of Gomel.

Italy Montgomery regroups his forward troops. Both V and XIII Corps are now in the line but there will be a pause while the reorganization is completed.

12 OCTOBER 1943

New Britain In a surprise attack 349 planes of Fifth Air Force drop 350 tons of bombs on Rabaul. Many of the defending aircraft are shot down and three destroyers and several merchant ships in the harbor are damaged.

12–13 OCTOBER 1943

Italy During the night Fifth Army starts its attacks on the Volturno line. On the left are the three divisions, 46th, 56th and 7th Armored, of McCreery's X Corps. Between the coast and Capua 46th and 7th Armored make some progress but are held by German counterattacks. Around Capua 56th Division can make no ground at all. The American VI Corps (General Lucas) does rather better. All three divisions, 3rd, 34th and 45th, make good advances. The German defense is energetically conducted throughout and in any case the river, swollen by recent rain, and the roadless hills would have been formidable obstructions. The combination of bad weather, inadequate roads and German demolitions means that, until the ground hardens in the spring, the Allied advance must hinge around the three or four major roads.

13 OCTOBER 1943

World Affairs Italy declares war on Germany.

14 OCTOBER 1943

Eastern Front The Soviets capture Zaporozhye. To the south they begin to assault Melitopol and farther south still they cut the railroad leading to the Crimea from Melitopol.

Europe, Air Operations A force of 291 Flying Fortresses from Eighth Air Force is sent to attack the German ball-bearing works at Schweinfurt. They do considerable damage to the target but lose 60 planes with a further 140 damaged. Most of the losses occur during the 400-mile round trip unescorted from Aachen. The Eighth Air Force has lost a further 88 aircraft in the last week. These losses are intolerable and the USAAF abandons long-range, unescorted daylight attacks for the time

being. They are not equipped to attack by night. The theories of the American airmen have been disproved on two counts. Bombers cannot fight their way to the target without prohibitive casualties and even carefully selected targets like Schweinfurt offer no great gains. Production in Germany is quickly switched to other areas, extra supplies are bought from Sweden and in any case an investigation ordered by Speer shows that stocks of ball bearings will last for several months.

Italy The battle on the Volturno goes on. The American V Corps continues to advance, especially on their right. The British 56th Division crosses the river east of its previous position and also pushes forward. In the Eighth Army sector 1st Canadian Division takes Campobasso.

15 OCTOBER 1943

Southeast Asia, Command The British General Pownall is appointed Chief of Staff to Admiral Mountbatten at SEAC. General Wedemeyer, an American, is to be his deputy Chief of Staff.

New Guinea The Japanese mount an air attack on Allied positions in Oro Bay. The attacking aircraft take heavy losses. The attack is repeated on 17 October with the same results.

Italy The Canadians from Eighth Army take Vinchiaturo. The battle on Fifth Army's sector has now moved north of the Volturno but the Germans are still defending expertly. They intend to fall back to two intermediate defense lines, the Barbara Line and the Reinhard Line, before the principal Gustav line defenses behind the Garigliano, Rapido and Sangro.

16 OCTOBER 1943

United States, Command General Brereton takes command of the US Ninth Air Force in the UK.

Italy In the Fifth Army sector the Germans begin to make a fighting withdrawal to the Barbara line according to the schedule that Kesselring has ordered.

16–18 OCTOBER 1943

New Guinea The Japanese counterattack from the few remaining outposts around Finschafen but the Australians hold them off.

17 OCTOBER 1943

German Raiders The last operational German auxiliary cruiser, *Michel*, is sunk by the US submarine *Tarpon* off the Japanese coast. *Michel* has sunk 17 ships during its cruise.

Eastern Front The Soviets break the German

line around Kremenchug and push forward once more. They also cross the Dniepr south of Gomel and take Loyev.
Italy The Americans take Liberi and Alvignano.

18 OCTOBER 1943
Italy The US 3rd and 34th Divisions reach Dragoni and prepare to attack it. Gioia is also taken.
Solomons There is a heavy air attack on the Japanese air base at Buin on Bougainville.
Eastern Front The fighting for Melitopol continues. The Soviets have now penetrated to the center of the town.

19 OCTOBER 1943
Italy The Germans pull out of Dragoni just before the attack from 34th Division goes in.
Eastern Front The Soviets attack Pyatikhatki, to the west of Dnepropetrovsk. Konev's forces are storming out of the Kremenchug bridgehead and making for Krivoy Rog. Manstein is desperately bringing up reserves to meet this attack and give the forces holding the bend of the Dniepr time to pull back. In the Kiev sector the Soviet units are busily consolidating their bridgeheads north of the city. They capture Vishgorod as well.

20 OCTOBER 1943
Pacific The aircraft from the Japanese carriers in Truk are transferred to Rabaul. The ships concerned are *Zuikaku*, *Shokaku*, *Zuiho*, *Junyo*, *Hiyo* and *Ryuho*. Although the aircraft are withdrawn from Rabaul in November they take heavy losses in the meantime, further signalling the decline of the Japanese naval air force as the number of experienced pilots dwindles.
Italy The US 45th Division takes Piedimonte d'Alife while on its left 3rd and 34th Divisions advance on either side of the Volturno.
New Guinea The 24th Brigade arrives at Finschafen to reinforce the Australian troops already there and to help clear the continuing Japanese resistance in the area.

21 OCTOBER 1943
Mediterranean, Command Admiral Sir John Cunningham succeeds Admiral Sir Andrew Cunningham in command of the RN forces in the Mediterranean.

22 OCTOBER 1943
British Command General Laycock becomes the British Chief of Combined Operations.
Italy Eighth Army comes into action once

more. Near the coast 78th Division seizes a small bridgehead over the Trigno during the night. Fifth Army is still fighting hard to make any sort of advance.

23 OCTOBER 1943
Eastern Front Melitopol falls to the Soviets after 10 days of fighting. The thrust from Kremenchug toward Krivoy Roy is still making good progress but slows as the opposition stiffens. The Soviets are now within 20 miles of the town and have cut the railroad to Dnepropetrovsk.
English Channel A German squadron protecting a blockade runner sinks the British cruiser *Charbydis* and the destroyer *Limbourne*.
Italy In the Fifth Army sector Sparanise is taken by the British 56th Division.

23–24 OCTOBER 1943
New Britain Rabaul is raided on both days. One destroyer is sunk in the harbor along with five merchant ships.

24 OCTOBER 1943
Italy The US 34th Division takes Sant'Angelo.

25 OCTOBER 1943
Eastern Front Malinovsky launches a powerful attack across the Dniepr at Dnepropetrovsk and Dneprodzerzhinsk. Both towns are taken comparatively easily because the German forces there have been weakened to meet Konev's attacks and Kleist's forces have not yet been brought into line from the Crimea.

26 OCTOBER 1943
New Guinea The Japanese outposts around Finschafen begin to withdraw toward Sattelberg.

27 OCTOBER 1943
Italy Eighth Army captures Montefalcone. Nearer the coast a night attack expands 78th Division's bridgehead across the Trigno but the main German defenses still hold out.
Eastern Front The Germans stage limited counterattacks south of Nikopol on the Nogaysk Steppe in an attempt to prevent the Soviets cutting off the Crimea.
Solomons New Zealand troops land on the Treasury Islands. The soldiers are from General Row's 8th Brigade and they meet no opposition on Stirling Island and only a few Japanese on Mono.

28 OCTOBER–3 NOVEMBER 1943
Solomons In Operation Blissful the 2nd Marine

Parachute Battalion is landed by sea at Voza on Choiseul. This is intended to be a diversion from the attack on Bougainville. After a series of sharp actions they are withdrawn from the operation.

29 OCTOBER 1943

Eastern Front The German forces between Orsha and Vitebsk come under renewed pressure from the Soviet armies. The brunt of the attacks is borne by General Heinrici's Fourth Army but he expertly organizes the defense to beat them off. His performance in these and later battles earns him the reputation as probably the best defensive tactician in the German army.

Italy Cantalupo is taken by troops from XIII Corps of Eighth Army.

30 OCTOBER 1943

Eastern Front In their advance across the Nogaysk Steppe, the Soviet forces reach Genichesk cutting one exit from the Crimea.

Italy On the west coast Fifth Army takes Mondragone, having penetrated the Barbara line there. Inland the other units of the army continue their advance over the difficult hilly terrain against tenacious defense.

31 OCTOBER 1943

Italy In the British X Corps sector Teano is taken in the course of attacks toward Monte Santa Croce. To the left attacks also go in against Monte Massico.

Eastern Front The Soviets capture Chaplinka and have now, therefore, cut all the railroad lines leading out of the Crimea, cutting off German supplies.

NOVEMBER 1943

Europe, Air Operations RAF Bomber Command drops 14,500 tons of bombs in various raids. Berlin is raided on three nights and is hit by more than 4000 tons of bombs. The 'Battle of Berlin' begins on the 18th. Dusseldorf and Frankfurt are other targets. American heavy bombers drop 6300 tons of bombs on a range of objectives in Norway and Germany. Ryukan and Knaben in Norway, and Wilhelmshaven and Munster are all attacked. The raid on Bremen on 26 November is the heaviest yet by the Americans. US medium bombers drop 1300 tons over France and the Low Countries. RAF aircraft also attack communications targets in these areas.

The Mediterranean forces attack a range of communications targets in Italy, especially later in the month to coincide with Eighth Army's attacks across the River Sangro. Strategic targets include Turin, Sofia and Toulon. Aircraft from the Middle East are active against shipping in the Aegean.

Pacific Japanese shipping losses reach a new high this month with the sinking of 265,000 tons, mostly by US submarines. Japan began the war with a merchant fleet of almost 6,000,000 tons capacity (not counting very small vessels). This has now been reduced, despite new construction, to less than 5,000,000 tons.

NOVEMBER–DECEMBER 1943

Battle of the Atlantic During these months 78 North Atlantic convoys pass across the ocean without loss. Seventeen U-Boats are sunk. During the six months up to November, 12 of the German U-Tanker fleet of 17 boats are sunk. Shipping losses in the two months total 60 ships of 313,000 tons.

1 NOVEMBER 1943

Solomons The US landings on Bougainville begin. The island is defended by General Hyakutake's Seventeenth Army with about 40,000 men and 20,000 naval personnel. Most are concentrated in the south of the island where the Japanese airfields are and where the sea conditions favor a landing. The Americans chose instead to land in Empress Augusta Bay at Cape Tarokina. The landing force is General Turnage's 3rd Marine Division, transported by Admiral Wilkinson's Task Force 31. The local Japanese garrison is only 200 men and is quickly overcome. Offshore a marine battalion lands on Puruata Island and takes it after a fight. By the end of the day 14,000 men are ashore. Admiral Merrill's Task Force 39, with four cruisers and eight destroyers, is in support and also shells Buka Island. Admiral Sherman has the carriers *Saratoga* and *Princeton* of Task Force 38 to the west and they add air attacks against Buka and the airfields at Buna.

After unsuccessful air attacks on the landings the Japanese send Admiral Omori from Rabaul with four cruisers and six destroyers to make attacks.

United States, Home Front President Roosevelt orders Ickes and his Solid Fuels Administration to take over the running of the country's coal mines. There are 530,000 men out on strike. There have been a number of disputes throughout October but from 28 October the strike gains momentum. The problem is resolved, for the moment, on 3 November.

Roosevelt urges Congress to continue food subsidies to encourage production and as a measure against inflation.

Eastern Front The Soviets take Perekop and advance to Armiansk, thus isolating the Crimea. Manstein's forces around Krivoy Rog begin a series of counterattacks which temporarily hold the Soviet advance. Part of the Soviet Fifty-sixth Army is landed in the Crimea near Enikale.

Arctic The first in a new series of Arctic convoys sails from the Kola Inlet to Loch Ewe and arrives without loss on 14 November. Of the next three convoys only one is attacked and the only damage is to an attacking U-Boat. These operations are completed by 9 December.

Italy The British X Corps continues its attacks against the German line between Monte Massico and Monte Santa Croce. Roccamonfina is taken by 56th Division in these attacks. The fighting along the Trigno in Eighth Army's sector continues.

2 NOVEMBER 1943

Solomons Just after midnight Omori's squadron steaming for Bougainville is detected by the radar of the American Task Force 39, led by Admiral Merrill. A confused night action ensues in which the American radar proves crucial. The Japanese lose one cruiser and one destroyer and most of their other ships are damaged. Two cruisers and two destroyers are damaged on the American side but the Japanese are forced to turn away. During the day, air attacks on Merrill's ships fail. On Bougainville itself the Americans extend their beachhead without difficulty, having wiped out the local garrison. Aircraft from Task Force 38 raid Buna and Buka.

New Britain The Japanese base at Rabaul is attacked by about 160 land-based aircraft from Fifth Air Force. Perhaps 20 aircraft on each side are lost. The US sinks three ships in the harbor.

United States Command General Spaatz takes command of all US Air Forces in the Mediterranean.

Italy Eighth Army's operations across the Trigno are stepped up into a full-scale attack. In the main coastal sector the advance of 78th Division is supported by a naval bombardment. On the west coast the Allied forces continue to make ground slowly. The 7th Armored Division from British X Corps reaches the Garigliano.

Eastern Front The Soviets take Kakhovka on the lower Dniepr and hold the German attacks around Krivoy Rog.

3 NOVEMBER 1943

Italy The British forces attacking near San Salvo meet heavy resistance from 16th Panzer Division (soon to be withdrawn to refit for the Soviet Union) but manage to break into the main defensive positions. In the Fifth Army sector Sessa Aurunca falls to X Corps.

4 NOVEMBER 1943

New Britain A fresh Japanese squadron led by Admiral Kurita with 10 cruisers and as many destroyers arrives in Rabaul. They are sighted en route and Task Force 38 is ordered to attack with its aircraft.

Eastern Front Vatutin's forces begin to break out of their bridgeheads over the Dniepr near Kiev. They find the weak spots in the inevitably thin German defense. In the south the Soviets are also attacking near Kherson.

Italy The British X Corps now holds Monte Massico and Monte Santa Croce and sends the 78th Division against Monte Camino. On the American VI Corps' sector Venafro and Roca-virondola are taken as the advance nears the Reinhard line. In the Eighth Army area the Germans are withdrawing to the Sangro. The two Allied armies now have full lateral communications through Isernia.

5 NOVEMBER 1943

New Britain Sherman leads *Saratoga* and *Princeton* to attack Kurita's squadron, newly arrived in Rabaul. Four heavy cruisers and two light cruisers as well as two destroyers from the squadron are damaged by the 107 attacking planes. The Americans only lose 10 planes. A second assault, this time by land based Liberators, adds to the confusion.

Solomons The marines on Bougainville beat off a counterattack by the Japanese 23rd Regiment. Few of the Japanese garrison of the island are being sent to oppose the landings, partly because of the difficult terrain that intervenes between the landing and the main Japanese concentrations but more because the Japanese commander judges that the attack is a feint.

France, Resistance Resistance workers set bombs in the Peugeot factory at Sochaux, destroying equipment used in the manufacture of tank turrets. When the Germans try to bring in new machinery that too is sabotaged. This factory is described by the British Ministry of Economic Warfare as the third most important target in France.

Eastern Front The Soviet threat to encircle Kiev grows as they cut the Kiev–Zhitomir railroad and continue to advance at practically pursuit pace. In the south they completely overrun the area between the lower Dniepr and the Crimea.

Italy Fifth Army begins major attacks against the Reinhard line. The most important efforts are in the center where the British 56th Division assaults Monte Camino and the US 3rd Division attacks near Mignano. The tenacious defense made by Hube's XIV Panzer Corps is aided by the extremely difficult terrain and the vile weather. The attacks make little progress but are continued. In the Eighth Army sector Vasto, Palmoli and Torrebruna are taken.

6 NOVEMBER 1943

Eastern Front The Soviet Union's third city, Kiev, is retaken by Vatutin's forces. Stalin issues a special order of the day and makes a broadcast to celebrate the achievement. Only 6000 prisoners have been taken, however. Once more the Germans have managed to slip away.

Italy Fifth Army's attacks are repeated but can gain nothing against stubborn defense.

7 NOVEMBER 1943

Eastern Front The Soviet attacks west of Kiev reach Fastov, 40 miles away, where there is a thin German defense line.

Solomons The carriers *Saratoga* and *Princeton* are attacked by 100 Japanese aircraft when 240 miles southeast of Rabaul but are not hit. Early in the day a Japanese battalion is landed just north of the American beachhead on Bougainville and immediately begins a fierce action. The Japanese also reinforce Buka Island.

8 NOVEMBER 1943

Italy The battle on the Fifth Army sector continues with no decisive success as both sides organize attacks and counterattacks. Troops from the left of Eighth Army reach the Sangro high up in the hills.

9 NOVEMBER 1943

France, Politics Generals Giraud, Georges and three others resign from the Committee of National Liberation. Giraud remains as Commander in Chief for the moment.

Solomons As the Americans advance inland on Bougainville to extend their bridgehead they meet up with the main body of the Japanese 23rd Regiment on the jungle tracks and a vicious battle develops. The second wave of the landings begins with the arrival of most of the 37th Infantry Division.

Eastern Front The Soviet forces have overcome the German resistance west of Kiev around Fastov, and are now advancing toward Zhitomir.

Italy Castiglione falls to the 8th Indian Division from Eighth Army.

11 NOVEMBER 1943

Mediterranean An Allied convoy east of Oran is attacked by about 50 German aircraft and loses three transports and one tanker.

Solomons On Bougainville the battle between the marines and the 23rd Regiment ends in defeat for the Japanese infantry, which is pushed back.

New Britain Admirals Sherman and Montgomery lead two separate carrier task forces to attack the Japanese base at Rabaul. Five carriers are involved and 185 aircraft attack altogether. The Japanese lose almost 70 of the defending Zero fighters to the American planes and one light cruiser and two destroyers in the harbor are put out of action. The strike aircraft sent against the carriers achieve no hits.

Eastern Front The Soviet forces driving west of Kiev take a crossing of the River Teterev and capture Radomyshl and other towns on the approach to Zhitomir.

Italy Montgomery's forces occupy Casalanguida as they push forward to the next German defense line on the Sangro.

12 NOVEMBER 1943

Eastern Front The Soviets capture Korostyshev, west of Kiev, and move on to enter Zhitomir. Zhitomir is a vitally important rail center on the last lateral rail line available to the Germans east of the Pripet marshes.

Aegean German forces from the 22nd Infantry Division under General Muller land on the Dodecanese island of Leros. They complete the capture of the island by 16 November and 3500 British and 5350 Italian troops surrender. In addition the British lose one destroyer offshore.

New Britain The remnants of the Japanese carrier aircraft transferred to Rabaul on 20 October are withdrawn because of their recent heavy losses. Of the 173 planes committed, 121 have been lost, with many irreplaceable pilots.

Italy The Allied attacks are grinding to a halt before the Reinhard line. The British 56th Division is forced to retire from some of its positions on Monte Camino.

13 NOVEMBER 1943

Gilbert Islands Flying Fortresses bomb Tarawa Atoll in the first attack in preparation for the coming landings. These attacks are repeated daily for the next week.

Solomons The third wave of the US landing force, the remainder of the 37th Infantry Division and the 21st Marines, begins to disembark on Bougainville. Merrill's Task Force 39 again provides cover with the cruiser

Denver taking a torpedo hit. There is a further action on the island on the Numa-Numa trail.

Italy Clark tells Alexander that he believes that Fifth Army's attacks should be halted for the present. Eighth Army continues to move forward to the Sangro and captures Atessa.

Eastern Front The Soviets complete the capture of Zhitomir and begin to extend their advance north toward Korosten.

14 NOVEMBER 1943

Eastern Front Manstein orders Manteuffel's 7th Panzer Division to counterattack south of Zhitomir from around Berdichev.

Italy Perano is captured by troops from 8th Indian Division supported by 2nd New Zealand Division. The New Zealanders have only just come into Eighth Army's order of battle and Montgomery now has five divisions and two armored brigades. His opponents, LXXVI Panzer Corps, have 65th Infantry Division, 1st Parachute Division and part of 26th Panzer Division.

Solomons On Bougainville the Americans continue to push the Japanese back along the jungle tracks, helped now by a few tanks.

15 NOVEMBER 1943

Italy Alexander calls off Fifth Army's attacks. Casualties have been heavy and the stubborn German defense, backed by rugged terrain and the shocking weather, shows no sign of cracking. In the east small units of Eighth Army succeed in crossing the Sangro but are fighting hard and do not yet have a solid hold.

16 NOVEMBER 1943

Eastern Front The Soviets continue to attack and make gains north of Zhitomir, which is threatened by a German attack from the south. Although the Germans only have a very small force in this attack, by widespread penetrations it gives the appearance of greater strength.

Italy The small British forces on the north bank of the Sangro consolidate their gains.

New Guinea The Australians have brought up tanks to help in their attacks on the Japanese strongholds near Sattelberg. These attacks now begin.

17 NOVEMBER 1943

Eastern Front The Soviets continue to advance toward Korosten and capture Novodichi. Farther north they also make gains near Gomel.

18 NOVEMBER 1943

Eastern Front The Soviets take Korosten and

Ovruch, a little farther north in the Kiev sector. West of Gomel they also take Rechitsa and cut the railroad in that direction. The Germans are still applying pressure south of Zhitomir.

Europe, Air Operations RAF Bomber Command begins the 'Battle of Berlin,' the third of Air Marshal Harris' well publicized campaigns. The campaign will include 16 major attacks on the German capital as well as others against different targets. In the attacks against Berlin itself about 9100 sorties are flown and 600 aircraft lost. The battle ends on 24 March.

19 NOVEMBER 1943

Central Pacific US carrier aircraft raid Mili, Tarawa, Makin and Nauru in preparation for the coming landings. Four carrier groups are involved from Admiral Pownall's Task Force 50 which includes 11 carriers, five battleships and six cruisers.

Italy The Germans withdraw the last of their forces north of the Sangro. Although Eighth Army also has troops north of the Sangro they hold only very little ground and a major, formal attack will be necessary to expand their tiny enclaves.

Eastern Front The Germans move in to take Zhitomir as the Soviets realize their danger and retreat.

20 NOVEMBER 1943

Gilbert Islands The American landing operations in the Gilbert Islands begin. There are US landings on Tarawa Atoll. General J C Smith leads 18,600 men from the 2nd Marine Division, escorted by Admiral Hill's Task Force 53 with a bombardment group of three battleships and four cruisers and air support of four escort carriers. The Japanese garrison comprises 4800 men led by Admiral Shibasaki. They have 50 artillery weapons and seven light tanks.

The landings are to be made on Betio Island which is little more than two miles long and is nowhere more than half a mile wide. The highest ground is only nine feet above sea level but the Japanese have added a formidable complex of bunkers and gun emplacements. The preliminary bombardment is massive – the supporting warships fire more than 3000 tons of shells and in addition there are air attacks. There are, however, some difficulties with the timing and coordination of the shelling and air attacks and the bombardment is lifted a little too early. The sandy ground absorbs much of the blast of the explosions and many of the Japanese bunkers remain intact. The reef around the island is also shallower in places than has been expected and many of the landing craft ground, leaving the marines to run through a vicious crossfire to the beach. In many of the Pacific operations a lack of precise topographical information is a problem. With this difficulty and the heavy Japanese fire many of the landing force do not reach the beaches and those who do are mostly pinned down at the water's edge. Of the 5000 who attempt to land, 1500 become casualties. Owing to the state of the tide, another unknown, and confusion in the chain of command, reserves are not sent at first and later cannot be sent. At nightfall the outcome of the battle is still in doubt. During the night the Japanese undertake some infiltrations but because of the bombardment are not able to organize an attack.

There are also US landings on the Makin atoll. The attack force here is drawn from General R C Smith's 27th Infantry Division. Naval support is provided by Admiral Turner's Task Force 52, which includes a bombardment group of four battleships and four cruisers and an air-support group with three escort carriers. The landings on Butaritari are fairly successful despite the energetic defense and the inexperience of the attackers.

The carrier *Independence* from the main carrier Task Force 50 is hit by a submarine torpedo.

Eastern Front In a new attack the Soviets cross the Dniepr near Cherkassy.

Solomons The Americans continue to push inland along the Numa-Numa trail parallel to the Piva River.

Italy Montgomery planned to attack the Sangro line today but heavy rain has swollen the river and made the ground even more difficult, so only a limited effort can be made. Only 36th Brigade is sent across and is quickly involved in a testing action.

Aegean The British evacuate Samos. The Germans move in on the 23rd and disarm 2500 troops on the island. This is the end of the brief campaign in the Dodecanese which has been too quickly improvised by the British with insufficient forces and as a result the British have taken a beating.

21 NOVEMBER 1943

Gilbert Islands The Americans send in new waves of marines to land on Betio Island, Tarawa Atoll. The first group take heavy casualties from Japanese positions established the previous night but at about noon there is a

Above: The beach at Tarawa after the landings. Casualties were very heavy.

significant change in the tide and the marines begin to flow ashore, both over the original beaches in the north and in the west of the island. Other American units land on Bairiki nearby.

The American forces are firmly ashore on Butaritari Island, Makin and push forward against fierce Japanese resistance.
New Guinea The attacks of the Australian 9th Division around Sattelberg are gradually gaining the upper hand.
Eastern Front Having taken Zhitomir the Germans now extend their attacks toward Korosten.

22 NOVEMBER 1943
Gilbert Islands There is now no question of the outcome of the battle on Tarawa although the Japanese are fighting fiercely for every inch of ground. During the night there are fanatical counterattacks by the Japanese at the east end of the island but they achieve nothing.

The American advance on Makin continues and by nightfall almost all of Butaritari has been taken. During the night a Japanese counterattack is wiped out.

There are US landings on Abimama, another atoll in the Gilbert Islands.
Italy The British forces have now won a fairly substantial bridgehead north of the Sangro about five miles wide and nearly 2000 yards deep. It is very difficult to bridge or cross the river in its present state and supplies and other help to the north bank are tenuous indeed.

22–25 NOVEMBER 1943
Allied Planning Roosevelt, Churchill and Chaing Kai-shek meet in Cairo. The discussions center on plans for Burma and China but no major decisions are reached. Equally there is no attempt, as the British want, to prepare a joint approach for the coming Teheran talks with Stalin.

23 NOVEMBER 1943
Gilbert Islands By noon the battle on Tarawa is over. The Americans have lost 1000 killed and 2000 wounded. The Japanese garrison has been annihilated. The only prisoners are 17 wounded soldiers and 129 Korean laborers. In proportion to the forces engaged it has been the most costly operation in the United States' military history. There have been important lessons for the organization of future attacks, particularly of the need for precise bombardment. Equipment can also be improved. In one respect it has been a successful trial for the new system of the fleet train which provides support and repair for the

naval units far from their bases.

The Americans complete the capture of Makin island also. They have about 200 dead and wounded. The Japanese have lost about three times as many, including prisoners. The escort carrier *Liscombe Bay* is sunk offshore by a Japanese submarine with the loss of 600 more lives.
German Planning The prototype of the Me 262 jet airplane is demonstrated before Hitler. He hails it as the ideal light bomber – a decision which is believed to have hindered its development and production for its true role as a fighter. The aircraft first flew in July 1942 and becomes operational in June 1944.

24 NOVEMBER 1943
Eastern Front The German attacks around Korosten now have increased strength and the Soviets are forced back.
Solomons The Japanese mount a small attack on the American positions on Bougainville which the marines easily drive off.

25 NOVEMBER 1943
Eastern Front The Soviets mount a new effort between Mogilev and Gomel. Propaisk is taken.
China, Air Operations Planes from Fourteenth Air Force attack Formosa for the first time, destroying 42 aircraft on the ground at Shinchiku airfield.
New Britain Five Japanese destroyers taking men to Buka in the Solomons are surprised by five US destroyers led by Captain Burke off Cape St George. Three Japanese ships are sunk in a night action. This is the last of the night sea battles which have characterized the Solomons campaign.
New Guinea The Australians at last capture the final Japanese positions at Sattelberg.

26 NOVEMBER 1943
Eastern Front The Soviets take Gomel which has been threatened with encirclement for some time.
Mediterranean A British troop transport is sunk off Bougie by a glider bomb and more than 1000 of the passengers are killed. Eight of the attacking aircraft are shot down.

27 NOVEMBER 1943
Italy The British manage to move a tank brigade across the Sangro to support their troops to the north who are still fighting hard.

28 NOVEMBER 1943
Italy A massive air and artillery bombardment

signals the start of Eighth Army's offensive across the Sangro. A new bridgehead is fairly quickly won and by the end of the day 8th Indian Division have penetrated nearly to Mozzogrogna. The defending German 65th Division is badly shaken by the shelling and is in any case unusually poorly trained and badly equipped. The attack was intended to follow up the initial advance on 20 November but has been delayed by bad weather. This has given the Germans time to assemble reserves behind 65th Division.

Eastern Front The Soviets make important gains northwest of Gomel, near Zhlobin, whereas farther south near Korosten they are in trouble.

28 NOVEMBER–1 DECEMBER 1943

Allied Planning Churchill, Roosevelt and Stalin and their staffs meet for the first time at Teheran. The decision to invade western Europe in May 1944 is confirmed and a now more definite plan for the invasion of southern France (Anvil) is agreed. This has been an American idea up to now, (the British prefer Balkan operations) but Stalin's support gives it increased weight. Churchill accepts it, believing that if there are landing craft in the Mediterranean for Anvil they might be available for other purposes. Perhaps the most important decision to emerge from the conference is Stalin's promise to join the war against Japan when Germany has been defeated.

There were problems of security at the conference and there is reason to believe that the Americans' accommodation was bugged. The Americans were solicitous throughout the proceedings not to appear to be with Britain and against the Soviet Union and in doing so perhaps gave too much ground.

29 NOVEMBER 1943

Italy Eighth Army's battle on the Sangro continues with reasonable progress for the attacks. Mozzogrogna is taken and Fossacesia also falls later in the day.

New Britain Four US destroyers bombard Japanese positions on the south coast, near Gasmata.

New Guinea The Australians capture Gusika and Bonga in their advance from Finschafen. Sio farther north is shelled by Allied warships.

30 NOVEMBER 1943

Eastern Front The Soviets pull out of Korosten in their second significant setback in this sector.

United States Command General Vandegrift is appointed to become commandant of the US

Marine Corps with effect from 1 January 1944.

Italy The attacks of Eighth Army have now cleared the first ridge beyond the Sangro. In the Fifth Army area diversionary attacks begin on the lower reaches of the Garigliano.

DECEMBER 1943

Europe, Air Operations The heavy bombers of Eighth Air Force and Bomber Command each drop about 12,000 tons of bombs. Bomber Command's targets include Berlin (7000 tons in four raids), Leipzig and Frankfurt. The USAAF attacks Kiel, Emden and Bremen. Both commands hit targets in the Pas de Calais area, especially after 21 December, against launching sites being built for flying bombs.

Bad weather is a problem for the Allied Mediterranean forces throughout the month but there are many sorties against targets including Turin, Innsbruck and Augsburg.

The new variant of the Mustang fighter with the Merlin engine is used operationally for the first time in a fighter sweep over Belgium on 1 December. The first escort mission flown by Mustangs is to Kiel on 13 December. This aircraft will transform the Allied strategic-bombing campaign by its unprecedented combination of range and performance.

1 DECEMBER 1943

Italy There is growing air and ground activity in Fifth Army's sector as diversionary attacks and other moves are made in preparation for the resumption of the offensive.

2 DECEMBER 1943

Eastern Front In their attacks south of Kremenchug the Soviets cross the River Ingulets and move on toward Znamenka.

Italy Units of the British X Corps and the newly arrived US II Corps (General Keyes) begin the Fifth Army attack on Monte Camino with massive artillery support. The US VI Corps pushes forward to the right of these attacks. In the east Eighth Army also advances and takes Lanciano and Castelfrentano.

New Guinea On the Huon Peninsula the Australians capture Huanko.

2–3 DECEMBER 1943

Italy During the night German bombers attack Bari. An ammunition ship in the harbor is hit and explodes, sinking 18 transports of 70,000 tons and destroying 38,000 tons of supplies.

3 DECEMBER 1943

Eastern Front The Soviets capture Dovsk

north of Gomel and make other gains around Rogachev in the same sector. To the south they also push forward west of Cherkassy.

Italy Units from X Corps nearly reach the summit of Monte Camino and to their right units of II Corps capture the slightly lower Monte Maggiore. Eighth Army takes San Vito but does not manage to exploit German weakness around Orsogna where the New Zealand Division is driven back by a desperate counterattack by 26th Panzer Division.

4 DECEMBER 1943

Marshall Islands Admirals Pownall and Montgomery lead six US carriers and nine cruisers to attack Kwajalein. Six Japanese transports are sunk and two cruisers damaged. Also 55 aircraft are shot down for the loss of five to the attackers. In a subsidiary operation *Yorktown* raids Wotje.

Solomons The marines on Bougainville receive a further reinforcement and are therefore able to extend their perimeter.

Pacific The Japanese escort carrier *Chuyo* is sunk by the US submarine *Sailfish* in Japanese home waters.

5 DECEMBER 1943

Italy Monte Camino is the scene of more fierce fighting as both sides dispute possession of its summit.

6 DECEMBER 1943

Eastern Front The Soviets advance a little to the north of Znamenka and cut the rail line to Smela.

Italy The British 56th Division captures Monte Camino after a bitter struggle. To the right II Corps now attacks Monte la Difensa, with some success. Eighth Army comes up to the River Moro.

7 DECEMBER 1943

Italy With the peaks south of the Mignano gap now in Allied hands the second phase of Fifth Army's attack can begin. Operating on a wider front, the US II and VI Corps move against Monte Sammucro and San Pietro but German resistance is strong. Eighth Army attacks Orsogna.

Europe, Air Operations In one of the wilder claims made by the protagonists of strategic bombing, Air Marshal Harris tells his superiors that he believes he can win the war if he is supported in his continuing attacks on Berlin and other targets so that he can send off 15,000 Lancaster missions in the next few months. He will be able to send 14,500 despite arguments

about the effectiveness of the bombing, but the war will not be won in this way.

8 DECEMBER 1943

Marshall Islands Kwajalein is bombarded by five battleships and 12 destroyers led by Admiral Lee. Two carriers give air cover. One Japanese destroyer is damaged.

New Guinea The Australians take Wareo and push on toward Wandokai.

Italy French troops begin to come into the Allied line, first the 2nd Moroccan Infantry Division. Italian troops are also being mobilized. Experienced units are being withdrawn, however, to be moved to Britain to join Operation Overlord. Fifth Army's attacks are making little ground but are continued. Canadian units with Eighth Army begin attacks over the Moro River, a few miles from the east coast.

Eastern Front The Soviets make more progress toward isolating Znamenka by cutting a second rail line out of the town.

9 DECEMBER 1943

Italy German counterattacks near Monte Sammucro are repelled and to the south the Allied line around Monte Camino is further consolidated.

Solomons The newly built American airfield at Cape Torokina on Bougainville becomes operational.

Eastern Front The Soviets take Mederovo near Znamenka and attack Znamenka itself.

10 DECEMBER 1943

United States, Home Front The long-running debate on the draft regulations ends when Roosevelt signs a revised bill which puts those who have been fathers since before Pearl Harbor at the bottom of the list.

Eastern Front Znamenka is taken by the Soviets and a little to the north Konev's troops begin a new series of attacks.

Italy Eighth Army is able to cross the Moro River in strength.

Solomons The first American planes arrive at the Cape Torokina airfield. Inland the marines are gradually extending American-held territory.

11 DECEMBER 1943

Italy The fighting in Fifth Army's sector has continued now for several days. There are as yet no decisive gains for either side and the Allied momentum is being worn down.

12 DECEMBER 1943

Diplomatic Affairs Dr Beneš visits Moscow to

sign a Czech-Soviet treaty of alliance providing for postwar cooperation and mutual assistance for the duration of the war.

Italy The 36th Division of II Corps is now attacking Monte Lungo near its former positions on Monte Maggiore.

14 DECEMBER 1943
Eastern Front Konev's troops take Cherkassy in the south. Yeremenko's Baltic Front begins a new major offensive just south of Nevel.

15 DECEMBER 1943
Italy A new phase of Fifth Army attacks begins. The II Corps renews the drive toward San Pietro and Monte Lungo. To the right VI Corps and the Moroccan Division also push forward with the Moroccans doing especially well.

New Britain General Cunningham's 112th Cavalry Regiment lands at Arawe off New Britain. This is a diversionary operation for the main landings on the island (*see* 26 December). The naval units in support are from Admiral Barbey's Task Force 76. An air attack on the Japanese airfield at Cape Gloucester provides further cover.

New Guinea The Australians take Lakona, 15 miles north of Finschafen.

17 DECEMBER 1943
Italy The Germans begin to withdraw some troops from San Pietro and from other positions a little to the north. Monte Sammucro is now in Allied hands.

18 DECEMBER 1943
Italy Fifth Army takes Monte Lungo, making the German position at San Pietro less secure. There are violent German counterattacks all along Fifth Army's front.

Early on, troops from US 36th Division enter San Pietro. To the north VI Corps is advancing all along its front as the Germans pull back a little way.

19 DECEMBER 1943
New Britain The US forces at Arawe take the nearby Japanese airstrip and beat off minor Japanese counterattacks.

21 DECEMBER 1943
Italy There is heavy fighting in the Eighth Army sector on the approaches to Ortona and in the Fifth Army area, especially near Monte Sammucro.

Eastern Front The Soviets eliminate a small German bridgehead east of the Dniepr near Kherson. There is heavy fighting in the north near Zhlobin.

22 DECEMBER 1943
Italy Eighth Army has now entered Ortona but the fight for the town goes on, from street to street and house to house. The town is defended by a unit of 1st Paratroop Division and the attackers come from 2nd Canadian Brigade.

23 DECEMBER 1943
Italy The 1st Canadian Division from Eighth Army seizes control of most of Ortona. Inland, other Eighth Army units take Arielli.

24 DECEMBER 1943
Solomons A Task Force of US cruisers and destroyers bombards Buka Island and the Japanese base at Buin on Bougainville, principally to divert attention from the imminent landings on New Britain.

Eastern Front The Soviets have prepared a major effort to retake the ground recently lost west of Kiev. Vatutin leads the reinforced armies of the 1st Ukraine Front in a massive assault. The lines of the defending Fourth Panzer Army are stretched too thin to hold this off, largely because their small reserve has been dissipated in the recent attacks. Once the Soviets succeed in breaking the front there will be little that the German commanders can do to prevent a deep penetration into their rear areas.

24–29 DECEMBER 1943
Allied Command A series of announcements in London and Washington makes known the leaders for the coming British and American campaigns. General Eisenhower is to be Supreme Allied Commander for the invasion of Europe, with Air Marshal Tedder as his deputy. Admiral Ramsay and Air Marshal Leigh Mallory will lead the naval and air forces. General Montgomery will lead the British group of armies in the operation. General Wilson becomes Supreme Commander for the Mediterranean with General Devers as his deputy. General Alexander commands in Italy. General Eaker commands the Mediterranean Air Forces. General Leese takes over Eighth Army. General Spaatz is appointed to command all the US Strategic Bomber Forces against Germany and General Doolittle will lead Eighth Air Force. General Paget becomes Supreme Commander in the Middle East.

25 DECEMBER 1943
Eastern Front The Soviet offensive south of

Nevel continues and the Vitebsk–Polotsk rail line is cut.

New Ireland Admiral Sherman's Task Group 50.2 raids Kavieng with 86 aircraft. Two carriers and six destroyers are in the attack force and they succeed in sinking only one transport ship.

Arctic The German battlecruiser *Scharnhorst* under Admiral Bey sails from north Norway to attack the convoy JW-55B which has been found by German air and submarine searches. Bey is unaware that the British battleship *Duke of York* is in distant support.

26 DECEMBER 1943

Arctic In the morning *Scharnhorst* and her destroyers search for the convoy but find instead the three-cruiser covering force led by Admiral Burnett. Visibility is extremely poor and early on *Scharnhorst*'s forward radar set is put out of action. Bey therefore breaks off the engagement and circles north to try to find the convoy. At midday *Scharnhorst* and the cruisers again fight but in better visibility which, combined with the disadvantage of the heavy seas for the smaller ships, should have made things easier for the Germans. If the attack had been pressed home Bey would almost certainly have got among the convoy which was only escorted by small ships with little torpedo armament. Instead the action is broken off. As *Scharnhorst* retreats, *Duke of York*, with Admiral Fraser aboard, comes up and a gun duel begins, surprising the Germans. The British battleship gains the upper hand and eventually the prolonged bombardment and torpedo attacks reduce the *Scharnhorst* to a wreck and she sinks. Only 36 out of her crew of almost 2000 are saved. The Germans now have no large surface ships operational to threaten the Arctic convoys and an important restraint on British dispositions is removed for the rest of the war.

Eastern Front In their offensive in the Kiev sector the Soviets capture Radomyshl.

New Britain After the usual preliminary bombardment, General Rupertus' 1st Marine Division begins landings near Cape Gloucester in three places. Admiral Barbey's Task Force 76 provides the transport and two other groups of cruisers and destroyers are in support. One of these destroyers is sunk by a Japanese air attack. The landing forces get ashore without incident although the terrain is extremely difficult. There are a few small Japanese attacks during the first night but they are driven off.

Italy Monte Sammucro and the surrounding hills are cleared of German defenders.

27 DECEMBER 1943

New Britain The US beachhead near Cape Gloucester is extended with little resistance from the Japanese. The weather and the ground prove more of a problem. The American forces at Arawe receive reinforcements which make them fairly secure against counterattacks.

27–28 DECEMBER 1943

Bay of Biscay The German blockade runner *Alsterufer* is sunk in the Bay of Biscay by Allied aircraft on the 27th. On the 28th the 11 German destroyers and torpedo boats which had been sent to escort her are met by two British cruisers, *Enterprise* and *Glasgow*. Three German ships are sunk and the rest break off the engagement. This is a notable achievement by the British against a superior force.

28 DECEMBER 1943

Eastern Front Vatutin's attacks west of Kiev are making good ground. Korostyshev and Kateyvka near Zhitomir are recaptured.

Italy The Canadians complete the capture of Ortona.

New Britain The marines begin to advance to attack the Japanese airfield at Cape Gloucester.

29 DECEMBER 1943

Eastern Front The Soviets retake Korosten and Chernakov northwest of Kiev, and Skvira to the southwest.

30 DECEMBER 1943

New Britain The US Marines complete the capture of the Japanese airfield at Cape Gloucester. It has been a surprisingly easy operation so far.

Eastern Front In the Kiev sector the Soviets take Kazatin near Berdichev.

31 DECEMBER 1943

Eastern Front The Soviets recapture Zhitomir. Farther north there is increased activity west of Nevel and south of Vitebsk where the road to Orsha is cut. Vitebsk is now almost surrounded.

Italy As the year ends both Fifth and Eighth Armies are battering wearily and almost fruitlessly against the German defenses.

JANUARY 1944

Europe, Air Operations RAF Bomber Command drops 18,000 tons of bombs this month, more than half on Berlin which is attacked by large forces on six nights. Brunswick and Magdeburg are also heavily hit. The American heavy bombers of Eighth and Fifteenth Air

Forces drop 22,000 tons as well as destroying many German planes in the air. Aircraft factories are among the main targets, especially at Brunswick, Halberstadt and Frankfurt. Both British and American heavy bombers are sent against the V-weapon sites in the Pas de Calais. Although the US Eighth Air Force now has Mustang fighters flying as escorts on its daylight raids, losses can be heavy. On 11 January a quarter of a force of 238 bombers is lost on a mission to Oschersleben. These losses do not reflect, however, the effects of attrition on the German fighter force. For night operations the Germans have now developed an airborne version of the radar-search receiver Naxos fitted to U-Boats to enable them to detect centimetric radar. This is fitted to night fighters using H2S transmissions to help them home into the bomber stream. It is not sufficiently precise for actual interception.

A whole range of communications targets in Italy and southern Europe is attacked by the Allied theater forces. After 22 January 11,000 tons of bombs are dropped in support of the Anzio operation.

Pacific, Air Operations The tempo of the Allied effort quickens here, as elsewhere. Rabaul is attacked on 13 occasions, the Marshall Islands on 11 and other targets also suffer heavy blows.

JANUARY–MARCH 1944

Battle of the Atlantic The efforts of the German U-Boats continue but with diminishing success. Altogether 54 Allied ships are lost to submarine attack during these months and 60 U-Boats are sunk. Some U-Boats try to operate in the Western Approaches close to the British Isles, relying on new radar receivers to give warning of aircraft but this does not prove successful. On 22 March Doenitz orders all U-Boats to disperse from groups and work singly. This is the final triumph for the Allied escort forces. The Germans decide to give up convoy attacks until the new experimental types of U-Boat are available.

1 JANUARY 1944

New Ireland Aircraft from Admiral Sherman's carrier task group attack a Japanese convoy off Kavieng.

2 JANUARY 1944

Eastern Front The Soviets capture Radovel, west of Korosten, just 18 miles from the 1939 Polish border.

New Guinea Admiral Barbey's Task Force 38 lands 2400 men of General Martin's 126th

Regiment of 32nd Division at Saidor. The airfield and the harbor are quickly captured. There is little direct air support because of bad weather but other targets are attacked. Admiral Crutchley leads an Allied cruiser and destroyer force as further cover. To the east the Australian advance reaches Sialum.

New Britain The US 7th Marine Regiment mounts an attack to expand the bridgehead near Cape Gloucester but it meets strong resistance and does not reach its objectives.

3 JANUARY 1944

Eastern Front The Soviets capture Olevsk and Novograd-Volynskiy, west and southwest of Korosten.

New Britain The fighting in the Borgen Bay area continues but the US forces are not yet able to bring up armor.

4 JANUARY 1944

Eastern Front The Soviet offensive in the Ukraine continues with the capture of Belaya Tserkov, south of Kiev.

New Ireland Sherman's carrier group attacks Kavieng yet again. The Japanese destroyer *Fumitsuki* is damaged.

4–5 JANUARY 1944

Italy Units of Fifth Army, particularly the British 46th Division, launch attacks on a 10-mile front toward the south end of the Gustav line.

5 JANUARY 1944

Eastern Front Before dawn Konev's Second Ukraine Front begins a new series of attacks toward Kirovgrad. Vatutin's First Ukraine Front captures Berdichev and Tarascha, southwest and south of Kiev.

New Guinea The American forces at Saidor meet their Japanese opponents in patrols to the west. The Australians advancing west along the north coast of the Huon Peninsula capture Kelanoa.

6 JANUARY 1944

Eastern Front The Soviets capture Rakitino, a few miles over the former Polish frontier.

New Britain The US forces manage to extend their bridgehead at Cape Gloucester southward to the Aogiri River.

7 JANUARY 1944

Eastern Front The attacks of both Ukraine Fronts make good progress around Kirovgrad and toward the former Polish town of Rovno.

CHRONOLOGY

Italy British and US units of Fifth Army take Monte Chiaia and Monte Porchia in their continuing attacks. San Vittore is also captured.

8 JANUARY 1944
Eastern Front The Soviets retake Kirovgrad – another major gain.

8–11 JANUARY 1944
Italy, Politics Mussolini's Italian Socialist Republic puts the members of the Fascist Grand Council who overthrew him on trial at Verona. Several are convicted in their absence. Those tried and executed include Ciano and de Bono.

9 JANUARY 1944
Italy Two divisions from US II Corps attack Cervaro and Monte Trochio, just east of the Cassino position.
Solomons On Bougainville the US engineers complete a second airfield at Piva, inland from the coast.
Eastern Front Vatutin's forces take Polonnoye, midway between Berdichev and Rovno, and farther south Konev's troops take Aleksandrovka.

10 JANUARY 1944
New Britain The Americans send reinforcements to their troops at Arawe. In the northern sector they make a small advance along the Aogiri Ridge despite considerable resistance.

11 JANUARY 1944
Eastern Front There are new Soviet attacks at Mozyr.
United States, Home Front Roosevelt appeals to Congress for a new national service law to prevent damaging strikes and to mobilize the whole of the adult work force for war work.
New Guinea The American forces at Saidor repair the airfield and it becomes operational.

12 JANUARY 1944
Eastern Front The Soviets capture Sarny, well inside former-Polish territory.
Italy The US 34th Division completes the capture of Cervaro and pushes forward toward Cassino. Farther north troops from the French Corps begin attacks toward Sant'Elia.

13 JANUARY 1944
Eastern Front Vatutin's troops take Korets between Novograd-Volynskiy and Rovno.

14 JANUARY 1944
New Britain The fighting around the Cape

Gloucester bridgehead continues. While the Japanese can score no positive success they do manage to hold up some of the American plans to expand their possessions.
United States, Home Front The major rail unions accept terms suggested by the president, avoiding a threatened strike. The railroads have in fact been run under the authority of Secretary Stimson since 27 December but they are returned to private ownership and operation on 18 January.
Eastern Front The Soviets recapture Mozyr and Kalinkovichi. In the north the troops of the Leningrad, Volkhov and Second Baltic Fronts begin a major offensive to relieve Leningrad.

15 JANUARY 1944
Eastern Front There is heavy fighting in the northern sector, especially just north of Lake Ilmen and just south of Leningrad itself.
Italy Troops of General Keyes' II Corps capture Monte Trocchio, the last important bastion before the defenses of the Rapido valley and the formidable Cassino position itself. Fifth Army has now closed up to the Gustav Line all along its front and despite the heavy fighting of the past weeks it must continue to attack to play its part in drawing off German reserves before the Anzio operation.
New Guinea The Australian troops on the north coast of the Huon Peninsula attack and capture Sio, but not before it has been evacuated by the Japanese.

16 JANUARY 1944
Allied Command General Eisenhower formally assumes his duties as Commander in Chief of the Allied Expeditionary Forces.
Eastern Front The Soviets break through in their attacks just north of Velikiye Luki.
New Britain There are considerable Japanese counterattacks toward Cape Gloucester but these are beaten off with heavy loss.

17 JANUARY 1944
Australia, Home Front Meat rationing is introduced.
Italy Late in the day the British X Corps from Fifth Army begins formal attacks on the German positions along the Garigliano. Three divisions make the assault. On the left 5th Division, aided by a small seaborne left hook, get successfully across the river as do 56th Division on their right. On the right flank of the attack, however, the efforts of 46th Division at Sant'Ambrogio and to the south are frustrated by the German defense. The defenders are from the 94th

24 JANUARY 1944

Infantry Division of Senger's XIV Panzer Corps.
Eastern Front Vatutin's troops take Slavuta, continuing the advance toward Rovno.

18 JANUARY 1944
Italy By daybreak both 5th and 56th Divisions have crossed the Garigliano, are soundly established on the north bank and are pushing forward. General Vietinghoff commanding the German Tenth Army gets permission from Kesselring, Supreme Commander in Italy, to start to move some of the reserve from the Anzio area to meet this attack.

19 JANUARY 1944
Eastern Front The troops of the Leningrad Front take Krasnoye Selo, Popsha and Peterhof, linking the sectors of Forty-second Army and Second Shock Army. A hundred miles farther south the troops of the Volkhov Front make further encircling advances near Novgorod.
Italy Minturno is taken by the British 5th Division in the continuing attacks by X Corps.

20 JANUARY 1944
Eastern Front The Soviet Fifty-ninth Army takes Novgorod in a brutal storming attack.
Italy The US II Corps begins attacks across the Rapido toward the Liri valley and Monte Cassino. The main effort near Sant'Angelo in Theodice is beaten off by the Germans with little difficulty. Farther south the attacks of the British X Corps are still making progress and capture Tufo.

21 JANUARY 1944
Eastern Front The Soviet attacks near Leningrad continue. In a new effort Mga is taken and the advance goes on toward Tosno.
Italy The attacks of US II Corps continue but only very small holdings across the Rapido can be gained and these are quickly attacked and eliminated by the Germans. The US 36th Division loses very heavily. The forces for the Anzio landing sail from Naples.

22 JANUARY 1944
Italy The Allied landings at Anzio begin. The landing forces are from General Lucas' VI Corps with the US 3rd Division and the British 1st Division providing the bulk of the assault troops. British commando and US ranger units are also involved. The Allied attacks on the Gustav Line, particularly those of X Corps, have been successful in drawing in some of the German reserves so that only light forces are in the Anzio area. Other units are quickly impro-

vised, however, and sent to join the defense. Kesselring calls for reserves from far afield. The landings against the initial light opposition are an exemplary success – of the 36,000 men landed by the end of the first day only 13 are killed and the port of Anzio is taken virtually intact. The naval forces involved include the usual selection of landing craft, cruisers, destroyers, mine-sweepers and other small vessels. Admiral Troubridge commands the British landing north of the town and Admiral Lowry the US landing to the south.

23 JANUARY 1944
Italy By the end of the day the Allies have 50,000 men ashore at Anzio but are only pushing forward very cautiously, inhibited more by the lack of drive from General Lucas than by the Germans. Kesselring insists that the Gustav Line and Anzio can both be held despite Vietinghoff's views to the contrary. Hitler allows reserve forces to be assembled from north Italy, France and the Balkans in the hope of dissuading the British and Americans from future amphibious operations elsewhere in Europe. Within a week eight divisions are in place. Fourteenth Army's headquarters arrives from north Italy to organize and lead them. In view of the scale of this rapid German reaction, criticism of Lucas for failing to push forward to Rome immediately is probably unfounded but a little more vigor could probably have secured better defensive positions before the Germans arrived in strength.
New Guinea The Australian forces in the Ramu valley advance up the slopes of the Finisterre Range toward Shaggy Ridge, capturing Maukiryo. Allied air superiority is an important factor here and in the rest of the campaign in New Guinea.

24 JANUARY 1944
Eastern Front In the Leningrad sector Pushkin and Pashovsk are captured and the rail line between Narva and Krasnogvardeisk cut. In the south the First and Second Ukraine Fronts begin a major offensive to encircle and eliminate the German salient around Korsun-Sevchenovsky. Five Soviet armies, three of them with large tank units, move in against little more than a corps from First Panzer Army. The attacking pincers are designed to meet at Zvenigorodka.
Italy The slow expansion of the Anzio beachhead continues. On the Gustav Line the French Corps attacks Monte Santa Croce while units of II US Corps attack over the Rapido toward Caira, a little to the south.

Above: German infantry fighting near Leningrad.

25 JANUARY 1944
Eastern Front The Soviet attacks around Korsun are driven forward ruthlessly. The south wing of the drive with the Fourth Guards Army and the Fifth Guards Tank Army makes good progress. In the north, Sixth Tank Army, led by an armor expert, General Kravchenko, does scarcely less well. Late in the day the Soviets begin an all-out assault in the Leningrad sector against Krasnogvardeisk. The town is carried early next morning.

New Guinea The Australians complete the capture of Shaggy Ridge, overlooking the Ramu valley.

Italy The fruitless attacks on the Gustav Line continue, especially by the US II Corps, 34th Division. The French Corps to the right makes some gains on Colle Belvedere. At Anzio the Allied forces attempt to extend their perimeter inland but only make a little progress.

26 JANUARY 1944
Italy The French Corps move on from Colle Belvedere toward Monte Abate. On their left the US II Corps at last manages to establish a small bridgehead over the Rapido.

New Britain There is a particularly heavy US air attack on Rabaul. Many Japanese planes are shot down and the base is gradually becoming worthless.

27 JANUARY 1944
Eastern Front General Govorov, commanding the Leningrad Front, issues a special order of the day announcing that the blockade of Leningrad has been completely lifted. Nearby, Tosno and Valosovo are taken. In the south Shpola is captured by Konev's forces as the encircling attacks proceed.

Italy The British X Corps renews its attacks near Santa Maria Infante. The 34th Division of II Corps takes Monte Maiola and Caira, just north of Cassino. The French around Monte

Abate are driven back by German counterattacks.

New Britain The Cape Gloucester bridgehead is further expanded by the marines' capture of Natamo in the northwest.

27–31 JANUARY 1944
War Crimes Britain, the United States and Australia formally protest about the ill-treatment of prisoners of war by the Japanese, as more information comes to light. All three nations promise that there will be tribunals to investigate and punish those responsible.

28 JANUARY 1944
Eastern Front In the Leningrad sector the troops of the Volkhov Front take Lyuban and several other small towns to the south. South of Kiev Manstein is assembling tank forces from both First Panzer and Eighth Armies to relieve the Korsun pocket. The movement of both sides is becoming difficult in this sector because occasional warm days turn the ground into a sea of mud. This freezes solid each night, trapping vehicles. The Soviet tanks are better suited for such conditions because they generally have wider tracks.

29 JANUARY 1944
Marshall Islands In preparation for the coming landings, Admiral Mitscher's TF 58 bombs and shells targets on Roi, Namur, Maloelap and Wotje. Land-based aircraft also attack Jaluit and Mille.

Italy At Anzio the Allies now have 69,000 men, 508 guns and 237 tanks ashore. Lucas is at last ready to attack but in fact faces eight German divisions. There have been intermittent German air attacks on the beachhead and shipping offshore. A token of the growing German strength is that on this one day a cruiser and a transport are sunk.

On the Gustav Line the US 34th Division is still pushing slowly but determinedly forward.

Eastern Front Hitler appoints Model to command Army Group North in place of Kuchler. The Soviet attacks continue. Chudovo is taken by Meretskov's men and Novosokolniki by Popov's.

30 JANUARY 1944
Indian Ocean The battleships *Queen Elizabeth* and *Valiant*, and the battlecruiser *Renown* with the carriers *Illustrious* and *Unicorn* arrive in Colombo from European waters. A battleship and a small carrier are already on the station and an increasing number of submarines are in

operation in the area.

Marshalls Task Force 58 continues its operations against Kwajalein, Roi, Namur and Eniwetok. Seven battleships are involved in bombardment missions and 400 bombing sorties are flown.

Italy At the south end of the Gustav Line the British 5th Division breaks through and captures Monte Natale. Nearer the main focus of action opposite Monte Cassino, the US 34th Division manages to maintain its holding on the west bank of the Rapido. At Anzio the planned Allied attacks begin. The British 1st Division pushes forward a little but takes heavy punishment. In the American sector, a Ranger battalion leading the attack has all but six men killed or captured. The attacks continue with further heavy loss and no worthwhile gains for the next three days.

31 JANUARY 1944

Eastern Front Soviet troops reach the outskirts of Kingisepp in their drive west from Leningrad.

Marshalls The landing operations against Kwajalein Atoll begin. Admiral Spruance is in overall command with General Holland Smith in charge of the various landing forces. The first landings are on Roi, Namur and some nearby islets. Admiral Connolly's TF 53 transports General Smith's 4th Marine Division and provides the support of battleships and escort carriers.

Fairly rapid progress is made on Roi but on Namur the Japanese resistance is more substantial. The Japanese counterattack on both islands during the night. Several neighboring islets have been seized and artillery landed to support the main attacks. There are also landings on Majuro Atoll by troops from 27th Infantry Regiment supported by Admiral Hill's Task Force.

Majuro is quickly made ready to become a major American base. It becomes operational on 2 February. The main carrier forces of TF 58 continue their attacks on these objectives and against Eniwetok and Maleolap.

Italy Caira is taken by II US Corps and on their right the French Corps retakes Monte Abate.

FEBRUARY 1944

Europe, Air Operations RAF Bomber Command drops 11,700 tons of bombs with the main efforts being against Berlin particularly, and Leipzig, Stuttgart and Schweinfurt. The US Eighth Air Force, based in Britain drops 18,000 tons and the Fifteenth Air Force from Italy drops 5900 tons both aiming at a range of targets connected with the German aircraft industry including Gotha, Leipzig and Oschersleben (*see* 20–27 February 1944). US medium bombers and aircraft of the RAF's 2nd TAF drop 4800 tons, mostly on V-weapon sites in France and Belgium.

In response to the growing Allied attacks the Germans revive their attacks on London but on a much less significant scale. These attacks are known as the 'Little Blitz' and are most intense between 18–25 February.

1 FEBRUARY 1944

Marshalls The US carrier operations continue. The land battle for Roi is virtually over but there is still heavy fighting on Namur. Admiral Turner's TF 52 with the usual complement of battleships and escort carriers lands troops from General Corlett's 7th Infantry Division on Kwajalein itself. The Japanese resistance is stubborn but the US forces are exceptionally well organized and by nightfall have overrun a third of the island.

Eastern Front In the north the Soviets take Kingisepp and push on to within one mile of the Estonian border. A little to the south between Luga and Utorgosh German counterattacks score local success.

Italy The US 34th Division continues to batter at the German positions north of Cassino around Monte Maiola. A little more ground is gained.

2 FEBRUARY 1944

Marshalls The American occupation of Roi and Namur is complete. The Japanese have lost virtually every man of the 3700 defenders. The American casualties number 740 killed and wounded. The battle for Kwajalein continues.

Eastern Front In the south, Third and Fourth Ukraine Fronts are pressing strongly against Sixth Army's salient around Nikopol. In the north Soviet troops penetrate into Estonia, capturing Vanakula.

Italy The Allied attacks around Anzio are brought to a halt. Although they have achieved no positive success and taken heavy losses the Germans have been forced to postpone their general attack planned to start now.

3 FEBRUARY 1944

Marshalls Admiral Ginder's TG 58.4 attacks Eniwetok with its carrier planes. Landings are made on Burton Island, one of the smaller islands of the Kwajalein group.

Eastern Front The encirclement of the Korsun pocket is announced and celebrated in Moscow.

Hitler has, as usual, ordered no retreat and Manstein is trying to assemble sufficient panzer forces to break through in relief.

Italy Mackensen's troops begin limited attacks against the British 1st Division's salient around Campoleone in the Anzio bridgehead. General Freyberg's New Zealand Corps joins the order of battle of Fifth Army and prepares to join the fighting in the Cassino sector.

4 FEBRUARY 1944

Marshalls All organized Japanese resistance in the Kwajalein Atoll is over. Almost all of Admiral Akiyama's 8700-strong garrison are dead, only 265 have been captured, many of them Korean laborers or wounded. Altogether the Americans have landed 41,000 men, of whom 370 have been killed and 1500 wounded.

Eastern Front The Soviets reach the mouth of the Narva in the north and on the east side of Lake Peipus they occupy Gdov. In the southern sector Hitler alters Manstein's dispositions, sending 24th Panzer Division back toward Nikopol rather than letting it join the counter-attack toward Korsun which has now started. It returns to Nikopol too late to affect that battle.

Italy Just north of Cassino the US 34th Division takes ground near Point 593 and Point 445 as well as attacking Colle Sant'Angelo. In the Anzio sector the German attacks continue and the British 1st Division is forced to give ground.

5 FEBRUARY 1944

Eastern Front The Soviets of First Ukraine Front occupy Rovno and Lutsk, pushing Fourth Panzer Army back once more. Inside the Korsun pocket General Stemmermann withdraws his forces slightly into a tighter perimeter. Air activity in this sector is very intense, with the Germans flying supplies fairly successfully to the trapped force from their airfields around Uman. The Soviets mount a considerable ground-attack effort as well as trying to cut off German supplies.

6 FEBRUARY 1944

Eastern Front The Third Ukraine Front captures Manganets, east of Nikopol. More significantly, the area west of the town Apostolovo also falls, threatening a further encirclement.

Italy The fighting in the hills just north of Cassino continues, with the American forces striving to recapture recently lost ground.

7 FEBRUARY 1944

Marshalls The US forces complete the mop-ping up of the last pockets of Japanese resistance on the Kwajalein Atoll. Various small groups have been found and wiped out.

Eastern Front Hitler has agreed to allow the troops in the Korsun pocket to try and break out. Stemmermann therefore pulls out of Gorodische and Yanovka to concentrate his forces.

Italy At Anzio, the German attacks against the British 1st Division are renewed. The objective is now Aprilia village and 'The Factory' nearby. The battle continues on 8 February. The British 56th Division and the US 45th Division have now arrived at Anzio.

8 FEBRUARY 1944

Eastern Front Troops of the Third Ukraine Front take Nikopol but most of the German defenders have managed to retreat. The area around Nikopol is important in the production of manganese.

9 FEBRUARY 1944

Eastern Front The Germans make renewed efforts to supply the Korsun pocket by flying large quantities of fuel and ammunition. They evacuate some of the wounded.

Italy The British 1st Division is driven out of Aprilia but manages to keep control of 'The Factory.'

10 FEBRUARY 1944

New Guinea The Australian forces advancing from Sio link up with the Americans near Saidor. The occupation of the Huon Peninsula is now virtually complete.

Eastern Front Vatutin's troops take Shepetovka.

11 FEBRUARY 1944

Italy The fighting at Anzio continues. 'The Factory' finally falls to the Germans after changing hands three times in the last two days. Around Cassino the US 34th Division makes a final, unsuccessful attempt to move forward the last few hundred yards to the Cassino monastery from the north.

Eastern Front Third Panzer Corps under General Vormann renews its attacks to relieve the Korsun pocket in the morning. It manages to capture a vital bridge over the Gniloy Tikich. The Germans inside the pocket begin their attempt to break out late in the day.

12 FEBRUARY 1944

Bismarcks The marines on New Britain take Gorissi, 25 miles east of Cape Gloucester. The Allies land on Rooke Island in the Dampier

Strait, Bismarck Sea.

Marshalls There are US landings on Arno Atoll.

Eastern Front The battle for the Korsun pocket grows in intensity. In the north the Soviet attacks also push forward and reach Luga.

Italy The New Zealand Corps replaces the exhausted US II Corps opposite Cassino. In the Anzio sector there is a comparative lull. The British 1st Division is taken out of the line because of its heavy losses and Lucas is busy organizing an inner defensive perimeter.

United States, Politics Wendell Willkie formally announces his candidacy for the Republican nomination for president. General MacArthur has also been suggested as a Republican candidate. Roosevelt's name has been put forward for several of the Democratic primaries but he has made no formal announcement himself.

13 FEBRUARY 1944

Eastern Front In the north the Soviet offensive drives on. Luga, Polna, and Lyady are recaptured. In the south the battles around Korsun-Sevchenkosky continue. The Germans in fact pull out of the town late in the day but do not make very much more progress in the break out attempt.

14 FEBRUARY 1944

Eastern Front The Soviets enter Korsun but can do no more to break down the resistance of the German pocket. A Belgian SS Brigade is especially prominent in the defense. III Panzer Corps is unable to break through the Soviet lines in relief.

15 FEBRUARY 1944

Solomons Part of General Barrowclough's 3rd New Zealand Division is landed by Admiral Wilkinson's III Amphibious Force on the Green

Islands, north of Bougainville. Admiral Merrill's TF 39 provides the escort. All the Japanese defenders have been overcome by 21 February.

Italy The monastery on the crest of Monte Cassino is heavily bombed at the request of the New Zealand Corps. The historic buildings are completely wrecked. Despite the reports by US troops formerly in the sector that no fire has come from the monastery, more recent reconnaissance has suggested a German presence. Freyberg and Tuker of 4th Indian Division, who have the responsibility of ordering their men to attack the position, decide that they must bomb. Freyberg's responsibility is heightened by his awareness that he leads a large proportion of New Zealand's military manpower. In fact the Germans have been scrupulous not to enter the monastery and have taken the trouble to transport some of its treasures to the safety of the Vatican. Once the abbey has been bombed, however, the Germans move in and find that the ruins and the cellars provide an excellent position – better than the undamaged buildings would have been. The bombers go in on the 15th to take advantage of good weather and so the follow-up attacks by the New Zealand Corps, designed to follow the bombardment, are badly coordinated. They achieve little because the preparations have not been completed.

16 FEBRUARY 1944

Marshalls The carriers of Admiral Ginder's TG 58.4 attack Eniwetok once more. The Japanese airfield on Engebi is virtually put out of action.

Eastern Front The final German attempt to escape from the Korsun pocket through the Soviet lines begins shortly before midnight.

Italy The Germans begin a major attack on the Anzio beachhead. Units of five divisions attack the relatively fresh 45th US and 56th British

Above: An aerial view of the devastation at Cassino after the bombing.

Divisions. The Luftwaffe has gathered its strength as well, operating in support of the attack and against the shipping offshore. The ammunition ship *Elihu Yale* blows up after one such attack. There is no decisive breakthrough on land but the Allied forces are pushed back. In the Cassino sector the attacks by the New Zealand Corps continue.

Diplomatic Affairs A Finnish diplomat arrives in Stockholm to receive terms for an armistice from the Soviet ambassador, Mme Kollontay.

17 FEBRUARY 1944

Eastern Front The battle of the Korsun pocket comes to an end when the bulk of the surviving German forces reach their own lines. Of General Stemmermann's original force of 56,000, 35,000 have escaped but with little equipment. Stemmermann is himself killed. All of the six divisions involved are totally unfit for further operations for the moment, leaving Manstein even more desperately short of manpower.

Italy The German attacks on the Anzio beachhead continue, with infantry divisions still leading the battle. The Germans almost achieve a breakthrough on the front of US 45th Division. There are heavy losses on both sides. In the Cassino sector Point 593 remains in German hands after being held briefly by 4th Indian Division.

Marshalls The first US landings on Eniwetok Atoll are carried out. Admiral Hill's TF 51.11 lands small parties on islets near Engebi with artillery to cover later operations. There are three battleships and three escort carriers in the supporting force. The total Japanese garrison of the islands is about 3400 men, led by General Mushida.

17–18 FEBRUARY 1944

Bismarcks American destroyers bombard Rabaul and Kavieng. Each of these ports is shelled twice more in the month on nights chosen to coincide with other operations, particularly the landings on Los Negros.

Carolines The Japanese base at Truk is attacked by three groups of Admiral Mitscher's TF 58 and a group of TF 50 led by Admiral Spruance, who is in overall command. Nine carriers (five fleet carriers and four light carriers) and six battleships are involved as well as cruisers and destroyers. Air attacks are mounted against Truk on both days (1250 sorties in all) and nearby shipping is also sought out. The Japanese lose a cruiser, two destroyers and several other warships to the air attacks, as well as 140,000 tons of shipping. Another cruiser and two

destroyers are sunk by the battleships *Iowa* and *New Jersey*. In the air the Japanese lose 250 machines. US submarines in supporting operations sink several more vessels. The Americans lose less than 30 planes and the carrier *Intrepid* is damaged.

18 FEBRUARY 1944

Marshalls With land-based artillery support as well as naval and air bombardment the American forces land on Engebi. The attacking force gets solidly established ashore and Japanese counterattacks are driven off.

Eastern Front In the north Popov's forces take the important town of Staraya-Russa. Meretskov's forces take Shimsk.

Italy The Germans commit 26th Panzer and 29th Panzergrenadier Divisions (their main tank reserve) to the attack at Anzio. The focus of the action is the 'Flyover' on the Anzio–Campoleone road and although some gains are made the strong Allied artillery holds off and blunts the attacks. Kesselring and Mackensen realize that the Allied beachhead cannot be wiped out. Offshore, the cruiser *Penelope*, damaged on 17 February by a torpedo attack, is hit again and sinks.

There are further attacks by Indian and New Zealand troops in the hills north of Cassino monastery and over the Rapido against Cassino town. Some gains are made but cannot be held in face of fire from dominating German positions.

United States, Home Front President Roosevelt vetoes the Bankhead Bill which had proposed to end food subsidies. His veto is upheld by the House.

19 FEBRUARY 1944

Marshalls The fighting continues on Engebi. The US forces now land at regimental strength on Eniwetok itself. Despite the usual heavy preparations, the Japanese resistance is strong.

Italy The front at Anzio becomes stable, with no further major effort planned by either side for some time. The fighting on the Gustav Line also dies down.

20 FEBRUARY 1944

Marshalls Aircraft from Admiral Reeves' TG 58.1 attack targets on Jaluit Atoll. The fighting on Eniwetok continues with the American forces gaining the upper hand. Parry, close to Eniwetok, is shelled.

Eastern Front Popov's Second Baltic Front sends Twenty-second Army on a new attack toward Kholm which is quickly successful.

Norway, Resistance A ferry carrying a stock of heavy water on the first stage of the journey from the Ryukan hydroelectric plant to laboratories in Germany is sunk and the cargo lost in an attack by resistance fighters acting on instructions from the British and Norwegian governments. Heavy water is used in atomic research.

20–27 FEBRUARY 1944

Europe, Air Operations During this period the US Strategic Air Forces launch a series of massive attacks against the German aircraft industry. Brunswick, Leipzig and Regensburg are among the targets. In the operations on the 20th, 940 bombers and 700 fighters are sent on attacks and 21 bombers are lost. Operations on the 25th are less successful, with 65 of a force of 800 bombers being lost. The series of attacks becomes known as 'Big Week.' The losses on the 25th are not typical of the present US operations and the continuing high German losses in the fighting are beginning to tell in the strength and quality of their forces.

21 FEBRUARY 1944

Eastern Front The Soviets in the northern sector take Soltsy, southwest of Shimsk, and Kholm, 60 miles farther south. In the Ukraine the Soviet advances around Krivoy Rog proceed apace.

Japan, Politics Prime Minister General Tojo takes on the office of Chief of the Army General Staff in place of Field Marshal Sugiyama. The navy minister, Admiral Shimada also takes on an additional office, replacing Admiral Nagano as Chief of Staff.

22 FEBRUARY 1944

Eastern Front Faced by another massive encircling threat the Germans pull out of Krivoy Rog.

Marshalls After another long bombardment the US forces land on Parry in the Eniwetok Atoll. The Japanese resistance is fierce.

23 FEBRUARY 1944

Eastern Front In the north the Red Army takes Strugi Krasnyye, midway between Luga and Pskov. It also begins to attack Dno.

Marianas The carriers of Sherman's TG 58.3 and Montgomery's TG 58.2 attack Rota, Tinian and Saipan. They sink 20,000 tons of Japanese shipping.

Marshalls The fighting for Parry comes to an end and with it the battle for the whole Eniwetok Atoll. The US losses are 300 dead and 750 wounded. Typically, the Japanese garrison has fought practically to the last man. There are 66 prisoners out of a force of 3400.

Italy General Truscott, for some time deputy, takes full command of VI Corps at Anzio, replacing General Lucas. Somewhat ironically the battle has now settled down to the sort of careful position warfare that Lucas is probably well fitted to control.

24 FEBRUARY 1944

Eastern Front In the north the Soviets take Dno and in the central sector Rogachev falls to the troops of the Second Belorussian Front.

New Guinea The US advance reaches Biliau near Cape Iris.

26 FEBRUARY 1944

Eastern Front In the north the Soviets take Porkhov, east of Dno.

27 FEBRUARY 1944

Admiralty Islands There are US air attacks on Momote and Lorengau in preparation for the planned reconnaissance in force shortly to be executed. The troops for this operation are now embarking in Oro Bay.

28 FEBRUARY 1944

Italy The Germans begin a second offensive at Anzio. The main weight of the attack falls on the 3rd US Division on either side of the Cisterna–Anzio road. The four attacking divisions fail to break through.

29 FEBRUARY 1944

British Planning RAF Fighter Command is reorganized and renamed Air Defence of Great Britain.

Admiralty Islands One thousand men of General Chase's 5th Cavalry Regiment are landed at Hyane Harbor on Los Negros. General MacArthur and Admiral Kinkaid, commanding Seventh Fleet, are present offshore and decide to convert the landings into a full-scale occupation. Japanese counterattacks during the night are beaten off.

Italy The Germans make a further limited effort against the Anzio defenses but it cannot be driven home in the dreadful weather.

MARCH 1944

Europe, Air Operations American heavy bombers drop 30,000 tons of bombs on a selection of targets including Berlin (*see* 6–8 March), Brunswick, Friedrichshafen, French airfields and V-weapon sites. RAF Bomber Command makes over 8000 sorties, including four 1000-bomber raids during which 27,000 tons of bombs are dropped. Objectives include Frankfurt, Stuttgart, Berlin, Essen, Nuremberg (*see* 30–31 March) and rail targets in France for Overlord. US and British medium and fighter bombers attack targets in occupied territory. The Mediterranean air forces also hit rail targets in north Italy.

1 MARCH 1944
Admiralty Islands On Los Negros the US forces eliminate some small Japanese units that have infiltrated their lines during the night.
Eastern Front The Soviets capture Russaki, near Pskov.

2 MARCH 1944
Diplomatic Affairs Owing to Turkey's reluctance to join the war or to make any other contribution to the Allied effort, Lend-Lease aid is cut off.
Admiralty Islands A second wave of 1000 men from the US 5th Cavalry Regiment arrives at Los Negros. The forces already established on the island take Momote airfield with the help of fire support from destroyers offshore.

3 MARCH 1944
Italy There is another flurry of activity in the Anzio sector where the American 3rd Division meets and holds an attack near Ponte Rocco. After this failure the German Fourteenth Army goes over to the defensive.
Admiralty Islands The Japanese send in a strong night attack against the American force on Los Negros. The attackers take heavy losses however, and much of the Japanese strength on the island is thereby dissipated.

4 MARCH 1944
Eastern Front The Soviets begin another series of massive attacks in the Ukraine with advances by Vatutin's forces in the area to the north and east of Tarnopol.
Admiralty Islands Admiral Crutchley's cruiser TF 74 shells Japanese batteries on Hauwei and Ndrilo which have been hampering access to Seeadler Bay.

5 MARCH 1944
Eastern Front The First Ukraine Front's attacks make rapid progress, fracturing Manstein's attenuated lines. Izyaslav, Yampol and Ostropol in the Shepetovka sector are all taken.
New Guinea Two battalions of the US 126th Infantry Regiment land at Yalau Plantation, 30 miles west of Saidor. There is almost no Japanese opposition.
Admiralty Islands The US forces move into the northern half of Los Negros. A third wave of 1400 troops arrives with destroyers which also give fire support.
Burma The 77th Long Range Penetration Brigade (LRP) is flown in to the landing area named 'Broadway,' 50 miles southwest of Myitkyina. A second Chindit Brigade, 16th LRP, has been on the march south from Ledo since 5 February heading for the 'Aberdeen' area.

6 MARCH 1944
Eastern Front The Third Ukraine Front begins a new offensive. Vatutin's attacks continue to make good advances, cutting the Odessa–Lvov rail line and capturing Volochisk.
New Britain The US 1st Marine Division is sent to land on the east side of Willaumez Peninsula with the aim of taking Talasea. The Japanese defense is not particularly formidable but the terrain is difficult and the advance inland is not very rapid.

6–8 MARCH 1944
Europe, Air Operations On 6 March US heavy bombers raid Berlin for the first time. A force of 660 bombers is sent and 69 are lost. The raid is repeated on the 8th when the 580 bomber force again loses about 10 percent of its number despite an escort of 800 fighters.

7 MARCH 1944
Solomons The Japanese have at last assembled large forces around the US beachhead on Bougainville and are preparing a major attack. On the Green Islands the Allied forces have now completed the construction of an airfield.
Admiralty Islands The Japanese batteries at the entrance to Seeadler Bay are bombarded once again by Admiral Crutchley's three cruisers and four destroyers.

8 MARCH 1944
Diplomatic Affairs The Finns reply to the Russian armistice terms asking for further guarantees. The principal difficulty is the Russian demand for the internment of German military personnel. This reply is rejected by the Russians on 10 March.
Solomons The Japanese begin attacks on the American positions on Bougainville. The airfields at Piva are shelled causing the Americans to withdraw some of their bombers. American artillery and naval vessels return the fire. Japanese infantry infiltrate the positions of 37th

13 MARCH 1944

Division. The attacking troops are mostly from General Hyakutake's 6th Division.

New Britain The attacks of 1st Marine Division make good progress toward Talasea as does the other American advance along the coast from Cape Gloucester.

Burma The Japanese offensive *U-Go* begins. The aim is to destroy the British forces around Imphal and Kohima and then push on through the passes to Dimapur, cutting off the Chinese and Americans in the north, and with the road to India ahead. Three divisions of General Mutaguchi's Fifteenth Army are to be employed in the initial operations. The offensive begins with advances by General Yamagida's 33rd Division against the positions of General Cowan's 17th Indian Division around Tiddim. These attacks are meant to commit the British reserves so that when the main attack goes in its task will be easier. The British are well aware that the Japanese plan to attack, but they underestimate the strength of the force to be used. The plan is for 17th and 20th Indian Divisions, both in fairly advanced positions, to fall back to around Imphal and protect and live off the large base organization there. The British forces at this stage are all from General Scoones' IV Corps. It is an essential part of the Japanese plan to capture large quantities of British supplies because most of their advances are to be made over jungle tracks impassable to supply vehicles. Food is the crucial element of the problem. It is precisely because of these difficulties that the British expect a smaller attack.

9 MARCH 1944

Eastern Front Vatutin's First Ukraine Front takes Starokonstantinov south of Shepetovka and reaches the outskirts of Tarnopol where there is bitter fighting.

Solomons On Bougainville the Japanese attacks on 37th Division make a few gains. The airfields at Piva and Torokina are shelled.

Admiralty Islands The first US planes begin operations from Momote airfield.

Burma News of the advance of 33rd Division reaches General Cowan's headquarters, but is not at first believed.

10 MARCH 1944

New Britain The American forces take Talasea.

Eastern Front The attacks of Konev's troops push forward up to 40 miles on a 100-mile front. Uman is taken. First Ukraine Front continues to advance north of Proskurov.

Solomons On Bougainville the Japanese gain Hill 260 but lose ground to American counter-attacks in other areas.

Burma The Japanese attack the rear of 17th Division's positions at Tongzang. It is becoming clear to the British command that the Japanese offensive is under way.

11 MARCH 1944

Eastern Front Troops of Third Ukraine Front take Berislav north of the Dniepr east of Kherson.

Admiralty Islands Advance guards are sent to scout landing places on Manus Island. One unit lands on Butjo Luo offshore and takes heavy punishment from the Japanese defenders.

Burma The Japanese 33rd Division as well as attacking 17th Division is infiltrating behind 20th Division but their advances in this sector are held near Witok. More Chindit forces are flying in to central Burma and are already disrupting Japanese communications with the forces facing Stilwell's Chinese and American troops. In the Arakan Buthidaung falls to the British.

12 MARCH 1944

Solomons On Bougainville the American forces begin to gain the upper hand over the attacking Japanese.

Admiralty Islands A small American force lands on Hauwei Island. There is strong Japanese resistance under the command of Colonel Ezaki.

Marshalls US forces occupy Wotho Atoll. There is no opposition.

Eastern Front Konev's forces reach the River Bug at Gayvoron. Other attacks capture Dolinskaya.

13 MARCH 1944

Eastern Front Kherson is taken by Third Ukraine Front after a hard struggle.

Solomons On Bougainville powerful American counterattacks with tank and air support retake almost all the gains made by the Japanese in the last few days.

Admiralty Islands Hauwei is completely overrun by the American landing force. Artillery is landed to support the coming operations on Manus.

Burma General Scoones authorizes 17th and 20th Divisions to withdraw from their advanced positions to Imphal. General Gracey with 20th Division has made better preparations for this move than Cowan with 17th. Scoones and his superiors Slim and Giffard agree that reinforcements are needed and Mountbatten therefore sends requests to the highest level for the use of

American aircraft (those normally used for ferrying supplies to the Chinese) to move 5th Division from the Arakan. The Japanese begin air attacks against the Chindits' Broadway airfield.

14 MARCH 1944

United States, Politics Willkie and Roosevelt top the polls in their parties' respective primary elections in New Hampshire.

Eastern Front The Russians have isolated a few German units North of Kherson. Eventually 4000 men are captured.

Burma The 17th Indian Division starts its withdrawal a crucial 24 hours late. The Japanese have created four roadblocks on the route it must take to Imphal. To the north 20th Division is pulling back in a more controlled manner.

15 MARCH 1944

Eastern Front Konev's forces have quickly crossed the Bug and now capture Vapnyarka cutting the Odessa–Zhmerinka rail line. Farther north near Vinnitsa Kalinkova falls to the Russians.

Italy Once more the Allied forces attack Cassino. The massive preliminary bombardment, 1400 tons of bombs and 190,000 shells, is mostly directed against Cassino town. The New Zealand Division moves in to attack the town with 4th Indian Division ready to follow up against the monastery. The advance of the Allied tanks is hampered by the mass of rubble created by the bombardment. The German resistance by a regiment of 1st Paratroop Division is very tenacious and well directed, but nevertheless some gains are made by the attacks in the town and on the lower slopes of the mountain at Castle Hill and Hangman's Hill.

Solomons The Japanese make another abortive effort against the American positions on Bougainville.

Admiralty Islands Units of 7th and 8th Cavalry Divisions are landed on the north coast of Manus Island near Lugos Mission. Once ashore they advance toward Lorengau by two routes.

Burma The main effort of the Japanese offensive begins with crossings of the Chindwin by 15th and 31st Divisions in several places north and south of Homalin.

16 MARCH 1944

Italy The heavy fighting around Cassino continues but the Allied forces can make no progress either in the town or on the slopes leading up to the monastery against the determined defense of the German 1st Paratroop Division.

Admiralty Islands The American advances on Los Negros and Manus proceed although the Japanese resistance on Manus is stiffening.

New Guinea American planes attack a Japanese convoy off Wewak. During the next few days it is almost completely destroyed.

17 MARCH 1944

Eastern Front Dubno is taken by the First Ukraine Front.

Admiralty Islands The US forces on Manus capture Lorengau airfield, their main objective.

Burma There are heavy Japanese air attacks on the Chindit's landing ground at Broadway. Several of the supporting Spitfires are destroyed on the ground.

17–19 MARCH 1944

Italy The battle for Cassino continues to be very fierce. The New Zealand and Indian troops mount unsuccessful attacks toward the southwest of the town and along Snake's Head Ridge to Point 593. The Germans similarly fail in efforts against Castle Hill and Hangman's Hill.

18 MARCH 1944

Admiralty Islands The village of Lorengau on Manus is taken by the US forces. On Los Negros there is a brisk engagement near Papitalai Mission.

Eastern Front Zhmerinka falls to the attacks of First Ukraine Front.

Marshalls Admiral Lee's TG 50.10 with two battleships and the carrier *Lexington* bombards the Mili atoll. The battleship *Iowa* is hit by return fire.

Diplomatic Affairs Admiral Horthy, the Regent of Hungary, is summoned to visit Hitler and is arrested.

18–19 MARCH 1944

New Guinea An Allied destroyer group bombards the Japanese base at Wewak.

19 MARCH 1944

Eastern Front Konev's forces have reached and crossed the Dniepr near Yampol capturing Soroki a little to the south. Near Dubno the Russians also take the town of Krzemienic.

Hungary The Germans move into Hungary (Operation Margaret) to prevent a collapse and ensure a line of retreat for their forces and continued access to the oil resources.

20 MARCH 1944

Eastern Front The Russians capture Mogilev Podolsky and Vinnitsa both important communications centers. The Russian advance in all sectors of the Ukraine is in considerable strength on a very wide front giving the Germans little opportunity for concentrated resistance.

Burma The first brigade of 5th Division has arrived at Imphal by air. A battalion is sent to Kohima.

Italy General Alexander agrees with General Freyberg that the losses in the battle for Cassino are growing too heavy and that it must be halted unless there are good gains in the next two days. The Germans are managing to bring their reserves into the battle while the Allies must move theirs over difficult ground under German artillery fire.

Bismarcks General Noble's 4th Marines are landed on Emirau Island in the Matthias group. There is no Japanese resistance. Admiral Griffin leads four battleships and two carriers in attacks on Kavieng as a covering operation. Four more carriers and seven cruisers are in direct support of the landings.

21 MARCH 1944

New Guinea The US forces moving west from Yalau Plantation make contact with the Australian units advancing north from inland on the Huon Peninsula.

Burma The 20th Indian Division has completed its withdrawal most successfully. It now holds positions on the Shenan Hills and between Palel and Wangjing. The 17th Division is still fighting its way back north through the Japanese road-blocks inflicting heavy casualties on 33rd Division as it does so.

22 MARCH 1944

Eastern Front Pervomaysk, southeast of Uman is taken by Konev's troops.

Axis Politics The Germans announce from Berlin that a new Hungarian Government has been formed and will be led by Field Marshal Szotjay.

22–23 MARCH 1944

Italy The New Zealand Corps makes a final effort against Cassino but to no effect. Afterward Freyberg calls off the attack. Some troops are withdrawn from the most advanced positions below the monastery and the remainder of the recent Allied gains consolidated.

23 MARCH 1944

Eastern Front In a new series of attacks First Ukraine Front drives south from between Proskurov and Tarnopol threatening to divide First and Fourth Panzer Armies from each other. Kapychintsy is taken.

Solomons The Japanese try another attack on the American positions on Bougainville but can still make no progress and again lose heavily.

St Matthias Islands US destroyers shell the Japanese seaplane base on Elouae.

24 MARCH 1944

Solomons The last significant Japanese effort on Bougainville comes to an end. There are various small skirmishes for a few months but the Japanese are worn out and the Americans are content merely to watch the Japanese weakness. In the past couple of weeks the Japanese have lost about 8000 casualties, the Americans only 300.

Burma General Wingate is killed in an air crash. The Senior Chindit brigade commander, Lentaigne, replaces him.

Eastern Front The advance of First Ukraine Front continues at speed. Chertkov and Zaleschik are taken in the drive southeast of Tarnopol. Third Ukraine Front takes Voznesensk northeast of Nikolayev.

25 MARCH 1944

Eastern Front Forces of First Ukraine Front take Proskurov. General Hube, commanding First Panzer Army is not obeying Manstein's orders to attack west to prevent encirclement resulting from the Soviet gains at Proskurov and to the southwest.

Admiralty Islands A final elaborate US attack on Manus crushes most of the remaining Japanese forces. On Los Negros too only scattered groups and individuals fight on.

26 MARCH 1944

Eastern Front A large part of First Panzer Army has been cut off around Kamenets-Podolski by the advances to the River Prut by First and Second Ukraine Fronts. Other units of Second Ukraine Front take Balta.

Italy There is a major regrouping of the Allied forces. The New Zealand Corps is taken out of the line and broken up. Units of Eighth Army are brought from the east side to replace it and the French Corps which has also taken heavy losses. The next Allied offensive will be in May when this regrouping and other preparations are complete.

27 MARCH 1944

Italy A small German coastal convoy is destroyed off Vado by a British torpedo boat squadron.

Eastern Front Kamenets-Podolski is taken by

First Ukraine-Front. Gorodenka is also taken by other units of this formation.

Burma General Stopford's XXXIII Corps is put under Slim's control and ordered to concentrate at Dimapur before advancing to Kohima. A second brigade of 5th Division arrives at Imphal by air and the third brigade is being sent to Dimapur also for Kohima.

27 MARCH–5 APRIL 1944

Arctic The convoy JW-58 sails from Iceland to Murmansk without loss. One feature of the battle is the number of German scout and bomber aircraft shot down by the planes of the escort carriers. In addition three U-Boats are sunk.

28 MARCH 1944

Eastern Front After a vicious struggle Nikolayev falls to Malinovsky's men.

29 MARCH 1944

Eastern Front Troops of the First Ukraine Front have crossed the Prut and taken Kolomya in Rumania (now part of the USSR) in the foothills of the Carpathians.

Burma The road between Imphal and Kohima is cut by Sato's 31st Division at Maram. Slim sticks to his plan to supply the garrison of Imphal by air.

30 MARCH 1944

Eastern Front Russian troops take Chernovtsy.

Hitler is furious with his generals and dismisses Manstein and Kleist from their commands of Army Groups North and South Ukraine. Model takes over from Manstein and Schoerner from Kleist. Lindemann takes Model's place at Army Group North.

Admiralty Islands US forces occupy Pityilu Island north of Manus. There is almost no opposition.

30–31 MARCH 1944

Carolines Spruance leads three groups of TF 58, including 11 carriers, in attacks on Palau Island. The Japanese have sighted the approaching Americans on 25 and 26 March and have therefore dispersed their warships. The battleship *Musashi* is hit by a submarine torpedo while moving away on 28 March however. Despite these precautions much ordinary shipping is hit. The operation continues on 1 April.

Europe, Air Operations The RAF raid Nuremberg and lose 96 planes from an attacking force of 795 – the worst losses for the RAF during the whole war. A combination of many factors accounts for this. Nuremberg is a rather more distant target than some of the usual ones and on a clear night the growing technical skill of the German night-fighter controllers and the new *Lichtenstein* airborne radar sets combine with German ability to track the RAF H2S and IFF transmissions in inflicting unacceptable punishment on the attacking force.

31 MARCH 1944

Eastern Front Malinovsky's troops take Ochakov southwest of Nikolayev.

Japanese Command Admiral Koga, Commander in Chief of the Japanese Combined Fleets, is killed in an air crash. Because of political differences no successor is appointed immediately. (See 3 May 1944).

APRIL 1944

Europe, Air Operations The US heavy bomber force drops 43,500 tons of bombs especially on aircraft factories throughout Europe. Steyr, Augsburg, Poznan, Duna and Oschersleben and many others are all attacked. The RAF heavy bomber force's main efforts are switched from German targets to transport centers in France and Belgium. Some attacks are still made on Germany including raids on Cologne and Essen. The rail targets include Laon, Tours, Rouen, Juvisy and Lille. This respite from all-out attacks on Germany is welcome to the crews if not to Air Marshal Harris because of the growing efficiency of the German night fighters. During the month 33,000 tons are dropped. USAAF Marauders add 8800 tons in attacks on French and Belgian rail targets.

Aircraft from the Mediterranean Air Forces attack oil and communications targets in southeast Europe including Ploesti, Sofia and Belgrade. These attacks are some help to the Russian forces advancing toward the Carpathians because they disrupt the rail network.

Indian Ocean During the month the British Eastern Fleet is reinforced by three more escort carriers and the French battleship *Richelieu*.

1 APRIL 1944

Carolines The carriers of TF 58 attack Woleai. In the three days of attacks 130,000 tons of Japanese shipping has been sunk as well as seven small warships. The Americans have lost 26 planes but have shot down 150.

Eastern Front A considerable German force has been surrounded near Skala between the advancing wings of First and Second Ukraine Fronts.

Admiralty Islands The US forces extend their

hold occupying Ndrilo and Koniniat.

2 APRIL 1944

Eastern Front The Soviets enter Rumania, crossing the Prut east of Chernovtsy.

Burma Mutaguchi's troops continue their advance. They now cut the road between Kohima and Imphal. South of Imphal 17th Indian Division has nearly completed its retirement to the main position.

3 APRIL 1944

Arctic The *Tirpitz* is attacked and damaged by Barracuda bombers from the carriers of the British Home Fleet. Four aircraft are lost but the *Tirpitz* is put out of action for a further three months. The *Victorious* and *Furious* and four escort carriers are involved.

4 APRIL 1944

Eastern Front There are local German counterattacks near Kovel and farther south where the Soviets are prevented from gaining routes through the Carpathians near Kolomya.

Burma The Japanese 31st Division begins to put real pressure on the British position at Kohima, cutting both routes out of the town toward the rear. It is vital for the Japanese to capture this British supply center as they are relying on its resources for their own replenishment.

France, Politics De Gaulle announces changes in the Committee of National Liberation. Two communists are appointed and de Gaulle himself becomes head of the armed forces. General Giraud is being sidelined. On 9 April he becomes Inspector General of the Army and on 14 April he is placed on the retired list.

5 APRIL 1944

Eastern Front Malinovsky's forces reach Razdelnaya, cutting the rail route from Odessa.

6–8 APRIL 1944

Eastern Front There is heavy fighting north of Razdelnaya as a small German pocket is wiped out.

7 APRIL 1944

Burma Near Kohima the Japanese encircle the 161st Brigade from Stopford's XXXIII Corps at Jotsoma and block the main road to the west near Zubza.

8 APRIL 1944

Eastern Front The Russian forces move to the attack in the Crimea. The defenders from

General Jaenicke's Seventeenth Army are attacked by a considerably superior force from Tolbukhin's Fourth Ukraine Front. Farther west the troops of Zhukov's and Konev's Armies penetrate well into Rumania taking Botosani and Dorohoi and Siret to the north. Konev's forces reach the River Siret on a 60-mile front. Patrols from Zhukov's armies reach as far as the Slovakian border.

10 APRIL 1944

Burma Slim now feels that he has a complete picture of the situation and that an offensive is practical and necessary. The troops surrounded at Imphal and Kohima are to continue to be supplied by air and particularly in the case of the Imphal garrison are to operate as offensively as possible. Stopford's XXXIII Corps are to break through and relieve Kohima.

Eastern Front The Russians take Odessa after a vicious battle. The Germans have managed to evacuate by sea 24,000 men, many wounded, as well as 55,000 tons of supplies. In the Crimea the initial German defense lines are being worn down. Armyansk is taken. The Rumanian troops holding the right of the line are in severe trouble. In Rumania itself Second Ukraine Front crosses the Siret and takes Radauti and Suceava.

11 APRIL 1944

Eastern Front In the Crimea the Russians make good progress capturing Dzhankoy and, in a new series of attacks in the east by Yeremenko's troops, Kerch is also taken.

12 APRIL 1944

Eastern Front Troops from Malinovsky's forces occupy Tiraspol. The Germans begin a further series of evacuations from the Crimea. In the next four days 67,000 men, Germans and their allies, are taken out with little loss from Russian air and naval attacks.

13 APRIL 1944

New Guinea The Australians take Bogadjim.

Eastern Front In the Crimea Tolbukhin's and Yeremenko's tank forces advance rapidly, capturing Feodosia, Evpatoriya, and Simferopol. The Germans and Rumanians are retreating in some disorder toward Sevastopol. Farther west Malinovsky's men take Ovidiopol at the mouth of the Dniestr.

14 APRIL 1944

Burma The Japanese road block at Zubza is broken and the 161st Brigade at Jotsoma relieved by the attacks of other units of the 2nd Indian Division.

15 APRIL 1944
Eastern Front After fighting for several weeks the Russians take Tarnopol.

16 APRIL 1944
Eastern Front The Russians take Yalta. To the west Malinovsky's troops cross the Dniestr north and south of Tiraspol.

18 APRIL 1944
Eastern Front There are important German attacks around Buchach which are designed to help free units trapped farther east. In the Crimea the Russians take Balaklava and begin operations in the outskirts of Sevastopol.
Operation Overlord The British Government bans all coded radio and telegraph transmissions from London and elsewhere in the British Isles. Diplomatic bags are to be censored and diplomats are to be forbidden to leave the country. The only exemptions are for the USA and USSR and, a tribute to their excellent security, the London Poles. The telephone service to Southern Ireland and the distribution of newspapers to there and to Gibraltar has already been stopped on 5 April. These measures are designed to help with the security of the preparations for D-Day.
Burma The advance guard of 5th Brigade makes contact with the Kohima garrison restoring its communications.

19 APRIL 1944
Indian Ocean Admiral Somerville's Eastern Fleet, reinforced for the occasion by the USS *Saratoga*, sends the carrier aircraft to attack Sabang and the nearby airfields. Only one of the attacking planes is lost and 27 Japanese are shot down.
Eastern Front Although the battle for Sevastopol continues, elsewhere on the front activity begins to die down. The recent Russian advances have stretched their supply lines and they need time to prepare their next moves. For their part the Germans and their allies have been so weakened as to welcome the respite.

20 APRIL 1944
Diplomatic Affairs In response to Allied pressure Turkey stops chrome exports to Germany.

21 APRIL 1944
New Guinea In preparation for the Hollandia landings Admiral Mitscher leads TF 58 including 12 carriers in attacks on Wakde Island, Sawar, Sarmi and Hollandia itself. The carrier planes attack during the day and there are cruiser bombardments during the night.

22 APRIL 1944
New Guinea The US operations against the Japanese positions at Hollandia and nearby begin. The landing forces are carried by the ships of Admiral Barbey's TF 77. Admirals Crutchley and Berkey lead cruiser forces in the covering group in which there are also two escort-carrier squadrons. Admiral Mitscher's carriers which made several of the preparatory raids remain in support. The landing force, I US Corps, is under the overall command of General Eichelberger and totals 84,000 men. The defenders are commanded by General Adachi and number 11,000. Initially there are three landings. One regiment is put ashore at Aitape; General Irving's 24th Infantry Division at Tanahmerah Bay; and General Fuller's 41st Division at Humboldt Bay. There is comparatively little resistance at first. The Japanese are taken somewhat by surprise and retire inland leaving for the moment only harassing forces. All the landings get well established ashore advancing in some sectors as much as eight miles.
Marshalls US forces occupy Ungelap Island completing the campaign for the group.

23 APRIL 1944
New Guinea The US forces take Hollandia without a fight. The advance inland continues meeting its first check near the village of Sabron. The only other problem is with the beach organization – there is some congestion. The subsidiary landing at Aitape is also going well. Tadji airfield is taken.

24 APRIL 1944
New Guinea The Hollandia operation continues to go well. Near Hollandia itself Lake Sentani is reached and there is also good progress at Aitape. Farther east the Australians advancing from the Huon Peninsula reach and capture Madang.

25 APRIL 1944
New Guinea The Allied forces, strengthened by further landings in Humboldt Bay, push forward.

26 APRIL 1944
Arctic The British Home Fleet in which Admiral Moore leads the battleship *Anson* and six carriers, tries again to attack *Tirpitz* but bad weather intervenes and instead a coastal convoy is found near Bodo and three ships sunk.

New Guinea The beachheads at Tanahmerah Bay and Humboldt Bay are linked up. The Australian forces to the east take Alexishafen.

28 APRIL 1944

New Guinea There is fighting near Aitape between the US forces and Japanese units moved west from Wewak.

United States, Politics The Secretary to the United States Navy, Frank Knox, dies. He has played a large part in the revival of the navy since Pearl Harbor.

29 APRIL 1944

New Guinea The captured Japanese airfields at Hollandia and Aitape are reopened.

29–30 APRIL 1944

Carolines On both days Admiral Mitscher's TF 58 sends heavy strikes against the Japanese base at Truk. Of the establishment of 104 aircraft 93 are shot down for the loss of 35 of the carriers' machines many of whose pilots are saved. On 30 April Admiral Oldendorf leads nine cruisers and eight destroyers to shell targets in the Sawatan Islands, southeast of the main Truk base.

30 APRIL 1944

Burma In the continuing battle for Imphal the Japanese attacks are being gradually worn down, especially as the food shortage becomes serious. The defense of 20th Division on the Shenam Ridge is particularly stout. The battle goes on.

MAY 1944

Europe, Air Operations The principal efforts of the Allied air forces based in Britain is directed to preparations for the Normandy landings. RAF Bomber Command only drops 8500 tons on targets in Germany with the major raids being on Duisburg and Aachen. Another 28,500 sorties are devoted to a range of small targets in France including stores dumps and rail and training centers. Mailly, Bourg Leopold and Boulogne are all hit with many others. The American heavy bombers drop 63,000 tons on three types of objective: rail centers, oil production areas and the more usual manufacturing towns. Among the oil targets are Bohlen and Poolitz; the aircraft manufacturing towns are Strasbourg and Poser; and the rail centers hit include Metz, Belfort, Mulhouse and Hamm. To round off the program Berlin and Brunswick are raided. The medium and fighter-bombers of the US Ninth Air Force drop 20,000 tons on targets in France mostly connected with communica-

tions. They hit 13 of the Seine bridges as well as road, rail and canal targets. The activities of the British light and medium forces follow the same pattern with redoubled strength this month. Planes of British Bomber and Coastal Commands step up mining operations in the Channel as well as their other tasks in preparation for D-Day. There is increased air activity here and off Norway to prevent U-Boats being on station in early June. The Mediterranean Air Forces contribute attacks on oil and communications systems in southeast Europe. Bucharest, Brasov and Ploesti are all struck.

English Channel During the month there is intense naval activity as both sides prepare for the coming operations. There are numerous small battles as patrols, coastal convoys and minelaying vessels meet.

1 MAY 1944

Carolines Admiral Lee leads seven battleships and 11 destroyers to bombard Ponape. The operation is covered by the carriers of Admiral Clark's TG 58.1.

3 MAY 1944

Japanese Command Admiral Toyoda is named Commander in Chief of the Japanese Combined Fleets. There has been a long delay in choosing a successor to Koga who was killed in an air crash on 31 March.

4 MAY 1944

United States, Home Front All meats are taken off the ration with the exception of steaks and certain choice cuts of beef for roasting.

6 MAY 1944

Eastern Front During the night the final Soviet assault on Sevastopol opens, preceded by the customary devastating bombardment. The southeast sector is most heavily attacked. In the last three weeks there have been intensive convoy operations in the Black Sea. Generally the Germans have managed to get sufficient supplies through as well as evacuate 40,000 men.

6 MAY–1 JUNE 1944

Arctic There is a series of six operations by the British Home Fleet off the Norwegian coast. Various air attacks on the *Tirpitz* are planned but are prevented by bad weather. As well as the inherent value of these raids they are designed to support one of the deception plans for D-Day, *Fortitude North*. This scheme principally involves false radio activity designed to suggest a coming landing in Norway.

CHRONOLOGY

7 MAY 1944
New Britain Units of the US 46th Division occupy Cape Hopkins Airfield without meeting any resistance.

8 MAY 1944
Eastern Front After refusing several earlier, timely requests, Hitler now gives his permission for full-scale withdrawals from the Crimea. During the next few days 37,500 men will be taken off but a further 8000 will be drowned in ships sunk by the fierce Soviet attacks from the air and submarines and surface naval units.

9 MAY 1944
Eastern Front Sevastopol falls to the Red Army. The remainder of the German garrison retreats toward Cape Kersonessky where evacuations are still being carried out.

9–13 MAY 1944
New Guinea There is constant skirmishing with occasional fierce engagements around the US beachheads at Hollandia, but the Japanese forces are ill supplied and weak and achieve little.

10 MAY 1944
United States, Politics J V Forrestal becomes Secretary to the US Navy.

11 MAY 1944
Italy Just before midnight the preparatory bombardment for the new Allied attacks, code named Diadem, begins and is quickly followed by the first infantry advances. Four Allied Corps are in the attack: II US, II Polish, XIII British and the French Expeditionary Corps. In the long lull since the last major operations the Germans have done much to strengthen their lines and provide other positions in the rear if a retirement is necessary. At first the Germans will be hampered by the temporary absence of Senger and Vietinghoff their Corps and Army commanders. The Allies have 12 divisions in the attack as well as ample reserves. The Germans are at a serious disadvantage, with only six divisions including reserves.

11–16 MAY 1944
Pacific In preparation for the attack on the Marianas which is imminent, the Japanese assemble practically all the heavy units of their Fleet in the Sulu Sea at Tawitawi. Their plan to defend the Marianas' line is code named *A-Go*. Admiral Ozawa is in command of the various squadrons.

12 MAY 1944
Italy Although the Allied attack is only one hour old at the beginning of the day even before dawn some gains have been recorded. The French Corps (General Juin) finds only the 71st German Division opposite its four and quickly seizes Monte Faito. Elsewhere the defense is more successful. The Poles are beaten back with heavy losses in their attack north of Cassino. To their left the British XIII Corps takes two small bridgeheads over the Rapido opposite Cassino. The two US divisions on the coastal flank to the left of the French can only make a little ground.

13 MAY 1944
Italy The US and British forces continue to push forward doggedly. Santa Maria Infante is taken by the Americans and Sant'Angelo by the British. The Poles are again bloodily repulsed by the parachutists defending Cassino. The French, however, are still doing well. On their left they take Castelforte and push on. In the center Monte Maio is captured and on their right they reach north to the Liri at Sant'Appollinaire.
Eastern Front The campaign in the Crimea is over. Altogether 130,000 Germans and Rumanians have been evacuated by sea and another 21,500 by air since 12 April but a further 78,000 have been killed or captured and many of those evacuated have been wounded.

14 MAY 1944
Italy The French break into the Ausente Valley, take Ausonia and push on over the Aurunci Mountains toward the next German line, hoping to break into it before the Germans can occupy it in strength. Their advance helps the American forces on their left to speed their own move forward against the German 94th Division.

15 MAY 1944
Italy The German position on the Gustav line is beginning to collapse. The French push on once more to take San Giorgio and farther north in the Liri Valley the British reach Pignaturo. The Canadian Corps is put in to the line to try to exploit this advance.

16 MAY 1944
Italy Of the five attacking Allied Corps only the Poles are still meeting really stubborn defense at Cassino. In the Liri Valley the British and Canadians are pushing toward Pontecorvo and Piumarola aiming later to reach Highway 6. The Americans on the coast are still doing well but the best gains are being made by the French who take Monte Petrella and advance on Monte

Revole as well as driving forward in other sectors.

New Guinea American units move on from Hollandia toward Wadke Island. The Hollandia operation has been a notable success. The local Japanese garrison has been quickly and cheaply neutralized and many more Japanese have been cut off to the east. There is hard fighting to come, however.

17 MAY 1944

Italy Although Kesselring, commanding Army Group C, has given Vietinghoff three more divisions they have been unable to halt the continued Allied progress in the Liri Valley and to the south. This continues with the capture of Piumarolo, Monte Faggeta, Esperia and Formia. Even near Cassino there are renewed Polish attacks which manage to take Colle Sant'Angelo. Although the French advance, the most threatening, is held up beyond Esperia especially near Monte d'Oro, the Germans decide on a general retreat.

Burma Merrill's Marauders help the Chinese forces to capture Myitkyina airfield.

New Guinea US forces are landed on Insumarai Island and on the mainland at Arare nearby. Artillery is quickly sent ashore to provide fire support for the next landings on 18 May. Admirals Crutchley and Berkey lead the cruisers and destroyers which give cover.

Indian Ocean The oil installations at Surabaya on Java are attacked by aircraft from the carriers *Illustrious* and *Saratoga*. The carriers are escorted by the battleships of Admiral Sommerville's Eastern Fleet, designated TF 65 for the occasion (the carriers are TF 66). The damage inflicted is not in fact as great as the attackers believe. One Japanese freighter is sunk and 12 aircraft are destroyed on the ground. Of the 85 attacking planes only one is lost. During the night there is a further attack by land based Liberator bombers.

18 MAY 1944

Mediterranean In sinking a ship from the convoy HA-43, *U.453* records the last success by a German submarine in the Mediterranean.

German Command Berlin announces that Field Marshal von Rundstedt is to be Commander in Chief West with Field Marshals Rommel and Blaskowitz his subordinates at Army Groups B and G in the north and south respectively. This arrangement is by no means ideal as Rommel and Rundstedt quickly develop diverging views on the necessary strategy and both put them to Hitler, who establishes a poor compromise.

Italy The Monte Cassino abbey is finally occupied by Allied forces as the Germans withdraw. In the Liri Valley the Canadian I Corps is now up to the Senger line before Pontecorvo. On their left the French, and on the coast the Americans, are meeting equally solid opposition.

New Guinea The main body of the 163rd Infantry Regiment (General Doe) is landed on Insoemar Island and quickly advances to take Wadke airfield.

Admiralty Islands The Sixth Army announces that the campaign is over. The Americans have lost 1400 dead and wounded, the Japanese 3820 dead and 75 prisoners.

19 MAY 1944

New Guinea On Insoemar the remnants of the Japanese forces retire to the northeast corner.

Italy The US forces take Gasta Itri and Monte Grande nearby while on their right the French push forward almost to Pico and begin fighting for Campodimele.

19–20 MAY 1944

Marcus Island On both days heavy air attacks are put in by the carriers *Essex*, *Wasp* and *San Jacinto* of Admiral Montgomery's TG 58.2.

20 MAY 1944

Poland, Resistance A V2 on test lands near the River Bug about 80 miles east of Warsaw. Polish resistance workers get to it before the Germans and hide and dismantle it. On the night of 25 July parts are flown out by Dakota and are in London seven weeks before the first V2 lands. Nothing effective can be done with this knowledge but it is an astonishing resistance achievement nonetheless.

Italy The French, Canadians and Poles assault the Senger line at Pico, Pontecorvo and Piedimonte San Germano respectively.

New Guinea The battle for Wadke is over with the small Japanese garrison being wiped out. There is a minor Japanese attack near Arare on the mainland.

21 MAY 1944

Italy A small force is sent by sea from Gaeta to Sperlonga and lands without difficulty. The US forces also take Fondi and the French Campodimele. In the Liri Valley and around Pico, the German opposition is stronger but the Allies are bringing forces forward for another blow.

New Guinea The beachhead at Arare is reinforced and offshore at Wadke the airfield is repaired and reopened by US engineers.

CHRONOLOGY

22 MAY 1944

Italy Keyes' II US Corps continues to push north along the coast and by Route 7. The French forces take Pico. Inland the fighting in the Liri Valley is still fierce.

Sulu Sea A US submarine reports the concentration of the Japanese Fleet around Tawitawi and in operations over the next two or three weeks various destroyers and tankers are sunk.

New Guinea The American positions around Aitape come under new and unexpected attacks and some withdrawals are made.

Wake Island A strong US destroyer force bombards the island. The same units are in action against Mili in the Marshalls on 26 May.

23 MAY 1944

Italy The Anzio beachhead bursts into new activity with a fierce bombardment followed by an attack on Cisterna by three divisions of US VI Corps. The German defense is strong and casualties are heavy but some gains are made. Advance guards of US II Corps reach Terracina while inland both the French and Canadians break into the Senger Line. The Canadian attack has been well prepared and by the end of the day they have broken through.

New Guinea The US forces meet heavy resistance on trying to advance west from Arare toward Sarmi. At Aitape the Japanese continue to force slight withdrawals.

Wake Island The destroyer bombardment of the previous day is followed up by heavy air attacks from the carriers of Montgomery's TG 58.2.

24 MAY 1944

Italy The attacks of Fifth and Eighth Armies continue. The Canadians take Pontecorvo and to the north their 5th Armored Division reaches the River Melfa. Terracina is occupied by II US Corps despite resistance from 29th Panzer Grenadier Division. At Anzio the attacks also continue. Cisterna is still held by the Germans but a little to the south Route 7 is reached near Latina. Hitler authorizes Kesselring to withdraw to the Caesar Line.

Burma There are strong counterattacks by units of the Japanese 18th Division south of Myitkyina.

25 MAY 1944

Italy Patrols of the II US Corps link up with units of VI Corps from Anzio. The main advance of VI Corps takes Cisterna and Cori. The obvious next move from here is toward Velletri and Valmontone and if this is executed quickly

most of the German Tenth Army may be cut off. Kesselring therefore sends his only remaining reserve, the Hermann Goering Division, to join the forces in this sector. General Clark, commanding Fifth Army, only keeps one division moving forward in this sector and despite direct orders from Alexander puts his principal effort into capturing the glory of freeing Rome. In the Liri Valley the battle is still going well for the Allies with Monte Cairo, Piedimonte and Aquino all being taken. Because of Clark's errors however, Senger is able to prepare a strong resistance around Arce and Ceprano which will enable his forces to pull back to the Caesar Line and even for a time look like making a stand.

New Guinea The US forces advancing from Arare cross the Tirfoam River after a brisk engagement.

Yugoslavia, Resistance A small German paratroop force is dropped at Tito's headquarters at Drvar in Bosnia. Tito and Major Randolph Churchill who is with him as a liaison officer both have a narrow escape.

26 MAY 1944

Italy The Allied advance continues despite stiffer German resistance. McCreery's X Corps takes Roccasecca, the Canadians take San Giovanni, and on their left the II US Corps reaches Priverno. At Anzio the main thrust of VI Corps makes some progress toward Lanuvio but 1st Armored Division cannot make much toward Velletri. The 3rd Division is held after taking Artena and is unable to reach Valmontono.

27 MAY 1944

Italy Artena is held by 3rd Division despite German counterattacks. In the Liri Valley Canadian units attack Ceprano and the British 6th Armored Division moves toward Arce.

New Guinea US Forces land on Biak Island. There is the usual preliminary bombardment before the men of 41st Infantry Division (General Fuller) land near Bosnek. At first there is little resistance but this is misleading, for the Japanese garrison at 11,000 men (Colonel Kuzume) is little weaker than the attack force. The close escort for the landing ships is provided by cruisers and destroyers led by Admiral Fechteler and as in the other landings on the north coast Crutchley and Berkey are in support. Elsewhere on the island the US troops make a little ground in their advance toward Sarmi.

28 MAY 1944

Italy Ceprano is taken by the Canadians. Here

and on all the other sectors the fighting remains fierce with the Allies everywhere attempting to push forward but in fact making few gains. Apart from rearguards the German XIV Panzer and LI Mountain Corps are falling back to the Caesar Line because of the threat to their rear posed by the Anzio forces.

New Guinea On Biak the Americans begin to extend their perimeter but one battalion is surprised by a fierce Japanese attack near Mokmer village and takes heavy losses. The US forces in that sector pull back. Similarly Japanese attacks cause retreats near Arare. General MacArthur is confident enough, however, to announce that strategically the campaign in New Guinea is over although some hard fighting is still to be done.

29 MAY 1944

Atlantic The US escort carrier *Block Island* is sunk by *U.549* which also sinks a destroyer in the same engagement before being hunted down.

Italy At Anzio Allied attacks by British and American units take Campoleone and Carroceto but here and near Lanuvio they are later held. The Canadians begin to advance up Route 6 from Caprano toward Frosinone.

New Guinea Both at Biak and at Arare the American beachheads come under heavy pressure. At Biak Japanese tanks are used to force back the 162nd Regiment almost to its landing ground.

30 MAY 1944

Italy Arce is taken by British troops of Eighth Army after a stubborn battle. In the Anzio sector the US forces are nearing the important position at Velletri.

Eastern Front In the first flurry of summer activity the Germans throw in powerful attacks against Konev's forces near Jassy.

31 MAY 1944

Italy The Canadians take Frosinone and X Corps takes Sora. In the Anzio sector Velletri and Monte Artemiso nearby fall to the US 36th Division while other units of VI Corps are attacking round Albano. By the capture of Velletri a gap is torn in the Caesar Line.

New Guinea The Americans narrow down their holdings near Arare. At all their beachheads on the north coast there is considerable skirmishing. To the east Australian troops take Bunabum.

JUNE 1944

Europe, Air Operations The Allied effort is directed mostly at tactical targets in very many fairly small raids. RAF Bomber Command drops 56,000 tons and the 25,600 sorties flown by Eighth Air Force add nearly as much. Light and medium forces contribute another 25,000 tons. A proportion of the heavy bomber raids are against strategic targets mostly connected with oil production. Objectives include Gelsenkirchen, Bohlen, Poolitz and others in Hungary and Yugoslavia. The Fifteenth Air Force from Italy joins these raids as well as attacking communications targets in southeastern Europe like Nish, Giurgiu and Brod. Railways in north Italy are also hit. German production of aviation fuel falls to one-third of the May figure as a consequence of the raids on oil producing centers. The first Me 262 jet fighters enter operational service with the Luftwaffe. Although these are vastly superior to all the Allied designs there will never be enough of them to cause any significant damage. They will be hindered by the continuing fall in fuel production and by attacks on the bases from which they operate.

Pacific, Air Operations The main targets are in the Marianas and Carolines. The First Superfortress raid on the Japanese mainland is on 15 June.

1 JUNE 1944

Italy Exploiting the success of 36th Division the US II and VI Corps begin to drive toward Rome at full strength attacking through the Alban Hills and toward Albano and Valmonte on either side. Since the Caesar Line has now been breached by these advances, Kesselring orders a fighting withdrawal north of Rome. The German forces still fight skillfully to delay the Americans, however.

Eastern Front Although the German pressure near Jassy is maintained Russian counterattacks are now succeeding in retaking and holding the disputed ground.

Mediterranean A German supply convoy bound for Crete from the Greek mainland is heavily attacked by RAF planes and several ships sunk. After this the Germans only sail occasional ships to the island.

Overlord The first code message, giving a general warning to the French resistance that invasion is imminent, is transmitted by the BBC in the evening. The Germans understand the rough significance of this verse (part of a poem by Verlaine) and alert some of their units.

New Guinea On Biak the American forces resume the offensive. They mount a strong tank and infantry attack and succeed in advancing despite sharp Japanese counterattacks. Around

Aitape on the mainland the Japanese are still attacking and forcing the Americans to contract their beachhead.

2 JUNE 1944

France, Politics The French Committee of National Liberation restyles itself the Provisional Government of the French Republic.

Italy As Kesselring's forces gradually pull back the Allies are able to advance all along the front. The US forces reach Route 6 at Valmontone, which they take, and also in other sectors. They also make good progress in the Alban Hills.

New Guinea The fighting on Biak continues. The US 186th Infantry Regiment is doing the bulk of the attacking supported by the 162nd. The objective is to reach and capture the airfields in the center of the island plateau. These airfields have been used as the base for attacks on Wadke.

Burma The final siege of Myitkyina begins.

3 JUNE 1944

New Guinea There are various Japanese attempts to bring reinforcements to Biak between now and June 12 but all are abortive. On Biak the US forces again advance. The 162nd Regiment meets heavy resistance.

Italy The US forces advancing on Rome take Albano and Frascati. Other American and French units move forward along Route 6. The Canadians to the southeast take Anagni. The German forces have already largely abandoned Rome, respecting its status as an 'open city' in return for a temporary truce with local resistance fighters.

4 JUNE 1944

Italy In the evening units of the US 88th Division enter Rome.

Above: Allied troops enter Rome.

Overlord The convoys for the invasion are already at sea but because of bad weather expected on 5 June they turn back to wait. Late in the evening Eisenhower decides, after consulting with the meteorological staff, that the invasion can take place on 6 June when a break in the weather is expected. It has long been decided that the first landings must be at dawn when there is a low tide. This should allow the engineering teams to work their way up the beach to the high-water mark clearing visible obstacles. These tidal conditions only occur on about three days every fortnight. Also desirable is for the moon to rise late to aid the airborne troops. These conditions pertain on 5 and 6 June and less ideally 7 June. If the invasion does not take place then the tides will be right about 20 June but the combination of moon and tides not until July. Eisenhower, therefore, has had to take a very difficult decision because any postponement would be bound to affect the troops morale; to give the Germans more time to improve their defenses; to upset relations with the Russians; and almost certainly jeopardize the security of the plan (for one thing the deception operation has been scheduled in line with the 5 June date).

The bad weather has helped in putting the Germans off their guard. Rommel has decided to take the opportunity to go to Germany for his wife's birthday on 6 June and to try to persuade Hitler to adopt his strategic ideas which include, among other things, strengthening the Normandy defenses. Other more junior commanders are also away from their posts – many at a training exercise in Brittany.

5 JUNE 1944

Italy The Allied forces make their triumphal entry into Rome and push on beyond in pursuit of the retreating Germans. There are problems of traffic congestion on the few good roads which prevent the Allied forces using their full strength. As usual the German retreat is accompanied by skillful rearguard actions and demolitions.

New Guinea On Biak the 162nd Regiment and 186th Regiment both continue to advance breaking down pockets of Japanese resistance. Near Aitape the Americans evacuate one of their outlying beachheads because of the Japanese attacks. Although the Japanese seem to be doing well here, they are taking dreadful losses.

Overlord The second message warning that the invasion is imminent is sent to the French Resistance. Again the Germans note its significance but in a glaring omission the Seventh Army in Normandy is not alerted. Just before midnight the airborne troops are sent on their way from their various airfields in southern England. The landing ships are, of course, already nearing France.

Burma At Kohima an outflanking attack at last forces the Japanese off the Aradura Spur and into retreat. It still remains to clear the road to Imphal.

6 JUNE 1944
D-DAY
The Allied Plans and Preparations
Briefly the Allies intend to land units of four army corps and three airborne divisions on the beaches of Normandy between Caen and Valognes. Normandy has been selected for a number of reasons. The topography of the

Above: The airborne landings were a vital part of the Allied plan at D-Day.

beaches and the area just inland is favorable. Normandy is within fighter range of southern England and is convenient for all the ports on the south coast. It is a less obvious choice than the Pas de Calais and is, therefore, less well defended.

The preparations have been enormous in scale and elaboration. There are nearly 3,000,000 men under Eisenhower's command and a mass of vehicles and stores have been accumulated. Not the least important items of equipment are the various parts of the *Mulberry* Harbors. There are old ships, assorted huge blocks of concrete and steel and all the metal roadways necessary to turn these into great artificial ports as soon as they are sunk off the beaches. This obviates the need to plan to seize a port as a first priority. All the ports are of course heavily defended, as the Dieppe experience has proved. The undertaking for the construction of the parts of the Mulberries (there are two – one British and one American) is so vast that it has absorbed a considerable proportion of the British war-production effort for several months. All the parts have been made in Britain because of their size and unwieldiness. The British have also produced a range of specially modified tanks and other armored vehicles mainly to help their engineers clear beach obstacles under fire. These 'Funnies' are organized as part of the 79th Armored Division which has been led and trained by General Hobart, one of the pioneers of tank warfare. All these devices are offered to the Americans, but they have chosen to accept only the amphibious tanks. This is a serious error.

As well as the preparations for the actual attack, a considerable effort has been put in to misleading the Germans as to the location of the landings. The main section of the deception plan has been designed to suggest a landing in the Pas de Calais by a fictional First United States Army Group (FUSAG) based in Kent and supposedly commanded by General Patton. At first real formations are based in Kent supposedly as part of this army, and when these transfer to France they are replaced by fictional units behind a screen of false radio traffic and reports from double agents. Some dummy installations, airfields and landing craft are also erected. A similar scheme is run to simulate the presence of a British Fourth Army in Scotland preparing for a descent on Norway. Again a real personality is chosen to command, a British General Thorne. It is essential for these schemes to have real commanders of sufficient stature reported to be in charge. After Patton goes to France he is

succeeded by another senior American General. The FUSAG scheme is a notable success in drawing attention away from Normandy and keeping alive the idea that the real landings might in fact be a feint.

The enormous number of air attacks on targets in France have been carefully orchestrated to avoid giving away the real location of the landings. Thus, destroying the Seine bridges, which has been done, will seem to the Germans to be just as necessary to prevent troops moving from Normandy to the Pas de Calais as the reverse. These and other air attacks have been a considerable success, but the real effect of the air operations is to come after the landing in the prevention of German reinforcements reaching Normandy in full strength or as quickly as might otherwise have been the case. Lorries and other types of 'soft' vehicles are particularly vulnerable.

The German Dispositions

Altogether in France, Belgium and Holland the Germans have 60 divisions including 11 armored. These figures are somewhat misleading, however. About half of the infantry divisions are not equipped for mobile warfare and all are understrength. Some are in France simply to refit after heavy losses on the Eastern Front and are hardly fit for action. To lead them they have, in Supreme Command, Field Marshal Rundstedt and commanding Army Group B in the northern half of the country, Field Marshal Rommel. Blaskowitz commands in the south. The landings will initially be opposed mostly by units of Dollmann's Seventh Army except on the British left flank where part of Salmuth's Fifteenth Army is stationed. However, this chain of command is made almost totally useless by Hitler's interference. As usual he insists on involving himself in even the most immediate tactical decisions. This difficulty is compounded by real doubts about the correct strategy both as to where the attack is going to fall, and how it ought to be met. As to the location both Hitler and Rommel have nursed a belief that Normandy might well be the target. Interestingly once the invasion has come where he predicted Hitler convinces himself that it is a feint. In the work Rommel has done to make the Atlantic Wall defenses a reality the Normandy area has received at least its fair share. The more important problem concerns how the armor reserve should be handled. Rundstedt wishes, in the classic style, to create a strong central reserve which can be used for a grand counterstroke once the focus of the Allied operation has been discerned. Rommel, on the other hand, believes that the invasion must be defeated as near to the beaches as possible and that the reserves should therefore be spread all along the front. He fears that Allied air power will prevent the sort of counterstroke that Rundstedt desires happening sufficiently promptly or in adequate strength. He realizes also that once solidly ashore the Allied material, quantitatively superior, is bound to tell. This belief can only be reinforced by the German intelligence appreciation that the Allies have 87 divisions in Britain, when in fact the total is 52 and only 37 are intended for France.

Both Rommel and Rundstedt put their views to Hitler and his decision gives a compromise result fatal to both schemes. He allows Rommel some of his way by releasing a few divisions from the reserve but not the three Panzer Divisions for Normandy that Rommel wants among his other plans. Rundstedt is left with an inadequate force for his strategic reserve, and to make matters worse he cannot call on it without permission from higher authority at OKW which in practice means Hitler.

The Forces Deployed

On the ground in Normandy the Germans have six infantry divisions. Two, 322nd and 716th, are wholly deployed on the beaches concerned along with parts of two more, 709th and 711th (from Fifteenth Army). In reserve on the left there is 91st Division and a parachute regiment and on the right, around Caen, 21st Panzer Division. Three more panzer divisions are within range farther inland but they are part of the OKW reserve and cannot be called in without permission. The fixed defenses are nowhere as formidable as has been planned because of shortages of transport, materials, especially concrete, labor, mines and other explosives. Partly because of these shortages and partly because of his belief that the invasion must be beaten on the beaches, Rommel has largely demolished what there was of a second defense line a little inland to use the materials for the beach defenses. This can only make the initial landings more crucial. The Allied air attacks have contributed to the difficulties with materials and construction.

At sea, the German Commander in Chief West, Admiral Krancke, is dreadfully over-matched. When in port his ships come under constant air attack and at sea are harried equally continuously. He has two large and two small destroyers, 31 motor torpedo boats and about 200 smaller vessels in the Channel. He has about 15 submarines under his direct command. In the air the situation is at least as bad. Sperrle's Third Air Fleet has less than 200 operational aircraft

from a paper strength of only perhaps twice that. Many of the pilots are almost complete novices. The Luftwaffe still absorbs a disproportionate fraction of the German manpower and by edict of Goering has only rarely been used to help in, for example, the construction of defenses. The Luftwaffe troops, several divisions, are not fully integrated in the army command structure. An indication of the German weakness in the air is that only one Allied aircraft is shot down by an enemy plane on 6 June. When the Allied plan is in turn examined, the list of participating units is massive. The naval forces include two battleships, two monitors, 23 cruisers, 105 destroyers and 1076 other warships (minesweepers and antisubmarine vessels especially) as well as 2700 merchant ships and 2500 landing craft. In the air 3500 heavy bombers, 1700 medium and light bombers, 5500 fighters and 2400 transport aircraft are employed. Despite this massive air and naval contribution the actual landing forces are by no means overwhelming in strength when compared to the German garrison in Normandy. There are three airborne divisions and five infantry divisions landed in the first waves as well as various independent Commando and Ranger units and, in the British and Canadian sector, three armored brigades. The principal limiting factor is the number of landing craft available. Partly because of the British commitment to produce *Mulberry*, almost all of the recent production of landing craft has been in the United States under the control of the US Navy. Admiral King has been most reluctant to release landing craft to the European theater and he still has a many times greater number in the Pacific. Altogether there are 21 American convoys and 38 British and Canadian.

The Airborne Landings

The two US airborne divisions, 101st and 82nd, begin to land shortly after midnight inland from the western flank beach, *Utah*. Just inland from *Utah* the ground is marshy and 101st Division therefore has the task of taking the exits on the various causeways through this area. The 82nd are to land somewhat farther inland and clear ground on either side of the Merderet between St Mère Eglise and Pont l'Abbé. Largely because of the inexperience of many of the pilots the men of both divisions are dropped in widely scattered groups. At dawn, for example, 101st Division only has 1100 men under command out of 6600. Groups of perhaps 50 men are attempting tasks planned for battalions. However, this scattering proves extremely confusing for the German defenders. By a stroke of luck the commander of the 91st Division is ambushed and killed by one such group. This Division, left leaderless, is intended by the Germans to deal with an airborne attack and has been specially trained. In a multitude of small gallant and successful actions the capture of St Mère Eglise stands out.

On the left, eastern, flank of the attack only one division, the British 6th Airborne, can be committed because of lack of aircraft. They have three main tasks. They are to take positions holding various crossings of the Orne and the Caen Canal between that town and Ouistreham. The large battery at Merville is to be stormed and finally various bridges over the Dives are to be blown up to protect the flank. Although, as on the opposite flank, many of the troops are not landed in the correct place, the drops are fairly good and all the objectives are achieved and where necessary held until reinforcements fight their way off the beaches. Even better, a large part of 21st Panzer Division is first attracted by the parachute landings and then held by the threat of a major break out from the beaches. They are unable to follow orders to move against *Omaha*.

Utah

The west flank landing beach is allocated to General Collins VII US Corps. The naval force is commanded by Admiral Moon and includes eight attack convoys and, for bombardment, a battleship, a monitor, five cruisers, and a dozen destroyers. The assault is carried out by the US 4th Infantry Division (General Barton). There are some problems with rough seas which are to some extent offset by a commander of tank landing craft in launching his amphibious cargo closer inshore than the normal American

practice. (The British operate differently.) The landings almost all take place by mistake on the southern sector of the beach and there is little resistance. The troops are quickly advancing inland held up mostly by the marshy ground. By the end of the day 23,250 men have gone ashore at *Utah* – an almost unqualified success. Less than 200 have died.

Omaha

The *Omaha* beach runs from Pointe de la Percee to St Honorine and has been allocated to General Gerow's US V Corps, like VII Corps from Bradley's First Army. The naval force is led by Admiral Hall with troops from 1st and 29th Infantry Divisions in the eight initial convoys. There are also two battleships, three cruisers and 11 destroyers to provide a preliminary bombardment which will be amplified by air attacks and rocket and gun fire from the landing craft. The terrain is not at all easy, with low hills just inland from the beaches interspersed with heavily defended gullies. The assault gets off to a poor start. The infantry, engineers and artillery are loaded into the landing craft and DUKWs fully 10 miles offshore in rough seas again contrary to British advice and practice. Some of the amphibious tanks are launched nearly four miles offshore and are swamped. Of the 446 Liberator bombers sent to attack only 329 arrive and most release their bombs too far inland. The rocket craft, designed to provide a final curtain of fire, are largely aiming short. As soon as the various barrages lift the return fire begins to come in and immediately there are heavy casualties. When the first wave reaches the beach they are totally

Above: Infantry landing craft at Omaha beach where Allied D-Day casualties were heaviest.

disorganized. Many of the troops are in the wrong sectors. The engineers have suffered as heavily as any in the run in and lack the specialized armor used by the British to get protection from the defensive fire while clearing the obstacles. At first the assault is held almost exactly at the water's edge, but as the tide comes in and with it subsequent waves of troops, the slow advance begins with certain individual leaders gradually inspiring forward momentum. This, combined with a renewed bombardment by destroyers at very short range against individual strongpoints, is the story for the rest of the day. By nightfall there are 34,250 Americans ashore at *Omaha* but none are as far as one mile off the beach. More than 1000 are dead and many more wounded but, although it is not clear at the time, they have broken the hard crust and there is for the moment easier going ahead.

Gold
This beach, from Arromanches to La Rivière, is the landing ground for the British 50th Infantry Division and the 8th Armored Brigade of Bucknall's XXX Corps. The transports and warships – 13 convoys and four cruisers and 13 destroyers – are led by Commodore Douglas-Pennant. Because of the tide the British landings here and to the east take place later than the Americans and there is therefore no possibility of meeting a startled enemy. Arromanches, La Rivière and Le Hamel especially are all heavily defended and fortified and many of the defending guns in these and other strongpoints survive the preliminary bombardment. The landings west of Le Hamel suffer most seriously, but even here the beaches are quickly cleared with the help of Hobart's armor. Because of the sea conditions the amphibious tanks are held back and landed a little later than planned directly on to solid ground. The advance inland is fairly rapid but the designated objectives of Bayeux and the road to Caen are not reached. Altogether 25,000 men are landed and about 500 are killed.

Juno
This beach runs from La Rivière to St Aubin. The landing force is 3rd Canadian Infantry Division and 2nd Canadian Armored Brigade which, like the *Sword* forces, are from General Crocker's I Corps. The naval group is led by Commodore Oliver including 13 convoys, 2 cruisers and 12 destroyers. The landings here are a little later than planned and partly because the tide has therefore come in somewhat the underwater obstacles are particularly troublesome. Here the amphibious tanks are launched sensibly within 1000 yards of the shore and as elsewhere

play an important part in silencing strongpoints. The specialized armor is also prominent. Once off the beach tanks and infantry quickly push inland reaching for Breteville and Caen. Here also there are traffic jams on the beaches. On the first day 21,400 go ashore.

Sword
The first landings on *Sword* are by the British 3rd Infantry Division, 27th Armored Brigade and several Marine and Commando units all under General Crocker's I Corps. The beach runs from Lion sur Mer to the Orne estuary. The naval force is led by Admiral Talbot and as well as the eight assault convoys there are two battleships, one monitor, five cruisers and 13 destroyers. Much of this strength would have been directed at the Merville battery if the paratroops had not succeeded in their mission. Again the amphibious tanks are launched rather too far out but they are well handled and most reach the shore. The 'Funnies' are put ashore safely also. Before 1000 hours most of the exits from the beach have been cleared after a sharp struggle. Commando units hurry inland to aid the paratroops along the Orne but the regular infantry are more cautious against the German resistance at Hermanville and along the Périers Ridge. This problem is compounded by the growing congestion on the beach with the supporting tanks unable to move forward. By late afternoon, however, Biéville has been reached when the counterattack of 21st Panzer comes in. It is beaten off here but there is nothing to stop it driving to the sea between *Sword* and *Juno*. It is too weak to achieve much there, however. By nightfall the British have 28,850 men ashore here and although the first day's objectives have not been reached the Orne bridges have been seized. It will take several weeks to take Caen and attain these first day objectives but there is no question of the solidity of this beachhead.

Overall the first day of the Overlord Operation has been a qualified success for the Allies. They have almost 150,000 men ashore and their aircraft are preventing the Germans having any chance of outstripping them in the buildup of forces in Normandy. If this can be maintained there can be only one result later if not sooner.

Italy French troops complete the capture of Tivoli. General Lemelsen becomes commander of the German Fourteenth Army in place of Mackensen. The recent Allied attacks have practically destroyed four German infantry divisions and the six mobile units have also been hard hit.

New Guinea On Biak the 186th Infantry

prepares for an attack to take Mokmer Airfield while the 162nd Regiment is engaged near Ibdi.

7 JUNE 1944

Italy The Americans take Bracciano and Civitavecchia. The docks there are sufficiently serviceable to be put into use immediately. The South African 6th Armored Division takes Civita Castellana and pushes on up the road to Orvieto. Other units of Eighth Army enter Subiaco.

Western Front Although the Allies have not reached the objectives set for the first day they are everywhere solidly established ashore. The priority is obviously to link up the four beachheads (*Gold* and *Juno* are joined already) and to expand inland to create room for the reinforcements now beginning to arrive. The *Utah* force, VII Corps, tries to link up with the scattered paratroop contingents and to advance toward Carentan and Montebourg. The V Corps from *Omaha* makes a general advance hoping to reach Isigny and Bayeux. They get as far as attacking Formigny. From *Gold* the British 50th Infantry Division takes Bayeux and other units cut the Caen–Bayeux road. Already the pattern for the battle is being established for the weeks to come.

The German reserves are being drawn and held committed by the British advance toward and on either side of Caen. This gives the Americans at *Omaha* especially a welcome respite to consolidate and expand. This is the plan that the Allied Commanders and particularly Montgomery had hoped to work to.

New Guinea The American forces on Biak capture the Mokmer Airfield. Elsewhere on the island the fighting is also fierce with various small groups of Japanese resisting strongly.

8 JUNE 1944

Western Front The second wave of Allied troops is now largely ashore. The US 4th Division (VII Corps) begins the advance toward Cherbourg and there is fierce fighting near Azeville. Units of V Corps take Isigny but cannot yet link with the *Utah* landings. With the capture of Port-en-Bessin by British Marines the link between *Omaha* and *Gold* is completed.

Italy The Allied advance continues in all sectors, but is gradually being slowed down by the German rearguards.

New Guinea On Biak the fighting around Mokmer continues in typical style with the Americans striving with the aid of heavy weapons to winkle the Japanese out of cave positions. On the mainland at Aitape the Americans push forward once more. A Japanese

attempt to bring reinforcements to Biak is intercepted and turned back after a sharp action with Admiral Crutchley's cruiser squadron.

9 JUNE 1944

Italy, Politics Marshal Badoglio resigns and Ivanoe Bonomi is invited to form a new government. The Cabinet now includes Count Sforza, Professor Croce and the Communist leader, Togliatti.

France In VII Corps' advance toward Cherbourg the German strongpoint at Azeville is taken. Other VII Corps attacks move west and toward Carentan. The troops from *Omaha* take Trévières and to the east around Caen the British and Canadian forces are in heavy action with the growing German reserves. Allied aircraft are now operating from landing grounds in France.

Italy US forces take Tarquinia, Viterbo and Vetrella. British units are advancing toward Terni and Orvieto. A small amphibious force lands at Santo Stefano. There are important reorganizations of the Allied forces. The divisions of the British X and XIII Corps are switched around and various American units, mostly of VI Corps, are pulled out of the line entirely in preparation for the invasion of the south of France.

10 JUNE 1944

Western Front The Utah and Omaha beachheads are linked up by the advance of the US 2nd Armored Division. The 101st Airborne Division is still fighting around Carentan. In the British sector the 7th Armored Division and the German *Panzerlehr* Division are heavily engaged near Tilly-sur-Seulles. General Montgomery establishes his headquarters in France.

Italy On the Adriatic coast Pescara and Chieti are taken by units of Keightley's V Corps. Inland the New Zealand Division enters Avezzano but fighting there continues.

10–13 JUNE 1944

Indian Ocean In a diversionary operation for the coming American attacks on the Marianas the British fleet carrier *Illustrious* and the escort carrier *Atheling* raid Sabang.

Eastern Front Cherepanov's Twenty-third Army begins attacks against the Finnish positions on the Karelian Isthmus. As always now in any Soviet operation the artillery support is massive. Terijoki and Yalkena are quickly taken.

11 JUNE 1944

Marianas Admiral Mitscher's TF 58 with nine

fleet and six light carriers sends fighter strikes against Saipan, Tinian and the other islands in the group. Thirty-six Japanese planes are shot down. The seven battleships of Admiral Lee's TG 58.7 provide close escort. Japanese shipping also comes under attack from TG 58.4. Three minor warships and 30,000 tons of merchant shipping are sunk by the aircraft. The operations continue. Admiral Spruance, in overall command of the Marianas campaign, is present on board the cruiser *Indianapolis*.

Western Front The main engagements are again at Carentan and Tilly. Carentan is taken by the US forces. At Tilly and elsewhere in the British sector the German resistance is becoming particularly strong. The US forces also take Lison.

Italy French troops capture Montefiascone, west of Viterbo. Farther inland British units are engaged near Cantalupo and Bagnoregio.

Europe, Air Operations The Rumanian airfield at Focsani is raided by planes from Fifteenth Air Force from Italy. After bombing the planes fly on to Russia. This is the first 'shuttle' raid on this pattern.

12 JUNE 1944

Western Front The US 4th Division is involved in a series of actions against German strongpoints at Montebourg, Crisbecq and near Azeville. The Germans only hold at Montebourg. Other units of VII Corps are fighting their way across the Cotentin Peninsula and southwest from Carentan. V Corps is helping in these attacks as well as advancing toward St Lô. In this sector Caumont is taken and the Foret de Cerisy and the Bayeux road reached.

The third wave of divisions is now largely ashore. At this stage there are 326,000 men, 104,000 tons of supplies and 54,000 vehicles from the Allied armies in France.

Italy In the Adriatic sector Popoli is reached by the British advance.

12–13 JUNE 1944

Marianas The operations of the US carriers go on. Three groups continue to attack Tinian and Saipan while the other concentrates on Guam. In response to these assaults the Japanese Fleets sail from Tawitawi and Batjan. The main force from Tawitawi is quickly sighted and reported by an American submarine. Altogether there are five fleet carriers, two light carriers and two seaplane carriers. In support there are five battleships and numerous cruisers and destroyers. In every department, therefore, they are outmatched by TF 58. Admiral Kurita leads

the Van Force which includes the two seaplane carriers, one light carrier and four of the battleships. Admiral Ozawa leads the main force with the remainder of the ships. The plan for their operation, devised by the Commander in Chief, Admiral Toyoda, intends to cope with their inferiority by relying on the help of land based aircraft from the Marianas and other nearby groups. Unfortunately from the Japanese point of view, the recent and present operations of the American carriers have drastically reduced these land based forces but the local commanders have left their superiors in ignorance of this when such knowledge will in fact prove vital in the coming battle.

13 JUNE 1944

V-Weapons The first V1 Flying Bomb lands in England. In the initial salvo 10 are fired of which four cross the Channel successfully. Only one lands in London, killing six civilians.

Kuriles Admiral Small leads a cruiser and destroyer group to bombard the Japanese on Matsuwa. The sortie is repeated on 26 June this time against Paramushiro.

Western Front After being switched to the far right of XXX Corps 7th Armored Division makes a rapid advance to Villers Bocage but a German counterattack quickly throws them back. There is also a fierce attack by 17th Panzer to retake Carentan which is only held off with difficulty. Elsewhere the US forces make some progress toward St Lô and in the Cotentin they take Pont l'Abbé.

Italy South African troops from Eighth Army take Bagnoregio just east of Lake Bolsena and other units take Narni between Orte and Terni.

New Guinea On Biak the Japanese cave positions in the east of the island are being gradually worn down. American aircraft are now operating from Mokmer Airfield.

14 JUNE 1944

Western Front A third US Corps, XIX, becomes operational in the sector between V and VII Corps. General de Gaulle visits the beachhead and takes measures to prepare for the restoration of French civil government in the captured territory.

Italy Orvieto, Terni and Todi all fall to units of Eighth Army. The US IV Corps on the west coast also pushes forward.

British Command The appointment is announced in London of Admiral Moore to be Commander of the British Home Fleet.

Marianas The preliminary bombardments for the invasion of Saipan and Tinian are made.

CHRONOLOGY

The two bombardment groups are commanded by Admirals Ainsworth and Oldendorf and their squadrons include seven battleships and 11 cruisers. There are eight escort carriers in support. The battleship *California* is hit by defensive fire. There are also intensive minesweeping operations.

14–15 JUNE 1944
Western Front During the night 325 RAF Lancaster bombers attack Le Havre. They sink 35 small naval vessels, a considerable proportion of the remaining German Channel forces.

14–17 JUNE 1944
Battle of the Philippine Sea The main US carrier forces which have been operating against the Marianas spend this period mostly replenishing. Two groups led by Admiral Clark do, however, attack Iwo Jima, Chichi Jima and Haha Jima on 15 and 16 June. By 17 all are on their way to rendezvous to the west of the Marianas. The Japanese carriers are sighted on 15 June on their way through the San Bernardino Strait while some of their battleships are also seen east of Mindanao. On 16–17 June the Japanese also link up and refuel and are sighted twice more. The Americans are therefore well informed as to the general Japanese intentions.

15 JUNE 1944
Western Front In the Cotentin the US VIII Corps becomes operational. Units of VII Corps take Quineville.
New Guinea On Biak there is a considerable but unsuccessful Japanese counterattack and on the mainland farther east, Australian troops occupy Hansa Bay.
Eastern Front The Finnish IV Corps withdraws, under pressure from the Soviet Twenty-first and Fifty-ninth Armies, to positions before Viipuri.
Far East, Air Operations Superfortress bombers from Twentieth Air Force in China are sent to bomb the Japanese homeland. Yawatta on Kyushu is attacked. This is the first such raid.
Marianas While the heavy ships of TF 52 keep shelling the main phase of the Saipan landings, Operation *Forager*, gets under way. Admiral Turner is in command of the support ships as well as the landing vessels and General H M Smith leads the V Amphibious Corps. Altogether there are 67,500 men in the land force mostly from the 2nd and 4th Marine Divisions (Watson and Schmidt). The defending forces come from both the Japanese Army and Navy. General Saito commands the reinforced 43rd

Above: On Saipan, Marines throw grenades.

Infantry Division and Admiral Nagumo leads the naval contingents, in all perhaps 30,000 men.

After three hours of air and naval bombardment the attacks go in north and south of Afetna Point. The landings are farther apart than has been intended and the fierce Japanese resistance prevents the beachheads being linked up. The Japanese artillery is especially destructive of the landing craft. The Marines do get well ashore during the day and by night they beat off the usual counterattacks.

15–16 JUNE 1944
Europe, Air Operations Bomber Command is again active over the Channel ports. This time 300 Lancasters attack Boulogne, sinking 14 small warships as well as other craft.

16 JUNE 1944
Western Front In the Cotentin the US forces advancing toward the west coast fight their way across the River Douvre and capture St Saveur after a fierce struggle. In other sectors all the Allied forces continue to press forward. King George VI visits the forces.
Italy Troops from the British X Corps take Spoleto and push on to enter Spoligno as well. On the west side American units take Grosseto.
Marianas Admiral Ainsworth's battleship squadron shells Guam but the Guam invasion is deferred because of the advent of the Japanese Fleet. On Saipan the two Marine Divisions succeed in linking their positions by taking Charan Karoa and Point Afetna. There is much artillery counterbattery work as well as the fighting on the ground.

17 JUNE 1944
Western Front Rommel, Rundstedt and Hitler meet at Soissons. Both Generals want to order

19 JUNE 1944

withdrawals to better positions but Hitler overrules them and going into a rage accuses the German army in France of cowardice and says that the V1s will force Britain out of the war.

In the fighting the 9th Division of the US VII Corps reaches the west coast of the Cotentin north and south of Barneville. The German divisions cut off to the north are refused permission to attempt a break-out.

Italy The French 9th Colonial Division (Senegalese), led by General de Lattre lands on Elba. They complete the occupation of the island on 19 June. On the main front the Polish II Corps replaces the British X Corps on the Adriatic sector. The advance here is now beyond the River Chieti in some places.

Marianas The US 27th Infantry Division is landed on Saipan to reinforce the American advance there.

18 JUNE 1944

Italy In the advance on Perugia units from Eighth Army take Assisi and to the west a French formation enters Radicofani.

Marianas The advance of the 4th Marine Division reaches the west side of Saipan at Magicienne Bay. The Japanese forces are thus separated into two. Part of the 27th Division, on the right of 4th Marines, captures Aslito airfield. Japanese air strikes sink one destroyer and two tankers offshore as well as damaging the escort carrier *Fanshaw Bay*. Much of the air cover and close support has been withdrawn to prepare to take part in the imminent fleet battle.

Battle of the Philippine Sea The US forces make their rendezvous west of the Marianas while the Japanese continue to approach. Late in the evening the Japanese scout planes sight the American fleet. This is the only advantage that the Japanese have and comes about principally because their scout planes have a longer range. The Japanese plan to launch their strike planes early the next day while still at very long range and, after attacking to have them fly on to Guam where the local forces can protect them while they refuel and rearm. Once this is done they can attack again on the return journey. The glaring weakness in this plan is that the air forces on Guam have suffered seriously from American attacks recently and have failed to inform the fleet of this. In fact this shortcoming is less significant than might have been the case as the American ships exact such a heavy price from the first attacks.

Eastern Front The Soviet attacks break through the main Finnish positions on the Mannerheim line and advance toward Viipuri.

19 JUNE 1944

New Guinea Reinforced American attacks go in against the Japanese strongpoints in the west of Biak.

Indian Ocean Port Blair in the Nicobars is attacked by aircraft from the carrier *Illustrious*. Admiral Power is in command and among the supporting heavy units are the *Renown* and the *Richelieu*.

Battle of the Philippine Sea Early in the morning the Japanese search finds TF 58, at the same time remaining unsighted themselves. At once the Japanese carriers launch four waves of attack aircraft numbering altogether 372. In numbers of planes the comparison is overwhelmingly in favor of the Americans – about 950 to 550 (including, for the Japanese, land-based aircraft). The American fleet is well disposed to meet air attack. The battleships are sailing slightly to the west to provide a large AA barrier and with the help of radar there is no question of surprise. Early on the Americans have time to send a strike against Guam further reducing the air force there. When the Japanese attacks are detected coming in fighters are sent out to meet them and the bombers are flown off to clear the carrier decks. The fighters make interceptions up to 50 miles out and shoot down many of the attackers. Still more are shot down by the ships' gunfire and only a handful actually make attacks. The battleship *South Dakota* receives the only damage – one bomb hit. The Japanese lose 240 aircraft and the Americans only 29. More Japanese planes are destroyed before landing on Guam and most of those that survive are hit on the ground – 50 machines in all. The list of Japanese misfortune is completed when, soon after launching their aircraft, the carriers *Taiho* and *Shokaku* are sunk by the US submarines *Cavalla* and *Albacore*. These have been two of the largest and most effective Japanese ships. The Japanese have succumbed so easily that the day is described by the American airmen and gunners as 'The Great Marianas Turkey Shoot.'

Italy British units reach the south and east side of Lake Trasimeno. The next German defense line, the *Albert* line, is just ahead.

Western Front Various American units complete the clearance of Montebourg and Valognes. From now until 22 June there are gales in the Channel which damage both the Mulberry harbors. The American one at Omaha is irreparable but with the help of sections from it the British harbor at Arromanches is made operable. Many landing craft are also sunk or damaged, especially DUKWs.

275

20 JUNE 1944
Western Front The American advance is about five miles from Cherbourg and is becoming embroiled in the outer defenses of the town.
Italy Perugia falls to the British 6th Armored Division.
Eastern Front Viipuri falls to the Red Army.
Battle of the Philippine Sea The Japanese do not realize the extent of their losses and begin to withdraw temporarily to refuel. They believe that most of their aircraft have landed safely on Guam. Mitscher, of course, pursues and in the late afternoon sends 216 planes to attack. They meet only 35 defending fighters and break through to sink the carrier *Hiyo* and damage two others, a battleship and a cruiser. In the action 20 American planes are lost. A further 72 crash in attempting to land back on their carriers in darkness despite the flight decks being bravely lit. A feature of the US operations in this and other engagements is the care taken of the pilots – only 16 flyers and 33 aircrew are not picked up and the story in the rest of the battle is similar. By contrast the Japanese have saved almost none of their pilots and although they still have a significant force of ships they cannot possibly train enough men to fly their aircraft. The pattern of all the previous fleet encounters in the Pacific is thus confirmed.

During the night the Japanese withdraw and are not followed.
New Guinea On Biak there is more heavy

Above: A Hellcat lands on Lexington.

fighting in the western caves area. The airfields and the villages at Borokoe and Sorido are also overrun.
Marianas On Saipan 27th Division has been given the task of clearing the south of the island while 2nd and 4th Marines advance to the north.

21 JUNE 1944
Italy The Eighth Army advance comes up to the *Albert* line at Chiusi to the west of Lake Trasimeno.
Eastern Front General Krutikov's Seventh Army begins a new phase of the Russian attacks against Finland. The advance is now against the Finnish VI Corps between Lake Ladoga and Lake Onega. The Russians also begin to occupy the islands off the Karelian Isthmus. This operation is complete in three or four days.

22 JUNE 1944
Western Front The final battle for Cherbourg begins with a two-hour air raid in which more than 1000 tons of bombs are dropped. Despite this preparation the three attacking divisions of VII Corps still meet fierce resistance.
United States, Home Front President Roosevelt signs the 'GI Bill' which introduces a range of benefits to give returned veterans a start in civilian life.
Denmark, Resistance An important rifle manufacturing plant is wrecked by saboteurs in Copenhagen.
New Guinea After a further series of attacks during the day the Americans believe that they have cleared the Japanese positions in the west of Biak, but during the night there is renewed Japanese activity. On the mainland fighting goes on near Aitape and Sarmi.
Marianas On Saipan 2nd Marines take Mount Tipo Pale and are engaged on Mount Tapotchau. The 4th Marines are making good progress farther east on the Kagman Peninsula.
Burma The siege of Imphal is raised when advance units of 2nd Indian Division link with 5th Indian at Milestone 107 on the Imphal–Kohima road. The Japanese are taking ever heavier losses both in combat and, more seriously, because of food shortages and illness as their supply system collapses.

22–23 JUNE 1944
Eastern Front During the night the bombardment for the first major Russian offensive of the summer begins. There are four fronts, First, Second and Third Belorussian and First Baltic, in the attack under the overall command of Marshal Zhukov. Among the massive concen-

tration of force Zhukov has amassed a huge quantity of artillery. The German defenders are from Busch's Army Group Center.

23 JUNE 1944

Western Front The outer defenses of Cherbourg are penetrated slightly in some sections but the battle continues to be intense. In the British sector of the Normandy front, 5th Division takes St Honorina to the northwest of Caen.

Eastern Front After the bombardment lifts the Russians begin their attacks in Belorussia. The front stretches from just north of Vitebsk in a long curve past Mogilev to the Pripet River. Advances of up to 11 miles are claimed in the first day. As well as their massive artillery superiority the Russians have almost complete dominance in the air to speed them on their way. They have been building such strength for some time but in recent weeks many Luftwaffe units have been transferred to fight the British and American bomber offensive.

In the Finnish sector Krutikov's troops manage to cross the Svir.

Marianas The battle for Mount Tapotchau continues with attacks and counterattacks being sent in by both sides.

24 JUNE 1944

Western Front The American attack on Cherbourg continues to grind forward slowly but surely. The German commander, General Schlieben, still refuses to surrender although he does not believe that he can hold out much longer.

Eastern Front Already, on the second day of the Soviet offensive, the strain on the German defenders in Army Group Center is considerable. The advance is as much as 25 miles deep in some places and the Orsha–Vitebsk rail line has been cut.

Marianas The 27th Division has completed the clearance of the southern part of the island and most of the component parts of the division join the main advance of the Marines to the north. The fighting here is fiercest, still, on Mount Tapotchau.

Bonin Islands The Japanese bases on Iwo Jima and Chichi Jima are attacked by American carrier aircraft. The Japanese lose 66 planes. The carriers involved are *Hornet*, *Yorktown*, *Bataan* and *Belleau Wood*. Admiral Clark is in command.

25 JUNE 1944

Western Front Units of the three attacking divisions have penetrated into the suburbs of Cherbourg. They have massive support from naval gunfire including three battleships, four cruisers and 11 destroyers. In the British XXX Corps sector 49th Division mounts an attack toward Rauray.

Italy The US 36th Division takes Piombino before it, like other units is taken out of the line to prepare for the *Anvil* landings in the south of France. Inland there are fairly successful British and French attacks against the *Albert* line west of Lake Trasimeno, especially at Chiusi.

Eastern Front The Russian advances in Belorussia continue, particularly near Vitebsk where five German divisions are now trapped. In this sector the troops of Third Belorussian Front have crossed the Bvina, and in the other sectors the fighting is nearing Mogilev and Bobruysk.

Marianas On Saipan the Marines fight their way to the top of Mount Tapotchau. There is also fierce fighting in the Hagman Peninsula and near the southwest tip of the island.

26 JUNE 1944

Western Front Most of Cherbourg, except the docks area, is taken by the US VII Corps. The garrison commander, General Schlieben and the local naval chief, Admiral Hennecke, are captured. The battleship *Rodney* and the monitor *Roberts* along with three cruisers give heavy gunfire support to the British forces attacking near Caen.

Italy The French troops are able to push forward north of Radicofani and on their right South African armored units are able to take Chiusi.

Eastern Front The Russian forces burst into Vitebsk after a heavy bombing raid. To the south near Rogachev they take the railroad town of Zhlobin.

Marianas A small Japanese reinforcement convoy for Saipan is met and turned away by US forces. On the island the American attacks grind forward a little more.

27 JUNE 1944

Western Front The capture of Cherbourg is completed and at last the Allies have access to a major port. It will, however, be some time before the port can be made operational because of booby traps and demolitions. Near Caen Rauray is captured by the British and slightly farther east there are new attacks by the British VIII Corps.

Eastern Front The Soviet advance goes on. Near Vitebsk the German pocket is whittled down still more. In the center of the offensive

Orsha is taken. To the left the Dniepr is crossed north and south of Mogilev and near Bobryusk another pocket is surrounded.

Axis Diplomacy The Germans announce that they have concluded successful talks with the Finns and promised them help against the Russians. On 28 June Keitel arrives in Finland to organize this.

28 JUNE 1944

United States, Politics At the Republican Party convention in Chicago Governor Thomas Dewey and Governor John Bricker win the nominations for president and vice-president respectively.

France, Resistance The Vichy Minister for Propaganda, Philippe Henriot, is assassinated in Paris.

Western Front In the Cotentin the US 9th Division is preparing for final attacks to eliminate the German resistance in the direction of Cap de la Hague. Just west of Caen advancing British troops cross the Odon on a two-mile front near Mondrainville.

Eastern Front In Finland the northern wings of the Russian advance reach Petrozavodsk and also cross the Murmansk rail line farther north. In the main battles in Belorussia Zakharov's troops take Mogilev and are now across the Dniepr nearby on a 70-mile front. Hitler dismisses Busch from command of Army Group Center. Field Marshal Model is appointed as his replacement.

New Guinea On Biak the US forces, now commanded by General Doe, have finally cleared the caves in the west of the island. The Japanese strength has now largely been dissipated and the main task for the Americans is mopping up.

29 JUNE 1944

Eastern Front Rokossovsky's forces take Bobryusk. To the west they also capture Slutsk and Lyuban and a little to the north they are across the Berezina. Near Polotsk Bagramyan's men seize Usachi.

New Guinea The Australian forces advancing from Wewak reach the River Sepik, 70 miles to the west.

30 JUNE 1944

Diplomatic Affairs The United States breaks diplomatic relations with Finland.

Denmark, Resistance A general strike begins in Copenhagen. On 1 July the Germans proclaim a state of emergency, but are forced to concede on some points on 4 July when the strike ends.

Western Front The last German forces in the Cotentin either surrender or are wiped out. The major British and American units are still battling on the approaches to Caen and St Lô respectively. Since D-Day the Allies have landed 630,000 men, 600,000 tons of supplies and 177,000 vehicles in Normandy. They have lost 62,000 dead and wounded.

Marianas On Saipan the US forces make ground north of Mount Tipo Pale and Mount Tapotchau. Other units clear the area known as Death Valley and the nearby Purple Heart Ridge. More than half of the island has now been taken.

Italy On the Tyrrhenian coast the US 34th

Above: Soviet T-34/85 tanks and infantry move into the attack.

Division is heavily engaged just south of Cecina, while inland the main Allied advance is being slowed by a new German defense line south of Siena and Arezzo.

JULY 1944

Europe, Air Operations The US Eighth and Fifteenth Air Forces drop 73,000 tons of bombs and RAF Bomber Command adds 57,000 tons more. Among the targets are, for the Americans, Munich, Friedrichshafen, Metz and Belfort and, for the British, Stuttgart and Hamburg. The German oil industry is heavily hit by both British and Americans especially at Wesseling, Bohlen, Merseburg, Vienna and Ploesti.

English Channel Throughout the month there are many sharp engagements, usually at night between German and Allied, mostly British, naval units. Both sides take some losses but the Allied preponderance of strength is normally decisive. The German submarine force suffers especially heavily.

1 JULY 1944

World Affairs An international monetary conference begins at Bretton Woods with an opening speech by the US Treasury Secretary, Morgenthau. The conference lasts until 22 July. Forty-four countries are represented. Agreement is reached on the establishment of an International Monetary Fund and an International Bank for Reconstruction and Development.

Western Front The German I SS Panzer Group mounts an armored attack around Grainville, but the British defense is very strong and little progress is made.

Italy Troops from Fifth Army take Cecina on the west coast and inland, in the advance to Volterra, Pomerance also falls. Farther inland still the German units opposite the British X and XIII Corps begin to pull back.

Eastern Front Berisov, midway between Orsha and Minsk, is taken by troops of Third Belorussian Front.

2 JULY 1944

Eastern Front The Russian forces cut several of the rail lines leading west from Minsk.

Marianas On Saipan the American forces manage a general advance. The remains of Garapan village are overrun.

New Guinea There are Allied landings on Numfoor Island. General Patrick commands 7100 men of the US 168th Infantry and some Australian units. Admiral Fechteler leads the naval force and TF 74 and TF 75 provide the escort and a preliminary bombardment. The

landings are on the north coast of the island near Kamiri Airfield. There is no resistance on the beaches. At Biak the skirmishing goes on.

Italy The Allied advance proceeds in the center and west. Foiano falls to the British 4th Infantry Division.

3 JULY 1944

Western Front The US forces begin a major drive south from the Cotentin Peninsula aiming to reach a line from Coutances to St Lô. The terrain here is very difficult with narrow lanes and high hedges canalizing the advance. The weather too is poor and at the start only a little ground is made toward St Jean de Daye and La Haye du Puits.

Italy French troops capture Siena. To their right in the advance toward Arezzo the British 78th Division takes Cortona, and on the left on the Tyrhennian coast the US forces reach Rosignano.

Eastern Front Troops of First and Third Belorussian Fronts complete the capture of Minsk. Many German units, particularly from Fourth Army are now isolated to the east and casualties and losses of equipment have been enormous. Already after less than two weeks of the Soviet offensive, Army Group Center is in total disarray and before long it will have practically ceased to be a coherent fighting formation. General Freissner replaces General Lindemann in command of Army Group North.

New Guinea On Numfoor the beachhead is expanded and a parachute battalion is dropped at the Kamiriz airfield and despite many casualties the area is occupied.

4 JULY 1944

Marianas and Bonin Islands Two groups of TF 58 send their carrier aircraft against the Japanese bases on Iwo Jima and Chichi Jima. The other two groups of the task force similarly attack Guam. The Guam attacks continue on 5 July.

Western Front The Canadian 3rd Division takes Carpiquet village just west of Caen but cannot yet capture the nearby airfield. The attacks of the US VII and VIII Corps continue.

Eastern Front There is a new series of attacks by First Baltic Front against the positions of Army Group North. The German armies here are in a very dangerous situation because of the Soviet advances to the south toward their right flank and rear. Polotsk is very quickly taken.

New Guinea On Numfoor the Kornasoren airfield is captured. A second parachute battalion is flown in and loses heavily because of inexperience.

CHRONOLOGY

5 JULY 1944
Western Front The US forces take La Haye du Puits.

New Guinea The Japanese garrison on Numfoor tries a counterattack but they are soon beaten off. The US forces are preparing to move against the island's third airfield at Namber.

6 JULY 1944
German Command Berlin announces that Field Marshal Kluge has replaced Field Marshal Rundstedt as Commander in Chief West.

Italy The Polish 3rd Division takes Osemo just south of Ancona on the Adriatic flank. Throughout the rest of July the German forces will fall back gradually from river to river, a few miles at a time. The next major delay will be on the Arno.

Eastern Front Troops of First Belorussian Front take Kovel, 70 miles east of Lublin. The Germans have pulled back in this sector. Svir, southwest of Minsk, is also taken.

New Guinea On Numfoor the Americans take the Namber airstrip after a short amphibious operation. Fighters are quickly flown in.

Marianas In Saipan the Americans continue to push forward toward the north end of the island. The senior Japanese commanders, Admiral Nagumo and General Saito both commit suicide while their remaining subordinates plan a final fanatical attack.

6–11 JULY 1944
Allied Diplomacy De Gaulle visits Washington for talks on the status of his administration and aid for the fighting French.

7 JULY 1944
France, Politics The former Cabinet Minister and anticollaborationist, Georges Mandel, is executed at Fontainbleu on the orders of the Vichy police chief, Darnand.

Western Front The US VIII, VII and XIX Corps are still attacking along a line from La Haye du Puits to just east of the Vire. The German opposition is still formidable. The British battleship *Rodney* shells German positions around Caen in preparation for the imminent British attack.

Italy Units of the US 34th Division take Pignano in their advance up the Tyrrhenian coast.

Marianas In Saipan practically the whole of the Japanese garrison, now reduced to about 3000 men, mount a wild attack on the American lines south of Makunsha Village. They succeed in coming to close quarters but by about midday they are being driven off with terrible losses.

8 JULY 1944
Western Front Early in the morning a major British and Canadian attack goes in around Caen. The preliminary bombardment includes 2500 tons dropped by 450 RAF heavy bombers. The advance enters the outskirts of the city. To the west the US forces' attack is reinforced by two more divisions newly arrived from Britain. The heaviest fighting in the American sector is along the line of the road from Carentan to Periers.

Eastern Front Rokossovsky's men take Baranovichi, midway between Minsk and Brest-Litovsk.

8–19 JULY 1944
Marianas Ainsworth's three battleships several times shell targets on Guam in preparation for the coming landings. There are also carrier attacks.

9 JULY 1944
Western Front Troops from 3rd Canadian Division and 1st British Division enter Caen and take most of the city north of the Orne. The Canadians also take Carpiquet Airfield. The American advance toward St Lô and farther west continues.

Italy The US 88th Division takes Volterra while on their right French units are advancing on Poggibonsi.

Eastern Front Troops from the Third Belorussian Front take Lida, 50 miles east of Grodno. Farther north other units reach the outskirts of Vilna.

Marianas The US forces reach Point Marpi and the final organized Japanese resistance is overcome. The Japanese have lost an estimated 27,000 dead as well as 1780 prisoners, both figures including a number of civilians. The US forces have a casualty list of 3400 dead and 13,000 hurt.

10 JULY 1944
Western Front The British VIII Corps begins new attacks toward Evrecy. Eterville is also captured.

Eastern Front Model, commanding Army Group Center, asks for Army Group North to be moved south behind the Dvina to bolster his front and to prevent them being cut off by the Russian drive to the Baltic. Hitler refuses to allow this sensible step. In the middle of Model's sector Slonim is taken.

New Guinea In the Aitape sector a series of Japanese attacks starts along the line of the Driniumor River.

11 JULY 1944

Western Front A counterattack by the German *Panzer Lehr* Division makes some progress against the US 9th Division southwest of St Jean de Daye but later the Germans are pushed back. In the British sector the slow advance continues. VIII Corps take the important Hill 112, southwest of Caen. The British around Caen are again supported by heavy naval gunfire.

United States, Politics President Roosevelt tells a Press Conference that he will run if nominated. He says, 'If the people command me to continue in office . . . I have as little right as a soldier to leave his position in the line.'

Allied Diplomacy Roosevelt announces that the US will recognize de Gaulle's French Provisional Government as the *de facto* authority for the civil administration of the liberated territory in France.

New Guinea In the Aitape sector the US forces pull back from the Driniumor River under pressure but are planning a counterstroke.

Eastern Front Second Baltic Front (Yeremenko) starts a new program of attacks on a 90-mile front east of Idritsa. Elsewhere the German pocket east of Minsk is wiped out.

12 JULY 1944

Western Front The US attack toward St Lô has now reached to within two miles of the town but is being slowed down by stubborn defense. A little east of the town Hill 192 is taken.

Italy A major sequence of Allied air attacks against the Po bridges begins. At the front the US 88th Division takes Lajatico.

Eastern Front Yeremenko's troops take Idritsa.

13 JULY 1944

Western Front The advance of the US First Army toward St Lô is practically brought to a halt. Plans are in preparation for a formal assault on the German lines east of the town. This is to be Operation Cobra.

Italy The French Corps is attacking around Poggibonsi and Castellina about 20 miles south of Florence.

Eastern Front After several days of vicious street fighting Vilna falls to the Russians.

New Guinea In the Aitape sector the US 128th Regiment pushes back to the Driniumor River. On Numfoor the final Japanese pocket comes under attack.

14 JULY 1944

Italy The French troops take Poggibonsi.

Eastern Front Konev's First Ukraine Front joins the attacks of the Belorussian Fronts to the

north. Troops from First Belorussian Front take Pinsk.

14–26 JULY 1944

New Guinea The Japanese positions near Aitape between Yakamul and But are bombarded on many occasions by the ships of Commodore Collins' TF 74. There are two cruisers and six destroyers involved in these operations, mostly Australian ships.

15 JULY 1944

Western Front The outskirts of Lessay are reached by the US forces. From here east to the River Taute the advance is halted while regrouping takes place. Nearer St Lô the fighting is heavy.

Italy Two divisions of Eighth Army begin a formal attack on the German positions at Arezzo. Nearer the west coast the Americans push forward toward Leghorn and the French take Castellina.

Eastern Front Second Baltic Front take Opochka, 30 miles north of Idritsa. Other Russian formations cross the Niemen in several places west and southwest of Vilna.

16 JULY 1944

Western Front The US forces continue their attacks near St Lô. In the British sector there are advances toward Hottot-les-Bagues and in the direction of Evrecy.

Allied Diplomacy The London Polish government publish a paper claiming territory in East Prussia, Danzig and the Polish Corridor for postwar Poland.

Italy Arezzo falls to the Eighth Army. Other British units from XIII Corps cross the Arno as the Germans fall back.

Eastern Front Russian tank units storm Grodno, southwest of Vilna. Farther south First Ukraine Front begin a new offensive toward Lvov on a 300-mile front.

New Guinea On Aitape the Japanese forces along the Driniumor River are losing ground.

17 JULY 1944

Western Front Field Marshal Rommel is severely wounded by the attack of an Allied aircraft on his car while he is returning to his Headquarters after an inspection trip. Field Marshal Kluge assumes Rommel's duties as well as his own as Commander in Chief. In the battle for St Lô the US forces have entered the town.

Arctic The British carriers *Formidable*, *Indefatigable* and *Furious* escorted by the battleship

Duke of York send attacks against the *Tirpitz* in the anchorage at Kaafiord. The attacks are detected on the way in and the Germans successfully conceal the target with smoke.

Japan, Politics A new Navy Minister, Admiral Nomura, replaces Shimada. On 18 July Tojo resigns his posts as prime minister and Chief of Staff. General Kuniaki Koiso and Admiral Yonai are chosen to form the new Cabinet. General Umezu becomes Chief of Staff. These changes are in fact manifestations of a growing desire on the part of many Japanese statesmen to end the war. They worry about an unfavorable peace, however, and wish to maintain the appearance of a strong front. The Allies are unable to recognize or correctly interpret these indications and the war therefore continues as before.

United States, Politics President Roosevelt announces that he will leave the choice of his running mate to the Democratic Party convention.

18 JULY 1944

Western Front St Lô is almost completely taken by units of the US XIX Corps. The British and Canadians begin a major push from east of the Orne southward in the direction of the high ground beyond Caen. This operation code named *Goodwood* is to become very controversial. Montgomery hopes that it will lead to a break out from Normandy, but even if this difficult aim is not achieved he believes the attack necessary to maintain the established pattern of drawing the German reserves to the British rather than the American sector. Montgomery has made some unfortunate, extravagant comments on the prospects for *Goodwood* (notably in arguing for heavy bomber support) which will backfire when in fact there is no breakthrough.

More than 2200 planes are involved in the massive bombardment which precedes the operation, including 1000 RAF heavy bombers which drop more than 7000 tons of bombs. The scale of the preparation does much to disorganize and demoralize the defense, and at first the attack goes well. Gradually severe traffic congestion problems develop in the rear. There are only four bridges available over the Orne and the Caen canal and in the dust raised by the bombardment and the advance the vehicles of the attacking and following divisions quickly become mixed and misdirected.

Italy Part of the US IV Corps begins to attack Leghorn on the west coast while a little inland other units reach the Arno at Pontedera which is taken. On the east coast the Poles also advance

taking Ancona. The capture of Leghorn and Ancona will ease Allied supply difficulties.

Eastern Front There are new Russian offensives by First Belorussian Front around Kovel and by Third Baltic Front toward Ostrov and Pskov. First Ukraine Front is beginning to make progress toward Lvov after two days of attacks.

19 JULY 1944

Western Front East of Caen the *Goodwood* battles continue with large numbers of tanks being engaged from both sides. The Germans usually have the advantage of better positions and this, combined with their armament, tips the balance in their favor despite the disparity of numbers. The Caen suburb of Vaucelles, however, is cleared by Canadian units who also take Louvigny and Fleury-sur-Orne.

Italy The US 34th Division takes Leghorn.

Eastern Front In their advance to Lvov First Ukraine Front surround five German divisions. Farther north, just east of Dvinsk, Russian units enter Latvia.

19–21 JULY 1944

United States, Politics In the Democratic Party convention at Chicago Roosevelt is selected by an overwhelming majority as the presidential candidate. He receives 1086 votes, Senator Byrd 89 and James Farley 1. Harry Truman is chosen as running mate by 1031 votes to Wallace's 105.

20 JULY 1944

Western Front The British attacks south and east of Caen continue, but the tenacious German antitank defense has worn down the advance units and cut their momentum.

Germany, Resistance Shortly after midday a bomb explodes in the conference room at Hitler's Headquarters at Rastenburg in East Prussia. Hitler, although badly shaken, is only slightly hurt. The bomb has been planted by Colonel Count von Stauffenberg who represents in this a wide-ranging conspiracy of senior officers and a few politicians. Immediately after the bomb goes off the conspirators act on the assumption that Hitler is dead. In fact the bomb, disguised in a briefcase has been moved slightly by accident by another officer and Hitler, shielded from the blast by the heavy leg of the map table, thus survives. Not all the elements of the conspirators plan are carried out with sufficient ruthlessness to achieve much success, and once it is clear that Hitler has survived the plot falls apart. On the first day several of the leading participants, including Stauffenberg, are shot in Berlin, and eventually the Nazi vengeance will encompass several thousand executions. Hitler later delights in watching film of these. Among those actively involved in the plot are General Beck, Carl Gördeler (formerly mayor of Leipzig), Field Marshal Witzleben, General Halder and others taken from aristocratic and Roman Catholic groups. Many others know of the plot including Rommel, Kluge and Canaris but have done nothing to help or hinder it. The security of the plot is easily penetrated and many of the conspirators are quickly rounded up. The effect of the incident on Hitler is first to increase his pathological distrust of the generals and second, when combined with the physical deterioration caused by the dubious combination of medicines he takes, the shock of the explosion further weakens his ability to concentrate and to remain stable in the face of reverses. He becomes less interested in his work and more prone to wild outbursts.

Marianas The bombardment of Tinian is stepped up a stage when army artillery based on Saipan adds its weight to the attacks from the air and by naval shelling.

21 JULY 1944

Italy The French Expeditionary Corps is taken out of line to prepare for the *Anvil/Dragoon* operation, which is to invade the south of France on 15 August 1944.

Marianas Troops of Geiger's III Amphibious Corps land on Guam. The naval force is commanded by Admiral Connolly and among the vessels in his TF 53 are six battleships and five escort carriers. Three groups of TF 58 also send their carrier aircraft to attack on 21 and 22 July. General Turnage's 3rd Marine Division is landed west of Agana at Asan and the 1st Marine (Shepherd) lands near Agat. Eventually in the campaign 54,900 American troops are landed. The Japanese defense is 19,000 strong under the command of 29th Infantry Division (Takashima). General Obata who commands the Thirty-first Army is also on the island.

When the landings go in there is only moderate resistance on the beaches.

New Guinea The Japanese send in another attack over the Driniumor River near Aitape. To begin with they achieve some success but later are held.

Eastern Front Troops from Maslennikov's Third Baltic Front take Ostrov in their continuing attacks.

German Command General Zeitzler resigns his post as Chief of Staff at OKH (the Army High Command with responsibility for the Eastern Front) and is replaced by Guderian.

22 JULY 1944

Eastern Front Rokossovsky's First Belorussian Front take Chelm in their advance on Lublin.

Marianas On Guam the Marines from both beachheads launch converging attacks in an attempt to link up. Both advance for about a mile despite heavy resistance.

23 JULY 1944

Eastern Front The Soviet forces capture Pskov – the last major town of the prewar Soviet Union in German hands. Farther south troops from First Ukraine Front enter Lublin. Fighting there continues.

In the German command Field Marshal Schoerner replaces General Friessner at Army Group North.

Poland, Politics The formation of a Polish Committee of National Liberation is announced from Moscow. The London based Polish government call it 'the creation of a handful of unknown communists.'

Italy Units of the US IV Corps enter the outskirts of Pisa but are only able to occupy the districts south of the Arno.

Marianas The Marines succeed in extending the northern beachhead on Guam to Point Adelup. Other units from the southern landing cross the neck of the Orote Peninsula cutting off the main Japanese airfield on the island.

Western Front General Crerar's First Canadian Army becomes operational.

24 JULY 1944

Marianas Admiral Hill's TF 52 lands General Schmidt's V Amphibious Corps on Tinian. Fire support is provided by the battleship groups led by Oldendorf and Ainsworth as in the earlier Marianas operations. The landing force is composed of the 2nd and 4th Marine Divisions and numbers 15,600 men. Colonel Ogata and Admiral Kakuta are the Japanese commanders and their force is approximately 6200 strong. The 2nd Marines are first involved in a feint landing on the southwest of the island while the 4th Marines in fact land in the northwest. The assault forces succeed in establishing a solid beachhead and heavy Japanese attacks are beaten off with great loss. Napalm is used in these engagements for the first time in the Pacific. It is also being introduced in Europe at this time.

Western Front The US *Cobra* attack just west of St Lô is scheduled to begin now but bad weather, hampering the air support, causes a postponement.

Eastern Front Lublin falls to Rokossovsky's troops. Other units of First Ukraine Front overrun the site of Majdanek Concentration Camp.

25 JULY 1944

Western Front Operation *Cobra* begins. The main attack just west of St Lô is made by General Collins' US VII Corps with VIII Corps on their right and XIII Corps to the left. There is a massive preparation, especially from the air. More than 3000 planes are involved including 1500 heavy bombers from Eighth Air Force. Some of the bombers aim short and cause many casualties including a general from HQ up to observe the operation. Despite this both VII and VIII Corps make good progress. The British attacks around Caen have contributed to draw away the German tank forces and reserves. South of Caen the Canadian troops are attacking along the road to Falaise but are meeting heavy resistance.

Eastern Front Russian units enter Lvov which is now also partially surrounded.

Germany, Home Front Goebbels is appointed Reich Plenipotentiary for Total War and new decrees are issued cancelling vacations for women involved in war work.

Allied Diplomacy Talks begin in Washington between British and United States representatives on arrangements for the control of oil production and trade in the postwar world.

Indian Ocean Admiral Somerville's British Eastern Fleet attacks Sabang. First planes from the carriers *Victorious* and *Illustrious* are sent against the airfield, then four battleships along with cruisers and destroyers move in closer to shell the harbor and oil installations.

Marianas The Americans are still unable to join their beachheads on Guam. Units from the southern landing force are also fighting on the Orote Peninsula.

After repulsing Japanese counterattacks during the early hours, 2nd and 4th Marines advance carefully to the south on Tinian.

25–28 JULY 1944

Carolines Two carrier groups from TF 58 attack Palau while a third sends its planes against Yap, Ulithi, Ngulu, Tais and Sorol. Mitscher is in command.

26 JULY 1944

Western Front The US attacks continue. Marigny and St Gilles are both taken by VII Corps and to the west VIII Corps is across the Lessay–Périers road.

Eastern Front Units of First Ukraine Front reach the Vistula west of Lublin and capture

Deblin. Farther north Narva is taken by troops of the Leningrad Front.

New Guinea The fighting in the Aitape sector continues. On Biak and Numfoor also the Japanese resistance still goes on.

United States, Planning Roosevelt meets MacArthur and Nimitz in Honolulu. MacArthur argues for an attack on the Philippines, but the navy suggests that they can be passed by and instead advocate Formosa as the next major strategic target. This debate is to become very heated and controversial.

27 JULY 1944

Western Front In the continuing American attacks VIII Corps makes an important breakthrough between Lessay and Périers, both of which are also taken.

Eastern Front The Soviets make good ground in several sectors. First Ukraine Front (Konev) takes Lvov and Stanislav 70 miles to the south; Second Belorussian Front (Zakharov) captures Bialystok after a harsh struggle; First Baltic Front (Bagramyan) takes Siauliai; and on their right Second Baltic Front (Yeremenko) takes Daugavpils and Rezekne.

Marianas On Guam the 77th Division is preparing to attack Mount Tenjo.

Work begins on the newly taken airfield at Ushi Point on Tinian.

28 JULY 1944

Western Front The US 4th Armored Division enters Coutances. This is the first objective for Operation *Cobra*.

Eastern Front The Russians take Brest-Litovsk and Przemysl.

Marianas Much of the Orote Peninsula of Guam is now occupied by the Marines. Inland a little the US forces take Mount Chachao and Mount Alutom in the continuing fight to join the beachheads.

29 JULY 1944

Eastern Front In a new offensive by Third Belorussian Front the Niemen is crossed.

Western Front The XIX Corps on the left of the US attack is advancing on Torigny and Tessy. In the center VII Corps reaches Percy and on the right VIII Corps is across the Sienne and moving toward Granville.

Marianas The Marines have now occupied rather more than the northern half of Tinian but the Japanese resistance is increasing again after a slight lull.

New Guinea On Biak the Americans complete the destruction of the Japanese pocket around

Ibdi. There is no more organized fighting. On the mainland near Aitape the US forces retire slightly at Afua.

30 JULY 1944

Western Front The advancing US forces take Granville and enter Avranches seizing the important bridges over the Sée. The left flank of the advance is, however, strongly counter-attacked by German forces from II Parachute Corps especially at Percy and Villedieu. Farther east there are successful British attacks near Caumont.

Marianas The main town on Tinian, also known as Tinian, is taken by the American forces. The Americans have now largely cleared the southern half of Guam.

Philippine Sea The American heavy cruiser *Indianapolis* is sunk by a Japanese submarine.

New Guinea General Sibert's 6th Division lands unopposed on the small islands of Amsterdam and Middleburg off Cape Sansapor. Admiral Berkey's TF 78 is in support.

31 JULY 1944

Western Front The US 4th Armored Division pushes on from Avranches and succeeds in taking crossings of the Sélune near Pontaubault. On the left of the advance the German counter-attacks continue around Tessy and Percy.

New Guinea One American battalion is moved from the offshore islands to land just west of Cape Sansapor. At Aitape the American forces go over to the attack along the Driniumor River.

Eastern Front In its advance from Vilna Third Belorussian Front now enters Kaunas. Farther south the First Belorussian Front is driving toward Warsaw. It takes Siedlice and Otwock only 12 miles southeast of the city.

British Command Admiral Fraser takes command of the British Eastern Fleet in succession to Admiral Somerville.

Marianas The Marines begin attacks on the last organized Japanese defenses in the south of Tinian.

AUGUST 1944

Europe, Air Operations The Allied bombing effort this month can be divided into four categories. First, general strategic bombing, area bombing, carried out solely by the heavy bombers of the RAF. Targets include Kiel, Bremen and Brunswick. Second, the attacks on particular target systems including oil, rail transport and aircraft manufacturing. Oil targets are attacked by both British and Americans and include Zeitz, Bohlen, Freital, Kolin,

Poolitz and Hamburg-Meerbeck. Rail centers hit are Saarbrucken, Mulhouse and Strasbourg and others. Aircraft works bombed are Anklam, Neustadt and Rakmel. The third type of operation is in direct support of the ground forces. British light and medium forces fly 33,000 sorties in this work. The American fighter-bombers fly 24,000 missions and their medium bombers a further 8500 in which they drop 10,500 tons of bombs. The lighter forces are in action everywhere and claim to destroy 12,000 vehicles, 850 tanks and much more. The heavy bomber forces are also involved in such attacks from time to time. The efforts of the RAF on 7–8 and 14 August are especially large. The final category of attacks is against the V-weapon sites. Most of these are carried out by British forces. The most notable raid is the 2000 tons dropped on the depot at Trossy St Maximin.

Developments during the month include shuttle raids by the Eighth Air Force in which planes fly to Russia and then Italy, attacking on each trip. Also large forces from Bomber Command are sent over Germany during daylight for the first time since the early months of the war. In all the US Eighth and Fifteenth Air Forces drop 75,000 tons and Bomber Command 65,000 tons. The German V-weapon effort also continues, causing 4000 casualties in Britain this month.

Far East, Air Operations There are Super-fortress raids on Nagasaki and Yawata. There are in addition the by now usual range of attacks on targets in New Guinea and the Marianas. Davao on Mindanao is also hit.

1 AUGUST 1944

Western Front General Patton's Third Army becomes operational and takes positions on the Allied right flank. The US forces are now organized as 12 Army Group (Bradley), First Army (Hodges) and Third Army. Dempsey's British Second Army and Crerar's First Canadian Army form 21 Army Group which Montgomery commands. As well as this post he still retains overall direction of the ground forces.

Patton's main task initially is to overrun Brittany, but some of his troops will head for Le Mans from the beginning. US First Army will advance on Mortain. The British and Canadians will continue to attack between Caumont and Caen. In this sector the British XXX Corps is at the moment advancing on Villers Bocage.

Finland, Politics President Ryti resigns. Marshal Mannerheim is chosen to replace him.

Eastern Front Troops from Chernyakhovsky's Third Belorussian Front take Kaunas, capital of

Lithuania. Many of the routes leading to east Prussia from the Baltic States, (described by the Germans as Ostland) are cut. In Poland the patriots of the Home Army (AK) begin open operations in Warsaw. This army is aligned politically with the exile government in London and, although by no means of one mind in political affairs, is generally anticommunist. The rising is timed so that when the Russians arrive in Warsaw, as they seem certain to do very shortly, they will find an established Polish government with the prestige of having liberated the national capital. However, the Russian advance almost immediately comes to a halt. This has since caused controversy. The Russian accounts claim that because of the long rapid advance they have made during July, they are unable, for the moment, to move further. The western position is that the Russians have stopped so that the Germans would do the job of wiping out the anti-Soviet forces in Poland. The most telling point on the western side is the reluctance of the Russians to lend any help to British and American plans and, after much negotiation, attempts to drop supplies to the Poles.

Marianas On Tinian the last organized resistance from the Japanese forces comes to an end. As usual the garrison has been completely wiped out. There are over 6000 Japanese dead and 250 prisoners, an unusually large proportion. The Americans have lost 390 killed and 1800 wounded.

2 AUGUST 1944

Western Front The VIII Corps of Patton's Third Army advances into Brittany, reaching Dinan and the outskirts of Rennes. On their left First Army units attack around Tessy and toward Mortain, taking Villedieu.

Marianas The American forces again attack on Guam. They make good ground on the west side of the island but are repulsed in the east.

3 AUGUST 1944

Western Front Part of Middleton's VIII Corps begins the attack on Rennes while other units bypass the city. Mortain falls to First Army units.

Eastern Front Konev's troops seize crossings over the Vistula just south of Sandomierz itself 110 miles south of Warsaw.

Marianas The 77th Division renews its advance on the east side of Guam where the Japanese have pulled back. Defensive positions are being prepared on Mount Santa Rosa and these are shelled by US warships.

Burma Mytkyina is finally taken by the Chinese

and American attack after the bulk of the Japanese garrison have managed to slip away.

4 AUGUST 1944

Western Front In Brittany the German forces, General Farmbacher's XXV Corps, pull back to the major ports, St Malo, Brest, Lorient and St Nazaire (these last two will hold out until May 1945). Middleton's troops complete the liberation of Rennes and advance on toward Vannes. From First Army V and XIV Corps also push forward while in the British sector Evrecy and Villers Bocage are taken.

Italy South African units of the British XII Corps enter Florence and take the districts of the river south of the Arno River. The Allied plans are revised according to proposals from General Leese that the next major offensive should be mounted by Eighth Army in the sector near the east coast.

Eastern Front In the north there are German counterattacks between Riga and Jelgava which reopen communication between Riga and the German forces in Lithuania.

Burma The British 2nd Division from XXXIII Corps takes Tamu.

4–5 AUGUST 1944

Volcano Islands Admiral Clark leads two groups of TF 38 in attacks on Iwo Jima and Chichi Jima. One Japanese destroyer is sunk and considerable damage done.

5 AUGUST 1944

Western Front In Brittany Vannes is liberated. Other VIII Corps units attack near St Malo and reach the outskirts of Brest. General Haislip's XV Corps, also from Third Army, is advancing rapidly to the southeast from the Sélune and reaches Mayenne and Laval. On their left VII Corps is also hurrying forward beyond Mortain.

Eastern Front The Russians bring a new army group, Petrov's Fourth Ukraine Front into their line in southern Poland and northern Hungary.

6 AUGUST 1944

Western Front The US VIII Corps extends its hold on Brittany. The 4th Armored Division reaches nearly to Loreint. Haislip's XV Corps takes Laval and advances on Le Mans. In the US First Army sector Vire is taken by 29th Division.

Marianas On Guam one regiment of 77th Division takes heavy casualties in a brief, fierce Japanese counterattack.

Italy The Allied forces in Florence begin to cross the Arno into the northern half of the city.

7 AUGUST 1944

Western Front The Germans begin an important counterattack just east of Mortain. The blow falls between VII and XIV Corps. The attackers are from 2nd and 116th Panzer Divisions. Mortain is retaken by the Germans but heavy Allied air attacks help to prevent any more serious loss. In Brittany VIII Corps is now attacking Brest, St Malo and Lorient.

During the night there are attacks southwest of Caen by Canadian forces after more than 1000 RAF heavy bombers have dropped in excess of 3000 tons of bombs on the German positions.

Eastern Front The Russian forces advance in the Carpathian foothills to take Sambor southwest of Lvov.

Marianas There are US attacks and fierce fighting all along the front on Guam. The difficult jungle terrain helps the Japanese defenders to concede only a little ground.

8 AUGUST 1944

Western Front The battles around Mortain continue with the Germans still trying to press their offensive home to Arromanches. Despite this threat Third Army goes on with its attacks to the south and southwest. The 79th Division from XV Corps enters Le Mans while on its right XX Corps newly in the line advances toward Nantes and Angers. The fighting around the Brittany ports goes on.

Marianas The remaining Japanese forces are compelled to retire toward the north end of Guam when the US troops manage to overrun Mount Santa Rosa.

Eastern Front The AK forces have now managed to seize control of most of Warsaw and have expanded their strength with much captured German equipment. SS General Bach-Zelewski is appointed to lead the German forces charged with defeating the Poles. The units employed by the Germans are mostly SS, police and punishment battalions, all alike in their liking for cruel and violent methods. After complaints from Guderian and others the worst offenders will be taken out of the fight and some of their leaders executed.

9 AUGUST 1944

Western Front The Canadian II Corps continues to attack along the Caen–Falaise road. The German attacks around Mortain are gradually being worn down. The XV Corps turns north from Le Mans heading for Argentan and eventually a junction with the Canadians between Argentan and Falaise. Allied fighter-bombers are very active.

10 AUGUST 1944

Western Front British troops operating as part of Canadian First Army take Vimont in the attack south of Caen. In the US Third Army sector all three corps are involved in vigorous fighting. In Brittany Middleton's troops have cleared most of St Malo and Dinard. In the main operations XX Corps takes Nantes and also reaches the Loire near Nantes and to the north XV Corps continues to advance on Alençon from Le Mans. Around Mortain the Germans pull back slightly, principally because of direct American pressure but also because of the growing threat to their rear.

Marianas The Americans wipe out the last serious opposition in the north of Guam. There are various small groups of Japanese holding out in jungle hideouts (one survivor at least will stay in the jungle until 1972). The Americans have taken 7000 casualties including 1300 dead. There are less than 100 Japanese prisoners out of a total garrison of at least 10,000.

Italy The advance of the Polish II corps reaches the Cesano River.

11 AUGUST 1944

Western Front The German Commander in Chief, Field Marshal Kluge wishes to pull back from Mortain but Hitler will only allow a partial retreat. Farther south the US forces cross the Loire.

Eastern Front Third Baltic Front begins a new offensive south of Lake Peipus. The German line is fractured and advances of up to 15 miles are made to the west and northwest.

12 AUGUST 1944

Western Front The US XV Corps takes Alençon and advances to the outskirts of Argentan where the German 116th Division is in position.

The first PLUTO (*Pipe Line Under The Ocean*) is in operation carrying fuel from the Isle of Wight to Cherbourg.

Italy The Allied forces complete the capture of Florence.

13 AUGUST 1944

Western Front Argentan is largely cleared by XV Corps attacks but General Bradley, commanding 12 Army Group, orders a halt here. To the south units of XII and XX Corps are advancing on Orleans and Chartres from around Le Mans.

14 AUGUST 1944

Western Front The Canadian advance has

reached to within about five miles of Falaise from the north. RAF heavy bombers drop 4000 tons of bombs in supporting attacks as the Canadian drive continues. The US XV Corps begins to move east from around Argentan toward Dreux. Other units are taking post at Argentan. In Brittany all of St Malo has been cleared except for the ancient citadel in the port area.

15 AUGUST 1944

Western Front In northern France the British VIII Corps enters Tinchebray from the north. Other British and Canadian units are attacking fiercely along a line from here to east of Falaise. From just south of Tinchebray to Argentan the US VII Corps and V Corps are attacking northward and trapped as meat in the sandwich are the divisions of the German Seventh Army and units of Fifth Panzer Army and Panzer Group Eberbach. These forces are now beginning a desperate retreat to the east. Field Marshal Kluge is forced to take cover from Allied air attacks for most of the day while attempting to visit the front. His long absence from HQ increases Hitler's suspicions that Kluge is disloyal and attempting to defect to the Allied side.

Southern France Allied forces land in southern France between Toulon and Cannes. This is operation *Dragoon*, originally and for most of the planning stage, known as *Anvil*. The code name has been changed because it is believed that the Germans have discovered it and its significance. The landing forces are from General Patch's US Seventh Army. Truscott's VI Corps provides the three divisions that make up the bulk of the assault force. The follow-up formation is General de Lattre's II French Corps. French commando units also land from the sea in the first wave and there is also an airborne attack. This involves 5000 men from a composite parachute group and they drop inland near Le Muy. Before these or the seaborne forces go in there are attacks by 1300 land-based aircraft and naval shelling. Admiral Hewitt is in command of the naval forces.

The largest group of special force troops lands on the island of Levante with cover from the battleship *Lorraine* and other vessels. General Daniels' 3rd US Infantry Division lands in the Baie de Cavalaire and among the bombardment group here is the battleship *Ramillies*. The fire support for General Eagle's 45th Infantry is provided by the battleships *Texas* and *Nevada*. This landing is in the Baie de Bugnon. The left flank division is the 36th Infantry, General

Dahlquist, with support from the *Arkansas*. As well as the land-based air cover, five British and two American escort carriers add fighter support (216 aircraft). In addition to the battleships mentioned fire support is also provided by 20 cruisers and 31 destroyers. A further four cruisers and 60 destroyers perform escort duties. There is almost no resistance to the landings and only 183 casualties are taken. Churchill has come to observe the operation from aboard a destroyer and, from his account in his memoirs, seems to have been bored by the lack of action. The German force in the south of France is General Weise's Nineteenth Army. This formation has only seven poor quality infantry divisions and the better trained and equipped 11 Panzer Division to cover the whole of the south and southeast of the country.

16 AUGUST 1944

Eastern Front The Russian attacks reach Ossow only seven miles northeast of Warsaw but they are pushed back by a German counterattack.

Northern France Canadian troops from II Corps enter the ruins of Falaise and a bitter battle develops. To their right Polish units of British I Corps begin to move west over the River Dives. To the south Chartres falls to the advance of US XX Corps.

Southern France The French II Corps (De Lattre) lands and passes forward through the US forces which are consolidating the beachhead.

17 AUGUST 1944

Eastern Front In Lithuania Army Group North sends in counterattacks all along the line but especially against Siauliai. The aim is to prevent Riga being cut off.

Northern France The capture of Falaise is completed by the Canadian 2nd Division. The damage to the town in the bombing and bitter fighting of the past few days has been so severe that in many places it is impossible to tell where the streets once were. The gap between the Canadian front to the north and the US V Corps to the south is now only a handful of miles.

To the south and west of these battles the American advance into the heart of France continues. Dreux, Chateaudun and Orleans are taken. In Brittany the defenders of the citadel at St Malo surrender.

Hitler dismisses Field Marshal Kluge. Model is appointed in his place. Kluge commits suicide on 18 August rather than face a treason trial.

Southern France Among the towns taken in the Allied advance are St Raphael, St Tropez,

Fréjus, Le Luq and St Maxime. There is little German resistance.

New Guinea The American holdings near Aitape are extended by a general advance. Japanese interference is negligible. On Numfoor the last significant Japanese force is brought to battle after several days maneuvering and is largely destroyed.

18 AUGUST 1944

Northern France The Falaise gap is closed by the junction of the Poles and Americans at Chambois. A considerable German force is still to the west. The German retreat through the Falaise gap in the past few days has provided unrivalled opportunities for the Allied fighter-bombers since there has been an enormous amount of vulnerable traffic compelled to travel by day on virtually one road.

In Third Army's advance toward the Seine forward patrols reach Versailles.

Southern France The US VI Corps is now moving toward Aix-en-Provence while on their left the French forces are attacking nearer the coast toward Toulon and eventually Marseilles. There is also a US advance north toward Gap.

Eastern Front In the north troops of Third Baltic and Leningrad Fronts advance north and south of Lake Peipus. In southern Poland Sandomierz, on the west bank of the Vistula, is taken by First Ukraine Front.

19 AUGUST 1944

Northern France The XV Corps from Third Army reaches the Seine at Mantes Grassicourt. The fighting between Falaise and Argentan is still very fierce and continues to go badly for the Germans. In Paris the resistance begin open operations against the Germans.

20 AUGUST 1944

Northern France The last units of the German Fifth Panzer and Seventh Armies which are to escape the Falaise pocket do so during the night by passing through the Allied lines around Chambois and St Lambert. Seventy or eighty miles to the east Patton's troops take crossings of the Seine at Mantes Grassicourt, thirty miles west of Paris. Farther up the river beyond Paris, XX Corps units enter Fontainbleau.

France, Politics Pétain is arrested by the Germans in Vichy for refusing to leave to go to an area safe from the Allied advance. General de Gaulle is in France and the FFI (resistance) forces claim to control eight departments.

New Guinea The Americans announce that the fighting on Biak has come to an end. The

Japanese have lost 4700 dead and 220 prisoners. The Americans have had 2550 casualties.

Eastern Front After a fierce artillery preparation during the night a major Soviet offensive begins in the south with two main attacks near Jassy and Tiraspol. Malinovsky's Second Ukraine Front advance south around Jassy and Tolbukhin's Third Ukraine Front southwest from Tiraspol. Their attacks fall on Third and Fourth Rumanian Armies and the German Sixth Army which in fact contains many Rumanian troops. These forces are all part of General Freissner's Army Group South Ukraine. In the north in Latvia the Russian attacks also continue fiercely. The fire of the German heavy cruiser *Prinz Eugen* helps beat off one important Russian advance near Riga.

21 AUGUST 1944

Northern France All the Allied armies begin a rapid advance to the northeast in pursuit of the broken and retreating German forces. Although at this stage, the invasion of France is behind the schedule set out in the *Overlord* plan, this will be corrected by the speed of the advance in the next few weeks. Third Army improves its bridgeheads over the Seine. On the right flank the advance reaches Sens.

Southern France Aix-en-Provence is taken by units of General Truscott's US VI Corps.

21-29 AUGUST 1944

World Affairs Senior Allied representatives meet at Dumbarton Oaks to discuss plans for maintaining postwar security. They agree that there should be an assembly of all nations backed up by a council of leading states. There should also be an International Court of Justice. The leader of the American delegation is Edward Stettinius, of the British team Sir Alexander Cadogan and for Russia Andrei Gromyko.

22 AUGUST 1944

Japan, Home Front The government introduces measures to conscript all women between the ages of 12 and 40 to do war work.

Arctic Admiral Moore leads three fleet carriers and two escort carriers of the British Home Fleet to attack the battleship *Tirpitz* in Kaafiord. The battleship *Duke of York* is in support. The attack is detected on the way in and loses heavily to the German barrage and to the defending fighters. No hits are achieved because of the smoke defenses. The attacks are repeated without result on 24 and 29 August.

Eastern Front Jassy is taken by Malinovsky's troops. Third Ukraine Front is extending its attacks northward toward Kishinev and has advanced up to 50 miles in the past two days.

23 AUGUST 1944
Northern France The resistance forces have, for the moment, largely freed Paris after a bitter struggle. To the east of the capital Melun falls to the American advance and to the south of the city French troops fighting with the US V Corps are brought forward to join the liberating advance. Montgomery's 21 Army Group and US First Army are hurrying forward to the Seine. Evreux is taken by units of US XIX Corps. Small Allied forces on the Atlantic coast link with resistance units near Bordeaux.

Southern France French troops reach the outskirts of both Marseilles and Toulon.

Rumania, Politics King Michael dismisses Marshal Antonescu and the new prime minister is General Senatescu. Rumania accepts the Russian armistice terms. On 25 August Rumania declares war on Germany. There is fighting near Bucharest.

Eastern Front The attacks of Second and Third Ukraine Fronts link up cutting off a large part, about 12 divisions, of the German Sixth Army. Second Ukraine Front also takes Vaslui, 35 miles south of Jassy. Many of the Rumanian troops formerly allied with the Germans have either simply deserted or gone over to join the Soviets.

New Guinea The battle for Numfoor is over

and most of the victorious American force is withdrawn to other sectors.

24 AUGUST 1944
Northern France The fighting in Paris flares up again as the Germans make a final effort. General Leclerc leads the French 4th Armored Division to the outskirts of the city.

Southern France An American force advancing east from the landing areas takes Cannes. Inland, in the drive north, Grenoble is taken and in the main advance west Arles is taken, on the Rhône south of Avignon, by the US 3rd Division.

Indian Ocean Admiral Moody leads the carriers *Victorious* and *Indomitable* in an attack on Padang in the southwest of Sumatra. The battleship *Howe* is one of the escorting ships. On 23 August Admiral Fraser has taken over command of the British Eastern Fleet from Admiral Somerville. In addition to the forces sent against Padang there are three battleships and two fleet carriers.

Eastern Front The Russian forces in the south advance at great speed. Freissner's Army Group South Ukraine has been shattered by the Russian attacks and the defection of the Rumanians. Kishinev is taken.

25 AUGUST 1944
Northern France General Leclerc's 4th Armored Division enters Paris. The German com-

Above: American troops march up the Champs Elysées, Paris, 26 August 1945.

mander General Choltitz disobeys orders to fight fiercely for the city and instead of causing such damage for nothing he surrenders. The British XXX Corps takes Vernon on the Seine and seizes river crossings nearby. On their left XII Corps is preparing to cross the river at Louviers and the Canadians take Elbeuf. In Brittany the US VIII Corps begins major attacks on Brest where the German garrison still resists stubbornly. The battleship *Warspite* shells targets in the town.

Southern France Avignon is taken by the US forces. The majority of General Weise's Nineteenth Army is now withdrawing rapidly northward up the Rhône valley. The fighting in Marseilles and Toulon continues, however.

Italy Eighth Army begins a new offensive over the River Metauro on the Adriatic sector. The German defenders are caught by surprise and good progress is made by the offensive. The V British Corps, the Polish Corps and I Canadian Corps provide the attacking units.

Eastern Front In Estonia Maslennikov's forces take Tartu, an important position in the German defense lines.

26 AUGUST 1944

Northern France Most of the Allied Armies now have units over the Seine and advancing to the northeast. General de Gaulle returns to Paris and joins a ceremonial parade despite the danger from a few remaining German snipers.

Italy Eighth Army establishes solid bridgeheads over the Metauro. The German 71st Division is pushed back rapidly by V Corps.

Eastern Front In the south the Russian advance reaches the Danube east of Galati. The main attacks are, however, west of the town between it and Focsani.

Bulgaria The Bulgarian government announces that it has withdrawn from the war and that German troops will be disarmed. On 29 August the Soviet Union announces that it cannot accept or recognize Bulgarian neutrality.

27 AUGUST 1944

Northern France The Allied attacks over the Seine continue. The advance of US First Army and the British and Canadian forces has not yet gone far beyond the river, but the US Third Army on the right takes Chateau Thierry on the Marne as well as reaching the Seine farther inland at Troyes.

Eastern Front In Rumania Focsani and Galati are captured along with a large part of their garrisons. The advance continues in the direction of Ploesti and Bucharest.

Europe, Air Operations The RAF raid on the Homberg-Meerbeck oil plant is the first large-scale daylight operation by Bomber Command over Germany since the early months of the war. Although Mosquito bombers have often made daylight attacks before this, the employment of the slower, more vulnerable heavy bombers shows the extent of the air superiority which has been established by the long-range fighters.

28 AUGUST 1944

Northern France US First Army units cross the Marne at Meaux. Third Army is moving toward Reims and west of Paris the Allied advance is also continuing.

Southern France The last German forces in Toulon and Marseilles surrender. In the Rhône valley some German units, particularly 11th Panzer Division, have been cut off south of Montélimar but in attacks northward they mostly succeed in breaking through, although they take heavy losses from Allied artillery and air power.

Eastern Front Some of Second Ukraine Front's attacking units swing west and move through the Oituz Pass over the Carpathians toward Transylvania. On the Danube Third Ukraine Front takes Braila.

Hungary, Politics A new government, led by General Lakatos, takes office. They announce that they are ready to negotiate with the Russians.

29 AUGUST 1944

War Crimes The Russians and the Polish communists jointly announce that they have discovered evidence that the Germans have murdered around 1,500,000 people in the former Majdanek concentration camp. This is the first of a series of such dreadful discoveries.

Northern France The Allied advance continues apace. The US VII Corps takes Soissons and crosses the Aisne. To the east Third Army units take Reims and Chalons-sur-Marne.

Italy The advance of Eighth Army reaches the River Foglia. The next obstacle is the German Gothic Line which lies immediately to the north.

Eastern Front The Russians take the important Black Sea port of Constanta. Buzau, east of Ploesti also falls.

Poland, Resistance The British and United States' governments declare that they recognize the Home Army (AK) as a responsible belligerent force and that it should be treated as such. The Germans officially reject this procedure. In Warsaw the fighting continues to be very fierce and brutal.

CHRONOLOGY

30 AUGUST 1944

France, Politics The Provisional Government of General de Gaulle is established in Paris and begins work.

Northern France The British XXX Corps takes Beauvais in its continuing and accelerating advance.

Italy The Eighth Army begins its offensive against the Gothic Line. The main attacks are by V Corps units with support from part of the Canadian I Corps. The Polish Corps is fighting on the coast at Pesaro.

Eastern Front The Russians take Ploesti. Most of the Rumanian oilfields are now in Russian hands further increasing the shortages which have been imposed on the Germans by the American and British air offensive.

31 AUGUST 1944

Italy In the east Eighth Army continues to attack in some places breaking in to the Gothic Line. In the west the US IV Corps pushes forward following a German withdrawal from some positions along the Arno.

Eastern Front The troops of Second Ukraine Front take Bucharest.

31 AUGUST–2 SEPTEMBER 1944

Volcano Islands As part of the preparation for the coming operation against the Palau Islands TG 38.4 attacks Iwo Jima and Chichi Jima. Admiral Davison commands the three carriers. On 1 and 2 September, in addition to the air attacks, the supporting cruisers and destroyers go in to shell the islands.

SEPTEMBER 1944

Europe, Air Operations The Allied Air Offensive continues to be very destructive. Altogether 112,400 tons of bombs are dropped by the heavy bombers this month. RAF Bomber Command drops just under half with targets including Frankfurt, Bremerhaven, and Karlsruhe. The Channel ports Calais, Boulogne and Le Havre are also strongly hit with Calais being the target for 6500 tons on two occasions. The US Eighth and Fifteenth Air Forces drop 60,000 tons in their attacks and strike at Mainz, Hamm and Ludwigshafen among the general targets and in the more specialized oil offensive they hit Sterkrade, Merseburg, Bratislava and Lutzkendorf among others. The lighter forces of both Allies continue to be very active in their tactical role. Their attacks are particularly heavy in support of the airborne Operation *Market Garden*.

German avgas production is now less than 10,000 tons per month, compared with the May figure of 156,000 tons.

Atomic Research Work on the atomic program at Los Alamos has now proceeded so far that a special bomber unit is established to begin training to drop a bomb when one can be made. Some of the scientists working on the project are now beginning to have doubts about the morality of continuing their work when the war seems to be well on the way to being won and when intelligence information suggests that there is little danger of any of the Axis powers making a bomb. There are also some suggestions that the knowledge that is being gained should not remain secret after the war but should be shared throughout the scientific world. Despite these doubts the work continues.

Far East, Air Operations The Superfortresses from China bomb targets in Manchuria on several occasions including Anshan and Penhsiku. There are also attacks on various Japanese-held islands in the Pacific.

1 SEPTEMBER 1944

Western Front Dieppe is liberated fittingly by Canadian units. Inland British forces take Arras in their advance north of the Somme. The attacks of US First Army come near St Quentin and Cambrai. On the right Third Army take Verdun and Commercy. Eisenhower officially establishes his HQ in France and takes over direction of the Allied land forces.

During the past few days there has been an increasingly acrimonius strategic debate among the Allied generals as to how to exploit the serious German collapse. Eisenhower believes in a 'broad front' advance with all the Allied armies having an approximately equal share of the supplies and other support. This is entirely safe because no part of the force will ever get far enough ahead to be in any danger of isolation. The alternative is for the majority of resources, especially in logistical support, to be placed behind a portion of the allied force and for this group to push forward at speed and, it is hoped, quickly cross the Rhine and win the war. The most forceful version of this argument is put forward by General Montgomery. He proposes a thrust by a force of about 20 divisions drawn from both his and Bradley's armies which should aim to cross Belgium and encircle the Ruhr. Of course, he wishes to command himself but he is prepared to work under Bradley. Eisenhower recognizes the risks inherent in this plan and the political difficulties which would arise if a large part of the US forces was compelled to halt to allow the narrow front attack. He argues too that there are simply too few lorries to carry the supplies needed for such a scheme. In fact there are probably just enough. This debate on strategy is to continue in various forms for several months. It is clear that many of the Allied supply problems which are making a strategic choice pressing stem from the lack of a major port near the advance. None of the French Channel ports are really large enough to fill the gap and they are in any case still in German hands. Antwerp is the obvious choice and will be the focus of much of the Allied efforts for the next two months and more once the excitement of the *Market Garden* parachute operation is over. In practice it may have proved impossible to have brought Patton's Army to a halt because his supply officers are already in the habit of commandeering any supply columns which fill their needs whether they have priority or not. They have also been less able to put captured railroad equipment into service than the other armies largely because of the troops' habit of wildly shooting up any such captures.

The advance in southern France continues. Narbonne and St Agrève are taken by French forces.

Italy Eighth Army continues its attacks on the *Gothic* line in the Adriatic sector. The advance of the Canadian I Corps around Tomba di Pesaro is particularly successful.

Eastern Front The Russian advance reaches the Bulgarian frontier at Giurgiu on the Danube. Calarasi is also taken.

Bulgaria, Politics The Prime Minister Bagrianov resigns and is replaced by Constantine Muraviev.

2 SEPTEMBER 1944

Western Front In southern France the Allied landings have now put ashore 190,000 men with 41,000 vehicles and 220,000 tons of supplies. The American advance has reached almost to Lyons. French units are being brought up to be the first into the city. In northern France the Allied advance continues rapidly, but supply problems and shortages are beginning to cause difficulty for US First and Third Armies. British troops enter Belgium. Among the towns liberated by various Allied forces are Douai, St Valery and Lens.

Finland The Finnish Prime Minister Antii Hackzell announces that Finland is breaking diplomatic relations with Germany and demands that all German troops are withdrawn.

Italy The Canadian forces in Eighth Army make a partial breakthrough and advance several miles to the Conca River west of

Cattolica. San Giovanni is taken. The Polish forces fighting in Pesaro have nearly completed the capture of the city. The eastern end of the Gothic Line has been overrun despite the arrival of some German reserves.

3 SEPTEMBER 1944

Western Europe Brussels is entered by the British Guards Armored Division. Other towns taken by 21 Army Group are Tournai and Abbeville. The US Third Army has advance units across the Moselle. Mons is taken by US First Army. In the advance in southern France Lyons falls to the French 1st Infantry Division.

Wake Island Admiral Smith leads three heavy cruisers and three destroyers to bombard the Japanese positions on the island. The light carrier *Monterey* provides air cover.

Italy Canadian units cross the Conca and continue their advance.

4 SEPTEMBER 1944

Western Front The British 11th Armored Division enters Antwerp but fails to push forward to take the important canal crossings which lead to ground dominating the approaches to this large and enormously valuable port. Other towns freed by the Allied advance are Lille, Louvain, Malines and Etaples.

Finland A cease-fire is agreed between the Russians and the Finns and comes into effect immediately. The armistice is signed on 10 September and provides for the restoration of the 1940 frontiers and for Finland to pay reparations. The Germans begin to pull out of Finland by land and sea. The bulk of their force will go to Norway, but about 7000 men will be taken off through the Baltic ports.

Eastern Front In their attacks through the Carpathians the Russians take Brasov. Senaia is also taken.

5 SEPTEMBER 1944

Western Europe The US First Army takes Namur and Charleroi. Hitler brings Field Marshal Rundstedt back to command in chief the armies in the west.

Italy Eighth Army's attacks continue but they are now up against the strong German positions on the Coriano and Gemmano ridges. Tank units have been brought forward but cannot break through. On the western side of the country units of US IV Corps take Lucca.

Bulgaria The Bulgarian attempts to stay out of the war prove unsuccessful. The Soviet Union today declares war. The Bulgarian prime minister broadcasts and declares war in turn on

Germany on 8 September.

Diplomatic Affairs The Benelux Customs Union (between *Bel*gium, *N*etherlands and *Lux*embourg) is established by agreement of the exile governments. This is one of the first moves which will lead eventually to the establishment of the European Economic Community.

6 SEPTEMBER 1944

Western Front The Canadian forces reach the Channel north of Calais and just south of Boulogne. The US First Army crosses the Meuse at several points south of Namur. Ghent, Courtrai and Armentières all fall to 21 Army Group. In southern France Chalons-sur-Saone is taken by the French II Corps.

Eastern Front The Russian advance through Rumania reaches the Yugoslavian border on the Danube at Turnu-Severin. Nearer the opposite end of the Russian front Ostroleka is taken only 25 miles from the East Prussian border.

United States, Home Front The army is able to announce that it will demobilize 1,000,000 men when the war with Germany is over.

Britain, Home Front The Minister for Home Security, Herbert Morrison relaxes blackout and other civil defense duties. The War Office ends compulsory training and drills for Home Guard units.

6–8 SEPTEMBER 1944

Carolines All four groups, 16 carriers in all, of Admiral Mitscher's TF 38 attack Palau. Admiral Halsey, commanding Third Fleet, is present aboard the battleship *New Jersey.*

7 SEPTEMBER 1944

Western Front In Belgium British and American units cross the Albert canal east of Antwerp. Other American formations from First Army have nearly reached Liège.

8 SEPTEMBER 1944

V-Weapons The first German V2 rocket weapon lands in the Chiswick area of London.

Western Front The VII Corps from the US First Army takes Liège. Troops from Canadian First Army capture Nieuport and Ostend. In southern France Besançon falls to US VI Corps.

Italy After two days of rain Eighth Army continues its attacks on the Gemmano and Coriano ridges without success.

9 SEPTEMBER 1944

Western Front In Belgium the Canadians take Bruges while in southern France Beaune, Le Creusot and Autun all fall to French units.

France, Politics General de Gaulle appoints a new Cabinet. The principal change is the appointment of Georges Bidault as Foreign Minister.

9–10 SEPTEMBER 1944

Philippines Mindanao. Three groups, 12 carriers in all, from TF 38 attack airfields on the island. There is little Japanese resistance.

10 SEPTEMBER 1944

Western Front Troops from US First Army enter Luxembourg. On the Channel coast Le Havre is shelled by the battleship *Warspite* and the monitor *Erebus*, in preparation for an Allied assault. Farther north the Canadians are attacking near Zeebrugge. Eisenhower accepts Montgomery's proposal that an airborne operation should be mounted to take the bridges over a series of canals and rivers in Holland. This operation will be known as *Market Garden* and is designed to allow a rapid advance into Germany. It is based on the assumption that the Germans have only light forces in the relevant areas and will not be able to prevent the advance of ground forces to link up with the paratroops. The operation will begin on 17 September.

Italy Fifth Army steps up its attacks with efforts by II US Corps toward the Futa and Il Giogo Passes north of Florence.

11 SEPTEMBER 1944

Western Front The attack on Le Havre by British I Corps goes in after a heavy RAF raid. US First Army units actually reach German soil north of Trier but they have little strength here. Malmédy is taken in this sector. The British Second Army enters Holland near Bourg Leopold and takes an important bridgehead over the Meuse-Escaut canal. The forces moving up from the south of France take Dijon and link with the French 2nd Armored Division of US Third Army near Sombernon.

Italy Fifth Army's advance continues. Pistoia is taken by South African units of British XIII Corps.

11–16 SEPTEMBER 1944

Allied Planning Churchill and Roosevelt and their staffs meet in Quebec for the Octagon Conference. There is little change made to the overall strategy. It is agreed to continue with the campaigns in northwest Europe and Italy along the established lines. Unusually there is no opposition even from the US Navy representatives to a vigorous policy in Italy. A program of attacks for Burma is agreed. Also after Churchill and Roosevelt have talked the matter over the US Navy concede that British forces should join their own for the final campaigns against Japan.

12 SEPTEMBER 1944
Western Front The 12,000-strong German garrison of Le Havre surrenders to the attacks of British I Corps. More units of the US First Army reach the German border between Aachen and Trier.
Aegean The Germans evacuate Mytilene.

The exiled Greek government moves from Cairo to Caserta in southern Italy to be nearer to home when the time comes for the return.

12–14 SEPTEMBER 1944
Philippines The three groups of TF 38 which attacked Mindanao on 9 and 10 September shift their attention to the Visayas or Central Philippine Islands. On 14 September one group again hits targets on Mindanao. More than 200 Japanese planes are destroyed in the 2400 missions flown.

13 SEPTEMBER 1944
Rumania The armistice between the Allies and Rumania is signed. The terms have been dictated by the Soviets and include reparations of $300,000,000 and the cession of territory to the USSR.
Western Front The US Third Army continues its attacks taking Neufchateau.
Eastern Front Second Belorussian Front take Lomza on the Narew west of Bialystok. The Soviets respond to British and American pressure and begin supply drops to the Polish Home Army (AK) forces fighting in Warsaw.
Italy Eighth Army has succeeded in clearing the Germans entirely from the Coriano Ridge and almost completely from the Gemmano positions.

13–14 SEPTEMBER 1944
Palau Islands The American forces begin their preliminary bombardment of Peleliu and Angaur. Admiral Oldendorf leads five battleships, nine cruisers and numerous destroyers in this operation. Also in support is an escort carrier force which varies in strength at different times from seven to 11 ships. Minesweeping operations also begin to clear the approach to the islands.

14 SEPTEMBER 1944
Italy With the capture of Zollara the Gemmano Ridge is finally cleared of German forces and the Eighth Army is able to push forward to the Marano River.
Eastern Front The Warsaw suburb of Praga is taken by Soviet troops of First Belorussian Front. There is no real attempt to break into the city proper to aid the AK.

15 SEPTEMBER 1944
Arctic A force of 28 British Lancaster bombers from a Russian base is sent to attack *Tirpitz* in the anchorage at Altafiord. Special 12,000-pound bombs are used but only one hit is obtained on the *Tirpitz*'s bows because of effective smoke screens shielding the target.
France, Politics Francois de Menthon, the Justice Commissioner, orders the arrest of Marshal Pétain and all the members of the Vichy Cabinet because of their alleged collaboration with the Germans.
Moluccan Islands American forces land on the southwest of Morotai at the Gila Peninsula. There is no Japanese resistance. The landing force is from Hall's XI Corps and includes the 31st Division and an additional regiment. The naval support is commanded by Admiral Barbey and includes six escort carriers as well as cruisers and destroyers. General MacArthur is present. On the first day 19,960 men go ashore and by the start of October the force has been built up by 26,000 combat troops and 12,200 in the construction units. Airfields are quickly built and until they become operational Fifth Air Force gives cover.
Palaus There are US landings on the southwest coast of Peleliu. The Japanese garrison of the island is made up of a regiment of the 14th Division commanded by Colonel Nakagawa. The main Japanese force in the area is on Babelthaup. The landing force is General Rupertus' 1st Marine Division from Geiger's III Amphibious Corps. The naval forces which carried out the preliminary bombardment remain in support.

The landings meet fairly moderate resistance on the beaches but as soon as they move inland the fighting becomes very fierce. The Japanese have constructed a formidable defense system based principally on the complex of caves with which the island is riddled. At the end of the day the beachhead is only a few hundred yards wide at the most.
Western Front The British Second Army takes a second crossing point over the Meuse-Escaut canal. Maastricht and Eisden are both taken by US First Army and Nancy and Epinal by US Third Army. The forces moving up from the south of France, General Patch's US Seventh Army and General de Lattre's French First

CHRONOLOGY

Army come under General Eisenhower's command.
Italy Eighth Army creates a bridgehead over the Marano.

16 SEPTEMBER 1944

Eastern Front There is a new large-scale Soviet offensive in the Baltic States involving principally attacks toward Riga and Tallinn. In the south in Bulgaria, Sofia is taken by that proportion of Third Ukraine Front which has crossed the Danube before turning west to threaten the retreat of the German forces in Greece.
Palaus The Marines consolidate and extend their beachhead on Peleliu. The island's airfield is partly captured.

16–20 SEPTEMBER 1944

Indian Ocean The British Eastern Fleet sends two carriers and one battleship to raid Sigli in northern Sumatra.

16–21 SEPTEMBER 1944

Denmark, Resistance There is a general strike in Denmark as a protest against recent deportations carried out by the Germans.

17 SEPTEMBER 1944

Western Front Operation Market Garden is begun. The Allied plan has as its chief proponent General Montgomery and is for airborne troops to seize a series of bridges over river and canal lines in Holland allowing the main Allied forces, or part of them, to continue their advance into Germany unimpeded by such natural barriers. The belief is that the German armies in the west have been so decisively weakened by the battles since D-Day that they will collapse if momentum can be sustained. In fact the German forces in Holland generally and especially around the Arnhem area in particular are not as weak as has been believed. It is indeed arguable that the effort put into Market Garden would have been better spent in clearing the Scheldt estuary and getting Antwerp working to create a solid basis for the future Allied campaigns.

In detail the plan provides for three airborne divisions to be dropped and five main bridges to be captured while the British XXX Corps attacks north to link up with each division in turn. The nearest bridges, over canals north of Eindhoven at Veghel and Zon, are the objectives of the US 82nd Airborne Division. These objectives are taken on the first day. The US 101st Airborne Division is dropped around Grave south of Nijmegen with the task of taking the bridges over

the Maas at Grave and the Waal at Nijmegen. The first of these is taken on the first day. The farthest bridge is at Arnhem over the lower Rhine. This is the objective of the British 1st Airborne Division. They are dropped deliberately a little distance away from the town to allow some organization before going into battle and on balance this proves to have been a mistaken tactic because of the time it gives the German forces to react. It is unfortunate that a SS Panzer Division, recovering from a mauling on the Eastern Front, is close by and is still a very formidable opponent. The airborne troops, of course, have only weapons light enough to be carried in gliders. One battalion manages to reach the bridge but is there cut off from the remainder of the force which is itself fighting for its life. The Germans retain control of one end of the bridge while the paratroops hold the other. Overall the first day of the operation has been fairly successful. All the bridges are still intact but the deciding factor will be whether XXX Corps can advance fast enough to aid the paratroops in the various landing grounds.

As well as the air support for this operation there is a heavy, 3500 tons, RAF attack on Boulogne before an assault by Canadian forces goes in.
Palaus General Mueller's US 8th Infantry Division lands on Angaur. The Japanese garrison is about 1600 strong. Resistance to the landings immediately and later during the first night is energetic but later during the first night is energetic but neither very powerful nor effective.

There are Japanese attacks by night but by day the Americans still hold most of the south side of Peleliu comfortably enough. They begin attacks on the Japanese positions on Mount Umurgrobol. Only a little progress is made here despite the support from heavy naval guns because of the strength and elaboration of the Japanese defenses.

18 SEPTEMBER 1944

Palaus On Peleliu the Marines try to extend their attacks on Mount Umurgrobol but they are thrown back by the Japanese and suffer heavy losses.

The American force makes a confident advance inland toward the center of Angaur. Although the Japanese infiltrations cause some problems, they are too heavily outnumbered to do much more.
Western Front The British XXX Corps links up with the 101st Airborne Division at Eindhoven and Veghel. These attacks continue, meeting gradually increasing resistance. To the north

both the other airborne divisions in the Market Garden operation are fighting fiercely to maintain their position.

Warsaw In the only major attempt to drop supplies allowed by the Soviets 1284 containers are dropped to the AK by a force of B-17 bombers, but only 228 fall in Polish held territory.

19 SEPTEMBER 1944

Western Front In the morning the continuing XXX Corps attacks link up with the 82nd Airborne Division at Grave. Together these formations move toward Nijmegen. At Arnhem the main body of the British paratroops still cannot reach the battalion which continues to hold its position at the north end of the bridge.

Back in Brittany the last resistance of the German garrison in Brest comes to an end.

Eastern Front In Estonia Valga falls to Maslennikov's troops. The Russian offensive here and throughout the Baltic States continues.

Palaus The heavy fighting on Peleliu around Mount Umurbrogol goes on. The American advance is being held fairly comfortably by the Japanese.

On Angaur the fighting is also intense.

20 SEPTEMBER 1944

Western Front A joint attack by the British Guards Armored Division and the US 82nd Airborne Division takes Nijmegen and the vital bridge over the Waal before it can be destroyed by the Germans. At Arnhem the British paratroops are driven away from the north end of the bridge despite a desperate fight.

In other attacks Polish troops of Canadian First Army make gains along the Scheldt estuary and US Third Army takes Châtel and Lunéville.

Italy The advance of British V Corps, Eighth Army, enters the Republic of San Marino.

Palaus On Angaur the main Japanese forces have been wiped out but a few units will hold out for some time in the northwest of the island.

21 SEPTEMBER 1944

Italy Eighth Army's advance reaches Rimini. The town is taken by Canadian and Greek units.

Western Front The British XXX Corps continues to attack northward from Nijmegen but can only make very slow progress because the advance must go along or very near to the roads and rail lines which are raised above the marshy surrounding ground and consequently exposed. It is, therefore, comparatively simple to meet these attacks. The British paratroops have been driven out of Arnhem and are now holding a

perimeter west of the town but still north of the Rhine. A Polish Parachute Brigade is dropped two miles south of this position on the opposite side of the river.

21–24 SEPTEMBER 1944

Philippines Twelve carriers from TF 38 attack targets on Luzon, especially near Manila and in Manila Bay on 21 and 22 September. On the 23rd there are no attacks, but on 24 September the Visayan islands are hit once again. In the operations since 31 August TF 38 has destroyed at least 1000 Japanese aircraft and sunk 150 ships of all types. The Americans have lost 72 aircraft including 18 accidents.

22 SEPTEMBER 1944

Western Front The Polish paratroops joined later by British 43rd Division try to reach the Rhine to help the British airborne troops still cut off on the north bank. Other XXX Corps forces continue to meet heavy resistance in their advance toward Arnhem. Elst five miles north of Nijmegen is taken. In other Allied attacks Boulogne falls to the Canadian 3rd Division.

Eastern Front Troops from Govorov's Leningrad Front take Tallinn the capital of Estonia. In Rumania the Russian advance reaches Arad.

Palaus General Geiger decides to bring in a regiment of 81st Infantry Division to replace some of the Marine units which have taken heavy losses in the attacks on Mount Umurbrogol. Later a second regiment of this division is committed.

23 SEPTEMBER 1944

Pacific Ulithi atoll, just north of the Palaus, is occupied by a part of the US 81st Division after a naval reconnaissance has suggested that it is not used by the Japanese. By the end of the war it will have become one of the main bases for the American fleets.

Eastern Front In Estonia the Russian advance reaches the Baltic at Pärnu. The Russian force in Rumania pushes on beyond Arad to the Hungarian frontier.

Western Front The battles in the Arnhem area continue with no real change in fortune for either side. To the west of the British XXX Corps advance, Canadian units cross the Escaut canal in the beginning of their offensive to clear the north bank of the Scheldt.

Italy Fifth Army's attacks north of Florence clear the Futa Pass through the Appenines.

24 SEPTEMBER 1944

Western Front XXX Corps advance reaches the

CHRONOLOGY

south bank of the Rhine west of Arnhem. North of the river the paratroops are still holding out despite many casualties from fierce attacks and shortages of food and ammunition. Other XXX Corps units enter Germany southwest of Nijmegen.

Palaus On Peleliu heavy naval and air bombardments herald new American attacks, but these too are thrown back.

25 SEPTEMBER 1944
Western Front Troops from British Second Army take Helmond and Deurne only a few miles east of Eindhoven. This illustrates well on how narrow a front XXX Corps has been compelled to advance to Arnhem. It is decided to evacuate as many as possible of the surviving Arnhem paratroops across the Rhine in small boats. During the night 2400 of the 10,000 who landed get away. About 1100 have been killed and 6400 taken prisoner. Some few more are sheltered by Dutch families until the Allies advance again despite dreadful food shortages and the terrible danger of discovery.

On the Channel coast the Canadian 3rd Division attacks Calais where the German garrison still holds out.

The Allied landings in the south of France which are still continuing have now contributed 324,000 men to the AEF along with 68,000 vehicles and 490,000 tons of supplies. Much of the supplies for the southern armies along the German border are still coming through Marseilles.

Eastern Front In Estonia the Baltic port of Haapsalu falls to the Russians. In Yugoslavia the Partisan forces take Banja Luka.

Palaus The Americans make some gains in the north of Peleliu on Mount Amiangal after attacks employing tanks and flame throwers.

The fighting continues around the Japanese pockets near Lake Salome on Angaur.

26 SEPTEMBER 1944
Greece, Politics At Caserta in Italy an agreement is concluded between the exile Greek government and the various guerrilla leaders in which the guerrillas undertake to obey the orders of the government. The government delegates military authority to the British General Scobie who has been appointed by General Wilson who has supervised the talks.

Italy Eighth Army units cross the Rubicon River as their advance goes on.

Western Front The Allied attacks in Belgium and Holland continue. Turnhout, in north Belgium midway between Antwerp and Eind-

hoven, and Oss, west of Grave, are both taken as the advance of XXX Corps to the Rhine is consolidated. This has been a considerable achievement even though the prize of the bridge at Arnhem has not been won.

27 SEPTEMBER 1944
Western Front The US XX Corps, Third Army, begins to attack the outer defenses of Metz. Much of Third Army's efforts will be devoted, perhaps wastefully, to this sector for some time to come.

Eastern Front German resistance on the Estonian mainland is largely over. The Soviets land on Vormsi Island just west of Haapsula. In Hungary there has been heavy fighting around Cluj for several days because of German counterattacks. These battles continue.

28 SEPTEMBER 1944
Palaus US forces from Peleliu land on Negesbus and Kongauru, other small islands in the group. There is little fighting on either.

On Peleliu itself the full-scale US attacks come to an end but bitter fighting continues all around Mount Umurbrogol as the Americans keep trying to eliminate individual Japanese positions.

29 SEPTEMBER 1944
Western Front In their continuing attacks at Calais the Canadian 3rd Division begins to make real progress against the stubborn German defense.

Palaus The US forces tighten their hold on the remaining Japanese pockets, still further confining them to a very small area in the northwest of Angaur.

Eastern Front Troops of the Russian Eighth Army land on Muhu Island in the Baltic. The German forces withdraw from this position to the nearby Saaremaa.

30 SEPTEMBER 1944
Western Front The attacks of First Canadian Army north and west of Antwerp continue. Calais surrenders to the Canadian 3rd Division. There are brief German attacks against the US XII Corps, Third Army, but these are held.

Palaus Admiral Fort takes over command of the American operations in this group and announces that Peleliu, Angaur, Ngesebus and Kongauru have all been completely occupied. The fighting is not over yet, despite this announcement.

OCTOBER 1944
Europe, Air Operations The American heavy

bomber forces drop 57,000 tons, most of it by Eighth Air Force. Among the targets are Kassel, Cologne, Hamm and Munster and in the oil offensive Buer, Sterkrade, Bohlen, Homberg and Regensburg. Synthetic manufacturing plants, refineries and stores are all hit. RAF Bomber Command drops 50,000 tons on German targets including Duisburg, 10,000 tons in two raids, Essen and Cologne. There are also heavy attacks in support of the armies and in these the RAF drops 10,000 tons mainly in the Walcheren area.

Far East, Air Operations Among the targets for the USAAF heavy bomber forces are the aircraft plants at Omura, military installations in many areas of Formosa and above all a range of objectives in the Philippines.

1 OCTOBER 1944

Italy General McCreery takes over command of Eighth Army from General Leese who is being sent to command Allied Land Forces, Southeast Asia. The US II Corps, Fifth Army, begins a new drive north in the direction of Bologna.

Greece British commando units land at Poros. Greek troops land at Mitilini, Lemnos and Levita.

2 OCTOBER 1944

Western Front US First Army begins a new offensive against the Siegfried Line between Aachen and Geilenkirchen to the north.

Eastern Front The brave resistance of the patriot forces in Warsaw comes to an end. At least 200,000 Poles have died in the brutal fighting. Much of the central part of Warsaw has already been destroyed and much more will be razed to the ground at Hitler's order.

Palaus On Peleliu the Japanese pockets on Mount Amiangal are mopped up. Resistance continues to be very fierce around Mount Umurbrogol.

3 OCTOBER 1944

Western Front The US First Army goes on with its attacks north of Aachen and succeeds in breaking through the Siegfried Line defenses in some areas.

The dikes around Walcheren Island are breached near Westkapelle by a heavy attack by RAF bombers. This causes much of the island to be flooded and is meant to hamper the German defense.

Eastern Front The Russians land on Hiiuma Island off the Estonian coast and practically overrun it.

4 OCTOBER 1944

Western Front There is a German counter-attack against the forces of US First Army which have broken through the Siegfried Line north of Aachen. The Americans hold their ground.

Eastern Front Pančevo on the north bank of the Danube just east of Belgrade is taken by troops of Third Ukraine Front. The Russian forces also reach Vladimirovac and link with Partisan units near there.

Greece Allied forces land on the Peloponese near Patras. There are other landings on the Aegean islands. Patras is occupied on 5 October.

5 OCTOBER 1944

Eastern Front Soviet forces land on Saaremaa Island in the Baltic. The German forces on the island make a fighting withdrawal toward the Syrve peninsula. The Russian offensive in the Baltic States proper is continuing. Army Group North is hard pressed on the approaches to Riga.

6 OCTOBER 1944

Western Front The Canadian II Corps begins attacks to eliminate the German forces holding out south of the Scheldt between the Leopold canal and the south bank of the river around Breskens. The ground conditions are very difficult with many wet and flooded areas. The attack makes a little progress.

7 OCTOBER 1944

Western Front The Canadians have managed to get some of their attacking forces across the Leopold canal into two small bridgeheads, but they are halted there by fierce German resistance. There is also heavy fighting in the US Third Army sector. The Americans gain some ground in Luxembourg and near Metz but between these areas there are effective German counter-attacks.

8 OCTOBER 1944

Western Front All along the front the attacking Allied troops are held by fierce resistance. The heaviest fighting is in the sectors of the Canadian II Corps and the US XII and XIX Corps.

Eastern Front Finnish troops retake Kemi at the head of the Gulf of Bothnia. This is the last port in Finland that has been held by the Germans.

Greece Corinth and Samos are taken by British forces. Part of the British 9th Commando also lands at Nauplion.

9 OCTOBER 1944

Western Front Troops from the Canadian 3rd

Division land at Breskens on the south bank of the Scheldt opposite Flushing. The fighting in the Aachen and Metz areas continues to be quite fierce.

Marcus Island A US Task Force of cruisers and destroyers is led to shell the island by Admiral Smith.

9–20 OCTOBER 1944
Allied Diplomacy Churchill and Eden visit Moscow for talks with the Russians on arrangements for the political future of eastern Europe. For some of the discussion there are representatives of the exile, London Polish government present. They achieve no real concessions from the Soviets. Similarly Stalin insists that Bulgaria and Rumania are to remain a Soviet sphere of influence entirely. Greece is to come under British sway and in Hungary and in Yugoslavia influence is to be divided. The western powers do not feel able to press Stalin any harder than this because they value his promise to join the war against Japan as well as his continuing help against a still undefeated Germany. Stalin will in fact scrupulously stick to his word about keeping out of Greece.

10 OCTOBER 1944
Ryukyu Islands The main American carrier force, TF 38 begins a series of operations with attacks by one of its four groups on Onami-O-shima, two on Okinawa and the fourth against Sakashima. Many Japanese aircraft are destroyed over the islands but the Japanese fail to find the American ships with their strikes. Ten Japanese merchant vessels are sunk around Okinawa.

TF 38 is led by Admiral Mitscher and includes 11 fleet carriers, six light carriers, six battleships as well as cruisers and destroyers. Admiral Halsey commands Third Fleet of which TF 38 is a part.

Western Front The attacks of US First Army around Aachen continue to press forward. The German garrison of the city is summoned to surrender.

Italy The US II Corps is still continuing its attack in the direction of Bologna, but the rugged terrain and the worsening weather help the vigorous German defense. To the east the British attacks are in most places over the Rubicon.

Eastern Front The advance of First Baltic Front reaches the sea north of Memel. In the south Third Ukraine Front continues to attack south of Belgrade. The rail line from there to Niš is cut around Velika Plana.

11 OCTOBER 1944
Philippines Two groups of TF 38 led by Admirals Cain and Davison carry out a small attack on airfields in the north of Luzon while the remainder of the force is refuelling.

Western Front Bardenburg is taken by units of XIX Corps (US First Army). Third Army take Parroy, having cleared the Forêt de Parroy nearby. In the Scheldt estuary the Canadians cut the causeway between the mainland and Beveland and Walcheren.

Italy The 91st Division of US II Corps is heavily engaged at Livergnano. Troops of Eighth Army take Lorenzo.

Eastern Front In Hungary troops from Second Ukraine Front, Malinovsky, cross the Tisza around Szeged which is taken. To the east there is fighting at Debrecen and Cluj, which falls after a long struggle.

12 OCTOBER 1944
Greece Allied paratroops land at Athens airfield. The Germans evacuate the Piraeus. There are other British landings on Corfu.

Eastern Front In Hungary Oradea is taken by Second Ukraine Front while a little to the north the battle for Debrecen goes on. Subotica, just west of Szeged, is taken by combined attacks by Tito's Partisans and the Russian forces.

Palaus On Peleliu the fighting here goes on, with 1st Marines heavily engaged with the Japanese defenses on Mount Umurgbrogol.

12–14 OCTOBER 1944
Formosa On 12 and 13 October all four groups of TF 38 send attacks against targets on Formosa. Altogether 2350 missions are flown by the carrier planes and in return the Japanese can only organize 190. Most of the Japanese attacks are intercepted and many more of their planes are destroyed over the island and on the ground. The Americans lose 48 aircraft. The carrier *Franklin* is slightly damaged and the Australian cruiser *Canberra* seriously hit. On 14 October one group continues the attack on Formosa, losing 23 planes from 246. The cruiser *Houston* is crippled in a torpedo attack. Superfortress bombers from Chinese bases join the assault.

13 OCTOBER 1944
Western Front Units of British VIII Corps begin an attack from south of Nymegen toward Venlo. Troops from the US 1st Division enter Aachen from the east and vicious street fighting begins.

The first V1's and V2's in what is to be a major part of the rocket campaign land on Antwerp.

Italy The British 46th Division (V Corps) takes Carpineta. Inland the fighting south of Bologna continues.

Eastern Front Troops from Second and Third Baltic Fronts break the German defense ring around Riga and reach nearly to the outskirts of the city.

Greece Advance guards of a major British and Greek force land at the Piraeus.

14 OCTOBER 1944

Western Front The advance of Canadian II Corps links up with the landing force at Breskens.

Greece Athens and the Piraeus are completely liberated. There are further British landings on Corfu. The main body of the British III Corps is about to land at Piraeus.

German Command Suspected of complicity in the 20th July plot against Hitler, Rommel is visited at home by two of Hitler's staff and given the choice of a humiliating public trial or a suicide by poison with a state funeral and a guarantee of immunity from persecution for his wife and family. Rommel decides to commit suicide and it is announced in Germany that he has died of wounds.

Palaus The 81st Infantry Division replaces the Marines at the front on Peleliu where the fighting is still fierce.

The American authorities announce that the occupation of Angaur is complete although skirmishing continues on the north of the island.

14–15 OCTOBER 1944

Philippines On Luzon the carrier forces of TG 38.4 send attacks on Aparri Airfield on 14 October and against other targets north of Manila on 15 October. In the operations of the whole of TF 38 between 10 and 15 October the Japanese have lost about 370 planes and the Americans less than 100.

15 OCTOBER 1944

Western Front The US VI Corps (Seventh Army) begins an offensive to the west of Epinal. The battles for Aachen and in the Scheldt estuary go on.

Italy The Polish 2nd Division takes Gambettola. American and South African units make some ground near Livergnano and Grizzana.

Eastern Front The Russian Fourteenth Army takes Petsamo in the far north of Finland. In Latvia Riga falls to Second and Third Baltic Fronts.

15–16 OCTOBER 1944

Hungary Budapest radio transmits a broadcast by Admiral Horthy, the prime minister and regent asking for an armistice from Russia. On 16 October it is announced on the radio that the request is void. Horthy resigns and is taken off to Germany. Ferenc Szalasy becomes regent and prime minister.

16 OCTOBER 1944

Western Front While the fighting inside Aachen continues, troops from US XIX and VIII Corps link up to the east, completing the isolation of the city.

The US VI Corps meets heavy resistance on the Moselle around Bruyères. On its right the French First Army begins a new drive.

Eastern Front In Yugoslavia the Russians take Niš recently evacuated by the Germans. In this sector Russian, Bulgarian and Yugoslav forces are all working together.

Greece British forces land on Lemnos.

16–19 OCTOBER 1944

Philippines The preliminary air attacks and fleet movements for the US landing on Leyte take place. On 16 October there are attacks by land-based aircraft of Thirteenth and Fifth Air Forces from Biak, Sansapor and Morotai against targets on Mindanao. The 18 escort carriers of Admiral T F Sprague's TG 77.4 also begin operations with attacks on Leyte, Cebu and Mindanao. These attacks continue on 17 October and are reinforced by the four carriers of Davison's TG 38.4 who attack Luzon. Also on 17 October minesweeping begins in Leyte Gulf. The small island of Suluan and Dinagat at the entrance to the Gulf are occupied by minor US Ranger units. On 18 October the escort carriers concentrate their efforts on Leyte while the large carriers, now 12 in three groups, still strike at Luzon. On 19 October the escort carriers maintain their attacks on Leyte. Fifth Air Force strikes at Mindanao.

The Japanese air forces lose heavily in these operations and in their own, unsuccessful attacks on the American naval squadrons. On 19 October the remaining units are concentrated in First Air Fleet under Admiral Onishi's command on Luzon.

17 OCTOBER 1944

Western Front Troops from the British Second Army take Venray in their drive toward Venlo. The US Seventh Army continues its battle around Lunéville and Bruyères.

Italy The Polish II Corps begins attacks just south of Forlí, while farther inland the offensive of US II Corps toward Bologna still grinds forward but only very slowly.

France, Politics The French War Ministry and the National Council for the Resistance reach agreement on the process for the integration of the resistance forces, FFI, into the regular army. This negotiation has not been easy because of the various political loyalties of the resistance groups.

17–19 OCTOBER 1944

Indian Ocean TF 63 from the British Eastern Fleet sends two carriers, one battlecruiser and lighter forces to attack the Nicobar Islands as a diversion for the US attack on Leyte. The carrier aircraft attack on 17 and 19 October and the islands are shelled on 17 and 18 October. Although considerable damage is done, as a diversion the operation fails.

18 OCTOBER 1944

Greece The Greek exile government returns home. Santorini and Scarpanto are occupied by British forces and the port of Patras is opened to shipping.

Germany, Home Front From now on all able-bodied males between the ages of 16 and 60 are to be liable for conscription into the home-defense force, the Volkssturm.

Western Europe General McClain replaces General Corlett in command of the US First Army.

Eastern Front Moscow announces that Red Army units from Petrov's Fourth Ukraine Front have entered Czechoslovakia. The Germans are rapidly retreating north from Greece and southern Yugoslavia, fearful of being isolated.

19 OCTOBER 1944

Western Front The attacks on Aachen are proceeding and the German resistance is being worn down. Farther south, in the Seventh Army sector, Bruyères falls to the US 36th Division. Nearby other units are preparing to assault St Dié.

Italy Troops from the 10th Indian Division are attacking over the Savio River.

20 OCTOBER 1944

Philippines There are US landings on the east coast of Leyte. All the escort and fleet carriers involved in the preparatory attacks and Fifth Air Force provide air support. The landing ships and the bombardment and escort groups are from Kinkaid's Seventh Fleet and the troops landed are from Krueger's Sixth Army. Four divisions from two corps are landed. Sibert's X Corps, 1st Cavalry and 24th Infantry Divisions,

land slightly to the south of Tacloban and Hodge's XXIV Corps, 96th and 7th Divisions, around Dulag. Each corps has fire support from three battleships as well as cruisers and destroyers. The cruiser *Honolulu* is badly damaged by aerial torpedo in these operations. There is little fighting on the beaches as the defending Japanese 16th Division soon retires to prepared positions inland to await reinforcements. The Americans are, therefore, able to take Tacloban Airfield but cannot link the beachheads of the two corps. By nightfall 132,000 men are ashore.

General MacArthur, who is in Supreme Command, lands a few hours after the assault troops and broadcasts to the Philippine people recalling his famous promise, 'I shall return.'

The Japanese have set in train a massive fleet operation, Sho-go, to counter the American landings. A carrier force commanded by Admiral Ozawa leaves Japan while other units are assembling at Brunei in North Borneo. (*See* 22 October for the Japanese plan and the composition of forces.)

Western Front The British I Corps, First Canadian Army, begins an offensive driving north from northeast of Antwerp. In the area opposite Patton's Third Army there is extensive flooding in the German rear after the 19th TAF have breached the dam at Dieuze.

Italy The 4th and 46th Divisions, British V Corps, enter Cesena. In the central sector, south of Bologna, the South African 6th Armored Division, serving with Fifth Army, repulses a German counterattack.

Eastern Front A combined attack by Tito's Partisans and Russian units completes the liberation of Belgrade. The Partisans also take Dubrovnik on the Adriatic coast while in Hungary Debrecen is taken by the Russians.

21 OCTOBER 1944

Philippines After a successful battle with Japanese night attacks, the US forces take Dulag Airfield and Tacloban village but they are still unable to link their bridgeheads. The ships of Seventh Fleet and one group of TF 38 give gunfire and air support. Two groups of TF 38 attack targets on Panay, Cebu, Negros and Masbate.

Western Front At midday Aachen is surrendered to the American forces. Much of the city has been ruined in the battle.

Italy The British V and Canadian I Corps continue to push troops over the Savio despite the river being in spate because of recent heavy rain.

Palaus The Japanese resistance on Angaur comes to an end. The Japanese have lost 1300 dead and 45 prisoners and the Americans 265 dead and 1335 wounded.

The larger islands in the group are left with their Japanese garrisons isolated and impotent. Already US heavy bombers are operating from Angaur.

22 OCTOBER 1944

Philippines On Leyte all the US forces push forward. The most notable gains are by the 7th Division on the right flank who advance toward Abuyog.

Battle of Leyte Gulf The main units of the Japanese Fleet sail from Brunei. The other two squadrons which are to take part in the operation are already at sea and approaching the Philippines from the north. The plan is for Ozawa's carriers to draw off the main American forces to the northeast while the battleships and cruisers pass through the San Bernardino and Surigao Straits to get among the invasion transports and their comparatively vulnerable escorts. Ozawa has one large and one small carrier, two seaplane carriers and two hybrid carrier-battleships as well as smaller vessels. They have only 100 aircraft with inexperienced pilots. The Center Force which is intended to pass through the San Bernardino Strait is led by Admiral Kurita from Brunei and includes five battleships, with the giant *Yamato* and *Musashi* among them, 12 cruisers, almost all heavy, and 15 destroyers. The Southern Force (Nishimura) also sails from Brunei with two battleships, a cruiser and four destroyers. They are to be joined in the Surigao Strait by Shima's Second Striking Force now approaching the Philippines from the northwest. This group is composed of three cruisers and seven destroyers. Although one group of TF 38 has left to replenish, Halsey still has 12 carriers and six battleships and Kinkaid has 18 escort carriers and the six older battleships which have been supporting the landings. Only in cruisers is there anything like an equality in numbers. In destroyers the Americans have three times the Japanese force.

Western Front The Canadians complete the capture of Breskens on the south bank of the Scheldt estuary. In southern Holland the British XII Corps is attacking toward Tilburg.

Italy Canadian troops from Eighth Army take Cervia.

Eastern Front In the far north advance units of the Russian Fourteenth Army from the Karelia Front reach the Norwegian border. In Hungary Malinovsky's forces reach Baja on the Danube south of Budapest.

France, Politics General de Gaulle's administration is recognized by the Allies as the *de jure* Provisional Government of France.

23 OCTOBER 1944

Western Front There are attacks by the British

Above: The hundreds of ships which made up the Leyte invasion force.

4th Armored Division at the east end of the Beveland Isthmus. The US Seventh Army is still engaged around Bruyères and St Dié.

Eastern Front In the far north the Russians complete the clearance of the Petsamo region.

Philippines The battles on Leyte continue. The 1st Cavalry Division attacks northwest from Tacloban. In the XXIV Corps sector a tank unit accompanying 7th Division takes Burauen.

Battle of Leyte Gulf Kurita's Center Force is sighted off Palawan in the early hours by two US submarines. Two heavy cruisers are sunk in the subsequent attacks and one more damaged and forced to retire. One of the submarines is lost but because of their reports the three remaining groups of TF 38 east of the Philippines prepare to attack when the Japanese squadron is in range.

24 OCTOBER 1944

Western Front The Canadian 2nd Division begins to advance along the Beveland Isthmus. Inland the attacks of the British XII Corps penetrate to 's Hertogenbosch.

Greece British troops enter Lamia.

Philippines A small force from 1st Cavalry Division crosses the San Juanico Strait from Tacloban to land on Samar. Other units from the division advance along the south side of the Strait to Guintiguian.

Battle of Leyte Gulf Land-based aircraft from Luzon attack Sherman's TG 38.3, fatally damaging the carrier *Princeton*. Kurita's Center Force, now in the Sibuyan Sea, is found by scout planes from TG 38.2 and attacked throughout the day by strike aircraft from the three US carrier groups. The battleship *Musashi* sinks in the early afternoon after taking at least six torpedo and 10 bomb hits. One cruiser is also forced to return to base. Kurita turns away because of the weight of the attacks, convincing Halsey that his withdrawal will be permanent. During the evening Kurita again reverses course. Nishimura's Southern Force is also sighted in the approach but takes only negligible damage from the resulting air attacks. Admiral Oldendorf who has been leading one of the bombarding squadrons assembles a considerable force in the Surigao Strait to intercept Nishimura. Ozawa's carriers locate Sherman's group and send the majority of their aircraft to attack. They do not find their targets and are forced to land on Luzon. Ozawa has only 25 planes after this. Late in the day Halsey orders his carriers and modern battleships to assemble before moving to attack Ozawa, believing that Oldendorf will handle Nishimura and that Kurita has withdrawn.

25 OCTOBER 1944

Philippines In the northeast of Leyte 1st Cavalry Division continues its advance. To the south, however, some US units are forced to be inactive because of lack of supplies.

Eastern Front In the far north Soviet troops enter Norway and take the port of Kirkenes. The advance in this region is supported by naval units who provide fire missions and transport for several small amphibious operations. In the south the Soviet and allied attacks have completely cleared Transylvania.

Italy The British V Corps advance reaches and in one sector crosses the River Ronco.

25–26 OCTOBER 1944

Battle of Leyte Gulf Between midnight and 0430 there is a running battle as Nishimura's and then Shima's forces try to pass through Surigao Strait. Oldendorf first sends PT Boats and then destroyers to attack with torpedoes while waiting with his six battleships and eight cruisers at the north end of the Strait. The PT Boats sink one cruiser and the destroyers twice hit the battleship *Fuso*, sinking it and three destroyers. The other battleship, *Yamashiro*, is damaged and, steaming on, is sunk by Oldendorf's heavy ships. In the gun action the cruiser *Mogami* is nearly wrecked and will be abandoned later after a collision with the *Nachi*. The surviving Japanese forces withdraw.

Battle of Samar Kurita's force, now four battleships, six heavy and two light cruisers and 11 destroyers, passes the San Bernardino Strait in the early hours and in the morning off Samar finds Admiral C A F Sprague's TF 77.4.3 which consists of six escort carriers and seven destroyers. The aircraft of this group have been used to support land operations and are not, therefore, provided with the torpedoes or armor-piercing bombs needed for attacks on heavily protected ships. The American force is immediately compelled to flee with some cover from smokescreens and rain squalls. The destroyers attempt torpedo attacks and Sprague's planes are reinforced by those of a second escort-carrier group, TF 77.4.2. For two hours between 0700 and just after 0900 the Japanese ships gradually close in despite being repeatedly forced to alter course to avoid torpedo attacks. In these attacks one of the Japanese cruisers is sunk but as the range shortens the American squadron begins to take punishment. Three destroyers and one escort carrier are sunk from Sprague's force. The second carrier group is sighted and engaged also at the same time as three more of the Japanese cruisers fall to the air attacks. At this stage some of the Japanese cruisers are within 10,000 yards of the escort carriers and are beginning to hit their targets regularly. Kurita, however, believes that the attacking aircraft may be from the much more powerful TF 38 and he decides that he must withdraw. This decision is probably an error since there is little doubt that Sprague's force, with all its destroyers damaged, could not have held out much longer. It is probable also that once this battle was completed, the Japanese could have reached and destroyed much of the transport fleet off Leyte. While Kurita is turning away there are Japanese Kamikaze air attacks on TF 77.4.3 in which four escort carriers are sunk (some are already damaged). At about the same time the third US escort-carrier group, not previously engaged, faces a similar attack in which three carriers are damaged. These are the first significant, premeditated suicide attacks. Kurita continues to retire toward the San Bernardino Strait and is attacked by more US aircraft on the way.

The Carrier Battle While the other actions are going on, Halsey is leading the modern battleships and the main carrier force north to intercept Ozawa who has therefore exactly performed his decoy mission. In the morning the first American strikes go in. There are two waves of attacks in the morning in which two of the Japanese carriers are sunk. Before midday Halsey hears news from the south and turns south with the battleships and one carrier group. The other two carrier groups continue the pursuit, sinking the remaining carriers *Zuiho* and *Zuikaku.* Two destroyers and a cruiser are also sunk. The only major units to escape are the carrier-battleships *Ise* and *Hyuga.* Halsey's return south is too late to catch Kurita.

On 26th October American air attacks sink three more cruisers from the various retiring Japanese squadrons. Overall the Leyte Gulf battle has been a shattering defeat for the Japanese as well as, in part, a tale of missed opportunities. The only important American units sunk have been the escort carriers of which there are many more in service. After Leyte the Japanese have few of their purpose-built carriers remaining, but this loss is of less consequence than the serious damage done to their battleship and cruiser force because of the already existing shortage of trained pilots. Three battleships and 10 cruisers have been lost, others have been damaged and all the survivors have been forced to retire without coming to grips properly with the American forces. In the action in the Surigao Strait there is none of the former night-fighting

expertise. Clearly, in the future, the operations of the Japanese Fleet will be even more circumscribed and their only hope now is in the new suicide attacks which have been very successful in their way so far.

26 OCTOBER 1944

Philippines On Leyte the Japanese positions on Catmon Hill just north of Dulag, are fiercely attacked by the US forces. The attacks are repulsed but the defenders later retire. The Japanese garrison on the island receives reinforcements at their base at Ormoc.

Western Front The British 52nd Division lands on the south side of Beveland near Baarland against heavy German resistance. The Canadian forces are still fighting along the Beveland Isthmus. To the south in the Seventh Army sector the battle for St Dié continues.

Eastern Front The pincers of Second and Fourth Ukraine Fronts link up at Mukachevo in the southern Carpathian foothills near Uzhgorod.

27 OCTOBER 1944

Philippines On Leyte the US 7th Division takes Buri Airfield.

Western Front The Canadian drive against Beveland goes on. The German positions just inland from here are also attacked. Bergen-op-Zoom is taken. Near Venlo, in the British Second Army sector, there is a sharp German counterattack.

Italy The Allied advance is gradually becoming bogged down as the winter weather sets in.

Eastern Front Fourth Ukraine Front takes Uzhgorod in northeast Hungary. In the northern sector there is a new Soviet drive in Latvia.

27–30 OCTOBER 1944

Philippines On 27 October one group of three carriers commanded by Admiral Sherman attacks Japanese shipping around Luzon, sinking two destroyers. They also send attacks against Luzon Island. The battleship *California* is damaged by the Japanese. On 28 October Davison and Bogan take over and in air operations and ground-attack missions on 28 and 29 October they destroy almost 100 Japanese aircraft for the loss of just 15. The carrier *Intrepid* is slightly damaged by a Kamikaze attack. On 30 October two more carriers are badly hit by suicide attacks as the ships of TF 38 begin to withdraw to Ulithi.

28 OCTOBER 1944

Western Front Tilburg is taken by troops from

Dempsey's Second Army while west of Venlo there is an Allied attack against the German paratroops who advanced the previous day.

Eastern Front The USSR-Bulgaria armistice is signed. Bulgarian troops now come officially under Soviet command. Such arrangements have already been operating.

Philippines Around Dagami the US attacks only make slow progress and there are heavy losses. In the north of the island there is a fierce engagement near Carigara where the advance of 1st Cavalry Division is held up.

29 OCTOBER 1944

Western Front On Beveland the 52nd Division reaches Goes. Inland Breda falls to Polish 1st Armored Division.

Philippines On Leyte Abuyag, south of Dulag, falls to the US forces. Elsewhere Catmon Hill is cleared of one or two final pockets of resistance and the advance to Dagami continues.

30 OCTOBER 1944

Western Front The Canadian forces succeed in fighting their way across south Beveland to reach the Walcheren Channel.

Philippines Dagami on Leyte is taken by an attacking regiment from 7th Infantry Division.

31 OCTOBER 1944

Denmark The Gestapo Headquarters in Aarhus is destroyed by the RAF in a precision attack designed to aid the resistance forces by wiping out many of the Gestapo records.

Greece The Germans evacuate Salonika. This means that the remaining island garrisons cannot be evacuated. In recent weeks many of the German Aegean forces have been taken off in small vessels despite Allied patrols.

NOVEMBER 1944

Europe, Air Operations The USAAF heavy forces drop 55,700 tons of bombs this month. Many German planes are destroyed in the air and on the ground especially on 2 and 27 November. The German railroad system also comes in for heavy punishment, Hamm, Coblenz and Saarbrucken being among the centers hit. The attack on oil production also continues. Leuna, Merseburg, Misburg and Gelsenkirchen are all targets for major raids. The British Bomber Command effort includes area attacks on Berlin, Hanover, Cologne, Essen and others as well as one particularly large attack on 16 November on Julich, Düren and Heinsburg which are almost obliterated in support of the American advance on the ground. The oil

offensive is also a part of the British operations with Homberg and Castrop-Rauxel being among the targets. Altogether Bomber Command drops 53,000 tons. The lighter forces of both allies provide copious escorts for the main bomber forces as well as performing tactical support missions and striking at V-weapon bases. Special RAF attacks breach the Dortmund–Ems and Mitteland canals which are important for the transport of industrial materials within Germany. This also hits at the continuing German efforts to build U-Boats because the prefabricated sections that are now being used have been transported on these canals. RAF mining operations in the Baltic are also hindering U-Boat training.

Pacific, Air Operations American Superfortress bombers hit Tokyo and Omura each three times. Although these attacks do not yet compare in scale to those being undertaken in Europe, they are still causing considerable damage. Other targets for the bombers are Singapore, Nanking, Shanghai and Bangkok.

1 NOVEMBER 1944

Western Front The battle for Walcheren begins. There are landings by a brigade of British 52nd Division and three commando groups. Flushing is partly taken by one landing force while the other is fighting near Westkapelle. Much of the planned air support has to be cancelled because of the bad weather. The landings receive gunfire support from the battleship *Warspite* and two monitors as well as other vessels. Many landing craft are lost on the approach, including gun-armed ships which have been intended to give close support. The German garrison of the island is the 70th Infantry Division commanded by General Daser.

Italy The fighting continues in some sectors and there is a small advance by British V Corps units near Forli.

Eastern Front Kecskemet, 50 miles southeast of Budapest, is taken by the Soviets.

Greece Distribution of food begins in and around Athens. Because of the war food imports to Greece have of course been drastically reduced and much damage has been done to the indigenous agriculture. Famine-relief measures are therefore highly necessary. The Germans evacuate Florina. All of their troops except isolated pockets and island garrisons will be gone by the middle of the month.

Yugoslavia, Politics Tito and the prime minister of the exile government sign agreements on the future constitution of the country.

Philippines The Japanese forces receive 2000

reinforcements at their base at Ormoc on Leyte. General Suzuki now commands the Thirty-fifth Army which includes the original 16th Division and the newly arrived 30th and 102nd. In the American advance 7th Division takes Baybay. Offshore one US destroyer is sunk and five badly hit in suicide and conventional bombing attacks.

2 NOVEMBER 1944
Western Front The fighting on Walcheren continues to be most intense. Flushing falls to the attacking troops of 52nd Division. The British 7th Armored Division from Second Army renews the activity on that front with a short advance. There is also an attack on the US Third Army front and on the Channel coast in the rear of the main attacks Zeebrugge and Heyst are cleared.
Eastern Front Partisan forces take Zadar.
Italy Casseta south of Bologna is taken in the Allied advance.

3 NOVEMBER 1944
Western Front The fighting at Breskens comes to an end. Over the river at Walcheren the battle is still very fierce but the British and Canadian assault forces manage to advance a little more. The Polish 1st Division and the Canadian 4th Armored Division are also pushing forward with some success.
Italy General McCreery is appointed to command Eighth Army.

4 NOVEMBER 1944
British Command General Dill, head of the British Chiefs of Staff Mission in Washington, dies.
Western Front The British I Corps continues to advance to the Maas estuary, capturing Geertruidenberg. The fighting on Walcheren continues. British minesweepers reach up to Antwerp as the work of clearing the port and approaches continues. Even at this stage many of the supplies for the Allied armies are still being landed in Normandy, many miles to the rear.
Eastern Front Southeast of Budapest Szolnok falls to the Soviets. They then push on to Cegled only 40 miles from the capital. In Dalamtia Sebenico is taken by the partisans.
Burma In Fourteenth Army's advance 5th Indian Division takes Kennedy Peak south of Tiddim.
Philippines On Leyte there are American advances west of Dagami around the feature known as 'Bloody Ridge.'

5 NOVEMBER 1944
Middle East Lord Moyne, British Resident Minister in the Middle East, is assassinated in Cairo by two members of the Zionist Stern Gang.
Greece British forces land at Salonika.

5–6 NOVEMBER 1944
Philippines Admiral McCain, who has replaced Mitscher in command of TF 38, leads three groups of the force in attacks on targets on Luzon and the waters nearby. Among the carriers involved is the new *Ticonderoga*. The Americans lose 25 planes and manage to destroy about 400 of the Japanese force. One Japanese cruiser is sunk by submarine attack and a second badly damaged and forced to beach. The US carrier *Lexington* is badly damaged by Kamikazes.

6 NOVEMBER 1944
Western Front On Walcheren Middleburg, the largest settlement on the island, falls to II Corps attacks.
Yugoslavia Tito's forces enter Monastir. They now control almost the whole of the Greece-Yugoslavia border.
United States, Politics In the presidential election Roosevelt is voted in for an unprecedented fourth term. He beats Dewey by winning 36 states with 53 percent of the vote. In the elections for the House of Representatives the results give 243 Democrats, 190 Republicans and 2 others.

7 NOVEMBER 1944
Philippines On Leyte the US 96th Division completes the capture of Bloody Ridge wiping out the last Japanese pockets. Near the north coast at Carigara the American advance is held for the moment.

8 NOVEMBER 1944
Western Front The last German resistance on Walcheren is overcome and the remainder of the garrison surrender. The US Third Army begins an offensive around Metz and to the south. The eventual objective is the Saar. South of Metz the Seille is crossed and Nomony taken.
Italy There are new British attacks south of Forlí by the VIII Corps of Eighth Army.
Burma Fort White, just south of Tiddim, is taken by the British advance.

9 NOVEMBER 1944
Western Front In the continuing Third Army offensive various units cross the Moselle around Metz while farther south XII Corps maintain its advance beyond the Seille taking Chateau Salins.

Italy Forlí is taken by the British 4th Division.

Philippines Further Japanese reinforcements, 2000 men of 26th Division land at Ormoc on Leyte but the transporting warships are forced to retire before all the supplies are ashore.

10 NOVEMBER 1944

Western Front Third Army's attacks go on. Good progress is made over the Moselle just south of Thionville and farther south beyond Metz the advance is even more rapid.

Philippines The fighting near Carigara is still fierce. There is a small amphibious move by units of 24th Division west along the north coast from Carigara toward Belen.

11 NOVEMBER 1944

Philippines A Japanese convoy is attacked off Ormoc by planes from eight carriers from TF 38. Four destroyers and one minesweeper are sunk as well as five transports with nearly 10,000 troops.

11–12 NOVEMBER 1944

Bonin Islands Iwo Jima is shelled during the night by a US destroyer and cruiser task force led by Admiral Smith.

12 NOVEMBER 1944

Norway The German battleship *Tirpitz* is attacked at anchor in Tromsofiord by 21 Lancasters carrying 12,000-pound bombs. There are several direct hits and other near misses and the *Tirpitz* capsizes.

Offshore a German coastal convoy is attacked by Royal Navy cruisers and destroyers.

13 NOVEMBER 1944

Western Front Third Army has now crossed the Moselle north of Thionville and built a bridge at Cattenom. South of Metz other Third Army units from XII Corps are attacking toward Morhange and Falquemont. Farther south still the Germans pull out of St Dié because of Seventh Army pressure there.

Eastern Front The Germans evacuate Skopje in southern Yugoslavia. The Bulgarian First Army is advancing in this sector.

13–14 NOVEMBER 1944

Philippines McCain's carriers once more attack shipping and targets on Luzon especially near Manila. One cruiser and four destroyers are sunk by the carrier planes.

14 NOVEMBER 1944

Western Front The British XII Corps begins attacks to eliminate the German holdings west of the Maas around Nederweert near Venlo. In the far south of the front the French First Army starts its Operation *Independence* to free Belfort.

Norway The Norwegian government in exile announces that Norwegian troops are operating alongside the Soviets in the far north.

15 NOVEMBER 1944

Western Front The attacks of Third Army around Metz press forward once more. South of the city the rail line to Saarebourg is cut and from here into the Seventh Army sector north of St Dié ground is gained all along the front. The French drive toward Belfort continues.

Eastern Front Jasberény, 30 miles east of Budapest, is taken by the Russians.

Mapia Island This small island 160 miles north of the west end of New Guinea is occupied by a regiment of the US 31st Division. The small Japanese garrison is overcome with little difficulty. The transport and covering squadron is made up of British and American ships and is commanded by Admiral Lord Ashbourne.

16 NOVEMBER 1944

Western Front There are heavy Allied air attacks in preparation for offensives by US Ninth and First Armies. Ninth Army attacks toward Geilenkirchen and Eschweiler with the intention of reaching the Roer. On their right First Army is moving toward Düren east of Aachen.

16–20 NOVEMBER 1944

Belgium, Politics There are political quarrels between the Belgian government and representatives of the resistance movement. On 16 November three ministers resign because of these problems. On the 17th there are meetings between Allied representatives and the ministers in which it is agreed to try to have the resistance surrender their arms. On the 18th the resistance agree to this and it is announced on the 20th.

17 NOVEMBER 1944

Western Front On the right of the Allied front the French offensive in the Belfort area reaches Montbéliard. To the north both Third and Seventh Armies advance following German withdrawals. Around Aachen First and Ninth Armies also push forward.

China Sea The Japanese fleet carrier *Junyo* is sunk by an American submarine.

18 NOVEMBER 1944

Western Front The Third Army advance

reaches close to the German border. Bouzonville on the River Nied is taken. Metz is entered from both north and south. Around Aachen the British XXX Corps joins the attacks of First and Ninth Armies. Jülich and Düren are entered.

Eastern Front The Eighth Army from Govorov's Leningrad Front renews its attacks on Saaremaa Island in the north of the Gulf of Riga.

19 NOVEMBER 1944

Western Front There are Allied attacks and advances all along the front. The British XII and VII Corps make ground near Venlo. In the Ninth Army sector a counterattack is beaten off and Geilenkirchen occupied. To the south Third Army completes the isolation of Metz. Farther south still the French attacks reach the outskirts of Belfort while on their right flank the advance has penetrated to the Swiss border North of Basle.

Philippines McCain's carriers carry out further attacks on Luzon and shipping targets in Manila Bay. They sink one cruiser and three other vessels.

20 NOVEMBER 1944

Western Front The fighting east of Aachen continues with units of US XIX Corps attacking near Jülich. In the Third Army sector the battle in Metz continues as other formations of the Army advance east taking Dieuze. To the south the French are still fighting in Belfort and advance patrols, passing the city on the right, reach Mulhouse and the Rhine.

Indian Ocean Two carriers from the British Eastern Fleet send two waves of attacks against airfields at Sabang and oil installations at Belawan Deli on Sumatra.

Greece The British General Scobie is placed in charge of measures for disbanding the guerrilla armies in Greece.

21 NOVEMBER 1944

Western Front In Holland the attacks of Second Army near Venlo. The efforts of US First and Ninth Armies can make little ground against the German resistance west of the Roer. The Third Army is still moving forward near Saarebourg.

Philippines On Leyte the US advance by 32nd Division from the north coast is strongly held in the Ormoc Valley. The 7th Division also begins to try to move toward Ormoc, attacking north from around Baybay.

China Sea The US submarine *Sealion* sinks the Japanese battleship *Kongo* as well as a destroyer in waters to the northeast of Formosa.

Eastern Front Tirana is occupied by Albanian resistance fighters. The Germans have pulled out on 20th November. Durazzo is also taken.

22 NOVEMBER 1944

Western Front In the southern sector of the front the French forces take Mulhouse after beating off a German counterattack in that area. The US Seventh Army, in line on the left flank of the French, advances at several points along its front. St Dié is taken and other units move toward Saverne. Farther north Third Army completes the capture of Metz.

23 NOVEMBER 1944

Western Front At the north end of the front the German Fifteenth Army pulls back a little deeper into Holland. By contrast the German Seventh Army begins a series of sharp attacks against US Ninth Army. In the advance of US Seventh Army French troops with the army reach Strasbourg.

Eastern Front In northern Hungary the Russians take Tokay. In the far north they are able to announce that, with Finnish help as the recent treaty has provided they have cleared Finnish Lapland of German troops.

24 NOVEMBER 1944

Western Front Patton's troops take crossings over the Saar about 25 miles north of Saarbrucken. Farther south the French 2nd Division completes the capture of Strasbourg.

Eastern Front The Russians expel the last German troops from Saaremo Island in the Gulf of Riga. The remaining heavy units of the German Navy, *Lutzow*, *Admiral Scheer* and *Prinz Eugen*, have covered the evacuation of the 5000 German troops that were on the island and given gunfire support to the land battles nearby in the past few days.

25 NOVEMBER 1944

Philippines The US advance is being held in most sectors of Leyte. One US paratroop unit is advancing in difficult terrain west of Burauen.

TG 38.2 and TG 38.3 again attack Luzon and the waters nearby. Seven American carriers are involved and they sink the cruisers *Kumano* and *Yasoshima*. In return Kamikaze attacks damage four of the carriers.

Western Front To the southeast of Aachen US forces from First Army advance beyond Hurtgen.

26 NOVEMBER 1944

Eastern Front Russian troops take Michaloyce

in eastern Slovakia.

Philippines The Japanese start a sequence of fierce night attacks in several parts of Leyte, but especially west of Burauen.

27 NOVEMBER 1944

Philippines The battleship *Colorado* and two light cruisers are damaged in suicide attacks in Leyte Gulf. On Leyte the Japanese attacks around Burauen continue and are reinforced by a small parachute unit. They come close to taking the Burauen airfield.

United States, Politics Cordell Hull resigns his post as Secretary of State. Edward Stettinius is appointed as his successor.

28 NOVEMBER 1944

Western Front The first Allied convoy reaches Antwerp. During the time the German troops and mines have been being cleared from the estuary much work has been done to put the quays and dock machinery in good order. There is still a problem, however, with transport for the stores once they have arrived. Nevertheless the opening of the port does totally alter the supply position of most of the Allied armies. There will be no more real shortages like those which limited the advance in the late summer. The German rocket attacks on the port do little to limit its capacity.

Philippines On Leyte there are more Japanese night attacks in all sectors. The heaviest pressure is at Kilay Ridge in the north and around Buri and Burauen.

Eastern Front The Soviet force on the Danube is just north of the confluence of the Drava. Mohacs is quickly taken on the west bank and the advance reaches Pécs.

29 NOVEMBER 1944

Philippines The Japanese attacks continue on Kilay Ridge on Leyte but in fact they lose ground to later US counterattacks.

The battleship *Maryland* and two destroyers are seriously hit in Kamikaze attacks in Leyte Gulf.

Pacific The US submarine *Archerfish* sinks the carrier *Shinano* in waters off Honshu. *Shinano* was originally designed as a sister vessel of the giant battleships *Yamato* and *Musashi*.

Western Front There is considerable activity in the US First, Third and Ninth Army sectors but little change in the position of the troops.

Eastern Front In Albania the last German forces leave Scutari. Lohr's Army Group E are now attempting to form a line along the Drina and then the Drava.

30 NOVEMBER 1944

Western Front There is a small advance in the Second Army sector west of the Maas near Venlo. North and south of Aachen Ninth and First US Armies continue their attack. In the Third Army sector units on the right of the advance have reached the Saar but on the left they are still some miles away from the river.

Eastern Front The Second Ukraine Front has begun a new offensive northwest of Debrecen in north Hungary.

DECEMBER 1944

Europe, Air Operations The US heavy-bomber forces concentrate on two target systems this month. Communications centers are attacked including Coblenz and Bingen. The effort on 11 December is particularly great with the targets being Giessen, Hanau and Frankfurt. The other range of targets is in the oil industry. Plants in Silesia and near Vienna are hit as are Harburg and Meiderich. On 24 December Eighth Air Force sends 2000 bombers on missions. The Allied Air Forces based in Italy contribute to these attacks as well as hitting targets on their own front and harrying the German retreat in Yugoslavia with bombing and arms drops to resistance forces. RAF Bomber Command drops 48,700 tons during the month. One third of the operations are made during the days and the targets are throughout Germany. Transport and oil systems are again favored targets. Hagen, Essen, Trier, Leuna and Poolitz are all hit.

Light and heavy forces of both British and American Air Forces also attack transport centers and troop concentrations during the German Ardennes attacks when weather permits. Altogether 35,500 tons are dropped in these operations.

Pacific, Air Operations US Superfortress bombers continue and extend their strategic bombing campaign from their bases in China and Saipan. Tokyo is attacked on four occasions during the month, Nagoya three times and Omura, Yokohama and Yokosuka once. Outside Japan targets include Mukden, Shanghai and Nanking.

Pacific, Naval War The American submarine fleet and mining campaign has now reduced the carrying capacity of the Japanese merchant fleet. The carrying capacity is now less than half the total possible at the beginning of the war. Food and oil imports from the East Indies are now down to a trickle.

1 DECEMBER 1944

Western Front In the Ninth Army area the

advance northeast of Aachen reaches Linnich which is taken by 102nd Division. The attacks by Third and Seventh Armies farther south are still proceeding but the advance here is, as in the north, very slow indeed.

Eastern Front In the attacks south of Budapest most of the Russian forces are held except around Pécs where Fifty-seventh Army is operating. Northeast of Budapest Fourth Ukraine Front attack the positions of First Panzer Army along the Ondava River.

2 DECEMBER 1944

Western Front Several Divisions of Patton's Third Army seize new crossings over the Saar. Saarlautern is entered by patrols of one unit.

Eastern Front In northern Hungary troops from Malinovsky's armies attack the well-defended German positions around Miskolc.

3 DECEMBER 1944

Greece Police open fire on demonstrations in Athens sponsored by the communist EAM party and the situation degenerates into open fighting. On 4 December martial law is declared as the fighting continues. During 5 December British tanks are used in the fighting and British warships shell EAM positions near Piraeus. The fighting goes on for most of the month but the former guerrillas are no match for the British troops in an open battle. Stalin keeps his agreement with Churchill and does not send any help to the communists.

Italy Eighth Army begins a new offensive on a three corps frontage with the right flank of the advance resting on the Adriatic coast. British, Polish and Canadian units are all involved.

Western Front The River Roer is reached by the advance of XIII Corps from Ninth Army.

Eastern Front Miskolc is taken by troops from Second Ukraine Front.

Britain, Home Front The volunteer defense force, the Home Guard, is 'stood down' from service since it is not now needed to watch for a German invasion.

4 DECEMBER 1944

Western Front The British Second Army clears out the last German pocket west of the Maas. To the right of the British forces the US Ninth Army ends its offensive toward the Roer. In the Third Army area units of XX Corps rush troops toward Saarlautern where a bridge over the river has been discovered intact.

5 DECEMBER 1944

Eastern Front The Russians take Vukovar on the Danube and to the northwest they also capture Szigetvar.

Italy Troops from I Canadian Corps take Ravenna as Eighth Army's attacks go on.

6 DECEMBER 1944

Western Front In the Third Army sector a division of XX Corps uses assault boats to cross the Saar near Patchen. Other units of the Army enter Saareguemines.

7 DECEMBER 1944

Eastern Front The Russian attacks in southern Hungary reach Lake Balatan. To the south Baros on the Drava is taken.

Rumania, Politics A new government takes office. Led by General Badescu they are pledged to implement fully the terms of the armistice, to help the Allies and to purge all pro-Nazis.

Philippines Early in the day the US 77th Division (General Bruce) land about a mile south of Ormoc on Leyte. The Japanese resistance is not particularly fierce. The escorting naval forces include 12 destroyers, one of which is sunk by a suicide attack. The US 7th Division which is already attacking north toward Ormoc along the coast, makes good progress in its advance.

8 DECEMBER 1944

Volcano Islands Three American heavy cruisers and their destroyer escorts bombard Iwo Jima. Admiral Smith commands. The operation is repeated twice more during December.

Eastern Front In Hungary the Russian troops of Third Ukraine Front attack near Szekesfehervar only 40 miles southwest of Budapest, the capital.

Philippines The newly landed 77th Division makes an important advance to within a mile of Ormoc. In the center of Leyte part of the Japanese 26th Division attacks near Buri but is beaten off.

Italy Eighth Army troops cross the Lamone River south of Faenza.

9 DECEMBER 1944

Western Front The northern half of the front is largely at rest. In the Third Army sector there is fighting around the various bridgeheads over the Saar. To the south of these battles both Seventh Army and French First Army are still pushing forward.

Eastern Front The Second Ukraine Front reaches the Danube north of Budapest at Vac. On the right of these attacks Balassagyarmat on the Slovak border is taken. The attacks southwest of Budapest also make progress.

Philippines The Japanese succeed in landing a small group of reinforcements at Palompon on the west coast of Leyte northwest of Ormoc. South of Ormoc the US 77th Division increases the extent of its holdings.

Britain, Home Front The black-out regulations are relaxed. There is as yet no question of restoring street lights but the rules for houses and other premises are not now so strict.

10 DECEMBER 1944

Philippines Ormoc is taken by the US 77th Division. Ormoc has been the main Japanese base on the island of Leyte. The main Japanese forces are now northwest of Ormoc, especially at and near Palompon.

Western Front The VII Corps from First Army starts a powerful attack west of Aachen in an attempt to take Düren. Third Army's battles on the Saar continue.

Diplomatic Affairs Following the recent visit of General de Gaulle, Bidault, the Foreign Minister and General Juin to Moscow a treaty of alliance is signed by French and Soviet representatives.

12 DECEMBER 1944

Greece After taking heavy setbacks in the recent fighting the Greek communists ask for terms for a cease fire. It is demanded that the communists surrender their arms. On December 16 General Scobie publishes the text of the Caserta agreement in which the guerrillas had promised to work with the established government (then in exile). (*See* 26 September 1944.) On 20 December Scobie warns civilians to stay away from areas occupied by the ELAS troops because he may find it necessary to bomb them. On 25 December, as the fighting begins to die down with the British very much in control, Churchill and Eden arrive for talks with the Greek leaders. It is decided to establish a regency.

Burma A British offensive begins in the Arakan. The attacking unit is XV Corps. The objective is Akyab. Three divisions are in the attack.

Western Europe First Army takes Düren.

13 DECEMBER 1944

Sulu Sea The American heavy cruiser *Nashville* and a destroyer, part of the force on the way to make landings on Mindoro, are both heavily damaged in Kamikaze attacks. *Nashville* is the flagship of the force and there are many casualties among the senior officers.

Italy In the Fifth Army sector units of British XIII Corps make strong attacks on Tossignano.

14 DECEMBER 1944

Italy Eighth Army is attacking to widen the bridgehead already established over the Lamone.

14–16 DECEMBER 1944

Philippines To cover the landings on Mindoro there are intensive attacks on airfields throughout Luzon by planes of TF 38. Admiral McCain now commands this force and it includes 13 carriers and eight battleships as well as the usual complement of cruisers and destroyers. Of the 1670 missions flown all but 250 are by fighters. The Americans lose 65 planes, the Japanese 170.

15 DECEMBER 1944

Philippines There are US landings at San Augustin on Mindoro. There is almost no resistance and the forces advance inland up to eight miles. General Dunckel is in command and his troops include part of the 24th Division and a parachute Regiment. The naval cover includes three battleships and six escort carriers. One of the carriers and two destroyers are hit by Kamikazes.

16 DECEMBER 1944

Western Front The Germans begin a major offensive in the Ardennes. The attack begins with a short, sharp artillery barrage along the chosen front between Monschau and Trier. Almost complete surprise is achieved. Allied intelligence has received some indications of the attack despite elaborate security on the German side but these signs have not been interpreted properly. Partly because of the enforced shortening of their front the Germans have been able to assemble a considerable reserve of armored divisions. They have chosen to strike here with the immediate aim of retaking Antwerp and splitting the British and American armies in two. In the longer term Hitler hopes to discourage and divide the British and Americans politically so that forces can be switched to the Eastern Front, perhaps even with help from anti-communist leaders who may emerge in Britain and America. Altogether the Germans have assembled 24 divisions, including 10 armored. These forces are distributed largely between Dietrich's Sixth SS Panzer Army and Manteuffel's Fifth Panzer Army. On the flanks of the attack are Fifteenth and Seventh Armies. All these forces are part of Model's Army Group B. Rundstedt has been brought back to have overall charge of the operation. To oppose the German forces are about six American divisions from V and VIII Corps consisting partly of inexperienced troops and partly of resting veterans. The terrain here in the same Ardennes area as was chosen for the start of the attack in 1940, is fairly rugged with many defiles and much heavily wooded country. Most of whatever movement is attempted must take place on the few major roads so, as will emerge, it is vital to seize the various junctions. The Germans hope to spread confusion in the American rear areas by infiltrating small groups of specially trained English-speaking troops with captured uniforms and equipment to perform sabotage and intelligence missions. This move is very successful at least in causing an atmosphere of suspicion and uncertainty. Many roadblocks and checkpoints are set in the American rear areas and they do something to hinder the movement of reserves.

The Germans are relying on bad weather to keep the Allied air forces grounded and for the moment this hope is fulfilled.

In the first day of the attack the Germans succeed in disrupting the Allied front and make good ground in many sectors.

In other areas US Third Army units are still attacking along the Saar but these operations are suspended when news of the Ardennes battle is received. The Ardennes battle is often popularly styled the Battle of the Bulge.

Italy Faenza is taken by units of the British V Corps.

Philippines There is considerable air activity with the Japanese attacking American shipping and the Americans replying with strikes against the Japanese air bases. On Mindoro the landing force does not attempt an advance but confines itself to construction work on an airstrip and to consolidating its perimeter.

17 DECEMBER 1944
Western Front The US 82nd and 101st Airborne Divisions are sent to reinforce the Allied troops in the Ardennes although these paratroops are officially still resting after the Arnhem operation. Various other armored and infantry units from several of the Allied armies are being rushed to the threatened sectors.

Indian Ocean The oil and harbor installations at Belawan-Deli in northern Sumatra are attacked by planes from the British carriers *Indomitable* and *Illustrious*. Admiral Vian is in command.

Italy Near Faenza 10th Indian Division manages to capture crossings over the Senio River.

Philippines On Mindoro the US forces take San Jose Airfield. There are advances by units of both X and XXIV Corps on Leyte.

18 DECEMBER 1944
Philippine Sea TF 38, retiring to refuel and replenish after the recent attacks on Luzon, is caught in a violent typhoon along with the units of the fleet train. Three destroyers are sunk and the damaged ships include three fleet carriers, four escort carriers and 11 destroyers.

19 DECEMBER 1944
Western Front At a meeting of the senior Allied commanders Eisenhower decides to appoint a single leader each for the areas north and south of the Bulge which is being created. Montgomery is appointed for the northern units and Bradley for the southern. This arrangement will not be made public until 5 January 1945.

On the ground the Germans have reached the Stavelot and Houffalize areas but between these advances some of the US forces are holding their ground around Gouvy and St Vith. Houffalize itself will be defended a little longer by 82nd Airborne Division while 10 miles to the south 101st Airborne is among the force which is preparing to hold the important road junction at Bastogne.

Philippines The Japanese decide that they can do no more to send reinforcements or supplies to Thirty-fifth Army on Leyte. The fighting continues north of Ormoc and throughout the northwest of the island.

20 DECEMBER 1944
Western Front On the northern flank of their Ardennes offensive the German forces attack northward from around Stavelot but, although they quickly make some gains, they are soon forced to retire. The units on the right of these in the German drive have not made much ground toward their objectives around Malmedy and to the north. The two vital junctions at St Vith and Bastogne are still being held despite deeper penetrations all around these towns. If the Germans are to develop their offensive much farther they must do so quickly before the weather clears and before the Allied reserves arrive in force. To maintain the momentum of the attack they must take the road junctions so they can easily speed their main forces and their supports forward.

21 DECEMBER 1944
Philippines The advances of US X Corps and XXIV Corps meet in the center of the Ormoc Valley on Leyte. There are still various groups of Japanese holding isolated positions in this area.
Western Front Bastogne is now almost completely surrounded. The 82nd Airborne Division

has been driven out of Houffalize in the continuing German advance between and behind Bastogne and St Vith. On the north flank of the advance American forces retake Stavelot and from here to Monschau the German LXVII Corps has been brought to a halt.

22 DECEMBER 1944

Western Front The American forces in Bastogne contemptuously reject a German demand that they surrender. It is said that General McAuliffe's reply to the demand consists of the single word 'Nuts.' The weather is beginning to change and all the German Generals involved in the attack, Rundstedt, Model and Guderian the Army Chief of Staff, recommend that the offensive be brought to an end because of the delays that have been imposed by the Allied resistance and the imminent arrival of the mass of the Allied reserves. To the generals it is clear that there is no question of reaching the grand objective of Antwerp. Although St Vith is taken late in the day this does not come close to curing the problems of delay that have been created.

Philippines On Leyte the main Japanese forces are now near Palompon, and this will be the main American objective for the next few days.

23 DECEMBER 1944

Western Front Although Bastogne still holds out against repeated German attacks they have been able to send forces past the town to advance to the west and northwest. These attacks are now beyond Rochefort and Laroche but have neither the necessary strength nor the logistical backing because of the blocks behind them and the growing effectiveness of the Allied air interdiction.

24 DECEMBER 1944

Western Front The German offensive in the Ardennes is brought to a halt by the end of the day. The longest advance is by 2nd Panzer Division to just outside Dinant. They form the point of the German wedge and on their flanks they have 116th Panzer to the north near Hotten and to the south Panzer *Lehr* Division west of St Hubert. Opposing the German units, now much weakened when compared with 16 December, are the main forces of US First and Third Armies, the British XXX Corps and, of course, the Bastogne defenders.

Eastern Front The Russians are now fighting in the outskirts of Budapest on the east side while other units advancing beyond the city have almost cut it off. The corridor from the city to the west is only about 25 miles wide.

United States, Home Front All beef products are rationed once more. New quotas are introduced for most other commodities also.

25 DECEMBER 1944

Western Front The Allies begin their counteroffensive against the German forces in the Ardennes. In this advance the attack of US 4th Armored Division from around Mortelange is to be designed to relieve Bastogne.

Philippines Part of the US 77th Division is moved by sea from Ormoc to San Juan on the west coast of Leyte north of Palompon. There is no opposition to the landing.

26 DECEMBER 1944

Western Front Bastogne is relieved by units of 4th Armored Division. Elsewhere in the Ardennes sector the Allied attacks have not yet really begun to have real effect.

Philippines A Japanese naval force which has come from Indochina bombards the American beachhead on Mindoro. There are two cruisers and six destroyers in the attack. One destroyer is sunk by an American PT-Boat. This is the last sortie by a Japanese naval force in the Philippines area.

Eastern Front Budapest is now almost completely encircled by Tolbukhin's Third Ukraine Front.

27 DECEMBER 1944

Western Front The German 2nd Panzer Division is driven out of Celles by the attacks of British XXX Corps. This division has pushed so far forward and is so isolated that it is bound to suffer severely in the Allied counterstroke.

29 DECEMBER 1944

Western Front There is something of a lull in the Ardennes battle. The Allies are busy preparing to extend their counterattacks.

Eastern Front There is fighting in Budapest. The Russians attempt to start negotiations with the garrison but there is a misunderstanding and some of the Russian emissaries are killed in the course of their mission.

Greece It is announced that a regency is to be established and that Prime Minister Papendreou will resign when a regent has been chosen. On 31st December Archbishop Damaskinos of Athens is sworn in and Papandreou resigns.

30 DECEMBER 1944

Western Front The VIII Corps from Patton's Third Army begins a new attack northward from a line between Bastogne and St Hubert. Houffalize is the objective.

Eastern Front The fighting in and around Budapest continues. Russian units from both Second and Third Ukraine Fronts are involved.

31 DECEMBER 1944

Philippines There are vicious Japanese counter-attacks in several parts of the northwest of Leyte, but the American forces beat them off with heavy losses. Elsewhere on the island the Japanese resistance is all but over. In the battle for Leyte Japanese casualties have been around 70,000, almost all killed. The American casualties have been 15,500 dead and wounded. The US Sixth Army which has fought the battle is now being prepared to move on Luzon and the Eighth Army is taking its place on Leyte.

Poland, Politics The Lublin-based Committee of National Liberation assumes the title of Provisional Government. The London exile government protest unavailingly.

World Affairs Hungary declares war on Germany.

Western Front The British XXX Corps takes Rochefort at the western end of the Ardennes salient.

JANUARY 1945

Europe, Air Operations Both the British and American heavy-bomber forces continue their operations. The Eighth Air Force drops 39,000 tons and Fifteenth Air Force 6,000 tons in various attacks. As well as tactical support missions, especially early in the month against targets in the Ardennes, there are mostly attacks on oil and communications targets. Berlin, Cologne and Hamm are all hit. The British heavy-bomber force attacks oil targets at Bochum and Leuna, some rail centers and general area targets at Hanau, Munich and Stuttgart. Bomber Command drops 36,000 tons in all operations. The Ninth Air Force, Second

Tactical Air Force and RAF Fighter Command all send many attacks against targets in the Ardennes and against V-weapon sites. A further 11,500 tons is dropped in these operations.

Far East, Air Operations US heavy bomber forces continue to attack targets in Japan. Nagoya is bombed three times, and Omura and Tokyo are also hit. In China there are attacks on Japanese communications and airfields. Singapore and Saigon are also hit by heavy bombers. There are, of course, many attacks against Japanese-held islands and shipping.

1 JANUARY 1945

Europe, Air Operations The Luftwaffe makes a series of heavy attacks on Allied airfields in Belgium, Holland and northern France. They have assembled around 800 planes of all types for this effort by scraping together every available machine and pilot. Many of the pilots have had so little training that they must fly in special formations with an experienced pilot in the lead providing the navigation for the whole force. The Allies are largely taken by surprise and lose many aircraft on the ground. Among the German losses for the day are a considerable number of planes shot down by 'friendly' anti-aircraft fire. Although the Allied losses of 300 planes are 100 greater than the German, the Luftwaffe comes off relatively worse. The Allied planes can be replaced immediately, but for the Germans neither the planes nor the pilots can be.

Western Front The land battle in the Ardennes continues with the Allied counterattacks gathering force. The most notable gains are in the US VIII Corps sector. Farther south in Alsace the German Army Group G begins an offensive in the Sarreguemines area. The US Seventh Army retires before this attack, on orders from Eisenhower.

2 JANUARY 1945

Western Front In the Ardennes Third Army troops take Bonnerue, Hubertmont and Remagne. Hitler turns down requests from Model and Manteuffel for withdrawals from the area west of Houffalize. In Alsace the German pressure and the Seventh Army withdrawals continue.

Eastern Front There are German counter-attacks northwest of Budapest which aim to relieve the siege of the city. The main forces involved in this offensive are two SS Panzer Divisions which have been withdrawn from the reserve in the more important Warsaw sector without the consent or knowledge of Guderian, the Army Chief of Staff.

Above: A damaged B-17 which made it home.

CHRONOLOGY

Allied Command Admiral Ramsay, Naval Commander in Chief of Allied forces in Europe, is killed in an air accident while on his way to meet Montgomery.

2–8 JANUARY 1945
Philippines From 2nd to 5th January the various transport, bombardment and escort carrier groups for the US landings on Luzon leave their bases on Leyte. There are six battleships, 16 escort carriers, 10 cruisers and many destroyers, landing craft and transports of all kinds. Several of the cruisers and destroyers are Australian. From 3 January the American movements are detected by the Japanese and attacks by midget submarines, Kamikaze planes and small surface ships begin. On 4 January the escort carrier *Ommaney Bay* is badly damaged by a Kamikaze and has to be abandoned. On the 5th two escort carriers, two cruisers and several smaller ships are damaged. The cruiser *Boise*, with General MacArthur aboard, has a narrow escape from a torpedo attack. One Japanese destroyer is sunk by US planes. On 6 January Admiral Oldendorf's battleship groups enter Lingayen Gulf to begin the preliminary bombardment and come under heavy attack. One minesweeper is sunk and two battleships, four cruisers and six destroyers are damaged. There are more attacks on the 7th and 8th, but these are less effective, hitting two escort carriers and the cruiser *Australia* for the second time. In the night of 7/8 January there is the last surface engagement of the Pacific campaign in which a single attacking Japanese destroyer is sunk by four US ships.

3 JANUARY 1944
Western Front In the Ardennes the fighting continues. There are desperate German attacks on the narrow corridor leading to Bastogne which manage to upset the timetable of the US attacks a little but achieve nothing else. Forces from US Third and now also First Armies are attacking toward Houffalize from the south and north.

In Alsace the German attacks and the American retreat continue. The US VI Corps is being pressed particularly hard in the area around Bitche. Farther south there is also fighting near Strasbourg.

Burma There are British landings at the northwest tip of Akyab Island in the Arakan area. A Commando and an Indian brigade are involved, but there is little resistance from the Japanese. Inland troops of XXXIII Corps take Yeu in their advance to the Irrawaddy.

3–4 JANUARY 1945
Formosa and Ryukyus There are attacks by three of the fleet carrier groups of the US Third Fleet against targets throughout Formosa and the southern Ryukyu Islands and the Pescadores. Bad weather prevents the operations from being fully effective, but about 100 Japanese planes are destroyed for the loss of just over 20.

4 JANUARY 1945
Western Front The fighting in the Ardennes continues. There are attacks by US VIII and III Corps and by the British XXX Corps. Some of the units of Dietrich's Sixth SS Panzer Army are withdrawn and sent to the Eastern Front. In Alsace the German attacks in the Bitche area continue.

Indian Ocean Three British carriers of Admiral Vian's TF63 attack the oil refineries at Pankalan Brandan on Sumatra.

Burma Akyab Island is completely occupied by the British forces.

5 JANUARY 1945
Western Front In the Ardennes there is less activity on the Third Army sector, but First Army maintains its attacks. There are German attacks just north of Strasbourg.

Bonins Admiral Smith leads a force of cruisers and destroyers to shell Iwo Jima, Haha Jima and Chichi Jima. There is a simultaneous attack by Superfortress bombers.

Burma Shwebo is taken by the British 2nd Division of Stopford's XXXIII Corps, as the advance of the corps to the Irrawaddy continues.

Kuriles Admiral McCrea leads three cruisers and nine destroyers to bombard Suribachi Wan.

Diplomatic Affairs The Soviets recognize the Lublin Committee as the Provisional Government of Poland. The USA and Britain announce that they continue to recognize the exile government in London.

Greece The fighting between the British and the Greek Communists comes to an end in the Athens area. General Alexander and British political representatives arrive in Athens for talks with the Communist leaders and the Greek government.

6 JANUARY 1945
Western Front There are various local actions all along the Ardennes front. Rundstedt again requests that the German forces be allowed to withdraw because of the Allied pressure. Hitler again orders no retreat.

Allied Planning Churchill asks Stalin if the Soviet forces can go over to the offensive in

Poland to take some of the pressure off the Allied armies in the Bulge. Stalin says that he will arrange for the Red Army plans for its next offensive to be brought forward.

6–7 JANUARY 1945

Philippines The American fleet carrier groups of TF 38 join in the operations by the escort carrier and land-based forces against the Kamikaze airfields on Luzon. Between 75 and 80 Japanese aircraft are destroyed for the loss of 28.

7 JANUARY 1945

Western Front The attacks of VIII Corps of First Army along the line of the Ourthe west of Houffalize make good progress around Laroche.

The German attacks in Alsace also continue with some success south of Strasbourg in the area around Erstein.

Italy There are some limited operations by Eighth Army to complete the Allied hold on the south bank of the Senio. Apart from these the wet weather and a lack of reinforcements and extra supplies means that the Allied armies are unable to go over to the offensive on any large scale. There will be some comparatively minor efforts in February and March but no big attack until April.

8 JANUARY 1945

Western Front The battles north and south of Strasbourg continue. The US Seventh Army is under considerable pressure near Rimling and Gambsheim.

9 JANUARY 1945

Philippines Operation Mike 1, the US landings on Luzon at Lingayen Gulf, is begun. General Swift's I Corps lands from the ships of TF 78 around San Fabian. The assault units are from 43rd and 6th Infantry Divisions. General Griswold's XIV Corps lands from TF 79 near Lingayen village. The assault units are from 37th and 40th Divisions. The Japanese commander in north Luzon is General Yamashita and he has decided not to contest the landing grounds. The nearest Japanese forces are from 23rd Division but they will not intervene in strength in the first two days. There are, however, continued Japanese air attacks in which the battleship *Mississippi* and two cruisers are hit. In a night attack by explosive boats several landing craft and transports are damaged. The American units are from Krueger's Sixth Army and the naval support is commanded by Admiral Kinkaid. As well as 150,000 men under his direct leadership in the north of the island

Yamashita commands the additional 110,000 men around Manila and to the south.

Formosa and Okinawa The fleet carriers of TF 38 attack targets on Okinawa and Formosa in conjunction with Superfortress bombers from bases in China. This is intended to give cover to the landings on Luzon. One Japanese destroyer is sunk along with seven other ships.

Western Front The US Third Army increases the force of its attacks northeast and southeast of Bastogne.

10 JANUARY 1945

Western Front In the Ardennes battle there is fighting near Laroche in an attack by the British XXX Corps. US First and Third Armies are also continuing to advance.

Philippines The US forces stream ashore on Luzon. Their beachhead is now several miles wide and deep.

Burma While the advance of XXXIII Corps to the Irrawaddy is attracting the Japanese attention, IV Corps is moving southward to the west of the Chindwin with the intention of crossing the Irrawaddy near Meiktila. Gangaw is taken in this advance.

11 JANUARY 1945

Western Front Units of the Third Army and the British XXX Corps join up near St Hubert as the German salient in the Ardennes is further reduced. To the south the fighting in the Seventh Army area around Bitche is also continuing, but the German attacks are being held.

Philippines The US 25th Division and an armored group are landed at Lingayen to reinforce the US bridgehead. The first serious fighting begins ashore. There are more Kamikaze attacks on the American shipping. Many smaller craft are damaged.

12 JANUARY 1945

Eastern Front A major Soviet offensive begins all along the front from the Baltic to the Carpathians. The principal attacks are by Rokossovsky's Second Belorussian Front with nine armies immediately north of Warsaw; by Zhukov's First Belorussian Front opposite Warsaw and to the south with seven armies initially; and by Konev's First Ukraine Front from the salient west of Sandomierz also with seven armies in the front line. There are additional efforts by Third Belorussian and both Baltic Fronts against the German forces in East Prussia and those cut off in Latvia. The defending German forces are mostly from Army Group Center and Army Group A. Second Army will bear the brunt of Rokossovsky's attack; Ninth Army faces Zhukov; and Fourth Panzer Army faces Konev. These German troops are outnumbered by at least four or five to one in all classes of equipment, and despite brave resistance they will have no answer to the Red Army's power.

Burma The 19th Indian Division takes bridgeheads over the Irrawaddy north of Mandalay at Kyaukmyaung and Thabeikkyin. Fierce Japanese attacks in these areas immediately begin. In the Arakan there are landings of British Commando troops near Myebon on the mainland between Akyab and Ramree.

Indochina There are air attacks from the planes of the carriers of TF 38 against Japanese installations at the naval base at Camranh Bay and other areas in Indochina. TG 38.5 continues the attacks from its specially trained carriers. Japanese shipping losses to the attacks amount to 29 ships of 116,000 tons. Eleven small warships are also sunk.

Western Front There are new attacks on the north flank of the Ardennes salient by VII and XVIII Corps of the US First Army.

13 JANUARY 1945
Eastern Front The German defense lines all along the front in Poland are shattered by the Soviet attacks.

Philippines The escort carrier *Salamaua* is badly damaged in a Kamikaze attack. These are now becoming rare, however, because most of the Kamikaze aircraft have been lost and the rest withdrawn. Ashore the US bridgehead is steadily being extended. Damortis is taken.

Western Front In the Ardennes units of US First Army from the north and of the British XXX Corps from the west, reach the Ourthe between Laroche and Houffalize. Third Army forces are also moving toward Houffalize from the south.

14 JANUARY 1945
Eastern Front The Soviet offensives in Poland begin to achieve important successes. Konev's forces cut the rail line to Krakow south of Kielce. Farther south in Hungary the Soviets resist German attempts to relieve Budapest and in eastern Czechoslovakia they take Lucenec.

Greece A cease-fire is agreed between the British and the Communist ELAS organization. ELAS agrees to release all hostages it has taken except for those accused of collaboration.

15 JANUARY 1945
Eastern Front Kielce falls to the First Ukraine

Front. To the south of Konev's forces Petrov's Fourth Ukraine Front also goes over to the offensive.

Philippines On Luzon the US XIV Corps continues to advance south from the beachhead and has now crossed the River Agno. The I Corps is attacking north and east but cannot take its objective of Rosario.

15–16 JANUARY 1945
Formosa The American fleet carrier groups attack targets mainly in Formosa but also in the Pescadores and along the south China coast. The weather is poor but some success is achieved and two Japanese destroyers sunk.

16 JANUARY 1945
Eastern Front Zhukov's forces take Radom while to the north some of his other units have encircled Warsaw and are fighting their way through the city. Most of the defending German troops have escaped to the west however. Konev's troops to the south are making even better progress than Zhukov's and have reached Czestochowa.

Western Front There are attacks by the British XIII Corps near Roermond aimed at eliminating the small German salient west of the Maas. In the Ardennes the First and Third Armies link up at Houffalize.

Burma Namhkam is taken by Chinese units which have advanced from Myitkyina along the Ledo Road. The road northeast from Namhkam into China is not yet clear.

17 JANUARY 1945
Eastern Front The totally devastated city of Warsaw is cleared of German resistance by Zhukov's forces. A Polish unit fighting with the Red Army is involved in the final attacks. To the north Rokossovsky's troops take Modlin.

Western Front The US Third Army captures Diekirch.

19 JANUARY 1945
Philippines On Luzon the US attacks are now being concentrated to the south of the beachhead with the aim of striking to Manila. Carmen is taken.

On Mindoro there is a brief flurry of activity as the Japanese try to slow the advance toward Calapan of the US 21st Infantry. Filipino guerrillas are active throughout the island in support of the US forces.

Eastern Front Konev's troops take Tarnow and Krakow. To the south of these attacks Nowy Sacz is taken by Fourth Ukraine Front while

Zhukov's forces take Lodz. Wloclawek on the Vistula also falls.

20 JANUARY 1945

Eastern Front The Soviet offensive against the German forces in East Prussia achieves an important breakthrough in the attacks from the northeast. Tilsit is taken. All the Soviet fronts in Poland are moving forward despite German resistance. In Hungary the fighting in Budapest continues, but the Soviets now control the Pest half of the town.

Western Front General de Lattre's French First Army begins an offensive in the Vosges area near Colmar. Bad weather hinders the advance and the defense by the German Nineteenth Army is strong. Progress is gradually made, however. In the Ardennes the advance of Patton's Third Army goes on. Brandenburg is taken.

Burma On the Ledo Road the Chinese forces have only a few more miles to clear. The advance from Yunnan has reached Wanting on the border and from the other direction Mu-se is taken only 10 miles away.

United States, Politics President Roosevelt is inaugurated for a fourth term. Vice President Truman is also sworn in. In his speech Roosevelt promises to continue to work for the Allied victory and for the establishment of peace and security for the postwar world.

Hungary, Politics The Hungarian Provisional Government concludes an armistice with the USSR, the USA and the UK. The Hungarians agree to pay reparations and to join the war against Germany.

21 JANUARY 1945

Eastern Front In East Prussia the Soviet attack pushes forward once more. Gumbinnen is taken.

Burma There are British landings at the northern tip of Ramree Island. The 4th British and 71st Indian Brigades are put ashore. The battleship *Queen Elizabeth* and an escort carrier are in support but there is little resistance. In the XXXIII Corps sector on the mainland Monywa on the Chindwin is taken by 20th Indian Division.

Philippines On Luzon the US 40th Division takes Tarlac and pushes south toward Clark Field.

Western Front Wiltz falls to the US III Corps in the Ardennes.

21-22 JANUARY 1945

Formosa and Ryukyus There are more opera-

Above: In the Ardennes sector an American half-track leads a cautious advance.

tions by the fleet carriers of TF 38. Over 1150 sorties are flown over Formosa on the 21st, and 104 Japanese aircraft are shot down and 10 ships sunk. The carriers *Langley*, *Ticonderoga* and *Hancock* are all hit in Japanese attacks. On the 22nd Okinawa is the main target. After this operation the carrier groups all return to Ulithi. Since they were last in port on 30 December 1944 the carriers have sunk 300,000 tons of shipping and shot down 615 Japanese planes. They have lost 201 planes and 167 pilots.

22 JANUARY 1945
Eastern Front As well as the attacks of First Baltic and Third Belorussian Fronts from the northeast the German position in East Prussia is being threatened by the northwest advance of Second Belorussian Front toward the Elbing and Danzig area. In the attacks from the northeast Insterburg falls while in the other advance Allenstein and Deutsch Eylau are taken. To the south Gneizo is taken in Zhukov's drive to Poznan.
Western Front The British second Army is continuing its attacks in the Roermond area and takes St Joost and other towns near Sittard. In the Ardennes US First Army attacks all along the front between Houffalize and St Vith.
Philippines On Luzon there is heavy fighting in the US I Corps sector near Carmen and Rosario.
Burma The British IV Corps takes Tilin in its continuing advance toward the Irrawaddy to the south.

23 JANUARY 1945
Eastern Front As well as the continuing attacks in Poland and East Prussia, there is a new advance from around Miskolc by Malinovsky's Second Ukraine Front with both Soviet and Rumanian troops involved.
Western Front St Vith falls to the attack of tank units from XVIII Corps. The German forces are falling back over the River Our from throughout the Ardennes salient but are losing heavily to Allied air attacks.
Burma Myinmu is taken by 20th Indian Division. This division, and the other XXXIII Corps units which have crossed the Irrawaddy north of Mandalay, are attracting important Japanese counterattacks because of Japanese fears of a threat to Mandalay. This is exactly what General Slim, commanding Fourteenth Army, has hoped for while IV Corps prepares the real advance farther south.
Philippines Units of Griswold's XIV Corps take Bamban in their continuing southward attacks and reach almost to Clark Field.

24 JANUARY 1945
Western Front Units from the French First Army take crossings over the River Ill in Alsace. In the Ardennes there are Allied advances north and south of St Vith. Third Army reaches the River Clerf.
Eastern Front Konev's troops are attacking near Breslau and Oppeln on the Oder. They take Gleiwitz. SS leader Himmler is appointed by Hitler to lead a new Army Group Vistula to oppose the main Soviet thrusts. Himmler has no experience or aptitude for operational command and his appointment is a further blow and insult to the German Army and General Staff.
Philippines Calapan is taken by the US forces on Mindoro. Japanese resistance on the island has now been totally overcome except for a few stragglers.
Cabanatuan is taken by the US forces on Luzon.
China The Fourteenth Air Force has to abandon its Suichuan airfield because of Japanese advances nearby.

24–29 JANUARY 1945
Indian Ocean The British carriers make their last attacks before sailing for Australia on the way to join the main US carrier groups in the Pacific. Admiral Rawlings leads the four carriers in attacks at the oil refineries at Plodjoe north of Palembang on the 24th and against Soengi-Gerong on the 29th. Over 130 Japanese aircraft are shot down and 48 British aircraft lost. The battleship *King George V* and cruisers and destroyers escort the carriers.

25 JANUARY 1945
Eastern Front The German forces in East Prussia are now virtually cut off and evacuation operations therefore begin. These evacuations continue into April and involve about 40 large passenger ships and many other transports as well as practically all the remaining surface ships of the German Navy including the cruisers *Emden* and *Hipper*. There are considerable losses to the many mines laid in the Baltic by RAF Bomber Command and to the submarines of the Soviet Baltic Fleet. General Reinhardt, who has been in command of the German Army Group Center in East Prussia, is dismissed and General Rendulic is appointed to the renamed Army Group North.

In the fighting on other fronts Ostrow is taken by Konev's left flank units. His troops also take crossings over the Oder near Breslau and Steinau.
Philippines The 37th Division of Griswold's

XIV Corps occupies a large part of the Clark Field air base.

Iwo Jima The island is bombarded by the battleship *Indiana* and force of cruisers and destroyers. There are also air attacks by B-24 and B-29 bombers. This is the first step in the preparation for the US landings in February.

26 JANUARY 1945

Eastern Front Rokossovsky's advance reaches the Baltic north of Elbing completely cutting off the German forces in East Prussia.

Western Front Units of Third Army in the Ardennes have now crossed the Clerf in several areas and are attacking all along the front of III and XII Corps.

Burma There are British landings on Chedube Island south of Ramree. A small force of Marines goes ashore on the first day and they are later reinforced by the 36th Indian Brigade. On the mainland to the north the 81st African Division takes Myohaung. Inland in the advance of IV Corps to the Irrawaddy. Pauk is taken by 7th Indian Division.

27 JANUARY 1945

Burma The Ledo Road into China is finally cleared when Chinese troops from Burma and Yunnan province link up near Mongyu. General Sultan, who leads the British, American and Chinese in this area, has in fact announced the road as open on 22 January. Sultan's forces are now moving south toward Mandalay and Lashio by several routes.

Eastern Front In Poland Zhukov's troops have swept round Poznan where the garrison still holds out and are maintaining their advance to the Vistula. Zhukov's forces are also attacking near Toruń and Bydgoscz. In Lithuania the port of Memel finally falls to the Soviets.

Western Front Troops from Patton's Third Army cross the Our and take Oberhausen. The gains made by the German Ardennes offensive are now almost completely eliminated.

Philippines The US 32nd Infantry Division lands at Lingayen Gulf to reinforce the American troops there.

28 JANUARY 1945

Eastern Front The advance of First Belorussian Front enters German Pomerania. Sepolno and Leszno are taken on the flanks of the advance. To the south Konev's troops complete the capture of Katowice.

29 JANUARY 1945

Eastern Front There are German counter-attacks from East Prussia against Rokossovsky's troops to the west, but toward the south of the German pocket Bischofsburg falls to the Soviets.

Philippines On Luzon General Hall's XI Corps is landed at San Antonio north of Subic Bay to join the American offensive. About 30,000 men go ashore on the first day of the landing. Their task is to advance across the neck of the Bataan Peninsula and clear it of Japanese.

30 JANUARY 1945

Philippines A US battalion is landed to take Gamble Island in Subic Bay. To the north XI Corps begins to advance inland quickly and takes Olongapo on Luzon.

30 JANUARY–2 FEBRUARY 1945

Allied Planning Churchill and Roosevelt and their advisors meet in Malta to make preparations for the Yalta Meeting with Stalin. They leave for Yalta on the 2nd.

31 JANUARY 1945

Eastern Front Zhukov's troops reach the Oder at Zehden and along a wide front to the south to beyond Frankfurt. The Oder here is less than 50 miles from Berlin.

Western Front Units of XVIII Corps from First Army enter Germany east of St Vith as they continue their advance from the Ardennes. In Alsace French attacks near Colmar also make some ground.

Philippines On Luzon two regiments of General Swing's 11th Airborne Division are landed by sea near Nasugbu southwest of Manila. Admiral Fechteler leads the naval support with a cruiser and eight destroyers. There is little opposition to the landing. North of Manila the US advance is still making progress. XIV Corps units have nearly reached Calumpit in a converging attack.

Diplomatic Affairs The Czechoslovakian Government in London recognizes the Polish Lublin Government as the Provisional Government of Poland.

FEBRUARY 1945

Europe, Air Operations The Allied strategic bombing effort continues. The US Eighth Air Force and RAF Bomber Command both drop over 50,000 tons of bombs and other US strategic bombers add a further 23,000 tons. Many towns throughout west Germany are hit for both strategic and tactical reasons. Communications targets are among the most common. The Eighth Air Force sends more than 1000 bombers on attacks on 15 days during the month. In Operation Clarion which begins on the 22nd tactical targets throughout Germany are attacked by up to 9000 planes including lighter forces. The US Ninth Air Force drops almost 20,000 tons in all missions and RAF tactical support further increases this figure. The Mediterranean Air Forces also attack communications in that theater as well as dropping supplies to Tito and his Partisans. The attack on Dresden by the strategic forces is particularly controversial (see 13–15 February).

Far East, Air Operations Among the major attacks by B-29 forces are those targeted on Kobe, Nagoya and Tokyo. Some of these are made in conjunction with the carrier forces of the Pacific Fleet. Allied heavy bombers and tactical support forces are active in all other Pacific fronts.

Battle of the Atlantic German U-Boat strength remains roughly about 150, but Allied material and technical superiority means that they can achieve very little. There is something of a revival in the campaign, however, in the inshore waters of the Western Approaches. The U-Boats sink 15 ships during the month but 22 of their number are lost.

1 FEBRUARY 1945

Eastern Front Toruń falls to attacks from Zhukov's and Rokossovsky's forces. Zhukov's troops which have reached the Oder opposite Berlin halt there to regroup while the many pockets of German resistance in their rear are being eliminated and while the units on their flanks broaden the advance by attacking into Pomerania in the north and crossing the Oder and moving toward the Neisse in the south.

Philippines The American advance on all fronts is slowed by fierce Japanese resistance. I Corps is heavily engaged near Rosario and San Jose while XI Corps is struggling to make more ground across the neck of the Bataan Peninsula.

Western Front The US VI Corps from Seventh Army crosses the river Moder and advances nearly to Oberhofen.

1–15 FEBRUARY 1945

Iwo Jima The US air attacks on the island are stepped up with B-24's and B-29's over the island every day. In this preparatory phase for the landings later in the month 6800 tons of bombs are dropped.

2 FEBRUARY 1945

Western Front First Army Units are attacking near Remscheid. British forces mount attacks over the Maas, north of Breda and near Nijmegen to put pressure on the Germans.

3 FEBRUARY 1945

Western Front French and American units complete the capture of Colmar. All formations of French First Army are now making good progress in this sector. The other Allied armies keep up the pressure on the Germans all along the front.

Eastern Front In East Prussia the Soviet attacks continue to confine and divide the German forces. Landsberg and Bartenstein are taken.

Philippines On Luzon in the Tagaytay Ridge area the uncommitted regiment of 11th Airborne Division is dropped to help the advance of the other regiments. The fighting north of Manila also continues.

4 FEBRUARY 1945

Philippines On Luzon advance units of 1st Cavalry Division reach the outskirts of Manila from the north while units of 11th Airborne Division approach from the south. Yamashita has not ordered his forces to defend the city, but the 20,000 Japanese troops under the local naval commander in the city are prepared to fight to the end.

Western Front The Allies announce that all German forces have been expelled from Belgium. First and Third Army units are attacking toward the Roer River around Düren.

4–11 FEBRUARY 1945

Diplomatic Affairs Roosevelt, Churchill and Stalin and their senior military and political colleagues meet at Yalta in the Crimea.

It is now clear to all that the war in Europe has been won but both Britain and the US believe that they still have much to do to defeat Japan. Partly because Roosevelt's illness seems to be weakening his negotiating powers and judgment, Stalin is able to obtain the promise of territorial concessions in Sakhalin and the Kurile Islands in return for a promise to declare war on Japan within two months of the end of the war in Europe.

The postwar borders of the countries of eastern Europe are also largely determined at the Yalta meeting. The most notable changes are in the position of Poland, with the whole country being effectively moved westward at the insistence of the Soviets. Stalin gives assurances that elections will be held in eastern Europe and that non-Communist parties will not be forbidden or persecuted; however, the Western powers will not be able to supervise any such elections and they will never take place in a form regarded by the West as free or democratic. The arrangements for the division of Germany into occupation zones for each of the major powers are confirmed and defined. In reality the arrangements for Europe, however distasteful for liberal western opinion, only reflect the predominant share the USSR has played in the defeat of Germany. For the war against Japan the British and American eagerness to bring the Soviets in is also easy to understand, bearing in mind the fanatical resistance of the Japanese garrisons yet fought and the large Japanese forces in Manchuria and China. The establishment of a United Nations Organization is also discussed, and it is agreed that the preliminary meetings to create the organization should be held in April in San Francisco. It is already clear that the Soviets will lead the other great powers in insisting that they be granted veto powers in votes on major issues.

5 FEBRUARY 1945
Western Front The German pocket near Colmar is cut in two by a link between French units and part of the US XXI Corps. Farther north US First Army extends its attacks, led by V Corps, toward the Roer aiming to take the Schwammenauel Dam.

Eastern Front The Soviet attacks on the surrounded city of Poznan make some progress. Soviet pressure continues in many other sectors.

Philippines The US forces close in tighter around Manila. The XI Corps has completed its attack across the Bataan Peninsula.

South China Sea The Japanese carrier/battleship *Ise* is damaged by a mine off Indochina.

Greece The Greek Communist Party accepts the Greek government terms for an amnesty. The communists have to surrender their arms. The amnesty comes into force on 12 February.

6 FEBRUARY 1945
Eastern Front Southeast of Breslau the Soviet forces begin to push out of their bridgehead over the Oder.

Italy Units of IV Corps from Fifth Army take Gallicano in a brief offensive designed to improve the Allied positions on either side of the Serchio Valley.

7 FEBRUARY 1945
Eastern Front Zhukov's troops on the Oder seize some small bridgeheads over the river in the Kustrin area and near Furstenberg. There are also attacks in Pomerania where Answalde and Deutsche Krone are among the main centers of German resistance.

Western Front In the V Corps' advance toward the Roer Schmidt is taken. To the south Third Army units move into Germany east of the Our.

8 FEBRUARY 1945
Western Front A new offensive is begun by the Canadian First Army and British Second Army from between the Maas and the Waal southeast of Nijmegen. There is considerable air support and the advance penetrates the Reichswald area on the first day. In the US Third Army sector the VIII Corps manages to advance beyond the Our.

Eastern Front In East Prussia the German forces have now been virtually split into three groups: the defenders of Königsberg, some forces trapped on the peninsula to the west of the town, and those to the south, the largest group, holding out around Keiligenbeil and inland.

Philippines The 1st Cavalry Division is heavily engaged in the eastern suburbs of Manila. The 37th Division is also fighting in the city.

9 FEBRUARY 1945
Western Front In the British and Canadian offensive near Nijmegen the Rhine is reached at Millingen, which is captured. The US Third Army is attacking near Prüm in the north of its sector while XII Corps to the south is also making gains. Farther south still the resistance of the German forces around Colmar comes to an end.

Philippines As well as the fighting in Manila there is an attack by 11th Airborne Division southeast of the city near Nichols and Nielson Fields.

Burma In the Arakan area 26th Indian Division completes the capture of Ramree Island.

10 FEBRUARY 1945
Western Front In the First Army sector German forces open the Schwammenauel Dam in an attempt, partly successful, to delay the advance of the US forces nearby. To the north there are unsuccessful German attacks on the British and Canadian units which have now advanced almost to Cleve and Materborn.

Eastern Front The last German resistance in Elbing comes to an end and the town is taken by Second Belorussian Front.

11 FEBRUARY 1945
Eastern Front Konev's troops begin to break out of their bridgehead over the Oder near Steinau and attack west and north threatening Glogau. Other units will turn south to help surround Breslau. Leignitz is also attacked.

Western Front British and Canadian units take Cleve in their continuing advance toward the Rhine. In the Third Army sector to the south the important road junction at Prüm is taken by VIII Corps units.

CHRONOLOGY

12 FEBRUARY 1945
Burma West of Mandalay XXXIII Corps units begin to take their second series of bridgeheads over the Irrawaddy. The advance here is by 20th Indian Division opposite Myinmu. To the south IV Corps has reached the Irrawaddy at Myitche and Seikpyu and is preparing to cross. British and US units of Sultan's Northern Area Combat Command are advancing south toward Lashio and Kyaukme, but are being held for the moment in heavy fighting near the River Shweli.
Philippines The US XI Corps has now closed the neck of the Bataan Peninsula and is advancing southward to clear the Japanese forces from it.

13 FEBRUARY 1945
Eastern Front After a battle lasting for almost two months the garrison of Budapest surrenders to Malinovsky's forces. Over 100,000 German prisoners have been taken in the city. The Soviet advance from the Oder to the Neisse begins to gain momentum despite desperate German efforts. Bunzlau on the River Bober is captured.
Philippines US Navy forces begin operations in Manila Bay, clearing minefields and shelling landing grounds. Corregidor is bombarded. In the ground fighting the 11th Airborne Division takes Cavite and completes the capture of Nichols Field.
Western Front The British forces clear the last German units from the Reichswald in the northern sector of the front.
Burma The 20th Indian Division has now established a solid bridgehead over the Irrawaddy despite fierce Japanese attacks.

13-15 FEBRUARY 1945
Europe, Air Operations On the night of 13/14 February there is a massive RAF attack on Dresden by 773 Lancaster bombers. This is followed up by daylight attacks by Eighth Air Force on the 14th and 15th involving 600 planes altogether. The greatest damage is done in the RAF attack when the city, crowded with refugees from the Eastern Front, is devastated in a horrific fire storm. Various authorities give different figures for the number of casualties ranging from 30,000 dead to 200,000 dead. The best estimates suggest a figure around 70,000 is most accurate. The raid becomes very controversial because Dresden is not an important military target and has been a city of much historical interest.

14 FEBRUARY 1945
Eastern Front In the Soviet attacks on Pomerania Schneidmühl falls. Deutsche Krone is also taken after being surrounded but Arnswalde holds out against a similar attack. In Konev's drive to the Neisse, Sorau and Grünberg are both captured.
Western Front The British and Canadian offensive reaches the south bank of the Rhine opposite Emmerich. Other British and Canadian units also make advances in this sector. The US forces farther south are mostly regrouping to prepare for the next series of attacks.
Burma The 7th Indian Division from IV Corps begins to cross the Irrawaddy near Myaungu. There is only slight Japanese opposition because most of the Japanese forces have been withdrawn to defend Mandalay. North of Mandalay 19th Indian Division takes Singu despite the efforts of the defenders.

15 FEBRUARY 1945
Philippines A regiment from XI Corps is landed at the southern tip of Bataan on Luzon to help in the operations of the remainder of the corps. The fierce fighting in Manila continues.
Eastern Front In Konev's attacks west of the Oder Breslau has now been surrounded.

16 FEBRUARY 1945
Philippines Two battalions, one seaborne and one dropped by parachute, land on Corregidor Island in Manila Bay. The attacking troops land successfully enough but a bitter struggle soon develops among the tunnels and gun emplacements of the island. The US troops are quickly reinforced. Since the battle for Luzon began 3200 tons of bombs have been dropped on Corregidor.

16-17 FEBRUARY 1945
Japan There are attacks by the 12 fleet carriers and four light carriers of TF 58, now returned to Spruance's command as part of Fifth Fleet, against Tokyo alone on the 16th and against Tokyo and Yokohama on the 17th. Over 2700 sorties are flown and 88 American planes and twice as many Japanese are shot down. The carriers are escorted by eight battleships, 15 cruisers and 83 destroyers as well as many other support ships and their escorts. The force moves off toward Iwo Jima when the strikes have been completed.

16-18 FEBRUARY 1945
Iwo Jima The preliminary bombardment for the American landings begins in earnest. Admiral Rodgers leads the six battleships, five cruisers and 16 destroyers of TF 54 in the

operation and the 10 escort carriers of TF 52 also make attacks including many with the new napalm bombs. On the 16th the bombardment is comparatively ineffective because of bad weather and poor observation, but on the 17th and 18th more is achieved. On the 17th there are also bombing raids by B-24 bombers. The battleship *Tennessee* is hit on the 17th, and a cruiser and several of the smaller ships charged with minesweeping and obstacle clearing duties are also damaged.

Kuriles On the 16th and 18th an American cruiser and destroyer force shells Kuraba Zaki.

17 FEBRUARY 1945

Western Front There are new attacks by XII and XX Corps of the US Third Army from southern Luxembourg and farther south around Saarlouis. US Seventh Army units are attacking near Saarbrücken while in the north Canadian troops have now reached the Rhine on a 10-mile front.

Burma The British operations in the Arakan continue with successful landings at Ru-Ya, 40 miles southeast of Myebon. Heavy fighting continues in the area of XXXIII Corps bridgeheads over the Irrawaddy and along the Shweli River farther north especially near Myitson.

Europe, Air Operations The Italian battleship *Conte di Cavour*, already damaged, and the unfinished *Impero* are sunk in Trieste harbor by the RAF.

18 FEBRUARY 1945

Western Front All US Third Army units are attacking. The Siegfried Line is broken north of Echternach by VIII Corps while both XII and XX Corps to the south are also gaining ground. In the continuing British and Canadian offensive the British XXX Corps attacks Goch.

Eastern Front Chernyakhovsky, commander of Third Belorussian Front, dies of wounds. His replacement will be Vasilievsky.

Italy There are new attacks by IV Corps of Fifth Army in the area of the front just west of the Bologna-Pistoia road.

Bonin Islands While most of TF 58 is replenishing, one group of four carriers commanded by Admiral Radford attacks Haha Jima and Chichi Jima.

19 FEBRUARY 1945

Iwo Jima Two Marine Divisions of the V Amphibious Corps land on Iwo Jima in Operation Detachment. Before the landing the bombardment groups step up their effort and are joined by the aircraft of two carrier groups and by two battleships, several cruisers and destroyers from TF 58. The assault forces are from 4th and 5th Marine Divisions with 3rd Marines in reserve. They are carried in Admiral Hill's TF 53 and land on the southeast of the island. About 30,000 men go ashore on the first day.

General Kuribayashi commands the Japanese

Above: Marines of the 5th Division display trophies after a few days on Iwo Jima.

garrison of about 21,000 men, and they have prepared exceptionally elaborate and tough defenses so that the eight square miles of the island is completely fortified. The topography of the island is dominated by the 600-foot high Mount Suribachi at the southern tip. The rest of the island is flat, sloping gradually upward toward the north end.

There is almost no resistance to the landings at first, but after about half an hour the defenders open fire. The increasingly fierce Japanese resistance fails to prevent the Marines consolidating their beachhead and fighting their way across to the other side of the island before the end of the first day.

The Americans are well aware that the island is going to be strongly defended since it is part of metropolitan Japan, but it is strategically important because it is within fighter range of Tokyo, and this means that the B-29 bombers from the Marianas can be escorted. Iwo Jima will also provide an emergency landing field for damaged bombers on their return from missions over Japan.

19–20 FEBRUARY 1945

Philippines There are US landings in the northwest of the island of Samar and on the small islands offshore of Dalupiri, Capul and Biri. There is some resistance on Biri.

20 FEBRUARY 1945

Eastern Front The Soviet forces are now moving northward into German Pomerania on a 200-mile front. The German forces opposing them are from Himmler's Army Group Vistula, and his incompetence has contributed to their plight.

Western Front The XX Corps of Third Army continues its attacks on the 'Saar-Moselle triangle.'

20–22 FEBRUARY 1945

Iwo Jima The fleet carriers of TF 58 and the bombardment groups continue to give lavish support to the Marines. On the 21st the escort carrier *Bismarck Sea* is sunk and the fleet carrier *Saratoga*, an escort carrier and other ships are all damaged by Kamikaze attacks. In the fighting on the island the US forces are inching their way forward on to Mount Suribachi in the south and taking most of the island's first airfield to the north of the beachhead. Every advance, however small, has to be prepared and accompanied with enormous firepower. There are Japanese attacks and infiltration attempts during each night.

21 FEBRUARY 1945

Burma The 17th Indian and supporting tank units begin to break out of IV Corps' bridgehead at Myaungu and advance toward Meiktila. The Japanese know of the presence of British units in this area, but do not realize such strong forces are involved because the advance of IV Corps has been well disguised. Farther north troops of the British XXXIII Corps step up their efforts to attract the main Japanese forces when the British 2nd Division crosses the Irrawaddy near Ngazun to link with 20th Indian Division who already have a bridgehead near there. Farther north still the British 36th Division takes Myitson.

Philippines The US XI Corps completes the capture of the Bataan area of Luzon. Fighting on Corregidor continues, as does the battle for Manila.

Western Front Goch falls to the attacks of 51st Division of the British XXX Corps.

22 FEBRUARY 1945

Western Front The US XX Corps largely completes its battle in the Saar-Moselle triangle with almost complete success.

Italy Fifth Army makes some gains in mountain fighting high up in the Reno Valley.

22–23 FEBRUARY 1945

Burma There are British landings near Kangaw carried out by 6000 men of the 3rd Commando Brigade and other units.

23 FEBRUARY 1945

Western Front A major new offensive by US First and Ninth Armies begins with heavy attacks along the Roer, especially in the Jülich and Düren areas. The river is crossed in several sectors. The attacks are opposed by the German Fifth Panzer and Fifteenth Armies which are part of Model's Army Group B. Farther south there are also attacks by units of US Seventh and Third Armies.

Eastern Front Poznan falls to the Red Army after a 28-day battle. In Silesia Konev's troops have largely completed their advance from the Oder north of Breslau to the Neisse. In Breslau the fighting continues. The German garrison of the city will not surrender until the end of the war, despite repeated Soviet attacks.

Iwo Jima Most of Mount Suribachi is taken by the US forces during the day and the US flag is hoisted on the summit. To the north of the beachhead the pattern of slow US advance after much effort is maintained.

Philippines The US forces attacking in Manila

Above: Marines employ flame throwers during the fighting on Mount Suribachi, Iwo Jima.

step up their offensive after a fierce bombardment. The Japanese resistance is now largely confined to the old walled section of the town, the Intramuros, but the fighting there is very fierce.

Arctic German Ju 88 bombers sink the SS *Henry Bacon* from the convoy RA-64. This is the last Allied merchant ship to be sunk by German aircraft during the war.

24 FEBRUARY 1945

Western Front Jülich is taken by units of the XIX Corps as the US Ninth Army begins to extend its advance over the Roer. To the north the British and Canadian attacks continue to drive southeast toward Udem and Weeze. The US First and Third Armies also push forward in their sectors.

Iwo Jima The US advance to the north takes part of the island's second airfield.

Burma In their advance on Meiktila 17th Indian Division takes Taungtha.

25 FEBRUARY 1945

Western Front Düren is taken by VII Corps of US First Army. Other bridgeheads over the Roer have been taken north and south of here and they are rapidly being extended. On the right flank of Third Army to the south, crossings over the Saar have also been made near Saarburg.

Iwo Jima The US advance continues but there are heavy losses in the area around the second airfield.

Eastern Front There is a German counterattack from south of Stettin toward Pyritz, but although some success is achieved its effect is only local and temporary.

25–26 FEBRUARY 1945

Japan The aircraft from the carriers of TF 58 again send attacks against Tokyo. Bad weather hinders their effectiveness.

26 FEBRUARY 1945

Eastern Front In the face of the Soviet attacks into East Pomerania and the Soviet's retention despite counterattacks of positions near Stettin, the Germans begin evacuations of wounded and refugees from Kolberg and other ports along the coast. These operations continue until the ports are taken during March.

Burma The advance of 17th Indian Division toward Meiktila continues to go well. Mahlaing and the Thabuktong airfield are taken. Reinforcements for IV Corps will be flown in to this airfield.

Western Front There are renewed British and Canadian efforts near Udem and Calcar. US First and Ninth Army units are moving rapidly from their bridgeheads over the Our.

Philippines The fighting on Corregidor comes to an end. The US forces find more than 5000 Japanese dead on the tiny island and others have been trapped in collapsed tunnels. There are 19 prisoners. US casualties are around 1000.

27 FEBRUARY 1945

Western Front Udem and Calcar both fall to the British and Canadian attacks. The advance in this sector reaches the Rhine northeast of Calcar. In the US First Army area units of VII Corps cross the Erft at Modrath in their advance toward Cologne. The US Ninth and Third Armies are both moving forward well, two of Third Army's Corps converging on Trier.

Burma Units of the 19th Indian Division begin to break out of their bridgehead over the Irrawaddy at Habeikkyin and advance south toward Mandalay against heavy Japanese resistance.

Iwo Jima The carriers of TF 53 again add their support to the ships aiding the Marines' attacks. The main focus of the advance is now the three Japanese positions overlooking the island's second airfield. Despite three days of attacks the Japanese defenders cannot be dislodged.

28 FEBRUARY 1945
Burma The British IV Corps begins to attack Meiktila in strength. The Japanese command has known of the presence of this force but has believed it to be only lightly armed in the Chindit pattern. They have, therefore, left it to the local troops at Meiktila to defend their own base. This is a serious error because Meiktila is a vital communications center, serving all the Japanese forces around Mandalay and to the north.

Philippines There are US landings at Puerto Princesa on Palawan by 8000 men of 41st Infantry Division. Admiral Fechteler leads a bombardment group of cruisers and destroyers and there is also support from land-based aircraft. There is little Japanese resistance to the landings.

MARCH 1945
Europe, Air Operations Both RAF Bomber Command and the US Eighth Air Force step up their efforts each dropping more than 73,000 tons of bombs. Among the RAF targets are Mannheim, Kassel, Essen and Dortmund. The raid on Dortmund on the 12th sees 4850 tons of bombs dropped – the heaviest attack on any target during the war. In an attack on the Bielfeld viaduct on the 15th the largest bomb dropped during the war is used for the first time, the 22,000-pound Grand Slam. The Eighth Air Force is able to send 1500 heavy bombers out on any one day and among its targets are Chemnitz, Osnabruck and Swinemünde. The German communications system and the synthetic oil industry are attacked by both British and American forces. Tactical targets are also hit by the heavy bombers. Ninth Air Force flies 55,000 missions and drops 33,000 tons of bombs in its support tasks. RAF tactical support forces fly 30,000 missions. The Mediterranean Air Forces also contribute to the Allied effort.

Far East, Air Operations This month there is a notable change in the American tactics for their attacks on targets in Japan. General Le May, commanding the bomber forces based in the Marianas, has become dissatisfied with both the weight and accuracy of attack achieved in precision bombing from B-29's at high altitude. The very high winds met at around 30,000 feet, which has been the operational altitude until now, mean that bomb accuracy is very difficult and attaining this altitude overstrains the aircraft and restricts the bomb load. The new tactics involve the attacks being made by night on city targets with the bombs being mostly incendiaries. The first and most horrific attack on this new pattern is aimed at Tokyo (*see* 9–10 March). Other targets hit in Japan include Nagoya, Osaka and Kobe.

Elsewhere there are many Allied air operations in the Philippines, Burma and over China where Fourteenth Air Force is maintaining its efforts.

1 MARCH 1945
Western Front München-Gladbach and Neuss fall to the US Ninth Army which is now advancing rapidly toward the Rhine. The attacks of First Army toward Cologne are continuing as are the efforts of Third Army near the River Kyll and south of Trier.

Eastern Front In Pomerania the northward attacks of Zhukov's forces achieve a breakthrough north of Arnswalde and move on in the Kolberg direction.

Iwo Jima The US forces now hold both the first and second of the island's airfields and have a foothold at the south end of the third. The fighting is still very fierce all along the line.

Philippines The Japanese resistance in Manila is now confined to only a few blocks in the administrative area of the city. Nearer the landing area at Lingayen Gulf there are renewed efforts by I Corps in the direction of Baguio and north along the coast.

Okinawa Part of the TF 58 carrier force attacks targets on Okinawa and shipping nearby. Two small Japanese warships are sunk.

2 MARCH 1945
Western Front Trier is captured by units of XX Corps from Patton's Third Army. First Army to the north is extending its advance beyond the Erft both toward Cologne and to the right also. Ninth Army captures Roermond and Venlo on the Maas on the left of its advance while on the right the Rhine is reached opposite Dusseldorf.

Ryukyu Islands Four cruisers and 15 destroyers

commanded by Admiral Whiting and drawn from TF 58 bombard Okino Daito Jima.

Rumania King Michael of Rumania is forced under pressure from the Soviets to dismiss his government and on 6 March to appoint a new government dominated by the Rumanian Communist Party. This is the first token since Yalta that Stalin will not hold to his assurances about doing nothing to hinder the process of democracy in eastern Europe.

3 MARCH 1945

Burma Meiktila is completely occupied by IV Corps units. They immediately dig in. The main route for supplies to the bulk of the Japanese forces in Burma is, therefore, cut and they will be compelled to turn away from the fighting farther north and try to clear their lines of communication. At the same time they must do something to hold off XXXIII Corps to the north.

Western Front Troops of Ninth and First Canadian Armies link up near Geldern. Farther south units of the US XII Corps from Third Army take a crossing over the Kyll. In the Seventh Army sector Forbach is taken.

Iwo Jima The area of the island which has become known as 'the Mincer' is finally cleared by the Marines' attacks after a vicious struggle. The third airfield is now completely in American hands.

Philippines Japanese resistance in Manila comes to an end after a bitter month-long fight. The 20,000 defenders have been wiped out and the town devastated.

Troops from the Americal Division are landed on Ticao and Burias Islands to the west of the San Bernardino Strait.

4 MARCH 1945

Western Front Geldern is taken by the British XXX Corps from First Canadian Army. US First and Ninth Armies continue their advance to the Rhine. VII Corps from First Army reaches the Rhine just north of Cologne.

Eastern Front The Soviet offensive in Pomerania continues to make gains especially toward the west near Stettin. There is also renewed fighting in East Prussia.

5 MARCH 1945

Western Front Units of the US VII Corps enter Cologne from the south and the east. The Allied advance in other sectors continues.

Burma Japanese counterattacks against IV Corps begin. The small town of Taungtha is retaken by the Japanese and 17th Indian

Division is almost cut off in Meiktila. Air supply continues, however.

Germany, Home Front Fifteen- and sixteen-year-old boys from the class of 1929 are called up to serve in the German army.

6 MARCH 1945

Eastern Front The German forces in Hungary launch a major counteroffensive in the area just north of Lake Balaton. Dietrich's Sixth SS Panzer Army, which was withdrawn from the Ardennes battle early in January, has been moved here to lead the attack. Other units from Wöhler's Army Group South also take part in the offensive. The operation is code named Frühlingserwachen or Spring Awakening. The Soviet Twenty-seventh Army bears the brunt of the attack initially and is forced to give ground but reserve units of Tolbukhin's Third Ukraine Front will soon arrive to slow the advance down. The optimistic German aim is to retake all the territory between Lake Balaton and the Danube.

In the fighting in Poland Second Belorussian Front completes the capture of the fortress town of Grudiadz which has been surrounded for some time.

Western Front The US Ninth Army has now reached the Rhine all along its front. Units of the Canadian First Army to the north are preparing to clear the final German pocket west of the Rhine around Xanten. To the south of Ninth Army First Army is fighting in Cologne and driving toward Remagen farther south. The 9th Armored Division leads the advance here. Farther south still units of Third Army are making a rapid advance in one section of the front toward the Rhine at Koblenz.

Burma In their slow advance down the Burma Road units of the Chinese First Army reach and capture Lashio.

7 MARCH 1945

Eastern Front In Hungary the German offensive continues and more gains are made. As well as the forces north of Lake Balaton there are attacks by units of Second Panzer Army toward Kaposvar to the south and from over the Yugoslav border by units of Löhr's Army Group E. In Poland evacuations begin from around Danzig. These last until the middle of April.

Western Front The leading tanks of III Corps reach the Rhine opposite Remagen and find the Ludendorff Bridge there damaged but still standing. Troops are immediately rushed across and brilliant staff improvisation sends more units hurrying to join them. Hitler is furious and sacks Field Marshal Rundstedt from command of the German armies in the west. Other Allied units complete the capture of Cologne while XII Corps units from Third Army continue to move forward particularly quickly.

Philippines There is fighting in the I Corps sector south of San Fernando. South of Manila the XIV Corps is fighting near Balayan Bay and Batangas against the defense lines of the south Luzon Shimbu Group of the Japanese forces.

Yugoslavia, Politics The two existing governments, Tito's and the royalist government, are merged into a new single government dominated by Tito and his followers.

8 MARCH 1945

Western Front American efforts to pass forces over the Remagen Bridge continue but there is unavoidably some congestion. German bombers, including some jets, begin all-out attacks on the bridge but fail to destroy it. To the north units of the Canadian II Corps take Xanten.

Burma The 2nd British and 20th Indian Divisions begin to break out of their bridgeheads over the Irrawaddy to the west of Mandalay.

Iwo Jima The US forces are still methodically pushing forward to the north of the island with continued heavy fire support. The Japanese forces are now all within one mile of the north end of the island.

8–9 MARCH 1945

France There are still German garrisons in the Channel Islands, and during the night they mount a raid on Granville on the west coast of the Cotentin. One small US warship is sunk and four merchant ships.

9 MARCH 1945

Western Front Bonn and Godesberg are taken by units of US First Army while others continue to expand the bridgehead beyond the Rhine at Remagen. Erpel is taken here. A little farther south toward Koblenz Third Army units reach the Rhine at Andernach.

Burma The southward advance of the 19th Indian Division reaches the outskirts of Mandalay. Other XXXIII Corps units are advancing toward the city from the west. The fighting around Meiktila is still very fierce as the Japanese continue to bring troops from the Mandalay area in a desperate attempt to free their communications.

9–10 MARCH 1945

Iwo Jima On both days the US attacks continue but during the night between there is an unusually fierce Japanese suicide attack. The attack achieves little and almost all those taking part are killed.

Far East, Air Operations There is a devastating attack by 279 Superfortress bombers on Tokyo. Over 1650 tons of incendiaries are dropped on the city in a new form of attack designed specifically to take advantage of the wood and paper construction of many Japanese houses. A massive fire storm is raised and many thousands of homes are completely destroyed. The death toll is at least 80,000 and probably as many as 120,000. It is the most damaging air attack of the war including the atomic attacks on Hiroshima and Nagasaki. This is only the first of many such raids on Japanese cities.

10 MARCH 1945

Western Front The last German forces are withdrawn from the pocket west of the Rhine between Wesel and Xanten. They have lost heavily to the British and Canadian attacks. US First and Third Armies link up near Andernach completing the Allied hold on the west bank of the Rhine everywhere north of Koblenz. Field Marshal Kesselring arrives from Italy to take command of the German armies in the west.

Eastern Front The German advance in the Lake Balaton area begins to be slowed by the fierce Soviet ground and air resistance, by the atrocious muddy conditions and by the lack of fuel for the tanks and other vehicles.

Philippines Most of the 41st US Infantry Division is landed at the southwest of Mindanao near Zamboanga. General Doe commands the troops and Admiral Barbey the naval support.

On Luzon fighting continues south of Laguna de Bay where the US forces are still trying to break through to the east.

Organized Japanese resistance on the island of Palawan comes to an end.

11 MARCH 1945

Burma Mongmit is captured by a converging attack by the two brigades of the British 36th Division which have moved south from Myitson and the third brigade of the division which moves in from the west.

Philippines There is more fighting in the Batangas area south of Manila and in the north toward Baguio.

Ulithi Atoll The carrier *Randolph* is damaged in a Kamikaze attack on the Pacific Fleet base at Ulithi.

12 MARCH 1945

Eastern Front Kustrin falls to Zhukov's forces

after a bitter struggle. Apart from a small area in the north near Stettin the Soviets now hold the whole of the Oder-Neisse line as far south as Görlitz.

Rokossovsky's forces continue to push forward toward the Gulf of Danzig. In the Polish Corridor they capture Tczew.

Western Front There is heavy fighting in the Remagen bridgehead where units of the German Seventh Army are counterattacking fiercely.

Burma Myotha, southwest of Mandalay, falls to the 20th Indian Division.

14 MARCH 1945
Western Front The XII Corps of Third Army begins an offensive southeast over the Moselle from near Koblenz and XX Corps expands its attacks from between Trier and Saarburg. To the north of these actions fighting around the Remagen bridgehead goes on but it is steadily being expanded despite the German efforts.

Burma Maymo, to the east of Mandalay, is taken by the 62nd Indian Brigade. The last rail line to Mandalay is, therefore, cut. Other units of 19th Indian Division are still fighting in Mandalay but have captured much of the city in a bitter house-to-house engagement.

Eastern Front The Soviets capture Zvolen in western Czechoslovakia.

15 MARCH 1945
Western Front The US Seventh Army goes over to the attack once more especially in the area around Saarbrücken and Bitche. Seventh Army is joining Third Army in the attempt to expel the Germans from the area between the Saar, Moselle and Rhine.

Burma The Japanese step up their efforts against Meiktila but can make no important progress against 17th Indian Division which is receiving supplies, reinforcements and ground attack support from the air.

Iwo Jima The fighting continues but the Japanese forces are now mostly confined in a small area in the northwest of the island.

Kuriles Admiral McCrea leads a squadron of US cruisers and destroyers in a bombardment of Matsuwa.

16 MARCH 1945
Eastern Front The Soviet forces in Hungary have regrouped following the German advance in the Lake Balaton area and now begin an offensive against the northern flank of the recently won German salient. The Third Hungarian Army takes the brunt of the first assaults and is soon in great difficulty.

Philippines Part of the US 41st Division lands on Basilan Island. Here, as on other small islands, the pattern will be for the US forces to subdue the Japanese in the first few days' fighting and then mostly to withdraw, leaving the mopping up to Filipino guerrillas.

Fighting continues along the Shimbu Line southeast of Manila and in the I Corps sector to the north, especially on the Villa Verde track.

Western Front Bitche is taken as Seventh Army continues its effort to break through the Siegfried Line.

17 MARCH 1945
Western Front The Remagen Bridge collapses under the combined strain of bomb damage and heavy use but US Army engineers have built several other bridges nearby and the advance over the Rhine continues. To the south the Third Army offensive over the Moselle takes Koblenz and Boppard on the left flank of the drive while farther forward the Nahe River has been crossed.

Burma Units of the Chinese Sixth Army take Hsipaw on the Burma Road, 50 miles southwest of Lashio. The Chinese First Army is still trying to advance along the road from Lashio to clear it of Japanese blocks.

18 MARCH 1945
Western Front Patton's offensive captures Bingen and Bad Kreuznach as the advance to the southwest continues. To the south Seventh Army is also beginning to accelerate its progress, most of its forward units having now crossed the German border.

Eastern Front Zhukov's troops take Kolberg on the Pomeranian coast. Other Soviet forces are closing in around Gdynia and Danzig to the east and making further inroads into the German positions in East Prussia.

Philippines There are US landings on Panay by 14,000 men of 40th Infantry Division commanded by General Brush in the area near Iloilo. There is little opposition from the Japanese at first.

Burma The British 2nd Division takes Ava on the bend of the Irrawaddy only a few miles south of Mandalay. The heavy fighting in Mandalay and round Meiktila continues.

18–21 MARCH 1945
Japan The carriers of Admiral Mitscher's TF 58 carry out a series of attacks on targets in the Japanese Home Islands. Admiral Spruance, commanding Fifth Fleet is also present. On the 18th Airfields on Kyushu are the main targets.

There are Kamikaze attacks by about 10 planes on the American ships in which *Intrepid Yorktown* and *Enterprise* are all hit but are not put out of action. On the 19th the carrier strikes are mostly sent against Japanese naval bases in the Inland Sea area. Kure is especially singled out. Six Japanese carriers and three battleships are damaged. The Kamikaze attacks in reply are very effective. The carriers *Franklin* and *Wasp* are both badly damaged and the *Enterprise* and *Essex* less so. The 832 dead on *Franklin* make this the heaviest ever casualty list on any US ship. On the 20th and 21st the carriers are replenishing to prepare for operations around Okinawa, but the Japanese attacks continue. They achieve little success on either day but a feature of the attacks on the 22nd is that many are made by manned rocket bombs.

19 MARCH 1945
Germany, Home Front Hitler orders a total scorched earth policy to be put into operation on all fronts. Industrial plants, buildings and food are to be completely destroyed. Speer, who remains in charge of German industry, does his best to prevent this decree being carried out. He is helped by many army leaders.
Western Front General Patch's Seventh Army completes the capture of Saarlouis. Fighting in Saarbrücken and the towns to the east continues. Third Army keeps up its rapid advance east and southeast toward the Rhine. Worms is reached, while to the left and right other units are near Mainz and Kaiserslautern.
Eastern Front There are renewed attacks by Third Belorussian Front against the German forces in East Prussia, especially in the area south of Königsberg. The drive lasts for a week until most of the German forces are eliminated or evacuated. About 38,000 are taken off by the many ships involved including many wounded and refugees.
Philippines In their northward attacks along the west coast I Corps takes Bauang south of San Fernando on Luzon.
Burma Mogok is taken by the British 36th Division.

20 MARCH 1945
Eastern Front Soviet forces in the Stettin area eliminate the German bridgehead over the Oder at Altdamm. In East Prussia Braundsberg is captured. General Heinrici, one of the best defensive tacticians in the German army, is appointed to command Army Group Vistula in succession to Himmler. Heinrici will have the task of building up defenses along the Oder for

when the Soviets extend their advance toward Berlin, but Army Group Vistula has already lost a large part of its original force in the fighting in Pomerania. It is perhaps unnecessary to point out that only the small pockets holding out near Danzig are anywhere near the Vistula.
Burma The 19th Indian Division completes the capture of Mandalay. The Fort Dufferin position has been among the most stubbornly defended by the Japanese.
Western Front Patch's forces take Saarbrücken and Zweibrücken a little to the east. In the Third Army sector Ludwigshafen and Kaiserslautern are captured. First Army is still fighting to expand the Remagen bridgehead. It is now almost 30 miles wide and 19 miles deep.

21 MARCH 1945
Western Front The main body of Third Army is now clearing the west bank of the Rhine everywhere north of Mannheim. Other Third and Seventh Army units are cooperating to take Annweiler, Neunkirchen, Neustadt and Homberg.

22 MARCH 1945
Western Front The US 5th Division from Patton's Third Army crosses the Rhine near Nierstein with none of the elaborate preparations which Montgomery is making in the admittedly more difficult sector farther north. It shows the contrast between their styles of generalship. Other Third Army units are completing the mopping up west of the Rhine and preparing to make crossings of their own.
Eastern Front In Silesia Konev's troops achieve a breakthrough in attacks over the Oder to the south of Oppeln and to the north of the town they extend an already existing bridgehead over the river. In the Polish Corridor the Soviet forces are still fighting to reach the Baltic between Gdynia and Danzig.

23 MARCH 1945
Western Front The British Second and Canadian First Armies mount a carefully prepared operation, code named Plunder, to cross the Rhine in the area from Emmerich to just south of Wesel. There is massive artillery and air support. Two parachute divisions are also to be dropped to aid the crossing. The operation begins at 2100 hours. US First Army and the small part of Third Army which has crossed the Rhine are also extending their hold.
Burma As well as capturing Mandalay, XXXIII Corps units have been striking south. Wundwin is taken by 20th Indian Division on one flank of

this advance.

Italy General Vietinghoff takes over command of German forces in Italy replacing Field Marshal Kesselring who has been withdrawn to the Western Front. Throughout March there have been small attacks by both II and IV US Corps of Fifth Army in the area around the Pistoia–Bologna road and to the west.

Philippines On Luzon San Fernando is taken by I Corps with help from Filipino guerrillas.

23–31 MARCH 1945

Ryukyu Islands There are various operations by US forces in preparation for the landings on Okinawa. Between 23 and 25 March the carriers of TF 58, now 14 organized in three groups, attack targets on Okinawa Island. On the 24th scout planes from the carriers find a Japanese convoy south of Kyushu and all eight ships in it are sunk. Also on the 24th Okinawa is bombarded by five battleships and 11 destroyers commanded by Admiral Lee. On 26/27 March the British Pacific Fleet, organized as TF 57 and commanded by Admiral Rawlings, makes attacks on airfields and other targets on Sakashima Gunto. There are four fleet carriers, two battleships, five cruisers and 11 destroyers in the British force. From the 25th, the 17 escort carriers of Admiral Durgin's TF 52 begin attacks on the same targets as the fleet carriers, both supplementing their efforts and giving them opportunities to refuel. On the 25th there is a bombardment of the small island of Kerama Retto just to the west of Okinawa itself. On the 26th General Bruce's 77th Infantry Division lands on Kerama Retto and overruns it against slight Japanese resistance. This landing is necessary to protect the waters that are going to be used for the main landings on Okinawa. Also on 26th March the main bombardment of Okinawa begins. Admiral Deyo leads the 10 battleships, 10 cruisers and 33 destroyers of TF 54 in this task. Also taking part are many rocket craft.

The Japanese reply to these Allied operations includes many unsuccessful submarine attacks in which two submarines are sunk and no torpedo hits achieved. The more deadly Kamikaze attacks start on the 25th. The Kamikaze attacks on the US naval forces are to be one of the dominating features of the Okinawa campaign. The planes are from various Air Fleets in the Japanese Home Islands and on Formosa. Admiral Ugaki commands. On the 25th 26 planes attack making eight hits including one on the battleship *Nevada*. On the 27th attacks by explosive boats are beaten off and on the 30th the cruiser *Indianapolis* is badly damaged by a suicide plane.

24 MARCH 1945

Eastern Front In Hungary Szekesfehervar falls to the attacks of Malinovsky's troops. The front line of the Soviet offensive in this area has already pushed farther to the west, taking Veszprem and Mor. The German and Hungarian forces are retiring in disorder after taking heavy losses. In north Poland the Soviets take Spolot on the coast between Gdynia and Danzig.

Western Front Montgomery's Rhine crossing operation goes well and by the end of the day the bridgehead is more than five miles deep. What remains of the town of Wesel after the preliminary bombardment is captured by British troops. The US Ninth Army, also part of Montgomery's Twenty-first Army Group, begins to cross the Rhine a little to the south of the British and Canadians.

25 MARCH 1945

Eastern Front In East Prussia Keiligenbeil falls to units of the Third Belorussian Front. In Hungary the Soviet offensive continues with the capture of Esztergom on the Danube. Just north of the Danube there are attacks by more of Malinovsky's troops.

Western Front The various crossings of Twenty-first Army Group are consolidated into one bridgehead 30 miles wide. Further south US First Army units, principally from III Corps, begin to break out of the Remagen bridgehead. The VIII Corps from Third Army begins to cross the Rhine near Boppard. To the south Darmstadt is taken by XII Corps units who crossed at Nierstein. Other formations have advanced farther east to the Main near Hanau and Aschaffenburg.

26 MARCH 1945

Iwo Jima The few hundred Japanese troops remaining on the island mount a final suicide attack. They are wiped out by the 5th Marine Division units which have been given the task of finishing off the last pockets. Only just over 200 of the Japanese garrison of 20,700 remain alive as prisoners of the Marines. The American casualties have been almost 6000 dead and 17,200 wounded. In addition 90 USN personnel have died.

Western Front The US Seventh Army begins to send units of XV and VI Corps across the Rhine between Worms and Mannheim. To the north all the Allied armies continue to push forward.

Philippines About 14,000 men commanded by

CHRONOLOGY

General Arnold and drawn from the units of the Americal Division land just south of Cebu City. Admiral Berkey leads a bombardment group in support.

27 MARCH 1945
Eastern Front The Soviets have now penetrated to the final defense lines at both Gdynia and Danzig. The attacks go on. In Hungary and Czechoslavakia Second and Third Ukraine Fronts continue their attacks. The heaviest fighting is along the line of the Rába River where Sixth SS Panzer Army loses heavily in fruitless attempts to stem the Soviet advance.

Western Front In the northern sector Twenty-first Army Group units are advancing along the line of the River Lippe and Ninth Army especially is beginning to penetrate south into the Ruhr area. Third Army has now crossed the Main both west of Frankfurt, where Wiesbaden is attacked, and to the east.

Philippines Cebu City is taken by the US landing force. As on the other islands the Japanese are beginning to withdraw to inland strongholds where they will be confined and worn down by Filipino guerrillas. Only on Luzon, Mindanao and Negros will the prolonged presence of US troops be necessary.

In Manila Bay an American force lands on Caballo Island, better known to the former defenders of the island as Fort Hughes. After struggling to penetrate the Japanese defenses until 5 April, the US forces will pour thousands of gallons of a diesel/gasoline mixture into the fort and set it on fire. Even after this treatment the Japanese resistance is not entirely finished.

Britain, Home Front The last German V2 rocket lands southeast of London at Orpington. The V2 campaign has killed over 2700 British civilians and injured 6500. As well as the 1115 launched at British targets a further 2050 were aimed at Antwerp, Brussels and Liège.

28 MARCH 1945
Western Front Marburg is taken by US III Corps which has made a rapid advance from the Remagen bridgehead.

General Eisenhower sends a controversial signal to Stalin giving details of his order of battle and saying that he intends to send the main weight of his advance across southern Germany and Austria. The main thrust is to be toward Erfurt and Leipzig and a secondary effort is to go for Nüremberg, Regensburg and Linz. The British protest very strongly about this signal suggesting that decisions of such importance should not be taken by Eisenhower

alone and that he is also overstepping his authority in communicating directly with the Soviets. The British would prefer the advance to be directed on Berlin as has been the plan up to now for the political value of this move. They believe that this plan is superior to one based on doubtful reports and worries of the preparation of a German National Redoubt in Bavaria. Both Churchill and the British Chiefs of Staff present this case to Washington. President Roosevelt has now become so weakened by his illness that most military decisions are left to General Marshall and the Joint Chiefs of Staff. Marshall has always been inclined to favor military rather than political reasoning in making strategic decisions and, therefore, confirms his support for Eisenhower. With the advantage of knowledge of future Soviet behavior, it is easy to comment that the war was fought for political and not military reasons, and that an advance to Berlin might have left the Western Allies in a stronger position in postwar Europe.

German Command After a blazing row with Hitler, General Guderian is dismissed from his post as Chief of the Army General Staff. His replacement is General Krebs, a far less talented officer. Although Guderian has only been able to achieve a fraction of his aims against Hitler's opposition he has managed to preserve some sanity in the actions of the German High Command. He is the last of the famous German leaders from the early war period to be dismissed.

Eastern Front Gdynia falls to Rokossovsky's forces. Just south of the Danube Györ is taken by troops from Second Ukraine Front.

Burma The Japanese have failed in their efforts to retake Meiktila and while they have been involved in this area XXXIII Corps has been making important gains to the north. General Kimura, commanding Japanese forces in Burma, decides that with his main communications cut, he must try to retreat as best he can. Many of the Japanese will manage to escape via Thazi to the east of Meiktila.

29 MARCH 1945
Philippines There are US landings in the northwest of the island Negros near Bacolod. The landing force is from 185th Regiment. The Japanese on this island will fight very fiercely.

30 MARCH 1945
Eastern Front On the Baltic coast the final German positions in Danzig are overcome by Soviet attacks. In Hungary the attacks of Third Ukraine Front beyond the Raba have made such good progress that the advance units enter

Austria north of Köszeg. To the north of these attacks Second Ukraine Front is closing in on Bratislava.

Western Front The US First Army advances north out of its salient around Marburg and reaches and crosses the River Eder. Third Army is attempting to strike east and north toward Gotha and Kassel.

Burma Kyaukse is taken by 20th Indian Division. The British forces now hold most of the important positions on the road between Mandalay and Meiktila. The Japanese forces in central Burma have been brought to battle and defeated exactly as General Slim has hoped. The Japanese have not been able to slip away largely intact as they intended, and instead have been compelled to fight the main action with improvised forces against the carefully organized British defense around Meiktila.

Europe, Air Operations In US attacks on the north German ports the cruiser *Köln* and 14 U-Boats are sunk.

31 MARCH 1945

Western Front Forces of French First Army begin to cross the Rhine near Speyer. To the north all the Allied armies maintain their advance.

Eastern Front Ratibor on the upper Danube is taken by Konev's troops.

Burma Northeast of Mandalay the British 36th Division and units of the Chinese Sixth Army take Kyaukme. The Burma Road from Mandalay to Lashio is now clear.

APRIL 1945

Europe, Air Operations Despite the progress of the Allied ground forces the efforts of the British and American Strategic Air Forces continue until almost the end of the month. The Eighth Air Force flies 18,900 sorties to drop 46,600 tons of bombs. The targets include jet airfields and communications centers. Nuremberg, Bayreuth, Neumark and Berlin are all hit. RAF Bomber Command drops 38,400 tons particularly against ports and shipping including Hamburg, Kiel, and Bremen. Leipzig is also attacked. Heavy bombers are used to drop food to parts of Holland and to evacuate freed prisoners of war from Germany. Tactical targets are attacked by the heavy bomber forces and other units. On 16 April American and Soviet ground attack forces meet near Dresden when they try to attack the same German train. On 30 April the British and American authorities announce that the strategic bombing offensive is over.

Far East, Air Operations The fire bombing attacks on Japanese cities go on. Tokyo is heavily attacked on six occasions during the month, and after 6 April land based escorts can be provided for the bombers. Kawasaki and Nagoya are among the other city targets. Also attacked are airfields in the Home Islands used by Kamikaze aircraft involved in the Okinawa operation. At the very end of March a major mining campaign in Japanese home waters has been begun by the B-29 forces and this now gets fully under way.

There are many air operations in support of the land forces in Southeast Asia Command and

Above: Men of a colored unit of Ninth US Army crew an AA machine gun at the Rhine crossings.

Fourteenth Air Force in China is active against rail targets particularly.

Battle of the Atlantic The German submarine strength still remains high at 166 operational and 278 on trials or in training at the start of the month. They sink 13 ships this month, but 27 are sunk at sea and 15 more destroyed by bombing. Only now does the first of the advanced Type XXI see service.

1 APRIL 1945

Okinawa The US forces begin Operation Iceberg, the invasion of Okinawa. It is the largest naval operation yet in the Pacific. Admiral Turner's TF 51 provides the 1200 transport and landing ships with over 450,000 Army and Marine Corps personnel embarked. The troops landed are from III Amphibious and XXIV Corps of General Buckner's Tenth Army. The landings are in the Hagushi area in the southwest of the island. Geiger's III Corps lands on the left with 6th and 1st Marine Divisions providing the assault units. Hodge's forces on the right are 7th and 96th Infantry Divisions. Hodge is to deal with the south end of the island and Geiger to advance to the north. There is almost no resistance on the first day and a solid beachhead three miles deep and nine miles wide is established. (Okinawa is 70 miles long and a maximum of 10 miles wide.) Kadena and Yontan airfields are taken.

The explanation for the lack of resistance is that the Japanese forces, 130,000 men of General Ushijima's Thirty-second Army, are entrenched in concealed positions and caves mostly to the south of the US landings on the Shuri Line. There are also 450,000 civilians on the island.

Throughout the battle at least two of the carrier groups of TF 58 will normally be available to give air support. The British TF 57 and the escort carrier groups will also be heavily involved. There will be almost daily bombardment by the heavy ships of TF 54. Japanese air operations, both conventional and Kamikaze attacks, will be equally plentiful. On the first day the US battleship *West Virginia* and the British carrier *Indomitable* are hit along with eight other ships.

Western Front The US First and Ninth Armies link up at Lippstadt, cutting off the German forces in the Ruhr which consist of 325,000 men mostly from Fifteenth and Fifth Panzer Armies under Model's command. Other First and Ninth Army units take Hamm and Paderborn. To the north British units have crossed the Mitteland Canal near Münster and are advancing toward Osnabruck.

Eastern Front Tolbukhin's forces capture Sopron in western Hungary south of Vienna. The advance here and by Malinovsky's forces to the north continues. On the Oder the resistance of the German pocket at Glogau is overcome by Konev's forces.

Philippines General MacNider's 158th Regiment lands at Legaspi in the southeast of Luzon and takes the town and airfield nearby. There is no Japanese resistance at first. Elsewhere on Luzon the US forces are beginning to make ground toward the southeast of Manila after much hard fighting against General Yokoyama's Shimbu Group. Yamashita's forces in the north of the island have also been fighting hard against both regular American units and guerrillas.

Italy British Guards and Commando units attack over the River Reno between Lake Comachio and the sea.

2 APRIL 1945

Western Front The British Second Army continues its advance north of the Ruhr. Münster is taken. The Canadian First Army also begins to move north and east from between Nijmegen and Emmerich.

Eastern Front In southeast Hungary Nagykanizsa falls to the Soviet advance while in Slovakia Kremnica is taken.

Okinawa The US forces on the island advance easily across to the east coast and make some progress to the north and south.

Philippines Part of the US 163rd Regiment is landed on Tawitawi in the Sulu Archipelago.

2–5 APRIL 1945

Okinawa, Air and Naval Operations On the 2nd as well as the normal bombardment and air support missions performed by the US forces there are attacks by the British carriers on Sakashima Gunto Island. In Kamikaze attacks four US transports are badly damaged with many casualties among the troops aboard. On 3 April one escort carrier and other ships are hit and on 5 April the battleship *Nevada* is damaged by fire from a shore battery. Bad weather which sets in from the 4th damages many landing craft.

3 APRIL 1945

Eastern Front In Austria the Soviet forces take Wiener Neustadt. Almost all of Hungary is now clear of Axis troops while in Czechoslovakia Bratislava is besieged.

Philippines Part of the US 40th Division lands on Masbate to help the Filipino guerrillas who have controlled part of it for several days.

4 APRIL 1945

Western Front British and Canadian units take Osnabruck and move on Minden. US Ninth Army units have reached the River Weser opposite Hameln. Troops from Third Army capture Kassel while other units of Patton's force are advancing near Erfurt after taking Gotha. French units take Karlsruhe.

Okinawa The US forces begin to meet the first real Japanese resistance on the ground. Hodge's troops are brought to a halt on a line just south of Kuba while Geiger's have reached the Ishikawa Isthmus.

Eastern Front Bratislava falls to Malinovsky's forces.

5 APRIL 1945

Philippines South and west of Manila the US forces on either side of Laguna de Bay are beginning to make significant gains in their attacks.

Italy On the west coast US units from Fifth Army begin to attack north near Massa, south of La Spezia.

Western Front Allied forces cross the Weser at several points.

Japan, Politics General Koiso and his cabinet resign. Admiral Suzuki forms the new government. Togo is Foreign Minister and Hiranuma President of the Privy Council. There is less military influence in this Cabinet than in Koiso's and all its members are agreed that no reasonable offer of peace should be turned down. Some even go so far as to think that any offer should be accepted if this is the only way that invasion can be avoided.

Diplomatic Affairs Molotov tells the Japanese ambassador in Moscow that the USSR does not propose to renew the 1941 Nonaggression Pact.

United States Command It is announced that General MacArthur will take control of all army forces in the Pacific and Admiral Nimitz all naval forces in preparation for the invasion of Japan.

6 APRIL 1945

Eastern Front The Soviet forces begin to besiege Vienna. In East Prussia Third Belorussian Front begins its final attacks on Königsberg after several days of preparatory bombardment and air attacks. Yugoslavian forces expel the Germans from Sarajevo.

Okinawa Geiger's Corps continues to advance to the north, but the other US units can make no progress against the first defenses of the Shuri Line.

6–9 APRIL 1945

Okinawa Air and Naval Operations/Battle of the South China Sea On 6 April the giant battleship *Yamato* leaves the Inland Sea accompanied by a cruiser and eight destroyers on a Kamikaze mission to Okinawa. *Yamato* only has enough fuel to reach Okinawa but not to return and the Japanese intention is to beach the giant ship off Okinawa and to fight from that position any US forces nearby. The *Yamato* is sighted several times and reported by US submarines. Also on the 6th there are many suicide plane attacks on shipping around Okinawa. The carriers *San Jacinto* and *Illustrious* are both hit along with 25 other ships. Ten small warships are put out of action. The British carriers are well served by their armored decks in this and all the actions off Okinawa.

On 7 April the *Yamato* is found by planes from the US carrier groups and in two waves of attacks involving 380 planes the battleship takes 10 torpedo and five heavy bomb hits before going down. Kamikaze attacks on the American shipping damages the carrier *Hancock* and the battleship *Maryland* as well as other units. On the 8th and 9th there are less concentrated attacks in which three destroyers and two other ships are badly hit.

7 APRIL 1945

Western Front Large parts of US First and Ninth Armies are heavily engaged around the Ruhr pocket while among the gains in the advance to the east is Göttingen.

8 APRIL 1945

Burma The British forces have regrouped following their success at Mandalay and Meiktila and are now ready for a rapid armored and motorized advance to finish the campaign in Burma. The British IV Corps is to advance down the Sittang Valley and XXXIII Corps by the Irrawaddy Valley. All units have been specially organized to make them more mobile.

Eastern Front In Austria the Soviet forces push on west of Vienna despite German counterattacks. There is very fierce street fighting in the Austrian capital. In East Prussia the Soviet attacks on Königsberg begin to break through the defenses.

Western Front In the southern sector of the front French troops take Pforzheim as they continue their drive to the southeast. To the north US Seventh Army units capture Schweinfurt. Other Allied armies farther north also advance.

Okinawa The III Corps advance has now cut

the neck of the Motobu Peninsula and 6th Marine Division begins operations to clear it of Japanese forces.

Philippines The US forces are reinforced by the landing of a second regiment in the northwest of Negros near Bacolod.

9 APRIL 1945

Italy The Allied spring offensive gets under way with attacks by General McCreery's Eighth Army. Fifth Army is also to attack but in order to make best use of the available air support in the assault phases of both attacks Fifth Army will not begin full-scale operations until the 14th. The main units of Eighth Army will be directed toward Ferrara but the left flank will reach to Bologna. Fifth Army is to advance with its right toward Bologna while other units penetrate past Modena to the Po.

Eighth Army's offensive begins with attacks by II Polish Corps along Route 9 toward Imola and by British V and X Corps to the right and left of the Poles.

Eastern Front The surviving defenders of the Königsberg fortress surrender to the Red Army. Some of the German troops in East Prussia fight on in the Samland Peninsula.

Western Front In the attacks against the Ruhr pocket Ninth Army units penetrate into Essen and reach the famous Krupp factories. Other British and US units, including some more from Ninth Army, are advancing near the River Leine to the east.

Okinawa There are unsuccessful XXIV Corps attacks in the Kakazu sector of the Shuri Line.

Philippines The 163rd Regiment of 41st Division lands on Jolo. There is no Japanese resistance. Other 41st Division units land on Busuanga in the Calamian group.

Europe, Air Operations In a RAF attack on Keil the German navy ships *Scheer*, *Hipper* and *Emden* are damaged beyond repair.

10 APRIL 1945

Western Front Hanover falls to the US XIII Corps from Ninth Army. Canadian forces are beginning to put pressure on the German positions in Holland. They begin operations to cross the River Ijssel. British Second Army is advancing toward Bremen, US Third Army toward Erfurt and Seventh Army to Nuremberg.

Italy Eighth Army's attacks make some good progress largely because the Germans have expected the main effort to come farther to the west. In the as yet limited efforts of Fifth Army on the west coast Massa is taken.

Philippines On Luzon the advance of XIV Corps reaches Lamon Bay and the coastal town of Mauban is captured.

Burma Thazi, east of Meiktila, is captured by the British IV Corps.

11 APRIL 1945

Eastern Front In Vienna Tolbukhin's attacks continue and have reached the Danube Canal near the city center.

Western Front Advance tank units of Ninth Army reach the Elbe south of Magdeburg.

Above: Supplies are unloaded at Okinawa while many more ships wait offshore.

Forces of Third Army take Weimar. The British cross the Leine near Celle.

Italy Carrara is taken by the US 92nd Infantry Division which has advanced on from Massa. Eighth Army's attacks have now pushed the leading units over the Senio to the Santerno and bridging operations there have begun.

Indian Ocean Sabang is shelled by the battleships *Queen Elizabeth* and *Richelieu* of Admiral Walker's British Eastern Fleet. Two escort carriers give air cover and attack installations and shipping at Port Blair and Emmahaven.

Philippines Units of the Americal Division land on Bohol.

11–14 APRIL 1945

Okinawa, Air and Naval Operations All four groups of TF 58 participate in operations against Okinawa and Japanese air bases. From 11 to 13 April the British carriers attack Sakashima Gunto. Japanese attacks score hits on the battleship *Missouri* and the carrier *Enterprise* on the 11th, on several of the radar picket ships on the 12th as well as two battleships and eight other vessels of the main forces, on the 13th only one destroyer is hit and on the 14th the battleship *New York* is damaged. The radar picket system provides for destroyer patrols to be stationed some way from the main forces to give warning of air attacks so that fighters can make interceptions before the attacking aircraft can close. Their advanced position makes the picket destroyers especially vulnerable to the Japanese attacks.

12 APRIL 1945

United States, Politics President Roosevelt dies of a cerebral haemorrhage at Warm Springs in Georgia. Vice-President Truman becomes President. Truman has so far had little involvement in the work of Roosevelt's administration (he was a surprising choice as running mate in 1944) and among the subjects on which he receives his first briefing in the next few days is the atomic-weapons project.

Roosevelt has been a president of whom strong opinions have been held. Most of the American people have valued his undoubted qualities of leadership both in bringing the United States out of the troubles of the Depression and in leading his country into war against the Axis dictatorships. A considerable number of Americans have held equally forceful opinions opposed to Roosevelt's ideas and methods. In the other Allied countries, especially in Britain, Roosevelt has been almost universally liked and respected.

Western Front US Ninth Army forces cross the Elbe near Magdeburg while in the rear of their advance Brunswick falls. Patton's troops take Erfurt. In the south French units take Baden Baden. The Ruhr pocket has been reduced by the capture of Essen by US attacks.

Italy Eighth Army has three separate bridgeheads over the Santerno. On the right of the attack V Corps is advancing along the north bank of the Reno.

Okinawa Fighting continues on the Motobu Peninsula and in the Kakazu sector of the Shuri Line but the US forces make little ground in these areas.

Burma The IV Corps advance is beginning to make progress in the Sittang Valley. There is fighting at Pyaubwe and Yamethin. To the west of Meiktila 7th Indian Division from XXXIII Corps takes Kyaukpadaung.

13 APRIL 1945

Western Front The full horror of the Germans crimes begins to become clear to the west, with the liberation of Belsen and Buchenwald by British and American forces respectively. Jena is taken by Third Army units. Patch's forces take Bamberg.

Eastern Front Vienna falls to Tolbukhin's Third Ukraine Front after a fierce street battle.

Okinawa The units of 6th Marine Division not engaged on the Motobu Peninsula continue their advance up the west coast and reach the northwest tip of the island at Hedo Point.

Philippines In Manila Bay US forces land on Fort Drum, 'the Concrete Battleship,' and begin to pour 5000 gallons of oil fuel into the fortifications. This is then set on fire and burns for five days eliminating the Japanese garrison. On 16 April a landing on Fort Frank finds it abandoned. This completes the capture of the islands in Manila Bay.

14 APRIL 1945

Italy Fifth Army joins Eighth Army in major offensive operations. The Fifth Army attacks are sent in on either side of the roads to Bologna from Florence and Pistoia. In this latter sector Vergato is taken.

Philippines The US XIV Corps continues its advance onto the Bicol Peninsula in the southwest of Luzon. Calauag is taken. In north Luzon I Corps is still attacking near Baguio, but can only make very slight progress.

14–20 APRIL 1945

France There are attacks by French land, sea and air units on remaining German positions in the southwest at Royan. The battleship *Lorraine* provides bombardment support. The Germans surrender on 20 April.

15 APRIL 1945
Burma In XXXIII Corps' advance Taungdwingyi falls to 20th Indian Division. Other units of XXXIII Corps are still fighting farther up the Irrawaddy than the next objectives for 20th Indian which now moves toward Magwe and Thayetmyo.

Western Front In Holland Canadian troops take Arnhem and attack toward Gronigen. The US First Army takes Leuna, but the units of Ninth Army which have crossed the Elbe near Magdeburg are forced to retreat.

Eastern Front The Soviets begin a final series of attacks against the German positions in Samland.

Okinawa The 6th Marine Division fights hard to capture Yae Take Hill but is driven back by the defense.

Italy Both Fifth and Eighth Armies continue their attacks. In the Eighth Army sector the Polish II Corps has now reached the Sillaro after crossing the Santerno.

15–26 APRIL 1945
Okinawa, Air and Sea Operations The escort carrier groups are active throughout the period while the fleet carriers rotate their duties with one group attacking targets on Okinawa, two attacking airfields on Kyushu and the fourth away replenishing. The British carriers mostly keep Sakishima Gunto neutralized. The Third major phase of the Japanese Kamikaze attacks occurs on the 16th and 17th. The carrier *Intrepid* and battleship *Missouri* are among the ships hit.

On the 18th and 19th there are especially intense attacks on targets on Okinawa itself from two fleet carrier groups and two escort-carrier groups. The positions of the Japanese 62nd and 63rd Divisions on the Shuri Line are hard hit in support of the ground offensive which begins on the 19th.

On 20th April the British carriers return to Leyte for a brief refit.

16 APRIL 1945
Eastern Front After receiving Eisenhower's 28 March message Stalin has become convinced that the British and Americans will not head for southern Germany but go for Berlin. He has, therefore, ordered preparations for the last great offensive to take the German capital to be hurried forward. Zhukov's First Belorussian Front and Konev's First Ukraine Front are to lead the attack with support from Rokossovsky in the north. Perhaps in an effort to divide the glory and retain credit for himself and not the army or any one of its leaders, Stalin has not made it clear whether Zhukov or Konev has to make the final assault on the city. Between them the two Soviet Marshals have well over 2,000,000 men, more than 6000 tanks and self-propelled guns, a similar number of aircraft and almost 16,000 guns – one gun for every 13 feet of the front on which the assault will take place. Although the Germans have about 1,000,000 men deployed in fairly strong and well-prepared positions overlooking the west bank of the Oder and Neisse, they are totally outmatched in the air and on the ground they have nothing to compare with the lavish scale of Soviet equipment. The German troops are organized in General Heinrici's Army Group Vistula and Field Marshal Schoerner's Army Group Center. After the massive artillery preparation Zhukov's attacks begin from the Soviet bridgehead already taken west of the Oder near Kustrin. Konev's attack begins a little later over the Neisse north and south of Triebel. By a well-timed short withdrawal the Germans have avoided the worst effects of the Soviet bombardment, but they have too little strength to do more than hold the Soviet attack temporarily.

Western Front US Seventh Army units reach the outskirts of Nuremberg. The special POW camp at Colditz is freed by other Allied units.

Okinawa The US 77th Infantry Division lands on the small island of Ie Shima. The island and its airfield are occupied by 21 April after a fierce battle in which 5000 Japanese are killed. The 77th Division is then ferried over to join the main fighting on Okinawa.

Burma In the Arakan, Taungup falls to the British forces.

17 APRIL 1945
Eastern Front The Soviet attacks east of Berlin continue. In the very fierce battles which have developed the Germans are fighting with skill and desperation but are slowly being forced to give ground.

In Austria and Czechoslovakia the Soviet attacks and German losses continue, Zisterdorf and Pölten are taken in Austria.

Italy All Eighth Army units are now making fine progress in the continuing Allied offensive. On the right Argenta falls to V Corps with help from an amphibious move across Lake Comachio. North and east of Argenta there are no more rivers before the Po and the British units are soon passing through this 'Argenta Gap.'

West of Argenta XIII Corps has now come into the line between V Corps and the Poles who are themselves moving northwest toward Bologna. Fifth Army attacks are also continuing, but with slightly slower progress because of the more difficult terrain south and west of Bologna.

Western Front German units in the Ruhr are beginning to surrender on a large scale. There is also fighting near Bremen and Nuremberg.

Philippines There are US landings in Moro Gulf at Cotabatu. The Assault units are from 24th Infantry Division from General Sibert's X Corps. Admiral Noble leads three cruisers and a destroyer force in support. The US forces which landed at Zamboanga early in March have already cleared a large part of the southwest of the island, but the majority of General Suzuki's Thirty-fifth Army remains in being. There is no opposition to the new landings at first.

18 APRIL 1945

Western Front The German forces in the Ruhr pocket surrender. Field Marshal Model commits suicide. Altogether 325,000 prisoners have been taken in this area by the Allied forces. Patton's troops cross the Czechoslovakian border after a whirlwind advance. The US Ninth Army takes Magdeburg.

Eastern Front Except in a small area in Konev's sector the Soviet forces have made less than 10 miles in their advance toward Berlin, but the German opposition is gradually being worn down.

19 APRIL 1945

Okinawa The XXIV Corps now has three divisions, 7th, 27th and 96th, in line and all three begin attacks after a heavy ground and air bombardment. The heaviest efforts are on either coastal flank.

Western Front The US First Army captures Leipzig. The British Second Army reaches the Elbe south of Namburg.

Burma In the Sittang Valley Pyinmana falls to the 5th Indian Division which now leads IV Corps' advance. Farther north between Meiktila and the Irrawaddy, XXXIII Corps completes the clearance of the Mount Popo area and takes Chauk also. Farther south along the Irrawaddy Magwe is taken by 20th Indian Division which has advanced southwest from Meiktila.

Philippines In the advance of US I Corps units on the northwest coast of Luzon Vigan is taken.

20 APRIL 1945

Eastern Front Rokossovsky's troops join Zhu-kov's and Konev's in the advance from the Oder. Rokossovsky's Second Belorussian Front attacks on a 30-mile front southwest of Stettin. To the south the German resistance on the Oder and Neisse has been smashed and the Soviet forces on both fronts are beginning to move forward more rapidly. Many of Konev's units are over the Spree while Zhukov's troops have taken Prötzel.

Western Front Nuremberg and Stuttgart are taken in the Allied advance. In the Stuttgart area the French First Army is advancing rapidly.

Okinawa III Corps completes the capture of the Motobu Peninsula and the whole of the main northern part of the island. The US attacks on the Shuri Line continue, but the few gains made cannot be held against the Japanese counter-attacks.

21 APRIL 1945

Eastern Front Some of Zhukov's leading tank units reach the eastern suburbs of Berlin.

Italy Bologna is captured by units of the Polish II Corps. Units of II US Corps also enter the town a few hours later. The main forces of Fifth Army have now fought their way down from the Appenines into the Lombard Plain and their advance to the Po, therefore, quickens. East of Bologna Eighth Army is also moving forward rapidly.

Burma The IV Corps advance in the Sittang Valley is beginning to pull ahead of the parallel efforts in the Irrawaddy Valley. Yedashe is taken by 5th Indian Division, while in the rear the airfields around Pyinmana are being cleared to be put into Allied service. In the Irrawaddy Valley Yenangyaung falls to XXXIII Corps units mopping up in the rear of the main advance.

Philippines The heavy fighting near Baguio is continuing, with the attacks of the US 37th Division making some gains near the River Irisan and the 33rd Division making ground to the west of the city.

Diplomatic Affairs A mutual assistance treaty is concluded between the Soviets and the Lublin Polish Government. This is a further indication that Stalin will not be scrupulous about his Yalta promises to arrange free elections and political processes in Eastern Europe.

22 APRIL 1945

Diplomatic Affairs Himmler meets Count Bernadotte of the Swedish Red Cross and gives him a message to pass to the Western Allies, offering a German surrender to the British and Americans but not to the Soviets. The message is passed to the Allies on the 24th.

Western Front Seventh Army units cross the Danube at Dillingen and Baldingen.

Philippines The US 31st Infantry Division is landed at Moro Gulf. The 24th Division is already advancing inland and has nearly reached Kabakan.

On Jolo the last Japanese resistance comes to an end as their final strongpoints fall to the US forces. Some scattered individuals remain at large but they can achieve nothing.

Italy Units of II and IV US Corps reach the River Penaro in their advance to the Po. On the left flank Modena is taken.

Burma In the Sittang Valley Toungoo falls to the 5th Indian Division.

23 APRIL 1945

Germany, Politics Goering sends a message to Hitler offering to take over the leadership of the Reich if Hitler is unable to continue with that task when he is besieged in Berlin. Hitler is furious at Goering's presumption and orders his arrest.

Eastern Front As both Zhukov's and Konev's troops continue to close in round Berlin in the rear of their advances Frankfurt (on Oder) and Cottbus are captured.

Italy Advance units of both Fifth and Eighth Armies reach the Po. Fifth Army units manage to cross the river south of Mantua.

Okinawa The attacks of XXIV Corps at last begin to make some ground. In the center of the front 96th Division does well.

Philippines Units of 37th Division reach the outskirts of Baguio.

24 APRIL 1945

Eastern Front Konev's troops penetrate into Berlin from the south joining with Zhukov's attacks from the east. Other units are moving round the city to the north and south to complete the encirclement. Large parts of the German Ninth Panzer and Fourth Armies have been cut off by Konev's advance.

Western Front Dessau on the Elbe is taken by First Army. The British forces begin attacks near Bremen. To the south on the Danube Ulm is taken and in the Black Forest area the French First Army continues its advance.

Italy Both Fifth and Eighth Army units begin to pour across the Po at several points near Ferrara and to the west. Ferrara itself is taken. On the west coast La Spezia falls to the US 92nd Division. Now that the Allied forces have burst free into open ground there is almost nothing that the Germans can do to slow their advance.

Okinawa The Japanese forces begin to pull back to the second section of the Shuri Line.

25 APRIL 1945

Eastern Front The encirclement of Berlin is completed near Ketzin. Zhukov's and Konev's units are still also driving into the city from south and east. South of the capital Konev's forces have also attacked east to the Elbe at Torgau where they link with American units.

In East Prussia Pillau is taken. There are still a few German troops holding out at the tip of the Samland Peninsula. Since early in the year 140,000 wounded and 40,000 refugees have been evacuated to the west from Pillau.

Italy Mantua, Parma and Verona are among the towns liberated by the Allies as the German resistance begins to collapse and large-scale surrenders begin. The extensive partisan operations are extended by risings in Milan and Genoa.

Western Front The US First Army meets up with the Soviet forces at Torgau on the Elbe. US Third Army crosses the Danube near Regensburg, which is attacked.

Burma In the Irrawaddy Valley mopping up operations continue. Salin is captured by the British forces. The main XXXIII Corps advance is closing in on Allanmyo. The spectacular progress of the 5th Indian Division in the Sittang Valley continues with the capture of Perwegen. The Japanese forces around Rangoon and in other parts of southern Burma are beginning to withdraw through Pegu to the east so as to be able to retreat into Thailand.

25 APRIL–26 JUNE 1945

World Affairs A conference is held at San Francisco to draw up the constitution of a United Nations Organization. It is decided that the UN should have a General Assembly of all nations and as a recognition of the difficulty and importance of unanimity among the major nations of a Security Council in which the great powers would have permanent seats and the power of veto. The permanent members of the Security Council are to be the United States, the Soviet Union, Britain, France and China. The Soviets have been among the stronger advocates of the major powers having a veto because they expect that they will be consistently outvoted by the memberships of the organization as it will stand at first. As well as the main bodies for international debate and peace keeping, there are proposals for the creation of an International Court of Justice and specialized social and economic agencies.

The text of the Charter of the United Nations is completed on 23 June, formally approved on

Above: Soviet T-34 tanks during a pause in the fighting in Berlin.

the 25th and signed on the 26th.

26 APRIL 1945
Eastern Front As well as the continuing advances in the Berlin fighting, Soviet units take Stettin in the Baltic and Brno in Czechoslovakia.
Western Front The British complete the capture of Bremen. Third Army units take Regensburg while other parts of Patton's force enter Austria. French First Army reaches Lake Constance.
Italy Fifth Army units are now heading north from Verona toward the Brenner Pass and west toward Milan. Eighth Army has crossed the Adige and is moving northeast toward Venice and Trieste.
Philippines There is a further US landing on Negros, this time by units of the Americal Division in the southwest of the island. The troops advance well inland before meeting the first Japanese resistance.
France, Politics Marshal Pétain is arrested when he crosses into France from Switzerland. He will be tried and condemned to death for treason and collaboration. De Gaulle will commute the sentence to life imprisonment.

27 APRIL 1945
Diplomatic Affairs The Allies reply to Himmler's peace proposals with a total refusal and a reminder of the already established demands for unconditional surrender.
Eastern Front In Berlin the Soviet forces have taken the Templehof airfield and are making progress in the Spandau, Grunewald and other areas. To the north of the capital Rokossovsky's troops begin to advance more freely, taking Prenzlau and Angermünde.
Italy Genoa, already largely controlled by partisans, is completely liberated by US forces.
Philippines Baguio is taken by the US forces. Fighting in other areas of the island continues, especially in the Bicol Peninsula.

27–30 APRIL 1945
Borneo Admiral Berkey leads a squadron of three cruisers and six destroyers in a preparatory bombardment of targets in the Tarakan area in the northeast of the island. On the 30th there is a small landing by a US force on the offshore island of Sadan.

27 APRIL–2 MAY 1945
Okinawa, Sea and Air Operations From the 27th to the 30th there is a fourth phase of Kamikaze attacks. About 125 planes make attacks, hitting nine destroyers and other smaller ships. Not all of the US carrier force is present to support the operations on the island until 8 May when the absentees return from a brief visit to Ulithi.

28 APRIL 1945
Italy Mussolini and his mistress Clara Petacci and other Fascist leaders have been caught by

partisans near Lake Como as they attempt to escape to Switzerland. They are now shot and their bodies are mutilated and hung up by the heels in the main square at Milan.

Brescia, Bergamo and Allessandria are taken by Fifth Army units.

Eastern Front The siege of Berlin proceeds with the Soviets now having penetrated to within a mile of Hitler's Bunker in the east and south. Most of the Potsdamer Strasse has been cleared by Konev's troops.

Western Front The US Seventh Army takes Augsburg in its advance south toward Austria. Other Allied units are crossing the Elbe in the north and others are advancing on Munich in the south.

Okinawa The fighting along the Shuri Line continues with the US forces employing tanks, flame throwers and artillery of all calibers in an attempt to destroy the Japanese defensive positions.

29 APRIL 1945

World Affairs Hitler marries Eva Braun and prepares his Political Testament, appointing Admiral Doenitz as his successor and describing how Germany has failed him in the struggle against Bolshevism.

Italy The surrender of the German forces in Italy is signed at Caserta in the south. The German representatives are present here because of a secret negotiation between the head of the OSS mission in Switzerland, Allan Dulles, and the SS General Wolff. These talks have been going on since much earlier in the year, but because of their clandestine nature the German representatives at Caserta cannot guarantee that the surrender will be ratified by Vietinghoff.

In the north the Allied armies continue to advance quickly. Venice is liberated by Eighth Army.

Eastern Front In Berlin the Soviets make gains in the Moabit district and in the Wilmersdorf area. North of the capital Red Army units continue their advance capturing Anklam and other towns. In the southern sectors of the front Soviet pressure in Austria and Czechoslovakia continues.

Western Front The concentration camp at Dachau is liberated along with 30,000 surviving inmates by troops from US Third Army. The advance then goes on toward Munich. South of the Danube US Third Army units reach the River Isar.

Burma In the Irrawaddy Valley Allanmyo falls to the advances of XXXIII Corps. The remaining Japanese forces in this area are becoming very disorganized by the British attacks. In the Sittang Valley the 17th Indian Division has now taken over the lead, and after capturing Nyaunglebim is attacking near Payagyi.

Philippines General Brush's 185th Regiment lands near Padan Point with support from a destroyer force led by Admiral Struble. There is little Japanese resistance.

29 APRIL–2 MAY 1945

Arctic The last convoy battle of World War II is fought around the convoy RA-66. This has 24 ships with an escort of two escort carriers, one cruiser, nine destroyers and 13 other ships – a very lavish force when compared with any Arctic convoy in 1942, for example. There are 14 U-Boats involved in attacks. Not one merchant ship is sunk but one escort is hit and two U-Boats sunk.

30 APRIL 1945

World Affairs Hitler and Eva Braun commit suicide in their rooms in Hitler's Bunker at 1530 hours. Their bodies are carried outside and cremated with gasoline.

Eastern Front The Soviet advance in Berlin reaches the Reichstag from the north. Other government buildings are also captured. In other sectors of the front Rokossovsky's troops advance toward Stralsund, Waren and Wittenberge. In Czechoslovakia Mor Ostrava is taken after a long fight. The Germans now hold only a part of Moravia and most of Bohemia. Slovakia has been completely overrun.

Western Front The advance in all sectors continues. The French forces enter Austria near Lake Constance and British units in the north push on toward the Baltic.

Okinawa Japanese counterattacks and infiltration attempts in the Shuri Line area are beaten off. There is particularly fierce fighting in the Maeda and Kochi Ridge positions. The 1st Marine and 77th Divisions take over at the front from the 27th and 96th Divisions.

MAY 1945

Far East, Air Operations The Superfortresses drop 24,000 tons of bombs on targets in Japan. Nagoya is the target for two very heavy raids on the 14th and 16th, both times by over 470 bombers. Tokyo is hit by 502 planes on the 25th. Otaka, Oshima and Tokuyama are also heavily attacked. The Pacific Fleet carriers also attack many targets in Japan.

In the SEAC area the operations are mostly restricted by the onset of the monsoon but there is some tactical support provided around Rangoon and against Japanese concentrations near Muolmein. In China Fourteenth Air Force strikes against tactical targets in many areas.

Europe, Air Operations The last operation by RAF Bomber Command is an attack by a Mosquito force on Kiel on the night of the 2/3 May. Many Allied aircraft are involved in food drops in Holland and in the evacuation of prisoners or war back to Britain.

1 MAY 1945

World Affairs Hamburg radio announces that Hitler is dead and that Doenitz is the second Feuhrer of the Reich. Doenitz himself broadcasts, announcing rather pathetically that 'it is my duty to save the German people from destruction by the Bolshevists.'

In Berlin Goebbels and his wife commit suicide after poisoning their six children. Martin Bormann disappears.

Eastern Front General Krebs visits Zhukov to try to negotiate surrender terms for Berlin, but is told that only unconditional surrender is acceptable. In the city the Soviet advance continues and only a tiny area remains in German hands.

Western Front The US First and Ninth Armies are firmly established along the line of the Elbe and Mulde. They have been forbidden to advance farther, into the zone designated for Soviet occupation. To the north the British continue their moves toward Lübeck and Hamburg while in the south the US Seventh Army presses on into Austria.

Italy General Vietinghoff agrees to the surrender terms signed at Caserta. Tito's Partisans take Trieste. Possession of this city will become a point of dispute between Italy and Yugoslavia after the war. Italy will retain the city but Yugoslavia will take much of the disputed land nearby.

Burma The British attacks in the Sittang Valley have now reached nearly to Pegu. The monsoon begins in southern Burma. As an alternative in case the land attacks have not made sufficient progress before this break in the weather, an amphibious operation to take Rangoon has been prepared and now goes into action, with parachute landings at the mouth of the Irrawaddy on the east bank.

Borneo There are Allied landings at Tarakan. General Whitehead leads 18,000 men of the reinforced 26th Australian Brigade in the landings. There is little Japanese opposition.

2 MAY 1945

Eastern Front The Soviet forces complete the capture of Berlin with the attacks from north and south linking up along the Charlottenburg Chaussee. North of Berlin Soviet units have taken Rostock and many other towns. The only large German forces which remain in contact with the Soviet armies are those isolated in Latvia and those in Austria and Czechoslovakia. These last are now under pressure from all sides, by forces from the Eastern and Western Fronts and from Italy.

Western Front The British Second Army takes Lübeck and Wismar on the Baltic coast. Canadian units take Oldenburg. US units continue their advances in Austria and Bavaria.

Italy At noon the German surrender becomes effective. The long, difficult and controversial campaign in Italy is over. Allied forces reach Trieste, Milan and Turin during the course of the day, while others are advancing north toward the Brenner Pass where they will link up with US Seventh Army forces from the north.

Burma The British carry out Operation Dracula, the amphibious attack on Rangoon. Admiral Martin leads the four escort carriers and other naval units involved and 26th Indian Division provides the landing force. There is no Japanese resistance. Admiral Walker leads TF 63 with the battleships *Queen Elizabeth* and *Richelieu* and two escort carriers as well as cruisers and destroyers in covering operations in which Port Blair and Car Nicobar are bombed and shelled.

The attacks of IV Corps against Pegu to the north of the landings finally complete the capture of the town.

Philippines The XIV Corps units advancing west along the Bicol Peninsula of Luzon link near Naga with units from the Legaspi area who have moved east. Only mopping up operations remain to be done in this part of the island.

3 MAY 1945

Eastern Front Soviet forces have now reached the Elbe west of Berlin and made contact with the US First and Ninth Armies and in the north with the British Second Army.

Western Front The British XII Corps occupies Hamburg. This virtually completes the British offensive operations. In Austria Innsbruck falls to the US Seventh Army while other units advance near Salzburg.

Burma Rangoon is taken by 26th Indian Division without any resistance from the Japanese. Farther north on the Irrawaddy, Prome is taken by XXXIII Corps.

Philippines Admiral Noble lands 1000 men near Santa Cruz in the Gulf of Davao. Davao City is taken by 24th Division units.

CHRONOLOGY

3–4 MAY 1945
Okinawa During the night the Japanese forces begin a large-scale counteroffensive from the south, but although the attacks are very fierce they do not break the American front. Much of the Japanese artillery, until now concealed from the overwhelming firepower of the American forces, gives its positions away by operating in support of the attacks.

3–29 MAY 1945
Okinawa, Air and Sea Operations TF 58 is now organized in three groups of 13 carriers altogether and two groups are present at all times in this period. The British TF 57 makes attacks on Sakashime Gunto on 11 days. Escort carrier groups continue this work when the British carriers are replenishing. Among the damage done in the Japanese attacks are hits on the *Bunker Hill, Enterprise, Victorious* and *Formidable*. The escort carrier *Sangamon Bay* has to be written off after Kamikaze damage incurred on the 3rd.

There are four main spells of Japanese attacks, 3–4 May, 10–13 May, 24–25 May and 27–28 May. Altogether the Japanese send 560 Kamikaze planes in these periods. As well as the carrier casualties the battleship *New Mexico* is hit on the 10th, several destroyers are sunk and many more small warships or transports badly damaged. On 24 May two groups of TF 58 attack the airfields used by the Kamikaze forces on Kyushu. On 28 May Admiral Halsey takes command of the US naval forces involved in the Operations and they return to being known as Third Fleet and TF 58 becomes TF 38.

4 MAY 1945
Western Front Doenitz sends envoys to Montgomery's headquarters at Luneburg Heath and they agree on the surrender of German forces in Holland, Denmark and north Germany. The surrender becomes effective at 0800 on 5 May.

In the fighting which continues on the 4th Salzburg is taken by US forces. Other units push into Czechoslovakia toward Pilsen.

5 MAY 1945
European War Zone In Prague resistance forces rise against the Germans and a very fierce battle begins with SS units in the city. The Soviets are closing in on Prague from the north and east but are not yet in striking distance. Other Soviet units take Swinemünde and Peenemünde on the Baltic coast. The German Army Group G surrenders to the US forces with the surrender being concluded at Haar in Bavaria. In Denmark

fighting breaks out in Copenhagen but is brought to an end when British units arrive by air in the evening.

United States, Home Front The War Department announces that about 400,000 men will remain in Germany to form the US occupation force, that 2,000,000 men will be discharged from the armed services and that this will leave 6,000,000 serving in the war against Japan.

Okinawa The Japanese counterattacks continue with some minor successes.

United States A woman and five children are killed by a bomb falling from a Japanese balloon near Lakeview, Oregon. The Japanese have been releasing these balloons for some time, hoping that they will drift in the wind over the United States before releasing their explosive cargo. This is the only success they will achieve.

5–6 MAY 1945
Indian Ocean There are attacks by aircraft from four British escort carriers on Japanese bases between Mergui and Victoria Point in southern Burma and on the 6th the battleships and cruisers of TF 63 shell Port Blair in the Andaman Islands.

6 MAY 1945
European War Zone Units of the US Third Army take Pilsen in Czechoslovakia but Patton is ordered, much to his disgust to halt his advance there and allow the Soviets to occupy the rest of the country as has been arranged. The fighting in Prague between the resistance and the German forces goes on.

Burma Troops from 26th Indian Division advancing north from Rangoon, link with units from IV Corps at Hlegu. Although many scattered Japanese forces remain in Burma west of the Sittang toward Thailand and in the southwest of the country, the campaign is virtually over. Mopping up operations will continue as far as the monsoon weather permits, but British attention will be directed more to preparations for the campaign in Malaya which is to be the next major move. This, of course, will never take place because of the Japanese surrender.

Okinawa The Japanese offensive peters out after taking very heavy losses of at least 5000 killed. Even while it has been going on US forces have made gains near Machinto airfield and Maeda Ridge. These gains are now confirmed.

7 MAY 1945
European War Zone Admiral Freideburg and General Jodl sign the unconditional German surrender at General Eisenhower's HQ. British,

French, Soviet and American representatives are all present. Operations are to end at 2301 on 8 May.

War at Sea Two merchant ships sunk by *U.2336* off the Firth of Forth are the last U-Boat victims of World War II.

8 MAY 1945

Europe The British and Americans celebrate VE (Victory in Europe) Day. Truman, Churchill and King George VI all make special broadcasts. In Prague the German forces surrender. The units of Army Group Kurland, long cut off in Latvia surrender also. Most of the German pockets which have been holding out in eastern Germany have also given in. Crown Prince Olaf and British and Norwegian troops land in Norway.

9 MAY 1945

Europe The German surrender is ratified in Berlin. For Germany Keitel, Freideburg and Stumpf sign, and for the Allies Spaatz, Tedder, Zhukov and de Lattre. The Soviets celebrate VE-Day.

The last German forces holding out in East Prussia and Pomerania capitulate. Among the prominent captives are Goering and Kesselring who surrender to the US Seventh Army.

10 MAY 1945

Philippines Part of the US 40th Division lands

in the north of the island at Macalajar Bay. The landing is successful, but everywhere else on the island there is heavy fighting between the US and Japanese forces already present.

Europe Quisling and some of his supporters are arrested by the resistance in Norway. Reichs Commissioner Terboven and the German Chief of Police in Norway both commit suicide. Quisling will be put on trial for treason by the Norwegians, and will be found guilty and executed.

11 MAY 1945

Europe Schoerner's Army Group Center, now confined to a pocket east of Prague, surrenders to the Soviets. Some German units in Yugoslavia keep fighting for a few more days but gradually they too give in. The war in Europe is over.

Okinawa After making some minor advances in the past four days the US Forces now go over to a more ambitious coordinated attack on the Shuri Line. The US forces are now deployed with the III Corps facing the right of the Line and the XXIV Corps to the left. In the attacks some of the III Corps units manage to make gains, but none of Hodge's force achieve any of their objectives.

13 MAY 1945

Philippines After more heavy fighting on Mindanao the Del Monte airfield is taken by

Above: Soviet troops distribute bread supplies to Berliners. All the Allies had similar tasks.

CHRONOLOGY

units of the US 40th Division.

15 MAY 1945
Okinawa The pattern of heavy fighting, slow US advances and costly and only partially successful Japanese counterattacks is maintained. There are particularly fierce battles on Sugar Loaf and Conical Hills.

15–16 MAY 1945
Indian Ocean After an attempt to reach the Nicobars on the 10th and 11th the Japanese cruiser *Haguro* and a destroyer try once more to get through with supplies for the Japanese garrisons on the islands. British battleship and escort-carrier forces try to make an interception, but it is achieved by a destroyer force, five strong, commanded by Captain Power. They make their attacks on the Japanese ships in the Malacca Straits area during the night 15/16 May, and in a classically delivered attack from all directions *Haguro* is sunk by the destroyers' torpedoes. This is the last surface action of the war involving major warships.

17 MAY 1945
Marshall Islands The carrier *Ticonderoga* attacks targets on the Japanese held islands of Taroa and Maleolap in what is virtually a training exercise in view of the weakness of the defense.

18 MAY 1945
Okinawa The US 6th Marine Division takes most of the Sugar Loaf Hill after several days of bitter fighting.

19 MAY 1945
Philippines In the I Corps sector Japanese resistance ends in the Ipoh Dam area of Luzon.

21 MAY 1945
Okinawa There are American successes near the Horseshoe, Half Moon and Wana positions in the III Corps sector, while on the east side 7th and 96th Divisions attack near Yonabaru. Faced with these US gains, the Japanese begin to pull out of the Shuri Line.

22 MAY 1945
Okinawa The US forces occupy Yonabaru.
United States, Politics President Truman reports to Congress on the Lend-Lease program. He announces that up to March 1945 Britain had received supplies worth $12,775,000,000 and the Soviets $8,409,000,000. Reverse Lend-Lease, mostly from Britain has been worth

almost $5,000,000,000 in the same period.

23 MAY 1945
Okinawa After advancing to take Naha very easily the 6th Marine Division tries to move on to the south but again meets very heavy resistance.
Britain, Politics The Labour Party has decided not to maintain the coalition government until after the end of the war and Churchill, therefore, resigns in order to prepare for the election. He forms a new caretaker government to hold office until the election.
War Criminals Himmler has been captured by the British forces, but he commits suicide before he can be searched or questioned properly.

27 MAY 1945
Okinawa The slow and meticulous US advance continues to be met by very fierce resistance.
Philippines Units of the US I Corps take Santa Fe on Luzon. There is still heavy fighting in several areas of Mindanao.

29 MAY 1945
Japanese Command Admiral Ozawa replaces Admiral Toyoda as commander of the Combined Fleet.

30 MAY 1945
Okinawa The US advance reaches Shuri south of the former Japanese positions.

JUNE 1945
Far East, Air Operations B-29 bombers fly 6500 missions over Japan and drop 42,000 tons of bombs. Osaka and Kobe are both attacked several times and other targets include Tokyo and Nagoya. Aircraft plants, naval bases and airfields are the favorite aiming points for precision attacks. In China Fourteenth Air Force attacks communications targets especially in the rail system. Planes based in the Philippines and on Okinawa join in these operations.

1–13 JUNE 1945
Okinawa, Air and Sea Operations The carrier groups of TF 38 now under Admiral McCain's command, continue to give support to the Okinawa operation. There are also attacks on 3/4 June on airfields on Kyushu and again on the 8th. On the 9th and 10th there are attacks on Okino-Daito-Shima and Minami-o-Shima. Both these targets are bombarded by battleship and cruiser forces.

The ninth wave of Kamikaze attacks on the US forces around Okinawa occurs between 3 and 7

June when one battleship, one cruiser and one escort carrier are all hit. The fast-carrier groups suffer heavily from the effects of a typhoon on the 5th. The cruiser *Pittsburgh* loses 110 feet from its bows and all the ships of TG 38.1 are damaged in some degree. After completing the program of attacks TF 38 returns to Leyte on 13 June after three months of nearly continuous operations in which the carriers and their supports have almost constantly kept the sea and been supplied and rearmed by the well-organized work of the fleet train.

4 JUNE 1945
Okinawa Two regiments of 6th Marine Division make landings on the Oruku Peninsula in an attempt to outflank some of the Japanese defense lines. Many of the Japanese troops formerly in the Shuri Line have in fact retired on to the Oruku Peninsula so it will be a hard fight.

5 JUNE 1945
Germany The Allied Control Commission meets for the first time in Berlin and announces that it is assuming the government of Germany.

6 JUNE 1945
Okinawa The 6th Marines have made good ground in the Oruku Peninsula following their landing. Other US units also push forward on the main front.

7 JUNE 1945
Philippines On Luzon forces from US I Corps take Bambang and move on northeast toward the Cagayan Valley. Other units are moving round the coast from the northwest to the north of the island.

8 JUNE 1945
Java Sea The Japanese cruiser *Ashigara* is sunk by the British submarine *Trenchant* after evacuating 1200 men from Batavia.

10 JUNE 1945
Okinawa Heavy fighting continues on the Oruku Peninsula and to the east and south, but it is becoming clear that the last stages of Japanese resistance on the island have been reached.
Borneo Almost 30,000 men of the 9th Australian Division land from a naval force commanded by Admiral Royal in Brunei Bay and on the islands of Labuan and Muara nearby. A preparatory bombardment has been fired by a force of cruisers and destroyers under the command of Admiral Berkey.

12 JUNE 1945
Okinawa Many of the Japanese troops on the Oruku Peninsula commit suicide believing that further resistance can achieve nothing.

13 JUNE 1945
Okinawa The Japanese resistance on the Oruku Peninsula ends. Almost 170 prisoners are taken – an enormous number when compared with previous totals of Japanese prisoners. The fighting continues to the southeast, especially in the Kunishi Ridge area.
Borneo US and Australian troops enter Borneo town.

14 JUNE 1945
Okinawa XXIV Corps units take Mount Yagu.

14–15 JUNE 1945
Caroline Islands Planes from the British fleet carrier *Implacable* and an escort-carrier attack the long isolated Japanese base at Truk on both days. There are also bombardments by some of the accompanying cruisers and destroyers of small islands nearby.

16 JUNE 1945
Okinawa Mount Yuza is taken by the US Forces.

17 JUNE 1945
Okinawa The American units begin to make gains in the Kunishi Ridge area which has been very stubbornly defended.

18 JUNE 1945
Okinawa General Buckner is killed by Japanese artillery fire while he is on a visit to the front line. General Stilwell is appointed to command Tenth Army in succession to Buckner.
Britain, Home Front William Joyce, Lord Haw Haw, is put on trial for treason in London. He will be convicted and executed for broadcasting propaganda from Germany.

18–20 JUNE 1945
Borneo In the north Australian troops take Tutong on the 18th and on the 19th there are Australian landings at Menpakul. On the 20th there are landings in Sarawak at Lutong.

19 JUNE 1945
Philippines In the Cagayan Valley Ilagan falls to the advance of I Corps.

20 JUNE 1945
Wake Island Admiral Jennings leads TG 12.4

with the carriers *Lexington*, *Hancock* and *Cowpens* in attacks on Wake. The carriers are en route to join TF 38 are using this opportunity to work up their skills with a real target. There are similar attacks directed against Wake on 18 July by the carrier *Wasp*, on 1 August by the *Cabot* and on 6 August by the *Intrepid*.

21 JUNE 1945
Okinawa The final Japanese HQ on Hill 69 is taken by the US forces. General Ushijima's body is found nearby.

22 JUNE 1945
Okinawa The fighting on Okinawa comes to an end. It has been a very bitterly fought campaign. The US forces have lost 12,500 dead and 35,500 wounded. The navy has had 36 ships sunk and 368 damaged. In the air the American forces have lost 763 planes. The Japanese losses are horrific. There are 120,000 military and 42,000 civilian dead and, if US reports are to be believed, they have lost 7830 planes and among other vessels the battleship *Yamato*. For the first time there is a significant number of Japanese prisoners – 10,755.

23 JUNE 1945
Philippines There is a US paratroop landing near Aparri on the north coast of Luzon at the mouth of the Cagayan River.

25 JUNE 1945
Philippines Tuguegarag is captured by the US forces in the Cagayan Valley. The surviving Japanese units on the island, about 50,000 strong. are now mostly concentrated in the Sierra Madre area to the east of the Cagayan Valley.
Borneo In Sarawak the Australian forces complete the occupation of the Miri oilfield area.

26 JUNE 1945
World Affairs The United Nations Charter is signed by representatives of 50 countries.

28 JUNE 1945
Philippines MacArthur announces that the operations on Luzon are over. It is now five months and 19 days since the invasion. Although there are still many Japanese on the island who will go on fighting until the end of the war, much of the mopping up will be left to Filipino units aided by US Eighth Army troops, who will take over responsibility for Luzon in addition to their present tasks in the other Philippine Islands in order to free Sixth Army to prepare for the invasion of Japan. Apart from on Luzon the only other significant bodies of Japanese resisting are on Mindanao.

29 JUNE 1945
United States, Planning The invasion plans for Japan are presented to President Truman and approved. They provide for landings in southern Kyushu on 1 November by forces already in the Pacific and on Honshu near Tokyo on 1 March 1946, when forces brought from Europe will participate. British and British Empire forces are to play a small part.

JULY 1945
Far East, Air Operations Among the targets for the US bomber forces are Akashi, Osaka, Kure and Kumamoto. A new tactic is tried starting on the 28th when 11 cities are told by leaflets that they are on the US target list and six of them are bombed on the 29th. Medium bombers join in the attack early in the month doing particular damage to shipping around the Japanese islands. There is much activity over China. In addition to the Fourteenth Air Force attacks there are two heavy attacks on Shanghai by planes based on Okinawa.

1 JULY 1945
Borneo After a preparatory bombardment beginning on 25 June by nine cruisers and 13 destroyers led by Admiral Barbey, 33,000 men of the reinforced 7th Australian Division land at Balikpapan. Three escort carriers give support to the landing for the first three days ashore. General Milford commands the troops.

3 JULY 1945
Borneo The troops landed at Balikpapan take Sepinggan airfield and by the 5th have cleared most of the oil producing area in the immediate vicinity.

5 JULY 1945
Philippines General MacArthur announces that the Philippines have been completely liberated.
United States, Command It is announced that General Spaatz will lead the US Strategic Air Force against Japan.
Britain, Politics The British election is held. The results are not available until 26 July because of the time taken to bring home and count the soldiers' votes.
Diplomatic Affairs Britain and the United States recognize a new Polish government of National Unity. Mikolajczyk, formerly leader of

the London exile government, is one of the deputy Premiers.

10–18 JULY 1945
Japan The American and British carrier forces send attacks on targets in the Japanese Home Islands. Admirals Halsey and McCain lead 15 carriers, eight battleships, 15 cruisers and 55 destroyers in the carrier groups alone and many more ships are on supporting missions.

On 10 July Tokyo is attacked by 1022 planes and after a break until the 14th attacks continue with targets on north Honshu and south Hokkaido being hit. Shipping is also a target and 50,000 tons is sunk in the Tsugaru Strait area. These attacks are repeated on the 15th. On the 14th three battleships lead a bombardment of steel works at Kamaishi and on the 15th another three head a bombardment of iron and steel works at Muroran. On 17 July the three carriers and one battleship of the British TF 37 join the American carriers in more attacks on the Tokyo-Yokohama area. The battleship *Nagato* is put out of action in these operations. During the night six battleships, two cruisers and 10 destroyers shell targets in the Hitachi area northeast of Tokyo, and on the night of the 18th there is a smaller bombardment of targets in the Cape Nojima area southeast of the Japanese capital. The Task Force then withdraws because a typhoon is forecasted.

11 JULY 1945
Germany There is the first meeting of the Inter-Allied Council for Berlin. The Soviets agree to turn over administration of the allocated areas to the British and Americans who have themselves made arrangements to allocate some of their sectors to the French.

12 JULY 1945
Borneo There is an Allied landing near Andus. Australian troops take Maradi in the north of the island.

14 JULY 1945
Europe General Eisenhower announces the closure of SHAEF (Supreme Headquarters Allied Expeditionary Force) and eases some of the restrictions on private contact between American soldiers and German civilians.

16 JULY 1945
Atomic Research The world's first atomic weapons test takes place at Alamagordo in New Mexico. The bomb used is based on the element plutonium and gives a yield of between 15 and 20 kilotons. It is mounted on top of a steel tower which is vaporized by the heat of the explosion which is greater than the temperature inside the sun. The explosion is visible and audible up to 180 miles away.

The type of bomb dropped on Hiroshima will not be identical to this but based on the isotope Uranium 235. The Nagasaki bomb will be a second Plutonium weapon.

17 JULY–2 AUGUST 1945
World Affairs Truman, Stalin and Churchill meet at Potsdam. There are further clarifying discussions of plans for dealing with defeated Germany and all the former occupied countries of Europe. Stalin confirms his undertaking to join the war with Japan but also tells the other Allies of peace moves that the Japanese have made via the as yet neutral USSR. There are no definite proposals contained in these approaches and it is therefore decided to do nothing direct to follow them up. On 26 July a broadcast is made to Japan with what has become known as the Potsdam Declaration. This repeats the demand for unconditional surrender, but states that the Allies do not want to reduce Japan to poverty in the postwar world. It says nothing of allowing or preventing the Emperor to remain at the head of the Japanese government.

On the 24th Truman and Churchill mention to Stalin that they have a new and powerful weapon for use against Japan but do not explain what it is. It is possible that Stalin already knows of the bomb through his espionage organization in the United States.

There is a recess in the conference between 25 and 28 July when the British delegation leave for their election results. Attlee is the new prime minister and Bevin the foreign secretary.

19 JULY 1945
United States, Politics Congress ratifies the Bretton Woods monetary agreement.

24 JULY 1945
Pacific War Truman takes the decision to use the bomb on Japan if they do not very soon come to terms. Whatever the later doubts about the morality of using the weapon, at the time there is very little doubt. It is simply a question of quickly persuading the Japanese to surrender in order to save the many lives on both sides that would be lost if the Allies invaded the Home Islands. No real thought is given to the possible forms of a demonstration use of the bomb to frighten the Japanese without having to destroy a city.

CHRONOLOGY

24–30 JULY 1945
Japan The British and American carriers continue their operations. There are now 15 US ships and four British. There are extensive air operations on the 24th, 27th and 30th. Many targets in the Inland Sea area are hit including Kure and Kobe. Several of the remaining large ships in the Japanese navy are hit and badly damaged. Three battleships and four carriers head the list. There are two bombardment operations. One, on the night of the 24th, is aimed at Kushimoto and Shionomisaki, and on the 29th the targets for five battleships and several cruisers and destroyers are aircraft factories at Hamamutsu in southern Honshu.

26 JULY 1945
Britain, Politics The election results begin to be announced. It is a massive victory for the Labour Party and a terrible defeat for Churchill's Conservatives. Attlee becomes prime minister. The reason for the Conservative defeat, despite Churchill's war record is that they have failed to convince the electorate that they would be active and original enough to prevent any return to the conditions of the 1930s when the Conservative governments did too little, it is felt, to mitigate the economic effects of the world depression and failed to stand up to Hitler. In the war years, too, it has mostly been the Labour politicians who have been responsible for the government departments charged with running the rationing system and organizing industry and it is felt that they have done this in a way that has benefitted the people in ways apart from helping the war effort.

28 JULY 1945
World Affairs The Japanese Premier Suzuki holds a press conference in which he says that the Japanese government will take no notice of the Potsdam Declaration. At least that is the interpretation that is put on his speech by the Allies, but it is possible that the word he used was intended to mean 'make no comment on for the moment' and that more might have been done to encourage a diplomatic response. It is upsetting to the Japanese that the declaration has not been delivered through the proper diplomatic channels via a neutral power and this contributes to their decision to take no immediate action on it.

29–30 JULY 1945
Pacific The US cruiser *Indianapolis*, returning to the United States after delivering the atom bomb to the Marianas air base, is torpedoed and sunk by the Japanese submarine *I.58*. It is not recognized that the *Indianapolis* is overdue for three days and many of the 316 survivors rescued are not found for several days after this.

31 JULY 1945
War Criminals Laval surrenders to the US forces in Austria. He is handed over to the French authorities and is later tried and executed.

AUGUST 1945
Far East, Air Operations The atomic attacks on Hiroshima and Nagasaki dominate the events of the month (*see* 6 and 9 August). There are also conventional strikes against many Japanese cities. Among the targets are Tokokawa, Yawata, Hikari, Nagoya and Toyama. The last strategic bombing raid is on the night of 14 August when Kumagaya and other targets northwest of Tokyo are bombed.

6 AUGUST 1945
Hiroshima The first atomic bomb is dropped on the city by a plane from the 509th Composite Group of the Twentieth Air Force piloted by Colonel Paul Tibbets. The plane is named by Tibbets after his mother, *Enola Gay*. The bomb is an uranium fission weapon and the yield is in the region of 20,000 tons of TNT.

Sixty percent of the city is destroyed in the blast or the firestorm that follows. There are about 80,000 dead, many of them being killed instantly. Many more will be horribly burned or will become ill in later years with the effects of the radiation. It is not the most devastating bombing attack of the war – the March fire raids on Tokyo have had a larger effect – but the economy of effort involved in sending only one plane on a mission to destroy a city shows only too well the complete change in military and political thinking which has been begun.

8 AUGUST 1945
World Affairs The Soviet Union declares war on Japan, citing as the reason Japan's failure to respond to the Potsdam Declaration.

Truman signs the UN Charter, making the US the first country to ratify its signature.

9 AUGUST 1945
Nagasaki The second atomic bomb is dropped on Nagasaki.

The attack is less devastating than at Hiroshima even although the bomb is of the technologically more advanced plutonium type. About 40,000 Japanese are killed.

Above: The atomic bomb explodes at Nagasaki.

Kamaishi. On the 13th there is a raid on Tokyo in which many Japanese aircraft are destroyed on the ground. On the 15th new attacks are under way when the order ending hostilities arrives and not all planes hear the recall. There is some air fighting also with Admiral Ugaki leading final Kamikaze attacks.

10 AUGUST 1945
World Affairs Japanese radio announces that a message has been sent accepting the terms of the Potsdam Declaration provided this 'does not compromise any demand that prejudices the prerogatives of the Emperor as sovereign ruler.'

On the 11th the Allies reply, saying that the Imperial authority would be subject to the decision of the Supreme Commander of Allied Powers in the occupation force. The Japanese are not yet ready to accept this demand which still seems very close to unconditional surrender.

14 AUGUST 1945
Japan At a government meeting Emperor Hirohito decides to end the wranglings of his politicians and orders that the war should end. He records a radio message to the Japanese people saying that they should 'Bear the unbearable.' During the night there is an attack by a group of officers on the Imperial Palace in an attempt to steal the recording and prevent it being broadcast. This is foiled by the palace guards. The Japanese decision is transmitted to the Allies and it is announced by them that Japan accepts unconditional surrender.

Since the event it has often been debated what the final cause was that made the Japanese decide to surrender. Examination of Japanese records and of the people concerned seems to show that it was from a combination of the threat of atomic attack, but also and perhaps predominantly from the defeat by the Soviets of the Kwantung Army.

15 AUGUST 1945
Pacific War This is VJ Day. Emperor Hirohito's broadcast is made to the Japanese people, many of whom cannot at first accept what has happened because the tight control of the government has prevented civilians knowing the full extent of the weakness of Japan's position.

Truman broadcasts threatening Japan with destruction by atomic bombs and the Japanese Supreme War Council agrees late that night that they should accept the Potsdam Declaration if the monarchy is to be allowed to be preserved. Some objections from the military are overruled by the Emperor himself.

Manchuria The Soviet forces begin a powerful offensive against the Japanese. The Soviets have assembled about 1,500,000 men in three fronts, First Far East Front, Second Far East Front and the Transbaikal Front. The 1,000,000 men of Yamada's Kwantung Army have no answer to the mechanized Soviet forces and are almost equally powerless in the air. The Japanese defense lines are almost immediately smashed.

9–15 AUGUST 1945
Japan The British and American carriers return to the attack after a replenishment period. The carrier *Wasp* and the battleship *Duke of York* have joined the force. Admiral Fraser is now present to command the British contingent. Airfields and shipping on Honshu and in the waters nearby are attacked with great effect on 9–10 August and there is a bombardment of

16 AUGUST 1945
Japan Prince Norukiko Higashi-Kuni forms a new government with himself as prime minister and war minister. The emperor issues a cease-fire order to all Japanese troops.

CHRONOLOGY

17 AUGUST 1945
Indonesia The Republic of Indonesia declares itself independent of Dutch colonial rule. No British forces will arrive to take over from the Japanese for six weeks.

In the postwar period there will be various spells of fighting between the Indonesian Nationalists and the Dutch before, in August 1950, the new republic is recognized worldwide.

18 AUGUST 1945
Manchuria Virtually the whole province has been overrun by the Soviet forces. They have taken Harbin and are closing in on Mukden and Changchun. In an advance from near Vladivostock they have entered northern Korea.

20 AUGUST 1945
United States, Home Front The War Production Board removes most of its controls over manufacturing activity. On the 14th all restrictions on the production of automobiles are removed. These and many other measures help the US economy to convert very quickly to a peace basis. It is stronger and more productive than before the war and with the impetus given by wartime inventions is ready to move into new fields also. The American standard of living, unlike that of any of the other major participants in the war, has increased.

21 AUGUST 1945
United States Policy President Truman orders the supply of Lend-Lease aid to stop immediately. Truman has been scantily briefed on this issue, and in its effects it contrasts very considerably with American generosity in settling Britain's Lend-Lease bill or in the establishment of the Marshall Plan.

22 AUGUST 1945
Manchuria The Japanese Kwantung Army surrenders. Soviet forces reach Port Arthur and Dairen.

27 AUGUST 1945
Japan The Allied fleets anchor in Tokyo Bay within sight of Mount Fujiyama.

2 SEPTEMBER 1945
World Affairs The Japanese surrender is signed aboard the battleship *Missouri* in Tokyo Bay. Foreign Minister Shigemitsu leads the Japanese delegation. MacArthur accepts the surrender on behalf of all the Allies. Admiral Nimitz signs for the United States and Admiral Fraser for Britain. There are representatives of all the other Allied nations. Also present are Generals Percival and Wainright who have been Japanese prisoners since they surrendered at Corregidor and Singapore.

Vietnam Ho Chi-Minh proclaims the existence of the Democratic Republic of Vietnam. As in the Dutch East Indies the colonial power will try to reimpose its control after the war and will eventually be forced to leave after much fighting. Even after the French have left, however, the history of Vietnam will continue to be troubled.

12 SEPTEMBER 1945
Malaya The surrender of Japanese forces in Southeast Asia is concluded before Admiral Mountbatten in Singapore. The Japanese garrisons in the various islands of the Pacific and in the East Indies will also surrender one by one in the next few days.

OCTOBER 1945
Germany General Patton is relieved of his post as military governor of Bavaria for not doing enough to remove former Nazi officials from the local government.

World Affairs On 24 October the United Nations Charter comes into force. There are 29 signatories at this stage.

NOVEMBER 1945
Europe There are elections in Austria, Hungary and Yugoslavia. In Yugoslavia Tito's National Front Party wins easily. In Austria all but five percent of the vote is roughly equally divided between the Catholic People's Party and the Socialists. The communists only win three seats out of 165. This effectively confirms Austria's place as a western nation, and although there will be no peace treaty or Soviet withdrawal until 1955 there is no real change in the situation. In Hungary the Small Landowners Party wins a majority of the votes with the Communists receiving about 20 percent. A coalition government is established.

War Crimes The trial of the major German war criminals begins at Nuremberg. Twenty-one are put on trial including Goering, Hess, Ribbentrop, Rosenberg, Speer, Jodl, Keitel, Raeder and Doenitz.

The trials are important particularly because the evidence produced gives a full and public account of the horrors of the Nazi treatment of the Jews and many other crimes. The evidence of Hoess, former commandant of Auschwitz, is particularly harrowing with its calm recital of perhaps 2,000,000 murders.

As an exercise in International Law the trials

have been much criticized because the offenses cited, preparing for aggressive war and crimes against humanity, had not been specifically recognized before. Equally there was some suggestion of 'victors' justice' in the way the evidence of Soviet aggression in the 1939 attack on Poland was carefully disregarded.

The trials will finish in October 1946.

DECEMBER 1945

War Crimes General Yamashita, former Japanese commander in the Philippines, is condemned to death by a US Military commission for maltreatment of prisoners by forces under his command especially during the famous Death March in 1942.

JANUARY 1946

World Affairs The first meetings of the General Assembly of the United Nations and of the Security Council are held in London. Immediately there are disagreements between the west and the Soviets. The Soviets are first to use the veto power.

MARCH 1946

India The British offer full independence to the Congress and Muslim League leaders. Talks to settle details begin and last until June, but no agreement is reached.

World Affairs In a public speech delivered in Fulton Missouri in the presence of President Truman, Churchill describes how an 'Iron Curtain has descended across Europe.' This is not yet a universally held view in the West.

Greece Elections are won by the conservative parties after a boycott by the communists. Civil war begins in May 1946 and lasts until October 1949 when the Western backed government comes out on top. The Communists receive aid from Tito and the government forces British and from May 1947 American help.

APRIL 1946

China Full-scale civil war begins between the communists and the Nationalists. Also this month the Soviets withdraw from Manchuria, leaving a vacuum which the Communists are quick to fill.

MAY 1946

Germany The British and Americans agree to end the taking of reparations payments from their zones of Germany and to unite their administrations and share costs. This is the first definite step toward the creation of a divided Germany. Western policy is beginning to move toward supporting German economic recovery as part of a European revival.

War Crimes The trial of major criminals begins in Tokyo. Tojo and four others will be sentenced to death at the end of trials in November 1947.

JUNE 1947

Italy In a referendum the Italian people confirm that they wish to live in a republic.

JANUARY 1947

Britain The coal industry is nationalized. This is only one of a series of socialist measures introduced by the Labour government which have a far reaching effect on British society. The welfare system is overhauled in line with the Beveridge Reports, the Bank of England, the gas and electricity industries are all nationalized. Perhaps the most ambitious scheme is the creation of a National Health Service providing for free treatment for all. This begins to operate in July 1948. All these changes arise out of wartime experience, which showed that the government could intervene in such affairs and run them in such a way that the worst miseries of the Depression could be avoided.

FEBRUARY 1947

Palestine Negotiations sponsored by the British between the Jewish and Arab leaders fail and under economic pressure Britain announces that the mandate will be returned to the United Nations. A United Nations Committee is appointed and reports in September that Palestine should be partitioned into a Jewish and an Arab state with Jerusalem staying international. Britain is to be in charge while this is created. The British are not altogether in favor of this plan and, therefore announce that the mandate will end on 15 May 1948. Both Arabs and Jews step up their military efforts before this time ignoring UN calls for a truce. The British continue with their plans for withdrawal despite the fighting.

Greece Also as a consequence of economic difficulties Britain tells the United States that she can no longer afford to stay in Greece supporting the government economically and militarily. The US agrees to take over Britain's role. This is the first sign of what will become known as the Truman Doctrine (*see* March 1947).

Eastern Europe The final peace treaties between the Allies and Finland, Rumania, Bulgaria, Hungary and Italy are concluded. This means that Britain and the United States are not even loosely involved through the Allied Control Commissions in these countries. The Soviet

CHRONOLOGY

presence in Eastern Europe remains.

MARCH 1947

United States Policy In a major speech to Congress on the 11th President Truman says,

'It must be the policy of the United States to support free peoples who are resisting attempted subjugation by armed minorities or outside pressures.'

This policy becomes known as the Truman Doctrine.

China In the Chinese civil war the Nationalists take the Communist capital at Yunnan. This success proves transitory and from this time on the Communists begin to gain the upper hand.

MAY 1947

Hungary There is a Communist-backed change of government in Hungary after Prime Minister Nagy is 'implicated' while on holiday in the disappearance of Kovács, another prominent member of the Small Landowners Party.

France and Italy In both countries governments are formed which exclude the Communist Parties.

JUNE 1947

Marshall Plan General Marshall, now Secretary of State, announces a plan to give economic aid to Europe and prepare a joint scheme for economic recovery. It is avowedly designed to encourage the formation of strong economies and free institutions. For the Soviets it holds a threat of German recovery as the dominant economic power in Eastern Europe and it is therefore unacceptable. The Soviets compel the other Eastern European nations to refuse Marshall aid.

Rumania The leader of the Peasant Party, Iuliu Maniu, is arrested, 'tried' and imprisoned at Soviet prompting.

AUGUST 1947

India and Pakistan Two new independent nations, India and Pakistan, are established on 15 August. The British government and the Viceroy in India, Lord Mountbatten, have decided that the timetable for granting independence should be speeded up from the original target of June 1948. This has avoided the period of tension being stretched out for so long, but inevitably in the haste not all arrangements have been made in the best way. Perhaps 250,000 die in the troubles between Muslim and Hindu which follow independence and about 12 million refugees cross the border to reach the appropriate state for people of their religion.

SEPTEMBER 1947

Eastern Europe As a response to the Marshall Plan, Stalin establishes the Cominform as an economic organization for Eastern Europe. The Eastern European and French and Italian Communist parties join the new organization.

OCTOBER 1947

Poland The Communist supremacy in Eastern Europe is confirmed when the former prime minister of the London exile government, Mikolajczyk, flees the country after striving unsuccessfully to protect the Peasant Party.

FEBRUARY 1948

Czechoslovakia The first postwar elections give the Communists 38 percent of the vote, the largest single share. The Soviets withdraw and a coalition government is established led by the Communist, Gottwald. Beneš becomes president and Jan Masaryk becomes foreign minister. Gottwald and Masaryk are in Moscow when Marshall aid is officially offered to Czechoslovakia, and they are told that they can chose between Soviet friendship and the Marshall aid. They refuse the American help. Nonetheless the West hopes that the Communists will do less well in the elections due in May and that they will be removed from the government as in France and Italy. On 21 March, however, a government crisis is precipitated by the resignation of some members over Communist monopolization of senior offices in the police. The social democrats, led by Beneš, do not respond decisively enough and a more predominantly Communist government is appointed. Masaryk remains a member of the government but early in March he is found dead after having 'fallen' out of a window in a government building.

Above: Czech leaders Beneš (seated) and Masaryk before they were deposed.

356

This sequence is particularly shocking to Western opinion because, even without violent tactics, the Communists fairly won the elections but were not content with this.

MARCH 1948
Marshall Plan Congress passes the Foreign Assistance Act on 31 March allocating $5,300,000,000 for aid to Europe.
Western Europe The Benelux countries and Britain and France conclude a mutual assistance agreement known as the Brussels Pact. Ostensibly it is aimed at preventing any future German aggression, but it is really an assertion of the principle of collective defense against the Soviets.

MAY 1948
Middle East As soon as the British mandate ends, the Jewish leader Ben Gurion proclaims the existence of the state of Israel. Israel is immediately recognized by both the United States and the Soviet Union. Fighting between Jews and Arabs continues intermittently until agreements with the Arab countries are concluded from February 1949 onward. The new state has been so successful in establishing itself that its frontiers are considerably wider than originally proposed by the United Nations.

JUNE 1948
Germany The Berlin blockade begins. After disagreements over currency reform beginning in March and the unilateral implementation of the rival schemes in the various zones, the Soviets close the border between Berlin and their zone because the western currency grows in strength and threatens their control of their zone. The blockade begins on 24 June. The western powers decide to airlift supplies into Berlin as a temporary expedient while they decide what action to take. The airlift proves so successful that it continues until the blockade ends in September 1949.
Yugoslavia The idea that all Communist Parties are dominated by the Soviets takes a serious knock when Yugoslavia is expelled from the Cominform because of Tito's independent policies over Trieste and Greece and manages to survive and after some difficulties to prosper without Soviet help or interference.

SEPTEMBER 1948
West Germany A Parliamentary Council meets in Bonn to draw up a constitution for West Germany as a new independent country. It is completed in April 1949 and the first elections in

August 1949 install Konrad Adenauer as Chancellor. In October 1949 East Germany is established under the leadership of Walter Ulbricht.

JANUARY 1949
China In the fighting Tientsin is taken by the Communists. After many defeats Chiang Kaishek resigns his post as President in the Nationalist government.

FEBRUARY 1949
Britain Clothes rationing comes to an end.

APRIL 1949
NATO The United States, Britain, Canada, France, the Benelux countries, Norway, Denmark, Italy and Portugal sign the North Atlantic Treaty agreeing on the principles of collective defense and that an attack on any party to the treaty should be regarded as an attack on all.

AUGUST 1949
Atomic Weapons The Soviet Union explodes its first atomic weapon. The American monopoly comes to an end.

OCTOBER 1949
China The Peoples Republic of China is proclaimed on 1 October. By December the Nationalists have completed their defeated withdrawal to Taiwan.

JUNE 1950
Korea Confirmation of the cold war hostility between the United States and the Soviet Union is made when the war in Korea begins. The United States reacts by mobilizing the United Nations to intervene and send forces to support the South Koreans. The Soviets happen to be boycotting the Security Council as a protest at the recognition of the Taiwan Government as the legal Chinese government and therefore miss their chance to use the veto. The United States regards Korea as a test case for the West's ability to resist Communist pressure throughout the world and believes it is valid to fight in Korea because the actions of the North Koreans are controlled from Moscow. Later appraisals do not confirm this view entirely since as Yugoslavia and China are to show the USSR cannot control national Communist Parties all the time. Korea is also taken as a sign of Communist intentions in Europe and this provokes rearmament programs throughout the west. Among the countries which will arm themselves is West Germany and thus one of the consequences of the Nazi defeat is removed.

Soviet JS-II tanks in Berlin in 1945.

LAND

LAND

PISTOLS AND REVOLVERS

Great Britain In the mid-1920s the British army decided to reduce the caliber of its pistols from 0.455 inches to 0.38 inches, and the pistol adopted to chamber this less-powerful round was the Enfield No. 2 Mark 1. The decision to change to a smaller round was taken partly to make weapon training easier, but it is significant that anyone who had any prospect of actually using his pistol against an opponent – as opposed to merely being armed with one – usually acquired a heavier-caliber weapon. There is no doubt that the heavier and slower-moving .45-inch round was markedly more effective at stopping an enemy than was the lighter and faster bullet.

The No. 2 Mark 1 was an Enfield-designed revolver based on the Webley commercial model. It was manufactured in two basic models, with and without a hammer comb. In its former condition the pistol could be cocked manually before firing (single action), or a single stroke of the trigger would both index a chamber and allow the hammer to rise and fall (double action). The Mark 1* deleted the hammer comb, apparently because operators in the AFVs found that it tended to catch on things, and thus made it impossible to fire with any accuracy.

Since RSAF Enfield Lock was unable to produce a sufficient number of standard pistols, the firm of Webley and Scott produced the Webley Mark 4 revolver from 1941 onward, and this augmented stocks of the Enfield. Webley revolvers from World War I (of .45-inch caliber) were often carried, and the USA supplied large numbers of the Smith and Wesson 38/200 revolver, many of which had a better finish and trigger pull than British weapons. Some were used by Commandos and Airborne troops, as were 9mm Browning FN and .450-inch ACP Colt Government Model 1911 semiautomatics.

The United States The most important pistol – and in the opinion of many experts far and away the best military pistol ever produced – used by the United States' forces during World War II was the Colt M 1911 A1. This semiautomatic pistol was based on the original commercial Model 1911 and incorporated various modifications to hammer tang, trigger length, grip shape and frame. The barrel was locked to the slide by means of a pivoting link and ribs, and the magazine held seven rounds of .45-inch ACP ammunition. So not only was the pistol extremely reliable – and capable of being stripped without the aid of special tools – but it also chambered the best service round.

The 230-grain bullet left the muzzle at a sedate 850fps. Although its range was limited by the amount the bullet dropped as it slowed down, in practice most pistol engagements took place over a matter of yards, and so this cannot be reckoned to be a serious military disadvantage. The Colt weighed 3 pounds loaded and had an overall length of 8.5 inches, of which the barrel represented 5 inches, so the weapon was both relatively heavy and large – unavoidable consequences of the power of its cartridge. Nevertheless, it was an outstanding weapon and continues in service to this day.

The United States also retained .45-inch caliber revolvers from Colt, and Smith and Wesson; the Colt M 1917 could chamber the rimless .45-inch ACP round by inserting six rounds in the half-moon clips which engaged the rims.

A crude single-shot .45-inch pistol, the Liberator, was designed for OSS as an assassination weapon; it was one of very few wartime designs.

The Soviet Union The Soviet Union produced such enormous quantities of submachine guns during the war that pistols played a decidedly secondary role. The standard revolver in use was the Nagant Model 1895 which is best remembered for its system of breech obturation. On cocking, the chamber slid forward to effect a seal with the rear end of the barrel and the cartridge case (which enclosed the bullet) completed the seal on firing. It fired a special 7.62mm cartridge, and the system worked; its value is questionable, however, since very little velocity is lost in orthodox revolvers without the obturation system.

The Tokarev Model TT 33 was based on the Colt's system of pivoting link. It was a strongly made semiautomatic pistol firing a powerful 7.62mm bottlenecked cartridge; it could also chamber the German 7.63mm Mauser cartridge which enabled captured stocks of ammunition to be used. The lockwork was easily removable for cleaning and the magazine lips were machined inside the pistol to obviate the major cause of malfunction in a semiautomatic pistol – damaged magazine lips.

Germany The Germans issued a far greater number of pistols than any other combatant during the war. The standard Wehrmacht pistol was the Walther P-38, a military derivative of the earlier AP. It fired the 9mm Parabellum round and was unusual in that it could be fired

RIFLES

single or double action. The pistol was well-balanced and comfortable – if loose – to fire. The magazine held eight rounds and the slide remained to the rear after the last had been fired. It proved a very satisfactory weapon and its modern counterpart, the P-1, equips the Bundeswehr today.

The 9mm P 08 (Luger) also saw widespread service throughout the war. Its toggle action was considerably more susceptible to malfunctions than the more robust P-38, but nevertheless it was in constant use. An even older design, the 7.63mm or 9mm Mauser Model 98 was also encountered, as were countless different types of Mauser, Walther, Sauer and Dreyse, manufactured in a variety of calibers. Mauser produced a crude last-ditch semiautomatic in the form of the Volkspistole, one of very few designs to actually originate during the war, and the Wehrmacht pressed several types of captured pistols, including the Belgian FN and Polish Radom, into service.

Italy The Italians used the 10.35mm M 1889 Bodeo revolver throughout the war, but the most important weapon in service was the 9mm Beretta Model 1934. This compact semiautomatic chambered the low-powered 9mm Short (.380 ACP) round which enabled it to dispense with locking systems, and it was a simple blowback pistol. The magazine base incorporated a tang to enable the firer's little finger to contribute toward the grip. The pistol was beautifully finished although somewhat underpowered, and it is interesting to note how the Italians refused to lower the standard of their small-arms production, unlike all other combatant nations. Overall length was only 6 inches and the magazine held seven rounds.

The 9mm Glisenti Model 1910 semiautomatic firing a special round also saw limited service.

Japan Although a 9mm revolver, the Meiji 26, was sometimes encountered, the Japanese mainly relied on three types of semiautomatic pistol during the war. The first was the 8mm Taisho 04 Nambu, a pistol based upon the Glisenti, whose major defect was the weakness of its striker spring. A smaller 7mm variant was also built, although neither pistol was an official issue despite being widely used.

The 8mm Taisho 14 Nambu, introduced in 1925, was a simplified Model 04. While doing nothing to improve the problems of the striker spring, it incorporated a safety catch which could only be operated by the disengaged hand, and magazine removal was awkward. Some

pistols had an enlarged trigger guard.

The last and worst Japanese pistol was the Type 94. This ugly weapon was dangerous in the extreme, since its sear bar was exposed, and a slight knock could cause it to fire. It could also fire when the breech was unlocked – in all, a dreadful design.

Other Nations The French army was equipped with revolvers of the M 1892 Lebel type and a semiautomatic pistol of rakish lines, the MAS 1935A. It chambered a 7.65mm cartridge but did not see widespread service.

The Poles produced an excellent semiautomatic prewar, the 9mm Radom. Designed as a cavalry pistol, it was beautifully made and had great strength imparted by the Browning locking action. It was adapted for German use when it became the Model 35 (P).

RIFLES

Great Britain The personal weapon of the British soldier during World War II was the bolt-action Lee Enfield design which his predecessors had used in World War I. The .303-inch Short Magazine Lee Enfield Mark 3 continued to equip many soldiers, although the Rifle No. 4 Mark 1 began to appear in 1939 and gradually replaced the earlier weapon. The No. 4 dispensed with the Mark 3's tangent sight and was an easier weapon to mass produce. The Mark 1* was a version built in the United States or Canada, the Mark 1 (T) was the sniper version and the No. 5 Mark 1 Jungle Carbine was a shorter derivative with butt pad to offset the increased recoil resulting from lightening the rifle. This last variant was by no means as unpleasant to fire as many critics suggest. All had a magazine capacity of 10 rounds loaded from chargers of five and all were sturdy, accurate and reliable weapons whose bolts were considerably faster to manipulate than the German Mauser design. The round was powerful and the .303-inch rifle of whatever mark was a successful design and performed well in all conditions.

The Home Guard received a motley assortment of rifles including the P 14 and M 1917 from the United States and the Ross from Canada. Many of the former were in .30–06 caliber and were distinguished by rings of red paint on the furniture.

The De Lisle carbine was a special-purpose weapon based on an SMLE .303-inch rifle rechambered for the .45-ACP round. It was fitted with a silencer and versions with folding and fixed butts were produced for silent killing at close range especially in secret operations.

The United States The US forces used two bolt-action rifles during the war, the M 1903 Springfield and the M 1917 Enfield. Both were chambered for the .30–06 round and the former M 1903 A 4 was a sniper variant. The standard weapon was, however, a semiautomatic rifle – the M 1 Garand. This attractive but weighty rifle was fed from eight-round chargers and entered service in 1936. One disadvantage was that no additional rounds could be added to the magazine, but the Garand performed well in rough conditions, and at least the US infantryman had a semiautomatic rifle when others did not.

Another exceptionally well-designed and compact weapon was the M 1 carbine. This fired a special round derived from the Winchester .32 commercial cartridge of limited power but, bearing in mind the M 1 Carbine was designed to replace the pistol, this was partially offset by the firer's increased prospects of hitting his target. The M 1A1 had a skeleton tubular butt for use by airborne troops. The M 1 itself resembled a sporting arm more than a military carbine, and its magazine held 15 rounds.

The Browning Automatic Rifle, or BAR, was a semiautomatic weapon dating from World War I, with limited magazine capacity of 20 rounds, and excessive weight and length. It was equipped with a bipod and used as a squad LMG. Another rifle to see limited service was the Johnson M 1941, a recoil-operated weapon with magazine capacity of 10 rounds.

The Soviet Union The Soviets employed a large and cumbersome bolt-action rifle of ancient design, the Model 1891/30g Mosin Nagant. This fired a rimmed 7.62mm round and was designed by the Belgian Nagant brothers in collaboration with a Colonel Mosin. The magazine capacity was a meager five rounds and the rifle was equipped with a long socket bayonet designed to remain fixed to the muzzle. Several varieties were in service, the most up-to-date of which was the Model 1938g, which had tangent leaf rear and hooded post foresight. Selected rifles were fitted with Type PU or PE telescopic sights for use as sniper rifles.

A shortened carbine version appeared in the closing stages of the war, the M 1944. This weapon had a folding bayonet, but represented little advantage otherwise.

Experiments had been carried out prewar with self-loading rifles and one design, the SVT-38, was in limited service alongside the improved wartime version, the Tokarev SVT-40. This fired the 7.62mm round and had a magazine capacity of 10 rounds. Some versions were fitted with muzzle brakes, but these were superfluous when one considers the weight of the weapon was some nine pounds. These weapons were susceptible to dirt, and many were converted to sniper rifles when they proved too vulnerable for general issue.

Germany The German Landser's personal weapon was the Mauser Karabiner 98K, a shortened derivative of the Gewehr 98 used in World War I. It retained the five-round internal box magazine and had tangent rear with hooded post foresight. While it was a robust weapon, recoil was sharp as the 7.92mm bullet left the muzzle. The Mauser front-locking bolt action was strong, but less rapid to manipulate than the British SMLE. However, from 1935 the German forces were equipped with a sound bolt-action rifle.

Several types of self-loading rifle were issued, the first of which was the Gewehr 41 (M) Mauser or the Gewehr 41 (W) Walther design. This muzzle-heavy weapon was superseded by the Gewehr 43 which adopted the piston gas operation system, and resulted in a more reliable rifle. Some were equipped with telescopic sights.

The St G 44 (Sturmgewehr, or assault rifle) was the first rifle to chamber the special 7.92mm Kurz short round (which was to reappear as the intermediate cartridge used in the Soviet AK 47 postwar), designed for ranges up to 400m. This radical concept resulted in two designs by Haenel and Walther, and the former's MP 43 was redesignated St G 44. The weapon was a success and greatly influenced Mikhail Kalashnikov's AK series.

The FG 42 (*Fallschirmjägergewehr*) was an advanced rifle firing the standard 7.92mm rifle cartridge from a lightweight weapon with bipod. Some 7000 were made. Recoil was excessive but the FG 42 included some interesting features, including the bullpup configuration, and a closed breech for firing single shots or an open one to promote cooling when firing fully automatic.

Italy The Italian infantryman was equipped with rifles of two different calibers: the 6.5mm cartridge was used in the Mannlicher-Parravicino Carcano Modello 91 rifle designed at Turin before the turn of the century and its derivatives, and the 7.35mm cartridge which appeared in 1938 for a similar rifle. The Fucile Modello 91 was rechambered and rebarrelled to accept the more powerful cartridge which had been deemed necessary after the Abyssinian campaign. The weapon was fed from six-round clips which then proceeded to fall from the box magazine after the last round had been chambered. Many variants to the basic design existed; the Moschetto Modello 91/24 carbine, the Fucile Modello 91/38 in both calibers, and a cavalry version of the larger. The rifles themselves were well made but the 6.5mm round was deficient in power; because of political wranglings, the 7.35mm-chambered weapons did not appear in any numbers. The involved name of the weapon comes from Mannlicher (the clip-loading system), Carcano (the safety mechanism) and Parravicino (head of the adoption committee), while the action is basically a Mauser.

Japan The Type 38 Arisaka rifle, again based on the Mauser action, was adopted by the Japanese in 1905 and was chambered for the 6.5mm cartridge. It incorporated a bolt cover which was designed to prevent the ingress of dirt into the action. The rifle was both long and heavy, considering the stature of its firers, but recoil was slight. A carbine version existed, known as the M 1938. Like the Italians, the Japanese planned to adopt a larger caliber – the 7.7mm – in the 1930s, and the Type 99 rifle was a Type 38 modified to accommodate the change. It featured an entirely superfluous monopod and a highly optimistic antiaircraft rear sight. The Type 2 was a parachutist's folding version with threaded barrel, and again with monopod; a similar weapon also existed based on the 6.5mm Type 38 carbine. Two further 6.5mm rifles also saw limited service. The Type 44 carbine was equipped with a folding bayonet, and the Type 97 was a sniper rifle fitted with a telescopic sight and modified bolt handle. The standard of

Above: Japanese troops with Arisaka 38 rifles.

workmanship deteriorated in the closing stages of war in Japan – as elsewhere – and some of the last weapons produced were of very poor quality and safety.

Other Nations Most of the other countries involved in the war produced their own weapons – the Belgians used the 7.92mm FN Mauser Modèle 1924, the French used a number of different types including the Gras and Lebel (8mm) and MAS 36 (7.5mm), which was an awkward weapon without a safety catch. The Germans captured large numbers of these and other Czech, Polish, Dutch and Norwegian rifles, and used them against their former owners in the hands of second-line or garrison troops. They had their own system of designation for captured weapons: for instance, the SMLE became the Gewehr 281 (e) – for englisch – and the Mosin Nagant became the Gewehr 254 (r) – russisch.

SUBMACHINE GUNS

Great Britain The submachine gun – which had begun life as a close-quarter trench clearing weapon in World War I – received little interest in Great Britain until the imminence of war revived the idea. Initially, quantities of American Thompsons were procured and an unnecessarily heavy and well-made design produced – the 9mm Lanchester. This equipped the Royal Navy because in 1941 the first 9mm Sten gun appeared. The Sten – which was named after the first letters of its designers Shephard, Turpin and the RSAF Enfield – was a simple blow-back weapon which ran to five marks, plus a sixth and silenced one. The Mark 1 retained unnecessary furniture and a flash hider; the Mark 2 had a removable barrel and rotating magazine housing; the Mark 3 a fixed tubular barrel casing; the Mark 4 (experimental) a folding butt; and the Mark 5 a wooden butt and No. 4 rifle-type foresight. The Sten was produced in millions – it had the advantage over its American counterparts of chambering Axis ammunition, and its only real weakness was the magazine feed. It was supplied to resistance groups all over occupied Europe. Toward the end of the war the 9mm Patchett, forerunner of the current British Sterling, was introduced in limited numbers.

The United States The standard US SMG until 1942 was the .45-inch M 1928 A or A 1 Thompson, whose worth had been proved in the days of Prohibition in the United States in the 1920s. The Thompson was a needlessly complicated and expensive weapon with a Blish delaying action centering round an H-shaped device which rose to lock the action. In practice this was an unnecessary refinement, as were the Lyman sights with windage scale and even the Cutts compensator on the muzzle. However, the Thompson was reliable, and thousands were shipped to Britain in 1940. Some models had vertical and some horizontal foregrips, and could accept 20-round box magazines or 50- or 100-round drum ones which tended to rattle. The .45-inch M 1 dispensed with most of the sophistications of the early guns in 1942, and the M 1A1 with even more in the interests of swifter production. All were solid enough to be readily controllable during prolonged bursts.

America's answer to the Sten was the .45-inch M 3. This basic weapon resembled and was known as the Grease Gun and had a telescopic tubular butt. Early models were cocked by cranking a handle, while later ones had a slot in the breech block for the insertion of the firer's finger. A spring-loaded ejection port cover was fitted, and the M 3 was a sound if unattractive gun. A minor SMG used by the USMC was the Reising Model 50 or 55 which fired from a closed bolt.

The Soviet Union The Soviets issued submachine guns very widely during World War II, and the most frequently encountered was the 7.62mm PPSh-1941. This was a development of the PPD 1940 simplified for mass production and the PPSh, though lacking in refinement, was one of the most practical SMGs produced. It employed stampings and pressings; to strip the weapon was simplicity itself and, unlike most of its counterparts, it was substantial enough to be used as a club in hand-to-hand fighting. The drum magazine held 71 rounds of the bottle-necked 7.62mm cartridge. Despite the urgency of its production a chrome-lined barrel was retained and, although it had a rough and ready appearance, the weapon functioned in mud and subzero conditions. It is estimated that over 6,000,000 PPShs were produced.

Another submachine gun, which improved upon the PPSh although never seeing wide-spread service, was the PPS-42. This was designed during the siege of Leningrad, and constructed of stampings and pressings spot-welded and with folding butt. The PPS accepted a 35-round box magazine (which also fitted the PPSh) and was the ideal answer to the need to produce a reliable gun at minimum cost.

The submachine gun epitomized the offensive spirit of the Soviet army, and never more so than

its use in the tank-rider battalions who closed with the Germans mounted on tanks and sprang off on reaching their objective.

Germany The Germans pioneered the submachine gun with the 9mm Bergmann MP 18 of 1918 – indeed, its derivative, the MP 28, was the weapon on which the Lanchester was based – and produced a variety of weapons between the wars. These included the Bergmann MP 34 and 35, the Solothurn S 1–100 and the Erma, all of which saw service with police or special formations, but the definitive German submachine gun of World War II – erroneously referred to as the Schmeisser – was the Erma-designed MP 38 and its developments.

The MP 38 incorporated some advanced features including a telescopic housing to the main spring and the use of stampings and plastics. The overall finish was excellent and the only modification found necessary was a locking device for the cocking handle to prevent in-advertent discharge if the weapon was jolted – a fault remedied likewise in the Sten. The muzzle had a cap, a hooded post foresight and a bar to enable the weapon to be fired from a vehicle with some degree of safety. The major production version after the modified MP 38/40 was the MP 40, which incorporated simplifications to facilitate production. The MP 40/2 had a magazine housing modified to accept twin magazines and the MP 41 had, for some unknown reason, a wooden butt. The MP 40 was a very good weapon – compact, since its tubular skeleton butt could be folded under the gun, reliable in feed (unlike the Sten), and able to operate under adverse conditions.

Italy The Italian army's most widely used submachine gun was the 9mm Beretta Modello 1938 A, an ingenious weapon equipped with two triggers to enable the firer to select single shots or fully automatic fire. Like all Italian small arms the finish was excellent, and various versions of the gun were produced. The first had a folding bayonet and slotted cooling jacket around the barrel; the second a jacket with round holes and the third deleted the bayonet and modified the compensator slots above the muzzle. In production the barrel underwent two further changes, initially a stamped and rolled jacket was fitted and finally the jacket was removed altogether. A choice of magazines was available in multiples of 10 up to 40 rounds, and a special high-powered cartridge was produced.

A number of other designs were used by the Italians, the earliest of which was the 9mm OVP, an unusual weapon dating from World War I with top-mounted magazine and cylindrical cocking sleeve surrounding the barrel. The Beretta Modello 1918/30 was encountered, and an SMG actually designed in 1943 – the FNAB Modello 1943 – was also built. Even this was well furnished and had a folding magazine housing as well as tubular butt. It fired from a closed bolt and was a compact and pleasant weapon to fire. A less well finished SMG was the TZ-45 and this, like the FNAB, was only produced in small numbers.

Japan Surprisingly enough the Japanese were decidedly slow in adopting a submachine gun; it was not until 1942 that the Type 100 appeared. This was a blow-back weapon with magazine feed on the left-hand side (an advantage when firing from the prone position) which had a 30-round box magazine for the 8mm Nambu cartridge. The Type 100 could accept a bayonet, and some had a rather superfluous bipod; a parachutist's model with folding butt was also produced.

In 1944 an improved Type 100 was built along simplified lines. It had an increased rate of fire, more or less doubling the earlier gun's 400rpm, but few if any reached front-line troops. Considering how suitable the submachine gun is for sudden close-range encounters in jungle conditions, it is remarkable how little attention the Japanese paid to the weapon.

Other Nations The French entered the war with the MAS 38, a neat weapon of good design, but chambering an underpowered 7.65mm pistol cartridge unique to the French. Australia produced two designs; the 9mm Owen and the 9mm Austen. The former was designed in 1940 and was of unusual configuration. A top-mounted box magazine containing 33 rounds

was fitted, and the sights were offset to the right. This positioning of the magazine has its advantages; it cannot catch in anything, and gravity assists the feed. Much care was taken to ensure that dirt was kept out of the action, and the barrel was readily removed by raising a spring-loaded catch; it also had a compensator. Various marks existed with skeleton butts and barrel, cooling fins and bayonet lugs. The Owen, though heavy, was a most pleasant weapon to fire. The Austen – Australian Sten – was, as its name implies, a weapon based on the Sten, but incorporating the telescopic main-spring housing of the German MP 38, and also a pistol grip and folding butt. A lightened version was produced in 1944.

LIGHT MACHINE GUNS

Great Britain The British army received in 1938 the first of many .303-inch Bren light machine guns which were to provide it with fire support at platoon and section level. The Bren was derived from the Czech ZB 30, a 7.92mm weapon designed at Brno, and its version specially supplied for evaluation, the ZB 33. The Enfield-produced gun (Br from Brno and En from Enfield) was to prove one of the most successful LMGs ever produced. The Mark 1 had a drum rear sight and an angled grip beneath the butt; the Mark 2 replaced the drum by a tangent sight and other simplifications were embodied; the Marks 3 and 4 had shortened barrels. All were fed from a top-mounted magazine usually filled with 28 rounds and fitted with bipods. The Bren finish was first-class, and it was almost too accurate. Reliability was good and the Bren – rechambered and rebarrelled for the 7.62mm NATO round – remains in British army service today as the L4 A 6.

The .303-inch Vickers Berthier outwardly

Below: British Bren Mark 1 light machine gun.

resembled the Bren and competed for adoption with it. It was in service with the Indian army and fought throughout the war in the Far East. The .303-inch Lewis gun which had been widely used in World War I continued to serve during World War II, mainly with the Home Guard and AA Command.

The United States The US forces employed, in addition to the BAR, the .30–06 Browning M 1919 A 6 as a squad automatic weapon. This was derived from the water-cooled Browning M 1917 medium machine gun, and featured a cylindrical barrel jacket with circular cooling holes, flash hider and bipod. It retained the belt feed of the parent weapon and had a long butt with pistol grip and a carrying handle. It was a compromise weapon, and both heavy and awkward. It could be employed in the sustained fire role by fitting a tripod.

The .30-inch Johnson M 1941 was a recoil-operated weapon used in limited numbers by the USMC. It had an adjustable rate of fire and fired from an open bolt during fully automatic fire to avoid rounds cooking-off between bursts; the bolt remained closed during single-shot fire. The Johnson had a folding bipod or, in later models, a monopod, and was light enough to be manageable as a rifle. The Americans never equipped their infantry with an LMG of any real merit during the war.

The Soviet Union The standard light machine gun employed by the Soviets was the 7.62mm Degtyarev DP 1928. It was a simple but highly effective gun of attractively slender lines fed from a top-mounted drum magazine containing 47 rounds; unfortunately, this was liable to distortion since it was made out of thin sheet metal. It was locked by flaps on the bolt being thrust outward to engage in recesses by the forward travel of the firing pin. A disadvantage was that, during sustained fire, the return spring became sufficiently hot to lose its tempering since its housing was located just below the barrel. Nevertheless, the Degtyarev was a reliable weapon issued in great numbers to provide fire support for the Soviet infantry. The DPM of 1944 remedied the spring problem and included a pistol grip, and the DT was an AFV version capable of conversion to the ground role if required.

Germany The German army had no light machine gun as such during World War II; both the MG 34 and MG 42 were belt-fed weapons and precursors of today's general purpose machine guns. Both could be used in the light role when fitted with bipod.

The MG 34 was a beautifully machined and finished weapon designed by Mauser along the original lines of the Solothurn MG 30. An interesting feature of the weapon was its trigger, which pivoted around a center point to provide fully automatic fire when the lower part was pressed and semiautomatic when the upper part was. Barrel changing was awkward but the MG 34 proved a sound design and continued in service until 1945. A saddle-drum magazine could be fitted containing 75 rounds.

The MG 42 was designed to include the maximum use of stampings and pressings, and introduced the roller locking system and pawl-operated belt feed. The gun was of excellent design – it was reliable in bad conditions, and barrel changing could be swiftly effected, which was as well since the rate of fire of over 1000rpm made it frequently necessary. This high rate of fire was not an advantage when the gun was being used on its bipod in the light role, although it imparted great moral effect. Both weapons were versatile, and the MG 42 remains in present-day Bundeswehr service, chambering the 7.62mm NATO cartridge.

The Germans also used the MG 15 aircraft gun converted to the ground role, and as many Czech VZ 53s and VZ 26s as they captured as substitute standard weapons. The Danish 7.92mm Madsen which had been supplied to Norway was also used, since it chambered the German service cartridge.

Italy The standard Italian light machine gun in service during World War II was the 6.5mm Breda Modello 1930. This weapon was based upon an earlier series of Breda guns and was blow-back operated. While this system works perfectly satisfactorily in submachine guns firing low-powered pistol cartridges, it is another matter in weapons firing full-power rifle rounds. To avoid the risk of case separation through difficult extraction, an oil pump was fitted to provide lubrication for the cartridges as they were fed from a 20-round box magazine which could be topped up from rifle chargers when pivoted forward. The barrel was not equipped with a carrying handle, which must have made it awkward to change when hot. The foresight was also mounted not on the barrel itself, but on the body of the gun. In all, the Modello 1930 was an ungainly weapon with considerable disadvantages, the most serious of which was the unavoidable adhesion of dust, sand and fouling to the oiled cartridge cases. The Modello 1938 was chambered for the larger 7.35mm cartridge.

Japan The Japanese, while neglecting the submachine gun, set considerable store by the LMG and employed several types. The 6.5mm Taisho 11 entered Japanese army service in 1922 and was a Nambu modification of the Hotchkiss design with unusual feed arrangements. A hopper fitted to the gun's left-hand side received six five-round rifle chargers and fed them one at a time, ejecting the charger after each five rounds fired. The sights and butt were offset to the right and the barrel was heavily finned to promote cooling. As extraction was violent, an oiling system was provided as on the Breda with all the attendant disadvantages.

In 1936 the 6.5mm Type 96 light machine gun entered service. This bore a striking resemblance to the Czech ZB series – the Japanese were never reticent about adopting other nations' ideas – and featured a curved top-mounted box magazine, ornate carrying handle on a finned barrel, and a drum rear sight. Since the primary extraction problem remained unsolved, the Japanese infantryman was expected to oil his cartridges as he changed his magazine, which, of course, led to much grit adhering to them. Two other points are worth noting on the Type 96 – it could accept a bayonet, which conforms to the offensive spirit of the Japanese, and it had a telescopic sight, whose fitting is incomprehensible.

The 7.7mm Type 99 light machine gun chambered a rimless cartridge which did not require oiling, since the primary extraction problem had been solved. Otherwise it was basically a Type 96, apart from an extension on its butt underside to assist firing on fixed lines in the medium role, and did not appear in any numbers.

Other Nations The French army replaced their poorly designed light machine guns dating from World War I with an altogether better design inspired by the Browning Automatic Rifle – the Fusil Mitrailleur Modèle 1924 Chatellerault. This was chambered for the new 7.5mm round – it seems extraordinary that the French have always retained a set of calibers different from everyone else – and was modified in 1928 to provide a well-designed and reliable light machine gun with top-mounted box magazine of 25 rounds. The Chatellerault, like the Beretta M 1938 A SMG, had two triggers to provide fire selection, and the Modèle 1931 was a version designed to accommodate a 150-round drum magazine for installation in the Maginot Line,

or, modified, in AFVs.

MEDIUM AND HEAVY MACHINE GUNS

Great Britain The .303-inch Vickers Medium Machine Gun entered British army service in 1912 and was derived from the American Maxim; the essential difference between the two weapons was that the British one inverted the Maxim toggle lock. From the start, the Vickers proved supremely reliable, and achieved feats of sustained fire during World War I which reflected the excellence of both design and manufacture. The Vickers fired from 250-round fabric belts and was water-cooled via water jacket and condenser can. During sustained fire there was a risk that the firing position might be betrayed by the ensuing clouds of steam.

The gun was fired from a tripod and the gunner held two spade grips; it was equipped with dial sights for firing along fixed lines. The water jacket could be grooved or straight. Seven marks of Vickers existed between 1912 and 1967, when the last gun was taken off charge amid some opposition. Many of these marks were specialized versions of the gun for air or armored use, and the basic Mark 1 remained in service throughout. A boat-tailed .303-inch Mark 8z cartridge enabled the gun to reach further than with standard Mark VII ammunition. The Vickers MMG was an excellent weapon; above all, it was reliable, and a fine piece of engineering.

The United States The American counterpart of the Vickers was the .30-inch Browning M 1917. The action was based on barrel and bolt recoiling together a certain way before the latter unlocked and an accelerator propelled it rearward, at the same time operating the belt feed mechanism. The gun entered service in 1917 somewhat belatedly, since official interest in it was initially slight. It functioned satisfactorily, and in 1936 the M 1917 A 1 appeared, incorporating essentially minor modifications. In appearance the weapon was similar to the Vickers but with straight water jacket and single pistol grip. Another variant was the M 1919 A 4, a dual-purpose weapon suitable for installation in AFVs or use in the ground role. It, too, took a 250-round fabric belt. The Browning family of medium machine guns extended to several versions designed for aerial use, and all proved reliable in operation and effective in action. The main disadvantage was weight, but this was offset by the weapon's sound design and consequent ability to keep firing.

The .50-inch M2 HB was a heavy machine gun

derived from the M 1921 gun which dispensed with water-cooling and sported a heavy barrel – hence the HB in its designation – to permit sustained fire. It was fed from a 110-round metallic link belt and was frequently pintle mounted on AFVs; air versions provided firepower for both fighters and bombers and, of course, it could also be employed in the ground role.

The Soviet Union The Soviets adopted the proven Maxim design in their 7.62mm Model PM 1910. Since no attempts at weight saving appear to have been made, the Soviet weapon weighed, without the tripod, over 52 pounds – which was 20 pounds heavier than the Vickers. As an aid to the unfortunate infantryman whose task it was to bring the Maxim into action, a wheeled mounting – known as the Sokolov, and itself weighing double the gun's weight – was designed to assist him. This had a detachable shield and could be fitted with runners for snow use. The 250-round fabric belt was employed, and a distinctive feature was the gun's enormous water-jacket filling cap.

In 1943 the Goryunov SG 43 appeared. This 7.62mm weapon was based on a tank gun and had a heavy barrel. It was unusual in having a sideways tilting locking block action and consequently complicated feed system from metallic link belts. The Goryunov was heavy, but reliable, and widely used in AFV mountings.

The 12.7mm DSh K 1938 was a heavy machine gun designed by Degtyarev and Shpagin; the latter designed the rotating cylinder feed mechanism, and the former the gas operation and locking system. The resulting weapon was fed from a 50-round belt, and saw widespread service in ground, antiaircraft and AFV roles. A modified version, the DSh KM, remains in Soviet service today. Because of the weight of the gun – nearly 80 pounds – it was equipped with a Sokolov-type wheeled tripod mounting which erected to form an antiaircraft mount.

Germany As has already been mentioned, the Germans did not have a medium or heavy machine gun per se; both the MG 34 and the MG 42 served in this purpose when mounted on tripods. The MG 34 was installed in an MG-Lafette 34 for firing along fixed lines and aligned by a dial sight. Owing to overheating the air-cooled barrel had to be changed after five 50-round belts had been fired. This was clearly a disadvantage, as was the narrowness of tolerances in the short-recoil operated action with rotating bolt, aided by a muzzle booster.

Barrel changing could be rapidly achieved and the very versatility of the MG 34 went some way toward compensating. The MG 42 was designed with a quick-change barrel which could be swiftly replaced when a release catch freed the breech end and enabled it to be withdrawn without, unfortunately, any form of handle. Nevertheless, the MG 42 was frequently carried into battle on its tripod by the gun group, and performed so satisfactorily that the Bundeswehr readopted the weapon in the guise of the MG 3 as soon as it could reasonably rid itself of the American M 1919 A 6s with which it was issued in 1956.

The 7.92mm MG 08/15, the standard water-cooled bipod mounted Maxim-type mainstay of World War I, was issued in limited numbers, but the philosophy had changed with the introduction of the first truly general-purpose machine gun, the Maschinengewehr 34.

Italy The 6.5mm Fiat-Revelli Modello 1914 medium machine gun was a water-cooled weapon inspired by the Maxim, as were most similar designs. The action was retarded-blowback operated, which meant that, to avoid primary extraction problems, the cartridge had to be oiled as it was chambered. The demerits of this system are apparent and have already been discussed, and to compound the felony, a strip-feed box magazine of 10 compartments of five rounds was fitted, and parts reciprocated outside the receiver. To attempt to remedy these defects, the Italians introduced the Modello 1935. This introduced a 50-round belt feed system in larger caliber of 8mm, and replaced the oiling system with a fluted chamber in which gases were designed to float the cartridge case off the walls and thereby ease extraction. For some unknown reason the gun fired from a closed bolt, which resulted in cook-offs when chamber temperature rose sufficiently to transfer its heat to the propellant of the chambered round and fire it. Since the water-cooling of the original Modello 1914 had been replaced by an air-cooled barrel, this was a regular occurrence after periods of sustained fire.

Breda manufactured a 13.2mm heavy machine gun in 1931, the RM Modello 31, originally designed for tank use, but also encountered in the ground role.

Japan The 6.5mm Taisho 3 1914 heavy machine gun was based on the French Hotchkiss Modèle 1900 which had proved highly satisfactory in the first real use of machine guns during the Russo-Japanese War of 1904–05. The gun had two spade grips, a strikingly finned barrel and a tripod equipped with sockets into which poles could be slotted to help the gun team during changes of position. The Taisho 3 was fed from 30-round metal strips and had a sedate rate of fire of some 400rpm. The real disadvantage was the eternal need to oil the cartridges because of the violence of the gun's extraction; provided they could be kept clean, the weapon functioned well.

The Type 92 machine gun introduced in 1932 was essentially a 7.7mm modification of the Taisho 3. In place of the spade grips it featured two pistol grips. A small flash hider appeared at the muzzle. The Type 92 could chamber both the 7.7mm semirimless and the 7.7mm rimless ammunition which, along with a rimmed round, the Japanese had seen fit to introduce in the 1930s. In 1941 a lightened version, the Type 1, was introduced which was only capable of chambering the rimless cartridge.

HAND GRENADES

Great Britain The standard British hand grenade in service during World War II strongly resembled the original Mills bomb of World War I. It weighed 1 pound 12 ounces and contained 2.5 ounces of Baratol HE which burst the serrated casing to provide splinter effect. In operation the No. 36 grenade relied upon a spring-loaded striker retained in position by a striker lever. On throwing, a cap was struck and initiated a four- or seven-second delay fuse.

A number of other grenades were available or developed during the war. The No. 68 was a finned rifle grenade for use with a cup discharger (which would also accommodate a No. 36 with gas check). The No. 69 was a bakelite-cased grenade armed by a tape and lead ball which unwound when it was thrown; this was a grenade designed for offensive use in the open. The No. 74 grenade which followed the weighty No. 73, was an antitank weapon consisting of an explosive-filled glass phial protected until use by two clam shells and held by a handle which housed the detonator. The phial was covered by a sticky substance which, with luck, would adhere to the target; hence its title Sticky Bomb. The No. 75 (Hawkins) was an antitank grenade operated by pressure – effectively a small mine. The No. 80 was a white phosphorus grenade with mousetrap igniter used for smoke or incendiary purposes. The No. 82 Gammon bomb consisted of a bag with igniter set into which plastic explosive could be inserted in quantities to suit the task in hand. Along with

these grenades – and others issued – the Home Guard employed Molotov cocktails in the form of glass bottles filled with inflammable liquids and phosphorus for use against armor.

The United States The US forces used two types of fragmentation grenades, the Mark II A1 and the Mark III A2. The former – unlike the British No. 36 – used a mousetrap igniter and was heavily serrated, which suited its use in defensive situations. The Mark III relied upon blast and consisted of a fiber cylinder filled with TNT. This enabled it to be thrown by advancing troops or used in house clearance where the heavy fragments of the defensive type of grenade would have placed the thrower at some risk.

The M 15 smoke grenade was filled with white phosphorus. In addition to providing a localized smoke screen, this grenade could also be used against troops with lethal effect. A series of purely smoke grenades with different color composition fillings was available, and an incendiary grenade, the M 14, was also made.

The Americans used rifle-launched antitank grenades in some numbers until the introduction of the bazooka. These were of the M 9 A1 type and had hollow-charge warheads which could penetrate side and rear armor at limited range. The British developed this as the No. 85 grenade but it saw limited service.

The Soviet Union The Soviet Model F 1 grenade was, like the American Mark II, based upon the standard French grenade of World War I and had, like the Mills, a fly-off striker, but one which operated axially and not vertically. In 1942 it began to be replaced by the RTD 1942. Both types were heavy and serrated, and could be thrown some 30 yards. A stick grenade, the Model 1914/30, was available in the early war, and was of interest because it was dual purpose; for offensive use, its cylinder provided blast effect, but a sleeve could be added to provide splinter effect for defensive purposes.

The RPG-43 was an antitank grenade with hollow-charge warhead. The way to ensure that the grenade struck its target in the right position was simply achieved – when the thrower released his grip on the handle, a sleeve attached to cloth strips trailed behind the grenade in flight and provided stability.

An unsuccessful attempt to improve the Model 1914/30 appeared. This Model RGD 33 was a complex weapon with a safety catch, and which required pulling and twisting to arm – not the easiest thing to do in the grime, sweat and activity of close-quarter combat.

Germany Germany had developed a stick grenade in World War I and had improved it afterward; in 1939 the Stielhandgranate 39 was available. This consisted of a cylinder of TNT filling on the top of a hollow wooden stick. When a cap on the handle's base was unscrewed a porcelain bead was exposed, and when this was tugged, a friction igniter lit the fuse which exploded the grenade some five seconds later. Subsequent grenades attached the striker cord direct to the cap. The Stielhandgranate was easy to throw with accuracy and a smoke version, the Nebelhandgranate 39, was also produced. Two auxiliary derivatives, the Behelfhandgranaten Holz and Beton, replaced the steel cylinder with wood and concrete ones respectively. A number of HE grenades could be clustered together to form a Geballte Ladung concentrated charge detonated by one of them.

The Eihandgranate 39 – Egg grenade – was an oval thin-cased grenade, again with pull-igniter system. Four to five second fuses were normal, but a one-second delay fuse provided a booby trap.

The Germans also had a variety of rifle grenades fired from a Schiessbecher discharger cup; some were HE and some hollow-charge for antitank use. A number of grenades could be fired from the two Kampfpistolen developed from flare pistols. Other grenades included Nipolit types of molded HE threaded to receive igniter sets, and the highly effective beehive hollow-charge of three kilograms which was attached to its target tank by three magnets – the Haft-Hohlladung.

Italy The Italian infantryman had three main types of hand grenade available, all bearing the designation Modello 35. These were manufactured by Breda, OTO and SRC and were fitted with all-way impact fuses. The first two were similar in construction and were operated by pulling a tab which released the safety cap and, on throwing, a safety pin was released to arm the grenade. The SRC also had a tab but had a wire coil fitted round the explosive-filled cylinder to increase fragmentation effect. All three grenades were painted bright red.

In use their reliability was uncertain and the Breda Modello 40 improved prospects of successful detonation by spring ejection of the safety cap when its wooden handle was released on throwing. The Modello 42 was an antitank stick grenade of similar configuration.

During the war the risk of booby traps was ever present; seemingly innocuous objects could be connected to concealed grenades or charges and the ensuing unexpected destruction could help to demoralize enemy troops. Grenades were particularly suitable for this purpose, and the Germans and Italians both made use of them, particularly in North Africa.

Japan The Japanese Type 97 hand grenade consisted of a serrated cylinder of TNT explosive with a somewhat primitive ignition system: once the safety pin had been withdrawn, the cap of the grenade was struck to ignite a safety fuse which exploded the grenade four to five seconds later. Similar to the Type 97 was the Type 91, which could accept a finned attachment to convert it into a rifle grenade with seven-second delay to allow for time of flight. A derivative of the Type 97 was designated the Type 00 – the principal difference being the lack of serrations which, in any case, bear little resemblance to the size or shape of splinters in any such grenades. Another type of grenade – designation unknown – had five grooves on its cylindrical body and a circlip for attaching it in booby-trap positions.

A very basic copy of the German Stielhandgranate was also made. Its 3 ounces of HE were contained in a rough cast-iron cylinder, and operation followed the German pattern of friction igniter on length of cord, but a ring

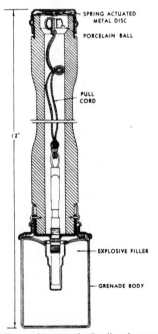

SPRING ACTUATED METAL DISC

PORCELAIN BALL

PULL CORD

12"

EXPLOSIVE FILLER

GRENADE BODY

Above: The mechanism of a Stielhandgranate 39.

replaced the bead. The Japanese also had 30 and 40mm antitank rifle grenades known as the Type 2.

Other Nations The French employed a number of grenades – their Grenade à Main F 1 was developed from their World War I grenade and influenced both American and Soviet types. The OF was a thin-cased offensive grenade and the D Modèle 1937 was a smooth-cased defensive type. The Dutch and Belgians had several types of offensive and defensive weapons, as indeed did most of the combatant nations of World War II. They were captured in large numbers and used against their former owners.

The essential with a grenade is that it must be safe – to use grenades is a fraught business and any unreliability of fuse length or operation requiring involved manipulation will serve to unsettle the thrower greatly. The British No. 36 was among the safest, and the Soviet RGD 33 a strong contender for the worst.

FLAME THROWER

Great Britain Little interest in the flame thrower was shown in Britain during the interwar period, and it was not until 1940 that the first British weapon, the Marsden Portable Flame Thrower No. 1 Mark 1, was developed. Like all such weapons, separate tanks housed compressed gas

Below: US Marine with a flame thrower on Iwo Jima.

and an inflammable liquid, which was ignited as it left the muzzle of the flame thrower. The Marsden had four cylinders of liquid and, like most early equipment, was decidedly heavy at 84 pounds. The effective range of the flame thrower was some 30 yards, and cumbersome and heavy equipment limited the operator's chances of closing with his target. The No. 2 Mark 1 of 1941 considerably improved the previous design and was known as the Lifebuoy because of its configuration. The liquid was carried in a circular container with the gas in a holder set in its center, and the Lifebuoy was worn on its operator's back. It weighed 64 pounds. The Mark II appeared in 1944 and incorporated several modifications designed for static defense and was a weird and complicated contraption mounted on a pair of iron wheels, and equipped with a hose. It was perhaps fortunate for its Home Guard operators that it was never used in action; indeed, all users of flame throwers had limited life expectancy if unlucky enough to be captured.

The United States The original US flame thrower was the E1 R1. This consisted of the usual backpack design with two cylindrical fuel containers and a third and smaller gas reservoir leading to an insulated flame gun. This weapon equipped the American infantryman until early 1942 when the Portable Flamethrower M1 entered service. At 70 pounds this was still on the heavy side, but it proved difficult to reduce the weight by much. The M1's tanks held four gallons of fuel which gave up to 10 seconds of fire, but normally only short bursts were necessary to ignite the target, which was, in the Pacific theater, frequently an underground bunker. The M1 A1 was a development of the M1 of 1942. It retained the tank configuration of the earlier types but ignited a more viscous fuel and increased the M1's range of some 30 yards by half as much again.

The M2-2 flame thrower was the last weapon introduced and appeared in early 1944. It slightly lightened its predecessor's weight and reduced its range, but was more reliable and replaced the earlier types. The Americans, engaged in close-quarter fighting often in jungle or heavily foliated areas, made considerable use of the flame thrower against the Japanese.

The Soviet Union The Soviet infantry was equipped with two types of flame thrower during World War II. The earlier type was the ROKS-2, and this consisted of a rectangular fuel reservoir attached to a carrying frame with shoulder straps, with gas cylinder mounted horizontally beneath it. The flame tube led to a long flame gun which was constructed from the Mosin Nagant M 1930 rifle and retained its butt. The weapon weighed some 50 pounds, but the reduced weight was the result of halving the normal fuel capacity of four gallons which, in turn, resulted in a maximum duration of fire of about seven seconds. The range was around 40 yards.

The ROKS-3 introduced the more conventional cylindrical fuel tank on the right-hand side of the backpack and the gas cylinder on the left. Both were mounted vertically and thus the weight was unevenly distributed. The flame tube led to a similar rifle-shaped flame gun, but this one had a rear pistol grip.

Germany The standard German flame thrower of 1939 was the Flammenwerfer 35, a weighty piece of equipment at 80 pounds with a fuel capacity of 2.5 gallons and range of some 30 yards. It was simply too heavy and the Flammenwerfer Klein Verbessert 40 was, as its name suggests, a smaller improved version. This was of double lifebuoy configuration and, at 47 pounds, an altogether better weapon, although weight savings were inevitably at the cost of fuel. The Flammenwerfer 41 reverted to the cylindrical tanks, but introduced a cartridge ignition system following ignition difficulties encountered on the Russian Front. Ten cartridges (*Strahlrohrpatronen*) were carried in a magazine and provided certainty of ignition in the coldest conditions.

In an attempt to lighten the weapon's weight still more, a 'fire and forget' flame thrower, the Einstossflammenwerfer 46, was developed. Although intended for airborne use, this single-shot weapon was encountered in the hands of ordinary infantry, and consisted of a single tube

with trigger mechanism and sling.

Two flame throwers were employed in static defensive positions. The earlier was a wheeled derivative of the Flammenwerfer 35 intended for two-man operation which in fact proved too awkward for front-line use, and the later one was the Abwehrflammenwerfer 42 with a nozzle fed from a central tank, to provide a 10-second flame jet once only. A trailer mounted weapon, the Flammenwerfer Anhänger, was also issued in limited numbers.

German flame-thrower operators frequently wore distinctive protective overalls and visors on their helmets which protected them from their equipment if not from their opponents. Most users were assault engineers.

Italy The Italian army had prewar experience of using flame throwers against tribesmen in Abyssinia, and their weapon of the late 1930s was the Lanciafiamme Modello 35. The equipment, which weighed 60 pounds, consisted of two vertically mounted cylinders with battery box, and provided 20 seconds worth of fire. It was operated by assault pioneers who, like the Germans, wore overalls and respirators. The Lanciafiamme Modello 40 featured a redesigned ignition system and consisted of three cylinders of similar size and redesigned flame gun. It had a reduced range and duration but weighed much the same as its predecessor. The operator's mobility was so hampered that the Italians, like most other participants in the war, resorted to reducing fuel capacity to reduce weight, and the Lanciafiamme Modello 41 – while weighing a mere 40 pounds – had a duration of only just over five seconds fire. The last Italian portable flame thrower in use was the Lanciafiamme d'Assalto Modello 41. This combined fuel and gas in a cylindrical container and halved the basic Modello 41's weight. The muzzle was at one end of the cylinder and the weapon was handy enough to allow its operator full mobility.

Japan The Japanese army was equipped with two flame throwers, the Model 93 and the Model 100 which, despite their separate designations, were essentially the same weapon. Neither displayed any outstanding features except that weight was reduced to 55 pounds for a capacity of over three gallons. The layout consisted of two cylindrical vertical reservoirs containing fuel and a third between them containing nitrogen gas. The hose led to a tap at the base of the flame gun, which was of slightly different configuration in the two models. Range was in the order of 100 feet and duration of fire around

10 seconds. Like the Americans, the Japanese utilized the flame thrower to good effect in the close confines of the Far East jungles.

Other Nations The French army used a portable flame thrower of orthodox construction, the Lanceflammes P. 4. The large fuel reservoir was vertically mounted on the pack frame and a slender gas cylinder fitted next to it. The corrugated hose led to a small flame gun which, unlike most other designs, was fitted with a lever trigger which was released by squeezing the palm of the hand. Range was limited to 50 feet.

While one cannot deny that all weapons are designed with the sole aim of destruction in mind, the flame thrower stands out as a barbarous weapon. While it is undeniably effective against strongpoints and dug-in infantry, it remains a terrible and inhuman weapon of war.

INFANTRY ANTITANK WEAPONS

Great Britain The British army began World War II equipped with an antitank rifle dating from 1934. This was the Boys, which had originally been known as the Stanchion, but received the name of one of the development team who died before it was completed. The Boys rifle weighed 36 pounds and projected a .55-inch solid-shot bullet at 3250fps. This could penetrate 25mm of armor at 500 yards which, by the standard of the mid 1930s, was quite good; but the Boys rifle was destined to be eclipsed by the increasingly thick German armor against which it was matched. The weapon was both heavy and unpleasant to fire – recoil was severe – and it did not take the infantryman long to realize its limitations. In 1942 a version with a short barrel was developed for airborne use which was, luckily for its users, never adopted. Both rifles were fed from a top-mounted five-round box magazine.

The Projector Infantry Anti-Tank, or PIAT, replaced the Boys in 1942. This was an ungainly weapon resting on a monopod and firing a 3-pound bomb with hollow charge warhead capable of penetrating 75mm of armor. It weighed 30 pounds and greatly improved on its predecessor's performance – the PIAT was a formidable if primitive-looking antitank weapon operated by its two-man team.

The Home Guard received numbers of a very basic weapon indeed – the Northover projector which hurled grenades or Molotov cocktails from its unrifled barrel by means of black-powder charges.

The United States The US Army did not possess an antitank rifle, but from 1942 it did have one of the most celebrated and effective antitank weapons of the war, the 2.36-inch Rocket Launcher M1, or Bazooka. This was a shoulder-fired recoilless weapon which sent a 3.4-pound rocket-propelled projectile out to 500 yards. It was named after a gadget used by the comedian Bob Burns and was first employed in North Africa. The original weapon was 54 inches long and served by a two-man team. Like all recoilless weapons a mighty back blast accompanied each firing and the smoke and dust raised could betray the firing position as well as endangering anyone inside the danger arc behind the weapon. Nevertheless, the Bazooka was capable of penetrating most Axis armor, and provided the infantry squad with something with which to hit back at the much-feared tank, as well as giving them a weapon which could take out strong-points and bunkers. The M 9, which had an electrical magneto firing mechanism inside the pistol grip, had a tube which separated into two parts for ease of transportation, and the M 9 A1 used aluminum to reduce weight. The caliber in these two was increased to 3 inches. Over 460,000 were produced during the war, and the Bazooka performed well.

The Soviet Union The Soviet infantryman had two antitank rifles at his disposal, one designed by Degtyarev and one by Simonov. Both were of 14.5mm caliber. The former, known as the PTRD 1941, was a single shot bolt-action weapon which fired two types of round. The first was solid AP and the second a tungsten-cored AP/Incendiary, and both were fired at a muzzle velocity of 3320fps from a 48-inch barrel. The overall length of the PTRD 1941 was an unwieldy 78.7-inches and it weighed over 38 pounds. It was operated by a two-man team and could penetrate 25mm of armor at 500 yards – a respectable enough performance per se, but one which did not take into account the increasing thickness of German armor.

The other antitank rifle in Soviet army service was the PTRS 1941. This was a semiautomatic gas-operated weapon with a magazine capacity of five rounds, which was 9 inches longer than the PTRD and 8 pounds heavier – both of which facts are of some relevance to the soldier who has to carry it.

The Soviets were conservative in weapon design, and neither weapon was really capable of tackling the kind of tanks it encountered later in the war. However, they were effective weapons against soft-skinned and lightly armored vehicles, as well as in ambushes and urban operations.

Germany The Germans used two antitank rifles early in the war, both firing 7.92mm hardened steel or later, tungsten-cored bullets from a necked-down 13mm case. The Panzerbüchse 38 had a falling block action, weighed 35 pounds and could penetrate 30mm of armor at 100 yards. The PzB 39 simplified the design and had a sliding breech. While it was lighter, the Germans realized the limitations of any antitank rifle, and by 1943 had developed the 8.8cm Raketenpanzerbüchse 43 – known as the Panzerschreck or Tank Terror – from a captured American Bazooka. To protect himself from the blast of this recoilless weapon the firer had to wear a respirator, and the 8.8cm RP 54 of 1944 was instead equipped with a shield to protect the firer's face. It fired a rocket-powered grenade out to 220 yards and could penetrate over 203mm of armor. The RP 54/1 was 3 pounds lighter at 21 pounds and a highly successful weapon.

The Panzerfaust of 1943 provided the individual infantryman at section level with the ability to engage tanks. The original Panzerfaust was the (Klein) 30m – the latter indicating range – and fired a hollow-charge bomb from a simple tube. The infantryman kept his head down until the tank was nearly upon him, then swiftly aimed through flip-up sights and fired the fin-stabilized round. The later Panzerfausts had increased ranges up to 100m and all bore the legend 'Achtung Feuerstrahl' – Beware Flame jet – to remind the firer of the danger of back blast. If the infantryman was composed enough he had an excellent chance of knocking out the tank, since the 3.5-pound charge could penetrate 203mm of armor. The Volkssturm received large numbers of Panzerfausts in 1945.

Italy The Italian army had neither indigenous antitank rifles nor recoilless antitank weapons during World War II. They did, however, receive stocks of the Polish Wz 35 Marosczek 7.92mm antitank rifle which the Germans had captured in 1939. This weapon had itself been inspired by the original German Mauser T Gewehr of 1918 and was of sound design. The Marosczek had a magazine capacity of five rounds of ammunition which was interchangeable with the 7.92mm German antitank round, and the Germans put both rifle and cartridge into service, the former as the PzB 770 (p). The rifle was 70 inches long, had a 47-inch barrel, weighed just under 20 pounds and had a muzzle velocity of 4200fps, which was exceedingly high. Penetration of the

tungsten-cored round was 20mm at 300 yards. The Marosczek was a good weapon and commendably light.

Japan The Japanese had a remarkably ugly as well as impractical antitank rifle in service, the 20mm Type 97. With this caliber it could hardly be called an antitank rifle in the accepted sense of the word, and, moreover, it was fully automatic. The design included a bipod, a monopod to prevent the weapon and firer moving rearward excessively, a shield (often removed), and a pair of handlebar shaped grips to enable its two or four man team to lift the 152-pound weapon. The barrel had the finning beloved of the Japanese, and the Type 97 used a combination of gas and blow-back operation. This may work with acceptable recoil forces with 9mm pistol cartridges, but must have been excruciating with even a low-powered 20mm round. The butt was angular and ugly, and a muzzle brake was fitted; a box magazine held seven rounds. Overall length was 80 inches, of which the barrel represented 47 inches. The 5.7-ounce solid AP shot or HE round could penetrate 30mm of armor at 250 yards. Not surprisingly the gun was not often met, and the increasing thickness of American tank armor reduced its effectiveness.

INFANTRY GUNS

Great Britain During World War II it was considered that the mortar provided sufficient fire support without burdening the infantryman with a lightweight gun. The 2-pounder which had equipped the infantry as an antitank gun was placed in the hands of the Royal Artillery in 1938. Its planned successor, the 6-pounder, did not begin to replace it until three years later because production emphasis was placed upon the 2-pounder. Even then it was not widely issued to the infantry, since antitank defense remained an artillery responsibility. The 6-pounder went to several marks: the Mark 2 was the first production model and it fired a 6-pound AP round out to over 5000 yards at a muzzle velocity of 2670fps. Penetration at 1000 yards was 75mm. The Mark 4 lengthened the barrel and upped the muzzle velocity to over 3000fps. APC, APCBC (ballistic capped) and later, APDS (discarding sabot) rounds were issued which could penetrate 150mm of armor. Although it was not generally issued to them, infantry used the lightweight 6-pounder to good effect. A 95mm Infantry Howitzer was planned in 1942, but a succession of problems arose which led to the gun never being issued, although numbers were completed.

The United States The Americans employed a number of antitank guns of 37mm and 57mm in the hands of their infantry which are covered in the Antitank Gun Section, and the 105mm Howitzer was the only gun purpose-designed for infantry use. This was a combination of shortened 105mm Howitzer barrel and 75mm carriage which reduced overall weight to 2500 pounds, but at the cost of range, since with maximum charges permissible only 7250 yards was attainable. The shell weight was 33 pounds, and its muzzle velocity 1020fps. The M 3 Howitzer was relegated to use with airborne forces from 1943 onward.

Two recoilless rifles were produced, the M 18 and the M 20. The former was based on similar German weapons and had a caliber of 57mm; it was light enough to be fired from the shoulder, but also had a tripod. Overall length was 60 inches and weight 40 pounds; it fired an HE, HEAT (antitank) or canister round to 4400 yards and could penetrate 76mm of armor. Its barrel was rifled, as was the heavier 75mm M 20's. The M 20 had a three-man crew and upped the range to 7000 yards, although its extra weight necessitated the use of a tripod. It entered service early in 1945.

The Soviet Union In 1941 the Soviets had a small 37mm Infantry Gun, the Model 15 R, and a 45mm Infantry Howitzer, the 29 K, both of which were obsolete. They, too, equipped their infantry with antitank guns of 45mm and 57mm calibers. However, heavier infantry guns were also widely used, including the 76.2mm Models 10 P and 1927, which was, like most Soviet equipment, an unpretentious, robust and efficient gun which fired a 14-pound shell out to over 9000 yards. The Model 1927 was a compact weapon served by a five-man crew, and had pneumatic tires and a neat shield. In 1943 the Model 1943 mounted the previous Model's barrel, suitably modified, onto a 45mm antitank gun chassis, and the combination weighed 1320 pounds, a reduction of 400 pounds on the Model 1927's weight. German Intelligence reported a 76.2mm recoilless gun on pedestal mounting for static defense, but this is all that is known about it.

Germany The Germans remained staunch advocates of the concept of providing their own infantry with organic fire support until the end of the war. Their two initial examples were the 7.5cm leichte Infanterie Geschütz 18, introduced in the 1920s, and of which mountain and airborne versions were produced; and the 15cm schwere Infanterie Geschütz 33, which, at over 3700 pounds, was hardly suitable for infantry employment. The le IG 18 weighed only 880 pounds and propelled a 13-pound shell nearly 4000 yards. The sIG 33 fired an 83-pound HE shell over 5000 yards and both saw widespread

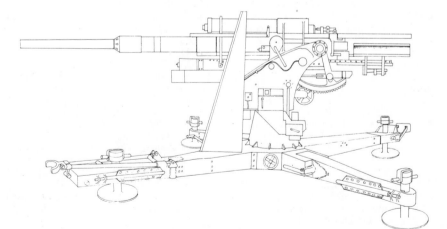

Above: A German 8.8cm antitank/antiaircraft gun.

use. The former was augmented by the IG 42 neuer Art and the IG 37 (of 1944) with longer barrel, muzzle brake and split-trail carriage.

Two recoilless light guns were in Wehrmacht service. The 7.5cm Leicht Geschütz 40 was a wheeled tripod-mounted weapon designed for airborne troops and hence only weighed 320 pounds. It fired a 12.8-pound shell out to 7500 yards and, like all such weapons, had a powerful back blast. The 10.5cm LG 40 and 42 were similar weapons which appeared in 1943 fitted with shields and fired a 32-pound shell to over 8600 yards. The Luftwaffe's parachute troops for whom these weapons were designed never received them in any numbers.

The Germans also placed many light antitank guns in the hands of their infantry, including the 3.7cm PAK 36, 5cm PAK 38, 7.5cm PAK 40 and PAK 41, and 8.8cm PAK 43. Captured Soviet Model 1927 guns were impressed in large numbers as the 7.5cm Infanterie Kanone 290 (r), latterly with German-manufactured ammunition.

Italy The Italians made use of the Cannone da 47/32 Modello 35 as an infantry gun, particularly in the hands of the Alpine divisions, where these weapons could be dismantled and carried in five loads by mule. The Modello 35 was an excellent design, fired a 5.2-pound shell over 4700 yards, and weighed a manageable 610 pounds. Two other older designs equipped the mountain divisions – the Cannone da 70/15, a rudimentary 76mm gun with spoked wheels firing a 10.6-pound shell; and the Cannone da 65/17, another ancient weapon with disproportionately large shield – frequently removed – which fired a 9.3-pound shell. Far and away the best design was the Obice da 75/18 M 34, a neat and useful weapon which could propel a 14-pound shell over 10,400 yards, and weighed 1720 pounds in action.

Japan The 37mm Type 11 Infantry Gun was a lightweight weapon with tripod dating from the early 1920s. It fired a 1.4-pound shell to some 2600 yards and weighed 205 pounds in action. In 1934 the 37mm Type 94 Gun entered service as an antitank weapon; its performance against Allied tanks was so dismal that it was pressed into service as an infantry support weapon, firing HE rounds, where its light weight of 714 pounds was advantageous. Its 1-pound shell carried 5000 yards.

The 70mm Infantry Howitzer Type 92 was ideally suited to operations in close country; its size enabled it to be swiftly brought into position

and its 8.3-pound shell could, if necessary, travel 3000 yards. The gun was light (468 pounds), and had a 24.5-inch barrel and was served by a five-man crew. A 75mm Regimental Gun Type 41 was designed for use by mountain troops and owed its origins to a Krupp design of 1906. It could be broken down into six loads and fired a 12.5-pound HE shell nearly 12,000 yards. In 1934 the Type 94 Pack Gun superseded it and both guns were encountered in use as close-range infantry support weapons, frequently firing over open sights.

Other Nations The original French lightweight infantry gun was the Canon d'Infanterie Modèle 1916 TRP on which the Japanese Type 11 gun was based. It had first seen the light of day during World War I and was really obsolete by 1940; nonetheless it did provide fire support and could propel a 1.2-pound shell to over 2600 yards. It rested upon a steel tripod and, despite its basic appearance, worked well enough. A whole range of mountain guns, mainly of 75mm and 105mm caliber, were captured by the Germans and subsequently used by them, as were some sound designs from the Czech firm of Skoda – mainly 75mm types – and some 7.5cm Norwegian M 11 Howitzers of original German manufacture.

The infantry gun was sometimes purpose built, but frequently co-opted when an antitank gun's performance was overshadowed by increased enemy armor. The prime requirement was lightness and in the quest for this, recoilless guns were designed whose successors are in use today. Many of the guns in service were old designs, but all provided direct fire support when required and augmented the mortar to this end.

MORTARS

Great Britain The mortar provides high-angle fire support for the infantry, and the platoon weapon employed by the British army from 1938 onward was the excellent 2-inch mortar. The first ones were unduly complicated and had base plates and collimating sights – these were soon dispensed with, and a white line helped alignment while a stirrup plate held the tube securely. A two-pound four-ounce HE, Smoke or WP bomb could be fired with a high degree of accuracy to 500 yards from a 21-inch barrel, and the mortar weighed only 10.5 pounds. The British army was lucky to have a mortar at all, since the decision to adopt one based on the 5cm Spanish model was taken with indecent haste. A 14-inch barrelled version appeared for Airborne use.

The 3-inch mortar provided longer-range fire support and was descended from the Stokes mortar of World War I. It consisted of three parts – 51-inch barrel, 37-pound base plate and bipod plus cradle weighing 45 pounds. Its bombs weighed 10 pounds and carried detachable chargers around their fins to alter the range: with four, 1600 yards was obtainable and with six, 2800 yards. The barrel weighed 44 pounds and thus three men could carry the mortar. Up to 80 degrees of elevation was provided, with limited traverse. The Canadians developed an 81-inch barrelled version and the Australians a 30-inch one, which, not surprisingly, lacked accuracy. A 4.2-inch mortar with range of 4100 yards and 20-pound bomb was also available.

The United States The United States Army's first mortar during World War I was the British Stokes, and experience with this led to the evaluation of the French 60mm Brandt weapon in the 1920s. A license-built version, the 60mm M 2, was fitted to an M 2 mount which consisted of base plate and collimator sight. The mortar weighed 43 pounds and sent a 2.9-pound bomb out to nearly 2000 yards from a 28.6-inch barrel. The usual range of bombs was available.

The 81mm Mortar M 1 was, like its smaller counterpart, an American derivative of the 81mm Brandt. Initially a sophisticated type of HE bomb was produced with folding fins which, theoretically, sprang out to stabilize the bomb in flight, but in practice, the explosion in the tube distorted them, and the opposite effect was produced. The improved M 56 bomb weighed 10.6 pounds and its range from the 49.5-inch barrel was 2500 yards. The mortar weighed 136 pounds and could be mounted in a number of self-propelled carriages. A 4.2-inch mortar, as well as 105mm T 13 and 155mm T 25 weapons, were used as heavy support mortars.

Above: An American 60mm mortar and crew during a training exercise.

The Soviet Union While the smallest Soviet mortar was a 37mm weapon which doubled up as a spade, a number of 50mm types provided firepower for the infantry at platoon level. The earliest, the 50mm PM 38, was of interest since it used a variable number of gas ports to regulate the range of the 1.8-pound bomb – a needless sophistication with which the PM 39 dispensed. The PM 40 was a robust weapon which reverted to the gas port system and weighed 20 pounds, its range was 440 yards and, like the PM 38, its barrel could be elevated to 45 degrees or 75 degrees only. The PM 41 dispensed with the previous types' bipod.

The 82mm PM 36 was based on the French Brandt, and the PM 37 introduced recoil springs and the circular base plate which was characteristic of subsequent Soviet mortars. The PM 41 was a wheeled derivative and, like the other types, fired a 7.5-pound bomb to just over 3000 yards.

A 107mm Mountain mortar, the PBHM 38, propelled a 17.5-pound bomb to nearly 7000 yards, but the standard heavy mortar was the 120mm HM 38. This excellent weapon – which was adopted and even produced by the Germans – fired a 35-pound bomb to 6500 yards and weighed 617 pounds. It had twin shock absorbers beneath its barrel. A 160mm mortar, the M 1943, fired a 90-pound shell and was a towed breech loading weapon more akin to a light gun.

Germany Germany began the war with the 5cm Leichter Granatwerfer 36, a neat but over-complex mortar on a baseplate equipped with telescopic sights. It fired a 1.9-pound bomb to 550 yards. The 8cm Schwerer Granatwerfer 34 was an altogether better weapon which replaced the GrW 36. It was well designed and constructed and provided the mainstay of mortars for the German infantry. It weighed 125 pounds and had a range of 2600 yards with 7.7-pound bomb. A short-barrelled version for airborne use, the Stummelwerfer or GrW 42, was also frequently encountered.

Two 10cm Nebelwerfer mortars firing smoke were issued, and the 12cm GrW 42 was a copy of the Soviet HM 38. The Nebelwerfer family provided a highly effective area weapon and the first employed was the 15cm Nebelwerfer 41 with six barrels on wheeled carriage with split trails. Operated by the Nebeltruppen, the six barrels could be fired in 12 seconds and sent 70-pound HE bombs out to over 7200 yards. Heavier weapons including the 15cm Panzerwerfer 42 battery on an Opel Maultier chassis, 21cm and 28/32cm weapons followed and the largest was a

30cm Nebelwerfer firing a 277-pound bomb. The one disadvantage of the Nebelwerfer was the amount of smoke generated on firing which could bring counter-battery fire.

Italy The Italian army's lightest mortar was the 45mm Modello 35 Brixia. This astonishingly complex weapon was magazine fed and employed the system of adjusting the gas port to alter range. The Brixia was manually breech loaded and even provided a seat for its gunner. The 1-pound bomb was sent out to nearly 600 yards, but the explosive charge was a mere couple of ounces.

The 81mm Modello 35 was a Brandt-inspired weapon which weighed 130 pounds and consisted of the usual three loads: barrel, bipod and base plate. It fired a 7.2-pound light bomb out to 4400 yards and also had a heavier one of 15 pounds which went less than half as far. The Brandt design was very sound and the various copies of it, including the Modello 35, performed well, and the smaller Brixia was ultimately worth replacing in Italian service.

Japan The 50mm Mortar Type 89 featured a novel way of adjusting range: the firing pin could be moved up and down the barrel by means of a threaded support rod. The spade-like base plate was misleadingly small and numbers of femurs were shattered when Allied troops took its nickname of Knee Mortar literally. Range was 700 yards and the bomb weighed 1.75 pounds, although ordinary grenades could be fired with unpredictable accuracy. Overall weight was 10 pounds and it was a compact and useful weapon.

The Type 98 was of more orthodox construction but had, for reasons best known to its designers, a fixed elevation of 40 degrees. The bomb was propelled by bagged charges ignited by friction igniters, while a second set initiated an explosive train which detonated the bomb seven seconds after it left the barrel irrespective of where it was along its flight path. It weighed 48 pounds and its 14-pound bomb was effective anywhere out to 400 yards.

The 81mm Type 97 appeared in 1937; another Brandt copy, it was redesignated Type 99 and made more compact in 1939. Overall weight was 52 pounds and it fired a 7-pound bomb out to 2200 yards – a very good mortar indeed. The 90mm Type 94 saw limited use and had a recoil mechanism not normally associated with a mortar where the base plate takes the full recoil.

Other Nations The French issued, in addition to their outstanding 81mm Brandt design, smaller mortars: the Lance Grenades 50mm Modèle 37 was a neat short-range weapon and the 60mm Modèle 1935 which inspired the American M 1 was also available. Numerous other mortars in service with the various Continental armies, Belgian, Czech and Polish types, were impressed into German service. The mortar was an extremely effective weapon in the hands of a well-trained team, and could reach behind high cover and provide almost immediate firepower in situations when conventional artillery was not available – in this respect the Soviets made particularly good use of it. Over short ranges mortars provided devastating firepower, smoke or battlefield illumination, and were very cost-effective weapons.

MINES

Great Britain Mines are a highly effective defensive weapon: they give no warning of their presence and, even when they have been detected, they can be fitted with antihandling or lifting devices designed to kill those who seek to neutralize them. Mines may be divided into two categories, antipersonnel or antitank, and many of the former were designed to maim rather than kill, since troops would be more unsettled by these. Antitank mines required more pressure to explode them – in the region of 350–500 pounds – as opposed to the 10–60 pounds required for an antipersonnel weapon.

The British Mark II Shrapnel mine typified the antipersonnel type; it was exploded when a trip wire was disturbed and had a lethal radius of 30 yards. The Mark V antipersonnel mine was, on the other hand, detonated by a pressure plate and contained seven ounces of HE.

The standard British antitank mine was the Mark V. This weighed 12 pounds, contained eight pounds of HE and was detonated by a pressure fuse with a shear pin. It could immobilize a tank by breaking its tracks, and was capable of being exploded by anyone unfortunate enough to run over it on foot. The mine's diameter was 8 inches and it was 4 inches high. Type C Beach mines were laid in large numbers in both charted and uncharted minefields along Britain's east coast.

A hybrid weapon was the No. 75 Hawkins grenade mine. This weighed 2.25 pounds and was in the shape of a buff-colored canister designed to end up flat when thrown. When laid, pressure on the striker plate crushed the detonator and initiated a chemical train to explode the main charge.

Mines were very frequently employed by all

combatants in North Africa where ease of concealment proved less difficult than in Europe.

The United States The Americans based their M 7 dual-purpose mine upon the British Hawkins, as well as having their own antipersonnel types. One, a bounding mine, was actuated when the unfortunate victim disturbed one of the three unobtrusive prongs of the buried weapon which blasted a grenade some 3 feet into the air, where it exploded with predictable results. The other and less sophisticated type merely exploded where it lay when trodden upon. In terms of antitank mines, they began by using a light steel cylindrical weapon filled with 5.5 pounds of HE which, as experience in North Africa highlighted, was insufficient to counter heavier tanks such as the Tiger. Consequently a heavier mine, the M 1 A 1, was introduced which owed much to the German Tellermine and contained 12 pounds of explosive.

The Soviet Union One of the most interesting ways of countering German armor was attempted in the Soviet Union. The Soviets strapped mines to the backs of dogs, which were then trained to crawl beneath tanks, whereupon a switch connected to an antenna was tripped to fire the mine. Their use was certainly attempted, but the operation was fraught with hazard, particularly if Soviet tanks were in the vicinity. More-orthodox antitank mines were the TM/39, a box-like weapon with a carrying handle weighing 11.2 pounds, of which 7 pounds was TNT explosive. A pressure of between 400–1500 pounds on the lid was sufficient to explode the mine. Another type encountered was the T–IV antitank mine; some of these pressure-operated weapons were wooden cased to render locating them with mine detectors more difficult.

Germany The Germans had a wide variety of mines available during World War II. Their antipersonnel mine was the Schrapnellmine 35, a weapon equipped with pull igniters for use as a booby trap, and a pressure switch too. It weighed 8.8 pounds and contained TNT which blasted out about 350 steel balls inside a cylinder designed to explode about 10 feet above ground level. The Schützenmine 44 was a derivative contained inside a wooden box. This and the Glasmine 43, an all-glass pressure mine, were very difficult to detect using mine detectors. An improvised Schü-mine, the A 200 Topfmine, entered service in 1944, and an Eismine 42 provided a bottle-shaped mine designed for use beneath ice.

The most widely encountered German antitank mine was the Tellermine type. The earliest was the TMi 29; the most widely used until 1943 TMi 35, and thereafter the TMi 42 or 43. All these mines were 12.4 inches in diameter and all had carrying handles. Fillings were 9–12 pounds and varied between TNT and Amatol. Tellermines were frequently laid with antilifting switches concealed beneath them, provision for which was made in their manufacture. A pull igniter was attached to a buried peg so that when the mine was disturbed, it exploded.

Other types of antitank mines were also available. A bar mine, the Riegelmine 43, existed, as did two types of Panzerschnellminen consisting of wooden boxes with pivoting lids. Another type of wooden mine was the Holzmine 42, while the Topfmine had a plastic body and was a very compact mine containing Amatol HE. The Leichte Panzermine was a lightweight mine designed for use by Airborne forces.

The Germans made great use of mines throughout the war, and made strenuous and successful attempts to prevent their being detected by the use of natural or undetectable materials. They also employed captured mines to augment their own plentiful stocks.

Italy The Italian Type B 4 antipersonnel mine contained four ounces of HE inside a canister with metal casing which fragmented to produce splinter effect. It was frequently encountered affixed to a stake and exploded when a trip wire was disturbed. The V 5 was a cylindrical derivative with two striker mechanisms and operated in the same way. A series of 1-pound AP mines was developed with different types of casing: the charge was 5.3 ounces of TNT housed inside a box which could be made out of wood or bakelite. The slightest pressure on the lid of the buried mine was sufficient to detonate it. The mine was under 6 inches long and, because of its casing composition, difficult to detect.

The B 2 antitank mine contained seven pounds of TNT which was housed in a sheet-metal box. The HE was located at each end and, when the center part was depressed, a guillotine cut a wire attached to the striker, whose spring drove it into the cap of the detonator and exploded the charge. The V 3 was a similar but smaller version of the B 2.

The Italians – like the Germans – were adept at booby trapping, particularly in North Africa. The Italian mines, another of which had spikes set into it to enable the weapon to be stuck into a wall or a tree, were widely encountered wired up as 'silent soldiers.' Another Italian weapon was the 4 AR Thermos Bomb which had an antihandling fuse and was also encountered in large numbers.

Japan The Japanese employed three main types of mine. The Model 93 of 1933 was a pressure mine which could be either antipersonnel or antitank. It superficially resembled the German Tellermine and could be adjusted to detonate at any pressure upward of 20 pounds by the insertion of different shear wires to suit the tank. The Model 99 (of 1939) was an antitank mine/grenade which was a flat cylinder containing 1.5 pounds of TNT which could be fixed to its target by means of four magnets located around its rim. It was a small weapon and easily transported by an infantryman who could employ it against Allied armor in the same way as the Germans used the Haft-Hohlladung. The Model 96 mine of 1936 was a mine containing 46 pounds of HE whose overall weight was over 100 pounds. This greatly destructive weapon had land or water application and relied upon the crushing of one of two lead-cased horns to initiate a chemical train which exploded the mine.

LIGHT ARTILLERY

It must be said straight away that the distinction between light and medium artillery is one of function rather than one of caliber or weight. Bearing this in mind the allocation of guns to specific sections, while not being arbitrary, is sometimes one of convenience.

Great Britain Two British guns from World War I may reasonably be included here, the 13-pounder and the 18-pounder field guns. The former, which fired a 12.5-pound shell to nearly 6000 yards, was employed for home-defense duties, but the 18-pounder, suitably updated, equipped the BEF in 1939. The 18-pounder was a sound weapon, firing an 18.5-pound shell over 11,000 yards, and was mounted on a variety of carriages with box and split trails. A certain number of ex-American 75mm guns were employed in beach defense positions, and used 18-pounder ammunition.

The 3.7-inch Pack Howitzer, dating from 1917, was employed as an infantry gun. This fired a 20-pound shell out to 6000 yards and weighed 1669 pounds in action; it equipped the airborne forces in the early days before the 6-pounder replaced it. As befits such a weapon, it was compact, effective and broke down into a number of loads.

As a replacement for the many guns abandon-ed in France in 1940, a 3-inch weapon known as the Smith Gun was swiftly produced. This rudimentary smooth-bore weapon had a two-wheel carriage and, when rolled onto its side, had 360 degrees of traverse, but very limited range. It is, perhaps, fortunate that it was never used against invading Germans.

The United States The 75mm Field Gun M 1917, hastily conceived after the United States entered World War I in 1917, had been modified in the 1930s and remained in service in 1941; although superseded by later designs, it was still in second-line service. The M 1917 fired a 15-pound shell 13,500 yards and, as has been mentioned already, was supplied to Great Britain in 1940. Because of production delays, original French 75mm guns were supplied to the Americans in 1917–18 and the Americans manufactured their own versions of these which received the designation M 1897 A 2. Modernized and mounted on carriages M 2 A 3, some remained in service in 1941 with training units.

The 75mm M 1 A 1 was a Pack Howitzer served by a crew of six and capable of being broken down into six loads. It was a robust and somewhat obsolete weapon on its carriage M 1 with spoked wheels, but on the carriage M 8 with pneumatic tires it provided an excellent close support weapon and was utilized by both American and British airborne forces. It fired a 13.7-pound shell out to 9750 yards.

The Soviet Union Apart from those described under Infantry Guns, the Soviets had two somewhat ancient weapons dating from the 1900s. The earlier was the 76.2mm Field Gun Model 00/02 which weighed nearly 2300 pounds in action and fired a shell weighing 16.4 pounds out to over 9500 yards. The gun saw widespread service in the 1930s but was being phased out by 1941, although it continued in service with several other countries including Rumania and Finland. The Model 02/30 was an attempt to modernize the old 00/02 by rebarrelling and changing propellant and shell on some weapons, but these remained in service alongside the original guns and must have provided a headache for those concerned with ammunition supply. The new shell weighed 14 pounds and had a maximum range with the L/40 barrel of 14,200 yards. The 76.2mm Field Gun Model 1933 was a new gun mounted on an old carriage, provided by the 122mm Field Howitzer Model 10/30. It was a longer-barrelled weapon than its predecessors and paved the way for the Model 1936.

Germany Germany had a wide variety of 7.5cm weapons which served with field, mountain and airborne formations. The leichtes Gebirgsinfanteriegeschütz 18 equipped mountain artillery battalions and provided a light weapon with spoked wheels and split trail until its replacement, the Gebirgsgeschütz 36, appeared in 1938. This weighed 1654 pounds in action and fired a 12.5-pound shell over 10,000 yards; since it could be elevated to 70 degrees it was, technically, a howitzer. It retained spoked wheels, had a muzzle brake, and could be broken down into eight loads.

Field guns of 7.5cm included a number of elderly Krupp designs and perhaps the first attempt at an update was the 7.5cm Feldkanone 16 nA (neuer Art-new type) which mounted a new barrel on the World War I Feldkanone 16 carriage. This weapon was designed to be horse-drawn, and it must be remembered that the Germans – and the Soviets – made widespread use of horses until 1945. The leichte Feldkanone 18 was designed by Krupps to replace it and entered service in 1938. A Feldkanone 38 with folding split trail and muzzle brake was also in service, and another compromise weapon mounted a 7.5cm Pak 40 barrel on a 10.5cm le FH 18/40 carriage to create a dual-purpose field gun known as the 7.5cm Feldkanone 7 M 85. This weighed 3920 pounds and had a range of 11,250 yards.

Italy The oldest Italian light gun was based on the M 06 Krupp design and was known as the Cannone da 75/27 Modello 06. The original carriage had spoked wheels but on some weapons these were replaced by rubber-rimmed steel ones. The 75/27 fired a 14-pound shell to a range of 11,200 yards. The Cannone da 75/27 Modello 11 weighed 4190 pounds (compared to the Modello 06's 2380 pounds) and could be fitted with either type of wheel. The carriage had a split trail and the barrel could be elevated to 65 degrees – like so many similar weapons, the Modello 11 was a gun-howitzer, which is to say that in the field-gun role it was capable of low-angle fire, while at barrel elevations of over 45 degrees it could deliver high-angle fire and reach behind cover. A third type of gun based on the M 06 was the Cannone da 75/27 Modello 12, but this was not produced in any numbers.

Japan The Japanese 75mm Type 94 Pack Gun has already been mentioned, and represented the last type of lightweight gun designed for use by mountain artillery troops, but the Japanese also employed a number of 75mm Field Guns again showing the influence of the Krupp M 06 design. The oldest was the Type 38, a gun which underwent several modifications to its carriage and trail, and formed the backbone of Japanese light/medium artillery during World War II. It fired a 13.2-pound shell to a range of over 13,000 yards and weighed 2500 pounds in action. The 75mm Type 41 Cavalry Gun was in service before 1914 and was used against the Chinese. In an attempt to update the Type 41, a new 75mm gun based on a French Schneider design and known as the Type 95 was introduced in 1935. This field gun had a range of nearly 12,000 yards and weighed 2438 pounds in action. For a weapon adopted in the mid-1930s it appeared rather archaic with its large spoked wheels and spades fitted to its trails.

Other Nations The French had several mountain guns designed by Schneider in service in 1939 dating from the First or interwar period. These included the Canon de 65 M Modèle 1906, the Canon de 75 M Modèle 1919 and the Canon de 75 M Modèle 1928. In addition, the Canon de 76 M Modèle 1909 – the Schneider-Danglis – was provided for use by the Soviet army in 1909. It continued in service with the Soviets and, when captured, received a Wehrmacht designation (as did all captured weapons) and continued in service as long as ammunition stocks remained. The Czech firm of Skoda also built a range of 75mm guns, many of which eventually fell into German hands via their former owners, the Yugoslavs and the Soviets.

The Australians modified the 25-pounder gun-howitzer in 1943 by greatly lightening and shortening it: the 25-pounder Short Mark 1 (Aust) weighed just over 3000 pounds and had a 49.8-inch barrel. The Baby 25-pounder was designed for jungle use and broke down into a number of loads. The reduced barrel length naturally reduced range and increased muzzle blast, but the Baby 25-pounder still had a range of over 10,000 yards and provided a weapon handy enough for use in close country.

MEDIUM ARTILLERY

Great Britain Foremost among British medium field guns was the 25-pounder, which owed its origins to the 18-pounder of World War I and the desire, in the 1920s and 1930s, to improve upon it. The first 25-pounder (Mark 1) was, in fact, a rebarrelled 18-pounder designed to accommodate a 25-pound shell and designated 18/25-pounder. Carriages were produced with both box and split trails, and it was with this gun that the Royal Artillery went to war in 1939. The weapon weighed 3570 pounds and its shell had a range of 12,000 yards.

The Mark II was conceived in the years immediately preceding World War II, but the first examples did not reach the gunners until 1940. It was to prove an excellent weapon. It was versatile, easy to manhandle, and with its humped box trail and circular firing platform which gave it 360-degree traverse, it served throughout the war and for long afterward. Range, with the new barrel with muzzle brake, was 13,400 yards and in action the gun weighed 3968 pounds. It fired a range of ammunition including APC and propaganda shells, and thanks to its trail could be elevated to 40 degrees which really put it in the gun-howitzer class. The Germans employed captured examples as the 8.76cm Feldkanone 280 (e), and over 12,000 were built.

The Vickers 105mm Model 1922 only saw limited service – it was a commercial gun – and is best remembered for its box trail with 360-degree firing platform which was employed on the Mark II 25-pounder.

The United States The most celebrated American medium artillery weapon in service during World War II was the 105mm Howitzer M 2 A 1 which began life in the immediate post-1918 review about what performance and configuration further guns should have. The M 1 Howitzer was modified and became the M 2 in 1934; it fired a 33-pound HE shell to a maximum range of just over 12,200 yards and weighed 4980 pounds in action. It was capable of elevation to 65 degrees and fired a range of ammunition which included the M 1 HE, M 60 Chemical (WP and smoke composition) and HEAT shell which could penetrate 115mm of armor – in all, a well-designed and versatile weapon of which more than 8500 were produced. The M 2 A 1 Howitzer rested on the M 2 A 2 carriage which had split trails and pneumatic tires. The M 3 was a lighter version weighing 2495 pounds which initially equipped Infantry Cannon Companies in the North African theater, but saw subsequent use with airborne forces. Both this and the M 2 Howitzer were mounted on a variety of self-propelled carriages which included the T 19 Howitzer Motor Carriage (on M 3 half-track), the T 32 HMC (on M 3 medium tank chassis, named Priest in British service) and the M 7, B 1 and B 2 HMCs based on the M 4 medium tank.

The Soviet Union The Soviets steadily developed their 76.2mm range of weapons and the last

prewar type to be introduced was the Model 1939. This was a more compact and slightly lightened derivative of the Model 1936, and was a neat weapon which sent a 14-pound shell out to a range of over 14,500 yards, and weighed 5180 pounds in action. It had a split trail, pneumatic tires and was capable of employment in the antitank role firing AP shot. The Germans employed it in this role as the Pak 36 (r) and found it extremely effective with German-made AP 40 ammunition. A hybrid weapon incorporating its barrel was the 76.2mm Field Gun Model 1941/Si S 3, whose carriage was that of the 57mm Model 1941/Si S 3 antitank gun. The range was in the region of 14,200 yards and a muzzle brake was fitted to assist in reducing recoil. The same carriage provided a base for the 76.2mm Tank Gun, fitted as an emergency measure to provide a field gun, in order to offset the massive losses of equipment which the Soviet army suffered.

Another stopgap field gun was the Model 1939/42, which had a lightweight carriage and from which the Model 1942/Si S 3 was developed. This gun's carriage had split trails and weighed 2470 pounds in action; it was a widely used and successful weapon.

Two 85mm Field Guns also saw service; the Model 1943 fired a 20-pound shell out to over 18,000 yards and weighed just over 3700 pounds in action, and the Model 1944 (D-44), despite being a Field Gun, was frequently employed in the antitank role and had a commendably low silhouette. It, too, had split-pole trails and continued in service long after the war.

Germany The 10.5cm leichte Feldhaubitzen 16, 18 and 18/40 provided the mainstay of German medium artillery during the war. The le FH 18 dated from 1935 and was universally employed, both as a field howitzer and mounted on a number of self-propelled carriages. It was an improvement upon its predecessor, the le FH 16, but retained spoked wheels on its split-trail carriage. It fired a 32-pound shell to a maximum range of 11,680 yards and, in action, weighed 4380 pounds. A derivative sported a muzzle brake designed to reduce recoil forces resulting from an increase in propellant in an attempt to increase range, and was designated the 10.5cm le FH 18 M – M standing for Mündungsbremse. Range was duly increased to just under 14,500 yards. The le FH 18/40 came into existence following the loss of many le FH18s in the mud in the Soviet Union – their weight resulted in guns becoming stuck fast and having to be abandoned. The weight reduction to 4310 pounds was negligible, however. The le FH 18/40 mounted a le FH 18 M's barrel on to a 7.5cm Pak 40 antitank gun's carriage with steel spoked wheels and split-pole trails.

Two 10cm schwere Kanonen – the 17/04 and the 18 – saw very limited use and suffered that fate accorded to obsolete pieces: relegation to static coastal gun positions. A derivative of the latter did appear in 1941 as the long-barrelled 10.5cm s K 18/40 and two years later the s K 42 followed it. Both fired a 33-pound shell out to 22,000 yards and in action weighed 12,500 pounds. They – like the British 5.5-inch Gun – were heavy weapons, but for a comparable gun-weight the latter's shell was three times as heavy.

Italy Italy's Ansaldo-designed Cannone da 75/32 Modello 37 was a well-designed field gun which fired a 13.9-pound shell to a maximum range of nearly 13,700 yards. Its carriage had split folding trails and wheels reminiscent of the later German le FH 18/40 type, and a neat square shield. In action the Modello 37 weighed a modest 2646 pounds and its barrel could be elevated to 45 degrees. Such was the inability of the Italian armament industry to gear itself up to produce the quantities of weapons which the army demanded, that sufficient numbers of the Modello 37 were never available, nor, indeed, were adequate numbers of the two howitzers described in the Howitzer section ever supplied.

Japan The French 85mm Modèle 1927 Schneider field gun provided the inspiration for the Japanese 75mm Type 90, a handy weapon featuring either spoked or pneumatic-tired wheels, a split trail and a shield. The Type 90 fired a 13.2-pound shell out to a maximum range of 16,350 yards, and weighed 3085 pounds in action. Its barrel was fitted with a muzzle brake which kept muzzle velocity to 2300fps.

Two rather archaic 105mm field guns also equipped the Japanese army in the 1930s and remained in second-line service during World War II. The Type 38 first saw the light of day in 1905, and fired a shell weighing nearly 40 pounds to a range of some 11,000 yards. At 7086 pounds it was decidedly heavy and could only be elevated to 15 degrees. The Type 14 was built only in limited numbers around 1925 but added nearly 4000 yards to the Type 38's range. It had a split trail with prominent spades and spoked wheels.

In 1932 the Type 92 105mm Gun Howitzer entered Japanese army service. This fired a 34.7-pound shell to 20,000 yards and, in action, weighed 8220 pounds. It was a very sound design

and provided the artillery with a gun light enough to be brought into action swiftly and with sufficient punch over a considerable range.

Other Nations France had several 105mm Schneider-designed guns in service, including the neat Canon Court Modèle 1934–35 and the solid-wheeled Modèle 1935 B, as well as the 105 L Modèle 1936; in German hands they formed part of the West Wall defense system. Czechoslovakian Skoda 100mm and 105mm guns, including the neatly proportioned 105mm Model 35 also equipped the Wehrmacht in some numbers, as did Belgian and Dutch 75mm guns of some obsolescence by 1940.

HEAVY ARTILLERY

Great Britain The 4.5-inch Gun Mark 1 was an interim weapon designed in the 1930s and consisted of a 4.5-inch barrel mounted on a 60-pounder carriage. The 55-pound shell was delivered to a maximum range of 21,000 yards and the gun weighed just under 16,000 pounds. On it was based the 4.5-inch Gun Mark 2, itself a transitional weapon mounted on the carriage which was to appear on the 5.5-inch Mark 3 Gun of 1940. The Mark 2 also incorporated the two distinctive vertical equilibrators and had a split trail. The 5.5-inch Gun fired a much heavier shell weighing 100 pounds and saw much more widespread service than its predecessor. In action it weighed 13,646 pounds, and, firing an 80-pound HE shell, had a maximum range of over 18,000 yards. The 5.5-inch continued in British army service until the 1970s and was a versatile and effective weapon.

Some 60-pounders Mark II saw limited service in the early days of the war, but not in any numbers, as did some 6-inch Mark XIX guns which also dated from World War I. The US 8-inch Gun M 1 also equipped the 4th Super Heavy Battery RA toward the end of the war.

The United States The US Army decided, shortly before World War II, to adopt a 4.7-inch Gun whose caliber, in the event, was reduced to 4.5-inch to enable it to accept British ammunition. The 4.5 Gun M 1, as it was designated, weighed 12,455 pounds and had a split trail. It fired a shell weighing 55 pounds to a maximum range of over 25,000 yards, a respectable enough range, but the explosive content of the shell was meager, which largely offset this advantage. The gun was mounted on the M 1 A 1 carriage.

The 155mm Gun M 1918 M 1 was an American-built version of the French 155mm

GPF gun dating from World War I. Its 94.7-pound shell had a range of 20,100 yards. It had a split-trail carriage and could be swiftly deployed – in all, a thoroughly useful weapon which was also mounted on the T 6 Motor Gun Carriage.

The 8-inch Gun M 1 was introduced in 1942 and was mounted on the 240mm Howitzer M 1 carriage, known as the M 2. Its maximum range of over 35,000 yards suited it to long-range bombardment and counter-battery fire missions, and its 240-pound shell had great destructive effect. The carriage was immensely heavy and was not provided with wheels – the M 1 was brought into action by means of a crane.

The Soviet Union Two 107mm field guns were in service with the Soviet army in 1941, the Model 1910/30r and the Model 1940 M 60. The former was an updated Schneider-carriaged weapon and the latter was designed to replace it. However, production emphasis was placed on still heavier weapons and so not many were produced. Both guns fired a 38-pound shell to a maximum range of around 18,000 yards and had split trails; the Model 1940 M 60 had pneumatic tires.

Two 122mm field guns were also employed. The Model 1931 was fitted with vertical equilibrators similar to the British 5.5-inch Gun and fired a 55-pound shell to a maximum range of nearly 23,000 yards. The Model 1931/37 was mounted on to a 152mm Model 1937 Gun-Howitzer carriage with split trail and spoked wheels and had a similar range; in action it weighed 15,700 pounds. With the designation A-19 S, the gun was fitted to the SU-122 assault gun.

There were 152mm field guns in service too. The Model 1910/30 was really somewhat dated by 1941, since it was based on a Schneider design of before World War I. Nonetheless it was in widespread use and fired a 96-pound shell out to over 18,000 yards, while in action it weighed 14,780 pounds. The 152mm field-gun Model 1935 was mounted on a tractor-type chassis and ran on tracks.

Germany The 12.8cm Kanone 44 was produced in two versions, one of which was built by Krupp on a four-wheeled cruciform carriage and the other by Rheinmetall on a six-wheeled one. The Kanone 44 had 360 degrees of traverse, steeply raked shield and a low silhouette, and was a versatile weapon also suited to antitank work. It fired a 62-pound shell to nearly 27,000 yards and, in action, weighed 22,400 pounds. Not many reached front-line service. A planned heavier

version, the 12.8cm Kanone 81, was mounted on a number of foreign carriages because German production of them was delayed. The Kanone 81 also had antitank application and its performance was similar to that of the Kanone 44.

Various 15cm Kanone types were in Wehrmacht service, the earliest of which was the Kanone 16. Its successor, the Kanone 18 of 1938, provided the mainstay of the German Divisional Artillery and rested on a two-piece platform. Its 96-pound shell had a maximum range approaching 27,000 yards and in action weighed over 28,000 pounds. The Kanone 39 was also employed, with a similar performance.

The 17cm Kanone 18 in Mörserlafette was mounted on the carriage of the 21cm Mörser 18. This gun had a dual recoil system and fired a 138-pound shell to over 32,000 yards. It weighed 38,630 pounds in action and was a thoroughly good weapon – swift to bring into operation and easy to manhandle.

The 21cm Mörser 18 itself had a similar recoil system and was another good design. Its 266-pound shell travelled 18,270 yards and it could accommodate several varieties of ammunition including Stielgranaten (spigot stick grenades) and fin-stabilized Röchling rounds. The last 21cm weapon, the Kanone 38, was an advanced Krupp design of which only seven were completed.

Italy Italy began the war with a 149mm gun, the Cannone da 149/35. This archaic weapon relied upon two ramps set behind the wheels to control its recoil, which resulted in the crew having to re-lay it before firing the next round. Its 101-pound shell had a range of just over 18,000 yards and in action its weight was a similar number of pounds; the Italian Divisional Artillery were indeed ill-equipped with it. A later development, the Cannone da 149/40 Modello 35, was a much better bet but only appeared in small numbers. It rested on a more-orthodox split trail carriage but, at 25,000 pounds, was appreciably heavier.

The heaviest Italian field gun was the Cannone da 152/45, a 152mm conversion of naval gun on wheelless carriage designed for firing from fixed emplacements. It fired a 103-pound shell to 21,000 yards and weighed a mighty 36,760 pounds in action.

Japan In addition to their range of 150mm Howitzers described in the next section, one field gun of the same caliber was in service with the Japanese army at the outbreak of war in 1941. This was the Type 89 Gun, dating from 1929. It had spoked steel wheels and a split trail, and

Above: German sIG 33, 15cm infantry-support gun.

fired a 101-pound shell to a maximum range of 21,800 yards. All things considered it was a dated weapon but all the Japanese had which was suitable for long-range bombardment tasks.

Other Nations The French army had a number of 155mm guns in service, most of which dated from World War I. Many were exported to the Soviet Union, from whence they came into German hands, as did those taken in 1940. Perhaps the best was the Canon de 155 Grand Puissance Filloux (GPF). In 1932 the Canon de 155 L Modèle 1932 Schneider appeared, firing a 110-pound shell to over 30,000 yards and capable of 360-degree traverse when in position. It was a very sound weapon. Czech Skoda guns of 149mm (including the successful K-series weapons of the 1930s) and 152mm were impressed into German service, as were fewer even heavier 210mm weapons. A few Norwegian 12cm Model 1932 heavy guns were also captured.

Most combatant nations still retained their heavy artillery weapons from the previous conflict. The British, Americans and Soviets all introduced new types as did the Germans, but the latter's lighter weapons often proved inferior in range, a tactical disadvantage.

HOWITZERS

Great Britain The 3.7-inch Pack Howitzer originated in World War I and was still in service at the outbreak of World War II, in somewhat modified form with its split-trail carriage fitted with pneumatic tires. The gun was very compact and the length of rifling was just under 36 inches; in action, the Howitzer weighed 1670 pounds and was served by a crew of seven. Its 20-pound shell had a maximum range of 6000 yards and because it could be broken down into light loads, it was adopted for airborne use. The 4.5-inch Howitzer Mark 2 was another World War I weapon in service during the early years of World War II. It was an effective and compact gun which sent a 34.5-pound shell to 6000 yards. In action it weighed just under 3300 pounds and its box-trail carriage was retro-fitted with pneumatic tires.

The 6-inch 26-hundredweight Howitzer served with medium-artillery regiments between the wars. It was an old weapon updated in the same way as the two previous guns and served throughout the war. It fired a 100-pound shell to a range of 11,400 yards and, in action, weighed 9260 pounds. The 7.2-inch Howitzer was a compromise weapon with 8-inch Howitzer barrel sleeved down to 7.2 inches. Such was the force of its recoil that ramps were needed similar to those used with the Italian Cannone da 149/35. Its 202-pound shell was, however, of good destructive effect. In 1944 a Mark 6 7.2-inch barrel was married to an American 155mm 8-inch Howitzer chassis to create a much better weapon.

The 8-inch Howitzer was a massive weapon weighing 20,050 pounds in action which saw little service, as did the elderly 9.2-inch and 12-inch Howitzers which were deployed in static defensive positions along the British coast.

The United States The Americans employed both 75mm and 105mm Gun Howitzers (which have been described elsewhere) on a widespread basis. The 105mm M 2 A 1 Howitzer's M 2 A 2 carriage was, however, modified and the M 3 Howitzer with M 3 A 1 carriage was a short-barrelled derivative whose carriage axles could be turned to allow the gun to fire from a stable platform. Limited elevation proved to be a problem.

The 155mm Howitzer M 1 appeared in 1942. This split-trail carriage weapon proved very successful and it sent a 95-pound shell out to 16,000 yards. In action the M 1 weighed just under 12,000 pounds and the gun was mounted in the T 64 E 1 Howitzer Motor Carriage. The 8-inch Howitzer M 1 was based on the similar British weapon and was mounted on the 155mm Gun M 1's carriage; its 200-pound shell carried over 18,500 yards and the weight in action was 29,700 pounds. It, too, was fitted to an HMC – the T 83.

The 240mm Howitzer M 1 was an excellent heavy weapon which, in action, weighed a massive 64,700 pounds. It propelled a 365-pound shell to over 25,000 yards and, for travelling, was provided with a six-wheeled trailer. It was fitted to the T 92 Howitzer Motor carriage and saw much action in the later war years.

The Soviet Union Like the Americans and the British, the Soviets used a number of dual-purpose weapons which could be employed as field guns or howitzers depending upon the tactical requirement. Nevertheless, they did employ certain howitzers, and the oldest of these was the 122mm Field Howitzer Model 1910/30. This weapon was really obsolete by 1941, featuring as it did spoked wheels and a box carriage, but it was a rugged weapon and fired a 48-pound shell to just under 9800 yards. In action it weighed 3230 pounds. The 122mm Model 1938 was an altogether better howitzer which increased the Model 1910/30's range by over 3000 yards. Its carriage had a split trail and, of course, pneumatic tires which greatly assisted mobility. The Model 1938 equipped heavy artillery units throughout the war and for long afterward. In German hands it received the designation 12.2cm sFH 396 (r).

In addition to the 152mm Gun-Howitzer Model 1910/34 r, the Soviets employed several other older weapons. The Model 09/30 and Model 1910/30 both fired 88-pound shells to a range of 10,800 yards and were short-barrelled and compact weapons. The Model 1938 r was a greatly superior weapon which added 3000

yards to its predecessors' range and weighed 9150 pounds in action. It was augmented by the 152mm Field Howitzer Model 1943 with distinctive muzzle brake which, like the 1938 r, fired a 112-pound shell.

The heaviest Soviet howitzer was the 203mm Model 1931. This existed in six variations, all of which were transported in two loads, and which were mounted on a tracked tractor chassis. Shell weight was 220 pounds and maximum range was in the region of 17,500 yards; in action, the Model 1931 weighed 39,000 pounds.

Germany The German army's field guns could, in most instances, be elevated sufficiently to permit their use as howitzers, but additional – mainly heavy – types were used, the oldest of which was the 15cm schwere Feldhaubitze 13. Most sFH 13s ended their days as part of the West Wall defenses along the French coast. The 15cm sFH 18 was an interwar development, a sound design whose 95-pound shell travelled to 14,600 yards. With boosted charges necessitating a muzzle brake on the barrel, the weapon became the sFH 18 (M) and it was mounted on the Sd Kfz 165 Hummel SP gun. The 15cm sFH 18/40 consisted of an sFH 40 barrel mounted on an sFH 18 carriage, but did not see widespread service.

An interesting heavy weapon capable of being elevated to 70 degrees was the langer 21cm Mörser – a World War I static mortar modified by the fitting of a carriage to render it mobile. In this form it weighed 20,330 pounds in action and hurled a 268-pound shell a range of 12,140 yards.

Italy Two Italian medium howitzers were in service during the war. The Obice da 75/18 Modello 35 was a useful lightweight weapon whose 14-pound shell could be sent to 10,500 yards. It consisted of a 75/18 Modello 34 mountain howitzer barrel on a split-trail carriage with spoked wheels. The Semovente M 40 and M 41 self-propelled guns mounted this barrel. The Obice da 105/14 was likewise not widely used, and its 36-pound shell had a maximum range of just under 9000 yards. In action the 105mm howitzer weighed 3090 pounds.

For heavier howitzers the Italians had the Obice da 149/19 Modellos 37 – 42 and the Obice da 210/22 Modello 35. The former dated from 1938 and three types were available, differing only in minor details – the 37, 41 and 42. The 149/19's shell weighed 94 pounds and travelled 16,740 yards. In action the weapon weighed 1130 pounds. The Obice da 210/22 was a well-designed and highly mobile heavy howitzer which fired a 293-pound shell to a range of 16,850 yards. In action it weighed over 35,000 pounds and the gun was capable of all-round traverse when resting upon its split-trail carriage.

Japan The lightest Japanese howitzer was the 105mm Type 91, a weapon dating from 1929 and showing marked Schneider influence. It had a split-trail carriage and ran on spoked wheels – in all, an unremarkable weapon with a range of 11,780 yards for its 35-pound shell and weighing 3306 pounds. A greater range of heavy howitzers was, however, available for divisional artillery. The earliest was the 150mm Type 38, a Krupp-designed howitzer from before World War I which had been superseded by more up-to-date weapons and was, therefore, only rarely encountered.

The 150mm Type 4 was a more mobile box-trail weapon firing a 79-pound shell out to 10,500 yards, which weighed 6160 pounds in action. In 1936 its planned replacement, the Type 96, appeared but by no means supplanted the Type 4 which continued in service until the end of the war. This Type 96 had a range of just under 13,000 yards and it fired a slightly lighter projectile.

Other Nations A French howitzer of the inter-war period was the Schneider-designed 149mm Obusier Modèle 1929. This was a box-trail weapon firing an 85-pound shell out to 16,400 yards. Another similar but heavier type was the Canon de 155 C Modèle 1917 Schneider which, despite its designation of 'canon,' was effectively an 'obusier' and dubbed as such by those to whom it was voluntarily or involuntarily supplied. Its 96-pound shell had a range of 12,360 yards and, in action, the Modèle 1917 weighed 7280 pounds. Skoda produced howitzers of 149mm, and various heavy types of 210mm which the Germans eventually used, since production continued after the German take-over in 1939. The most widely used was the K 39/40 series which fired a 298-pound shell to 32,800 yards. The German annexation of Czechoslovakia practically doubled their strength in heavy artillery – at a stroke.

ANTITANK GUNS

Great Britain The development of British anti-tank guns epitomizes that of all participants in World War II: a move from lightweight guns firing small-caliber solid-shot AP projectiles, toward sophisticated weapons with ammunition to match as enemy armor thickness steadily increased. Britain began the war with the 2-pounder, introduced in 1938 and designed to fire from its platform which bestowed 360 degrees of traverse, and to be carried by portee vehicles or towed. Its 40mm solid-shot round could penetrate 53mm of armor at 500 yards – sufficient to defeat the early German targets. It weighed 1850 pounds and, as far as it went, was a success until the Desert War proved its obsolescence. There, the 2-pounder was of little use, but better than nothing. Its planned replacement – the 6-pounder – was delayed because production emphasis continued to be placed on the proven 2-pounder, and it did not enter service until 1941. Its 6.2-pound solid shot could penetrate 70mm at 1000 yards and it weighed 2470 pounds. The 6-pounder was eclipsed by the introduction of the German Tiger tank with its 100mm frontal armor and it, in turn, was replaced by the excellent 17-pounder. This entered service in late 1942 and proved to be a splendid antitank weapon; its low silhouette and ability to penetrate 130mm of armor at 1000 yards were major advantages. The first 17-pounders were mounted on 25-pounder carriages but this proved an unsatisfactory arrangement and the Mark 2 improved matters.

All these guns were mounted in various self-propelled carriages: the 6-pounder was mounted in the Deacon and the 17-pounder in the Archer.

The United States The lightest US antitank gun was the 37mm M 3 A 1, a weapon owing much to its German counterpart. It fired a solid-shot projectile weighing just under 2 pounds which could penetrate 25mm of armor at 1000 yards, and an APC one which could defeat 53mm; at 912 pounds it was extremely light – a great virtue provided safety is not endangered by excessive recoil forces, since the lighter the weapon, the easier it is to be brought into action or to change its position. The Americans only just got this fine balance right, and retrofitted muzzle brakes to some weapons to make them more controllable. All too soon its performance was overtaken by increases in German armor thickness, but it remained in service in the Pacific Theater, and over 18,000 were produced. It provided the armament for a host of self-propelled Gun Motor Carriages, including the M 29 C Weasel and jeep carriers.

Its successor was the 57mm M 1, based on the British 6-pounder. Its AP projectile had a muzzle velocity of 2700fps and could penetrate 70mm of armor at 1000 yards. At 2700 pounds it was still light enough to manhandle, but the

Americans sought to improve upon it and the 3-inch Antitank Gun M 5 was the result. This weapon combined elements of several other weapons including the Antiaircraft Gun M 3 and the 105mm Howitzer. It considerably improved the 57mm M 1's performance with 96mm penetration at 1000 yards, but also greatly increased its weight at 5850 pounds. The AP shot weighed 15.4 pounds. Like the 57mm which was fitted on the M 3 Half-Track and the T 49 GMC, the M 5 was carried by several self-propelled carriages including the successful M 10 GMC and a range of T-series ones.

The Soviet Union The Soviets had purchased a number of German 3.7cm Rheinmetall Pak 35/36 antitank guns prewar as the Model 30. These fired solid-shot rounds weighing 1.5 pounds which could penetrate 38mm of armor at 400 yards and weighed a commendably light 952 pounds. The 45mm Model 1932 had a carriage with wire-spoked pneumatic wheels – like the 37mm – and both it and the similar Model 37 fired 3-pound projectiles which could defeat 38mm of armor at 1000 yards. A lighter version for horse traction weighed 992 pounds and one with carriage for vehicle towing 1125 pounds. The 45mm Model 42 increased barrel length and fitted solid wheels, but otherwise did little to improve upon the other 45mm weapons.

The 57mm Model 1941 was mounted upon the 76mm Si S 3 field-gun carriage of the same year. Its 6.8-pound solid shot could penetrate 140mm of armor at 500m, and in 1943 its barrel was mounted upon another field-gun carriage – that of the 76mm Model 42/Si S 3 – to create the Model 1943.

The heaviest Soviet antitank gun was the 100mm Model 1944, a heavy weapon with double-tired carriage and low silhouette whose 34-pound projectile would defeat just under 200mm of armor at 450m. In action it weighed 3.4 tons and it had a muzzle velocity of just under 3000fps.

Germany The lightest German antitank guns were the 2.8cm sPzB 41 and its lighter, airborne version. These squeezebore weapons fired 2.8cm tungsten-cored projectiles which were fired down a tapered bore to emerge at 2cm diameter at 4600fps and could penetrate 56mm of armor at 400 yards. The airborne version weighed a mere 260 pounds. The 3.7cm Pak 35/36 (*Panzerabwehrkanone*) provided the standard antitank weapon in 1939 and continued in service until 1945 with performance enhanced by the use of AP 40 tungsten-cored ammunition. In 1941 the

4.2cm le Pak 41 appeared – this was a scaled-up sPzB 41 Gerlich squeezebore weapon which did not see widespread service. The weapon designed to replace the 37mm Pak 35/36 was the 5cm Pak 38 – an excellent antitank gun which fired an AP 40 projectile weighing just over 2 pounds which could penetrate 86mm of armor at 500 yards. In action the Pak 38 weighed 2174 pounds and was thus both highly mobile and effective. It was augmented in late 1941 by the 7.5cm Pak 40, another first-class design with performance to match; with AP 40 shot weighing 7 pounds it could defeat 115mm of armor at 500 yards and only weighed 3300 pounds. Its Gerlich equivalent was the 7.5cm Pak 41 whose service life was limited by the increasing shortage of tungsten ammunition.

The heaviest antitank guns were 8.8cm weapons. The Pak 43 rested on a cruciform platform and was a superlative gun developed from the antiaircraft weapon. With 16-pound AP shot it could penetrate 226mm – nearly 9 inches – of armor at 500 yards and could thus defeat the heaviest Allied tanks. The Pak 43/41 version was based on it and had a split-trail carriage. The '88,' in this and earlier forms, gained a fearsome reputation among British and American tank crew. Although it was a very fine weapon, many of the successes attributed to it were in fact achieved, through adept tactics, by other weapons in the German armory.

Italy Italy produced no indigenous types of antitank gun during World War II. The Cannone contracarro da 37/45 was a license-produced version of the German Rheinmetall-Borsig Pak 35/36. This 37mm weapon was employed in North Africa both in the conventional and the portee role – in this case the light gun is mounted on the back of a truck which is then indistinguishable from other ordinary vehicles and can thus provide mobility and surprise.

The Cannone da 47/32 M 35 was a license-built version of the Austrian 4.7cm Böhler antitank gun of 1935. This had the disadvantage of being produced without a shield for its crew, who must have felt somewhat exposed when facing an Allied tank attack, even if conventional shields only provided scant protection. The gun fired an AP shot projectile weighing 3.2 pounds which could penetrate 43mm of armor at 550 yards.

Japan The Japanese began the war with two 37mm antitank guns, one purpose-built and one a field gun employed in the antitank role. The former was the 37mm Type 97, which was the

German Pak 35/36 license-built in Japan. The latter was the 37mm Gun Type 94, which fired a 1.5-pound AP projectile capable of penetrating 24mm of armor at 1000 yards, a mediocre performance but, *faute de mieux*, at least something. The 47mm Type 1 appeared in 1941 and was a conventional weapon of low silhouette firing a 3-pound AP shell which could defeat 50mm of armor at 500 yards. At 1660 pounds it was a useful weight to manhandle in difficult terrain.

Other Nations France's lightweight antitank gun in 1939 was the Canon Leger de 25 antichar SA-L Modèle 1934. Its 25mm projectile was inefficient even by interwar standards, and it proved of little use; neither did its successor of 1937 improve things. The Canon de 47 antichar SA Modèle 1937 was an altogether better gun which fired a 3.8-pound shell. Although it did not achieve much before France capitulated in 1940, the Germans appreciated the weapon's potential and mounted it on a number of self-propelled antitank carriages.

Czechoslovakian Skoda-produced guns of 37mm (M 37) and 47mm (M 36) were pressed into German service and the former continued to be of use when firing the Stielgranate 41 spigot grenade. The 47mm M 36 fired a 3.6-pound shell capable of penetrating 51mm of armor at 700 yards, a respectable performance for a prewar gun, and respectable enough for the Germans to make use of it in the field, in static defenses, and on self-propelled carriages.

Other antitank guns in service in 1939 were the Belgian Canon de 47 antichar SA-FRC, used more in German than in Belgian hands, and the neat little Swedish 3.7cm Bofors which saw service with both British (in North Africa) and German formations.

ANTIAIRCRAFT GUNS

Great Britain Britain, like most other participants in World War II, began it equipped with some antiaircraft guns developed from World War I weapons. Several 20mm guns had been added to the inventory, including the Polsten and Hispano-Suiza on light mountings which were effective up to some 6500 feet, but much more widely issued was the 40mm Bofors of Swedish descent. This was a versatile and well-designed weapon used by just about all combatant nations during the war, and which fired a 1.96-pound shell to an effective ceiling of 23,500 feet. The Bofors was highly mobile and weighed 5420 pounds. Vickers also produced

40mm (2-pounder) guns, as well as a 75mm commercial venture.

Among the medium guns were the 3-inch 20 hundredweight – which fired a 16-pound shell to 23,500 feet – and the 3.7-inch which began to enter service in 1938. This was a useful weapon which added nearly 10,000 feet to the 3-inch gun's ceiling and fired a 28.5-pound shell. It was equipped with a mobile mounting, but was more frequently emplaced in static positions. The 3.7-inch Mark VI was a 4.5-inch naval gun lined down to the smaller caliber and capable of engaging targets up to some 55,000 feet – and highly effective it was. Both the 4.5-inch and the 5.25-inch guns were naval weapons employed in static positions as heavy antiaircraft guns with effective ceiling of 42,500 and 55,500 feet and shell weight of 54.5 and 80 pounds respectively.

The United States The lightest and simplest US antiaircraft weapon was a quadruple mounting of .50-caliber Browning M 2 machine guns on a wheeled trailer, which was highly mobile and laid down a heavy weight of fire against low-flying enemy aircraft. The lightest single-barrel weapon was the 37mm M 1 A 2 on a wheeled platform carriage which was effective up to 18,500 feet, to which height it sent a 1.3-pound shell. The 37mm combined with two .50-caliber M 2s to create the Combination Mount M 54.

The US medium antiaircraft weapons were the 3-inch M 3 with performance similar to the British 3-inch, although the shell was lighter, and the 90mm M 1, M 1 A 1 and M 2. These fired 23.4-pound shells to just under 40,000 feet and had a variety of mounts both mobile and static, and the M2 Mount enabled the M 2 Gun to be used as a dual-purpose weapon.

The 105mm M 1 was only produced in small numbers. Its 33-pound shell was effective up to 42,000 feet but in service it was replaced, after 1940, by the 120mm Gun M 1. These were not employed outside the United States and the United Kingdom. Their 50-pound shells had an effective ceiling of 56,000 feet and with their four-wheeled carriage with folding platform they were mobile weapons.

The Soviet Union The smallest Soviet antiaircraft guns were three types of 25mm (Models 1939–41) which were based on a similar Bofors weapon and were effective to a ceiling of some 15,000 feet. Another Bofors-inspired weapon was the 37mm Model 1939, which was fed by five round clips – as opposed to the four round ones of the Bofors – and proved a mobile and successful gun.

Medium antiaircraft guns existed in 76.2mm and 85mm calibers. The 76.2mm Model 1931 was a light and easily transportable gun which fired a 14.5-pound shell to an effective ceiling of just over 30,000 feet. It weighed 10,600 pounds travelling and shed its wheels when set up on its platform. The Germans used it as the 7.62cm Flak M 31 (r). In 1938 an updated weapon appeared, the Model 1938, which incorporated a modified and lightened carriage. The 85mm Model 1939 was a very sound design which fired a 20.2-pound shell to nearly 35,000 feet. It was fitted to the SU-85 assault gun carriage. Like some captured 76.2mm weapons, it was rebored by the Germans to fire the 8.8cm round. In 1944 the 85mm Model of that year incorporated modifications to the recoil mechanism.

For heavy antiaircraft artillery the Soviets employed the 105mm Model 1934 which had an effective ceiling of over 42,500 feet and sent a 33-pound shell to that height.

Germany The Germans devoted much energy to the development of highly effective anti-aircraft guns throughout the range of calibers. The lightest 2cm weapons included the Flak (*Fliegerabwehrkanone*) 30, a gun with a five-man crew and wheeled carriage; the Flak 38 – which increased the Flak 30's rate of fire of 120rpm by 100 and was a Mauser-designed gun; the 2cm Gebirgsflak 38, a pack weapon for mountain troops; and the 2cm Flakvierling 38, the most effective light weapon with a rate of fire of some 900rpm from its quadruple barrels. All had a ceiling of 6500 feet and posed a formidable threat to low-flying aircraft, particularly when fitted with the later generation of sights.

The 3.7cm weapons included the Flak 18. 36 and 37, the last two of which saw widespread use as medium weapons with an effective ceiling of 11,500 feet and shell weight of 1.4 pounds. The Flak 43 was fitted with a new breech mechanism which doubled the other guns' rate of fire to 160rpm. It was considerably lighter and more mobile, and a Flakzwilling two-barrelled type was derived from it. There were also 5cm and 7.5cm guns but they did not see widespread service.

A series of excellent 8.8cm weapons – which doubled as antitank guns – were in Wehrmacht use during the war. The Flak 18, 36 and 37 all fired a 20.3-pound shell to an effective ceiling of over 26,000 feet and were highly mobile weapons mostly with 10-man crews. The Flak 41 only existed in small numbers but was a sophisticated gun with an excellent performance and ceiling of over 49,000 feet.

To engage high-altitude targets the Germans used the 10.5cm Flak 38 and 39 and the 12.8cm Flak 40 guns. The former had a ceiling of 42,000 feet and fired a 33-pound shell, while the latter – and its twin-barrelled Flakzwilling 40 counter-part – fired a 57.3-pound shell to 48,500 feet and, like all types, was frequently installed in Flak towers and on railroad mountings.

Italy The lightest Italian AA guns were 20mm weapons designed by Breda (the Cannone-Mitragliera da 20/65 Modello 35) and Scotti (da 20/77). Both were light and maneuverable guns with effective ceiling of 8000 feet. The Cannone-Mitragliera da 37/54 Modello 39 was a Breda weapon which fired a 1.75-pound shell to 13,500 feet and, like some Scotti versions, was clip-fed. At 70rpm its rate of fire was half that of the lighter guns.

Various 75mm Cannone CA weapons were in Italian service: the 75/27 and 75/46 Modello 34 were prewar guns firing 14.3-pound shells to over 27,000 feet. The 76.2mm Cannone da 76/40 CA added to the medium-gun inventory. The Cannone da 90/53 entered service in 1939 and proved to be an outstanding weapon. Designed by Ansaldo, the gun was encountered in static and coastal emplacements, on mobile mounts and doubled up as an antitank weapon. It fired a 22.7-pound shell to just over 39,000 feet.

The heaviest guns were 102mm weapons, the Cannone da 102/35 and 102/47 Modello 29, which fired 25-pound shells to over 30,000 feet and provided heavy antiaircraft defense.

Japan Japan had 20mm and 25mm AA weapons – the lightweight Type 98 with two-wheeled carriage and the statically mounted Type 96 naval adaption. The former was a versatile and particularly effective weapon fed by 20-round box magazines and a rate of fire of 120rpm.

Medium Japanese antiaircraft guns included the 75mm Type 88 and the 8cm High Angle Gun Type 3, whose caliber was really 76.2mm. Of the two, the former was the better weapon and fired a 14.5-pound shell to an effective ceiling of nearly 24,000 feet.

Among heavier artillery the 105mm Type 14 was an army gun which had an effective ceiling of over 30,000 feet for its 35-pound shell. Several naval guns – adapted for ground use – were employed in static emplacements. The 100mm Type 98 was a two-barrelled mounting and the 120mm Type 10 had a single barrel and fired a 45-pound shell. The 127mm Type 89 was another two-barrelled naval gun which provided a dual-purpose weapon when installed in a static location. In the antiaircraft role it propelled a 50-pound shell to 25,000 feet.

Other Nations The best French medium AA gun was the 75mm Canon de DCA Modèle 1936. This, like others and many Belgian and Czech guns, was pressed into German service but two weapons, the Swiss 20mm Oerlikon and the Swedish 40mm Bofors, deserve special mention since both were highly effective weapons and saw considerable use in the hands of gunners of almost all armies engaged in the conflict, whether as license built or captured equipment.

COASTAL AND RAILWAY GUNS

Great Britain A number of Coastal Guns dating from World War I were augmented in 1940 by many different types of weapon hastily set up to defend the British Isles. There had been, however, a deployment of such weapons in the Far East and the Mediterranean; Malta, for instance, had twin six-pounder Coast Guns with a maximum range of over 5000 yards. Around Britain many naval guns were emplaced of 12-pounder, 4.7-inch, 6-inch and 8-inch types, while with 9.2-inch and 13.5-inch guns, two 14-inch guns – dubbed Winnie and Pooh – were operated by the Royal Marines at Dover; and *King George V* Class battleship weapons were used to bombard German gun positions in France. The heaviest guns were two 15-inch weapons also located at Dover. Countless intermediate caliber ex-naval guns were emplaced around Great Britain in the Emergency Batteries. Maunsell Forts in the Thames and Mersey Estuaries provided AA defense.

Little British interest was shown in railway guns, because the few that were developed were eclipsed by the power of aerial bombardment and played a very minor role in the war. Examples included the 9.2-inch Railway Gun, the 12-inch Railway Howitzer and the 13.5-inch Gun and 18-inch Howitzer, all of which saw service in Kent, and the penultimate of which could send a 1250-pound shell 40,000 yards – which took it across the Channel. The weapons were unwieldy and cumbersome and, frankly, did not contribute greatly to the prosecution of the war.

The United States The US forces likewise possessed a range of coastal artillery guns and howitzers, the smallest of which was the 3-inch Seacoast Gun. This, like other and heavier weapons, was emplaced in the Philippines, Corregidor and Manila as well as on the Atlantic and Pacific seaboards of the USA. The 6-inch, 8-inch and 10-inch guns were backed up by heavy weapons such as the M 1890 Seacoast Mortar which fired a 1046-pound shell out to over 12,000 yards. The heaviest weapons were the 12-, 14- and 16-inch Seacoast Guns on turret mountings or Barbette or Disappearing Carriages. They hurled a 2240-pound shell a distance of 45,100 yards. The heaviest howitzer, the 16-inch, fired a slightly lighter shell to 24,500 yards and was Barbette mounted in its emplacement.

The Americans, like the British, did not set much store by railway guns although they, too, retained some from World War I of 8-inch, 12-inch and 14-inch caliber. The 12-inch railway howitzer was the M 1890 Howitzer mounted upon a railroad flat car, and the M 1920 14-inch Railway Gun was used in the Panama Canal Zone. The Americans made little use of any of these weapons which had been designed to act as mobile coastal defense guns.

The Soviet Union The most famous Soviet battery of coastal defense guns was the 20.3cm L/45 Maxim Gorki Battery which was located on the Black Sea coast near Sevastopol and battered into submission by the Germans in 1942. Little is known about other Soviet coastal-defense weapons – it is reasonable to assume that, as in other nations, naval guns on land service mountings were used. It was likewise in the case of Soviet railway guns; armored trains were certainly in service, mounting a variety of guns and point defense weapons, and it is possible that heavier weapons specifically mounted on railroad carriages existed as well.

Germany Coastal Artillery defense was a Kriegsmarine responsibility during World War II, although manpower shortages led to the army providing crews for the many weapons emplaced along the West Wall and Baltic coasts. As in Britain and the United States, many German coastal guns were ancient weapons, but Germany added enormous numbers of captured field guns to the Atlantic coast defenses to augment the larger and heavier ex-naval weapons. A host of weapons of German origin including 5, 7.5, 8.8, 10.5, 12.8, 14, 15, 17, 24, 28, 30.5 and 40.6cm types were mounted on or in a great variety of mountings and emplacements, including naval turrets and, of course, reinforced armored bunkers and casements, many of which survive to this day. Many batteries carried names, and the Batterie Todt on the Channel coast which fired at Dover had four

38cm SK C/34 guns with reinforced-concrete overhead protection. These guns had originally been intended for the later *Bismarck* Class battleships which were never completed.

The German Eisenbahnartillerie employed a great variety and number of railway guns during the war, the first of which were Krupp-produced weapons under the Sofort-programm of 1936. These weapons were the 15cm and 17cm Kanonen (E), the 24cm Theodor Bruno and Theodor Kanonen and the 28cm kurze Bruno and large Bruno Kanonen – none of which were produced in any numbers. Newer weapons followed, including the very successful 215-ton 28cm Kanone 5 (E) which fired both orthodox and 560-pound rocket-assisted projectiles – the range of the former was 39 miles and of the latter 53. This weapon was employed with devastating effect at Anzio in 1944. In an effort to improve the performance a 31cm fin-stabilized projectile-firing version was developed to propel the Peenemünder Pfeilgeschosse (Arrow Projectile) an astonishing 93 miles. Some 25 K5 (E) guns were built before 1945, but many other types were also in service. In addition to various heavy Haubitze weapons, the heaviest guns included 38cm and one 80cm Kanone (E) known as Gustav or Dora which ran on two sets of railroad lines and saw service in the Crimea. It fired a seven-ton concrete-piercing shell and was used with devastating effect for bombardment along the Black Sea coast. The Germans were certainly the major exponents of railway guns and used them to good effect to back up coastal artillery weapons, although accuracy at range was never their strong point.

Italy Italian heavy guns employed in static defensive positions have already been covered, but one remains which was encountered in Italy and has not been described. This was the Mortaio da 218/8 D.S. – a siege mortar dating from World War I which sent a 224-pound shell to a maximum range of just over 9200 yards.

While the Italians did not have any railway guns, as far as can be ascertained, they did provide the Germans with some Ansaldo-built armored trains armed with 47mm guns and machine guns which entered service in 1944.

Japan The Japanese Home Islands were well defended by a number of ex-naval guns of 25, 30 and 41cm caliber which, in the event, took no part in the eventual defense of Japan. These were installed in lavishly equipped and well-designed emplacements; many of the bunkers in which guns were sited on countless Pacific islands showed a high degree of sophistication and skill in concealment, and these were to prove formidable obstacles to the Americans.

Other Nations France had some railway guns in service in 1939, the lightest of which fired a 24cm and the heaviest a 52cm shell. When the Germans occupied France in 1940 they utilized these weapons until ammunition supply was expended. The French had pioneered railway guns and among their more successful designs which still remained in service was the 9.2-inch weapon.

Whereas most nations had a variety of mostly obsolescent coastal defense guns at their disposal, it is interesting to note how only the land-orientated Continental powers concentrated on railway guns to any real extent, and then went on to employ them in support of the coastal-defense guns. The main problems with them were their very size and consequent lack of mobility, and the difficulty of stabilizing them. This was solved by allowing recoil to be absorbed by the carriage mount which rolled rearward; by sliding mounts, or by outriggers in which jacks bore the brunt of the recoil and the wheels were lifted clear of the tracks.

SHELLS

It is worth considering the various types of ammunition which were available to fulfill the various specialist requirements of the artillery, and of many of which mention has already been made.

The British 25-pounder Gun Howitzer used a representative selection of ammunition. It fired a 25-pound shell with range adjustment provided by the number of the propelling charges. Normal charges 1–3 consisted of three bags of propellant with different amounts of propellant to alter range; Super Charge provided increased range. All these varieties were contained in a brass cartridge case. The separate shells themselves were HE (of various types), HE with tracer element, Smoke (with white phosphorus and base ejection), Colored Smoke, Chemical (designed for gas but never employed), Target Recognition, Incendiary, Star-Shell and Propaganda. Armor Piercing (AP) and Armor Piercing Capped (APC) were also available for anti-tank use, and Percussion, Time and Proximity Fuzes could be fitted.

Many guns in use throughout the war – mainly of older design or smaller caliber – used fixed ammunition. The disadvantage of this system was that range could not be adjusted since the propellant remained firmly enclosed inside the shell case, and the shell itself could not be removed.

Antitank guns employed a variety of ammunition, the earliest type of which was the Solid Shot projectile (AP Shot) designed to be fired at high velocity and able to simply punch through thin armor. The AP Shell contained a relatively small explosive charge and a base fuze designed to explode the shell once it had penetrated. AP Shell had a tendency to disintegrate on striking reinforced armor plate, and APC (Armor Piercing Capped) went some way toward solving this problem by the fitting of a hardened cap, while a ballistic cap shaped version (APCBC) improved streamlining.

As the war progressed, armor thickness increased and the Germans came up with the tapered-bore antitank gun named after one of the idea's developers, Gerlich. The theory behind the Gerlich principle was as follows: a shot projectile was squeezed as it progressed down a tapered bore to emerge from the muzzle at an extremely high velocity and reduced in diameter. Acceleration was dramatic and the German APCR (Armor Piercing Composite Rigid) round encapsulated a tungsten core within a softer outer casing. A device fitted at the muzzle of the British 2-pounder and the US 37mm antitank guns which served to squeeze the skirted projectile as it emerged was known as the Littlejohn adaptor. The British APDS round (Armor Piercing Discarding Sabot) employed a solid core within a sabot which disintegrated at the muzzle to allow the core to continue toward its target at very high velocity – in the case of the 17-pounder antitank gun, at 3950fps.

The High Explosive AntiTank Shell was a hollow charge projectile fired at low velocity which employed a concave nose cone with explosive enclosed within a ballistic case which, on detonation, was focused into a jet of gas and molten metal with a velocity of some 25,000fps which simply bored its way through any known tank armor. This principle was employed on the Bazooka and the German Panzerfaust. Since the effect of a HEAT round depended on its explosive charge, it was unnecessary to fire it at a high velocity. Low-powered rocket launchers like the Bazooka were, therefore, more than adequate. A further antiarmor round was the HEP (High Explosive Plastic) or, in the more descriptive British designation, HESH (High Explosive Squash Head). This shell employed a bagged HE charge whose case gave way, on striking the target, to allow the explosive to squash outward and be detonated by a base fuze. At this point a scab broke away inside the vehicle. The first use of HESH was in the Wallbuster shell.

In the early days of the war antiaircraft fire was more of a morale booster than a deterrent; but with the advent of increasingly efficient predictors and the VT (Proximity) fuse matters changed considerably. The latter relied upon the completing of an electrical circuit to detonate the shell when its own emitted radio waves responded to any object in its lethal area. The first ones were used in the Pacific in 1943 and later proved of great use against Kamikazes and during the V-1 Flying Bomb attacks on England. When employed in the ground role they could provide air-bursts above the heads of enemy infantry.

ROCKETS

Great Britain To provide cheap if only moderately effective barrages of antiaircraft fire the British employed several types of unguided rockets including 2-inch and 3-inch types. The latter was far more widely used and carried a 4.3-pound HE warhead to a ceiling of 22,000 feet – the unrotated rocket was fin-stabilized and launched from various projectors to accommodate up to 20 rockets. The artillery also employed 3-inch rocket launchers known as Land Mattress equipments which provided 30 barrels on a trailer and could saturate an area several hundred yards square at 6000 yards. Another weapon, designed for taking out Japanese bunkers, was the 3-inch LILO rocket capable of accepting warheads of different weights to suit the task needing to be tackled.

The United States After a slow start, rockets were produced for the US forces in vast numbers. The standard type was the 4.5-inch HE Rocket M8, which carried 4.3 pounds of HE to a range of 4600 yards and weighed 38.5 pounds. These rockets were fired from a wide variety of launchers mounted on trucks, tanks and DUKW's. The M16 was a more accurate spin-stabilized rocket with enhanced range and a heavier type, the T37 7.2-inch rocket, was introduced for demolishing hard targets at close range. One launcher for these rockets was the M17, a box of 20 tubes fitted on top of the turret of an M4 Sherman tank.

The Soviet Union The Soviet army employed a number of different caliber fin-stabilized rockets to good effect during World War II. The M-8 launcher carried 36 82mm rockets and could be fitted to the back of a truck. The rockets and their launchers – known as Katyushas – provided an effective and cheap area weapon and each rocket carried 6.7 pounds of HE to a range of over 6000 yards. The 132mm rocket had a 40-pound warhead and range of over 9200 yards, and was frequently launched from the 16-rail M-13 launcher. Heavier types included 300mm and 310mm rockets launched from M-30 racks, ground-mounted and holding four rockets. The rocket launcher was much favored by the Soviets who – like the West Germans – continue to employ it to this day.

Germany The Germans had a considerable number of rockets in wartime service. Early 7.3cm types included the Propagandagranate 41 (which distributed leaflets) and the Sprenggranate with more hostile antiaircraft intent. The 8cm spin-stabilized rockets launched from Raketen-Vielfachwerfer multiple launchers saw limited use pending the introduction of heavier types such as the 15cm Wurfgranate 41. This was used in the Nebelwerfer, and Panzerwerfer 42 10-barrelled launcher on the Sd Kfz 4/1 Maultier or Schwerer Wehrmacht Schlepper self-propelled carriages. The Wurfgranate 41 carried 5.5 pounds of HE and could be propelled over 7700 yards.

The 21cm Wurfgranaten 42 carried 22.4 pounds of HE and were spin-stabilized; in flight the rocket motor vented through a number of venturi to impart the spin, as in the case of the 41. Heavier rockets included 28, 30, 32 and 38cm Sprenggranaten and among their launchers was the Schwerer Wurfrahmen 40 fit for the Sd Kfz 251 half-track. Various frames both mobile and static were also employed. The Germans found these heavier types of rocket invaluable for fighting in built up areas and made much use of them in the Soviet Union. Their 32cm M Fl 50 was an incendiary bomb and the 38cm Sprenggranate 4581 delivered 270 pounds of HE to over 6000 yards – a powerful punch which could be launched from the Raketenwerfer 61 Sturmtiger based on the Tiger tank chassis.

Italy The Italians employed no indigenous rocket equipment during the war.

Japan The Japanese had a 20cm army rocket weighing some 200 pounds (of which 35 was HE) which, when thrown from a Type 4 launcher which strongly resembled a conventional mortar, had a range of around 3000 yards. The navy also employed a 20cm rocket which was often launched from rudimentary rails and frequently employed for beach defense in the Pacific Theater. A more sophisticated wheeled tube launcher also existed. A 45cm rocket was also encountered which carried nearly 400 pounds of HE out to 2000 yards when launched from a simple wooden trough.

A rather ad hoc device was a rocket motor attached to standard aerial bombs which propelled the combination along a launcher resembling a length of gutter with a bipod. The same idea was tried with heavier bombs, too. While they might have lacked sophistication, these weapons nevertheless posed a threat when used in conjunction with others in the defensive systems the Japanese so skillfully employed in the Pacific islands.

LIGHT TANKS

Great Britain The British army began World War II with a number of light reconnaissance tanks dating from Vickers designs of the 1920s. Various Marks existed. The earliest Mark II was steadily developed until the last mark, the VI, which had a variety of light gun armament. The Mark VI B had machine guns installed and the VI C had a 15mm Besa with co-axial 7.92mm machine gun. The vehicles weighed 5.2 tons and had a crew of three; armor thickness was up to 14mm and the tanks were capable of a maximum speed of 25mph from a Meadows engine which developed 88hp. The length was just under 13 feet. These light tanks were already outclassed in the early campaigns of the war but saw service in the desert until 1942.

The Mark VII Light Tank known as the Tetrarch was designed in 1937 and dispensed with the Horstmann coil-spring suspension of the earlier marks. It featured instead four road wheels incorporating the suspension and weighed 7.5 tons. Its Meadows engine developed 165hp and gave a top speed of 40mph, and armament consisted of a 2-pounder with 7.92mm Besa machine gun. The Tetrarch first went into action in 1942 in Madagascar and was adopted by the airborne forces. The Hamilcar glider was designed to accommodate it and it saw limited action.

The Mark 1 Infantry Tank Matilda 1 was designed for infantry support tasks and provided with a .303-inch machine gun mounted in a turret. Powered by a Ford V-8 engine developing 70hp, small numbers of Matilda 1s saw service with the BEF in France in 1940, but remained there after Dunkirk. They weighed 11 tons, had a two-man crew, and paved the way for the heavier and better known Matilda II series.

The United States The Americans had a range of light tanks in service, the earliest of which was the M2A4. This 11-ton tank had a four-man crew and was powered by a 250hp Continental W-670 engine which gave it a maximum speed of 25mph. The main armament of 37mm gun was augmented by no less than five .30-caliber Browning machine guns. The M3 was basically an uparmored version and, as the Stuart or Honey, went into battle with the British army in North Africa. Armor thickness doubled the M2A4's and was 51mm. Weight was increased to 13.4 tons and a succession of improvements, mainly to turret design and gun stabilization, were made. In 1941 the M3A1 appeared with alterations to fighting-compartment layout and the M3A3 of 1942 featured additional improvements. Length was slightly increased to 16 feet 6 inches, and secondary armament reduced to two machine guns.

The M5 had welded-plate hull armor and was powered by two Cadillac V-8 engines developing 220hp. Maximum armor thickness was 67mm and weight was 16.2 tons. The M5A1 was the final modified version with more spacious turret, and was introduced in late 1942.

The M22 Light Tank – Locust – was adopted in 1943 to provide an air-portable tank which could also be carried in Hamilcar gliders. The M22 had a three-man crew, weighed eight tons and was powered by a 162hp Lycoming 0-435T engine which gave it a road speed of 40mph. Attempts to reduce overall weight included reducing maximum armor thickness to 25mm, and the armament to one 37mm gun with single .30-caliber machine gun. M22s were used in the crossing of the Rhine in 1945 by the British.

The M24 Chaffee carried a 75mm gun with pintle-mounted .50-caliber and three .30-caliber machine guns. Two Cadillac V-8 engines provided a top speed of 35mph and a power-operated turret was fitted. The M24 weighed 19 tons and had torsion-bar suspension; it was a highly mobile tank and represented a considerable advance on earlier types when introduced in 1944.

The Soviet Union The Soviet army employed a wide variety of light tanks. The T-26 series was based upon a British six-ton Vickers design and included a radio-fitted command tank and versions with twin turrets. Armament varied but a 37mm or 45mm gun was carried. Weight was around eight to nine tons and it had a three-man crew. A 91hp engine provided a road speed of some 30mph and armor thickness was up to 25mm. Over 12,000 were produced.

The Soviets introduced the first of a series of amphibious tanks in 1933. This was the T-87, which weighed three tons and was powered by a 40hp engine. Armament for the two-man crew was a single 7.62mm machine gun, and their maximum armor protection was 9mm. The T-88 of 1938 was a lowered and improved design and was succeeded in 1941 by the T-40. This weighed 5.5 tons and had a 85hp engine. Main armament consisted of a 12.7mm D Sh K machine gun or 20mm Sh VAK cannon and the T-40 had independent torsion-bar suspension.

The BT Light Tank was based on an American Christie design of the 1930s and proved a highly successful design. It went to seven marks, during the course of which its main armament was increased to 45mm, and numerous modifications were made. The BT-5 had a three-man crew and weighed 11.3 tons. With a road speed of over 68mph it lived up to its Fast Tank designation, and was powered by an M-5 engine developing 350hp. The BT-7 had a 500hp V-12 engine and armor thickness of 22mm.

The T-50, -60 and -70 light tanks were intended as replacements for the previous types. The T-50 had a 300hp engine, 45mm gun and weighed 13 tons; the T-60, at 5.5 tons, proved suitable for reconnaissance and the T-70 of 1942 had increased armor thickness of 60mm and weighed nearly 10 tons.

Germany The Germans, who had been slow starters in the tank field, more than made up in the 1930s, and the Panzer divisions which spearheaded the advances of 1940 were well equipped and trained formations. Their German-designed PzKpfw I and II types were supplemented by the Czech-designed PzKpfw 35 (t) and 38 (t) vehicles.

The PzKpfw I was designed as a training tank in 1932 and, to circumvent Versailles Treaty restrictions, was designated Landwirtschaftsschlepper – agricultural tractor. It was powered by a 57hp Krupp engine initially, but the Ausführung B had a 100hp Maybach engine and armor thickness of 13mm. Armament was two 7.92mm machine guns in a turret, and in this form they saw action in the early campaigns of the war. The PzKpfw II went to several marks; the Ausf. F was powered by a 140hp Maybach gasoline engine providing a speed of 25mph for the 9.3-ton vehicle. The three-man crew was protected by a maximum of 35mm armor and their armament consisted of a 2cm KwK 30 cannon and 7.92mm MG 34. The vehicle was highly mobile and its length was 15 feet 9 inches. Although deficient in protection and firepower the PzKpfw II was used as a reconnaissance tank and its last variation, the Ausf. L – Luchs – was conceived as such.

The Czech Skoda and CKD-designed LT 35 and LT 38 were adopted by the Germans as PzKpfw 35 (t) and 38 (t) respectively – t standing for tschechisch and showing their origins. The latter saw more widespread service and proved an excellent addition to the Wehrmacht inventory. The 8.4-ton vehicle was powered by a 125hp Praga engine and had a road speed of 35mph. Maximum armor protection for the four-man crew was 25mm and a Skoda 3.7cm gun was backed up by two 7.92mm machine guns. Their one disadvantage was the riveted hull but otherwise they were well-designed and useful tanks.

Italy Italy developed British Carden Lloyd light tanks in the 1930s as fast tanks with the designation Carro Veloce. The CV 33 series incorporated a number of improvements and the 1935 CV 33/11 tank version had two 8mm machine guns, in line with its role as an infantry-support vehicle. Command versions with radio fit, bridging and flame-thrower variants were also produced.

In 1936 the CV 35 was introduced, and two years later the designations of the light tanks were changed to Carro Armato L3/33 and L3/35 respectively. The L3/35 was armed with 8mm Breda Model 38 machine guns and weighed 3.4 tons; its two-man crew was protected by a maximum of 13.5mm of armor and the 10-foot 5-inch long vehicle was powered by a 43hp FIAT-SPA gasoline engine. A flame-thrower version – the L3/35 Lanciafiamme – was also produced to provide additional support for the infantry.

The Italians also employed another light tank, the L6/40 of 1940. This six-ton vehicle was armed with a 20mm Breda gun and equipped reconnaissance elements of the Italian cavalry both in the North African campaigns and in the Soviet Union. The most frequently encountered type remained the L3, however.

Japan The Type 95 Light Tank series was developed following experiences with the Type 89 Medium Tank of 1929 and appeared five years later. Designed by Mitsubishi, the Type 95 HA-GO weighed 7.5 tons and carried a three-man crew. Attempts were made to improve its armament and an amphibious derivative appeared, but the basic tank was the one most frequently encountered. Its main armament was a 37mm Type 94 gun and secondary armament consisted of two 7.7mm Type 97 machine guns. Its 110hp engine gave it a maximum speed of 28mph and its crew had 12mm maximum armor protection. The hull was riveted and the suspension system was two pairs of bogie wheels mounted on bell cranks. The Type 95 was 14 feet 4 inches long and was widely used by the Japanese.

In 1942 the Type 98 KE-N1 Light Tank entered production with the aim of improving the HA-GO's performance and firepower, but only limited numbers were made.

France France had two types of light tank in service in 1939: the Renault-designed R-35 and the Hotchkiss H-35 or H-39. The former weighed 9.8 tons and had a two-man crew. With 40mm frontal armor it had good protection but its speed was a meager 13mph since it had an 82hp engine, and the commander was expected both to command and operate the 37mm gun. The Hotchkiss weighed 11.8 tons and had a two-man crew. The H-39 had a 120hp engine and carried a 37mm gun; its protection and shape were very good and the Germans put captured examples to use.

Other Renault designs included the D 1 and D 2, but not many were operational in 1939.

MEDIUM TANKS

Great Britain Included in this section are the Cruiser series of tanks designed to counter enemy armor; the Infantry tanks are covered in the Heavy Tank section which follows. The Cruiser series began with the Mark 1 (A.9), a Vickers-designed medium tank dating from 1937. The Mark 1 had a crew of six, weighed 12 tons and was armed with a 2-pounder gun in hydraulically powered turret. Fitted with a 150hp AEC engine and capable of 25mph, the Mark 1 Cruiser was used in the early battles in North Africa. Two auxiliary turrets were equipped with .303-inch machine guns at the forward part of the 19-foot long hull. The Cruiser Mark II (A.10) doubled the armor thickness, now 30mm, and was conceived as an Infantry Tank. The weight was increased to 13.75 tons.

The Cruiser Mark III (A.13) introduced Christie suspension to the Cruiser range in 1938 and was powered by a 340hp Nuffield Liberty engine which produced a road speed of 30mph. The crew consisted of four, and they were protected by 14mm of armor. Armament remained a 2-pounder with .303-inch machine gun. The Cruiser Mark IV (A.13 Mark II) featured 30mm armor and distinctive V-shaped spaced armor turret sides; the increase in armor was paid for by an increase of weight to nearly 15 tons.

The Cruiser Mark VI Crusader (A.15) went to three marks; with a 2-pounder it had insufficient firepower and with 40mm armor inadequate protection by the time it was introduced in 1941. The Mark III increased this to 51mm. The Mark VIII (A.27 M) Cromwell went to eight marks; basically it was a 24–30 ton development of the previous types armed with a 6-pounder gun and increased armor thickness of 76mm, and introduced in 1943. A 600hp Rolls Royce Meteor engine provided 32mph and the Cromwell had a crew of five. The final development of the Cromwell line – the most widely used British tank – was the Comet (A.34) armed with 77mm gun. This was a development of the 17-pounder and the first satisfactory British tank gun. The Comet weighed 32.5 tons, had a crew of five, and had 101mm armor. The A.41 Centurion arrived too late to see action but was also equipped with the 17-pounder gun.

The United States In 1939 America was still using the M2A1 medium tank, and in 1941 work began on a replacement for this 37mm gun-armed vehicle. The M3 Medium Tank was equipped with a 75mm weapon mounted in a sponson on the right of the tank, while a 37mm in hydraulically operated turret was accompanied by two .30-caliber machine guns. In subsequent British service, the M3 was known as the Lee, while versions with British-designed turrets became the Grant. The M3A1 featured a cast hull in place of the riveted type of its predecessor and the M3A2 had a welded hull. A 340hp Continental R-975 engine propelled the 29.4-ton tank at 26mph, and its crew of six had 37mm armor protection. The M3A3 had two 375hp GM engines and the A4 a 370hp Chrysler. The M3A5 reverted to a riveted hull.

The M4 Sherman Medium Tank which was to achieve so much success in the war was designed, in 1941, to replace the Lee/Grant series. The essential differences were in the deletion of the sponson gun and its replacement in a turret with power-operated traverse, and a height reduction of 15 inches. Countless modifications were introduced to hull construction, suspension and gun mounts. The original Sherman had a welded hull which, in the M4A1, was replaced by a cast type. The tank weighed 32.6 tons and had a five-

man crew. Maximum armor thickness was 75mm which was the same as the main armament's caliber, and one .50-caliber Browning and two .30-caliber weapons were also carried. The 353hp Continental R-976 engine produced a road speed of 24mph, and the Sherman was 19 feet 6 inches long.

The M4A2 introduced GM 6-71 engines and the M4A3 of 1942 a 500hp Ford engine. The M4A4 had a Chrysler engine and elongated hull. The 75mm was installed in an M34 A1 mount.

The M4 also carried a 76mm gun to bring its firepower more into line with that of its opponents and, in British use, the M4 was equipped with a 17-pounder gun and known as the Sherman VC Firefly – the sole British tank capable of taking on the heavier German tanks in 1944.

The Soviet Union The Soviet army introduced a Medium Tank, the T-28, in the 1930s and gradually increased its armament and armor until its weight had doubled from that originally specified. The 32-ton vehicle had a six-man crew and was powered by a 500hp M-17 L engine which gave it a road speed of 23mph. Armor thickness was 80mm and a 76.2mm gun was mounted in the later versions.

The definitive Soviet tank of World War II was, however, the T-34. This appeared in 1941, much to the consternation of the Germans, and original examples were armed with a 76.2mm gun and two additional 7.62mm machine guns. The T-34/76 had a four-man crew and weighed 26 tons; powered by a 500hp V-2-34 engine it enjoyed a high degree of mobility, while firepower was well looked after, and protection of 45mm was adequate.

In 1943 the T-34/85 appeared. This upped the main armament to an 85mm gun and increased armor thickness to 60mm which, in turn, added five tons to the weight. The T-34 was an excellent tank and its 85mm gun could penetrate 95mm of armor at 1000 yards, even if by German standards its armor was thin. A total of over 40,000 T-34s were produced during the war which, considering the disruption to industry caused by the German advance, was enormous.

In 1943 the design was given additional armor to a maximum thickness of 110mm and the resulting tank was known as the T-43. It retained the 76mm gun and the T-44 introduced a transverse engine in a newly designed medium tank. Neither saw widespread use.

Germany The PzKpfw III first appeared in 1936 and was designed as a highly mobile and versatile medium tank. In service in limited numbers in 1939, the PzKpfw III was to go on to several Ausführungen. The Ausf E had a 3.7cm Kw K gun and weighed 20 tons. Its five-man crew had maximum armor protection of 30mm and, in the Ausf F, a 5cm KwK L/42 gun to improve firepower. A 300hp Maybach HL 120 engine gave a road speed of 25mph. Armor protection – or lack of it – was to prove a problem with the PzKpfw III and subsequent Ausführungen steadily increased thickness to 50mm in the case of the J and M, whose turret had 57mm. Guns of both calibers continued in service until 1942, the crews of the 3.7cm weapon being considerably disadvantaged. Tropical versions were the G (Tp) and L (Tp) which had various filters for desert operations. The Ausf J introduced a short-barrelled 5cm Kw K 39 gun, and the final Ausf N was a close-support version with 7.5cm L/24 gun.

The PzKpfw IV was designed in the early 1930s as an artillery support vehicle armed with 7.5cm gun. The original armor thickness was increased from 30mm by the use of appliqué plates on the Ausf D, while the Ausf F had 50mm armor as standard. The D weighed just under 20 tons and had a five-man crew. It was powered by a 300hp Maybach HL 120 engine which gave it a road speed of 26mph, and was 19 feet 4 inches long; its short-barrelled 7.5cm Kw K L/24 gun was replaced in later models by a longer 7.5cm L/43 gun. This last-mentioned gun was well capable of defeating the T-34's relatively thin armor and the Ausf G introduced a muzzle brake to it. The PzKpfw IV remained in production throughout the war.

Italy The Italian army's medium tank at the outbreak of war was the Carro Armato M 11/39, a Fiat-Ansaldo design of 1935. It weighed a modest 10.8 tons and its main armament consisted of a 37mm Vickers-Terni gun with two 8mm Breda Model 38 machine guns for its three-man crew. The 37mm weapon was mounted in a turret on the tank's right-hand side, and a second and higher turret housed two machine guns. A 43hp FIAT-SPA engine gave a road speed of 21mph to the tank, whose length was 15 feet 6 inches. The tank's 30mm frontal armor was outclassed by British 2-pounders in the desert and reliability proved suspect; the design was simply eclipsed and most M 11/39s which had not been destroyed fell into Allied hands on Italy's capitulation in North Africa.

The M 13/40 series improved on its predecessor's design and featured a 47mm gun in a conventional rotating turret when introduced in 1940. Its four-man crew was housed in a compartment similar to the M 11/39's, and was really inadequately protected by the standards of the day. The M 14/41 introduced a more powerful engine and the M 15/42 another, plus different 47mm gun. They formed the basis of the more successful Semovente da 75/18 SPG.

Below: A German PzKpfw III with 3.7cm gun in the desert in 1941.

Japan Japan's Type 89 Medium Tank was produced by Mitsubishi and first appeared in 1929. The vehicle weighed 12.8 tons and, with 115hp engine, enjoyed good mobility; but this is where its advantages stopped. Maximum armor thickness was a meager 17mm, which mattered little in the Type 89's early actions against the Chinese, but was to prove hopelessly inadequate when pitted against the smallest Allied antitank guns. The gun was a 57mm type which could not fire AP projectiles and was thus suited only to infantry close support tasks. The tank was solidly built but quite simply outdated by the outbreak of war.

The Type 97 was a better tank but still not the equal of Western designs. The Type 97 was a 15.6-ton vehicle with the turret offset to the right, and this housed a 47mm Type 1 gun backed up by two 7.7mm Type 97 machine guns. The tank had a five-man crew and was powered by a 170hp Mitsubishi diesel engine which gave a road speed of 24mph. In an attempt to improve its firepower, a 75mm Type 90 field gun was adapted to fit the turret, but it remained inferior to the Sherman against which it was matched. Armor thickness was a maximum of 30mm, which was under half the Sherman's, but *faute de mieux* the Type 97 was employed throughout the Pacific War.

France France adopted the Char Moyen de Bataille (Char B) in 1934 and produced several variants of it. The major production version (B 1-*bis*) was a 31-ton vehicle with a four-man crew, powered by a 307hp Renault engine and armed with a 75mm and 47mm SA 35 gun, the former on a right-hand sponson and the latter in a top turret. Armor thickness was 60mm maximum.

The three-man Char de Cavalerie Somua 1935 S entered service in 1935 and was a very good design. It was of fully cast construction with excellent ballistic protection. At under 20 tons and with 190hp engine it was mobile and with 47mm SA 35 gun it was well armed. The turret's frontal armor was 55mm and the suspension was protected by armored skirts. That the tank was badly used in 1940 was not the fault of its designers.

Canada A Canadian medium tank, the Ram, was an indigenous design based on American M3 components but armed with a British 2-pounder gun. It weighed 29 tons, had a five-man crew and was upgunned to carry a 6-pounder in 1942. In many respects it was superior to the M4 Sherman, apart from its gun, but was never used in action; many were converted to Ram Kangaroo APCs.

HEAVY TANKS

Great Britain The Infantry Tank Mark II Matilda II bore little resemblance to the Mark I; it was, at 26.5 tons, twice its weight and it carried a crew of four. The inadequate armament of the Mark I was replaced by a 2-pounder with an additional 7.92mm Besa machine gun and it entered service in 1939. Its two 87hp AEC engines provided a road speed of 24mph. A particularly important feature was its maximum armor thickness of 78mm which protected it from German Pak weapons under 8.8cm. The Matilda II went to five marks – principal differences were to engine and two marks were close-support versions with a 3-inch howitzer.

The Infantry Tank Mark III Valentine was a prewar Vickers design, a contemporary of the Matilda, conceived as a 16-ton AFV based on existing components when possible. It was a successful tank and saw widespread service, notably in the desert, until its 2-pounder gun became obsolete and was eventually replaced by a 6-pounder. With maximum armor of 65mm the Valentine was well protected and its 135hp AEC engine gave it reliability and a good performance. The original version had a two-man crew, but in the Valentine III a third man was added. The Mark II, IV and V had GMC diesel engines and the VI was produced in Canada. A 6-pounder gun was installed from the Mark VIII and the XI and final version had a 75mm weapon.

The Infantry Tank Mark VI Churchill (A.22) entered service in 1941 but suffered from unreliability because of its hurried introduction. The first two marks had a 2-pounder gun but the Churchill III introduced a 6-pounder in 1942. The 39-ton tank had a crew of five and its 350hp Bedford engine produced a road speed of 25mph. The protection was good, since 101mm frontal armor was fitted. The Mark IV had a cast turret and the Mark IV (NA 75) installed 75mm guns cannibalized from M4 Shermans in North Africa to good effect. The V was a close support version with 95mm gun, and by the VII weight had increased to 41 tons. Subsequent marks up to XI carried a variety of guns and turret designs.

The United States The US Army's heavy tank, the M28 Pershing, was designed following the successful employment by the Germans of their Tiger tanks, and was the final development of a series of experimental tanks starting in 1942. The T26 – which became M26 in the spring of 1945 – was a 41-ton vehicle with a five-man crew.

Its main armament was a 90mm M 3 gun backed up by a .50-caliber Browning M 2 and two .30-caliber Browning machine guns. Its frontal armor thickness of 102mm afforded a high degree of protection. It was powered by a 500hp Ford GAF engine which gave the tank a road speed of 20mph, and individually sprung torsion-bar suspension was fitted. The Pershing – like the British Centurion – arrived in north-west Europe in the closing stages of the war, but unlike the Centurion it was involved in the fighting, and some 2500 were produced by May 1945.

The Soviet Union The Soviet army's earliest heavy tank was the T-35. This was equipped with a formidable armament. One 76.2mm and two 37mm or 45mm guns were augmented by seven 7.62mm machine guns mounted in a total of five turrets on the original version. The T-35 weighed just under 50 tons and was powered by a 500hp M-17 T engine. Initially it had 30mm armor, but this was later doubled. Some were in service in 1941, but had already begun to be replaced by the KV heavy-tank series. The KV-1 A was a 42.8-ton tank powered by a 550hp V-2K engine and manned by a crew of five. Its main armament was a 76.2mm M 1938/39 or M 1940 gun which, in the less successful and unwieldy KV-2, was replaced by a 152mm howitzer for fire-support tasks. Armor thickness on the KV-B and C was 106mm but this was reduced in the KV-1s briefly to 82mm in the interests of a weight reduction of four tons, and increased mobility. The final version was the KV-85, which carried an 85mm M 1943 gun with the previous models' three 76.2mm machine guns. Weight returned to 45 tons and the maximum armor thickness for the four-man crew was 110mm. The KV-85 was the precursor to the JS (Josef Stalin) series.

The JS-1 was a 43.3-ton heavy tank which entered service in 1943. Its main armament was the same as the KV-85's and it was powered by a 513hp V-2-15 engine which gave a maximum speed of 23mph. The gun was increased to 100mm in the JS-100 and a 122mm M-43 weapon replaced this in 1944.

The JS-II featured a hull and turret with improved ballistic shape and increased rate of fire. It weighed 45.2 tons and its maximum armor thickness of 150mm afforded good protection. In the JS-III this was increased to 230mm but the tank's well-shaped armor had little opportunity to prove itself since it arrived in the last weeks of the war.

Germany The remarkable German PzKpfw VI

Tiger was the culmination of a series of designs by Porsche and Henschel leading to the adoption of the Henschel version. It weighed 54 tons and carried a crew of five; a 694hp Maybach HL 230 P gasoline engine gave the compact vehicle an adequate maximum speed of 23mph and its torsion-bar suspension aided mobility. Of all-welded construction, the Tiger had a maximum armor protection of 100mm and its main armament was the 8.8cm Kw K 36 gun with two 7.92mm MG 34 machine guns. In 1942 its gun could outperform those of Allied counterparts and its armor deflect their projectiles, but the design was complex and in particular, the turret could only traverse slowly. The improvements in Allied tank guns gradually reduced the tank's invulnerability, but it still presented a formidable obstacle in defense until the end of the war. Only 1350 were produced.

The Tiger II Ausführung B – known as the Königstiger which was incorrectly translated as King Tiger – appeared in late 1943 and incorporated armor improvements with a maximum thickness of 185mm, as well as improved suspension. The tank was fitted with two types of turret – an angular Henschel version and a more rounded Porsche design. The 8.8cm Kw K 43 could penetrate 180mm of armor at 500 yards and the crew enjoyed excellent protection. However, in the eternal triangle of firepower, mobility and protection a price must always be paid, and at nearly 70 tons the Königstiger's mobility suffered, so the tank proved better in defense than in attack.

The PzKpfw V Panther was introduced before the Königstiger in 1942. It weighed 44.8 tons, had a five-man crew, and mounted a 7.5cm Kw K 42 gun. The 690hp Maybach engine improved the tank's sluggish performance with the original MAN engine, but was constantly beset by problems, as was the transmission which was not robust enough for the vehicle's weight. The Panther existed in various Ausführungen, but the revised Ausf A and G provided the majority of 5500 built. The Panther was really inspired by the advantages evident in the Soviet T-34; with its armament and 120mm maximum armor protection it was a powerful opponent wherever encountered.

Italy The Italians did not possess a heavy tank; they received a small number of German PzKpfw VI Tiger tanks and doubtless operated other types which had been captured.

Japan The Japanese army had very few heavy tanks, the first of which appeared in 1933. This was the Type 91, an 18-ton vehicle powered by a 224hp BMW engine with five-man crew. Its 70mm main armament was housed in a top turret while secondary turrets housed machine guns. Armor thickness was a maximum of 20mm. The Type 91 was succeeded by the Type 95, a 26-ton AFV whose 70mm gun was backed up by a 37mm and two 7.7mm machine guns. It was powered by a 290hp engine and armor thickness was increased by 15mm. Neither type entered production in any numbers.

France France entered the war with modified Char Lourd FCM 2 Cs which had originated from a World War I design, and several FCM 2 C-*bis* types. Both designs were well and truly obsolete by 1940 and weighed 67 and 74 tons respectively. They were powered by 250hp engines and had a road speed of 8mph. Over 33 feet in length, they were poorly armored and armed with main turrets housing, in the 2 C, a 75mm gun and in the 2 C-*bis* a 155mm howitzer, with secondary turrets for machine guns. Six 2 Cs were matched against the German armored thrusts of 1940 and it is reasonable to suppose their life expectancy was limited.

SPECIAL-PURPOSE TANKS

This section includes tanks modified to perform tasks other than their prime one but not those acting as carriages for antitank weapons or medium to heavy guns and howitzers, which will be covered later.

Great Britain To provide a mobile platform for four 7.92mm Besa machine guns in a power-operated turret, Mark VI Light Tanks were adapted to fulfill a pressing requirement for antiaircraft protection in 1940. They then carried the designation Light Tank AA Mark 1 or Mark II. Three marks of Crusader Tank were also converted into AA tanks. The first carried a 40mm Bofors, usually in a turret and was served by a three-man crew; the second had two 20mm Oerlikons; and the third carried the same weapons with improved sights.

Cruiser and Infantry Tanks were also adapted to perform a number of essential battlefield tasks. These included modifications to provide Command or OP vehicles, which frequently carried dummy guns to prevent their being singled out for special treatment. Bulldozer and Dozer/Crane conversions were made, as were ARV Recovery and AMRA Anti-Mine Roller Attachment versions to clear paths through minefields.

Most tanks were capable of conversion to some or all of these roles, and only certain examples will be singled out for mention. The Cromwell was fitted with a device for clearing hedgerows in the bocage country of Normandy and carried the designation Cromwell Prong. The Valentine Snake towed an explosive device through minefields, the Crocodile provided a flame thrower and the Scorpion a flail, again for minefield clearance. An interesting variant was the Valentine DD, or Duplex Drive, which provided floatation by the erection of canvas screens around the tank and whose use had been pioneered on the Tetrarch Tank in 1941.

The Churchill was modified to create AVRE (Assault Vehicles Royal Engineers), ARV and BARV (Beach Armored Recovery Vehicles for clearing tanks stranded on beaches) tanks. A whole range of various Track-laying and Bridging variants also existed. These Churchill variants were the most effective of the vehicles employed by the British 79th Armored Division on D-Day.

The CDL Tank concept was a prewar idea resurrected for intended use in the Middle East, but which was not actually employed until 1945. CDL stood for Canal Defence Light, and the first tank modified for this battlefield illumination task was the Matilda. American M 3 Grants were also adapted and retained their 75mm main armament, whereas the Matilda's turret gun was replaced by a powerful searchlight.

The United States The Americans possessed a range of antiaircraft guns mounted on half tracks, but only one full-tracked AA Gun Motor Carriage. This carried twin 40mm M 2 guns and was known as the M19. It was a dual-purpose weapon which had an antitank role too, while accompanying armored formations. The M19 was based on the M24 Chaffee Light Tank and was served by a crew of six. Powered by two Cadillac engines, it had a maximum speed of 35mph and proved a versatile weapon.

Both M2 and M3 Medium Tanks were modified into flame gun equipped vehicles as well as Gun Motor Carriage chassis. The M3 Grant was converted into a CDL tank which, in the interests of secrecy and to effectively disguise its true nature, carried the designation T10 Shop Tractor. In the event this aura of secrecy was largely wasted, since neither American nor British CDL types were used to any great extent.

The M4 Sherman was adapted to perform similar roles to those of British tanks: Dozer, Mine-Exploder, Flame-gun and Rocket-launcher equipped versions all saw service. The

M4 was also converted to DD configuration and used on D-Day by both British and US units. The British modified their Shermans to ARV, BARV, and Rocket status – the latter in small numbers firing 60-pound aircraft rockets in a locally effected conversion of 1944. The Kangaroo was a turretless Armored Personnel Carrier, the Crab a flail and the Crocodile threw a jet of flame 100 yards.

The Soviet Union The Soviets only employed one self-propelled tracked antiaircraft carriage, namely the SU-37 which, as its designation suggests, mounted a single or twin 37mm Model 89 gun on a T-70 Light Tank chassis. The vehicle was manned by a crew of three and weighed 10.5 tons; two GAZ-203 engines of 70hp propelled it at a speed of 28mph and armor protection for the crew was up to 35mm.

Germany As the war progressed, the Germans developed their light and antiaircraft guns mounted on lorries or half-tracks into fully armored and tracked antiaircraft tanks. The first, introduced in 1943 and based on the ex-Czech PzKpfw 38 (t) chassis, was the Leichter Flakpanzer 38 (t) Sd Kfz 140. This vehicle weighed just under 10 tons and had a crew of four to operate it and the single 2cm Flak 38 gun which it carried. It was a highly mobile vehicle which provided its crew with up to 25mm of armor protection.

The Flakpanzer IV was a 25-ton vehicle which mounted a quadruple-barrelled 2cm Flakvierling 38 on a PzKpfw IV chassis to provide a potent air-defense weapon which could lay down a barrage of 800rpm and whose five-man crew had up to 85mm of armor protection. It was christened the *Möbelwagen* (furniture van). The Wirbelwind (Whirlwind) derivative afforded better protection to the crew in the form of an octagonal turret, while the Ostwind variation of this had a single 3.7cm Flak gun, and the Flakpanzer IV (3.7cm) – also known as the Möbelwagen – had a single gun set inside a square armored compartment. This had a seven-man crew with up to 85mm armor protection, and the 25-ton vehicle was capable of 25mph. The PzKpfw IV was a sound tank design and the antiaircraft tank versions of it provided mobile support to the excellent Flak defenses put into the field by the Germans, particularly toward the end of the war.

Italy The Italians, while having no tracked antiaircraft vehicles, did employ a number of truck-mounted guns to good effect. The L3/33 Lf and L3/35 Lf flame thrower versions of the light tank have already been mentioned, and Command/OP versions of the M 13/40 were built with dummy guns.

Japan The Japanese had three types of antiaircraft tank in service during the war. The SO-K1 had twin 20mm cannon with shield on top of the superstructure of a modified KE-GO chassis; the SA-TO had a single 20mm gun in an enclosed turret mounted on a Type 97 chassis suitably altered, and the TA-HA carried twin 37mm antiaircraft guns on a Type 1 Medium Tank chassis.

SELF-PROPELLED GUNS

This section includes Antitank guns and self-propelled guns and howitzers which were designed during the war to provide mobile firepower.

Great Britain Such was the effectiveness of the 17-pound antitank gun that it was mounted in a number of self-propelled carriages in British service. The Archer, which entered service in 1944, was a 16.5-ton vehicle with a four-man crew which carried its 17-pounder in a superstructure mounted aft. Maximum armor protection was 60mm and the Valentine tank provided the chassis. Some Archers had a fully enclosed compartment for their crews.

The Avenger SP gun was based on a Challenger tank chassis and weighed 30 tons; however it arrived in service too late to see action. Another 17-pounder-armed vehicle was the Achilles, which was based on the American M10 Gun Motor Carriage supplied to the British. These were operated both in the 17-pounder Achilles version and the Standard M10 SP 3 configuration with 3-inch gun – the latter designated 3-inch SP Wolverine.

The American M7 Howitzer Motor Carriage was armed with a 105mm Howitzer, and, in British service, was known as the Priest. It was a very successful and mobile weapon which arrived in North Africa in time for the Battle of El Alamein in October 1942. A Canadian-built version of the M7 Priest was armed with a 25-pounder gun and operated by a six-man crew. It was named the Sexton. The earlier Bishop was inspired by the successful employment of SP guns by the Germans in the desert, and consisted of a 25-pounder gun in tall box-like superstructure mounted on a Valentine tank chassis. It was replaced by the Priest. The Churchill was also equipped with a 3-inch gun to form the Gun

Carrier Mark 1, but was never used operationally.

The United States The Americans employed several Gun and Howitzer Motor Carriages designed to provide self-propelled fire support for armored and infantry divisions. The M3 HMC and M10 GMC have already been described in British use; the Americans operated these 29.5-ton vehicles with their five-man crews from 1942 onward. The M10 had counterweights on its turret to compensate for the weight of its 105mm gun, and this, the M10A1 and the M7 were based on the M4 Sherman tank chassis.

The M36 GMC, introduced in 1944, provided a 90mm gun which was capable of engaging German Tiger and Panther tanks with considerable success, and gradually replaced the less efficient M10s. Some versions had muzzle brakes fitted to the gun. The heavier GMCs, both carrying 155mm guns, were added to the inventory in the latter part of the war. These were the M12 and M40 and they were designed for long-range bombardment.

The M18 Gun Motor Carriage, the Hellcat, was an excellent and highly mobile weapon. Its 76mm M1A1 gun was mounted in an open turret and operated by a crew of five. A 400hp Continental R-975 provided a top speed of 50mph but the all-welded hull's maximum armor thickness was only 12mm. The Hellcat relied upon high mobility to extricate itself from difficulties and, with low silhouette and torsion-bar independent suspension, was able to do so.

The Soviet Union Inspired by the Germans, the Soviets placed considerable emphasis upon self-propelled antitank guns, the earliest of which were based upon the Komsomolets tractor. The SU-45 had a high superstructure and carried a 47mm tank gun – it weighed some six tons and had a crew of three. The SU-57 was another Komsomolets-tractor based vehicle but its Model 1941 57mm gun was exposed, apart from a small shield.

The SU-76 entered Soviet service in 1942 and was based on the T-70 light-tank chassis. It carried a 76mm M 1942 gun with 60 rounds in an open superstructure which, in the later SU-76 M, was covered. The latter vehicle was powered by two 85hp GAZ 203 engines which gave it a road speed of some 30mph. Its maximum armor thickness was only 25mm. The SU-85 was a 29.5-ton vehicle with four-man crew who enjoyed considerably more protection from the 75mm frontal armor. The SU-85 was of commendably low silhouette and had a respectable top speed of 35mph. It was based upon the T-34 chassis which partly accounted for its success. The SU-76 i was another SP gun based on captured German PzKpfw III chassis. The SU-100 was also based on the T-34 and featured a 100mm gun which increased the punch of the smaller weapons previously fitted. It was powered by a 500hp engine which gave it a road speed of 35mph and the principal recognition feature was a cupola on the right-hand side of the superstructure. It weighed 32 tons and the four-man crew was well protected behind 100mm

Above: A British Bishop SP gun with 25-pounder gun on Valentine chassis.

armor.

The KV Heavy Tank provided the basis for the SU-122 antitank vehicle which weighed 44 tons and was powered by a 600hp engine. It carried a 122mm gun. A later version of this weapon was subsequently employed on the heaviest Soviet SP gun, the ISU-122 with massive firepower and protection of up to 200mm. This was based on the Josef Stalin tank.

These Soviet SP guns were solid and unpretentious and played an indispensable part in defeating German armor.

Germany The Germans put much of the equipment they captured to use in the form of the Panzerjäger or tank-hunting vehicles which enabled mobile antitank guns to be brought into action far more swiftly than was possible with conventional wheeled guns. One of the earliest was a Czech 4.7cm antitank gun mounted on a French Renault R-35 Tank chassis. The same gun was fitted to a German PzKpfw 1 Ausf B chassis to form a 7.5-ton lightly armored vehicle with a powerful punch. The 7.5cm Pak 40 gun was mounted on a French Lorraine ammunition carrier in a cumbersome superstructure, but was effective enough; it was designated Marder 1. The Marder II was based on a PzKpfw II chassis and was armed with the same gun, as was the Marder III, in which it was carried in a superstructure fitted to a PzKpfw 38 (t) chassis. This also formed the basis for the Panzerjäger 38 (t) Ausf M which used the 7.5cm Pak 40/3 gun, and enjoyed improved stability. This gun's APC round was capable of penetrating 102mm at 1000 yards. The Pak 40 was also fitted to the French Hotchkiss H.39 chassis, and the Raupenschlepper Ost tractor to provide a 4.5-ton vehicle powered by a 70hp Steyr engine. Captured Soviet 7.62cm Pak 36 (r) guns were mounted on Czech PzKpfw 38 (t) and German PzKpfw II chassis to provide fast, mobile and 30mm armored tank hunters. The 8.8cm Pak 43/1 on a PzKpfw III/IV chassis was originally designated Hornisse (Hornet) but this was changed to Nashorn (Rhinoceros). It weighed 24 tons, had a five-man crew, and its gun could penetrate 170mm of armor at 1000 yards.

In the later war years the Germans introduced a number of Jagdpanzer, tank destroyer, vehicles designed to be employed more aggressively than the lighter tank hunting types. The earliest of these low-slung and well-armored vehicles was the none-too-well designed Jagdpanzer 38 (t) Hetzer (Infuriator), which was constructed around the familiar PzKpfw 38 (t). It offered good protection for its four-man crew and

weighed 15.8 tons; its 7.5cm Pak 39 was offset to the right and it entered service in 1944. The Jagdpanzer IV carried the same gun on a PzKpfw IV chassis and provided a low-silhouette tank destroyer, as did the upgunned long-barrelled 7.5cm Stu. K 42-armed version which had 80mm frontal armor protection and was externally coated in Zimmerit antimagnetic compound.

The Jagdpanther was an excellent tank destroyer which entered service in 1944; it weighed nearly 49 tons and provided good protection for its crew of five. As its name implies, it was based on the Panther Ausf G chassis and its 8.8cm Pak 43/3 gun could defeat 169mm of armor at 1000 yards. It was preceded by the Ferdinand – later Elefant – tank destroyer based on the Porsche contender for the Tiger's chassis. It was very heavily armored – 200mm maximum – and weighed 65 tons. The Jagdtiger was an even more potent hunter and carried a 12.8cm Pak 44 gun which put it in a class of its own. It weighed over 70 tons which greatly hindered its mobility, but in defense it was a formidable opponent and its six-man crew had 250mm of frontal armor to protect them.

The Germans also employed several types of assault guns – Sturmgeschütze – for infantry-support tasks. The 11.5-ton Wespe (Wasp) was based on the PzKpfw II chassis and had a 10.5cm le FH 18/2 gun. The same chassis was used for the s IG 33 15cm gun, while the Sturmgeschütz III Ausf G was based on PzKpfw III chassis and was armed with a 7.5cm Stu. K 40 gun. It was a mobile assault gun and provided 80mm of armor protection for its four-man crew. The 10.5cm Sturmhaubitze 42 Ausf G was also based on the PzKpfw III chassis and, like most Sturmgeschütze, frequently carried additional protective Schürzen (apron) armor plates.

The *Brummbär* (grizzly bear) was a heavy assault howitzer carrying a 15cm Stu H 53 gun introduced in 1943 to destroy strongpoints and for street-fighting operations. It weighed over 27 tons and its four-man crew had frontal armor protection of 100mm. The *Brummbär* was based on the PzKpfw IV tank chassis. Various modifications were incorporated but the thick-set outline remained with stubby gun barrel set in a frontal ball mount. The Sturmpanzer VI – Sturmtiger – was designed around the 38cm Raketenwerfer 61 rocket launcher. Ten examples, based on the Tiger chassis, were produced in 1944. They proved victims of their own immobility, since they weighed just under 70 tons, and were never employed in the street-fighting operations for which they had been designed.

Italy The Italian army's experiences in North Africa led them to adopt a series of Semoventi-self-propelled guns – to take on Allied armor. The earliest was the Semovente da 47/32, based on the L.6/40 light tank chassis, which weighed 6.5 tons and was capable of 42mph. The M.42 medium tank provided the chassis for the Semovente da 75/34 M.42 which carried a 75mm gun and provided armor protection of up to 70mm for its three-man crew. Most were used by the Germans in Italy.

The Semovente da 75/46 M.43 was a 15-ton vehicle on the M.43 medium tank chassis which carried a longer-barrelled 75mm gun. In March 1943 orthodox tank production ceased in Italy and effort was devoted solely toward the manufacture of Semoventi. Foremost was the Semovente da 75/18 based on the chassis of the M.41 tank. This 13-ton vehicle had proved very successful in North Africa and was powered by a 125hp FIAT-SPA engine. It carried a 75mm Model 34 gun.

The Semovente da 90/53 was based on the M 14/41 tank chassis with 101mm frontal armor protection and four-man crew. The Germans acquired large numbers of Semoventi following the Italian armistice in 1943 and continued to use them against the Allies.

Japan The Japanese had three types of SPG in service, all based on the Type 97 medium tank. The Type 1 HO-NI 1 carried a 75mm Type 90 antitank gun in a three-sided superstructure. The HO-NI had a 105mm howitzer and was powered by a 170hp Mitsubishi engine. The HO-NI I and II both had a maximum of 50mm armor protection. The Type 3 HO-NI III was equipped with a 75mm Type 88 gun and additional armor protection. All three types weighed around 16 tons.

ARMORED AND SCOUT CARS

Great Britain The British army employed light scout cars for reconnaissance purposes in considerable numbers and utilized several designs; they effectively replaced the light tank in this role. The earliest type was the improved Beaverette, based on a Standard 14hp car chassis, but this was a temporary measure and the Guy Armored Car of 1940 – developed from the Guy Quad-Ant artillery tractor – set the standard for subsequent types, which included Alvis-Straussler and AEC designs. The latter

carried either a 2-pounder or 75mm gun depending upon mark and weighed 12 tons.

Humber produced an armored car based on the Karrier artillery tractor. It weighed just over seven tons, was 15-feet long, and its six-cylinder engine developed 90bhp. The Daimler weighed over seven tons and had a crew of three. It carried a 2-pounder gun and proved a first-class design. It epitomized all the requirements of an armored car – it was quiet, mobile, had swift acceleration and offered 16mm of armor protection to the crew.

In the Desert War the British army made considerable use of American-designed and South African-built Marmon-Herrington armored cars. These were based on a Ford chassis and went to four marks with a variety of gun armaments. Canada produced the Fox armored car which resembled the British Humber, but which was based on a General Motors chassis.

A number of lightly armored Scout Cars were also in use: these included the Morris Mark 1, a machine-gun armed vehicle of nearly four tons with a crew of three, the three marks of Humber with four-wheel drive and the Daimler with 2520cc engine and three-ton weight which carried the name of Dingo. Canada also built the Lynx (a copy of the Dingo), and the Otter Light Reconnaissance Cars. The Australians produced yet another version of the Dingo.

The United States The Americans built a variety of armored and scout-car prototypes but many did not progress beyond the experimental stage. Attempts were made to provide armor for the Jeep chassis, and Willys and Ford produced other designs, but the Standard American Scout Car was the 4 × 4 White M3. This was powered by a Hercules JXD engine developing 110bhp and weighing 8900 pounds. The M3 half-track was based on it.

The M8 Armored Car was originally designed by Fords to provide the Tank Destroyer Force with a 37mm Gun Motor Carriage. It was the only armored car used by the Americans during the war. It had an unusually high top speed of 56mph – which perhaps led to its designation of Greyhound by the British to whom it was supplied – and was a quiet and versatile vehicle. It, too, had a Hercules rear-mounted engine and over 8500 were produced. The M8 had a four-man crew and drive was provided to all its six wheels. A 37mm M6 gun was mounted in a cast turret and augmented by a .30-caliber Browning machine gun, while provision was made for a .50-caliber Browning pintle mount.

The M 20 Armored Utility Car was, in effect, an M8 Armored Car with its turret removed and replaced by a turret ring on which was fitted a .50-caliber Browning M2 machine gun. It was used as a highly mobile armored personnel carrier, cargo transport and command vehicle. It provided frontal armor protection of 22mm. Just under 4000 were built and some formed the basis of the T 69 Multiple Gun Carriage equipped with quadruple .50 Brownings.

The Chevrolet M6 Armored Car was designed to British requirements and known as the Staghound. Its original mark had a 37mm gun, but subsequent types had twin .50-caliber Brownings, 3-inch Howitzer or 75mm gun armament. The eight-wheeled Heavy Armored Car T 18 produced by General Motors carried a 57mm gun and was known as the Boarhound by the British, for whom it was built.

The Soviet Union The Soviets produced several types of armored cars during the 1930s which were based on Soviet Ford chassis. The GAZ BA-20 M of 1936 strongly resembled a sedan car with turret tacked on. It supplanted the earlier Bronieford GAZ-A but retained its rear-wheel drive. It was powered by a 50bhp engine and armed with a single 7.62mm machine gun. The GAZ BA-10 M was a heavy six-wheeled armored car developed from a series of similar vehicles dating from the early 1930s. It entered service in 1937 and was based on the GAZ-AAA commercial truck chassis. It weighed just over six tons, carried a four-man crew and was armed with a 45mm gun with two additional machine guns. Spare wheels were carried just aft of the front pair and, despite its ungainly appearance, the BA-10 M was an adequate design. An amphibious version, the BAZ, was also built.

In 1943 a new armored car appeared: this was the GAZ BA-64. It was powered by a 3280cc four-cylinder engine developing 50bhp and weighed 5290 pounds. Based on a GAZ-67 B chassis, the BA-64 provided up to 10mm armor protection for its two-man crew and carried a 14.5mm antitank rifle in a neat turret at the rear of the vehicle, as well as a secondary 7.62mm machine gun. The BA-64 had four-wheel drive and was 11 feet 1 inches long.

Germany A series of armored-car types throughout the early 1930s led to the adoption of six-wheeled designs in the late 1930s. These had been pioneered by Mercedes in 1931 by the G 3a/P Heavy Armored Car and were the Magirus-built SdKfz 263 6 × 4 and the Krupp designed Command Armored Car, the L2H 143 SdKfz

247. The former carried a bedstead radio aerial above it in the manner favored by the Germans.

The Mercedes-Benz G 3a/P – the SdKfz 231 – carried a 2cm gun in its rear-set turret. It was a 6 × 4 vehicle powered by a six-cylinder engine developing 68bhp, and parallel development took place of the SdKfz 232 (Fu), a communications variant. Fu was the abbreviation for Funk, or wireless.

The same designation SdKfz 231 was applied to eight-wheeled armored cars. These 8 × 8 types entered Wehrmacht service in 1937 and saw widespread use. The SdKfz 232 (Achtrad) was the eight-wheeled communications variant with characteristic integral frame aerial mounted sufficiently high on top of the vehicle to enable the turret, housing its 2cm KwK 30 or 38 gun, to rotate beneath it. A 150hp Büssing-NAG gasoline engine drove the 8.8-ton vehicle and produced a maximum speed of 53mph. They were built until 1942 by Deutche Werke AG at Kiel, and had a four-man crew, whose maximum armor protection was 14mm. The SdKfz 263 succeeded the 232, and the SdKfz 233 was armed with a 7.5cm gun.

Light armored cars were also produced. In 1936 the Horch Sd Kfz 221 was designed to provide reconnaissance elements of armored battalions with a 4 × 4 vehicle powered by a 81hp Horch V-8 gasoline engine and weighing four tons. In 1938 the Sd Kfz 222 entered Wehrmacht service. This carried a 2cm KwK 30 gun, had a crew of three protected by up to 30mm of armor, and weighed nearer five tons. The Sd Kfz 223 was a radio-fitted version for use in armored recce battalions with frame aerial necessitating the fitting of an MG 34 machine gun in place of the 2cm weapon. The Sd Kfz 260 Funkwagen and Sd Kfz 261 with rod aerial were unarmed signals vehicles on the same chassis. A small 4 × 4 armored command car, the Sd Kfz 247 built by Auto-Union, was also employed.

The heaviest German armored car was the Sd Kfz 234/2 Puma. This outstanding 8 × 8 design entered service in 1943 in answer to a specification of 1940 for a monocoque chassis-designed vehicle of 11 tons armed with a 5cm KwK 39/1 gun. The four-man crew had 30mm frontal armor protection, and their 19-foot 6-inch long vehicle could reach 52mph and climb 30-degree gradients. The Puma was powered by a 220hp 12-cylinder Tatra engine and, with six forward and six reverse gears, was a highly mobile and effective vehicle.

Italy The Italian armored car in service in the prewar campaigns in Africa was the Fiat

Above: French-crewed but US built M8 Armored Cars.

Ansaldo 611, but Italy began the war with the Autoblinda (AB) 40, a 4 × 4 Fiat/Spa design weighing 6.5 tons and based upon an artillery tractor chassis, the Trattore Medio (TM) 40. The AB 41 retained the rear-engined configuration of its predecessor and small frontal turret housing two Breda 8mm machine guns. These vehicles had low rear decking and carried spare wheels on their sides. Weight remained the same, and the third and last model was the AB 43. These vehicles were also built without turrets. They were powered by 80 or 100hp Spa engines and had the ability to retire rapidly when placed at tactical disadvantage by the expedient of carrying a second driver who faced aft. The AB 41 was mostly used in North Africa but also occasionally on the Western Front. The crew consisted of four, and the vehicles were 16 feet 5 inches long. They were well designed and nimble armored cars well suited to desert operations.

Fiat/Spa also produced a 4 × 4 Reconnaissance Car based on the AB-41. This open vehicle carried two rows of jerrycans along its sides to provide long range for its desert operations, and a distinctive feature was the recessed front deck which housed the spare wheel. A variety of armament could be fitted. The Lince – strongly resembling the British Daimler Dingo scout car – was also built in prototype form.

Japan The Japanese employed various types of 4 × 2 armored cars and several 6 × 4 models. The 6 × 4 Type 2592 of 1932 was powered by a six-cylinder engine developing 85bhp and was a vehicle of high silhouette and angular appearance. The Type 2593 produced by Sumida and others had a more powerful engine developing 100bhp and weighed seven tons. Its silhouette was lower and its turret was mounted midway along the top. The Type 2593 carried a crew of six and was unusual in that along its sides it carried rims which enabled the vehicle to be lifted on to and run along railroad tracks.

Other Nations France had various 4 × 4 armored cars (Automitrailleuses) in service in 1939 including the Berliet and the better Panhard 178 B design. This weighed eight tons and its engine developed 115bhp. Berliet also produced a 6 × 6 armored car, the UDB 4, in the mid-1930s. The Czech firm of Tatra produced the VZOR 30 6 × 4 design which resembled the French Berliet.

HALF-TRACKS

Great Britain While the British appreciated the half-track's virtues, and had used the type in the interwar period, they never prolonged its development, and the only half-track vehicles produced in Britain during the war were prototypes of vehicles which never achieved production status. These included the three-quarter-Track Bedford BT Traclat which was powered by two Bedford engines and appeared in 1945. However, large numbers of American half-tracks were acquired and served with the British army, including Gun Motor Carriages which were employed, not as artillery tractors, but as general-purpose transport vehicles.

The United States The Americans, unlike the British, devoted much attention to half-tracks and a wide range of them, built by White, Autocar, Diamond T and International Harvester, was available before the end of the war. The smallest was a conversion of the Willys jeep into a snow tractor. Other types of armored half-tracks included the Mack T 19, Autocar, White T 17 and Diamond T 16 (which were experimental models) and the Autocar 2.5-ton truck. Among the combat vehicles were to be found the Carriers M2 and M3 – which saw widespread service in all theaters – and their derivatives the M5 and M9. The M3 or M3A1 was a personnel carrier powered by a White 160 AX engine which developed 147bhp. It could carry 13 infantrymen. It weighed 14,800 pounds and was 20 feet 2 inches long. The M3A2 was a version equipped with a special AA mounting. The M5 was produced by International Harvester and was powered by an IHC engine – Britain received over 4000 of this type. The M9 Car, Half-Track, was also supplied to the UK.

These Carriers and Cars formed the basis for weapons carriers including the M4A1 81mm Mortar Carrier based on the White M3, as was the M13 Multiple Gun Motor Carriage. The T 12 Gun Motor Carriage was based on the M3 and carried a 75mm Gun, while the T 30 GMC was equipped with a 75mm Howitzer. Others carried 37mm and 40mm AA guns.

These half-tracks proved of great use, particularly over rough ground where the traction provided by their rear tracks and Kégresse bogies was greater than could have been provided by trucks. As well as this their configuration allowed them to be in the thick of the battle and provide their infantrymen with some protection behind 6mm of armor plate. Such was the success and longevity of the American half-track that examples were still in front-line military service in the late 1970s.

A whole range of half-tracks manufactured by Linn, Ford/Marmon Herrington and General Motors during the 1930s was also available.

The Soviet Union The Soviet Union received large numbers of American half-tracks under the Lend-Lease scheme and used them alongside as many German types as they could capture. The Soviets had pioneered half-track development in World War I when a Frenchman called Kégresse effected some conversions to Czarist vehicles to provide them with the ability to operate on snowy ground. It is, therefore, surprising that more emphasis was not placed by the Soviets on the genre during World War II.

The half-tracks which were in use were modifications to standard trucks. The GAZ-60 was a 1.25-ton vehicle developing 50bhp and the range of 2.25-ton Cargo Half-Tracks included the ZIS-42 and ZIS-33 (which incorporated the original rear wheel within the framework of the track). One ZIS-42 variant had an engine developing 88bhp – the standard type developed 73.

Germany German interest in half-tracks (Halbketten) vehicles began in the early 1930s, and the initial light one-ton range made provision for the design to be expanded for vehicles of up to 18 tons. The early Demag D 11 one-ton leichter Zugkraftwagen was built in 1934 and powered by a BMW engine, while the D 7 (Sd Kfz 10) was another light vehicle carrying an eight-man crew. From it was developed the D 7 p Sd Kfz 250/1 which dispensed with the windshield of the D 7 and provided a lower silhouette. The concept of a standardized le WS (leichter Wehrmachtsschlepper) or light tractor was mooted in 1942, but never came to anything, and light German half-tracks were mostly manufactured by Demag or Adler. The latter company's HK 300 series included the A 1 prototype powered by a 2540cc Maybach engine, and A 2, while the HK 301 had an engine of over 3000cc. Hanomag also produced a three-ton half-track, the Sd Kfz 11 H kl 6, and Borgward even produced a half-track embulance for the German coastguard based on this Sd Kfz II chassis design.

The medium half-track range included five-ton types, and heavier types in this category of Mittlerer Zugkraftwagen included the Büssing-NAG BN 1 7 with crew of 15, and a Czech-built Sd Kfz 6 Praga model. Eight-ton Sd Kfz 7 series half-tracks included the Krauss-Maffei KM m range of which some were used as carriages for AA guns. Large numbers were produced throughout the war.

As an intermediate measure pending the arrival of better purpose-built all-wheel drive vehicles, a program of standard lorry conversion was undertaken in 1942 to enable the Wehrmacht to remain mobile in the conditions prevalent on the Eastern Front. These Maultier (Mule) conversions were made to Opel Blitz and Klöckner-Humboldt Deutz chassis; some Opel versions were armored and employed as Panzerwerfer 42 launcher vehicles (qv).

In 1943 the Schwerer Wehrmachtsschlepper – or heavy tractor – was introduced in an attempt to reduce the number of various types of medium tractor in service, such as the Sd Kfz 6 and 7. The firms of Büssing-NAG and Tatra thereafter built a standard vehicle capable of various body configurations.

Heavy semitractors included the 12-ton Sd Kfz 8 range – the Mercedes-Benz DB 9 and DB 10 – which carried 13 personnel and were powered by Maybach HL 85 engines developing 185bhp. The heaviest of all was the 18-ton Sd Kfz 9 Famo F 2, an enormous vehicle whose Maybach engine developed 230bhp and which was employed either as an artillery tractor or, more usually, as a tank recovery vehicle. Both these heavy half-tracks were in German army service at the outbreak of war in 1939.

Italy The Italians designed one heavy half-track vehicle which they intended to employ as an artillery tractor. This was known as the Fiat 727 SC – semicincolato – but such was the time lag between conception and development that only the prototype had been constructed by the time the Italians surrendered in 1943. Both Fiat and Breda constructed lighter half-tracks in small numbers, the former a truck conversion and the latter a low-slung armored personnel carrier.

Japan The Japanese employed a half-track APC designated HO-HA Type 1. This seven-ton vehicle carried 12 infantrymen plus a three-man crew, and was powered by a diesel engine developing 130bhp. It entered service with the Imperial Japanese Army in 1941 but, as far as can be ascertained, did not see widespread use.

Other Nations France developed half-track personnel carriers and numerous artillery tractors in the 1930s; the Citroën-Kégresse type had a fully enclosed rear compartment. Some were converted by the Germans into Panzer-werfer 42 carriers, or used as artillery tractors, as were captured Unic vehicles. Poland also provided a half-track ambulance, the Polski Fiat 62-1 L, and several artillery tractors.

CARRIERS AND ARTILLERY TRACTORS

Great Britain In the early 1930s the forerunner of the Bren Gun Carrier was designed as the Carden-Loyd Carrier Full Track Mark VI. Developed by Vickers-Armstrong into the Carrier, Full Track, MG in 1934 and powered by a V-8 engine developing 65bhp, this in turn was succeeded by the Carrier, Full Track, Bren, in 1938. This sound design was manufactured by a number of firms including Ford, Thornycroft and Wolseley and went to several marks as a Universal and Armored OP vehicle. The Carrier

weighed some four tons, was 12 feet long and most marks were powered by engines developing 85bhp. Canada also built over 30,000. They normally carried a three-man crew.

A number of trucks were modified to act as tractors for Bofors and 2- and 6-pounder antitank guns. Bedford QL's and Austin K 5s were converted to act as portee vehicles, as were AEC Matadors – known as Deacons – camouflaged to provide portee carriages for 6-pounders. Various manufacturers provided 4 × 4 Quads or FATs (Field Artillery Tractors), squat purpose-built vehicles whose task was to tow 17-pounder and 25-pounder guns. Morris-Commercial built the square-set C 8, Guy the Quad-Ant, and these proved well suited to the task of bringing gun, limber with ammunition supplies and crew into action. Heavy and medium artillery tractors included the 4 × 4 AEC Matador truck and Scammell and Albion 6 × 4 designs.

The United States The Americans produced Ford T 16 Universal Carriers for Britain as well as the M29 Studebaker Weasel and LVTs which are described elsewhere. Another full-track Utility design was the M39 Armored Carrier which served as an APC and artillery tractor. For the towing of guns the Americans mostly employed standard 6 × 6 trucks, but 4 × 4 prime movers such as the five-ton Walker ADUM and the 6 × 6 7.5-ton Minneapolis-Moline GTX were also manufactured for the task.

High-speed full-track tractors provided cross-country mobility and examples were the International M5 13-ton vehicle with crew of nine; the Allis-Chalmers M6 38-ton design which had a 10-man crew; and the 18-ton M4 from the same manufacturer. These vehicles were based on tank chassis and the M4 and M6 were powered by two six-cylinder engines developing a total of 380bhp.

The Soviet Union The Soviets placed much emphasis upon full-tracked artillery tractors which enabled them to transport their guns over the kind of terrain which could defeat wheeled vehicles. Many were based upon commercial agricultural tractor designs. In this category were the DT-54, STZ and Stalinets SG-65.

Purpose-built tractors were also produced, however, including the Komintern with central cab and the Komsomolets tractor which was employed to tow antitank guns. The Stalin was another large artillery tractor with frontal cab and the STZ and KT-12 provided examples of artillery tractors whose cab was situated forward over the engine.

Wherever conditions were suitable the Soviets moved their artillery by all available types of vehicle including the range of trucks described in other sections.

Germany The Germans employed several types of Radschlepper, or wheeled tractors, to perform a variety of towing tasks. Faun and Hanomag produced 4 × 2 heavy tractors, powered by 13,540cc and 8553cc engines respectively developing 150 and 100bhp, and Skoda built a large-wheeled 4 × 4 tractor, the Radschlepper Ost, for service in the Soviet Union. Famo and Austro-Daimler produced tractors and the Wehrmacht also utilized captured French Latil and Laffly types.

The Germans employed their extensive range of half-tracks as artillery tractors, while among full-track tractors a number of interesting designs emerged. Sachsenberg designed the Land-Wasserschlepper, an amphibious tractor powered by a Maybach HL 120 engine developing 300bhp and weighing 16 tons. It served as an engineer vehicle and landing craft, carried a crew of 20, and was designed by Rheinmetall-Borsig in 1936.

The Raupenschlepper Ost (RSO) was a tracked tractor designed by Steyr for service on the Eastern Front. Powered by a 3517cc Steyr V-8 engine developing 70hp, the RSO had a payload capacity of 1.5 tons and weighed 7713 pounds. It proved a successful design and ran to three variants, the last of which dispensed with the enclosed cab, and was manufactured by Klöckner Humboldt Deutz/Magirus.

The Czechs produced several full-track artillery tractors, including the Praga T 4, T 6 and T 9 whose development spanned the years between 1938 and 1944. Any such vehicles captured from the Russians or the French were also impressed into Wehrmacht service, while the Austrian-produced Saurer Räder-Kettenwagen RK 7 with combined wheels and tracks, and the unusual Austro-Daimler ADMK of similar configuration, the Maschinengewehr Traktor – a kind of Austrian version of the Bren Gun Carrier – were also used.

Italy The Italians concentrated on the development of wheeled artillery tractors in the 1930s and by the time war broke out had a number of types in service. Breda, Fiat, Fiat/Spa and Pavesi all produced vehicles. Breda's Model 40 was a 4 × 4 heavy design, and the Fiat/Spa Pavesi P 4-110 was a large-wheeled short wheel-base heavy tractor weighing 8816 pounds. Fiat/Spa

also produced 4 × 4 light and medium artillery tractors: the Trattore Leggero TL 37 was powered by a 4053cc engine developing 57hp and, weighing 7270 pounds, had a payload of 1763 pounds. Several types of body were fitted to its chassis. In 1940 the Trattore Medio TM 40 appeared which was a well-designed vehicle powered by a six-cylinder engine developing 108bhp and weighing 12,120 pounds. This, too, provided the basis of several types of body.

Fiat introduced the OCI 708 CM, a full-track light artillery tractor, in the mid-1930s but the Italians mostly opted for highly mobile wheeled vehicles.

Japan The Japanese army made extensive use of half and full-track artillery tractors. Among the former were designs by Isuzu, whose Type 98's diesel engine developed 120bhp and which, carrying a crew of 15, weighed six tons. The KO-HI Type 98 was designed for towing antiaircraft guns and carried a similar number of crew. Its engine developed 110bhp. The HO-HA Type 1 half-track served as an armored personnel carrier and also towed antiaircraft weapons.

Full-track vehicles included the gasoline-engined Type 94, a four-ton tractor towing field artillery pieces, and the Isuzu Type 98 six-ton tractor which was equipped with a winch, crewed by seven, and had a diesel engine developing 120bhp. The Type 92 B was an eight-ton tractor which, unlike the earlier Type 92 A, was powered by the standard diesel engine installed in almost all later Japanese artillery tractors.

France In France Citroën-Kégresse's VBTT was a half-track armored personnel carrier designed in the early 1930s to augment earlier types produced by the same company. Renault also provided a full-track APC and a supply version.

France developed half-tracks to an advanced state in the 1930s and many types of artillery tractor were on the inventory in 1939. These included the Citroën-Kégresse P 75, the Somua MCG 5 and MCL 5 designed to tow the 155mm GPF and MSCL 5. There were various other types including the P 107 and TU 1.

Full-track artillery tractors included the Renault Y 1 and YK of 1933. The Germans employed all the above types following the defeat of France in 1940.

Other Nations Czechoslovakia also produced several types of artillery tractors, including the Praga T 4, T 6 and T 9. These well-designed full-track vehicles had canvas-covered super-structures and the most powerful, the T 9, had a 14,500cc gasoline engine developing 140bhp. The Belgians had several types of wheeled artillery tractors in service, including the French-designed Latil TL 6 medium tractor, the Brossel and FN 4 × 4 heavy types and also half and full-track designs. Poland employed several Polski-Fiat half-tracks and full-track vehicles, including the CZP lighter tractor and C7P heavier types.

UTILITY VEHICLES

Great Britain In 1939 the British army had at its disposal a variety of light utility vehicles and cars for general purposes. There were mostly conversions of standard civilian vehicles and the utility vehicles were equipped with canvas tilts and rear space for the transportation of person-nel or supplies. Vehicles of this type included Austin, Hillman and Morris 10 HP cars, and the Standard 12 HP. The Austin 8 HP provided a light car with open-tourer body. A number of heavier 4 × 2 cars were also in service as staff cars, and these included Humber Snipes with both saloon and open-tourer coachwork, while larger vehicles still included Ford WO A 2 models – heavy utility types – and a longer-bodied Humber Snipe. The Humber FWD was, as the name implies, a four-wheel drive type of robust design.

Light trucks included vehicles of eight, 15 and 30 hundredweight. Here again the Humber Snipe and FWD provided the basis for eight-hundredweight vehicles, while Ford and Morris-Commercial also produced canvas-topped cab vehicles with half doors to act as light load-carrying or wireless trucks. The 15-hundred-weight range included the Bedford MWD on which a variety of body types could be fitted; Morris-Commercial and Fordson types; and the Guy Quad-Ant on whose chassis the Guy armored car was based, and which served as a field-artillery tractor. Both the 15- and the 30-hundredweight trucks played a large part in the early days of the war, but were superseded by types with greater payloads. In the 30-hundredweight category, the 4 × 2 Austin K 30, its two-tonner enclosed cab version, the K 2, Bedford, Thornycroft and Commer vehicles were to be found.

The United States The 'Truck, .25-ton, 4 × 4, Command Reconnaissance' began life as the Bantam in 1940. This was powered by a 45hp Continental engine at first but the Willys pilot Model of November that year had a 54hp power plant. The next Willys Model, the MB, was awarded the production contract and this became the celebrated Jeep. The vehicle weighed 4250 pounds and proved enormously versatile and rugged. Ford produced over 250,000 GPW versions alone of the total wartime production of just over 639,000, and the 11-foot long vehicle – capable of 65mph – was encountered in every theater in a multitude of different versions. Jeeps featured prominently in the Lend-Lease pro-gram and were supplied to the Soviet Union and Britain, where they were put to use with the SAS and Airborne Forces as well as more con-ventional units. The Jeep even provided the basis for an experimental rotor-powered flying machine.

So important was the part played by the Jeep – whose name is reputed to come from the abbreviation GP (General Purpose) – that it is easy to overlook other less spectacular vehicles used by the US forces. Light and medium sedans served as staff cars and included Ford, Chevrolet, Plymouth and Packard types, mostly powered by eight-cylinder engines of around 85bhp. Light cargo transport vehicles, .5-ton 4 × 2 and 4 × 4 trucks, were manufactured by, among others, Dodge, General Motors, Chevrolet and Ford. Dodge's 4 × 4 .5-tonner served as a weapons carrier, command reconnaissance and radio vehicle.

There were .75-ton trucks, manufactured mainly by Dodge and by Ford. The Dodge .75-ton 4 × 4 T 214-WC 56 resembled an enlarged Jeep. The same chassis provided the basis for weapons carriers and command trucks, while the 4 × 4 Ford GAJ was designed as a cargo vehicle. In the .5-ton range both two and four-wheel drive trucks were manufactured; Ford, Chrysler, Dodge and General Motors produced tens of thousands of such vehicles for Allied use during the war. The 4 × 4 vehicles included the Chevrolet YP-G. Some 6 × 6 types were also constructed, typified by the Dodge T 223-WC 62 canvas-topped cab cargo truck.

The Soviet Union The Soviet army's GAZ-67 B was a 4 × 4 Field Car based upon the American Jeep, copious quantities of which had been provided under the Lend-Lease scheme. Al-though it was not of the same standard as the original, it nevertheless proved most useful and continued in service after 1945. Various Ford-inspired sedans provided tramsport for person-nel and staff officers, among them the GAZ-61 and the GAZ-M-1.

Large numbers of angular trucks were in service with the Soviet army. Among the 1.5-ton vehicles were the 4 × 2 GAZ-AA, -MM, -42, and -44; the first mentioned was inspired by a similar Ford model and built until 1945. ZIS vehicles of 2.5-ton payload were also widely used. The 6 × 4 trucks included the 1.5-ton GAZ-AAA (which formed the basis for the BA-10 armored car), and the 2.5-ton ZIS-6, rugged vehicles of similar appearance and with 50 and 73bhp engines respectively. Both provided the basis for special-purpose bodies, and on the ZIS-6 was mounted the 16-barrelled M.13 132mm rocket launcher.

Germany Germany's equivalent to the Jeep was the leichter Geländewagen K 1 Typ 82 – the 4 × 2 Kübelwagen manufactured by Volkswagen. Powered originally be a VW 998cc air-cooled engine, later models had a 1131cc type developing 25bhp. Over 50,000 Kübelwagen were produced; they weighed 2170 pounds and were 12 feet 2 inches long. The vehicle was of squat and purposeful appearance and could be rapidly converted into open-tourer configuration; special tropical equipment included filters and wider than normal tires which were later adopted as standard. Variations on the basic Kübelwagen theme included the Kfz 2 Funkwagen (radio equipped), the Kfz 2/40 Instandsetzungstruppkraftwagen (maintenance vehicle), the Verwundeten-Transportwagen (ambulance) and the Messtruppkraftwagen (survey vehicle). The Kübelwagen had an excellent cross-country performance and was a reliable and strong vehicle. Other types of light open cars were built by BMW, Opel, Hanomag and Volkswagen as well as a Czech-produced Tatra design. Medium cars included Horch 830, Wanderer, and Mercedes-Benz 4 × 2 and 4 × 4 types which weighed around 4408 pounds and of which some were used as light artillery tractors. The 4 × 4 Kfz 15 (Horch 40) was a typical staff car manufactured by Horch and Auto-Union and provided the basis for a radio vehicle.

Heavy cars of 4 × 2, 4 × 4 and 6 × 4 types included designs by Auto-Union, Horch, Phänomen and Mercedes-Benz as well as the Austrian firm of Steyr. These were robust models which served as a basis for armored cars and command vehicles, and provided artillery tractors as well as, in the case of the Mercedes-Benz 6 × 4 G 4/W 31, staff cars for the Nazi Party leadership.

An abundance of light trucks included 4 × 2, 4 × 4, 6 × 4 and 6 × 6 types with payloads of around two tons. The Schell program of 1938 attempted to rationalize matters by standardizing designs and largely succeeded in allocating and building vehicles to two specifications, cargo

Above: Rommel used this captured 'Mammoth' command truck.

and military, the latter class having four-wheel drive. Such vehicles were built by Auto-Union (1500 A), Phänomen (Granit) and Mercedes-Benz (1500 A), while cargo vehicles included Adler, Mercedes and Auto-Union 4 × 2 designs.

The 6 × 4 vehicles included the Krupp LZH 143, the Büssing/NAG G 31 and the Magirus M 206, as well as products of numerous other manufacturers; 6 × 6 types were built by the last two mentioned manufacturers as well as MAN, Mercedes-Benz and Henschel.

Italy Italy's equivalent to the Jeep was the 4 × 2 Fiat 508 C Torpedo Militare light car, powered by an 1100cc engine developing 32bhp, which followed Fiat's 508 C Colonial light field car of prewar design. Both vehicles performed well over rough going, and were encountered in the desert war. Bianchi also produced two light field cars, the 54 and 56, while the Fiat 2800 Mil Col was a solidly constructed five-seater powered by a six-cylinder engine developing 85bhp and equipped with open-tourer body. Italian military vehicles, incidentally, had right-hand drive.

A light truck version of the Fiat 508 C Mil was fitted with a canvas tilt. Other and larger light trucks included the 4 × 2 Fiat 618 Mil Col, the 4 × 4 Fiat/Spa CL 39 with one-ton payload, and the Fiat/Spa TL 37. This was powered by a four-cylinder 57bhp engine and based on the TL 37 artillery tractor and the OM Autocarretta 32, a highly mobile prewar design with independent suspension, which also influenced the CL 39. These vehicles were well-designed and engineered and proved very suitable for operations in North Africa. Fiat/Spa produced the 4 × 2 Autocarro 38 R with 2.5-ton payload capacity and upon which several special body variants were based.

Japan The Japanese army's scout car was the Kurogane-designed 4 × 4 Type 95, powered by a two-cylinder 1400cc engine developing 25bhp and with a weight of 2204 pounds. Under 5000 were built. Types of saloon were used as staff cars, including the Nissan 70 and several American or American-inspired models, while Command Cars included 4 × 4 types from Isuzu, Mitsubishi, and Sumida, and 6 × 4 designs were in service from the last two mentioned manufacturers, and Chiyoda.

The most widely used Japanese light truck was the 1.5-ton 6 × 4 Isuzu Type 94 A (gasoline) or 94 B (diesel)-powered vehicle. This had a slatted rear compartment and a canvas cab top and was employed as an artillery tractor as well as for the transportation of personnel and supplies. Toyota produced a light truck, while 1.5-ton vehicles included the 4 × 2 Toyota KB – a Chrysler-inspired vehicle – and Isuzu Type 94. The same company built the Type 97, a conventional two-tonner, while the Nissan 80 was a 2.5-ton cargo truck based, as almost all Japanese vehicles were, upon original American designs.

Other Nations The French used Renault, Peugeot and Hotchkiss saloon cars impressed for military service, and had a range of VTT (Véhicule Tout Terrain) cross-country field cars. These included 4 × 4 Latil, Hotchkiss and Laffly types, while Laffly also built a 6 × 6 VTT. A large number of light 1.5-ton trucks – many by Citroën, Renault and Latil – were also available. The Czech firms of Skoda, Tatra and Praga built saloon and command cars as well as cargo trucks.

MEDIUM AND HEAVY TRUCKS AND TANK TRANSPORTERS

Great Britain In addition to countless civilian trucks impressed, in Britain as in all combatant countries, for military use there existed a multitude of 4 × 2 and 4 × 4 medium trucks of three-ton capacity. Manufacturers of 4 × 2 types included Bedford, Commer, Austin and Thornycroft, as well as a host of others; and three-tonners made up the bulk of British military vehicles. Typical were the Austin K 3, the Bedford OYD and the Commer Q 4; many served as the basis for bowsers, searchlights, workshop and for other purposes. The 4 × 4 three-tonners included the Austin K 5, Bedford QL/QLD, and Albion FTII N, which was powered by a 4500cc engine developing 90bhp. These, too, provided wireless vehicles and several other specialist tasks. The 6 × 4 three-tonners – such as the Austin K 3/YF and K 6 types – also carried a range of special bodies.

Heavy trucks were manufactured by ERF, Dennis and Foden in the five- and six-ton 4 × 2 range, while 10-ton 6 × 4 vehicles provided for heavy lift and included the Leyland Hippo, Foden and Albion types which, like the six-ton range, owed their origins to prewar commercial trucks. The British used numbers of American trucks and the Canadians and Australians both manufactured large numbers of American designs, notably Chevrolet and Ford vehicles.

For the transportation of tanks to and from base workshops or to recover them from the battlefield the British relied upon indigenous as well as American designs. The Scammell TRMU/30-ton 6 × 4 or 6 × 8 tractor powered by an eight-liter Gardner diesel, and a smaller version of 20 tons, and the Albion CX 245 of 15 tons and CX33 were in service, while the 40-ton Mark I and Mark II trailers carried the actual tanks. The American Diamond T 981 M 20 12-ton 6 × 4 prime mover was designed for British use in the desert, while the Mack 6 × 4 weighing 22,112 pounds and a smaller 13-tonner version, along with the White 920 18-ton 6 × 4, also saw service in North Africa and elsewhere.

The United States The American 2.5-ton 6 × 6 Light/Heavy truck saw widespread use during the war in every theater. Most of the massive total of 800,000 produced were from General Motors, and to them a number of specialist bodies, including bowsers and winch platforms, were fitted. Some four-ton 4 × 4 trucks were also used but more commonly employed were four-ton 6 × 6 vehicles, manufactured by White (950) and Diamond T (968 A), many of which carried a frontal winch. Five- and six-ton 4 × 2 trucks were, like their British counterparts, mainly militarized civilian vehicles from Mack, Diamond T and many others, while six-ton 6 × 6 ones provided a heavy lift capability and were augmented by 7.5-ton, eight-ton, 10-ton and 12-ton types. The 7.5-ton range mostly provided prime movers for trailers and bowsers, while eight-ton and 10-ton 6 × 4s were used for long-distance haulage, and were typified by the White 1064 and Mack NR 9. The Diamond T 981, which has already been mentioned, equipped the American forces as a prime mover, and the heaviest type of vehicle in use was the 8 × 8 range of eight- and 12-ton trucks which enjoyed a fair cross-country performance.

In addition to the tank transporters supplied to Britain, the Americans utilized several other types themselves, including the successful Diamond T M 20 with its 45-ton M 9 trailer with 12 wheels, and the M 26 armored prime mover in conjunction with the 45-ton M 15 trailer with light.

The Americans also had, of course, a whole range of specialist vehicles, including cranes, wreckers and buses which were either purpose-built military vehicles or simply civilian types impressed. They also provided enormous numbers of all types of military vehicles to Britain and the Soviet Union under the Lend-Lease program.

The Soviet Union The Soviet army employed the usual variety of medium and heavy trucks during the war. The series of three-ton 4 × 2 vehicles included the ZIS-5 or Ural ZIS-5 produced in the Urals factory to which the company had retreated in 1941, and a four-ton type was the YAS-3. The YAG-6 was a five-ton 4 × 2 truck powered by a ZIS engine developing 73bhp. The 6 × 4 eight-ton truck was the YAG-10 powered by a six-cylinder engine developing 60bhp, which in addition to providing heavy lift was also converted into a platform for mobile AA guns. The Soviet Union was also the recipient of many hundreds of thousands of US trucks.

Germany Like all other nations, the Germans impressed civilian vehicles but the 1938 Schell program ensured that the Wehrmacht would have a range of standardized military designs, the A-vehicles. Also produced were S-vehicles – commercial variants lacking specialized military equipment and frequently with two-wheel drive. Medium trucks in the 4 × 2 range were three-ton Mercedes and Borgward types, initially with canvas-topped cabs, although the unattractive Einheits cab introduced in 1944 provided an enclosed structure of compressed paper and wood. Among the 4 × 4 vehicles were the widely used Opel Blitz 6700 A with three-ton payload, the Magirus Klöckner A 3000, the Borgward B 3000 A and the Mercedes-Benz L 3000 A/066. The 6 × 4 and 6 × 6 designs were produced by, among others, Büssing-NAG, Henschel and Mercedes-Benz.

In the Heavy Truck (schwerer Lastkraftwagen) range were to be found MAN, Henschel and Mercedes-Benz designs – the latter's L 4500 A serves as an example – while 6.5-ton vehicles abounded. The 6 × 4 and 6 × 6 types were manufactured by Büssing-NAG and Mercedes-Benz (the LG 4000 LG 68 6 × 6) as well as by the Czech firms of Tatra and Skoda. Whereas the heavy ranges were used for transporting troops and material, medium LKw chassis also provided the basis for specialist wireless, command and tanker variants. The Wehrmacht made widespread use of captured vehicles, too.

Italy The Italians had, like the Germans, a similar standardization program for medium and heavy trucks. The Autocarro Unificato Medio range had a three-ton payload, and the Pesante, a six-ton one, as a minimum. Manufacturers built vehicles conforming to these specifications. Fiat/Spa built a three-ton 6 × 4 cross-country truck, the Dovunque 35, while in the same range Fiat produced a 4 × 2 vehicle, the 626 BL, and OM a similar type. Various specialist bodies were also fitted to these.

Among 4 × 2 types of greater payload capacity were the five-ton Fiat 665 NL or NM with half-doors (an Italian preference) and the six-ton Alfa-Romeo 800 RE. A 6.5-ton capacity was produced by Lancia's 3 RO N Mil, and the heaviest Italian truck was the Fiat 634N with a 7.5-ton payload. The heaviest in the Dovunque series was the 6 × 6 Fiat/Spa 41. This was sometimes employed to pull trailers when acting as a tank transporter, as were other heavy types.

Japan The Japanese employed several types of medium and heavy trucks. Examples in the three-ton range included the 6 × 4 Isuzu TU 10 and TU 23 or Type 1 Cargo Truck which was powered by either a diesel or a gasoline engine developing 85bhp or 70bhp respectively. Isuzu also produced a 4 × 2 seven-ton Type 2 truck with twin rear wheels to provide for heavy transportation, and the largest 20-ton truck, the TH 10. To ensure that a supply of trucks suitable for military use would be forthcoming, the Japanese introduced a subsidy scheme before the war for suitable commercial vehicles with military potential, which, in the event, was a good example of forward planning.

Other Nations France made use of a large variety of medium and heavy trucks until 1940; thereafter the survivors were utilized by the Germans. Citroën, Matford, Laffly, Latil and Renault all produced 4 × 2 designs with varying payload capacities and Berliet built a 30-ton 6 × 4 tank transporter. Czech designs included the four-ton 6 × 4 Praga SV and Skoda 65T6-L, -T and -H, while the Tatra T 22 was a prime mover. Numerous Czech vehicles were used by the Germans.

AMPHIBIANS

Great Britain Amphibious vehicles were a great asset during littoral operations and landings, and Britain produced several indigenous designs during the war, including Morris and Thornycroft types. The only one to be introduced into

Above: A US Marine LVT heads for the beach after being unloaded from a landing craft.

(limited) service was the Terrapin Mark 1, a four-ton 8×8 amphibian designed by Morris-Commercial.

The British army also used American-built DUKWs and LVT Buffaloes, particularly in the fighting in Northwest Europe in 1944–45.

The United States The Americans began experiments with an amphibious version of the .25-ton 4×4 Jeep in 1941, the Ford GPA. The body consisted of a boat-shaped hull which reappeared more important on the 2.5-ton 6×6 amphibian of 1942, better known as the GMC-produced DUKW. The abbreviation DUKW stood for the year of design (D-1942), the type of vehicle (U-amphibian), the type of transmission (K-all-wheel drive) and the axle configuration (W-dual rear). The DUKW is one of the success stories among wartime developments and was to prove a most versatile and useful vehicle. Powered by a six-cylinder engine developing 104bhp, it weighed just over 15,000 pounds and was 31 feet long. The postwar Soviet BAV was a copy of it. Over 21,000 DUKWs were produced in the United States.

Studebaker also produced the M 29 C Weasel Cargo vehicle which, unlike the DUKW with its propeller, relied upon the rotation of its tracks for water propulsion. The Weasel weighed 4780 pounds and was also used by the British, as was the LVT series of Landing Vehicles, Tracked, known as Alligators or (Water) Buffaloes. The LVT went to four marks; the LVT (3) could carry 6000 pounds and was powered by two Cadillac V-8 engines. The LVTs were used in the Pacific and European Theaters, and over 18,000 were built. Some were fitted with armor and the LVT (A) 1 carried a turret with 37mm gun, while the (A) 4 version had a 75mm howitzer.

The Soviet Union The Lend-Lease scheme provided the Soviets with numbers of the Ford GPA amphibian and a Soviet-built copy, the GAZ-46 MAV was also produced. They also received DUKWs which, as has already been mentioned, were likewise copied.

Germany The Germans developed several types of leichte Schwimmfähige Personenkraftwagen, or light amphibians, the earliest of which was Porsche's Typ 128, a 4×4 design of 1940. This had a four-cylinder engine developing 24bhp and preceded the Kfz 1/20 K 2 S Typ 166 designed by Volkswagen and introduced two years later. The 166 weighed 2006 pounds and was a neat vehicle with spare wheel stowed on its hood, and propeller-driven once in water. Over 14,000 were built before production ceased in 1944. A mittlerer schwimmfähiger Pkw, the Trippel SG 6 series, was in production from 1940. This 4×4 vehicle was powered by a six-cylinder Opel engine developing 55bhp and weighed 3860 pounds. Subsequent variants had Czech Tatra engines and an armored version was also built.

Italy The Italians did not possess any amphibians during the war.

Japan In 1943 the firm of Toyota produced the SUKI two-ton 4×4 amphibian, which superficially resembled an angular American DUKW. Its six-cylinder engine produced 63bhp and overall weight was 14,110 pounds. The SUKI vehicle was based upon the KCY truck chassis and was 25 feet long. Just under 200 examples were built. They proved of use for transferring material from ship to ship in the Pacific, a role which all amphibians performed to good effect.

The escort carrier Guadalcanal in 1944.

SEA

SEA

BATTLESHIPS

When World War II broke out in September 1939 battleships were still acknowledged to be the most powerful of all warships. Their numbers were governed by international agreements, principally the Washington Treaty and the two London Treaties. Displacements of the various battle fleets were limited at Washington in 1922 to totals over 500,000 tons for Britain and the United States, 300,000 tons for Japan, 220,000 for France and 180,000 for Italy. Also in 1922 the size limit had been fixed at 35,000 tons displacement, with guns no greater than 16-inch caliber, but the Japanese refused to ratify the 1936 London Treaty in order to build much bigger ships in secret, and in reply to this the United States announced its intention of building to a new limit of 45,000 tons.

Each of the major navies' battleships reflected national preferences and strategic necessities. The French and British were constrained by lack of money and so had not spent the large sums of money expended by other navies on modernizing old ships. Nevertheless a belated British program of rebuilding to improve protection and antiaircraft defense had started in 1933, and HMS *Warspite* and *Renown* were to be followed by two more battleships in 1940–41. In contrast the Americans had rebuilt all but five of their battleships by the early 1930s, while the Japanese rebuilt all 10 of theirs. The Italians went furthest down this path, rebuilding four rather weak World War I dreadnoughts into formidable, fast battleships.

Although a number of ships had been completed after the signing of the Washington Treaty in 1922, most had been designed before the full lessons of war experience had been digested. The only exceptions were the British *Nelson* and *Rodney*, laid down after exhaustive tests against surrendered German ships; although ugly they embodied several advanced features and were the only truly modern front-rank capital ships in service in September 1939. They displaced nearly 40,000 tons in fighting trim and had three triple 16-inch turrets in a unique disposition, all forward of a massive block of superstructure. The French copied the arrangement but cured the problem of excessive blast by putting the guns in two quadruple turrets well forward.

The *Nelson*s and their contemporaries were relatively slow, achieving 22–24 knots, as they did not sacrifice armor to gain speed, unlike the older battlecruisers such as the *Hood* (31 knots), *Renown* (30 knots) and *Kongo* Class (27 knots).

Thus, when the Germans produced a replacement for their aging coast-defense battleships, all that they were allowed under the Treaty of Versailles, they made a point of striving for a decisive margin of speed. When the *Deutschland* appeared in 1933 she was apparently superior in gunpower (six 11-inch guns) to any cruiser and, at 26 knots, faster than any battleship. Small wonder that she was known as a 'pocket battleship' to the world's press, although the Germans themselves referred to her as an armored ship (*panzerschiff*). She was in fact a hybrid, an overgunned heavy cruiser.

The laying down of two more *panzerschiffe* and plans to build a further three caused great alarm to the French. Their battleships were particularly slow and weakly protected and their parlous financial state after World War I had prevented them from building up to the numbers allowed by the Washington Treaty. To combat the threat of pocket battleships operating against their lines of communications they laid down two 26,000-ton battlecruisers or fast battleships, the *Dunkerque* and *Strasbourg*. Like the British *Nelson* Class, they saved weight by concentrating the armament in two quadruple mountings forward, but devoted all the weight saved to speed, both reaching 31 knots on trials.

By abrogating the Treaty of Versailles Hitler freed the German navy to build two replies to the French ships, the *Scharnhorst* and *Gneisenau*. Although nominally equal in tonnage to the *Dunkerque* Class they displaced 5000 tons more and could match the speed of the French ships without such light armor. This was helped by having to make use of six triple 11-inch gun mountings originally ordered for three cancelled *panzerschiffe*, but as a result they were somewhat undergunned for their size.

The European arms race was in full swing by 1936. The Italians started two fast battleships of the *Littorio* Class armed with nine 15-inch guns and steaming at 30 knots, to which the French replied with the *Richelieu* and *Jean Bart*, enlarged editions of the *Dunkerque* Class with quadruple 15-inch guns. The Germans announced their intention of building up to the 35,000-ton limit, at least nominally, with the *Bismarck* and *Tirpitz* and the British replied by laying down two *King George V* Class armed with 10 14-inch guns (originally 12 guns were to be fitted) and steaming at 28 knots. These were not the only capital ships planned. By September 1939 the British had laid down another three *King George V* Class and were planning four *Lion* Class of 40,000 tons with nine 16-inch guns, the Germans were planning six monsters of 56,000 tons, the French had plans for two modified *Richelieu* Class and the Italians had started two more of the *Littorio* Class.

In the Pacific the rivalry was just as intense. Baulked by the naval treaties of numerical parity with the United States, the Japanese went to great lengths to modernize their old capital ships to a very high standard. This was hindered by the fact that eight of the Japanese ships were considerably inferior to the American ships, and no amount of rebuilding could overcome their deficiencies. All that could be done was to build in secret and flagrantly violate the treaty limitations to produce a class of ships with absolute superiority over anything afloat. It was reasoned that a ship of 64,000 tons, armed with nine 18-inch guns, could not be matched without widening the Panama Canal, a facile argument put forward in favor of the British *Dreadnought* with regard to the Kiel Canal in 1906, with equally little justification. It did make some sense in the short term, however. With some casuistry the Japanese could even claim that the ships would not appear until the Treaties had lapsed. The rationale behind the *Yamato* and *Musashi* and two planned sisterships was that they would be kept back in home waters until the American superiority in numbers had been whittled down by attacks from carrier aircraft and submarines, and they would then form the backbone of a powerful counterattacking force.

For their part the Americans contented themselves at first with laying down two classes of 35,000-tonners armed with 16-inch guns in 1937–39. The first pair, the *Washington* and *North Carolina*, did not compare very favorably with their German and British contemporaries, having comparatively light protection, but the four *South Dakota* Class can claim to be the best all-round design built under Treaty limitations. Their speed was 28 knots, as in the British ships, but they carried a heavier armament of three triple 16-inch gun mountings and had superior underwater protection. Like the British, the Americans suspected that the Japanese intended to breach the current international limits of 45,000 tons and 16-inch guns, but they were confident that their own fast carriers would provide the necessary firepower to offset any Japanese superiority of gunpower. Therefore the next class of battleships was given lighter protection, the same armament as the *South Dakota* Class and a massive increase of speed to 33 knots to permit them to keep pace with the *Essex* Class carriers. Two of these magnificent ships, the *Iowa* and *New Jersey*, were ordered in

1939 but only two more out of a planned total of six were built.

The one remaining major navy was the Soviet navy. Its three battleships were veterans of Czarist days, completely outclassed by foreign ships. The Soviet Union's internal troubles and the need to regenerate heavy industry made it impossible to start any new construction until the late 1930s, but this did not prevent enquiries being made in Germany, the United States and Italy for complete capital ship designs. None of these was accepted but in 1938 two 59,000-ton ships were laid down. Although more-lightly armed and armored than the Japanese giants, the Soviet ships were in fact slightly larger and a good deal faster. When the Allies found out about them in 1943 Stalin insisted that they had been intended for the Far East to oppose the Japanese, but the question was academic as ships of such complexity were beyond the capacity of Soviet industry. They fell victim to the German army's successes on land; *Sovietsky Soyuz* had most of her armor removed during the siege of Leningrad to provide steel for more important munitions, while *Sovietskya Ukraina* was destroyed by German forces when they evacuated Nikolayev in 1944.

It is often assumed that the battleship was an anachronism in World War II and that navies were somehow reactionary in continuing to build them. There is little evidence for this, for battleships continued to play an important role right up to the end, even after they had been surpassed in effectiveness by aircraft carriers. What finally robbed them of their overriding importance was simply that their principal weapon, the big gun firing at ranges of up to 25–30 miles, was quite outclassed by carrier bombers, which were capable of hitting targets 300 miles away. Although battleships could not be risked in waters dominated by hostile air power, neither could lesser warships, and when shore-based bombers were too far away or simply not available there was no substitute for the accuracy and weight of fire of a battleship's guns.

British battleships engaged their French opposite numbers in July 1940 at Mers-el-Kebir, but it was a very one-sided action with the French penned in a constricted harbor. The *Bretagne* blew up and the *Provence* and *Dunkerque* suffered serious damage from the 15-inch shells of the *Hood*, *Valiant* and *Resolution*, a feat which the Swordfish torpedo bombers could not have emulated in the same time and under the same circumstances. Later that month Admiral Cunningham's Mediterranean Fleet met the

Above: The German battleship Tirpitz *berthed in a Norwegian fiord.*

Italian Fleet off the coast of Calabria and the flagship HMS *Warspite* scored a hit on the Italian flagship *Giulio Cesare* at 26,000 yards – a record not broken by any other battleship in action at sea. Although the Italian ship suffered severe topside damage, she and her squadron mate were able to use their higher speed to disengage under cover of a smokescreen.

What air power could do when given the right circumstances was demonstrated when the Italian battle fleet was attacked in its main base at Taranto in November 1940. For a loss of only two aircraft the British were able to sink the new battleship *Littorio* and the older *Duilio* and *Conte di Cavour* at their moorings. In complete contrast, when the *Bismarck* and the heavy cruiser *Prinz Eugen* broke out into the Atlantic in May 1941, torpedo planes could slow the *Bismarck* down but capital ships were needed to bring her to action. Similarly, when the *Scharnhorst* and *Gneisenau* sortied into the North Atlantic in 1940–41 the British were able to defend their shipping by adding an old battleship to the escort of each convoy. Although in theory two fast battlecruisers should have been able to run rings around 22 or 24 knot veterans of Jutland, one crippling hit from 15-inch guns at long range would put the German ships at risk of being intercepted by the Home Fleet.

The *Bismarck* action was a classic set-piece battle. Cruisers shadowed the German force in the Denmark Strait, allowing the fast ships *Hood* and *Prince of Wales* to intercept. The *Hood* was shooting accurately but before she could register on the *Bismarck* she was hit amidships by an 8-inch salvo from the *Prinz Eugen*. The huge explosion which followed destroyed the *Hood*, but its cause remains a mystery. In all

probability a fire detonated the warheads of above-water torpedo tubes, but other possibilities cannot be ruled out. Both German ships rapidly shifted fire to the *Prince of Wales*, and hit her seven times, but the brand-new British ship stood up remarkably well. Only two out of the seven hits did any damage, the only significant one being a hit on the compass platform which failed to burst but shattered the binnacle and caused heavy casualties among the bridge personnel. However, she recovered quickly and used her air warning radar to get 'straddles' on the *Bismarck*. Two of these inflicted underwater damage on the fuel bunkers, contaminating her oil fuel and ultimately sealing her fate. Three days later, her steering irreparably damaged by a torpedo hit from a carrier aircraft and leaving a massive oil slick, the pride of the Kriegsmarine was caught at dawn by the *Rodney* and *King George V*. Pounded into silence within half an hour, she was finally sunk by a salvo of torpedoes from a cruiser.

The last big ships engaged in the European Theater were the *Scharnhorst* and *Tirpitz*. Although both ships posed a threat to convoys from Britain to North Russia it diminished as each month went by. In 1943 the *Tirpitz* was badly damaged by midget submarines, but repeated air attacks were frustrated by the high sides of the fiord in which she lurked. She was finally sunk by bombing in 1944 when she had been moved southward to a more exposed anchorage. At the end of 1943 the *Scharnhorst* was ordered to sea to make a last attempt to intercept a north Russian convoy. It proved a disastrous operation; the British cruisers fought an heroic holding action to allow the battleship *Duke of York* time to come up, and the German battlecruiser got the worst of the ensuing gun duel. After being hit repeatedly, the *Scharnhorst* was sent to the bottom by a brilliant torpedo attack from destroyers.

The Taranto attack certainly inspired the Japanese in their planning for a knockout blow against the American Pacific Fleet at Pearl Harbor, but American unpreparedness reduced the margin of risk even further. Two waves of carrier bombers and torpedo bombers wrought havoc in 'Battleship Row,' sinking the *Oklahoma, Arizona, West Virginia* and *California* and seriously damaging the *Tennessee* and *Nevada*. Only two battleships escaped serious damage, but fortunately the carriers were away on other missions, and in their zeal to get at the big ships the Japanese pilots also failed to destroy the fuel supplies stored ashore.

The British also suffered a catastrophe when three days later the *Prince of Wales* and *Repulse* were sunk with apparent impunity off the coast of Malaya by land-based aircraft. The two capital ships had been sent out to the Far East to 'overawe' the Japanese, but without tactical coordination with the land-based air forces and no strategic plans to join forces with the Americans in the Central Pacific, the task force was pathetically isolated and would have succumbed to attack by one means or another within a few weeks. The sinking of the powerful *Prince of Wales* was aided by a tragic error in damage control early in the action, but given their complete lack of air cover there could be little doubt about the eventual outcome.

Although the US Navy responded to the destruction of its battle fleet by forming fast carrier task forces, these still relied heavily on battleships to provide antiaircraft firepower and to ward off any surface attack. The new fast battleships were assigned to these groups as soon as they were commissioned, but even so some big-ship engagements were fought without the presence of carriers. In November 1942 the *Washington* and *South Dakota* fought a close-run action against the Japanese *Kirishima* and a force of cruisers and destroyers off Guadalcanal. An electrical fault knocked out all electrical power in the *South Dakota* at the outset, leaving her blind and careering closer to the Japanese, who hit her repeatedly. Fortunately, her squadron mate kept her searchlights switched off and fired steadily on radar. The *Kirishima* was so heavily punished that she failed to score a crippling hit on the *South Dakota* and was herself reduced to a flaming wreck.

The main Japanese battle fleet had not been risked in a trial of strength, the bulk of losses being taken by the carriers, and so when in October 1944 the Combined Fleet made a final sortie to wipe out the American landings on Leyte in the Philippines it included, in the various groups, the 64,000-ton *Yamato* and *Musashi*, the *Nagato* and the older *Kongo, Haruna, Fuso, Yamashiro, Hyuga* and *Ise*. Admiral Kurita's six carriers had only 30 aircraft between them and even the converted 'battleship-carriers' *Hyuga* and *Ise* carried no aircraft.

The *Musashi* was the first to go, sunk by waves of bombers and torpedo bombers in the San Bernardino Strait on 24 October. That night the Southern Group, the *Fuso* and *Yamashiro* and a cruiser and destroyers, ran into a force of six old American battleships in the Surigao Strait. Appropriately enough, five of them had been at Pearl Harbor but were now modernized and equipped with the latest fire-control radar. First the *Fuso* was sunk and then fire shifted to the flagship *Yamashiro*, setting her ablaze. Her sinking marked the end of the last battleship-versus-battleship duel, but later that day Admiral Kurita's force broke through to find the American invasion force off Samar. For the first and last time the *Yamato*'s 18-inch guns were used against an enemy fleet, but Admiral Kurita withdrew without realizing what an opportunity he had missed.

The *Yamato* finally succumbed to waves of American carrier aircraft while steaming on a suicide mission to Okinawa the following April. After three hours of ceaseless attack she went down with most of her company. The long reign of the battleship was over, although nobody could deny the contribution they had made to the victory at sea. The Japanese surrender was signed on board the flagship USS *Missouri* in Tokyo Bay in August 1945.

Yet battleships proved finally that with proper air cover they could operate almost with impunity. In 1943–44 British battleships carried out constant bombardments off the Italian coast, and only the veteran *Warspite* was damaged by glider bombs. In August 1945 American and British battleships bombarded the Japanese home islands without undue risk. Throughout the war only two battleships were sunk by submarines at sea, as against six sunk by aircraft and seven by gunfire and torpedoes. The remaining 12 were sunk in harbor in one way or another.

SPECIFICATIONS

The ships built after the Washington Treaties

BATTLESHIPS AND BATTLECRUISERS

Class	Number built	Years built (and modernized)	Tonnage	Armament Main, Secondary, AA	Speed (knots)	Armor (max.) inches
United States						
Arkansas	1	1912 (1926)	26,000	12 12-inch, 16 5-inch, 8 3-inch	21	11
New York	2	1914 (1927)	27,000	10 14-inch, 16 5-inch, 8 3-inch	21	12
Nevada	2	1916 (1929)	29,000	10 14-inch, 12 5-inch, 8 5-inch	20	13½
Pennsylvania	2	1916 (1931)	33,000	12 14-inch, 12 5-inch, 8 5-inch	21	14
New Mexico	3	1917–8 (1932–4)	33,000	12 14-inch, 12 5-inch, 8 5-inch	21	14
California	2	1920–1	33,000	12 14-inch, 12 5-inch, 8 5-inch	21	14
West Virginia	3	1921–3	32,000	8 16-inch, 12 5-inch, 8 5-inch	21	16
Washington	2	1941	37,000	9 16-inch, 20 5-inch	28	12
South Dakota	4	1942	37,000	9 16-inch, 20 5-inch	28	12¼
Iowa	4	1943–4	46,000	9 16-inch, 20 5-inch	33	12¼

Several of the older ships sunk at Pearl Harbor were raised and refitted for service later in the war. They then had massive antiaircraft batteries.

Class	Number built	Years built (and modernized)	Tonnage	Armament Main, Secondary, AA	Speed (knots)	Armor (max.) inches
Britain						
Queen Elizabeth	5	1915–(1937–41) (two ships not modernized)	31,000	8 15-inch unmodernized – 12 6-inch, 8 4-inch modernized – 20 4.5-inch	24	13
Royal Sovereign	5	1916–7	29,000	8 15-inch, 12 6-inch, 8 4-inch	22	13
Renown (Repulse not modernized)	2	1916 (1939)	32,000	6 15-inch Renown 20 4.5-inch Repulse 9 4-inch, 8 4-inch	29	9
Hood	1	1920	41,000	8 15-inch, 10 4-inch	31	12
Nelson	2	1927	34,000	9 16-inch, 12 6-inch, 6 4.7-inch	23	14
King George V	5	1940–2	38,000	10 14-inch, 16 5.25-inch	28	15
Japan						
Kongo	4	1913–5 (1934–40)	32,000	8 14-inch, 14 6-inch, 8 5-inch	30	8
Fuso	2	1915–7 (1935)	35,000	12 14-inch, 14 6-inch, 8 5-inch	24	12
Ise	2	1917–8 (1934–7)	36,000	12 14-inch, 14 6-inch, 8 5-inch	25	12
(both Ise Class converted to hybrid carriers 1943)						
Nagato	2	1920–1 (1936)	38,000	8 16-inch, 18 5.5-inch, 8 5-inch	25	13
Yamato	2	1941–2	65,000	9 18.1-inch, 12 6.1-inch	27	16
Germany						
Deutschland	3	1933–6	12,000	6 11-inch, 8 5.9-inch, 6 3.9-inch	26	2½–3
Deutschland renamed Lutzow. Slight differences between the three ships built						
Scharnhorst	2	1938–9	32,000	9 11-inch, 12 5.9-inch, 14 4.1-inch	31	14
Bismarck	2	1940–1	42,000	8 15-inch, 12 5.9-inch, 14 4.1-inch	29	12½
Italy						
Conte di Cavour	2	1914–5 (1937)	24,000	10 12.6-inch, 12 4.7-inch, 8 3.9-inch	28	10
Duilio	2	1915–6 (1940)	24,000	10 12.6-inch, 12 5.3-inch, 10 3.6-inch	28	10
Littorio	3	1940–2	41,000	9 15-inch, 12 6-inch, 10 3.6-inch	30	14
Littorio renamed Italia in 1943 in Allied service						
France						
Courbet	2	1913–4	22,000	10 13.4-inch, 22 5.5-inch, 5 2.9-inch	20	10½
Provence	3	1915–6 (1933–6)	23,000	10 13.4-inch, 14 5.5-inch, 8 2.9 inch	21	10½
Dunkerque	2	1937–8	26,000	8 13-inch, 16 5.1-inch	31	9½
Richelieu	2	1940	39,000	8 15-inch, 9 6-inch, 12 3.9-inch	30	13
Jean Bart was never completed during the war but her guns were in action						

expired differed from the World War I veterans in the distribution of their armor, the power of their engines and the attention paid to defenses against air attack. The modernization programs of all navies introduced changes in line with these developments. The old ships normally had separate batteries of antiaircraft and secondary guns. The more modern vessels had dual purpose types. All nations crammed as many additional light antiaircraft guns as they could fit on their ships during refits throughout the war as experience showed them to be needed. Modernization of old ships also increased passive defense against air and submarine attack. Deck armor and antitorpedo bulges were fitted in many cases and in the newer ships more attention was paid to these factors in the design. The more modern ships also had their armor disposed in such a way that only the more vital parts of the ship were protected but these had very heavy armor.

In the tables opposite where two batteries of secondary guns are listed, the first is the low-angle armament and the second the heavy anti-aircraft battery. All ships carried many smaller guns.

AIRCRAFT CARRIERS

Although the aircraft carrier had made its appearance in World War I, it was still unproven as a weapon of war when war broke out in 1939, and only a few dedicated aviators believed that it was more important than the battleship. Yet in little more than two years it became the new capital ship and completely transformed the nature of sea warfare.

It is symptomatic of the relatively low prestige of carriers that they were less affected by the international disarmament treaties than battleships. At Washington in 1922 little objection was raised to the conversion of very large battlecruiser and battleship hulls into carriers, and opinion was divided about the respective merits of big or small carriers. Apart from the conversions, standard displacement of new construction was to be limited to 27,000 tons; vessels below 10,000 tons were exempted and ratios were fixed at 135,000 tons each for Britain and the USA, 81,000 tons for Japan and 60,000 tons for both France and Italy. The London Naval Treaty of 1935 reduced the limit further to 23,000 tons, reflecting a consensus that the type had grown too large.

The early British lead in the design and construction of carriers was thrown away in the 1920s, partly because the newly independent Royal Air Force had control of naval flying, but equally because so many air-minded naval officers had switched allegiance to the new service in order to keep flying. By the time senior naval officers again recognized the potential of naval air power, the material state of British naval aviation was so poor that little could be done to improve matters quickly. The worst problem was the sheer obsolescence of the aircraft, for the RAF had little enough money for its own purposes. Its senior officers were too concerned with the concepts of strategic bombing to divert their limited resources, except on the smallest scale, to the construction of specialized naval aircraft.

In contrast the American and Japanese navies had retained control of their naval air forces, and pushed ahead with new high-performance aircraft capable of developing the most advanced theories of defense and offense. Both realized that the carrier's strike aircraft were the ship's main weapon, and concentrated their design efforts on expanding the carrying capacity of succeeding designs. From this came the concept of the 'open' hangar, which was basically a lightly constructed box superimposed on the main hull; because it was lightly stressed with a timber flight deck laid on steel it could be spacious and provided with big roller shutters for ventilation.

The Japanese navy had followed the British lead by laying down its first carrier, the 7000-ton *Hosho* in 1919, and got her into service in 1923. She was not particularly successful but she provided invaluable experience for the conversion of the 41,000-ton battlecruiser *Akagi* and the slightly smaller battleship *Kaga*, permitted under the terms of the Washington Treaty. Their next step was, however, not a great success. Hoping to profit by the Treaty's exclusion of limits on carriers of less than 10,000 tons, they tried to build the *Ryujo* within the limit but with a capacity for 48 aircraft. She was only a qualified success but she paved the way for the *Soryu* and *Shokaku* Classes.

The Americans made a more modest start by converting a fleet collier into a carrier in 1920–22. The *Langley* was slow but she carried 55 aircraft on a displacement of only 11,000 tons. The wreckage left by the Washington Treaty yielded the 33,000-ton *Lexington* and *Saratoga*, big ships in which these ideas could be developed further. Like the Japanese, the Americans found that the big air group enabled more aggressive tactics to be pursued; the proportion of strike aircraft to defending fighters could be increased.

From a series of war games the US Navy evolved the concept of the carrier task force, and each year's Fleet Problem yielded better techniques, both in the air and on board.

Although the British had a head start in carrier design they were not so fortunate as the Americans and Japanese in what they got out of the Washington Treaty. Seduced by the apparent cheapness of smaller hulls, they chose to reconstruct three 18,000-ton light battlecruisers, the *Furious, Glorious* and *Courageous*, and so never reaped the benefits of a big air group. This, coupled with the lethargic policy of the RAF towards the design and procurement of naval aircraft, meant that British carrier aircraft were tied to the humdrum task of reconnaissance and spotting for battleships' guns. However, the technical details of British carrier design remained excellent. Fire precautions were tighter than in other navies, thanks largely to the 'closed' hangar. This differed from the 'open' type favored in the United States and Japan in being separated from the ship's side by workshops and offices. Air locks permitted the hangar to be sealed off and a separate ventilation system took care of avgas vapor.

The only other country to build a carrier was France; the former battleship *Béarn* was converted in 1922–27 but suffered from lack of speed, much like the British *Eagle.* Aircraft were getting heavier, and until the catapult became standard an adequate 'wind over deck' speed was essential, quite apart from a margin of speed over the rest of the fleet. Carriers needed to turn into wind to launch and recover aircraft, which meant that they often had to catch up with their squadron.

After an attempt to keep size down with the 13,800-ton *Ranger* (launched 1933) the US Navy decided to return to 20,000 tons for the *Enterprise, Hornet* and *Yorktown.* In these ships a good balance of speed, aircraft capacity and defensive armament was achieved and paved the way for the later *Essex* Class. Even when a further small carrier, the *Wasp*, was authorized to use up the remaining 14,500 tons allowed under the second London Naval Treaty, the best features of the big carriers were retained. The Japanese, however, went to 25,000 tons in the *Shokaku* and *Zuikaku*, which were ordered under the 1937 Fleet Replenishment Program. They too formed the basis of subsequent developments and were probably the most balanced Japanese design.

The British returned to the carrier business in 1934 when they authorized a new 22,000-tonner, to be launched in 1937 as the *Ark Royal.*

She embodied many unusual features; apart from a double-storied closed hangar she had an aerodynamically shaped flight deck and island to reduce turbulence. She was to have been the prototype of a new class, but the growing fear of high-level bombing led to her successors being totally different. The basic design was retained but an armored hangar was provided, with armor on the roof and sides to keep out 1000-pound bombs. As the displacement was only 23,000 tons the penalty in top-weight was very heavy, and the new *Illustrious* had only one hangar and half the capacity of the *Ark Royal.* Six of this new type were ordered in 1937–39 as part of Great Britain's long-deferred rearmament program. The armor was judged especially important for Mediterranean operations because carriers there would always be within range of land-based air attacks.

The French also allocated funds to carrier construction in the mid-1930s. They toyed with the idea of converting two heavy cruisers and finally ordered two 18,000-ton ships in 1938. In the same year the German Navy launched the 23,000-ton *Graf Zeppelin*, but neither she nor the French *Joffre* and *Painlevé* were completed. The rivalry between air force and navy was more virulent in Germany than in other countries, and Field Marshal Goering was able to block the supply of aircraft to the navy.

Aircraft carriers differ from other warships in that they are, in effect, designed around specific aircraft. In this respect Japanese and American aircraft were incomparably superior to British types. Japanese aircraft, particularly the A6M Zero, deliberately sacrificed such 'luxuries' as self-sealing fuel tanks and pilot-armor to achieve higher speed and endurance, whereas American aircraft emphasized ruggedness and survival. British carrier aircraft were far slower than their contemporaries, and in addition they were limited in numbers. Even after control of naval aviation had been removed from the RAF priority was inevitably given to production of landplanes.

Despite these drawbacks the Royal Navy and its Fleet Air Arm scored a well-deserved victory in November 1940, when 21 torpedo bombers attacked the Italian Fleet in its main base at Taranto. The 90-knot biplanes hit the battleships *Conte di Cavour, Littorio* and *Duilio*, set oil-storage tanks alight and destroyed the seaplane base, all in the space of two hours. The strategic and tactical benefits were immediate; the Italians were forced to handle their heavy ships very cautiously and the British were able to dominate the central Mediterranean, running supplies through to Malta and Alexandria. The Germans were forced to respond by sending a specially trained anti-shipping strike group, *Fliegerkorps X*, to the Mediterranean to knock out the armored carrier *Illustrious*. She was hit by six bombs in a brisk attack off Sicily in January 1941 and badly damaged, but her armored flight deck and stout construction saved her from being sunk.

The lessons of Taranto were studied closely by the Japanese, who were planning a decisive stroke against the Americans. Aware that they had to reduce the odds against them, but also entertaining the dangerous delusion that an effete American public would be so dismayed by a sudden defeat in the Pacific that they would sue for peace, the Japanese decided to launch six carriers against the US Pacific Fleet in its anchorage at Pearl Harbor, Hawii. For a variety of reasons the great naval base turned out to be quite unprepared for attack, and two waves of torpedo bombers from the carriers *Akagi, Hiryu, Kaga, Shokaku, Soryu* and *Zuikaku* were able to sink the battleships *Arizona, California, Oklahoma* and *West Virginia* and damage the *Maryland, Nevada, Pennsylvania* and *Tennessee* more or less seriously. In addition, numbers of aircraft were destroyed on the ground but Admiral Nagumo refused to allow a third strike, and in their exuberance the Japanese carrier pilots had failed to hit the massive fuel-storage tanks.

By what seemed a miracle the American carriers were away from Pearl Harbor exercising on 7 December 1941, and they now formed the only major striking force left to the Americans in the Pacific. With no battleships available for at least six months the carrier had to become the new capital unit and so the prewar concepts of fast carrier groups were brought into use sooner than they might have been. For the first few months nothing seemed to be able to stop the Japanese. They swiftly occupied Malaya, the East Indies and the Philippines, and moved into the Indian Ocean to strike at Ceylon (now Sri Lanka).

Despite their losses at Pearl Harbor the Americans were not inclined to sue for peace and in January 1942 their carriers launched the first strikes against the Marshall Islands and the Gilberts. In April the *Hornet* launched 16 army B-25 twin-engined bombers for a raid on Tokyo, flying them on to land in China. The military results were negligible but the Japanese, who had not foreseen the use of such big aircraft from carriers, were stunned by the raid.

The pattern of a new type of sea warfare became apparent in the Battle of the Coral Sea early in May 1942. The Americans suffered a tactical defeat in that they lost the big *Lexington* in return for the much smaller *Shoho* but succeeded in their strategic aim of preventing the Japanese from gaining a foothold in New Guinea as a prelude to an attack on Australia. There were other less obvious benefits. The Japanese were convinced that they had inflicted serious damage on the USS *Yorktown* and did not realize that she had survived the battle. Their own *Shokaku* and *Zuikaku* were damaged, the former quite seriously, and so the two best carriers were not available for the Battle of Midway a month later.

Below: The carrier Ark Royal *was sunk by a German submarine in 1941.*

Midway followed the pattern of the Coral Sea battle, with virtually no contact between surface units and massive blows delivered by the rival carrier air groups over distances of hundreds of miles. The difference was that Midway was a massive and clear-cut defeat for the Japanese. Not only did they fail to capture the strategically important outpost of Midway Island but they lost the crack carriers *Akagi, Hiryu, Kaga* and *Soryu* and in addition their magnificent air groups, probably the best-trained force of naval aviators ever seen. Although the Americans were helped immeasurably by having broken the Japanese cipher, the outcome of the battle finally turned on the ability of the US carriers to survive battle damage. The Japanese carriers were quickly gutted by fires from bomb hits, whereas the *Yorktown*, which had been hurriedly repaired after her Coral Sea damage, survived three bomb hits before diverting her remaining aircraft to another carrier, and would have been saved if an enemy submarine had not torpedoed her the following day.

The Americans were to be roughly handled by the Japanese in two more carrier-versus-carrier battles in the Solomons, losing the *Wasp* and the *Hornet*, but the tide of battle had already turned in their favor. The Japanese were prodigal in their waste of carrier planes and aircrew, and to make matters worse their shipyards were not prepared for rapid production. In contrast, the Americans matched the large output of their aircraft factories with a truly staggering expansion of pilot training and built large numbers of carriers. In January 1942 work started on converting nine light cruisers to carriers (CVLs), the *Independence* Class. In mid-1940 Congress had authorized a dozen of the 27,100-ton *Essex* Class (CV9-20) and followed them with another 21 ships. By the end of 1943 the new Fast Carrier Force, then known as Task Force 50, could muster five *Independence* Class CVLs and the first four *Essex* Class CVs. The *Essexes* quickly showed themselves to be outstandingly successful, and they must qualify as one of the most effective and potent class of warships ever built.

Meanwhile the British were desperately locked in combat with the Germans for domination of the Atlantic. The lack of air cover for convoys made itself felt in two crucial areas: between Gibraltar and the British Isles, and in the so-called 'Black Gap' in the mid-Atlantic. Gibraltar–UK convoys suffered primarily from the depredations of long-range bombers operating from airfields on the Biscay coast of France, whereas in mid-Atlantic antisubmarine aircraft

were needed. To fight the shore-based FW 200 Condor bombers the Royal Navy conceived the idea of catapult-launching a single fighter aircraft from the forecastle of a merchant ship. This became the Catapult-Aircraft Merchantman, or CAM-Ship, but the aircraft was forced to land in the sea each time. In mid-1941 work began on converting a captured German merchant ship into an 'escort carrier.' The ship, HMS *Audacity*, only sailed with three convoys before being torpedoed in December 1941 but she proved so useful that both British and American shipyards started to convert more hulls. The US Navy designated them CVEs and their arrival on the scene from mid-1942 onward helped to stem the tide against the U-Boats.

The value of a CVE in antisubmarine warfare was that she could sail with a convoy, flying off aircraft when needed, to sink shadowing U-Boats or merely force them to submerge. As more of them were commissioned they were put to wider uses, however. During the early phases of an amphibious landing CVEs provided air cover until air strips could be established, and as carrier task forces began to operate deeper into the Pacific a number of CVEs were used to ferry spare aircraft out to them. Although the first escort carriers were all converted from merchant hulls, either after launch or on the stocks, later classes were designed from the keel up. The British took the process to its logical conclusion by building a class of 'light fleet' carriers, 14,000-ton ships with a fair turn of speed and capable of operating with the fleet. Five of these ingenious utility ships were completed before the end of the war, despite having been designed as late as 1942.

Despite their production problems the Japanese completed a number of carriers. They had designed a large submarine tender and two fleet oilers for rapid conversion to small fleet carriers, and these emerged as the *Ryuho, Shoho* and *Zuiho* in 1941. Three requisitioned liners followed in 1941–42 as the *Taiyo, Chuyo* and *Unyo* but they lacked arrester wires and catapults and so were useless for working with the fleet. Two more big liners were converted and joined the fleet in 1942 as the *Hiyo* and *Junyo*. Intrigued by reports of the British *Illustrious* Class, the Japanese laid down their own armored type, the *Taiho* in 1941, and she came into service in 1944.

The conversion program took up all the dockyard resources and so no carriers were ordered under the 1940 Program, but in 1941 the first of an improved version of the *Hiryu* Class was ordered. Midway caused a sharp

AIRCRAFT CARRIERS

Class	Year built	Displacement	Aircraft	Speed (knots)
United States				
Saratoga	1927	33,000	120	33
Ranger	1934	14,000	75	29
Yorktown	1937–41	20,000	80	34
Wasp	1940	14,700	80	30
Essex	1942–5	27,100	80	33
Independence (CVL class conversions)	1942	11,000	33	32
Japan				
Hosho	1922	7500	20	25
Akagi	1927	36,500	90	30
Kaga	1928	38,200	90	28
Ryujo	1933	10,600	48	29
Soryu*	1937–9	18,800	71	34
Shokaku	1941	25,675	84	34
* Hiryu similar but a little larger.				
Britain				
Courageous	1925–7	22,500	35	31
Ark Royal	1938	22,000	60	30
Illustrious	1940–1	22,500	54	31
Indomitable	1941	25,500	65	31
Implacable	1944	26,000	72	32
Furious	1918	22,500	35	30

Note. The aircraft capacity of all types of carriers varied from time to time depending on the models of aircraft carried and how they were stored.

reappraisal of the carrier program; five *Taiho* Class and 13 *Unryu* Class were ordered and no fewer than seven conversions were authorized. Two of these were warship hulls, the heavy cruiser *Ibuki* and the giant battleship *Shinano*. The former was never completed but the *Shinano* was nearly ready for sea in 1944. She was not a full conversion to a fleet carrier but was intended to act as a 'spare deck' for other carriers, and had elaborate maintenance facilities for servicing and repairing aircraft. However, she was to be given a small fighter air group for self defense and a massive antiaircraft armament. The concept was also tried by the British in the much smaller *Unicorn* but it was not tried in action by the Japanese as the *Shinano* was ignominiously torpedoed by an American submarine as she made her way to the Inland Sea to be completed.

Mussolini had scoffed at the idea of carriers for the Italian navy on the grounds that the whole of Italy could function as a carrier, but after Taranto this facile judgment was reversed and two liners were taken in hand. The Italians were plagued by shortages of steel and labor and neither the *Aquila* nor the *Sparviero* was ready by the time of the collapse in September 1943. The Germans also found it impossible to complete the *Graf Zeppelin* and sent her catapults to Italy in a vain attempt to speed up the construction of the *Aquila*. A conversion of the heavy cruiser *Seydlitz* began in 1942 but was never finished.

Returning to the Pacific, two carrier battles remained to be fought. In June 1944 Task Force 58 attacked the Marianas and precipitated the Battle of the Philippine Sea, in which the Americans sank the *Taiho, Shokaku* and *Hiyo* and destroyed some 400 carrier aircraft. For the Americans the worst moment came when the exultant pilots found themselves almost too far from their carriers to get back. About 80 of the returning aircraft had to 'ditch' into the sea but as they were close to the carriers the loss of pilots was relatively light. At Leyte Gulf four months later the real extent of the Philippine Sea victory became apparent; the Japanese could still send a force of carriers to sea but some of the ships carried no aircraft of any kind. The series of battles which make up Leyte were not classic carrier engagements but when the US fast carriers were decoyed away the CVEs were left to face a powerful surface force which included the 64,000-ton battleship *Yamato*. However, even the little 'jeep carriers' proved surprisingly tough.

In April 1945 the assault on Okinawa gave the Japanese a final chance to defer, if not avoid, disaster. The Kamikaze tactic, a suicidal dive onto an enemy warship, was intended to knock out carriers, and the *Enterprise, Intrepid, Bataan* and *Bunker Hill* were all heavily hit. The British Task Force 57 was also attacked but its armored decks and closed hangar systems stood up better to direct hits and in no case were they gutted by fire. In contrast the *Bunker Hill* was so badly damaged that she was never repaired, while a low-level bombing attack on the *Franklin* killed 832 of her crew.

Although all three services played their full part in defeating Japan, there is little doubt that the fast carrier task groups contributed a major part to that defeat. Their aircraft destroyed not only most of the Japanese navy but also a large section of the air force. Without them the 'island-hopping' strategy could not have become so sophisticated, and even the final assault on Japan needed airfields in the Marianas for the B-29 bombers to fly from.

In retrospect the American *Essex* Class proved to be the most farsighted design, although late in the war the possibility of exchanging six of them for six British *Illustrious* and *Implacable* Class was discussed. For the British, given the poor performance of their naval aircraft and the fact that they would be operating close to two powerful land-based air forces, the armored hangar made sense. However, in the long run, events proved the Americans right; the main armament of a carrier was her aircraft, and so the bigger the air group the more offensive and defensive power she had.

CRUISERS

The cruiser had been the subject of as much political controversy as the battleship or the carrier between the two world wars. With battleship construction halted by the Washington Treaty and carriers proving very costly there was an understandable tendency to channel resources into cruisers. Although not capable of taking severe punishment in battle they were still hard-hitting ships with one supreme advantage, they could be built in reasonable numbers.

Historically, the role of the cruiser was to scout for the main fleet and to protect shipping

on the trade routes, but in World War I a new breed of light cruisers had done a very good job spearheading light forces in the North Sea. This accentuated a tendency to divide cruisers into 'heavy' and 'light' categories, the former to work on the trade routes and the latter to scout for and work with the fleet.

Any natural evolution was doomed to failure by the outcome of the Washington Conference. The United States Navy had already decided that it wanted to build 10,000-ton cruisers armed with 8-inch guns for the Pacific, and by using the existence of four new British cruisers as a pretext, persuaded the delegates to accept this as a new limit for heavy cruisers. Accordingly numbers were fixed in a similar ratio to capital ships, while the light-cruiser category was restricted to ships with 6-inch or lighter guns, but without a limit on numbers.

The first generation of 'Washington Treaty' heavy cruisers proved a disappointment by and large, for they were a complete break with previous ideas. All had weaknesses of one sort or another, in seakeeping, endurance or protection, but the Japanese appeared to find the most ingenious solution in their *Furutaka* Class. These two ships were intended to carry six single 8-inch guns, make 35 knots and have 3-inch side armor, all on a displacement of only 7100 tons. These requirements were impossible to meet, and the ships actually displaced 2000 tons more, but the Japanese published only the original design figures and these were believed by Western intelligence agencies. Nevertheless they were very fast and other navies' heavy cruisers compared badly with them on paper.

The faults of the first generation were partly cured in their successors, but the 10,000-ton limit had been chosen arbitrarily by the Americans without realizing that it would lead to a cruiser too large to be built cheaply but not big enough to carry efficient protection. The British, who had a large Empire and mercantile fleet to protect, fixed their needs at a minimum total of 70 cruisers, and clearly these could not all be heavy cruisers. They worked ceaselessly to get the tonnage reduced to 8000 tons and produced the experimental *York* and *Exeter* with the same armament as the *Furutaka* type to show that it could be done. Royal Navy opinion really favored the 6-inch gunned cruiser, for recent war experience showed that a concentration of light cruisers would be more than a match for one heavy cruiser. The higher rate of fire of the 6-inch gun would enable a smaller cruiser to 'smother' the heavy cruiser with salvoes, enabling her to close the range.

Right from the outset the Italians showed little respect for the Washington Treaty limit. Although their first heavy cruisers, the *Trento* and *Trieste*, were within the limit this was achieved by having only the flimsiest armor. To cure this fault and still have the high speed so dear to Italian designers it would be necessary to go to 15,000 tons. When it was pointed out that this would violate the Treaty the designers were permitted to compromise on 11,500 tons, an overrun of 15 percent. As in Japan, this excess tonnage was not published and when the *Zara* reached 35 knots on trials rival navies were amazed. What was not mentioned was that the builders did not install the armament, and so contractors' sea trials were run without the four twin 8-inch gun turrets on board. The Italian navy also paid an incentive bonus for every knot over the designed speed, and this tempted designers to push speeds ever higher, however artificial the conditions. In wartime this was to prove disastrous, for the speed of Italian cruisers in full-load condition fell far below the published trial speed.

True to their doctrine of matching the best foreign design with one better the Japanese expanded the original *Furutaka* design to include five twin 8-inch guns and more armor. Once again the Treaty limit could not be met and the four *Ashigara* Class averaged nearly 12,500 tons on trials. To make matters worse there was no margin of stability and so when an improved design was ordered, the *Atago* Class, their standard tonnage rose to 11,350 tons and the trials were run at nearly 13,000 tons. Yet the world was told that the ships displaced only 9850 tons, and cheating had become the norm.

The Germans had been permitted to build replacement tonnage for the ancient light cruisers retained under the Treaty of Versailles, but the first ship, the slow and underarmed *Emden* was useful only for training, and the following three *Köln* Class were short on endurance and seakeeping. Two more light cruisers, the *Leipzig* and *Nürnberg* were enlarged versions of this trio but still lacked the endurance necessary for extended operations.

The building of 'pocket battleships' or *panzerschiffe* has already been mentioned (see Battleships), but their impact on cruiser design was even more profound. A *Deutschland*-type ship might run away from a battleship but she would pound any heavy cruiser with her 11-inch guns, it was argued. The framers of the Washington Treaty had labored long and hard to avoid this category, the big, well-armored and heavily gunned commerce-raider, and yet German ingenuity had apparently outflanked the provisions with ridiculous ease. Yet, despite the fact that the *Deutschland* and her sisters *Admiral Graf Spee* and *Admiral Scheer* exceeded the Treaty limit by a considerable margin, they were poorly protected and five knots slower than contemporary American and British cruisers. This lack of speed, plus the slow rate of fire possible from two triple 28cm (11-inch) gun turrets, put them at a disadvantage against fast-moving targets. After much initial publicity the German navy came to realize its shortcomings and the planned total of six ships was cut back to three. In 1940 they were reclassified as heavy cruisers, a more appropriate designation for these expensive hybrids.

In 1934 two conventional heavy cruisers were ordered for the *Kriegsmarine*, the *Admiral Hipper* and *Blücher*. This time the departure from the treaty limits was even more flagrant, and standard displacement proved to be 13,900

Below: The USS Boston, *a* Baltimore *Class heavy cruiser, in 1944.*

tons. They were formidable ships, armed with four twin 8-inch guns and a heavy antiaircraft armament but they had poor endurance and a troublesome propulsion system. Three more were authorized but only the *Prinz Eugen* was completed in 1940.

The British and French were very worried by the growing threat of cruiser warfare against their shipping, and each took steps to deal with it. The French went for an expensive solution, the battlecruisers *Dunkerque* and *Strasbourg*, whereas the British fell back on the tried-and-tested method of concentrating large numbers of smaller cruisers. Quantity became more important than quality, particularly as the Royal Navy was hamstrung by a provision of the London Naval Treaty of 1930, which permitted the construction of a fixed total of 91,000 tons of light cruisers.

The British would have been content to build 7000-ton cruisers, but their hand was forced by the appearance of a new and even more unorthodox Japanese design. In 1931, having reached their quota of 12 heavy cruisers allowed by Treaty, the Japanese laid down a new type of 8500-ton light cruiser armed with five triple 6-inch gun turrets, capable of 35 knots. Here was a 'light' cruiser which would pose a serious threat to any heavy cruiser, using her speed to close the range and smother her opponent with rapid salvoes. Inevitably this combination of offensive powers could not be achieved on such a small displacement, and the weight-saving measures adopted proved to be inadequate. On their trials the first two ships, the *Mogami* and *Mikuma*, suffered splits in their welded seams from the shock of their own gunfire, and subsequently it was found that the weight of the turrets was too much for the supporting structure.

The world at large knew little of the problems with the *Mogami* Class, and the US Navy felt constrained to produce a reply. This resulted in the *Brooklyn* Class, laid down in 1935, with the same armament as the *Mogami* Class. The British, by now aware that they were also likely to be fighting the Japanese, had to depart from their policy of keeping down size, and their reply to the *Mogami* was just under 10,000 tons. The *Southampton* Class struck a good balance of fighting power with adequate protection, speed, radius and a strong antiaircraft defense, all at the cost of one less triple 6-inch turret than the *Brooklyn* or *Mogami*.

In 1936 the British introduced a new concept, the antiaircraft cruiser. Faced with the threat of heavy air attacks in the Mediterranean and

with the problem of what to do with a series of small, light cruisers left over from World War I, they rearmed two prototypes, the *Coventry* and *Curlew*, with light antiaircraft guns. The purpose of these ships was to provide AA fire for a squadron or convoy, not to operate independently, and when the conversions proved successful four more were taken in hand. Design work also started on a bigger purpose-built AA cruiser, based on the successful small light cruisers of the *Arethusa* Class. In all 16 of the *Dido* type were authorized, and they were given a new type of 5.25-inch dual-purpose antisurface and antiaircraft gun. This allowed them to function as proper cruisers rather than escorts.

The US Navy was impressed by the AA cruiser concept and produced the *Atlanta* Class. The ships resembled the *Dido* in layout, with three tiers of twin 5-inch gun mountings forward, but their purpose was different. They were given very high speed to allow them to work with destroyers, the idea being to neutralize the powerful Japanese Special Type destroyers by strengthening the American destroyer squadrons.

In 1940 Congress passed the Two-Ocean Navy Bill and this permitted a logical development of cruisers, unfettered by treaties. The *Brooklyn* idea was developed into the *Cleveland* Class, in which the fifth triple 6-inch turret was dropped, like the British *Southampton* Class. The successful *San Francisco* Class heavy cruiser design was expanded into the 13,600-ton *Baltimore* Class, giving for the first time a balanced ship with good armament, protection and range. However, none of these would be ready until the middle of 1942 at the earliest. The new British cruisers had been started three years earlier, but few of them would be in service before 1941. Apart from the antiaircraft cruisers, production was centered on a diminutive of the *Southampton* design, the 8000-ton *Fiji* Class.

To make up the numbers of cruisers the British intended to take up 50 big liners for conversion into Armed Merchant Cruisers (AMCs), just as they had done in 1914. The Germans also intended to repeat their conversions of auxiliary cruisers (*hilfskreuzer*) or disguised raiders, fast cargo vessels fitted with concealed 15cm guns. They would cruise on the distant trade routes, sinking unescorted merchantmen while, it was hoped, the disguise would permit them to bluff their way past enemy cruisers.

When war broke out in 1939 the *Admiral Graf Spee* and *Deutschland* were already at sea

CRUISERS

Class	Years built	Tonnage	Guns (main)	Guns (antiaircraft)	Torpedo tubes	Speed (knots)
United States						
Omaha	1923–5	7050	10/12 6-inch	8 3-inch	6	35
Salt Lake City	1929–30	9100	10 8-inch	8 5-inch	0	32
Northampton	1930–1	9200	9 8-inch	12 5-inch	0	32
Portland	1932–3	9900	9 8-inch	12 5-inch	0	32
San Francisco	1934–7	10,000	9 8-inch	12 5-inch	0	32
Brooklyn	1938–9	10,000	15 6-inch	8 5-inch	0	32
Wichita	1939	11,000	9 8-inch	8 5-inch	0	32
Atlanta	1942–5	6000		12 or 16 5-inch	8	34
Cleveland	1942–5	10,000	12 6-inch	12 5-inch	0	33
Baltimore	1943–5	13,600	9 8-inch	12 5-inch	0	33
Britain						
Kent	1928	10,000	8 8-inch	8 4-inch	8	32
London	1930	10,000	8 8-inch	8 4-inch	8	32
Norfolk	1930	10,000	8 8-inch	8 4-inch	8	32
York	1930–1	8300	6 8-inch	4 4-inch	6	32
Leander	1933–5	7200	8 6-inch	8 4-inch	8	32
Perth	1936	7000	8 6-inch	8 4-inch	8	32
Arethusa	1935–7	5200	6 6-inch	6 4-inch	6	32
Southampton	1937–9	9400	12 6-inch	8 4-inch	6	32
Edinburgh	1939	10,000	12 6-inch	12 4-inch	6	32
Dido	1940–2	5600		10 5.25-inch	6	32
Diadem	1943–4	6000		8 5.25-inch	6	32
Fiji (sometimes known as *Colony* Class)	1940–3	8500	9/12 6-inch	10/8 4-inch	6	32
Japan						
Furutaka	1926–7	9000	6 8-inch	4 4.7-inch	8	33
Ashigara	1928–9	13,400	10 8-inch	8 5-inch	16	33
Atago	1932	13,200	10 8-inch	8 5-inch	16	34
Mogami	1935–7	12,500	10 8-inch	8 5-inch	12	34
All *Mogami* Class had triple 6-inch replaced by twin 8-inch by 1941						
Tone	1938–9	11,200	8 8-inch	8 5-inch	12	35
Agano	1942–4	7000	6 5.9-inch	4 3-inch	8	35
Oyodo	1943	8200	6 5.9-inch	8 3.9-inch	0	36
Italy						
Trento	1928–9	10,000	8 8-inch	12 3.9-inch	8	35
Bolzano	1933	11,000	8 8-inch	12 3.9-inch	8	36
Zara	1931–2	11,800	8 8-inch	12 3.9-inch	0	32
Giuseppe Garibaldi	1937	9500	10 6-inch	8 3.9-inch	6	35
Duca d'Aosta	1935–6	8500	8 6-inch	6 3.9-inch	4/6	37
Alberico da Barbiano	1931–3	5300	8 6-inch	6 3.9-inch	4	37
Attilio Regolo	1942–3	3750		8 5.3-inch	8	39
Germany						
Emden	1925	5600	8 5.9-inch	3 3.5-inch	4	29
Koln	1930	6650	9 5.9-inch	6 3.5-inch	12	32
Leipzig	1931	6700	9 5.9-inch	6 3.5-inch	12	32
Nurnberg	1935	7000	9 5.9-inch	8 3.5-inch	12	32
Admiral Hipper	1939–40	14,000	8 8-inch	12 4.1-inch	12	32

undetected, and they immediately began to prey on shipping in the South Atlantic. Powerful hunting groups were formed of British and French heavy cruisers and three months later the Germans played into their hands by choosing to attack shipping at a focal point off the River Plate in South America. The *Admiral Graf Spee* was sighted early on 13 December 1939 by the heavy cruiser *Exeter*, which was accompanied by the light cruisers *Ajax* and *Achilles*. In the battle the *Exeter* was badly knocked about, with both forward turrets put out of action. The two smaller cruisers darted in and out of range, distracting the German gunners and forcing them to shift target repeatedly. Finally the *Graf Spee* gave up, and sought sanctuary in the Uraguayan port of Montevideo. Misled by skillful propaganda into believing that the carrier *Ark Royal* and the battlecruiser *Renown* were very close, Hitler ordered the *Graf Spee*'s captain to scuttle his ship four days after the battle. The first phase of cruiser warfare was over, for the *Deutschland* had already returned home after sinking only two ships.

There were very few cruiser-versus-cruiser duels in the European theater, but HMAS *Sydney* caught and sank the Italian *Bartolomeo Colleoni* off Crete in July 1940, and HMS *Sheffield* and HMS *Jamaica* drove off the *Lützow* (formerly the *Deutschland*) and the *Admiral Hipper* after they had unsuccessfully tried to attack a convoy in the Arctic in December 1943. German cruisers fared badly in the Norwegian campaign in 1940, with the *Blücher* sunk by coastal batteries, the *Königsberg* sunk by British dive bombers, the *Karlsruhe* torpedoed by a submarine and the *Leipzig* badly damaged by a torpedo. One of the biggest surprises was the effectiveness of 8-inch shellfire against battleships, for it had been believed that a capital ship had nothing to fear from a heavy cruiser. The British battlecruiser *Hood* was set on fire by 8-inch shellfire from the *Prinz Eugen*, and the *Bismarck* and *Scharnhorst* both had their fire control knocked out by 8-inch shells.

Cruisers found a new role in amphibious operations. Not only were their guns useful for providing fire support but they had sufficient space on board to accommodate extra staff. Their AA batteries and radar provided AA defense off the beaches, where they could be risked closer inshore than battleships. Several cruisers were used as flagships during amphibious operations, although it was found subsequently that the gunfire support mission tended to conflict with their command role, as they were so frequently required to provide covering fire.

In the Far East Allied cruisers showed none of the superiority that they did in the Atlantic and Mediterranean. The first actions were at Pearl Harbor, in which the USS *Raleigh* was damaged, and the occupation of Shanghai, in which the old armored cruiser *Idzumo* sank the gunboat HMS *Peterel*. Then came the disastrous fighting in the East Indies in February 1942, in which the American-British-Dutch-Australian (ABDA) force was wiped out by Japanese cruisers. The Dutch *De Ruyter* and *Java*, the American *Houston*, the British *Exeter* and the Australian *Perth* were all sunk, having inflicted very little damage on the Japanese in return. Then the carriers made a lightning strike into the Indian Ocean and sank the British carrier *Hermes* and the heavy cruisers *Dorsetshire* and *Cornwall*.

Even when the Allies moved back to the offensive things did not go well. The landings on Guadalcanal in the beginning of August 1942 provoked an immediate riposte by the Japanese at Rabaul. Five heavy and two light cruisers under Admiral Mikawa attacked a force of Allied cruisers lying off Savo Island on the morning of 9 August 1942, sinking the USS *Quincy, Vincennes* and *Astoria* and HMAS *Canberra* and blowing the bow off the *Chicago*. Surprise was total but fortunately the Japanese failed to reach the amphibious transports off Lunga Point and a submarine managed to sink the heavy cruiser *Kako* on the way home. Subsequent battles showed how superior the Japanese were at night fighting: Cape Esperance, Guadalcanal, Tassafaronga and others showed that the only way to beat the Japanese was to use long-range gunfire with radar control, this keeping the dreaded Long Lance torpedoes at maximum range. In the hard-fought series of battles around Guadalcanal the US and Allied navies lost six heavy and two light cruisers and the Japanese three heavy and two light.

The rapid fire of the 6-inch gun was best suited to this sort of action and the new *Cleveland*s were well equipped to take up the role, leaving the big *Baltimore* Class 8-inch gunned ships to escort carrier task forces. They proved ideal for that task, having the range and speed to keep up with the fast carriers, and also the space for adequate AA firepower. In contrast the small *Atlanta* Class AA cruisers proved less suited to Pacific conditions, lacking the range for extended operations.

Unlike the battleship, the cruiser ended the war in even greater demand than before, and 50 percent larger. Both the British and the Americans produced designs for 6-inch and

8-inch gunned cruisers displacing 15–17,000 tons, although only the US Navy went ahead with these plans. They even produced a freakish pair of 'large cruisers' (CB), the *Alaska* and *Guam*, displacing 29,000 tons and armed with nine 12-inch guns. They were born of fears that the 8-inch gun might prove inadequate to defend carriers from attack by Japanese cruisers, and although a total aberration they proved magnificent carrier escorts. The final development of the cruiser was the 17,000-ton *Des Moines* Class, armed with nine 8-inch guns using automatic loading to fire 10 shells per minute. In this class, not completed until long after the war, the cruiser overtook the battleship to become a new breed of capital ship.

DESTROYERS

Unlike most other warships the destroyer's function had remained virtually unchanged since first introduced in 1893; protecting the battle fleet from torpedo attack and in turn attacking the enemy's battle fleet. To achieve this they were armed with quick-firing medium-caliber guns and torpedo tubes and given a big margin of speed over other warships.

There had, however, been fierce competition among the major navies to improve destroyers, and this led to a big disparity in performance and armament. This trend had started with the Italians in World War I, when they armed the *Carlo Mirabello* Class with a 6-inch gun forward and seven 4-inch guns. Although the design followed the basic form of a destroyer, the ships were intended to act as fleet scouts, and had actually been scaled down to 1780 tons from 5000-ton light cruisers. As such they were hybrids; too light to act as cruisers and too heavily loaded to be able to function effectively as destroyers. This did not deter the Italians from continuing to build big destroyers, otherwise known as *esploratori* (scouts), such as the *Leone* Class.

The French kept a wary eye on Italian developments, and in 1922 they authorized six *contre-torpilleurs* or 'destroyers of destroyers' in addition to conventional destroyers. These were the first of a series culminating in the six *Fantasque* Class ordered under the 1930 Fleet Law. They were intended to displace 2610 tons and develop 74,000 horsepower for 37 knots, but on trials reached speeds of more than 40 knots with as much as 50 percent more power. It was a staggering technical achievement but the cost was high: weak armament, very low endurance and poor reliability.

Italy responded to the challenge with the 'Navigatori' type and when Germany began to rearm after 1934 she too built very big destroyers. The British, however, gave priority to escort duties and insisted on building larger numbers of cheaper and more cost-effective destroyers. Nine classes of destroyers, lettered 'A' to 'I' were built from the late 1920s onward and even when policy changed in 1936 the new 'Tribal' Class were modest in comparison with the super-destroyers built for other navies.

An equally fierce rivalry developed in the Pacific. In 1923 the Japanese ordered the first of their Special Type or *Fubuki* Class, displacing a nominal 1750 tons and capable of 38 knots. Unlike the French and Italian boats, however, they carried a very heavy armament of guns and torpedoes. Development of the type proceeded and in 1923 the first oxygen-driven torpedoes, nicknamed Long Lance, were issued. What made these destroyers even more formidable was the provision of deck-mounted reloads, so that they could retire behind a smokescreen, reload and then make a second attack.

Finally the Americans responded with their own superdestroyers, the *Porter* Class, which were nearly as big as the *Fubuki* type. However, trying to match the nominal displacement showed that the Japanese could not have

Below: The USS Van Valkenburgh *(DD656), one of the very successful* Fletcher *Class.*

DESTROYERS

Class	Displacement	Years built	Armament	Torpedo tubes	Speed
United States					
Selfridge	1850	1936–7	8 5-inch	8	37
Mahan	1500	1936–7	5 5-inch	12	36
Gridley	1500	1938–40	4 5-inch	16	36
Bristol & Benson	1650	1940–3	4 5-inch	10	36
Fletcher	2100	1942–4	5 5-inch	10	35
Gearing and Sumner	2200	1944–5	6 5-inch	10	36
Britain					
A–I Classes	1400	1930–40	4 4.7-inch	8 or 10	36
Tribal	1900	1938–9	8 4.7-inch	4	36
J, K & N Class	1700	1939–42	6 4.7-inch	10	36
L & M Class	1950	1941–2	6 4.7-inch	8	36
Hunt	1000	1940–3	4 or 6 4-inch AA	0–3	27
O & P Class	1550	1941–2	4 4 or 4.7-inch	8	34
War Emergency Classes	1750	1942–4	4 4.5 or 4.7-inch	8	34
Japan					
Kagero	2000	1939–41	6 5-inch	8	35
Germany					
Z-1 Class	2400	1938–9	5 5-inch	8	38
Z-23 Class	2600	1942–3	5 5.9-inch	8	38
T-1 Class	1100	1940–2	1 4.1-inch	6	33
T-22 Class	1300	1942–4	4 4.1-inch	6	33
Italy					
Aviere	1650	1938–9	4 4.7-inch	6	39
France					
Mogador	2900	1938	8 5.5-inch	10	38

mounted so much topweight without severe problems and neither the *Porter* Class nor their successors were as seaworthy as the smaller conventional destroyers. In theory the super-destroyer should have had the advantages of a bigger and more-seaworthy hull and heavier armament, but in practice the extra weight of armament coupled with the impossibility of providing adequate fire control nullified the benefits of size.

The German superdestroyers provide a classic example of this predicament. After building 22 destroyers in 1934–39 the Kriegsmarine decided to revive an idea it had tried in 1918, arming destroyers with cruiser-caliber (15cm) guns. The *Z23* Class did not come into service until World War II was well under way, but apart from their heavy guns they were nothing more than an extension of the previous designs. In action they proved a liability, partly because the 15cm shell was too heavy for hand loading in rough weather but equally because the ultrahigh-pressure steam plant was very difficult to maintain.

At the start of the war the British were in the middle of a big destroyer-building program, divided between standard or 'fleet' destroyers and escort destroyers. The former was a simple design intended for mass production, known as the Emergency Type, displacing some 1700 tons and armed with four single guns and eight torpedo tubes. The escort destroyers were a diminutive of this design, and were known as the 'Hunt' Class. They were armed with a purely antiaircraft armament and were intended primarily to defend coastal convoys. At the same time a program of converting old destroyers for escort duties was in hand, and this was to prove invaluable. From the outset fleet destroyers were used as antisubmarine escorts, having been fitted with sonar since the mid-1920s, and as many as possible were diverted from escorting the main fleets to support the convoys.

Apart from skirmishes, the first important destroyer battles took place during the Norwegian Campaign in April 1940. In a brisk action at Narvik on 9 April five British destroyers attacked the German flotilla in the fiords, sinking two and losing two themselves. Four days later nine destroyers returned to the attack, supported by the battleship *Warspite*, and sank all eight Germans with only minor damage to HMS *Eskimo*.

Probably the most outstanding achievement of British destroyers was their work in rescuing a large proportion of the 338,000 troops evacuated from France in May–June 1940. In many cases destroyers lifted 900 men at a time, and at least one is recorded as having 1400 soldiers on board. Out of 162 destroyers in service in mid-June 1940 only 74 were undamaged. Fortunately, the German destroyer force had been severely depleted in Norway, and only eight of them remained – one of the factors inhibiting the Sealion invasion plans. In response to a plea from Winston Churchill, President Roosevelt authorized the US Navy to lend 50 old destroyers to the RN in return for a 99-year lease on bases in the Caribbean and elsewhere. Although old, these 'four-stackers' proved very useful as convoy escorts and released more-modern destroyers for work with the Fleet.

To cure the lack of endurance in escort destroyers the British converted many of the older 'V & W' Class to Long-Range Escorts, replacing one boiler with a fuel tank and strengthening the armament with new weaponry such as the Hedgehog mortar. Otherwise war construction concentrated on the Emergency and 'Hunt' types until 1943. Then a much bigger destroyer was designed for service in the Pacific, with a powerful dual-purpose armament and greater range. War experience also showed that destroyers could be made less vulnerable to battle damage by dividing the machinery and boilers into double units, and so the final wartime designs reverted to two funnels after a lapse of 10 years.

Several actions in the Atlantic and Arctic showed that the British policy of putting seaworthiness before armament and high speed was fully justified. Thus Vian's 4th Flotilla was able to shadow and attack the *Bismarck* in May 1941, while British and Norwegian destroyers torpedoed the *Scharnhorst* in December 1943 after bad weather had forced the German admiral to send his destroyers back to base. In the Mediterranean the story was much the same, and in December 1941 three British and one Dutch destroyer wiped out two Italian light cruisers in a brilliant night action.

Destroyer actions in the Pacific at first went decidedly in favor of the Japanese. Not only was the range and speed of the Long Lance a complete surprise to the Americans but also the tactic of retiring to reload proved successful in the confused night actions. A force of American, British and Dutch destroyers was completely outfought in the East Indies in January–February 1942 and US destroyers were roughly handled in the fierce night actions which were fought in the Solomons after the landings on Guadalcanal in August 1942.

A feature of operations in the Solomons in 1942–43 was the conversion of older destroyers to fast transports. The Japanese introduced them to run the 'Tokyo Express' under Admiral Tanaka, high-speed runs from Rabaul to Guadalcanal, bringing food, ammunition and reinforcements for the hard-pressed garrison. The Americans did the same, converting old four-stackers and DEs to assault transports or APDs. The Japanese torpedoes' phenomenal range, coupled with superb night-fighting techniques, made the night encounters in the Solomons a terrible time for the Americans, but the answer finally proved to be long-range gunfire from cruisers, controlled by radar, a technique which the Japanese could not match.

Fortunately the US Navy had been farsighted in its destroyer policy, and had developed the first-class 5-inch/38 caliber dual-purpose gun as the main armament. With the Mk 37 fire control system, US destroyers had a good antiair and antisurface armament, although the 21-inch torpedo was very poor, and no match for the Long Lance in reliability, let alone destructiveness. In 1940 the first of a magnificent new class of destroyers was ordered, the *Fletcher*. With five 5-inch guns and 10 21-inch torpedo tubes, she could make 35 knots and was big enough to take all the extra AA guns and equipment needed. With their balance of firepower, speed and size the *Fletcher*s rank as the most successful destroyers used in World War II, and the type was expanded into the *Allen M Sumner* and *Gearing* types, with twin 5-inch guns instead of singles.

The toughest test for American destroyers came in April 1945, when the force covering the invasion of Okinawa was attacked by Kamikazes. The destroyers and DEs were organized in a radar picket line around the islands, far out at sea and therefore more exposed to air attack. By the time the attacks finished at the end of July, 13 destroyers and DEs had been sunk and another 88 damaged, many of them seriously. Frantic efforts were made to improve the AA defenses of destroyers but in the time available little could be done. The destroyers were forced to take most of the punishment intended for the amphibious transports.

Ironically the last classic destroyer action in the Far East was fought by the British. In May 1945 a force of five destroyers encountered the heavy cruiser *Haguro* north of Sumatra and sent her to the bottom in a brilliantly executed attack from all points of the compass.

By the end of hostilities the destroyer had been transformed from a surface-warfare vessel into a general-purpose fleet escort. Daylight attacks with torpedoes had been virtually suicidal at the beginning of the war, and now radar and improved fire control made night attacks nearly as hazardous. Despite its hard work escorting convoys, the destroyer was not an ideal anti-submarine escort and that function tended to devolve more and more to specially designed frigates and DEs. Armament altered to reflect this change in function, with dual-purpose and even purely antiaircraft guns replacing the former low-angle weapons and light antiaircraft guns replacing half the torpedo tubes. Extra fuel was also carried whenever possible.

Weight being crucial, destroyers pushed ship technology further than most warship types. Thus, longitudinal framing was rapidly established after its introduction in Britain and the United States in the 1930s. Welding was adopted on a large scale, both to save weight and to speed up construction. The lead taken by the Japanese and Americans in providing dual-purpose antisurface and antiaircraft gun mountings was followed in other navies, and by 1945 destroyers were much less vulnerable to air attack than they had been. Although the Americans and British found that speed was much less significant in action than they had thought, the Japanese continued to pursue the goal of higher and higher speeds, culminating in the 40-knot *Shimakaze* in 1943.

The losses tell the most dramatic tale of destroyers' contribution to the War:

American	99
British	169
Dutch	9
French	60
German	25
Italian	134
Japanese	134
Soviet	33

Excluding 36 French destroyers scuttled in 1942, a total of 87 percent of these destroyers were sunk in action.

SUBMARINES

Any doubts about the power of submarines had been dispelled by the experiences of World War I, so when the British tried to get the submarine banned as inhumane at the various disarmament conferences, other nations, notably France, were reluctant to discard such a cost-effective weapon.

In the years immediately after World War I nearly all navies had dabbled in the design of cruiser-submarines, based on the long-range, heavily armed U-Boats built in 1917–18. Despite the fact that the Germans themselves had found them to be clumsy and less effective than the standard 'Mittel-U' and UB-III types, navy after navy built submarines armed with 6-inch and even 8-inch guns. Another aberration was to equip submarines with hangars and catapults to enable them to fly off reconnaissance aircraft. Gradually, however, common sense asserted itself, and apart from the Japanese, moderate dimensions became the norm once more.

The British, with the benefit of war experience behind them, built only one cruiser-submarine, the giant *X.1*. and converted the *M.2* to carry a float plane, and soon reverted to developments of the successful 'L' Class design. The first designs were not a complete success as their riveted external fuel tanks leaked oil, but the basic design was sound, and in 1929 the first of a highly successful series, the 'S' Class was authorized. In this design the fuel tanks were inside the pressure hull but this did not inhibit rapid diving – an 'S' boat could dive in 24 seconds or less, as it was assumed that British submarines would be operating off a hostile coast, under constant surveillance from the air. These boats were intended for restricted waters, and they were supplemented by a small class of mine-layers. The need for the latter type disappeared with the introduction of a mine which could be ejected from torpedo tubes, and only six were built. In 1935 the first of a larger 'patrol' type, the 'T' Class, was authorized, and a year later the first of a small 540-ton type, the 'U' Class, was started to provide cheap boats for training.

British submarines did not adopt welding until World War II but habitability was comparatively good and the value of a heavy bow salvo of torpedo tubes was appreciated before most other navies. The six-tube salvo of the 'S' Class gave way to an eight-tube salvo in the 'T' Class to improve the chances of obtaining a hit at maximum range. Above all, British submarines had the advantage of a reliable torpedo; the 21-inch Mk 8 with its highly efficient Brotherhood Cycle engine remained an outstanding torpedo throughout the war.

The US Navy was permitted the same tonnage of submarines (52,700 tons) as the British and the Japanese under the 1930 London Naval Treaty, and so it was necessary to find an optimum size for Pacific operations. A series of giant submarines in the early 1920s had not proved successful, but in 1933 four prototypes were laid down, the *Porpoise, Pike, Shark* and *Triton*. These four boats tested various diesels for future classes, and so by 1940 the latest *Gato* Class were the outcome of steady development, 1520-tonners capable of 20 knots on the surface and armed with six torpedo tubes forward and four aft. Special attention was paid to habitability, with air conditioning a necessity for extended operations in the Pacific.

Unfortunately, American submarines were handicapped by a torpedo which had a faulty exploder, as well as other faults. As late as 1943 submarines were reporting that their torpedoes were running wild or failing to detonate on impact. It was to cause a major scandal and undoubtedly robbed Pacific Fleet submarines of many successes.

France had always shown great interest in the submarine, but as in the years before 1914 the detailed design was not up to the standards achieved by other navies. Although fast diving, they were unreliable and the torpedoes were not particularly good either. The obsession with a trade war against the British led to the building of large numbers of 1500-ton submarines, more suited to commerce raiding than offensive operations against enemy surface warships, but there were also 600-ton coast-defense submarines. The French could also boast of having the world's largest submarine, the 2880-ton *Surcouf*, armed with two 8-inch guns and a seaplane.

Like the French, the Italians built a large fleet of submarines but they were not particularly well designed. Although avoiding the extremely large cruiser-submarines favored in other navies, the Italians built a number of clumsy, slow-diving boats with a heavy armament of deck guns. Mindful of creature comforts, they also provided big conning towers with galleys and toilets, all at the expense of efficiency, and when a flotilla of submarines was sent to Bordeaux in 1940 the Germans insisted that they should all be modified to enable them to operate in the Atlantic on something like equal terms with the U-Boats.

The Japanese remained wedded to the idea of big cruiser-submarines and went to great lengths to perfect a means of housing and launching float planes from them. As they were prepared to be 'flexible' in their interpretation of tonnages they were not as inhibited as the Americans in choosing an optimum displacement. A 21-inch version of the oxygen-driven Long Lance torpedo was produced for use in submarines but in other respects Japanese submarines were not as good as the American boats, being unable to dive as fast or as deep. Above all, the tactical doctrine was faulty, with commerce destruction given a much lower priority than attacks on enemy warships.

The Japanese were the first to build midget submarines, having built two prototypes in the mid-1930s and put them into mass production in 1938. They were intended for penetrating enemy harbors, and could be transported aboard fleet submarines, major warships or specially converted tenders.

Germany was forbidden to possess U-Boats under the Treaty of Versailles but took immediate steps to preserve the expertise of her design teams by moving them to Holland. There, the front organization *Scheepsbouwkantoor* designed submarines for Turkey, Finland and Spain but also developed designs for the day when Germany would need U-Boats once more. In 1934 Hitler gave his new *Kriegsmarine* permission to stockpile material for a dozen U-Boats, ready to start building as soon as he renounced the Treaty of Versailles.

Despite their introduction of cruiser-submarines in the previous war, the German naval staff decided against such unwieldy boats and settled on medium-sized designs for the North Atlantic. The first boats ordered were 250-ton coastal boats, followed by a pair of 860-ton seagoing boats. The latter were not a success, and when the Anglo-German Naval Agreement of 1935 fixed the total of U-Boat tonnage at 35 percent of the Royal Navy's total it was decided to go for a smaller type to get maximum numbers. The result was the 750-ton Type VII, developed from the successful UB-III of 1917, and was the prototype of the standard U-Boat used with such deadly effect in the Atlantic. A bigger ocean-going boat, the Type IX was also put in hand, so that by September 1939 there were two Type I boats (862 tons), 32 Type II (250 tons), 21 Type VII (750 tons) and 10 Type IX (1000 tons). In only five years a fleet of 65 U-Boats had been created and it was possible to expand production immediately.

It is often suggested that the Germans should have devoted more resources to U-Boat construction than they did, and Admiral Doenitz later claimed that with 200 U-Boats in commission instead of 58 he would have won World War II for Hitler. This claim must be treated with reserve, for there were several factors working against such a possibility. First, there was the Anglo-German Naval Agreement, entered into by Hitler to avoid provoking the British; any sudden expansion of the U-Boat Arm would have meant cancelling orders for surface ships. Second, there was the problem of which U-Boat to build, and agreement for a program of 200 U-Boats given too early could have resulted in too many of the unsuccessful Type I or the small Type II boats. Third, the German Navy needed its big surface warships as much to restore its own morale vis à vis the Luftwaffe and the Wehrmacht as for national prestige, for in their eyes it had disgraced itself by its surrender and scuttling at Scapa Flow. All these factors combined to give the German navy too small a U-Boat Arm at the outbreak of World War II, and in any case war came about five years earlier than planned.

The Soviets had a very large fleet of submarines, a few of them veterans of the Czarist navy but many of them built in the 1930s. They included four basic types, the small 'M' or coastal type, the seagoing 'Scha' and 'S' types and the 'K' cruiser type, of which the 'S' Class resembled the Type VII U-Boat, having been designed with German technical assistance. When the Germans attacked in June 1941 a surprisingly large number of the 213 submarines officially complete and on the strength of the Soviet navy were laid up and did not get to sea at all. The material state of those which did see active service was not bad but the crews were badly trained and there were no technical advances such as sonar or gyro-angling for torpedoes until they were supplied by the Soviet Union's British and American allies.

The Germans scored two quick successes before the end of 1939, torpedoing the carrier HMS *Courageous* in September and then penetrating Scapa Flow to sink the battleship *Royal Oak* the following month. The Norwegian campaign in the spring of 1940 proved very disappointing because the new magnetic exploder for the standard torpedo proved to be faulty. In northern latitudes the exploder was affected by the earth's magnetic field, and so target after target escaped unscathed because the warhead failed to detonate. In contrast British submarines enjoyed a lot of success, damaging the battlecruiser *Gneisenau* and the light cruiser *Leipzig* and sinking the light cruiser *Karlsruhe* and the torpedo boat *Luchs*

between April-July 1940.

The fall of France in June 1940 transformed the naval war and tilted the balance in favor of the U-Boats. Hitherto they had been operating out of the North Sea, but as soon as bases became available on the Atlantic coast the U-Boats were sitting astride the British shipping routes in the Western Approaches. From Lorient, La Pallice and Bordeaux they could range far into the Atlantic, and British shipping losses began to rise sharply from August. Priority was now given to U-Boat building, and large numbers of Type VIIC boats (as well as smaller numbers of Type IXB) were put in hand. A total of 54 were commissioned in 1940, rising to 202 in 1941 and 238 in 1942, and although losses were inflicted on a growing scale by Allied antisubmarine forces, U-Boat building far outstripped these losses. Fortunately for the Allies the rapid expansion of the U-Boat arm meant that a growing number of U-Boats had to be kept back in the Baltic for training. Another problem inherent with submarines is that they make heavy demands on maintenance, and a surprisingly low proportion of the U-Boats were actually in the Western Approaches at any given time.

In 1941 Doenitz introduced the *rüdeltaktik* ('wolf pack'). Although not original, having been proposed by Bauer in 1916, it was forced on Doenitz by the rising number of losses among the highly trained prewar U-Boat commanders, and required less individual skill. It relied on concentrated attacks on convoys at night, and the concentration of as many as 20 U-Boats was achieved by the shore-based HQ 'homing' U-Boats on to a convoy already located. Any U-Boat which reported a convoy was told to tail it on the surface, noting any changes of course, and only when all available U-Boats within reach had been brought into position was the order given to attack.

Until the escorts had radar it was possible to attack on the surface at night, and this proved devastating. Even when this tactic had to be abandoned, submerged attacks at night were very successful, and until the spring of 1943 Doenitz hoped to be able to destroy an entire convoy. Although this never happened there were some terrible convoy battles in which scores of ships were sunk without the escorts being able to sink any of the attackers.

Throughout 1941 the British battled on alone, but the long-awaited entry of the United States into the war at the end of that year did not bring the respite that had been expected. Instead, the shipping losses rose even higher because ASW

Above: The USS Tinosa *in 1944.*

provisions on the East Coast proved to be woefully inadequate. The U-Boats reaped a grim harvest for the first half of 1942 until US countermeasures began to take effect. From then on it was more and more a war of technology and shipbuilding, with scientists on both sides developing new weapons and sensors, and in this respect the Germans were badly placed to coordinate their scientific efforts. A near-fatal strategic error was made by the Allies late in 1942, when they withdrew the cream of their ASW forces to protect the 'Torch' landings in North Africa. The U-Boats quickly took advantage of the weaker opposition in the Atlantic and losses began to climb, topping 700,000 tons in November 1942 and reaching nearly that figure in March 1943.

Admiral Doenitz was sure that victory was in his grasp, but in April and May 1943 the tables were dramatically reversed, and losses of U-Boats suddenly rose. The causes were complex, for much new equipment came into service, US shipbuilding, both of escorts and merchant ships, was getting into top gear, and the escort carriers and escorts allocated to the 'Torch' operations were fed back into the Atlantic battle in the nick of time. The result was in no doubt and Doenitz withdrew his U-Boats for re-grouping and retraining with new weapons. When these were available later that year it was too late, for the initiative had passed to the Allies.

The U-Boats remained dangerous for the rest of the war but were never the threat that they had been. New devices, particularly an electric homing torpedo, made them more deadly in attack, while the *schnorchel* air mast gave them some respite from the unceasing air attacks, but these could not restore the balance. That, it was hoped, would come from two radically new designs, the 'Electro U-Boat' and the Walther hydrogen peroxide propulsion system. The former, known as the Type XXI, was a stream-lined U-Boat with enlarged batteries, capable of high underwater speed in short bursts, while the latter was independent of outside oxygen, and promised to turn the U-Boat into a 'true submarine,' with no need to recharge her batteries. Fortunately, the Allies were to be saved a new onslaught on their shipping by the chronic administrative inefficiency of the Third Reich; a failure to get priorities right ensured that resources were wasted on developing the Walther turbine instead of pushing ahead with the simpler but equally deadly Type XXI. As a result only three Type XXI boats and a handful of the smaller Type XXIII were ready by the last month of the war.

The Mediterranean was also the scene of much submarine activity, but this time it was German and Italian communications which suffered at the hands of British submarines. The 10th Flotilla at Malta scored a dazzling string of successes in 1940–42, even though bombing made Grand Harbor almost untenable for some months. In fact, the pressure on the Italians became so great that Hitler ordered a dozen of his precious U-Boats into the Mediterranean to take some of the pressure off his allies. All of those U-Boats were sunk, but not before they had torpedoed the carriers *Eagle* and *Ark Royal* and the battleship *Barham*. In contrast, Italian submarines proved to be badly handicapped by their technical problems, and achieved comparatively little.

In the Pacific submarines were used to even greater effect than they were in the Atlantic. The American submarines proved to be well designed for their role and their tactical and strategic direction proved equally good. Although Japanese carriers were given priority as targets, oil tankers were next on the list and merchant ships were not neglected. As a result the Japanese island empire was strangled for lack of shipping. Another important role for American submarines was reconnaissance, and time and time again they gave timely warning of Japanese fleet movements.

There were several outstanding examples of aggressive handling. During the Battle of the Philippine Sea in June 1944 the USS *Cavalla* sank the carrier *Shokaku* while the *Albacore* got the *Taiho*. During the prelude to the Battle of Leyte Gulf the following October, the *Darter* and *Dace* not only reported the departure of Admiral Kurita's First Strike Force from Brunei but also managed to sink the heavy cruisers *Atago* and *Maya* and cripple the *Takao*. In November that year the *Archerfish* torpedoed the giant carrier *Shinano* before she had even

SEA

SUBMARINES

Class	Displacement (tons)	Torpedo tubes	Surface speed (knots)	Underwater speed (knots)
Germany				
Type VIIc	750	5	17	7
Type IXc	1150	6	18	7
Type XXI	1620	6	$15\frac{1}{2}$	16
Type XXIII	232	2	$9\frac{3}{4}$	$12\frac{1}{4}$
Type XVIIb	312	2	$8\frac{1}{2}$	$21\frac{1}{2}$
United States				
Gato and *Balao* Classes	1520	10	20	9
Britain				
S Class	670	6	14	10
T Class	1100	10	15	9
U & V Classes	540	4	12	9
Japan				
RO-100 Class	600	5	14	8
I-15 Class	2200	6	23	8

been completed. It was against Japanese shipping that US submarines were deadliest. Operating in a modified version of the German wolf pack, with three boats to a pack, they inflicted heavy losses on the Japanese mercantile marine and eventually forced the Japanese to resort to sending cargoes in small coasters and junks in shallow waters, hugging the coastline all the way. Submarines also contributed to the mining of harbors and shipping routes, and it can be claimed that the United States Navy is the only one to have won an outright offensive against shipping.

In direct contrast the Japanese showed a very poor appreciation of how to use submarines against the Americans. Imbued with a sense of fanaticism, they scorned attacks on shipping and supply lines as too defensive and devoted their efforts to attacks on warships. As their equipment was not particularly good, apart from the torpedoes, this meant that Japanese submarines were exposed to the heaviest counterattacks. This was reflected in the enormous losses suffered, and these grew worse when submarines were switched from naval operations to supplying remote army garrisons.

Despite their shortcomings Japanese submarines achieved some outstanding successes, including the sinking of the carriers *Yorktown* and *Wasp*, the cruisers *Juneau* and *Indianapolis* and a considerable number of lesser warships, but their failure to attack lines of communication left the US Navy relatively unhampered.

Homing torpedoes were introduced in most navies during the war, some of them homing actively but the majority homing passively on propeller noise. Another improvement was the magnetic influence exploder, which permitted a 'near miss' underneath the keel of the target, but both the Americans and the Germans experienced severe technical problems with these. The Germans led the way in designing an electric torpedo, principally to speed up production and to save strategic materials. The G7e, for example, took 1707 man-hours to make and cost 13,500 Reichsmarks as against 3730 man-hours and 24,000 RM for the G7a.

Aircraft proved the biggest menace to submarines, and all front-line boats were progressively armed with light AA guns on the conning tower. The Germans took this to extremes by trying to stay on the surface in the Bay of Biscay to fight it out with RAF Coastal Command bombers, but it proved an expensive mistake. Although a few unwary Liberators and Sunderlands were shot down in the early days they soon learned to fly round and round out of range, while summoning the nearest group of warships; no U-Boat dared to linger for too long, and was soon forced to dive, at which point she was most vulnerable to damage.

The *schnorchel* air mast, copied from a Dutch design captured in 1940, enabled a submarine to recharge its batteries while running on diesels at periscope depth, but this procedure was extremely wearing for the crew. It also had the effect of making the U-Boats 'keep their heads down,' and although it cut the savage rate of losses experienced in mid-1943 it did little to add to the number of merchantmen sunk. The problem was that airborne radar and the fitting of powerful searchlights to aircraft had made it all but impossible to recharge batteries on the surface at night.

World War II showed that the submarine had lost none of its deadliness since 1918. Although countermeasures temporarily got the upper hand against the U-Boats in 1943, new technology almost restored the balance in their favor two years later. Postwar evidence was to show how close the Allied margin of victory had been.

A feature of World War II was the widespread use of midget submarines. The Japanese tried to coordinate an attack on Pearl Harbor with the main air strike but this failed miserably. Two other attacks were carried out against defended harbors, Sydney and Diego Suarez, and the latter caused severe damage to the battleship *Ramillies*. Later, however, opinion veered to using midgets for local defense, and the *Koryu* and *Kaiten* types were developed for this purpose.

The Italian 'human torpedoes' or 'pigs' were two-man midgets driven by the operators astride the body. Their most notable achievement was the disabling of the battleships *Queen Elizabeth* and *Valiant* in Alexandria at the end of 1941, but after the surrender of Italy Italian crews attacked Italian warships in German hands, under British operational control. The cruiser *Bolzano* was sunk in this way in June 1944. Other midget submarines operated against the Soviets in the Black Sea, but with no great success.

The British, apart from copying the human torpedo idea from the Italians and calling it the 'Chariot,' built a series of midgets to penetrate the anchorage of the battleship *Tirpitz*. Known as X-craft, six were used in September 1943 to penetrate Altenfiord and succeeded in placing two-ton charges under the target. They were used later to attack targets such as floating docks in Norway. An enlarged type, the XE-craft, was built for the Pacific. Two of these succeeded in damaging the Japanese cruiser *Takao* in Singapore in July 1945.

The Germans designed a whole series of midgets known as *Kleine Kampfmittel* (small battle units) for harbor and coastal defense to ward off amphibious assault. First tried at Anzio, they were widely used at Normandy but without conspicuous success. The most successful of these types was the *Seehund*, which was a proper miniature submarine, whereas many of the others were nothing but 'human torpedoes.'

Although many claims were made of Allied shipping sunk, the results were meager in comparison to the effort expended.

PT-BOATS, MTBs AND E-BOATS

Patrol Torpedo Boats, otherwise known as PT-Boats, and their equivalents in other navies, Motor Torpedo Boats (MTBs), were small high-speed craft relying on speed to avoid damage while delivering torpedo attacks against hostile shipping.

Although other navies had developed them during World War I, the United States had been a relative latecomer to the field, and it was not until 1937 that the US Navy's General Board authorized a modest program of development and evaluation. Two years later contracts were awarded for six experimental boats, *PT.1–6*, followed by two more, *PT.7–8*. A British prototype, the wooden *PT.9* was bought for comparison, and she and *PT.3* and *PT.4* formed the first PT-Boat Squadron in mid-1940.

The success of the British Power Boat design led to an immediate order for an American-built version, the 70-foot Elco design, 10 of which had been ordered at the end of 1939. From these was developed the highly successful 77-foot Elco design, while the similar 78-foot Higgins design proved nearly as fast and slightly more sea-worthy. From these were to stem some 800 boats, as scores of small shipyards took over wartime production.

After Pearl Harbor training intensified, and as the new PT-Boats came from the yards they practiced running in formation and offensive tactics, but their chance of action did not come until the decision was made to land on Guadalcanal. The Solomon Islands were ideal for mosquito-craft operations, with the narrow channels offering ideal positions for ambushes. Only two squadrons were ready by July 1942, and they found the reality very different from the theory. Without radar they were virtually blind, and therefore very vulnerable to the Japanese destroyers, whose crews had excellent training in night fighting. Despite great bravery they were only able to sink one cruiser, and losses were heavy, but as the Japanese grip on the Solomons loosened they were able to inflict greater casualties.

Apart from the Mediterranean, where PT-Boats were under British operational control, they were used off the coast of New Guinea and in the Philippines. In both theaters they proved most useful in dealing with the coast-wise shipping used by the Japanese to supply their garrisons. However, they did take their toll of destroyers, and performed a fine service for the amphibious assault forces in the Philippines by rooting out the Japanese *Shinyo* suicide boats which had been dispersed in various hiding places around the islands.

The Japanese had shown interest in motor torpedo boats much earlier, having bought four British CMBs in 1922, but thereafter they ignored the type until 1938. An Italian MAS-Boat was bought and a prototype was ordered from the Tsurumi shipyard in 1940, but plans for mass production were not drawn up until 1941. By the time that the shipyards were beginning to turn them out the supply of gasoline engines was failing, and this meant that a weird variety of power plants had to be used.

The first motor gunboats (MGBs) were developed by the Japanese, as a parallel program to the MTBs, but they were never as heavily armed as their British counterparts, and they suffered from the same production problems as the MTBs. Some 6000 of the 1.5-ton *Shinyo* suicide motor boats were built by August 1945, but apart from the sinking of two US destroyers in the Philippines they had no significant successes.

Germany had dabbled unsuccessfully in motor torpedo boats in World War I, but turned to them during the time of the Versailles Treaty to strengthen the meager forces permitted under the Treaty. A good round-bilge hull form was developed, but more important was a development contract given to MAN and Daimler-Benz to produce a lightweight diesel engine. This finally resulted in a 20-cylinder V-form unit from Daimler-Benz, which became standard from *Schnellboot* (fast boat) *S.18* onward.

Having evaluated designs so thoroughly, it was easy to put the type into production in 1938–39, and the initial order ran to 105 boats, followed by orders for 446 more. Although lightly armed with two single 21-inch torpedo tubes and two 20mm guns, the S-Boats were rugged and seaworthy. From *S.62* onward a 37mm gun replaced the after 20mm and later boats had twin 20mm. Throughout the war they remained equal to their contemporaries, both in performance and the ability to take punishment.

S-Boats were used to good effect in the English Channel and the southern North Sea, where they fought many pitched battles against the British. The busy coastal shipping route on the east coast of England was a favorite target. For some reason they were known to the British as 'E-Boats'. A squadron was sent down to the Mediterranean through the French rivers and canals, and when the Soviet Union was invaded more were sent to the Black Sea. Although heavily outnumbered in the Black Sea they gave a good account of themselves, and they were similarly involved with Soviet light forces in the Baltic.

One of their biggest successes was the torpedoing of the destroyers *Wakeful, Jaguar, Cyclone* and *Sirocco* during the Dunkirk Evacuation, of which the British *Wakeful* and the French *Jaguar* and *Sirocco* were sunk. In attacks on east coast convoys they sank the destroyers *Exmoor, Eskdale, Penylan* and *Vortigern*. In the Mediterranean they sank the destroyers *Hasty, Lightning* and USS *Rowan*, and damaged the cruiser HMS *Newcastle*. However, when command of the air passed into Allied hands they began to suffer increasingly heavy losses. By May 1945 only about 100 S-Boats survived out of the large total built.

The Italians had started it all in 1915 by building *Motoscafi Armato Silurante* (torpedo-armed motor boats) or MAS-Boats. These had carried out many daring raids on the Austro-Hungarian navy's ships and bases, and to Luigi Rizzo belongs the credit of sinking an Austro-Hungarian dreadnought battleship *at sea* – one of the few times small torpedo craft have achieved such a feat. Development continued between the two world wars, with the firms Baglietto and SVAN predominating. Unfortunately, the Italians were preoccupied with maximum speed, and so they kept displacement down, which in turn limited the payload and seakeeping. The result was that the later MAS-Boats which served in World War II were lightly built and lightly armed.

The achievements of the MAS-Boats and the bigger *Motosiluranti* built during the war were meager. Their biggest successes were the sinking of the British cruiser *Manchester* during the 'Pedestal' convoy action in August 1942, and damaging the Soviet cruiser *Molotov* off the Crimea in the same month. Their least successful operation was an attempt to penetrate Grand Harbor in Malta in July 1941; they were spotted by aircraft and then driven off by well-directed fire from the coast-defense artillery. Many fell into German hands in September 1943 and were subsequently sunk in the Aegean. As with the Japanese, the increasing disruption of industry made it very hard to find sufficient engines for wartime production, and it proved difficult to expand the light forces or to introduce new types better suited to wartime conditions.

Above: British MTB's at high speed.

The British, having developed the Coastal Motor Boat (CMB) during World War I then lost interest until the late 1930s, when growing pressure from commercial designers forced the Admiralty to buy a series of prototypes for evaluation. This resulted in the Vosper 70-foot type being selected, but an immediate problem was the lack of suitable engines. As no development work had been done in the 1920s and 1930s the only suitable lightweight unit was the Italian Isotta-Fraschini gasoline engine, but this supply was cut off in mid-1940 when Italy became an enemy, and the situation was only remedied when the United States made Packard engines available under Lend-Lease.

Both Vosper and British Power Boats relied on a short, hard-chine hull, unlike the long-hulled round-bilge German S-Boat, and this limited the amount of payload. To offset this and to meet tactical needs the Motor Gunboat (MGB) was developed, with heavier automatic weapons in place of torpedo tubes. Eventually, longer round-bilge boats were built, but the final outcome of this development process was a 'semihard chine' hull known as the Fairmile 'D' Type which was slower than the short-hulled MTBs but much more robust and powerful.

An antisubmarine design had been built by British Power Boat, but these Motor Anti-Submarine Boats (MA/SBs) found few targets in coastal waters, and so in 1940 they were converted to Motor Gunboats (MGBs). As tactics for convoy battles evolved it was found necessary for MGBs to draw the fire of the enemy S-Boats so as to allow the MTBs to dash in for a torpedo attack. The next step was to merge the types, and from 1943 convertible hulls were built to perform both functions. The British Coastal Forces organization expanded enormously during the war, and under Lend-Lease many Elco and Higgins PT-Boats were transferred from the United States.

The biggest problem for light attack craft in all navies was the noise of their engines at full speed. The German S-Boats were well silenced by having their exhausts underwater, but the big Packards of the American and British boats had to be specially muffled (they were also a worse fire hazard than diesels). To avoid the excessive noise and to provide a more powerful armament the British designed the Steam Gunboat (SGB), virtually a 138-foot miniature destroyer capable of 35 knots. Seven of these handsome craft were built, of which the most famous was the *Grey Goose* (SGB.9), but their light steel hulls and steam turbines proved vulnerable to gunfire at close range. As more and more armament was added their speed fell, the last straw being the provision of .75-inch armor plating over their machinery.

The Soviet navy also made a major effort in fast attack craft. After a strong impression had been made on them by the British CMB attack on Kronstadt in 1919, the aircraft designer A N Tupolev was asked to design MTBs, and by 1933 there were 59 boats in service, mostly the *Shya-4* type. These led to the more successful *G-5* and *D-3* types. When Germany invaded the Soviet Union in June 1941 the impressive total of 269 MTBs was claimed to be in commission.

With the major warships trapped in harbor by minefields or circumscribed in their movements by German air superiority for much of the time, the naval war in the Baltic and Black Sea was inevitably one of small units. Lack of suitable gasoline engines was a great problem, and some of the MTBs were completed with engines of such low power that they were downgraded to patrol boats. They also suffered from poor equipment and had poor seakeeping, and to remedy these deficiencies some 200 American PT-Boats were transferred under Lend-Lease. Despite these, large numbers of craft Soviet MTBs were handled bravely rather than skillfully, and heavy losses were incurred without corresponding damage to the enemy. Their most outstanding successes were the sinking of a Finnish minelayer in August 1943 and a German torpedo boat in June 1944, and in all they sank not more than 30 Axis warships and merchant ships.

In general it can be said that in World War II small attack craft proved a disappointment in action, and although they performed heroic feats the results never lived up to the claims made on their behalf. The basic problem was that the boats required massive maintenance and support to keep even a small number ready to go to sea. Furthermore, the dash and noise of PT-Boats and MTBs tended to disguise their limitations. War experience was to show that they could best be used in ambush, running slowly on silenced engines and only using full power to get away after the attack. Even so, their lack of size restricted them to relatively calm weather or sheltered waters, and any attempt to use them in the open sea was doomed to failure. They lacked the navigation and command facilities to be able to keep track of a fast-moving action, and so the fighting rapidly degenerated into a melee in which boats could easily fire on their squadron mates or miss the target completely. This accounts for the inflated claims made by small attack craft of all navies, for even a small trawler could be mistaken for a destroyer from the bridge of a motor torpedo boat.

RAIDERS AND ARMED MERCHANT CRUISERS

The tradition of arming fast passenger liners with medium-caliber guns dates back to the nineteenth century. The Declaration of Paris in 1856 had outlawed privateering, but during the Civil War fast steamers were fitted out as blockade runners and the idea of using such vessels to attack mercantile shipping was the next development. It was believed that fast ocean liners could function as commerce raiders, and as this role supplemented the work of cruisers they became known as Armed Merchant Cruisers or AMCs. With their big margin of speed it was hoped that they would be able to catch and sink slow freighters, while eluding enemy cruisers with ease.

Apart from a few ships converted during the war against Spain and still on the strength in 1917–18 the US Navy had not made use of AMCs on any scale, and felt no need to do so in 1941. The Japanese, on the other hand, had made excellent use of AMCs in their war against Russia in 1904–05, and converted 13 ocean liners in 1941–42 to release regular cruisers for work with the Fleet. The nature of the war in the Pacific left them with little to do and in 1942–43 the seven survivors were converted back into transports, more-useful employment for Japan's dwindling reserves of shipping.

The British, following the precedent established in the previous conflict, requisitioned no fewer than 56 ocean liners in 1939–40 and, as before, their primary role was the enforcement of the blockade. The Northern Patrol examined neutral ships for contraband and kept watch for any German warships trying to slip out into the Atlantic. It was arduous work, involving lengthy patrols in all weathers, with the constant risk of submarine attack. If any AMC were to be attacked by a German warship the outcome was predictable, for she would be outgunned and outmaneuvered, with no resistance to even the smallest shell hits.

On 23 November 1939 the *Rawalpindi* fell victim to the battlecruiser *Scharnhorst* which sighted the AMC at dusk, between the Faeroes and Iceland. The *Scharnhorst*'s 11-inch guns opened fire at 8000 yards, and within 15 minutes the liner was overwhelmed, having scored only one hit on her adversary. A year later, on 5 November, a convoy of 37 ships escorted by HMS *Jervis Bay* was attacked by the pocket battleship *Admiral Scheer* in the North Atlantic. Once again the result was a foregone conclusion, but the AMC put up sufficient resistance to win time for the convoy to scatter. By the time the *Admiral Scheer* had sent the *Jervis Bay* to the bottom all but five of the merchant ships were out of range and a major catastrophe had been averted.

Typically, armed merchant cruisers were 15–20,000-ton twin-screw passenger liners capable of a minimum of 15–17 knots. Armament was limited to eight single 6-inch guns taken from World War I cruisers, with rudimentary fire control and backed up by a pair of antiaircraft guns. Although as much inflammable material was stripped as possible, their former passenger accommodation was a major fire risk, while their high silhouettes made them conspicuous targets. As the war progressed it was possible to give them refinements such as radar but nothing could make them robust enough to take much punishment.

As in World War I, AMCs fought several hard actions against their opposite numbers, the German mercantile raiders. In July 1940 the *Alcantara* inflicted slight damage on the *Thor* but sustained serious damage herself in a brief action. In December that year the *Thor* met the *Carnarvon Castle*, inflicting such severe damage that the AMC was forced to break off the action, and in April 1941 she sank the *Voltaire*.

U-Boats took a heavy toll of AMCs, and 10 were torpedoed in the North Atlantic between June 1940–May 1941. These heavy losses led the British to withdraw them from the North Atlantic, and even the numbers in the South Atlantic and West Indies declined until by the beginning of 1943 only 17 were left. The rising demand for troop transports and infantry carriers for amphibious operations accelerated the decline, and by mid-1944 the last AMC was out of service.

The original concept of the armed liner had outlived its usefulness but there was a new role for the heavily armed merchant ship, that of auxiliary antiaircraft escort. Although not classified as AMCs, these freighters were armed with the equivalent of a 10,000-ton cruiser's AA battery, complete with radar and full fire control. Their task was to sail with convoys, providing them with AA defense and allowing the valuable cruisers to operate well clear of the convoy. Eight of these conversions were commissioned in 1940–42, and they must be regarded as the legitimate successors to the armed merchant cruiser in that they released the real cruisers for other work.

The only other navy to commission any number of AMCs was the French, with 22 large liners converted in 1939–40. Most fell victim in one way or another to the catastrophe which overwhelmed France in June 1940, and they were decommissioned in various ports by the end of 1940.

The German navy revived the highly successful concept of the *Hilfskreuzer* (disguised mercantile raider). These were sturdy cargo liners, equipped with elderly medium-caliber guns in concealed positions, intended to operate independently on the distant shipping routes. The disguise was partly to help them slip through the British blockade but also to allow them to approach unescorted merchant ships, and this was facilitated by each ship having several outfits. The presence of a raider on the trade routes caused untold confusion, and on average each of the nine raiders which got to sea required 14 cruisers to track them down.

Although the *Hilfskreuzer* was only a merchantman and therefore as lightly built as a passenger liner, it had several advantages over the Armed Merchant Cruiser. She presented a much lower silhouette, being a fast freighter, and she had no large passenger accommodation to act as a fire trap. With plenty of hold space available it was possible to site the six or eight 5.9-inch guns to best advantage, making it harder for the ship to be knocked out by battle damage. The Kriegsmarine lavished considerable care on their design and equipment, which meant that their gunnery was always good.

The only counter to these raiders was to ensure that their victims were able to make a distress call before being sunk, and the British devised a brief 'Q-Q-Q-Q' signal to increase the chance of a radio call being made in time. To back this up it was eventually necessary to keep a much closer check of worldwide shipping movements, so that a cruiser could check the whereabouts of the ship whose 'alias' was being used. These disguises often fooled Allied warships. The New Zealand cruiser *Leander* was very nearly sunk by the Italian raider *Ramb I* in February 1941, but fortunately the raider's opening salvo went wide. A major disaster befell the Australian cruiser *Sydney* in the Southwest Pacific in November 1941, when she intercepted the German raider *Kormoran*. The raider's bluff was so good that the cruiser rashly approached too close, only to be greeted by a hail of accurate gunfire and a hit from a torpedo. The Australian cruiser gamely hit back and inflicted sufficient damage on the *Kormoran* to make certain that she sank, but was herself on fire and mortally hit. Nothing was ever heard of HMAS *Sydney* again, but months later a handful of *Kormoran* survivors told how the cruiser had drifted away over the horizon in a mass of flames.

The *Hilfskreuzer* were all commissioned ships of the *Kriegsmarine* manned by naval crews, but to the Allies they were known by a series of symbols. Thus *Orion* was Raider 'A,' *Komet* Raider 'B,' *Atlantis* Raider 'C,' *Widder* Raider 'D,' *Thor* Raider 'E,' *Pinguin* Raider 'F,' *Kormoran* Raider 'G,' *Michel* Raider 'H,' *Stier* Raider 'J' and *Coronel* Raider 'K.' The *Coronel* never broke out of the Channel and neither did an eleventh ship, the *Hansa*.

Raiders did not always get the upper hand. In September 1942 the *Stier* caught the American Liberty ship *Stephen Hopkins*, but with only a single 4-inch gun the freighter fought back before being sunk. Despite having six 5.9-inch guns and two torpedo tubes, the *Stier* was severely damaged by 15 hits and eventually caught fire and sank. In November 1942 the Japanese AMCs *Hokoku Maru* and *Aikoku Maru*, armed with eight 5.5-inch guns apiece, tried to sink the Dutch tanker *Ondina* in the Indian Ocean. The tanker was escorted by the 733-ton Indian Navy minesweeper *Bengal*, each armed like the *Stephen Hopkins* with nothing more than a single small gun, and because both captains kept their heads a remarkable fight ensued. While the *Ondina* maneuvered independently *Bengal* steamed for the two AMCs and closed to 3500 yards, setting the *Hokoku Maru* on fire. The tanker was eventually sunk, but not until the *Bengal* had inflicted severe damage on the *Aikoku Maru* as well. It was one of the most remarkable single actions of the entire war.

In the final analysis the armed merchant cruiser did not prove as cost effective as the disguised raider, but each was intended to fulfill a quite different role. In 1940–41 the British had all too few cruisers to spare for trade protection, and only when sufficient escort carriers (CVEs) were available to patrol the distant shipping routes did the AMC finally lose its utility. By making up numbers at a crucial stage the AMCs strengthened the effect of the blockade and diminished the likelihood of a large-scale breakout into the Atlantic by German heavy units. A conversion program to CVEs might well have given better value but in 1939–41 there were neither the aircraft nor the pilots available.

For the disguised raider matters were simpler, for she merely had to avoid trouble. Her effectiveness was measured not so much by the tonnage of shipping sunk as the amount of disruption caused. Even so the totals are impressive. The *Orion* sank six ships totalling 39,000 tons and then shared seven ships totalling 43,000 tons with the *Komet*. On a second cruise the *Komet* sank three ships of 21,300 tons. The most successful were the *Atlantis* with 22 ships totalling nearly 146,000 tons and the *Thor* with the same number of ships totalling 152,000 tons in two cruises. Next came the *Pinguin* with 28 ships totalling 136,600 tons. The *Stier* sank four totalling 30,700 tons, the *Kormoran* 11 totalling 68,200 (excluding HMAS *Sydney*) and the *Michel* 18 ships totalling 127,000 tons in two cruises. Another means of causing disruption was laying random minefields and eight ships (42,000 tons) were sunk by them.

Three of the raiders were sunk by cruisers, the *Atlantis* on 23 November 1941 by HMS *Devonshire*, the *Pinguin* on 8 May the same year by HMS *Cornwall* and the *Kormoran* on 19 November 1941 by *Sydney*. The *Stier*, as already mentioned, sank on 27 September 1942 after her duel with the Liberty ship *Stephen Hopkins*, showing how vulnerable the raiders could be to gunfire. Two were torpedoed, the *Komet* on 14 October 1942 in the English Channel by the British motor torpedo boat *MTB.236* and the *Michel* on 17 October 1943 off Yokohama by the US submarine *Tarpon*. The *Thor* suffered irreparable damage while lying in Yokohama in November 1942, when another ship blew up alongside. When it became virtually impossible to get through the Allied patrols the surviving raiders were converted to other uses, bringing to an end one of the German navy's most successful campaigns.

WEAPONS

When World War II began, the range of naval weapons was virtually unchanged since 1918. The prime weapon of surface ships was still the heavy gun, with a range of 20–30 miles, and although twin mountings had been superseded by triple and quadruple mountings in modern ships, the basic design of guns and mountings had changed little since 1914. The multiple mountings were needed to save weight but war experience was to show that the twin turret was still the best. The range of older guns was increased by modifying the turrets to give greater elevation and by the use of modified projectiles and more-powerful charges. A British battleship, HMS *Warspite* achieved a hit on the Italian *Giulio Cesare* at the record distance of 26,400 yards with such a modified weapon.

Although the Washington Treaty limited gun caliber to 16 inches, the Japanese secretly armed their two largest battleships with 18-inch guns, but as these ships never engaged the US battle-fleet their advantage in range and hitting power was never put to the test. On the other hand the 8-inch limit for heavy cruisers was adhered to, and apart from special ships like AA cruisers the cruisers on both sides were armed with 6-inch or 8-inch guns.

Some navies favored above-water torpedo tubes for cruisers but others, notably the US Navy, had discarded them in the early 1930s. The British and Japanese, on the other hand, reckoned that poor visibility such as that found in the Solomons and the North Atlantic, favored the use of torpedoes, and experience proved them right. The advent of radar gradually overcame the torpedo's special advantages. Even destroyers, whose raison d'être was to torpedo enemy surface ships, began to sacrifice torpedo tubes in favor of light antiaircraft guns by 1944.

The torpedo never lost its importance in submarines, but the technology of design advanced out of all recognition during the war years. Although the 'steam' or compressed-air driven torpedo remained in use with all navies the Japanese led the way to higher performance with their oxygen-driven Long Lance. The Germans were equally keen on faster running and long-range torpedoes but chose hydrogen peroxide instead for a series of experimental weapons which never entered service. As early as 1923 work started on an electrically driven torpedo, the G7e, to replace the standard compressed-air G7a, and this was used in World War II. The main advantage was simpler production, for the G7a was very difficult to mass produce; in all the German navy fired over 10,000 torpedoes in action, about 2300 G7as and 7000 G7es, the remainder being special types. The most important of these special types was the *Zaunkönig* acoustic homing torpedo, intro-

ANTISUBMARINE WARFARE

duced in 1943 primarily as an antiescort weapon, but it was only moderately successful.

The other important innovation was the magnetic or influence exploder, which allowed a torpedo to explode as it passed underneath the target's keel. The Germans set great store by their exploder but it was faulty and as the British and the Americans were developing their own devices they were able to develop counter-measures quickly. Both the Americans and the Germans had great trouble with faulty tor-pedoes, for prewar inspection procedures had failed to highlight their technical weaknesses.

Antiaircraft weapons underwent rapid de-velopment as soon as the air threat became apparent. With few exceptions prewar apprecia-tions of the problem had been less than adequate and there were very few good dual-purpose gun mounting or fire-control systems to go with them. The best light AA gun proved to be the Swedish 40mm Bofors gun and this was adopted first by the British and then by the Americans, in single, twin, quadruple and even six-barrelled mountings. It was backed up by the 20mm Oerlikon gun from Switzerland, which was mass produced to provide close-range firepower in all classes of ships. The best medium-caliber AA gun was undoubtedly the American 5-inch/38 caliber, which had the good fortune to be provided with an outstanding fire-control system, the Mark 37.

By the end of the war the 20mm and 40mm guns were failing to cope with the latest aircraft, and stood in the same relation to their targets as the heavy machine guns of 1939. To cope with the Kamikaze threat the US Navy called for a new design a 3-inch/50 caliber automatic twin mounting but this did not appear until after the war. Radar and better fire control made all AA weapons far more effective than they had been, and by the latter part of the war it was accepted that numbers of fire-control sets was more im-portant than numbers of guns in providing defense against air attack.

By far the biggest advances took place in the evolution of antisubmarine weaponry. In September 1939 the standard weapons were relatively ineffective aircraft bombs and ship-dropped depth charges which were only slightly more sophisticated than the ones used 20 years before. The first improvement made by the British was to adapt the naval depth charge for air dropping, giving aircraft a reasonable chance of sinking a U-Boat, but several minor technical problems had to be overcome before the RAF was happy with it. The standard naval depth charge was also modified to make it sink

faster, and a one-ton version was used in small numbers in the Atlantic.

The biggest problem was to find weapons which could be fired ahead of an escort while she still held the U-Boat in the narrow beam of her sonar. This resulted in the Hedgehog, a multiple-spigot mortar firing 32-pound contact-fuzed bombs. In 1944 the British produced the Squid, a mortar firing three full-sized depth charges on a wide bearing. Escorts were also modified to allow them to drop as many as 14 depth charges in a pattern at varying depths to increase the likelihood of a kill.

The development of acoustic homing devices provided the deadly Mark 24 Mine, otherwise known as Fido. This was a slow-running air-launched torpedo which homed on the propeller noise of a diving U-Boat. It was first used in 1943, at about the time the Germans first used their own *Zaunkönig* homer in U-Boats. Homing torpedoes were not used by surface escorts, although their use in that role was under consideration in 1945.

Many of the improvements were minor. Better reloading gear enabled more depth-charge patterns to be dropped and new lightweight and compact explosives extended the lethal radius of bombs and depth charges. Even the addition of a heavy weight to the standard depth charge made it sink faster and reduced the margin of error.

ANTISUBMARINE WARFARE

Antisubmarine warfare (ASW) proved to be one of the most important aspects of the war at sea, not only in terms of resources which had to be devoted to it but in terms of its influence on strategy. Yet paradoxically the four major navies, American, British, German and Japanese had to a great extent underestimated the vital role it was to play. This was all more puzzling in the case of the Americans and British for in 1917 the British, with the world's largest navy and an enormous mercantile fleet, had been brought to their knees by the unrestricted U-Boat campaign against shipping. Only the combined exertions of the Royal Navy and the US Navy had averted catastrophe by the belated introduction of convoys and a massive building program of merchant ships and escorts.

By the end of World War I the US Navy therefore had a first-class antisubmarine capa-bility, with the latest tactics and weaponry as well as sufficient escorts. It was also in possession of the latest technology, the new sonic method of detecting underwater targets, and its prototype sonar was ready in the early 1920s.

Yet American interest in ASW stagnated for a variety of reasons. Not only was there the grinding parsimony of the depression but also the influence of isolationism, which bred the idea that the United States would never go to war again to protect British shipping. Being self-sufficient in raw materials the US had laid up most of its own war-built mercantile marine and there seemed little need to devote funds to the protection of commerce. In 1927–28 exercises were staged with the aircraft carrier *Langley* to test ways of protecting slow convoys but nothing further was done.

The British were more aware of their vulnerability to submarine attack, still possessing the world's largest mercantile fleet, but they also allowed tactical thinking to atrophy. They consoled themselves with the thought that unrestricted submarine attacks on shipping were now banned by international treaty and so exercises were directed to the protection of warships against attack. The RN's Asdic sensor was technically superior to the USN's sonar but it bred a degree of overconfidence in the ability to contain the U-Boat threat.

Hitler's repudiation of the Versailles Treaty's restrictions on U-Boat construction was a clear warning that a U-Boat war against British commerce was a definite possibility. Between 1936 and 1938 plans were drawn up to strengthen the British ASW effort, a new class of utility escort, the 'Flower' Class corvette was designed, and stockpiling of Asdic sets began. The corvette went into mass production within a month of the outbreak of war while a number of old destroyers were refitted for escort work. Unlike the previous conflict there was no disagreement about the value of convoying as a countermeasure and plans existed for the immediate introduction of convoys. Both tactics and the building program were closely coordinated with the Canadians, who undertook to build their own corvettes and shared the running of the convoy organization. Another far-reaching decision made at the end of 1937 was a directive to the Royal Air Force making ASW equal in importance to reconnaissance in the duties assigned to Coastal Command. At the time it was only a gesture, for Coastal Command lacked an effective antisubmarine weapon and had very few effective aircraft, but it paved the way for expansion.

The Germans were aware of the existence of Asdic, but British security had prevented any details of its mode of operation or its capabilities from leaking out, and so they had no oppor-

tunity to develop tactics to counter it. Although Hitler declared himself bound by International Law and the treaties, his U-Boat Arm was fully aware that it could only function effectively if it was allowed to wage 'unrestricted' warfare, or in other words, if it could sink merchant ships on sight. Only the fear of American and other neutral opinion kept the Prize Ordinance in force. The Japanese had no such scruples about international opinion but their adherence to the dogma of the offensive blinded them to the need to develop effective ASW measures, both for their warships and their vital mercantile fleet. Their submarines were dedicated to attacking enemy warships and virtually no attention was paid to the development of ASW tactics or to the design and building of escorts.

Early ASW operations in British waters seemed to justify prewar confidence; although the carrier HMS *Courageous* was torpedoed by a U-Boat, when one of her sisters tried to do the same to the *Ark Royal* the escorting destroyers sank her very quickly. The coastal patrols by aircraft and the efficiency of the escorts forced the U-Boats to move further afield but even so convoying kept the losses within bearable limits, so that by May 1940 852,813 tons of shipping had been sunk in return for 24 out of the original 58 U-Boats destroyed.

All this changed dramatically with the fall of France in June 1940. With bases on the Atlantic coast of France the U-Boats could now strike directly at the Western Approaches and use shore-based aircraft for reconnaissance. The results were immediately apparent, and by May 1941 a further 2,000,000 tons of shipping had been sunk for the loss of only 13 U-Boats. Driven out of coastal waters, the U-Boats could now range deep into the Atlantic, beyond the 15 degree West limit at which escorts left the convoys to sail on undefended except by armed merchant cruisers. This was the significance of the dreaded 'Black Gap' in mid-Atlantic, where ships were beyond the reach of shore-based aircraft and small warships from either side, but within the operational radius of the Type VII U-Boat.

The long-term solution was to build high-endurance escorts and aircraft but for the moment all that could be done was to base aircraft and escorts in Iceland, since Eire would not permit the British to use their former bases at Cobh and Berehaven. In September 1940 the US Government transferred 50 old destroyers in exchange for base rights, and these were all used as escorts. Other old destroyers were converted into long-range escorts by the simple expedient of replacing the forward boiler with an extra fuel tank, the loss of speed being an acceptable trade off. It was also possible to strengthen the anti-submarine armament by removing some guns and torpedo tubes and increasing the number of depth charges.

In September 1940 the U-Boats started to use a new tactic, that of the wolf pack. Any U-Boat which sighted a convoy merely followed astern at a discreet distance, and reported its course, speed and numbers back to base. From there other U-Boats were 'homed' onto the convoy, and only when all the available U-Boats were in position was a simultaneous night attack launched. As often as not the defenders were swamped and many daring U-Boat commanders got inside the convoy while remaining on the surface, trusting that the small silhouette of the U-Boat's conning tower would not be spotted. Since the Asdic sensor could not detect a submarine on the surface, surface attack could only be dealt with by a shipboard radar, and this was fitted for the first time early in 1941. The loss of Asdic contact during the last moments of a depth-charge attack was countered by the Hedgehog, a mortar which fired 24 small contact-fuzed bombs ahead of the ship. An even more important innovation was the provision of a high-frequency direction-finding device (H/F-D/F or 'Huff-Duff') which allowed escorts to track the range and bearing of a U-Boat from her radio transmissions. Although not as accurate as radar it enabled an escort to pinpoint the area in which a surfaced U-Boat was operating. One of its most important uses was in frustrating the wolf pack, for if the U-Boat sending her sighting reports could be forced to dive it was often possible to route the convoy away and shake off the rest of the pack. All the while, Allied cryptographers wrestled with the German ciphers to harvest a growing volume of intercepts, which yielded priceless information about Admiral Doenitz's orders to his U-Boats.

Building of 'Flower' Class corvettes was increased and eventually nearly 300 were completed. A new long-range escort, known as the 'River' Class frigate was put in hand but did not appear until mid-1942. By June 1941 Coastal Command had 10 specially modified Liberator bombers, known as the Very Long Range type (VLR), and the first Catalina flying boat became available. The value of aircraft in protecting convoys was now apparent, for they could at the very minimum ensure that U-Boats dived instead of trailing astern of the convoy, reporting back to HQ. As early as January 1941

work had begun on converting a captured German freighter into the first Merchant Aircraft Carrier by the simple expedient of cutting off her superstructure and laying a wooden flight deck from bow to stern. As HMS *Audacity* she sailed on her first convoy in September 1941, and although intended only to provide fighter defense against air attack she proved so successful that more were immediately ordered.

The US Navy was kept fully in the picture by the British, and its own prototype escort carrier or CVE, the USS *Long Island*, was completed in June 1941. The second ship went straight to the RN as HMS *Archer* in November 1941, followed by five more. After Pearl Harbor the urgent need for ships for the Pacific slowed down the CVE program and so the British reverted to the *Audacity*-type limited conversion in the summer of 1942. These Merchant Aircraft Carriers or MAC-Ships were oil tankers and grain carriers with a plywood flight deck; the aircraft were parked on deck and a normal cargo could still be carried in the holds. Only 12 ships were completed by May 1943, by which time the CVE program was back in top gear, but both types performed a vital role in giving convoys air cover all the way across the Atlantic.

The entry of the United States into the war on 7 December 1941 signalled a dramatic increase in escort building. A month before Pearl Harbor orders had finally been placed for a new destroyer escort (DE) for the RN, and these were soon followed by enlarged types. Even so it was April 1943 before the first DE commissioned. In the meantime the U-Boats were sinking large numbers of ships off the East Coast for the US Navy's ASW preparations appeared to be almost nonexistent. Despite close liaison with the British on tactics Admiral King was reluctant to bring in convoying, but after six months of mounting losses he was forced to do so. As a stopgap the British and Canadians transferred some trawlers and corvettes but only after a local convoy system was introduced did the losses fall to an acceptable level.

During the summer of 1942 U-Boats were still being built faster than they could be sunk, but improved airborne radar and better weapons enabled Allied ASW forces to hold the balance. The Germans introduced a new radar receiver, the Metox, to allow U-Boats to detect radar transmissions, but the Allies brought in a new centimetric radar which could not be detected by the Metox. From now on the war against the U-Boats increasingly became a battle of technology, with scientists on both sides trying to match each new development. An important tactical innovation was the formation of the first support groups late in 1942. There were now enough CVEs and escorts to provide independent hunting groups which could attack U-Boats before they reached the convoys or they could reinforce hard-pressed convoys. They also contributed to the number of U-Boats sunk in another way, for whereas a convoy escort frequently had to leave a contact and rejoin her convoy the support group was free to continue the hunt until a kill was made.

Fortunately for the Allies, all the important improvements in tactics and weaponry were in service by the time the Battle of the Atlantic reached crisis point in March 1943. At the worst moment it looked as if the ASW measures had failed, and the disbandment of the convoy system seemed to be the next step, but just in time the extra ASW forces diverted to cover the North African landings returned to the Atlantic. More important, a long wrangle between the advocates of strategic bombing and the Anti-U-Boat Warfare Committee was resolved and six more squadrons of bombers were allocated to antisubmarine work. The initiative swung back in favor of the Allies as suddenly as it had gone the other way. In the first 20 days of March 1943 97 merchant ships were sunk for the loss of only 16 U-Boats, and yet in May only 50 ships were sunk for a total of 41 U-Boats. On 22 May Doenitz tacitly admitted defeat by ordering the U-Boats to withdraw from the North Atlantic for reequipment.

Although the U-Boats had only been checked and not totally defeated, the Allies could now move to offensive ASW on a large scale for the first time. Coastal Command could switch some aircraft from close support of convoys to reinforcement of its patrols in the Bay of Biscay. Here they could attack U-Boats in transit to their patrol areas, and as Doenitz for several months mistakenly advised his U-Boats to stay on the surface and fight it out with the bombers, their losses became unbearably high.

The U-Boats returned to the North Atlantic in September 1943, hoping that their new *Zaunkönig* acoustic homing torpedo would redress the balance. Life proved as hard as ever, for the Allies now had base rights in the Azores and had provided countermeasures to the new torpedoes. A change of the convoy cipher also robbed the Germans of hitherto reliable information about the whereabouts of convoys. American escort-carrier groups stationed in the mid-Atlantic played havoc, especially as Ultra was now providing a constant stream of accurate intercepts giving positions of U-Boats. Bombing of the U-Boats' bases had proved totally ineffective but early in 1944 Bomber Command was asked to switch to disruption of the building program of the new fast Type XXI and Type XXIII U-Boats. Raids were carried out on the factories making electric motors and periscopes, while other raids on the canal system disrupted deliveries of the prefabricated sections. Offensive minelaying was another tactic used in ASW, with deep fields laid under convoy concentration points.

In the closing months of the war the use of the *schnorchel* air mast cut down the number of kills made by aircraft, while escorts found it very difficult to locate U-Boats in coastal waters. The increasing disruption of the German economy, as well as the fact that the Allied armies were closing in on the shipyards themselves, meant that the war against the U-Boat was nearly won. By May 1945 a total of 807 out of the 1150 U-Boats launched had been destroyed and 85 percent of their crews were dead or taken prisoners. At the end of 1944 no fewer than 880 ocean-going warships were serving as escorts and a further 2200 craft were serving as coastal escorts. Shipping losses totalled 2882 ships of 14,400,000 gross register tons.

In the Pacific Japanese submarine tactics never reached the proficiency shown by the U-Boats, but this did not mean that the US Navy could neglect ASW. On several occasions Japanese submarines were able to sink or damage major warships, while the lengthy lines of communication across the Pacific were highly vulnerable. The battleship *North Carolina* and the carrier *Saratoga* were both damaged in 1942, the latter twice, while the carriers *Yorktown, Wasp* and *Liscombe Bay* and the cruisers *Juneau* and *Indianapolis* were sunk. Although the Japanese submarines wasted their efforts in attacking heavily defended formations of warships this did not mean that the vast number of troopships, oilers and transports of all kinds sailed without escorts.

There was no major difference in ASW tactics and equipment in the Pacific and all the experience gained in the Atlantic was available to the USN escorts. In May 1944 they gave a convincing demonstration of their proficiency when a Hunter-Killer Group of three DEs stumbled across a patrol line of 25 Japanese submarines north of New Guinea and New Ireland. On 19 May the newly arrived USS *England* detected and sank *I.16*. Moving westward the group found more of the Japanese patrol line and on 22 May the *England* once again made contact, this time destroying *RO.106*. Next day she sank *RO.104* and the day after that *RO.116*, but two days elapsed before she got another, *RO.108*. To cap this unique achievement on 31 May while screening an escort carrier she detected and sank *RO.105*. In less than two weeks she had sunk six submarines, a feat without parallel in the entire war.

The Japanese submarine arm suffered a catastrophic defeat at the hands of US and Allied ASW forces. Out of 193 boats in commission between December 1941 and August 1945 (including midgets and suicide craft) a total of 120 were sunk by surface escorts, submarines, aircraft or mines. The disaster was more complete than the defeat of the U-Boats, for whereas the U-Boats had brought the British and Americans to the brink of defeat the Japanese submarines had achieved very little.

Nor did Japanese ASW methods prove effective against American submarines. There are many examples of US submarines completely dominating the escorts, destroying them before going on to wipe out the convoy. The problem was once again faulty doctrine, for in spite of having an island empire and a large mercantile marine the Japanese made very few preparations to defend themselves against an all-out attack on their communications. There was no research into sonar prewar, very little into radar and no program for mass production of escorts until 1943. Only 14 escorts were ordered in 1941 and eight more in 1942. The prewar escorts of the *Shumushu* Class were equipped mainly with spare and obsolescent equipment and had a useless ex-army trench mortar and six depth charges as antisubmarine weapons. Not until late 1942 did the four ships receive an underwater sensor.

Convoying of merchant ships had not been considered before the war, as far as we know, and even after American submarines began their depredations against shipping there was a reluctance to admit that the real danger lay within the defensive perimeter. Tentative convoying began in 1943, but there were nowhere enough escorts. Postwar exchanges of information revealed that the Japanese thought they had sunk 486 American submarines – the real figure was only 42!

AIR POWER AND SHIPS

Second only to the submarine, the aircraft had the most profound influence on naval warfare. This did not come as a surprise, for since the end of World War I there had been a constant and acrimonious dispute between the advocates of traditional sea power and the disciples of air power, the newcomers claiming that the power of the airplane had rendered armies and navies obsolete.

The best known of the 'bomber-versus-battleship' protagonists was Brigadier General Billy Mitchell, who had commanded the US Army's Air Service during World War I. Convinced by Trenchard's success in establishing the Royal Air Force as a separate service, he demanded the abolition of the army and the navy, but in particular he aimed his invective at the battleship. In 1921 he was allowed to conduct a series of trials against obsolete ships and surrendered German units, the most spectacular of which culminated in the sinking of the dreadnought battleship *Ostfriesland*. Ignoring the fact that the army bombers had perfect visibility, exact knowledge of the target's whereabouts, no alterations of course or antiaircraft gunfire to throw off their aim, and the fact that the old ship was in a poor state of repair, Mitchell claimed that the end of the battleship was at hand.

The US Navy was understandably angry at what it regarded as a piece of showmanship which obscured the truth, and subsequent controlled tests showed that ships could take much more punishment. Ultimately, however, the dispute had a beneficial result, for it gave a much needed shot in the arm to the arguments for naval aviation, and the US Navy developed the doctrine that carrier aircraft were the best defense for warships, and that torpedo bombers and dive bombers could reinforce the guns of the battle fleet. However, trials with the carriers *Langley, Lexington* and *Saratoga* did nothing to shake the faith of senior admirals in the battleship as the capital unit of the fleet. Given the relatively primitive state of aircraft design it seemed reasonable to pin faith in antiaircraft gunnery as the main defense against air attack.

The Japanese developed very similar doctrines to the Americans, experimenting with fast carrier task forces but continuing to rely on the battle fleet as the ultimate arbiter of sea power. Like the USN the Imperial Japanese Navy retained control of its naval air arm and refused to be swayed by the more extreme air-power advocates. Peacetime exercises showed both navies that the often-repeated claim that 'air power is indivisible' was only true in the most superficial sense. Flying over the featureless sea requires special techniques of navigation and the exacting needs of flying off carriers called for specially designed aircraft.

The British with a world lead in naval aviation, swallowed the strategic air-power doctrines whole in 1918 and paid a heavy price for their decision. Naval aviation was starved of funds, resulting in poor aircraft and a failure to develop the right doctrines. What was worse was that the majority of air-minded naval officers had transferred to the RAF in 1918, making it even harder for the claims of naval air power to be advanced. The battleship lobby reigned supreme for many years in the Royal Navy and as the RAF did very little to test some of its more extravagant claims, fleet exercises against air attack were unrealistic and poor preparation.

The experiences of 1940 proved a rude awakening. Off Norway British and French ships were under incessant air attack and although losses were not heavy the constant threat of dive bombers restricted their freedom of action. Both sides had their problems, however; the Allies found that existing guns and fire control were not adequate in the face of enemy command of the air but the Luftwaffe also found that its pilots had overestimated the ease with which they could hit a moving ship. The evacuation from France in May-June was another nightmare, for the Allied ships were usually attacked in congested water with their decks crowded with soldiers. In the Mediterranean the British had to contend with high-level bombing, which proved less accurate than dive bombing but was still a constant threat.

The lessons of 1940–41 were that ships were very vulnerable if the enemy had undisputed command of the air, for the primitive fire control and inadequate AA armament of ships could not cope with wave after wave of attacks from every point of the compass. Even a single aircraft carrier, such as HMS *Illustrious*, with the Mediterranean Fleet, flying a few slow Fulmar fighters was a major deterrent. From September 1940–January 1941 not a single major unit of the Mediterranean Fleet was damaged in a daylight air strike. This was recognized by the Luftwaffe, who had created Fliegerkorps X as a ship-busting force to remedy the deficiencies shown up in Norway. As soon as Fliegerkorps X put the *Illustrious* out of action the pendulum swung back in favor of the Axis.

It was not all one-sided, for in November 1940 British carrier aircraft put a large part of the Italian Fleet out of action at Taranto. No more than 21 Swordfish biplanes, some with torpedoes and others with bombs, sunk the battleship *Conte di Cavour* and damaged the *Littorio* and *Duilio*, all for the loss of two aircraft. At a most crucial stage of the war the British had freed themselves of a major threat.

The evacuation of Crete in May 1941 showed just how vulnerable warships could be in the Mediterranean when command of the air was lost. A carrier and two battleships were hit and a large number of cruisers and destroyers were sunk or damaged. Crete fell to an airborne assault and the central Mediterranean came under Axis control, apart from the small British island of Malta.

The lessons of Taranto were not lost on the Japanese, who were already planning a similar knockout blow against the American battlefleet in the Pacific. While their diplomats continued to negotiate in Washington six carriers steamed for Hawaii, and by a combination of circumstances the great base at Pearl Harbor was taken totally by surprise when 140 aircraft suddenly attacked. Within five minutes all seven of the battleships moored along 'Battleship Row' had been hit by bombs or torpedoes and an eighth lying in a dry dock had been damaged. The rest of the base took severe punishment as well, nearly 250 aircraft being destroyed on the ground. A second strike added to the chaos but inflicted comparatively little major damage, and suffered considerable casualties from defending AA fire, but at a cost of only 29 aircraft out of the 350 involved the Japanese wiped out the US Navy's Pacific Fleet. Three days later land-based bombers completed the destruction of Western sea power in the Far East by sinking the British *Prince of Wales* and *Repulse* with equal ease.

It seemed that Billy Mitchell had been right, for the world's most powerful battleships had only lasted minutes against air attack. However, the Japanese had failed to get the American carriers, which were away on an exercise on 7 December and they had also failed to destroy the oil fuel reserves at Pearl Harbor. Six of the battleships could be repaired and new ships were already under construction, but with hindsight Pearl Harbor was a blessing to the US Navy. It forced Admiral Nimitz to rely on the carriers, and so the concept of carrier task forces became a reality far sooner than any naval aviator had dreamed possible.

All this was in the future, and for the moment the Japanese appeared invincible. The fast carriers switched to the East Indies as soon as the conquest of the Philippines had been achieved, and ranged as far afield as Ceylon and Northern Australia. By 10 March 1942 the Japanese were in possession of the Philippines, Malaya and the East Indies at a cost of three destroyers, fewer than 100 naval aircraft and a number of merchant ships. The Allies had lost four battleships, five cruisers and 14 destroyers.

For six months the Japanese reigned supreme but early in May 1942 the carriers *Lexington* and *Yorktown* administered a check to them in the Battle of the Coral Sea. Although the *Lexington* was sunk, the Japanese lost the *Shoho* and a large number of aircraft and they failed to consolidate their foothold in New Guinea. Then a month later came Midway, when three American carriers sank four out of the six Japanese carriers, losing the *Yorktown* at the end. This was the second carrier-versus-carrier battle, fought over great distances between the rival air groups, and it set the pattern for the rest of the Pacific War. Although the Japanese seemed to get the best of two later battles in the Solomons, they were increasingly prodigal with their highly trained aircrews. The *Wasp* and *Hornet* were lost but the United States was turning out large numbers of pilots and new ships were in hand, whereas the Japanese would have no new carriers until 1943 and their training program was inadequate.

Radar proved absolutely vital to the development of air power and to the defense of warships against air attack. In carriers and their escorts it could track hostile aircraft and allow defending fighters to position themselves correctly for interception. When combined with the latest mechanical fire-control computers it enabled antiaircraft gunfire to become much more effective, so that major warships had a good chance of beating off attacks.

During the long campaign across the Pacific the US Navy fought a battle of attrition against the Japanese, one which the Japanese could not ultimately win. The former superiority in aircraft performance was reversed, and as the standard of US carrier pilots' training improved while that of the Japanese rapidly decreased, the wastage of Japanese aircrew became crippling. The Battle of the Philippine Sea in June 1944 showed how big the disparity had become, and during the Battle of Leyte Gulf the Japanese had to send carriers to sea with amost no aircraft because there were no pilots to fly them.

Only right at the end did Japanese air power seem to challenge US sea power, when Kamikaze tactics nearly overwhelmed the defenses of the ships around Okinawa. The problem was that a Kamikaze pilot was not deterred by accurate gunfire; unless shot down by defending fighters or literally shot to pieces by a series of direct hits, his final dive onto a ship was fairly easy to achieve. The Kamikaze attack foreshadowed the era of the guided missile, with a human brain directing the final dive rather than an electronic system.

The Kamikaze threat was met by a combination of an extended radar screen, the hasty issue of proximity fuzes for AA ammunition and a sophisticated fighter defense. Between 26 March–22 June 1945 there were 1900 Kamikaze attacks which sank 26 ships and damaged 176 more, but the defenders did not find the complete answer. Fortunately Japan was running out of fuel and food and the long struggle which had begun at Pearl Harbor ended suddenly with the dropping of two atomic bombs. From start to finish it had been decided by air power, not the unilateral air power envisaged by Douhet, Mitchell and Trenchard but in a balanced partnership with traditional sea power.

THE SEA WAR IN THE ATLANTIC

Although not termed the Battle of the Atlantic until after 1940, the naval war in the Atlantic was the longest single campaign of the war. It was also the most important strategic theater, for ultimately by linking the United States with Great Britain and Western Europe it combined what might otherwise have been two separate wars, a European civil war and a Pacific war between the United States and Japan. In other words, the Atlantic was the only battleground in which all the protaganists (even Japan peripherally) had a stake. If the US joined the war, clearly Hitler's only hope lay in severing the supply lines between the British Isles and North America, for without them the British were impotent and the Americans could never hope to fight in Europe.

The titanic struggle to dominate the Atlantic can best be divided into eight phases: Phase 1 lasted from September 1939–May 1940, Phase 2 from June 1940–March 1941, Phase 3 from April 1941–December 1941, Phase 4 from January 1942–July 1942, Phase 5 from August 1942–May 1943, Phase 6 from June 1943–August 1943, Phase 7 from September 1943–May 1944 and Phase 8 from June 1944–May 1945.

When the first phase opened, the German U-Boats were bound by the Prize Ordinance, under which merchant ships had to be examined to see if they were enemies or neutrals or whether their cargoes were destined for the enemy. Hitler worried that, as in 1917, unrestricted use of the German submarine fleet might bring the United States in. However an overzealous commander torpedoed the liner *Athenia* within hours of the declaration of war, and the Admiralty acted on the assumption that unrestricted warfare was in force. Thereafter the restrictions on the U-Boats were removed one by one, until by mid-1940 the U-Boats were free to sink all ships in British waters.

During this phase the U-Boats scored two impressive sinkings of warships, the carrier *Courageous* in September 1939 and the battleship *Royal Oak* in Scapa Flow a month later, but losses of French and British merchant ships did not reach a crippling level. In addition the sinking of the pocket battleship *Admiral Graf Spee* off Montevideo in December 1939 seemed to signify that the German navy would prove no greater threat than it had in the previous war.

The invasion of Norway was closely followed by the invasion of France, and the ensuing defeat of the British and French armies brought about a disastrous reversal of the strategic position in the Atlantic. Not only did the U-Boats have bases on the flank of the Atlantic convoy routes but the British faced the threat of invasion by the German army. This fear proved to be exaggerated but it had to be countered by withdrawing every available warship from the Atlantic, thereby allowing the U-Boats to make heavy inroads into shipping. There was also the problem of the Mediterranean, for Italy had entered the war on 10 June and some British warships had to be diverted to strengthen the Mediterranean Fleet.

This second phase was marked by savage losses in the Western Approaches as the U-Boat wolf packs perfected their tactics against poorly escorted convoys. Only American support enabled the British to win through this grim period, notably the passage of the Lend-Lease Act in March 1941, and the exchange of 50 old destroyers for a 99-year lease of bases in the Caribbean, the Bahamas, and Newfoundland. Even so, the war material had to reach the British Isles and shipping losses were critical. The hard-pressed escorts gained their first break in March 1941 when they sank the three ace U-Boat captains Kretschmer, Prien and Schepke. Then in May they recovered vital cipher material from *U.110* which enabled the cryptographers to make immediate progress with the Enigma ciphers. In May 1941 the last serious attempt to operate major warships against the Atlantic convoys was defeated when the battleship *Bismarck* was sunk, and although the heavy cruiser *Prinz Eugen* and the battle-cruisers *Scharnhorst* and *Gneisenau* remained at Brest they ventured out from there only to withdraw to Germany to avoid air attacks.

The third phase saw the introduction of the first limited attempts to get aircraft to sea with convoys. The Catapult-Aircraft Merchant Ships (CAM-Ships) carried a Hurricane fighter for defense against marauding bombers, but a refinement was the first escort carrier, HMS *Audacity*, which went to sea in September 1941. From that month also there was a series of incidents involving U-Boats and US warships, first the *Greer* and later the *Kearney* and *Reuben James*. However these were not enough to bring America into the war.

The fourth phase of the Battle of the Atlantic was expected to be an alleviation of the British position but the unnecessary and unexpected losses of British and US shipping off the eastern United States added to the burden of both navies, and only after an agonizing six months was the balance restored. Shipbuilding and weapon production were now getting into their stride and the two Allies reached agreement about the best dispositions to defeat the U-Boats.

The fifth phase was a period of balance, with both sides building up for a decisive battle to decide the outcome. Undoubtedly the Allies were getting stronger but they decided to reduce escort strength in the Atlantic to provide cover for the big 'Torch' amphibious landings in North Africa. Whatever the strategic wisdom of the North African landings it nearly brought disaster in the Atlantic for the U-Boats were able to take advantage of the weakened convoy escorts. There was also a conflict of priorities in Britain, with the RAF refusing to divert four-engined bombers from Bomber Command to Coastal Command. The RAF believed, almost certainly wrongly, that it was best to bomb the U-Boat bases and factories.

The first weeks of March 1943 were terrible times for the Allies, with shipping losses rocketing to 68 percent of ships in convoy. For a bleak period of 20 days it looked as if the combined might of two navies and their respective air forces could not stave off defeat but suddenly the escorts gained the upper hand. The factors were complex: the superior Allied arrangements for the cooperation between scientists and the armed forces; the return of all the escorts and escort carriers diverted to North Africa and a change of the convoy cipher all played a part in preventing the U-Boats from destroying the convoy system. When it is remembered that there were over 100 U-Boats at sea daily throughout this period, the danger to the Allied cause can be imagined. The extent of the victory lay in the total withdrawal of the U-Boats at the end of May for reequipping with new weapons.

The next phase began in June 1943 with a concerted air offensive against the U-Boats' transit routes through the Bay of Biscay. The U-Boats responded by trying to fight it out on the surface with enhanced AA armament and the Luftwaffe sent out groups of Ju 88 twin-engined fighters to deal with the Allied anti-submarine aircraft. Both expedients failed and U-Boat losses continued to rise, whereas shipping casualties were dropping.

In September 1943 the U-Boats returned to the attack armed with a new homing torpedo, an improved radar detector and the *schnorchel* air mast. These were a great help in reducing losses, particularly the *schnorchel*, which allowed batteries to be recharged while running submerged, but they could not stop the convoys getting through. In the same month the battleship *Tirpitz* was finally immobilized in Altenfiord by British midget submarines. Since late 1941 she had maintained a baleful watch over the convoys carrying war material to the northern Soviet Union, and the mere threat of a move to sea had resulted in disaster for convoy PQ-17. Service in these Arctic convoys was probably the most arduous and unpleasant task given to any seamen during the war. The convoys to the Soviet Union left from either Iceland or northern Scotland and for almost all of their 10–14 day passage were within range of attack from German aircraft, surface ships and U-Boats. In winter the weather was always bitterly cold, with ships often becoming dangerously unstable because of the weight of ice coating their upper works. In summer the almost continuous daylight meant that there might be no respite from any form of attack. Although only about 40 convoys sailed in each direction, the strain on Allied resources was considerable. Only the most modern merchant ships could be used in this theater because of the terrible weather and the need for high speed. With average losses of 7.5 percent compared with about one-tenth of this in the normal Atlantic service, the burden was very great. As so much of the convoy route was within range of German air attack the Royal Navy was faced with the very difficult problem of whether the heavy ships of the Home Fleet and valuable escorts should be risked if the Germans sent their surface ships out. At the time of PQ-17 it was decided that the merchant ships were more expendable than the necessary covering force. For the convoys after PQ-17 a rather bolder policy was followed and in December 1943 the last German capital ship, the battlecruiser *Scharnhorst*, was brought to action by the British Home Fleet. After an attempt to get past the cruisers escorting a convoy she was caught by the battleship *Duke of York* and finally torpedoed by British and Norwegian destroyers.

The last phase of the Atlantic battle coincided with the long awaited opening of the Second Front in Normandy, for Admiral Doenitz ordered all available U-Boats to concentrate on cross-Channel shipping. This was anticipated by the Allies, who stationed very strong surface and air patrols at either end of the Channel to 'cork the bottle.' These were so effective that out of 25 U-Boats ordered to the invasion area only four reached their objective.

Although the invasion of Normandy was principally necessary for far broader reasons it was also needed to bring the battle of the Atlantic to an end. Strategic bombing had failed to prevent a rise in the rate of U-Boat production in 1944 and the Allies were aware that work had begun in 1943 on the new Type XXI and XXIII boats and on the Walther-engined Type XVII; all capable of reversing the tide of battle in Germany's favor.

Fortunately for the Allies industrial production in Germany was becoming disorganized under the competing pressures of the Wehrmacht and the Luftwaffe. Too much time was spent on the Walther turbine boats, which were too unsafe to be used operationally, and production of the outdated Type VIIC was continued in parallel with the urgently needed Type XXI. To make matters worse the prefabrication of the complex Type XXI and Type XXIII boats was entrusted to foreign labor, thereby increasing the risk of sabotage and poor workmanship. Personnel shortages were acute, and officers were transferred from the Luftwaffe to the U-Boat Arm to keep the new boats manned.

With hindsight it is clear that the Kriegsmarine's dream of dominating the Atlantic was a delusion. Especially after the losses sustained during the invasion of Norway its surface forces were far too small to take on the Royal Navy. The victories on land provided a magnificent range of bases but only the U-Boat fleet took full advantage. The surface raiders often wasted golden opportunities. By contrast the British and Americans stuck to their task, eventually winning the struggle by their tactics and training as much as their technology.

THE SEA WAR IN THE PACIFIC

The campaign in the Pacific between the United States and Japan was like no other in the history of sea warfare. Fought over immense distances, it marked the introduction of radically new techniques and battles on a scale never imagined.

Japan won the first round by striking at the Pacific Fleet's base at Pearl Harbor in Hawaii, sinking or putting out of action seven of the eight battleships lying there. The damage was done by two strikes of bombers and torpedo planes from a fast carrier task force, exactly the sort of tactics that US Navy aviators had been proposing for years. The secondary objective of the Japanese, the American carriers, escaped because they were away on exercises. Although the original American strategy was now in ruins a new one could be built around the carriers, and this Admiral King as COMINCH and Admiral Nimitz as CINCPAC proceeded to do.

Nimitz refused to remain passive while the Japanese rampaged through the Pacific, and in February 1942 launched strikes against the Gilbert and Marshall Islands, followed by the Doolittle Raid on Tokyo, in which B-25 bombers took off from the carrier *Hornet*. These were only pinpricks but they kept the Japanese aware that the US Navy had not been beaten.

With the fall of the Philippines and Singapore there was no main base to support fleet operations in this area and so the remnants of the British and Australian forces fell back to the Dutch East Indies, where they joined Admiral Thomas C Hart's Asiatic Fleet and the Dutch in a new American-British-Dutch-Australian (ABDA) Command. ABDA was doomed from the start but it fought a tenacious rearguard action, culminating in the Battle of Java Sea in which the Allied ships were annihilated.

The Japanese now dominated the Southwest Pacific from Burma down almost as far as Australia, and had established the defensive perimeter of island bases which they regarded as essential to protect their conquests in Asia. Then things began to go wrong, and 'victory fever' seemed to grip the Japanese military hierarchy. Having dismayed their enemies by a series of outstanding victories they began to believe themselves invincible and instead of consolidating the defensive perimeter they drew up plans for fresh conquests. The first was to be New Guinea, the stepping stone to Australia, followed by the Solomon Islands. However, the Americans had broken the Japanese ciphers and were fully aware of their plans to thrust against Port Moresby and move to occupy Tulagi. In May 1942 the rival carrier task forces met in the Battle of Coral Sea, the first in history in which the rival fleets never saw one another. Coral Sea was a tactical defeat for the Americans for they lost the big carrier *Lexington* and suffered damage to the *Yorktown* in exchange for sinking

the small *Shoho*, but strategically it was a victory, for the attack on Port Moresby was blocked and two big carriers were damaged.

Numbers of carriers now became crucial, for when the Japanese made their momentous decision to occupy Midway they had four large carriers operational against only three American CVs. The American ships were the *Yorktown*, hurriedly patched up after the Coral Sea battle, and her sisters, *Hornet* and *Enterprise*. The Americans had the advantage of foreknowledge, thanks to the efforts of their cryptanalysts, and Admiral Spruance ignored the feint attack on the Aleutians to concentrate on Midway.

The battle which followed is one of the turning points of history, for in the second carrier-versus-carrier battle all four Japanese carriers were destroyed by air strikes, in return for the loss of the *Yorktown*. At the time Midway seemed no more than a check to the Japanese, but with hindsight it was clearly the beginning of a steady decline.

The Americans could now cautiously move over to the offensive, and when they learned that the Japanese were strengthening their positions in the Solomons they decided to move to occupy Guadalcanal. While the US Marines fought desperately to hold their bridgehead the navy fought equally desperately against a series of night attacks by Japanese warships. Only two days after the first landings the Allied forces were roughly handled in the Battle of Savo Island, losing four heavy cruisers. Another six battles were to be fought, until the number of casualties caused the channel off Savo to be nicknamed Ironbottom Sound.

The Japanese success was partly because their night-fighting drill was excellent but also because they had a magnificent 'secret weapon' in the oxygen-driven Long Lance torpedo, which had phenomenal speed and range. Time and again the Japanese turned the tables on the Allies, even when they had been detected on radar. Many of these fierce actions were attempts to stop Admiral Tanaka's 'Tokyo Express,' nightly trips by light cruisers and destroyers to run supplies, ammunition and reinforcements to the Japanese garrison on Guadalcanal. The culminating battle took place on 13–14 November, when on the first night the US cruisers and destroyers got the worst of the exchange and suffered heavy losses; on the second night the battleships *Washington* and *South Dakota* frustrated an attempt to shell Henderson Field and sank a Japanese battleship. Gradually the US Navy learned to use radar to the best advantage, and although losses continued the Japanese found Guadalcanal an increasing drain on their resources. When in February 1943 the starving survivors were evacuated by Tanaka's ships, the American foothold in the Solomons was secure and the threat to Australia was removed. While one thrust moved up from the Solomons to the Philippines the main offensive by the fast carrier task forces was launched across the Central Pacific. From then on the strategy was 'island-hopping', leaving the toughest Japanese bases to wither on the vine. Once the heavily defended Gilbert, Marshall and Mariana Islands were in American hands, still stronger bases like Rabaul and Truk could be dealt with at leisure.

November 1943 saw the first moves in the new offensive, when the Fifth Fleet attacked Tarawa in the Gilberts. In a bloody three-day assault the US Marines took the island and killed every defender. Tarawa taught some painful lessons, and when the next assault was made on Kwajalein and Eniwetok in the Marshalls it was preceded by a prolonged bombardment, from the air and by naval gunfire. The fortress of Truk was raided but not assaulted, and instead in June 1944 Saipan became the next objective.

The Japanese did their best to defend the Marianas, but against no fewer than 15 carriers they had only nine. However, the real disparity was in trained pilots, and green pilots were slaughtered in the 'Great Marianas Turkey Shoot.' The Battle of the Philippine Sea was the last of the great carrier battles, and the final remnant of Japan's great force of naval aviators was all but wiped out.

The next assault, the big landing in Leyte Gulf in the Philippines four months later, brought on another pitched battle. This time the Japanese surface fleet was destroyed in a series of actions, having nearly achieved its aim of destroying the amphibious transports. Only the valor of the escort carriers and their escorting destroyers saved the transports off Samar from disaster, while in Surigao Strait Admiral Olden-dorf's elderly battleships inflicted a shattering defeat on Nishimura's force. It was the last battleship engagement and the end of all Japanese hopes of stopping the Americans.

While the carriers ranged far and wide across the Pacific another, more insidious, war was being waged. Submarines from Pearl Harbor harried Japanese shipping and reported on the movements of their fleets. In conjunction with this campaign extensive mining was carried out from the air, and the combined effect on Japanese shipping was catastrophic. By the end of hostilities some 4,800,000 tons of shipping

had been sunk by submarines and a further 2,250,000 tons had been sunk by mines. On many occasions timely warning was given of fleet movements by US submarines, and eight carriers were torpedoed. To make things easier for the US submariners the Japanese failed to foresee that their shipping would be attacked. As an island empire they were exceptionally vulnerable to such an attack and they paid the penalty for the oversight. By 1945 it was almost impossible to move fuel supplies in bulk and shipping had been shifted to coastal craft because of the relentless depredations of Allied submarines.

The last battles of the Pacific war were for the islands of Iwo Jima and Okinawa. The garrisons of both resisted fanatically and the battles were hard for the supporting Allied naval forces also. Nearly 10,000 sailors were killed or wounded during the three-month Okinawa campaign, mostly by Kamikazes, and 34 ships were sunk and 368 damaged. By this time, however, Japan's cities were being relentlessly bombed with the culminating efforts being the atomic raids on Hiroshima and Nagasaki. Whatever wider issues are raised by President Truman's decision to drop the bomb, it certainly helped bring the war to an end and saved the many thousands of American and Japanese lives which would have been lost in an Allied invasion. On 2 September 1945 the last act of the Pacific war, the Japanese surrender, was staged, appropriately, on the fantail of the battleship *Missouri* in Tokyo Bay. Japan had become great through sea power and she was finally overcome by it.

In retrospect the strategy followed by Admiral Nimitz (a refinement of the prewar Orange plans) proved very sound. Once the Central Pacific was finally under American control it was possible to push forward and attack the vast defensive perimeter set up by the Japanese. Conversely, the Japanese had set themselves an impossible task in trying to hold down a chain of bases from the Aleutians down to New Guinea, but by the time they finally elected to withdraw to a more sensible line they had left it too late. On the American side the only strategic complication was the difference of opinion between Nimitz and MacArthur over the army's insistence on liberating the Philippines rather than destroying the Japanese empire. With hindsight we can see that both were right, since the United States had a political commitment to the Filipino people that overrode military expediency. Unlike Japan the Americans had the resources to pursue more than one objective.

A B-17 Flying Fortress over Guadalcanal.

AIR

AIR

AIR POWER IN 1939

World War I (1914–18) was an unfortunate conflict in many respects, not least for its effect on the military use of rapidly developing technology. The war, particularly in Western Europe, saw the introduction of a range of new weapons systems, but did not continue long enough for their full potential to be realized. Nowhere was this more true than in the case of air power, for although most of the military roles of aircraft had been recognized by 1918, few, if any, had been assessed completely or correctly, leaving a plethora of half-formed ideas, myths and dubious doctrines which the interwar period, with its lack of major conflicts to act as convincing proving grounds, did little to change. By the start of World War II, therefore, not one of the major air forces had developed a fully formed air weapon with the flexibility and adaptability inherent in the new dimension of war.

Potentially the most damaging of the interwar air doctrines, affecting the air forces of Britain and, to a slightly lesser extent, the United States, was that of strategic bombing. This was based on the belief, arising from the incomplete evidence of a confused German campaign against Britain in 1917–18, that the manned bomber, flying unmolested over the enemy homeland and dropping high explosives onto unprotected cities, could win the next war on its own. The destruction of key industries and the killing of industrial workers would, it was argued, undermine any modern state's ability to continue hostilities, for without the products of industry, a war economy would be impossible to sustain. Such was the force of this belief that for much of the interwar period the Royal Air Force concentrated almost entirely on its bomber arm, viewing all other air roles as unnecessary diversions. Even when fighter or interceptor aircraft were developed in earnest after 1935, their task was seen as protecting the homeland from enemy bomber fleets and not as one of air superiority, destroying hostile air forces wherever they might appear. A very similar set of beliefs was beginning to gain a firm hold in the United States Army Air Corps by the late 1930s, with the added requirement that, as the United States was so far away from any potential enemy, air defense of the homeland was even less important. Thus, when two of the major Allied nations entered World War II in 1939 and 1941 respectively, their air forces were excessively oriented toward strategic air power, lacking the doctrines, capability and, most importantly, specially designed machines for a whole range of tactical tasks. The correction of this imbalance was to be a difficult and costly process.

Other air forces took the opposite view, stressing tactical rather than strategic roles, and this imbalance was to prove just as difficult to rectify. By 1939 both the German and the Soviet air forces were dedicated to close support of ground forces. In the German case this was part of the brilliant short-term offensive capability known as Blitzkrieg, in the Soviet part of a defensive doctrine designed to inflict maximum punishment on anyone foolish enough to attack the country, but in both air forces the resultant lack of strategic, long-range capability and naval support as specific roles was to cause problems. A similar state of affairs was apparent in Italy and a host of smaller European countries.

Finally some air forces, recognizing the vastness of ocean which was to be their battle-field, chose to stress naval aviation at the cost of other roles. Japan was the most obvious proponent of this doctrine and, although her air elements were capable of land-based tasks, the aircraft carrier and its weapons became the center of attention, diverting resources and manpower from other areas. Fortunately for the Allies, the United States Navy, and to a lesser extent the Royal Navy, had not ignored their air potential, but the fact that both were able to develop in this diametrically opposite way to their land-based compatriots shows the lack of cooperation and coordination which pertained in most of the major combatant nations.

The picture in 1939 is therefore one of unfortunate emphasis, varying according to the air force involved but indicative of the half-formed appreciation of the full potential of air power in all the nations of the world. World War II is the watershed, a period during which this full potential was gradually (and often painfully) realized. Tracing the process of such realization, chiefly through the development of the various aircraft types, is the primary purpose of this section.

FIGHTERS

The fighter or interceptor aircraft (known as 'pursuit plane' in American parlance) was very much a development of World War I. When that conflict began in 1914 the embryonic air forces of the combatants were based primarily upon the support role of reconnaissance, being expected to aid ground units by reporting observations from 'the other side of the hill.'

It did not take long for countermeasures to be developed. At first the reconnaissance machines were attacked by ground fire, but it soon became obvious that a far more effective method was to engage them from other air machines. Consequently fighter aircraft, designed to intercept or pursue the slow-moving 'spy planes,' appeared, only to be countered in turn by other fighters intent upon protecting the reconnaissance capability. By 1916–17 air-to-air combat between protecting and intercepting fighters had become accepted practice, the purpose being to attain and maintain 'air superiority' which would enable reconnaissance missions to be flown. As bombers made their appearance over both the battlefield and the homeland, this concept was extended to include all air space of value to the war effort.

The growing interwar belief that 'the bomber will always get through' undermined the confidence afforded to the fighter, but by the mid-1930s most air forces were accepting the efficacy of such machines. Their duties were ostensibly two-fold – to protect the homeland, paradoxically against incoming bombers whose invulnerability was widely presumed, and to achieve air superiority over the battlefield by destroying attacking aircraft – but the emphasis varied according to the air force concerned. As World War II progressed, both roles began to emerge as equally important and this necessitated the development of specialist aircraft designs. In the fight against bombers, for example, new techniques of interception were required, covering, in daylight, a mix of speed, altitude and destructive firepower and, at night, an additional ability to find and destroy unseen targets. Similarly, in the acquisition of tactical air superiority it was necessary to produce robust, maneuverable aircraft which enjoyed speed, altitude and firepower as well as an ability to be easily maintained on battlefield airstrips. As a final development, notably in the American case, it was necessary to introduce long-range fighters to protect bomber formations flying by day into a hostile air environment. In the event, few air forces had the time or the industrial capacity to develop new designs to satisfy these required roles and had to make do with adaptations to existing types. The lesson was well worth the learning.

Britain In the British case, the interwar emphasis was placed firmly on the interception of enemy strategic bomber fleets. As late as 1938 the RAF's Manual of Air Tactics was stating quite seriously that air-to-air combat between attacking and defending fighters – a popular conception of air warfare inherited from World War I – was 'not now practicable,' given the speed of the aircraft involved. Interceptions would be too fleeting for either machine to loose off destructive fire and too fast for the human frame of the pilots to survive wild maneuvers. The key design was therefore the bomber, a relatively slow-moving machine. It was hoped that the bomber could be shot down by fighters, enjoying the ability to climb quickly to its operating altitude, the ceiling to outmaneuver it by attacking from above and the firepower to hack it out of the sky in one destructive pass. Such emphasis, into which neither speed nor survivability against hostile fire really entered, was reflected in the fighter designs available in 1939. Although both the Supermarine Spitfire and Hawker Hurricane were to enter popular legend as superb fighting machines, they had to be adapted to fit the newly discovered needs of air combat and, at the beginning of hostilities, were part of a fighter arm which included obsolete and archaic designs.

The most obvious manifestation of obsolescence was the Gloster Gladiator, a single-engined biplane fighter which seemed to owe more to World War I than to modern air thinking. First flown in 1934 and delivered to front-line squadrons of the RAF as recently as 1937, this aircraft was an anachronism for much of its service life. Its 840hp Bristol Mercury radial engine gave it a reasonably high performance, enabling it to climb at the rate of 2300 feet per minute, and its four .303-inch Browning machine guns did provide a respectable punch for the time, but its speed of 253mph was slow and it was clearly of use against slow-moving bombers only. Nevertheless it saw active service in Norway and France in 1940, contributed to the Battle of Britain by helping to defend Plymouth and did sterling service in the Mediterranean against equally obsolete Italian designs. The pity is that it had to be used at all.

A similar sentiment may be expressed over the Boulton Paul Defiant, for although this was a monoplane, both its speed (304mph) and rate of climb (1900 feet per minute) were sacrificed by the addition of a hydraulically operated dorsal gun turret. This increased drag and necessitated the provision of a two-man crew, coordination of whose efforts was essential but not always possible in the fast-moving melee of air combat. As a result, this machine experienced a short and costly service life, entering front-line squadrons in December 1939 and being relegated to largely unsuccessful night-fighting duties within 12 months, after suffering appalling daytime casualties.

It was thus extremely fortunate that both the Spitfire and Hurricane were available in 1939, for both offered significant improvements in speed and maneuverability. Of the two, the Hurricane was the more numerous when the war began. First flown in November 1935, it entered service two years later and proved to be both versatile and adaptable. With a maximum speed of 316mph, a rate of climb of 2530 feet per minute and an armament fit of eight wing-mounted .303-inch Browning machine guns, the Hurricane Mark I was one of the few fighter aircraft to satisfy the needs of bomber interception. During the Battle of Britain in 1940 it was able to engage and destroy incoming German bombers and could comfortably outfly the twin-engined Messerschmitt Bf 110 escort fighter. Thereafter, in the Mark IIB, the Hurricane was upgunned to take 12 Brownings and in the Mark IIC boasted four 20mm cannon. However, as it proved difficult to increase its speed to match that of other aircraft types coming into service, by 1942 the role of interceptor was gradually dropped in favor of ground support. In this guise the Hurricane continued to fly in all theaters until the end of hostilities.

As the war progressed, therefore, the Spitfire assumed importance as the premier British fighter aircraft. Designed by R J Mitchell and incorporating the newly developed Rolls-Royce Merlin 12-cylinder in-line engine, the prototype first flew in March 1936, and entered RAF service as the Spitfire I just over two years later. It was a superb machine, combining grace and aerodynamic lines with a good top speed (362mph), rapid rate of climb (2530 feet per minute) and effective armament fit (eight wing-mounted .303-inch Brownings). It was this model, together with a small number of Mark IIs (characterized by their 1175hp Rolls-Royce Merlin XII engines), which successfully challenged the German air threat of 1940, displaying an ability to adapt to air-to-air fighter combat. Further models appeared in late 1940, fitted with progressively more powerful Rolls-Royce Merlins, but it was not until March 1941 that the next important variant entered service. This was the Spitfire V, equipped with the 1450hp Merlin 45 (which pushed the speed up to 374mph) and a choice of three wing designs, each with a different armament fit, including 20mm Hispano cannon. The Mark V proved useful in fighter sweeps over occupied Europe, but with the introduction of the

Messerschmitt Bf 109F and Focke-Wulf Fw 190A was, for a time, outclassed. An emergency improvement program produced the Spitfire IX, the most numerous of the 24 marks, with 1660hp Merlin 61, four-bladed propeller and varied cannon/machine-gun armament. This proved capable of 408mph and a rate of climb of 3950 feet per minute, but did not regain immediate supremacy over its Luftwaffe opponents. This was not achieved until the Merlins had been replaced by 2050hp Rolls-Royce Griffons – a change which took place from the Mark XIV onward and necessitated quite radical structural alterations. The final wartime variant was the F 21, capable of over 450mph and a rate of climb of about 4500 feet per minute, although the Spitfire did eventually reach Mark 24 before production ceased in 1947. Taking all the models together, it was probably the most versatile fighter design of World War II, flying in all theaters and engaging nearly every type of enemy machine.

It is never wise to stick rigidly to one design, however successful that may be, and while Supermarine were progressively improving the Spitfire, attempts were being made to produce a successor. The fact that none was found before the advent of the turbojet is proof of the effectiveness of Mitchell's original idea, but it also reflected a lack of clear thinking over the fighter's true role.

The least successful design which emerged was the Westland Whirlwind, a single-seat, twin-engined day fighter which first flew in October 1938, and entered service in June 1940. Despite a fair top speed (360mph) and a healthy punch (four nose-mounted 20mm cannon), its Rolls-Royce Peregrine engines were unsatisfactory. It was withdrawn from service in 1941 after delivery to only two squadrons. Similar engine problems bedevilled a Hawker design of October 1939 which was meant to produce a single-seat, single-engined replacement to the Hurricane. With a top speed of 412mph and a rate of climb in excess of 2775 feet per minute, Typhoon (originally called the Tornado) should have offered significant advantages, but its 24-cylinder Napier engine proved something of a disappointment. The project was almost cancelled in 1941 but the Typhoon soon showed its worth at low-level operations, chasing and destroying the fastest German fighters over Britain and France. It then came into its own as a ground-support machine. Its successor and stablemate, the Tempest V, followed an almost identical pattern of development in 1943–44.

Adaptation to new roles was in fact a

characteristic of quite a few British-designed fighters during the war years, for even before the Typhoon had reached front-line service the twin-engined Bristol Beaufighter had followed a similar pattern. Designed in the late 1930s without official backing from the Air Ministry, this machine was an attempt to create a long-range fighter, capable of effective bomber escort and armed with a devastating array of 20mm cannon slung beneath the forward fuselage. It was such an impressive design that it was hastily adopted by the RAF in 1940, but its original role was quickly supplemented and then largely overridden by a variety of other tasks, including ground support, torpedo carrying and night interception. In the event, such flexibility gave the RAF a superb fighting machine at just the right time, but as a pure fighter aircraft its service life was short.

In fact it was not until July 1944 that a potential replacement to the Spitfire appeared, and even then it was only the revolutionary development of the turbojet which swung the balance. The aircraft concerned was the Gloster Meteor I, a pleasing machine which combined twin Rolls-Royce centrifugal turbojets with four nose-mounted 20mm cannon to produce a fighter of unprecedented power. In 1944 this power was largely unrealized, for although the Meteor enjoyed considerable success against the fast-moving V1 flying bombs, it was beset with teething troubles. Nevertheless, it did act as a useful instrument in the RAF's development of aerial flexibility in the immediate postwar years, a development which probably constituted the most important air lesson of World War II.

Day fighters were not the only machines which were required as the war progressed, for as soon as the Luftwaffe switched to night bombing in autumn 1940, some form of night fighter became essential to protect British cities. Unfortunately, few people had contemplated the possibility of night combat before the war, and no specific designs existed. At first Hurricanes and Defiants were committed to the night skies to seek out the enemy bombers unaided, but success was understandably virtually non-existent. Experiments had been conducted in 1939, however, into the possibilities of AI (Air Interception) radar and this proved to be the key. Early sets were fitted to Defiants, Beaufighters and even Bristol Blenheim light bombers to produce the first effective British night interceptors. Many commentators express the opinion that the night blitz over Britain was virtually defeated by the Beaufighter with AI fit. However, the most famous British night

fighter, the De Havilland Mosquito, did not appear until mid-1941. A revolutionary twin-engined aircraft of wooden construction, the Mosquito was designed, again without official Air Ministry backing, as a fast intruder bomber. It was to excel in this role as the war progressed, but its speed (Mark VI, 380mph), high maneuverability and apparently infinite adaptability lent it naturally to other roles. When fitted with AI radar, four 20mm cannon in the belly and four .303-inch Browning machine guns in the nose, the Mosquito was a lethal aircraft in the night skies of Europe. Modified during the later years to take AI Mark VIII centimetric radar, which enabled successful contacts to take place at a variety of altitudes, the night-fighter version eventually went to nine marks with improved speed, rate of climb, armament and range. Like many other countries Britain did not pursue the development of single-engined night fighters (it was felt that a two-man crew was essential for radar operation and that nose-mounted, forward-looking radar was the best design), but with an aircraft like the NF Mosquito, many would argue that this hardly mattered. As in so many other aspects of warfare, the British produced what was needed in the end, after a series of experiments, failures and private ventures.

The United States The years 1939–41 were traumatic ones for the United States. Although ostensibly neutral, she found herself drawn increasingly into support for beleaguered Britain, offering Lend-Lease aid and moral encouragement, while at the same time realizing that her armed forces were ill-equipped for modern war. In terms of air power this led to a drastic reassessment of American requirements, which became even more necessary as relations with Japan deteriorated and war in the vastness of the Pacific became inevitable. The advocates of strategic bombing used the opportunity to press for more and better long-range daylight bombers and the US Navy continued to stress the importance of the aircraft carrier. Both weapons systems seemed to satisfy the basic needs of American strategy, being capable of taking the war to enemy forces many hundreds of miles from the USA, but for the same reason land-based pursuit planes failed to attract the attention they deserved. This did not mean that no development took place, but it did put an enormous strain on the aircraft industry as the need for fighters, initially as tactical air-superiority machines and then as long-range escorts to vulnerable day bombers, became obvious. Fortunately, American manufacturers had maintained an interest in fighter design before 1941 and a variety of firms produced aircraft, firstly for the French and then, after June 1940, for the British markets. Many of these types were hurriedly pressed into US Army service when the United States entered the war in December 1941, but in most cases a process of rapid adaptation was needed to satisfy specific US needs.

Perhaps the leading manufacturer for the European markets was the Curtiss-Wright Corporation, who enjoyed close contacts with the French up until 1940. A Curtiss design of 1934, known to the Americans as the P-36, was supplied to the Armée de l'Air in 1939 as the Hawk 75, and after courageous service against the Luftwaffe in May-June 1940 remaining stocks were transferred to Britain as the Mohawk. A single-engined, single-seat monoplane, the P-36 was characterized by a retractable undercarriage and a high speed by contemporary standards (300mph), but by the beginning of World War II it was outclassed. It was not until the Pratt and Whitney radial engine had been replaced by an Allison V-1710-33 in-line engine in 1938 that a more effective pursuit-plane emerged. Known to the Americans as the P-40, this aircraft enjoyed a top speed of 345mph and a rate of climb of 2650 feet per minute. The Europeans showed interest and, although by the time the P-40B had been cleared for service in late 1940 the French market was closed, it did join RAF and Commonwealth squadrons as the Tomahawk. Unfortunately, despite modifications to the engine – an improved Allison changed the appearance of the aircraft to such an extent that the RAF renamed it the Kittyhawk – and the addition of such combat aids as armor protection and self-sealing fuel tanks, weight became a problem and performance suffered. By 1941 even the ultimate development machine, the P-40N/Kittyhawk IV, could not compete on equal terms with either the Spitfire or the Luftwaffe's Bf 109, and, in common with many other types, it was relegated to ground support. Nevertheless, the US Army did receive the later marks of the P-40 in quantity (calling them collectively the Warhawk) and it undoubtedly helped to sustain American fighter strength during the early months of war.

The P-40 was joined by the Bell P-39 Airacobra, an unconventional single-engined, single-seat fighter which enjoyed the useful top speed of 385mph. Characterized by a tricycle undercarriage and an Allison V-1710-63 in-line engine situated aft of the pilot, this aircraft was designed initially as a Company venture, with no official backing. Early models incorporated a massive armament fit of 37mm cannon in the propeller boss and fuselage-mounted .30-inch and .50-inch machine guns. These impressed the British sufficiently to produce an order in 1940, but when these aircraft entered RAF service as the Airacobra I, they proved neither popular nor effective, The main problem was speed, for when combat aids such as armor plate and self-sealing fuel tanks were added, this dropped significantly to 358mph maximum while adversely affecting handling characteristics. These problems led to their early replacement, but this did not deter the US Army from acquiring large numbers of P-39s in the early wartime period. With drop tanks attached, a ferry range of over 1000 miles could be attained and this gave tremendous advantages in both the Atlantic and Pacific theaters. It was at best only a stopgap weapon, requiring replacement as soon as more reliable machines appeared, and although Bell followed the basic design trend to produce the P-63 Kingcobra in 1943, problems persisted and it is a sad fact that neither the P-39 nor its stablemate was an outstanding success. Large numbers of both types were supplied to the Soviet Union under Lend-Lease, but even the Soviets were obliged to transfer the machine to ground-support tasks.

Fortunately for the Americans this was not all that was available in late 1941. As early as 1937 the US Army Air Corps had issued one of its few official pursuit-plane specifications, calling for a long-range machine capable of speeds in excess of 375mph. Despite a complete lack of previous experience, the Lockheed Aircraft Corporation won the contract and produced an innovatory design known as the P-38 Lightning. This twin-engined, twin-boom fighter with an array of armament in the nose first flew in January 1939. It more than satisfied the specification, but the two Allison V-1710 liquid-cooled engines, fitted with revolutionary GEC turbochargers, caused problems, leading in fact to a prototype crash less than two weeks after the initial flight. Despite this, the US Army had seen enough to be impressed, and development went ahead. In March 1940 the British ordered 143 P-38s, but when the State Department vetoed the export of turbochargers the resultant aircraft was unsatisfactory. The RAF rejected the design, although their interest did at least ensure the availability of the aircraft in its original form when America entered the war. Problems with the Allison engines continued –

in many ways they were too sophisticated for hard combat usage – but the P-38's range was an immediate asset in both the European and Pacific theaters, where it was used as a bomber escort and long-range interceptor for the duration of hostilities. As always, reliability and endurance led to a plethora of adaptations, notably to reconnaissance and ground-support tasks, but the primary role of interception remained throughout. The P-38's potential was perhaps shown to the full in April 1943 when 16 machines of the 339th Fighter Squadron shot down the Japanese aircraft carrying Admiral Yamamoto over 500 miles from their base at Guadalcanal.

The effect of British purchasing power upon American fighter design was further shown, this time with happier results for the RAF, in the case of the P-51 Mustang. In April 1940 North American Aviation was approached by British representatives to produce an entirely new fighter aircraft. The result, designed, tested and flown in the incredibly short period of 117 days, was a single-engined, single-seat monoplane capable of 390 mph, with a rate of climb of around 2600 feet per minute and an armament fit of two .50-inch machine guns in the nose, two .50-inch and two .30-inch machine guns in the wings. The RAF immediately purchased a total of 620, altered the wing-mounted armament to four 20mm cannon and christened the aircraft the Mustang. It was a pleasing machine with plenty of potential, but its one major drawback at this stage was its operational range, which could barely exceed 450 miles. As RAF fighters by 1941–42 were beginning to fly well into occupied Europe to seek out the Luftwaffe, this was a severe drawback. When the existing Allison V-1710-81 engine was replaced by a Rolls-Royce Merlin in late 1942, a truly great aircraft emerged. The US Army, which had taken the P-51 into service as soon as the US entered the war, saw the advantages, especially for bomber escorts, and began to equip the fighter squadrons sent to England as part of the Eighth AAF. A revised airframe, characterized by a 'bubble' canopy, produced the Merlin-equipped P-51D in late 1944, and when equipped with drop tanks this aircraft was capable of escorting B-17 and B-24 bombers all the way to Berlin and beyond. In addition, with armament of six wing-mounted .50-inch machine guns, a top speed of 437mph and a high degree of maneuverability, the P-51D was able to engage and destroy a wide range of enemy aircraft, contributing enormously to the demise of the Luftwaffe in 1944–45.

Indication of this contribution may be gauged from the record of the P-51 in Eighth AAF service. When the bombers of the Eighth were first sent to England the Allison-engined Mustang was thought to be suitable for only the most short-range operations, and even when the Merlin-engined P-51B became available in 1943, it was earmarked for the Ninth rather than the Eighth AAF. Fortunately, the potential of the aircraft as an escort fighter was recognized in December 1943, when the 354th Fighter Group of the Ninth AAF operated temporarily under command of the Eighth, and thereafter, as a result of pressure from the England-based airmen, the policy was reversed. The Eighth AAF was given priority of supply, not only of the P-51Bs but also of the C, D and K variants as they appeared, with the result that, by the end of hostilities in Europe in May 1945, 14 out of the 15 Fighter Groups in the Eighth AAF were operating Mustangs. Their range enabled them to fly freely, deep into Germany (the first fighter air-to-air combat over Berlin, involving P-51s, took place on 4 March 1944), and for the first time the B-17s and B-24s were given effective aerial protection. It was a remarkable achievement and contributed significantly to eventual Allied victory in the air.

The P-51 was not the first European-based escort fighter, however, for from March 1942 the task was carried out by the P-47 Thunderbolt, popularly known as the 'Jug.' This aircraft had been designed in 1940–41 by the Republic Aviation Corporation in response to the lessons of air combat emerging from the war in Western Europe, as it became clear that a machine which combined power, speed, rate of climb and heavy armament fit was needed. The P-47 had an enormous engine, the Pratt and Whitney R-2800 Double Wasp 18-cylinder radial, which caused both design and technical problems when Republic received official backing for the project in 1941. The engine required an enormous four-bladed propeller, ground clearance of which necessitated a large landing gear, and weight was theoretically excessive. The gamble paid off; the extremely powerful engine gave a top speed of over 427mph, the rate of climb was over 2600 feet per minute and, with drop tanks attached, it had the potential range to escort bombers to Berlin. Eight wing-mounted .50-inch Colt-Browning machine guns added the final touch to produce a fighter which was to contribute significantly to air victory, particularly over Europe. The P-47D was in fact the most numerous subtype of any fighter in history (12,602 were eventually manufactured) and, as with so many other designs, the aircraft was

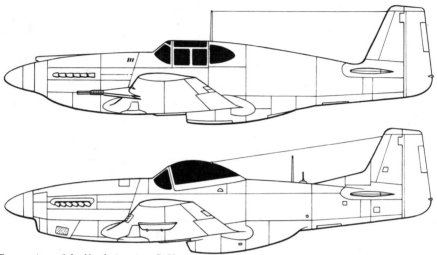

Two versions of the North American P-51.
Above: P-51D and Top: P51A.

adapted to a variety of other roles, particularly ground support.

Neither the P-51 nor the P-47 was replaced by more modern designs before 1945, although the US experimented with turbojets in an effort to produce a new generation of aircraft before hostilities ceased. The first development was the Bell P-59 Airacomet, which first flew in October 1942, but the results were disappointing and it never saw front-line service. Problems also affected the Lockheed P-80 Shooting Star, for although production began in January 1944 it was not ready for service before V-J Day. In both cases, however, valuable experience of use in the postwar aviation world had been gained.

The American need for night fighters was understandably less acute than that of Britain, yet paradoxically the US authorities were the first in the world to authorize a specific design. The Northrop P-61 'Black Widow' – named because of its color scheme – reflected American interest in the RAF's AI-equipped night fighters in 1940. It resulted from a specification put forward in January 1941. First flown in May 1942, the P-61 was a twin-engined, twin-boom machine which enjoyed a top speed of 440mph in later production versions and was equipped with the new SCR-720 AI radar in the nose. This enabled it to seek out enemy aircraft in the night skies of both Europe and the Pacific, while its four fixed 20mm belly-mounted cannon, supplemented in early versions by four .50-inch machine guns in a dorsal turret, constituted a devastating punch against which few hostile aircraft could survive. The P-61 was in fact the only purpose-built night fighter produced by any nation during World War II, and although the Americans experimented with adaptations to other machines – notably the single-engined Grumman F6F Hellcat naval interceptor – the Black Widow was a unique and effective aircraft. Lessons drawn from its development were to stand the West in good stead in the growing confrontation with the Soviet Union after 1945.

The Soviet Union The military potential of the Soviet Union between the two World Wars was largely ignored by commentators in the West. A widespread anathema to the Communist regime, coupled with a deliberate policy of isolationism emanating from Moscow, led to a mixture of ignorance and underestimation. Occasional shafts of enlightenment from the East – particularly the Kiev Maneuvers of 1936, to which foreign representatives were invited and where such innovations as massed parachute attacks were seen – were conveniently written off as Soviet attempts to disguise inherent political weakness. The relatively poor showing of Soviet 'advisers' in Spain (1936–39) and soldiers in Finland (1939–40) were taken as reinforcement of existing preconceptions. No doubt there was an element of truth in such judgments, but in terms of air power there is much to suggest that, by the late 1930s at least, the design and production of aircraft for tactical roles in support of ground forces was comparatively well advanced.

This was particularly the case with fighter aircraft, whose purpose was to attain and maintain air superiority, chiefly through a policy of aggressive action at all times. This role demanded a mix of speed, maneuverability, a good rate of climb and heavy armament. The aircraft also needed to be rugged to counter the relative unsophistication of both pilots and ground facilities. All this was answered to good effect in the mid-1930s by the design bureau of Nikolai N Polikapov which produced a world-beating machine in the I-16 fighter. Developed at the same time as (and actually entering service before) the I-15 biplane, the I-16 was a stumpy single-engined monoplane of almost 'homemade' appearance. Its large radial engine – originally the 480hp M-22, based on the British Bristol Jupiter, but later the M-25, based on the American Wright Cyclone – gave the aircraft not only its distinctive appearance but also a speed which eventually reached 326mph, a respectable achievement for the late 1930s. Its climb-rate was also good, at nearly 2700 feet per minute, and its fine maneuverability in the hands of experienced pilots made it an air superiority machine of some value, as Spanish Nationalists discovered when over 400 I-16s were shipped to Spain to equip the Republicans during the Civil War. Its most dramatic and effective feature was its armament which, by contemporary standards, was unprecedented. The I-16 Type 17 (eventually succeeded by the Type 24) had two 7.62mm ShKAS machine guns on the engine cowling and two 20mm ShVAK cannon in the wings; with rates of fire of 1600 and 800 rounds per minute respectively this was a formidable punch, better than that of any other fighter at the time. The I-16 fought in Finland in 1939–40 and against the Luftwaffe in 1941–42. By then it was outclassed, but it showed the potential of Soviet designs of the future.

These designs began to appear in 1940 in response to the 'Winter War' with Finland, and received an understandable boost from the German invasion of the Soviet Union in June 1941. They emanated from three main design bureaus – Lavochkin, Gorbunov and Gudkov (LaGG), Mikoyan and Gurevich (MiG), and Yakovlev (Yak) – and it would seem convenient to take each in turn, if only to show how, during the Great Patriotic War of 1941–45, Soviet fighter needs were largely standardized to satisfy the tactical air-superiority role. The total lack of long-range and night fighters in Soviet

service reinforces the point.

The LaGG designs had their origins in the I-22 fighter prototype of 1938. A single-seat, single-engined monoplane, the I-22 was unusual in being built largely of wood. Unfortunately, its 1050hp Klimov M-105P 12-cylinder in-line engine was not satisfactory and, even though a large number of I-22s entered squadron service as the LaGG-1, the aircraft was a disappointment. Nevertheless, with a combination of one 20mm cannon in the propeller hub and two 12.7mm machine guns above the engine, its armament was respectable and it gained a reputation for ruggedness in 1941 when the Germans invaded. By then, however, the engine had been replaced by a 1240hp M-105 PF in-line to produce the LaGG-3. This was still not a perfect machine – even with the new engines its top speed was less than 350mph – and further refinements soon followed.

Development was concentrated on the engine as the key to improvement and the designer, S A Lavochkin – by now working on his own, which altered the preface of future machines of this stable from LaGG to La – decided to try a radial instead of an in-line power pack. He may have had no choice, as there is evidence that the Soviet High Command had transferred existing in-line designs to what they considered to be more promising Yak fighters. The result, utilizing the 1330hp Shvetsov M-82A 14-cylinder two-row radial, was known as the La-5. A low-wing monoplane, it resembled the LaGG-3 in airframe terms, but had a better cockpit design and improved armament fit of two 20mm cannon on the engine cowling. The aircraft was certainly comparable to the German Bf 109 when it entered squadron service in late 1942 and when a better engine, the fuel-injection ASH-82FN radial, was added, a better all-round performance was achieved. With a maximum speed of 403mph and a rate of climb of over 3000 feet per minute, the Soviets were clearly producing a competitive fighter aircraft. It was made even more effective in 1943, when a process of weight reduction and drag elimination boosted the top speed to 423mph and gave a rate of climb of 3900 feet per minute. These improvements led to it being redesignated La-7. The design trend continued in 1944 and 1945 with the La-9 and La-11, both of which refined existing ideas still further, but neither saw active service in World War II.

The wartime record of the MiG partnership is less dramatic. The designs produced were, on the whole, disappointing. Tracing their history from the I-61 fighter prototype of 1939, the main purpose of the MiG machines seems to have been high-altitude interception. The I-61 was capable of operating at up to 37,000 feet, drawing its power from a 1200hp Mikulin AM-35A 12-cylinder in-line engine, but even though this entered service in the MiG-1 in 1940, it had distinct disadvantages. Armament was poor initially, comprising one 12.7mm cannon and two 7.62mm machine guns, and the pilot must have been somewhat uncomfortable at high altitudes in the open cockpit. Work on a replacement design began in 1941, entering service as the MiG-3. Engine size was increased to 1350hp, an enclosed cockpit was fitted and extra machine guns enhanced the armament. A top speed of 398mph and a rate of climb of 3700 feet per minute resulted but although performance above 15,000 feet was good, at lower altitudes the aircraft was sluggish. Production probably ceased in 1943 as available engines were switched to the Il-2 ground-attack machine, and later developments, known as the MiG-5 and MiG-7, do not appear to have been important.

The last of the three bureaus to be considered is that of A S Yakovlev. This was undoubtedly the most important bureau during the war years. Yakovlev himself had gained a prewar reputation for glider design, so it was something of a surprise when, in 1939, his answer to a government fighter-plane specification was chosen for production. This was the I-26, a single-engined monoplane equipped with a 1100hp VK-105 PA 12-cylinder in-line and capable of a top speed of 373mph and a rate of climb of 3940 feet per minute. Armament of one 20mm ShVAK cannon in the propeller boss and two 7.62mm ShKAS machine guns above the engine gave the aircraft a reasonable punch for the time, and it was cleared for production as the Yak-1 in June 1941. It enjoyed the added advantages of easy maintenance and good handling characteristics, and very little modification was needed to produce one of the classic fighters of World War II. Minor changes to the rear fuselage to improve pilot-view led to a redesignation in 1942 to produce the Yak-7. This in turn evolved into the Yak-9 when an improved engine (the 1260hp Klimov VK-105PF) was fitted and armament enhanced to take 12.7mm instead of 7.62mm machine guns. In 1944 performance was further enhanced by yet another new engine, the 1650hp VK-107A, to produce the Yak-9U. This aircraft, with a top speed of 435mph and rate of climb of 4900 feet per minute, outclassed both the Bf 109 and Focke-Wulf 190 fighters on the Eastern Front.

While all this was going on, Yakovlev followed a conscious policy of improvement rather than a gradual process of evolution and in 1942 he produced what became, rather confusingly, the Yak-3. This took the basic Yak-1, reduced its weight and drag by cutting down the airframe and from it developed a fighter of tremendous potential. With a top speed of 447mph, a rate of climb of 5250 feet per minute and improved maneuverability, the Yak-3 probably did more to destroy the air superiority of the Luftwaffe in the East than any other single type. In close combat it was formidable, enjoying (according to Soviet reports) a speed advantage of 35–45mph over its piston-engined rivals. In concert with its contemporaries, the Yak-3 constituted the ultimate in Soviet wartime fighter design, satisfying the needs of the tactical air superiority role almost exactly. In terms of speed, rate of climb, maneuverability and robustness, the Yaks were superb. Although by 1944–45 their armament was comparatively light, this was more than compensated for by the skill of their pilots. Altogether an estimated 37,000 Yak fighters were produced during World War II. It is interesting to note that, large though such figures were, they did not satisfy Soviet demands for fighter aircraft. Between 1941 and 1945 the Americans provided, under the Lend-Lease program, a total of 9438 fighters to the Soviets. These were joined by a further 4283 from Britain. The breakdown was:

United States	Britain
P-39 – 4,719	Hurricane – 2,952
P-40 – 2,097	Spitfire VB – 143
P-47 – 195	Spitfire IX – 1,188
P-63 – 2,427	

Germany According to the terms of the Versailles Treaty, which was imposed on Germany at the end of World War I, no German air force was permitted to exist. As early as the 1920s, this particular restriction was being covertly ignored and, under the guise of civilian and sporting aircraft, a number of aviation firms maintained both an interest and a tradition in military designs. At the same time a new generation of pilots and technicians was trained in the Soviet Union, where, through an unofficial agreement between Berlin and Moscow, German expertise in military design and organization was exchanged for the training aids forbidden at Versailles. This, when Adolf Hitler assumed power in January 1933, the basic tools for rapid rearmament already existed. The Allies were expected to react to the fundamental political changes within Germany, but when they did not,

Hitler felt free to ignore the Versailles settlement. In March 1935 he authorized the formation of the Luftwaffe, destined to become, for a short time in the late 1930s and early 1940s, the most powerful and effective air force in the world.

Of the firms involved in maintaining design expertise, the Ernst Heinkel Flugzeugwerke had been the most active, and so far as fighters for the nascent air force were concerned, it was its ideas which prevailed in the early months. Heinkel had begun experiments with what, in retrospect, was clearly a fighter design in the 1920s. By 1928 it had produced a biplane, known as the He 37, which was faster than anything then in service with either the British or the French. This naturally led to further development, geared progressively to the demands of the secret rearmament program, so that when the Luftwaffe emerged in 1935 a number of prototype designs were in a very advanced state. The most important was the He 49, a biplane fighter which first flew in November 1932, and this in turn was refined to produce the He 51, the first fighter to be openly ordered for the Luftwaffe. A single-engined, single-seat biplane, the He 51 first flew in May 1933 and entered squadron service with Jagdgeschwader (JG) 'Richthofen' two years later. Powered by a 750hp BMW VI 7.3Z 12-cylinder in-line engine, it was capable of speeds of up to 205mph and a rate of climb of 1850 feet per minute. Armed with two 7.92mm Rheinmetall MG 17 machine guns above the fuselage, the He 51 fought in Spain with the Condor Legion and was still in service when Hitler invaded Poland in September 1939. As a stopgap weapon to cover the development of more modern designs, it was more than successful, indicating to the Allies that a resurgent Germany was by no means weak in either technology or expertise.

More modern designs were needed if the Luftwaffe was to develop at the speed and in the directions desired and, once again, the groundwork had been laid by 1935. Early in 1934 the Luftwaffenfuhrungsstab (Luftwaffe Operations Staff) had issued a specification for a single-engined fighter aircraft of monoplane configuration armed with two 7.92mm machine guns and capable of high speed and maneuverability. The challenge was taken up by a number of aviation firms, including Heinkel and the Arado Flugzeugwerke, both of which had experience in the relevant fields, so it was something of a surprise when the relatively new Bayerische Flugzeugwerke, under the direction of Professor Willy

Messerschmitt, produced a revolutionary design. Based upon the Bf 108 high-speed monoplane which was to take both fifth and sixth places in the 4th Challenge de Tourisme Internationale of 1934, the Messerschmitt Bf 109 was in reality the smallest airframe it was possible to fit around the most powerful engine (a Rolls-Royce Kestrel V) then available. First flown in September 1935, the prototype impressed the Luftwaffe staff sufficiently to win a production contract, although no one at the time expected this to result in an eventual total of 35,000 machines.

The initial production model was the Bf 109B, equipped with a 635hp Junkers Jumo 210.D engine. A top speed of 292mph was disappointing, but a rate of climb of about 2200 feet per minute was promising. Armed with three 7.92mm MG 17 machine guns, one in the propeller boss and two on the engine cowling, this model was blooded in Spain with the Condor Legion, surprising many with its effectiveness. C and D models followed, increasing top speed to a more respectable 340mph, but it was the E, fitted with a Daimler-Benz DB 601 engine and four MG 17s (two on the cowling and two on the wings) which helped to destroy the European air forces in the early months of World War II. Popularly known as the 'Emil,' this aircraft finally met its match when pitted against the Spitfire over England in the summer of 1940. By 1941 the F (Friedrich) model had appeared, pushing the top speed above 370mph and, for a time, outflying the Spitfire V. This was replaced in turn by the G (Gustav), which first appeared in the late summer of 1942. It was this model which saw the most widespread service. Fitted with a 1475hp DB 605 A-1 engine, the G could reach 428mph and achieve a rate of climb of almost 4000 feet per minute. Armament varied according to need, but standard fit by 1944 included 15mm MG 151 machine guns, 30mm MK 108 cannon and even 210mm wing-mounted rocket tubes. Further variants were produced, notably the K with a top speed of 452mph, but it was the E, F and G models which contributed the most to Luftwaffe operations. They constituted some of the most effective and versatile fighters of World War II.

Single-engined machines were not the only requirement of the new air force in the mid-1930s, and concurrent with the specification which produced the Bf 109 went a call for a twin-engined fighter design. Once again, despite considerable opposition from more experienced firms, the contract was awarded to Messerschmitt's Bayerische Flugzeugwerke for a design which was to become the Bf 110 Zerstörer (destroyer). A twin-engined, two-seat monoplane, the prototype of which first flew on 12 May 1936, this aircraft was an attempt to produce what was known as a 'strategic fighter,' capable of escorting bombers on raids deep into the enemy homeland. Range was therefore a key consideration, with speed, maneuverability and firepower taking subsidiary places. Even so, the early Bf 110s showed considerable potential. Despite unimpressive maneuverability, the two 1100hp Daimler-Benz DB 601 engines produced a top speed of 352mph – comparable to most single-engined fighters then in service – and operational range was reckoned to be about 700 miles. Armament was also good, comprising two 20mm Oerlikon MGFF cannon and two 7.92mm MG 17 machine guns in the nose with a third, manually operated MG 17 in the rear cockpit. A strategic fighter requires a large degree of air superiority and, although the Bf 110 did well in the European campaigns of 1939–40, it was badly mauled by both Spitfires and Hurricanes during the Battle of Britain. By 1941–42 most had been refitted as ground-support machines or night fighters.

The failure of the Bf 110 as a fighter highlights one of the most important requirements of any armed force – the need for replacements to existing designs, preferably coming into service before disaster strikes. In many ways the wartime record of German fighter design follows this pattern. There was a constant search for replacements to the 109 and 110. In single-engined terms, the Luftwaffe was fortunate, for as early as June 1939 the firm of Focke-Wulf had test flown a back-up design to the Bf 109. Unusual in the fact that it sported a radial rather than an in-line engine, the prototype Fw 190 displayed all the characteristics of a dependable and effective fighter. Its 1700hp BMW 801 Dg 18-cylinder engine gave a top speed of 408mph, the rate of climb was a respectable 2350 feet per minute and, with a total of six machine guns (two on the engine cowling, two in the wing roots and two in the outer wings), its destructive capacity was impressive. Production began slowly but by early 1941 the Fw 190A was appearing over France and shooting down the more sluggish Spitfire V. Successive models, reflecting the priorities of the Eastern Front, concentrated upon ground-support roles, but in 1943 the Fw 190D (Dora) entered service. Powered by a 1776hp Junkers Jumo 213 in-line engine – a fit which produced a characteristic 'long nose' – this aircraft could reach 440mph and achieve a rate of climb of

3300 feet per minute. Later versions of this model were further modified under the designation Ta (for the designer Kurt Tank) 152, which produced sleeker and faster machines. With nitrous-oxide fuel injection, the Ta 152H high-altitude interceptor could reach 472mph and, theoretically, outfly most of the Allied opposition. However, this was toward the end of the war, when German resources and priorities did not permit a major production run. As a result, the Ta 152 was not encountered in significant quantity. Even so, it represented a peak of fighter design during World War II, indicating the tremendous technological advances engendered by that conflict.

Attempts to produce a successor to the Bf 110 were less successful, for although Messerschmitt and his team began work on the next generation as early as 1937, the result, the Me 210, was disappointing. First flown in September 1939, this twin-engined, two-seat monoplane disproved the theory that good-looking aircraft perform well. Powered by two 1395hp Daimler-Benz DB601F in-line engines, it was capable of 385mph but it had stability problems. These were not solved by changes to the airframe, which included replacing the original twin tail fins with one tail fin, and, despite an official Luftwaffe order for 1000 of these machines, production ceased in April 1942, by which time only 350 had been built. Later in the same year a successor – the Me 410 Hornisse (Hornet) – was flown with 1720hp DB603A engines, but the design was still not satisfactory. The vast majority of these aircraft were rapidly relegated to other roles and did not fly as day fighters after 1942.

By that time, with the balance of the air war gradually swinging away from the Luftwaffe, a touch almost of desperation crept into fighter designs as unconventional and revolutionary ideas were explored in a desperate attempt to gain advantage. In piston-engine terms, this trend was exemplified by the highly unorthodox Dornier Do 335 Pfeil (Arrow) a twin-engined machine based on the center-line thrust concept, in which one engine drives a tractor propeller conventionally in front of the pilot while another drives a pusher screw to the rear. It had a very respectable speed of 474mph and heavy armament fit (30mm MK 103 cannon in the front propeller boss and two 15mm MG 151 machine guns on the fuselage top) but there is no evidence that the Pfeil flew in combat and resources could have been better applied elsewhere.

The Do 335 was, however, a one-off design

and a far more promising area of wartime research centered on rocket and jet engines. At first the rocket seemed to offer the most advantages and, once again, it was Messerschmitt who led the way. His Me 163 Komet, which first flew on 2 October 1941, was an arrowhead, delta-shaped aircraft powered by a single Walther HWK 508 A-1 rocket motor which produced the incredible top speed of 596mph. The practical problems inherent in this futuristic research were enormous. The motor was fuelled by an exceedingly dangerous mixture of T-Stoff (hydrogen peroxide) and C-Stoff (alcohol/hydrazine), which had a predilection toward premature explosion. Takeoff was frightening, to say the least, as the slightest following wind would overturn the aircraft and the smallest bump would explode the fuel. Endurance was never more than 12 minutes and landing was death defying, as the wheels had been discarded at takeoff. Nevertheless, with a rate of climb in the region of 16,000 feet per minute, it was possible to launch the Me 163 against high-flying bombers with some success. Accidents were common, but combats did take place, albeit with little recorded success.

A more promising design trend was the turbojet, as both the British and Americans were discovering at much the same time. Messerschmitt was once more in the forefront, this time with his Me 262 Schwalbe (Swallow). A twin-engined, single-seat fighter with futuristic swept-back wings, the Me 262 offered tremendous potential when first flown in July 1942. Its two 1980-pound thrust Junkers Jumo 004 single-shaft turbojets gave it a top speed of 540mph, a rate of climb of almost 4000 feet per minute and an operational range of 500 miles. Unfortunately, the engines proved less than reliable and the landing gear was prone to collapse. When this was combined with political interference in its development – Hitler insisted that it should be produced as a fighter-bomber and not as an interceptor – it is hardly surprising that the Me 262 did not reach front-line squadrons before July 1944. Even so, about 100 high-flying US day bombers fell victim to this aircraft and it was among the most effective of the early jets. This is less than can be said about the only other jet fighter to enter service – the Heinkel He 162 Salamander or Volksjäger (People's Fighter). Test flown on 6 December 1944, only 37 days after design plans were begun, this single-seat interceptor with its 1760-pound thrust BMW 003 turbojet seated incongruously on its back was meant to be an expendable piece of kit, easy to produce and fly,

in a last frantic effort to halt the Allied bomber fleets. Unfortunately for the Luftwaffe, by the time the first examples had been delivered to front-line squadrons in spring 1945, Allied bombers had destroyed all remaining fuel stocks. So far as is known, the Salamander never flew in anger, although at least fifty aircraft were in service.

The shift in emphasis away from tactical air superiority and toward bomber interception was the most important aspect of wartime German fighter design, and nowhere was this exemplified more than in the area of night interception. In common with nearly every other air force, the Luftwaffe had given no thought at all to night fighters before the war. Although by 1942–43 the RAF's night-bombing offensive forced a change of thinking, no specific night-fighter designs were produced. All the night fighters in service by 1945 were modifications of existing designs, incorporating airborne interception radars, particularly the Lichtenstein SN-2 set, and heavy armament fit. The distinctive AI nose-mounted aerial arrays appeared on Bf 110 G-4s, Me 210 and 410 variants, Fw 190s and even Me 262s from the fighter stable, and on Dornier Do 217E and N series machines, Junkers Ju 88G-7 and Ju 188 bombers, to produce a hodgepodge of designs and capabilities. When tied into the elaborate radar early-warning system known as the Kammhuber Line, and later when ground control introduced more flexibility, such aircraft were effective, as RAF Bomber Command found to its cost. However, the opportunity to standardize and produce just one type appears to have been lost in 1943, when the Heinkel He 219 Uhu (Owl) was not developed to the full. A twin-engined, two-seat machine, designed in 1940 to replace the Bf 110 as a long-range fighter, the He 219 fitted well into the nighttime role when it was finally issued in summer 1943. Powered by two 1750hp DB 603 engines which gave it a maximum speed of 416mph, this aircraft proved well able to adapt to the addition of radar and heavy armament fit (including, by 1944, the deadly, upward-firing *schräge musik* twin 30mm MK 108 cannon). Its potential was shown by the commanding officer of 1 Gruppe/Nachtjagd-geschwader 1 on the night of 11/12 June 1943, when, in an He 219A-0, he destroyed five Lancaster bombers single-handed. Fortunately for the RAF, a mere 268 examples of the Uhu were produced – a derisory figure given the scale and urgency of its task, and an indication of the confusion in German fighter design by the latter half of the war.

AIR

Italy The Italian armed forces were not fully prepared for war in 1940, when hostilities began against a weakened Britain and a defeated France. Despite an apparent wealth of combat experience during the 1930s – in Ethiopia (1935–36), Spain (1936–39) and Albania (1939) – motivation was weak and equipment was, in certain important areas, obsolete. Furthermore, Italian industry was never fully mobilized in support of the war effort, and even when new equipment designs appeared, they were rarely produced in quantities sufficient to affect the military balance. In many respects this was surprising, for Italian ideas, particularly on air warfare, had dominated European thinking since the early years of the century. For example, the Italians had led the world in the use of offensive air power during their war with Turkey in 1911, and the theories of Giulio Douhet in the 1920s were of seminal importance to the evolution of doctrines of strategic bombing. Nor did the problem lie in a lack of design capability, for in the 1920s and 1930s a number of Italian engineers were regarded as leaders in their particular fields. Yet between 1940 and Mussolini's overthrow in 1943, no Italian aircraft succeeded in catching the imagination of the combatant nations and none was produced which radically upset the air balance. This was mainly because of the failure to produce sufficiently reliable and powerful engines, but also it is perhaps a classic case of theoretical capability not being translated into practice.

So far as fighters were concerned, part of the reasons for this lay in a dogged determination, especially among the pilots of the Regia Aeronautica, to stick with designs which had already proved useful, despite the obvious advances in air technology. As proof of this, Italy has the distinction of being the only major combatants to retain biplane fighters in front-line service for the duration of hostilities, regardless of the development of new, more modern monoplane machines. Although these did sterling service in a variety of roles, the stubborn adherence to their use must be a major reason for their lack of overall success. The earliest of such types still in front-line service in 1940 was the CR 32, designed by Celestino Rosatelli and built by Aeronautica d'Italia SA Fiat. First flown in August 1935 as the latest in a long line of Rosatelli designs, the CR 32 was blatantly obsolete by the beginning of World War II. Although robust, pleasant to fly and remarkably maneuverable, this single-engined, single-seat biplane, sporting such outmoded features as open cockpit and fixed undercarriage, was slow (at 224mph) and was hopelessly undergunned (two 12.7mm Breda-SAFAT machine guns in fixed positions above the engine). It saw action in Ethiopia and Spain, where its success against minimal opposition undoubtedly led to its retention, and continued in front-line service during the Mediterranean campaigns of 1940–41. The fact that it was consistently outflown by almost every Allied design, including the equally obsolete Gloster Gladiator, should have proved its archaic nature, but unfortunately it was not the only biplane on issue to Italian fighter squadrons. Its stablemate, the CR 42, was also in full production, and was eventually to be built in greater numbers than any other Italian fighter, a total of 1781. It retained all the disadvantages of open cockpit, fixed undercarriage and poor armament fit. First flown as late as January 1939, the CR 42, with its 840hp Fiat A-74 RC 38 radial engine, was underpowered, attaining a top speed of only 280mph, and although maneuverability was still good there was little chance of such an outmoded aircraft holding its own. Despite disastrous clashes with Allied monoplanes over southern England and North Africa in 1940, and over Malta in 1941–42, the type was retained in service until the Italian surrender in 1943.

The failure of these designs was predictable, but their continued deployment is made even more surprising by the fact that monoplane fighters, incorporating many of the features of developing air technology, were available before the war began. Fiat had designed and flown the G50 Freccia as early as 1937, producing a single-seat, single-engined machine of some potential. With enclosed cockpit and retractable undercarriage, the prototype should have represented the jump in technology which both the Spitfire and Bf 109 were making at much the same time elsewhere. However, the G50 used the same radial engine as the CR 42, producing a top speed of only 293mph, and, as with so many other Italian designs, lacked destructive firepower. In addition, many pilots openly preferred the CR 32 which the G50 was meant to replace, and succeeded in forcing design changes which delayed production. As a result, fewer than 500 G50 fighters saw front-line service and, despite constant engine improvements in the G50 *bis* and *ter* models of 1940–41, the type did not contribute as much as it might. A follow-up design, the G55 Centauro, with license-built Daimler-Benz DB605A in-line engine and enhanced armament, never reached full production.

Above: In the foreground a Fiat G50 Freccia and behind a Me Bf 110 of ZG 26.

Fiat was not the only Italian firm to design fighters, nor the only one to explore the potential of monoplanes. Aeronautica Macchi, for example, provided three related models to front-line squadrons, the first of which, the MC 200 Saetta (Lightning), flew as early as December 1937. A highly maneuverable single-seat, single-engined interceptor, with retractable under-carriage and, at first, an enclosed cockpit, the MC 200 suffered from the usual Italian problems of lack of both power and heavy armament. Pilot conservatism also affected the design, obliging Macchi to reintroduce an open cockpit in the first production run. The machine was modified in 1940 under the new designation MC 202 Folgore (Thunderbolt), chiefly through the substitution of a German-designed DB 601 in-line engine which altered the airframe profile, but despite an increase of maximum speed to 370mph, overall performance was still moderate. It did not compare too badly with the RAF Hurricanes and P-40s. It was not until the development of the MC 205V Veltro (Grey-hound) in 1942 that the Regia Aeronautica achieved anything approaching parity with the best Allied fighters, but weak industrial back-up produced nothing but delays. With a DB 605A engine, giving a top speed of 399mph, and a reasonable armament fit of two German MG 151 wing-mounted cannon to augment the normal engine-mounted machine guns, the MC 205 could have tilted the balance of the air war in the Mediterranean, but few reached front-line squadrons before September 1943.

The same depressing pattern was followed with the third of the Italian fighter-design teams, that of the Officine Meccaniche 'Reggiane' SA, a subsidiary of Caproni. In 1938 they produced, in the Re 2000 Falco I (Falcon), a single-seat, single-engined monoplane of modern design. The familiar problems persisted. Despite maneuverability, the Re 2000 sported an underpowered engine (the 1025hp Piaggio PX1 *bis* RC 40 radial) which produced a disappointing top speed of 329mph and was, with the usual two engine-mounted machine guns, lightly armed. In 1940 a DB 601 in-line engine changed the shape of the airframe to produce the Re 2001 Falco II, but it was still outclassed. Further engine improvements, each of which put progressively more strain on an already overloaded aeroengine industry, produced the Re 2002 Ariete (Ram) and Re 2005 Sagittario (Archer) in 1941 and 1942 respectively, but few of these reached the front line before the Armistice. The Re 2005, capable of 421mph and fitted with three 20mm cannon as well as the normal machine guns, was in fact a potentially formidable aircraft, showing what could have been achieved. The few available examples, together with what remained of other designs, were transferred to the Cobelligerent Air Force in 1943 and fought on the Allied side.

Allied air superiority and technical expertise tended to disguise the continuing shortcomings and problems which the Italian aircraft suffered. Despite an apparent need, the Italians developed neither long-range fighters nor night fighters during World War II. They used existing models to carry out such roles, with a predictable lack of success.

Japan In December 1941 the Western Allies, catapulted into a war in the Far East by a series of coordinated Japanese attacks, were astounded by the air strength of their new enemy. Through a combination of factors, chiefly a belief that all Japanese equipment was based on designs imported from abroad and a rather arrogant feeling that anything from the East was by definition inferior, a dangerous degree of complacency had taken root in the 1920s and 1930s. This was shattered not only by the success of the aerial strike on Pearl Harbor (7 December) but also by the ease with which the aircraft of both the Imperial Army and Navy achieved air superiority throughout the Pacific and Far Eastern theaters. Owing to Pearl Harbor it is the navy machines which tend to be remembered in the West – aircraft such as the Mitsubishi A6M Zero-Sen fighter and the Aichi D3A dive bomber – but it is worth remembering that the types in service with the Japanese Army Air Force (JAAF) contributed just as much to the early victories. (It is difficult, and in many ways rather false, to draw a sharp distinction between Japanese army and navy aircraft – many of the latter were, for example, land-based – but only fighters which saw service with the JAAF are covered here. All army aircraft were characterized by a Kitai (Ki) or airframe number, while those used by the navy were assigned type numbers, so the distinction is at least logical on paper.)

All Japanese fighters, designed primarily to win and maintain air superiority by destroying enemy aircraft, had a high degree of combat maneuverability, often at the cost of speed, protection and firepower, and those on issue to the wartime JAAF were no exception.

One of the main problems, as with Italy, lay with the engines. Japan had done little experimental work before the war on streamlined in-line power packs and was forced to depend almost exclusively on big, heavy radials. Thus, despite some extremely graceful airframe designs, which provided maneuverability, the squat profile of a radial engine often affected speed to a significant extent. It also meant that, in order to mount such an engine, the rest of the aircraft had to be kept as light as possible to retain a useful power-to-weight ratio, and for this reason many Japanese fighters lacked such 'necessities' as self-sealing fuel tanks or armor protection. This was a factor which was to prove decisive, for although in 1941 the Allies were often caught with obsolete aircraft in the Far East and Pacific, once improved designs became available Japanese fighters were found to be extremely vulnerable as soon as they could be outperformed, and outmaneuvered by the opposition.

Kawasaki and Nakajima appear to have monopolized army fighter design and their ideas can be traced back at least to the early 1930s. Few of the early designs saw widespread service in the Pacific War – an indication of the rapid development of Japanese air technology so badly assessed by the Allies before 1941 – but one which did was the Kawasaki Ki-10 (Army Type 95 Fighter). This single-seat, single-engined biplane had all the characteristics of Japanese design – high maneuverability, under-powered 850hp in-line engine, low speed (about 250mph) and light armament (two 7.7mm Type 89 machine guns above the engine). However, the JAAF pilots liked it, and although monoplane designs were available as early as 1937, only two years after the prototype Ki-10 had first flown, the aircraft saw widespread service against the Chinese (after 1937) and the Soviets (1939). It surprised many with its agility but contributed significantly to Allied complacency. Its replacement, the Nakajima Ki-27 (Army Type 97 Fighter), followed much the same pattern, for although this was a monoplane with high maneuverability, it did not compare in other ways to Allied fighter designs. With fixed undercarriage, low speed (about 290mph), poor engine (650hp Army Type 97 radial) and inadequate armament (two 7.7mm machine guns above the engine) the Ki-27 (code named Nate by the Allies) appeared to be obsolete in 1941. However, it was used in quantity during the attacks upon the Philippines, Malaya and the Dutch East Indies in 1941–42 and was still being encountered as late as 1943 in the interceptor role.

The Ki-27 represented the first step in modernization for the JAAF, and the fact that it first flew as early as 1936 put it in the same design class as the Spitfire and Bf 109, but follow-up machines, which were more sophisticated, were coming off the drawing boards by 1939. In single-engined terms the most important was undoubtedly the Nakajima Ki-43 Hayabusa (Peregrine Falcon, or Oscar to the Allies). This single-seat monoplane, equipped with retractable undercarriage and 950hp Nakajima Ha-25 14-cylinder radial engine, promised a great deal, particularly in the traditional area of maneuverability. Unfortunately the prototype turned out to be heavy on the controls and rather disappointing, and many JAAF pilots preferred the Ki-27. This delayed deployment of what turned out to be one of the best combat fighters of World War II, for in the Ki-43-II series a 1105hp Ha 115 radial pushed the top speed to a more respectable 313mph, a special 'combat maneuver flap' under the wings gave tremendous agility and the addition of 12.7mm machine guns improved the armament fit. Some disadvantages remained, notably the notoriously poor protection, but the Oscar was produced in greater quantities than any other JAAF fighter of the war years (5919 by 1945) and was the preferred mount of many Japanese fighter aces.

The Ki-43 was complemented, and many of its shortcomings solved, by another Nakajima design produced in 1940. This was the Ki-44 Shoki (Devil-Queller or Tojo to the Allies), which was produced specifically to provide speed and climb rather than maneuverability. Pilot conservatism delayed full-scale production until mid-1942, but when the prototype first flew in August 1940 it was obvious that improvements had been made. Powered by a 1260hp Nakajima Ha-41 radial, the Ki-44 could achieve 360mph and a rate of climb of around 3900 feet per minute at prototype stage, and performance improved as the war progressed. Armament was still poor by Western standards (two 12.7mm machine guns in the wings and two 7.7mm, later improved to 12.7mm, in the fuselage) but it came into its own, particularly utilizing its rate of climb, against Allied bombers in 1944–45.

Meanwhile, Kawasaki had not been idle, producing its contribution to single-engined design in March 1941. This was the Ki-61 Hien (Swallow, or Tony to the Allies), a fighter based firmly upon expertise imported from Germany, Japan's Axis partner. It was designed around a license-built Daimler-Benz DB 601 in-line engine (so making it the only Japanese fighter of the war years to forsake the radial) and equipped initially with Mauser 20mm MG 151 cannon, brought into Japan by U-Boat. The result was promising. The prototype achieved 348mph and had a rate of climb of 2200 feet per minute. The Ki-61 entered squadron service in August 1942, and was encountered by the Allies for the first time eight months later over New Guinea. Dependence on a foreign-designed engine caused problems of production and reliability, leading eventually to the substitution of a 1500hp Mitsubishi Ha-112-11 14-cylinder radial in a desperate attempt to maintain deployment. This makeshift solution was given the new designation of Ki-100 and proved remarkably good, meeting Allied bombers and fighters with something approaching combat superiority. Unfortunately for the JAAF, the experiment was not tried until early 1945, so few Ki-100s entered service. By comparison, the Ki-61, despite the engine problems, completed a production run of over 2600 machines and saw combat in all areas of hostility.

The Ki-61 was joined in the later war years by yet another Nakajima model, the Ki-84 Hayate (Gale, or Frank to the Allies), and this was perhaps the best all-round fighter to equip the JAAF. First flown in March 1943, it sported a 1900hp Nakajima Ha-45 Model 11 18-cylinder radial engine fitted with fuel injection, and this gave it the enhanced speed of 392mph together with a rate of climb of 3600 feet per minute. Constant problems with the engines and a general decline in Japanese industrial standards as the Allies blockaded the home islands combined to undermine reliability, but when it entered service in April 1944 the Ki-84 outflew most of the opposition. Armament was for once quite respectable, comprising two 20mm Ho-5 cannon in the wings and a 12.7mm Type 103 on the fuselage top, and if this aircraft could have been produced in quantity, the air war in the Pacific might well have taken a different course. American bombing of the engine factories in 1944–45, together with a shortage of steel, prevented a large production run, but the Ki-84 remained as the zenith of Japanese single-engined fighter design during World War II.

The JAAF was, however, equally interested in twin-engined, long-range interceptors, particularly as most of their campaigns were fought over immense distances. As early as January 1939 Kawasaki had designed and test flown the attractive Ki-45 Toryu (Dragon Killer, or Nick to the Allies) in an attempt to satisfy this need. Powered by two 1080hp Mitsubishi Ha-102 14-cylinder radials, the production Ki-45-1 was capable of a top speed of 340mph, a rate of climb of 2300 feet per minute and, most important of all, a range of 1400 miles with full combat load. Once again, however, armament was inadequate (two 12.7mm machine guns in a fixed nose position and two 7.7mm manually operated in the rear cockpit) and engine problems persisted. Modifications and improvements delayed full production until late 1942 (and, even then, only 1698 Ki-45-1s were manufactured) and it was not a popular aircraft. Its major claims to fame are that, in the Kai-B, it provided the first Kamikaze or suicide planes and, in the Kai-C, the most effective Japanese night fighter. As the former was a sign of tactical desperation and the latter a hurried modification beset with problems, the Ki-45 was not a great success.

The same was true of a follow-up design, the Kawasaki Ki-102 (Allied code name Randy). This twin-engined, high-altitude interceptor, first flown in March 1944, never really had the time to be produced in quantity and, despite its sleek appearance, had little effect in its designated role. Powered by two 1500hp Mitsubishi Ha-112 14-cylinder radials, it could reach a top speed (in the c series) of 373mph, but it was only when modifications produced a night-fighter version, equipped with a rudimentary AI radar, forward-firing 30mm cannon and upward-firing 20mm, that it posed anything like a potential threat. But time had run out for the JAAF by then (mid-1945) and production was curtailed. It was a familiar story.

France The history of the French air force between the two World Wars is not a happy one, constituting a record of technological flair spoiled by staff indecision about air roles, a plethora of conflicting designs and, up to 1936, governmental indifference. Much of this resulted from the large number of small aircraft-producing companies which had grown up during World War I, for, despite a shortage of funds and resources in the 1920s and 1930s, they continued to compete for contracts which, in the end, they could rarely satisfy. Realizing this, the French government nationalized large portions of the industry in 1936. Although this sorted out many problems, the aircraft produced thereafter by SNCASO were not ready, in terms both of technology and numbers, for the war which broke out three years later. So desperate was the situation, in fact, that during the Munich Crisis of late 1938 the French were forced to order large numbers of Curtiss Hawk fighters and Douglas DB-7 light bombers from America as part of their rapid rearmament program.

French designs did exist, however, and in terms of fighters these varied widely in effectiveness and availability. The least effective was the oldest, reflecting the tremendous surge of effort in the aero industry after 1936, and was in fact a design taken over from a private company on nationalization. This was the Morane-Saulnier MS406, a single-engined, single-seat monoplane of somewhat foreshortened appearance, the only saving feature of which was that it was available in some numbers in 1939–40. Fitted with an 860hp Hispano-Suiza 12Y-31 in-line engine, the MS406 was underpowered and consequently rather slow at 304mph. Nor was it heavily armed, for with one 20mm Hispano-Suiza HS-9 cannon in the propeller hub and only two 7.5mm MAC machine guns in the wings, it could not achieve a great deal against the invading Luftwaffe in May-June 1940. Despite the fact that 19 out of 26 French fighter groups were MS406-equipped, the aircraft proved too slow to catch the Bf 109, less than adequate in terms of

combat maneuverability and too lightly armed to do much damage.

Even the more modern French designs had their drawbacks, exemplified by the early history and combat record of the second most available fighter in 1940, the Bloch MB-152. Designed by SNCASO and first flown as the MB-150 in October 1937, this single-seat, single-engined monoplane had already caused a scandal when the test pilot had refused to fly the prototype when it was first wheeled out in July 1936. Modifications had persuaded him to change his mind and by December 1938, when the first MB-152 took to the air, it looked as if an effective design had at last appeared. Powered by a 1080hp Gnome-Rhône 14N-25 radial, the 152 could achieve a top speed of 316mph and a rate of climb of about 2600 feet per minute. But production problems emerged, to the extent that when World War II began fewer than 100 examples were available, a proportion of which lacked propellers and gunsights. A massive production boost ensured a delivery of 593 MB-152s by May 1940, but teething troubles persisted, reducing their effectiveness against the invader. Surviving machines were taken over by the Luftwaffe for use as trainers.

The record of the third major design, the Dewoitine D520, is even more depressing, for although this was undoubtedly the best fighter available to the French, the familiar production problems almost prevented its appearance in the 1940 campaign. This could have been unfortunate, for this single-seat, single-engined monoplane was potentially an effective machine, large numbers of which could have tilted the balance against the Luftwaffe. Powered by a 910hp Hispano-Suiza 12Y-45 in-line engine, the D520 could achieve a top speed of 332mph and a rate of climb of 2350 feet per minute, while its armament fit of single 20mm cannon in the propeller hub and four 7.5mm machine guns in the wings, was respectable. In the event, a crash production effort did manage to provide 101 D520s by May 1940 and thereafter up to 10 a day (an incomparable record) were produced. The figures speak volumes for what might have been achieved prewar if the French aircraft industry had been properly organized. As it was, with a loss rate of 85 D520s for the destruction of 147 Luftwaffe aircraft in the short campaign of 1940, the fighter gave a good account of itself. It is therefore small wonder that both the Luftwaffe and the Vichy air force used the machine.

French indecision about air roles and confusion over needs is shown to good effect in the only twin-engined fighter available to them in 1939 – the Potez 63 series. Designed by Avions Henri Potez in answer to a 1934 specification for a two/three-seater long-range day and night fighter, the first production machine, the 630, appeared in May 1937, powered by two Hispano-Suiza 14 hbs radials. Top speed of 275mph was disappointing and the engines proved particularly unreliable, but when these were replaced by 700hp Gnome-Rhône 14M models to produce the 631, a very useful aircraft emerged. With a range of 1500 kilometers and a heavy armament fit of two 20mm cannon in the propeller hubs and anything up to seven 7.5mm machine guns in a variety of placings, the original specification would appear to have been satisfied. Unfortunately, the aircraft seemed so good that it was immediately modified to answer a host of other needs, so that, although a number of fighter-squadrons flew the 631 in 1940, the full potential of the series was never realized.

Australia The Australian armed forces during World War II were heavily dependent for equipment upon the British and Americans. Attempts were made, however, to manufacture indigenous weapons designs in certain key areas, in an effort to achieve some independence of supply. So far as aircraft were concerned, the Commonwealth Aircraft Corporation of Fishermen's Bend, Melbourne, was created as early as 1936, producing in March 1939 the single-engined Wirraway, a general-purpose machine based upon the American NA16 series of trainers. The experience thus gained was put to good effect in early 1942 when, under the pressure of Japanese advances and in the incredibly short period of 14 weeks, Commonwealth designed and flew a monoplane fighter. Known as the Boomerang, this was a single-seat, single-engined aircraft of sturdy appearance, powered by a 1200hp Pratt and Whitney Twin Wasp radial (the largest engine available) and with a top speed of only 305mph. Many felt that the design would be outclassed even before it entered service, but in fact it was a surprising success. Delivered to front-line squadrons in August 1942, the Boomerang proved particularly well suited to the rugged terrain of the southwest Pacific and, armed with two 20mm Hispano cannon and four .303-inch Browning machine guns, all in the wings, was capable of carrying out its interceptor role.

Czechoslovakia Although completely dismembered in March 1939, Czechoslovakia has a place in the history of fighter design because of the excellence of its prewar manufacturers. In 1933 the firm of ASPRL Avia produced what many regard to have been the best biplane interceptor of the time, affecting design trends elsewhere in Europe. Owing its origins to the B34, an experimental fighter which was used to test a variety of engine fits, the Avia B534 emerged to enjoy speed (252mph as early as 1933) and maneuverability. An Avia-built Hispano-Suiza 12 Ydrs in-line engine provided the power, while four 7.92mm MK 30 machine guns, two on the lower wings and two in blisters below the cockpit, constituted a useful punch. Modifications proved difficult, however, and although over 300 were in Czech service in 1938–39, they were by then outclassed by Luftwaffe monoplanes. Nevertheless, the Luftwaffe took them over as trainers and a number fought on the Eastern Front in the German-controlled Slovak fighter squadrons between 1941 and 1944.

Holland The greatest asset of the Dutch in airpower terms was the firm of N V Fokker – one of the most famous names in air history. Having gained a wealth of experience during World War I, building biplane fighters for the German air force, the firm went on to produce a whole series of clean, maneuverable and record-breaking designs during the interwar years. Two of these designs were fighters, one single-engined and one twin-engined, and although the Dutch air force was not prepared for a war in which Holland was supposed to be neutral, both did good service against hopeless odds in May 1940.

The single-engined fighter was the Fokker DXXI, designed initially for the Netherlands East Indies air force but taken into service not only by the Dutch domestic force but also by the Danes and Finns. First flown in March 1936, this single-seat monoplane was powered by an 830hp Bristol Mercury VIII radial engine, giving a top speed of 286mph and a rate of climb of about 2600 feet per minute. Armament was respectable for the time (four 7.92mm FN-Browning machine guns, two in the fuselage and two in the wings) but a number of archaic features, notably the fixed undercarriage, precluded a modernization program to keep it in line with other European designs. On 10 May 1940 29 DXXIs were available to help defend Holland; they fought well until their ammunition ran out two days later.

The twin-engined design, the Fokker G1, was no less remarkable. The prototype, featuring such innovations as eight nose-mounted machine guns, retractable undercarriage and twin-boom configuration, caused something of a stir at the 1936 Paris Air Show, even though it had yet to fly. Its design probably contributed to similar developments in France (the Breguet 690 series) and Germany (the Focke-Wulf Fw 189). Powered by two Bristol Mercury VIIIs, the G1 eventually achieved a top speed of 295mph and enjoyed a range in excess of 800 miles. It was supplied to Denmark and Sweden before being taken into Dutch service in 1938. Twenty-three G1s were available in May 1940 and 18 more, earmarked for export to Spain, were hurriedly pressed into service. All but one were destroyed.

Poland Created in 1928, the PZL (Panstwowe Zaklady Lotnicze, or National Aero Factory) of Poland produced a number of impressive aircraft during the interwar years. Their most innovatory designer, Zygmund Pulaski, began to develop fighters with the P7a, a distinctively gull-winged monoplane of remarkable quality. This was further developed to produce the P11, first flown in August 1931. Retaining the gull-wing configuration, the P11 eventually achieved a top speed of 242mph and a rate of climb of 2600 feet per minute – both reasonable figures for the time. Early models experimented with a variety of engines and it was not until the P11a went into production in June 1933 that a 500hp Polish-built Skoda Mercury IV 52 radial became standard fit. In 1934 the engine was lowered and the cockpit raised, thus enhancing pilot vision, to produce the P11c and, with two 7.7mm KM Wz 33 machine guns in the sides of the fuselage and two more in the wings, this was the main Polish fighter to face the Luftwaffe in 1939. By then it was, of course, obsolete, as its fixed undercarriage and open cockpit showed, but the 12 squadrons available did a tremendous job, destroying 126 enemy aircraft before being virtually wiped out. Replacement designs were on the drawing board or in prototype stage, but the defeat and subsequent dismemberment of Poland spelled the end of the PZL concern.

GROUND ATTACK

The concept of 'ground attack' – the use of aircraft to provide close support to troops in the battle area – had its origins, as did so many air power roles, in World War I. The advantages of such support are obvious: aircraft, operating in a three-dimensional setting, can spot targets from above and attack them instantaneously. In an offensive land situation they can weaken enemy defenses, support hard-pressed ground troops by destroying defensive positions and, if victory is gained, add to the general demoralization of the retreating enemy forces. Conversely, in a defensive battle they can contribute to the containment of an enemy by attacking his advancing troops, destroying his forward supply dumps, force concentration and communications and, if retreat is unavoidable, may protect the ground forces as they retire. Clearly, in both cases an element of local air superiority is essential, indicating the importance of interdependent air capability with fighters protecting the ground-attack machines, but enough may be achieved to justify the design and deployment of specialist battlefield-support aircraft.

This point was noted and acted upon during World War I, principally by the British and the Germans. The Royal Flying Corps appears to have been the first to appreciate ground attack, for during the Somme Offensive of 1916 British aircraft were used not only to locate enemy strongpoints but also to attack them using machine guns and light bombs. As the war progressed, this tactic was gradually extended into the enemy rear areas, but it was not until 1918 that specific air designs, incorporating a mixture of speed, hitting power and protection from ground fire, began to emerge for the nascent RAF. None of these entered squadron service before hostilities ceased, although their contribution to future campaigns was being seriously considered. The tank pioneer, Major-General J F C Fuller, for example, envisaged the use of fighter-bombers in his revolutionary 'Plan 1919,' for while the tanks found and exploited a line of least resistance in the enemy defenses, the RAF would contribute to the general chaos and demoralization by hitting the enemy 'brain' – his GHQ. As with the aircraft designs, this plan was destined never to be put into practice and the RAF, intent upon proving its independent viability, concentrated after 1918 upon strategic bombing, to the detriment of tactical roles. By 1939 the doctrines and the specialist designs needed for successful ground attack had been forgotten in Britain. A whole new learning process had to begin, under the pressure of war. It was to prove costly.

This was not the case with the Germans. They had been quick to realize the potential of the RFC attacks on the Somme and by 1917 had not only introduced very similar tactics but had also begun to develop heavily armed and armored ground-attack aircraft such as the Junkers CLI. Indeed, by the autumn of 1917 special Schlachtstaffeln (Battle Squadrons) had been organized on the Western Front with the specific duty of battlefield support and, when these were used in close cooperation with General von Hutier's stormtroops in March 1918, the Allies came dangerously close to defeat. The doctrine of infiltrating selected squads of heavily armed infantry through weak spots in the enemy lines, by-passing strongpoints and receiving close support from the air, was one of the most important tactical innovations of World War I. It was not forgotten by the Germans after 1918 and, when the new Luftwaffe was unveiled in 1935, ground-air cooperation was still a feature. Although von Hutier's stormtroops were soon to be replaced by tanks, the resultant policy of Blitzkrieg was heavily dependent upon air support for its speed and demoralizing power. (Air power was intended to supply heavy fire support in the event of artillery being unable to keep up with a rapid tank advance.) By 1939 air support for ground forces was a high priority in the Luftwaffe Air Field Manual, reflected in the aircraft designs available.

The same priorities were apparent in the Soviet air force, although appreciation of the importance of ground attack had not emerged before the late 1930s. Drawing lessons principally from the Spanish Civil War – a conflict in which strategic air power played an apparently minor part – the Soviet High Command had restructured their air elements as an adjunct to ground forces by 1939, stressing ground attack as an integral part of the process. This led inevitably to the development of specialist aircraft, which were to contribute significantly to the eventual Russian victory in World War II.

No other major air force appears to have afforded a great deal of thought or effort to battlefield support before World War II. The French had some experience from the previous conflict, but their aircraft designs were either unsatisfactory or poorly produced; neither the Italians nor the Japanese paid much attention to the role. Even the United States, whose air forces were to make great strides in ground-attack technique during World War II, had no specific aircraft designs available in 1941. The general recognition of these shortcomings was to constitute an important air lesson, leading the way to more balanced and effective air forces by 1945.

The Western Allies Both the British and the French were forced to recognize their lack of doctrines and aircraft designs applicable to

ground attack in May 1940. The military leaders of both countries had not appreciated the development of new techniques of war in Germany during the 1930s and had laid too much stress upon defensive roles for their forces – roles which, by definition, required only passive air support. Thus when the Blitzkrieg mix of fast-moving armor and aggressive, ubiquitous air power swept through France and the Low Countries, Allied surprise and confusion ensued. Despite Allied air supremacy in numerical terms, no aircraft existed which were designed to blunt an enemy advance. The machines hastily committed to ground attack were therefore, inevitably, massacred.

The RAF had virtually nothing suitable for the rediscovered role and was forced to commit as a last resort the Fairey Battle, a slow-moving, single-engined, unprotected light bomber which had first flown in March 1936. At the time it had been hailed as a revolutionary design, combining the clean lines of a monoplane with the power of a 1030hp Rolls-Royce Merlin II in-line engine, and was intended as a fast intruder bomber. Its range of just over 1000 miles and its bomb-carrying capacity of 1000 pounds seemed to make it well suited to this task, but by 1940 it was rapidly approaching obsolescence. Its speed of 241mph maximum made it highly vulnerable to interception by the new monoplane fighters and its lack of armor protection and good defensive armament made it a deathtrap in all but the most favorable air situations. A less suitable ground-support machine would be difficult to describe, yet the Battle was committed in large numbers to the task of trying to halt the German advance. In one strike alone, against pontoon bridges at Sedan, 40 Battles were lost without affecting the course of the campaign.

The French were slightly better off, in that they had more than one light-bomber design available, but the problems of role adaptability, combined with those of a confused air industry, produced the same outcome of defeat. This may be seen to good effect with the Potez 633, developed as a light bomber from the potentially effective 631 fighter design in 1936. The 633 maintained the top speed of its predecessor (273mph) as well as its engines (two 690hp Gnome-Rhône 14M radials) but, in order to save weight to enable a bomb load to be carried, lost most of its armament, having to make do with two 7.5mm machine guns only, one in the nose and one in the rear cockpit. The eventual bomb load of 1323 pounds was useful, but the absence of protection, both integral and from escorting fighters, made the 633 less than adequate when hurriedly thrown against battle-field targets.

The same was true of the Breguet series of light bombers, developed in 1938–39. First flown as an experimental fighter design in March 1938, the twin-engined, two-seat Breguet 690, fitted with 700hp Hispano-Suiza 14AB radials and capable of a top speed of 295mph, had seemed promising, but was soon bedevilled with problems. Breguet was not part of the state-owned SNCASO, so was not given aid or industrial priority and, in the best French traditions of the prewar period, the machine was accepted only as a light bomber. This eventually emerged as the 691 in March 1939, capable of carrying eight 110-pound bombs over 840 miles, but engine problems then emerged. Gnome-Rhône 14M7 radials were substituted to produce the 693 in October 1939, followed six months later by the 695 with imported Pratt and Whitney Twin Wasps. By June 1940 a total of 270 Breguets had been delivered to the Armée de l'Air, but the different engine fits posed maintenance problems and, despite a very heavy armament, particularly on the 693 (one 20mm cannon and two 7.5mm machine guns in the nose, one machine gun fitted to fire obliquely to the rear, two more in side nacelles and one in the rear cockpit) lack of air superiority doomed the design to destruction in the ground-attack role.

The final light bomber available was the SNCASO-produced Bloch 174. Powered by 1140hp Gnome-Rhône 14N radials, this twin-engined monoplane was capable of a top speed of 329mph and could carry eight 110-pound bombs over 1025 miles. In normal circum-stances, this would have been a useful addition to French air strength, but only 50 had been delivered by May 1940, the majority of which were wasted in the long-range reconnaissance missions so graphically described by Antoine de Saint-Exupéry in his book *Flight to Arras*.

Once the Franco-German Armistice had been signed at Compiègne on 22 June 1940, Britain was left alone to continue the war. At first, as the Battle of Britain took place, little thought was devoted to ground attack or to the lessons of the late campaign, but things began to change as the year drew to a close. The British offensive against the Italians in Libya (December 1940–February 1941) led to urgent calls for close air support, while at the same time the need for some sort of aggressive action in Europe was passed on to the RAF. In both cases the answer was seen in the development of 'fighter-bombers' – aircraft which would combine the speed and

firepower of the interceptor with the hitting power of the light bomber – but, as always, the designs were not available. Thus, in a move which was to characterize Allied reactions to ground attack throughout the war, a number of fighter aircraft were hurriedly modified to carry bombs or heavier caliber weapons. At first this was a barely satisfactory compromise, sacrificing speed and maneuverability for dubious destructive capability. It was not until a large measure of tactical air supremacy had been achieved, close ground-air cooperation established and more instantaneously destructive weapons developed that ground attack became a viable proposition.

These factors did not begin to come together before mid-1943, and until then ad hoc fighter modifications were all that were available. Some success was achieved in 1941 by re-arming the Hawker Hurricane, now fast approaching the end of its useful life as an interceptor, for both the Mark IIC (with four 20mm cannon and up to 1000 pounds of bombs on external wing racks) and IID (with two wing-mounted 40mm Vickers S guns) began to hurt enemy ground forces in North Africa, the latter in the novel 'tank-busting' role. In this they were aided by fighter-bomber variants of the American-produced P-40 series in RAF service – the Kittyhawk II/P-40F with six .50-inch machine guns and 1000 pounds of bombs and the Kittyhawk IV/P-40N with four .50s and up to 1500 pounds of bombs. By the time of Alamein (October 1942) these aircraft were causing significant damage to Axis ground targets.

But limitations were apparent. Whenever local ground or air defenses were active, the fighter-bombers suffered heavy casualties, lacking the capability to defend themselves adequately. If ground fire was heavy, armor protection to the aircraft was essential, but this merely increased weight and reduced speed; if enemy fighters appeared, the already-obsolete RAF machines were outclassed. In both instances the ground-attack mission was invariably abandoned in the interests of survival, leaving ground forces without support. Furthermore, even when an attack did go in, it was obvious that the weapons being used – cannon and machine guns for strafing and bombs for precise destruction – were inadequate. If a fighter-bomber was to be effective it had to destroy ground targets instantaneously, for there was often no time for a second try. A strafing run could achieve short-term results but, unless completely accurate, would not disable armored vehicles or knock out strongpoints. Theoretically the bombs should have done this, but the chances of placing a small piece of ordnance onto an equally small target with precision were remote. By 1942 it was only the sustained and repeated use of fighter-bombers – a use dependent upon air supremacy – which achieved results.

Attempts to solve some of these problems were made throughout the early years of the war. To achieve a mixture of speed, range and integral protection, more modern fighters were pressed into service. In some cases the results were poor, most notably when the Supermarine Spitfire was modified for ground attack in 1941. In the Mark V, powered by a 1440hp Merlin 45, a confusing mix of weapons fits (eight .303-inch machine guns in the VA, two 20mm cannon and four .303s in the VB and a choice of guns plus two 250-pound bombs in the VC) proved unsatisfactory, the loss of speed and maneuverability leaving the aircraft inferior to both the Bf 109F and Fw 190A. Similar shortcomings affected the Westland Whirlwind when a 500-pound bomb-carrying capacity was introduced at much the same time. It was not until inherently more robust twin-engined fighters had been added to the list that speed and hitting power began to be successfully combined. The Bristol Beaufighter, for example, did not lose its chief characteristics of strength and maneuverability when underwing bomb racks were added, while the De Havilland Mosquito fighter-bomber variant, the FBVI, took the state of the art to new heights. Four 20mm cannon beneath the cockpit, four .303-inch machine guns in the nose and up to 1000 pounds of bombs, carried both internally and externally, gave the aircraft tremendous hitting power without leading to a loss of speed (the FBVI could still achieve 380mph).

Even the Mosquito could not solve the most persistent problem – that of poor bomb accuracy. Fortunately for the Allies, a solution appeared in mid-1943 in the shape of the unguided rocket missile. Comprising a length of tubing with fins for stabilization and a propellant at one end, and an armor-piercing or high explosive warhead at the other, this simple weapon substituted concentrated, 'swamping' fire for random bomb accuracy. Its introduction, coming at a time when Allied air supremacy was beginning to appear over Europe and the Mediterranean, revolutionized the ground-attack role. Fitted in groups of four on special racks beneath each wing, the RAF's 3-inch rockets were immediately added to all existing fighter-bomber variants. Aircraft such as the

Hurricane and Beaufighter received a new lease of life and the Mosquito suddenly blossomed into a truly formidable ground-attack machine. The rockets' real contribution to victory, however, came when they were added to the unsuccessful fighter designs from Hawker, for both the Typhoon and Tempest proved well suited to modification. These aircraft, combining robustness, speed, survivability and fire-power, were used to particular effect in support of the Allied forces in Europe after June 1944. With forward air controllers accompanying the ground troops and calling up rocket strikes from a 'cab rank' of aircraft available, instantaneous and destructive missions could be flown, knocking out enemy armor, strongpoints and lines of communication. Air supremacy was still essential, but the RAF had come a long way since the disasters of 1940. The Typhoon was in fact first modified to carry two 250-pound bombs under the wings in late 1942 and the Mark IB's armament fit was gradually increased as the war progressed, finally reaching a total of 2000 pounds, the bulk of which was made up of rockets (four under each wing). Ground-attack missions carried out by such aircraft included those against the Dieppe/Caudecote and Cap de la Hague radar stations on 2 and 5 June 1944, just before D-Day, as well as the destruction of the HQ of the German Fifteenth Army at Dordrecht on 24 October. The Tempest was less important – fewer examples were produced – but with a similar offensive armament fit it joined its stablemate in providing one of the most effective ground-attack forces ever established.

The United States Army Air Force followed an almost identical process of development. When America entered the war in 1941 she possessed no land-based ground-attack aircraft, although it is interesting to note that two types of dive bomber were available. The first of these was designed as a carrier-based aircraft, the Douglas SBD Dauntless, but the army had acquired nearly 800 as the A-24. First flown in July 1935, the Dauntless could reach a top speed of only 245mph but was reasonably armed for the time – two .50-inch machine guns in the nose, two .30-inch machine guns in the rear cockpit and a bomb load of up to 1500 pounds. By 1941, however, it was felt to be obsolete and, although the SBD was to contribute enormously to the naval war in the Pacific, the A-24 version was not a major weapon. It was replaced in mid-1941 by the Vultee A-31 Vengeance, a dive bomber built in 1940 to a British specification, although many people began seriously to doubt the efficacy of dive bombers once the German Junkers Ju 87 Stuka suffered casualties over Britain (1940) and Russia (1941). As a result, nearly all the A-31s were passed over to the RAF, who used them principally in the Far East in a variety of tactical roles. Its lack of speed (279mph maximum) and comparatively poor bomb load made it a less than adequate ground-attack machine.

This left the Americans facing similar problems to those of the British in 1941–42, and their initial solution was exactly the same – the modification of existing fighters to produce fighter-bombers. Thus the Lockheed P-38 Lightning was fitted with inner-wing pylons for 1000 pounds of bombs as early as March 1942 to produce the F model. This retained a top speed of over 380mph and enjoyed both effective range and good survivability, making it quite a success in the first phase of ground-attack development. North American followed with modifications to the P-51 Mustang, actually producing a specific fighter-bomber design, known to the USAAF as the A-36. Six .50-inch machine guns and wing racks for two 500-pound bombs gave a reasonable hitting power, but the problems of accuracy and destructive capability remained. Once again, an answer was found in the development of unguided rockets – in the American case of 5-inch caliber – and when wing racks were added to the Republic P-47, producing the D model in 1943 and the N two years later, a most effective ground-attack aircraft finally emerged. These versions of the Thunderbolt flew in all theaters of war, having much the same impact as the Typhoon and Tempest and emphasizing to the Americans the need for multirole air capability. With eight .5-inch Colt-Browning machine guns in the wings (the firing of which was likened to 'driving a five-ton truck straight at a wall at 60mph') and three or five racks for bombs or rockets up to 2500 pounds, the P-47D and N ground-attack variants were formidable machines.

The Soviet Union The prewar Soviet decision to develop a tactical air force, geared almost entirely to the needs of ground forces, produced the doctrines and aircraft designs applicable to battlefield support far earlier than was the case in the West. Indeed, by the time of the German invasion in June 1941, sufficient background work had been done to avoid the traumas which affected the British and Americans at much the same time, and although the Red Air Force was virtually annihilated during the early months of war on the Eastern Front, the experience and

expertise already amassed acted as an invaluable base which the enemy could not destroy. By 1945, after four years of further development and new aircraft designs, the Soviets possessed the strongest tactical-support air force in the world, having defeated their only serious rival.

The process of development was never easy, however, as the aircraft available in 1941 serve to show. The decision to abandon strategic air power was taken only in 1939, and although various design bureaus were quick to produce purpose-built ground-attack machines, quantity manufacture took time to organize. During the interim the Russians were forced to follow the familiar path of modification to existing fighter and light-bomber designs, with all its attendant problems. The oldest machines thus converted to the fighter-bomber role were the stubby Polikarpov fighters, the I-15 and I-16. The former had first taken to the air as long ago as 1933 and suffered all the disadvantages of its age, but when a 1000hp M-63 radial engine was introduced in early 1939 this apparently obsolete biplane received a remarkable boost. Known as the I-153, its robustness and survivability, already proved in Spain, lent it naturally to fighter-bomber duties and its armament fit was enhanced accordingly to include RS-82 unguided rockets (the first to enter service in any air force) and underwing 165-pound bombs as well as its normal four 7.62mm machine guns. Used in its new role in Manchuria in 1939 it proved so successful that it replaced the similarly modified I-16 monoplane in some squadrons. Both Polikarpov designs were still in front-line service in June 1941, being flown in an extremely hostile air environment against German ground targets with amazing courage but predictable results. At the same time long-range bombers such as the Ilyushin Il-4 twin-engined machine, designed in the mid-1930s to answer an air role no longer seen as important, were also converted to ground attack, but with little real effect. Specific designs were clearly essential.

Fortunately for the Soviets, development of such designs was already well advanced, having been initiated as early as 1937 with the Sukhoi Su-2 single-engined, two-seat tactical attack bomber. Although this predated the restructuring of the Red Air Force and so tended to reflect outmoded air thinking, the Su-2 did have a number of design features which were to be refined and developed over the next few years. Powered by a 1000hp Shvetsov M-88B radial engine, it enjoyed the reasonable top speed (for time and type) of 288mph, a range of 746 miles and a bomb or rocket-carrying capacity of

1323 pounds. Armament was a little inadequate, comprising four 7.62mm ShKAS machine guns in the wings and one in a manually operated dorsal turret, but most significantly of all it had substantial armor protection, particularly in the crew and engine compartments. This enabled it to survive a certain degree of ground fire, even at low level, and although the majority of the 1500 Su-2s in front-line service in 1941 were eventually destroyed in action, they did contribute to the early campaign of Russian defense.

The lessons drawn from the development and use of the Su-2 were put to good effect by the design bureau of Sergei Ilyushin in 1939 when they produced the remarkable Il-2 Bronirovanni Shturmovik (armored attacker) single-engined close-support aircraft. First flown in December 1939, the single-seat prototype was not perfect, for despite a clean aerodynamic shape and a 1300hp M-38 in-line engine, it proved to be underpowered, capable of a top speed of only 251mph. The reason for this was that Ilyushin had designed what was, to all intents and purposes, a flying battleship, complete with unprecedented armor-plate protection and a formidable array of weapons (two 20mm ShVAK cannon and two 7.62mm ShKAS machine guns in the wings, plus underwing racks for eight RS-82 rockets and four 220-pound bombs). A more powerful engine – the 1680hp AM-38 – pushed the speed up to a more useful maximum of 281mph and quantity production was undertaken. The first examples reached front-line squadrons in time for the early campaigns of 1941, indicating with their mix of armament, survivability and range (373 miles with full load) that an effective ground-attack machine had emerged.

In spring 1942 a conference was held between the design team and representatives of the combat pilots to discuss possible modifications. A number of suggestions were made and acted upon to produce the Il-2M3. The cockpit, with its armor plating, was redesigned to make room for a second crew member, armed with his own 12.7mm machine gun, and VYa 23mm cannon replaced the ShVAKs in the wings. The engine was boosted to 1750hp by adjusting the compression ratio of the AM-38 and, although this did little to alter either speed or range, the Red Air Force had now acquired a superb machine. Il-2M3s were used from August 1942 exclusively for ground attack. Their tactics varied according to the circumstances. The most favored approach in open country and against enemy vehicles or infantry was for a pair of Shturmoviks to go in low (between 15 and 30 feet above the

ground) and release their weapons horizontally. Against more substantial targets, such as buildings or prepared positions, up to 12 Il-2s, with fighter escort, would attack in the conventional dive-bombing way, placing bombs or rockets with as much accuracy as possible. But the most important and effective tactic was undoubtedly the 'Circle of Death.' The Il-2s would cross the front line to either side of the assigned target, circle round and come in from behind. This circle would be repeated by each aircraft until ammunition was expended, so producing a situation in which at least one Il-2 was attacking the target for anything up to 30 minutes. This proved particularly effective against tanks; in the Battle of Kursk in mid-1943, for example, the German 9th Panzer Division lost 70 tanks in 20 minutes to the 'Circle of Death,' and this was by no means an isolated case. To the Soviets the Il-2 was the most important aircraft of World War II, a belief reflected in the fact that its replacement, the Il-10, with 2000hp AM-42 engine, top speed of 315mph and bomb or rocket load of 2200 pounds, was merely the next logical development stage. The Il-10 did in fact enter squadron service in 1944, but was overshadowed for the rest of the war in Europe by its predecessor.

A less specific ground-attack design, but one which supported the Il-2 throughout the war on the Eastern Front, was developed by the design bureau of V M Petlyakov in 1938. Intended initially as a high-altitude fighter, the twin-engined, three-seater Pe-2 first flew sometime in 1939 and was quickly modified to become an attack bomber. Powered by two Klimov 1100hp M-105R in-line engines, it enjoyed the very good top speed of 336mph, a range of over 900 miles and a useful bomb load of 2200 pounds, carried either externally or in special bays built into the rear fuselage and engine nacelles. Defensive armament was not heavy, comprising only four 7.62mm ShKAS machine guns in the early production models, and bombing accuracy was not good from high altitude, leading to the addition of dive brakes just before squadron delivery in August 1940. Armor protection was added in 1942 and the machine was upgunned to produce the Pe-3 *bis*, ostensibly a fighter but used extensively for ground attack up to 1945. Armament by then consisted of two 7.62mm ShKAS machine guns in the nose and two in beam positions, one 12.7mm BS machine gun in the cockpit, one in a dorsal turret and one in a ventral position, as well as up to 6600 pounds of bombs. The Pe-2 and Pe-3 were therefore formidable machines.

An estimated 11,400 were built, leaving little industrial capacity to spare for the development of replacement designs.

In some respects this was a pity, for another twin-engined attack bomber was available but did not see the action it deserved. This was the Tupolev Tu-2, test flown as early as October 1940. It was a sound, robust and capable design, powered by two 1850hp Shvetsov ASh-82FN radial engines. It was capable of carrying up to 5000 pounds of bombs over 1550 miles and could achieve a top speed of 340mph. In addition, armament was good (one 12.7mm BS machine gun in the cockpit and one each in mid-fuselage dorsal and ventral positions, as well as two 20mm ShVAK cannon in the wing roots) and armor-plate protection was included. But the Petlyakov designs took production precedence and fewer than 1000 Tu-2s entered squadron service before 1945. The fact that the Soviets could afford virtually to ignore a ground-attack aircraft which most Western air forces would have welcomed with open arms merely reinforces the success of the Il-2 and Pe-2/Pe-3 designs.

Germany From its secret inception in the early 1930s, the Luftwaffe was always strongly geared toward tactical strike support of ground forces. At first the aim seems to have been the development of a balanced air force, capable of both strategic and tactical roles, but time, industrial capacity and a strong army lobby ensured an emphasis upon ground attack, particularly after June 1936 when the Luftwaffe's chief proponent of strategic bombing, Lieutenant-General Walther Wever, was killed in a flying accident. Such an emphasis suited Hitler, who saw his conquests being achieved quickly using concentrated ground and air forces on the battlefield, and by 1939 the Luftwaffe was potentially strong in two main ground attack areas – the Stukageschwader (dive-bomber groups) and Schlachtgeschwader (battle or attack groups). Both had their distinctive, specially designed aircraft, some of which dated back to before the official establishment of the Luftwaffe in 1935.

The Stukageschwader concept had always taken priority, partly because of experiences during 1918 and partly because some of the most influential men in the Luftwaffe hierarchy – notably Hermann Goering and Ernst Udet – were committed advocates of the dive bomber. A program of development was initiated in 1933, to cover two distinct phases. In the first, known as the Sofort-Programm (immediate program)

a single-seat biplane was to be designed and produced as quickly as possible, purely as an interim measure to equip the first dive-bomber squadrons. While this was going on, however, a Sturzbomber program was to be followed through to produce a modern, advanced warplane equipped with all the latest dive-bombing aids and with performance equal to that of contemporary fighters. This design would, it was hoped, be sufficient to see the Luftwaffe through the campaigns of conquest. Only when that program had been completed would the Schlachtflugzeug machines be called for, and relatively small, heavily armed and armored close-support aircraft developed. It was an ambitious projection.

The specifications of the Sofort-Programm were answered by two aviation firms – Fieseler Flugzeugbau and Henschel Flugzeugwerke – who produced the Fi 98 and Hs 123 biplanes respectively. The Henschel design was obviously superior and quickly accepted for production, despite the need for extensive modification when two of the prototypes failed to recover from diving attacks. First flown in May 1935, the Hs 123 single-seat, single-engined biplane turned out to be well suited to its role. Its 880hp BMW 132 Dc radial engine gave a top speed of 213mph and an operational range of 530 miles. Armament comprised two 7.92mm MG 17 machine guns in front of the pilot and underwing racks were fitted to take four 110-pound bombs. The production version, the Hs 123A, was used in Spain during the Civil War and was delivered to the first of the Luftwaffe's Stukagruppen in 1937. Despite enthusiastic reports from Spain, the interim nature of the Hs 123 was adhered to and the design had been virtually phased out by the beginning of World War II. Such was the success of the few remaining examples in Poland, however, that they were retained as a Schlacht unit, operating in the Balkans in 1941 and even in the USSR until they were finally wiped out in 1944. The Hs 123 was one of the last biplanes to see front-line service.

Work on the Sturzbomber program also began in 1933, although the official specification was not issued to Arado, Heinkel and Junkers until January 1935. The result was a foregone conclusion, for Junkers had been developing a single-engined monoplane dive bomber for some time. Their design was chosen without serious competition in mid-1935 and was to become one of the most famous and evocative aircraft of the wartime Luftwaffe – the single-engined, two-seat Ju 87, universally known by the abbrevia-

Above: A Stuka formation over the desert.

tion of its role name – the 'Stuka.' It was an odd design, with characteristic angled wings and fixed spatted undercarriage. First flown in May 1935, the prototype, with Rolls-Royce Kestrel V in-line engine and twin tail fins, was not very satisfactory, suffering overheating problems and tail-assembly failure which led to its destruction. A second prototype adopted the Junkers Jumo 210A engine and single tail-fin design which was to remain basically the same thereafter. Production began in 1937 with the Ju 87A, and early examples were used to equip home-based Stukagruppen and the Condor Legion in Spain in the same year. Engine problems persisted, however, leading to the substitution of a 1100hp Jumo 211 Da to produce the Ju 87B in 1938, and it was this model which contributed so brilliantly to the Blitzkrieg campaigns of 1939–40. With a top speed of 242mph, an operational range of 373 miles and an armament fit of two 7.92mm MG 17s in the wings, with another in the rear cockpit, one 1102-pound bomb on special cradle beneath the fuselage and two 110-pound bombs under each wing, it did not seem to be a natural war winner, lacking both speed and protection. But in the absence of serious opposition over Poland, Scandinavia, the Low Countries and France, the steep dive and screeching air brakes of the Stuka struck terror into enemy ground forces, affecting their psychology as much as

their military hardware. Success continued under similar conditions in Greece, Crete, parts of North Africa and the early campaigns in Russia, up to 1942, when mounting casualties, presaged by the destruction of the Stukagruppen in the Battle of Britain (1940), led to a serious reassessment of the dive bombers' role.

As a result most Ju 87s after 1942 were transferred to Schlacht duties, principally on the Eastern Front. The D model, with 1300hp Jumo 211J engine, top speed of 250mph and enhanced armor and armament protection, was used initially, having been developed as early as 1940, but it was not until the G appeared in 1943 that a new lease of life was afforded to what had rapidly become a dangerously obsolete aircraft. The G was designed specifically as a 'tank buster,' being a conversion of the D-5 model to take a pair of underwing 37mm Flak 18 anti-tank cannon. It was still very slow and fell easy prey to Russian fighters by now enjoying air supremacy, but in the right hands the Ju 87G was capable of inflicting enormous damage. Hans-Ulrich Rudel was the greatest Stuka pilot of them all. Flying a Ju 87G-1 for much of his career on the Eastern Front, he was eventually credited with the destruction of 519 Soviet tanks.

The fact that both the Hs 123 and Ju 87 transferred from dive bombing to close-support Schlacht duties implies that the final part of the Luftwaffe's prewar projection was never fully realized. The official specification, calling for a small, heavily armed and armored close-support aircraft, was issued in 1937 and both Focke-Wulf and Henschel produced designs. But problems over performance – small aircraft demand small engines and by definition they produce little power – together with a production emphasis upon the Ju 87, led to delays and neither design was really given the impetus it deserved until it was almost too late.

The Focke-Wulf design was the twin-engined, three-seat Fw 189 *Uhu* ('Owl'), an aircraft of unusual twin-boom configuration with extensively glazed central crew nacelle. First flown in July 1938, its potential was underestimated when its two 465hp Argus As 410 A-1 in-line engines produced a top speed of only 215mph. Production was grudgingly authorized, however, with the first Fw 189As entering squadron service, chiefly as tactical reconnaissance machines, in September 1940. It was not until the invasion of Russia in June 1941 that the aircraft came into its own, displaying a toughness and maneuverability which suited it well to close support. Armed with one 7.92mm MG 17 in each wing root, two 7.92mm MG 81 machine guns in the rear cockpit and underwing racks for four 110-pound bombs, it was able to deliver telling blows against enemy ground targets, especially infantry, and survive defending fire. Unfortunately, most Fw 189s were built in occupied France, so production ceased abruptly in 1944 as the Allies took over the factories, and only 840 examples saw service.

The winner of the 1937 Schlacht specification was in fact the Henschel Hs 129, a single-seat, twin-engined aircraft of more conventional configuration. It too had its problems, having been fitted originally with the same underpowered engines as the Fw 189 and, although production was authorized after flight trials in 1939, the early Hs 129A models were almost all turned over to the Rumanian air force in 1941 for service on the Eastern Front. The Henschel design team did not give up, however, and, after a number of experiments, succeeded in fitting captured 690hp Gnome-Rhône 14M radials to the basic design. This provided enough power to give a top speed of 253mph and, aware of the shortcomings of other available Schlacht aircraft, production of the newly designated Hs 129B went ahead. It turned out to be a remarkable aircraft, particularly on the Eastern Front where, by 1944, it was the most effective antitank machine in service with the Schlachtgeschwader. Its main features were its superb survivability – the pilot occupied a very small, heavily armored cockpit – and its flexibility as a weapons platform. Normal armament consisted of two 7.92mm MG 17s and two 20mm MG 151/20s, usually in side-fuselage fairings, plus two wing-carried 110-pound bombs, but as the war progressed a wide range of weapons, principally of the antitank variety, were fitted. These included the first 30mm cannon to see service in any air force, 8.8-pound SD4 hollow-charge bombs and 280mm rocket tubes. Most impressive of all, however, was the single 7.5cm BK antitank cannon, slung beneath the forward fuselage with barrel protruding far beyond the nose of the aircraft. This formidable weapon could literally slice through the thickest armor then in Russian use, and the Hs 129Bs so equipped inflicted heavy damage right up to the end of the war. But there were never enough of them, since full production had begun too late to swing the balance of the air war.

With so few purpose-built Schlacht aircraft available, particularly during the middle years of the war, it is hardly surprising to find that the Luftwaffe, in common with its enemies in the West, experimented with a variety of fighter-bomber modifications, none of which was sufficiently successful to preclude the Fw 189 or Hs 129 from front-line service. As early as 1940–41, for example, the Henschel Hs 126, a high-wing, single-engined army cooperation machine, was fitted with the means to carry a single 110-pound bomb beneath the fuselage, and was actually used in the close-support role as late as 1944, but with predictably mediocre results. Similar modifications were made to the Bf 109E and F models, with subsequent loss of speed which made them easy prey to interceptors, and to the Bf 110C, again with poor results. The Fw 190F, with its heavy armament fit and centerline 3968-pound bomb, was slightly more successful, as was the Junkers Ju 88 when transferred from its bombing duties to close support, but all such conversions merely showed the failure of the Luftwaffe's prewar ground-attack development projection. Too much emphasis was placed upon the Ju 87, even after its vulnerability had been made obvious, and too little upon the Fw 189 and Hs 129. As early as 1942 the Luftwaffe was struggling to satisfy demands for close support, its most important declared role.

BOMBERS

The first recorded example of aerial bombardment took place in the summer of 1911, when Italian aircraft, sent to North Africa to fight the Turks, dropped modified grenades onto an enemy camp near Tripoli. Damage was slight and world reaction insignificant, but an important air role had been initiated. As always, it was to take World War I for the role to become firmly established.

Between 1914 and 1918 two distinct types of aerial bombardment emerged. The first, practiced eventually by all combatants, involved the fairly simple concept of dropping high explosives onto enemy rear areas, hitting lines of supply, command networks, fuel dumps and military concentrations. This became known as tactical or, if it entailed isolating enemy forces from their support echelons, interdiction bombing. Exactly where close support/ground attack ended and tactical bombing began was, and often still is, a debatable point. For purposes of clarity and convenience, a distinction may be drawn between attacks in direct support of forces actually on the battlefield (ground attack) and independently mounted air assaults designed to weaken or destroy the enemy before he enters the battle area (tactical/interdiction bombing). In many ways it is a question of distance from the front line, and for this reason aircraft-design requirements for both roles tend to be similar, stressing maneuverability, weapon-carrying capacity and survivability. However, tactical bombers do require, in addition, the ability to carry large bomb loads relatively long distances, if only to avoid the necessity for repeated attacks and to enhance flexibility. By 1939 most of these specifications had been recognized by the major air forces and purpose-built aircraft, usually multiengined to give the required performance, had appeared. World War II was to witness refinement to this role rather than initiation or rediscovery.

The second form of aerial bombardment established by 1918 did not enjoy such universal support during the interwar period. The concept of strategic bombing – aerial attacks upon the enemy homeland, designed to destroy industry and demoralize civilian populations – was in fact seriously adhered to by only two of the major air forces in 1939: the RAF and the United States Army Air Corps. This was surprising. The potential of strategic bombing had been explored as early as 1917–18 by the Germans when they had sent Gotha and 'Giant' bombers against targets in London and southern England. A worrying degree of civilian panic had occurred as, for the first time, the noncombatant sectors of society found themselves in the 'front line,' and this had manifested itself in a significant diminution of war production. Furthermore, very few of the bombers had been destroyed by defending air or ground forces, implying that cities were completely vulnerable target areas. It did not take long for a number of theorists, notably Guilio Douhet in Italy, Brigadier General 'Billy' Mitchell in America and Lord Trenchard in Britain, to postulate that the bomber was a potential war-winning weapon; if raids could be sustained, industrial plant would be destroyed and civilian morale undermined, to the extent that the enemy would be unable to continue the war. So persuasive did these arguments appear that by 1939 it was a widely held fear, particularly in Britain, that city areas were doomed to destruction within days of the outbreak of war.

In retrospect, it is easy to appreciate why this should be so. Most of Britain's centers of population and administration were concentrated in the southeast, within easy flying distance of European airfields and, of course, the experiences of 1917–18 were fresh in the collective memory. This does not explain why the RAF was intent upon providing the capability to inflict the same sort of damage upon its enemies. For this, one has to go back to the establishment

of the RAF as an independent force in 1918, when, in direct response to the German raids on Britain, the specific role of mounting a strategic counteroffensive was afforded to it. This was never, in fact, carried out before the end of World War I, but was used as the weapon to counter interwar moves to disband the RAF. Thus, by 1939, merely in order to survive as an independent entity, the RAF had to emphasize its strategic bombing capability, calling for the design and deployment of long-range, self-defending bombers which could fly by day to destroy the heart of the enemy. Similar calls were beginning to be heard from the USAAC, although in this case the reason lay in an attempt to gain rather than preserve air-force independence.

Other countries did not stress strategic bombing at all, and few had any suitable aircraft designs available by 1939. Both the Germans and the Russians had made the conscious decision to concentrate upon tactical support roles for their air forces; Japan was oriented toward naval aviation. Only France and Italy had toyed with the idea of strategic capability, but neither had developed really viable machines. The concept, and the relevant aircraft development, was left to the British and Americans.

Britain With the emphasis so firmly upon strategic bombing, it might be expected that the RAF was well equipped with long-range, multi-engined aircraft in 1939. This was not the case. Although the financial stringency of the inter-war years had been relaxed in 1936 and an expansion to the RAF authorized, most of the bomber designs available at the beginning of World War II were light or medium models, with restricted range and/or bomb-carrying capacity. Four-engined, long-range 'heavy' bombers, despite substantial development programs, were not yet in front-line service.

The first of the light bomber designs to emerge during the 1936 Expansion Scheme was the single-engined Fairey Battle, used so disastrously for ground attack in 1940. Almost immediately, it was joined by the more promising Bristol Blenheim, a twin-engined monoplane which had started life as a private civil-transport venture. Its most remarkable feature when first flown in June 1936 was its speed, for at 260mph the prototype was faster than most of the fighters then in RAF service. The Air Ministry immediately ordered 150 of the snub-nosed Mark I and these began to equip home-based squadrons in 1937. Powered by two 840hp

AIR

Bristol Mercury VIII radial engines, the Mark I, together with its longer-nosed stablemate the Mark IV, enjoyed an operational range of 1125 miles carrying a bomb load of 1000 pounds, figures which tied the aircraft inexorably to the tactical bombing role. Defensive armament comprised one fixed forward-firing .303-inch Browning and one dorsal turret-mounted .303-inch Vickers K machine gun. The Blenheim Mark IV, with redesigned asymmetric nose and 920hp Mercury XV engines, appeared in 1938 to give an enhanced speed of 266mph and extended range of 1460 miles, but armament and bomb load remained virtually unchanged. These variants, each with three-man crew, saw useful service as tactical bombers, chiefly in North Africa, up to 1942.

In the medium-bomber range, which of necessity included aircraft earmarked for strategic bombing, the designs were initiated as early as September 1932 by Air Ministry Specification B.9/32. Two twin-engined monoplane bombers emerged in answer to this in 1936 and both were to be pressed into strategic service in the early war years. The first to be test flown (by a margin of six days) was the Vickers Wellington, a design based very much upon a single-engined general-purpose bomber, the Wellesley, which had first flown in June 1935 and was itself to see active service in East Africa in 1940–41. The Wellesley had introduced some novel features to bomber design, notably the ingenious geodetic, web-like airframe construction invented by Barnes Wallis. This was found to impart enormous strength to the aircraft and was used to equal effect in the Wellington when the prototype first flew on 15 June 1936. Powered by two 1000hp Bristol Pegasus radial engines, the Mark I entered squadron service in October 1938. With a top speed of 235mph, and a range in excess of 1200 miles with a bomb load of 4500 pounds, this was clearly a bomber of some potential. But defensive armament was weak – twin .303-inch Brownings in nose and tail turrets – and when the Wellington was used for daylight attacks against German shipping in 1939 casualties were heavy. Nevertheless, the design was eventually taken to 14 marks, gradually increasing speed to over 255mph and defensive armament to a more respectable six or eight Brownings (four of which were together in a power-operated rear turret) and the aircraft was still in operational service as late as 1945. A successor, the Warwick, was produced to increase range and bomb load but, by the time it was ready for squadron delivery in 1942, the four-engined designs had taken precedence. It

was used instead as a transport and anti-submarine patrol aircraft, leaving the Wellington to make its mark as a night bomber, a role for which it had never in fact been designed but for which its range, bomb load and survivability made it well suited.

The second bomber to result from Specification B.9/32 was the Handley Page Hampden. This aircraft, with twin 965hp Bristol Pegasus XVIII radials and long, thin fuselage, was an unorthodox design which seemed barely capable of withstanding active service, but the Air Ministry was sufficiently impressed by the maiden flight on 21 June 1936 to order 180. In retrospect it was not a sound decision. Although both speed (265mph maximum) and bomb load (up to 4000 pounds, some of which was carried externally) seemed adequate, the four-man crew was cramped, range was comparatively poor (1200 miles with 4000 pounds of bombs) and defensive armament was inadequate (fixed, forward-firing .303-inch machine gun in front of the pilot, plus twin Vickers in dorsal and ventral positions). Casualties were heavy during the early daylight raids of 1939, and although a better survivability rate was experienced once the decision was taken to switch to night raids in 1940, the Hampden never achieved a great deal, chiefly, one would imagine, because strategic bombing was not really its intended role beyond a certain, very restricted range. An attempt to improve performance by substituting 1000hp Napier Dagger in-line engines (so producing the Hereford) was unsuccessful and all variants had been phased out of front-line service by 1942.

The only purpose-built 'heavy' bomber in service in 1939 was the Armstrong Whitworth Whitley, produced in response to Air Ministry Specification B.3/34 and first flown, before either the Wellington or Hampden, in March 1936. A twin-engined, five-seat monoplane with a very thick wing, the positive incidence of which caused a characteristic 'nose heavy' flying attitude, the Whitley I was powered by 795hp Armstrong Siddeley Tiger IX in-line engines. It began to equip front-line squadrons in March 1937 and appeared to be a formidable machine. With top speed of 220mph, normal operational range of 1650 miles and maximum bomb-carrying capacity of 7000 pounds, it certainly answered the original specification; as with so many of its contemporaries it was under-powered and, with only three .303-inch machine guns (one in a nose and two in a tail turret), inadequately protected. Engine changes produced the Marks II and III in 1937–38, but it was not until the Mark IV appeared in late 1938,

488

fitted with 1145hp Rolls-Royce Merlin Xs and a four-gun tail turret, that an adequate design emerged. Slight airframe changes resulted in the Mark V and, between 1939 and 1943, this was the model which saw most active service. Used initially for nighttime leaflet raids over Germany, the Whitley was robust and reliable, characteristics which made it a useful interim design in the night-bombing offensive before the four-engined machines appeared. It was gradually relegated to transport and glider-tug duties after 1943.

The first of the four-engined strategic bombers to equip front-line squadrons, and the only one actually designed from the outset to carry four engines, was the Short Stirling. First flown in May 1939 in answer to Air Ministry Specification B.12/36, this was a huge and impressive aircraft, unfortunately marred by a number of design problems. Powered by four 1595hp Bristol Hercules XI radial engines, performance looked good on paper: maximum speed of 270mph, operational range of 2000 miles, maximum bomb load of 14,000 pounds and strong defensive armament of eight .303-inch Brownings (two in a nose, two in a mid-dorsal and four in a rear turret). Its short wing span (99 feet – purposely designed to enable the aircraft to be kept in existing RAF hangars) affected service ceiling, restricting it to operational altitudes of around 17,000 feet only, and the divided bomb bay did not have room for anything bigger than a 2000-pound weapon. The Mark II was an unsuccessful attempt to gain power by substituting American 1600hp Wright Cyclone radials, but the Mark III, with 1650hp Hercules XVIs, did improve performance. The Mark III was in fact the major production model, equipping squadrons from February 1941, when the Stirling made its operational debut, until 1943 when the type was withdrawn

to transport and glider-tug roles.

The Stirling was followed into operational service by the Handley Page Halifax in March 1941, an aircraft designed initially as a twin-engined machine in answer to Specification P.13/36. Early problems with intended Rolls-Royce Vulture engines led to changes, however, and when the prototype Halifax first flew on 25 October 1939 it was fitted with four Merlin X in-line powerpacks which gave a good performance. With top speed of 265mph, operational range of 1860 miles with 5800 pounds of bombs and maximum bomb load of 13,000 pounds, the production Mark I, with seven-man crew and good defensive armament (up to eight .303-inch Brownings in nose, tail and beam positions) seemed a weapon well suited to the needs of Bomber Command. The first raid, carried out on the night of 11/12 March 1941, reinforced this and squadron expansion to take the Halifax began immediately. The Mark II appeared later in 1941, characterized by the substitution of Merlin 20s and a mid-dorsal two-gun turret, and as the development went on the nose turret was gradually replaced by a large molded plexiglass nose, housing bomb-aimer and single machine gun. These aircraft appeared in bulk in 1942, equipping No. 4 Group based in Yorkshire, and proved to be useful night bombers as the offensive built up. Casualties were heavy, however, caused in part by a lack of engine power which restricted the operating ceiling to 22,600 feet and, as the range with full bomb load was only about 1100 miles anyway, in September 1943 the Mark II was withdrawn from hazardous missions. This ruling was cancelled five months later when the Mark III, with 1650hp Bristol Hercules radials fitted, overcame many of the previous problems (the ceiling was raised to 24,000 feet and the range to 1260 miles with full load, 1985 maximum) and it

Above: A Handley Page Halifax Mark I, Series 3.

was this model which was used by No. 4 Group in the interdiction raids against northern France in preparation for *Overlord* in early 1944. The Mark III also proved able to hold its own in night raids and remained in service until the end of the war. Subsequent marks were used mainly for transport and glider-tug duties.

Handley Page was not the only firm to answer Specification P.13/36, for on 26 May 1940 A V Roe unveiled its Vulture-equipped prototype of the Manchester. A twin-engined monoplane of powerful lines, it was not a successful design, for despite a top speed of 265mph, a maximum bomb-carrying capacity of 10,350 pounds and a range of 1630 miles with 8000 pounds, it suffered from chronic engine problems. Nevertheless, it was ordered for front-line service, equipping its first squadron in February 1941. Initial production models had triple fins, but in the Mark IA the central fin was deleted and it was in this guise that the majority of Manchesters operated up to their hasty withdrawal in June 1942. The aircraft was never popular, although many of its features were, for the time, remarkably good. Of special note was its heavy defensive armament of eight .303-inch machine guns in nose, dorsal and tail positions.

The Manchester was important, however, for out of its failure emerged the superb four-engined Lancaster – arguably the best strategic bomber of the war, with outstanding weight-carrying and endurance qualities. The result of a fortuitous marriage between the Manchester airframe and the Rolls-Royce Merlin engine, the prototype, known initially as the Manchester III, first flew on 9 January 1941. Its four 1460hp Merlin 20s gave it a top speed of 287mph and an operational range of 1660 miles with a bomb load of 14,000 pounds. It retained the defensive armament of its predecessor and, as the war progressed, displayed robustness, reliability and, most usefully, almost infinite adaptability. Squadron delivery began in early 1942 and both day and night operations began immediately. Casualties were heavy during daylight at this stage in the offensive, however, and although one of the first Lancaster raids was the daring low-level daylight attack on Augsburg on 17 April 1942, the aircraft really came into its own at night. Between 1942 and 1945 Lancasters dropped nearly 600,000 tons of bombs, two-thirds of the overall total dropped by Bomber Command during World War II, on German industrial and population centers, contributing not only to the 'area' destruction of cities but also to the precise destruction of selected targets. Such raids as that on the Ruhr

Dams on 15 May 1943 (for which the Lancasters were specially modified to carry Barnes Wallis' 'bouncing bomb'), the sinking of the battleship *Tirpitz* in Tromsofiord on 12 November 1944 (for which the 12,000-pound 'Tallboy' bomb was used) and the destruction of the Bielefeld Viaduct (with 22,000-pound 'Grand Slam' bomb) on 14 March 1945, all ensured a permanent place for the Lancaster in RAF history. Subsequent modifications to the original production series included substitution of 1650hp Bristol Hercules VI or XVI radials to produce the Mark II, and the use of Packard-built Merlins to produce the Mark III, but the basic configuration remained unchanged. By 1945 a successor design was well advanced, but the longer-range Lincoln, with 1680hp Merlin 85s, did not see wartime service.

With such a useful four-engined design available by 1942, it might be felt that the twin-engined strategic bomber concept was dead, but this was not so. On 20 November 1940 a small design team working for the firm of De Havilland test flew a remarkable twin-engined monoplane, constructed largely of wood, as a fast day bomber. This was the Mosquito, one of the most impressive and ubiquitous aircraft of any air force in World War II. Powered by two 1230hp Merlin 21 in-line engines, the early models enjoyed a top speed of 380mph and could carry 2000 pounds of bombs over 1300 miles. With performance figures such as these, the aircraft was immediately and quite naturally transferred to a plethora of other roles, including night fighting, reconnaissance and ground attack, but several specific bomber variants saw front-line service. Issued to squadrons from November 1941 the BIV, characterized by its clear plexiglass nose, contributed significantly to the offensive against Germany, proving an ideal platform for radar aids (especially the 'Oboe' blind-bombing device) and being used for night-intruder missions, pathfinding and target marking. By 1944, with alterations to the bomb bay, a single Mosquito could carry 4000 pounds of bombs to Berlin – more than was the usual load of an American four-engined B-17. It was a most effective machine.

The United States The USAAC (renamed the United States Army Air Force – USAAF – in June 1941) displayed a growing interest in both tactical and strategic bombers during the 1930s, gradually developing a number of designs which were to be extensively used not only by the Americans but also by a number of other Allied nations. These designs were characterized by a useful mix of speed, maneuverability and fire-power (although some proved unable to carry very large bomb loads); they were divided, in the same way as British bombers, into light, medium and heavy categories, with a fourth – very heavy – added in 1943 specifically to cater for the B-29. By 1945, in terms both of numbers and effectiveness, the USAAF Bombardment Groups were to constitute a weapon of awesome destructive capability.

So far as light bombers were concerned, seven Bombardment Groups were in existence in December 1941, equipped almost entirely with the Douglas A-20, a twin-engined, two or three-seat monoplane of clean lines and outstanding maneuverability. First flown on 26 October 1938 as the Douglas 7B, an unofficial design venture, it had attracted the attention of a French Purchasing Commission who eventually ordered 380, suitably modified for European service, for the Armée de l'Air. Powered by two 1200hp Pratt and Whitney Twin Wasp radials, these export models, known as the DB-7, were formidable machines for their time, capable of 295mph maximum and of carrying up to 1764 pounds of bombs over an operational range of 1000 miles. With tricycle undercarriage, armor protection to crew area and fuel tanks, and defensive armament of four forward-firing 7.5mm MAC machine guns, as well as two more of similar caliber in dorsal and ventral positions, 100 DB-7s were in French hands by the end of 1939, some of them seeing active service six months later. The remainder of the order was transferred to Britain in June 1940 where the aircraft was known, in its original form, as the Boston I or II and, when modified for night-fighter or intruder duties, as the Havoc. The latter, armed with four forward-firing .303-inch Browning machine guns and a Vickers K gun in the rear cockpit, could carry up to 2400 pounds on intruder raids and were used extensively for low-level daylight sweeps over northern France in 1941. Night-fighter equipment included four additional .303-inch Brownings in a 'solid' nose, AI radar and, in the Havoc III, such devices as cable-towed mines and 'Turbinlite' aerial searchlights. In 1941 a number of DB-7s were produced for a specific order from Britain and these light bombers, known as Boston IIIs, were used for intruder and tactical missions by the RAF for the rest of the war.

Meanwhile, the US Army had not been idle, ordering 123 DB-7s in July 1939, to be known as the A-20. Early production models were transferred to night-fighter and photoreconnaissance duties and the first of the light-bomber designs was the A-20A. Powered by two 1600hp Wright Double Cyclone raidals, this version could reach a top speed of 350mph, was heavily armed (four forward-firing, two upper, one lower and two rearward firing .30-inch machine guns) and capable of carrying 1100 pounds of bombs. Modifications produced the A-20B (with .50-inch machine guns) and A-20C (the same aircraft as the RAF's Boston III) in 1941–42, but the major production variant was the G, characterized by a solid nose housing 20mm cannon and .50-inch machine guns, increased bomb load of 4000 pounds (half of it carried externally under the wings) and range of 1000 miles. H, J and K variants followed, the latter two as 'lead bombers' with transparent nose, but it was the G which saw the widest service, equipping USAAF and Russian squadrons in quantity after 1942. Eventually known as the Havoc to the Americans as well as the British, it was a reliable and potent machine.

The success of the DB-7/A-20 program tended to overshadow its equally effective successor, the Douglas A-26 Invader. First flown on 10 July 1942, this twin-engined, three-seat light bomber was to have a remarkable history, seeing active service not only throughout World War II but also in Korea (1950–53) and even Vietnam (1964–73). Powered by two 2000hp Pratt and Whitney Double Wasp radials, it could reach a top speed of 355mph, was capable of carrying up to 6000 pounds of bombs and enjoyed an operational range of up to 1800 miles. Armament was, once again, heavy (in the main production A-26B, 10 .50-inch Browning machine guns, six in the solid nose and two each in dorsal and ventral positions) and well over 2000 of these effective tactical bombers were in service by 1945. The A-26C, characterized by its transparent nose, was used as a lead bomber, with solid-nosed A-26Bs following up, in both the European and Pacific theaters.

The familiar pattern of American aircraft design in the late 1930s – foreign requirements initiating or boosting production capability and building up a base of expertise which was then translated to USAAF needs – is also apparent so far as medium bombers are concerned. The Glenn L Martin Company produced a prototype XA-22 attack bomber in 1939, had it rejected by the US Army but immediately ordered in quantity by the French. Known by this stage as the Martin 167, this twin-engined, three-seat monoplane, powered by Pratt and Whitney Twin Wasp radials, was quite fast (278mph maximum) and capable of carrying out a useful

Above: A North American B-25J Mitchell, the most common version of this successful plane.

bombing role (bomb load of 2000 pounds could be carried 1080 miles). As with so many American designs, it was well armed (four machine guns in the wings with a further two in dorsal and ventral positions) and did good service in 1940 with the Armée de l'Air. Surviving machines were transferred to the RAF as the Maryland, serving principally in the Middle East, and were useful enough for the RAF to order an improved design as part of the Lend-Lease agreement. Powered by two 1600hp Wright Cyclone radials, this modification, known to the British as the Baltimore, to Martin as the 187 and to the USAAF as the A-30, first flew in June 1941, entering RAF squadrons four months later. Initial performance figures were little different to those of the Maryland, but as the Baltimore developed through a total of five marks, speed and firepower were enhanced. The ultimate production model, the Mark V, could reach a top speed of 302mph, packed a tremendous punch (up to 12 machine guns in a variety of positions) and enjoyed a range of nearly 1200 miles. Used exclusively in the Mediterranean and never, in fact, taken into USAAF service, the Baltimore performed well in the tactical bombing role.

The same cannot be said for the Lockheed Vega-37, known to the RAF as the Ventura. A twin-engined medium bomber, produced in 1940 specifically for the British, this aircraft proved unsatisfactory and was never ordered in bulk. The USAAF did not take it on for operational duties, although some were passed to the US Navy as the PV-1 patrol bomber.

Even if the Vega-37 had been a useful machine, however, the USAAF would still have hesitated about its deployment, for by 1941 it was already in possession of two excellent medium bomber designs which were to remain in front-line service throughout the war. The first, and

marginally the more impressive, was the North American B-25 Mitchell, a twin-engined, four- or six-seat monoplane of reliability, flexibility and power. First flown on 19 August 1940, the B-25 was fitted with 1700hp Wright R-2600s which gave it a top speed of 315mph and the ability to carry 3000 pounds of bombs over a range of 1500 miles. Initial armament was, by American standards, poor (one .50-inch machine gun in the glazed nose, three .30-inch in beam and tail positions) and immediate modification, introducing dorsal and ventral turrets while deleting tail armament, produced the slightly slower B-25B. It was with suitably modified versions of this that Lieutenant Colonel James Doolittle mounted the daring carrierborne Tokyo raid on 18 April 1942. External bomb racks were added to produce the C model, supplied under Lend-Lease to Britain, China and Russia, but it was the G, produced in 1942, which was the next major variant. This introduced the 'solid' nose, with 75mm cannon and up to six forward-firing .50-inch machine guns, and led naturally to the H, which sported the grand total of 14 machine guns in nose, dorsal and ventral positions. Both G and H variants were used extensively for antishipping strikes in the Pacific. Finally, so far as wartime deployment was concerned, came the J, which existed in both glazed- and solid-nose configuration, and this was the most-produced version to see service. Formidably armed with up to 18 machine guns and capable of carrying up to 4000 pounds of bombs, over 4000 B-25Js had been built by 1945, seeing active service in all theaters of war. Taken overall, the B-25 was probably the best medium bomber of World War II.

It was followed closely, in terms both of time and performance, by the Martin B-26 Marauder, a compact and streamlined twin-engined design which first flew on 25 November 1940. At first enormous problems beset this advanced machine, for with unprecedented wing loadings designed to give enhanced high-speed cruising capabilities, inexperienced pilots found it a difficult plane to handle. Indeed, accidents had become so common by 1942 that a special Board of Enquiry had to be convened, but when this concluded that it was crew training and not the aircraft which was at fault, the B-26 slowly began to shed its unfortunate image. This was just as well, for it was an effective medium bomber. Its twin Pratt and Whitney Double Wasp radials gave a top speed of 305mph, enabling a bomb load of 3000 pounds to be carried over ranges in excess of 1150 miles. In addition, it was heavily armed, the later F and G models mounting 11 .50-inch Brownings in nose, waist, dorsal and tail positions. Making its operational debut over Rabaul in April 1942, the B-26 went on to serve in all theaters, often alongside the B-25, and eventually emerged as one of the safest and most accurate bombers in the Allied air forces.

The virtual standardization of USAAF medium-bomber design which concentration upon the B-25 and B-26 implied was repeated in the heavy or strategic category with the B-17 and B-24. The first of these, dubbed the 'Flying Fortress' because of its heavy defensive armament, began life as early as 1934 when the Boeing Airplane Company entered a USAAC competition for a new long-range bomber. Their Model 299, first flown on 28 July 1935, was a revolutionary design, for whereas the emphasis in all air forces at the time was upon twin-engined bombers, the 299 sported four. The result was impressive: powered by 750hp Pratt and Whitney Hornet radials, this prototype of the B-17 proved capable of speeds in excess of 236mph, could carry up to 4000 pounds of bombs over 1100 miles and could operate comfortably at the high altitude of 24,000 feet. In addition it was, as its name implied, well protected by as many as five machine guns, mounted in nose, dorsal, ventral and side blister-type positions. Unfortunately, immediate development was restricted, firstly by a prototype crash and then by a bitter controversy between the army and navy over the concept of strategic bombing. Although preproduction YB-17s were authorized and tested, full-scale manufacture did not begin until 1939. This concentrated to begin with upon the B-17B, a machine little different from the YB models, but soon passed on to the C with uprated engines, redesigned gun positions and improved

performance. A number of B-17Cs were delivered to the RAF as Fortress Is in 1941, but they were not a success. Maintenance problems, a rash of accidents and the discovery that, in such areas as self-sealing fuel tanks, armor protection and rear-firing armament, the aircraft was not adequately geared to modern air war, led to drastic modifications.

These were manifested in the D model, which took account of most of the shortcomings so far as armor protection was concerned, but defensive problems, particularly a 'blind spot' to the rear, continued, as the Ds caught in the Philippines in early 1942 found to their cost. This led to the development of the E, in which machine-gun protection was considerably enhanced. The entire tail assembly was redesigned to incorporate a manually operated turret housing twin .50s, side blisters were replaced by open gun platforms and both dorsal and ventral turrets appeared. It was this model, together with the improved F variant of 1942, which was sent to England to build up the Eighth AAF for strategic daylight precision attacks upon Germany. Losses were heavy, however, particularly when a new defensive blind spot in the nose of the B-17 was discovered and exploited by the Luftwaffe, and chin turrets, housing twin .50s remotely fired from within the aircraft, had to be hastily added. When these and other modifications were incorporated into the production process, the result was the B-17G, the ultimate design model. With 1200hp Wright Cyclones fitted, the G could reach a top speed of 280mph, could carry a bomb load of 6000 pounds, enjoyed a range of 1140 miles at an altitude of 32,500 feet and was very heavily protected by up to 13 .50-inch machine guns. Nearly 8700 examples were built, contributing not only to the bombing of Germany but also to operations in the Mediterranean, Far East and Pacific.

The B-17 was joined in all these theaters by another equally famous four-engined design, the Consolidated Vultee B-24 Liberator, first flown on 29th December 1939. Enjoying an effective range almost double that of the B-17 but restricted to a lower cruising altitude (factors which made it impossible to fly mixed formations of these two types of bomber) the B-24 was eventually produced in greater numbers than the Fortress, and certainly saw more widespread service in a variety of guises. Powered by 1200hp Pratt and Whitney Twin Wasp radials, the B-24 was a tough, impressive bomber with very high aspect ratio wings, elliptical engine nacelles and twin vertical tail surfaces. Early models suffered from the same combat deficiencies as the B-17C and were in fact relegated to long-range reconnaissance and transport roles by the RAF, but modifications to include such things as self-sealing fuel tanks and armor plating were put into effect in 1941 to produce the first major production model, the D. This equipped USAAF Bombardment Groups in Europe and the Mediterranean during the early stages of the campaign against Germany, and experience, particularly against Luftwaffe day fighters, led to refinements in the E, G and H variants. But the major production version, bringing all these improvements together, was the J, introduced in 1942, and this was the model which saw the most active service. Uprated Twin Wasps gave a top speed of 290mph, an operational range of 2100 miles, a bomb-carrying capacity of 5000 pounds and a cruising altitude of 28,000 feet. In addition, as one might expect, defensive armament was comprehensive, comprising 10 .50-inch machine guns in nose, dorsal, ventral, waist and tail positions. Some 2738 B-24Js were built as part of a grand production total of over 19,000. The soundness of the design is indicated by the fact that many B-24s were still in service with allied air forces as late as 1952.

Despite the obvious effectiveness of these machines, however, the USAAF still sought substantial improvements, particularly to range and bomb-carrying capacity. As early as March 1938 the Air Staff authorized a study into the feasibility of a VLR (Very Long Range) bomber, able to carry up to 20,000 pounds over 3000 miles. Boeing, with the B-17 experience behind them, produced their Model 345 and the design was so impressive that 500 were ordered for the USAAF even before the prototype had flown. This was unfortunate, for although what became known as the B-29 Superfortress was an impressive machine, it was technologically extremely advanced, incorporating such innovations as pressurization and very high wing loadings, and beset with problems. Most of these stemmed from the engines, for the four 2200hp Wright R-3350 Duplex Cyclones were themselves a new development, the sheer size and power of them producing persistent (and often fatal) cooling problems. Nevertheless, after a maiden flight on 21 September 1942 and despite a prototype crash, production went ahead, spurred by the need for VLR bombers to hit Japan. A mass of modifications, ranging from the addition of self-sealing fuel tanks to the incorporation of a novel computer-guided, remotely controlled gun system, delayed deploy-

ment, and the first B-29 raid, from eastern China, did not take place until June 1944. The bases were moved to the Marianas Islands of the Central Pacific in November, and from then until August 1945 up to 20 Bombardment Groups flew regularly over Japanese cities in both day and night operations. Engine problems persisted, but with a top speed of 358mph, a normal range of 2850 miles and a bomb load of up to 20,000 pounds carried at over 32,000 feet maximum altitude, the B-29 was clearly a formidable machine. Modifications to remove the gun system, and so increase speed and range, produced the B-29B, but the aircraft will be remembered for all time as the first atomic-bomb delivery platform. The destruction of Hiroshima and Nagasaki in August 1945 stands as an awesome reminder of destructive capability, but also indicates the heights which aircraft and weapon design had reached by the end of World War II.

The Soviet Union The emphasis upon fighter and close-support aircraft in the Russian air force by 1939 was reflected in the small number of purpose-built bomber designs available. The majority dated from the early or mid-1930s and, although four-engined machines had been developed, they had not been uprated and were, together with the twin-engined tactical bombers, approaching obsolescence by the beginning of World War II. In addition, industrial priority was afforded to other designs and those bombers which did exist were often used as much for ground attack as for their designated roles. The overall result was a lack of design experience which, many would argue, was to affect the Russian air force until well into the postwar period.

The oldest design still in service in 1941 was the four-engined Tupolev TB-3, an archaic monoplane with open cockpit and fixed undercarriage, which had first flown in December 1930. At the time, it had had much to offer – a top speed of 179mph, a maximum bomb load of 12,000 pounds and a normal range of 1939 miles – and as the 1930s progressed, various modifications, partricularly to the in-line engines, had been put into effect. Examples of the 1936 model, with 950hp M-34 RN engines, saw service against both Japan and Finland three years later, but by 1941 the machine was clearly outclassed. It had already been replaced in some squadrons by the more advanced Petlyakov Pe-8, but this was never produced in sufficient quantity to be effective. Powered by a bewildering number of different in-line and radial packs, the four-engined Pe-8 was theoretically very effective – a top speed of 272mph, a maximum bomb load of 11,600 pounds and a range of almost 3000 miles with 8000 pounds were all very useful features – and the fact that examples did bomb Berlin on a number of occasions, beginning in August 1941, shows what might have been achieved if the Russians had developed strategic bombing potential.

Twin-engined bombers were given a little more emphasis, chiefly because they could be of use on the battlefield, and the oldest model of these still in service in 1941 was also a Tupolev design – the SB-2. With a top speed of 280mph, developed from twin 750 or 840hp M-100 or, in the *bis* model, 1100hp M-103 in-line engines, the SB-2 was fast, but both range (990 miles) and payload (a mere 1200 pounds) were poor. About 6000 examples are thought to have been built between the prototype flight in 1933 and 1941, when the chaos of invasion shifted production elsewhere. The same pattern was almost followed by its successor, the Ilyushin Il-4. First flown in 1935, this twin-engined monoplane, powered by 1100hp M-88B radials in its final versions, enjoyed a top speed of 254mph and could carry 2200 pounds of bombs up to 1610 miles. But armament was poor (three manually operated machine guns in nose, dorsal and ventral positions) and production almost ceased in 1941. A reasonable ground-attack capability saved the design, but even so the machine was not given the attention it deserved and moves to replace it in front-line service were initiated. The chosen design was the Yermolaev Yer-2, characterized by its cranked wing and offset cockpit, and this did have the advantage of very long range for a twin-engined bomber, being capable of carrying 2000 pounds of bombs up to 3000 miles. As only 430 of these machines appear to have been built, however, the priorities were clearly elsewhere. Yer-2s probably bombed Berlin, but the lack of development indicates how the Russian mind was working; bombers were just not the aircraft that were needed.

Germany During the early 1930s, before the Luftwaffe officially existed, a great deal of emphasis was placed upon the bomber as a war-winning weapon. This resulted primarily from a belief that a fast, maneuverable bomber could easily outfly existing fighters to achieve either tactical or strategic advantages, but was also a logical preference given the restraints imposed upon German aircraft development at the time; after all, a bomber could be disguised as a

civilian transport or airliner, permitted under the terms of Versailles, whereas a fighter was obvious to all. Thus when the Reichsluftfaht-ministerium (State Ministry of Aviation) looked around for bomber designs they turned naturally to the commercial sector of the air industry for ideas and protection from prying eyes, and followed existing trends toward relating small, fast and highly loaded aircraft. Most of these were, of necessity, twin-engined, so that for the entire period of World War II few bombers emerged which could be included in a 'heavy' or strategic category. In addition, bomber development tended to follow the same pattern as that of fighters – a persistent emphasis upon existing designs, with replacements not being given priority until it was too late. Part of this may have been a result of engine-manufacturing problems, for it is a noticeable fact that the Luftwaffe experienced persistent difficulties in achieving good production runs of the best powerpacks; difficulties exacerbated to a tremendous extent once the Anglo-American strategic bombing campaign began to bite in 1944. Thus, although basic airframe designs tended to remain unchanged, subtypes – incorporating new or different engine fits – proliferated.

This may be seen to good effect with one of the earliest of the twin-engined bombers to enter Luftwaffe service – the Dornier Do 17, a machine which started life specifically for commercial use, as a fast mailplane for Lufthansa. The prototype flew in autumn 1934 and showed such potential that it was an obvious contender for bomber selection. Characterized at this stage by a long, aerodynamically clean fuselage (which earned it the nickname of the 'Flying Pencil'), it entered Luftwaffe squadrons in 1937 as the Do 17E. Designed to carry 1650 pounds of bombs, this model – the first to sport the twin tail fins which were to be a recognition feature – could reach a top speed of 220mph and was protected by three 7.92mm machine guns, situated in nose, dorsal and ventral positions. Examples of the E, together with a few F (reconnaissance) models, served in Spain, where their speed and operating altitude (over 18,000 feet) made them virtually invulnerable to interception. K models, in which the existing 750hp BMW VI engines were replaced by Gnome-Rhône 14Ns, were produced for export to Yugoslavia, and further engine modifications produced M and P variants for the Luftwaffe, some of which saw service in World War II.

But problems did begin to appear. Defensive

armament was found to be poor against more modern fighters and performance suffered from inadequate engines. S and U models began a process of modification, indicated most obviously by an enlarged and deepened nose which housed extra armament and destroyed the 'Flying Pencil' profile, and this was taken further in the Z when 1000hp Bramo Fafnir 32B engines were fitted. With a top speed of 255mph and a range of 932 miles, the Do 17Z was a more effective machine, capable of carrying over 2000 pounds of bombs, and was used extensively in both day and night operations against Britain in 1940–41. An export version, with 1075hp DB 601 in-line engines, was given the new designation of Do 215 and was, in fact, used by the Luftwaffe.

The enhanced performance of the 215 led to more modifications, which in turn produced an entirely new 'family' of medium bombers, initiated as early as August 1938. Known collectively as the Do 217, these aircraft bore superficial resemblance to earlier models but differed in a host of details, most notably engine fit (usually 1580 or 1700hp BMW 801s) and, in the K and M variants of 1942–43, completely redesigned nose configuration which did away with the original stepped windshield and introduced a rounded, fully glazed shape. The Do 217K was, perhaps, the best Luftwaffe bomber of the war years, achieving speeds in excess of 320mph with a bomb-carrying capacity (with wing racks) of 8000 pounds and a formidable defensive armament of up to 12 machine guns. Unfortunately, in a move so typical of German wartime aircraft design, Dornier terminated production in late 1943 to concentrate on a high-altitude heavy bomber, the abortive Do 317.

A similar story emerges from the firm of Junkers. They, too, had been active in commercial aircraft design after World War I, producing in 1934 a civil airliner which was taken into Luftwaffe service. This was the Ju 86, employed eventually as a bomber and reconnaissance machine. Early D models, which saw service in Spain, proved to be underpowered, being fitted with two 600hp Junkers Jumo 205C engines only, but when 800hp BMW 132s were substituted to produce the E, the aircraft became an effective machine, capable of a top speed of 202mph, carrying over 2000 pounds of bombs over operational ranges of 900 miles. Examples were in action in Poland in 1939 but production was then switched to a high-altitude version, the Ju 86P, fitted with turbocharged 1000hp Jumo 207s and pressurized cabin. This was a

bold idea – the few Ju 86Ps which flew over Britain and Russia in 1940–41 were virtually impossible to intercept at their operating height of over 40,000 feet – but the potential of the original design was lost.

Fortunately for the Luftwaffe, Junkers had by then produced a new design, the Ju 88, arguably the most versatile aircraft of the war. This also began life as a civil venture, being accepted by the Luftwaffe in 1936 as a Schnellbomber – a medium bomber with the speed and maneuverability of a fighter. Production began in 1939 and early examples were just entering squadron service when World War II began. These were inadequately armed, however, and it was not until the Ju 88A-4 appeared in early 1940 that the true value of the design was appreciated. Powered by two 1340hp Junkers Jumo 211J engines, the A-4 could reach a top speed of 269mph, carry a bomb load of 1100 pounds over ranges of 1120 miles and defend itself well using up to seven machine guns, all concentrated forward in the crew compartment. But such performance figures, combined with the excellent combat maneuverability which soon became apparent, undermined its impact as a bomber by leading, inevitably, to its use in other roles. Production of a bomber version continued until 1943, culminating in the S model with 1700hp BMW 801G engines, but by then the emphasis of Ju 88 design had shifted, principally to night-fighter variants. These contributed significantly to the defense of Germany in the middle years of the Allied bombing offensive but, once again, a worthwhile bomber design had been lost to the Luftwaffe. Junkers tried to improve matters by developing a faster and more streamlined Ju 88 – known as the 188 – for intruder bombing missions, but despite some impressive performance statistics (the Ju 188S, for example, could reach the incredible speed of 435mph), full production never got under way. Further follow-up designs – the 288, 388 and 488 – were unsuccessful, representing a considerable waste of time, resources and research.

The final twin-engined bomber to emerge from the prewar commercial sector was the Heinkel He 111, an aircraft remembered for its part in the bombing of Britain but one which was not, in fact, an outstanding success. This was not apparent to begin with. When the He 111B first entered squadron service in 1936, it seemed to be a useful design. Powered by 950hp DB 600 CG engines and characterized by a long, slim nose and broad wing, the aircraft was relatively fast (230mph maximum) and could carry a large bomb load (up to 3300 pounds) – figures which ensured both survivability and hitting power in the favorable air environment over Spain. But that same environment caused the problems which were to lead to early obsolescence, for against minimal opposition the inadequate defensive armament of only three 7.92mm MG 15 machine guns was neither realized nor rectified. Thus, as the bomber was developed through D and E variants before 1939, extra guns were not added and the same was true in the major production version, the He 111H. Powered by two 1200hp Junkers Jumo 211 D-2 engines, this model, fitted with asymmetric 'bubble' nose, could reach a top speed of 252mph and carry up to 4400 pounds of bombs over ranges of 750 miles, but it was dangerously vulnerable to interception, as casualties over Britain in 1940 showed. In response Heinkel added extra machine guns and tried to improve both altitude and speed, but to no avail. By 1942 the He 111 was a vulnerable, obsolete design. The short-sightedness of the German aircraft industry was shown by the fact that no replacement was available. The type was still in service in 1945, with predictable results.

The problems experienced by these twin-engined bombers, particularly during the bombing of Britain, suggest in retrospect that what the Luftwaffe needed were long-range, strategic machines. Indeed, it has often been argued that the lack of such aircraft was one of the major weaknesses of the wartime Luftwaffe, implying that none was developed or deployed. This is not strictly true, however, for at least two usable designs existed in 1939 and one other was developed before the end of hostilities. All were potentially effective long-range, strategic bombers, yet none was produced in quantity as such and, with the exception of a few intruder raids against Britain in 1943–44, none flew strategic missions, being employed instead as transports, maritime patrol aircraft or reconnaissance machines.

The two prewar designs began life, as might be expected from their size and range, as civil aircraft, both taking to the air for the first time in 1937. The more famous of the two was produced by Focke Wulf as the Fw 200 and saw widespread service as a long-range commercial transport for Lufthansa, establishing a number of flight records and winning substantial export orders before the Luftwaffe, rather belatedly, showed interest. It was a natural long-range bomber. Powered by four 1200hp BMW-Bramo Fafnir 323 engines, it could reach a top speed of 224mph, carry over 4000 pounds

of bombs on ranges up to 2175 miles, operate at 19,000 feet altitude and, when produced for squadron service, defend itself adequately, using eight machine guns or cannon. Severe structural problems later led to some spectacular wing and fuselage failures, but the Fw 200 'Condor' was almost never deployed as a strategic bomber, being used instead for transport or maritime patrol. It carried out these duties admirably – the British called it the 'scourge of the Atlantic' for its contribution to the battle for the sea lanes – but could probably have achieved far more if bombing had been its primary role.

The Fw 200 was joined in its oceanic duties after 1942 by an aircraft which was, if anything, even more impressive. This was the Junkers Ju 290, a four-engined, ex-Lufthansa airliner which had in fact been developed in 1936 (when it was known as the Ju 90) specifically as a strategic bomber, only to be cancelled on the death of General Wever. Powered by BMW 801 radials, with a top speed of 273mph, the Ju 290 could carry 6600 pounds of bombs over ranges of nearly 3700 miles and was armed with an unprecedented 13 machine guns or cannon. It was wasted on maritime patrol and transport duties and the fact that it did not even enter squadron service until 1942 indicates the low priority afforded to it. Production ceased in October 1944, by which time only a small number had been built.

This depressing picture of missed opportunities is further highlighted by the history of the only heavy bomber developed during the war years – the Heinkel He 177 Greif (Griffon). Designed in answer to a rather odd specification of 1938 which called for a heavy bomber capable of dive bombing, the He 177 was almost an experimental machine, incorporating a wealth of new ideas which, naturally, led to problems. At first glance the aircraft appeared to be twin-engined, having only two nacelles and propellers, but it was in fact equipped with four DB 601s, linked in pairs on each wing. This gave some useful performance figures, notably a top speed of 295mph and a bomb-carrying capacity of 4500 pounds on the prototype as early as 1939, but a series of disastrous engine fires (which earned the aircraft the nickname of the 'Flaming Coffin') delayed production. Even so, official support for the machine was sustained and early examples saw action over the Eastern Front in late 1942. Altogether nearly 800 He 177s were built, being used as transports, antishipping aircraft, missile carriers (two Hs 293 guided bombs could be carried beneath the wings by 1944) and, almost unbelievably, as day and night

Above: A V1, ready for launch.

fighters. A small number were even used as bombers, although their deployment came too late in the war to be effective.

A similar story of 'too little too late' emerged with the Arado Ar 234 Blitz (Lightning), the only jet-engined bomber to be fully developed. First flown in June 1943, the Ar 234 was powered by two 1980-pound thrust Junkers Jumo 004B turbojets, giving a top speed of 457mph, a bomb-carrying capacity of 3300 pounds and an operational range of 1013 miles. These figures were impressive, making the aircraft virtually invulnerable to interception and capable of hitting targets which mattered in the final months of the war, as indicated by its employment in the Battle of the Bulge (December 1944) and against the intact Rhine bridge at Remagen (March 1945). But production did not get under way until 1944, and even though over 200 examples are known to have been completed, shortages of fuel, airfields and pilots precluded their squadron deployment. It was a situation which typified the weaknesses of German aircraft development during World War II.

Even if the Ar 234 had been successfully deployed, however, it is unlikely that it would have been used for long-range bombing, for by 1944 the Germans were laying great stress, not upon aircraft, but upon missiles for that role. The so-called Vergeltungswaffen (reprisal weapons) were frightening developments which, if deployed in quantity earlier in the war, could have tilted the balance against the Allied powers. The V1, the first of the two designs to be used in action (against London in June 1944) was a pilotless, rocket-powered bomb carrying a warhead of 1870 pounds. Developed at the research establishment in Peenemünde on the Baltic coast and tested in 1942, the V1 worked on the ram-jet principle, consisting of a combined fuselage and warhead with an Argus As 014 jet with 600-pound thrust mounted aft. It was

guided by a gyroscopic preselector, could reach a maximum speed of 350mph and travel about 600 miles before plummeting to the ground. Over 9000 were launched against Britain, of which 5000 reached their target, and a further 20,000 were built, fortunately too late in the war to be really effective. By September 1944 they had been joined by the infinitely more formidable V2, a liquid-fuel rocket which followed a delivery curve taking it to an altitude of 50 miles at its peak, carrying a one-ton warhead. It weighed 13.6 tons altogether and was, by virtue of its supersonic speed, invulnerable to any form of interception. Altogether 1115 were aimed at London before the war ended, causing 2700 deaths and a host of injuries, and some were used as SSMs (surface-to-surface missiles) on the battlefield. The existence of the V2 may have represented a misuse of German resources in 1944–45, but it augured ill for the future of mankind. In modern terminology the V1 would be described as a cruise missile and the V2 as a ballistic missile.

Italy Despite the importance of Guilio Douhet in the evolution of a theory of strategic bombing between the two World Wars, this was not a role which was stressed by the Regia Aeronautica. As Mussolini tried to carve out a new 'Roman Empire' in the 1930s the requirement was for what were termed 'colonial' bombers, capable of contributing to the subjugation of native peoples. Characteristics such as range, robustness and bomb-carrying capacity were therefore developed, often at the cost of speed and defensive armament, and when these same bombers were called upon to carry out both tactical and strategic missions in World War II they often proved to be ill-suited, suffering significant casualties as ground and air opposition emerged. For this reason, they are often dismissed as inferior designs, reflecting the poor state of Italian technology, and although an element of truth may be found in such beliefs, this does scant justice to the aircraft themselves, most of which were designed for tasks far removed from those which they eventually carried out.

This may be seen to good effect with the Savoia-Marchetti SM 79 Sparviero (Heron), a three-engined medium bomber which saw widespread service throughout World War II. First flown as an eight-seater commercial transport in October 1934, this ungainly looking aircraft, with its distinctive hunched back and braced tail plane, was taken into military service two years later. It proved to be both robust and reliable under combat conditions in Ethiopia and Spain and was successfully adapted to torpedo carrying in 1939, a role in which it was to be used extensively between 1940 and 1943. As a bomber it had some useful features: a top speed of 267mph, an operational range of 1200 miles and a bomb-carrying capacity of 2200 pounds. But it was not well protected with, at best, only three 12.7mm Breda-SAFAT and one .303-inch Lewis machine guns, and, as the war progressed, it began to lack power. Attempts to solve this second problem led to the substitution of 1000hp Piaggio PX1 RC 40 radials for the original 780hp Alfa-Romeo 126 RC 34s, but performance was never good. Allied fighters were able to destroy SM 79s comparatively easily and the type was dismissed as inferior. Its stablemate, the SM 81 Pipistrello (Bat) was treated in the same way, although in this case one can appreciate why. First flown in 1935 as a development of the SM 73 airliner, the SM 81 was an obsolete design by 1940. With three low-powered Piaggio PX radials and fixed undercarriage, the aircraft was slow (211mph maximum), poorly protected and vulnerable. Even so, it was used as a night bomber by the Regia Aeronautica – a role for which it had not been designed – as late as 1942.

Even more dramatic as examples of Italian bomber-design shortcomings were the aircraft which emanated from Società Italiana Caproni during the interwar period. They constituted a long and varied line of 'colonial' bombers, dating back to the early 1930s and reflecting their designated role. The Caproni Ca 101 and 111, flown in 1932 and 1933 respectively, were single-engined utility aircraft which were used as bombers and transports in Ethiopia, but the first multiengined design was the Ca 133, test flown in 1935. Powered by three 460hp Piaggio PVII RC 14 radials, this was not a bomber to be committed to a hostile air environment. With a top speed of only 174mph and defensive armament of four light-caliber machine guns, Ca 133s were vulnerable and obsolete by 1940. The RAF found them simple to destroy and most were relegated to transport roles. A follow-up design, the Ca 135, was more promising, being developed specifically as a medium bomber, but the original fit of two 800hp Isotta-Fraschini Asso engines proved disappointing. By the time they had been replaced by more powerful Piaggo PXI bis RC 40 radials in 1937, the Regia Aeronautica had purchased its bombers elsewhere. The Ca 135 therefore never served in Italian squadrons and the only examples to see action during the war did so in Hungarian

colors on the Eastern Front. With a top speed of 273mph, bomb load of 3500 pounds, range of 745 miles and, for once, an adequate armament fit (twin-gun turrets in nose, dorsal and ventral positions), the Ca 135 would seem to have been a reasonable machine.

The main reason for the lack of official Italian enthusiasm over the Ca 135 was that when it was experiencing engine problems in 1936–37 other, more reliable designs were available for immediate production and deployment. One of the best was the Rosatelli-designed Fiat BR (Bombardamento Rosatelli) 20 Cicogna (Stork). First flown in February 1936 and delivered to squadrons only seven months later, the BR 20 was an advanced design of some potential. Powered by two 1000hp Fiat A80 RC 41 radials, it was capable of 270mph and could carry 3500 pounds of bombs over ranges of 1700 miles. It was, in addition, adequately armed, with machine guns in nose, dorsal and ventral positions, and did well in Spain where it often operated in conjunction with He 111s in Nationalist service. Examples were purchased by Spain, Venezuela and even Japan, and the Regia Aeronautica deployed some 250 when Italy declared war in June 1940. Two groups of BR 20s attacked Britain in October 1940 but, like their escorting CR 42 fighters, proved a poor match for the defending Spitfires and Hurricanes. This suggested a degree of obsolescence, and from 1941 remaining examples were relegated to oceanic patrol and reconnaissance, indulging in tactical bombing only when the opposition was known to be light. An improved BR 20 bis was not produced in quantity.

Another promising design which became available in the immediate prewar years was the Cantieri Ruiniti dell'Adriatico (Cant) Z1007 Alcione (Kingfisher). First flown in May 1937, this three-engined medium bomber was a land-based version of the successful Z506B seaplane. Powered by 840hp Isotta-Fraschini Asso engines and built almost entirely of wood, the Z1107 was well accepted by Regia Aeronautica test pilots and rushed into service. The 1000hp Piaggio PXI bis radials were substituted to produce the Z1007 bis in 1939, and this was the major model to see wartime action, appearing in the Mediterranean and over Russia. With a maximum speed of 280mph, bomb load of up to 4000 pounds and operational range of nearly 1200 miles, it was an impressive and underrated machine. A successor, the more powerful Z1018 Leone (Lion) was planned, but few examples had been produced by 1943.

Another Italian design consistently underrated by the Allies was the Piaggio P 108B (Bombadiere) – the only truly 'heavy' bomber employed by the Regia Aeronautica during World War II. Developed as part of a design series which included transports and anti-shipping machines, the four-engined P 108B was an extremely powerful aircraft, used in some numbers over North Africa, the Mediterranean, Russia and the Balkans. Powered by 1500hp Piaggio PXII RC 35 radials, it could reach a top speed of 267mph and carry a bomb load of 7700 pounds over a range of 2200 miles. Eight 12.7mm Breda-SAFAT machine guns, four of which were situated in remotely fired turrets above the outer engine nacelles, provided adequate armament. The potential of this aircraft – largely unrealized and unrecorded – may be gauged from the fact that examples which were not surrendered to the Allies in September 1943 were willingly taken over by the Luftwaffe.

Japan The JAAF employed its bombers in two distinct roles, both of which were tactical in concept. For short-range, close-support missions reasonably fast, robust and maneuverable 'light' bombers were used, while for longer-range interdiction strikes, so-called 'heavy' machines, emphasizing survivability, endurance and bomb-carrying capacity, were preferred. As with fighters, many Imperial Navy bombers carried out exactly the same roles, often at the same time as their JAAF compatriots, but for purposes of convenience a distinction between the two arms will be made.

The design trend which produced many of the army light bombers destined to see service in the Pacific War began in May 1936 when, as part of a JAAF modernization program, the firms of Mitsubishi and Kawasaki were instructed to produce prototypes of single-engined monoplane machines. The official specification was fairly strict, laying down such capabilities as 248mph maximum speed at 9800 feet, bomb load of 660 pounds and dive-bombing potential. Both firms submitted designs in early 1937 which were to see some service in the early campaigns of conquest in 1941–42.

The Mitsubishi prototype flew first, in February 1937, and was a light bomber of conventional lines for the time. Known to the JAAF as the Ki-30 Army Type 97 Light Bomber and to the wartime Allies as the Ann, this two-seat, mid-wing monoplane, powered by a 950hp Mitsubishi Ha-5 Zuisei radial, answered the original specification but had a number of features which doomed it to early obsolescence.

With a maximum speed of 263mph, bomb load of the requisite 660 pounds and range of 1056 miles, it clearly had a useful role to play, as was shown when it was deployed to China in 1938, but it was inadequately armed with only two 7.7mm Type 89 machine guns and, with fixed undercarriage, was not well suited to modification. A few examples flew in the Philippines campaign of 1942, but it was relegated to training duties very soon thereafter. Its rival in 1936, the Kawasaki Ki-32 Army Type 98 Light Bomber (Allied code name Mary), suffered a similar fate. First flown in March 1937, this was unusual in that it had an in-line engine (a Kawasaki Ha-9-II), and this in fact delayed production, as problems multiplied. Otherwise, however, its basic configuration of single wing and fixed undercarriage was the same as the Ki-30 and performance figures were little different. It too saw limited service at the beginning of the Pacific War – over Hong Kong in December 1941 – before being relegated to more mundane tasks.

Thus by early 1942 the JAAF was short of light bombers and was forced to depend upon the only other design initiated in the prewar years – the Kawasaki Ki-48 Army Type 99 (Allied code name Lily). Fortunately this proved to be an adequate machine, seeing service in China and the southwest Pacific until 1944. First flown in July 1939 and powered by two 980hp Nakajima Ha-25 radials, the Ki-48-I was designed specifically to counter the Soviet SB-2. In the event, it was inferior in bomb load but adequate in all other departments, enjoying a maximum speed of 298mph, defensive armament of three 7.7mm machine guns (in nose, dorsal and ventral positions), bomb load of 660 pounds and operational range of 1491 miles. Modifications improved engine performance, speed and bomb load to produce the Ki-48-II in 1942, but defensive armament was unchanged, leading to vulnerability and heavy losses. By 1944, when remaining examples became suicide planes or missile test beds, JAAF light bombers had virtually ceased to have any effect at all. Their duties were taken over by more robust navy designs, although they too were finding the going hard in the face of Allied air and equipment superiority.

JAAF 'heavy' bombers enjoyed a slightly better record of success, at least in the early war years. The most important design in 1941 was the Mitsubishi Ki-21 Army Type 97 Heavy Bomber (Allied code name Sally), a twin-engined, seven-seat machine which had resulted from the modernization program of 1936.

Powered by 850hp Nakajima Ha-5-Kai radials, the Ki-21-I, developed from a prototype flown in November 1936, was by no means inferior to its Western counterparts. A maximum speed of 268mph was useful, as was its bomb-carrying capacity of 1700 pounds and its range of 1680 miles. But, as with many Japanese bombers, defensive armament was poor, comprising three manually operated 7.7mm machine guns only, although for once this was recognized and attempts at improvement made. In 1938 armament was increased to five machine guns (one of which could be remotely fired from the tail) and crew armor was added to produce the Ib, while a sixth gun, in beam position, produced the Ic. A year later work began on the Ki-21-II, powered by 1490hp Mitsubishi Ha-101 engines, and development was completed in 1942 with the IIb, characterized by the addition of a dorsal turret. All variants saw widespread service in World War II, although by 1944 they were showing their age.

Specifications for a replacement to the Ki-21 were issued by the army as early as 1938, but the result – the twin-engined, eight-seat Nakajima Ki-49 Donryu (Storm Dragon – Allied code name Helen) – was disappointing. First flown in August 1939, the prototype was drastically underpowered and even when 1250hp Nakajima Ha-41 radials were substituted to produce the Ki-49-I, performance figures were little better than those of the Ki-21 (speed was increased to 306mph maximum, and maximum range was now 1833 miles). In addition, armament was inadequate – one 20mm cannon in the nose and two 7.7mm machine guns in the nose and tail – and although 129 were built (some of which bombed Port Darwin, Australia, in February 1942), they fell easy prey to Allied fighters. An improved Ki-49-II, powered by 1450hp Nakajima Ha-109-II engines and sporting one 20mm cannon and five 7.7mm machine guns, appeared in 1942. This was the main production model and should have sustained the JAAF bomber squadrons during the middle years of the war. It failed to do so.

An adequate replacement for the Ki-21 did not appear until 1943, when the Mitsubishi Ki-67 Hiryu (Flying Dragon – Allied code name Peggy) first took to the air. This was an impressive machine. Powered by two 1900hp Mitsubishi Ha-104 radials, it could reach a top speed of 334mph and carry a bomb load of 1764 pounds over ranges in excess of 1500 miles. With one 20mm cannon in a dorsal turret and 12.7mm machine guns in nose, tail and beam positions, it could defend itself, but its main feature was its

excellent maneuverability, comparable to that of many contemporary fighters. Unfortunately for the JAAF, it appeared at a time when Japanese industry was beginning to suffer the effects of the Allied blockade. Although an amazing total of 727 examples were produced, many were never deployed, being kept back as suicide planes against an Allied invasion of the home islands which never came.

France In addition to the Bloch, Breguet and Potez light bombers so disastrously used for ground attack in 1940, the Armée de l'Air had at its disposal a number of bomber designs when World War II began. All were used to good effect in their designated roles during the campaign of 1940, but the familiar problems of industrial chaos after the nationalization of 1936, coupled with the lack of clear air doctrines, meant that their efforts were in vain.

The oldest design still in front-line service was also the heaviest – the four-engined, five-seat Farman F222/223 series, which traced its origins to the F210 or 1930. This established the curious configuration of the aircraft, with box-like body, very high wing and unusual engine layout (the 800hp Gnome-Rhône GR14Kbrs radials were mounted in back-to-back pairs, so that the single nacelle under each wing housed a 'pusher' and a 'puller' propeller). The F222, first flown in June 1935, introduced retractable undercarriage and enjoyed reasonable performance figures – a cruising speed of 196mph, bomb load of 5500 pounds and range of 1240 miles – and was used extensively for both long-range tactical and strategic raids in 1940. This was followed into service by the redesigned SNCA du Centre-produced F223, with 1100hp Hispano-Suiza HS 14 engines and, although only small numbers had been produced by June 1940, this was one of the best Allied bombers of the time. One F223 actually bombed Berlin on 7/8 June 1940.

Also used for nighttime strategic raids, although designed originally as a five-seat reconnaissance bomber, was the twin-engined Amiot 143. First flown in April 1931 in answer to a specification of 1928, this aircraft began to equip the Armée de l'Air in 1935. It was therefore obsolete by 1940, as indicated by its poor top speed (for a medium bomber) of 193mph, its angular appearance and fixed undercarriage. Nevertheless, with a maximum bomb load of over 3000 pounds (half of which was carried on external wing racks) and range of 1200 miles, it could not be ignored and a series of quite effective night operations was carried out before the fall of France. Unfortunately, large numbers of 143s were lost when committed to daylight tactical missions and by June 1940 few remained.

The final design available was the SNCASE/ Lioré et Olivier LeO 45, a twin-engined medium bomber of attractive appearance and some potential. The prototype, powered by Hispano-Suiza 14A radials, gained world speed records of 310mph level and 388mph in a dive in September 1937 and production began immediately. The 1030hp Gnome-Rhône 12N engines were substituted to improve reliability and endurance (so producing the 451) and 180 were in squadron service in May 1940. With bomb load of 4400 pounds, operational range of up to 1800 miles and impressive armament fit of 20mm cannon in dorsal turret and 7.5mm machine guns in the nose and retractable ventral positions, it is hardly surprising to find that the 451s did well against hopeless odds in the subsequent campaign. The Luftwaffe took over captured examples as transports and the Vichy air force deployed 150, some of which saw action against the Allies in Syria in 1941. As with fighters, the French had produced their best design too late.

Czechoslovakia At the time of the German invasion in March 1939, the Czech air force was deploying only one type of light bomber – the S328, produced by Vojenska Tovarna na Letadla (Letov). It was an obsolete, single-engine biplane, first flown as early as February 1933. With 635hp Walter Pegasus II radial, its top speed was only 174mph and its bomb-carrying capacity an ineffective 500 pounds. Its operational range was about 435 miles and defensive armament, comprising four 7.92mm MK 30 machine guns, was poor. Yet this aircraft, employed originally as a reconnaissance bomber, saw extremely widespread service. The Luftwaffe used the S328 as a trainer and issued examples to both the Slovak and Bulgarian air forces. A few even found their way into Soviet hands when Slovak pilots changed allegiance in 1944, and the type was still in use, as a counter-insurgency machine, when hostilities ceased. It was a remarkable record.

Holland The Dutch, like the Czechs, had only one light bomber design available when their country was invaded. This was the single-engined, two-seat Fokker CX biplane which, like the Letov S328, was obsolete and vulnerable. Versions in Dutch service, powered by 650hp Rolls-Royce Kestrel Vs, were capable of 199mph, could carry about 800 pounds of bombs

over a range of 516 miles and were poorly armed with three 7.9mm machine guns. None survived the German invasion, although license-built Finnish examples, with 835hp Bristol Pegasus XX1 radials, were still in action in 1945. Robustness and reliability made up for some of the obvious shortcomings of the design.

Poland During the 1930s the Poles produced some remarkable bomber designs, introducing techniques and capabilities well in advance of most other states. One of their best was the PZL P23/43 Karas (Carp) three-seat, single-engined reconnaissance bomber, a machine which paved the way for some of the ground-attack aircraft developed, principally in Germany and Russia, during World War II. Powered by a 580hp PZL Pegasus II, the prototype was first flown in August 1934, achieving a top speed of 198mph and range, with 1500 pounds of bombs, of 410 miles. A 680hp PZL Pegasus VIII was substituted to produce the P23B, pushing the top speed up to 217mph, and the development trend continued to improve performance right up to 1939. The P43, with 930hp Gnome-Rhône 14 Kfs radial, appeared in 1936 and by the time of the German invasion three years later 14 Polish bomber regiments had been issued with this version. A feature of all variants was the good defensive armament (up to five 7.7mm machine guns in nose, dorsal and ventral positions) but this was not enough to defeat the Luftwaffe. Surviving examples fled to Rumania where they were interned, a few actually being used by the Rumanians against the Soviet Union in 1941.

The same thing happened to the second of the Polish designs, the PZL P37 Los (Elk) twin-engined medium bomber. It was first flown in June 1936, powered by 875hp PZL Pegasus XIIB radials, but production was delayed by a political scandal and insufficient numbers were available to be effective in 1939. This was unfortunate, for the machine, with a top speed of 277mph, range up to 2800 miles and maximum bomb load of

Above: A Grumman F6F Hellcat lands on an

5688 pounds, had much to offer. Those which were available, including a very small number of P37Bs, with 925hp Pegasus XX engines, proved to be effective in their designated role but were soon overwhelmed. A few survivors saw action on the Eastern Front in Rumanian colors.

NAVAL SUPPORT

The advantages of air power, illustrated so far solely in relation to the destruction or defense of land targets, have always been equally applicable to a naval setting. When air capability was first discovered in the years before 1914, the maritime nations were quick to realize its potential in the spotting and shadowing of enemy vessels at sea. To begin with, because of problems of range and endurance – qualities which early aircraft lacked – lighter-than-air rigid or semirigid airships were used, being carried with the fleet to be inflated and sent aloft whenever the need arose. Such machines were frequently dangerous or unreliable, however, and it did not take long before experiments with heavier-than-air aircraft were carried out. By 1914 rudimentary seaplanes and even ship-launched aircraft were in naval service, particularly in Britain and Germany,

Essex *Class carrier late in the war.*

but it was not until August 1917 that the first successful launch and recovery took place, on the converted warship HMS *Furious.* This marked the birth of the aircraft carrier, a vessel of integral importance to the development of air support at sea. Early aircraft types carried were designed principally for reconnaissance although, in parallel to developments on land, the protection of reconnaissance potential and the destruction of enemy observation machines led inexorably to their use as fighters. Thereafter it was only a small and logical step to develop naval bombers, for if you are going to the trouble and expense of finding the enemy fleet, you might as well try to destroy it at the same time, using the same means of transport.

Thus by the beginning of World War II naval aircraft were designed to carry out three major roles – reconnaissance, air interception and bombing. In many respects the criteria of design for such aircraft were exactly the same as for their land-based counterparts, but there were some essential differences or refinements. A successful naval reconnaissance aircraft, for example, needed the normal capabilities of altitude and speed to escape interception, but also had to enjoy operational endurance, either because of the large areas of ocean to be covered or because of the need to remain in contact with discovered enemy vessels until naval or air units could close in for the kill. This in itself produced further design requirements. Oceanic patrol aircraft, employed in the lengthy and often fruitless task of finding enemy ships or submarines at sea, needed to be able to remain in the air for anything up to 14 hours at a stretch. They could not, therefore, be small machines, carried on board ship; by 1939 all the major combatants had developed large, multi-engined flying boats or land-based, long-range maritime bombers for this task. Fleet shadowing, by comparison, needed to be more flexible, using aircraft which could be launched at sea, either from conventional warships or carriers; by 1939 float planes were in widespread service, whereas in Britain, the USA and Japan, modified ship-borne machines had also been developed.

The same need for modification may be seen with the naval fighters, which had to be capable not only of fleet defense, shooting down enemy reconnaissance aircraft or attackers, but also of offensive operations, escorting bombers to the target and fighting through its defensive screen. Endurance was therefore added to the normal prerequisites of speed, maneuverability and firepower, while the cramped conditions on board the carriers necessitated small, compact

AIR

and ideally standardized designs to ease stowage and maintenance problems. The same applied, naturally, to the bombers, which could appear in three different guises: as level, dive or torpedo attackers. Level bombers (those which delivered their loads while flying straight and level over the target) needed robustness, range, bomb-carrying capacity and accuracy; dive bombers needed, in addition, a degree of integral protection during their vulnerable periods of approach and recovery; torpedo bombers needed all this, plus an ability to fly low and fast so that their weapons would not just sink to the bottom of the ocean when released.

Such a multiplicity of different requirements was to cause persistent headaches to designers throughout World War II, particularly in Britain, the USA and Japan – the major naval combatants and the only ones to deploy large numbers of aircraft carriers. These headaches were not eased when a fourth naval-air role, that of close support to invading troops during amphibious landings, was gradually developed, especially by the Americans, for this introduced even more refinements to existing designs. Attempts were made to combine various of these roles in one basic aircraft, but by 1945 the naval demands were so precise that this proved impossible. Such a solution is still being sought.

Britain Until April 1941, when the Admiralty rather belatedly gained direct operational control of RAF Coastal Command, the Royal Navy suffered all the disadvantages of a split in the sources of its air support. The reason for this dated back to the formation of the RAF as an independent entity in 1918, for part of the *raison d'être* of independence was complete control of all air elements, including those of the fleet. Unfortunately, with strategic bombing taking precedence, little time or effort was devoted to Coastal Command or carrier aircraft for much of the interwar period, and it was not until 1937 that the navy managed to regain full control of its Fleet Air Arm (FAA) squadrons. Even then, the RAF retained responsibility for long-range maritime reconnaissance and protection of coastal shipping. It was an unsatisfactory and unnecessary division of duties.

The RAF's lack of serious interest in naval support is indicated most markedly by the fact that in 1939 many of the necessary aircraft had to be hurriedly acquired from a wide variety of sources. In terms of long-range reconnaissance, for example, a number of civilian flying boats, particularly the Short 'C' and 'G' Empire-class

machines of Imperial Airways, were pressed into service, new designs were requested or purchased from the Americans and, as a real sign of desperation, heavy bombers were transferred from the hitherto sacrosanct Bomber Command. In fact, only one purpose-built maritime reconnaissance machine was available from British sources – the Short S25 Sunderland. Fortunately, this turned out to be a classic aircraft, performing its designated tasks of oceanic patrolling and antisubmarine warfare superbly. First flown in October 1937, this four-engined flying boat was developed from the commercial 'C'-class machines in answer to an RAF specification of 1933. The Mark I, powered by 1010hp Bristol Pegasus 22 radials, was the first production model, followed by the Mark II (with uprated Pegasus XVIII engines and a dorsal turret in place of beam guns) and virtually similar Mark III. The latter was the main wartime model, enjoying a top speed of 210mph, a range of over 2900 miles, endurance of up to 16 hours and, most impressively of all, a formidable weapons fit, comprising eight .303-inch machine guns (in nose, dorsal and tail positions) as well as 2000 pounds of bombs, mines or depth charges. Dubbed the 'Flying Porcupine' by Luftwaffe pilots who found its defensive armament almost impossible to penetrate, the Sunderland III was able to operate effectively over the vast areas of the Atlantic and Indian Oceans throughout the war. It was joined from September 1941 by the American-produced B-24B (RAF Liberator I) which, with a range of nearly 2400 miles, was the first of the land-based VLR (Very Long Range) aircraft to enter British service. Its introduction, together with that of other American designs such as the PBY-5 Catalina and Lockheed Hudson, helped to close the Atlantic 'air gap,' where convoys were devoid of air cover, a factor which greatly improved Allied chances of victory in this crucial area.

For shorter-range reconnaissance and attack, Coastal Command had the Avro Anson, a twin-engined monoplane developed from a commercial light transport (the Avalon) and first flown in 1935. When it entered squadron service a year later, it was widely regarded as an advanced design, incorporating such innovations as retractable undercarriage and closed cockpit, but by 1939, despite the reliability which earned it the nickname 'Faithful Annie,' it was approaching obsolescence. The Mark I, powered by 355hp Armstrong Siddeley IX radials, could achieve a top speed of 188mph only, enjoyed an operational range of just over 650 miles and was not well armed, even with the provision of a dorsal turret. Later marks introduced uprated engines, but performance figures did not improve significantly. Most were relegated to transport or training duties by 1941.

The Anson was replaced in Coastal Command attack squadrons by the Bristol Beaufort, a twin-engined, four-seat torpedo bomber, derived from the Blenheim. Powered by 1130hp Bristol Taurus VI radials and first flown in October 1938, the Beaufort offered some improvements over its predecessor. With a top speed of 265mph (reducing to around 220mph when an 18-inch torpedo was carried externally), a range of 1600 miles and a heavy armament fit (up to eight .303-inch machine guns in wing, dorsal and beam positions, plus 2000 pounds of bombs and one torpedo), this aircraft performed well in a variety of coastal roles. Australian-built examples were particularly active in New Guinea and the Solomons in 1942–43. But the effectiveness of the Beaufort was restricted by a comparatively small production run: just over 2000, some of which were transports and trainers, were built before production ceased in 1944.

It was therefore incumbent upon the navy to develop its own machines to satisfy most of the support roles. They were clearly never in a position to compete with the RAF over long-range reconnaissance capability, but did have a tradition of design so far as shipborne, short-range amphibians were concerned. Not that this was immediately apparent in 1939, for the main design then in FAA service, and one which was to remain in the front line throughout World War II, was an ungainly looking biplane – the Supermarine Walrus. With its origins in the Seagull amphibian series of the 1920s and first flown, in fact, as the Seagull V in June 1933, the Walrus began to equip FAA squadrons when they were still under RAF control, in July 1936. The Mark I, with a single 635hp Bristol Pegasus II M2 radial engine mounted as a pusher between the wings, was employed as a fleet spotter, reconnaissance and patrol aircraft and was often embarked on battleships or cruisers for catapult launching. The Mark II, with 775hp Pegasus VI, could reach a top speed of 135mph and enjoyed a range of 600 miles: it was used, in addition to the other roles, for air-sea rescue missions. Both marks were fitted with two .303-inch Lewis or Vickers machine guns for defense and up to 760 pounds of bombs for attack. A retractable undercarriage gave the aircraft an ability to alight on land, but the twin floats and flying-boat hull usually meant

recovery at sea. The Walrus proved to be so successful, despite its archaic design and performance figures, that an improved replacement, the Sea Otter, never fully ousted it from front-line service during World War II.

The existence of the Walrus, however, implied a prewar lack of official priority toward naval support aircraft, and this is further highlighted in the case of FAA carrier-borne fighters. Available designs in 1939 were archaic and ill-suited to their role. Six FAA squadrons were equipped with Gloster Sea Gladiators, 'navalized' versions of the RAF's obsolete biplane design; others deployed the unsatisfactory Blackburn Roc single-engined turret fighter, based on the same mistaken concept as the ill-fated Boulton Paul Defiant. Although the Roc was a monoplane, fitted with four .303-inch Browning machine guns in a power-operated dorsal turret, its underpowered 905hp Bristol Perseus XII radial engine produced a top speed of only 190mph and the type was soon withdrawn from service. A replacement, the single-engined, two-seat Fairey Fulmar, offered the advantages of eight wing-mounted .303s, a reliable Rolls-Royce Merlin in-line engine, a top speed of 280mph and improved combat maneuverability, but it did not enter service until June 1940. It went on to see widespread service, particularly in the Mediterranean, where it operated well against the Italians, but was at best an interim design, soon outmoded by more modern (and faster) opposition.

Attempts to produce a purpose-built fighter, incorporating all the lessons of modern air combat, began with Specification N.5/40 in 1940, but squadron deployment of the chosen design could not be expected for at least two years. In the meantime, the navy turned to other sources for interim designs. The first of these was, predictably, the American aircraft industry, and for much of the early wartime period the FAA was virtually dependent upon this source for its fighters. Sea Gladiators were gradually replaced from October 1940 by Grumman F4F-3s, known in FAA service as Martlets Marks I–III, and these began to go to sea on board escort carriers within the year. Thereafter the Martlet and its replacement F4F-4 development (known as the Wildcat, Marks IV–VI) continued in service throughout the war. A total of 215 Martlets and 902 Wildcats performed well in all theaters, showing a particular adaptability to cramped conditions on board small carriers and an inherent robustness and reliability which went much of the way to satisfying the needs of the FAA. They were followed in 1943, by which time it was apparent that British industry could not cope with the enormous demands imposed upon it by both the RAF and FAA, by the Grumman Hellcat (originally known as the Gannet to the FAA), of which 2112 were delivered by the end of the war. Most of these, together with about 900 Chance Vought Corsairs, also delivered between 1943 and 1945, served in the Pacific and Far Eastern theaters. The contribution of all these types cannot be overstated. Their provision by the Americans undoubtedly saved the FAA during the crucial years 1940–42 and bolstered it significantly thereafter, although it should not be imagined that no British designs existed. In 1940 another interim source was available – the already-proven fighter designs of the RAF.

FAA modifications to such RAF aircraft were surprisingly successful, beginning in early 1941 when combat-weary Hawker Hurricane Is were 'navalized' by the addition of arrestor hooks and catapult launching points. They were never purpose-built. All Sea Hurricanes in service were merely modifications to a design which was, by 1941, becoming outclassed as an interceptor, and although performance was not altered significantly by the process of 'navalization,' something more modern and effective was clearly needed.

Fortunately for the FAA just such a fighter emerged when the modification idea was applied to the Supermarine Spitfire. In late 1941 a Spitfire VB was fitted with arrestor hooks and tested on board the carrier HMS *Illustrious*, emerging successfully as the Seafire IB. Over 180 of these excellent conversions entered squadron service in 1942, to be followed by purpose-built Seafire F Mark IIIs, powered by 1470hp Merlin 55s and suitably adapted to carrier deployment with catapult attachments, arrestor hooks and folding wings. All retained the speed, maneuverability and firepower of the parent design but also shared the Spitfires' short range. Despite this disadvantage the Seafire rapidly became an integral part of Britain's carrier force. Wartime development culminated in the Mark XV, with 1850hp Griffon engine, top speed of 383mph and heavy armament fit, and examples of this superb machine saw some service, from May 1945, in the Far East.

By that time the navy's choice in answer to Specification N.5/40 had been in front-line service for two years as a useful and effective fighter. First flown in December 1941, the Fairey Firefly was a two-seat, single-engined design, based upon, but significantly more powerful and maneuverable than, the Fulmar. Fitted with a 1730hp Rolls-Royce Griffon IIB in-line engine, the Mark I (the main wartime production version) incorporated all the obvious naval features, such as strengthened airframe and folding wings, and enjoyed creditable performance figures: top speed of 316mph, operational range of 760 miles and excellent maneuverability, particularly at low speed. Armament fit of four wing-mounted 20mm Hispano cannon and up to 2000 pounds of bombs or other weapons was more than adequate. Subsequent modifications (some of them postwar) increased the speed to 386mph and range to 1300 miles, and the type saw service not only in World War II but also in Korea. It had taken a long time, but in the Firefly the FAA at last had a proper, home-produced carrier fighter.

A similar process of gradual development may be seen with the bombers of the FAA. In 1939 two design trends were apparent, with both dive-bomber and torpedo-strike aircraft in squadron service. The dive bombers were unsatisfactory, represented by the unimpressive Blackburn Skua. First flown in February 1937 and powered by the same 905hp Bristol Perseus XII radial engine as its stablemate the Roc, the Skua was obsolescent by the beginning of hostilities two and a half years later. With a maximum speed of 229mph and a bomb load of only one centerline 500-pound weapon, the aircraft was barely capable of carrying out its main role and, when four wing-mounted .303-inch Browning machine guns were added in an attempt to produce a fighter, the results were disastrous. By 1941 most Skuas had been relegated to target-towing and little serious attempt appears to have been made to maintain dive-bombing potential within the FAA.

Responsibility for offensive operations therefore rested almost entirely upon the torpedo bombers, represented in 1939 by an extremely archaic-looking biplane, the Fairey Swordfish. A three-seat, fabric-covered machine with a top speed of only 139mph and restricted range of 546 miles with full load, the Swordfish was in theory a dangerously obsolete piece of equipment. Yet, in one of the most remarkable stories of the war, this aircraft, which first flew as early as April 1934, was not only to remain in front-line service until 1945 but was also to contribute significantly to Allied naval victory. Powered by a reliable 690 or 750hp Bristol Pegasus radial engine and armed with one 18-inch torpedo or 1500 pounds of bombs, mines or depth charges, the exploits of the 'Stringbag' are legion. On 11 November 1940 Swordfish crippled the Italian Fleet at Taranto; in May 1941 they slowed down the German battleship *Bismarck*, enabling British warships to close in for the kill; by 1944–45 they were being widely and successfully used as radar-equipped submarine hunters and even, when fitted with 3-inch rockets on underwing racks, as ground-support machines. The Swordfish eventually equipped a total of 26 FAA land-based torpedo squadrons. It also appeared on board carriers and as a float plane.

Naval Specification S.41/36, designed to provide a replacement, was issued as early as 1936. In response Fairey produced another biplane, the three-seat, single-engined Albacore carrier torpedo bomber. Although first flown as early as December 1938 and despite poor performance figures, including a top speed of only 161mph, the Albacore saw service in all theaters of war. Torpedo- or bomb-carrying capacity was similar to that of the Swordfish.

The Albacore was withdrawn from front-line service in 1943, when it was replaced by yet another Fairey design, the three-seat, single-engined Barracuda monoplane torpedo bomber. Produced in answer to Naval Specification S. 24/37 of 1937, the Barracuda had an unfortunate gestation, caused primarily by engine problems. Nevertheless, it was eventually an effective aircraft, with top speed of 228mph, range of about 600 miles and offensive armament of one 18-inch torpedo or 2000 pounds of other stores. It was, in fact, employed occasionally as a dive bomber – most notably in April 1944, against the German battleship *Tirpitz* – but its normal role was torpedo strike. In this it was adequate, although the continued deployment of the Swordfish implies that the Barracuda was never fully accepted as an ultimate design, lacking power and defensive armament. RAF Coastal Command flew the torpedo-carrying version of the Bristol Beaufighter, equipped with one centerline torpedo or 2127 pounds of bombs, plus wing racks for eight rockets or a further 1000 pounds of free-fall ordnance. With performance figures similar to those of the fighter-bomber version of this aircraft (top speed of 330mph, rate of climb of 1700 feet per minute and range of 1500 miles) the Beaufighter was clearly an effective naval-support machine, but, with priority being given to production for other roles, numbers in service were never large. American designs were acquired for the FAA and a total of 958 Grumman Avengers were delivered to satisfy the torpedo-bomber role.

The United States The US Navy (USN) has always played an important part in the defense of the United States, protecting the seaward approaches to the country and projecting national influence into other areas of the globe. These tasks are enormous, involving the use of naval vessels to cover huge tracts of ocean, and it was not until the advent of air power that any degree of effectiveness could be guaranteed. Long-range aircraft gave the USN the ability to patrol a far wider area of sea with greater chance of intercepting potential threats; carrier-borne aircraft improved the striking power of fleets operating many hundreds of miles from their base facilities. Such enhanced flexibility was recognized during the interwar period, partly as a result of American experience of major war in 1917–18 and partly in response to the growing power of Japan in the vastness of the Pacific. By 1941 the USN was provided with a wide range of modern aircraft designs, deployed both on land and aboard a number of purpose-built carriers. The expertise that this represented was to develop effective air support not only for the USN but also for a number of Allied navies during World War II.

Indeed, the importance of carrier warfare, particularly in the Pacific, cannot be over-emphasized. Left without its battleship fleet after Pearl Harbor, the USN was forced to depend for its continued effectiveness upon the aircraft carrier and the major sea battles of the Pacific War revolved around these ships and their air squadrons. These battles gradually wore down the Japanese naval air service by imposing irreplaceable losses upon it. The statistics speak for themselves; at Midway in June 1942 the Japanese lost four fleet carriers and 253 aircraft to the American carrierborne squadrons; at the Philippine Sea (including the Great Marianas Turkey Shoot) two years later they lost a further two carriers and 545 aircraft; and at Leyte Gulf in October 1944 the process of destruction was completed when they lost the last four of their major carriers together with an estimated 500 aircraft. The USN did not escape without casualties, of course, but these could be replaced by a rapidly expanding war industry, with the result that by early 1945 the American carriers had gained both sea and air supremacy right up to the shores of Japan itself – a unique and decisive feat.

In terms of long-range maritime patrolling, the advantages of flying boats were appreciated as early as 1933, when the USN called for a monoplane design to operate principally in the Pacific. The Consolidated Aircraft Corporation obliged with what turned out to be an enormously successful machine – the PBY Catalina. First flown on 21 March 1935, the prototype was powered by two 825hp Pratt and Whitney Twin Wasp radials, positioned close together on a very high wing, and these gave it the exceptional speed, for time and type, of 184mph. The USN immediately ordered 60 as the PBY-1, fitted with slightly uprated Twin Wasps and redesigned vertical tail surfaces, and these began to equip navy squadrons in October 1936. PBY-2 and -3 models followed in 1937, incorporating few obvious changes to design, but the -4 model of 1938 was the first to feature characteristic transparent beam blisters instead of side hatches. It was gradually superseded by the PBY-5, and this was the major production version, seeing service not only with the USN but also with RAF Coastal Command and, as the license-built GST, with the Soviet navy. It was an impressive machine. Powered by 1200hp Twin Wasp radials, it enjoyed a top speed of 200mph, operational range of 3100 miles and a good armament fit (usually four .50-inch or .30-inch machine guns in nose, ventral and beam positions, plus up to 2000 pounds of bombs or other stores). The PBY-5A was an amphibian, fitted with retractable undercarriage as well as the wingtip stabilizing floats which were a feature of all variants. The contribution of the Catalina in all theaters, and in a wide variety of maritime reconnaissance and strike roles, cannot be overstated.

The PBY was joined in USN service in 1940 by the PBM Mariner, another twin-engined monoplane flying boat. Designed by the Glenn L Martin Company as a medium-range maritime reconnaissance bomber, the prototype first flew on 18 February 1939, two years after the navy had placed its initial order. Characterized by a shoulder-mounted gull wing and retractable stabilizing floats, the production PBM-1 was powered by 1600hp Wright Double Cyclone radials, enjoying a top speed of 205mph, useful range of nearly 3500 miles and a good armament fit (four .50-inch machine guns in nose, dorsal and beam positions) plus a bomb load of 4000 pounds. A plethora of design changes culminated in the PBM-5 of 1943, powered by 2100hp Pratt and Whitney Double Wasps, and this was the first to operate as an amphibian. Performance had by this time improved all round and armament increased to eight .50s, but the type was always overshadowed in the public eye by the Catalina. A small number of PBM-3s were issued briefly to RAF Coastal Command.

The USN also deployed a four-engined flying boat – the Consolidated PB2Y Coronado – for very long-range tasks, but it was never a great success. First flown in December 1937, the PB2Y was always a heavy machine and, although its 1200hp Twin Wasps could produce a top speed of 223mph, takeoff was difficult, even when assisted by special rocket packs, and it was sluggish in the air. Even so, with an operational range of 3900 miles (in the PB2Y-5 model of 1943) and excellent armament fit (eight .50s in nose, beam and tail positions) plus up to 4000 pounds of bombs, mines or depth charges, the aircraft could not fail to perform some useful duties, particularly in the Pacific. A greater degree of overall success was achieved by its land-based stablemate, the PB4Y-2 Privateer. Developed from the B-24D of 1943, the Privateer was a larger, more powerful version of the Liberator, designed to act as a maritime patrol bomber. Powered by four 1200hp Twin Wasps, it could reach 237mph, operate over ranges in excess of 2800 miles and deliver up to 6000 pounds of bombs or other stores. Defensive armament was formidable, comprising 12 .50s in a variety of positions. Examples saw effective Pacific service in 1944–45, representing the zenith of American maritime patrol design during World War II.

Before leaving such aircraft, however, mention must be made of the Lockheed Model 414 Hudson. A twin-engined medium bomber, developed hurriedly from Lockheed's Model 14 airliner in answer to requests from Britain in 1938, this machine saw little operational service with the Americans but proved a decided asset to RAF Coastal Command in the early, difficult, years of the naval war. Enjoying respectable endurance, unprecedented crew comfort (including automatic pilot) reasonable defensive armament of five .303-inch Browning machine guns (two in a dorsal turret, two in beam and one in a ventral position) and adequate bomb load of 1500 pounds, the Hudson was a potent warplane. Known in restricted US service as the A-28 (when fitted with Twin Wasp radials) or A-29 (with Wright Cyclones), the aircraft was yet another example of timely American design.

The influence of European requirements may also be seen in the case of USN fleet fighters available in 1941, although not to the extent already noted with their land-based counterparts. The navy had a strong tradition of acquiring effective carrierborne interceptors during the interwar period, and there is evidence that by the mid-1930s they had options on more designs than they needed. Thus in 1936, when a specification was issued for a new single-engined, single-seat monoplane naval fighter, the designs

Above: Corsair F4U fighters of the US Marines silhouetted against an antiaircraft barrage.

produced by the Brewster Aircraft Company and the Grumman Aircraft Engineering Corporation were both potentially excellent. In the event, Brewster won the contract, but Grumman continued its program as a private venture, eventually attracting a substantial order from the French in 1939. Known at this stage as the G-36A, surviving or undelivered examples were transferred to Britain in June 1940, entering FAA squadrons as the Martlet and helping to fill the carrierborne fighter gap then so apparent.

Meanwhile, however, the USN had shown interest and in August 1939 an order for 54 of what became known as the F4F Wildcat (a name also given to British examples in 1944) was authorized. Powered at this early stage by a 1200hp Wright Cyclone radial, this stubby, short-winged fighter proved to be ideally suited to carrier deployment, seeing widespread service during the early months of the Pacific War. Modifications were continually put into effect, but the F4F-4, with uprated engine and folding wings, was the most important Grumman-produced variant. With a top speed of 318mph, range of 900 miles and armament of six wing-mounted .50-inch machine guns as well as racks for two 250-pound bombs, the F4F-4 was an effective fighter. In 1943 the Eastern Aircraft Division of General Motors took over production, leading to new designations of FM-1 and, when 1350hp Wright Cyclone engine was fitted, FM-2. These variants were still in service in

1945, sharing with their predecessors a well-deserved reputation for robustness and maneuverability.

The design which won Brewster the 1936 USN contract was the F2A Buffalo, and, although it took until January 1938 for the prototype to be flown, this proved to be a good choice as the navy's first monoplane fighter. Powered by a 1100hp Wright Cyclone radial, the Buffalo was a compact, barrel-like aircraft, well suited to life on board cramped carriers. It also turned out to be a fairly effective interceptor, with a top speed of 321mph, range of up to 950 miles and armament of four .50s, two in the wings and two in the fuselage. Early production F2A-1s saw widespread land-based service with the Finns from 1940 to 1944, but USN examples, even the more powerful -2 and -3 models, were outclassed when pitted against the remarkable Japanese A6M Zero in the early months of the Pacific War. The Buffalo took part in the defense of Midway in 1942 and served with the RAF in Malaya.

The Zero was, in fact, the major problem confronting the USN in 1941–42, for neither the Buffalo nor the early-model Wildcats could match its combat performance. Fortunately, follow-up designs did appear quickly – an indication of the strength of the US aircraft industry at the time – and the first of these, the Chance Vought F4U Corsair, entered squadron service in mid-1942.

In spite of early problems, it was a superb naval fighter. First flown on 29 May 1940, the prototype gave notice of its potential by achieving a top speed of 395mph and this feature alone ensured its immediate production. F4U-1 models, with 2000hp Pratt and Whitney Double Wasp radials and six wing-mounted .50-inch machine guns, were powerful machines in their own right, but -1C (with four 20mm cannon) and -1D (with drop tank and two 1000-pound bombs) variants ensured a continued position of superiority over the opposition throughout World War II. Later models included reconnaissance, night-fighter and, with 5-inch rockets on underwing racks, ground-attack machines, some of which saw action in Korea. Altogether over 12,500 Corsairs were built, some for the British and New Zealand naval air arms, before production ceased in 1952.

Nor was the Corsair alone in its major role of regaining and maintaining air supremacy in the Pacific, for in October 1942 USN squadrons began to receive the equally effective Grumman F6F Hellcat. A bigger and more powerful development of the Wildcat, the F6F was arguably the best naval fighter produced by the Allies in World War II. With top speed of over 375mph, provided by a 2000hp Pratt and Whitney Double Wasp radial, range of over 1000 miles and armament of six wing-mounted .50s, performance statistics were not dissimilar to those of the Corsair, but the Hellcat was more maneuverable and better suited to carrier warfare, enjoying a robustness and strength which has rarely been surpassed. Examples took part in all the naval battles of the Pacific War after 1943, destroying over 6000 Japanese aircraft (many of them the now outclassed Zeros) in the process. Night-fighter and reconnaissance versions also existed.

The quality of all these fighter designs was matched by the bombers in USN wartime deployment. In terms of dive bombers, the Douglas SBD Dauntless was the front-line carrierborne machine in 1941. Rejected as obsolescent by the USAAF, who deployed it as the A-24, naval versions were to make a significant contribution to eventual Allied victory in the Pacific. Because it was the only design available, the Dauntless was thrown against the Japanese from Pearl Harbor onward and, although its maximum bomb load of 1500 pounds could never be made up of more than three pieces of ordnance (one 1000-pound weapon on center-line, with two 250-pound bombs on outer wing racks), its ability to absorb tremendous punishment, combined with the bravery of its crews,

produced remarkable results. Still in squadron service as late as June 1944, the Dauntless suffered fewer casualties per mission than any other single USN type and sank more Japanese shipping than any other Allied weapon. Its successor in dive-bomber squadrons was the Curtiss SB2C Helldiver. First flown on 18 December 1940, the SB2C-1, powered by a 1700hp Wright Cyclone radial, was a powerful yet unpopular machine. With a top speed of 281mph, range of 1110 miles and armament of four .50s in the wings and two .30s in the rear cockpit, as well as bomb load of 1000 pounds carried internally, the Helldiver entered the fray over Rabaul in November 1943. It was to remain in constant action, often in conjunction with the Dauntless it was meant to replace, until the end of hostilities.

The pattern was slightly different in the case of the torpedo bombers, for the main design available in 1941 – the Douglas TBD Devastator – was clearly outmoded and vulnerable as soon as the war began. First flown as early as January 1935, this three-seater, single-engined machine was slow (206mph maximum), underpowered (by its 850hp Pratt and Whitney Twin Wasp radial) and poorly protected (by just two machine guns, one to the right of the nose and one in the rear cockpit). Furthermore, range was restricted to 435 miles and offensive armament was only one 21-inch torpedo and 500 pounds of bombs. Despite sustained action up to June 1942, the Devastators were quickly replaced by a much more effective design – the Grumman TBF Avenger. Initiated in 1940, first flown in August 1941 and in action with some of the US forces at the Battle of Midway in June 1942, the Avenger was an excellent carrierborne torpedo bomber. Powered by a 1700hp Wright Double Cyclone radial, it could achieve a top speed of 278mph, enjoyed a range in excess of 1200 miles and could deliver one 22-inch torpedo or 2000 pounds of bombs. Adequately defended by up to five machine guns, one of which was in a power-operated dorsal turret, the aircraft could also fight through enemy defenses to make its attack. Eastern Aircraft took over production in December 1943, under the new designation TBM, and some of their models, equipped with 5-inch rockets, were also used for ground attack. Once again, the USN had been provided with the right aircraft at the right time. It was the key to success.

Japan Of all the countries involved in World War II, Japan was the one most dedicated to naval aviation. The reasons are obvious. If the inhabitants of such a small group of islands were to defeat the Americans and the Western colonial powers in the vastness of the Pacific, they needed to destroy the 'heart' of enemy military capability quickly, before superior industrial might could be mobilized and concentrated against them. The discovery and destruction of the heart could not be carried out by land forces because of the huge areas of ocean involved, not could it be achieved by naval vessels alone, since they lacked the requisite flexibility and coordinated long-range hitting power. If such targets as the US Pacific Fleet at Pearl Harbor were to be taken out, the attack needed to be a complete surprise and a complete success. Aircraft were the only weapons capable of carrying out the preliminary reconnaissance and instantaneous destruction so essential, and for this reason the Japanese Naval Air Force (JNAF) was a strong and effective part of the Imperial Navy by 1941.

Long-range maritime reconnaissance was clearly an important JNAF role in the search for enemy force concentrations, and this was reflected in the existence of two flying-boat designs in December 1941. The first of these, the four-engined Kawanishi H6K (Allied code name Mavis), had appeared in July 1936 in answer to a specification calling for a flying boat with operational range of around 2500 miles. Powered by 840hp Nakajima Hikari 2 radial engines in early production models, the H6K, characterized by its large parasol wing supported by V-struts, satisfied the range requirement but was underpowered and poorly defended (with only three 7.7mm machine guns). Uprated Kinsei 43 radials helped to rectify the first of these shortcomings in the H6K-2 variant of January 1938, but the problem of protection was never adequately solved. Even the H6K-4, with increased range of 2981 miles and blister beam positions and tail turret for extra machine guns, was always vulnerable to Allied fighter attack. Fortunately for the JNAF, a far superior design began to equip reconnaissance squadrons in late 1941. This was the Kawanishi H8K (Emily), another four-engined flying boat, but one which was almost certainly the best of its type developed for service in World War II. When first flown in January 1941 the prototype had proved unstable, but when extra hull depth was added it turned into a very effective machine. Powered by 1530hp Mitsubishi Kasei 11 radials, production H8Ks could reach a top speed of 269mph and enjoyed a normal operational range of 3000 miles. (Provision was made for extending even this long range up to a massive 4475 miles.)

In addition, they were adequately armed (five 20mm cannon in nose, dorsal and tail turrets, three 7.7mm machine guns in beam and rear ventral windows) and could deliver either two torpedoes or up to 4400 pounds of bombs. The Emily was almost impossible to shoot down, and for this reason examples continued to operate right up to the end of the war.

For shorter-range reconnaissance work, carried out from island bays or from ships at sea, the JNAF developed a series of single-engined float planes. The earliest design still in frontline service in 1941 was in fact a biplane – the Mitsubishi F1M (Pete). Developed in answer to a specification of 1934 for a new shipborne observation machine and first flown in June 1936, the F1M seemed at first glance to be obsolete. But with a top speed of 230mph, and range of up to 670 miles, it clearly still had much to offer and, during the early campaigns of the Pacific War this robust and maneuverable aircraft was encountered in a wide variety of roles. Armament fit of three 7.7mm machine guns (two above the engine and one in the rear cockpit) even enabled it to act as a fighter.

The Pete was supported in its reconnaissance duties by the Aichi E13A (Jake), a monoplane float plane which had first flown in late 1938. Powered by a 1080hp Kinsei 43 radial, this aircraft could reach 234mph and enjoyed the useful range of 1300 miles. It was very poorly armed, however (one 7.92mm machine gun in rear cockpit) and, although large numbers saw service, their contribution and effect naturally declined as Allied air superiority increased. The same happened to another Aichi design, the E16A Zuiun (Auspicious Cloud – Allied code name Paul), which did not enter front-line service until early 1944. Powered by a 1300hp Kinsei 51 radial, with top speed of 273 miles, normal range of 731 miles and improved defensive armament (two 20mm cannon in the wings and one 13mm in the rear cockpit), this would have been an adequate machine in the early months of war, but was doomed to swift extinction in the face of powerful Allied opposition.

The JNAF did not confine its reconnaissance potential just to waterborne machines, however, for in a unique development program it explored the possibilities of deploying carrier-borne aircraft capable of acting as the 'eyes' of the fleet. An effective landplane, entering service, in late 1942, was the Nakajima J1N1 (Irving), a twin-engined monoplane which started life as a long-range escort fighter. First flown as such in May 1941, its top speed of 315mph and range of more than 1500 miles lent it naturally to reconnaissance work, and this was its designated role up to spring 1943. By that time, unarmed aircraft had become dangerously vulnerable and surviving examples were converted to night fighters by the addition of four 20mm cannon. A similar fate befell the only purpose-built carrierborne reconnaissance machine, for although the Nakajima C6N Saiun (Painted Cloud – Allied code name Myrt) enjoyed excellent performance figures (a top speed of 379mph and range of 1914 miles), its lack of armament forced a change of role when it entered service in July 1944. C6N-1-B Variants, with torpedo-carrying capacity and forward-firing cannon, saw some action in 1944–45, as did -1-S night fighters, but the original idea behind the design had been lost.

The JNAF enjoyed infinitely more success with its carrierborne fighters, and it was in this role that some of the most famous Japanese aircraft of World War II appeared. One of the earliest to see service was the Mitsubishi A5M (Allied code name Claude), developed in response to a 1934 specification which called for a speed of 217mph and an ability to climb to 16,400 feet in 6.5 minutes. The prototype, flown on 4 February 1935, achieved far more – a top speed of 270mph and a climb to the required altitude in just under six minutes – and production began immediately. Powered by a single Nakajima Kotobuki radial and armed with two forward-firing 7.7mm machine guns on the engine cowling, this maneuverable little monoplane achieved dramatic success in China in 1937 and Mongolia two years later. A fixed undercarriage was a drawback, but examples of the A5M did see action in the early part of the Pacific War.

The expertise amassed by Mitsubishi during this development program was put to good use in 1937, when the JNAF called for a new carrier fighter, to be capable of 311mph and to be armed with two cannon and two machine guns. The result, first flown on 1 April 1939, was the single-seat, single-engined A6M, an aircraft better known by its type number – Zero Sen or Type 0, to denote its service acceptance in the Japanese year 5700 (1940) – even to the Allies, despite an official code name Zeke. The Zero was a most effective machine. Early A6M1 versions were powered by 780hp Mitsubishi MK2 Zuisei 13 radial engines and could achieve a top speed slightly in excess of the required specification, a rate of climb of over 4000 feet per minute and a combat maneuverability unequalled at the time. A modified

version with 925hp Nakajima NK1C Sakae 12 radials, the A6M2, quickly appeared and examples of this type were deployed with great success in China after July 1940. They were well armed with two wing-mounted 20mm cannon and two fuselage-mounted 7.7mm machine guns. A further variant was the clipped wing A6M3. Both types saw widespread and successful action in the early months of the Pacific War, sweeping aside all Allied fighters in a campaign which both shocked and surprised the Western powers. In fact it was not until the JNAF had been considerably weakened by heavy pilot losses at such battles as Midway (June 1942) and Guadalcanal (August 1942–February 1943) that the Allies were able to counter the growing myth of Zero invincibility, and not until such American fighters as the F4U Corsair and F6F Hellcat had been deployed in late 1942/early 1943 that the Zero began to lose its potency. This did not mean that its career was over: far from it. A lack of suitable replacement designs led to the emergence of the A6M5 in late 1943, powered by a 1130hp Sakae 31 radial and characterized by enhanced armament fit (12.7 or 13.2mm machine guns, in addition to the normal cannon), and this was in fact the most-produced variant of the war years. In the end, however, the twin pressures of Allied bombing and blockade began to close down the factories and, although even more variants were planned, few saw active service. Late models were converted into suicide planes and a float-plane version, the A6M2-N (Allied code name Rufe) did appear in some numbers, but in the final months of war the Zero had met its match. A combination of poor production, badly trained pilots and superior Allied machines doomed it to destruction.

The existence of such a good fighter undoubtedly delayed the development of replacements and, although these did exist and see action, they appeared too late in the war to be fully effective. The first to reach front-line squadrons was another Mitsubishi design, the J2M Raiden (Thunderbolt – Allied code name Jack), which had been initiated as early as 1938 but not flown until March 1942. A dumpy, single-seat, single-engined fighter, it experienced tremendous problems, chiefly with its 1430hp Kasei radial engine, and production was delayed. The prototype was in fact virtually rebuilt to take a 1820hp Kasei 23a and the first models did not enter service until December 1943. Nevertheless, with a top speed of 363mph, rate of climb of 3800 feet per minute and armament fit of two wing-mounted 20mm cannon and two fuselage-mounted 7.7mm machine guns, the production J2M2 clearly had much to offer. Indeed, when the armament was concentrated solely in the wings to produce the J2M3, the aircraft was capable of tackling the B-29s over Japan, achieving sufficient success for the Americans to rate it one of the best enemy interceptors of the war. But, as with the Zero, the problems of national defeat negated much of its advantage.

The same was true of a Kawanishi fighter design – the N1K1-J Shiden (Violet Lightning – Allied code name George). Developed, unusually, from a float plane (the N1K1 Rex), the George was potentially a very effective machine. Powered by a 1990hp Nakajima Homare 21 radial, and first flown in July 1943, it could reach 363mph, achieve a rate of climb of 3300 feet per minute and was armed with up to four 20mm cannon and two 7.7mm machine guns. In addition, it turned out to be one of the most maneuverable aircraft of the war years. Performance was enhanced in 1944 with the development of the N1K2-J Shiden-Kai, a much lighter and simpler aircraft. The ailing aeroengine industry could not cope with demand, however, and this, together with all the other problems besetting Japan in 1944–45, meant that few examples saw front-line service.

Fighters alone could never satisfy the strategic needs of Japan and, understandably, there was a strong emphasis placed upon bombers as well. In the dive-bombing role, the JNAF in December 1941 was fortunate in having at its disposal the two-seat, single-engined Aichi D3A (Val). Developed in answer to a specification of 1936, and influenced quite markedly by designs from the German firm of Heinkel, the D3A first flew in January 1938, achieving a top speed of 240mph despite the provision of a fixed undercarriage. Production D3A1 models, capable of carrying 683 pounds of bombs (fixed on a centerline cradle and under the wings) over ranges of 1131 miles, were delivered to carriers in 1939. Many examples took part in the attack on Pearl Harbor, being credited, there and elsewhere in the early Pacific campaigns, with 80–82 percent bomb-hitting accuracy. The 1075hp Kinsei 44 was replaced by an uprated Kinsei 54 in August 1942 to produce the D3A2 version, but by then the aircraft was outclassed, proving vulnerable to Allied air opposition. The Val was supposed to be replaced by the Yokosuka D4Y Suisei (Comet – Allied code name Judy), but this was never an entirely satisfactory design. First flown in November 1940, production D4Y1 models should have

been effective, with top speed of 343mph, bomb load of 683 pounds and range of 978 miles, but the original in-line 1200hp Aichi Atsuta 21 engine was poor and defensive armament inadequate (three 7.7mm machine guns only). A switch to the 1400hp Atsuta 32 in the D4Y2 variant did not improve matters, and it was not until the 1560hp Kinsei 62 radial was used that a useful aircraft began to emerge. By then it was 1943 and Japanese air superiority – a vital prerequisite for dive-bombing success – was no longer guaranteed.

An almost identical pattern of events affected the JNAF torpedo bombers. In December 1941 the main design in service was the Nakajima B5N (Kate), an effective machine so long as air superiority pertained. Powered initially by a 770hp Nakajima Hikari 3 radial engine, the B5N1 entered production in 1937 with useful performance figures: a top speed of 229mph, bomb load (torpedoes were not fitted to begin with) of 683 pounds and range of 679 miles. The B5N2 entered service two years later, fitted with a 1115hp Sakae 21 radial and, although this increased the speed to 235mph, range was reduced when one 18-inch torpedo was carried externally. Nevertheless, the new range of 608 miles was sufficient for 103 B5N2s to take part in the Pearl Harbor attack as well as a host of subsequent actions. By 1942, however, the type was clearly outclassed and new designs were initiated. These were never satisfactory. The first to enter service, in June 1944, was the Nakajima B6N Tenzan (Heavenly Mountain – Allied code name Jill), an aircraft which should have been effective, with top speed of 299mph (in the B6N2 variant), bomb load of 1300 pounds in addition to one 18-inch torpedo and range of 1890 miles. But the original 1870hp Nakajima Mamori 11 radial was prone to overheating and replacements were little better. In addition, with poor crew training and, by 1944, an absence of carriers from which to operate, the Jill was never a major threat. Nor was its contemporary, the Aichi B7A Ryusei (Shooting Star – Allied code name Grace) which, although the most powerful Japanese dive bomber produced, suffered all the familiar problems of wartime development. First flown in May 1942, examples did not enter service until 1944 and had little effect on the Pacific War.

Finally, the JNAF employed land-based bombers for longer-range naval support, deploying two twin-engined designs during World War II, both of which were effective during the years of air superiority. The earlier model was the Mitsubishi G3M (Nell), first flown in July 1935. Powered by 910hp Kinsei 3 radials, production G3M1s had a top speed of 216mph, bomb load of 1764 pounds and an exceptional range of 2700 miles, while being reasonably well protected by up to four 7.7mm machine guns (in cockpit, ventral and retractable dorsal positions). Service delivery took place in late 1936 and examples saw action in China. The G3M2 variant, with uprated Kinsei 42s and increased speed of 232mph, soon followed, but the G3M3, with Kinsei 51s and enhanced armament fit (one 20mm cannon in dorsal fairing, 7.7mm machine guns in cockpit, beam blister and tail positions) was the best model to see service. By 1943, however, Allied air strength began to tell and the type was relegated to second-line duties. It should perhaps have been joined by its stablemate, the G4M (Betty), a machine which, through an insistence on bomb load (2205 pounds maximum) and range (over 3700 miles, was poorly protected and extremely vulnerable. In addition, its two 1530hp Kasei 11 radials did not produce the necessary power (Mitsubishi always insisted that it should have been a four-engined bomber, but were overruled by the JNAF) and, despite constant modifications, the G4M was obsolete and outclassed as early as 1942, only a year after its delivery to squadrons and two after its first flight. By 1942–43, therefore, the JNAF was desperately short of level bombers and no replacement designs were produced in quantity. The degree of desperation may be gauged not only from the continued deployment of the G4M but also from the development in 1945 of the Yokosuka MXY-7 Ohka (Cherry Blossom – Allied code name Baka) single-seat suicide bomb. Powered by a three-barrel Type 4 Model 20 rocket motor, the Ohka was designed to be released from a parent craft (usually a G4M) about 12 miles from the target at an altitude in excess of 18,000 feet. The doomed pilot, seated behind a 2645-pound warhead, would then glide down until he reached a good attack position, upon which he would fire the rockets to take him in. The first Ohka attacks, upon American shipping off Okinawa, took place in March/April 1945, but they were the tactics of a defeated nation.

Germany Naval support was not an air role stressed by the Luftwaffe during World War II. Although an aircraft carrier, the *Graf Zeppelin*, was launched in December 1938 and squadrons of Bf 109 fighters and Ju 87 dive bombers prepared for deployment, the ship was never taken into service. This left maritime reconnais-

sance and long-range, land-based naval bombing as the only feasible support tasks. Both were carried out: for bombing the Fw 200 and Ju 290 four-engined aircraft were used; for reconnaissance a number of flying-boat and float-plane designs existed.

The largest of the flying boats to see active service was the six-engined Blohm und Voss Bv 222 *Wiking*. This monstrous machine, powered usually by 1000hp Bramo Fafnir 323R radials and weighing anything up to 108,000 pounds fully loaded, was developed initially as a commercial transatlantic boat for use by Lufthansa. With a top speed of 242mph, range of 3790 miles, flight endurance of an incredible 28 hours and heavy armament fit (C models of 1941 had machine guns in a wide variety of positions, including special remotely fired turrets on the wings), the *Wiking* was clearly an impressive aircraft. However, development problems were enormous, the engines were not satisfactory and, despite useful service ferrying supplies to many areas of war, the design was not a success. An attempt to improve matters led to the Bv 238, another six-engined flying boat, but the prototype of this did not even fly until 1944 and the project was cancelled soon afterward.

Of the smaller, shorter-range flying boats, the oldest in service in 1939 was the Dornier Do 18, an unusual and unsatisfactory machine. With tandem push/pull Junkers Jumo 205C diesel engines fitted above a high wing, the early production Do 18D models, which entered service in 1938, were underpowered (top speed was only 160mph) and poorly protected (by two 7.92mm machine guns in open cockpits at bow and aft). About 100 examples, including slightly more powerful G, H and N variants, were produced, but they were barely capable of active service. They were replaced by the three-engined Blohm und Voss Bv 138, a more promising design but one which took time to develop. The prototype, flown in July 1937, was not very impressive (chiefly because of problems with its 600hp Jumo 205C diesels), and it was not until the machine had been radically altered that a viable aircraft emerged. This was the Bv 138C-1, delivered to squadrons in 1941. Powered by 880hp Jumo 205 Do and adequately protected not only by 20mm cannon in bow and stern power-operated turrets but also by 7.92mm machine guns in open positions, this was a useful flying boat, enjoying a top speed of 170mph and range of 2500 miles. Known to its crews as the 'Flying Clog' because of its distinctive hull shape, the Bv 138C-1 performed well as a reconnaissance, mine-laying, mine-detecting and rescue aircraft. It was joined after 1940 by another good design – the three-engined, parasol-winged Dornier Do 24, a flying boat developed originally, in 1937, for the Dutch. With a top speed of 211mph, range of 2920 miles and adequate defensive armament (7.92 or 20mm machine guns in bow, dorsal and tail turrets) this was an aircraft of some potential. Unfortunately, only just over 200 saw service.

The same sort of half-hearted commitment is apparent with the float planes, for although two reasonably effective designs existed in 1939, capable of reconnaissance, mine-laying and even torpedo-strike missions, they were never used to their full capacity. The better of the two was undoubtedly the Heinkel He 115, first flown in October 1936 and fitted with two 865 or 970hp BMW 132 radials. The performance figures of this aircraft were quite good: a top speed of 203mph, range of 1300 miles and a flexible weapons load (five 550-pound bombs or bombs/torpedo or 2028-pound mine). In addition, when the improved C model entered service in 1941, defensive armament was adequate (one 20mm cannon, plus two 7.92mm machine guns) and the type saw widespread wartime action, usually from coastal bases. By comparison, the single-engined Arado Ar 196 was designed originally as a shipborne, catapult-launched observation seaplane. Consequently it had folding wings and restricted range (670 miles), but was well armed (two 7.92mm machine guns and one 20mm cannon in the C series) and could deliver two 110-pound bombs. Examples served on board such capital ships as the *Graf Spee*, *Scharnhorst* and *Gneisenau*. Once again, however, a relatively small production run (about 400) and a lack of development to such roles as antisubmarine warfare (ASW) indicated a lack of real interest in naval support. It was a major German weakness.

Italy The Italians, surprisingly, deployed few aircraft specifically for naval support during World War II, depending upon modifications to existing land-based designs for such tasks as torpedo strike or interception at sea. As with the Germans, however, maritime reconnaissance was catered for and, although a multiplicity of different aircraft existed, only two – one a flying boat and the other a float plane – saw widespread wartime service.

The flying boat was the single-engined Cant Z501 Gabbiano (Gull), and its operational career was not a success. First flown in August 1934 and powered by a 900hp Isotta-Fraschini Asso X1R2 C15 in-line engine, it had a top speed of 171mph and maximum range of 3000 miles, but proved to be underpowered and extremely vulnerable. With, at best, only three 7.7mm Breda-SAFAT machine guns (in engine-nacelle, dorsal and bow positions) the Z501 was easy prey for Allied fighters and few survived the early months of the war.

The best of a plethora of float planes available was the Cant Z506B Airone (Heron) a three-engined design first flown in 1936. Powered by 750hp Alfa Romeo 126 RC34 radials, it enjoyed a top speed of 227mph, range of 1243 miles and useful offensive weapons load (2205 pounds of bombs or one 1764-pound torpedo). Its crew was adequately protected by up to five 7.7 or 12.7mm Breda-SAFATs (in retractable dorsal and beam positions) and later models proved capable of ASW tasks. Many survived until the armistice in September 1943 and remained in service thereafter with the Cobelligerent Air Force.

The Soviet Union The Soviet navy was not an impressive organization during World War II, having been significantly weakened by the 'purges' of the 1930s and denied an oceanic role by a distrustful Stalin. Consequently naval support was virtually unnecessary as a specific air role and, although the Soviet naval air service boasted 2500 aircraft (including 763 fighters) in 1941, divided between the four fleets – Baltic, Black Sea, Northern and Pacific – the vast majority were land-based machines, such as the Ilyushin Il-4 and Polikarpov I-16, issued without modification to the navy. Indeed, only one specifically maritime aircraft appears to have been provided – the Beriev MBR-2 single-engined coastal patrol float plane, first flown as early as 1931. Powered by a 680hp M-17B or 830hp AM-34N radial, positioned on top of a high shoulder wing, the MBR-2 was not particularly effective, being capable of a top speed of only 136mph and a range of 600 miles. It could carry up to 661 pounds of bombs or depth charges under the wing and was protected by two 7.62mm ShKAS machine guns (one in an open bow cockpit and the other in an enclosed dorsal turret) but few offensive operations were carried out. Most examples appear to have been used as transports.

LAND RECONNAISSANCE

When heavier-than-air machines were first put to military use in the years before World War I, reconnaissance was seen as their only worthwhile role. It is therefore surprising to find that

Above: A Fieseler Storch *over a desert camp. Rommel made much use of a Storch for scouting.*

by the time of World War II the major combatants (with one exception) had no purpose-built reconnaissance aircraft in front-line service. All were forced to modify existing designs to answer this important need, and this set the trend for the duration of hostilities. In the RAF, for example, Supermarine Spitfires (Marks IV, X, XI and XIX) were given uprated engines and sent on unarmed photoreconnaissance missions at both high and low levels, and a similar process was applied to the De Havilland Mosquito (Marks PRI, VIII, 32 and 34), all with a great deal of success. Both the Americans (with modified versions of the Douglas A-20 and Boeing B-29) and the Germans (with the Junkers Ju 86P and Dornier Do 17Z) enjoyed similar results with converted bombers, but neither the Italians nor the Russians appear to have stressed the role.

The exception was Japan and the reconnaissance machine in question – the Mitsubishi Ki-46 (Allied code name Dinah) – was superb. Developed for the JAAF as a strategic reconnaissance aircraft and first flown in November 1939, the Ki-46 was one of the most aerodynamically clean designs of World War II and this was reflected in its capabilities. Early production Ki-46-I models had a top speed of 335mph, service ceiling of 35,000 feet and range of 1300 miles, and were able to penetrate Allied air space with virtual impunity, despite a complete lack of defensive armament. In the Ki-46-II version of March 1941, the existing twin 870hp Mitsubishi Ha-26-I radials were replaced by 1080hp Ha-102s, and this increased the speed to 375mph and range to 1537 miles. Allied countermeasures, particularly in the field

of radar, forced the development of an even faster and cleaner Ki-46 III in 1943, capable of 391mph and with a range of 2500 miles, and it was not until the B-29 raids upon Japan began to hurt in 1945 that this excellent machine disappeared from the reconnaissance squadrons. Because of its ceiling, the Ki-46 was converted to night-fighter duties, although success was poor. Nevertheless the history of the design in its designated role shows what could (and perhaps should) have been achieved if other air forces had followed the Japanese example.

TRANSPORT

The advantages of using aircraft to ferry men and supplies, either around a battle area or over long, intertheater distances, began to be recognized only during the interwar period. In a tactical setting, transport aircraft could be used to move units to answer a perceived threat, to supply beleaguered troops or to drop specially trained parachutists or gliderborne elements behind enemy lines, to disrupt or weaken his defenses. In a strategic setting, reinforcements and supplies could be flown from one theater of war to another to ensure an adequate military effort or to bolster up an ailing defense. Whatever the role, however, specialized aircraft were needed, combining robustness, reliability and carrying capacity but heavily dependent, because of their inherent lack of speed, upon air superiority. During World War II, Britain, the United States and Germany appear to have been the only major combatants to devote time and effort to the transport role, with varying degrees of success.

Britain So far as strategic transport aircraft were concerned, the RAF had no purpose-built designs available in 1939, being obliged to gather what they needed from a variety of sources. Civil airliners were pressed into service, American firms were approached with a view to purchasing modified versions of their civilian freight or passenger aircraft and a number of existing bomber designs were transferred to the transport role. In the early war years, therefore, machines such as the Lockheed Hudson, Armstrong-Whitworth Whitley, Vickers Warwick and Short Stirling were all used, not only by the RAF but also by the newly formed British Overseas Airways Corporation. It was not until 1942 that a purpose-built, home-produced transport aircraft – the Avro York – appeared, and even that bore a striking resemblance to its stablemate, the Lancaster heavy bomber. Nonetheless, the York was a useful machine. Powered by four 1620hp Rolls-Royce Merlin T-24 or 502 engines, it could carry up to 10 tons of military stores in its deep and capacious fuselage. Nicknamed 'Noah's Ark' by the RAF, it was used in all theaters of war to deliver guns, ammunition, spares and people, and went on, after 1945, to be used as a passenger plane for BOAC. A top speed of 298mph was respectable, as was the range of 2700 miles, but it was perhaps fortunate that the York entered service only when Allied air supremacy could be achieved.

For shorter-range tasks, the RAF depended heavily upon the American-produced C-47 Dakota, but did deploy some of its own designs. The most distinctive (and ubiquitous) was the single-engined, two-seat Westland Lysander, a short takeoff and landing (STOL) aircraft designed in answer to Specification A.39/34 of 1934 as an army cooperation machine. Powered by an 890hp Mercury XII radial, the prototype flew for the first time on 15 June 1936, entering service two years later, basically as an artillery observation aircraft. With a top speed of 237mph, range of 600 miles and fixed undercarriage, it seemed to be an archaic design by the beginning of World War II, but in fact the Lysander developed under the pressures of war into a very effective utility machine. Marks II (with 950hp Perseus XII radial) and III (with 870hp Mercury XX or XXX) were produced to answer a number of needs. Army cooperation remained high on the list, but other duties included air/sea rescue, rudimentary ground attack (for which up to 500 pounds of bombs could be fitted to small stub wings on the wheel arches) and target towing, in addition to

the role of transport. In the latter context the delivery and recovery of secret agents to and from occupied Europe was an important contribution to the covert side of war. The Lysander's ability to land and take off from confined and uneven areas was invaluable in this work.

Finally, for airborne landings the RAF deployed a number of transports and glidertugs. Once again, the C-47 was widely used, but a variety of converted bombers also played a crucial part. Such aircraft as the Whitley, Stirling and Handley Page Halifax appeared in this role, often with few modifications to the machines used by Bomber Command. They were joined by the twin-engined Armstrong Whitworth Albemarle – the nearest the British came to a specialized glider-tug. First flown in March 1940 as a bomber, but converted to transport duties after only 32 examples had been produced, the Albemarle proved well suited to towing lighter, man-carrying gliders such as the Army's Airspeed Horsa (capable of lifting 30 fully armed men or their equivalent weight in supplies or equipment – for example, an antitank gun or a jeep). Powered by 1590hp Bristol Hercules XI radials, the Albemarle could reach a top speed of 265mph and operate over a range (without glider attached) of 1300 miles. It was used, with the Horsa, at Sicily (July 1943), in Normandy (June 1944) and at Arnhem (September 1944), leaving the four-engined Stirlings and Halifaxes to tow the much bigger, vehicle-carrying General Aircraft Hamilcar glider (capable of carrying loads such as a 17-pounder antitank gun and towing vehicle, a single Tetrarch or Locust light tank, two Universal Carriers or a wide range of other necessary stores).

The United States The USAAF was extremely fortunate to have available in 1941 a trio of well-designed, reliable, long-range transport aircraft, all of which enjoyed the common feature of having originated as civil airliners in the prewar period. The oldest still in service was the twin-engined C-47, known to the Americans as the Skytrain and to the British as the Dakota. This remarkable machine was initiated in 1935 as the Douglas Sleeper Transport, the latest in a successful series of commercial passenger transport aircraft from the Douglas Aircraft Company. It was first flown on 17 December 1935 and soon in regular service as the DC-3; its obvious capabilities led to its adaptation for military use in 1938. Powered usually by 1200hp Pratt and Whitney Twin Wasp radials, production C-47s, characterized by specially strengthened cargo

AIR

Above: Douglas C-47s at an airfield in New Guinea in December 1943.

floor and undercarriage and by wide loading doors on the port side, could reach a speed of 229mph and operate over a range of 2125 miles. Wartime production totalled just over 10,000, of which some 1200 were supplied under Lend-Lease to the RAF, and the type appeared in all theaters as a cargo aircraft, glider-tug and paratroop carrier, being redesignated the C-53 Skytrooper (RAF Dakota II) in the latter role. Its reliability and performance were excellent under all conditions and numerous examples are still flying today.

The C-47 was joined, principally in the Far East and Pacific theaters, by another twin-engined transport, the Curtiss C-46 Commando. Designed originally as the CW-20 airliner, the prototype flew on 26 March 1940 and was immediately adopted by the USAAF. Powered by 2000hp Pratt and Whitney Double Wasp radials, giving a cruising speed of 227mph and a top speed of 269mph, the C-46 was an ideal cargo carrier, being able to accommodate small vehicles and light guns as well as the normal supplies of food, fuel and passengers. Most of the 3330 produced during World War II were deployed to the notoriously difficult 'Hump' route from eastern India to China, where they performed sterling service, although a few did see action in Europe, towing gliders such as the Waco CG-4A (known in RAF service as the Hadrian and capable of carrying freight or 15 fully armed troops, including pilot and copilot) for the crossing of the Rhine (March 1945).

The final member of the USAAF transport trio was also the largest – the Douglas C-54 Skymaster. First flown as the DC-4 airliner on 21 June 1938, this four-engined machine was never a commercial success but was taken over by the military in 1941. With 1350hp Pratt and Whitney Twin Wasp radials, the C-54 could reach a top speed of 239mph and operate over the very useful range of 3900 miles. Most of the 1242 examples produced were fitted with large freight doors and strengthened floors and saw service principally from bases in the United States, ferrying supplies and personnel to and from the various theaters of war. One model, known as the C-54C, was converted into a VIP transport, fitted with an electric hoist for a wheelchair, and used by President Roosevelt on his visits to other Allied leaders. The C-54 remained in widespread military service after 1945, the first of many strategic transports which are now such an integral part of the air forces of the world.

Germany By far the most common transport aircraft in German wartime service and one which, with the Junkers Ju 87 Stuka, became something of a symbol of Blitzkrieg in 1940, was the Junkers Ju 52/3m. This distinctive machine, with its three 830hp BMW 132T radial engines and unusual corrugated fuselage, was first flown in May 1932 as a civil airliner, having been developed from an abortive single-engine design known simply as the Ju 52. With a top speed of 180mph, range of 808 miles and fixed undercarriage, the Ju 52/3m clearly had its shortcomings, but its strength, reliability and versatility ensured it a military role. To begin with, in 1935, modified versions of the airliner appeared as Luftwaffe bombers, protected by two 7.92mm machine guns (in dorsal and ventral positions) and capable of carrying 3300 pounds of bombs, but it is in the transport role that the type is best remembered. Used in all theaters to carry up to 18 fully armed troops (usually parachutists), a variety of freight loads or, in an air ambulance version, 12 stretchers, the *Tante Ju* (Auntie Ju) was a popular and capable machine. A total of 4845 were produced in Germany, with many more license-built elsewhere. Float-plane and mine-detecting variants also existed, while in the glider-tug role the aircraft was often paired with the troop-carrying DFS (Deutsche Forschungsinstitut für Segelflug – German Research Institute for Gliding) 230, capable of lifting a pilot and nine fully armed troops.

The ubiquity of the Ju 52/3m tended to preclude the need for replacement designs, although as the war progressed a number of experiments were attempted to increase the flexibility of the transport arm. These were not successful, chiefly because the trend was not toward purpose-built machines but toward modifications, usually to glider designs. Thus the twin-boom Gotha Go 242 transport glider, a machine of moderate capabilities which first appeared in late 1941, was fitted with two radial engines (invariably captured French Gnome-Rhône 14Ms) to produce the unsatisfactory Go 244. With top speed of 290mph and range of only 430 miles, this aircraft, despite an ability to carry up to 21 troops, stores or light vehicles, clearly had little to offer. A similar process of glider conversion produced the Messerschmitt Me 323, a six-engined monstrosity of limited usefulness. Its parent design, the Me 321 Gigant, developed in 1941, had had severe limitations as a glider, particularly in the area of launch (at 74,856 pounds fully loaded, it took a trio of Messerschmitt Bf 110s or a specially built three-engined Heinkel He 111Z to force it into the air), and the addition of 1140hp Gnome-Rhône 14N radials did little to solve the problems. With a top speed of only 177mph and range of 680 miles, the Me 323 proved exceptionally vulnerable to fighter attack. Even so, it could carry up to 48,000 pounds of stores or a complete company of infantry: an un-precedented feat.

The Luftwaffe had much more success with its light transports, of which the best by far was the single-engined Fieseler Fi 156 Storch (Stork). This amazing aircraft, first flown in May 1936, appeared as a battlefield taxi, air observation platform, air ambulance and even ground-support machine in all theaters of war and in the colors of most Axis air forces. Powered by a 240 or 270hp Argus As 10 in-line engine, the Fi 156 could achieve a top speed of only 109mph and could not be expected to operate over ranges much in excess of 200 miles, but its remarkable STOL capabilities, combined with its excellent pilot/passenger vision in extensively glazed cockpit area, meant that it was a useful and effective machine. Among the first of its type to be developed anywhere in the world, it acted as progenitor to a wide variety of military and civil light aircraft designs.

HELICOPTERS

The mid-1930s was a period of great experimentation with the concept of rotary-wing flight and, although World War II is not associated in the public mind with helicopter conflict, a number of designs were deployed by the major combatants. In 1939 the Germans held most of the helicopter records – for duration (1 hour 20 minutes), distance (143 miles), speed (76mph) and height (11,247 feet) – with the Focke Achgelis Fa 61, a twin-rotor machine with enclosed cockpit and nosewheel configuration. From it was developed the Fa 223, and this was the first helicopter to enter military service, being used for observation and light transport by the Luftwaffe from 1940 onward, although never in large numbers. Later designs included the jet-powered Doblhoff WMF 342 and the rotor-powered naval reconnaissance Fa 230, but neither saw widespread action.

A similar restricted development program took place in Britain, where the emphasis was upon autogyros and rotaplanes rather than true helicopters, but these were used by the RAF as early as 1935. The main design was the C-30 Autogyro, invented by the expatriate Spanish designer Cierva and manufactured by Avro. Powered by a 140hp Genet Major radial engine which drove a large three-bladed rotor, accelerating it until sufficient speed was attained to generate lift after a short takeoff run, the C-30 had a top speed of 110mph, range of 285 miles and ceiling of 8000 feet. A partially enclosed, two-seat version, the C-40, saw some service as an army cooperation and communications machine, as did a rival design, the Westland C-31 Rotaplane, powered by a 90hp Pobjoy radial and capable of 100mph maximum. In fact the only true helicopter to see service with the RAF was an American design, the Sikorsky Hoverfly R-4B. Developed in the early 1940s and delivered to the USAAF and USN in 1943, this machine, powered by a 200hp Warner R-550-3 engine driving the now familiar dorsal-mounted rotor, was widely used in the closing months of the Pacific War, enjoying the distinction of being the first helicopter to land on board a warship at sea. Further development produced the R-6 version in 1945, and this foreshadowed the typical look of the postwar helicopter, with streamlined tadpole fuselage and bubble cockpit. Active service may have been restricted, but the door had been opened to a new dimension of air warfare.

Front row, from left, Goering, Mussolini, Hitler and Ciano. Other prominent Nazis behind.

BIOGRAPHIES

BIOGRAPHIES

Adachi, Lieutenant General Hatazo, 1890–1947
Adachi was the Japanese Commander in New Guinea. In November 1942 Adachi took over as Commander of the Eighteenth Army and fought the desperate battle to hold on to New Guinea. His headquarters was at Rabaul which meant that all his supplies had to come by sea; this became a severe problem because the US had air superiority and was trying to encircle Rabaul. His army was forced to retreat down the Kokoda Trail and shortly thereafter was pushed back from Buna, Salamaua and Madang. Adachi would not give up and was determined to reach Hollandia to establish a base from which he could fight the Americans and Australians. He reached Wewak but in April 1944 the US anticipated him and made an amphibious attack on Hollandia. Adachi and his men were now cut off at Wewak and their attempt to break out was contained by General Hall's XI Corps. They faced death from disease and starvation but Adachi determined 'not to set foot on my country's soil again but to remain as a clod of earth in the southern Seas with 100,000 officers and men.' He made another brave but pointless attempt to break out in May 1945. This time the Australian 6th Division repulsed his men and the Japanese lost 9000. When news of the Japanese capitulation reached him, he surrendered on 13 September 1945 with 13,500 men. In 1947 he was sentenced to life imprisonment for war crimes.

Ainsworth, Rear Admiral Walden, 1886–1960
Ainsworth held numerous commands in the Pacific but he is remembered for his part in the Battles of Kula Gulf and Kolombangara. Ainsworth was in command of a task force of three cruisers and five destroyers which was escorting the invasion force to New Georgia. On 4–5 July 1943 his guns shelled Vila and Bairoko but he lost a destroyer in this action. On the night of 5/6 July Ainsworth's force was patrolling the Kula Gulf when it ran into Japanese transports on a reinforcement mission to New Georgia. The 'battle' was very confused: the US ships did not stay in formation and one cruiser, the *Helena*, was sunk. It was thought that Ainsworth had repulsed the transports but the Japanese had landed on New Georgia.

On the night of 12/13 July Ainsworth took part in his fifteenth combat mission up the Slot, the channel dividing the Solomons in two. The US had the advantage of radar but the Japanese had an antiradar tracking device. The Japanese were also equipped with Long Lance torpedoes which had greater range and higher speed than

US torpedoes. Ainsworth did not know of the potential of these torpedoes and was lucky to lose only one destroyer in this action. Ainsworth continued to serve in the Pacific and supported the amphibious operation in the Marianas. He retired in 1948.

Alexander, Field Marshal Sir Harold, 1891–1969
Alexander was one of the outstanding Commanders of the British army, who was called in by Churchill in times of trouble. In 1940 he went to France to command the 1st Division of the British Expeditionary Force and at Dunkirk was chosen to command the last corps to remain on the beach. In January 1942 he was appointed Commander of the I Corps and sent to Burma, where he could do little against the Japanese air superiority, except withdraw troops to India.

Appointed Commander in Chief, Middle East, in August 1942 by Churchill, he directed the great campaigns in which Montgomery's 8th Army triumphed over Rommel at Alamein and thereafter. After the US and British troops joined forces in Tunisia, Eisenhower was appointed Supreme Allied Commander in North Africa, and Alexander was his deputy and commander of the 18th Army Group. By May 1943 Tunisia had been cleared and the Allies' next target was Sicily and Italy. When Eisenhower was appointed Supreme Commander Allied Expeditionary Force (SCAEF), Alexander became the Supreme Allied Commander in the Mediterranean. The Allied campaign in Italy was drawn out and handicapped by the fact that Overlord and the campaign in France had top priority. Alexander complained frequently about his lack of landing craft and other essential equipment. He received the surrender of German troops in Italy on 29 April 1945.

Alexander's success lay in his ability to achieve cooperation between soldiers of different nationalities and between the services. His easygoing manner disguised a very tough inner discipline and Churchill found it difficult to find fault with him. Although some, for example General Brooke, felt that he had allowed Montgomery too much independence, their partnership led to a welcome success, for which Alexander will always be remembered.

Ambrosio, General Vittorio, 1879–1950
Ambrosio was Chief of Staff of the Italian army and took part in the plot to overthrow Mussolini. He was a professional soldier who held a series of staff appointments and eventually succeeded Cavallero as Mussolini's Chief of Staff on 31

January 1943. This was an anti-German move because Ambrosio wanted to ensure that Italy was not treated as Germany's satellite. The North African campaign was drawing to a close and there was little Ambrosio could do to restore the situation, especially since Generals von Arnim and Kesselring would not consult him.

Faced with an impossible military situation Ambrosio decided to convince Mussolini to withdraw from the alliance with Germany and negotiate with the Allies. Ambrosio accompanied Mussolini to conferences with Hitler at Salzburg (April 1943) and Feltre (July 1943) and saw that Mussolini was incapable of speaking out against Hitler. Ambrosio claimed that he had been preparing a coup for several months and he was even considered as a replacement for Mussolini. On 24 July the Fascist Grand Council passed a vote of censure on Mussolini and on 25 July the king appointed Badoglio as prime minister. Ambrosio had the regular army Piave Division stationed in Rome and had sent Mussolini's elite bodyguard on maneuvers. He maintained the pretense of loyalty to Germany and sent an envoy to negotiate with the Allies. The negotiations were protracted and the formal surrender was eventually signed in Malta on 29 September by Badoglio and Ambrosio. This had given the Germans enough time to occupy Rome and all of northern Italy. After this fiasco Ambrosio was dismissed by Badoglio because the Allies did not trust him.

Anders, Lieutenant General Wladyslaw, 1892–1970

Anders was in command of the Nowogrodek Cavalry Brigade stationed in south Poland when the German Blitzkrieg hit his country. He was captured by the Soviets and interned in Lubianka jail where the Red Army tried to recruit him. After the German invasion of the USSR he was freed and set about tracing the Poles who had been held in camps after 1939. The Soviets were uncooperative and Anders was faced by a bureaucratic wall of silence. He asked Stalin twice to help him trace officers who were missing but received no assistance. Stalin wanted the Polish Corps to fight for the USSR but would not arm them. Eventually he agreed to allow the Poles, about 60,000 men and 100,000 women and children, to leave via Persia for Palestine in 1942. The Polish 'army' received extensive training in Palestine and was ready for combat in late 1943 and joined the British Eighth Army in Italy. The Poles were noted for their courage and the Polish II Corps was involved in the close hand-to-hand fighting at

Monte Cassino and eventually took the hill on 18 May 1944 after suffering very high casualties. His corps was withdrawn for a while to build up its numbers. Soon after Anders led his corps in the Adriatic sector, fought at Pescara and Ancona and liberated Bologna.

After the death of Sikorski in July 1943 the Poles looked to Anders as their national leader. Although it seemed as if the Soviets would install a puppet regime in Poland after its liberation, Anders was determined to fight until Hitler was finally defeated and *then* to look at the political problems. After the war his army was 112,000 strong and was a considerable embarrassment to the western Allies. There was talk of using it to garrison Germany but it was finally decided to disband it. Anders and all but seven officers and 14,000 men decided not to return to Poland. Anders was head of the Polish community in England until his death.

Anderson, General Sir Kenneth, 1891–1959

A brigade and divisional commander in the Dunkirk campaign, Anderson was appointed in 1942 to command the British First Army which was to undertake the invasion of North Africa under Eisenhower's command. He proved less than wholly successful in the post, or at least did not satisfy Churchill's and Alexander's exacting standards, and from June 1943–45 held inactive commands in Britain and East Africa.

Anderson, Sir John, 1882–1958

Anderson was a very influential figure in Churchill's Cabinet and had been British home secretary in Chamberlain's cabinet. His name became a household word when he introduced a scheme to build special steel shelters – called Anderson shelters – to protect 20,000,000 people in 1940. From 1943–45 he served as chancellor of the exchequer. He was also put in charge of Tube Alloys, the atomic bomb project.

Antonescu, Marshal Ion, 1882–1946

Antonescu was a stupid rather than sinister Rumanian dictator throughout the war. He was an army leader who had assumed leadership of the Fascist Iron Guards. King Carol II, who was afraid of his power, had him imprisoned but when faced with growing territorial demands from Germany and the USSR (he had ceded Bessarabia and northern Bukovina to the USSR and more territory to Hungary and Bulgaria), Carol abdicated and appointed Antonescu prime minister. Antonescu came to power with the support of the Iron Guards on 4 September 1940 and immediately sent messages of loyalty to Hitler and Mussolini. He called in German troops to protect the Ploesti oilfields. On 23 September 1940 he signed the Axis Pact and by this time had won Hitler's trust. In January 1941 he asked Hitler for permission to suppress the Iron Guards who had been persecuting the Jews and committing other atrocities, and Hitler readily assented. Antonescu secured his hold on Rumania by using the army to put its citizens down. Later that year Rumanian divisions joined Army Group South in the invasion of the USSR. These divisions went on to fight at Stalingrad and after their defeat Antonescu was soon thinking in terms of getting Rumania out of the German alliance. He sent his prime minister, Mihai Antonescu, to Mussolini to discuss the possibility of the withdrawal of Italy, Rumania and Hungary from the alliance but although Mussolini agreed with this scheme, he never took any action against Hitler. As the Red Army swept through the Ukraine there was little Antonescu could do. On 23 August 1944, King Michael summoned him and after a stormy interview Antonescu was arrested and replaced by Sanatescu. He was tried for his war crimes and executed after the war.

Aosta, Duke Amadeo of, 1898–1942

Governor of Italian East Africa and Commander in Chief of the Italian armies in Eritrea and Ethiopia, Aosta, a cousin of the king of Italy, undertook the invasion of British Somaliland in August 1940. His campaign was initially highly successful but as soon as the British were able to concentrate reinforcements, the tide swung in their favor. In April 1941 they reoccupied the Ethiopian capital, Addis Ababa, and a month later Aosta himself was forced to surrender at Amba Alagi. He died the following year in captivity in Kenya. He was liked and respected by friend and enemy alike as a gentleman, a patriot and a brave man.

Arnim, Colonel General Jurgen von, 1889–1971

Arnim was the offspring of a traditional Prussian military family. He became a member of the elite German General Staff and commanded a corps in the USSR. At the end of 1942 Hitler selected him at short notice to command the Fifth Panzer Army in North Africa. He took over command in early December 1942 in Tunisia and secured lines of communications with Rommel on the Mareth Line. In March Arnim was made Commander of Army Group Afrika but he never received enough supplies and fought a depressing retreat until he had run

out of space, ammunition and equipment. The Germans had orders to fight until their last round of ammunition was fired but the spirit of defeatism that spread through the ranks led them to take their orders literally: they fired their last shots in the air. Arnim was captured on 12 May 1943 but only after he had severed communications with his units so he could not call for the surrender of all his troops. He spent the rest of the war in prisoner of war camps.

Arnold, General Henry 'Hap,' 1886–1950

Arnold was the US general who commanded the USAAF in all theaters throughout the war. In 1936 he was appointed Assistant Chief of the Air Corps and became Chief of Air Staff in 1938. Although no funds were available he persuaded the US aviation industry to step up the production of airplanes and to prepare plant and training facilities in anticipation of the rush for new aircraft, thereby insuring production capacity. Aircraft production in the USA grew from less than 6000 per annum to 262,000 during the years 1940–44. World War II saw a massive growth in the USAAF and Arnold was behind every change. He supervised training programs for pilots and by the end of the war, Air Force personnel had grown from 21,000 in 1935 to over 2,000,000 in 1944.

He served on the US Joint Chiefs of Staff Committee and the Combined Chiefs of Staff Committee of the Allies. He recommended strong support for the British and was opposed to the policy of American isolationism. He considered air power would prove the decisive factor in any future conflict. Arnold firmly believed in the war-winning capability of strategic bombing of specific targets and this brought him into conflict with his British counterparts who favored area bombing.

He was a popular figure whose nickname 'Hap' or 'Happy' was well-deserved. He managed to develop a working relationship with the solitary British Chief of Air Staff, Portal, which was essential to Allied success. In 1944 he was made a full General of the Army and when the USAAF was made into a separate force equal to the army and navy, he was its first Five-Star General.

Attlee, Prime Minister Clement, 1883–1967

Leader of the Labour Party in parliament at the outbreak of the war, Attlee became deputy prime minister to Churchill on the formation of the coalition government in May 1940. The two men were temperamental as well as political opposites, Attlee being dry, unemotional and self-effacing almost to the point of disappearance. In education and background, however, they were closer than their party affiliations would have suggested, Attlee being a public-school socialist who had been drawn into the Labour Party through his interest in social work in London's East End before World War I (in which he, like Churchill, served as an infantry officer). Thus, although never friends they were able to find much common ground in the direction of the war and worked together without disharmony. A superb party manager, Attlee insured the complete support of the Labour minority for Churchill's policies and, with Bevin, the cooperation of the trade unions in the untroubled production of war material. In the general election of July 1945 he was swept to the prime ministership by the landslide victory of his party and replaced Churchill as the British representative at the Potsdam Conference.

Auchinleck, Field Marshal Sir Claude, 1884–1981

Auchinleck, affectionately known as 'the Auk,' was one of the most respected commanders in the British army. He made his early career as a soldier in the Indian army and was brought home to command the IV Corps in 1939. He spent some time as Commander in Chief in northern Norway and of Southern Command in 1940 but was then appointed Commander in Chief, India in 1941. In June 1941 he was then chosen by Churchill to be Commander in Chief, Middle East, replacing Wavell. He arrived in Egypt at the point when British fortunes were at their lowest; Rommel had successfully defeated the British Battleaxe Operation. Auchinleck immediately set about planning a counterattack, which was code named Crusader, for November 1941. Crusader was a hard-fought battle and ended in a victory for the British and the relief of the besieged Tobruk. However, Rommel did not give the British a chance to consolidate their victory and he counterattacked, forcing the British to make a strategic withdrawal to Gazala and Bir Hacheim. In May 1942 fighting was renewed and Rommel outstripped the British and took Tobruk. Although the first Battle of El Alamein, in July 1942, was a decisive victory and a tremendous setback for Rommel and the Italian army, Churchill decided it was time to replace Auchinleck with Alexander. Churchill could not forgive Auchinleck for the fall of Tobruk and Auchinleck could not alleviate Churchill's fears about the desert campaign. Auchinleck returned to India and served as Commander in Chief of the Indian army until 1947.

Bader, Group Captain Sir Douglas, 1910–1982

Bader was a British pilot who became a legend in his own time because he overcame the physical disability of having artificial legs. In December 1931 he lost both legs in a flying accident and was invalided out of the RAF. He argued his way past the RAF Volunteer Reserve Medical Board and in November 1939 was flying again. In June 1940 he was given command of Fighter Squadron 242, which was manned by Canadians. His outstanding leadership qualities were rewarded during the Battle of Britain when he was given five squadrons. However, he was often in disagreement with Fighter Command Headquarters and often ignored their orders, especially over his development of the 'Big Wing' Formation, which earned him the respect of his German adversaries. In August 1941 he collided with an enemy aircraft over Béthune and was captured. He spent the rest of the war in POW camps.

Badoglio, Field Marshal Pietro, 1871–1956

Badoglio was a veteran of Italy's colonial wars, having fought in the disastrous campaign of 1896 in Ethiopia and in that of 1911–12 against Turkey in Libya. He made a considerable reputation for himself during World War I in the fighting against the Austrians on the Isonzo. He was the Italian Chief of Staff after the war, governor of Libya 1928–33, commanded the army which annexed Ethiopia in 1935–36 and subsequently became Viceroy of Ethiopia. He was reappointed Chief of Staff on Italy's entry into World War II but resigned on the failure of the invasion of Greece in December 1940. Long an opponent of Mussolini, he was the principal instigator of the dictator's downfall in 1943 and signed the armistice with the Allies in September. He became the first prime minister of the anti-Fascist government.

Baruch, Bernard, 1870–1965

Baruch was one of Roosevelt's economic advisers and was an extremely influential businessman. In 1941 he put forward his criticisms of the war economy and was appointed special adviser to Byrnes' Office of War Mobilization. In 1943 he produced a comprehensive report on how industry should adapt to wartime requirements. In 1946 President Truman appointed him US representative to the United Nations Atomic Energy Commission and Baruch produced a plan to establish control of all atomic energy activities dangerous to the world, but this plan was not acceptable to the USSR.

BIOGRAPHIES

Bazna, Elyesa 'Cicero'

Bazna was a Turkish subject of Albanian origin who became the highest paid spy in World War II. Before the war he had worked as the valet of the German ambassador in Ankara, Jenke, Ribbentrop's brother-in-law. He had transferred to the British Embassy without difficulty and served as valet to the British ambassador, Knatchbull-Hugessen during the war. In October 1943 he visited the German embassy and saw the Intelligence attaché, Moyzisch, to whom he offered secret British documents for £20,000 (US$80,000 at the time). Cicero, as he was code named by the Germans, had obtained a key to the embassy safe and was photographing all the papers that passed through the embassy. He supplied the Germans with many important documents including the minutes of the Teheran and Cairo Conferences and details of the planned Allied invasion of Europe. He was paid some £300,000 (US$1,200,000 in the currency of the time) in bank notes but British embassy officials became suspicious and Bazna disappeared. The information he had given the Germans was treated with suspicion by the Germans who thought it was planted, and was never presented to Hitler because Ribbentrop and Kaltenbrunner argued as to who should present it. Bazna was traced after the war to South America where he was arrested for trying to pass counterfeit money – the Germans had given him forged bank notes. Neither side profited from this coup in espionage.

Beaverbrook, Lord Maxwell Aitken, 1879–1964

A Canadian self-made multimillionaire and the founder of a great press empire, Beaverbrook had played a major part in British coalition politics during World War I when he had directed the government's information services and had become a close friend and political ally of Winston Churchill. On the latter's assumption of the premiership in 1940, Beaverbrook was made Minister of Aircraft Production, with the task of increasing the output of desperately needed fighters. By ruthless simplification of production methods he did succeed in keeping the numbers of replacements ahead of losses during the Battle of Britain. Subsequent investigation suggested, however, that the disruption he caused in established procedures resulted in an eventual net shortfall of aircraft by the end of 1940. Then, however, the crisis was over. He subsequently acted as Minister of Supply (1941–42) and Lord Privy Seal (1943–45), and also as administrator of the Lend-Lease scheme in America in 1942. A 'political gadfly' with an irrepressible urge to create mischief around him, Beaverbrook was valued by Churchill less for his administrative skills than for his creative unorthodoxy.

Beck, General Ludwig, 1880–1944

A former chief of staff, Beck had resigned in 1938 in protest against Hitler's plans for aggressive war which he believed would bring about disaster for Germany. He then became the focus for the 'military opposition' to Hitler, which maintained a timorous existence during the early years of the war. A man of genuine moral courage, however, he gladly joined with Stauffenberg in the active conspiracy which culminated in the Bomb Plot of 20 July 1944, was arrested in the War Office by the opportunist Fromm, and committed suicide under his supervision that evening.

Bedell Smith, General Walter, 1895–1961

A staff officer who had risen from the ranks, he became, at the outbreak of the war, secretary of the US Joint Chiefs of Staff and American secretary of the Anglo-American Combined Chiefs of Staff. In September 1942 he went to England to become Chief of Staff to Eisenhower, with whom he remained to the war's end. Eisenhower enormously valued his services and talents which were those of the perfect soldier-diplomat. He laid the basis for the negotiation of the Italian armistice of 1943 and arranged the surrender of the German forces in the west in May 1945.

Beneš, President Edouard, 1884–1948

Beneš was the President of the Czech republic-in-exile during World War II. Beneš was President of Czechoslovakia at the time of the Munich Agreement, which compelled the Czechs to cede fortified Sudetenland to Germany. After this defeat for the Czech republic, Beneš resigned and left for the West. In 1939, after the German occupation of Czechoslovakia, Beneš formed the Czech National Committee in Paris. In 1940 it transferred its base to London and Beneš immediately started trying to get the Allies to repudiate the Munich Agreement and get recognition for his government. He organized refugees into units which served in the British army and RAF. He was unwilling to encourage sabotage and guerrilla warfare so long as Czechoslovakia was far from the front but he gave the order for the operation to assassinate Heydrich. When this was accomplished it increased his standing in the eyes of the Czechs. Beneš' government was finally recognized by

Britain in July 1941 and the Munich Agreement was repudiated in August 1942. He negotiated with the USSR because he felt he had to accommodate the Communists in Czechoslovakia. Beneš signed a Pact of Friendship and Mutual Assistance with the USSR in December 1943. At the end of the war he obtained agreement to massive transfers of Czechoslovakia's Germans to Germany which made for stability in postwar Czechoslovakia. Beneš returned to Prague and was elected President of the Republic in 1946. After the Communist takeover in 1948 he resigned and died shortly afterward.

Bennett, Air Vice-Marshal Donald, 1910–

Bennett was an Australian-born RAF officer. In August 1942 he was appointed to command the newly created Pathfinder Force of Bomber Command. He remained in command of the Pathfinders until the end of the war, by which time the original small force had expanded into the elite group of Bomber Command. He was the youngest officer of his rank in Bomber Command.

Beria, Lavrenty, 1899–1954

Beria was head of the Soviet Intelligence, NKVD, during World War II. He did not have a particularly high standing within the Communist Party organization but Stalin appointed him member of the GKO and he took part in the day-to-day running of the war. Through his intelligence network he often gave Stalin more up-to-date information on activities on the front than front commanders were able to. He was also in charge of partisan activities behind German lines and his units used terror tactics to make the civilian population undertake anti-German action. His NKVD men also ran the prisoner of war camps.

Bernadotte, Count Folke, 1895–1948

Bernadotte was the nephew of Gustavus V of Sweden and Vice-Chairman of the Swedish Red Cross. Using his position he was able to arrange the exchange of sick and disabled German and British prisoners at Gothenburg in October 1943 and again in September 1944. In February 1945 Bernadotte arranged for the transfer of Danish and Norwegian political prisoners and came into contact with Himmler. Himmler decided to approach him with terms to make a settlement with the Allies. Bernadotte agreed to transmit the terms but the Allies rejected the proposal. He published his account of this episode in *The Curtain Falls*.

Beveridge, Sir William, 1879–1963

Beveridge was a British economist who produced the Beveridge Report on Social Insurance and Allied Services. He was a respected figure whom Churchill called into his administration to be undersecretary of labor. When his report came out in December 1942 it was widely acclaimed as the foundation for a future social-welfare system. It provided benefits for unemployment, health, marriage, maternity, widowhood, old age and death. However, Churchill and his Cabinet decided that the report could not be implemented and only introduced plans for a national medical service, training benefits and child allowances. Beveridge had always stood above party politics but in 1944 he stood as a Liberal candidate and became an MP, but in 1945 he lost his seat in the Labour Party landslide.

Bevin, Ernest, 1881–1951

Bevin was a British Labour Party politician who served as minister of labor and national service in Churchill's war cabinet. An Emergency Powers Act was passed in 1940 which gave Bevin dictatorial powers to help mobilize manpower. He suspended the 48-hour week and the right to strike. Workmen were forbidden to leave or change jobs without official approval. In 1941 he introduced a measure which conscripted into industry all men over 30 not serving in the armed forces and all women between 20–23. By 1943 he had successfully completed his mobilization plan and thanks to his work only one hour per worker per year was lost in industrial stoppages. He began drafting plans for postwar demobilization. After the war Bevin became Attlee's foreign secretary and attended the Potsdam and United Nations Conference. His main concern was to decolonize British possessions and 'leave behind for ever the idea of one country dominating another.'

Billotte, General Gaston Herve Gustave, 1875–1940

As Commander of the First Army Group in 1940, Billotte was effectively chief of the principal front of operations, being directly subordinate to Georges (Commander in Chief, North East) and Gamelin (the Supreme Commander), and having under him the best of the French field armies (the 1st and 7th) as well as the British Expeditionary Force. He was also said to be the only French General who knew Gamelin's mind (for what that was worth) and in whom General Lord Gort and King Leopold of Belgium had full confidence. On the German invasion of Belgium he supervised the advance to the Dyle and the subsequent withdrawals to the Escaut and the Dendre but, at the moment of his death, in a road accident, was planning a counterattack. His death could not have come at a worse moment for the Allies. His son, Pierre, rallied to De Gaulle and commanded a Free French armored formation in the liberation of Normandy and Paris in 1944.

Blakeslee, Colonel Donald, 1915–

Blakeslee was a US fighter ace who joined the Royal Canadian Air Force (RCAF) and was posted to 401 Ram Squadron in the UK in May 1941. He later commanded USAAF 4th Fighter Group which was responsible for the destruction of 1016 aircraft. Blakeslee himself shot down 15 enemy aircraft in the air and destroyed two planes on the ground.

Blamey, General Sir Thomas, 1884–1951

Blamey was GOC of the Australian Imperial Forces during World War II. He had served as chief of staff to Monash during World War I but during peacetime he was commissioner of the Victoria police. In February 1940 he was called up to take command of the AIF, Middle East, mainly because he was a well-known figure. In 1941 he arrived in Greece where he took command of the Anzac Corps and he supervised the evacuations from Crete and Rhodes. He then transferred to Egypt and became Deputy Commander in Chief, Middle East. He returned to Australia in March 1942 and was appointed Commander in Chief of Allied Land Forces, under General MacArthur's overall command. He faced a constant stream of unjustified complaints from MacArthur about the Australians' fighting ability but he did not stand up to them. In September he had to take personal command of the troops fighting on the Kokoda trail to pacify MacArthur. He supervised the recapture of Buna and retained command of Australian Land Forces in New Guinea. The Australians had to patrol Japanese troop concentrations at Wewak and in the Solomons. Under pressure from MacArthur he planned operations by Australian troops to reduce the pockets and to recapture Borneo at the end of the war.

Blaskowitz, Field Marshal Johannes von, 1883–1945

Blaskowitz was a German General who served in 1940 in France and afterward became Commander of the Army of Occupation in Poland. He was very independent-minded and prepared two memos protesting against SS brutality and treatment of the Jews. In 1944 Blaskowitz was given command of Army Group G covering the Biscay area and the Mediterranean coast of France. After the success of Operation Dragoon he was relieved in September 1944. He was to be put on trial at Nuremberg but committed suicide beforehand.

Blomberg, Field Marshal Werner von, 1878–1943

As war minister in Hitler's first cabinet, Blomberg quickly abandoned the role of watchdog which President Hindenburg had intended he should play and became a devotee of Germany's new leader. In return he was promoted to become the first Field Marshal of the new regime in 1936. In February 1938, however, he was forced from office, an unwise second marriage he had just made having provided Hitler with the pretext he needed to humiliate the high command of the army, shave its self-confidence and allow him to replace its leaders with soldiers completely subservient to himself. The 'Rubber Lion' as Blomberg was known – an apt comment on the divergence between his martial appearance and fiberless character – went quietly, consigning the once fiercely independent German army to Nazi hegemony.

Bock, Field Marshal Fedor von, 1885–1945

Bock had risen through the ranks of the German army to become, alongside Rundstedt and Leeb, one of the three army group commanders in the early campaigns. In the Polish Campaign, Bock was in command of Army Group North which swept aside the Polish units. In the campaign in the west he commanded Army Group B which overran Belgium and Holland and broke the line of the Lower Seine in the Battle of France. Bock's next command was of Army Group Center, which advanced from Poland to Moscow in the second half of 1941. Bock hopelessly overextended his lines and his men were completely exhausted, Bock himself was suffering from stomach cramps and could not properly exercise his command. Along with Rundstedt and other senior generals he was purged following the Soviet counteroffensive outside Moscow in December 1941. However, early in 1942 Reichenau suffered a stroke at his Headquarters and Bock was recalled to take command of Army Group South in the USSR. While in command of the German drive into the Caucasus in July 1942, he was dismissed following a dispute with Hitler.

Bong, Major Richard, 1920–1945
Bong was a US pilot who achieved the greatest number of victories in the USAAF. He served in New Guinea with the 5th Air Force and in 1942 was flight leader of the 'Flying Knights' Fighter Squadron of P-38s. During his career he managed to shoot down 40 planes and was awarded the Congressional Medal of Honor. He died in 1945 while testing a P-80 jet in California.

Borghese, Commander Prince Valerio, 1912–
Borghese was an Italian naval commander who led the Tenth Light Flotilla on numerous missions in the Mediterranean. This flotilla specialized in individualistic operations and sank 73,000 tons of Allied shipping. For his services, Borghese was awarded a gold medal by Mussolini. His most successful raid was on 18 December 1941 when he sent out three chariots (human torpedoes) from his submarine the *Sciré*. They entered the port of Alexandria and crippled the battleships *Valiant* and *Queen Elizabeth*. In 1943 he was given command of a destroyer flotilla and land-based assault craft off Anzio but he achieved disappointing results before the Italian government decided to come to terms with the Allies.

Boris III, King of Bulgaria, 1894–1943
Boris III was the King of Bulgaria, who eventually joined the Axis side after pressure from Hitler. Bulgaria's position initially was difficult because Boris had married an Italian princess which had made him oppose a Balkan anti-Italian pact. He was anxious to conserve Bulgarian neutrality but was too weak to stand alone. In November 1940 Boris met Hitler at Berchtesgaden and was able to leave without committing himself but eventually agreed to sign a pact with Germany. In March 1941 Boris declared war on Great Britain and six months later on the USA but refused to declare war on the USSR. On 28 August 1943 he died under mysterious circumstances shortly after an interview with Hitler. It is probable that he died of natural causes, possibly a heart attack.

Bor-Komorowski, General Tadeusz, 1895–1966
Count Komorowski, code named Bor, led the Polish partisans in the Warsaw Uprising of 1944. Bor-Komorowski stayed in Poland after the German invasion in 1939 and was put in charge of resistance in southern Poland. In June 1943 Rowecki, the AK leader, was arrested and Bor took over. He immediately put into action the first stage of his anti-German strategy, Fly

(sabotage and the collection of intelligence). This was to be followed by Tempest (local revolts, diversionary guerrilla tactics and ultimately by Rising, a general insurrection when Germany's defeat in Poland was imminent). On 1 August 1944 he gave the order for the Rising in Warsaw. The AK and Communists fought together in a desperate battle but never had enough supplies or ammunition to make victory possible. On the first day the Poles seized control of three-quarters of Warsaw but the Germans brought in their special antipartisan units led by Bach-Zelewski and captured the city street by street. The USSR only began to make air drops on the city in mid-September and by then it was too late. On 2 October Bor and his forces surrendered to the Germans and obtained POW status. Some 200,000 Poles had died in the fighting and the remaining 800,000 were evicted. Bor was interned in Colditz and the Polish government-in-exile appointed him Commander in Chief of Polish Armed Forces. Bor's aristocratic manners earned him respect but he did not have the qualities necessary to lead a partisan uprising.

Bormann, Martin, 1900–1945
A member of the same Freikorps as Goering and Hess in 1918, Bormann was one of the first recruits to the infant Nazi Party and rose to become its Reichsleiter (national organizer). After the defection of Hess to Britain in May 1941 he succeeded him as head of the Party Chancery and in April 1943 was named secretary to the Fuehrer, in which capacity he turned himself into the watchdog at the Fuehrer's door allowing entry only to those whom he wished the Fuehrer to see. Functionaries as powerful as Goering were later to complain that it became virtually impossible to speak to Hitler without Bormann's assent, particularly if he suspected that they had news or opinions to voice which he did not wish Hitler to hear. At the same time he had policies of his own to put forward. His strategic and diplomatic viewpoint was as intransigent as his master's, and he is believed to have been the moving spirit behind some of the Fuehrer's most mistaken decisions. At the very end of the war, however, he adopted a foreign policy of his own of seeking accommodation with the Soviets. The policy failed to come to fruition, but was kept secret from Hitler at whose side Bormann remained to the end. He made his escape from Hitler's bunker on 1 May 1945 but was reported to have been killed in the streets outside. The West German government officially declared him dead in 1973.

BIOGRAPHIES

Bradley, General Omar, 1893–1981

A protégé of Eisenhower, who had been in the same class as he at West Point, Bradley's career was also linked with Patton's. Bradley first rose to prominence when he took command of the II Corps, from Patton, in North Africa. He immediately showed his mettle, when troops under his command stormed Bizerta on 7 May 1943 and took 40,000 prisoners. The II Corps then took part in operations in Sicily, landing at Gela and Scoglitti. Bradley's greatest contribution to the Allied victory was the part he played in Operation Overlord. He was chosen by Eisenhower to command the US landings on D-Day, as Commander of the US First Army. After the landings, Patton arrived to take command of the new Third Army and Bradley became his superior, as Commander of the 12th Army Group. Although Bradley had served under Patton and was susceptible to his influence, this turned out to be a workable relationship, beneficial to both men. Bradley's great moment came during the German Ardennes Offensive, when his men were completely taken by surprise. However, he kept his head and was able to prevent a decisive breakthrough by the Germans. After breaking through the Siegfried Line, his troops crossed the Rhine at Remagen in March 1945 and in the following month met the Soviet troops on the Elbe. Bradley was a quiet and calm man, with a sound grasp of tactics, who inspired the confidence of his superiors and also of his men.

Brauchitsch, Field Marshal Walter von, 1881–1948

Hitler appointed Brauchitsch Commander in Chief of the German Army after he had had Fritsch dismissed on a trumped-up charge of impropriety. Brauchitsch was chosen because he was a more pliable person, who was susceptible to Hitler's powers of persuasion. He was also respected in the army and refused to join a plot to have Hitler arrested if he took action against Czechoslovakia. Brauchitsch had operational control of the Polish campaign but he was not consulted over the decision to attack France and the Low Countries. He and Halder led the army opposition to the scheme in October and November 1939 but bad weather intervened to make their protests and Halder's plans for a coup unnecessary. Brauchitsch's control of the Battle of France was less complete and during the planning for the attack on the USSR which followed, Hitler began to take more decisions himself. During the Barbarossa Operation Brauchitsch suffered a heart attack and when

Zhukov opened the Soviet counterattack outside Moscow, Brauchitsch was in no fit state to respond. He offered his resignation to Hitler within 36 hours and this time it was accepted. Hitler blamed him for this setback and called him 'a vain, cowardly wretch.' Hitler's success in preserving the German army in this first Soviet winter further confirmed his belief in his own ability. Brauchitsch was not employed again.

Braun, Eva, 1912–1945

Eva Braun was Hitler's mistress from 1932 until their suicide. Hitler had had an ascetic image of himself built up by Nazi propaganda and the great demand that he made of his mistress was that she remain discreet and self-effacing. She met Hitler shortly after the death of his beloved niece, when Eva was working as an assistant to Hoffmann, Hitler's staff photographer. Hitler soon installed her in his house but very few people knew of her existence and it was only toward the end of the war that she was invited to attend receptions – and then only because her sister had married General Fegelein, Himmler's representative with Hitler. She was very jealous of Hitler and on two known occasions, November 1932 and May 1935, attempted to commit suicide because of other women. During the war she had no reason to get jealous because although Hitler did not see much of her he did not have enough time to see other women. Braun came to Berlin to be with Hitler during his last days and as a sign of gratitude for her devotion and loyalty to him he married her between 0100–0300 hours on 29 April. He said she was 'the woman who after many years of true friendship came of her own free will to this city, already almost besieged, to share my fate.' They discussed suicide for some time and died together on 30 April 1945.

Braun, Wernher von, 1912–1977

Braun was one of Germany's leading scientists during the war. At the age of 25 (1937) he was appointed Technical Director of the German army's Rocket Research Center at Peenemünde on the Baltic. Within a year he had produced a self-propelled rocket which could carry an explosive warhead 11 miles. Experimentation continued but major development and production of the rockets were hindered by Hitler's decisions on priorities. It was not until 1943 that the V-2 rocket was given the full go-ahead. Variations were tested which could travel more than 200 miles to target and mass production began in earnest. The first V-2 rocket was fired against Britain on 8 September 1944 and in the following few months more than 3600 were 'deployed' to the UK and the Allied bases in the Netherlands and Belgium. Although the range of these rockets was more than adequate, they carried too small a warhead to yield the results Hitler had anticipated. Braun surrendered himself, his staff and research to the Americans in 1945. His expertise aided the US in its development of intercontinental ballistic missiles and in its space program.

Brereton, Major General Lewis Hyde, 1890–1967

Brereton was an American flying and fighting general who fought on most fronts in World War II. First and foremost an aviator, in 1941 when Japan threatened war Brereton was appointed Commander of the US Far East Air Force under General MacArthur. Unfortunately he only had a limited number of B-17s in the Philippines and the Japanese were able to destroy most of them on the ground. He was transferred to India and became commander of the newly established US Middle East Air Force and had to build up supplies and supervise the training of inexperienced American pilots. In October 1942 he was sent to command the US Ninth Air Force and made a valuable contribution to the end of the Tunisian campaign. In October 1943 he transferred to the UK to build up the Ninth into a formidable tactical air unit. His groups attacked the German transport network prior to Operation Overlord, attacking the bridges over the Seine, the Oise and the Meuse. In August 1944 he became the first Commander of the First Allied Airborne Army and took part in planning operations, coordinating airborne and troop carrier units. The biggest operation he was involved in was Operation Market Garden at Nijmegen, Eindhoven and Arnhem.

Brooke, Field Marshal Sir Alan, 1883–1963

Brooke was sent to France in May 1940 to command the British II Corps and carried out the evacuation from Dunkirk with great skill. At the end of 1941 he was appointed Chief of General Staff, replacing General Dill, at a particularly low point in the war for the British. Brooke was ideally suited to the job because he presented Churchill with a calm and competent exterior, keeping for his diary his fears and frustrations. He recognized Churchill's virtues as a war leader but was equally conscious of his faults. He had an excellent grasp of strategy and was able to turn many of Churchill's ideas into

practical military operations. He maintained good relations with the US but was very disappointed when he was not made Supreme Commander of Overlord. His diaries, *The Turn of the Tide* and *Triumph in the West*, are an invaluable source on the British conduct of the war.

Buckner, Lieutenant General Simon Bolivar, 1886–1945

The son of a Confederate General of the Civil War, born to his father in old age, Buckner commanded the American forces in the Aleutians for most of the war. He was eventually appointed to lead the Tenth Army in the assault on Okinawa, the final stepping stone for an amphibious assault on the Japanese Home Islands themselves, and rapidly established a reputation as a dynamic and intelligent leader. He was killed in action on 18 June, almost at the very end of the battle.

Budenny, Marshal Semyon, 1883–1973

During the early part of World War II Budenny was Commander in Chief of the Soviet armies in the Ukraine and Bessarabia. He survived the Purges of 1937–38 thanks to his association with Stalin and Voroshilov, dating back to the Civil War. He had been a Czarist cavalry officer but had held a series of staff appointments and had little experience of command in the field. When the Germans invaded in June 1941 the Soviet High Command fused the Southern and Southwestern groups and put Budenny in command. Budenny could not respond to the speed of the German attacks and set into motion a series of piecemeal measures which could not alter the situation. He was removed from his command on 13 September in disgrace and was transferred to the Reserve Front. He never returned to active command but remained as Commander in Chief of the various Caucasian Fronts until January 1943 when he was made Commander of the Cavalry of the Soviet Army.

Busch, Field Marshal Ernest, 1885–1945

Busch was one of Hitler's many Field Marshals whose main talent was his subservience to his master. He was Commander of the Sixteenth Army which would have taken part in Operation Sealion had it been implemented. He was then given command of Army Group Center on the Eastern Front from October 1943 to June 1944 but was replaced by Model shortly before the collapse and destruction of that Army Group in the Belorussian Campaign. Busch was then appointed Commander in Chief Northwest,

BIOGRAPHIES

stationed in Norway, where he remained until he surrendered with his troops in April 1945.

Bush, Vannevar, 1890–1974
Bush was a distinguished American scientist. As the USA approached war, Bush put forward the policy that the USA should mobilize all scientific resources and he convinced Roosevelt to set up the Office of Scientific Research and Development (OSRD) on 28 June 1941 with himself as Director. Through his activities in promoting scientific research, Bush became involved in coordinating research into the atomic bomb. Two principles formed the bases of his policy: to delegate supervision of specific research projects to others which left him free to give overall direction, and to keep research channelled into the war effort. He had to ensure smooth relations between civilians and army personnel, and overcame his own objections to General Groves' appointment as head of the Manhattan Project. He was a gifted scientist and was President of the Carnegie Institute of Washington during the war.

Byrnes, James, 1879–1972
Byrnes was an important behind-the-scenes operator in Washington throughout the war. A Supreme Court judge, he directed the Selective Service and the Lend-Lease Acts through Congress. In 1942 he was made director of war mobilization and put into operation various schemes to keep the cost of living low: he froze salaries to a ceiling of $25,000 and cut down on horse racing and civilian rail travel. He was a candidate for the vice-presidency in 1944 but was persuaded to stand down in favor of Truman. After Roosevelt's fourth electoral victory Byrnes accompanied him to the Yalta Conference.

He resigned from office before Roosevelt's death but Truman convinced him to return to become secretary of state and he assisted in drafting the Potsdam Declaration and at the London Conference proclaimed the United Nations Charter. He was a conservative and a hard-liner who was first to reject Japan's initial *conditional* offer to surrender in August 1945.

Campbell, Major General John 'Jock,' 1894–1942
A Royal Artillery officer famed for his bravery, Campbell was commanding the 4th Regiment, Royal Horse Artillery in the Western Desert at the outbreak of war with Italy and quickly demonstrated flair in a harassing role during the retreat which the British were obliged to make

before the Italian advance. His most successful enterprise was his handling of the Support Group of 7th Armored Division against an Italo-German force at Sidi Rezegh, 21–22 November 1941; for his success he was awarded the Victoria Cross. He had just been appointed Commander of 7th Armored Division (the famed 'Desert Rats') when he was killed in a car accident.

Canaris, Admiral Wilhelm, 1888–1945
The son of an industrialist, Canaris was a U-Boat commander in World War I. At the outbreak of World War II he was Head of the Abwehr, the Intelligence Department of the German Armed Forces High Command. Canaris is one of the most enigmatic figures of the war. It is known that information often reached Germany's enemies through Abwehr channels and that the Abwehr organization was involved in many of the plots against Hitler and the Nazis generally. What part Canaris played in all this is not at all clear. He was certainly not a Nazi himself and he despised many of their ideas and practices. Perhaps the best interpretation of Canaris is that he had too much of a liking for intrigue and clandestine operations for their own sake and that he wanted personally to participate in too many such schemes to be effective either as an intelligence chief or as an anti-Nazi conspirator. Canaris was arrested after the July Plot and was sent to Flossenberg concentration camp. The Abwehr was dissolved, its operations now under Himmler's direction. Canaris was executed at Flossenberg on 9 April 1945, weeks before the camp was liberated.

Carol II, King of Rumania, 1893–1957
Carol II was the Hohenzollern king of Rumania before World War II. Although of German extraction he favored alliance with Britain and France and on 13 April 1939 he received a guarantee that Rumania's border would be defended by them. Three months later he proclaimed himself dictator. Rumania faced increasing pressure from the USSR and Germany after the fall of Poland. Germany's invasion of France led Carol to declare himself in favor of the Axis and in June 1940 Hitler forced Carol to cede Bessarabia and northern Bukovina to the USSR in order to keep the USSR out of the war. In August he handed over Transylvania to Hungary and in September southern Dobruja to Bulgaria. These losses were very unpopular and on 6 September 1941, in view of his considerable unpopularity, Carol abdicated in favor of his son Michael.

Cavallero, Marshal Ugo, 1880–1943

Cavallero was the Italian Chief of General Staff who succeeded Badoglio after Italy's disastrous campaign in Greece. He was a man of considerable energy and drive and made every attempt to try to modernize the Italian army. He was a great admirer of German efficiency and as such was distrusted by his colleagues who felt he was pro-German and only in power thanks to German support. He did improve Italy's conduct of the war and forced the navy to cooperate by sending supplies to Libya. However, he was at the mercy of Mussolini's whims and knew he would fall when the war turned against Italy. Ciano detested Cavallero and De Bono said of him 'Cavallero is optimistic. That's the only reason the Duce prefers him . . .' so neither were displeased when Mussolini dismissed him in January 1943 after the fall of Tripoli. He was interned for a while but tried to make a comeback when Mussolini fell and found that he was not trusted by either the Fascists or their opponents. He was found dead on a garden bench in the early morning of 14 September 1943.

Chamberlain, Prime Minister Neville, 1869–1940

Chamberlain, a member of one of the leading Conservative Party families, became prime minister of Great Britain in May 1937. Although his experience had been in home affairs, he made the direction of foreign policy his principal concern. The line he adopted in his dealings with dictators quickly attracted the description of 'appeasement' but the term did not at the time carry any suggestion of the disreputable; Chamberlain himself regarded it as an accurate expression of his desire to preserve peace. His opponents were later, somewhat unfairly, to accuse him of desiring to do so at any price. Though prepared in 1938 to sacrifice the national territory of Czechoslovakia – 'a far-off country of which we know little' – he regarded that capitulation as unavoidable in Britain's current state of military unreadiness, which he was simultaneously working to change, through a program of rapid rearmament. By 1939 he had accepted that Germany's territorial ambitions could no longer be tolerated by the Western powers and, with France, issued guarantees of protection to Poland. When Germany attacked Poland in September 1939 he stood by those guarantees and, if with the heaviest of hearts, brought Britain into the war against Hitler. His credibility as a war leader had been hopelessly compromised, however, by his appeasement

policies and his position was further undermined by the defeat of the British Expeditionary Force to Norway in April 1940. Criticism of his leadership was publicly and widely expressed in the House of Commons in May, notably by Leo Amery, and on 10 May he surrendered the premiership to Winston Churchill. He remained a member of the War Cabinet but was broken by his humiliation and the failure of his honest search for peace, and died in November 1940. His reputation, though now assessed more charitably, has never fully recovered.

Chennault, Major General Claire Lee, 1890–1958

In 1937 Chennault had retired from the USAAF because of faulty hearing and had left for China to become an adviser on aviation and the supervisor of a training program. In November 1940 he returned to Washington to recruit pilots and was able to get 100 veteran army, navy and marine corps fliers to join him and a further 100 engineers to maintain equipment. The unit, nicknamed the Flying Tigers, was operational in 1941 and in the skies over Burma destroyed nearly 300 Japanese aircraft in six months fighting. In April 1942 he was called to active duty in the US Army and became leader of the 14th US (Voluntary) Army Air Force in China. In May 1943 at the Washington Conference Chennault came into conflict with General Stilwell, Chiang Kai-shek's Chief of Staff, over the distribution of resources and over strategy. Chennault wanted to build up the Air Force and, having secured a larger share of material and supplies than Stilwell, launched an attempt to drive the Japanese back. This was accomplished too successfully by July 1944 and the Japanese launched a counteroffensive, *Ichi-Go*, to reconquer the lost territory. In July 1945 Chennault resigned in disagreement over the decision to disband the Chinese-American joint wing of the Chinese air force. Chennault was a rough man, who was nicknamed 'old leatherface' because of the burn marks on his face received during the days of open cockpits.

Chernyakhovsky, General Ivan, 1906–1945

Chernyakhovsky was the youngest High Commander of the Soviet army. He was one of the few Jews to serve in the army and owed much to Zhukov's early recognition of his talents. As Commander in Chief of the Sixtieth Army he recaptured Voronezh on January 1943 and then recaptured Kursk. He was given command of the 3rd Belorussian Front and in the Belorussian Offensive led the right pincer against Minsk and attacked the Third Panzer Army near Vitebsk. His armies then swept over Latvia and took Vilna and Kaunas on the east Prussian border. After a break in action he renewed the offensive against Königsberg and broke through heavy German defenses. He was killed, however, in action near Mehlsack in February 1945 when he was hit by a shell fragment in close fighting.

Cherwell, Lord, 1886–1957

Born Frederick Alexander Lindemann, Lord Cherwell was a close personal friend of Churchill. Taken from his professorial position at Oxford University to become a member of Churchill's War Cabinet (Paymaster-General from 1942–45), Cherwell played an influential part in the direction of the war, one of the first scientists to do so. A strong-willed man whose opinions brooked no argument, Cherwell favored strategic bombing and insisted that all RAF strategy should be directed to that end, even at the expense of other war efforts. His judgment and opinions were often faulty but were proclaimed with such vigor that they were often upheld, even if incorrect.

Cheshire, Group Captain Leonard, 1917–

Cheshire was one of Britain's leading bomber pilots and commanders. Cheshire learned to fly as a member of the Volunteer Reserve Air Squadron at Oxford University where his father was Vinerian Professor of Law. Despite his inexperience in the service, on joining the Royal Air Force he quickly demonstrated that he was a leader of outstanding flair and intelligence and, as commander of 617 (Pathfinder) Squadron, established new standards of accuracy in the marking of targets in Germany for the massed bomber fleets of the RAF to strike. He was sent to the Far East at the end of 1944 and on 9 August 1945 was present in the camera plane at the atomic bombing of Nagasaki as official British observer.

Chiang Kai-shek, Generalissimo, 1887–1975

Chiang Kai-shek was the leader of the Kuomintang and head of state of nationalist China. He became prominent in Kuomintang affairs in the 1920's and with the support of sections of the army attained the leadership. He was faced with the problem of consolidating the position of the Kuomintang internally, especially against the Communists, and at the same time responding to the growing nationalist feeling against the Japanese. His problems were compounded in 1937 when the Japanese extended their control and forced his government to move to Chung-king. Although Roosevelt wished to aid the Chinese in their war with the Japanese, he was bound by various laws which prevented him from helping warring states. To circumvent this law, Roosevelt did not recognize that a state of war existed in China, and sent supplies. Chiang's main problem in fighting the Japanese was that his own control of the Chinese central government was tenuous. He had been involved in fighting the Chinese Communists prior to the Japanese invasion and the loyalty of some parts of the army was in doubt: commands were divided into war areas and the local commanders could be bought off by the Japanese. Chiang was constantly suspicious of his own commanders and tried unsuccessfully to direct operations from Chungking, which was too remote.

Chiang's first direct involvement in the series of wars known as World War II, was in the Japanese invasion of Burma in 1942. Chiang appointed Stilwell, his US Chief of Staff, as Commander of the two Chinese armies which he sent to Burma. Stilwell was treated like all Chiang's subordinates and by-passed over crucial decisions. The antagonism between Chiang and Stilwell dates from this time because Stilwell could not direct operations effectively in Burma and because Chiang felt let down over the volume of US aid. Chiang decided to back Chennault and accepted the latter's view that air power would win the war in China. By maintaining a constant flow of demands for aircraft and supplies, Chiang eventually received Allied agreement to an air offensive in China in 1943. However, the strategy did not succeed because it provoked, as Stilwell had pointed out, a counterattack by the Japanese, who overran the US Fourteenth Air Force's bases in east China. After this disaster the US Joint Chiefs wanted Stilwell appointed commander of all Chinese troops because he had achieved success in his campaign in northern Burma. However, Chiang asked for Stilwell's dismissal.

Chiang's main concern was political survival and his Nationalist armies did not have the strength to fight the Japanese armies in an all-out offensive. The most they could achieve was to keep Japanese troops tied up in China away from the battlefields of the Pacific. For this purpose, Chiang received massive Lend-Lease aid from the USA, aid which did not get used in the fight against the Japanese but in the fight against the Communists. Although Chiang was recognized by the Western powers as the head of state in China in 1945, his power was declining and soon after World War II ended, civil war in China started again.

Chuikov, General Vasili, 1900–

A Red Army volunteer in 1918, he served against Kolchak and in the Russo-Polish War of 1920, attended the Frunze Academy, acted as military adviser to Chiang Kai-shek between 1926–37, served at the Ministry of War in 1941–2, and in 1942 was appointed commander of the Sixty-second Army in the defense of Stalingrad. His army held the foothold on the right bank of the Volga throughout the German siege and was the mainstay of the defense. Redesignated the Eighth Guards Army, it remained under his command until the end of the war and took part in the Battle of Berlin. His account of the Battle of Stalingrad, *The Beginning of the Road*, is a masterpiece of military literature and the most interesting war memoir published by any Soviet general.

Churchill, Prime Minister Winston Spencer, 1874–1965

'What is our policy? I will say it is to wage war by land, sea and air with all our might and with all the strength that God can give us . . . Victory at all costs, Victory in spite of all terror, Victory however long and hard the road may be.'

In September 1939 Winston Churchill held the post of First Lord of the Admiralty (the same post he had held in World War I) in the Conservative government of Neville Chamberlain. After the disastrous Norwegian Campaign, for which the country and parliament blamed Chamberlain, Churchill succeeded Chamberlain as prime minister and formed a National Government and became minister of defense on 11 May 1940. Churchill's contributions to World War II and the Allied cause are numerous. A strong leader, dedicated to Britain and to total victory over the Germans, he banished any thought of surrender.

The mutual friendship between Churchill and the President of the United States, Roosevelt, which had developed before the start of World War II, led to the sharing and trading of war supplies and personnel even before the US officially joined the war. The Lend-Lease Act of March 1941 allowed the UK to order and 'borrow' war goods on credit – ownership remained nominally in American hands. Everyday communications between Roosevelt and Churchill were carried out by telephone and by letter but the decisions on war strategy were made at a series of international conferences with or without the presence of other leaders such as Stalin or Chiang Kai-shek. The first conference attended by Churchill and Roosevelt was at Argentia Bay in August 1941 where the

Above: Churchill, Gamelin and Gort early in 1940.

Atlantic Charter was signed. The Washington Conference in December of that year established the 'Germany First' policy. The two leaders were able to weather many disagreements on strategy, which arose from the conflicting advice of their advisers. The US was naturally suspicious about Churchill's constant postponements of Overlord in favor of intervention in the Mediterranean and the Balkans. However, the US agreed to the Torch landings and then the invasions of Sicily and Italy but once Overlord was under way it received top priority. Roosevelt and Churchill also did not see eye to eye over how to deal with Stalin. Churchill's anti-Communism led him to treat Stalin with great suspicion but Roosevelt felt that he understood Stalin and could reach an understanding with him over eastern Europe. History has vindicated Churchill's view and shown him to have been the wiser. Churchill's negotiations with Stalin at Yalta in February 1945 show that he realistically expected Stalin to take over eastern Europe and so Churchill tried to retain a British interest in Yugoslavia in more than name.

Churchill was above all a politician and his gifts as a military commander have been called into question. He made errors of judgment – often seeking the advice of inspired amateurs such as Cherwell and Wingate – much to the dismay of his military advisers, such as Brooke. Churchill always tried to have his commanders maintain an enterprising, attacking attitude. It was one of his chief merits as a leader that this aim led him constantly to produce new ideas and question old assumptions. Often his keenness led him into advocating impractical plans from which he could only be dissuaded by long arguments with his staff, but it can generally be said that on the major issues his judgment and sense of priorities were sound. His treatment of Wavell and Auchinleck and his failure to do more to protect British territory in the Far East in 1941 are the issues on which he is most often criticized, but in each of these cases there is a great deal to be said for Churchill's point of view. Neither Wavell nor Auchinleck had succeeded in their tasks despite a considerable effort being devoted to strengthening their forces. The decision to leave Singapore weak was in many ways a calculated risk. Theaters nearer home were also in need and if Japan attacked any losses would be balanced by an almost-certain US entry to the war.

Churchill's personality and dynamism helped him maintain successful relations with parliament and the country. He survived two votes of no confidence which were overwhelmingly defeated in parliament. He kept the morale of the country up by broadcasting to the people on significant occasions. One such memorable occasion was on 22 June 1941 after the German invasion of the USSR, when Churchill pledged British support to the Soviets. Had Churchill died on one of his many trips abroad, British morale would have been greatly damaged. However, after the war, the British people who had admired and depended on him, rejected his leadership in the general election of July 1945. Although often viewed as an ungrateful choice, the decision to allow Attlee to assume leadership should not be considered as such. The people of Britain regarded Churchill as a *war* prime minister but thought that someone else should help with the reconstruction of a war-torn Britain.

Ciano, Count Galeazzo, 1903–1944

A career diplomat, Ciano's marriage to Edda Mussolini, daughter of the dictator, procured his rapid promotion to foreign minister in 1936. In that capacity he signed the 'Pact of Steel' with Germany in May 1939. He was rightly fearful, however, of the consequences for Italy of going to war. He gradually fell out with his father-in-law and resigned from the foreign ministry in February 1943. He remained a member of the Fascist Grand Council and in that capacity voted for Mussolini's removal on July 25. In August he was tricked by the Germans into putting himself in their hands, was imprisoned and executed, with Mussolini's acquiescence.

Clark, General Mark, 1896–1984

Clark was Eisenhower's deputy during Operation Torch. He was involved in the secret negotiations with various French leaders, trying to persuade them to join the Allies. When the landings took place and Admiral Darlan was taken, Clark and Eisenhower recognized his potential value as a French leader. Opinion in Britain was uncertain about negotiating with a Vichy leader but it was accepted by the British Parliament. However this potentially embarrassing commital was ended when Darlan was assassinated shortly afterward.

In January 1943 Clark was appointed Commanding General of the Fifth Army and prepared for the invasion of Italy. On 9 September 1943 the invasion of western Italy began at Salerno. The troops established a bridgehead and managed to take Naples. The terrain in Italy considerably hampered Allied mobility and the Fifth Army was held up at Monte Cassino. His troops took part in the Anzio Landings in January 1944 but this did not succeed in cutting off communications from Cassino to Rome. The British Eighth Army reached the American positions and joined in the attempts to break through the Gustav Line. The stalemate continued for three months and Clark asked for permission to bomb the monastery at Cassino; however this did not help the Allies as the rubble was easier to defend. Finally British, American, Polish and French troops defeated the Germans at Cassino in very bitter fighting in May, and on 4 June Clark's Fifth Army entered Rome.

Clark's decision to go straight for Rome, disobeying direct orders from Alexander, gave the Germans a chance to escape north and regroup. The main Allied advance on Germany was through France and resources for the Italian Front were now diverted to the Anvil/Dragoon Landings in the south of France. The Fifth Army continued its advance but was stopped short of Bologna in October. In December Clark was elevated to command the 15th Army Group in the Mediterranean under Alexander who then became Supreme Allied Commander in the Mediterranean Theater. In the last months of the war Clark achieved a decisive victory and in April 1945 he received the surrender of 230,000 German and enemy troops in Italy, the Tyrol and Salzburg. After the war Clark became commander of the US occupation force in Austria.

Clay, General Lucius, 1897–1977

A military engineer who had worked on dam construction in the United States before the war, Clay acted as manager of the US Army procurement program from 1942, then as a base commander in Normandy, then as deputy director of the Office of War Mobilization until April 1945 when he moved to Germany as deputy to Eisenhower for the military government of Germany. He quickly became convinced that the United States must work to restore civilian government in the occupied zones, and was a major architect of the postwar Federal Government.

Collins, Lieutenant General 'Lightnin' Joe' Lawton, 1896–1963

A leader of consequence, Collins, in December 1942, led the 25th Infantry Division in Guadalcanal, relieving the 1st Marine Division, and he cleared the island of Japanese. In January 1943 he led part of the XIV Corps in driving the Japanese off New Georgia.

In December 1943 he went to England to take command of the VII Corps and landed at Utah beach in Normandy. He drove his men hard to keep the enemy on the defensive. His energy earned him the name 'GIs General' and by exerting constant pressure his troops took Cherbourg on 24 June. His troops closed the Falaise Gap, crossed the Seine and drove north into Belgium and took Mons, Namur and Liège. Collins participated in the counterattack and capture of Houffalize during the Battle of the Bulge and crossed the Rhine at Remagen. His troops drove through Germany, enveloped the Ruhr and met the Soviet XXXVI Corps on the Elbe.

Coningham, Air Marshal Sir Arthur, 1895–1948

Coningham was an extremely hard-working and efficient air commander. He first saw action in World War I as a Commander of New Zealand troops, where he gained the nickname 'Maori.' He then became a flier and during the interwar period became an expert on long-range flying. In 1939 he was in command of 4 Group of long-range bombers, based in Yorkshire. He then spent several years in the Desert Campaign, eventually becoming Commander of the Western Desert Air Force and conducting many joint air-ground operations in conjunction with Montgomery's Eighth Army. He was then given command of the British and US Air Forces in Tunisia and during 1943 his forces took part in raids and operations in Pantelleria and Sicily. He later commanded the 2nd Tactical Air Force (British and Canadian), which took part in the campaign in Normandy – July 1944 and other operations in northwest Europe until the end of the war.

Crerar, General Henry, 1888–1965

In July 1940 Crerar was sent by the Canadian government to London as Chief of General Staff to plan training programs for Canadian troops. He worked seven days a week to set up

the programs but in November 1941 resigned his post and took a lower command in order to see action in the field. He led the I Canadian Corps in Sicily where his troops distinguished themselves at Catania. In 1943 he was recalled to Britain to take command of the First Canadian Army, which in fact consisted also of Poles, Belgians, Dutch and British units. The army landed near the mouth of the Orne river and was employed to 'break in' to Falaise in August 1944. The troops succeeded and then were used to assault the Channel fortresses of Le Havre, Boulogne, Calais and the mouth of the Scheldt. Crerar decided to take each in turn and by 1 October had reached his objective and taken 72,000 prisoners. After clearing the Scheldt and Antwerp his troops moved on to the offensive, southeast of Nijmegen. On 27 February 1945 the army stormed Udem and broke through the Siegfried Line.

Cripps, Sir (Richard) Stafford, 1889–1952

Cripps was a British Labour Party politician who had had a varied career before the war. Churchill's coalition government made extensive use of his services, first in 1940 as ambassador to Moscow where it was believed his left-wing views would give him greater influence than a career diplomat could command, then in 1942 as emissary to Indian nationalists whom he tried to win to a policy of wartime cooperation with an offer of postwar independence, and finally in November 1942 as minister of aircraft production. Though Churchill, like many others, found his coldness and self-possession deeply antipathetic, he readily recognized his intellectual and administrative qualities.

Cunningham, General Sir Alan, 1887–1983

Cunningham was the younger brother of Admiral Cunningham. He led the forces that liberated Ethiopia from Italian occupation. In December 1940 the offensive opened and Cunningham and his troops marched into Italian Somaliland and began the long march for Addis Ababa. Displaying great skills of leadership and exploiting his forces' mobility to the full, Cunningham entered the capital of Ethiopia in triumph on 6 April 1941 and a month later the emperor, Haile Selassie, returned to the throne.

In August 1941 Cunningham left for the Western Desert to take command of the new Eighth Army. He had some 630 tanks at his disposal and he immediately set about preparing for Auchinleck's Crusader Operation, which would lead to the relief of Tobruk. However, Rommel was prepared for the British offensive and Cunningham failed to press the attack through. Auchinleck lost confidence in him and he was replaced on 26 November 1941 by a younger man, Ritchie. Cunningham spent the rest of war in administrative posts.

Cunningham, Admiral of the Fleet Sir Andrew, 1883–1963

An outstanding British naval commander, in 1939 Cunningham was the Acting Commander in Chief of the Mediterranean Fleet. His main task was to harass the Italian Fleet and after the fall of Greece, ensure that supplies got through to Malta. He was a man of action and immediately set out to establish British naval supremacy. One important move was to establish good relations with Vice-Admiral Gode-froy's French squadron at Alexandria and they had a sufficiently good working relationship that Godefroy agreed to disarm his ships peacefully after the fall of France. Since the Italian fleet was reluctant to leave its harbor, Cunningham decided to attack it in Taranto and sent a squadron of Swordfish to bomb Italian battleships. On 11 November 1940 the battleships *Littorio, Conte di Cavour*, and *Duilio* were put out of commission and the Italian fleet was never to regain the initiative in the Mediterranean. Cunningham followed this up by engaging the Italians in the Battle of Cape Matapan in March 1941 where he was able to sink the heavy cruiser, *Pola.* Cunningham was then involved in the naval actions off Crete where, despite the lack of air cover, he risked his fleet to prevent German reinforcements reaching the island. The British lost Crete and Cunningham lost three cruisers and six destroyers; this coincided with a difficult situation in North Africa and the siege of Malta. British naval power was stretched to its limits. Cunningham was then sent to Washington to attend Chiefs of Staff planning meetings and was then appointed Eisenhower's deputy for the Torch landings. He was also naval commander for the landings in Sicily but after the death of Admiral Pound in October 1943, he was recalled to London and was appointed First Sea Lord. He continued to advise Churchill on naval strategy but his main talent had been as a fighting admiral.

Curtin, Prime Minister John, 1885–1945

Curtin was prime minister of Australia from 1941 until shortly before the end of the war. As leader of the Australian Labour Party he had opposed conscription in the early days of the war and had resisted offers to join in a National government. In 1941 he brought down the Fadden government and came to power with a majority of one. He immediately found that he had to increase conscription because Australia declared war on Japan after Pearl Harbor. From this point he set about reorienting Australia's foreign policy and became a firm advocate of partnership with the USA. He had difficult relations with Churchill and had rows over Britain's lack of naval support in the Far East. Curtin was a firm advocate of air force power and gave MacArthur his full support. In 1942, while Australia feared a Japanese invasion, Curtin became his own Minister of Defense but as the threat receded he relinquished this post and took greater interest in diplomacy and the postwar situation. He was a popular figure and led the Labour Party to electoral victory in 1943. He became ill in November 1944 and died in July 1945. His deputy, Chifley, became acting prime minister in April 1945 and full prime minister in July.

Daladier, Prime Minister Edouard, 1884–1970

Daladier came to power in France as a leader of the Radical Socialists when the Popular Front began to disintegrate. He was supposed to be acceptable to all parties but after he signed the Munich Agreement in September 1938, he lost the support of the socialists and had to rely on the right wing. He led France into war in 1939 but the preparations made by his government were weak and little was done to invigorate the listless army command. In March 1940 his government fell on these issues, with the failure to provide adequate aid to Finland being the immediate cause. He retained a post in Reynaud's government and continued to champion the incompetent Gamelin. Following the German invasion of France he tried to help resistance in North Africa but was captured and taken back to Vichy France. He was put on trial by the Vichy authorities at Riom, charged with leading France into war unprepared. He was later interned in Buchenwald and Dachau but was freed in April 1945.

Darlan, Admiral Jean Francois, 1881–1942

In 1939 Darlan was Commander in Chief of the French navy. When his country was defeated in the Battle of France, Darlan was faced with the problem of disposing of the navy, the second strongest fleet in European waters. He met Churchill and promised not to let the fleet fall into German hands but seemed unsure about exactly what to do with it. Eventually he accepted the office of minister of the navy in Pétain's government and sent his navy to North

Africa. Churchill ordered the ships of Somerville's Force H to destroy the French navy by bombardment in July 1940. The operation became known as the Mers-el-Kebir incident. In February 1941 Darlan became vice-premier to Pétain in the Vichy government. He tried to cooperate with Hitler to better conditions in France and to achieve more concessions and freedom for France but was all but ignored by Hitler. In spring 1942 he lost his ministerial posts when Laval returned to power but was appointed Head of the French Armed Forces and High Commissioner in French North Africa. The Allied Torch landings in November 1942 caught him in Algiers on a private visit to his son. Recognizing that he could be a useful figure in persuading at least the local French forces to join the Allies, Eisenhower and Clark began talks with him. Although they agreed to support the talks the British were not keen to negotiate with a representative of Vichy. However, Darlan was recognized as head of the French government in North Africa, but he was assassinated by a young French monarchist on Christmas eve 1942 before he had rendered any lasting damage to Allied relationships.

Darnand, Joseph 1897–1945

Darnand was notorious for his organization of the Milice, the militarized police force of the Vichy Regime. Darnand was a collaborator by conviction rather than through convenience. He was an enthusiastic supporter of Vichy's connection with the Nazis, went to Germany after the liberation of France in 1944 and took office in the puppet Sigmaringen 'French Government.' At the end of the war he was repatriated, tried and shot for treason. His persecution of opponents of Vichy and the excesses of his hated Milice undoubtedly justified his execution, but he regarded himself quite genuinely as a patriot.

De Gaulle, General Charles, 1890–1970

De Gaulle had served as a subaltern in Petain's regiment during World War I and after the war had made himself a reputation as a military writer and theorist. Among his works was *The Army of the Future* and in this he predicted the nature of armored warfare and preached the need for mechanization. In 1940 his views were finally recognized and he was given command of the 4th Armored Division which was in the process of being set up and was completely inexperienced. Although he was only given his command after the German attack began he was able to lead two attacks against the flank of the German advance. Both were beaten off after

some success. In recognition of his success, de Gaulle was appointed under-secretary for war and attended the last desperate Cabinet meetings. He left for England on 17 June and on the following day made a broadcast to the French people 'Believe me! Nothing is lost for France! The same methods which have defeated us may one day bring us victory.' The war had to go on in the colonies. He declared the existence of 'Free France' and made himself head of that organization. Few people joined him at first because he was regarded as a traitor but he determined to try to annex France's colonies and continue the fight against Germany. The first attempt was to take the port of Dakar, Operation Menace, in September 1940, but this ended in disaster when the French forces under Boisson refused to surrender and the British ships off Dakar suffered extensive damage.

De Gaulle also convinced Churchill that the French in Syria were ready to desert Germany but when the joint British and Free French forces invaded in June 1941 they faced stiff opposition from the local French armed forces under the command of General Dentz. It was only when the Vichy government began to collaborate openly with the Germans that the French began to look to de Gaulle for leadership. Although the British gave him their full support, de Gaulle did not receive recognition from the US until after the Torch landings. Even then the US wished to promote Giraud as an alternative leader so de Gaulle was forced to cooperate with him until 1943 when he forced Giraud to resign.

De Gaulle returned to France on 13 June 1944 but his moment of triumph came on 26 August, when he entered a liberated Paris to a tremendous reception by the people. A Committee of National Liberation was set up with de Gaulle as its president but the postliberation situation was still difficult. De Gaulle was not invited to the conferences at Yalta and Potsdam and he resented the fact that France was not treated as an equal partner by the Allies. He was the most dynamic leader France had at the time but he was overly concerned with reestablishing France as a great power. Unfortunately his decision to reassert France's rule in Indo-China led to a very costly war, which the country could ill afford.

De Guingand, Major General Francis, 1900–1979

De Guingand was a British general and Chief of Staff to Montgomery in North Africa and in northwest Europe. De Guingand had a lot of experience of staff work before he began working with Montgomery and proved invaluable in the detailed negotiations with the other service chiefs in the desert. Montgomery used him as a representative at planning conferences. In northwest Europe de Guingand's main contribution was to smooth relations between Montgomery and Eisenhower, particularly when they disagreed over the broad- or narrow-front advance toward and into Germany.

De Lattre de Tassigny, General Jean, 1889–1952
In 1914 cavalry officer de Lattre de Tassigny was severely wounded by a sword in a mounted duel with a German Uhlan. By 1939 he was a general and Chief of Staff of the French Fifth Army and led the 14th Division on the Aisne. In 1940, after the French capitulation, he remained dedicated to the army and to the Vichy government which sent him to Tunisia. He was soon recalled because of his Allied sympathies and was awarded 10 years imprisonment for protesting against the German occupation of the *zone libre* in 1942. In 1943 he escaped from Riom prison and went to the UK where he allied himself to de Gaulle and became the Commander of the First French Army in North Africa. In 1944 he led the First French Army in the liberation of France. He signed the German surrender on behalf of France.

Dempsey, General Miles, 1896–1969
Dempsey was a British general who led the 13th Infantry Brigade at Dunkirk and because of his excellent organizational ability was selected in June 1941 to form a new armored division. He was then appointed XIII Corps commander in Montgomery's Eighth Army and quickly impressed Montgomery with his skill. Montgomery said he was a 'soldier who can describe foreign terrain so vividly from a map that it becomes almost a pictorial reality for his listeners.' Dempsey led his XIII Corps in many difficult landings in Italy and Sicily. He was so successful that he was promoted and given command of the Second Army in the D-Day Landings. He had a quiet, unassuming manner and kept his corps commanders under control. His army landed at Juno and held the area between Caen and Bayeux, keeping German armor away from the US forces so they could break out of Normandy. Dempsey's army fought at Falaise and Mortain and then dashed over northern France to Brussels and took part in Operation Market Garden. Their advance faltered at this point and they were unable to reach the British paratroops at Arnhem in time. After the German surrender Dempsey was appointed Commander in Chief of Allied Land Forces in Southeast Asia.

Dentz, General Henri, 1871–1945
Dentz was the Vichy High Commissioner in Syria in June 1941. When Britain and the Free French army invaded Syria on 8 June 1941 Dentz's men fought bitterly and held out for as long as possible. He had insufficient air cover and the Vichy government was reluctant to ask for German assistance, so on 11 July Dentz signed an armistice with the British. He was arrested a few months later when it was discovered that he had broken the terms of the armistice by sending prisoners of war out of Syria after the armistice had been signed.

Devereux, Major James, 1903–
Devereux was the US Commander of Ground Forces on Wake Island in 1941. Although the garrison was very small they beat off one Japanese landing, sank two destroyers and shot down several aircraft. They were overwhelmed by a second landing and Devereux spent the rest of the war as a prisoner.

Devers, General Jacob, 1887–1979
Devers was the US General who directed Operation Dragoon in August 1944. He started his war career as commander of armored forces and was appointed commander of US forces in the UK in 1943. Since he did not have sufficient battle experience he was made General Maitland Wilson's second in command in the Mediterranean Theater. The Allies argued over strategy in this theater and the British gave way and agreed to a landing in southern France to link up with Overlord forces in northern France. Devers was put in charge of the landings which took place on 15 August 1944. His troops only met pockets of resistance at Montélimar and Marseilles, which they bypassed. The US troops travelled at great speed up the Rhône Valley and reached other Allied forces in September. Devers was then given command of the 6th Army Group: the US Seventh Army and the French First Army. They successfully held on to Strasbourg during the Alsace counteroffensive and swept into Germany to take Munich and Berchtesgaden.

Dietrich, SS General Josef 'Sepp', 1892–1976
One of the closest and oldest comrades of Hitler to whom he acted as bodyguard before the accession to power, Dietrich took a major part in the Blood Purge of 30 June 1934. During World War II he became a general in the Waffen

SS, commanded the I SS Panzer Corps in the USSR and in December 1944 the Sixth SS Panzer Army in the Battle of the Bulge. He was given the latter command by Hitler to emphasize his mistrust of army officers following the Bomb Plot of July. In 1946 he was sentenced by an American military court to 25 years imprisonment for the murder of American prisoners at Malmédy by soldiers of the Sixth Panzer Army.

Dill, Field Marshal Sir John Greer, 1881–1944
An outstanding and popular member of the British army, Dill served as Director of Military Operations and Commandant of the Staff College before the outbreak of World War II. In 1939 he commanded I Corps in France. In October of that year he was promoted to General and in April 1940 he returned from France as Vice-CIGS (Chief of Imperial General Staff) only to succeed Ironside as CIGS in May. A cautious man at all times, Dill advised restraint, a policy at odds with Churchill's more impulsive nature. Suffering from overwork and nervous strain Dill was replaced as CIGS by Alan Brooke in December 1941. He accompanied Churchill to Washington where he remained as Head of the British Joint Staff Mission. In the US he enjoyed total diplomatic and personal success and his relationship with the Americans was so favorable that they arranged for him to be buried in Arlington National Cemetery.

Doenitz, Admiral Karl, 1891–1980
Commissioned into the German navy as an officer in 1919 Doenitz was Flag Officer U-Boats until 30 January 1943. Convinced that the U-Boat alone could win the war for Germany, he was in fact almost proved correct: he was responsible for sinking 15,000,000 tons of Allied shipping. By early 1943 he had more than 200 U-Boats operating in 'wolf packs' and 181 in production. After vicious battles in March 1943 the Allied convoy escorts gradually gained the upper hand. Doenitz was promoted to command the German navy replacing Raeder. Although the German navy was now in decline, Doenitz never lost the admiration and respect of Hitler, perhaps because the navy alone remained loyal. Leaders in the army had proved themselves treacherous and the Reich Marshal of the Luftwaffe incompetent. Hitler chose to name Doenitz as his successor and head of state. Doenitz assumed the leadership on 30 April 1945 and negotiated the capitulation of the German forces in the west. He was imprisoned at Flensburg until he was tried at Nuremberg where he was sentenced to 10 years for war crimes.

Donovan, William Joseph, 1883–1959
'Wild Bill' Donovan was a US lawyer who was head of the OSS (Office of Strategic Services), the forerunner of the CIA (Central Intelligence Agency). In 1940 Donovan was the unofficial observer for the Secretary of the Navy, Knox, in Great Britain. Knox was very pleased with his reports and he was sent on several missions by President Roosevelt to southeast Europe and the Middle East to observe resistance movements. On his return he was made coordinator of intelligence and on 13 June 1942 became director of the newly created OSS. The OSS had three branches – intelligence, operations and research – and had many influential people working for it. It was said to have employed 13,000 Americans but it also recruited agents in North Africa, Burma and Europe for its clandestine operations.

Doolittle, Lieutenant General James, 1896–
Doolittle, the only nonregular officer to command a major combat air force, began his military-aviation career in 1917 in the US Army Air Service. In 1922 he made the first flight across the continent of North America in less than 24 hours. Then followed a period of highly successful air racing. Working as an experimental engineer in the Air Corps Materiel Division, he played a major part in the development of aircraft instruments, making the first successful flight using these devices. He was awarded the Harmon Trophy in 1930 in

Above: Doenitz (right) and Raeder before the war.

recognition of this work.

Having left the air corps of the US Army in 1930 he returned in 1940 as a major with the unenviable job of converting the automobile industry to aircraft production. In 1942 he led the raid on Tokyo in which squadrons of B-25s were launched from aircraft carriers and landed on airfields in China. Although the military results of this raid were of little or no consequence, the moral and political effects were very great and probably contributed to the Japanese navy's decision to overreach itself and attack Midway. Doolittle received the Medal of Honor for his actions in the Tokyo raid.

In 1942 Doolittle was given command of the US Fifteenth Air Force in preparation for Operation Torch, the Allied invasion of North Africa. In 1943 he became Commander of the Northwest African Strategic Air Force, part of the Mediterranean Air Command.

In 1944 he was given command of the Eighth Air Force which carried out the strategic-bombing campaign against Germany and bombed the flying-bomb bases prior to D-Day. In 1945 Doolittle and his Eighth Air Force sought action in the Pacific and enjoyed equal success against the Japanese.

Skillful, aggressive and versatile, Doolittle was admired by his men and colleagues.

Douglas, Air Marshal Sir William Sholto, 1893–1969

Douglas was Assistant Chief of Air Staff at the outbreak of the war but succeeded Dowding as commander of RAF Fighter Command when it shifted to the offensive. His aircraft were involved in fighter battles over the Channel and northern France. In January 1943 Douglas was transferred to RAF Middle East Command and a year later became head of Coastal Command when he helped plan the strategies for D-Day and also antisubmarine operations.

Dowding, Air Chief Marshal Sir Hugh C T, 1882–1970

Dowding was a British air marshal who led RAF Fighter Command during the critical period of the Battle of Britain. Dowding had spent a long and successful career, first with the Royal Flying Corps and later with the RAF, with command of squadrons in France during World War I, as Director of Training at the Air Ministry and Air Officer Commander in Chief in Transjordan and Palestine. Between 1930–36 he was a member of the Air Council for Supply and Research where he vigorously supported both the development of the new monoplane

aircraft types, and inventive research, especially in the field of radar.

In July 1936 he became the first Air Officer Commanding in Chief of RAF Fighter Command, a force which he transformed from a single group operating in southeast England to a highly organized defense system covering the whole of the British Isles. Utilizing the scientific advances of the day, he developed a system of fighter control in which radio and radar communications played a fundamental role, enabling up-to-the-minute information regarding enemy activity to be passed directly from ground to air.

Dowding was a man of single-minded determination who was able to exploit all available resources, however scant, to maximum advantage. His clear appreciation of operational needs was to bring him into conflict with the British Cabinet as he fought to preserve his limited squadrons in the UK during the Battle of France, but his planning undoubtedly saved Britain during the massive Luftwaffe offensives of July, August and September 1940. At the time he received little of the credit he deserved and from November 1940 onward his only service was in a comparatively unimportant capacity. He retired in 1942.

Dulles, Allen Welsh, 1893–1969

Dulles was the American Chief of OSS (Office of Strategic Services) in Switzerland. He was an experienced diplomat who arrived in Switzerland via Vichy France in November 1942 and soon built up a large network of resisters and informers. He achieved a famous coup at the end of the war when he was able to negotiate the surrender of German troops in Italy by talks with SS General Wolff. There were many problems to be overcome but an agreement was reached. It came into force on 2 May 1945 and probably saved many lives and helped shorten the war.

Eaker, General Ira, 1898–

Eaker was a US Air Force general and a leading advocate of the strategic bombing of Germany. He led the first US bombing raid in Europe, on marshalling yards outside Rouen on 17 August 1942. As commander of the Eighth Air Force he attended the Casablanca Conference where he convinced the Combined Chiefs to allow the US bombers to continue their policy of daylight precision bombing alongside the RAF's nighttime area bombing offensive. In June 1943 he was promoted to lieutenant general and a year later succeeded Tedder as

Commander in Chief of the Mediterranean Area Command. His air force was based in Italy and he continued the strategic bombing offensive against Germany and the Balkans. In March 1944 Eaker planned the bombing of the monastery at Monte Cassino. In August of the same year he was Air Commander in Chief of Operation Dragoon, the Allied invasion of southern France.

Eden, Anthony, 1897–1977

Eden was a British statesman and Churchill's foreign secretary for most of the war. Eden was Britain's youngest foreign secretary and served from 1935–38, but resigned because he did not agree with Chamberlain's policy of appeasing Hitler. When Britain entered the war Eden was recalled to be dominions secretary and then secretary of state for war (1940) but he did not serve in the War Cabinet at first. Churchill was very close to him and eventually had him appointed to the Foreign Office where he remained until 1945. Churchill considered Eden his successor and Ismay said that he (Eden) 'bore a close resemblance to Churchill in methods and hours of work.' As foreign secretary Eden travelled extensively: to Greece (February 1941) and to Moscow (December 1941) in his first year of office. He was a man of inflexible principles and was often involved in arguments with the USSR. In December 1941 he refused to recognize the USSR's prewar frontiers but he still managed to negotiate the 20 year Alliance Treaty which was signed in May 1942. Eden tried to dissuade Churchill from making any concessions to Stalin over eastern Europe. In September 1944 he arrived too late to stop Churchill agreeing to the Morgenthau Plan and there was a public outcry against this plan to dismantle all of Germany's industrial plants after the war. Eden was a very talented foreign minister who was able to achieve concessions from other parties in unequal negotiations by persuasion.

Eichelberger, Lieutenant General Robert Lawrence, 1886–1961

Given command of the US I Corps in 1942, Eichelberger directed its operations during one of the most crucial periods of the Pacific war when he helped to stem the tide of the Japanese advance on Australia through New Guinea and won the small but significant victory of Buna in January 1943. In September 1944 he was appointed to command the Eighth Army and directed it in the successful invasion of the Philippines.

Eichmann, Adolf, 1906–1962

Eichmann was a German SS officer who was head of the Gestapo's Section IV BG, the Department of Jewish Affairs. After the Wannsee Conference (January 1942) it was decided to put into effect the final solution to exterminate all Jews. On 1 July 1943 Eichmann got the final decree signed by Bormann which deprived Jews of all rights of appeal. Eichmann introduced the convoy systems to extermination camps and had gas chambers installed because they were the most efficient means of execution. Although a member of the SS, he was known to have Jewish relations and probably had a Jewish mistress when he lived in Vienna. He disappeared in 1945 and went to South America and settled down in Buenos Aires. In 1960 he was discovered by Israeli agents and kidnapped. He was put on trial in Israel and in his defense said he was merely doing his job. He was found guilty and hanged.

Eisenhower, General Dwight D, 1890–1969

The son of a poor family from Texas, Eisenhower paved the ground for his military success at West Point where he became a football star and was universally popular. His army career made slow progress between the wars, but he had the good fortune to attract the favorable attention of General Marshall, the Chief of Staff, who early in 1942 brought him to head the Operations Branch in Washington. He was then sent to lead the American staff in Britain and was shortly afterward chosen to command the Allied landings in French North Africa, Operation Torch. In Washington, Eisenhower had been a leading exponent of the policy of opening a second front in Europe in 1942, and he naturally regarded Torch as a diversion. He nevertheless put his heart into making it the spectacular success that it became and at once demonstrated the many qualities – of imperturbability, professional skill, wise judgment, public charm and gentle conciliation – which were to make him the natural choice for Supreme Allied Commander in Europe throughout the war. During 1943 he oversaw the final conquest of North Africa and the launching of the invasions of Sicily in July and of Italy in September. In December he was recalled to Britain to assume the Supreme Allied Command of the projected invasion of Europe with Montgomery as his operational Commander. Until 1 September his role was that of strategic overlord, but on that day he assumed direct control of operations and was almost immediately confronted with a

BIOGRAPHIES

major crisis of command decision, perhaps the greatest with which he was faced during the war. The Germans were in full retreat to their own frontiers and Patton and Montgomery, commanding the right and left flanks respectively of the Allied advance, were each clamoring for a disproportionate share of supplies strictly limited by the destruction of the French railroads and the unavailability of ports beyond Normandy. Urged by each to sanction a 'narrow-front' advance which each claimed would win a speedy final victory, he decided instead to pursue a 'broad-front' strategy which allowed all armies to advance at a uniformly slower pace. He made to Montgomery, however, the concession of allowing him to mount a risky airborne operation (Market Garden), which Patton was later to claim robbed him of promising opportunities in Lorraine. Market Garden, considered in a later judgment to have been aimed at capturing 'a bridge too far' failed. Montgomery forever claimed that the failure was the result of Eisenhower's 'broad-front' strategy. Although modern research suggests that the logistic resources to support a narrow-front advance might just have been found it would certainly have caused enormous political difficulties if either Montgomery or Patton had been forced to halt to allow the other to advance. No one can now tell whether a narrow-front advance could have ended the war. Eisenhower appears to have realized this and to have decided that his best policy was to support both an American and a British dash to the frontier in the general interest of good inter-Allied relations even though neither general could achieve the success he expected. In that assessment he was certainly accurate for, though his subordinates seethed with frustration, the British and American publics both saw the advance to the German frontier as a triumph of Allied arms. Eisenhower certainly did not undervalue Montgomery's skill as a battlefield commander and during the crisis of the Battle of the Bulge, judged him the right man to take over direction of the counteroffensive, even at the cost of sore feelings among American commanders. Thereafter the course of Allied strategy, both on the British and American fronts, ran smooth – during the Rhine crossing and in the advance to the Elbe and into Austria. Eisenhower ended the war as much a hero of the British people as of the American, who elected him president in 1952. Though not perhaps a great soldier in the technical sense, he proved himself very able in the direction of inter-Allied campaigns.

Esmonde, Commander Eugene, 1909–1942

Esmonde was a British naval airman. In May 1941 he led a strike force of Swordfish torpedo planes from the carrier *Victorious* against the *Bismarck*. They achieved one hit. In February 1942 his squadron was based in southern England. When *Scharnhorst, Gneisenau* and *Prinz Eugen* sailed up the channel, Esmonde led a brave but unsuccessful Swordfish attack, during which he was killed.

Falkenhorst, Colonel General Nikolaus von, 1885–1968

Falkenhorst was the Commander in Chief of German troops in Norway. He had been chosen in February 1940 at very short notice to prepare for the invasion of Norway. He was given a few hours to submit detailed plans of invasion which he completed with the aid of a Baedecker guide. He was then allotted no more than five divisions and by April the invasion force was ready. Falkenhorst was directly responsible to Hitler and remained in command of troops in Norway until 1944. The only military operation he took part in was a limited invasion of the USSR from Norway in 1941. He was hated by the Norwegian population because he used terror tactics to keep them under control. He was condemned to death after the war but was spared and released in 1953.

Fletcher, Vice-Admiral Frank, 1885–1973

'Black Jack' Fletcher was the US admiral in tactical command at the Battle of Coral Sea. Fletcher's flagship was the USS *Yorktown* and after trying to sight the Japanese forces in Coral Sea for several days, he sent out a strike force on 7 May 1942 which sank the *Shoho* and hit the *Shokaku*. The US lost the *Lexington* and the *Yorktown* was badly damaged which was a tactical defeat but a strategic victory because it knocked the *Shokaku* and *Zuikaku* out of the Battle of Midway. Fletcher was also in tactical command at Midway but his flagship was hit by three bombs early in the battle. In August 1942 Fletcher was in command of three carriers, the *Saratoga, Wasp* and *Enterprise*, off Guadalcanal; however, he was so nervous about being attacked that he withdrew early to the annoyance of ground troops. Fletcher retained command of the carrier force in the Battle of the Eastern Solomons when the *Enterprise* was badly damaged but the Japanese lost the *Ryujo* and at least 90 aircraft. In 1943 Vice-Admiral Fletcher was transferred to command the north Pacific forces and remained at this post until the end of the war.

Forrestal, James, 1892–1949

Forrestal was Roosevelt's extremely vigorous secretary of the navy. In 1940 he had been taken on as an administrative assistant and was appointed undersecretary of the navy shortly afterward. He launched a new building program and solved the problem of establishing priorities regarding resources through a Controlled Materials Plan. In 1941 Forrestal went to London to negotiate Lend-Lease deals. In May 1944 he became acting secretary of the navy and set about rationalizing the service. He visited the Pacific area three times and twice visited Europe – he watched the Allied landings in the south of France. He recommended the unification of the three services into a Department of Defense in the Eberstadt Report and at the end of the war he spoke out with intense feeling against too rapid demobilization.

Frank, Anne, 1929–1945

Anne Frank is known to millions because of the record she left of her experience of the war. In her diary she described how her family and some friends lived in an attic from July 1942, when they feared they might be sent to concentration camps because of their Jewish origins, until they were discovered by the Gestapo in August 1944. The family was hiding in rooms above Mr Frank's office which was busy during the day; thus the occupants of the attic could not make a sound during working hours. She wrote her diary in the form of letters to an imaginary friend, Kitty, and in it she described the difficulties of living as a family in the cramped conditions and falling in love with the boy, Petr, who was also trapped. After their arrest Anne and her sister Margot were sent to Belsen where they died of typhus two months before the Liberation. After the war the only survivor of the family, Anne's father, returned to the attic where he discovered her diary on the floor. Her diary has been published in many languages and the stage version has been performed around the world.

Frank, Hans, 1900–1946

Frank was a Nazi lawyer who rose to the top administrative post in Poland. When Hitler invaded Poland part of it was annexed to Germany, part of it went to the USSR, but central Poland was put under Governor-General Frank's control. He worked in direct association with the commanders of the German occupation forces, the SS and the Security Police. He was a ruthless, emotionally unstable man and his avowed aim was to make the Poles understand that 'a master race is reigning over them.' Frank divided the country into four districts, set about stripping the country of food and supplies and undertook the liquidation of the Polish educated class. He also had the Jews rounded up and sent to the concentration camps of Auschwitz and Treblinka which were outside his jurisdiction. He tried to commit suicide on several occasions as the Red Army overran Poland and finally resigned in August 1944 at the height of the Warsaw Uprising. He was tried at Nuremberg where he said 'It was too comfortable to live on the system, to support our families in royal style, and to believe it was all right.' He was hanged on 16 October 1946.

Fraser, Admiral Sir Bruce, 1888–1981

Fraser was Commander in Chief of the Royal Navy Home Fleet from May 1943 to June 1944. In December 1943, from his flagship, *Duke of York*, he directed the operation in which the *Scharnhorst* was intercepted and sunk. In 1944 Fraser was promoted to admiral and became Commander in Chief of the Eastern Fleet and took part in some of the naval operations off Japan. On 2 September 1945 he signed the Japanese surrender documents on behalf of the United Kingdom.

Freyberg, General Sir Bernard, 1889–1963

Freyberg was the extremely competent Commander of New Zealand troops in World War II. After delaying the German invasion of Greece, Freyberg and his troops withdrew to Crete in May 1941 and there inflicted heavy casualties on General Student's crack parachutists. The New Zealanders nearly reversed an inevitable victory for the Germans but in the end conceded defeat and withdrew to Egypt. Freyberg's forces then fought heroically in many operations in the Desert War. Freyberg had to insist that his troops remain as a New Zealand division and as the 2nd NZ Division they fought in the Crusader Operation, November 1941, where they were nearly overrun by Rommel's forces who resealed Tobruk. In fighting round Minqar Qaim in June 1942, Freyberg was wounded in the neck by a shell splinter but he recovered in time to fight in the Second Battle of El Alamein, where he led the 'Supercharge' break out. His forces pursued the Axis troops into Tunisia and fought on the Mareth Line. In November 1943 the New Zealanders moved to Italy, and were transferred from the British Eighth Army to the US Fifth Army of General Clark. Freyberg was the Corps Commander leading the attacks on Monte Cassino and it was he who urged the

BIOGRAPHIES

Allies to bomb the monastery with the words 'any higher commander who refuses to authorize the bombing will have to be prepared to take the responsibility for the failure of the attack.' The bombing of Monte Cassino protracted the offensive as the Germans were able to use the rubble as defensive positions. However, in May 1945 Freyberg led his troops in triumph into Trieste.

Frick, Wilhelm, 1877–1946

Frick was a senior Nazi civil servant. He was Minister of the Interior in Hitler's first Cabinet and was responsible for putting into effect measures to extend the Nazi Party's control of the state. As Chief of Police he came into conflict with Himmler who wished to control the security forces of the regime and Frick was forced to give Himmler responsibility for law and order. Frick's influence dwindled but he retained his post until 1943 when he became Reichs Protector of Bohemia and Moravia but he had very little power and Frank, his deputy, was the real ruler. Frick was found guilty of crimes against humanity at Nuremberg and was executed in October 1946.

Friedeburg, Admiral Hans von, 1895–1945

Friedeburg succeeded Admiral Doenitz as Commander in Chief of the Navy in April 1945. Doenitz became Chancellor of the Reich in Hitler's political testament and sent Friedeburg to negotiate surrender with the Allies. Friedeburg went to Montgomery's Headquarters at Lüneburg on 3 May and after some negotiation signed a surrender document covering German Armed Forces in northern Europe and Germany effective on 7 May.

Fritsch, General Werner von, 1880–1939

Fritsch was one of the few men in power who might have stood up to Hitler in 1938. He was Commander in Chief of the German Army in 1938 and would have succeeded General Blomberg as Minister of War. Blomberg was in disgrace for having married a woman who was reputedly a prostitute and he was forced out of office by pressure from Goering and Himmler. Fritsch, who was next in line to succeed Blomberg, was then accused of being homosexual after the Gestapo had convinced a blackmailer, Schmidt, to name him as one of his customers. Fritsch maintained an indignant silence and resigned from his post. This gave Hitler his chance to subordinate the Army High Command to his authority: 16 high-ranking Generals were prematurely retired including

von Leeb and von Rundstedt; a further 44 were transferred to new commands. Although Schmidt later admitted to a court of inquiry that he had lied because of Gestapo pressure, Fritsch was never reinstated. He was given an honorary colonelcy with Artillery Regiment 12 and while he was on duty in Poland in September 1939, Fritsch was killed by a stray bullet.

Fromm, General Friedrich, 1888–1945

Fromm's notoriety derives from his equivocal role in the 1944 Bomb Plot. A staff officer by training and career, he held throughout World War II the post of Commander of the Home Army (*Ersatzheer*) to which Stauffenberg was appointed as Chief of Staff in June 1943. He became aware of the conspiracy to overthrow Hitler which his new subordinate had begun to organize and appeared to lend it his support. On the morning of July 20 he allowed preliminary orders to be issued in his name for the occupation of Berlin by anti-Nazi forces. But as soon as he learned of Hitler's escape from death he 'sought to rehabilitate himself in the eyes of the winning side' by eliminating the chief conspirators, ostensibly as part of his undying loyalty to the Fuehrer but actually to destroy the incriminating evidence against himself. He instituted a drumhead courtmartial, condemned the conspirators to death and had them shot in the courtyard of the War Ministry. 'It is of some satisfaction,' Wheeler-Bennet concluded, 'to know that it profited him nothing.' He was arrested by the Gestapo, tortured and tried before the People's Court in February 1945 and hanged at Brandenburg Prison on 19 March.

Fuchida, Commander Mitsuo, 1902–1976

Fuchida was a veteran pilot of the China War who was selected to lead the Japanese air attack on Pearl Harbor. Fuchida coordinated all the preparations for the attack and led the first wave personally: it was unusual to have a single flight commander and it was a tribute to his skill and courage. Fuchida would have led the flying operations at Midway but was prevented by appendicitis and his friend, Genda, replaced him.

Galland, Lieutenant General Adolf, 1912–

Galland was one of the Luftwaffe's most successful fighter aces. He held a staff post in Poland in 1939 but was then transferred to an active command in France. During the Battle of Britain he led III Gruppe of Jagdgeschwader 26 and took part in many fights over the Channel. In November 1941 he became Mölders' successor as Commander of the Fighter Arm.

His task was to organize the defense of Europe and to this purpose he wanted Messerschmitt to build the new 262 fighter. Galland took the side of the pilots in demanding better equipment and this frequently led him into arguments with Hitler. He was eventually dismissed in January 1945 and was given command of an elite jet-fighter squadron. He was shot down on 26 April 1945, captured and taken to England for debriefing.

Gamelin, General Maurice Gustave, 1872–1958
A military bureaucrat rather than a soldier, Gamelin had made his name as Head of the Operations Section of the French General Headquarters during World War I. An interwar Commander in Chief, he was Commander of Land Forces in 1940, responsible for the direction of strategy and the coordination of the French and British forces in the defense of France. He proved unable either to give firm and clear directions to his subordinates or to react energetically to events and had to be removed from office in the first days of the German offensive of May 1940.

Gandhi, Mohandas Karamchand, 1869–1948
The Mahatma (great soul) had been frequently arrested for acts of civil disobedience against the British government of India before 1939. He did not, however, endorse political action against the British on the outbreak of war, but chose to work on Britain's 'sense of fair play' by arguing more and more strongly that only a free India could give Britain effective moral support in her war against the dictators. The failure of his urgings, and his dissatisfaction with Sir Stafford Cripps' offer of a new constitution and with the war itself led him in August 1942 to embark on a campaign of civil disobedience which led in turn to violence among his millions of followers and to his arrest. He remained in custody until May 1944.

Geiger, Major General Roy, 1885–1947
Geiger was a tough Marine commander who fought in the Pacific. He first saw action in Guadalcanal in September 1942, but was recalled to the Marine Corps Headquarters to become Director of Aviation. In November 1943 he returned to active service and led the I Marine Amphibious Corps on Bougainville. Thereafter he commanded the redesignated III Marine Amphibious Corps and led the invasion of Guam in July and August 1944. Before the invasion Geiger warned his troops 'it will be a tough and bitter fight against a wily, stubborn enemy who will doggedly defend Guam against this invasion.' He also led the III Corps at Okinawa.

Genda, Commander Minoru, 1904–
Genda was a Japanese fighter commander. He was recruited by Rear Admiral Onishi to plan a feasibility study for the attack on Pearl Harbor and with Fuchida prepared the attack. He served in Nagumo's carrier fleet and gave him tactical advice on his use of air power. Genda led the first wave at Midway.

George VI, King of Great Britain and Northern Ireland, 1895–1952
George was the titular head of the British Commonwealth and Empire and during World War II wanted to present himself to the public and the world as a symbol of Britain's upright resistance against the evil forces of Fascism and Nazism. In May 1940 the question was often raised about transferring the British Government and Monarch to Canada, but George and his queen, Elizabeth, would not hear of it. They remained in Britain and spent much of their time touring the country. On 13 September 1940, a few minutes after their return to Buckingham Palace, a bomb exploded a mere 80 yards from the king and queen but they were unharmed. After the bombing raid on Coventry the king visited the city on 16 November 1940. George made a point of having cordial relations with Churchill, who dined at Buckingham Palace once a week. Churchill kept the king informed about the war effort. The king also maintained the morale of the armed forces by visits to the navy and army: he would have liked to have seen the men go ashore in Normandy and had to be dissuaded. The king overcame his natural shyness and stammer and came very close to the hearts of his people.

Georges, General Joseph, 1875–1951
Georges, immediately subordinate to Gamelin, held the position of Commander of the Northeast Front in 1940 and it was his troops which faced the German onslaught in May that year. Although he had command of Giraud's Seventh Army, Billotte's 1st Army Group, Pretelat's 2nd Army Group and the British Expeditionary Force, he was completely unsuited to his very great responsibilities and reacted too slowly to the German advance. Georges gave evidence at Pétain's trial after the war and said that he thought France could have fought on.

Ghormley, Vice-Admiral Robert Lee, 1883–1958
Ghormley was the American Naval Com-

BIOGRAPHIES

mander of South Pacific during the first stage of the Guadalcanal Campaign. In the summer of 1940 he served as a liaison officer in London and examined British naval tactics. In March 1942 he arrived in Auckland, New Zealand, to take up his command in the South Pacific and shortly afterward was told to organize the simultaneous seizure of Tulagi and Guadalcanal for 1 August 1942. The task facing him was formidable and he expressed his displeasure and asked for a postponement. His superiors, Admirals Nimitz and King, allowed him one week's delay and the expedition set off for a landing on 8 August. The planning of the operation was hurried and the troops did not have sufficient transports or landing craft – half their supplies had to be left behind. Intelligence reports and maps were lacking and the expedition was soon named Operation Shoestring.

Ghormley made the controversial decision which allowed Vice-Admiral Fletcher's aircraft carriers to withdraw shortly after the landings and this contributed to the destruction of four cruisers in the Battle of Savo Island. Ghormley's lack of confidence in the mission and the bad publicity the operation received led to his replacement in October 1942 by Vice-Admiral Halsey. Ghormley returned to Washington for the rest of the war.

Gibson, Wing Commander Guy, 1918–1944
Gibson led one of the war's most spectacular bombing attacks in World War II. In May 1943 he was given command of the special 617 Squadron which was formed to drop Sir Barnes Wallis' special bouncing bomb on the surface of dams in Germany. He had 18 Lancaster bombers which he divided into three squadrons. Gibson led 617 Squadron on the most important mission to attack the Möhne and Eder Dams. Gibson was the first to approach the dam on a very narrow and difficult flight path and although he dropped his bomb accurately, the dam held. It was only on the fifth attempt that the Möhne dam was breached. The survivors of this raid proceeded home but Gibson led the three bombers which still had their load intact to the Eder dam which was breached on the last attempt. Gibson was awarded a Victoria Cross for his bravery and skill. Gibson was killed when returning after a mission to the Netherlands in September 1944.

Giffard, General Sir George, 1886–1964
After early service in West Africa and the Middle East, Giffard transferred to India where he was made General Officer Commanding Eastern Army. His main task was to organize units for an offensive in Burma and he faced a considerable logistical problem. Communications in Assam were primitive and techniques of supplying land forces by air were devised. In August 1943 South East Asia Command (SEAC) was set up and Giffard became Commander in Chief of the 11th Army Group. He was in charge of all land forces which would be involved in the Burmese offensive and began planning the Arakan offensive for January 1944. Although he worked very well with General Slim, Giffard did not get on at all well with Stilwell, who was also under his command. Despite Giffard's support to Slim during the battles of Imphal and Kohima, he was replaced toward the end of 1944 by General Leese.

Giraud, General Henri, 1879–1949
Giraud was in command of the Seventh Army when the German offensive in France opened in May 1940. His army collapsed and was merged with Corap's Ninth Army but it failed to make an impression on the German advance and Giraud and his men were taken on 19 May. He was interned in Königstein in Saxony but escaped in April 1942 to Switzerland and then Vichy France. Giraud was approached by the US who wanted to negotiate with him over their invasion of French North Africa. They did not realize that Giraud was out of touch with the political situation and did not have the power to stop French resistance in North Africa. Nonetheless Giraud was smuggled out of France in November 1942, a few days before the Torch landings, in the submarine *Seraph* and taken to Gibraltar. After Darlan's death, Giraud was made High Commissioner of French North and West Africa. De Gaulle, head of the Free French, did not wish to see Giraud rivalling him for his position as leader of the French Resistance, but the US felt de Gaulle was too controversial and they continued to promote Giraud. They code named him King-Pin in all their dispatches. Eventually de Gaulle and Giraud were forced by Churchill and Roosevelt at Casablanca, in January 1943, to make a temporary reconciliation and became joint Presidents of the Committee of National Liberation, which was set up in June 1943. Giraud soon found himself outmaneuvered by de Gaulle and resigned from the Committee in October. In April 1944 he also resigned from his positions in North Africa and then faded into obscurity.

Goebbels, Dr Joseph, 1897–1945
The son of a clerk, Goebbels was an educated

man with literary pretensions who joined the Nazi Party in 1924. He was soon mesmerized by Hitler's leadership and became the Gauleiter of the Berlin Nazi Party. During the Nazi struggle for power Goebbels was in charge of publicity and edited *Der Angriff* in which he attacked the Jews, the Communists and the big capitalists. With Hitler in power Goebbels became minister of propaganda and he controlled all aspects of communications through his ministry – press, radio, publishing, theater and cinema. He was completely cynical and a compulsive liar: at various times he attributed his limp to World War I or to a spell in prison; however it was much more likely to have been caused by infantile paralysis. In the first years of the war Goebbels' reported Hitler's successes but he always stressed that the USSR was not an easy country to conquer. After the surrender of the Sixth Army at Stalingrad, Goebbels took the step of making a speech about defeat and using a question and answer technique, pledged Germany's desire to continue fighting the war wholeheartedly. Goebbels also had to keep the nation's morale going in the face of the bombing of the cities and his constant theme was that if Germany surrendered she would be at the mercy of the USSR and her Allies. Goebbels was appointed Plenipotentiary for Total War in 1944 and he extended working hours, conscripted women, and cut entertainment and education. He did not hide from the Germans the fact that things were bad but he never let them give up hope, especially through his last invention, the 'National Redoubt,' where the Nazis would fight to the last. Even the Allies believed him and feared a last stand in Bavaria. Goebbels retained Hitler's trust until the end. He witnessed Hitler's marriage in the bunker. Goebbels shot himself and his wife on 1 May 1945 after poisoning their six children. He was perhaps the only one of Hitler's senior subordinates who could be described as genuinely able and talented.

Goering, Reichsmarschall Hermann, 1893–1946
A member of the Richthofen Fighter Squadron during World War I, Goering was a flying ace who had shot down 22 planes. He was a welcome recruit to the Nazi Party in 1922 and took part in the Munich putsch in November 1923. On Hitler's accession to power he became Minister of the Interior in Prussia, organized the Gestapo and built up Germany's new air force. He was the only Nazi leader with upper-class pretensions: he had an estate, called Karinhall after his first wife, which he ran as a model for conser-

vationist policies, where he entertained politicians with hunting and shooting parties. Nevile Henderson, who accompanied Goering on some of these hunts, said of him 'of all the Nazi leaders, Hermann Goering was for me by far the most sympathetic. . . . I had a real personal liking for him. . . .'

In 1939 Goering's fortunes reached their peak when Hitler named him Reichsmarschall and his successor. However, Goering was not the best choice for leadership of the Luftwaffe. He lacked concentration and was given to making extravagant claims for the air force which it was unable to fulfill. During the Polish campaign in 1939, the Luftwaffe had demonstrated its power, but Goering took risks and committed all available aircraft, never keeping sufficient reserves. In May 1940 Goering convinced Hitler that the Luftwaffe could finish off the encircled British Expeditionary Force at Dunkirk. The Luftwaffe managed to sink a few British ships but 338,226 British and French troops were successfully evacuated, when the Wehrmacht's tanks could have achieved the surrender of the mass of the BEF. Goering took a considerable interest in the details of the German tactics during the Battle of Britain, often interfering in an ill-advised manner. Nonetheless the Germans were coming close to victory when, with prompting from Hitler he switched the attack from the airfields to London. While it dented civilian morale, the Luftwaffe lost the initiative and Hitler was forced to cancel Operation Sealion, the invasion of Britain. Goering's next serious miscalculation was at Stalingrad, where he promised to supply Paulus' Sixth Army with 500 tons of fuel and food per day. This was an impossible task to fulfill and it was the last time Hitler allowed himself to rely on Goering's judgment.

Goering withdrew from active participation in High Command decisions and turned to drugs and fantasies. He blamed his subordinates, Milch and Jeschonnek, for the continuing failures of the Luftwaffe, but the fatal weakness of the Luftwaffe dated from before the war when Goering neglected the possibilities of longer range aircraft and only commissioned aircraft which could be used to aid ground operations. Living in his dream world Goering reemerged in the final days of the war when, conscious of his position as Hitler's heir, he sent the Fuehrer a telegram in which he suggested that he should assume power in the event of Hitler's death or capture. Hitler was furious and ordered Goering's immediate arrest. Soon after he was captured by the Americans and was put on trial at Nuremberg, where his old vigor returned. He conducted himself with great dignity, assuming responsibility for all crimes. However, a showman to the end, he cheated the hangman by poisoning himself with a carefully concealed capsule on the eve of his execution.

Gort, Field Marshal John, 1886–1946

Highly decorated in World War I, Lord Gort served the military between the wars as Director of Military Training India (1932) and Commandant of the Staff College at Camberley (1936–37). In 1937 Hore-Belisha, minister of war, promoted Gort to be Chief of Imperial General Staff (CIGS). In 1939 he became Commander in Chief of the British Expeditionary Force (BEF) and went to France. Although unimaginative and overly concerned with trivial matters of organization, Gort's guidance of the BEF in the Battle of France showed a great deal of foresight. In spite of instructions to remain in position, Gort chose the right moment to withdraw, allowing the army to be evacuated from Dunkirk with no time to spare. Gort was removed from the field after Dunkirk and became first Governor of Gibraltar and then Governor General and Commander in Chief in Malta (1942). He conducted the defense of Malta with vigor and resolution. He finished the war as High Commissioner in Palestine.

Govorov, Marshal Leonid, 1897–1955

Govorov was the architect of the liberation of Leningrad. An artillery specialist, Govorov had served with the Western Front in the summer of 1941. He experienced the devastation of the German onslaught and emerged to become a tough commander. He was given command of the Fifth Army outside Moscow and took part in the great counterattack of December 1941 which saved the Soviet capital. He was then made Commander of the Leningrad Front and wore down the German troops besieging Leningrad in a protracted offensive lasting over a year. He broke the blockade of Leningrad by hacking a corridor from Lake Ladoga through to Schlüsselburg and shortly afterward was promoted to Marshal. His Leningrad Front swept over the Baltic states and then, alongside General Chernyakhovsky's Front, isolated the remnants of German Army Group North in East Prussia after taking Riga. Govorov was one of the lucky Generals who survived the purges and went on to make a great contribution to the Soviet victory.

Griswold, Major General Oscar, 1886–1954

Griswold was Commander of the US XIV Corps which fought in Guadalcanal, New Georgia and the Philippines. The XIV Corps took over on Guadalcanal after the toughest fighting was over and its task was to mop up the last resistance. In New Georgia its task was more one of containing Japanese troops; however, in January 1945 the XIV Corps was in the front line, fighting the Japanese in the reconquest of Luzon. Griswold was a cautious commander who advanced slowly so that his flanks would remain secure. His corps was involved in bitter fighting at Clark Field and at Manila, where Japanese naval troops fought a suicidal last stand to save the capital which lasted a month. Griswold's men proceeded to the area east of Manila where members of the Japanese Shimbu group were holding out in caves. This was costly in casualties and the Corps was relieved on 14 March 1945 and sent south to clear the rest of Luzon.

Groves, General Leslie, 1898–1970

Groves was the US general appointed to supervise the Manhattan Project: the building of the atomic bomb. Groves was a West Point engineer with no competence in atomic physics and after Bush's first interview with him, Bush exclaimed, 'We're in the soup.' However, Groves proved an extremely competent director who dealt with all the bureaucratic problems arising from the scientific research. He arranged the purchasing of uranium and selected the site for the bomb-making project at Los Alamos. He was convinced the bomb would win the war; his scientific colleagues, however, had misgivings. Groves strenuously urged its use to end the war. He was almost obsessively security conscious and was strongly opposed also to sharing any atomic information with the British.

Guderian, Colonel General Heinz, 1888–1954

Guderian was the architect of Germany's Panzer victories in France in May 1940, and in the USSR in June 1941. In 1937 he published a widely acclaimed textbook, *Achtung! Panzer!* in which he advocated his ideas about high-speed warfare. Most of the other officers in the German Army High Command were skeptical about his ideas. He commanded XIX Panzer Corps with distinction in Poland and, when leading the same unit in the Battle of France he confounded his critics and gave a perfect demonstration of his theory, breaking through at Sedan, crossing the Meuse, and travelling so fast that the German High Command felt it had to put a brake on him. In June 1941 Guderian led the Second Panzer Army in the invasion of the USSR, which accomplished the encirclement of the Soviet Armies in Kiev and Uman. Guderian's Army was then assigned to advance on Moscow and approached from the south. Guderian, however, did not see eye to eye with his superior Kluge, whom he persistently ignored and disobeyed. In December he was dismissed by Hitler in the purge of the eastern generals for disobeying his orders and making a timely withdrawal. In February 1943 he was recalled to build up the morale of the Panzer corps and given the title of Inspector General of the Armored Troops. He made reforms and reorganized the Panzer army but what gains he had achieved were largely squandered at the great tank battle at Kursk in July 1943. On the day after Stauffenberg's Bomb Plot Guderian replaced Zeitzler as Chief of General Staff but Hitler ignored his advice. Guderian applied pressure on Hitler to withdraw forces to a defensive line round Germany but Hitler would not countenance any withdrawal. On 28 March 1945 Guderian was finally dismissed. Hitler had never fully recognized Guderian's great gifts as a military commander and theorist.

Haile Selassie, Emperor of Abyssinia, 1891–1976

Haile Selassie was crowned King of Ethiopia in November 1930. In 1935 the Italians invaded Ethiopia and successfully drove Haile Selassie into exile in Britain in 1936. In 1940 he returned to Anglo-Egyptian Sudan to lead a refugee army and by January 1941 he once again had a foothold on Ethiopian soil. Together with Generals Cunningham and Platt who attacked from the southeast and the north, he was able to claim the whole country by the end of 1941. By January 1942 he had attained independence from Britain and in 1945 overcame British resistance both to his joining the United Nations as a full charter member and to his signing the peace agreement ending World War II as a national leader.

Halder, General Franz, 1884–1971

During World War I Halder was a member of the staff of the Crown Prince of Bavaria where he left his mark as an outstanding officer. In 1938 Beck resigned as Chief of the Army General Staff and Halder was appointed to replace him. Halder was *not* an admirer of Hitler and lent his support to various conspiracies to have him arrested, none of which materialized. Halder helped plan the invasions of Poland and of France. He warned Hitler against pursuing his Western offensive in 1939

but Hitler went ahead in May 1940, in spite of Halder's advice. Halder helped to plan the invasion of England and the attack on the Soviet Union in 1941. In December 1941 Brauchitsch resigned and Hitler took over as Commander in Chief of the German Armed Forces. Halder continued as Chief of General Staff but was finally replaced by Zeitzler in September 1942. He was arrested after the 1944 Bomb Plot against Hitler and was interned at Dachau. He was freed in 1945 and gave important evidence at Nuremberg.

Halifax, Earl of (Edward Wood), 1881–1959

Halifax was the British foreign secretary from 1938–40 in Chamberlain's government. In total agreement with Chamberlain's policy of appeasement, Halifax was considered as a possible successor to Chamberlain in 1940 but because he was a member of the House of Lords and not an elected member of the Commons Churchill was preferred. Halifax remained as foreign secretary until the end of 1940 when he was replaced by Eden. (He remained a member of the War Cabinet until 1945.) In 1941 Halifax was appointed Ambassador to the United States of America, a position in which he excelled himself. Admired by the Americans, his integrity and diplomacy won him a large circle of friends which included Roosevelt and Hull.

Halsey, Admiral William 'Bull,' 1882–1959

Halsey played a leading part in defeating the Japanese in the Pacific War. He was a leading exponent of naval air strategy, well known for his flamboyance and quick temper. As Commander of Task Force 16, the carriers *Hornet* and *Enterprise*, he had arrived at his Hawaiian base in April 1942 and had immediately set off to launch Lieutenant Colonel Doolittle's raid on Tokyo. He could have made a valuable contribution to the Battle of Midway but he was hospitalized because of a nervous skin disease. However, he was soon fit and was called in by Admiral Nimitz to break the stalemate in the Solomons campaign. Halsey was immediately involved in the Battle of Santa Cruz Island in October 1942 when the Japanese outmaneuvered the US. The Japanese anticipated all the American tactics and succeeded in sinking the *Hornet*. Halsey realized that the assignment to get the Guadalcanal campaign moving was a tough one. However, the next major encounter between Japanese and American naval forces was the naval battle of Guadalcanal on 12–13 November 1942. In this case the US emerged successfully having sunk two Japanese battleships, two destroyers and six transport ships for the loss of two cruisers and four destroyers. Halsey realized that although the US had the advantage of radar it could not exploit it to the full because of the superior night-fighting skills of the Japanese. Together with Vice-Admiral Kinkaid he drew up guidelines for night-fighting tactics which contributed to later successes in halting Japanese efforts to supply their troops in the Solomons.

Halsey realized that the step-by-step strategy in the Solomons would lead to increased resistance and so he suggested leapfrogging over concentrations of Japanese troops and on his suggestion Kolombangara was by-passed. However, his forces were still used in 1943 for assaults on the Russell Islands, two islands of the Trobriand group and then Bougainville. Nimitz then decided to transfer him to the leapfrogging campaign in the Central Pacific and he became Commander of Third Fleet. Halsey and Spruance alternately took command of the Central Pacific Fleet (which was alternately called the Third or the Fifth Fleet). Spruance held the command at the Battle of the Philippine Sea and Halsey at the Battle of Leyte Gulf. In October 1944 Halsey's fleet was off the coast of Leyte guarding the San Bernardino Strait. He was determined to get a crack at destroying the Japanese carrier fleet and waited for a sighting. When he was given the position of Vice-Admiral Ozawa's carrier fleet, Halsey went steaming off north with all his 64 ships, leaving the San Bernardino Strait unprotected. This was the Japanese plan: they were short of naval aviators and aircraft and so the carrier force's only value was as a decoy. Admiral Kurita's battleships passed the San Bernardino Strait and but for the spirited fighting of elements of Vice-Admiral Kinkaid's Seventh Fleet, they might have inflicted greater damage than the loss of one escort carrier and three destroyers. Halsey's pursuit of the carriers was highly successful and he either sank or damaged what remained of Japan's carrier fleet.

Halsey proved himself a brilliant director of naval aviation, liable to take unnecessary risks in contrast with Spruance who tended to be overcautious.

Harriman, William Averell, 1891–

Harriman was a distinguished businessman turned diplomat, who served as US ambassador in Moscow from 1943–46. He first arrived in London in March 1941 to negotiate Lend-Lease arrangements. He was given the rank of ambassador and accompanied Lord Beaverbrook on an Allied mission to Moscow in September 1941. Harriman had to reassure Stalin that the USA would send supplies and aid. In 1942 Harriman served on various Joint Allied Commissions in London, including the Combined Production and Resources Board. In October 1943 he became Ambassador to Moscow and his main duty was to keep Roosevelt informed of Soviet attitudes. Harriman seems to have impressed Stalin, who had frequent meetings with him. Harriman became particularly concerned with the Polish problem, fearing that the Soviets would impose a Communist government on the country. In August 1944 he tried to get Soviet permission for US planes to use Soviet airfields to supply the Warsaw Uprising, however, Molotov and Stalin adamantly refused this request. At the Yalta Conference Harriman conducted private negotiations with Molotov to settle the question of Soviet participation in the war in the Far East and is considered to have obtained the best possible solution. He was also made a member of the three-power committee to organize a new provisional government in Poland. With Sir A Clark Kerr, Harriman tried very hard to increase the percentage of non-Communists in the new government but Molotov did not give much ground. The USA and Great Britain had to concede that Soviet influence in Poland would be excessive and Harriman also warned that the USSR would wish to achieve the same results in other East European countries.

Harriman was a skilled negotiator, but faced with Soviet intransigence there was little he could achieve.

Harris, Air Chief Marshal Sir Arthur, 1892–1984

The commander of 5th Bomber Group at the outbreak of war, Harris became disillusioned with the effects of precision bombing and, when appointed head of Bomber Command in February 1942, began to both advocate and institute 'area' bombing. This technique required the assembly of very large bomber fleets, up to a thousand or more, and the drenching of whole areas with high explosives and incendiaries. The aim was to use statistical probability rather than selectivity to destroy military targets and at the same time to make a direct assault on German civilian morale. Later in the war, as sophisticated navigational aids became available and target marking techniques improved, it would have been possible to return to a policy of precision bombing which with the resources then available might well have shortened the war. Harris vigorously opposed a return to precision attacks, dismissing such ideas as impractical panaceas, and even when ordered to concentrate on the German transport and oil-production systems he largely went his own way. He was also at times reluctant to take the advice of scientists on measures to deceive the German defenses. This undoubtedly cost the lives of many bomber crews. By the propaganda success of his '1000 bomber raids' in 1942, Harris established himself in the public eye and it was, therefore, difficult for him to be replaced when his shortcomings became apparent later in the war. He remained at Bomber Command until the German surrender but was given no further RAF post.

The bomber offensive absorbed a considerable proportion of Britain's war effort and, although many Germans were killed or made homeless as a result, postwar research, accompanied by a mass of statistics, has shown that the extravagant claims of Harris and the American airmen were a long way from fulfillment until the long-range Mustang fighter entered service. If the effectiveness of the bombing was uncertain, equally difficult was the problem of the morality of the attacks. Harris has been much criticized for continuing area attacks in 1945 and in particular for the Dresden raids. Whatever questions may be asked about Harris as a commander, he was personally well liked by his subordinates, despite his forceful and abrasive character.

Heinrici, Colonel General Gotthard, 1889–

Heinrici was a German general who built up a reputation as a brilliant defensive fighter. After Field Marshal von Kluge was promoted to command Army Group Center, Heinrici became Commander of the Fourth Army which held a line from Orsha to Rogachev. Between October–December 1943 the Soviets mounted several offensives against this line but did not break through. Heinrici achieved this by concentrating his forces at Orsha and also by bringing in, daily, a fresh battalion to man the sector under greatest pressure. He only had 10 depleted divisions but by putting three and a half of them at Orsha and by moving them round, battalion by battalion, so they all experienced front-line fighting, Heinrici was able to withstand forces six times greater than his own. However, Hitler's orders not to retreat did not make this easy. Heinrici was transferred to Slovakia in 1944 and fought a retreating battle in command of the First Panzer Army. In March 1945 General Guderian prevailed on Hitler to replace

Himmler with Heinrici as Commander of Army Group Vistula but it was too late. Heinrici could do little more than delay the obvious. He was captured by the Soviets who jailed him until 1955.

Henderson, Sir Nevile, 1882–1942

Henderson was the British ambassador to Berlin from 1937 until the outbreak of the war and was a leading supporter of Chamberlain's appeasement policy. Henderson was blind to the excesses of the Nazi regime and said in 1938 that Hitler 'would not dare to make war if we really showed our teeth.' Henderson had a good relationship with Goering, with whom he went hunting. Henderson persistently ignored Foreign Office instructions to express his own opinions: for example he condemned Schuschnigg's behavior during the Austrian *Anschluss* and later played down the help Britain would give Poland. After the *Anschluss* Lord Halifax criticized his behavior. Eventually on 3 September 1939 Henderson handed Ribbentrop Britain's ultimatum at 0900 hours giving the Germans two hours to withdraw from Poland. Britain was at war. Henderson was very disappointed and wrote an account of his experiences in *Failure of a Mission*. During the war Henderson founded a British War Refugees Fund. He also offered to return to Belgrade as ambassador but this was turned down. He died shortly afterward.

Herrmann, Major Hajo, 1913–

Herrmann was the German bomber commander who masterminded the use of the Messerschmitt Bf-109G as a free-ranging night fighter. The Germans were having little success in shooting down Allied bombers with flak and Herrmann suggested to Field Marshal Milch that daytime fighters could be used to shoot down the bombers over their target areas because flares, fire and spotlights could give enough light to pick out the bombers. This method was first tried out in July 1943 and achieved some success during the great raids on Hamburg that month. The tactic became known to the Germans as 'Wild Boar' and remained an important part of night-fighter operations until 1945.

Hess, Rudolf, 1896–

A close friend of Hitler dating from the 1920s, Hess was figuratively second in line to the Fuehrer and his deputy in the Nazi Party. In May 1941 Hess took it upon himself to act as a peace emmissary and left Germany, alone, in a Messerschmitt 110 and crash landed in Scotland.

He intended to locate the Duke of Hamilton, whom he had met in more peaceful times, and make him persuade Churchill to surrender before Britain was annihilated. Hess was astonished to find himself treated as a POW. Interned in England until after the war he was tried at Nuremberg, sentenced to life imprisonment and incarcerated at Spandau Prison in Berlin, where he still remains.

Hewitt, Vice-Admiral Kent, 1887–1972

Hewitt was the US expert on amphibious landings. His first major operation was the North African landings in November 1942 when he sailed from Hampton Roads in Virginia in command of 102 ships. He had to put the 24,500-strong all-American force under Major General Patton ashore in three separate landings. As the Western Naval Task Force approached the North African coast the weather was very stormy and the forecast was not favorable but Hewitt decided to take a chance and fortunately was rewarded with a calm sea on 8 November. Hewitt was then given command of the US Eighth Fleet off the North African coast and his next major operation was the landing on Sicily in July 1943. Hewitt was in command of the Western Naval Task Force and had 580 vessels under his command. Although there was an unpleasant swell on the day of the landing, the troops achieved surprise and met little opposition on the beaches. In September Hewitt commanded the US landings in southern Italy near Salerno, which nearly turned into a disaster; although the Allied forces had foregone shore bombardment in order to achieve surprise, the Germans were prepared to resist them. Hewitt was then chosen to command the last major amphibious landing in Europe: the Anvil landings in southern France.

Heydrich, Obergruppenfuehrer Reinhard, 1904–1942

By birth and training, Heydrich belonged to the 'other side' of Hitler's Germany, the officer class which the Nazis both envied and disliked. However, cashiered from the navy for trifling with the affections of a superior officer's daughter, he transferred his loyalties firmly to the new force in German life, joined the SS and was quickly chosen by Himmler as his deputy. He became head of the Reich Main Security Office, the central agency for internal counter-espionage and repression, arranged the Gleiwitz incident on the Polish border, which provided Hitler with his pretext for war in September 1939, and, after the invasion of the USSR, took charge of the operations of the extermination squads (*Einsatzgruppen*) which murdered the Jews of the occupied eastern territories in hundreds of thousands. It was his hand which drafted the protocol for the 'Final Solution of the Jewish Problem,' endorsed by the Wannsee Conference in January 1942, which led to the systematic murder of European Jews in the extermination camps of the east in 1942–44. He was then appointed Reich Protector (governor) of Bohemia-Moravia (occupied Czechoslovakia) and was assassinated in Prague by a team of Czech agents, specially parachuted into the country. He eventually died 4 June 1942. By way of reprisal, the Germans destroyed the Czech village of Lidice and murdered its adult population. Heydrich stood out from the majority of the Nazi leadership by reason of his remarkable self-assurance, intense ability and apparently total inhumanity, a combination of qualities possessed otherwise only by Hitler himself, whom Heydrich, it is suspected, intended eventually to succeed. He frightened all who knew him, even Himmler.

Himmler, Reichsfuehrer-SS Heinrich, 1900–1945

After Hitler, Himmler is probably the most notorious of the leaders of the Third Reich. In the popular imagination he is indeed generally held responsible for all the terror and repression which the Reich visited on its victims. Popular belief is, in this instance, not very far from the truth. By a diligent and unrelenting pursuit of power, Himmler had made himself by the last year of the war not only head of the SS, and so chief of the criminal and political police, of the concentration camp system and of a private army, the Waffen SS, but also Minister of the Interior, Commander of the Replacement Army and an army group commander on the Eastern Front. He was second in power to Hitler himself and widely regarded as his obvious successor, even though title to the succession was held by Goering. Himmler had begun his ascent to power early. The son of a Bavarian schoolmaster, he had just missed war service in 1918 but joined a right-wing Freikorps in the Bavarian civil war which followed the armistice. He made a natural transition to the infant Nazi party and was with Hitler at the Munich putsch. He became head of the Schützstaffel (SS), originally a party strong-arm squad, in 1929, and quickly turned it into an efficient, disciplined rival to the SA, the party's Brownshirt militia. A decisive incident in his rise was the ruthlessness with which he and his SS subordinates, particularly

Above: Himmler and SA leader Roehm, killed in the Blood Purge in 1934.

Heydrich, liquidated the leadership of the SA, which Hitler had judged had grown overmighty, in the Blood Purge of 30 June 1934. His usefulness to Hitler was further confirmed by his provision of evidence against Blomberg and Fritsch in the crisis of 1938, when the two generals were removed from the Ministry of War and the Army High Command, thus preparing the way for Hitler to subordinate the army to his direct control. On the outbreak of war he became responsible for the administration of the party's racial (anti-Semitic) policy, and, holding fanatical personal views on the subject, applied all his remarkable powers of organization to the extermination of the Jews of Poland and later of the occupied Soviet Union. In 1943 he succeeded Frick as minister of the interior, thus consolidating in his hands all the judicial, police and other disciplinary powers of the German state. The attempt against Hitler's life by the military conspirators in the following year further increased his power, as Hitler looked to the Waffen SS to provide generals and soldiers of stronger loyalty. In January 1945 he was even appointed to command Army Group Vistula, in the hope that he might by his devotion to the Fuehrer stem the Soviet advance where the army generals had failed. In the last resort, however, he became impressed by his own position, suggested to Hitler, on the latter's incarceration in the Reich Chancellery, that power be passed to him and was instantly demoted by radio signal. True to his old loyalty, he at once obeyed the order. He was captured by the British after the war disguised as a private soldier but, as soon as his identity was discovered, took poison and committed suicide. His character has continued to baffle historians. Despite his direct and freely admitted responsibility for monstrous cruelties, he was a retiring, even timid personality, kind to subordinates and animals, and apparently more interested in the rites and ideology of Nazism – runes, Nordic myths and Aryan genealogy – than in the pursuit of ultimate power. His loyalty to Adolf Hitler was certainly the mainspring of his actions, and he collapsed when accused of having violated the bond of trust.

Hirohito, Emperor of Japan, 1901–

Hirohito, the Imperial Son of Heaven of Great Japan, was held by many Westerners to have been responsible for the war in the Far East. He was a shy and ineffectual-looking man who was more interested in the study of marine biology than in politics and war. The emperor's position in the constitution was not powerful: he presided over all cabinet meetings but, according to tradition, he never joined in discussions and merely gave his assent to decisions. He was not associated with any political party or group of men and his ministers would have never asked him his opinion on anything because that would have been embarrassing. The Japanese people loved their Emperor and he was respected as a deity: once the war had begun they felt they were fighting the war for him and would gladly die for him.

Hirohito could see that Tojo's policy would lead to war and he tried to exert some pressure on Tojo to be more cautious. However, when war broke out it was in his name and all proclamations and orders were issued in his name. Tojo, Yamamoto, and the other leading figures kept Hirohito informed of the events of the war but he chose to remain in the background. However, as the war dragged on and the Japanese homeland was in danger of being invaded, the emperor, acting on the Marquis Kido's advice, decided to speak out. On Hirohito's initiative Prince Konoye was asked to go on a peace mission to the USSR. Hirohito saw the situation become even more critical: he witnessed the bombing of Tokyo, and the dropping of the two atomic bombs created a profound impression on him. On 9 August 1945 the Cabinet was deadlocked in the discussion on whether to accept the Potsdam Declaration: the main stumbling block was fear over the emperor's status after the war. Hirohito was on good terms with his prime minister, Suzuki, and he decided that he was willing to risk his position to facilitate peace negotiations. For the first time Hirohito expressed his views when Suzuki appealed to him and he said 'I cannot but swallow my tears and sanction the proposal to accept the Allied Proclamation on the basis outlined by the foreign minister [Togo].' On 14 August the decision to surrender was finally taken and again Hirohito made an emotional speech about the inevitability of peace. The emperor also made a recorded speech giving the reasons for the surrender which was broadcasted the next day. It was the first time in history that the emperor had addressed his people directly, and he used the words of his predecessor, Emperor Meiji, that Japan had to 'accept the unacceptable, endure the unendurable.' After the war Hirohito remained on the throne because MacArthur realized that to remove him would create bitter anti-American feelings and make it difficult to control Japan. However, MacArthur was determined to destroy the emperor's divinity and in January 1946 Hirohito made a declaration of nondivinity.

Hitler, Fuehrer Adolf, 1889–1945

Whether or not Hitler is regarded as the author of World War II, its character and course can only be understood in terms of his own extraordinary personality and overpowering will. He himself had served as a junior soldier on the Western Front in World War I (he did not serve on the Eastern Front), and his experience of the trenches was as formative an influence upon his outlook as his indulged but unsuccessful youth and his years of adult vagrancy in prewar Vienna. He believed that he and his generation of Germans – though he was German only by adoption, having been born a subject of Franz Josef – had been betrayed by their country's peacemakers and that it was their task to reverse the betrayal. In the aftermath of war he was drawn into extreme right-wing politics in Bavaria, joined and then took over one of the many small nationalist parties, the National Socialists. Hitler's party and some allied groups attempted a coup d'état in Munich in November 1923. Its crushing by the police and army convinced him that he must henceforward gain power through constitutional means, which he eventually succeeded in doing at the election of January, 1933. Within 18 months he had persuaded parliament to vote him dictatorial powers and had inherited the presidency. He had already fostered Germany's economic recovery by advanced fiscal policies and he next

Above: Hitler and von Reichenau in 1939.

began the work of rearmament. By 1936 he judged himself strong, and the Western Powers weak, enough to risk reoccupying the demilitarized Rhineland and in 1938 he embarked on outright measures of territorial aggrandizement: first the annexation of Austria, then of the Czech Sudetenland, then in 1939 of the rump of Czechoslovakia itself. His policies had by 1939, however, driven the Western Powers themselves to rearm and to guarantee the integrity of his next probable victim, Poland. When he attacked her on 1 September, France and Britain declared war. His generals viewed the outcome with anxiety, despite his last-minute diplomatic triumph in neutralizing the Soviet Union, but he proved their fears groundless by the speed of his victory in Poland. In the following spring his armies achieved effortless victories in France, Belgium and Holland. Strategic logic, as he saw it, next dictated that he should attack the USSR, lest Stalin eventually attack him, and in June 1941 he launched his armies on Moscow. Leningrad and the Ukraine. By the winter they were seriously overextended and, despite the taking of vast numbers of prisoners, still locked in combat with the Red Army. In the summer of 1942 they resumed their progress, but were checked and defeated at Stalingrad that winter. Hitler's strategy, always vulnerable at its narrow industrial and economic base, now lost its impetus and he was forced to fight defensively. He nevertheless succeeded in retaining absolute mastery over his own subordinates, in part by an apparatus of terror and repression, in part by a clever division of responsibilities. He always played a large part in military affairs but from the winter of 1941 he considerably increased his dominance over his

HOMMA

generals. He made it an offense for an officer to try to obtain military information that did not directly concern his own command. Even Army Group Commanders were kept ignorant of developments elsewhere in the theater in which they were employed. Thus no one man had sufficient knowledge to argue with him whether or not the war was being lost. From the middle of 1943, when he lost his armored reserve in the USSR, in the Battle of Kursk, it was undeniably being lost. He nevertheless continued to wage a tenacious defense, believing that the development of miracle weapons and the appearance of rifts in the alliance of his enemies, whom he believed ideologically incompatible, would eventually bring Germany victory. After the army officers' attempt on his life in July 1944, he directed the war more or less alone, and with sufficient acumen, despite his deteriorating health, mental capacity and stability, to achieve a humiliating defeat of the Americans in the Ardennes Offensive (Battle of the Bulge) in December 1944. By April, with the enemy's armies on German soil in both east and west it was clear even to him that he was beaten. Refusing the chance to escape from Berlin, he remained in his command bunker to the end, committing suicide only when his rearguards were actually locked in combat with the Soviets on the surface above. He had fought, as promised until 'five-past-midnight.'

Ho Chi Minh, 1890–1969
Ho Chi Minh was the leader of the Vietnamese resistance to Japanese rule during the war. He had been associated with the Chinese Communist movement in Canton and had set up in China the Communist-dominated Viet Minh, which was to fight for Vietnamese independence. However, Chiang Kai-shek had him interned in jail from 1942–43 and it was only on the insistence of the OSS (Office of Strategic Services) that he was released to fight in Vietnam. He turned to the US in Kunming to help his movement and received arms and supplies from the Americans but instead of pursuing an out and out offensive against the Japanese, the Viet Minh remained in the highlands of Tonkin building a network of support and waiting for the defeat of the Japanese. In August 1945 his forces were strong enough to march into Hanoi and set up the Provisional Government of the Democratic Republic of Vietnam.

Hodges, General Courtney Hicks, 1887–1966
An expert in infantry warfare, Hodges was Chief of Intelligence in 1941–42 but was commissioned

to lead the X Army Corps late in 1942. Promoted to lieutenant general of the Third Army in 1943, he soon was appointed by Eisenhower to be deputy to Bradley, commander of the US First Army, which was preparing for the invasion of Europe. When in 1944 the Normandy forces were joined together into the 12th Army Group under Bradley, Hodges took over full command of the US First Army. He breached the Siegfried Line, captured Aachen and helped in winning the Battle of the Bulge by holding the northern half of the American line. His Army captured the bridge at Remagen and helped to encircle the Ruhr. Although not one of the most famous American commanders, Hodges was perhaps one of the best.

Hoeppner, General Erich, 1886–1944
One of the Wehrmacht's tank experts and Panzer leaders, Hoeppner led the Fourth Panzer Group into the USSR in June 1941. As part of Army Group North, he headed first toward Leningrad but was then deployed to Moscow where his tanks penetrated enemy lines and almost reached Moscow, breaking through past Mozhaysk. He contracted dysentry in December 1941 when the Soviet counterattacks began. He was dismissed by Hitler in the purge of the eastern Generals and he was held responsible for the failure to take Moscow. Hoeppner was involved in Stauffenberg's July Plot of 1944 to kill Hitler and was at the War Office in Bendlerstrasse to direct a military takeover of power. When the news broke that Hitler was alive, he was arrested that evening by Fromm. He chose to go on trial and was hanged on 8 August.

Homma, General Masaharu, 1888–1946
Homma was the Japanese General who led the invasion of the Philippines. Homma was an intelligence officer who was selected to lead the operation to take Luzon despite his lack of battle experience. He landed in northern Luzon a few days after Pearl Harbor and found that the Filipino troops melted away when faced by his seasoned veterans from the war in China. He had orders to take Manila first and hesitated over whether to block off the US and Filipino withdrawal to the Bataan Peninsula or march into Manila knowing that General MacArthur had already left the city. Homma decided to take the capital and wasted valuable time. He then underestimated the numbers in Bataan and left only nine battalions to complete the capture of Luzon: his best division, the 48th, was withdrawn to take part in the invasion of the

5

57

Dutch East Indies. His forces launched their first offensive against Mount Rosa in Bataan on 9 January 1942 and after a month of fierce fighting the offensive was halted. Homma was relieved of his command for incompetence and replaced by General Yamashita although Homma remained as a figurehead. In April 1942 75,000 US and Filipino troops surrendered but the Japanese army had not prepared for a surrender on this scale and took the most expedient course: they marched the troops 60 miles to a railroad line and then shipped them to Camp O'Donnell. En route the Japanese treated their prisoners badly: giving them no food or drink for five days, shooting stragglers and inflicting other hardships. This was the infamous Bataan Death March in which about 16,000 US and Filipino troops died and for which Homma was held responsible. In September 1945 Homma was arrested in Tokyo. He was tried in Manila and executed by firing squad.

Honda, Lieutenant General Masaki

Honda was the Commander of the Japanese Thirty-third Army in Burma and one of the most able army commanders of the Burma Campaign. Honda's army fought in the long battle of retreat following the failure of the Kohima and Imphal offensives in 1944. He had orders to hold a line from Lashio to Mandalay in January 1945 but his troops fought as far north as Mogaung and Myitkyina and held up the combined US and Chinese troops trying to open the Burma Road. In mid-February 1945 General Slim's Fourteenth Army made a brilliant maneuver which threatened to cut off Honda's forces and take Meiktila. The Japanese Commander Kimura put Honda in charge of operations outside Meiktila and Honda nearly cut off the British troops who had broken through to the city. The British had superior resources and Honda was forced to fight a long and bitter retreat through southern Burma.

Hopkins, Harry, 1890–1946

Hopkins was a close friend and adviser of President Roosevelt. He had served as Secretary of Commerce and played a leading part in the direction and strategy of the war as Chairman of the Munitions Assignment Board and as a member of the Pacific War Council, the War Production Board and the War Resources Board. He was also Roosevelt's special adviser to the Allied leaders: in January 1941 he had talks with Churchill to set the Lend-Lease arrangements in motion; in July of the same year he visited Stalin to discuss the USSR's needs. He visited London twice in 1942 and also attended all the major Allied conferences that took place. During these conferences he often acted as Roosevelt's spokesman and was called in to deal with tricky questions. At the Casablanca Conference he tried to mediate between Generals de Gaulle and Giraud. At Yalta and Teheran he was particularly concerned with the future of Europe after the war. Hopkins's last important mission was after Roosevelt's death when President Truman asked him to go as his special envoy to Moscow for talks with Stalin. Hopkins's poor health caused him much pain throughout the war but even on this last mission he overcame his suffering to get an agreement on the future government of Poland. He died shortly after the war.

Horrocks, General Sir Brian, 1895–1984

Field Marshal Montgomery felt that Horrocks was one of the best corps commanders available for World War II and appointed him to command XIII Corps in the Battles of Alam Halfa and Alamein in the Western Desert. He accompanied Montgomery to Europe where he commanded XXX Corps in the Battle of Normandy, the advance to Brussels, Operation Market Garden to take Arnhem and the drive into Germany. An outstanding commander, Horrocks led his corps and armies with drive and ability.

Horthy, Admiral Miklos, 1868–1946

A former Admiral in the Austro-Hungarian navy, Horthy served as Regent of Hungary from 1920–44. During World War II his main preoccupation was to keep Hungary's contribution to the war to a minimum. At first he decided to join the Axis because he would never fight on the side of the USSR, but on the other hand he was reluctant to condemn Great Britain and the USA. In August 1941 he sent an army into Yugoslavia and also one to the USSR. However, in May 1943 Horthy refused to send in reinforcements. In March 1944 he tried to persuade Hitler to allow Hungarian troops to return but Hitler refused and threatened to occupy the country. Horthy continued trying to decrease the Hungarian contribution to the war by stopping the persecution of Jews but Hitler brought him to heel again with threats. In August 1944 Rumania collapsed and Horthy began negotiations with the Allies, and in October he announced Hungary's withdrawal from the war. Hitler immediately dispatched Skorzeny, who kidnapped Horthy's son and took the citadel in Budapest. Horthy gave in, abdicated and was taken to Germany where he remained until the US freed him in May 1945. Horthy was a Hungarian nationalist and – caught between the two power blocks Germany and the USSR – had the misfortune to join the losing side, leaving Hungary to a Communist coup.

Horton, Admiral Sir Max, 1883–1951

An expert in the field of submarine warfare, Horton was given command of the Reserve Fleet from 1937 to 1939. At the beginning of World War II he was in command of the difficult and dangerous Northern Patrol and in January 1940 became Flag Officer Submarines. In 1942 he was appointed Commander in Chief of the Western Approaches which meant that he was responsible for seeing that the convoys carrying supplies to and from North Africa could cross the Atlantic safely. Confronted with 400 German U-Boats, this was to prove a difficult task. Fortunately the 'air gap' in the mid-Atlantic was closed and more escorts were made available. By May 1943 the shrewd and competent Horton was able to turn the Battle of the Atlantic to the Allies' favor.

Hoth, General Hermann, 1885–1971

In June 1941 Hoth led the Third Panzer Army in the invasion of the USSR. His group was to penetrate along the River Niemen to Kaunas and Vilna and link up with General Guderian's Panzer group at Minsk. In the first few weeks of the war Hoth and Guderian sealed off the pocket at Bialystok which led to the surrender of about 290,000 Soviets. Hoth's forces regrouped east of Vyazma and continued the advance on Moscow but his Panzers were fighting in severe cold and in difficult terrain. However, they reached the Moscow–Volga canal and were only 12 miles from Moscow when they faced the Soviet counterattack and were pushed back. The other Panzer commanders, Guderian and Hoeppner, were dismissed but Hoth retained his command and led the Fourth Panzer Army in the advance on Stalingrad. When it became clear that General Paulus' army was trapped in Stalingrad, Hoth led the valiant attempt to break through and relieve them. He only just failed. At Kursk Hoth led the Fourth Panzer Army in the southern pincer but he had insufficient artillery to achieve a breakthrough. Hitler finally lost confidence in him after the fall of Kiev in November 1943 and he was dismissed. Less volatile and colorful than Guderian, Hoth was a thoroughly competent tank commander.

Hull, Cordell, 1871–1955

Hull was Roosevelt's Secretary of State from 1933–44. He was a confirmed internationalist and played a large part in founding the United Nations. Before the USA declared war on Japan, Hull was involved in protracted negotiations with the Japanese over the situation in the Far East. He had the advantage of having all Japanese messages from Tokyo to Washington decoded and this meant that he could see that the Japanese were preparing for war. In September 1941 Hull persuaded the president not to meet Prime Minister Konoye because he felt that there would have to be a diplomatic agreement to prepare the ground. The final stage of negotiations opened on 22 November 1941 when the US and Japanese considered draft proposals for an interim agreement which outlined a timetable for Japanese withdrawal from Indochina and eventually from China. This could have saved the day but the Chinese did not like the proposal, fearing that they were being abandoned by the US. After consultations with the President, Hull submitted a final demand that Japan withdraw from all of mainland Asia. This was unacceptable to the Japanese and they handed Hull the Declaration of War two hours after Pearl Harbor had begun.

During the war Roosevelt conducted much of US foreign affairs himself through his special envoys, Hopkins and Harriman. Hull had no more than weekly meetings with the president. However, he had his own concerns and pursued a policy of trying to win over the Vichy Regime in France which led to the Darlan Agreement. US relations with the Free French movement of de Gaulle were soured by this and Hull refused to recognize de Gaulle's Committee until August 1943. He suffered from ill-health but was able to lead the US delegation to the Foreign Ministers' Conference at Moscow in 1943 which solved many postwar problems. Hull also did much work for the Dumbarton Oaks Conference in which the workings of the proposed United Nations were discussed. He retired shortly afterward because of ill-health.

Hyakutake, General Haruyoshi, 1888–1947

Hyakutake was the Commander of the Japanese Seventeenth Army which fought in Guadalcanal in 1942. In early August 1942 it became clear that the US troops on Guadalcanal were planning on staying on the island and Hyakutake was given orders to recapture the island. He had some 50,000 men under his command but they were scattered in the Solomons, Philippines, New Guinea, Manchuria, Guam and Java so he

BIOGRAPHIES

decided to send the 2nd Division under General Ichiki. Ichiki launched an attack on the airstrip on Guadalcanal, Henderson Field, but lost most of his 900 men on 21 August. Hyakutake decided to send a stronger force, about 4000 men, under General Kawaguchi, but again they were massacred at the Battle of Bloody Ridge on 12–13 September 1942. Hyakutake put off plans to take Port Moresby and decided to take over operations on Guadalcanal himself. He had 30,000 men landed on the island and on 21 October launched a complicated operation which again failed. His troops did not attack as planned and their communications were bad. He continued to plan the destruction of Henderson Field but after the navy failed to knock it out in the Battle of Guadalcanal (12–13 November) his troops' morale slumped. His men were disease-ridden and starving but continued to fight the Americans despite the lack of air support. On 31 December 1942 the Japanese High Command decided to order Hyakutake to withdraw. His men were withdrawn in secret over the next few weeks.

Ickes, Harold, 1874–1952

Ickes was President Roosevelt's Secretary of the Interior and had responsibility for protecting national resources: coal mines, fuel, fisheries and so on. In July 1943 he was appointed Director of the Petroleum Reserves Corporation and set about safeguarding US oil supplies by acquiring the rights to oilfields outside the USA, especially in the Middle East.

Ironside, Field Marshal Sir Edmund, 1880–1959

A soldier of the old school, Ironside was an intelligence officer in the Boer War (1899–1902) and Commander of the Allied Forces in north Russia in 1918–19. In addition he was fluent in seven languages. In 1939 Hore-Belisha found that he could not work well with Gort, his Chief of Imperial General Staff (CIGS), and replaced him with Ironside who at that time was Inspector General of Overseas Forces. Gort became head of the British Expeditionary Force, a position that Ironside had always wanted. In May 1940 Ironside was replaced as CIGS by Dill and assumed the post of Commander in Chief Home Forces. Ironside was very much a man of action rather than a staff officer. He might well have proved a good commander for the BEF but he was not a success as CIGS or as Commander of Home Forces.

Ismay, General Sir Hastings, 1887–1965

During World War I General Ismay sought but never found action in a major theater but did serve in Somaliland. In 1939 he became head of the Secretariat of the Committee of Imperial Defense and when Churchill became prime minister and minister of defense in May 1940, Ismay became his Chief of Staff. In this post the diplomatic and politic Ismay served as the interpreter and communicator of information between Churchill and the people who ran the machinery of war. Terse, tactless questions and answers were intercepted, rephrased and transmitted so that no one was offended. Ismay became the accepted channel of communication between Churchill and his Chiefs of Staff and generals. He liaised with the Americans on behalf of Churchill and attended several conferences including the Foreign Secretaries' Conference in Moscow. Admired by everyone, he was once toasted by Admiral King 'Pug Ismay, whose contribution to our victory could never be properly rewarded.'

Iwabuchi, Rear Admiral Sanji, 1893–1945

Iwabuchi was a Japanese commander who led a suicidal attempt to keep US troops from taking Manila. Yamashita, the general in command of Japanese troops in the Philippines, had ordered a general withdrawal from Manila and a last stand was to be fought in the north. Iwabuchi and his 15,000 naval forces did not come under Yamashita's control and they determined to fight to the end for the city. Iwabuchi's men demolished sections of the city and held it street by street. It took the US 37th Division over a month to clear the resistance in which none of the Japanese survived and approximately 100,000 Filipino civilians died.

Jeschonnek, General Hans, 1899–1943

Jeschonnek served as the German Chief of Air Staff from 1939–43. He was a World War I flying ace who had been picked by Goering to help build up the Luftwaffe. He was very hardworking and anxious to prove the value of air power. As German fortunes declined so the pressure on Jeschonneck to counter the bombing offensive increased. Jeschonnek was not used to planning defensive operations and too often his fighters arrived too late to intercept a bombing mission over the Reich. Goering lost confidence in him and very rarely consulted him. Finally the situation became intolerable: Jeschonnek gave orders for the Berlin air defenses to fire on 200 German fighters who had mistakenly assembled there during a raid on the Peenemunde Rocket Station. Jeschonnek shot himself on the next day.

Jodl, General Alfried, 1890–1946

Jodl originally was a Bavarian artillery officer. In 1938 he became head of the Operations Section of OKW, the organization which replaced the War Ministry and the High Command. In 1939 he became Chief of Staff to Keitel, chief of OKW. In this position Jodl directed all the Nazi campaigns except the Soviet campaign as Keitel was a somewhat weak and ineffectual leader, leaving all policy decisions to the dynamic and talented Jodl. Jodl attended the twice-daily conferences over which Hitler presided and turned Hitler's strategy into concrete tactical operations. In 1944 Jodl was promoted to colonel general. On 7 May 1945 only one week after Hitler's suicide, Jodl signed the surrender of the German army at Rheims. He was tried at Nuremberg for war crimes and pleaded 'soldier's obedience' as his defense for his actions but he was convicted and hanged in 1946.

Johnson, Group Captain James, 1916–

'Johnnie' Johnson was the RAF official top fighter pilot with a score of 38 planes shot down during the war. He flew in the Battle of Britain, the Dieppe Raid and during the D-Day buildup. In the last year of the war he flew with a Canadian fighter-bomber formation.

Joyce, William 'Lord Haw-Haw,' 1906–1946

Possessing a style and personality totally different from his Pacific equivalent, Tokyo Rose, William Joyce (Lord Haw-Haw) subjected the British population to propaganda that was a curious mixture of fact and fiction with a preponderance of the latter. Amusing but vicious, Joyce did all that was possible to undermine the confidence of the Allies beginning each broadcast with 'This is Jairmany calling,' a parody of his public-school accent. His mother was English and his father Irish. He was born in Brooklyn in New York City and moved to England in 1921. At the outbreak of war he and his wife went to Germany where he offered his services to the Nazis. Just after the end of the war he was arrested at Flensburg by the British and was taken to London to be tried at the Old Bailey for high treason. His only defense was that he was an American citizen and therefore not legally able to perform acts of treason against Britain. The prosecution, however, stated that for the first nine months of the war he had a British passport and therefore did owe allegiance to the crown. He was found guilty and sentenced to death. All appeals were turned down and he was executed in 1946.

Juin, Marshal Alphonse Pierre, 1888–1967

Juin graduated from St Cyr Military Academy at the top of his class, a class which also claimed Charles de Gaulle as a member. In 1940 while leading a division of the French First Army, Juin was captured but was released at the special request of Pétain. He was offered the position of Minister of War in the Vichy government but turned it down, accepting instead the position of Commander in Chief in North Africa, replacing Weygand. Disillusioned with the Vichy government, he enthusiastically joined the Allies in November 1942 and distinguished himself in North Africa against Rommel and in Italy against Kesselring, who held Juin in high esteem as a military commander. In 1944 he became Chief of Staff of the French National Defense Committee. He helped to liberate France and was posthumously appointed Marshal of France by de Gaulle.

Kaltenborn, Hans V, 1878–1965

Kaltenborn was an American writer and broadcaster. Kaltenborn covered all the major theaters of war from Britain and France to West Africa and the Pacific and dramatized the war for Americans in his daily radio broadcasts.

Kaltenbrunner, Ernst, 1902–1946

An initiator and perpetrator of many of the Nazi atrocities, Kaltenbrunner was Head of the Austrian SS before the *Anschluss*. In 1943 he was appointed to replace the assassinated Heydrich as Head of the Reich Main Security Office. He was responsible for the Gestapo, the Security Service, the extermination squads and the concentration camps. A favorite of Hitler, he sanctioned the brutal inhumanities of the Nazi regime, murdering POWs, Jews, enemies and rivals indiscriminately. It was said that although Himmler was technically his superior Himmler himself was afraid of the malicious and malevolent Austrian. Refusing to recognize even his own signature at Nuremberg, he was the third of 10 Nazis hanged on 16 October 1946.

Keitel, Field Marshal Wilhelm, 1882–1946

Keitel was brought in by Hitler to be head of the unified defense staff to replace the War Ministry and the Army Command, the *Oberkommando der Wehrmacht*, in 1938. He was selected for his lack of personality and lack of intellectual ability. He carried out Hitler's orders without question and was known as *Lakaitel* (*Lakai* means lackey). He was involved in most strategic decisions but only to the extent of giving Hitler advice, and then only when it was sought. Jodl, his deputy, took on most of the real work of the OKW. Keitel was arrested after the war and although his defense was that he was obeying orders, he was found guilty of war crimes at Nuremberg and hanged.

Kenney, Lieutenant General George, 1889–1977
Kenney was MacArthur's air commander for the operations in New Guinea and the Solomons. When he arrived to take up his appointment as Commander in Chief of the US Far East Air Force in the southwest Pacific, he found the situation was confused. US-Australian rivalry led him to separate the USAAF and RAAF, and he made the administrative side more efficient. For the New Guinea campaign he developed the use of air transport for troops in the jungle. He took part in the massive invasion of the Philippines and started to use napalm bombs in the operations in Corregidor. He was a man of tremendous energy and ambition and attended the Japanese surrender ceremony in Tokyo Bay.

Kesselring, Field Marshal Albrecht, 1885–1960
Kesselring is considered one of the half dozen most talented generals of World War II. Like Halder and Jodl he was by origin a Bavarian artillery officer but had transferred in 1933 to the embryo Luftwaffe. He commanded air fleets in the campaigns over Poland and Belgium in 1939 and 1940, and during the Battle of Britain commanded the Luftflotte II which was stationed in northeast France and the Low Countries. His air fleet was on the verge of knocking out Fighter Command when Goering decided that the bombing offensive be diverted to London. Kesselring launched daylight raids on London but aircraft losses were excessive and their failure led to the indefinite postponement of Operation Sealion.

In·1941 Kesselring was sent to Italy and made Commander in Chief South, sharing with Rommel the direction of the North African campaign. In Rome where his headquarters was situated, Kesselring often lost touch with events on the front but his constant theme was the need for more aircraft in the Mediterranean which would have been decisive. The lack of air cover speeded up the withdrawal from North Africa as it became impossible to keep the troops adequately supplied. However, once fighting shifted to Sicily and Italy, Kesselring came into his own and conducted a brilliant defense of the peninsula. Without adequate reserves in Italy he held up the Allies in Sicily by gradually moving his line back into the northeast corner of the isle, thus giving the Allies no room to maneuver. In

Italy his persistent defense gave rise to frustration in the Allied camp and even after the eventual breakthrough he was able to halt General Alexander's forces south of the Po.

In March 1945 Hitler transferred him to the west to replace Rundstedt as Commander in Chief but the front there was beyond holding. He eventually negotiated surrender with the Americans but he remainded loyal to Hitler until he had news of his death. Imprisoned in Italy after the war he was tried for war crimes. His death sentence was commuted to life imprisonment. He was released in 1952 owing to ill health.

Khrushchev, Nikita, 1894–1973
During the war Khrushchev served as a political commissar on various fronts and his duty was to keep an eye on the military and make sure they obeyed Stalin's orders. As Marshal Budenny's political commissar on the Southwest Front in June 1941 he witnessed the failure of the massed Red Armies to subdue the Germans. Khrushchev had strict orders not to allow valuable industrial installations to fall into the hands of the Germans and dismantled as much equipment as possible and sent it east. He also blew up the Dniepr Dam and effectively disrupted all industrial activity in the Ukraine. He saw the fall of both Budenny and Timoshenko for incompetence but their replacement, Yeremenko, finally managed to reverse the trend of German victories. Khrushchev built up a good relationship with Yeremenko which continued after the war. In 1944 Khrushchev served on the 1st Ukrainian Front and undertook purges in the Ukraine so he could build a solid power base for the future political struggles.

Kido, Marquis Koicho, 1886–1977
Kido was the Japanese Lord Privy Seal and the Emperor Hirohito's closest adviser during the war. Early in 1944 he decided that Japan could not win the war and he began to talk to senior politicians about peace. After the fall of Tojo in July 1944 and the fall of Koiso in April 1945, Kido was behind the appointment of the peace-seeking Suzuki as Premier. Kido's main concern was that the peace would not mean an end to the emperor's position and power. Toward the end when it was clear that the emperor's position was not guaranteed, Kido still pressed Suzuki into getting agreement on that clause in the surrender terms. Kido was a friend of Anami but in the last days of the war these two were completely opposed. After the war Kido was tried and sentenced to life imprisonment.

Kimmel, Admiral Husband, 1882–1968

Kimmel had been unexpectedly appointed Commander in Chief of the US Pacific Fleet on 1 February 1941. Although he had received a warning from Washington that war was approaching, the only action he took was to send his carriers on maneuvers. He had not been properly briefed on the seriousness of the situation and expected the Japanese to attack the Philippines first. He did not liaise with General Short, the army commander at Pearl Harbor, who controlled land-based aircraft and had radar. By the time the message that Japan was about to declare war arrived from Washington, Pearl Harbor had been under attack for several hours. Kimmel was held responsible and was removed from his command on 17 December 1941. The subsequent investigation censured Kimmel and he applied for retirement and took no further part in the war.

King, Admiral Ernest, 1878–1956

King was one of the giants of US strategic planning. When the USA entered the war, King was appointed Commander in Chief of Naval Forces and then in March 1942 took over the duties of Chief of Naval Operations, making him the most important figure in the US Navy. He was a member of the US Joint Chiefs of Staff Committee and also of the Combined Chiefs of Staff Committee with the British and never failed to expound his point of view. His constant theme was that the US Navy could win the war in the Pacific if it were given a greater share of resources. This often brought him into conflict with the British; he only received Marshall's support if the British were dragging their feet over operations in Europe.

As Chief of Naval Operations King was behind Nimitz and helped to make the fleet train system work. This system helped to keep carriers and their battleship escorts at sea without needing to return to base for repairs or servicing. King stayed in Washington throughout the war leaving operational command to his subordinates, but he is remembered as the architect of the victory in the Pacific.

King, Prime Minister William MacKenzie, 1874–1950

King was the Liberal Party prime minister of Canada throughout the war. King was elected in 1940 with a huge majority. He soon decided to win over the Canadians to war gradually and in this he was successful. By April 1942, he initiated and passed a measure to allow conscription. King liked to play the intermediary between President Roosevelt and Prime Minister Churchill and he was the host at two conferences in Quebec in August 1943 and in September 1944. Toward the end of 1944 he faced a crisis because of the rising number of Canadian casualties but he resolved this by getting his Defense Minister to resign.

Kinkaid, Admiral Thomas, 1888–1972

Kinkaid made his reputation as an aggressive naval commander off the shores of Guadalcanal. In October 1942 he was in command of Task Force 16, the *Enterprise* and the *Hornet*, which took part in the Battle of Santa Cruz Island. In this encounter the *Hornet* was lost, but huge losses of aircraft were inflicted on the Japanese. Kinkaid was then made Commander of Task Force 67, a cruiser squadron, and set about improving night-fighting techniques so that he could prevent the Japanese supplying their men by the 'Tokyo Express' by night. After a successful operation as commander of the Northern Forces in the Aleutian Campaign, Kinkaid was appointed Commander of the Seventh Fleet, which was a fleet of transports and converted carriers. It transported the Sixth Army to Leyte in October 1944 and during the Battle of Leyte Gulf came under attack from Vice-Admiral Kurita's battleships. However, his escort carriers put as many aircraft as possible in the air and held off the Japanese until Kurita lost his nerve and withdrew.

Kleist, Field Marshal Paul Ewald von, 1881–1954

Kleist was a top Panzer commander in the German army. In May 1940 he was in command of the Panzer group which included the corps Guderian and Hoth, which crossed the Meuse at Sedan with such masterful efficiency and speed. In 1941 Kleist held the command of First Panzer Group which was part of Army Group South's advance into the Ukraine. Kleist's advance was slowed down by tank opposition from Kirponos' forces and had to be speeded up by the division of Guderian's Panzer group from Army Group Center. The largest encirclement was achieved at Kiev and Uman and some 665,000 men were taken but valuable time was lost and the advance to Moscow was held up. Kleist's First Panzer Army was given orders in 1942 to take the oilfields in Baku and drive through the Caucasus. Although Kleist's troops reached Mozdok they ran out of gasoline and were forced to withdraw in a hurry, leaving equipment behind because the Soviet Stalingrad offensive threatened to cut them off. Kleist was then given command of Army Group A which fought in the long retreat in the southern Ukraine in 1943–44. He was taken prisoner by the Soviets and died in jail. Kleist was a reliable Panzer commander, without the brilliance of Guderian.

Kluge, Field Marshal Gunther von, 1882–1944
Kluge was a respected figure in the German army who commanded the Fourth Army with great success in the Polish and French campaigns. In 1941 he led that army in its advance in the USSR as part of Army Group Center. He was technically superior to Guderian, who refused to act as his subordinate and did not consult Kluge concerning his actions. Kluge feared Hitler's wrath and in the wake of the Soviet counteroffensive in December 1941 he evolved a technique for dealing with Hitler about the latter's prohibition on retreat. He would telephone Hitler repeatedly and negotiate a limited retreat. A series of repeated 'little retreats' eventually constitutes a full retreat. He managed to keep Hitler's confidence and he was appointed Commander in Chief of Army Group Center, distinguishing himself in the defensive battles to keep his front stable. On 1 July 1944 he became Commander in Chief of the West after Hitler had lost confidence in Rundstedt. Kluge worked hard to mount a counterattack at Avranches but he did not have sufficient forces to stop the US VII Corps breaking out. Kluge became very depressed about the situation on the Western Front and at the same time he was under pressure from Stuelpnagel to join the Generals' Plot against Hitler. On the day of the July Plot Kluge refused to commit himself until he had absolute proof of Hitler's death and when this was not forthcoming he refused to join. Hitler was suspicious about his participation and thought that Kluge had tried to negotiate with the Allies. On 17 August Kluge was dismissed and recalled to Berlin but he swallowed poison on the way back, leaving a testament affirming his loyalty to Hitler.

Knox, W Frank, 1874–1944
Knox was a Republican who held the post of secretary of the navy from July 1940 until his death in April 1944. He was an experienced politician and administrator on whom Roosevelt could rely to do the job well. As secretary of the navy he supervised the expansion of the navy and insured that the fleet in the Pacific was supplied.

Koenig, General Marie Pierre, 1898–1970
Koenig gained some of his military expertise in

the French Colonial wars and served as a captain in the Norway campaign in 1940. When the Allies were forced to withdraw from Norway he returned to France only to be compelled to retire to England when France fell. He joined de Gaulle's Free French Army and was sent to North Africa to command a force largely made up of members of the Foreign Legion. An enthusiastic and dynamic leader he conducted the defense of Bir Hacheim in June 1941. After the invasion of Europe he became commander of the Forces of the Interior. His major task in this post was to bring the resistance groups under the control of the government of de Gaulle. When Paris was liberated he became the military Governor of the city.

Koga, Admiral Mineichi, 1885–1944
Admiral Koga replaced Admiral Yamamoto as Commander in Chief of the Combined Fleet after the latter's death on 18 April 1943. Unflamboyant, efficient and cool, he was nonetheless seduced by the idea of the 'Decisive Battle' with the Allied Fleet, a do-or-die conflict which would decide the nation's fate. He completed plans for this battle (Operation Z) on 8 March 1944 but he knew the chances of victory were slim. On 31 March 1944 his plane disappeared in a storm without trace.

Koiso, Lieutenant General Kuniaki, 1880–1950
Koiso, a reserve general with experience in intelligence but not in combat, was appointed prime minister after the resignation of Tojo in July 1944. He was to share power with Admiral Yonai (navy minister and assistant prime minister) who was associated with Konoye, Kido and the Emperor Hirohito, and therefore with the peace faction. Koiso was never more than an unstable interim leader, having the support of neither the peace faction nor the militarists, and therefore having no influence on the prosecution of the war or on the preparations for peace. He believed Japan could not win the war but felt the US would not give acceptable terms. In this position he presided over defeat after defeat. He had publicly committed his government to victory in Leyte in a radio broadcast on 8 November 1944. The December decision to abandon Leyte, followed by the defeat at Iwo Jima, brought his government near collapse.

Koiso was ignored by the military and not involved in decision-making. When the Americans landed on Okinawa, Koiso demanded that the military structure be reorganized so that he, the prime minister, would be consulted. When the admirals and generals refused, Koiso resigned in April 1945 and he was succeeded by Suzuki.

Kondo, Vice-Admiral Nobutake, 1886–1953

In December 1941 Kondo and his Southern Fleet were on patrol off the shores of Malaya and when news reached him that Force Z, the *Repulse* and *Prince of Wales*, was in the vicinity, he sent out the aircraft which sank this British naval presence in the Far East. At Midway he was in command of the Main Support Force for the invasion of the island, but when Nagumo's Carrier Force had been put out of commission by the US, Kondo's fleet withdrew without seeing any action. Kondo was then given command of a unit of cruisers and given tactical control of the fleet in the battle known as the Eastern Solomons on 24 August 1942. Kondo tried to engage the US fleet off Guadalcanal by day in order to give Tanaka a chance to get supplies to the Japanese on the island, but both operations failed. In October Kondo was sent to try to coordinate his fleet with the land offensive and in the Battle of Santa Cruz Island that followed, sank the *Hornet*. The last action in which he was engaged was the naval Battle of Guadalcanal in which his cruisers tried to shell Henderson Field. He did not accomplish this mission because he ran into US forces off Savo Island and although he sank the *Preston* and the *Walke* the main object of the exercise, the reinforcement of Guadalcanal, failed.

Konev, Marshal Ivan, 1897–1973

By 1945 Konev had become one of the Soviet Union's two leading soldiers. Konev attended the Frunze Military Academy and graduated in 1926. An exceptionally competent commander, Konev served in the Smolensk sector in August 1941 and from October 1941 throughout 1942 he was commander of the Kalinin Front which stayed the German advance on Moscow. In July 1943 he checked the German attack at Kursk and swept on to take Orel, Belgorod and Poltava. From 1943–44 he led the Steppe Front (which eventually became the 2nd Ukrainian Front) which liberated Kirovograd in January 1944. Konev was responsible for one of the most famous of Soviet victories: he encircled 10 German divisions at Korsun-Sevchenovsky. Although this was a masterful stroke, the Germans managed to break out but only with terrible losses – 20,000 men. Konev then led the 1st Ukrainian Front and captured Lvov. In February 1944 he was appointed marshal. Accompanied by Zhukov and his army, Konev's Front advanced from the Vistula to the Oder and eventually reached Berlin. He continued to the Elbe where he joined US forces at Torgau. He then swept south and entered Prague in May 1945.

Konoye, Prince Fumimaro, 1891–1945

Konoye was a member of the peace-seeking faction in Japan. In July 1940 he had been recalled to serve as prime minister. He had a history of opposition to the militarists but did not have effective political power. Although he had envoys in the USA trying to secure a compromise over the issue of Indochina and of China itself, he could reach no agreement because the military leaders refused to countenance any withdrawal from China. He was forced to resign in October 1941 and was replaced by Tojo. After the fall of Tojo in July 1944 Konoye began to campaign for an end to the war and was saying in private that Japan had lost the war and there was nothing Japan could do to avoid a total military collapse. Konoye was chosen to lead a peace-seeking delegation to the USSR but Molotov refused to see him as he was preparing to leave for the Potsdam Conference. In the postwar Cabinet Konoye served as vice-president but the US threatened to try him as a war criminal so he poisoned himself rather than face trial.

Kretschmer, Lieutenant Commander Otto, 1912–

Kretschmer was one of the leading German U-Boat Commanders in World War II and is credited with having sunk more than 200,000 tons of Allied shipping between 1939 and 1941. In 1939 he commanded *U.23*, a small coastal submarine, which sank the HMS *Daring* among others. After nine patrols in *U.23* he was given command of the ocean-going submarine, *U.99*. With this U-Boat, Kretschmer perfected his technique of infiltrating convoys and then committing a surface attack. On one patrol alone he sank seven ships. He was awarded the Knights Cross with Oak Leaves for his exploits. On 17 March 1941 *U.99* and *U.100* (the latter commanded by Schepke) were encircled by HMS *Walker* and HMS *Vanoc*. Kretschmer and his crew scuttled their U-Boat and surrendered. Kretschmer was incarcerated in Britain and Canada for the duration of the war.

Krueger, General Walter, 1881–1967

Krueger was a skilled tactician, who was one of MacArthur's principal ground commanders. He took command of the Sixth Army in early 1943 and turned it into a superb fighting force which saw action in New Guinea, New Britain, the Admiralties, Biak, Numfoor and Morotai. The army was expanded and took part in the reconquest of the Philippines in 1944. In January 1945 the Sixth Army landed in Luzon where it faced conditions it had not experienced before. The army had fought in jungles and swamps and now faced long dusty roads through open spaces, then cities and also mountains. MacArthur was also pressing for the offensive to be speeded up but Krueger kept his commanders advancing steadily until they reached Manila, which had to be fought for street by street and was only taken at the beginning of March. The Sixth Army spent the last few months of the war clearing the Philippines of the Japanese. Krueger was an extremely competent commander who did not seek the public eye.

Krupp von Bohlen und Halbach, Alfried, 1907–1967

At the outbreak of World War II Krupp was one of three deputy directors of the massive Krupp industries which included the Essen armament factories and various mining, energy and steel-making concerns. Between 1939–43 Krupp 'incorporated' industries from occupied countries into the Krupp organization. In some cases processing plants were totally dismantled and then transported to and reassembled in Germany – such as the Mariupol electro-steel works which were reconstructed at Berthewerke in Breslau. Krupp was not selective about the labor he used in his many factories: prisoners of war, civilians from occupied countries and inmates from concentration camps. He even went so far as to establish factories near concentration camps because of the availability of 'cheap' labor. By 1943 Krupp had become the sole owner of the company, had been awarded the Nazi Cross and had been appointed the war economy leader. In 1944 he was arrested by an American patrol and in 1948 was tried as a war criminal. He received 12 years' imprisonment.

Kuribayashi, Lieutenant General Tadamichi, 1885–1945

On 30 June 1944 Kuribayashi was appointed commander of ground forces on Iwo Jima. With his 109th Division he set about building a formidable network of caves and pillboxes which made the island immune to aerial bombardment. The Japanese defenses on Iwo Jima were consistently bombed for months before the invasion by the US Marines in

February 1945. Kuribayashi was a cavalry officer who had lived for three years in the USA and had great admiration for US industrial power but this did not deter him from his desire to fight to the last. He was tireless in his efforts to resist the Marines and bitter fighting continued until 26 March when the final suicidal attack by the Japanese failed. One of his last messages to Japan was sent on 15 March: 'Have not eaten or drunk for five days. But fighting spirit is running high. We are going to fight bravely to the last moment' – and this he did.

Kurita, Vice-Admiral Takeo, 1889–1977

Kurita commanded the Close Support Force at Midway but his major engagement was the Battle of Leyte Gulf in October 1944. Here he commanded the formidable First Striking Force. On his way to Leyte Gulf, he was spotted by US forces, attacked and forced to take evasive action losing the *Musashi*. He therefore arrived at Leyte six hours late, but he still took the heavily outnumbered US transports and escorts completely by surprise. Kurita's forces went into battle and sank three destroyers and an escort carrier; however, when they finally gained the upper hand in the two-hour battle Kurita decided to withdraw. Although his ships might have been able to sink more US ships they would still not have scored the decisive victory required by the outnumbered Japanese navy.

Langsdorff, Captain Hans, 1890–1939

Langsdorff was the commander of the 'pocket battleship' *Graf Spee*. Before he was trapped by the Royal Navy in 1939 he sank nine British commerce ships totalling 50,000 tons. But on 13 December 1939 the British cruisers *Ajax*, *Exeter* and *Achilles* cornered the *Graf Spee* near Montevideo Harbor off the coast of Uruguay. The ensuing battle was called the Battle of the River Plate. Realizing that escape was impossible, Langsdorff landed his crew and 300 prisoners of war before scuttling his ship and committing suicide. An honorable man, Langsdorff had ensured that not one British life was lost on any of the British merchant vessels he had destroyed.

Laval, Pierre, 1883–1945

Laval first became infamous on an international level when he, as French foreign minister, accompanied by Sir Samuel Hoare, the British Foreign Secretary, made a secret agreement with Italy to surrender Abyssinian territory to her. Once the Hoare-Laval Plan was made public both ministers resigned. Laval surfaced again as deputy head of state and foreign minister when Pétain was appointed head of state by the National Assembly on 11 July 1940, after the fall of France. He had reached the conclusion early in the Battle of France that German victory was imminent and thus continued to woo Germany even if it meant having to repress dissident Frenchmen. Accused of plotting, Laval was ousted from office in December 1940 but was reinstated in April 1942. When France was liberated by the Allies he withdrew to Germany accompanied by the now-puppet regime. At the end of the war Laval was found in Spain, was deported, tried in France, found guilty and shot at Fresnes prison. Disliked by the Allies and most Frenchmen and distrusted by his German 'friends,' he saw himself as a French patriot, a view which finds little support.

Leahy, Admiral William, 1875–1959

Leahy was Roosevelt's personal military representative and Chief of Staff from 1942 onward. His precise duties were never defined but he presided over meetings of the Joint Chiefs of Staff and acted as a liaison officer between that body and the president. He had daily conferences with the president and made sure that the president's opinions were made known. When Roosevelt died Leahy proved an invaluable adviser to Truman in the last months of the war.

Leclerc, General Philippe, 1902–1947

An officer in the French army, Leclerc was captured in May 1940 at Lille. He escaped once, was recaptured and escaped again and joined de Gaulle in England. He went to Africa as the first military governor of Chad and Cameroun and General Officer Commanding in French Equatorial Africa. In December 1942 he commanded a Free French force and led it across the Sahara Desert to join the British Eighth Army in Libya. In 1944 he led the 2nd French Armored Division for the Normandy invasion and was the official who received the formal surrender of the Germans in Paris in August 1944. He fought in several other campaigns, notably in Alsace and in southern Germany. Always a French patriot, he was unfortunately killed in an airplane accident shortly after the armistice.

Leclerc's real name was de Hautecloque but he did not use this in order to protect those members of his family who remained in France.

Leeb, Field Marshal Wilhelm Ritter von, 1876–1956

Leeb began his military career as a Bavarian artillery officer as had Halder, Jodl and Kesselring. An intelligent man, he soon rose to the top of the prewar army and retired after the Blomberg-Fritsch crisis in 1938. Author of a theoretical text on defensive warfare, he was recalled to command Army Group C in the Polish campaign. In 1940 Army Group C attacked the Maginot Line. In the USSR he led Army Group North in the advance to Leningrad (1941). In January 1942 Leeb was purged and was never recalled.

Leese, General Sir Oliver, 1894–1978

In 1942 Montgomery brought in Leese to command XXX Corps of the British Eighth Army in North Africa. Leese was an exceptionally competent leader, distinguishing himself at El Alamein and leading the Allied invasion of Sicily. As Commander in Chief of the Eighth Army, having succeeded Montgomery in January 1944, Leese went to Italy where he succeeded in pushing Kesselring into retreat. In November 1944 he gave command of the Eighth to McCreery and became Commander in Chief of the Allied land forces in Southeast Asia.

Leigh-Mallory, Air Marshal Sir Trafford, 1892–1944

Leigh-Mallory was a controversial figure but a very successful fighter commander. At the outbreak of the war Leigh-Mallory was in command of No 12 (Fighter) Group which was responsible for the defense of the Midlands and the east coast shipping routes. He favored the use of 'big wing' formations in the Battle of Britain, which meant that a massive concentration of intercepting forces had to be available inland. The Commander in Chief of Fighter Command (Dowding) and the Commander of No 11 Group in the south of England were against this and there were bitter disputes. In December 1940 Leigh-Mallory became Commander of No 11 Group and with Douglas as head of Fighter Command was able to shift Fighter Command onto the offensive. In November 1942 Leigh-Mallory was appointed head of Fighter Command and in 1943 Commander in Chief of the Allied Air Forces for the coming invasion of Europe. Again he became involved in a dispute because he wanted control of the British and US strategic bomber forces, but their commanders, Harris and Spaatz, insisted on their operating independently. Leigh-Mallory's greatest contribution to Operation Overlord was his Transportation Plan, which advocated a concentrated bombing of German communications prior to the landings. On the whole he was successful in this role and the 9000 aircraft under his command denied free use of the air to the Luftwaffe.

In November 1944 Leigh-Mallory was appointed Commander in Chief of Southeast Asia Command but he was killed with his wife in an air crash while en route.

LeMay, General Curtis, 1906–

LeMay was the architect of the US bombing offensive against Germany and Japan. He was sent to England in 1942 with the Eighth Air Force and instituted a daylight-bombing campaign against specific targets. He led many raids himself and devised the best defensive formation: aircraft flying at staggered heights. In July 1944 LeMay went to the China-India-Burma Theater to take command of the 20th Bomber Group and greatly improved the bombing offensive against Japan. He used B-29s and flying long distances from China they were able to hit targets in western Japan and Formosa, providing there was good visibility. In November 1944 the Marianas was ready to be used as an air base and LeMay now sent out missions to bomb the Imperial homeland. Since bomber losses were high in daylight raids, LeMay switched to nighttime low-level area bombing using fire bombs. The most spectacular raid was the Tokyo raid on the night of 10 March which destroyed 16.5 square miles of the Japanese capital.

Leopold III, King of the Belgians, 1901–

On 10 May 1940 Germany invaded Belgium and King Leopold assumed command of the Belgian army. Leopold requested aid from the Allies who sent troops to aid the Belgian forces. However, after two weeks of difficult fighting which had cornered the Belgians in the northeast of their country, Leopold made the decision to surrender on 28 May 1940. The army, the people and the government, led by Prime Minister Pierlot, opposed this admission of defeat and declared his capitulation illegal. But it was too late to reverse the action. The Germans confined Leopold to the Palace of Laeken near Brussels. He further antagonized his citizens by contracting a morganatic marriage during the war. When the US invaded Belgium in 1944, Leopold was taken by the Wehrmacht to Germany where he was found by the Americans in 1945. The Belgian people refused to let Leopold return to the throne and would not even allow him to return to Belgium until 1950.

List, Field Marshal Wilhelm, 1880–1971

List was an engineering officer in the Bavarian army. In 1939 he commanded the Fourteenth Army and led it into Poland. In 1940 he led the Twelfth Army which led the advance into Belgium by crossing the Meuse between Namur and Dinant. On 19 July 1940 he became field marshal and in the spring of 1941 was Commander in Chief of German Forces for Operation Marita (the invasion of Greece). In the USSR he commanded Army Group A (July–September 1942) as it advanced into the Caucasus. His failure to break through the line caused him to be dismissed by Hitler. He was tried for war crimes at Nuremberg and sentenced to life imprisonment but was pardoned and released after five years.

Litvinov, Maxim, 1876–1952

A Bolshevik from his early days, Litvinov was Soviet commissar for foreign affairs from 1930. He was in favor of Soviet cooperation with the west and advocated the use of the League of Nations, as an anti-Fascist organization. However, he was replaced on 3 May 1939 by Molotov who reversed Litvinov's policies and made a pact with Germany. From 1941–43 he was Soviet ambassador to the USA. At the same time but continuing until 1946 he was deputy commissar for foreign affairs.

MacArthur, General Douglas, 1880–1964

MacArthur was one of the most colorful and controversial figures in the US Army in World War II. He had served for several years before the war as an adviser to the Philippine government but in July 1941 was recalled to active duty with orders to mobilize forces in the Philippines and prepare for war. By December he had raised the number of men at arms from 22,000 to 180,000; however these consisted mainly of untrained Filipinos who would desert as soon as the fighting broke out. MacArthur was handicapped in his defense of the islands by lack of naval and air support. Within a week of the main Japanese landings, MacArthur had abandoned Manila and withdrawn to the Bataan peninsula. The final battle was protracted with the last US troops surrendering in May 1942. MacArthur left the Philippines at the president's request on 11 March with the words 'I shall return.'

MacArthur felt he and the USA had reneged on their word by leaving the Philippines to the Japanese and determined to recapture it as soon as possible. His ambition was fulfilled three years later and these years were spent gradually wearing down Japanese concentrations in the islands to the north of Australia. In the spring of 1942 MacArthur had only 25,000 troops and 260 obsolete aircraft in Australia and he had a tough job persuading the Joint Chiefs of Staff to send reinforcements. The United States' policy was Germany first and the defeat of Japan was not considered as urgent. MacArthur saw the defeat of Japan as an important venture and pressed his views. In this he could count on some support from Admiral King, Commander in Chief of the navy, whose main concern was that his navy win the war in the Pacific. The first operation the Joint Chiefs agreed to undertake was the recapture of Guadalcanal in August 1942 but this first step was allocated to Admiral Nimitz's fleet; MacArthur would accomplish the next step in the Solomons campaign and also retake New Guinea.

The fight to take Guadalcanal was hard and costly in casualties. In early 1943 MacArthur presented his Elkton Plan which proposed by-passing the major troop concentrations and taking airfields in the Huon peninsula, New Georgia, New Britain, Bougainville and an attack on Kavieng and Rabaul. MacArthur's tactic was known as island-hopping by the army and succeeded because the Japanese troops lost their air cover and were isolated and left to die. By hopping from coastal town to coastal town, New Guinea was eventually secured by mid-1944 and some 44,000 Japanese troops under General Adachi were by-passed at Wewak. The Solomons campaign was also protracted and Rabaul was by-passed. By mid-1944 the Joint Chiefs were ready to consider the next step. Nimitz thought this should be the capture of Formosa and destruction of Japanese air power, but MacArthur advocated his long-cherished dream of recapturing the Philippines and in September it was finally agreed on. On 9 January 1945 the US troops landed at Lingayen Gulf on Luzon and MacArthur waded ashore accompanied by Osmeña and Romulo and one month later he entered Manila. The fighting in the Philippines continued until the Japanese surrender and MacArthur spread his activities to the Dutch East Indies. He was convinced the Japanese would fight to the last and advised President Truman accordingly. It fell on MacArthur to accept Japan's formal surrender on Nimitz's flagship the USS *Missouri* in Tokyo Bay on 2 September 1945.

MacArthur was a flamboyant character who made sure the people back home knew what he was doing to win the war. He was a great publicist but he made many enemies. Generals

Above: General MacArthur in 1945.

Marshall and Eisenhower disliked him and even President Roosevelt, resentful of his popularity, did not wish him to have the limelight. After the war he ruled Japan as an all-powerful potentate but he overstepped the mark in Korea which led to his downfall.

McCreery, General Sir Richard, 1898–1967

In 1940 McCreery served with the British Expeditionary Force in its disastrous campaign in France. In May 1941 he was sent by Brooke to North Africa to serve as Chief of Staff to Auchinleck. However, their relationship was stormy and McCreery was dismissed. He returned to serve as Alexander's Chief of Staff in August 1942 and played a major role in drawing up the plans for the last stages of the Battle of El Alamein.

McCreery went on to a successful career as a corps commander with the X Corps of the Eighth Army, which he led in the Salerno landings. The corps played a crucial role in the Battle for Monte Cassino and McCreery was promoted in November 1944 to lead the Eighth Army in its final offensive in Italy.

Malenkov, Georgi, 1902–1983

Malenkov pursued a successful career working on the security and political aspects of the military from 1920–41. At the start of the German invasion of the Soviet Union he was appointed to the newly formed Committee for the Defense of the State (GKO). This committee was composed of Stalin, Molotov, Voroshilov, Beria and Malenkov. Malenkov was responsible for technical equipment for the army and air force. He was closely involved in the massive Soviet evacuation of industrial materials to the east. During the first two years of the war he also served as political commissar on a number of different fronts. From 1943–45 he served as chairman of the Committee for the Restoration of the Economy which dealt with countries recently liberated from the Germans. At the end of the war Malenkov became deputy chairman of the Council of Ministers and briefly took power after Stalin's death, to be ousted shortly thereafter by Khrushchev.

Malinovsky, Marshal Rodion, 1898–1967

Malinovsky was commanding an army at Odessa at the start of Barbarossa (June 1941) and in December 1941 was given command of the Southwest Front. In December 1942 at Stalingrad, Malinovsky prevented Manstein from freeing Paulus' encircled Sixth Army. From 1943–44 Malinovsky was commander first of the Southwest Front and then of the 3rd Ukraine Front with which he cleared out the Donbass and west Ukraine. Later in 1944 he became commander of the 2nd Ukraine Front and, in conjunction with Tolbukhin, invaded Rumania, totally defeating the Germans, taking 200,000 prisoners and causing Rumania to defect to the Allies. Malinovsky continued on to Hungary and took Budapest in February 1945. In April 1945 he liberated Slovakia. Malinovsky then led the Soviet armies in Manchuria in August.

Mannerheim, Marshal Carl von, 1867–1951

Mannerhiem was a Finnish officer in the Czar's army at the time when Finland was a part of the Russian empire. He returned to Finland in 1917 to lead the White Army to victory over the local Red Army. In 1939 Mannerheim was recalled by Finland to resist the Soviet invasion. The brilliant Finnish defense could not hold out long against the superior Soviet forces but, largely thanks to Mannerheim's military prowess, the armistice terms were comparatively mild. In 1941 Hitler invaded Soviet territory and Finland chose to resume hostilities against the USSR to regain the territory she lost in 1940. When defeat yet again seemed inevitable in 1944 Mannerheim, as head of state, was able to secure terms for the armistice propitious to Finland. Finland's national hero was a statesman of tact, intelligence and diplomacy.

Manstein, Field Marshal Erich von, 1887–1973

Along with Guderian, Manstein is regarded as the most successful and most brilliant field commander of the German army in World War II. Manstein's reputation rests on two pillars: his ability to frame excellent plans and his skill at executing difficult orders in the teeth of the enemy's opposition. He first made his name in World War II when, as Chief of Staff to Rundstedt of Army Group A in 1939, he proposed an alternative to the High Command's plans for invading France and the Low Countries. This was for a drive to the Channel through the wooded hills of the Ardennes, aimed at separating the British and French field armies from their static supporting armies. Already notorious for his arrogance and tactlessness to superiors, his temerity in challenging the High Command view brought him appointment to a less influential post but en route he was called to visit Hitler, to whom he outlined his scheme and who thenceforth supported it. In the attack on the USSR he was given command first of LVI Panzer Corps and then of the Eleventh Army, which he handled brilliantly in the capture of the Crimea. In July 1942 he was promoted to command Army Group Don and in December very nearly succeeded in relieving Stalingrad in an operation known as Winter Storm. On 15 March 1943 he achieved the greatest German success in counteroffensive operations of the whole war by recapturing Kharkov. Thereafter, like all German generals, he was driven steadily into retreat, with the difference that he constantly asked Hitler for permission to 'maneuver,' by which the Fuehrer understood him to mean give up ground when not under pressure to do so. In fact, his idea was to force the Soviets off balance and then counterattack, but Hitler's suspicions always overcame the logic of his arguments. He was eventually dismissed in March 1944 and spent the rest of the war on his estate. He is still regarded as a master of modern warfare.

Mao Tse-tung, 1893–1976

Mao was chairman of the Chinese Communist Party from 1931 until his death. He broke with Stalin in 1927 after Comintern directives led to a massacre of Communists by the Kuomintang in Shanghai. In 1937 a new alliance between the Kuomintang and the Communist Party was forged in the face of Japanese aggression, but only lasted until 1940 when Mao decided to fight Chiang Kai-shek rather than the Japanese. Mao directed his wartime operations from Yenan, in Shensi Province. One last attempt at an alliance negotiated by US Ambassador Hurley, between Chiang and Mao failed in 1944. After the defeat of Japan, civil war began.

Mao was a brilliant innovator of new revolutionary techniques and a master of guerrilla warfare. His strategy was to base his revolutionary movement on the peasantry, moving his forces through friendly territory and organizing these areas as he progressed. Only Tito led a comparable resistance movement during the war with such success.

Marshall, General George, 1880–1959

At the outbreak of World War II, Marshall had just been appointed Chief of Staff of the American army, then only 200,000 strong. He had formerly acted as aide to Pershing, after World War I, in which he had fought as a junior officer, but otherwise had had no training in the raising of a great army for war, toward which America seemed inevitably to be drifting. Nevertheless he succeeded, by the time of Pearl Harbor, in more than doubling the army's size and, as soon as war broke out, on carrying through a major reorganization, which divided it into three: the Army Ground Forces, the Army Air Forces and the Army Service Forces. He proved himself to be more than an organizer. He had already done much to aid American preparedness for war by his prewar planning and appointment of trusted subordinates, like Eisenhower, to key positions. Immediately after Pearl Harbor, he became chairman of the new Joint Chiefs of Staff Committee to advise the president on strategy, a post he held throughout the war. He consistently supported the principle of 'Germany First' and, though irritated by what he regarded as British prevarication over the invasion of Europe, steadfastly supported the Anglo-American strategic line in the face of American naval opposition. He accompanied the president or represented the Chiefs of Staff at most of the major inter-Allied conferences of the war, and maintained a creative relationship with Roosevelt until his death. Despite suggestions that he should eventually take over command of the American armies in Europe, the president eventually decided that he was too valuable in Washington to be spared and he remained Chief of Staff until the war's end. In postwar years he became secretary of state and the architect of the Marshall Plan to rebuild the war-shattered economies of Europe, foe's and friend's alike. A cool and distant figure, with whom few could claim to be intimate, he impressed all who worked with him by his total unselfishness and impartiality of judgment and by a sort of Roman nobility of character.

Masaryk, Jan, 1886–1948

Masaryk was an important Czechoslovakian statesman and foreign minister of the Czech government-in-exile in London. At the time of the Munich Agreement and the partition of Czechoslovakia, Masaryk was ambassador to London. He became foreign minister of the government-in-exile under Edouard Beneš. His first major task was to act as mediator between Beneš and the British government in the Czechs' attempt to gain full recognition for their government. This was achieved in July 1941 and was followed in 1942 by Eden's formal renunciation of the Munich Agreement. Masaryk also went on extensive speaking tours of Britain and the United States and made daily BBC broadcasts to Czechoslovakia. These were extremely successful, partly because of the symbolic value of his name; his father, Thomas Masaryk, was the hero of Czech independence. Relations between the Czech government-in-exile and the USSR were extremely good. Masaryk signed a mutual aid agreement with the USSR on 18 July 1941 which provided for Czech units within the Soviet army and later signed a friendship pact.

Masaryk died having 'fallen' out of a window in Prague under mysterious circumstances.

Matsuoka, Yosuke, 1880–1946

Matsuoka was foreign minister of Japan from 1940–1941. He was a westernized man, brought up in Portland, Oregon, by a Methodist family and holding a degree in law from the University of Oregon. However, he was at the same time extremely xenophobic, greatly mistrusted America and Britain, and was primarily concerned with not allowing Japan to lose out in the approaching Great Power crisis. He is best remembered for coining the phrase, Greater East Asia Co-Prosperity Sphere.

His main experience was in business but he turned to foreign affairs as Japanese delegate to the League of Nations, 1932–33. He staged a dramatic walk out when Japan was censured for its invasion of Manchuria. A close friend of Konoye's, Matsuoka became foreign minister in his Cabinet in September 1940. His first achievement was to complete a Tripartite Pact with Germany and Italy (27 September) which was primarily aimed at inhibiting the United States. In the spring of 1941 he travelled to Germany and the USSR and was so impressed with Stalin and with the USSR's strength that he signed a neutrality pact with Molotov on 13 April 1941. The Japanese were outraged by the conclusion of such an agreement with their traditional enemy and by Matsuoka's un-Japanese-like direct action. In July 1941 the entire Cabinet resigned in order to get rid of him. Matsuoka was tried and executed by the Allies for his part in initiating the war.

BIOGRAPHIES

Mauldin, William H, 1921–
An American cartoonist, Mauldin served with the 45th Infantry Division (and the magazine *Stars and Stripes*) in Sicily, Italy, France and Germany. His cartoons and sketches of the war as seen through the eyes of his two immortal character, the infantrymen 'Willie' and 'Joe', won a Pulitzer Prize in 1944.

Menzies, Robert, 1894–1978
Menzies was prime minister of Australia from April 1939–28 August 1941, as head of the United Australia Party's minority government. Thus it was Menzies who organized Australia's preparations for war, announced its entry into the war (3 September 1939) and deployed three Australian divisions to the Middle East. In August 1940 he formed a coalition government with the Country Party but had only a very small majority over the opposition Labour Party. From January–May 1941 Menzies travelled back and forth to London, visiting troops along the way. Menzies resigned on 28 August 1941 and his party only remained in power until 6 October when it was succeeded by a Labour government under Curtin.

Meretskov, Marshal Kirill, 1897–
Meretskov was Chief of General Staff at the start of the war but was soon superseded by Zhukov. In the Russo-Finnish war he had commanded an army on the Vyborg flank and led the breakthrough of the Mannerheim Line. He again made a name for himself as commander of the Volkhov Front in the defense of Leningrad in December 1941 by driving the Germans out of the town of Tikhvin, thereby keeping supply lines open. In January he and General Govorov broke the German Blockade and reestablished railroad lines from Moscow to Leningrad. In February 1944, Meretskov was appointed commander of the Karelian Front to drive the Germans out of Finland. He had by this time lost touch with Stalin and was out of favor. In August 1945 he was given command of the 1st Far Eastern Front.

Merrill, Brigadier General Frank, 1903–1950
Merrill trained a led a long-range penetration group called 'Merrill's Marauders.' They were modelled on Wingate's Chindits but were considerably more effective.

Merrill was in Rangoon at the start of the war and was Stilwell's most trusted subordinate during his retreat from Burma. In May 1942 Merrill became a Lieutenant Colonel and began training his guerrilla force for operations in jungle conditions behind Japanese lines. The Marauders' most notable battle was in 1944, when after setting out in February they reached the Japanese rear areas at Maingkwan and severed their supply line at the Hukawng Valley by March. Although Merrill himself was hospitalized from April–July, his Marauders continued living off the land, harassing the enemy's communications and attacking isolated outposts. On 17 May, together with some of Stilwell's Chinese troops, they captured the Mytkyina airstrip. The town of Myitkyina held out till 3 August 1944.

Merrill then became deputy US commander in Burma-India and, later, Chief of Staff of the US Tenth Army in the Pacific.

Metaxas, General Joannis, 1871–1941
Metaxas was the dictator of Greece from 1936–41. He was a staunch royalist who was thought to be pro-German but when Mussolini invaded Greece in October 1940, Metaxas immediately mobilized all his reserves. By November the Greeks had gained the upper hand and were able to repel the Italians and occupy half of Albania. Metaxas died shortly after his success and he did not see the final invasion of Greece.

Michael, King of Rumania, 1921–
Michael became king when his father Carol II abdicated in his favor in September 1940. His accession to power coincided with Antonescu's seizure of power and Michael could do nothing to prevent it. However, in August 1944 Michael was able to turn the tables and had Antonescu arrested and locked away in a closet in his palace. His attendants disarmed Antonescu's bodyguard and a new government was formed that evening, 23 August. The government's first act was to declare war on Germany. Michael remained King until the end of 1947 when he decided he could no longer lead a Communist state.

Mihajlović, General Draza, 1893–1946
Mihajlović was a Yugoslavian resistance leader who was superseded by Tito in the middle of the war. He was a Royalist army officer in charge of the Operations Bureau of the General Staff when the Germans invaded in April 1941. Following the invasion, Mihajlović left for Serbia with a small following and established a resistance group called the Cetniks. In the fall of 1941 Mihajlović was widely publicized by the Allied press and was even supported by the Soviets. However, the Cetniks were not only dedicated to Serbian interests but were also

staunchly anti-Communist. Attempts at co-operation between Mihajlović and Tito's partisans foundered during the first campaign against the German occupation (fall 1941). Mihajlović and his Četniks attacked Tito in Serbia and were soundly defeated. Mihajlović then decided not to launch an active campaign against the Nazis but rather to wait for the Nazis to wipe out Tito and his partisans. Not only did he decide not to attack the Germans but decided to collaborate with them as well. In January 1942 he was appointed Commander in Chief of Armed Forces and war minister of the Yugoslavian government-in-exile. It was not until late in 1942 that the Allies found out what was happening and they soon shifted their support to Tito who rapidly became a national leader. The Yugoslav government-in-exile dismissed Mihajlović in May 1944 and he had no part in the postwar coalition government. Mihajlović was tried and executed in 1946.

Mikolajczyk, Stanislaw, 1901–1967

Mikolajczyk was a Polish statesman who headed the Polish government-in-exile from 1943–44. He had been the leader of the Polish Peasant Party and left Poland in 1939 to join the Polish National Council in Paris. In 1941 he was appointed deputy prime minister and minister of the interior in Sikorski's government in London. He was charged with maintaining contact with the Resistance in Poland. After Sikorski's death, Mikolajczyk became prime minister but lacked his predecessor's authority both with his own people and with his Allies. In November 1944 he resigned because of the lack of Allied support over the Warsaw Uprising and the question of Poland's eastern frontier. He was the only major Polish politician in the west to return to Poland after the war, where he joined the Lublin Committee. However, he was soon purged by the government.

Milch, Field Marshal Erhard, 1892–1972

Milch had been a fighter squadron commander in World War I and had then gone on to work in the commercial aviation industry. In 1926 he was made chairman of Lufthansa, the newly formed state airline. He used Lufthansa as a cover behind which he developed the skilled manpower and tested the techniques and machinery which would form the new German air force. When the Luftwaffe was officially recognized in 1935 it had 1000 aircraft and 20,000 trained men, and Milch was placed at the head of the Air Ministry. Working with Udet and Wever, Milch directed the organizational

side of the business for which he had tremendous talent. He had been a close friend of Goering, but they fell out and Udet was temporarily in the ascendant until he committed suicide in 1941. Milch was the dominant figure in German aircraft production until 1944 when he had to share his power with Speer. He was convicted of war crimes and was released on parole in 1955.

Mitscher, Vice-Admiral Marc, 1887–1947

Mitscher was the US navy's main aviation expert and a commander of carrier forces in the Far East throughout the war. In 1941 he was given command of the carrier USS *Hornet* which was used to launch Doolittle's bomber raid on Tokyo (18 April 1942). In June the *Hornet* was one of the three US carriers at the Battle of Midway. Mitscher was made air commander of Guadalcanal on 1 April 1943 and had control over the air force units of the US army, navy, and marines and of the New Zealand RAF.

In January 1944 Mitscher took command of the Fast Carrier Force, Task Force 58, part of Spruance's Central Pacific Force. From January to October 1944 it was responsible for destroying 795 enemy ships and 4425 planes. This force had its own fleet train and could therefore remain in operation for long periods at a time. It was used to provide an air umbrella for the invasions of the Marshalls and Hollandia and in June 1944 went to the Marianas. Mitscher and his force played a crucial role in the Battle of the Philippine Sea where Mitscher made the daring decision to send his planes out although they could only be recovered from the raid after dark. From August–September 1944, Task Force 58 was involved in raids on the Bonin Islands, Palau, Mindanao and Formosa. Finally they provided air cover for the campaigns in Iwo Jima and Okinawa where they had to contend with Kamikazes and other enemy planes flown from Japan.

Model, Field Marshal Walther, 1891–1945

Model represented a new middle class in the German army and was one of Hitler's more trusted army commanders. He built himself a reputation as an energetic and forceful commander at the head of the 3rd Panzer Division in France and the Sixteenth Army in the USSR. As the older army commanders lost Hitler's confidence, Model was given greater responsibilities. He helped plan the great tank battle at Kursk which ended in a defeat for the Germans; however, Model held the front together with his tireless energy. In 1944 Hitler used him as a trouble-shooter, transferring him from front to front. In early 1944 he commanded Army Group North and stopped the Soviet advance into the Baltic States. He also commanded Army Group Center after the opening of the Belorussian Campaign and the collapse of all resistance on that front. Model succeeded in restoring stability to the front and stopped the Soviet armies outside Warsaw. On 17 August he was transferred to replace Kluge as Commander in Chief of the west but found there was little he could do to repair the front. In September he was replaced by Rundstedt and given command of Army Group B in Belgium, which was driven back to Holland shortly afterward. However, he was in the vicinity of the British paratroop attack on Arnhem and successfully prevented the Allies gaining an early bridgehead over the Rhine. Through careful reorganization of his forces he was able to mount the Ardennes offensive which nearly broke the back of the Allied advance. However when the offensive petered out, Model found himself trapped in a pocket in the Ruhr. He tried in vain to break out and decided to disband the Army Group on 15 April 1945. He shot himself on 21 April because he felt it was a disgrace for a field marshal to surrender.

Moelders, Colonel Werner, 1913–1941
Moelders was one of the Luftwaffe's leading fighter pilots with a score of over 150 planes downed. He commanded fighter groups in the Battle of France and the Battle of Britain. In 1941 he went to the Eastern Front as inspector of fighter aircraft. He died in November 1941 when his plane hit a factory chimney on the way to the state funeral of Udet.

Moelders was outstanding both as a tactician and as a pilot. He invented the 'Four Fingers' formation which was later adopted by the RAF.

Molotov, Viachislav M, 1890–
Molotov succeeded Litvinov as Soviet commissar for foreign affairs on 3 May 1939 and retained this post until 1952. In August 1939 he successfully negotiated the Nazi-Soviet Non-Aggression Pact which specified the partitioning of Poland between Germany and the USSR and defined their spheres of influence in the Baltic and Balkans. The basis of this agreement was overturned when Molotov received reports of German activities in Finland and Rumania. Molotov confronted Hitler with these reports, negotiations broke down and Hitler's plans for *Barbarossa* were set in motion in late 1940. On 13 April 1941 Molotov won a diplomatic victory

by signing a nonaggression pact with Japan, but he had to announce the news of the German invasion on 21 June 1941. He was appointed to the five-man State Defense Committee shortly afterward.

Throughout the war Molotov attended all the major Allied conferences and many meetings with heads of state in Moscow. He took on many of Stalin's reponsibilities at various times owing to the latter's overwork or ill-health. In May 1942 he visited Washington and London, charged with pressuring the Western Allies into opening up a second front in Europe at the earliest possible date and resuming the sending of convoys of equipment to the USSR. Roosevelt actually promised Molotov that an Allied invasion of Europe would take place in 1942 but had to back down later in the year. Molotov also signed a 20-year treaty with England at this time, pledging support against Hitler.

In June 1943 Molotov was engaged in secret negotiations with Ribbentrop through intermediaries. Though they did not come to an agreement, news of the Soviet attempt to make a separate peace leaked to the Western Allies. It was not allowed to disrupt their relations, however, and convoys to the USSR were resumed in November 1943. Molotov hosted the Foreign Ministers' Conference in Moscow in October 1943 and was the USSR's first delegate to the United Nations in San Francisco in June 1945.

Montgomery, Field Marshal Bernard, 1887–1976
Montgomery's willfulness, egocentricity and arrogance were dominant traits of his character as a young officer. Despite them, he had risen at the outbreak of World War II to general's rank and to command 3rd Division, which he took to France in 1939 and evacuated from Dunkirk, battered but intact, in June 1940. He was one of the last officers to leave the beaches, and brought home an enhanced reputation, which won him command first of V and then of XII Corps. His rise to fame began in 1942 when he was chosen by Churchill to replace Auchinleck in command of Eighth Army in the Western Desert. He had the good luck to take over at a time when the Eighth Army was receiving its first plentiful consignment of modern equipment and reinforcements and when Rommel's forces had almost outreached their own supplies by the speed and depth of their advance. It was Montgomery's remarkable ability to infuse his new command with confidence and belief in his powers of command, as much as these material benefits, which fitted it, however, to undertake

the task of defeating the enemy for good at the Battle of El Alamein. Montgomery's conduct of the battle, and particularly of the pursuit toward Tunis which ensued, has been criticized. However, he was the undoubted victor and thus, to that date, the first British general to have defeated a German commander in a major battle. The British people accepted him as a hero overnight and he never subsequently lost that cachet. After the landing of the Anglo-American armies in French North Africa he became subject to Eisenhower's command and fought successfully to destroy what remained of the German-Italian army in Africa, particularly at the Battle of Mareth. He commanded the British land forces in the invasion of Sicily during which he and Patton competed in a 'race' for the honor of taking Messina in the northeast of the island. Subsequently he led the Eighth Army in the invasion of Italy as far as the line of the River Sangro. In January 1944 he was recalled with Eisenhower to plan the invasion of Europe, in which he was to command the ground forces under the latter's supreme direction. He rightly insisted on the reinforcement of the planned seaborne landing force from three to five divisions and, once they were ashore on 6 June, conducted a well-judged offensive against the Germans which culminated in the breakout of the Allies from the bridgehead in July. In September he surrendered control of the ground forces to Eisenhower, but continued in charge of the British 21st Army Group until the end of the war. During the Ardennes campaign, he was once again summoned by Eisenhower to take charge of an Anglo-American force on the northern flank of the breakin, which he handled with great skill if less tact. His organization of the Rhine Crossing was his last major command achievement before the end of the war, when he accepted the surrender of all German forces in northern Europe. After the war he was Chief of the Imperial General Staff and Deputy Supreme Allied Commander in Europe.

Morgan, General Sir Frederick, 1894–1967

Morgan was the chief planner of the Allied invasion of Normandy. In January 1943 he was appointed Chief of Staff to a Supreme Allied Commander who was not yet appointed, and was ordered to produce a detailed plan for an invasion of Europe. Morgan was not given sufficient resources, especially landing craft, and could not get any until Eisenhower was appointed Supreme Allied Commander. Morgan's final plan was adopted at a conference in June-July 1943 and for the next year,

until D-Day, the plans for Operation Overlord were worked out in great detail under Morgan.

Morgenthau, Henry, 1891–1967

Morgenthau was President Roosevelt's secretary of the treasury from 1934 until the end of the war. During the war his one overriding task was to finance a mammoth war economy and war production without prompting correspondingly great inflation. This he did by maintaining high taxes and by selling Defense (later called 'War') Savings Bonds. Morgenthau was also responsible for the freezing of Japanese assets before the war in the Far East and for organizing economic measures against the Axis Powers. He also put the Lend-Lease Program into operation.

At the Quebec Conference of September 1944 Morgenthau put forward a plan to settle the long-disputed fate of postwar Germany. The Morgenthau Plan advocated enforcing agrarianism on Germany, in which most industry would be dismantled and the sites turned into arable land. This plan actually had the support of Churchill and Roosevelt but not of their Cabinets. Thus when the plan was leaked to the public they abandoned it quickly. The fact that Morgenthau was a Jew allowed Goebbels to use both him and his plan for anti-Allied propaganda – a warning to Germans of what would happen should Germany surrender.

Morrison, Herbert, 1888–1965

Morrison was a member of Churchill's Cabinet throughout the war, first as minister of supply and then simultaneously as home secretary and minister of home security.

In 1940 he was a leader of the Labour Opposition in Parliament and was responsible for the 'No-confidence' motion which felled Chamberlain's government on 8 May 1940. Churchill then made Morrison minister of supply in his new government with special emphasis on securing raw materials. In October 1940 he was made home secretary and minister of home security. Morrison organized the National Fire Service and a system of fire watching by the Civil Defense and the Home Guard. As home secretary he had to take responsibility for decisions regarding censorship of news and internment and arrest of suspected enemies of the state. In 1945 he played a large part in organizing the Labour election campaign. The new government adopted his proposals on nationalization, health and education.

Moulin, Jean, 1899–1943

Moulin was an important French resistance

BIOGRAPHIES

leader responsible for fusing dozens of rival guerrilla groups into one organization loyal to de Gaulle. Moulin was prefect of Chartres, in which capacity he entered a dispute with the Germans in the summer of 1940 over certain arrests. He tried to commit suicide on 17 June but was saved and retired to Provence. There he made contact with resistance groups and managed to unite three of them under the name of *Combat*. In late 1941 Moulin managed to get to London to confer with de Gaulle as representative of *Combat*. He could have presented himself as a major rival to de Gaulle but instead gave him his complete loyalty. He was parachuted into France on 1 January 1942 as de Gaulle's delegate-general and spent the next 18 months on the move throughout France, discussing, negotiating and persuading in order to bring about a unified resistance. By March 1943 he had achieved a fusion of all non-Communist groups in the former Vichy areas into the Mouvements Unis de Résistance, and in May 1943 succeeded in effecting a national link-up called the Conseil National de la Résistance, all loyal to de Gaulle, whose first meeting he chaired on 27 May 1943. However, at a meeting of 21 June at Caluire, near Lyons, Moulin was arrested by the Germans and died after being horribly tortured. Moulin had been one of the most talented and politic of resistance leaders and there was no one who could completely take his place.

Mountbatten, Admiral Lord Louis, 1900–1979
Mountbatten was an expert in communications in the Royal Navy when the war began. In 1939 he was given command of the 5th Destroyer Flotilla assigned to the defense of Britain, and participated in the evacuation of Allied troops from Norway. In April 1941 he took his ships to Malta and in May saw action off Crete, in which his flagship, HMS *Kelly*, was sunk. Shortly after he became Chief of Combined Operations and was involved in preliminary planning for the projected invasion of Europe. He continued his planning activities as a member of the Chiefs of Staff Committee, working on the raids at St Nazaire (March) and Dieppe (August) and the Allied North Africa Landings of November 1942. Mountbatten also attended the Casablanca Conference in January 1943 and the Quebec Conference (July) at which the Allied command in Southeast Asia was reorganized.

Mountbatten became Supreme Allied Commander of this new Southeast Asia Command in October 1943. He lacked ships, landing craft and other equipment and therefore decided to concentrate on a land campaign. He spent the remainder of 1943 building up a secure base in India with improved communications which could be used for the campaign in Burma which began in December 1943. Mountbatten carried out these preparations with flair and a real feeling for public relations which enormously increased morale. The campaign itself, directed by General Slim, was very successful despite limited resources, highlighted by the countering of a major Japanese offensive at Kohima and Imphal in March–April 1944 and the capture of Mandalay in March 1945. Burma was completely reconquered by May 1945. In September Mountbatten accepted the surrender of 750,000 Japanese at Singapore.

Mountbatten was a popular leader because of his showmanship and a successful one because of his great capability, belief in science and technology and his ingenuity in confronting problems.

Mueller, Heinrich, 1896–1945?
Mueller was head of the Gestapo throughout the war. The name Gestapo derives from the initial letters of its full German title, *ge*heime *Sta*ats*po*lizei (secret state police). The Gestapo was Department IV of Heydrich's and later Kaltenbrunner's RHSA (Reich Main Security Office). Eichmann's Jewish section was part of the Gestapo. Mueller was not a typical Nazi leader and, indeed, he only joined the party at a comparatively late date. He is perhaps best described as an anonymous, zealous and unscrupulous policeman. Little is known about his background. In April 1945 he disappeared without trace in Berlin. It has been suggested that he escaped to South America or that he defected to the Soviets. Supporters of the latter theory suggest that he had long been in Soviet pay and that he died in Moscow in 1948.

Murphy, Robert, 1894–1958
Murphy was an American diplomat who acted as Roosevelt's political representative in North Africa from 1941–43. In this capacity he gathered much useful intelligence and set up an intelligence network in preparation for Eisenhower's landings at Casablanca in November 1942. On 22 November 1943 Murphy was appointed member of the Advisory Council to the Allied Control Commission for Italy.

Murrow, Edward R, 1908–1965
Murrow was an American radio correspondent and European Director of CBS 1937–45. His daily broadcasts from London through the Blitz

brought the horrors of war home to Americans before Pearl Harbor. After the war he made a series of documentaries for television, including the expose of Senator Joseph McCarthy.

Mussolini, Benito, 1883–1945

Mussolini's international importance was already in decline by the outbreak of World War II. His seizure of power in 1922 had inspired Hitler by its demonstration of what a Fascist party, properly led, could achieve. By his seizure of Ethiopia in 1935 and massive intervention in the Spanish Civil War in 1936, he succeeded in making himself seem the equal, if not the superior, of the German dictator on the international stage even after Italy's real power had begun to wane. But, as he himself knew all too well, Italy was industrially too weak and geographically too exposed to wage aggressive war against the Western Allies, and he carefully avoided involving himself in World War II until both had been brought to the brink of defeat by the Blitzkrieg of May, 1940. Thereafter he was cast as Hitler's junior partner. His desert army was humiliatingly defeated by a minor British force in December 1940, and the invasion of Greece which he launched from Albania in November came to an even more shameful end. He had to be rescued from the debacle in April 1941 and thereafter played no independent role in the war. He lost the greater part of his field army in the Tunisian defeat of 1943, when his expeditionary force in the Soviet Union was also almost completely destroyed. By July, when it was clear that the Allies were preparing an invasion of mainland Italy, his position at home had been fatally weakened and he was deposed at a meeting of the Fascist Grand Council on 24 July. Imprisoned on the Gran Sasso in the Abruzzi, he was rescued by a parachute coup de main, led by Otto Skorzeny, on 12 September and taken to the north of Italy, where he attempted to refound a sovereign government at the head of a so-called Italian Social Republic. Germany had by then, however, taken Italy under effectively military government and Mussolini wielded little power. In April 1945 he was captured, with his mistress, Clara Petacci, by partisans and executed. Their bodies were exhibited, hung by the heels, in a Milan square. It was a squalid end to a life which, though marred by much miscalculation, great vulgarity and some cruelty, compared in no way with the calculated inhumanity of Hitler's.

Nagumo Vice-Admiral Chuichi, 1887–1944

Nagumo commanded First Carrier Strike Force *Kido Butai*, from his flagship the *Akagi* for the first 11 months of the war. This was the Japanese navy's corps d'élite, but Nagumo was a torpedo expert, not an aviation specialist, unhappy in his position and overcautious. He led his force at Pearl Harbor in December 1941 and decided against sending his planes in for a third attack, thought it could have been decisive. He then commanded *Kido Butai* at Midway where he showed hesitation and an inability to adapt to this new form of battle in which enemy fleets never made contact. Nagumo then fought two unsuccessful naval battles off Guadalcanal: the Battles of the Eastern Solomons and of Santa Cruz Islands. He was relieved of that command and posted to the Marianas. There he organized the defense of Saipan. He committed suicide on 6 July 1944 when it was clear that all was lost.

Nimitz, Admiral Chester, 1885–1966

Nimitz was Commander in Chief of the US Pacific Fleet from 17 December 1941 until the end of the war. An outstanding strategist, he was responsible for bringing the US Fleet from its weak and dejected situation after Pearl Harbor to a position of initiative and offense within the first year of the war in the Far East. Taking command shortly after Pearl Harbor, Nimitz's first task was to protect the US Hawaiian bases and maintain communications with the mainland. To this purpose he gathered the large Midway Fleet. At the Battle of Midway Nimitz was considerably aided by the cracking of the Japanese Fleet code some months earlier and by the American victory at Coral Sea in May 1942. After Midway, Nimitz had a considerably freer hand.

Commands in the Pacific were now rationalized, in order to ease interservice tensions.

Above: Nimitz and Fraser in 1945.

BIOGRAPHIES

MacArthur was given command of the Southwest Pacific up to 160° East longitude and Nimitz commanded the Central Pacific from 160° East, including Guadalcanal, the site of his next offensive. After initial difficulties and heavy losses, Vice-Admiral Halsey was able to rally US forces and regain the initiative as the US increased war production and superior resources were taking effect.

Nimitz was a great believer in amphibious operations and felt that these would be more successful if used not to attack central Japanese troop concentrations directly but to take less-well-defended islands behind the Japanese main lines thereby cutting them off, a strategy known as leapfrogging to navy men. This was to be organized as an approach to Japan by way of the Central Pacific Islands. The Joint Chiefs of Staff agreed to this in 1943 and the operations opened up with November 1943 assaults on Makin and Tarawa in the Gilbert Islands and in February 1944 on the Marshalls. Nimitz then divided his fleet into two teams which he employed alternately: Spruance's 5th Fleet and Halsey's 3rd. While one of these two was commanding an operation the other and his staff would be planning the next move. After the taking of the Marianas it was agreed that Nimitz should aid MacArthur's landings at Luzon. Okinawa and Iwo Jima were next. Fanatical Japanese resistance was overcome and air bases for the attack on Japan established. One of the mainsprings of Nimitz's strategy throughout the war was his rivalry with MacArthur: Nimitz and his superior, King, were always arguing that the navy should have priority in the Pacific campaign and the lion's share of the resources available. The Joint Chiefs gave way to MacArthur's campaign to recapture the Philippines; Nimitz had argued for the taking of Formosa. However, Nimitz's Central Pacific route to Japan was accepted for the final assault. In the last months of the war Nimitz's staff were planning this operation. The two rivals joined together in the final ceremony of victory: MacArthur accepted the formal surrender of the Japanese on board Nimitz's flagship the USS *Missouri* in Tokyo Bay on 2 September 1945.

Novikov, Colonel General Aleksandr, 1900–1976
Novikov was Commander in Chief of the Soviet Air Force (VVS) from 1942–46. After serving as Chief of Staff to Leningrad VVS from 1938–40 and as Chief of Staff of VVS on the Karelian Front during the Russo-Finnish War, Novikov became Commander in Chief and undertook the major reorganization of the air force following serious defeats by the Luftwaffe. During the war Novikov attended most Stavka meetings and was in charge of all air operations at the Battles of Stalingrad, Kursk, Belorussia and Königsberg and in the 1945 operations against the Kwantung Army in Manchuria.

O'Connor, General Sir Richard, 1889–1981
In September 1939 O'Connor was in command of the 7th Division and was governor of Jerusalem. In June 1940 O'Connor and his division were sent from Palestine to Egypt where he was appointed commander of the Western Desert Force, under the overall command of his friend, General Wavell. In September 1940 Marshal Graziani's Italian forces from Libya invaded Egypt. In three months Wavell had launched an offensive which was to take Tobruk and to reach Benghazi and El Agheila by 9 February 1941. O'Connor was in tactical charge of this brilliant operation. O'Connor had been pulled out of the front line when Rommel's first offensive began but he was soon sent forward as an adviser to General Neame. He had only just arrived at the front when he was captured. He was taken to Italy but escaped and by June 1944, O'Connor was again in command, this time of VIII Corps for the invasion of Normandy. O'Connor was a brilliant commander. His operative motto was 'offensive action wherever possible.' Many of his colleagues and comrades-at-arms felt that if he had not been captured so unluckily he would have attained an even more enviable reputation.

Oldendorf, Vice-Admiral Jesse, 1887–
Oldendorf was the commander of Task Group 77.2 at the Battle of Leyte Gulf. His task was to prevent the Japanese forces from passing through the Surigao Strait. Early in the morning of 25 October 1944 Oldendorf's ships were able to devastate Vice-Admiral Nishimura's force with torpedo and radar-controlled gunfire. This was the first clear victory achieved by the Americans in surface action against the Japanese. Oldendorf remained as commander of Combat Formations of the 7th Fleet and when on duty off Luzon in January 1945 bore the brunt of the Kamikaze attacks.

Onishi, Vice-Admiral Takijiro, 1891–1945
Onishi was a fanatical Japanese militarist and something of a cult figure among his staff. In 1941, as Chief of Staff of the Eleventh Air Fleet under Yamamoto, Onishi and his friend, Commander Minoru Genda, carried out an

important feasibility study on Pearl Harbor in preparation for the attack. In the first days of the war Onishi led an attack on Clark Field near Manila, and despite bad weather and against the advice of his subordinates, destroyed all US air power in the Far East.

In October 1944 Onishi was made Commander of the Fifth Base Air Force on Luzon which was to support Admiral Kurita's attack on the US invasion force at Leyte. He had only 100 planes at his disposal and, wanting to maximize their effectiveness, he set up the Special Attack Group – the first formal Kamikaze corps. Their first operations proved remarkably effective and for a time the Japanese looked on them as the answer to all their problems, which put Onishi very much in the limelight. Onishi was a die-hard to the end and adamantly opposed surrender. After the Japanese surrender of 15 August he committed suicide.

Oppenheimer, J Robert, 1904–1967

In 1936 Oppenheimer was a professor of atomic or nuclear physics at the University of California. In 1942, when the USA joined the war, he was appointed director of the government laboratory at Los Alamos and head of the team which was to build the first atomic bomb. A dynamic leader with a brilliant mind, Oppenheimer was able to complete his project in time to use it against Japan. Some have argued that this was done in the 'nick of time' as many lives were spared because the Allies did not have to invade the Home Islands.

Ozawa, Vice-Admiral Jisaburo, 1896–1966

Ozawa was commander of the Japanese Mobile Fleet from November 1942 until the end of the war. Ozawa was one of the first to realize the possibilities and significance of carriers but he did not take over the carrier force until after Japan had lost its superiority at sea and most of its trained aviators. Appointed after the dismissal of Nagumo, Ozawa was commander at the Battle of the Philippine Sea in which he lost his flagship, the carrier *Taiho*, and 340 planes. Two other carriers were damaged and on the next day Ozawa made the mistake of lingering near the battle site, which cost him three more ships. The Japanese could never again face the US navy with equal strength; Ozawa wanted to resign but was persuaded to stay.

At the Battle of Leyte Gulf, 25 October 1944, Ozawa's Mobile Force was to act as a decoy to lure Admiral Halsey's fleet away from the San Bernardino Strait. This Ozawa accomplished with tremendous skill, but the battle had already been lost – the Japanese navy could no longer challenge the US.

Papagos, General Alexander, 1883–1955

Papagos was the Commander in Chief of the Greek army on 28 October 1940 when the Italians invaded Greece from Albania. He repelled the attack and sent the Italians back to Albania. The Allies instructed General Wavell to send large reinforcements to help Papagos. At a joint meeting between the Greek and British military leaders it was agreed to defend the Aliakmon Line on 23 February 1941 but a week later the British found that Papagos and his army had not withdrawn to the Aliakmon Line but were waiting to see what position Yugoslavia was going to take. On 9 March the Italians attacked and in early April the Germans arrived to reinforce them. The British-Greek armies were forced to retreat and by 27 April Greece was under German control. Papagos was taken to Dachau concentration camp as a hostage in 1943 and was freed by the Americans in 1945. He returned to his original position as Commander in Chief to wage war against the left-wing guerrillas in northern Greece in the years immediately following World War II.

Park, Air Marshal Sir Keith, 1892–1975

Park was an extremely inventive and energetic British air marshal who commanded in the Battle of Britain, Malta and the Far East. A New Zealander, Park became Air Officer Commanding (AOC) 11 Fighter Group under Dowding in 1939. In June 1940 he was in charge of providing air cover for the Dunkirk evacuation. In the Battle of Britain Park's tactics were much criticized and led to great tension with Air Vice-Marshal Leigh-Mallory, but they were generally successful. In particular he urged that the RAF should meet attacking German planes well before the German planes reached their targets; this put the RAF fighters at great risk but made the German bombing less effective. Neither Park nor Dowding, his chief, received the credit they deserved and all Park's later appointments were less important.

In the fall of 1941 Park became AOC at Allied headquarters Egypt and on 15 July 1942 was appointed AOC Malta. Malta was a vital strategic base for the Allies but from late 1941 it had been on the defensive and was constantly short of supplies. Park pushed the campaign onto the offensive by attacking German convoys and aircraft at sea. In November 1942 he provided air support for Allied landings in

North Africa, as he did for landings in Sicily in July 1943, and Italy in September 1943. In January 1944 Park became Supreme Commander of Air in the Middle East and in February 1945 he was appointed Air Commander in Chief of Southeast Asia Command, in which capacity he provided vital air support for the British offensive on Rangoon.

Patch, General Alexander McCarrell, 1889–1945

In 1941, before the Americans had joined the war, Patch commanded the Infantry Replacement Center at Camp Croft in North Carolina. In spring of 1942 he was sent to help the French defend New Caledonia in the South Pacific and was appointed commander of that Task Force. In the very early days of 1943 Patch, as commander of American forces, led his troops to their first major land victory at the Battle of Guadalcanal. In March 1944 he became commanding general of the US Seventh Army which landed between Cannes and Toulon on 15 August as part of the invasion of France (Dragoon). Fighting steadily, the Seventh Army advanced up the Rhône Valley capturing Alsace in the winter and the Saar by 15 March 1945. The German Army Group G was now in retreat and Patch crossed the Rhine on 26 March. He then prevented the Germans from forming a national redoubt by making a headlong advance into southern Germany. On 5 May 1945 Patch received the formal surrender of Balck's Army Group G.

Patton, General George, 1885–1945

Patton belonged to the small band of American officers who cherished a belief in the future of the tank through the long years of interwar stagnation. He had seen action in the American tank corps in World War I and distinguished himself. He had also impressed by his ability in the more-conventional activities of army life and had been appointed superintendent of West Point. Patton was not at heart conventional. His manner was extrovert, his appearance flamboyant and his dealings with people emphatic to the point of theatricality. He was given command of II Corps in the Torch landings in North Africa in 1942 and was then promoted to lead the Seventh Army in the invasion of Sicily, where he lost patience with Eisenhower's plan, which allotted the decisive role to Montgomery, and took over the lead himself. Unfortunately, he also lost patience, not once but twice, with soldiers whom he found in hospital for 'combat fatigue' and on the second occasion was reported in the newspapers for having slapped a man's face. As a result he was demoted and, when reemployed for the invasion of Europe, had to serve as commander of the Third Army under his old subordinate, Bradley. He nevertheless succeeded in making himself the star of the breakout from Normandy by the speed and force of his advance to Lorraine and the German frontier in July-September. It was an advance conducted against the background of a bitter strategic debate with Eisenhower over the proportion of supplies to be allotted to his and Montgomery's forces. Like Montgomery, Patton remained convinced that he had been robbed of the chance to invade Germany and perhaps end the war in 1944. He spent the winter of that year fighting a bitter battle of attrition on the frontier, interrupted by his decisive intervention in the Battle of the Bulge, conducted a masterly crossing of the Rhine in the spring and repeated his whirlwind success of the previous summer by the audacity of his advance to Czechoslovakia, from which he withdrew with the greatest reluctance. He was killed in an accident in December 1945. Patton was no great theorist of tank tactics, but he was the founder of the armored tradition in the American army.

Paul, Prince Regent of Yugoslavia, 1893–1976

Paul served as regent for King Peter II from 1934 until he was deposed on 27 March 1941 in a bloodless coup. Paul worked for Yugoslav neutrality, believing the country militarily unfit to fight the Germans. However, despite Allied pressure and contrary to the sentiment of large sections of his people and armed forces, Paul bowed to German threats and signed a secret pact with the Axis on 25 March 1941. Two days later the leader of the Yugoslav Armed Forces, Simović, put into operation plans for a military takeover and gave Peter II power to rule the country. Paul and his family left for Greece that night.

Paulus, Field Marshal Friedrich, 1890–1957

Paulus was a bright young staff officer who served as Chief of Staff of the Sixth Army in its campaigns in Poland, Belgium and France. He was picked out and made Deputy Chief of General Staff to Halder with the brief to examine the possibilities of an attack on the USSR, and was responsible for much of the detailed planning of Operation Barbarossa. In January 1942 he was made commander of the Sixth Army and led it on the advance to Stalingrad. He planned to surround the city and encircle the Soviet troops within it. Although he succeeded in capturing almost all of the city by November 1942, he was running short of supplies and his men were exhausted but Hitler insisted that he continue to fight and promised that Goering's Luftwaffe would keep him adequately supplied. These promises were never kept and the Soviet troops under Chuikov fought street by street, giving Paulus no respite. In December Manstein launched an offensive to try to relieve Paulus' army but Paulus refused to break out because Hitler had given him orders not to withdraw. In recognition of his bravery Hitler made him a field marshal on 30 January but on the next day he surrendered, much to Hitler's anger. He was kept in captivity for the remainder of the war. In mid-1944 he began giving broadcasts urging German soldiers to give up and his name became synonymous with traitor. He decided to settle in the Soviet zone of Germany after the war and appeared as a key witness for the Soviet prosecution at the Nuremberg trials.

Pavlov, General Dimitry

Pavlov was commander of the Western Front when the Germans invaded the Soviet Union. A tank expert who had served in Spain and in Finland on the Mannerheim Line, he believed that tanks had a merely subsidiary role as infantry support. In 1940 Pavlov was appointed commander of the Western Military District (renamed the Western Front on 23 June 1941) which covered northeastern Poland, and the Bialystok and Brest Litovsk regions. In June 1941 Pavlov faced Guderian's 2nd and 3rd Armored Groups with equal infantry strength but low numbers of tanks, one half of which he lost in the first day's encounter. By 28 June his defenses had collapsed and he was replaced by Yeremenko. Pavlov, his Chief of Staff, and his Fourth Army commander, Korobkov, were all shot for incompetence.

Percival, Lieutenant General Arthur, 1887–1966

Percival was GOC (General Officer Commanding) Malaya when the Japanese invaded on 8 December 1941. After serving in France under General Dill, Percival was sent to Malaya in July 1941. British defense of the area depended on command of sea and air, yet there were few fighters in Malaya in 1941 and after the loss of Force Z, the RN, too, was almost powerless. The Singapore base did have considerable fortifications but these had been designed to protect against sea attack. Percival had been aware of these problems when he had served in

Malaya in 1936–38 but nothing had been done since to rectify the problem as the European fronts had top priority. Furthermore Percival's troops were ill-trained and badly led, regarding the jungle territory as totally inimical to military operations, and their defense in north Malaya was simply a series of retreats. By 27 January Percival ordered a general withdrawal to Singapore Island and on 8 February the Japanese landings began. Churchill ordered Percival to fight to the death, but Singapore was rapidly running out of water supplies, had no hope of reinforcements or air support and the troops were quite demoralized. Percival and 85,000 men surrendered to General Yamashita on 15 February 1942. Percival was interned in Manchuria throughout the war but was flown in to be present at the Japanese surrender in Tokyo Bay on 2 September 1945.

Pétain, Marshal Henri Philippe Omer, 1856–1951

A remarkable and patriotic soldier, Pétain was much honored for his defense of Verdun in 1916. In 1939 he was appointed ambassador to Spain but was recalled to Paris by Reynaud in 1940 after the German invasion of France and appointed deputy premier. Convinced that Britain was destined to lose the war, he rejected Reynaud's proposal (which was supported by de Gaulle and Darlan) to ally with Britain and continue to fight the Axis invasion. Pétain was heard to utter 'To make union with England was fusion with a corpse.' Laval and some Cabinet ministers supported Pétain and Reynaud resigned on 16 June 1940. Pétain assumed control and offered the Germans an armistice on 22 June. Laval petitioned the National Assembly to grant Pétain emergency powers. Pétain established his government at Vichy in the unoccupied part of France and pursued a policy of collaboration with the Germans, who allowed him to have 10,000 men to keep the peace in his sector. In December 1940 Pétain dismissed Laval because Laval not only wanted to be on peaceful terms with Germany but wanted to support the Axis actively and declare war on the United Kingdom. Although Laval's influence was for a while partly curbed, he was reinstated on the Germans' insistence in April 1942. In November the Allies invaded French North Africa and the Germans occupied the Vichy-ruled part of France; Pétain's government became powerless. He was removed to Germany in August 1944 but voluntarily returned to France in April of the following year to stand trial. He was sentenced to death but de Gaulle commuted the sentence to life imprisonment as they had served in the same regiment in World War I. Pétain died on the Atlantic island, Ile d'Yeu, at the age of 95. Pétain was not a treacherous leader but one who suffered rather from defeatism; he inevitably chose the policy he thought best for France.

Peter II, King of Yugoslavia, 1923–1970

Peter ruled through his regent, Prince Paul, from 1934 until Simović's coup of 27 March 1941 placed him on the throne. The coup was a reaction to Paul's collaborationist policy with the Nazis, embodied in a pact with the Axis signed on 25 March. However, Germany invaded on 6 April and all resistance collapsed within two weeks. Peter and his government went to Athens and then to London where they spent the duration of the war. Peter supported the non-Communist guerrilla force in Yugoslavia called the Četniks, which were led by Mihajlović. The Allies, however, seeing that the Četniks spent most of their time fighting other partisans and collaborating with the Germans, supported Tito's partisans. Peter was therefore a diminishing force in Yugoslav and Allied affairs. Peter bowed to the inevitable and signed an agreement with Tito on 1 November 1944 which involved representing himself through a regency council. However, Tito declared a Republic on 29 November 1945 and Peter never returned to his country.

Phillips, Admiral Sir Tom, 1888–1941

Phillips was the commander of Force Z which was sunk off Malaya in the first days of the war against Japan. In July of 1941 Churchill decided to cut off oil supplies to Japan and to provide a deterrent force in the area. Rather than send a large fleet he sent the *Prince of Wales*, which was a new-style battleship, and the *Repulse*. Phillips arrived in Singapore on 3 December to take command and set off on 8 December to attack a large Japanese convoy which had been reported unloading at Singora and Kota Bharu. Phillips had no aircraft carrier (it was originally planned to send one) and no air support from land bases. On 9 December the weather cleared and Force Z was spotted by Japanese planes. Phillips turned south to return to port but then turned toward Kuantan when he received reports (which turned out to be false) of a Japanese landing there. Force Z was attacked by the Japanese elite 22nd Air Flotilla on the morning of 10 December and the *Prince of Wales* and the *Repulse* were both sunk by midday. Most of

the men were rescued but Admiral Phillips was one of those lost.

Popov, General Markian, 1902–1969

Popov began the war as commander of the Leningrad Military District (which became the Northern Front in late 1941). He took part in the Battle for Stalingrad in 1942 as a commander of armored divisions. On 16 February 1943 as part of Timoshenko's drive after Stalingrad, Popov captured Kharkov but was driven out by the massive German counterattack. In July 1943 at the Battle of Kursk, Popov commanded the Bryansk Front which with Sokolovsky's Western Front was to wait in reserve until after the German offensive had been repulsed. On 12 July, two days after Kluge ordered the German army onto the defensive, Popov came down from the north onto Kluge's army in the Orel area and delivered a mighty blow. Popov advanced from Orel in the second half of August to Bryansk. In 1944 Popov was given the command of the 2nd Baltic Front which with two other fronts could only advance slowly because of the fortifications they encountered in the north. He was replaced by Yeremenko when he failed to take Riga. Although he was a competent general he was never really trusted by Stalin.

Portal, Marshal of the RAF Sir Charles, 1893–1971

Portal was the British Chief of Air Staff from 1940–45. Formerly chief of Bomber Command, Portal was a wise and competent commander of the RAF and his chief contribution to the winning of the war was the influence he wielded over Churchill and in Anglo-American strategic decision making. He was much liked by the Americans, to whom he was remarkably successful in presenting the British point of view at the major inter-Allied conferences. Portal was a firm advocate of strategic area bombing and this brought him into conflict with the Americans who advocated daylight precision bombing. Following the Casablanca Conference both strategies were continued.

For the Allied invasion of France in 1944 it was decided that the combined British and American heavy bomber forces should give direct support. It was Portal's task to make sure that Harris at Bomber Command obeyed this and other instructions on target selection. Portal was not completely successful in this but felt unable to dismiss Harris because of his standing with the public and Bomber Command.

Pound, Admiral of the Fleet Sir Dudley, 1877–1943

In 1939 Pound was promoted to Admiral of the Fleet and First Sea Lord, and he also acted as chairman of the British Chiefs of Staff Committee until March 1942 when Brooke succeeded him. His regime as First Sea Lord was marked by increasing centralization which often worked to his good. However, he worked too hard and his judgment was sometimes called into doubt. In July 1942 he took the decision to order the convoy PQ-17 to scatter because it was threatened by a powerful German surface force. The decision to scatter left the convoy vulnerable and only 13 ships reached the USSR out of 37. It was not unusual for the Admiralty, with access to complete intelligence information, to interfere in the direction of operations and this was often done with success. In the case of PQ-17 Pound overreacted and could, in fact, have waited before taking his decision. He remained First Sea Lord until forced to resign because of illness late in 1943. He died three weeks later. Although he often found himself opposing Churchill's offensive schemes, Pound retained the prime minister's confidence throughout.

Prien, Commander Gunther, 1908–1941

During the first two years of the war Prien was a U-Boat Commander who became a German national hero. As commander of submarine *U.47* he was ordered by Admiral Doenitz to plan and execute an attack on Scapa Flow, the British anchorage in Scotland. In the early morning of 14 October 1939 Prien's U-Boat penetrated a narrow passage into the anchorage. Though most of the fleet had been removed to Loch Ewe, Prien managed to sink the HMS *Royal Oak* with 833 men on board. Occurring only six weeks after Britain had entered the war, it was a blow to morale but led to a tightening up of anchorage defense which was much needed.

Prien then served with distinction on the Atlantic convoy routes in 1940 until, on 7 March 1941 *U.47* was sunk with all hands by the corvettes *Arbutus* and *Camellia* and destroyer *Wolverine*.

Pyle, Ernest, 1900–1945

Pyle was a famous American war correspondent who spent more than three years in combat areas in Europe and the Far East. Already a successful and syndicated columnist before the war, Pyle was stationed in London in 1941 where he covered the Blitz. He went on to cover the campaigns in North Africa, Sicily, Italy and France. He also accompanied the assaults on Iwo Jima and Okinawa. He was killed by Japanese bullets on 18 April 1945 while visiting the island of Ie Shima. Pyle won many awards including the Pulitzer Prize for his vivid eyewitness accounts which concentrated on the experiences of the ordinary soldier.

Quezon, Manuel, 1878–1944

Quezon was President of the Commonwealth of the Philippine Islands from 1935 until his death in 1944. He was strongly in favor of US-Philippine cooperation. When war began the Philippines were a prime Japanese target and they made their first landings on the mainland on 22 December 1941. Quezon, who did much to raise Philippine morale throughout this time, left for Corregidor on 24 December on MacArthur's advice. He kept in close contact with the struggle, however, and was inaugurated into his second term of office as president in an air-raid shelter in Corregidor. In March 1942 Quezon left for Australia and then went on to the US where he spoke before the House of Representatives on 2 June, and offered assurances of Filipino determination to fight to the end. Quezon was ill with tuberculosis and died on 1 August 1944 at Saranac Lake, New York, a few months before the liberation of his country.

Quisling, Vidkung, 1887–1945

A former army officer and government minister, Quisling was the leader of the Norwegian Nazi Party, the *Nasjonal Samling*. In December 1939 he visited Hitler and showed him his plans for a coup in neutral Norway. Hitler, while stalling Quisling, prepared his own plans for an invasion of Norway which would depend not on the ability of the Norwegian Nazi Party followers but on the strength of the German army for its success. On 9 April 1940 the Germans invaded Norway and Quisling became the head of the puppet government; most Norwegian ministers and officers in the government resigned within a week of his appointment. In September even the Germans were having difficulty agreeing with him and he was ousted. In February 1942 he was reinstated by Reichskommissar Terboven as Minister President but he had no real authority. At the end of the war he surrendered himself to the police and was tried for high treason. He was found guilty and executed on 24 November 1945. Considered by the Norwegians, the Allies and most of the world as a traitor of the worst type, there is little

BIOGRAPHIES

doubt that he regarded himself as a patriot who tried to achieve the best 'deal' possible for Norway.

Raeder, Admiral Erich, 1876–1960

Raeder was Commander in Chief of German naval forces until 1943 and was the architect of the German navy of World War II. He had the 'pocket' battleships built and laid the foundations for the German U-Boat fleet. In October 1939 he put forward a plan to rival British naval supremacy in the North Sea using bases in Norway and shortly afterward was planning the naval aspects of the Norwegian campaign of April 1940. The next operation he was given to plan was the invasion of England, which Raeder thought was far too ambitious a project for the German navy. For the next two years Hitler and Raeder were involved in a constant argument over how the German navy should be used and over the general course of German strategy. Raeder was probably one of the best strategists in the German High Command but his sensible arguments in favor of completing the domination of the Mediterranean were set aside after the beginning of Barbarossa. Raeder's influence declined and after the failure of the Battle of the Barent's Sea he was dismissed by Hitler although Hitler's own instructions were the principal cause of that defeat. Raeder was found guilty of war crimes at Nuremberg and sentenced to 10 years' imprisonment.

Ramsay, Admiral Sir Bertram Home, 1883–1945

At the beginning of the war Ramsay was on the retired list but was brought back to serve as Flag Officer, Dover. He had served in the Channel squadrons in World War I. In 1940 he masterminded the superbly successful naval side of the Dunkirk operation and was clearly marked out as a brilliant commander of amphibious operations. He was deputy to Admiral Cunningham for the Torch Operation in 1942. In July 1943 he prepared the amphibious landings in Sicily as Naval Commanding Officer, Eastern Task Force. In 1944 he was appointed Naval Commander in Chief for Operation Overlord, much to Eisenhower's relief as he thought Ramsay an exceptionally able Commander. The naval section of the Overlord file was code named Neptune and involved an enormous amount of detailed work to ensure that the enormous variety of shipping involved was protected in transit and arrived with the soldiers' needs when required. Even when bad weather disrupted the Mulberry

harbors Ramsay and his staff kept things moving. His next project involved the invasion of the Isle of Walcheren. On 2 January 1945 Ramsay was on his way to meet Montgomery in Brussels when his plane crashed, killing all hands. Ramsay was a brilliant Admiral who commanded the respect of both his superiors and his men.

Reichenau, Field Marshal Walther von, 1884–1942

Reichenau was one of the few army commanders who was a definite supporter of Hitler and his Nazi regime. In fact Hitler had considered making him his Commander in Chief of the army after Fritsch's dismissal, but Rundstedt managed to talk him out of this. In 1939 he led the Tenth Army into Poland and then in 1940 the Sixth Army into Belgium, entering Brussels in triumph. In 1941 he led the Sixth Army in the invasion of the USSR and his army accomplished the encirclement of Kiev, although this took longer than anticipated. After the purge of the eastern generals in December 1941, following the failure of the offensive against Moscow, Reichenau was made commander of Army Group South. However, he had a heart attack at his Headquarters and died after being flown back to Leipzig – a premature death for such a skillful Commander.

Reynaud, Paul, 1878–1966

Reynaud was prime minister, foreign minister and minister of war of France until 16 June 1940. He succeeded Daladier on 21 March 1940. One of his first acts was to meet Churchill and on 28 March to issue a declaration in which both England and France pledged not to make a separate peace with Germany. Although Reynaud soon quickened the tempo of the French war effort he had little time before the German attack began. He was in fact about to replace Gamelin and strengthen his cabinet on the eve of the attack but this had to be deferred. On 18 May Reynaud did carry out these measures, replacing General Gamelin with the aged Weygand and appointing the even more aged Pétain as deputy prime minister. Reynaud was to regret this decision, for both Weygand and Pétain were strongly in favor of surrendering to Germany. Reynaud wanted to continue the fight but there was little he could do except negotiate with Britain for aid which it could not give. On 13 June he asked Britain to release him from his pledge not to make a separate peace. Two days later he proposed moving the government, air force and fleet to North Africa but no action was taken. On 16 June Reynaud finally resigned and Pétain took over.

Reynaud was arrested by the Vichy government on 6 September 1940. Early in 1942 he was one of the defendants at the famous show trial at Riom in which the Vichy government tried former government leaders for their alleged failure and negligence during the fight against the Germans. The defendants managed to turn the tables on their accusers laying the blame on the military establishment who were now among the staunchest supporters of the Vichy regime. Reynaud was deported to Germany in 1943 and released at the end of the war.

Ribbentrop, Joachim von, 1893–1946

Ribbentrop became Hitler's foreign minister in 1938 because he had impressed the Fuehrer with his veneer of social graces. In fact his arrogant airs made him many enemies within Germany and abroad. Ciano, Italy's foreign minister, despised him and said he was 'vain, frivolous and loquacious.' He laid the foundations for the German-Soviet Non-Aggression Pact partitioning Poland, which he signed with Molotov in August 1939. However, Ribbentrop warned Hitler that the invasion of Poland would probably lead to war with England and he was proved right. His influence declined steadily during the war but Hitler retained him; however, in 1943 Ribbentrop had secret discussions with Molotov at Kirovograd about ending the war on the Eastern Front. The discussions faltered on the question of where to draw a new frontier. Ribbentrop maintained a low profile throughout the war and disappeared after the fall of Berlin. He was captured by the Allies, put on trial at Nuremberg and hanged as a war criminal.

Ridgway, General Matthew Bunker, 1895–

Ridgway was a daring Commander of airborne infantry operations in Sicily and in northwestern Europe. Assigned to the US 82nd Infantry Division, he organized airborne landings as part of the assault on Sicily in 1943. Ridgway successfully accomplished the aims of his mission, but the casualties were high; bad weather and insufficient training of the glider pilots forced a large number of the planes to land in the sea. In September he was brought with his division to Salerno immediately following the Italian capitulation and fought his way up to Naples.

Ridgway was then sent to Britain to participate in the preparations for D-Day. During the invasion Ridgway and his 82nd led the assault on the Cotentin peninsula on 6 June 1944. Ridgway was then put in command of the XVIII Airborne Corps which fought in the airborne invasion of the Netherlands at Eindhoven, in the defense against the Germans' Ardennes offensive and in the Allied offensive against the Siegfried Line. His last engagement was the crossing of the Elbe.

Rokossovsky, Marshal Konstantin, 1896–1968

Rokossovsky was one of the Soviet Union's most able and successful front commanders of the war. A veteran of the Far East, he was arrested during the purges of 1938 but was subsequently released and reinstated. In June 1941, after the German invasion, he led the first tank counterattack in the Ukraine. Transferred north, he helped the trapped and inexperienced Sixteenth and Twentieth Armies to break out of their encirclement at Smolensk on 6 August. He distinguished himself in November and December in the defense of Moscow as Commander of Southern Section, Siberian army.

In 1942 Rokossovsky served as commander of the Don Front at the defense of Stalingrad. Here his armies achieved a decisive breakthrough against the Rumanian and Italian armies, enabling the Soviets to move southward to encircle Paulus' Sixth Army and later to mount an offensive against it. At the Battle of Kursk Rokossovsky commanded the Central Front while Vatutin commanded the Voronezh Front. Opening the battle on the night of 4 July with an artillery barrage, the Central Front held its ground throughout the Germans' week-long onslaught until on 12 July Field Marshal Kluge and General Model went onto the defensive, leaving behind them 50,000 German dead, 400 tanks and mobile guns and 500 aircraft. In the counteroffensive beginning 3 August, Rokossovsky broke through to the Dniepr and in the fall continued through to the Pripet Marshes.

In June 1944 Rokossovsky was given command of the 1st Belorussian Front which moved against the German center to take Lublin and Brest Litovsk. On 29 June Rokossovsky trapped two German Panzer corps and took Bobruysk with 24,000 prisoners. By July 1944 he had advanced nearly to Warsaw but when the Polish AK in the city rose in August he did little to help them, alleging that supply and transport problems prevented his advance continuing. The Soviets were not only reluctant to help the Poles themselves but also refused to allow the

BIOGRAPHIES

Western Allies to use Soviet airfields to supply the Warsaw insurgents. The uprising was put down by late September. In January 1945 the fronts were reorganized and Rokossovsky, now commanding the 2nd Belorussian Front, resumed his advance, first taking Warsaw and then heading north to sweep through northern Poland and take Danzig on 30 March. This trapped the Germans in East Prussia. On May 1945 his troops made contact with the British at Wittenberg. After the war Rokossovsky became Chief of Armed Forces in Poland.

Rommel, Field Marshal Erwin, 1891–1944

Rommel excelled at every level of command he held, from platoon to army group commander. As a lieutenant in World War I, he led his platoon with great dash in the Battle of the Frontiers. As a company commander he won the *Pour le mérite*, Germany's highest decoration for bravery, in the Battle of Caporetto. Between the wars Rommel wrote an important textbook on infantry tactics, in which the theory or doctrine of 'forward control' was first developed, and at the outbreak of war he was given command of the 7th Panzer Division, which he commanded in the Battle of France. He perhaps owed his command to a lucky acquaintanceship with Hitler, but he justified his appointment by the brilliance with which he handled the division in the field (slightly marred by his unsure reaction to the British counterattack at Arras on 21 May 1940). In February 1941, when the rest of the German army was preparing for the invasion of the Soviet Union, he was chosen to lead the Afrika Korps which Hitler had decided to send to the rescue of Mussolini's army in Libya, and his handling of it in the next 18 months laid the foundation of a military legend. On his arrival he immediately halted and then turned back Wavell's advance into Cyrenaica. He was pushed back by Auchinleck's Crusader offensive but in January 1942 he returned to the attack. His advance into Egypt was only just halted during the summer. His keenness to make this advance led him to overextend his lines of communication when it would probably have been better to look for more-limited gains in Africa and to carry out the planned attack on Malta. Although he was soundly beaten at El Alamein in October, he made Montgomery pay a high price for his victory. His retreat to Tunisia was a well-conducted delaying action and his defense of the territory when he arrived far stronger than the Allies had expected. He was ordered home by Hitler before the final collapse and then sent to

Above: Rommel in Africa in 1942.

prepare France against the threat of Allied invasion. His strengthening of the coastal defenses made the landings, when they came, costlier than they would have been, even though he had not been allowed by Rundstedt to deploy his troops as he wished. On 17 July, however, he was wounded by a British fighter's attack on his car and evacuated. He then came under suspicion of implication in the Bomb Plot and was offered by Hitler the choice of standing trial, with the inevitable danger that threatened his family, or of committing suicide. He took the proffered poison and was given a state funeral, having died of his wounds, it was announced.

Roosevelt, Eleanor, 1884–1962

Eleanor Roosevelt was the wife of President Roosevelt and an extremely popular public figure in her own right. In September 1941 she was made director of the Office of Civilian Defense. Throughout the war she travelled widely on goodwill trips to build morale, visiting Britain, Australia and the South Pacific. She was several times a delegate to the United Nations General Assembly and was chairman (1947) of the UN Committee on Human Rights.

Roosevelt, President Franklin Delano, 1882–1945

Roosevelt had been president of the United States for nine years before Pearl Harbor, years which he had devoted chiefly to leading America out of economic collapse. His political interests were domestic, his instincts pacific, and he was conscious of the extent and intensity of American unwillingness to become involved in the European war of 1939–41. He nevertheless felt it of vital interest to the United States that Britain and her Allies be saved from defeat and he was able, notably by the Lend-Lease Act of March 1941, to assure her supplies of whatever war material she needed. He also began to agree with Winston Churchill, an old acquaintance, on a common set of war aims, formalized by their meeting in Argentia Bay, Newfoundland, in August 1941, and known as the Atlantic Charter. When war came, through Japan's surprise attack on Pearl Harbor, America was materially unprepared for it, but Roosevelt at any rate had decided the broad lines on which it should be fought. Germany was to be defeated first, since only she among the Axis powers possessed the industrial and technical capability to win a victory single-handed; Britain was to be preserved from defeat at all costs, since her territory provided the essential springboard for an invasion of Europe; America would support all enemies of the Axis, whatever their political creed; she would make a massive military effort on land, sea and in the air, but would principally work for victory by making herself the 'arsenal of democracy.' Roosevelt, crippled by polio, seemed physically unfit for the effort of a war presidency, but he sustained the burdens with remarkable vitality. He won a fourth presidential election in 1944 by a vast majority, and devoted much time to maintaining effective relations with Congress. He also travelled to meet Churchill and the other wartime leaders at a succession of exhausting and widely scattered conferences: Casablanca in January 1943, Quebec in August, Cairo in November, Teheran in December, Quebec again in September 1944, and Yalta in February 1945. Roosevelt played an independent role throughout, often at odds with Churchill over means, if not over long-term ends. His diplomacy was, in particular, designed to diminish the scope of the colonial system in the postwar world, and to tame the USSR by the administration of sympathy and concessions. Churchill felt, but did not say, that he found Roosevelt's estimation of Soviet intentions naive. Postwar opinion in the west has tended to support Churchill's point of view. There was a generosity in Roosevelt's philosophy of international relations which nevertheless commands respect, and he was clearly more farsighted on the colonial issue, particularly in the Far East, than the British leader. His worldwide appeal was enormous, his character, opinions and achievements in themselves a demonstration to neutral opinion that right was on the Allied side. When he died, on 12 April 1945, he was mourned throughout the Allied and neutral nations, and perhaps nowhere more than in Britain.

Rosenberg, Alfred, 1893–1946

Rosenberg was born into one of the overseas German communities at Reval in Czarist Russia, and trained as an architect in Moscow before the revolution. On its outbreak he made his way to Germany, filled with violent anti-Bolshevik and anti-Semitic sentiments, to which he was able to give full vent when he joined the Nazi Party and became editor of its newspaper, the *Völkischer Beobachter*. During Hitler's imprisonment after the 1923 Munich Putsch he was temporarily party leader. He lacked executive skills, however, and was relegated to theoretical and educational activities when Hitler resumed the leadership. Hitler had, nevertheless, a sort of reflexive respect for him as an intellectual and old comrade, and made him minister for the Occupied Eastern Territories in 1941, on the grounds of his special knowledge of and interest in the region. However, Rosenberg exercised little real power there. It was Goering and Himmler who put into practice the theories of racial superiority and exploitation that he had advanced. As a prophet of the excesses of Nazism, and an accessory to its crimes, he was tried and executed at Nuremberg.

Rundstedt, Field Marshal Gerd von, 1875–1953

Rundstedt was retired from the German army after the Fritsch-Blomberg crisis but returned to command Army Group A which invaded Poland in September 1939. In May 1940 he held the same command for the invasion of France and it was his Panzer spearhead which broke through at Sedan and cut off the British Expeditionary Force. He persuaded Hitler to allow Army Group A to halt its offensive and to leave the reduction of the Dunkirk pocket to the Luftwaffe. This crucial decision allowed the evacuation of the BEF. In 1941 Rundstedt was given command of Army Group South which moved through the Ukraine in September but was relieved of the command two months later when Hitler refused to allow him to withdraw. In 1942 he was reinstated and made Commander in Chief, West, and was responsible for the defense of Fortress Europe. He and his subordinate Rommel disagreed over how the defending forces should be deployed and the compromise ordered by Hitler ruined both schemes. On 1 July 1944 he was replaced by Kluge, who was then dismissed on 17 August, and replaced by Model. Rundstedt was recalled in September but at that point there was little he could do to stop the Allied advance over northwest France. The Battle of the Bulge is sometimes known as the Rundstedt Offensive but in fact it was far more Hitler's brain child and Rundstedt had little confidence in its outcome. He retired in March 1945 after its failure, but to the end Hitler respected his judgment. It has been said that this was because Hitler was impressed by his aristocratic presence, and the Prussian military tradition which he represented.

Rydz-Smigly, Marshal Edward, 1886–1943

Rydz-Smigly was the virtual ruler of Poland and Commander in Chief of the Polish armed forces when the Germans invaded in 1939. He did not mobilize his country in time and then conducted a defense which did not take account of the Germans' speed of advance. His army was in confusion within a week and unable to mount any delaying actions. Two weeks after the invasion, Rydz-Smigly ordered a withdrawal into southeastern Poland hoping to establish a concentrated center of resistance which could wait until British or French aid arrived. However, at this point the Soviets invaded eastern Poland and the army caved in. Rydz-Smigly and his government escaped to Rumania, where they were imprisoned. Rydz-Smigly was dismissed from his posts by Sikorski and his government-in-exile in London. He escaped from Rumania in 1941 and returned to Poland to join the underground. He was probably killed by the Germans in 1943.

Sauckel, Fritz, 1894–1946

Sauckel served as Nazi plenipotentiary general for the Allocation of Labor from 1942 until the end of 1944. He organized the deportation of over 5,000,000 people to Germany to maintain the war effort and himself estimated that perhaps only 200,000 of these came voluntarily. He had enormous problems after 1943 when all available manpower was used up and he resorted to by-passing local governments to kidnap labor off the streets. In one affair his men kidnapped 1000 French police officers in Marseilles while they were out on exercises. He encountered great resistance in which men in many occupied areas took to the hills and forests. Nonetheless Sauckel managed to produce enough labor to actually increase war production until 1944 when the German economy began its final collapse. He was tried at Nuremberg after the war and executed for crimes against humanity.

Schacht, Dr Hjalmar, 1877–1970

Schacht was Hitler's brilliant minister of the economy who engineered Germany's recovery and rearmament in the 1930s. In 1923 he was appointed special commissioner to restore Germany's currency and managed to defeat inflation by the summer of 1924. He warned against the shaky foundations of the 1920s' prosperity and accurately foresaw the advent of the economic world crisis. In the winter of 1928–29 Schacht was one of two chief delegates to the Young Committee on reparations and protested violently against the resulting Young Plan. He joined Hitler's camp (though he never joined the Nazi Party) in 1930 as an economic adviser and brought with him his enormous prestige and the support of his many influential industrial contacts. A respectable bourgeois conservative, he believed that Hitler would bring stability to Germany but that he could be controlled and was therefore instrumental in bringing him to power. He became president of the Reichsbank in 1933 and economic minister in 1935 in which capacities he masterminded German economic recovery without inflation, especially through fiscal manipulations and foreign-trade operations. Though he believed that rearmament was essential to Germany he disagreed with Hitler in the subordination of all other matters to this objective. On these grounds he resigned in 1937 as economic minister and his functions were taken over by Goering. Similarly in 1939 he was dismissed as bank president after protesting against Hitler's extravagant military expenditure. Schacht also maintained that Germany could not hope economically to sustain a prolonged war. In 1943 he left the Cabinet and public affairs completely.

Schacht had been involved in German opposition circles since his participation in the abortive military coup of 1938 and the Nazis had never trusted him. After the July 1944 Bomb Plot he was arrested on suspicion and imprisoned in Flossenberg. Released by the Americans he was tried at Nuremberg, acquitted and went on to become an influential adviser to Third World countries.

Schellenberg, SS General Walther, 1911–1952

Schellenberg was an SS General and secret service officer who became head of Combined Secret Services in 1944. A law graduate of Bonn with a strong interest in and command of several languages, he was much prized by the SS and SD for his culture and intelligence. This won him the patronage of Heydrich, Head of the SD, when Schellenberg joined in 1934. He was involved in a vast number of plots and subterfuges which he enjoyed enormously and performed well. In 1938 he organized the Einsatzgruppen of combined SS, SD and Gestapo under Heydrich's orders. He was one of the first to enter both Austria and Poland after their takeovers, to carry out operations planned by Himmler. In 1939 he was involved in investigating British intelligence, an operation in which he posed as a resistance agent to gain the confidence of three MI6 agents in Holland. This led to their kidnap by SS troops. This was one of the most successful operations by German counterintelligence.

In 1944 Schellenberg became head of all the secret services after the arrest of Canaris and the dismantling of the Abwehr. In 1945 he took a leading role in Himmler's attempt to arrange an armistice with the Western Allies. Schellenberg arranged meetings between Himmler and Count Bernadotte in April 1945. When the Reich finally fell, Schellenberg was in Denmark still trying to arrange a surrender.

Schoerner, Field Marshal Friedrich, 1892–1973
Inordinately ambitious, Schoerner was also an able leader, but feared as well as admired by his men because of their suspicion that they would pay with their lives for his offensive zeal. It nevertheless brought him rapid advancement in the German army, which accelerated as prominence allowed him to display his ostentatious Nazism and ready agreement to obey impossible orders – which both commended him to Hitler. By July 1944 he had been appointed to command Army Group North, at the head of which he remained unprotestingly until January 1945, though it had by then been surrounded for several months without reason or hope of rescue. He then moved to the command of Army Group Center in Czechoslovakia. In the last 10 days of the war, following Hitler's suicide, Schoerner inherited the title of Commander in Chief, which he had always thought that he deserved.

Scobie, General Ronald, 1893–1969
In October 1941 Scobie's Division replaced the besieged Australian garrison at Tobruk. In the major winter offensive to reconquer Cyrenaica, Scobie, under Cunningham's command, led the breakout from Tobruk on 20 November 1941. In 1942 Scobie became GOC at Malta which was strategically crucial because of its use as a base to attack German supply convoys to North Africa. In 1943 he was given the post of Chief of Staff, Middle East Command. Finally, in 1944 Scobie became GOC in Greece and directed the final operations leading up to the German withdrawal from Athens on 12 October. However, when the British entered the capital two days later they found the Communist National Liberation Front (EAM) and its military wing (ELAS) ready to take over the government. This was a particularly sensitive issue to England and France who were at the time faced with the imminent Soviet occupation of all eastern Europe and the Balkans. Scobie was ordered by Churchill to hold Greece at all costs and found himself in the middle of a civil war by December. EAM, however, was not receiving any external aid because they constituted a purely indigenous group and because the Soviets had promised not to interfere. They were forced to make a truce on 14 January 1945. A constitutional regime was set up and the Communists brutally repressed.

Scoones, General Sir Geoffrey, 1893–1975
Scoones was a British corps commander involved in the intense fighting in Burma in 1944. From 1939–41 he was on the General Staff at Allied HQ in India and then Director of Military Operations and Intelligence. On 19 July 1942 he was given command of the IV Corps stationed at Imphal near the Burmese frontier. The British were unable to mount an offensive, however, as command and communications were being reorganized and the Burma front was low on the list of Allied priorities. In November 1943 SEAC was established and Scoones was placed under Stilwell's command, assigned to cross the Chindwin River into Burma. However, the Japanese were planning an offensive on Imphal in January 1944 and in February Scoones put forward a plan to withdraw to Imphal which was strategically strong. Against all odds he got all his forces there by April and possessing only five weeks' worth of supplies managed to defend the area until the Japanese ran out of supplies. Scoones began his advance into central Burma on 23 June.

On 7 December 1944 Scoones was appointed General Officer Commanding, Central India Command.

Seyss-Inquart, Artur von, 1892–1946
Seyss-Inquart was an Austrian Nazi who prepared the way for the Anschluss and later became Reich commissioner of the Netherlands from 1940–45. Acting as secret Austrian representative for the Nazis while the party was still illegal, Seyss-Inquart finally came to the fore in 1938 when Hitler demanded on threat of invasion the legalization of the Nazi Party and the appointment of Seyss-Inquart as minister of interior with control over the police. This was accomplished in February 1938 and Seyss-

BIOGRAPHIES

Inquart began taking his orders directly from Berlin, acting independently of the Austrian Chancellor. On 11 March 1938 with German troops at the Austrian border, he was appointed chancellor and organized the Nazi takeover of power.

In October 1939 Seyss-Inquart was made deputy governor-general of the Polish general government which comprised territories not officially annexed by Germany or the Soviet Union. In May 1940 he became Reich commissioner of the Netherlands with total control of the entire Dutch administration which he subordinated completely to the demands of the German war effort. Directly responsible to Hitler and without interference from even the Dutch Nazis whom he excluded from government, in March 1941 he was given power of summary justice in any case of suspected resistance or dissension. He issued heavy collective fines and reprisals, confiscated the property of Jews and all enemies of the Reich. He deported 117,000 Jews, forced 5,000,000 Dutch to work for the Germans and in 1943 seized textiles and consumer goods for Germany. In May 1945 Seyss-Inquart was arrested by the Canadians and executed for war crimes after a trial.

Shaposhnikov, Marshal Boris, 1882–1945

Shaposhnikov was a brilliant military theorist, who at various times in the war was a member of the Stavka and Chief of General Staff. Throughout the 1930s he was extremely influential as deputy people's commissar for Defense. In 1940 he was made head of the Stavka with Zhukov as his deputy and in August of that year was put in charge of fortifications. He put forward a plan to withdraw the Red Army behind the old borders, the Stalin Line, rather than allow them to be thinly spread over the new Polish frontier. This plan was overruled and Shaposhnikov was dismissed as Chief of Staff and replaced by Meretskov. On 10 July 1941, following the German invasion Stalin reformed the Stavka and once again included Shaposhnikov who was also reinstated as Chief of General Staff. However, he counselled withdrawal as part of a policy of strategic defense and thereby courted Stalin's anger. After a tour of duty in Belorussia, Shaposhnikov fell ill and was replaced by Vasilievsky in November 1941, but nevertheless helped plan the defense of Moscow and the counterattack which followed. In June 1942 Shaposhnikov advised against an offensive at Kharkov considering it premature and once again argued for strategic defense. In the same

month he was again appointed deputy people's commissar of defense in charge of revising military regulations. From June 1943 until his death, Shaposhnikov served as commandant of the Voroshilov Military Academy.

Shirer, William L, 1904–

An American journalist and broadcaster, Shirer lived in Berlin during 1940–41 and broadcast his opinions over CBS radio. His experiences in Germany were subsequently published as *Berlin Diary*. His other books include the best-selling *The Rise and Fall of the Third Reich*.

Sikorski, General Wladyslaw, 1881–1943

Sikorski was head of the Polish government-in-exile and Commander in Chief of Free Polish Forces from 1939 until his death in 1943. He was refused a command in the Polish army when the Germans invaded because Rydz-Smigly distrusted him. Sikorski was in Paris when Poland collapsed and became premier of the provisional government and commander of the Polish armed forces then in France, an army which grew to a body of 100,000 by the spring of 1940. When France fell Sikorski went to England with his army and government.

In England Sikorski opened negotiations with the Allies for recognition and aid for the underground movement. He also established close rapport with Churchill which was to be of much use. In July 1941 when the Soviet Union was at its lowest point, following the opening of Barbarossa, Sikorski began negotiations which led to the Sikorski-Maisky agreement. This was a joint Soviet-Polish declaration of alliance which included a recognition of Poland's pre-1939 borders and a repudiation of the Soviet-German partition. It also provided an amnesty for Polish prisoners and deportees and permission for General Anders to form a Polish army in the USSR. The central issue at this time and throughout the war was the fate of the 14,500 Poles who had been deported in 1939, 8000 of whom disappeared into Soviet camps after April 1940. Anders was unable to trace the vast majority of these and tension between the Polish government-in-exile and the Soviet Union increased by the year. In 1943 Sikorski presented Churchill with evidence that the 4100 Polish officers buried at Katyn had been murdered by the Soviets. Churchill, however, wanted to keep his relations with Stalin smooth at all costs and therefore smothered the issue. Sikorski died in a plane crash at Gibraltar on 4 July 1943 and the Polish government in London became progressively impotent. Sikorski was the only

Polish leader who had sufficient stature and skill to secure the confidence of his people and to achieve the close relations with both Churchill and Stalin, which were necessary to maintain a united and effective Polish government with substantial influence in Allied affairs.

Simović, General Dušan, 1882–1962

Simović was head of the Yugoslav government when Germany invaded in 1941. A staunch Serbian nationalist and anti-German, he became Chief of Army General Staff in 1939 and then Chief of Air Force Staff in 1940. From December 1940 he became a leader of resistance both to the Germans and to the impotent policies of the Yugoslav government, then headed by the regent, Prince Paul. Urged by the Allies to resist and to attack the Italians in Albania and pressured by the Germans to join the Tripartite Pact, events came to a head when in February 1941 Hitler demanded the right to move military materials across Yugoslavia. Simović openly warned Paul that the Serbian people would not accept his deferring to Hitler's pressure. However, the government signed a secret pact with the Axis on 25 March. Two days later in an efficient and bloodless coup the army put Simović at the head of the government and declared Peter II King. The Allies immediately pledged their support to Simović and renewed their attempts to bring Yugoslavia into the war. Simović, however, wanted to concentrate on internal problems and maintain strict neutrality so as not to antagonize Hitler. Hitler, on the other hand, decided to invade as soon as he had news of the coup. An army which included seven Panzer divisions and 1000 aircraft was assembled to invade Yugoslavia on 6 April. Belgrade fell on 12 April after intensive bombing and heavy casualties; the government fell on 17 April and resistance was over by 20 April. Simović fled to Greece with Peter and served as Premier of the government-in-exile in London until his resignation in 1942. Although nominated by Peter to head his government after the war, he was rejected by Tito. He retired in May 1945.

Skorzeny, Lieutenant Colonel Otto, 1908–1975

Skorzeny was one of Hitler's most successful irregular soldiers. He had been invalided out of service in December 1942 and found himself appointed to organize a special commando unit. As an unknown he had been appointed by the German Army High Command to sabotage the outfit which Hitler had specially requested, but in fact, he succeeded in establishing a most successful unit. Their first coup was in September 1943 when Skorzeny and about 90 soldiers landed on the plateau of the Gran Sasso in the Abruzzi mountains and succeeded in abducting Mussolini. His unit was expanded and his next mission was to bring the Hungarian dictator, Horthy, to heel. Skorzeny decided the best method to accomplish this would be to kidnap Horthy's son, who was negotiating an armistice with the Soviet Union. Once he had sent Horthy's son to Berlin, Skorzeny brazenly marched into Castle Hill, the citadel of Budapest and took control of the city. Horthy was forced to abdicate and a pro-Nazi regime was established. All this had been done for the loss of only seven Germans killed. In December 1944 Skorzeny took part in another daring raid when he and his men dressed up as US troops and went behind the lines during the Ardennes Offensive. Although they could not turn the battle into a victory, their actions severely shook the Americans, who instituted stringent security measures which only confused the situation more. After the war Skorzeny was tried at Nuremberg but he was acquitted.

Slessor, Air Marshal Sir John, 1897–1979

Slessor was an RAF commander who played a major role in the battle against the German U-Boats. When war broke out he was director of the Plans Branch of the Air Ministry. In 1940 he participated in a conference of US and British army, navy and air force officers in the United States. The conference established the 'Germany first' policy. Slessor then became Air Officer Commanding 5 Bomber Group, RAF Bomber Command. In 1942 he was given the newly formed post of Assistant Chief of the Air Staff (Policy) and attended all the major Allied conferences. In 1943 Slessor became head of RAF Coastal Command cooperating with the Royal Navy and the US forces in an intensive effort to defeat the U-Boats in the Battle of the Atlantic. The use of aircraft in this fight turned out to be crucial. Convoys escorted by planes were rarely attacked because they made it impossible for the German boats to operate in wolf packs. Victory in this struggle was essential both to maintain the merchant fleet and to make an Allied landing in France possible. In January 1944 Slessor became Commander in Chief of RAF units in the Mediterranean and Deputy Commander in Chief of Allied Air Forces in that theater. In his capacity as Deputy Commander in Chief he was involved in the Riviera landings of August 1944. After the war he became Chief of Air Staff.

BIOGRAPHIES

Slim, General Sir William, 1891–1970

At the beginning of the war Slim was given command of the 5th Indian Division in the Sudan where he led the offensive against the Italians at Gallabat. He was wounded in this engagement but returned to command the 10th Indian Division in Iraq in 1941. In June 1941 he conducted a successful campaign in Syria and then led a force into Iran (25 August) to enforce Allied demands for the removal of German agents operating there. He routed the enemy and continued on to Teheran where he joined Soviet troops. In 1942 he was sent to command the Burma I Corps (Burcorps) which comprised virtually all of Alexander's forces. He arrived in the middle of a desperate situation in which he had to maintain order and morale during a 900-mile fighting retreat from Rangoon to India and to accomplish this before the monsoons began. Once in India he commanded XVIII Corps and his main task again was to build morale.

Late in 1943 Slim was put in charge of the newly formed Fourteenth Army which was organized to mount an offensive in Burma, although this was low on the list of the Allies' priorities. The campaign opened in December 1943 and the British forces struggled to take and retain Arakan. The Japanese mounted an impressive counterattack to take Kohima and cut off the road to Imphal. Slim's army held them off and forced them to withdraw when their supplies ran out. The Japanese did not collapse but withdrew to Mandalay and Meiktila. Slim followed them through the jungle, crossed the Irrawaddy and took Mandalay in late March 1945 and raced to reach Rangoon before the monsoon. He arrived in May to find the Japanese had already evacuated.

Slim's campaign made extensive use of guerrilla groups: Merrill's Marauders and Wingate's Chindits. He achieved his successes by using air supply to maintain communications with his rapidly moving troops. He was greatly admired and liked as a commander and achieved the greatest land victory over the Japanese in World War II. Late in the war, Slim was made Commander in Chief of Allied Land Forces in Southeast Asia.

Smith, General Holland, 1882–1967

Holland 'Howling' Mad' Smith is considered the father of amphibious warfare. As marine commander of the V Amphibious Corps, he trained and led his troops in the assaults on Kiska and Attu in the Aleutians, Tarawa and Makin in the Gilbert Islands, Kwajalein and Eniwetok in the Marshalls, and Saipan and Tinian in the Marianas. In August 1944 he was made commanding general of Fleet Marine Force Pacific, directed operations at Guam and led Task Force 56 on Iwo Jima.

Smith developed the techniques that became the standard for amphibious assaults involving the complex coordination of land, sea and air forces. All of his operations resulted in extremely high casualty figures which did not deter Smith at all. He was a very tough and hard-driving leader. However, after the enormous losses on the Gilbert Islands, Smith maintained that the struggle was unnecessary and the islands could have been by-passed. Smith often had problems obtaining cooperation between the army and the marines, a difficulty which came to a head during the Okinawa invasion. However, Smith's skillful administration of amphibious techniques he had developed, rendered the differences unimportant and the landings and battle at Okinawa successful.

Smuts, Prime Minister Jan Christiaan, 1870–1950

A South African soldier of the old school, Smuts had been a member of the British War Cabinet during World War I and had been present at the signing of the Peace Treaty at Versailles in 1919. In the decade before the outbreak of World War II South African politics had rested on the mutual cooperation between the two major parties: the National Party with Hertzog as prime minister and the Union Party with Smuts serving as deputy. When Poland was invaded in 1939, the coalition divided. Smuts, who was in favor if South African involvement, won a difficult parliamentary debate on the subject and soon was elected prime minister. By 1940 he had assumed the leadership of South Africa's war effort including her armed forces. South African soldiers fought bravely on many fronts especially in the Ethiopian, North African and Italian campaigns. Smuts supported Churchill in his policies and decisions at every turn. He attended the San Francisco Conference in 1945 to draft the United Nations' Charter and was present for the signing of the peace agreement at Versailles in 1946, the only person to attend both Versailles peace conferences.

Sokolovsky, Marshal Vasiliy, 1897–1968

Sokolovsky served as Chief of Staff of the Western Front under General Konev from 1941–43. He took part in the planning of Operation Kutuzov (the Battle of Kursk) and commanded the Western Front there. He led the

Western Front to Smolensk which he captured on 25 September 1943. He was also involved in the campaigns at Lvov and the Vistula-Oder. From 1944–45 Sokolovsky was Chief of Staff of the 1st Ukranian Front and was held responsible for this army's failure to advance north from the Pripet Marshes. He was nonetheless posted to serve as Marshal Zhukov's deputy front commander on the 1st Belorussian Front in its final assault on Berlin. After the war he was made commander of the Soviet forces of occupation in Germany.

Somervell, General Brehon, 1892–1955
Somervell served as US Commanding General of Army Service Forces from 1942 until the end of the war and as a presidential adviser. He was involved in problems of mobilization and war production and attended all major planning meetings. He was responsible during the war for supplies, equipment and for the allocation of resources.

Somerville, Admiral Sir James, 1882–1949
In 1940 Somerville was appointed Commander of Force H in the Mediterranean based at Gibraltar. In July of that year it was his unpleasant task to threaten the French fleet under Admiral Gensoul at Oran and Mers-el-Kebir with annihilation unless it proceeded to sail out of range of Axis control. The French government had promised the Allies that no French ship would fall into enemy hands. Somerville delivered an ultimatum and when the French failed to respond, the British were obliged to fire and 1297 French lives were lost. In 1941 Somerville shelled Genoa and was active in the pursuit and ultimate defeat of the *Bismarck*. Throughout his service at Gibraltar his forces were involved in sending aircraft and supplies to Malta as well as protecting the occasional convoys going right through the Mediterranean. Between 1942–44 Somerville was Commander in Chief of the Eastern Fleet which was based in Ceylon. In 1943 he attended the Washington Conference with Churchill and Roosevelt and in 1944 he was head of the British naval delegation in Washington.

Sorge, Richard, 1895–1944
Sorge was a German journalist who ran a very successful spy network for the USSR in Japan. Sorge had been a field commander of Soviet spies in the Far East as early as 1929. As a journalist for the *Frankfurter Zeitung* he made contacts in the German Embassy, first through Herbert von Dirksen and then through the

military attaché, Colonel Eugen Ott. In 1934 Sorge built up a network of agents who collected intelligence throughout Japan. His most important agent was Ozaki Hozumi, who was an expert on Chinese affairs and adviser to Prime Minister Konoye. Ozaki was able to photograph top-secret documents and Sorge would exchange information with his friend Ott who was promoted to ambassador in 1935, and thus receive confirmation. He sent advance warning of *Barbarossa* to Stalin, and although this was ignored he received a note of thanks from Moscow. Sorge supplied the USSR with important information that Japan would not invade the USSR and Stalin was able to move his Siberian divisions to the defense of Moscow. By 1941 the Japanese secret service had intercepted the transmission of a signal and knew about the network. The Japanese arrested one of Sorge's organizers who confessed and implicated Sorge and Ozaki. They were both arrested in October 1941 and tried and hanged on 9 October 1944.

Spaatz, General Carl 'Tooey,' 1891–1974
Spaatz was a US general who commanded air forces in Europe and the Pacific. Spaatz was an official observer in London during the Battle of Britain. In July 1942 he arrived in London again as Commander of the Eighth Air Force, which was to be the principal arm of the strategic air offensive against Germany. He favored day-time precision bombing, believing that the bombers could fight their way through to the target unescorted. In fact losses were very heavy until the Mustang fighter was available and bombing accuracy was never as impressive as was claimed. Although Spaatz always claimed to be making precision and not area attacks, in cloudy conditions the US bombers were restricted to the same navigational aids and accuracy as RAF Bomber Command. He set the Eighth Air Force campaign on its way and was then sent to the North African Theater to coordinate air operations of Eastern Air Command and the 12th Air Force. He then became commander of the Northwest Africa Air Force during the Tunisian campaign and later in Sicily. In January 1944 he returned to Britain as Commanding General of the Strategic Air Force, whose campaign in northern Europe was now in full swing. He directed the aerial preparation of the Normandy landings and then switched to the destruction of the synthetic oil plants, followed by the transportation system within Germany itself. By March 1945, when Spaatz left Europe, production of oil and

movement of inland transport in the Reich had been almost completely halted. In July he took command of the Strategic Air Force in the Pacific and directed the bombing of Japan's major cities. His planes also carried the atom bombs which fell on Hiroshima and Nagasaki.

Speer, Albert, 1905–1981

Speer is generally recognized as the most able of Hitler's subordinates and the most interesting, in that he retained throughout his membership of Hitler's court, a clear-sighted understanding of its essentially Byzantine character. An architect by training, he first came to Hitler's notice in the planning of the Nuremberg party buildings. In 1942 on the death of the armaments minister, Todt, in an air crash, he was promoted to succeed him at the age of 37, and at once began to demonstrate the most remarkable talent for the administration of war industry. Despite the rising tide of the Allied Bombing Offensive on the armaments factories, he was able, through a policy of rationalization and dispersal, to make output rise for every month until September 1944, and to maintain a flow of war material, if on a diminishing scale, to the very end of the war. It was the destruction of the transportation system, rather than of his dispersed factories, which eventually defeated his efforts. Tried at Nuremberg, he was sentenced to 20 years for his use of slave labor in war industry, and wrote during his captivity the most revealing of all the Nazi memoirs.

Sperrle, Field Marshal Hugo, 1885–1953

After commanding the German Condor Legion in the Spanish Civil War, Sperrle became general of aviators in 1937. Appointed to the command of Luftflotte III in January 1939 he provided air support for the Blitzkriegs. During the Battle of Britain, from July 1940 to May 1941, Luftflotte III was stationed in northern France and Sperrle was in Paris. His unit was given the operational sphere of eastern Britain and Kesselring's Luftflotte II, stationed in northeast France and the Low Countries, was assigned to western Britain. Both being self-contained, coordination between the two was poor. After heavy losses through the summer they settled down to constant night bombing from high altitudes.

Luftflotte III took the brunt of the Allied air offensive before and during D-Day but took little part in opposing the invaders.

Spruance, Admiral Raymond, 1886–1969

Spruance was probably America's greatest and most successful naval commander from the historic victory at Midway to his triumph at the Philippine Sea. He began the war as commander of a cruiser division at Midway Island and was promoted in June 1942 to commander of Task Force 16 assigned to prevent any invasion of Midway Island. At the Battle of Midway Spruance took over direction of the battle when Fletcher's flagship, the *Yorktown*, was put out of action and later sunk. His brilliant execution of bomber attacks on the Japanese fleet disabled 10 of their ships, including four carriers. After this decisive battle, Spruance was appointed Chief of Staff to Nimitz and was involved in strategic planning.

In August 1943 he returned to active combat as commander of the Fifth Fleet (Central Pacific Fleet) and in November of that year commanded the bombardment of Tarawa in the Gilbert Islands prior to its reconquest. In January 1944 Spruance led the successful leap-frogging operation which resulted in the capture of Kwajalein in the Marshalls. This was followed by his attack on Truk in the Carolines which was coordinated with Turner's attack on Eniwetok, 17 February 1944.

Spruance conducted the naval bombardment which opened the campaign in Saipan on 11 June 1944. His fleet was stationed off the Marianas to protect the invasion force. On the 18 June he was attacked by Japanese aircraft but these were shot down by Mitscher's planes. On the next day Spruance ordered Mitscher to send out a strike force against the Japanese fleet including Ozawa's carriers. This engagement was known as the Battle of the Philippine Sea; after it the Japanese navy could no longer challenge the Allied fleets. Spruance was criticized for being overcautious in not deploying Mitscher's strike force earlier, which might have finished off the Japanese fleet.

Spruance directed the naval side of the Allied invasion of Iwo Jima in mid-February 1945 and then went on in the same month to conduct the first carrier strike on Tokyo. At the end of the war, he was involved in planning the invasion of the Japanese mainland.

Spruance was cautious but effective and always achieved his victories at the minimum cost. He pioneered many naval techniques including the fleet train (which enabled carrier forces to remain in operation for long periods at a stretch) and the circular formation of carriers. Spruance was an unassuming man, unshakable in battle.

Stalin, Joseph, 1879–1953

Stalin was the dictator of the USSR and Commander in Chief of the USSR's armed forces. Stalin was suspicious of the army and its commanders and in order to get their complete loyalty in 1937 he had purged all those he considered suspect. In 1939 Stalin knew that the USSR was not ready for war so he made a nonaggression pact with Germany. He abandoned his traditional allies in eastern Europe and in September 1939 annexed part of Poland. Stalin's dreams of expansion received a setback in November 1939 when the invasion of Finland ran into unexpected opposition. The lesson that was learned was that the Red Army was not the formidable fighting unit it was previously thought to be.

Hitler's invasion in June 1941 went smoothly and Stalin's massed armies could not stop the German troops who had superior weapons, tanks and training. In the first months of the war Stalin's lack of experience as a war leader showed. He relied on his friends from the First Cavalry Army of 1920: Budenny, Voroshilov and Timoshenko and they were not brilliant army commanders. Finally Zhukov was called in and he executed the counter-attack which saved Moscow in December 1941. Stalin's tactics had been to rely on scorched-earth policy and the Soviet winter. As much industrial plant as possible was moved east of the Urals and the Ukraine and Belorussia were left ravaged. Millions of people had perished in the first six months but the USSR recovered as its armies became more experienced and because the T-34 tank which appeared on the battlefield in 1941 was vastly superior to anything the Germans had produced. The second turning point in the war on the Eastern Front was at Stalingrad where the Soviets cut off General Paulus' Sixth Army and scored a tremendous victory.

Stalin's confidence as a military commander grew and he relied heavily on his staff officers Vasilievsky and Zhukov, who prepared plans and issued directives. It is unlikely that Stalin originated operational concepts but the choice of plans was his. If Stalin disliked a front commander he would dismiss him without warning and this meant some generals were reluctant to report setbacks. In 1944 the Soviet armies swept over the Ukraine, Belorussia and the Baltic states and eventually took Berlin in April 1945.

Stalin's other main role was as a political negotiator and he showed great cunning in his dealings with Churchill and Roosevelt. From

Above: Stalin and Voroshilov at a party meeting.

the first Moscow Conference held in December 1941, Stalin kept up the pressure on the Western Powers to open up a second front in Europe as soon as possible. At various points he threatened to make a separate peace with Hitler and maintained that if Britain and France had opposed Hitler more effectively, the USSR would not have had to suffer such terrible losses. These constant demands for a second front created much suspicion among the Allies: Churchill thought that as few concessions as possible should be made while Roosevelt thought he could reason with Stalin and accommodate him. In mid-1944 it became clear that Stalin wished to settle the political future of eastern Europe. In Poland he promoted the Lublin Committee and recognized it before attending the Yalta Conference (February 1945). At Yalta Churchill and Stalin divided up countries into spheres of influence and Stalin made promises to hold free elections in Poland which he never kept. At the Potsdam Conference he also staved off pressure to hold elections in Poland from the inexperienced Truman and eventually set up puppet Communist regimes in eastern Europe, the last country to fall being Czechoslovakia.

Stalin was a violent man, bent on acquiring as much for the USSR as he could get. The eastern European countries were milked for equipment and supplies after the war to pay back the USSR for all its suffering. Stalin insured that the USSR was a force to be reckoned with in world politics, not to be isolated as in the first years of the revolution. Her military might was feared the world over.

Stark, Admiral Harold, 1880–1972

In 1939 Stark was appointed Chief of Naval Operations and was in charge of the immense expansion of the American navy immediately prior to the war. At this time he also took part in secret discussions with the British regarding the coming war and organized naval patrols to protect US shipping from German submarine and surface ships. Toward the end of 1941 as Japanese-American negotiations reached a critical point, Stark put the navy on war alert and it was able to move into action immediately after Pearl Harbor. However, he failed to give Admiral Kimmel of Pearl Harbor sufficient warning and was criticized in the government inquiry. In March 1942 Stark was made commander of all US naval forces in the European area. This post was an administrative and diplomatic one, involving him in all the Allied conferences and planning sessions during the rest of the war. Stark was from the start one of the principal advocates of giving the war against the Germans top priority. In the lead up to Operation Overlord, Stark played a major role in keeping Anglo-American relations smooth and cooperative.

Stauffenberg, Colonel Claus von, 1907–1944

Stauffenberg was a brilliant young officer who had served with great bravery in the Polish campaign, France and North Africa. In April 1943 he was severely wounded by bullets from a low-flying aircraft in the Western Desert. He lost an eye, his right hand and forearm and some fingers on his left hand, but as he lay in hospital he told his wife, 'I feel I must do something now to save Germany. We general staff officers must all accept our share of the responsibility.' When he left hospital he was given a staff appointment àt the Reserve Army Headquarters and as Chief of Staff to Olbricht was drawn into the conspiracy against Hitler. In June 1944 he was promoted and had to attend briefing sessions at Hitler's Headquarters at Rastenburg. He decided to use this opportunity to try to assassinate the Fuehrer and after several false alarms left a bomb in his briefcase during a staff conference on 20 July 1944. No one had thought to search the briefcase because Stauffenberg was a cripple but the explosion failed to kill Hitler, mainly because the conference was taking place in a temporary hut rather than in the usual conference bunker so the blast was diffused and because an officer had knocked the briefcase away from Hitler. Stauffenberg left for Berlin (at 1240 hours) as soon as he heard the explosion and arrived at the war office to find Olbricht, Hoeppner and Beck unable to take decisions. Stauffenberg assured them that Hitler was dead but the conspirators had lost the initiative and

at 2250 hours they were overpowered by loyal officers and Fromm took control. He had Stauffenberg shot in the courtyard. Stauffenberg will long be remembered for his courage and valor and as the personification of the German resistance against Hitler.

Stettinius, Edward, 1900–1949

Stettinius was an American industrialist (chairman of US Steel) who became a leading government adviser on industrial problems in a war economy and eventually became secretary of state. He was first brought into government affairs as chairman of the War Resources Board which investigated the industrial problems which would occur in case of war. In May 1940 he was made a member of the National Defense Advisory Commission and in January 1941 was made director of the Office of Production Management. From October 1941–September 1943 Stettinius was special assistant to Roosevelt on matters concerning war production, allocation of raw materials and war economy. He was also a Lend-Lease administrator. In 1943 he was appointed undersecretary of state and was involved in Anglo-American negotiations in London in April 1944. He also helped organize the Dumbarton Oaks conference. In November 1944 Roosevelt appointed Stettinius secretary of state to replace Cordell Hull. Stettinius remained in this position until July 1945 when he was replaced by Byrnes but he became the first US delegate to the United Nations, a body he worked with great diligence to promote.

Stilwell, General Joseph, 1883–1946

Stilwell served as Chiang Kai-shek's Chief of Staff from 1942–44 and commanded Chinese and American forces in Burma. Stilwell had a long experience of the Far East, having served as military attaché to the US Embassy at Peking from 1932–39. In 1941 he was appointed by the War Department to command US forces in China, Burma and India and to improve the fighting efficiency of the Chinese army, which meant ensuring the proper use of American aid. On 11 March 1942 he became Chief of Staff to Chiang. At this time Stilwell campaigned in Burma with the Chinese Fifth and Sixth Armies, unsuccessfully attempting to hold the Burma road against the Japanese. Stilwell rescued the Chinese garrison which was encircled at Toungoo but after intense fighting Stilwell retreated into India. In August 1943 the Southeast Asia Command was organized and Stilwell was appointed Deputy Supreme Allied Commander under Vice-Admiral Mountbatten.

Stilwell had been extremely critical and mistrustful of the British and this appointment enabled them to keep him under control. It also gave the Chinese some official recognition and guaranteed a minimum of cooperation in the attempt to recapture Burma and restore overland communications with China.

During 1943 Stilwell prepared an offensive into Burma and on 21 December he took personal command of the operation to take Myitkyina which only fell in the following August. Stilwell blamed the British units, Wingate's Chindits, for not fighting well yet they had to be withdrawn because of heavy losses. In China the air offensive conducted by Chennault had provoked the Japanese to launch operation Ichi-Go and they overran US air bases in East China. The joint chiefs decided to appoint Stilwell commander of all Chinese troops in order to deal with the crisis. However, Chiang used the opportunity to have Stilwell recalled in October 1944. Stilwell had one last command: he replaced Buckner as head of the US Tenth Army on Okinawa.

Stilwell was a brilliant soldier but he was too independent a commander and not tactful or diplomatic in dealing with people he disliked. He thought his mission was to press a reluctant Chiang into direct military action against the Japanese. However, Chiang did not have the political power he sought and preferred to use US aid to fight the Communists. Stilwell understood this, mistrusted Chiang and yet had to contend with strong, unrealistic Sinophile sentiments in the USA and among his superiors. At the same time had had a low opinion of the British and saw no reason to help them reestablish their empire. Stilwell, nicknamed 'Vinegar Joe,' roused controversy and antagonism wherever he went.

Stimson, Henry, 1867–1950

Stimson was American secretary of war throughout World War II. He had been Hoover's secretary of state from 1929–33 and was appointed to Roosevelt's Cabinet in July 1940 despite being a Republican and already 72 years old. His initial preoccupations were overseeing mobilization and training. Stimson was strongly against America's isolationist tradition and championed Lend-Lease and increasing aid to Britain. He sought the repeal of the Neutrality Act which would enable merchant ships to be armed and introduced the US's first compulsory military service in peacetime in 1940. After Pearl Harbor Stimson was in favor of putting Germany first and was especially vocal in advocating the initiation of a 'second front' in northwest Europe as soon as possible. However in 1943 he bowed to Churchill's arguments to postpone Operation Overlord. Stimson attended all the major Allied conferences.

Stimson was also very active in organizing scientific research during the war. In particular he was involved in exploring the possibilities of atomic warfare from a quite early date and was personally responsible for the Manhattan Project. Stimson strongly recommended the use of the atom bomb against Japan. He resigned in September 1945.

Stirling, Colonel David, 1915–

After Dunkirk Stirling, transferred from the Scots Guards to the newly raised commandos, was sent to the Middle East and there hit upon the idea of organizing deep penetration raids into the enemy lines with the object of destroying aircraft. He received official backing and a small allotment of men and, first by parachute, then by Long Range Desert Group, began a series of descents on enemy airdromes. By 1942 this unit had been transformed into a regular regiment, called the Special Air Service (SAS), and he had become a lieutenant colonel and a legend to both sides in the desert, where he was known as the 'Phantom Major.' Early in 1943, however, he was captured by a unit of German soldiers especially trained in anti-SAS operations, and, despite numerous attempts at escape which eventually consigned him to Colditz, remained in enemy hands until the end of the war. While active, he had seen to the destruction of 250 enemy aircraft, and created a novel and now much imitated form of military organization.

Stopford, General Sir Montagu, 1892–1971

Stopford commanded the XXXIII Indian Corps which reopened the Imphal Road into Burma and captured Mandalay. He was posted to this command in November 1943 and was sent into action when the Japanese mounted their offensive across the Chindwin on Manipur in early 1944. Stopford was ordered to this new front and mobilized and transported his men there with enormous speed. The Japanese had successfully cut the Kohima-Imphal road which stopped communications and supplies to British troops in that part of Assam. Furthermore the British garrison at Kohima, a small force of 1500, was outnumbered four to one and subjected to an intensive barrage. Stopford arrived in time to clear out the roadblock, raise the siege of Kohima and continue along the Imphal road to join Scoones' IV Corps and help relieve the siege of Imphal. Stopford immediately pressed into Central Burma to take Meiktila and then into the Burmese mountains to attack Mandalay from the north in March 1945. The XXXIII then followed the Irrawaddy River to capture the Yenangyaung oilfields. When Slim left Burma, Stopford became commanding officer of the Fourteenth Army and accepted the Japanese surrender in Burma. Stopford was a highly respected general and very sucussful in this, the most intense campaign of the Far Eastern Theater.

Streicher, Julius, 1885–1946

Streicher was one of the most violent and crude Jew-baiters of the Nazi Party. His career began when he helped to found the Nuremberg German Socialist Party immediately following World War I. This party was a major rival of Hitler's fledgling National Socialist Party until Streicher was persuaded by Hitler to change sides with a large body of supporters. Hitler was extremely grateful for this and remained loyal to Streicher for the rest of his life. Streicher played a role in the Beer Hall Putsch of 1923 and in the same year founded *Der Stürmer* which he edited until 1943. This paper had a semiofficial status and specialized in the most scurrilous and pornographic sensationalism, mainly directed against Jews and Communists. In 1935 Streicher staged the Nuremberg rallies.

Though dedicated to Hitler and always protected by him, Streicher was too corrupt and disreputable to be given high government posts. In 1940 he was tried and found guilty of misappropriating confiscated Jewish property. Streicher was removed from his position as Gauleiter of Franconia, but Hitler allowed him to spend the duration of the war on his farm. Streicher was tried for war crimes after the war, was found guilty and executed.

Student, General Kurt, 1890–1978

Student had flown as a pilot in the German air force in World War I and joined the Luftwaffe on its formation in 1934. Goering, who was much impressed by the potential of the parachute and the success the Soviets were having in adapting it to military use, chose him to raise an experimental force of parachute infantry (Fallschirmjäger), which was soon expanded to divisional size. He also oversaw the development of gliders for the transport of air landing troops. This airborne force contributed considerably to the success of the Blitzkrieg in 1940, particularly by its descents in Holland, at Eben Emael and the crossing of the Meuse which opened the way for the German armored forces to penetrate deep into the Low Countries. The descent on Crete in the following year, though brilliantly conceived and executed, was far more costly in lives and forced Hitler to forbid large-scale parachute operations in future. The parachute force continued to grow, however, since it was valued for its high morale, and in 1944 numbered 10 divisions. By then Student, who had had the good fortune to be present at the Arnhem Operation and to read its character correctly, had been appointed to command Army Group G in Holland, a position which he held until May 1945.

Stuelpnagel, General Karl von, 1886–1944

Stuelpnagel, the military governor of occupied France, was a leading member of the military opposition to Hitler and a key participant in the attempted putsch of 20 July 1944. He had been an active opponent of the Nazis since 1938. In 1939 he was made quartermaster general and then Deputy Chief of Staff, in which capacity he argued strongly, but without effect, on military grounds against Hitler's proposed Western Offensive. Stuelpnagel planned the abortive coup of November 1939. Stuelpnagel continued his search for upper echelon army support throughout 1940 and 1941. In 1941 he was sent to the Eastern Front where he commanded the encirclement of Kiev and in 1942 went to France.

Stuelpnagel's next venture was planned in May 1944 and its purpose was to arrange an armistice without Hitler's consent. It faltered when Rundstedt, Commander in Chief, West, refused to take part in it. By July Rundstedt had been replaced by Kluge who gave his conditional agreement to participate: he would move only if Hitler was definitely dead. On 20 July 1944 Stauffenberg's bomb went off at Rastenburg but Hitler escaped injury. The signal for Operation Valkyrie (to take over the state) went out and Stuelpnagel began rounding up SS, Gestapo and Nazi officials in Paris; however, when Kluge heard Hitler was still alive he refused to help the coup and Stuelpnagel tried to cover his steps. He claimed he had rounded up the SS and Gestapo for their own security but he was summoned to Berlin and en route shot himself. He was found floating in a river and rescued. Stuelpnagel lived in spite of his terrible head wounds and was put on trial and hanged as were other conspirators including Fromm, Carl Gördeler and Witzleben.

Sugiyama, General Hajime, 1880–1945
Sugiyama was commander of the First Imperial Army and of the Home Defense Army and was Army Chief of Staff from 1938–44. He attended the Disarmament Conference in Geneva from 1926 to 1928 and became a member of the Japanese supreme war council in 1935. As war minister from 1937–38 he oversaw the 1937 China campaign and was then appointed army Chief of Staff. He was an extremely militant member of the Strike South faction of the military and along with Nagano, the navy Chief of Staff, played a critical role in bringing Japan and America to the point of war. During the Japanese negotiations with the US in the fall of 1941, these two set deadlines as to when war must begin. Throughout the war Sugiyama directed operations from Tokyo. In February 1944 he was made a field marshal and resigned as Chief of Staff in favor of Tojo who was then attempting to consolidate his power. Following Tojo's fall, Sugiyama was appointed war minister under Koiso, a post he held until the end of the war. After the surrender he played an important part in getting the army to lay down its arms. He committed suicide on 12 September 1945 despite appeals from the emperor to put national interest first.

Sultan, General Daniel, 1885–1947
In April 1942 Sultan was appointed Deputy Commander in Chief of US troops in the China-Burma-India Theater. After General Stilwell's recall in November 1944 Sultan succeeded him as Commander in Chief of that theater. He led the advance from Myitkyina in February 1945 and reopened the Burma–Ledo Road. He reached Lashio in March 1945 and took part in planning the reconquest of Malaya, an operation which never took place because of the Japanese surrender in August 1945.

Suzuki, Prime Minister Kantaro, 1867–1948
Suzuki was an antimilitarist and symbol of peace who led the Japanese peace-seeking Cabinet from April 1945 until the end of the war. A veteran of Korea in the 1890s and of the Russo-Finnish War, Suzuki was already in retirement by 1927. Nonetheless as a military man who was involved in neither the army nor navy cliques, he was already a valuable compromise figure at that time. In 1929 he was appointed grand chamberlain, an advisory post quite close to the emperor, and was made a member of the supreme war council. He was a prime target of the 1936 coup in which he barely escaped death.

In August 1944, after the fall of Tojo, Suzuki was appointed president of the Privy Council as a first step to bringing him back into public affairs. When Koiso's government fell on 5 April 1945 following the American invasion of Okinawa, Suzuki was made prime minister. Although he was a universally popular figure, committed to peace and convinced the war was lost, he was extremely old and perhaps too respected a figure to conduct a vigorous leadership. However, he was also engaged in a difficult juggling act in which either Japan would be annihilated or the military would mutiny in order to pursue their fight to the death. Suzuki nonetheless made two grave mistakes. One was to try to negotiate via Stalin. The other was to issue an extremely ambiguous answer to the Potsdam Declaration which seemed to say that the Japanese would not even consider it seriously. This was not in fact his intention. On 14 August 1945 Suzuki obtained agreement to take the revolutionary step of asking the emperor to decide the question of war or peace. He resigned the same day as the surrender was confirmed.

Tanaka, Rear Admiral Raizo, 1892–1969
Tanaka was a commander of destroyer flotillas, the most highly trained units of the Japanese navy, and particularly expert in night action. Commanding from his flagship, the *Jintsu*, he was involved in every major battle of the first 18 months of the war. At Midway, Tanaka commanded the transport group of the Midway Occupation Force. He was especially notorious for running the 'Tokyo Express' which operated nighttime supply runs to the Japanese on Guadalcanal and regularly slipped through the greatly superior American naval forces equipped with radar. At the Battle of Guadalcanal 12–14 November 1942, Tanaka escorted by Kondo attempted to land 11 transports at Guadalcanal. He was only able to land 2000 soldiers and paltry amounts of rice and ammunition. On 30 November, while trying to float barrels of supplies ashore to Guadalcanal, Tanaka was surprised by a larger American force and was able to inflict a humiliating defeat on them due to the superior training and experience of his men in night action. In July 1943 Tanaka was still trying to reinforce troops on Kolombangara in the Solomons. US methods of night fighting had improved and Tanaka's flagship was devastated by gunfire and sank. Shortly after, Tanaka protested about the waste of resources in trying to supply these islands; in reply he was dismissed.

BIOGRAPHIES

Tedder, Air Chief Marshal Sir Arthur, 1890–1967

Tedder was a British air marshal who served as deputy supreme commander of Operation Overlord. In 1941 he came to the fore when he was appointed Commander in Chief of the Middle East Air Force. He stressed the importance of gaining air superiority in the Desert War, feeling particularly vulnerable because it was easier for the Axis forces to receive reinforcements from other fronts. Churchill found him too cynical and nearly sacked him in October 1941 but he had the full confidence of General Auchinleck and retained his command. By the time of the Battle of El Alamein, Tedder's air force had achieved air superiority and he had designed a system of pattern bombing, 'Tedder's Carpet,' to soften up Axis defense positions prior to an offensive. He also learned of the need to establish good relations with army commanders and won their respect in the North African campaign.

After the Casablanca Conference, January 1943, Tedder was appointed General Eisenhower's army and air force deputy in Tunisia and thereafter was responsible for coordinating land and air operations in the invasions of Sicily and Italy. In 1944 he returned to Britain to become Eisenhower's deputy in the run up to the D-Day landings. He was also the supreme air commander and had to coordinate Leigh-Mallory's air offensive with the strategic bombing offensives of Harris and Spaatz. Tedder favored Leigh-Mallory's plan to knock out the German transportation system. In November 1944 he took over the direction of the tactical air force when Leigh-Mallory left for the Far East. On Eisenhower's behalf he signed the instrument of surrender of the German forces in the west in May 1945. His real talent was as a strategist rather than a commander and his great contribution to winning the war in Europe was to isolate the Normandy battlefields from the hinterland of France.

Terauchi, Field Marshal Hisaichi, 1879–1945

Terauchi was supreme commander of the Japanese Southern Army throughout the war. He took the command on 6 November 1941 with instructions to seize all American, Dutch and British possessions in the 'southern area' starting on 8 December. The invasions were accomplished more quickly than anyone expected, enabling Terauchi to order the invasion of Java a full month ahead of schedule. In 1942 Terauchi was given responsibility for constructing the 250-mile Burma Road. Though it would normally have taken five years to build, he resolved to build it in 18 months. Living in appalling conditions, a full third of his work force of 50,000 POWs died (as well as a considerable number of Japanese). Terauchi at one point censured Homma, responsible for the Bataan Death March, and Immamura, for pursuing too liberal a policy regarding natives.

In May 1944, Terauchi moved his HQ from Saigon to Manila and was charged with defending a vast area from New Guinea to Burma with his Southern Army. In July 1944 he was one of the three men suggested to replace Tojo as prime minister. Terauchi also commanded at Leyte, where he refused to surrender a lost battle despite a shortage of troops on Luzon and the loss of a convoy of 10,000 men sunk by Allied aircraft. In September 1945 Terauchi suffered a stroke and was therefore unable to attend the surrender of Southeast Asian troops on 12 September in Singapore.

Ter Poorten, General Hein, 1887–1948

Serving as Commander in Chief of land forces in the Dutch East Indies from October 1941, Ter Poorten had to organize its defense against the Japanese, who invaded Sarawak, the Celebes and Tarakan (Borneo) in January 1942. Ter Poorten had 125,000 well-trained men and American backing but he had insufficient artillery, planes and transport and the US bombers were of little use because of the lack of fighter support. Aware of this in advance, he blew up all the oil wells in these territories and surrendered in March 1942 near Bandung.

Tibbets, Colonel Paul, 1915–

Tibbets commanded and trained the men who dropped the atom bombs on Hiroshima and Nagasaki, and himself piloted the *Enola Gay* which dropped 'Little Boy' on Hiroshima on 6 August 1945. As a bomber pilot he had been decorated many times and was one of the first to fly a B-17 mission over Europe, at a time when the Luftwaffe still ruled the air. He was then transferred back to the US to lead modification work on the new B-29s. In September 1944 at the age of 29, he was called upon to train a special unit to drop the atomic bomb. He developed the technique to be employed and played a part in the selection of the targets to be attacked.

Timoshenko, Marshal Semyon, 1895–1970

Timoshenko was an experienced and effective general who took the full brunt of the German invasion of Soviet Russia in 1941. A man of peasant origins with a long career in the cavalry and a friendship with Stalin dating back to the Civil War, he participated in the occupation of Poland and commanded Karelian troops in the Russo-Finnish War. In May 1940 he was made a marshal and replaced the less able Voroshilov as commissar of defense in charge of reorganizing the Red Army with special reference to the training and discipline of recruits. On 23 June 1941 Stalin called the Stavka (a large committee of Soviet High Command) and Timoshenko initially chaired it. He was given command of the Western Front when the Germans invaded, but at first could do little to halt their advance and at one point his army was encircled by the Germans at Smolensk. Nonetheless he was able to delay the Germans which prevented them from reaching Moscow before winter. In September 1941 Timoshenko was transferred to the command of the Southwestern Front but failed to prevent the Germans from breaking through to the Crimea and was unable to mount a counteroffensive. In May 1942 he mounted a major offensive at Kharkhov, unaware that the Germans had planned their own offensive a week later and were consequently well prepared. Timoshenko was routed and transferred to the much quieter North Western Front.

Tiso, President Joseph, 1887–1946

Tiso served as the president of separatist Slovakia from 1938–44. Slovakia was included in the new Czechoslovak Republic after World War I but was underdeveloped economically and politically and the Slovaks felt the Czechs were doing nothing to alleviate their problems. When Monsignor Tiso became leader of the Slovak People's Party the government pressed for full independence rather than autonomy. The Czech government tried to arrest Tiso but Hitler saw that a satellite state would be useful to him in dismantling the Czech government. He therefore forced them to give up control of the new Slovak state which was then given recognition by the USSR, France and Great Britain. Tiso signed a pact with Germany in March 1939. He constructed a number of concentration camps but did not use them to intern Jews until forced to by Hitler. In August 1944 Tiso was deposed during a partisan uprising preceding Slovak liberation by the Red Army. Tiso was tried and hanged on 3 December 1946.

Tito, Marshal Josip Broz, 1892–1980

Tito was the Communist leader of the Yugoslav resistance during the war. He was able not only to become a national leader and maintain a large and well-disciplined army throughout the occupation but also to keep thousands of badly needed Axis troops tied up fighting the Partisans in Yugoslavia.

Tito was almost 50 at the outbreak of war and had gained experience in the Russian Revolution, Spanish Civil War and Comitern. When Germany invaded Yugoslavia he organized resistance quickly, and was able to mount sabotage attacks by July 1941 and a full-scale campaign in Serbia in the fall. He succeeded in capturing a number of Serbian towns, including Uzice, where he set up an arms factory and printing press. However, he soon came to blows with the rival resistance group, the Četniks, led by Mihajlović who collaborated with the Nazis in order to try to defeat left wing forces. Tito defeated Mihajlović but was then driven out of Serbia by the Germans. This was the first of seven major Axis offensives against the partisans. In each case, Tito followed a policy of fighting as long as he was able, then disappearing into the hills still maintaining tight communication and organization and assuming governmental functions in areas under his control. In November 1942 he held an assembly in Bihać. In May 1943 Tito was attacked by forces six times his size, lost a quarter of his men and half his equipment but managed to keep his men together.

The Allies had little idea of what was happening in Yugoslavia throughout this period. They had given their support to Mihajlović early in the war, but late in 1942 they obtained better intelligence and began shifting their support to Tito. After Fitzroy Maclean's clandestine visit to Partisan headquarters, Tito became the single largest recipient in the Allied aid program. His fortunes further improved when the Italians pulled out of the war in September 1943. This allowed him to obtain Croatia, the Dalmatian coast and a vast quantity of Italian arms. Tito now had an army of 250,000 men. In May 1944 the Yugoslav government-in-exile dismissed Mihajlović and began negotiating with Tito. In the same month the Germans launched another massive assault on the Partisans but with adequate Allied air support and the approach of the Red Army. Tito managed to take Belgrade by the 20 October 1944. Tito then took part in a coalition government under a temporary regency, but the Communists won the first elections with a large majority and abolished the monarchy.

Tito was one of the greatest and most successful leaders of the war. Because of his

BIOGRAPHIES

aggressive policies, he became the symbol of his country's unity and was able to institute an indigenous Communist government without Soviet support or control.

Tizard, Sir Henry, 1885–1959

Tizard was a British scientist and an important adviser to the government throughout the war. From 1933 he was chairman of the Aeronautical Research Committee and was one of the pioneers in the development of operational radar, a technique of great importance to the war effort. He was also a member of many other committees which dealt with air warfare. He served as scientific adviser to the Chief of Air Staff for the first year of the war, but resigned this and most of his other posts in June 1940 because of his opposition to Lindemann (known as Lord Cherwell), the scientific adviser to the new Churchill government. Nonetheless Tizard was active throughout the war. He led a group of scientists to America to initiate profitable Anglo-American scientific cooperation for war purposes. From June 1941 he represented the Ministry of Aircraft Production on the Air Council. In 1943 he spent three months in Australia giving advice on the use of scientific techniques. Later in the war he was a strong opponent of Lindemann's advocacy of area bombing of German towns, believing this to be less successful than more limited operations such as those waged against the U-Boats.

Togo, Shigenori, 1882–1950

Togo was twice foreign minister: at the start of the war and at the end. He was vigorously anti-militarist and antiwar and while he was minister under Tojo he made every effort in his negotiations with the Americans to avoid war. However, he was not able to do anything in the face of the entrenched power of the military leaders and in reality served as little more than a cover for Tokyo's preparations for Pearl Harbor. (It was in accord with this interpretation of his actions that he was tried and convicted as a war criminal despite the sincerity of his efforts.) He resigned shortly after war was declared.

Togo lived in retirement throughout the war until Suzuki appointed him foreign minister in April 1945. He only accepted the job when assured that his sole task would be to seek peace. In this pursuit he was still severely hampered by die-hards in power and was in fear for his life throughout the summer. He was opposed to negotiating through the Soviets and his mistrust was justified. He favored publication of the Potstam Declaration in Japan to show that it was taken seriously and advocated its immediate acceptance providing the emperor's status was guaranteed. He resigned from the Cabinet in August 1945, after the surrender had been agreed on. He was a brilliant intellectual, extremely blunt, independent and harsh.

Tojo, General Hideki, 1884–1948

Tojo was the Japanese prime minister who initiated the war in the Pacific and directed it until 1944. A military man with tremendous support in the army as the man who would give them the opportunity to fulfill all their ambitions, his first important post was as Chief of Staff to the Kwantung Army in Manchuria in 1937. In 1938 he was given a special Imperial dispensation to hold a military and a cabinet post simultaneously. He served as vice-minister and then in 1940 minister of war, under Konoye. It was in 1940 that he played a leading role in negotiating the Tripartite Pact with Italy and Germany. On 16 October 1941 Tojo became prime minister on the resignation of the more moderate Konoye.

Tojo's task was to bring Japan into the war. As a first step he forced the French Vichy government to allow Japan to occupy all of French Indochina. At the same time Tojo was negotiating with the Americans up till the last moments before Pearl Harbor.

Tojo had concentrated onto himself the three posts of prime minister, war minister and Chief of Army Staff and was therefore wholly responsible for the conduct of the war. Thus his position became increasingly weak as events turned against Japan. He tried to diffuse some opposition by handing over the ministry of war to Umezu, but when the Marianas fell he could no longer hold on. He resigned on 18 July 1944, the day that Saipan fell.

Tojo attempted suicide after Japan surrendered but survived to be one of the seven Japanese war criminals to be hanged by the Allies. Nicknamed 'the Razor,' he was a hard-working and authoritarian man whose regime was indistinguishable from a military dictatorship. However, as Professor Butow put it, 'He somehow failed to fit the pattern. Unlike the Fuehrer or Il Duce, Tojo was a selector not a creator, of national thought. His word was not law. It was not his to command or dictate. He was one among equals. He was a militarist – misguided, naive and narrow in outlook. . . .'

Tokyo Rose (Mrs Iva Ikuko Toguri d'Aquino), 1916–

Throughout the war Tokyo Rose made propaganda broadcasts attempting to demoralize the Allied troops in the East. Speaking in a bright and sexy voice she would tell the troops about Japan's successes and imminent victory, about how easy and pleasant life was at home and about how the girls they had left behind were busy getting themselves other men. These remarks would be interspersed with light music. Tokyo Rose was an American citizen with Japanese parents. She had a degree from UCLA in zoology. She had been visiting a sick relative in Japan when the war broke out and chose to join the Japanese Broadcasting Company rather than be conscripted into factory work. She was trained in broadcasting by an American POW. In 1948 she was sentenced to 10 years in jail and a $10,000 fine for treason. Mrs d'Aquino is now living in Chicago and still denies being Tokyo Rose. She was pardoned by President Ford in January 1977.

Tolbukhin, Marshal Fyodor, 1894–1949

Tolbukhin was commander of the armies which forced the Germans out of the Crimea, the Ukraine, Rumania, Yugoslavia and Hungary. A graduate of the Frunze Military Academy in 1934, from 1942–43 he was commander of the Fifty-seventh Army defending Stalingrad. In 1943 as commander of the South Front he was responsible for capturing a number of towns at the mouth of the Donets. In April 1944 Tolbukhin, in conjunction with Yeremenko, led the offensive which recaptured the Crimea and took 67,000 German and Rumanian prisoners by 13 May. In August 1944 Tolbukhin and Malinovsky, with 38 divisions between them, were charged with clearing out the Balkans. Together they defeated a German army of 200,000 at Jassy-Kishinev and Tolbukhin was made a marshal. They now cleared Rumania and Tolbukhin went on to Yugoslavia to recapture Belgrade with the help of Tito's partisans in October 1944. He then turned north to meet Malinovksy in Hungary and settle down to the long winter siege of Budapest. In the spring he led the offensive which drove the fanatical Sixth SS Panzer Army out of the west of Hungary into Austria (March 1945).

After the war Tolbukhin was made supreme commander of troops in Bulgaria and Rumania.

Tovey, Admiral Sir John, 1885–1971

From 1940–43 Tovey was Commander in Chief of the Home Fleet which was based at Scapa Flow. The Home Fleet's main purpose was to protect and guide convoys across the Atlantic. Tovey's greatest achievement was the hunting,

chasing and sinking of the *Bismarck* in May 1941, an act he accomplished with the aid of Somerville's Force H from the Mediterranean. From 1942–43 Tovey's Home Fleet was responsible for guarding the northern passages across the Arctic to make them safe for convoys to Murmansk. To achieve this end he was forced to concentrate a large number of his ships near Iceland. Ordered to protect convoys at all costs he tried several times to destroy the *Tirpitz* but was always forced to abandon the chase in favor of covering the convoys.

Toyoda, Admiral Soemu, 1885–1957

Toyoda, originally the commander of the Yokosuka naval base, succeeded Admiral Koga as Commander in Chief of the Combined Navy in May 1944. He was firmly committed to the policy of luring the Americans into the 'Decisive Battle' to destroy their entire fleet and had his first attempt at this in June 1944. In May 1944 the Americans had made a landing at Biak and Toyoda, believing this to be the main US offensive, set Operation Kon into action, which involved transporting troops from the Marianas to Biak. This was unsuccessful and in the meantime the American Central Pacific Fleet attacked the unprepared Marianas. Toyoda therefore ordered operation A-Go, which involved luring the American Fleet from near the Marianas to a point near the Palaus. This resulted in the catastrophic Battle of the Philippine Sea, in which the Japanese lost over 400 planes, many ships and their last chance to confront the American navy with equal force.

Toyoda, however, did not renounce his belief in the 'Decisive Battle' which he now planned for Leyte Gulf. This battle, which occurred in October 1944, was well planned by the Japanese and they could have succeeded in inflicting great damage on the US fleet, but due to bad coordination, inflexibility and lack of air power, they lost their last aircraft carriers while inflicting little damage on the Americans. Toyoda ordered the last action of the Japanese navy in April 1945 when he sent the *Yamato* on a suicide mission to Okinawa. It was sunk, however, before it arrived there.

Toyoda was a member of the triumvirate of die-hards (the others were Umezu and Anami) who rejected any form of unconditional surrender, including the Potsdam Declaration. Nonetheless he was able to continue as Navy Chief of Staff after the war.

Truman, Harry, 1894–1972

A Senator from Missouri at the outbreak of

World War II, Truman was asked to chair the Senate Special Committee to investigate the National Defense Program which was under suspicion of misappropriation of funds and misallocation of contracts. Although many were against the formation of this committee, General Marshall and others were so outspokenly in its favor that it was convened. With tact and care Truman saved the country millions of dollars with very few scandals as the problems were solved with a minimum of publicity. In 1944 he became vice-president in Roosevelt's government and became president immediately upon the death of Roosevelt in April 1945. At first he relied heavily on Roosevelt's advisers but soon replaced them with Cabinet members of his own choosing. He continued to pursue Roosevelt's policies, including the organizing of the San Francisco Conference to outline the United Nations Charter at the end of April 1945. Truman also had to confront Stalin regarding the latter's treatment of Poland. Truman sent Harry Hopkins on a mission to Moscow to negotiate with Stalin about this negation of the Yalta Agreement but the meetings were unsatisfactory. In July 1945 Truman, Churchill and Stalin met at the Potsdam Conference and Stalin stubbornly confirmed his intention to continue with his Poland policy. On the return journey from Potsdam Truman announced his determination to drop an atomic bomb on Hiroshima on the 6 August 1945 to insure the speedy completion of the Pacific War. He continued as president for a further seven years.

Turner, Vice-Admiral R Kelly, 1885–1961

Before the war Turner was with the War Plans Division (Navy) and involved in negotiations with the Japanese. In July 1942 he was posted as commander of the South Pacific Amphibious Force (TF62) although he had never before been in active combat. He was chosen as an expert in amphibious operations, which were vital in the Pacific, and was to command transport, escort and bombardment forces. Turner's first operation was the 7 August 1942 landing of 11,000 troops at Guadalcanal. In the aftermath of the landing, Turner was caught completely by surprise by the fleet of Admiral Mikawa, and in the Battle of Savo Island which followed, suffered a humiliating defeat.

Turner was then stricken with malaria, but returned to the scene to oversee the invasion of New Georgia. On 20 November 1943 he directed the landings in the Gilbert Islands in which the Americans suffered the worst casualties of the war up to this point. In 1944 he was transferred to the Central Pacific Area under Spruance, and took part in the Marshall Islands operations. In the first of these, on Kwajalein, Turner took the Japanese completely by surprise. He was subsequently made a vice-admiral. On 17–18 February, while Spruance attacked Truk, Turner landed 8000 men at Eniwetok and the island was taken in four days. Turner landed the 2nd and 4th Marine Divisions on the Marianas, in June 1944.

In August 1944 Turner was assigned to set up an air base on Saipan which was to be used by B-29s bombing the Philippines in preparation for landing there. In February 1945 he led the expeditionary force which took Iwo Jima.

Tyulenev, General Ivan, 1892–

Tyulenev was general in charge of the defense of the Caucasus during the Germans' 1942 campaign to break through to the Baku oilfields and to the Black Sea. He was sent to the Caucasus in October 1941 and began building the defensive fortifications which were to prove decisive. The Germans made spectacular advances throughout August and September 1942, driving the Soviets back into the mountains, into excellent defensive positions. During the fall the Germans attempted three further offensives: Grozny in the east, Tuapse in the west and an attempt to cross three mountain passes to the Black Sea. All of these failed and in January 1943 Tyulenev, well supplied with fuel, men and bombers, was able to launch a counteroffensive on two fronts and drive the Germans out by February.

Udet, Lieutenant General Ernst, 1896–1941

Udet was a World War I flying ace whom Goering appointed head of the Luftwaffe's Technical Department. He had been a close friend of Milch and had taken over many of Milch's former responsibilities, as inspector general of the Luftwaffe. However as Milch stated, 'Hitler recognized in Udet one of our greatest pilots, and he was right. But he also saw him as one of the greatest technical experts, and here he was mistaken.' Udet became the head of a vast bureaucracy but did not exercise sufficient control over aircraft production. He was responsible for equipping the Luftwaffe with tactical rather than strategic aircraft and placed great emphasis on the Messerschmitt 109. However in 1941 aircraft production dropped and Udet came under extreme pressure to improve the situation. He became suspicious of everyone and committed suicide in November 1941 after an unpleasant conference with Milch. His death was reported as an accident while testing a new weapon and Udet was given a hero's funeral.

Umezu, General Yoshijiro, 1880–1949

Umezu, a veteran of the Kwantung army in Manchuria and China from 1931–40, was made Chief of Army Staff after Tojo's fall in July 1944 and played a major role in the internal government maneuverings preceding Japan's surrender. Tojo had himself taken the posts of prime minister, Chief of Army Staff and minister of war. When the news of Saipan arrived and his position was tenuous, he ended this unpopular arrangement and Umezu became minister of war. When Tojo fell in July 1944 Umezu became Army Chief of Staff.

In the latter days of the war, Umezu was one of the triumvirate of die-hards in the Cabinet, the others being Toyoda and Anami. They were fierce opponents of unconditional surrender. Umezu was the first of these to relent and see the impossibility of their position. He was persuaded to accept the Potsdam Declaration though he wished to negotiate further conditions. Umezu was under constant and heavy pressure from the army not to surrender.

Umezu was one of the few top Japanese politicians present at the surrender on the USS *Missouri*. Unwilling to go, he had been personally ordered by the Emperor to represent the army.

Ushijima, General Mitsuru, 1887–1945

Ushijima, the former commandant of the Military Academy, after service on Iwo Jima was sent to Okinawa in late 1944 as commander. Instructed to keep the island at all costs, he made excellent use of its rugged terrain, building defense lines in depth, making use of caves and building forts. In addition he correctly predicted the Americans' invasion strategy. Starting with a force of 21,000 men he built it up into an army of 130,000 by conscripting men of all ages from among the natives.

On 1 April 1945 the Americans began a landing of 170,000 combat troops and 115,000 service troops. Ushijima led a primarily defensive campaign except for two counterattacks which were carried out virtually against his will (13 April and 3 May). Both failed with very heavy losses. Full use was made of Kamikaze aircraft. Throughout May Ushijima retreated southward through heavy rain and continued fighting from caves, against which the Ameri-

cans' air power could do little. Ushijima and his subordinates committed suicide on 22 June as US forces approached their cave. Those of his troops that remained continued fighting until 2 July. The final toll of the campaign was 120,000 Japanese dead, 42,000 civilian dead and 50,000 US casualties (including 12,500 dead), the heaviest US loss of the Pacific War.

Vandegrift, Lieutenant General Alexander, 1887–1972

Vandegrift led the 1st Marine Division in the first months of the campaign to take Guadalcanal. He was chosen to lead this campaign at very short notice and given a few months to prepare it. He had little time to collect Intelligence and in his own words 'there was no time for a deliberate planning phase.' On 7 August 1942 Vandegrift and his men landed unopposed on the island and immediately began building an airstrip, which was later called Henderson Field. His men stayed there for four months facing continued attempts by the Japanese navy, army and air force to recapture the island. On 9 December Vandegrift and the 1st Marine Division were withdrawn for a well-earned rest and left with more than a third of the men unfit for combat duty. Vandegrift returned to the USA and was made commander of the I Marine Amphibious Corps and took part in the landings on Bougainville in November 1943. He was posted back to Washington in 1944 and made commander of thd marine corps and built it up by another 25,000 men. He supervised the demobilization after the war.

Vasilievsky, Marshal Alexander, 1895–1977

Vasilievsky served as Chief of General Staff for most of the war, took part in all major planning conferences and was responsible for coordinating the operations of many different fronts and strategic flanks. In the 1930s he held a number of different posts in the Commissariat of Defense. From 1941–42 he was Deputy Chief of Operations Control and then Chief of General Staff, USSR Armed Forces. His masterpiece was probably his coordinating of the three different fronts which participated in the Stalingrad offensive of November 1942, which he planned with Zhukhov and Voronov. At Kursk, in July 1943, Vasilievsky with Zhukhov personally supervised the Red Army preparations and the building of the defensive fortifications at the Kursk salient. He also vetoed the suggestion of Vatutin and Khrushchev that the Soviets should take the first offensive. He claimed that the Germans should be made to attack first and wear themselves out.

Vasilievsky had a major role in the final Soviet offensive against Germany. From 1944 he was in charge of coordinating the operations of the 2nd and 3rd Fronts in East Prussia and Belorussia and organized the final advance from Warsaw to Berlin. He was in constant contact with Stalin throughout this period, especially through his representative in Moscow, Antonov. In March 1945 when front commander Chernyakhovsky was killed in action, Vasilievsky took over his command and led the East Prussian campaign himself. Vasilievsky also took Stalin's place in Moscow when the latter was at the Yalta Conference in February 1945.

After the European war was over Vasilievsky was posted to the Far Eastern Front as Commander in Chief. He led his troops across the Manchurian border on the day the second atom bomb was dropped and led a vigorous and fast moving campaign.

Vatutin, General Nikolai, 1901–1944

Vatutin led the armies which recaptured Stalingrad, the Ukraine and Kiev. A graduate of the Frunze Academy in 1929, he rose to become one of Stalin's advisers on the Stavka and, in 1941, head of General Staff Operations. In 1942 he was given his first important military command, the Voronezh Front. In November of that year he led his Southwest Front in the famous Stalingrad offensive in which he, in conjunction with Generals Rokossovsky and Yeremenko cut off and trapped Paulus' Sixth Army. Vatutin went on to threaten the German's line of retreat.

In the Kursk Campaign of July 1943, Vatutin managed to halt Von Manstein's advance and then counterattacked to take Kharkov. He then led his army into the Ukraine and in a campaign launched on Christmas Eve 1943 took Kiev in January 1944. In early March 1944, Vatutin, leading an expedition to take Rovno, was ambushed by Ukrainian anti-Soviet partisans and fatally wounded.

Vian, Vice-Admiral Sir Philip, 1894–1968

Captain Philip Vian was the perpetrator of the daring *Altmark* raid. In February 1940 in HMS *Cossack*, commanding a destroyer flotilla, Vian boarded the German prisoner ship *Altmark* in a Norwegian fiord and rescued 299 British prisoners who had been captured during the *Graf Spee*'s commerce raids. In May 1940 he led the evacuation of Namsos aboard HMS *Afridi* which was sunk during the exchange.

In May 1941 he was commander of the 4th Flotilla which helped to sink the *Bismarck*. Now an admiral, Vian led the successful raid on Spitzbergen in July 1941 and in December commanded a squadron in the First Battle of Sirte. He helped protect the convoys bound to and from Malta and the Second Battle of Sirte was a success mostly because of his decisive leadership. He led an assault force for the invasion of Sicily in July 1943 and a squadron of aircraft carriers for the Italian landings at Salerno. In June 1944, as naval commander of the Eastern Task Force, he participated in the cross-Channel invasion of Europe (Operation Neptune). On D-Day he watched the daylight operations and controlled the night surface patrols.

Late in 1944 he was appointed commander of the Eastern Fleet's aircraft carrier squadron in Ceylon and joined the British Pacific Fleet in Australia for the assault on Okinawa. An energetic and tireless leader, Vian was always in the thick of battle.

Vlasov, Lieutenant General Andrey, 1900–1945

Vlasov was the leader of an anti-Stalin movement among Soviet prisoners in Germany. He had served the USSR well before his capture by the Nazis. He was a military adviser to Chiang Kai-shek from 1938 to 1939. In August 1941 he showed great courage in the defense of Kiev when completely surrounded by the Germans. Stalin allowed him to withdraw and gave him command of the 2nd Assault Army defending Moscow. In May 1942 he was captured by the Germans near Leningrad. He felt that the Soviet High Command had abandoned him and as a result he had refused to escape. He soon began to make propaganda broadcasts in which he gave voice to the Soviet army's mistrust of Stalin. In November 1944 Himmler gave him permission to form the Anti-Stalinist Committee for the Liberation of the Peoples of the Soviet Union. He drew recruits to this organization from German POW camps and from among Soviet civilian prisoners brought to Germany for forced labor. On 14 November he published in Prague a manifesto denouncing Stalin on the grounds of his annexation of foreign territory and of his policy regarding nationalities. At the same time he was allowed to form a Russian Liberation Army (the ROA), which Hitler, however, used mostly for political propaganda purposes rather than for combat. At the end of the war Vlasov was in charge of two divisions totaling 50,000 men. One division was fighting the Red Army at Frankfurt on the Main; the other accompanied by Vlasov entered Prague before the US, defeated the SS, made contact with the Czechs and attempted to turn Czechoslovakia over to the Americans. They unfortunately declined the offer and allowed the Russians to take it over. Many of Vlasov's troops surrendered to the Americans and committed suicide when the Americans repatriated them. Vlasov himself was unable to escape and was arrested by the Soviets in May 1945. It was announced on 2 August 1946 on the back page of *Pravda* that Vlasov and several of his officers had been tried for espionage and treason against the USSR and had been executed accordingly.

Vlasov was in fact an idealistic man who hated the tyranny of Stalin and made the mistake of seeing the Germans as potential liberators. He was far from alone in this view: the German's greatest mistake in the Soviet Union, perhaps, was that instead of making use of the great anti-Stalin feeling of the people they showed themselves to be far more brutal than the Soviet government.

Voronov, General Nikolay N, 1899–1968

Voronov was a marshal of artillery and member of the Stavka for the entire war. He played a major role in the reequipping of the artillery and in the development of its tactical application. During the Russo-Finnish War in 1939 he was able to use artillery to breach the Mannerheim Line. He also directed artillery on the Leningrad Front in 1941. His crowning achievement was probably the Stalingrad offensive of November 1942 which he planned with Zhukov and Vasilievsky, an offensive which opened with sustained pounding of the German position with 2000 of Voronov's guns. He went on to plan the deployment of artillery and antiaircraft guns at Kursk and other later battles.

Voroshilov, Marshal Kliment, 1881–1969

Voroshilov had been an associate of Stalin and Budenny during the Civil War when the three of them served in the 1st Cavalry Army. In 1934 he was appointed commissar for defense in charge of the mechanization of the Red Army. In this capacity he also met with the Anglo-French military mission of 1939 to discuss, inconclusively, the defense of Poland. In May 1940 as part of the reorganization of the Red Army, Voroshilov was replaced by the more able Timoshenko and appointed Deputy Chairman of the Defense Committee. In July 1941 in response to the German invasion, Stalin set up the State Defense Committee (GKO) composed of himself, Voroshilov, Molotov, Malenkov and Beria. They were in charge of both the overall conduct of the war and mobilization of Soviet resources. Voroshilov was given command of the armies of the Northwest Front. There he failed to check the German advance or to save Leningrad, partly because of his lack of military knowledge and partly because his troops were ill-trained and inexperienced. Because of his defeats and because he and Zhdanov had set up a military soviet for the defense of Leningrad without Stalin's orders, Voroshilov was replaced by Zhukov and assigned to staff positions until the end of the war.

As a member of the State Defense Committee he played a diplomatic role. In August 1942 he served as military spokesman in talks with Brooke and Wavell over the possibility of an Anglo-American air force in Transcaucasia. In November 1943 he attended the Teheran Conference. Voroshilov signed the armistice with Hungary on behalf of the Allies and later became head of the Soviet Control Commission of Hungary.

Wainwright, Lieutenant General Jonathan, 1883–1953

Wainwright conducted the heroic defense of Bataan and then of Corregidor after MacArthur left the Philippines. He had been posted to the Philippines before, in 1909–10, and had served in France during the Great War. He was sent to the Philippines in September 1940 and in December was ordered to defend northern Luzon. When the Japanese landed at Lingayen Gulf on Luzon in December 1941, Wainwright retreated to Bataan in order to avoid being cut off from the main US forces. When MacArthur was ordered to leave Luzon, Wainwright took over the command and was made a lieutenant general on 19 March 1942 by Roosevelt. He managed to hold out far longer than expected against great Japanese air superiority until ordered to retire to Corregidor on 8 April. There Wainwright and his 15,000 men held out under continuous heavy bombardment from across the straits. On 4 May the Japanese hit the island with 16,000 shells and landed 2000 troops on the night of 5 May. Wainwright surrendered on 6 May and ordered a general surrender of all US and Filipino troops in the Philippines. Guerrilla activities, however, continued throughout the war.

Wainwright accompanied his men on the Bataan Death March, surviving this to be held as a POW in Manchuria until the end of the war. Still suffering the effects of imprisonment,

BIOGRAPHIES

he stood next to MacArthur on the USS *Missouri* when the Japanese officially surrendered on 2 September 1945. He was awarded the Congressional Medal of Honor.

Wallis, Sir Barnes, 1887–1979

A British aeronautical engineer, Wallis was responsible for the design and construction of many of the Allied 'super bombs.' Before World War I he was a designer for Vickers and after a brief period with the Royal Navy Air Service returned to Vickers as an airship designer. In the 1920s he designed and built the R.100 airship. As an airplane designer he invented the 'geodetic' fuselage used on the Vickers Wellington. During the war he specialized in developing new and different types of bombs. On 16 May 1943 Wing Commander Gibson led the RAF on a mission to destroy the dams on the Möhne and Eder. It was the first known use of the 'bouncing bomb,' one of Wallis's more famous and useful weapons. It had to be dropped from 60 feet and then it bounced on the water up to the dams where it exploded. His other big success was the development of the Grand Slam bomb. The first of these was dropped on the Bielefeld Viaduct and weighed 10 tons. He was also responsible for the development of the 'Tallboy,' a 12,000-pound deep penetration bomb which was used to sink the *Tirpitz* on 12 November 1944. There were 854 Tallboys and 41 Grand Slam bombs dropped during the war.

Warlimont, General Walther, 1894–

Warlimont held the post of deputy chief of OKW Operations Staff under General Jodl from September 1939 to September 1944. His importance lies in his postwar writings on the activities and operation of Hitler's HQ. As a close observer of and participant in many of the important military decisions of the war his evidence and accounts have been invaluable.

An officer since World War I, and with service in the Spanish Civil War, Warlimont was appointed chief of the National Defense Section (General Staff) in the OKW in September 1938 and the following year was promoted to deputy chief of the Operations Staff. Warlimont was only a few feet away from Hitler, when Stauffenberg's bomb exploded on 20 July 1944 and he received minor injuries. Warlimont continued working until September when he collapsed from the delayed effects of the bomb and remained on sick leave for the rest of the war.

Watson-Watt, Sir Robert, 1892–1974

A scientist and inventor of worth, Watson-Watt was a pioneer in the field of experimental radar. In 1935 under the auspices of the Air Ministry he was able to prove that an airplane could be detected by its echo as it passed through radio waves. By 1936 employers of this method were able to detect the height and distance of approaching aircraft up to 75 miles away.

By the outbreak of World War II a series of defense stations had been built along the coast of England which used radar as their means to detect the approach of enemy aircraft. Throughout the war Watson-Watt developed additional uses for his 'invention.' The accuracy of anti-aircraft guns was improved; fighters were able to locate other aircraft; bombers could locate targets; reconnaissance planes could pin-point U-Boats and report their position to naval vessels; identification between friendly ships and planes was perfected. Tedder called Watson-Watt 'one of the three saviors of Britain.'

Wavell, Field Marshal Sir Archibald, 1883–1950

Wavell was a highly respected and brilliant general who had the misfortune of being consistently sent to impossible situations, yet always acquitted himself well. In July 1939 he was appointed Commander in Chief of the Middle East and North Africa, a territory which also covered the Eastern Mediterranean and East Africa. The Italian Tenth Army invaded Egypt on 13 September 1940 and had penetrated over 60 miles inside the border within the week. Wavell with his Western Desert Force, though heavily outnumbered and undersupplied, managed to drive the Italians out of Egypt by 4 January 1941 and to recapture Tobruk on 22 January. His 6th Australian Division captured Benghazi on the 6 February by which time the Allies controlled all of Cyrenaica and had taken 130,000 prisoners. In February Wavell followed up his Egyptian victory with a series of offensives in East Africa which led to the Italian surrender of Addis Ababa on 6 April. Unfortunately in February Wavell agreed to send part of his force to Greece. They arrived there too late to be of any use and in the meantime Rommel had invaded and outmaneuvered the one infantry and one armored division which Wavell had kept to defend Cyrenaica. By 11 April, Rommel was on the Egyptian border.

By July 1941 Churchill had little confidence in Wavell and was tired of his inability to launch an offensive against Rommel. He was, therefore, transferred to the post of Commander in Chief in India. In November 1941 the Japanese began their invasions of Malaya and the Dutch East Indies. Wavell was made Allied Supreme

Commander of the joint American-British-Dutch-Australian Command but was unable to prevent the Japanese victories because of the weakness of his forces. He therefore resigned shortly after in February 1942.

Wavell then returned to India to prepare an offensive against Burma. This began in December 1942 with an advance through Arakan but achieved no breakthrough partly because of Wavell's reliance on a strategy of frontal assault. In January 1943 he was made a field marshal and in June of that year Churchill, still doubtful of his military capability, gave him the purely political post of Viceroy of India. In this capacity Wavell was closely concerned with the internal political and economic problems of India, in particular with the Bengal famine.

Wavell had suffered many disadvantages in his career: Churchill's dislike, lack of adequate supplies and military machinery and impossible assignments, nonetheless he was much loved by his men and associates. Rommel's tribute was that he always kept a copy of Wavell's book *Generals and Generalship* with him.

Wedemeyer, Major General Albert, 1897–
Wedemeyer became Chiang Kai-shek's Chief of Staff, replacing Stilwell, in October 1944. He had served in the War Department, General Staff as an expert in war plans from 1941–43. In August 1943 he was appointed US Deputy Chief of Staff under Lord Mountbatten at his new Southeast Asia Command (SEAC) planning the invasion of Japanese-held bases. In October 1944 when Stilwell was recalled from China at Chiang's request, Wedemeyer was sent in. Stilwell's post had been Commander in Chief of land forces in China, but Roosevelt decided that America would no longer take responsibility for the worsening situation there. Wedemeyer was therefore sent as Chief of Staff to Chiang Kai-shek. His task was to attempt to establish some cooperation between Chiang and the Communists and to insure that US aid was correctly used by the Kuomintang.

Weygand, General Maxime, 1867–1965
Weygand was not French by birth – indeed his paternity is a mystery, though it is widely suggested that he was an illegitimate son of Leopold II of Belgium – but was trained at St Cyr Military Academy and chosen by Foch at the outbreak of World War I to be his Chief of Staff. Foch's success guaranteed his own and between the wars he rose to the highest ranks of the French army. Age, however, enforced his retirement before 1939 but he was recalled in the

August of that year to command French forces in the Lebanon and Syria. On 19 May with the home front collapsing and Gamelin's incompetence demonstrated for all to see, he was brought back to France to take over as Supreme Allied Commander. Despite his age, he remained vigorous and incisive and began at once an attempt to create a new front ('the Weygand Line') south of the Somme. But the French First Army and the British Expeditionary Force had already been isolated, and the rest of the French army was not of the best quality. The Weygand Line, against which the German forces turned on 5 June, did not hold and by 12 June Weygand had decided that they must be asked for an armistice, which Pétain signed on 22 June.

Weygand was then made delegate general in French North Africa and commander of local French forces, which stood outside the armistice arrangements. So resolutely anti-Axis was the spirit in which he exercised command that, at German insistence, he was relieved in November 1941 and a year later, on the German occupation of the Vichy zone, he was arrested and imprisoned in Germany. Re-arrested on his return to France in May 1945, he was tried for treason in 1948 but acquitted. The charge was unfounded. Weygand was tainted by the defeat of 1940 but in no way responsible for it, and demonstrated throughout his life profound devotion to his adopted country.

Wilhelmina, Queen of the Netherlands, 1880–1962
When the Germans invaded the Netherlands in May 1940, the Queen left the Hague for the safety of the extreme south of the country. However the Germans got there before her, so she hastily left for London on 13 May and was soon joined by her government. She was welcomed in London and continued to see to the affairs of state and look after the welfare of her subjects in exile. She also spoke to those who were left behind on Radio Oranje on the anniversary of the invasion and on other special occasions. Wilhelmina visited the Netherlands in March 1945 as a guest of the Allied authorities but finally returned on 2 May.

Willkie, Wendell, 1892–1944
Willkie was notable both as Roosevelt's opponent in the 1940 election and as his goodwill envoy to the world. As a former democrat who switched to the Republican Party in opposition to the New Deal in 1938, Willkie was a surprise candidate in 1940. However he

did surprisingly well at the polls. He was a visionary and idealistic internationalist in opposition to America's habitual isolationism and wrote a book advocating these views, *One World*, which turned out to be a best seller. He called for a postwar world which was a union or commonwealth of free nations. Such ideas laid the groundwork for the founding of the United Nations. In January 1941 Willkie went to the United Kingdom, met with its leaders and brought back messages for Roosevelt. He followed this up in August 1942 with a 31,000-mile trip which took him as far as the Near East, USSR and China. Again he met with leaders and kept in very close contact with Roosevelt. Willkie announced that he would again run for the presidency in 1944, but withdrew after being heavily defeated in the Wisconsin primary in April. He died a few months later in October 1944.

Wilson, Field Marshal Sir Henry Maitland, 1881–1964

Almost the whole of Wilson's service in World War II was spent in the Mediterranean, where he presided over a successsion of crises, defeats and withdrawals, but maintained Churchill's confidence throughout. Large in frame and hearty in manner, he was known as 'Jumbo,' but was far from elephantine in his thought processes. At the outbreak he was commanding in Egypt and oversaw Wavell's early campaign in the desert and Cunningham's in Ethiopia. He then directed both the intervention in and retreat from Greece, where he did much to minimize British losses. His next crisis was the pro-Axis coup in Iraq, which he occupied successfully with a skeleton force, and he was then called on to carry out the most sensitive operation of the Middle Eastern War, the occupation of Syria, held by Vichy French forces. From 1942–43 he commanded the Persia-Iraq Theater and Ninth Army, and then succeeded Alexander as Commander in Chief, Middle East, on the latter becoming Eisenhower's deputy. In January 1944 he became Supreme Allied Commander Mediterranean, though by then executive control of the main fighting in Italy had passed to the national commanders, Alexander and Clark. On the death of Sir John Dill in November he moved to Washington in charge of the British Joint Staff Mission, and in that capacity was present at the Yalta and Potsdam Conferences. Though credited with no great strategic decisions, Wilson was a rock of sound military sense in difficult situations.

Wingate, Major General Orde, 1903–1944

Wingate fired the imagination of the public and of many politicians with his guerrilla forces in Burma called the Chindits. He had much experience in guerrilla tactics, starting with his service with the 'Special Night Squads' in Israel in 1936. After he had been seconded to Africa, he took up his guerrilla activities again in Ethiopia in the fall of 1940 with his very successful 'Gideon Force,' which after capturing many Italian forts, accompanied the victorious Haile Selassie into Addis Ababa.

Wingate was then sent home to a desk job, was extremely depressed and attempted suicide during a bout of malaria. While recovering he was summoned to the Far East by General Wavell who offered him the opportunity to organize his 'Long Range Penetration Groups.' These were brigade-sized units which were to be dropped behind the Japanese lines, supplied by air, communicating by wireless and whose purpose was to disrupt enemy communications, attack outposts and destroy bridges. He called them the Chindits after *Chinthe*, a mythical beast.

The Chindits began their first operation in February 1943, crossing the Chindwin River into Burma. They managed to cross the Irrawaddy by March but by then the Japanese, aware of their presence, counterattacked forcing Wingate to withdraw to India, having lost a third of his equipment. Despite this limited success, Wingate became a popular hero and was made much of by Churchill. His operations however had no strategic impact and inflicted only light casualties.

Wingate now prepared a second Chindit operation, this time with six brigades, far more ambitious aims and supplied by its own air unit, 'Cochran's Circus.' This expedition was air dropped into Burma in February 1944 and ran into difficulties. Wingate, however, died before the outcome of the expedition became clear, in an air crash in the jungle on 24 March 1944.

Witzleben, Field Marshal Erwin von, 1881–1944

Witzleben belonged, with Beck, to the small group of German officers who consistently opposed Hitler and who began to plot his downfall before the outbreak of the war. His disaffection was not suspected, however, and he was given command in 1940 of the First Army, which penetrated the Maginot Line. He was promoted to field marshal at the victory celebrations of 18 July 1940 and appointed Commander in Chief, West, in May 1941, by then a backwater post. He retired sick in 1942 but kept in touch with the circle of military conspirators, who intended to appoint him Commander in Chief if their plans succeeded. Ironically it was a false report that Witzleben had been seen that morning in uniform which, on 20 July 1944, alerted the security forces in Berlin to the possibility of a Bomb Plot. He was present later in the day at the War Ministry, while the Berlin conspirators attempted to marshal army units in the city and was arrested by Fromm that evening. Arraigned before the People's Court where he was systematically humiliated, he was sentenced to death and hanged by strangulation in August.

Wolff, General Karl, 1900–1984

As senior SS Commander in Italy, Wolff secretly negotiated the surrender of Italy to the Allies in March and April 1945. Wolff was a very close friend of Himmler and served as his Chief of Staff until the war and as his liaison with Hitler's HQ until 1943. He had had experience in Italian affairs since 1930 and accompanied Hitler to Rome in 1940. When Italy surrendered to the Allies on 8 September 1943 Wolff was appointed military governor of north-Italy. When Mussolini returned to Italy on 27 September, Wolff accompanied him and helped to reestablish a Fascist regime under German domination, the Salo Republic. He served as liaison officer with Mussolini, organized the transport of Italian troops to Germany for training and fought the partisans.

However in March 1945 Wolff opened negotiations with Allen Dulles of the Office of Strategic Services (OSS) in Switzerland for the surrender of the German army in Italy. He released an OSS agent and a partisan leader as sign of good faith. By the end of April the negotiations were almost complete and Wolff had already visited Switzerland twice. At this point however the Soviets began pressuring the Allies for excluding them and almost ended the project; Wolff's family were arrested on suspicion and Wolff had to send them out of the country. Finally, however, on 23 April Wolff and Vietinghoff, the general in command, agreed to disregard Berlin, call off resistance and allow the partisans to take over; on 29 April they signed a surrender and on 2 May it went into effect. Wolff had managed to negotiate secretly while maintaining relations with Berlin, Mussolini and with the partisans.

Yamamoto, Admiral Isoroku, 1884–1943

Yamamoto was Japan's greatest naval strategist and commander. As minister of navy from 1938 and Commander in Chief of the First Fleet from 1939, he was responsible for the great buildup and improvement of the Japanese Imperial Navy and naval air forces before the war. Although opposed to war with the United States on the grounds that Japan must inevitably lose a protracted war against such a powerful opponent, Yamamoto saw that Japan's only chance lay in a preemptive strike to cripple the US Navy from the start. Thus he began planning the operation against Pearl Harbor in early 1940, which succeeded in crippling the US Pacific Fleet on 7 December 1941.

Despite this success the US carriers were still operational, having been sent out on maneuvers on the weekend of the Pearl Harbor attack. After the Battle of the Coral Sea, in which the US lost the *Lexington*, and shocked by the Doolittle raid on Tokyo, Yamamoto decided to try to wipe out what was left of the US Pacific Fleet in a decisive battle. The next stage of Japanese High Command strategy was to take Midway Island, which was a US base and could be used to attack Hawaii. Yamamoto devised an extremely complex plan which involved the movement of eight separate task forces, including a diversionary attack on the Aleutian Islands. However the US had the key to the Japanese fleet code and knew of the attack on Midway on 4 June 1942. Nagumo, the overconfident Japanese carrier fleet commander, was totally outmaneuvered and lost four carriers, so the Japanese, deprived of air cover, had to withdraw.

Yamamoto never fully recovered from the shock of this defeat but continued to command fleet movements in the Solomons campaign. The Japanese fleet suffered from huge losses of aircraft and pilots which it could never make good although several victories were scored in the waters off Guadalcanal. His

Above: Admiral Yamamoto.

last plan was for a massive naval air counter-strike, I-Go, designed to smash Allied advances, in the spring of 1943.

In April 1943 the US intercepted advance reports of Yamamoto's tour of inspection in the Western Solomons. His aircraft and escort were shot down by aircraft from Guadalcanal on 18 April 1943. Yamamoto's death was a considerable blow to Japanese morale and he received the full honor of a hero's funeral.

Yamamoto's great contribution to naval strategy was his early recognition of air power and the development of long-range aircraft.

Yamashita, Lieutenant General Tomoyuki, 1885–1946

Yamashita was known as the 'Tiger of Malaya' for his dramatic capture of Malaya and Singapore, which Churchill described as the worst British military disaster in history. He also directed the Japanese defense of the Philippines at the end of the war.

Yamashita had been sent on a military mission to Germany in 1940, as inspector general of the Imperial Army Air Forces. He reported that Japan should not declare war on either Britain or the the United States until its army and air forces were drastically modernized. When the war broke out however, Yamashita was commander of the Twenty-fifth Army. He invaded the Thai Peninsula in early December and within 70 days had overrun all of Malaya, mainly because of his great speed and use of surprise. At Singapore, although he had outrun his supplies, he bluffed General Percival into believing that the Japanese had vastly superior forces. Percival surrendered on 15 February 1942.

Yamashita was then retired by Tojo to command of the 1st Army Group in Manchuria to train soldiers. He was not given another active post until Tojo's fall in July 1944, when he was appointed commander of the Fourteenth Area Army assigned to defend the Philippines. Yamashita had only just arrived there when the Americans invaded Leyte in October 1944; he had no time to prepare defenses and had no control over the air force. He was ordered to make a stand there but all Japanese resistance was over by January 1945. When the Americans invaded Luzon in January 1945 Yamashita at first could only retreat; yet he managed to organize a counterattack within a week. He left Manila to the Americans, but Iwabuchi disobeyed his orders and defended the city. Yamashita continued his operations despite the failure of supplies until news of the Japanese surrender reached him on 2 September. He was arrested, tried as a war criminal and executed in February 1946.

Yeremenko, Marshal Andrey, 1892–1970

Yeremenko was a front-line general at Stalingrad, Smolensk, in Czechoslovakia and the Crimea. Recalled from a tour of duty in the Far East at the start of the German invasion, he was appointed commander of the Bryansk Front in August 1941. He was severely wounded during the retreat from Bryansk (13 October) and was out of action for a year. In August 1942 he was made commander of the Southeast Front and participated in the encirclement operations at Stalingrad.

In 1943 Yeremenko was involved in the advance on Smolensk. He was then posted as commander of the Independent (Black Sea) Maritime Front and ordered to clear out the Crimea, which was occupied by a mixed force of Germans and Rumanians. Yeremenko and Tolbukhin began their offensive on 8 April 1944 and had captured 67,000 men, mostly German, by the time the enemy surrendered on 13 May.

Yeremenko took charge of the 2nd Baltic Front in 1944, captured Dvinsk (in Latvia), joined the offensive against the German Army Group North and threatened Riga. He was then assigned to the Carpathian Front until 1945.

Zeitzler, General Kurt, 1895–1963

Proof of exceptional ability in staff appointments at Corps level in the Polish and French campaigns led to Zeitler's promotion to Chief of Staff of First Panzer Army, with Kleist's command, in the invasion of the Soviet Union. On Halder's dismissal in September 1942, he succeeded him as Chief of Staff of the army, with responsibility for the prosecution of the war on the eastern front. He and Hitler at first worked well together, since Zeitler admired the Fuehrer greatly, but they fell out over the management of the Stalingrad operation. Zeitzler wanted to allow Paulus to retire from the city once he was encircled, but Hitler adamantly refused permission for the necessary orders to be given. When the error of Hitler's judgment was demonstrated by Paulus' capitulation, Zeitzler's position was consequently strengthened and he exercised considerable powers of command during 1943. He was first of all, able to make Hitler agree to 'adjustments of the front,' that is withdrawals, in the spring and then in the summer to a strategic counter-

Above: Marshall Zhukov and Air Chief Marshal Tedder ratify the German surrender.

offensive at Kursk in July. Because Hitler took little part in the debate over Kursk, Zeitzler wasted time persuading his fellow generals to accept his plan, and the attack was eventually launched too late for it to succeed. The failure weakened his position, and it was further undermined by the defeats in the Soviet Union in spring and summer 1944. On 1 July 1944 he and Hitler had a bitter dispute, Zeitzler left his headquarters and succumbed to a complete physical and nervous collapse. He was succeeded by Guderian.

Zhukov, Marshal Georgi, 1896–1974

Zhukov was Deputy Supreme Commander in Chief of the Red Army for almost the entire war, taking a major role both in planning overall strategy and in directing many effective campaigns in the field. His rise to prominence began with a successful operation against the Japanese in Mongolia in 1939, during which he learned much about Japanese military techniques. He was then appointed Chief of Staff of the Red Army in 1940.

Following the German invasion of the USSR, Zhukov was installed as director of the Soviet Army High Command. He served well but unsuccessfully in the defense of Smolensk in August 1941. In October 1941 he replaced Voroshilov as commander of the northern sector, in personal charge of the defense of Leningrad. He was then sent to Moscow as Commander in Chief of the entire Western Front and defended the capital successfully against two German offensives. On 6 December 1941 Zhukov counterattacked and forced the Germans back but reached a standstill by

February 1942. He was then appointed deputy commissar for defense.

In the 1942 campaign Zhukov was in command of the defense of Stalingrad. He directed and shared in the planning of the counteroffensive of November in which his forces broke through from the northwest and south of the city at the River Don, encircling Paulus' Sixth Army which surrendered on 31 January 1943. Zhukov was also involved in the Battle of Kursk (July 1943), a major German defeat and the largest tank battle of the war.

Zhukov directed the Soviet sweep across the Ukraine, and had to replace Vatutin as commander of the 1st Ukrainian Front. The Front advanced at the rate of 30 miles per day during February and March 1944, though he was forced to a halt when supplies failed in April. He then took overall command of the Fronts in June 1944 for the USSR's greatest breakthrough: the collapse of Army Group Center in Belorussia. This offensive stopped short of Warsaw in August but was resumed in January 1945. After the fall of Warsaw, Zhukov's Fronts advanced at the rate of 100 miles per week through Prussia until he again had to stop because of supply problems. On 16 April Zhukov crossed the Oder, launching the final offensive which led to the Battle of Berlin on 2 May. On 8 May after a week of intensive fighting, Zhukov signed the German surrender in Berlin.

As a General Zhukov was imaginative and very successful, overly cautious at the beginning of the war but daring and decisive by the end. Stalin recognized his ability but worried that Zhukov might prove a political opponent.

CASUALTIES

The human cost of World War II was enormous. Precise figures for the losses of the various participants are not always available and, of those that are, some are generally regarded as being unreliable. The best estimates put the death roll as approximately 50,000,000.

Undoubtedly the losses of the Soviet Union were the most serious. The most likely total of military and civilian deaths is perhaps 20,000,000. In addition, in the areas occupied by the Germans about two-thirds of the houses and productive capacity was destroyed. The Western Allies escaped comparatively lightly. The United States lost less than 300,000 dead. Britain lost under 500,000, and the countries of the British Empire an additional 120,000, considerably less than the British Empire casualties in World War I.

The major Axis powers both lost heavily. German losses were in excess of 4,500,000 of whom 1,000,000 were civilians. Many of these deaths were inflicted by the Nazis on their own people. Japanese casualties were in the region of 2,000,000. The Italians lost about 500,000.

Outside the Soviet Union the heaviest loss was probably borne by China. Estimates of the Chinese losses vary from less than 3,000,000 to up to 15,000,000. The higher figures are probably nearer the truth. Particularly disturbing in China was the number of refugees displaced from their homes during the war and the civil war that

followed. The Chinese culture has traditionally laid much emphasis on caring for and maintaining family graves and traditions and refugees are of course unable to do this.

There are very few figures for deaths elsewhere in Asia but it is known that 1,500,000 died in Bengal in the famine in the summer and fall of 1943. More could have been done to mitigate this disaster if shipping and railways had been free from the demands of war.

In Central and Eastern Europe the death toll was also very heavy. Dominating the list of losses are the more than 5,500,000 Jews murdered by the Nazis but many non-Jewish civilians were also killed. The distinguished record of the Yugoslav Partisans was not achieved without a price. Perhaps 1,000,000 Yugoslav civilians died at the hands of the Germans and the .rious factions struggling for control of their country. About 4,000,000 civilians of other Eastern European countries also died. The armed forces of Yugoslavia, Hungary, Poland and Rumania all lost between 300,000 and 400,000. Bulgaria had fewest casualties – 20,000. In Western Europe France lost 500,000, half of them civilians. Holland lost 200,000 civilians and Belgium and the Scandinavian countries all suffered heavily in relation to their comparatively small populations.

World War II was the most dreadful conflict in human history.

Tarawa after the battle. Proportionately casualties were the heaviest in US history.

INDEX